The Hoover Library on War, Revolution, and Peace
Publication No. 15

The Bolsheviks and the World War

The Hoover Library on War, Revolution, and Peace
Publication No. 15

THE BOLSHEVIKS AND THE WORLD WAR

THE ORIGIN OF THE THIRD INTERNATIONAL

By

OLGA HESS GANKIN

and

H. H. FISHER

STANFORD UNIVERSITY PRESS
STANFORD, CALIFORNIA

STANFORD UNIVERSITY PRESS

STANFORD, CALIFORNIA

Copyright 1940 by the Board of Trustees of the
Leland Stanford Junior University

Library of Congress Catalog Card Number 40-14271

Printed in the United States of America

First published, 1940
Second printing, 1960

PREFACE

THE PURPOSE of this book is to make available in English a collection of documents on the origin of the Third or Communist International. During the decade before 1914 the groups which composed the Russian Social Democratic Labor party were in a turmoil of dissension caused mainly by conflicting theories of organization and tactics. These disputes greatly distressed the leaders of the Second International, and they tried, without success, to persuade the Bolsheviks to accept the kind of compromise by which other socialist parties maintained the formal unity required by the International. Lenin and his friends viewed with no less disapproval what they considered to be the opportunism of the socialist leaders. Certain documents are given which relate to these matters, to Lenin's defense of the Bolshevik viewpoint and his attempts to organize the Lefts within the International.

A great majority of the documents which we reproduce originated during the World War. Among the countless casualties of this war was the Second International. It was not destroyed, but it was put out of action as an effective international force. The failure of its constituent parties to oppose the war measures of their governments or to take advantage of the situation to advance the cause of socialism was interpreted by the Bolsheviks as proof of the bankruptcy of the leadership of the socialist and labor movements. The Bolsheviks and their allies denounced this betrayal, as they regarded it, of the workers and urged the Lefts of all countries to break with their party majorities and to join in the establishment of a new and truly revolutionary International. This campaign was carried on under great difficulties in small gatherings, by letters, by pamphlets, and in fugitive periodicals which reached the readers to whom they were addressed only when they escaped the vigilance of the police. The advocacy of self-determination, defeatism, and the transformation of the international war into a civil war was opposed, sometimes contemptuously and sometimes violently, by many socialist and labor bureaucracies; and even among the small party of its adherents it aroused bitter contention.

The campaign derived its chief impetus from the Russian Bolsheviks and had its organizational base in the Zimmerwald movement. The documents which we give for the period relate to Bolshevik party affairs, to the international conferences of the Zimmerwald movement, the activities of its executive body, the International Socialist Committee at Berne, and particularly the affairs of the Zimmerwald Left. Materials relating to a few other groups are included where their activities were of concern to the Bolsheviks or their allies. The documents in this volume do not go beyond the autumn of 1918. Preparations for the establishment of the Third International and its first congress in 1919 are discussed in a forthcoming volume in this series entitled, *The Bolsheviks and World Revolution: The Founding of the Third International.* This volume will also include information on activities within the Zimmerwald movement in certain countries, propaganda among the war prisoners in Russia and among the soldiers of the intervention forces, the campaign in Russian borderlands in support of world revolution, and, finally, the establishment of the Third International.

Polemical statements, such as very many of the documents in this book are, do not in themselves carry on a narrative of the events to which they relate. For this reason we have thought it desirable to give with each group of documents an account of the activities of the organization or groups involved during the period under consideration. The activities and interrelations of these groups were often complicated, and the sources of information are scattered and sometimes conflicting. They exist principally in contemporary publications, in reminiscences, and in the memory of participants who have been kind enough to give us their help. The purpose of editorial notes is not to interpret the documents but to supplement them with as much factual and bibliographical information as space and the sources at our disposal permit.

Also supplementary to the documents are the chronology and the biographical notes, which with the bibliography follow the text. The chronology is chiefly concerned with events in the history of the socialist movement, particularly in Russia, from the middle of the nineteenth century to the spring of 1918. The biographical notes have been assembled in order to furnish information concerning those whose names are mentioned in the text. Unfortunately we have not been able to secure this information for all those whose names appear. In a number of cases the information we give has been provided by the subject of the note or by a friend or associate, and we are very grateful for the information so received. In the other cases we have used the available reference works.

The bibliography contains the titles of the primary sources used, of the books and articles cited, and of certain other works which are relevant to the topics treated in the following pages. Where not obvious from the title, the character, origin, and point of view of the book are indicated in its accompanying note. With this bibliography is a list of newspapers and periodicals which have been cited or from which material has been quoted. Revolutionary journalism is a hazardous business. Such publications are often suppressed or they cease publication for lack of funds and readers; sometimes they are revived under the familiar name, or with the old name slightly modified, or under entirely new names. They are moved from place to place, editors are changed, and policies are revised or even reversed. We have thought it advisable to give a brief sketch of the history of those publications on which we have been able to get information. For much of this information we are indebted to libraries and organizations which possess complete files. In some cases we have not been able to secure this information; in other cases it is incomplete.

The very considerable research which has gone into the preparation of this book has been done by Dr. Gankin, who has also made the translations. To her belongs the credit for whatever this volume may contribute toward making more easily accessible these source materials on the history of the Bolshevik party during the World War. For the selection of materials and their presentation and for such errors of judgment and fact as the book may contain, we are jointly responsible.

We are under obligation to a number of individuals and institutions for the assistance they have been kind enough to give us. Dr. Angelica Balabanoff, former secretary of the International Socialist Committee and first secretary of the Third International, has been kind enough to read portions of the manuscript and to make many valuable suggestions.

We are indebted to Mr. Boris Nikolaevsky, Paris representative of the Institute for Social History at Amsterdam, for copies of materials and for other information secured through his wide acquaintance with the literature and membership of the socialist movement. The former Library of the Communist Academy, now the Main Library of the Department of Social Sciences of the Academy of Sciences of the U.S.S.R. at Moscow, the Russian Historical Archive at Prague, the Bibliothèque de Documentation Internationale Contemporaine et Musée de la Grande Guerre at Vincennes, the Schweizerische Landesbibliothek at Berne, the Library of the Palace of Peace at The Hague, the Belgian-American Educational Foundation, Inc., at Brussels, and the American-Scandinavian Foundation at New York have courteously and helpfully responded to our requests for information. The Library of Congress, the New York Public Library, the Harvard University Library, and the Stanford University Library have generously permitted us to use volumes from their shelves. International Publishers have very kindly permitted us to quote from the translations of Lenin's works published by them.

Our principal sources are, however, in the Hoover Library, and we are deeply indebted to Miss Nina Almond, Librarian and Consultant in Research, and to our other colleagues in the administrative and research departments of the Library for their aid. Dr. J. E. Wallace Sterling has aided us in many ways in the preparation of the manuscript of this book, and we are grateful to him and to Dr. Easton Rothwell, Mr. Paul L. Hanna, and Mr. Benjamin Bock for many valuable suggestions and to Miss Helene von Damm for her valuable assistance in preparing the index.

H. H. FISHER

STANFORD UNIVERSITY, CALIFORNIA
April 15, 1940

PREFACE TO THE SECOND PRINTING

The first printing of this volume was sold out in 1953. In view of many requests for further copies, the Hoover Institution has accepted the suggestion of the Stanford University Press that the volume be reprinted. It must be emphasized, however, that this is not a new edition, but merely a reprint of the original edition, in which a few errata have been corrected and a few easily ascertained death dates added to the Biographical Notes. We are aware that since 1940, when this volume was prepared for print, a number of new documents pertinent to the topics covered by this collection have become available. Unfortunately, it is not practicable to include them in this reprinting.

W. GLENN CAMPBELL

January 1960

TABLE OF CONTENTS

The Bolsheviks and the World War

CHAPTER I

THE BOLSHEVIKS, THE MENSHEVIKS, AND THE SECOND INTERNATIONAL

During the 'eighties of the last century the revolutionary labor movement in Europe began to recover from the reaction which followed the tragic end of the Paris Commune. Despite Bismarck's antisocialist laws the German Social Democratic party, unified at the Gotha Congress in 1875, grew in numbers and influence. In France with the return of the Communard exiles the socialist movement revived in a tumult of factional controversy. During this decade the Social Democratic Federation and the Fabian Society appeared in England as the propagandists of very diverse brands of socialism. A Social Democratic League was founded in Holland in 1878, and in Belgium the discordant socialist groups organized in 1885 the Belgian Labor party, socialist in everything but name. The prohibition against socialist activity in the Habsburg Empire was lifted in 1869, but only in 1888 did the socialists succeed in capturing the leadership in the Austrian labor movement and in organizing a united socialist party. An Italian Workers' party organized early in the 'eighties fell into the hands of the anarchists and was promptly outlawed, but in 1892 a socialist congress laid the foundations of the Marxist party of Italian Workers. The Danish Social Democratic League was founded in 1878, the Norwegian and Swedish Social Democratic parties in 1887 and 1889, and the Swiss in 1888. Across the Atlantic in the United States various socialist groups which had been active since 1850 succeeded in 1874 in establishing the Social Democratic Workingmen's party, which three years later became the Socialist Labor party of North America. Like many European parties it had to settle accounts with the anarchists during the 'eighties and in 1892 it nominated its first presidential ticket.

In Russia Marxian socialism came somewhat later. When the movement began to develop in the inhospitable climate of Tsarism there was already a long-established, indigenous, revolutionary socialist movement, reflecting in its aims and tactics the influence of the social and political environment in which it had been born. The disappointment and disillusionment of peasants and young intellectuals after the emancipation in 1861 found expression among the radical intelligentsia in a movement to overthrow not only Tsarism but the existing social order. To accomplish this end secret societies, among them the "Zemlia i Volia" ("Land and Freedom"), were formed and great numbers of students went "to the people," that is, to the peasants, who were counted upon to rise in an "elemental" revolt as they had done in the seventeenth and eighteenth centuries. This elemental rising, guided by the radical intelligentsia, it was expected, would succeed where the earlier risings had failed and, existing institutions having been swept away, Russia would be able to establish a socialist society based on the peasant commune without having to pass through the stage of capitalism.

The peasants did not respond to the propaganda of those who went to the people, the Narodniks; but the government did, and with such severity that by the end of the 'sixties the secret revolutionary societies were broken up and great numbers of the Narodniks were imprisoned or exiled. The government's repressive measures did not destroy the Narodnik movement, and in the 'seventies, particularly after the recall of Russian students from abroad in 1873, it revived. In these years two tactical tendencies disturbed the unity of this movement. Some favored the tactic of permeation by propaganda among the peasants; others held that terrorism directed against officials and particularly against the Tsar was the only effective tactic in the existing circumstances. When in 1879 the "Zemlia i Volia" was revived, these two tendencies proved irreconcilable and within a few months the society split into the "Narodnaia Volia" (the "People's Will"), which advocated and practiced terrorism, and the "Chernyi Peredel" (the "Black Partition"), which did not. The former group carried out many acts of terror against individual officials and finally after several failures succeeded, in 1881, in assassinating Alexander II.

In the meantime with the growth of industrialism in Russia, industrial conflicts became more frequent and the Narodniks began to spread revolutionary propaganda and to organize the workers for political as well as economic ends. Thus in the mid-'seventies the South Russian Workers' League was formed and at the end of the decade a North Russian Workers' League. These organizations were soon broken up by the police; but the Narodniks learned from experience that the workers were far more receptive to revolutionary propaganda than the peasants. By this time, too, Marxism was beginning to penetrate circles of the radical intelligentsia. The Communist manifesto had been translated some years earlier, and in 1873 the Tsarist censorship had permitted the publication of a Russian edition of the first volume of *Das Kapital*. But to the great majority of the Narodniks Marx's doctrines were applicable to the West where industrialism was well advanced, but not to Russia where, it was hoped, the industrialist stage would be skipped.[1]

Soon after the accession of Alexander III the government dispersed the organizations of both the "Narodnaia Volia" and the "Chernyi Peredel." Several members of the latter organization, among them G. V. Plekhanov, Vera Zasulich, and P. B. Axelrod, went abroad, where they at first remained faithful to Narodnik ideas. But, separated as they were from Russian conditions and in close contact with the socialist movement in the West, they gradually moved toward the Marxist position. In 1883 Plekhanov and his friends formed

---

[1] It is interesting to note that in 1870 N. Utin, a member of the original "Zemlia i Volia," organized in Geneva a Russian section of the First International and that Marx accepted Utin's invitation to serve as "secretary for Russia" on the General Council of the International.

in Switzerland the "Emancipation of Labor" group, and in the following year published a program which, though not entirely free of Narodnik ideas, was in reality the first program of the Russian Social Democrats.

In Russia meanwhile, despite the government's measures, industrial strife continued, strikes were frequent, and workers' "circles" were formed, broken up and reformed in various industrial centers. One of these circles, organized in St. Petersburg by the Bulgarian Blagoev and called "The Party of Russian Social Democrats," established brief contact with Plekhanov's group abroad. Along with this development in the labor movement Marxism steadily gained ground among Russian intellectuals both at home and abroad. The "Emancipation of Labor" group under Plekhanov's leadership became more definitely Marxist and in 1890 began the publication of *Sotsial-Demokrat* for the dissemination of Marxist ideas. In St. Petersburg in the early 'nineties there were the so-called "legal Marxists" who used Marxist theories to explain and defend the inevitability of the industrialization of Russia. There were also revolutionary Marxists, among them V. I. Lenin, whose objectives were quite different but who were temporarily allied with the legal Marxists in combating the prevailing ideology of the Narodniks.

This alliance soon came to an end. The legal Marxists for the most part became exponents of Russian liberalism; the revolutionary Marxists and the surviving workers' circles were the founders of the Russian Social Democratic Labor party. As for the Narodnik movement, it survived both the attacks of the police and the onslaughts of the Marxists and at the beginning of the century joined both its propagandist and terrorist tendencies in the Socialist-Revolutionist party.

In the West meanwhile, with the revival and spread of the socialist movement the international organization of revolutionary labor came back to life. In July 1889 the Second International came into being at a congress in Paris called by German socialists and organized by the followers of Guesde. Like its predecessor, the new International was destined to endure storms of conflicting currents in socialist thought. Congresses at Brussels in 1891 and at Zürich in 1893 were disturbed by the anarchists and those who advocated the general strike as a substitute for political action; but at the London Congress of 1896 the anarchists were expelled and plans were laid for a permanent international socialist organization. This expulsion of the anarchists did not bring unity to the International. During the late 'nineties other tendencies took shape. A Right wing, the "opportunists," began to question the validity of revolutionary tactics and to advocate the attainment of socialism by gradual steps through legislative enactment of reform measures. Eduard Bernstein's *Die Voraussetzungen des Sozialismus und die Aufgaben der Sozialdemokratie* (1899), urging the revision of certain Marxian theories, gave a name, "revisionism," and a theoretical basis to this tendency.

The more orthodox Marxists opposed revisionism as a false interpretation of Marxist doctrine. Later two tendencies developed among the opponents of revisionism. A small number of Lefts became increasingly critical of what they regarded as the reformist opportunism of the party majority. A Center group opposing both the so-called "Russian" tactics of the Lefts and the heretical deviations of the revisionists, maintained a doctrinal orthodoxy, but in tactics tended toward compromise and expediency.

At the Paris Congress of 1900, where the International Socialist Bureau with headquarters at Brussels was established, revisionism became an issue before the International. In 1899 Millerand entered the ministry of Waldeck-Rousseau. Jaurès and others of the Right tendency approved, but the French orthodox Marxists, notably Guesde and Vaillant, and the Blanquists strongly disapproved. When Millerand's case came before the International at Paris, Kautsky, who with Bebel had been a leading opponent of revisionism in Germany, introduced a "Centrist" compromise resolution to the effect that the entrance of a socialist into a bourgeois cabinet was not a normal but merely a transitional and exceptional emergency measure; that Millerand's action raised a question of tactics rather than of principle; and that it was a dangerous experiment, profitable only if approved by a united party and if the socialist minister continued to hold the mandate of his party.[2] This resolution was adopted by a vote of 29 to 9 over Guesde's demand for an unconditional condemnation of ministerialism.

In the midst of this controversy, which had its echoes in the socialist movement in Russia, the Russian Social Democratic Labor party (R.S.D.L.P.) was organized at a congress in Minsk in 1898. But before the new party had an opportunity to establish itself it was suppressed by the government and many of its leaders were exiled to Siberia. In the meantime, economism, the Russian counterpart of revisionism, was agitating the Russian socialists both abroad and at home. The League of Russian Social Democrats, an organization of émigré groups founded in 1895 on the initiative of the "Emancipation of Labor" group, began to turn to the economist position, and in April 1900 Plekhanov and his followers withdrew from the League and made an open fight against economism. A month later the Social Democrats in Russia held an illegal conference at Pskov, laid plans for rebuilding the party organization, and decided to get in touch with the "Emancipation of Labor" group for the purpose of issuing a party newspaper. This contact led to the publication, at first in Munich and later in London, of the paper *Iskra* and the establishment of a group under the same name, which later drafted a party program and called the Second Congress in 1903. It was in connection with the publication of *Iskra* that V. I. Lenin, who had organized the League of Struggle for the Liberation of the Working Class in St. Petersburg, went abroad in 1900.

Lenin thus became acquainted with the international socialist movement and its European leaders at the time when revisionist tendencies were in full swing. There was no question about his attitude. He had been fighting economism and its variants in Russia, and he immediately carried the fight into the larger international arena, joining Plekhanov, who had been one of the first to denounce revisionism. In his articles and pamphlets of this period, Lenin attacked not only revisionism but the attitude toward it taken by the International at the Paris Congress.[3] And naturally he, like Plekhanov, was particularly anxious that the program of the reconstituted Russian Social Democratic Labor party should be free of these heresies.

The Second Congress of the R.S.D.L. party met in July 1903, first in Brussels and later in London. The party program drafted by *Iskra* and adopted by this Congress was notable for its consistent adherence to orthodox Marxian principles. It formulated clearly the Marxian postulates of a social revolution, the transfer of power to the laboring class, and the expropriation of the expropriators; and of all the European socialist party programs it alone contained a paragraph on the dictatorship of the proletariat: "The dictatorship of the proletariat—i.e., the seizure of political power by the proletariat—power by which the proletariat would be able to crush all resistance on the part of the exploiters—is a necessary condition for a social revolution."[4]

At the Second Congress also occurred the historic split in the Russian social democratic movement. Within the *Iskra* group which dominated the Congress a conflict arose over paragraph one of the party constitution dealing with party membership. One group headed by Lenin held that actual personal participation in a party organization should be required of all members, whereas another group headed by

---

[3] Translations of certain of Lenin's writings during this period are given in *Selections from Lenin*, Vol. I; *The Fight for the Programme, Party Organisation and Tactics, 1893–1904*; in Lenin's *Collected Works*, Vol. IV, *The Iskra Period 1900–1902*; in his *Selected Works*, Vol. II, *The Struggle for the Bolshevik Party (1900–1904)*; and in Elizabeth Hill and Doris Mudie (eds.), *The Letters of Lenin*, pp. 100–179. The last-named will hereafter be cited as *The Letters of Lenin*.

[4] *Vtoroi ocherednoi sezd ross. sots.-dem. rabochei partii. Polnyi tekst protokolov*, p. 2.

L. Martov maintained that anyone who merely co-operated with a party organization should be eligible for membership. The struggle thus precipitated generated very bitter feeling in the Congress, for it involved far more than the matter of eligibility for party membership; it touched the fundamental conflict of revolutionists versus moderates, which was an issue throughout the socialist movement.

When the debate ended Martov's proposal was accepted, but the victory was short-lived. First the representatives of the Bund (the All-Jewish Workers' League of Lithuania, Poland, and Russia) withdrew when their demand for a federative affiliation with the R.S.D.L. party was refused. They were soon followed by the delegates of the League of Russian Social Democrats, chiefly economists, who objected to the decision of the Congress to dissolve their organization. With the departure of these delegates who had supported Martov's resolution, his majority became the minority (i.e., *Mensheviki*) and Lenin's group became the majority (*Bolsheviki*). As a result of this victory the Bolsheviks elected two of the three members of the editorial board of the party Central Organ—Lenin and Plekhanov versus Martov. Martov's request that the board be enlarged to include three former editors of *Iskra*—Axelrod, Zasulich, and Potresov—was voted down, whereupon the Mensheviks declined to participate in any of the central institutions of the party. The Bolsheviks thereupon came to occupy all of the positions on the editorial board of the Central Organ, on the Central Committee of the party, and on the Party Council.

A month after the London Congress of the R.S.D.L. party, the German Social Democrats met at Dresden. The party, developing rapidly in numbers and political influence, had raised its membership from 2.1 millions to three millions and its representation in the Reichstag from thirty-two to fifty-six. This growth raised great hopes, particularly among the revisionists, who foresaw the election of a social democrat as Vice-President of the Reichstag and further political triumphs. But at Dresden, after fiery denunciations of revisionism by Bebel and Kautsky, the Congress by the overwhelming vote of 288 to 11 adopted a resolution definitely condemning this heresy and strengthening Kautsky's 1900 resolution on participation in bourgeois ministries. There were two significant things about this vote. First, many pronounced revisionists voted for the resolution condemning their own activities; and, second, the orthodox majority, stronger in this Congress than ever before, took no organizational measures to compel the revisionists to observe the party's orders. Rosa Luxemburg's suggestion that the heretics be expelled from the party was not even mentioned. Throughout the remainder of the prewar period the German party repeatedly declared by large majorities its adherence to orthodox Marxism and at the same time condoned the steady growth of the revisionist tendency within the party. This in general was the policy of the other parties of the International. In the pre-war period only the Bolsheviks of the R.S.D.L. party, the Bulgarian "Narrow" socialists, and the Dutch Lefts definitely organized a Left wing hostile to the accommodating spirit of the Center and to the revisionism of the Right.

At the Amsterdam Congress of the International in 1904 the Germans pressed for the adoption of their Dresden resolution and after a four-day debate, in which the protagonists were Bebel and Jaurès, the resolution was accepted and with it the declaration of the Guesdists against ministerialism. Of particular significance to the Russian Mensheviks and Bolsheviks, who were both represented at the Congress, was another resolution which demanded that in every country there should be only one socialist party and thus the unity of the movement should be preserved. On the strength of this resolution the Presidium of the International presently began to interest itself in the struggle then going on within the R.S.D.L. party.

By the summer of 1904 the complexion of the Russian party had so changed that the Mensheviks now controlled all the central party institutions and even on the Central Committee a majority of the Bolsheviks favored reconciliation with the Mensheviks. In this situation Lenin and his followers began to organize independently of the central party institutions. They began to agitate for the calling of a third congress of the party, for which purpose they set up a Bureau of the Majority Committees in St. Petersburg in November 1904 and in 1905 began to publish in Geneva their own paper, *Vpered*. This Bureau and the party Central Committee, having come to an agreement, set up an organization committee to call the party congress.[5] The leaders of the Second International, who observed with disfavor this violent dissension in the Russian party, regarded it as primarily a matter of organization and personalities and thus underestimated its significance. Most of the leaders of the Second International sided openly with the Mensheviks, who were better known in Western Europe than Lenin and his supporters and whose position was more in line with that of the majority of the International.[6] At this time Lenin's policies apparently had no supporters in the international socialist movement and even Rosa Luxemburg opposed his organizational plans.[7] In

[5] From available memoirs it would appear that this Bureau of the Majority Committees was decided upon at the meeting in August 1904 in Geneva of "22" Bolsheviks who nominated the members of the Bureau. These nominations were confirmed by the Northern, Southern, and Caucasian Conferences of the S.D. Committees in Russia; and the Bureau was set up with a section in Russia and one abroad, the latter consisting of the editorial board of *Vpered*, i.e., Lenin, Lunacharsky, Olminsky, and Vorovsky. The Bureau was abolished in March 1905, when an organization committee for calling the Third Congress of the party was formed, partly from members of the Bureau and partly from the Central Committee of the R.S.D.L. party. (R. Khabas, "Sozdanie bolshevistskogo tsentra [B.K.B.] i gazety *Vpered*," in *Proletarskaia Revoliutsiia*, 11 [34], 1924, pp. 19–32.)

[6] Kautsky expressed his opinion in an article in *Iskra*, in which among other things he said: ".... If at your congress I had had to choose between Martov and Lenin, on the basis of the entire experience of our activity in Germany, I would have pronounced myself definitely in favor of Martov. Lenin's manner of action—the elimination of Axelrod, Starover and Zasulich from the editorial board of *Iskra*—is to me no less an error. .... Had Lenin not wished a split, but had he wished instead to uphold party unity, he should have endeavored to come to an agreement with the former editors, who have made *Iskra* as great as it is now.... [and] in this case the responsibility for the initiation of this ill-fated discord falls upon Lenin." (*Iskra*, No. 66, May 15, 1904, pp. 3–4.)

[7] Her point of view was expressed in her article, "Organizatsionnye voprosy russkoi sotsial-demokratii," in *Iskra*, No. 69, July 10, 1904, pp. 2–7; also published

these circumstances the Bolsheviks declined Bebel's proposal, in February 1905, that both groups submit their differences to a court of arbitration over which he would preside.

The Third Congress of the R.S.D.L party met in the spring of 1905 at London in an atmosphere of excited anticipation, generated by the rising revolutionary tide in Russia. There were representatives of twenty Bolshevik committees present, but the representatives of nine committees delegated to the congress went not to London but to Geneva, where they took part in a separate conference with the Party Council and the editorial board of *Iskra,* which were both controlled by the Mensheviks. Thus the Third Congress was a purely Bolshevik affair. Taking advantage of this situation the Bolsheviks abolished the Party Council, made their own paper, *Proletarii,* the party organ in place of *Iskra,* and elected a new Central Committee (Lenin, Krasin, Bogdanov, Postolovsky, and Rykov) with plenary powers between conferences and with authority to name the editorial board of the central organ. Other measures taken at this Congress included the substitution of Lenin's formula regarding party membership for that of Martov which had been adopted at the Second Congress, and the addition to the party constitution of certain amendments designed to democratize its organization and increase the membership among workers. Bebel's arbitration proposal was barely touched upon, the delegates seemingly accepting Lenin's attitude that this was a purely Russian question to be settled by the party itself. But the Congress did not close the door to an understanding with the Mensheviks but adopted a resolution "not to be published" directing the new Central Committee "to adopt all necessary measures for the preparation and elaboration of conditions on which fusion with the section of the R.S.D.L. party which has split off can be accomplished. The final approval of these conditions must be left to a new party con-

in German in *Neue Zeit,* Nos. 42 and 43, 1903–1904, pp. 484–92 and 529–35. This was a reply to Lenin's pamphlet, *Shag vpered dva shaga nazad,* in which he discussed the events of the Second Congress of the R.S.D.L. party.

gress. . . . ."[8] Another resolution of this Congress, significant in the light of events of 1917–18, was the authorization
for all party organizations to support the peasantry in all
revolutionary measures including the confiscation of lands
of landowners, the state, churches, and monasteries.

With the spread of the revolutionary movement in Russia
in the summer of 1905 the differences between the Bolsheviks
and Mensheviks diminished in importance and when the International Socialist Bureau proposed a conference of representatives of both groups under its auspices the Bolsheviks
accepted and selected their representatives. Events in Russia
and the return to Russia of many of the party leaders made
it necessary to postpone the conference indefinitely. Moreover the revolutionary current was sweeping the two groups
together regardless of outside intervention. Without waiting
for the leaders to settle their disputes, the Mensheviks and
the Bolsheviks in the provinces were joining forces. In December 1905 during the Moscow uprising the Menshevik
group made certain concessions to the Bolsheviks on several
issues, including the question of party membership. A Bolshevik conference at Tammerfors in the same month voted
for unification, and in January 1906 the Bolshevik Central
Committee and the Menshevik Organization Committee were
fused into a single body for the purpose of calling a unification congress. This, the Fourth Congress, met at Stockholm
in April–May, 1906. Once again the Mensheviks had a majority, which was reflected in the resolutions of the Congress
and in the election of seven Mensheviks and three Bolsheviks
to the Central Committee. The Congress declared the hostility of the party to the new State Duma, but voted for
participation in the elections over the protest of the Bolsheviks, who favored a boycott. The Congress also revised the
Bolsheviks' resolution on the agrarian question demanding
"municipalization" rather than outright confiscation of the
privately owned, church, and state lands.

[8] *Tretii ocherednoi sezd rossiiskoi sotsial-demokraticheskoi rabochei partii 1905
goda. Polnyi tekst protokolov*, p. 394.

Shortly after the return of the delegates to Russia in July 1906 the Tsar dissolved the First State Duma. There followed the Viborg manifesto in which a majority of the Duma members including Constitutional Democrats, Trudoviks, and others, but not the Social Democrats, appealed to the people not to pay taxes or furnish recruits to the army until a new Duma was summoned. The Central Committee of the R.S.D.L. party called for a general strike and the Socialist-Revolutionists urged a peasant rising. Mutinies broke out at Sveaborg and Kronstadt but these disturbances were soon put down.

With the ebb of the revolutionary tide the differences among the Russian Social Democrats revived, and such unity as had been achieved during the revolution and at the Stockholm Congress was soon completely destroyed. The years which followed were full of ideological confusion and bitter factional strife. The R.S.D.L. party continued nominally to exist; however, it was no longer a party with two major tendencies—Bolshevik and Menshevik—but a congeries of groups, large and small, continually shifting and maneuvering for tactical advantage and bitterly debating the issues of revolutionary doctrine, tactics, and organization in press and pamphlet and at occasional conferences. The Fifth Congress in 1907 was the last congress in which all the principal groups which were recognized as a part of or affiliated with the Russian Social Democratic Labor party took part. Basically the cause of this party disintegration was the subsidence of revolutionary sentiment in Russia during the period of generally increased prosperity from 1907 to 1913 and the success of the government under Stolypin's efficiently ruthless guidance in breaking up revolutionary party organizations in Russia. The differences among the party leaders who were abroad and thus escaped imprisonment or exile to Siberia were due to irreconcilable interpretations, first of the lessons of the revolution of 1905, secondly of the reasons for the failure of the revolution to spread during and after the uprising in December 1905, and thirdly of the situation after the dissolution of the Second State Duma in 1907 and the promulgation of the new electoral law. These divergent interpretations not only kept the main currents of Bolshevism and Menshevism from achieving any degree of unification but also split these two main tendencies into discordant factions.

One issue which added much fuel to the flames of intraparty controversy concerned the relation of the party to the labor movement. As early as the summer of 1905 Axelrod had proposed the calling of a nonpartisan labor congress for the purpose of bringing the broad masses of the workers into the socialist movement. In 1906 the proposal was revived. Certain Mensheviks urged that the formation of nonpartisan labor organizations and the holding of a nonpartisan labor congress were the best means of broadening contacts with the workers and influencing them in the direction of the party's aims. The Bolsheviks condemned this proposal on the ground that its practical effect would be not to reorganize and strengthen the party but to destroy its identity and in fact to liquidate it.

The issue came up again at the Fifth Congress of the party, which met in London in the spring of 1907, the last party congress until the summer of 1917. At London the Bolsheviks slightly outnumbered the Mensheviks, but the balance of power was held by the delegations from the Social Democracy of Poland and Lithuania, the Lettish Social Democratic party, and the Jewish Bund,[9] which had affiliated with the R.S.D.L. party at the Stockholm unification congress. The Central Committee elected by the Congress consisting of five Bolsheviks, four Mensheviks, and six representatives of the national parties reflected the distribution of voting strength. The Congress declined to endorse the Bolshevik criticism of the Mensheviks in the Duma and in the outgoing Central Committee and adopted the Menshevik resolution disbanding the fighting squads and forbidding

[9] Brief accounts of these parties and their relations with the R.S.D.L. party are given in *The Bolsheviks and World Revolution*. For the formation of the Social Democracy of Poland and Lithuania, see also below, p. 501.

armed raids and "expropriations." On the other hand, the Congress voted against the Menshevik labor congress proposal and adopted with amendments the Bolshevik resolutions on the attitude toward nonproletarian parties and on the abolition of the neutrality of the trade unions. The Congress declared it the policy of the party to make clear the futility of the Duma as a means of realizing the demands of the workers, peasants, and petty bourgeoisie, the impossibility of securing freedom by parliamentary means, and the inevitability of open conflict with the armed forces of absolutism—a conflict aiming at the transfer of power to representatives of the people and the calling of a constituent assembly elected by universal, equal, direct, and secret suffrage.

In the years following the Fifth Congress certain Mensheviks tended to minimize illegal party activity and to emphasize the importance of developing connections with such legal organizations as trade unions, co-operatives, etc. Some even suggested the abolition of the party Central Committee. The advocates of this line denied that they were "liquidators," as they were accused of being. They insisted that they were seeking the best and most effective method of promoting the cause of Social Democracy in the face of the destruction of the old party apparatus by Stolypin's police. The Bolsheviks maintained that those whom they called "liquidators" were straying from the straight and narrow revolutionary path into the swamp of opportunism and that their object was to transform the party from a revolutionary organization into a reformist party like those dominating the Second International. Plekhanov also opposed this tendency and in 1909 organized a group of Menshevik "Party Men" (or "Party Mensheviks") and withdrew from the *Golos Sotsial-Demokrata*, which had been established in Geneva the preceding year as the leading Menshevik organ abroad.

While this controversy was at its height the Bolsheviks were beset with internal dissensions. Lenin had originally advocated a boycott of the Duma elections. Later, in the light of the changed situation in Russia, he abandoned this position and urged the utilization of the Duma, the elections, and other legal means of propaganda along with illegal activities as the most effective party tactics. A number of leading Bolsheviks regarded this as a Menshevik heresy. Some demanded an immediate recall of the party deputies in the Duma; others proposed an ultimatum to the deputies and then their recall.

At about the same time another tendency was reflected in the writings of Lunacharsky and Bogdanov and propagated in a school for party workers organized at Capri under the patronage of Gorky. This movement sought to harmonize Marxism with the empirical monism of Mach and Avenarius, and against it Lenin wrote his treatise, *Materialism and Empirio-Criticism; Critical Notes concerning a Reactionary Philosophy.*[10] In 1909 the advocates of recall and the Machists formed a literary group which took its name from the publication *Vpered* issued by the group in Paris in 1910. The *Vpered* group, among whom were Gorky, Lunacharsky, Bogdanov, Aleksinsky, and Pokrovsky, claimed that they and not Lenin and his friends were the true representatives of pure Bolshevism. Further they charged that the intolerance and personal ambitions of certain party workers, among whom they presumably included Lenin, were responsible for the factional strife.

The efforts of a nonfactional group of Bolsheviks and of Trotsky and his associates in Vienna to neutralize these complicated antagonisms accomplished little except to invite condemnation by Lenin, whose formula for unification was to purge the party of the liquidators who deviated to the Right and of the *Vpered* partisans who deviated to the Left from the attitude on party tactics maintained by his own and Plekhanov's groups.

The warfare waged by these various groups abroad and the wholesale arrests of party workers in Russia made it

[10] Volume XIII of Lenin's *Collected Works*. The circumstances under which this controversy arose are discussed by A. Deborin in the introduction to that volume.

practically impossible for the party apparatus to function. The Central Committee elected in 1907 was supposed to meet every three months. It held one meeting in 1908 and none in the following year. In the meantime some of the members of the Committee had left the party, others were inactive, and not all the vacancies were filled. But finally in January 1910 the Central Committee held what proved to be its last plenary session and made another and last attempt to compose these differences. The resolutions emphasized the necessity of winning the masses by both legal and illegal activities, of strengthening the illegal party, and of setting up an efficient Central Committee. The extreme Right tendency (liquidationism) and that of the extreme Left (the advocates of recall of the Duma deputies) were condemned and all the factions were urged to abolish their organizations. Two Bolsheviks, two Mensheviks, and a Polish Social Democrat were appointed editors of the Central Organ, the *Sotsial-Demokrat,* which was expected to replace the Bolshevik *Proletarii* and the Menshevik *Golos Sotsial-Demokrata.* The Central Committee delegated Kamenev as its representative on the editorial board of *Pravda,* published in Vienna by Trotsky's nonfactional group, and promised financial support to this paper. The *Vpered* group was permitted to continue as a publishing group. The Central Committee proper was transferred to Russia and a Bureau of the Central Committee was set up abroad, consisting of a Bolshevik, a Menshevik, a Pole, a Lett, and a member of the Bund, with Karl Kautsky, Franz Mehring, and Klara Zetkin to supervise the use of the funds placed at the disposal of the party center by the Bolsheviks. All these concessions, compromises, and modifications of the party machinery failed to achieve their purpose. Within a few weeks after their adoption charges began to fly back and forth of sabotage and violation of the decisions of the conference, of factionalism, of duplicity, of betrayal of principles, and of violation of agreements and the struggle between the discordant factions went on in even deeper bitterness.

During the period we have been discussing, the three tendencies within the German social democratic movement which have already been referred to became more clearly established. The revisionists, despite official party denunciation, continued to flourish. A Center led by Bebel and later strengthened by Kautsky's support waged theoretical warfare with the reformists and presently had to do battle against the Left which, under Rosa Luxemburg's leadership, was steadily increasing its forces.[11] The German Lefts, however, in spite of their increasing strength, did not set up a separate organization during the prewar period.

During the years in which Lenin was a representative of the R.S.D.L. party on the International Socialist Bureau, where his motions were usually defeated by the more conservative majority, he tried to strengthen his ties with Rosa Luxemburg and her supporters on the basis of their opposition to opportunism. But the German Lefts were critical of the Bolsheviks for their alleged "Blanquism," for their part in the split in the R.S.D.L. party, and for their advocacy of a united front of the proletarians with the movements for national self-determination which Lenin understood as involving the right of separation. Rosa Luxemburg, moreover, was an advocate of the doctrine of permanent revolution.

While the Bolsheviks and their natural allies in Germany and elsewhere remained somewhat alienated from each other by these points of difference, there was a growing rapprochement between the Mensheviks and the German Center and during the same period a general strengthening of reformism throughout the labor movement in Europe, Russia, and America. Because of the strength of the Right and Center, the Lefts were usually voted down at the international so-

---

[11] In a letter to Klara Zetkin written upon her return from Russia in 1907 Rosa Luxemburg said that Bebel and the other "old men" at the head of the party had gone over entirely to parliamentarism and would oppose any attack from the Left on opportunism or any attempt to give expression to the discontent of the rank and file with leadership of the party officials. (I. Lents [J. Lenz], *Istoriia Vtorogo Internatsionala*, p. 137, and in German in *Illustrierte Geschichte der deutschen Revolution*, p. 62.)

cialist congresses. An exception was the adoption at the Stuttgart Congress in 1907, under circumstances described below, of four amendments endorsed by Lenin, Rosa Luxemburg, and Martov to Bebel's resolution on militarism. At this Congress Lenin attempted without much result to bring together the revolutionary Marxists of the different national parties. At the Copenhagen Congress in 1910 Lenin made another attempt to draw more definitely the lines between the revolutionary and the opportunist wings of the Second International but accomplished little more than at Stuttgart. Resolutions were adopted at Copenhagen on recent events in Persia and the suppression of the Turkish revolution with a general condemnation of capitalist colonial policy and an appeal for struggle against the reactionary forces of Russian Tsarism, but the Congress did not accept Lenin's evaluation of the significance for the international labor movement of the rising opposition to imperialism and of the importance of the beginnings of revolutionary action in the East to the revolutionary movement in Russia and Europe. Lenin's amendments to the resolution on co-operatives were also defeated and in an article on the outcome of the Congress he stressed the weakness of the Center before the Right on this issue and declared that the settling of accounts with the reformists was merely postponed.

Along with the more general issues affecting the International as a whole, the tangled affairs of the Russian factions came before the Congress. Lenin and Plekhanov protested against the attacks of the Menshevik liquidators; and the Central Committee of the R.S.D.L. party, then under Bolshevik control, issued a report in French on the state of affairs in Russia with an analysis and refutation of the program of the liquidators.

The years 1910 to 1913 saw a revival of social unrest marked by strikes, demonstrations, and an increased activity in the more revolutionary groups of the socialist movement. There were bitterly contested strikes in France, England, America, Germany, and Russia and revolutionary movements in Mexico, China, and the Near East. These events stimulated the action of the more revolutionary elements of the socialist parties. In Germany, against the background of workers' demonstrations over the inadequacy of the government's proposed reform of the Prussian franchise, Rosa Luxemburg, Karl Radek, and Pannekoek engaged Kautsky in a debate on revolutionary tactics. Luxemburg advocated the use of a general strike in Germany, citing in support of her argument the success of the general strike in the Russian revolution of 1905 and the fact that this strike had developed into an armed uprising. She held that to postpone the seizure of power on the ground that it was premature was equivalent to renouncing such an attempt altogether.[12] On the other hand, Kautsky advocated the "strategy of attrition" (*Ermattungsstrategie*), a defensive struggle of the working class, instead of the "strategy of overthrow" (*Niederwerfungsstrategie*) for which Germany was not prepared.[13]

In the midst of this debate the Baden Social Democracy, one of the strongholds of revisionism, voted for government credit. This was done against the orders of the party and in violation of one of its fundamental principles.

Kautsky asked Rosa Luxemburg to postpone the discussion of the general strike until he had dealt with the Badeners; but she refused, and Kautsky had to carry on his fight on two fronts. He characterized the situation in this fashion: "If we look up the duchies of Baden and Luxemburg on the map we shall find that the town of Trier—Karl Marx's native town—is situated between them. If we go from there to the left across the border we shall come to Luxemburg, but if we take a sharp turn to the right and cross the Rhine we shall then come to Baden. This relationship on the map symbolizes the present situation within the German Social Democracy."[14]

[12] R. Luxemburg, "Die Theorie und die Praxis," *Neue Zeit*, No. 43, July 22, 1910, pp. 564–78; No. 44, July 29, 1910, pp. 626–42.

[13] K. Kautsky, "Was nun?" *Neue Zeit*, No. 28, April 8, 1910, pp. 33–40; No. 29, April 15, 1910, pp. 68–80.

[14] K. Kautsky, "Zwischen Baden und Luxemburg," *Neue Zeit*, No. 45, August 5, 1910, pp. 652–67.

The Baden and Luxemburg issues were debated at the Magdeburg Congress of the German S.D. party, September 18–24, 1910. The Congress condemned the conduct of the Baden socialists and on Rosa Luxemburg's motion approved the use of the general strike by the Prussian Social Democrats. The second part of her amendment dealing with propaganda for the general strike was withdrawn with her consent.[15]

Martov and other Mensheviks seized the occasion of this controversy in the German party to justify their own attitude in their conflicts with the Bolsheviks. They sought to identify Kautsky's position with their own and claimed his concurrence in their views of the Russian revolution of 1905. Kautsky denied the latter claim, but articles by Trotsky and others appeared in *Neue Zeit* and other German periodicals in what became a general offensive against the positions of Rosa Luxemburg and Lenin.[16]

Apparently Kautsky asked Lenin not to engage in a polemic on this issue in the German press, but Lenin replied to the attacks in an article which he outlined but which was written and signed by Marchlewski and published in *Neue Zeit*.[17]

In his letter telling Marchlewski what to put in his article Lenin said: "What a pity Kautsky and Wurm do not see the vileness and meanness of such articles as those of Martov and Trotsky. I shall try to write Kautsky at least privately to explain matters. It is simply scandalous that Martov and Trotsky are lying with impunity and write libels under the guise of 'scientific' articles!! . . . . All the Mensheviks (especially *Nasha Zaria, Vozrozhdenie,* and *Zhizn*) have joined

[15] "Die Wahlrechtsdebatte," *Vorwärts*, No. 224, September 24, 1910, pp. 1–2. For the proceedings of the Congress see "Parteitag der deutschen Sozialdemokratie zu Magdeburg," *Vorwärts Beilagen*, Nos. 220–225, September 20—September 25, 1910. Also *Vorwärts*, No. 224, September 24, 1910, p. 3.

[16] *Pisma P. B. Akselroda i Yu. O. Martova*, I, 202–203. Martov's "Die preussische Diskussion und die russische Erfahrung," *Neue Zeit*, No. 51, September 16, 1910, pp. 907–19, and in Russian as "Konflikty v germanskoi rabochei partii," in *Nasha Zaria*, No. 7, 1910; "Erklärung," in *Neue Zeit*, No. 1, October 7, 1910, p. 27.

[17] J. Karski [Marchlewski], "Ein Missverständnis," *Neue Zeit*, No. 4, October 28, 1910, pp. 100–107.

the dispute between Rosa Luxemburg and Kautsky in order
to proclaim K. Kautsky a 'Menshevik.' Martov is sweating
blood in order to deepen the gulf between Rosa Luxemburg
and K. Kautsky by resorting to *kleinliche und miserable Di-
plomatie*. These *elende* tricks cannot succeed. The revolutionary social democrats can argue about when the *Niederwerfungsstrategie* should be applied in Germany, but not
about the adequacy of *Niederwerfungsstrategie* for Russia
in 1905. To deny this strategy for Russia in 1905 has not
even occurred to Kautsky. Only liberals and the German and
Russian Quessels can deny this."[18]

The Moroccan diplomatic crisis of the summer of 1911
was the occasion of another flare-up in the German Social
Democratic party when Rosa Luxemburg criticized the party
Presidium for refusing, as requested by the I.S.B., to take
a stand in the early days of July against German intervention.
Only at the Jena Congress in September was a resolution
against intervention adopted. At the same time Bebel and the
Center joined the revisionists in deploring Luxemburg's criticism of the party Presidium, and she was charged with "un-
comradely"[19] action before a meeting of the International
Socialist Bureau at Zürich on September 23, 1911. According to Zinoviev, when Lenin came to Rosa Luxemburg's defense "the thunder and lightning descended upon him as well.
Vladimir Ilich [Lenin] appealed to Plekhanov . . . . but . . . .
Comrade Plekhanov replied that the ear should not grow
beyond the forehead, that we [Russians] should keep silent;
that when we had millions of members as the German Social
Democracy had, then we should also be considered. But for
the time being we were merely 'poor relations.' After listening to Plekhanov, Vladimir Ilich slammed the door and left
the meeting. Thereupon Comrade Lenin began to approach

---

[18] Lenin, *Sochineniia*, XIV, 352–56. Lenin's letter was dated October 7, 1910.
Ludwig Quessel was a revisionist.

[19] In an article, "Um Marokko," in No. 168 of *Leipziger Volkszeitung*, July
24, 1911, pp. 1–2, Rosa Luxemburg had quoted Molkenbuhr's letter to Huysmans
as an example of the attitude of the party Presidium toward intervention.

more and more the elements which supported Rosa Luxemburg."[20]

At about this time there was apparently a plan on foot for Kautsky, Mehring, and Klara Zetkin, the so-called "depositors," under whose trusteeship the R.S.D.L. party funds had been placed, to call a unification conference of all contending Russian groups. Such a plan Rosa Luxemburg wrote at the time was a "fool idea." "At this conference, naturally, only a handful of fighting cocks *living abroad* would rival in clamoring for the ear and soul of the German trustees, and to expect anything of *these* cocks is pure delusion. They are already so involved in quarrels and so embittered, that a general confab will merely give them an opportunity to unburden themselves of their old, oldest and freshest insults, so that oil will merely be poured into the flames. *The only way* to preserve unity is to bring about a general conference with delegates *from Russia,* for the people in Russia all desire peace and unity, and they are the only power that can bring the fighting cocks living abroad to reason. Therefore, to do nothing else than to insist upon *this* general party conference and as for the rest to hold ears, eyes and noses shut, would in my opinion be the only correct attitude to take. Unfortunately, the idea of that new conference with the Germans has already caused great confusion among the Russians. Trotsky brags in 'strictly confidential' letters that *he* is the big man who will get everything back on the right track. The Mensheviks who stick to him have taken courage and are boycotting the general party conference that has been prepared, and the Bolsheviks together with the Poles have been greatly confused by this gossip."[21]

[20] G. Zinoviev, "Lenin i Komintern," *Sochineniia,* XV, 254. Safarov, who was present, also mentions the incident and adds that "Returning home from the meeting, Ilich swore violently, called everybody 'scoundrels,' and was especially indignant over the conduct of the Germans." (G. Safarov, "O tovarishche Lenine," in *O Lenine, Sbornik vospominanii,* I, 75.)

[21] Luise Kautsky [ed.], *Rosa Luxemburg Letters to Karl and Luise Kautsky from 1896 to 1918,* pp. 163–64. There is evidence that during the Jena Congress the Mensheviks held private conferences with Kautsky and Haase regarding the Russian party funds and that pains were taken to keep these conversations from the

The proposed party conference to which Rosa Luxemburg referred was being prepared on the initiative of the Leninist Bolsheviks with the co-operation of the Poles and some of the Party Mensheviks. Plekhanov and most of his followers soon withdrew from the preparatory commission, and the Bolsheviks on their own responsibility called the Conference which met in Prague in January 1912. The Conference, which included party workers from Russia, was entirely controlled by the Leninist Bolsheviks, who had eighteen of the twenty delegates. The Conference adopted a number of resolutions, all of which were edited or in part written by Lenin, dealing with the current situation and the tasks of the party, the work of the party deputies in the Duma, trade unions, and strikes. On the ground that the old Central Committee had ceased to function and was therefore incapable of calling a new party congress, the Conference assumed the powers of a party congress, denounced the liquidators and expelled those so charged from the party, elected a new Central Committee,[22] and established a new Central Organ—*Pravda.*[23]

The preparations of the Leninist Bolsheviks for the Prague Conference caused great indignation among the other party factions. The leaders of these groups thereupon set up in January 1912 their own organization committee for the purpose of calling a "general" party conference. This committee, supported by Mensheviks (but not the Plekhanovists), the Caucasian Regional Committee, the Letts, the Bundists, the *Vpered* group, and Trotsky's Non-factional Social Democrats, held a meeting in Paris in March 1912, and in resolu-

---

knowledge of Zetkin and Luxemburg. (*Pisma P. B. Akselroda i Yu. O. Martova,* I, 217.)

[22] Among the members of the new Central Committee were Lenin, Zinoviev, Ordzhonikidze, and Malinovsky. Stalin was soon afterward co-opted to the committee. Malinovsky was later exposed as a police agent and on his return to Russia after the November revolution was tried by the Soviet government, condemned, and executed.

[23] This newspaper began to come out in St. Petersburg on April 22, 1912, and hence the name *Pravdists,* denoting allegiance to the resolutions of the Prague Conference and adherence to the Leninist Bolshevik line.

tions denounced the Prague Conference as a *coup d'état,* accused the Leninist Bolsheviks of forcing a party split, and urged all party groups to refuse to recognize the acts of the Prague Conference. Following these preliminaries a conference met in Vienna in August 1912, attended by representatives of groups in the Organization Committee and delegates from several other factions, including several party workers from Russia. Aleksinsky, representing the *Vpered* group, disagreed with the platform and withdrew. The Plekhanovists refused to attend. The Conference adopted resolutions on the platform for the elections to the Fourth Duma, universal suffrage, the land problem, and cultural national autonomy. The Organization Committee was re-elected as a permanent body,[24] the Menshevik rival of the Central Committee named by the Bolsheviks at Prague. Out of this Conference came what was known in party literature as the "August bloc" against the Bolsheviks. This alliance was short-lived. Trotsky soon withdrew, others did likewise, and the bloc gradually disintegrated.

While these alliances, blocs, and conferences were forming and reforming with a steady rise in the temperature of the contending factions, the Germans made further efforts to establish unity among the Russians. The German S.D. party proposed a unification congress in connection with the election campaign for the Fourth State Duma in the spring of 1912. Nothing came of this nor of a similar proposal made in October of the same year by Plekhanov and supported by Haase at a meeting of the International Socialist Bureau. The conflict continued unabated and in the autumn of 1913 the last connecting organizational link between the Mensheviks and the Bolsheviks was broken when the Bolshevik deputies withdrew from the R.S.D.L. party group in the Fourth State Duma and organized an independent group. This action had been decided upon at the Bolshevik confer-

---

[24] During the World War the Menshevik Organization Committee in Russia was represented abroad by a Secretariat, members of which attended various socialist conferences on behalf of the Organization Committee of the R.S.D.L. party.

ence at Poronino in October of that year. At about this time
Rosa Luxemburg brought up before the International a new
proposal to call a unification conference of representatives of
all the Russian groups, and in December 1913 the International Socialist Bureau adopted a resolution to that effect. All
the Russian factions agreed to the conference, and the Bolsheviks even urged that preparations for it be completed as
rapidly as possible. To prepare the way for the meeting
Vandervelde visited Russia in June 1914. The Conference,
attended by representatives of all the Russian organizations
calling themselves social democratic, met in Brussels under
the chairmanship of Vandervelde and Kautsky, July 16–17,
1914. Little was accomplished beyond declaring the feasi-
bility of unification of all factions and deciding to publish a
manifesto urging unity and condemning the schismatic policy
of the Bolsheviks. Thus, despite a decade of effort within the
party and outside to re-establish some kind of unity, no central
party organization guided the reviving revolutionary movement of the Russian workers in 1913 and 1914 and no generally recognized leader or group held the allegiance of Russian party workers living in a score of cities and towns of
Western Europe. Instead, the Russian Social Democrats
faced the issue of the war with their leadership split into a
dozen factions.[25]

Before any further action could be taken in this matter
the International was overwhelmed by the events of the last
week of July and the first days of August. On July 23 Austria-Hungary sent its ultimatum to Serbia and five days later
declared war. On the following day, July 29, the International Socialist Bureau held an extraordinary session in Brussels attended by representatives of socialist parties in France,
Germany, Great Britain, Poland, Russia, Italy, Holland,
Switzerland, Denmark, Spain, and Austria-Hungary. At
the sessions of the I.S.B. the delegates reported on and discussed the situation in the countries actually at war or on the
verge of it, and it was unanimously decided not to postpone

---

[25] *Pisma P. B. Akselroda i Yu. O. Martova*, I, 292–93.

the international socialist congress scheduled to take place in
Vienna August 23 but to advance the date to August 9 and to
hold the meeting at Paris with "the War and the Proletariat"
as the first topic on the agenda. It was further decided that
the proletarians of all countries, and especially those of Germany, France, Great Britain, and Italy, should extend and
intensify their demonstrations against war and for the settlement of the Austro-Serbian conflict by arbitration.

The proclamations, appeals, and demonstrations of socialist and labor organizations failed to check the spread of
war. On August 1, Germany declared war on Russia, and
two days later on France. On August 4, after German troops
had entered Belgium, came the British declaration of war.
There was, of course, no congress of the International in
August 1914 nor any further attempt to restore unity among
the Russian Social Democrats.[26]

[26] In addition to the works cited in this section see also: Lenin, *Sochineniia,*
VII and VIII; "Die Resolution zur Marokkoangelegenheit," *3. Beilage des Vorwärts,* No. 213, September 12, 1911, p. 2; "Sozialdemokratischer Parteitag," *3.
Beilage des Vorwärts,* No. 213, September 12, 1911, p. 1; "Sitzung des Internationalen Sozialistischen Bureaus," *Vorwärts,* No. 254, October 30, 1912, pp. 2–3 and
1. Beilage des Vorwärts, No. 256, November 1, 1912, pp. 1–2; *Londonskii sezd
rossiiskoi sots. demokr. rab. partii sostoiavshiisia v 1907 g. Polnyi tekst protokolov; Protokoly obedinitelnogo sezda rossiiskoi sotsial-demokraticheskoi rabochei
partii sostoiavshegosia v Stokgolme v 1906 godu; Prazhskaia konferentsiia RSDRP
1912 goda. Stati i dokumenty;* V. Vaganian, *G. V. Plekhanov. Opyt kharakteristiki sotsialno-politicheskikh vozzrenii;* L. Martov, *Istoriia rossiiskoi sotsial-
demokratii. Period 1898–1907 g.* (3d ed.); *Izveshchenie o konferentsii organizatsii
R.S.-D.R.P.* (published by the Organization Committee of the R.S.D.L. party, September, 1912); V. N. Nevsky, *Istoriia R.K.P. (b). Kratkii ocherk* (2d ed.); N.
Popov, *Outline History of the Communist Party of the Soviet Union,* I; O. Veiland, "Avgustovskii blok (1911–1914 g.g.)," *Proletarskaia Revoliutsiia,* No. 1 (60),
1927, pp. 125–83; D. Kardashev, "K istorii zarozhdeniia biuro komitetov bolshinstva," *Proletarskaia Revoliutsiia,* No. 10 (93), 1929, pp. 80–95, and No. 1 (96),
1930, pp. 47–67; O. Bosh, "Prazhskaia konferentsiia (Yanvar 1912 g.)," *Proletarskaia Revoliutsiia,* No. 4 (39), 1925, pp. 179–206; and the following articles based
on documentary sources and dealing directly with the topics discussed in this
section: S. Bantke, "V. I. Lenin i bolshevizm na mezhdunarodnoi arene v dovoennyi period," *Proletarskaia Revoliutsiia,* Nos. 2–3 (85–86), 1929, pp. 3–57; G. Beshkin, "Borba s likvidatorstvom na mezhdunarodnoi arene v dovoennye gody,"
Proletarskaia Revoliutsiia, No. 9 (104), 1930, pp. 3–34; M. M. Mikhailov, "Lenin
v borbe s opportunizmom v mezhdunarodnoi sotsial-demokratii (do 1904 goda),"
Krasnaia Letopis, Nos. 1–2 (46–47), 1932, pp. 5–21; K. Pol, "Bolsheviki i dovoennyi II Internatsional," *Proletarskaia Revoliutsiia,* Nos. 2–3 (109–110), 1931,
pp. 22–58 and 4–5 (111–112), 1931, pp. 35–79; A. Slutsky, "Bolsheviki o germanskoi

A. The International Socialist Bureau and the
Menshevik-Bolshevik Controversy

The first attempt of outsiders to bring the Mensheviks and Bolsheviks together was Bebel's proposal, February 3, 1905, of a court of arbitration to which each party should nominate two arbitrators, who, with Bebel as chairman, should constitute the court. The Mensheviks accepted and nominated Kautsky and Zetkin.[27] Lenin replied, on February 7, in the letter given below, that neither he nor his associates could take the responsibility of accepting or rejecting the proposal, which would be referred to the forthcoming Third Congress of the party. He also called Bebel's attention to the letter to Greulich containing an explanation of the split in the Russian party. The Bureau of the Majority Committees also replied to Bebel, emphasizing that the split was not a matter of personalities but "a clash of political ideas" and this could be remedied not by a court of arbitration but only by a party congress.[28] On February 22 Lenin wrote another letter to Bebel signed by "N.N.," an unidentified member of the Russian section of the Bureau, in which the German social democratic leader was urged to attend the Third Congress of the R.S.D.L. party and to prevail upon the Mensheviks to do likewise.[29] Neither Bebel nor the Mensheviks appeared at the

S.-D. v period ee predvoennogo krizisa," *Proletarskaia Revoliutsiia,* No. 6 (101), 1930, pp. 38–72. Slutsky's article called forth strong criticism on the part of the Russian Communist party leaders. Stalin denounced the author as having written an "anti-Party and semi-Trotskyan article." In a letter to the editorial board of *Proletarskaia Revoliutsiia,* translated and published in his book *Leninism,* II, 446, Stalin wrote that he could not "refrain from protesting against the publication of Slutsky's article .... as a discussion article, since the question of Lenin's Bolshevism ...., the question as to whether Lenin *was* or *was not* a real Bolshevik cannot be converted into a subject of discussion." A bibliography of Russian sources, such as articles, recollections, and documents dealing with Lenin as the organizer and leader of the party during the various stages of its development, was compiled by A. D. Eikhengolts and published under the title "Lenin-vozhd VKP (b) (Bibliograficheskie materialy)," in *Proletarskaia Revoliutsiia,* No. 3, 1934, pp. 273–94.

27 *Iskra,* No. 86, February 3, 1905, p. 8.
28 *Leninskii Sbornik,* V, 172–74, 171.
29 *Ibid.,* 182–83.

Third Congress, held in London in May, and no action was taken on the arbitration proposal. The delegates who referred to the matter echoed the sentiments expressed by Lenin in his reply to Bebel. Arbitration was in effect declined, and the new Central Committee notified the International Socialist Bureau that pending the selection of a successor to Plekhanov as Russian representative on the International Socialist Bureau all official business should be done with Lenin.[30] The International Socialist Bureau, however, asked Plekhanov for his version of what had taken place and, having received it, continued to recognize him as the Russian representative. The Bolsheviks strenuously objected to this decision, to Plekhanov's version, and to the attitude of the German socialist papers.

Referring to Plekhanov's own statement[31] that he could not represent the party in the International unless confirmed in that office by both groups, Lenin urged the Central Committee to revoke Plekhanov's appointment as representative of the party and to appoint a Bolshevik to take part in a conciliation conference (newly proposed by the I.S.B.) on condition that this conference should be merely a preliminary discussion.[32] The Central Committee acted according to Lenin's recommendation and appointed its representatives. But the conciliation conference never met. Revolutionary events in Russia overshadowed party disputes and called home from abroad the leaders of both factions.

---

[30] Lenin, "Pismo Mezhdunarodnomu Sotsialisticheskomu Biuro," *Sochineniia,* VII, 310.

[31] In a letter to the I.S.B., May 29, 1905, *Iskra,* No. 101, June 1, 1905, p. 8, reprinted in Lenin, *Sochineniia,* XXVIII, 472. English translation in *The Letters of Lenin,* pp. 240–41.

[32] *Leninskii Sbornik,* V, 479–82; 483–86; Lenin, *Sochineniia,* VIII, 206. Bebel had suggested that the conflict could be more easily settled by referring it to a small group rather than to the plenum of the I.S.B., but added that it "might take several days." (Mikhailov, "Lenin v borbe s opportunizmom v mezhdunarodnoi sotsial-demokratii [do 1904 goda]," *Krasnaia Letopis,* Nos. 1–2 [46–47], 1932, p. 16.)

BEBEL'S PROPOSAL TO ARBITRATE THE BOLSHEVIK-MENSHEVIK DIFFERENCES

[Bebel to Lenin, February 3, 1905][33]

RESPECTED COMRADE!

From various sides the Presidium of the German Social Democracy is being asked to attempt to intervene in the sad conflict between the partisans of *Vpered* and *Iskra*. The conflict, which originated long ago, now has an especially detrimental effect upon the condition of the party, in view of the state of affairs in Russia.

I have been commissioned to preside over the court of arbitration which must be composed of two representatives of each of the disputing parties and myself. The court will announce a verdict concerning the disputed points.

The two representatives whom each party nominates, however, must belong to neither the Russian nor the Polish nationality, nor to any of the nations which are subject to the Russian government (Letts, Finns, etc.) in order that there may be no suspicion of the judges' impartiality.

The court of arbitration must examine this matter objectively.

At the same time I presume that should you and your friends accept this court of arbitration and elect judges to that court, you and your friends will be willing also to submit to the verdict of this court of arbitration.

The court of arbitration must be held at *Zürich*.

You will be notified of the time of the sitting of the court as soon as the arbitrators are appointed by both sides and both sides express their agreement to the conditions under which the court of arbitration will sit.

A further condition is that *from the day when you and your friends decide to accept the court of arbitration, all polemics with the side, against' which you have struggled until now, must be discontinued.*

It stands to reason that identical promises will be demanded from the opposite side.

I presume that you and your friends will be glad to put an end to the split and mutual struggle between the party comrades, who adhere to the same fundamental basis. The news about this split has stirred up great confusion and definite discontent in the international social democracy and everybody expects that after a free discussion both sections will find a common basis for struggle against the common enemy.

I beg you kindly to notify me as soon as possible of your own and your friends' decisions.

With a social democratic greeting.   A. BEBEL

---

[33] *Leninskii Sbornik*, V, 169–70. Bebel's letter in Russian was published in *Iskra*, No. 86, February 3, 1905, p. 8.

Kindly *seal* your letter to me and address it to me at the German Reichstag in Berlin.

LENIN'S REPLY

[Lenin to Bebel, February 7, 1905][34]

DEAR PARTY COMRADE!

On the same day on which you wrote to me, we were preparing a letter to Comrade Hermann Greulich in which we explained how and why the split within the Russian Social Democratic Labor party has become an accomplished fact. We shall forward a copy of this letter to the Presidium of the German Social Democratic party.

The Third Congress of our party is convened [now] by the Russian Bureau of the Majority Committees [without the sanction of the official central institutions of the party (*Iskra,* the Central Committee, the Party Council)]. The editorial board of *Vpered* and the Russian Bureau of the Majority [which have been given, by the committees, the task of defending the standpoint and the political interests of the majority] are merely provisional centers [which have been authorized by the committees for definite and special purposes]. Neither myself nor any of the editors, contributors, and partisans of *Vpered,* who are known to me, would take upon ourselves at this time, without the sanction of [this] the party congress, the responsibility for new, important steps [referred to] which would bind the entire party. Thus your proposal can be communicated only to this party congress.

In conclusion permit me to express profound regret that probably the German Social Democracy's attempt at intervention is too late. I speak here about intervention in general, and not about special forms of intervention, such as, for example, a compulsory court of arbitration, which it is especially difficult to realize. A few months ago, when possibly this would not have been too late and when there was yet a slight hope that the Third Congress of the party would unify both groups and would be able to *restore* party *unity*—at that time the German Social Democracy did its best to block this path. Kautsky tried in *Iskra* to

[34] *Leninskii Sbornik,* V, 172–74. Translated from the German text. Portions of the text in brackets were crossed out by Lenin. "We do not know the real text of Lenin's letter to Bebel. But among Vladimir Ilich's [Lenin's] papers his reply written in German was preserved. . . . . A reply to Bebel was sent also on behalf of one of the members of the Bureau of the Majority Committees and the text of this reply was also composed by Lenin. . . . . The Bureau of the Majority Committees answered Bebel also. This answer was published in *Vpered,* No. 11, March 23 (10) 1905." *(Leninskii Sbornik,* V, 171.) The letter of the Bureau of the Majority Committees to Bebel is reprinted in *Raskol na II sezde R.S.D.R.P. i II Internatsional,* pp. 105–106.

weaken the value of a *formal* organization [i.e., of an organization in general].[35] The weekly of the German Social Democracy extolled disorganization and treachery (Rosa Luxemburg in *Die Neue Zeit*) under the ingenious and "dialectic" pretense that organization is merely a process, only a tendency. The irritation in this connection was very great among our ranks. Comrade Riadovoi,[36] a very influential member of the majority, said that Kautsky would publish my reply. I wagered with him that the contrary would happen. My "defense" was written briefly and to the point, was limited to a correction of the actual errors and opposed the mockeries directed against our party, with a statement of facts. Kautsky rejected my article for the remarkable reason that the attacks against us had been published by *Neue Zeit* not because they were directed against us, but in spite of this![37] This was simply a mockery! Thus, *Neue Zeit* (and not it alone) wished to acquaint the German Social Democracy with the points of view of the minority only. Indignation in this connection was boundless. To my mind, it was natural that German Social Democrats would follow the easily understood human wish to see persons who were long known to them as the representatives of the Russian Social Democracy abroad; that they would ridicule the Russian party congress and its decisions, the Russian committees and their activity. But after all this [it would also be natural] it will not surprise me if [every attempt at] intervention on the part of [official] representatives of the German Social Democracy encounter [specific] difficulties within our ranks.[38]

I apologize for my bad German.

With a social democratic greeting ——

[35] Kautsky's article was published in the form of a letter in *Iskra*, No. 66, May 15, 1904, pp. 2–4.

[36] A. A. Malinovsky.

[37] In returning Lenin's manuscript Kautsky wrote that since Lenin had been criticized in *Neue Zeit* he had a right to answer but in the article submitted Lenin had made an analysis of the dispute in the Russian Social Democracy. This, Kautsky considered unnecessary and harmful, since the dispute was of a nature which the Germans could never understand and the result would be a decrease in sympathy for Russian Social Democracy of both tendencies. Luxemburg's article was published, Kautsky said, because it dealt theoretically with organizational questions of general interest and only incidentally with the Russian disputes. Lenin had the right to answer criticism; but if his article, which raised many questions never yet mentioned in *Neue Zeit*, were published, Plekhanov, Axelrod, and others would demand the right to present their points of view. In order to prevent *Neue Zeit* becoming the arena for Russian disputes, Kautsky asked Lenin to rewrite his article dealing with the organization question only in principle. Full text of Kautsky's letter is given in *Leninskii Sbornik*, XV, 224–26.

[38] After making the revisions indicated in the last paragraph Lenin omitted this paragraph altogether.

A BOLSHEVIK ACCOUNT OF THE SPLIT IN THE RUSSIAN SOCIAL DEMOCRATIC LABOR PARTY

[Editors of *Vpered* to Hermann Greulich, February 4, 1905][39]

In a letter of February 1, 1905, to the editorial board of *Vpered* (the Russian Social Democratic Labor party), a prominent leader of the Swiss Social Democrats, Hermann Greulich, expressed among other things his regret about the new split among the Russian Social Democrats. He also remarked: "Who is the more guilty in this split, I shall not decide. I have proposed to the Presidium of the German Social Democratic party that it settle this question by international means." The editorial board of *Vpered,* together with Comrade Stepanov, authorized representative abroad of the Russian Bureau of the Majority Committees, replied with the letter given below.

In view of the fact that Comrade Greulich intends to secure an international solution, we inform all the foreign friends of the newspaper *Vpered* about our letter to Greulich and ask them to translate this letter into the language of the country in which they live and to acquaint as large a number of foreign Social Democrats as possible with this letter. It is also desirable to translate into foreign languages Lenin's pamphlet *Zaiavlenie i dokumenty o razryve tsentralnykh uchrezhdenii s partiei* [The declaration and the documents concerning the split between the Central institutions and the party] as well as the resolutions of the Northern, Southern, and Caucasian conferences.

"Vpered"—the Berne Group of aid to the R.S.D.L. party—publishes this letter, considering that it is very important, especially for the comrades in Berne, to have a brief review of the split. We ask foreign comrades to reforward this letter to Russia.

BERNE, February 15, 1905

DEAR COMRADE!

In your letter you touch upon the question of the responsibility of one of the groups of our party—the R.S.D.L.P.—for this split. You say that you have asked the opinion of German Social Democrats and the International Bureau on that question. Therefore, we consider it to be our duty to tell you how the split occurred. We shall confine ourselves to a statement of *facts, which have been authentically proved,* omitting if possible every evaluation of these facts.

---

[39] *Leninskii Sbornik,* V, 176–81. This letter to Hermann Greulich was not published. It was distributed in mimeographed form among the groups of Social Democrats abroad, who sympathized with the Bolsheviks. The Berne group re-edited this letter by supplying it with a brief introduction and the heading: "Kratkii ocherk raskola v R.S.-D.R.P.," *ibid.,* p. 176. This is a translation of the Berne edition of the letter.

Until the end of 1903 our party was a body of disunited local social democratic organizations, called "committees." The Central Committee and the Central Organ, which had been elected at the First party congress (1898), were lacking. The police had destroyed them and they had not been restored. A split had taken place abroad between the League of the Russian Social Democrats (organ *Rabochee Delo,* hence Rabochedeltsy) and Plekhanov. *Iskra,* which was founded in 1900, took the side of the latter. During the three years, from 1900 to 1903, *Iskra* acquired an overwhelming influence upon the Russian committees. *Iskra* defended the ideas of revolutionary social democracy against economism (*Rabochee Delo* tendency—a Russian variety of opportunism) ; lack of party unity depressed everybody. Finally, in August 1903, it was possible to call the Second party congress abroad. All the Russian committees as well as the Bund (an independent organization of the Jewish proletariat) and both sections abroad, *Iskra* and *Rabochee Delo,* took part in it.

All participants of the Congress considered it to be legally constituted. The struggle at the Congress was between *Iskra* supporters and adversaries of *Iskra* (Rabochedeltsy and Bund). The so-called "swamp" was in the middle. The *Iskra* partisans won. They introduced the party program (the draft program of *Iskra* was adopted). *Iskra* was recognized as the Central Organ, and its orientation as that of the party. Several of the resolutions on tactics were in the *Iskra* spirit, the statute of organization (drafted by Lenin) which was adopted, was that of *Iskra,* and was weakened by the *Iskra* adversaries, with the co-operation of the minority of the *Iskra* partisans only in small details. The grouping of the votes at the Congress was as follows : 51 votes in all ; 33 votes of the *Iskra* partisans (24 *Iskra* partisans of the present majority, 9 *Iskra* partisans of the present minority) 10 of "the swamp" and 8 of *Iskra* adversaries (3 Rabochedeltsy and 5 Bundists). At the end of the Congress, before the elections, 7 delegates (2 Rabochedeltsy and 5 Bundists) left the Congress (the Bund withdrew from the party). Then the minority of the *Iskra* partisans, which, thanks to the mistakes it had made, was supported by the *Iskra* adversaries and "the swamp" proved to be a *minority at the Congress* (24 as against 9 + 10 + 1, i.e., 24 and 20). In electing the central institutions it was decided to elect three persons to the editorial board of the Central Organ and three to the Central Committee. Of the six persons of the old editorial board of *Iskra,* Plekhanov, Axelrod, Zasulich, Starover, Lenin, Martov, the following were elected : Plekhanov, Lenin, and Martov. It was intended to elect to the Central Committee two from the majority and one from the minority. Martov refused to enter the editorial board without the three comrades who were eliminated (not elected) and the entire minority refused to vote in the election to the Central Committee. Nobody has yet disputed nor do they now dispute the legitimacy of the elections, but after the Congress the minority refused to work under the leadership of the centers elected by the Congress. This boycott lasted for three months: from the end of August to the end of November, 1903. Six issues (Nos. 46 to 51) of *Iskra* were *edited by Plekhanov and Lenin*. The minority formed a secret organization within the party (*a fact* which has been acknowledged now *in the press* by the minority partisans themselves and which *nobody* now repudiates).[40] By an overwhelming majority (12 out of 14 committees that had an opportunity to state their position) the Russian committees pronounced themselves against this disorganizing boycott. But after the stormy congress of the "League Abroad" (the organization of the party abroad) held at the very end of October 1903, Plekhanov decided to yield to the minority, declaring before the entire party in the article "Chego ne delat" ["What should not be done"] (*Iskra*, No. 52, November 1903), that to avoid a split it was necessary to make concessions even to those who, by mistake, tend toward revisionism and act as *anarchist individualists* (the underscored [italicized] expressions are the actual words used by Plekhanov in the article "Chego ne delat"). Lenin withdrew from the editorial board not wishing to act against the decisions of the Congress. Whereupon Plekhanov co-opted all the four former editors. The Russian committees declared that they would wait and see what the orientation of the new *Iskra* would be—whether the Mensheviks had entered the editorial board for "peace."

Things turned out as the Bolsheviks had predicted, namely that the orientation of the old *Iskra* did not continue, and that the new Menshevik board did not establish peace in the party. The orientation of *Iskra* had switched so much to the old orientation of the *Rabochee Delo* partisans, an orientation which was rejected by the Second Congress, that *even* Trotsky, a prominent member of the minority who published the pamphlet on program matters, *Nashi politicheskie zadachi* [Our Political Tasks], a pamphlet which came out under the *editorship of new Iskra*, declared literally: "An abyss lies between the old and the new *Iskra.*" We confine ourselves to this statement of our opponent in order to avoid going into lengthy explanations of the fundamental instability of *Iskra*. On the other hand, "the minority's secret organization" did not dissolve, but continued to boycott the Central Committee. This secret split of the

---

[40] In *Iskra*, No. 83, January 7, 1905, p. 5–6, a resolution was published in the section, "Iz Partii." This resolution was adopted at a conference of the Central Committee and representatives of the minority. It read as follows: "We, members of the minority, in view of the agreement which has been concluded between our authorized representatives and the Central Committee, and in view of the possibility of an actual unification of the party, ... discontinue our isolated existence within the party." In the same issue the Central Committee made the statement that the Mensheviks had transmitted to the Central Committee their organizational contacts and had declared that the organizational isolation of the minority had been abolished.

party into an open and a secret organization hampered activity intolerably. A large majority of the Russian committees, which had declared themselves on the issue, resolutely condemned the orientation of the new *Iskra* and the disorganizing conduct of the minority. From all sides there were demands for an immediate calling of a Third congress in order to find a way out of this intolerable situation. According to our party constitution, a declaration of party organizations supported by half of the complete number of votes was required, for the calling of an extraordinary congress (the regular congresses are called every two years if possible). *Half of the votes have already been secured.* But here the Central Committee betrayed the majority. Under the pretext of "reconciliation," the members of the Central Committee, who had not been arrested, *made a deal with the secret organization of the minority* and declared that this latter organization was dissolved. Furthermore, stealthily and in spite of the written declarations of the Central Committee, *three Mensheviks were co-opted* into the Central Committee. This co-option took place in November or December 1904. Thus from August 1903 to November 1904 the minority was fighting and breaking up the entire party over the question of co-option of three members to the Central Organ and three to the Central Committee. The Central institutions, which had been thus disguised, replied to the demand for a congress either with abuses or with silence.

At this time the patience of the Russian committees was exhausted. They began to call separate conferences. Up to that time three conferences had been held : conferences of (1) the four Caucasian committees,[41] (2) the three southern committees (Odessa, Nikolaev, and Ekaterinoslav), and (3) the six northern committees (Petersburg, Moscow, Tver, Riga, "the North," i.e., Yaroslavl, Kostroma, and Vladimir, and, finally, Nizhni Novgorod). All these conferences declared in favor of the "majority" and decided to support its literary group (composed of Lenin, Riadovoi [A. A. Bogdanov], Orlovsky [V. V. Vorovsky], Galerka [M. S. Olminsky], Voinov [A. V. Lunacharsky] and others) and elected *their own bureau.* This bureau was commissioned by the third, that is, the northern conference, to transform itself into an organization committee and call a congress, i.e., the Third party congress of the Russian committees apart from the centers abroad, which had split away from the party. That is how the matter stood on January 1, 1905 (new style). The Bureau of the Majority Committees began its work. (On account of police conditions in Russia, the business of calling the Congress will of course last for several months. The announcement about the calling of the Second Congress came out in December 1902, whereas

---

[41] Baku, Tiflis, Batum, the Imeritia-Mingrelia. V. Nevsky, *Istoriia RKP (b), Kratkii ocherk* (2d ed.), p. 246.

the Congress actually met in August 1903). The literary group of the majority established an *organ of the majority,* the newspaper *Vpered,* which has come out each week since January 4, 1905 (new style).

Up to the present (February 4, 1905) four numbers have come out. The orientation of the newspaper *Vpered* is the *orientation of the old Iskra.* In the name of the old *Iskra, Vpered* struggles resolutely against the new *Iskra.*

Consequently, there are two Russian Social Democratic parties. One has the organ *Iskra,* which "officially" is being called the Central Organ of the party, and it has the Central Committee, which represents four *of the twenty* Russian committees (committees in Russia other than the twenty which attended the Second Congress were formed thereafter and the question of recognizing them as legitimate committees is a disputed one). The other party has the organ *Vpered,* and the Bureau of Russian Majority Committees, representing fourteen committees in Russia. (The thirteen committees which were named above, the Voronezh committee, and most probably the Saratov, Ural, Tula, and Siberian committees also; the last four at least declared in favor of the "majority" after the Second Congress of the party).

All opponents of the old *Iskra*—all the *Rabochee Delo* partisans and a large part of the near party intelligentsia—are on the side of the "neo-*Iskra* partisans." All fundamentally convinced partisans of the old *Iskra* and a large part of the class-conscious advanced workers and practical party workers in Russia are on the side of the *Vpered* partisans. Plekhanov, who at the Second party congress (August 1903) and at the congress of the League (October 1903) was a Bolshevik, but who, since November 1903, had been struggling desperately against the majority, declared publicly, on *September 2, 1904* (this statement has been published), that the forces of the two sides are approximately equal.[42] We Bolsheviks assert that the majority of real Russian party workers are on our side. We consider that the chief reason for the split and the chief obstacle in the way of unification is the disorganizing conduct of the minority, which refused to submit to the decisions of the Second Congress and preferred a split to the calling of the Third Congress.

At the present time the Mensheviks are causing splits in the local organizations all over Russia. Thus, in Petersburg, they prevented the committee from organizing a demonstration on November 28 (see *Vpered,* No. 1).[43] Now they have broken away in Petersburg as a sepa-

---

[42] This refers to the Menshevik pamphlet, *Kratkii otchet o sobranii chlenov R.S.-D.R.P. v Zheneve 2 sentiabria 1904 g.* (published by the party club at Geneva), which contains Plekhanov's recognition of the equality of forces. (*Leninskii Sbornik,* V, 181, note 3.)

[43] Lenin's article, "Pora konchit," in *Sochineniia,* VII, 40–43.

rate group, which is called a "group attached to the Central Committee" and which acts against the local party committee. Recently they formed a similar local group "attached to the Central Committee" in Odessa for struggle against the party committee. The Menshevik Central institutions of the party were compelled on account of the falsity of their position to disorganize the local party work, for these Central institutions did not wish to submit to the decision of the party committees which had elected them.

The fundamental differences between *Vpered* and the new *Iskra* are essentially the same as those which prevailed between the old *Iskra* and *Rabochee Delo*. We consider these differences to be important, but on condition that we have the right to defend our own points of view, the points of view of old *Iskra,* we would not consider these differences to be a hindrance to joint work within one party.

ON BEBEL'S MEDIATION PROPOSAL

[Excerpts from the Minutes, Third Sitting, Third Congress of the Russian Social Democratic Labor Party, May 1905][44]

Liadov: .... I wish to note that one omission was made in the reports: namely, the question of Comrade Bebel's proposal to replace the Congress by a court of arbitration. I request the Bureau[45] to explain whether or not this question is subject to consideration right now.

(*The Bureau confers as to whether the Bebel matter is relevant to the question of constituting the Congress.*)

Chairman: One member of the Bureau did not express an opinion, two agreed that it was relevant.

Valerianov: I propose that the assembly decide this question.

Chairman: I put it to a vote, does the Congress wish within the limits of these debates to express an opinion on Comrade Bebel's proposal?

Votes: in favor, 13; against, 4 votes.

(Second ballot. Adopted)

Liadov (continues): Only the Bureau of the Majority Committees has replied to Comrade Bebel's proposal. It may appear to the German comrades that this matter had been settled by a "small, but a brisk company." I propose that the party, as represented by its congress, should express an opinion concerning this question. The German comrades

---

[44] *Tretii ocherednoi sezd rossiiskoi sotsial-demokraticheskoi rabochei partii 1905 goda. Polnyi tekst protokolov,* pp. 62–74.

[45] The Bureau of the Presidium made up of Lenin, chairman; Maximov (Litvinov) and Zimin (Krasin), vice-chairmen; and Andreev [N. A. Alekseev] secretary. (*Ibid.,* p. 20.)

sympathize very much with our struggle and our sufferings, but at the same time their attitude toward our party is very disdainful. Comrade Bebel's proposal is an illustration of this disdain. Compare, for instance, his attitude toward the French dissensions: there Comrade Bebel did not propose a court of arbitration. He regards the French as adults, whereas he treats us like children. . . . .

Maximov: . . . . Let me say a few words with regard to Comrade Liadov's remark concerning Comrade Bebel's proposal. I consider it superfluous to touch upon this question in my speech, for to my mind this proposal was not addressed to the party or to the Congress and had no direct relation to the question of constituting the Congress. I think, that for that very reason it is not necessary for the Congress to discuss this matter now.

I shall note in passing, that, if the Congress itself solves the questions which Comrade Bebel proposed to solve by a court of arbitration, it would amount to an actual sanctioning of the position taken in this matter by the Bureau of Majority Committees. . . . .

Kamsky: I am against passing a resolution on Bebel's proposal. When we really do split, then it will be necessary to speak of unification, and then Comrade Bebel's services may be useful to us. . . . .

Barsov: . . . . Finally, I wish to say a few words in connection with Comrade Bebel's proposal on behalf of the Presidium of the German Social Democratic party for conciliatory mediation between the two hostile groups of our party. Of course, we must be grateful and give our comradely "thanks" for this proposal to the German comrades and to their glorious, unyielding leader, Bebel ——. But the rejection of this proposal by the Bureau of Majority Committees was entirely correct, and very partisan-like, whatever our comrades of the editorial staff of *Iskra* may mutter ——. Our party is still a very young organization; it requires and needs the solution and settling of its problems from within, independently, and with the participation of real party workers from Russia; this is made possible only at an assembly like the Congress. It is true that our "dissensions" are possibly not great, but our actions, our conduct during the one and one-half to two years since the Second Congress being very harmful precedents, are very dangerous for the future of our party ——. Therefore, we must cure our own internal wounds. Apparently our German comrades have not too good an opinion of us; they wish to teach and punish us, as minors, through the authority of a court of arbitration, at which so renowned a leader of German Social Democracy as Bebel would preside. We are willing to learn and learn over again from our renowned comrades of the German Social Democracy by imitating them in many things ——, but only we ourselves shall be able to build our party, to establish order in it and to develop it —— and in all this the German comrades can help us little though they might wish sincerely and ardently to do so ———. Apparently they have been misled by our dignified comrades of the editorial staff of *Iskra,* who became confused in the factional struggle and have lost both rudder and compass ———. For the German comrades were unable to use our services, or the services of stronger parties of other countries either in their struggle against Bernstein, or in composing their famous Dresden resolution ———. Whereas the Dresden resolution[46] was adopted at the Amsterdam Congress, also by the international Social Democracy. Why? Because our German comrades are a force, they have matured through an inexorably critical, internal struggle against all forms of opportunism at party congresses and other meetings—and we must mature in the same way in order to play our great role, independently forging our own organizations into a party, not merely ideologically but in reality. We must prove by this congress our maturity for party activity, for disciplined party work. We must become active leaders of the entire proletarian class of Russia, by uniting and organizing ourselves immediately for struggle against autocracy for the glorious future of the reign of socialism. Only as a party of this kind shall we enter the international social democratic army of the proletariat as one of the detachments of the advance guard of sharpshooters ———.

When the Report on the Third Congress of the R.S.D.L. party appeared in German, Kautsky wrote in the *Leipziger*

---

[46] The following passages of the resolution which was adopted by the German Social Democratic party at Dresden from September 13 to 20, 1903, were included in the resolution of the Amsterdam International Socialist Congress:

"The party congress condemns most resolutely the revisionist endeavors to alter our heretofore proved and victorious tactics based on class struggle so as to replace the seizure of political power after the defeat of our opponents by a policy of adaptation to the existing state of affairs.

"This revisionist tactic would result in that a party which strives to bring about as quickly as possible a transformation of the existant bourgeois order into a socialist order—hence a revolutionary party in the best sense of this word—will be replaced by a party which confines itself to reforming the bourgeois society.

"The party congress condemns furthermore every endeavor to gloss over the existing and ever-growing class antagonisms in order to facilitate a rapprochement with the bourgeois parties.

"The party congress expects that in accordance with the principles of the party program the Reichstag group will make use of its additional power—which it has gained by the increase in its membership as well as through the tremendous increase in the number of the voters who back it—in the interests of the laboring class, will pay attention to the expansion and assurance of political freedom and of equal rights of all and will struggle more energetically than ever against militarism and marinism, against colonial and world policy, against injustice, oppression and exploitation of every kind." (*Protokoll über die Verhandlungen des Parteitages der sozialdemokratischen Partei Deutschlands. Abgehalten zu Dresden vom 13. bis 20. September 1903,* pp. 133–34.)

Volkszeitung[47] that this was not a report at all but simply a collection of resolutions presented in a form which would be incomprehensible to a majority of German readers and which would give "an entirely false conception of the relations within the Russian Social Democracy." The dissensions, according to Kautsky, were less significant than those within the German Social Democracy and concerned chiefly whether party members should take part in the future revolutionary government. "Surely," said Kautsky, "it should be possible to discuss very peacefully within a united party the sharing of a live bear's skin." Since the split, caused by the Third Congress, had occurred just when the revolutionary situation in Russia was developing and there was less dissension than before, Kautsky urged that the resolutions and their preliminary history be forgotten rather than distributed: "Let us be cautious about further spreading over Germany the attacks by Lenin and his adherents, as we would be if the attacks came from the other side." Lenin, naturally, was incensed. He wrote an open letter, which the *Leipziger Volkszeitung* did not publish, in which he declared that Kautsky committed a "grave error" in writing of things of which he had only hearsay knowledge and that his description of relations in the Russian Social Democracy was "very inaccurate." He protested against "the attempt to muffle our voice in the German social democratic press by such an unheard-of, rude, and mechanical device as the boycott of the pamphlet" containing the resolutions. "Kautsky," Lenin said, "has no right to talk of his own impartiality. He has always been biased in this struggle within the Russian Social Democracy. Certainly he has every right to be so. But he who is partial would do better to refrain from speaking too much about impartiality in order to avoid being accused of hypocrisy." Lenin objected to the description of the resolutions as "attacks by Lenin and his friends on Plekhanov and his friends," and in conclusion warned the German Social Democrats: "Do not believe a word of what the so-called impartial Germans tell

[47] No. 135, June 15, 1905, p. 2.

you about our split. Demand documents, authentic documents. And do not forget: prejudice is further from truth than ignorance."[48]

THE STATUS OF THE RUSSIAN SOCIAL DEMOCRATIC LABOR PARTY ORGANIZATIONS AFTER THE THIRD CONGRESS

[A Statement by Huysmans with a Letter from Plekhanov, June 16, 1905][49]

Because the state of affairs [in the R.S.D.L. party] has been pictured in some German newspapers in an entirely different light I at once addressed a letter to Comrade Plekhanov in which I asked him to make a statement on the authenticity of the information with which Ulianov had supplied me.

In reply to my inquiry I received the following letter. I omit a few words, the publication of which might offend some comrades.

"GENEVA, June 16, 1905

"DEAR COMRADE!

"I hasten to answer your letter. Here are the facts: the Second Congress of our party, which was held in 1903, formed new central institutions; the Council, the Central Committee and the Central Organ. But at the Congress there were differences on the question of organization. These differences were caused by the fact that some comrades were more in favor of centralization than others.

"These differences became gradually accentuated, so that after a few months a split in our young party appeared imminent.

"Understanding the fatality of this split, the Central Committee did everything in its power to prevent it. Unfortunately, at the beginning of 1905, all members of the Central Committee except two, disappeared ——. The two remaining members took the side of ultra-centralists and decided to call the Third Congress which is mentioned in the letter to which you refer.

"According to the constitution, the congress could be called only by virtue of a decision of the Council, the supreme party institution, and at the demand of half of the committees active in Russia.

"Thus the actions of the Central Committee were entirely arbitrary

---

[48] For a Russian translation of Kautsky's letter, see *Raskol na II sezde R.S.D.R.P. i II Internatsional*, pp. 146–49. For Lenin's reply, see "Offener Brief an die Redaktion der Leipziger Volkszeitung," *Leninskii Sbornik*, XVI, 109–11.

[49] P.K. i Sh. L. "Lenin i Mezhdunarodnoe Sotsialisticheskoe Biuro v 1905 godu," *Krasnaia Letopis*, No. 1 (12) 1925, pp. 119–20.

(*entièrement arbitraire*). But the ultra-centralists, who were openly opposing the Council, gladly followed the Central Committee. They arrived at the Congress, at which only part of the committees were present; these committees were called 'the swamp' by the ultra-centralists themselves. Owing to this union of the ultra-centralists with 'the swamp' the delegates at the new Congress represented something like half of the recognized organizations.

"It is this half of the party which adopted the resolutions mentioned in Comrade Ulianov's letter. It is this half that is now publishing in the name of the entire party the 'central' organ *Proletarii*. The other half is rallied around the old central organ *Iskra*.

"Thus, we have carried out in our own way the resolution of the Amsterdam Congress:[50] we have split. For this reason I beg you to note that neither section has the right to speak in the name of the entire party. For this same reason the funds which I shall receive henceforth for the benefit of the Social Democratic party, I shall divide into two equal parts. Both groups asked me to continue as representative of the R.S.D.L. party in the International Bureau. I did not decline. It is not hard for me to be impartial in this question.

"I am not in favor of one or the other and think that under the present circumstances a split is a great mistake, and perhaps an irreparable mistake.

"On my part I beg you to inform me as quickly as possible whether you consider that, under the circumstances which you now know, I can continue to represent my party in the International [Socialist] Bureau.

"Accept and so forth,

"G. Plekhanov

"P.S. Since at present unity is imperative and since the differences between the two groups are insignificant, you would do well if you proposed that you mediate to restore unity."

The Executive Committee of the International Socialist Bureau believes that the question raised in these letters can be settled only by a general meeting of the Bureau, and for the time being Comrade Plekhanov must continue to fulfill his mandate.

Since a commission for the working out of a new method of representation was appointed at the meeting of January 15 of this year, all Russian groups may soon be satisfied.

Accept and so forth,

Secretary G[C]. Huysmans

[50] The Amsterdam International Socialist Congress in 1904 demanded that in every country there should be only one socialist party.

ON PLEKHANOV AND GERMAN INTERVENTION IN THE RUSSIAN PARTY CONFLICT

[Lenin to the Secretariat of the International Socialist Bureau, July 24 (11), 1905][51]

DEAR COMRADES! Several days ago we received your letter of June 28 and with it the interesting documents (letters of Comrades Bebel and Plekhanov) but, being very busy, we were unable to answer you immediately.

I. We are compelled to make the following remarks concerning Comrade Plekhanov's letter:

1. Comrade Plekhanov's statement that after our party Congress (August 1903) the differences among us concerned only questions of organization, does not entirely correspond to the facts. Actually "the minority" of the Second Congress (headed by Comrades Axelrod, V. Zasulich, and Martov) split the party immediately after the Congress by declaring a boycott of the central institutions elected by the Congress and by forming a secret organization of the "minority" which was dissolved only in the autumn of 1904. Comrade Plekhanov himself, who was on our side at the Second party congress and the Congress of the League of the Russian Social Democrats Abroad (October 1903), was apparently of a somewhat different opinion about our dissensions when, in No. 52 of *Iskra,* he announced publicly (November 1903) that in order to avoid a party split skillfully worked out concessions to "revisionists" (Plekhanov's expression) would have to be made.

2. Likewise the statement that the Third party congress was called "entirely arbitrarily" does not correspond to the facts. According to the party constitution it is the duty of the Council to call a congress, whenever half of the committees demand it. The Council, as you know from the resolutions of the Third Congress translated into French, ignored the party constitution. The committees of the party and the Bureau of the Majority Committees were obliged morally and officially to call the Congress even against the will of the Council, which was evading that task.

3. From the same resolution of the Third Congress you know that at this Congress it was not "nearly half of the organizations with full rights" which were represented but a significant majority of the largest committees.

4. There actually are in our party comrades who are being called jokingly "a swamp." During the party discords the members of this "swamp" passed repeatedly from one side to the other. Comrade Ple-

---

[51] Lenin, *Sochineniia,* VIII, 9–12. First published in *Krasnaia Letopis,* No. 1 (12), 1925, pp. 120–22.

khanov was the first of these turncoats who as early as November 1903 passed from the "majority" to the "minority" only to forsake the "minority" again in May of this year by withdrawing from the editorial board of *Iskra*. By no means can we approve of these vacillations, but we think that we cannot be blamed for the fact that comrades from the "swamp" have decided to join us after endless combinations.

5. In the letter to the Bureau (June 16 [3], 1905) Comrade Plekhanov has rather inopportunely forgotten to mention his letter of May 29, 1905, published in *Iskra* (No. 101), with the complete and exact translation of which we have already supplied you.[52]

6. In speaking of the other *Iskra* party group, Comrade Plekhanov once more forgets to add that the conference of the "minority" (May 1905)[53] has revoked the constitution elaborated by the Second Congress, but has not formed a new Central Organ. We presume that the International Socialist Bureau has a complete translation of all the resolutions of this conference. If *Iskra* is unwilling to send them to the Bureau, we are ready to take it upon ourselves to do so.

7. Comrade Plekhanov says that only two remaining members of the Central Committee (the other members have been arrested) have expressed themselves in favor of calling the Third Congress. Comrade Plekhanov's letter is dated June 16 (3), 1905. On the following day, the 17th (4th), in No. 4 of *Proletarii*, the Central Organ of the party created by the Third Congress, the following declaration was published: "Having familiarized ourselves with the open letter of the Central Committee to the chairman of the Council, Comrade Plekhanov, and being in complete agreement with the Central Committee, we believe it imperative—for reasons which the comrades who are informed of developments in the intra-party life will understand—to declare publicly our solidarity with the Central Committee." The signatures are pseudonyms: Ma, Bem, Vladimir, Innokentii, Andrei, Voron. We can inform you confidentially that these pseudonyms are those of the arrested members of the Central Committee.[54] Consequently, as soon as these mem-

---

[52] In this letter Plekhanov resigned as fifth member of the Party Council and as editor of the Central Organ and further asked the Bolsheviks if they wished him to continue as representative on the International Socialist Bureau. ("Iz Partii," *Iskra*, No. 101, June 1, 1915, p. 8.)

[53] The conference of Mensheviks at Geneva.

[54] The enumerated pseudonyms are those of the Central Committee members—conciliationists: Ma—V. A. Noskov, Bem—M. A. Silvin, Vladimir—L. Ya. Karpov, Innokentii—Y. F. Dubrovinsky, Andrei—A. A. Kviatkovsky and Voron—L. E. Galperin. They were all arrested (together with three Mensheviks—V. N. Krokhmal, E. M. Aleksandrova, and V. N. Rozanov who were co-opted in the Central Committee) at the Central Committee meeting on February 22 (9). 1905 in Moscow at the home of the writer, L. N. Andreev. (Lenin, *Sochineniia*, VIII, 474, note 11.)

bers of the Central Committee found out about the conflict between the Central Committee and Comrade Plekhanov (and hence also the Council) over the question of calling the Congress, the majority of them at once declared in favor of the Central Committee and against Comrade Plekhanov. We urgently request the International Secretariat to notify us whether Comrade Plekhanov has deemed it necessary to inform the Bureau of this important declaration of the arrested members of the Central Committee, which entirely refutes Comrade Plekhanov's statement in his letter of June 16 (3).

8. Comrade Plekhanov is mistaken when he says that both groups have asked him to continue as party representative in the International Bureau. So far, the Central Committee of our party has made no request to that effect. As we informed you a few days ago, this question has not yet been finally settled, though it has been placed on the order of the day.

9. Comrade Plekhanov believes that it is not difficult for him to be impartial in the question of our differences. But after all that we have mentioned we believe that this is rather difficult for him, and, at least at the present moment, almost impossible.

II. I pass to Comrade Bebel's proposal relating to this question. Here I must say:

1. I am only one of the members of the Central Committee and the responsible editor of *Proletarii*, the Central Organ of the party. For the entire Central Committee I can settle only foreign questions and some other matters which I have been specially commissioned to settle. Moreover, all my decisions can be revoked by the general assembly of the Central Committee. Consequently, I cannot settle the question of the Bureau's intervention in our party affairs. But I at once forwarded your letter to all the Central Committee members in Russia, as well as the letters of Comrades Bebel and Plekhanov.

2. In order to hasten the reply of the Central Committee it would be very beneficial to receive from the Bureau some necessary explanations: (*a*) should we understand the word *intervention* as merely a conciliatory mediation and advice which has only a moral but no binding force? (*b*) or does the Bureau imply that the decision of a court of arbitration would be binding? (*c*) does the Executive Committee of the Bureau propose to grant to a general assembly of the International Socialist Bureau the right finally and peremptorily to solve the question concerning our differences?

3. I consider it to be my duty to inform the Bureau that some time before the Third Congress, Comrade Bebel made me and my partisans a similar proposal, offering his services or the services of the entire Presidium of the German party (*Parteivorstand*) as arbitrator in the dispute between the "majority" and the "minority."

I replied that a party congress would soon be held and that personally I could not make any decisions for the party and on its behalf.

The Bureau of the Majority Committees rejected Bebel's proposal. The Third Congress adopted no decision with regard to this proposal and thereby expressed its silent agreement with the reply of the Bureau of the Majority Committees.

4. Since the International [Socialist] Bureau considers it possible to obtain information from "some German papers" I am forced to declare that almost all German socialist papers, and especially *Die Neue Zeit* and *Leipziger Volkszeitung* are completely on the side of the "minority" and present our affairs very partially and incorrectly. Kautsky, for example, also calls himself impartial, whereas in reality he went so far as to refuse to publish in *Neue Zeit* the refutation of one of Rosa Luxemburg's articles in which she defended party disorganization. In *Leipziger Volkszeitung* Kautsky advised against circulating the German translation of the resolutions of the Third Congress. After this it is easy to understand why many comrades in Russia are inclined to consider the German Social Democracy partial and extremely prejudiced on the question of the split within the ranks of Russian Social Democracy.

Accept, dear comrades, our brotherly greeting.

Vl. Ulianov (N. Lenin)

PROPOSAL FOR TWO RUSSIAN REPRESENTATIVES ON THE INTERNATIONAL SOCIALIST BUREAU

[Lenin to the Central Committee of the Russian Social Democratic Labor Party, October 8 (Sept. 25), 1905][55]

Dear Friends!

I hasten to notify you of one important development in the matter of representation in the International Socialist Bureau. The South Russian Conference of Mensheviks[56] adopted a resolution. . . . . They asked Plekhanov to represent *their section of the party*.

This is precisely what we want! Plekhanov, of course, will satisfy their request. His quasi-neutrality, which is so detrimental to us, will be put an end to, which was the thing to be done. Let there be two persons in the International Socialist Bureau: one from the majority and one from the minority. This is best. And *it would be better still* if Plekhanov should represent the minority. This is a wonderful precedent to a future unification. I sincerely, explicitly beg you: discard now entirely the idea of having Plekhanov, and appoint your own delegate from the majority. Only then shall we be completely protected. It would be well to appoint

[55] Lenin, *Sochineniia,* VIII, 254. First published in *Leninskii Sbornik,* V, 515.

[56] On September 3 to 6 (August 21–24), 1905, at Kiev. (Lenin, *Sochineniia,* VIII, 498, note 116.)

Orlovsky. He knows languages, is a good speaker, and possesses dignity. The greater part of almost all communication is in writing and of course we would confer with one another, though there is really nothing to confer about. I assure you from experience that this representation is *pure formality*. In former times Plekhanov many a time commissioned Koltsov with this representation and there was never any mishap on account of this, though Koltsov is a good-for-nothing "parliamentarian" and in general an impossible, clumsy fellow.

With a handshake,

N. LENIN

BOLSHEVIK ACCEPTANCE OF THE INTERNATIONAL SOCIALIST BUREAU MEDIATION PROPOSAL

[Lenin to the International Socialist Bureau, October 27 (14), 1905][57]

DEAR COMRADE!

On June 28 (15) you sent us Comrade Bebel's proposal with regard to our party dissensions.

On July 24 (11) I wrote you that I could not give you an answer on behalf of the Central Committee of our party, for I am only one of the members of the Committee. I had asked the Bureau to give me certain explanations. In reply I received a letter, August 5, from citizen Huysmans in which he writes that the intervention of the Executive Committee will be only for moral effect. I immediately informed the Central Committee of our party of the exact character of Bebel's proposal. Now I am in possession of the reply of the Central Committee[58] which accepts your proposal and names Comrades Vasilev, Schmidt, and Lenin as its representatives. Comrade Schmidt is in Russia. Therefore, we must decide the day assigned for the conference (at least three weeks in advance).

The other delegates are in Switzerland.

Accept and so forth.

V. ULIANOV (LENIN)

B. THE INTERNATIONAL SOCIALIST CONGRESS AT STUTTGART, 1907

The Second International did not immediately renew its offer of mediation after the subsidence of the revolution of

---

[57] Lenin, *Sochineniia*, VIII, 321. Mimeographed publication, in French, in 1905.

[58] The letter of the Central Committee of October 16 (3), 1905 is preserved in the archives of the Marx-Engels-Lenin Institute. (Lenin, *ibid.*, VIII, 505, note 144.)

1905. There was, for one thing, the evidence of a more conciliatory spirit among the Russian Social Democrats at the unification congress of 1906. It is true that it soon began to appear that this was only a suspension of hostilities and not a lasting peace; but when the Second International held its Seventh Congress at Stuttgart in August 1907 the attention of the delegates was in the main focused on issues of more general significance.

Since the Amsterdam Congress of 1904, where revisionism and ministerialism had been paramount issues, the Russian 1905 revolution had provided many questions such, for example, as the general strike for debate among socialists in the West. But it was not the lessons of the Russian revolution that chiefly concerned the Stuttgart Congress. The International, dominated as it was by Western socialists, was primarily interested in events nearer home which threatened European peace. The French policy in Morocco, the Tangier incident, the diplomatic crisis that followed, the Algeciras conference with its inconclusive results, and the general surge of militarism among the Great Powers combined to make colonialism and militarism the chief items of the Stuttgart agenda.

With respect to the first of these items, a majority of the commission on the colonial question supported a resolution which included a sentence whereby the International would for the first time endorse a "socialist" colonial policy. The voting on the paragraph containing this statement revealed the interesting fact that a majority of the delegations from large countries possessing colonies and all the delegations of the small colonial powers favored retention of the paragraph. They were, however, defeated by the close vote of 127 to 108, with the ten Swiss votes not cast.[59] David defended the socialist colonial policy on the ground that it was futile to condemn capitalist colonial policy without offering an alternative. The colonies must pass through capitalism, and the socialists

[59] *Internationaler Sozialisten-Kongress zu Stuttgart, 1907*, pp. 38–39.

could mitigate this "painful passage" by the reform of the capitalist methods.[60]

In opposition to this point of view Kautsky declared: "I contend that democracy and social policy have nothing in common with conquest and foreign rule. . . . . If we wish to exert a civilizing influence upon primitive peoples, the first requirement is to gain their confidence. This we can do only by granting them freedom. . . . . I beg you not to adopt the introductory sentence which is so new, and which is at such variance with our entire socialist and democratic thinking. . . . ."[61]

In the final ballot all the delegations except the Dutch, which abstained, voted for the amended resolution. According to the minutes, "a commotion broke out among the German delegates because David had at first cast a negative vote for the delegation. A lively protest arose against this action and Singer took a poll of the German delegates. By a large majority the delegation voted in the affirmative."[62]

ON COLONIAL POLICY

[Resolution of the International Socialist Congress at Stuttgart, 1907][63]

The Congress is of the opinion that, by virtue of its inner nature, capitalist colonial policy must lead to enslavement, compulsory labor or extermination of the native population of colonial territories. The civilizing mission referred to by capitalist society serves only to camouflage its desires for exploitation and conquest. Only a socialist society will give to all peoples the opportunity to develop their culture completely. Capitalist colonial policy, instead of increasing the collective forces, destroys through the enslavement and impoverishment of the natives, as well as through murderous, devastating wars, the natural riches of the territories into which it transplants its own methods. Thereby, it slows down and hampers even the development of trade and the consumption of the industrial products of the civilized states. The Congress condemns the barbarous methods of capitalist colonization and

[60] *Internationaler Sozialisten-Kongress zu Stuttgart,* 1907, pp. 30–31.

[61] *Ibid.,* pp. 34–35. Lenin's observations on this issue are given on pp. 61–62 of this volume.

[62] *Internationaler Sozialisten-Kongress zu Stuttgart, 1907,* p. 40.

[63] *Ibid.,* pp. 30–40.

demands, in the interests of development of productive forces, a policy which would permit a peaceful, cultural development and which would place at the service of the progress of all mankind the natural riches of the soil.

The Congress again confirms the resolutions on the colonial question passed at Paris (1900) and Amsterdam (1904) and once more denounces the present colonization method, which is capitalist by nature and which has no other purpose than to conquer and subjugate foreign peoples in order to exploit them unmercifully for the benefit of a vanishing minority, while simultaneously the burdens of the proletarians at home increase.

As an enemy of every exploitation of man by man, and as a defender of all the oppressed, without racial discrimination, the Congress condemns this policy of robbery and of conquest which consists in nothing but shameless application of the right of the strong and which is the trampling underfoot of the right of the vanquished peoples.

The colonial policy increases the danger of military conflicts between the states which practice colonization and increases burdens through the maintenance of an army and a navy.

Financially, the colonial expenditures for which imperialism is responsible, as well as those which are made in the interests of the economic development of the colonies, should fall only upon those who profit from the plunder of foreign territories, whose wealth comes from these territories.

The Congress finally declares that it is the duty of the socialist delegates to combat implacably in all parliaments this method of unmerciful exploitation and enslavement which reigns in all the existing colonies.

For this purpose they [the socialists] must support all reforms in order to improve the fate of the natives, must prevent every infringement upon the rights of the natives, prevent them from being exploited and enslaved, and must endeavor by all means at their command to educate the natives for independence.

ON A SOCIALIST COLONIAL POLICY

[Resolution of the Majority in the Commission on Colonial Affairs
of the Stuttgart Congress][64]

The Congress records that the benefit derived from the colonies in general—and especially by the working class—and the necessity of maintaining them are being strongly exaggerated. But the Congress does not denounce on principle and for all time any colonial policy which might have a civilizing effect under a socialist regime.

[64] *Internationaler Sozialisten-Kongress zu Stuttgart, 1907*, p. 24.

[The second, third, fourth, fifth, sixth, and seventh paragraphs are the same as the resolution adopted.]

For this purpose the delegates of socialist parties should propose to their governments that they conclude an international treaty in order to adopt a colonial statute by which they would protect the rights of the natives and which would be entirely guaranteed by the states which conclude this treaty.

Absorbing an even greater share of the attention of the Congress than colonial policy was the question of militarism. This was not the first time the Second International had considered this question. Militarism had been denounced a number of times at preceding congresses, though there was always in the ranks of the Second International a tendency to distinguish between offensive and defensive wars. At Stuttgart the great predominance of moderate elements which inevitably clashed with Hervé's antipatriotic point of view caused heated debates in the commission on militarism. The Right and the Center of the German delegation dreaded every mention of agitation among the soldiers; nor did they wish to endorse a resolution which would bind them to a definite method of struggle against the war which everyone expected. They combined a Marxist evaluation of the causes of war with opportunist tactics. Bebel's resolution, which he proposed in the commission on behalf of the German delegation, was very vague as to the definite tasks of the proletariat. That passage of his resolution read as follows: "If a war threatens to break out it is the duty of the workers in the countries involved and of their parliamentary representatives to exert every effort to prevent the outbreak of war by means they consider most effective. In case war breaks out notwithstanding these efforts, it is their duty to intervene in favor of its early termination."[65]

In reply to Hervé's demand for insurrection and a military strike as a means of preventing wars, Bebel concluded his lengthy speech by saying: "We cannot permit ourselves to be pushed beyond this [i.e., beyond what has already been done

[65] *Internationaler Sozialisten-Kongress zu Stuttgart, 1907*, p. 86.

by the German Social Democracy on the question of combating militarism] and toward the adoption of fighting methods which might prove to be fatal to the party life, and under certain conditions, to the very existence of the party. I hope that after these general debates a subcommission will succeed in arriving at an understanding."[66]

In the subcommission Bebel's draft resolution was drastically changed. Four amendments proposed by Rosa Luxemburg, Lenin, and Martov (Rosa Luxemburg represented the Russians in the subcommission) were included in the resolution.[67]

This altered resolution as given below was then unanimously and without further debate adopted by the entire Congress, despite Hervé's attempts to have the German Right and the Center "show their true colors." Hervé called everybody's attention to the difference between what was said by the German representatives in their speeches and the resolution, which was adopted by acclamation.[68]

The two paragraphs of the resolution as amended and adopted by the Congress contain the basic principles of the Bolshevik tactics during the World War, and reflect the experience of revolutionary struggle during the Russo-Japanese War according to the Bolshevik interpretation of that experience. Lenin relates that the original draft of the amendments contained much more open statements about revolutionary action and agitation. Bebel refused to accept them, because, as he said, they would result in the dissolution of the German S.D. party organizations by the government. After many consultations and revisions of the text "in order to express the same thought" in less provocative language, Bebel agreed to accept the amendments.[69]

The adoption of the amendments to Bebel's resolution was the first victory for the small Left nucleus within the Second

[66] *Internationaler Sozialisten-Kongress zu Stuttgart, 1907*, p. 83.

[67] See below, p. 59, note 74.

[68] *Internationaler Sozialisten-Kongress zu Stuttgart, 1907*, p. 70.

[69] Lenin, *Sochineniia*, XXX, 378.

International. It is also notable as one of the few occasions on which Martov and Lenin supported the same proposal.

ON A GENERAL STRIKE AGAINST WAR
[Rosa Luxemburg's Speech at the Stuttgart Congress][70]

Rosa Luxemburg: I have asked for the floor in order to remind you, on behalf of the Russian and the Polish Social Democratic delegation, that we all should think of the Great Russian revolution in connection with this point of the agenda [militarism and war]. When at the opening of the Congress, Vandervelde, with his inherent eloquence, contented himself with expressing thanks to the martyrs, we all rendered homage to the victims, the champions. But after hearing many a speech, and especially that of Vollmar, I must say openly that the thought dawned on me, if the bloody ghosts of the revolutionaries were here, they would say: "We give you back your homage, but learn from us!" And it would be treason against the revolution if you were not to do so. At the last Congress, in 1904 at Amsterdam, the question of mass strike was raised. A decision was adopted which declared us to be immature and unprepared for the mass strike. But the materialistic dialectics, to which Adler has referred with such conviction, have suddenly accomplished what we had considered to be impossible. Unfortunately I must turn against Vollmar and Bebel, who are saying that we are not in a position to do more than we have done up to now. The Russian revolution sprang up not merely as the result of the war; it has also served to put an end to the war. Otherwise Tsarism would surely have continued the war. For us the importance of the dialectics of history is that we should not wait with folded arms until it brings us ripe fruits. I am a convinced adherent of Marxism, and for this very reason I consider that it is very dangerous to express the Marxian conception in a rigid fatalistic form which would only cause such reactionary excesses as Hervéism. Hervé is an *enfant*, an *enfant terrible* to be sure. (*Cheers.*) When Vollmar said that Kautsky spoke only in his own name, this is even more true of Vollmar. It is a fact that a large part of the German proletariat has disavowed Vollmar's points of view. This happened at the party congress at Jena at which a resolution was adopted, almost unanimously, to the effect that the German party was a revolutionary party which has learned from history. In this resolution the party declared that a general strike, which it has been denouncing for years as anarchistic, is a means which under certain circumstances may be applied.[71] But it was not the spirit

[70] *Internationaler Sozialisten-Kongress zu Stuttgart, 1907,* pp. 97–98.

[71] At the Jena Congress of the German Social Democracy held from September 17 to 23, 1905, Bebel's resolution on the "mass strike and the social democracy" was adopted by 287 votes against 14. Among other things this resolution said: "The

of Domela Nieuwenhuis, it was the red ghost of the Russian revolution which hovered over the deliberations at Jena. To be sure, we had in mind at that time a mass strike for suffrage and not against the war. But we cannot swear that we will carry out a mass strike if we are deprived of suffrage. And no more can we swear that we will carry out the strike for suffrage only. After Vollmar's speech and partly after Bebel's speech we consider it necessary to sharpen Bebel's resolution and we have elaborated an amendment which we shall later submit. I must also add that in our amendment we are to a certain degree going beyond Comrades Jaurès and Vaillant in contending that in case of war the agitation should be directed not merely toward the termination of war, but also toward utilizing the war to hasten the overthrow of class rule in general. (*Applause.*)

ON MILITARISM AND INTERNATIONAL CONFLICT

[Resolution of the International Socialist Congress at Stuttgart,
August 18–24, 1907][72]

The Congress ratifies the resolutions against militarism and imperialism adopted by previous international congresses[73] and declares once more that the struggle against militarism cannot be separated from the socialist class struggle in general.

Wars between capitalist states, generally, result from their competitive struggle for world markets, for each state strives not only to assure for itself the markets it already possesses, but also to conquer new ones; in this the subjugation of foreign peoples and countries comes to play a leading role. Furthermore, these wars are caused by the incessant competition in armaments that characterizes militarism, the chief instrument of bourgeois class rule and of the economic and political subjugation of the working class.

Wars are promoted by national prejudices which are systematically cultivated among civilized peoples in the interest of the ruling classes

party congress declares that in case of an assault upon the general, equal, direct and secret ballot or upon the right of organization it is the duty of the entire laboring class to make use of every adequate means of defense against this assault. In this connection the party congress considers that the widest use of mass strikes is one of the most efficient means of struggle to prevent this political crime from being committed against the laboring class or to win an important fundamental law for the liberation of the laboring class." (*Protokoll über die Verhandlungen des Parteitages der sozialdemokratischen Partei Deutschlands abgehalten zu Jena vom 17. bis 23. September 1905,* p. 143.)

[72] *Internationaler Sozialisten-Kongress zu Stuttgart, 1907,* pp. 64–66.

[73] All the resolutions of the Second International on militarism adopted prior to 1907 are given in their original French texts. C. Grünberg, *Die Internationale und der Weltkrieg,* pp. 5–10.

for the purpose of diverting the proletarian masses from their own class problems as well as from their duties of international class solidarity.

Hence wars are part of the very nature of capitalism; they will cease only when the capitalist economic order is abolished or when the number of sacrifices in men and money, required by the advance in military technique, and the indignation provoked by armaments drive the peoples to abolish this order.

For this reason, the working class, which provides most of the soldiers and makes most of the material sacrifices, is a natural opponent of war, for war contradicts its aim—the creation of an economic order on a socialist basis for the purpose of bringing about the solidarity of all peoples.

The Congress therefore considers it the duty of the working class, and especially of its representatives in the parliaments, to combat with all their power naval and military armaments and to refuse the means for these armaments by pointing out the class nature of bourgeois society and the motive for maintaining national antagonisms. It is also their duty to see to it that the proletarian youth is educated in the spirit of the brotherhood of peoples and of socialism and is imbued with class consciousness.

The Congress sees in the democratic organization of the army, in the substitution of the militia for the standing army, an essential guaranty that offensive wars will be rendered impossible and the overcoming of national antagonisms facilitated.

The International is not able to mold into rigid forms the antimilitarist actions of the working class because these actions inevitably vary with differences in national conditions, time, and place. But it is its duty to co-ordinate and strengthen to the utmost the endeavors of the working class to prevent war.

Actually, since the International Congress at Brussels, the proletariat, while struggling indefatigably against militarism by refusing all means for naval and military armaments and by endeavoring to democratize military organization, has resorted with increasing emphasis and success to the most diverse forms of action so as to prevent the outbreak of wars or to put a stop to them, as well as to utilize the disturbances of society caused by war for the emancipation of the working class.

This was evidenced by the agreement concluded after the Fashoda incident by the English and French trade unions for the maintenance of peace and for the restoration of friendly relations between England and France; by the conduct of the Social Democratic parties in the German and French parliaments during the Moroccan crisis; by the demonstrations conducted by the French and German socialists for the same purpose; by the joint action of the socialists of Austria and Italy, who met in Trieste for the purpose of thwarting a conflict between these two countries; further, by the emphatic intervention of the socialist workers of Sweden for the purpose of preventing an attack upon Norway; and, finally, by the heroic, self-sacrificing struggle of the socialist workers and peasants of Russia and Poland waged against the war unleashed by Tsarism and then for its early termination, and also for the purpose of utilizing the national crisis for the liberation of the working class.

All these endeavors are evidence of the proletariat's growing power and increasing strength to render secure the maintenance of peace by means of resolute intervention. This action of the working class will be all the more successful if its spirit is prepared by similar actions and the workers' parties of the various countries are spurred on and consolidated by the International.

The Congress is convinced that, under pressure exerted by the proletariat and by a serious use of courts of arbitration instead of the pitiful measures adopted by the governments, the benefit derived from disarmament can be assured to all nations and will enable them to employ for cultural purposes the enormous expenditures of money and energy, which now are swallowed up by military armaments and wars.

If a war threatens to break out, it is the duty of the working class and of its parliamentary representatives in the countries involved, supported by the consolidating activity of the International [Socialist] Bureau, to exert every effort to prevent the outbreak of war by means they consider most effective, which naturally vary according to the accentuation of the class struggle and of the general political situation.

Should war break out none the less, it is their duty to intervene in favor of its speedy termination and to do all in their power to utilize the economic and political crisis caused by the war to rouse the peoples and thereby to hasten the abolition of capitalist class rule.[74]

ON THE GERMAN ATTITUDE TOWARD THE RESOLUTION ON MILITARISM

[Excerpt from Hervé's Speech][75]

The elegant manner of concluding the resolution does credit, which I have never doubted, to the skill of the Subcommission. But this elegant

---

[74] The four amendments proposed by Luxemburg, Lenin, and Martov were embodied in the following parts of the resolution as given above: (1) The first clause of the first sentence and the second sentence in paragraph two beginning: "Furthermore, these wars are caused ...." (2) The last part of the third paragraph beginning, "for the purpose of diverting the proletarian masses ...." (3) The last sentence in the sixth paragraph beginning, "It is also their duty ...." (4) The last two paragraphs beginning, "If a war threatens to break out ...." and "Should war break out none the less ...." (*Internationaler Sozialisten-Kongress zu Stuttgart, 1907*, p. 102.)   [75] *Ibid.*, p. 70.

form is much too transparent not to be merely a lame excuse. Whom do you wish to fool anyway? Do you believe, perhaps, that the entire world will not see the difference between the resolution which is now being adopted unanimously and the speeches which were delivered in the hall upstairs [i.e., in the commission]? The difference is so striking that I, by no means a diplomat or a tactician (*laughter*), have voted with both my hands in favor of the resolution and wish that Vollmar had signed it with equal joy. For Bebel and Vollmar's speeches in the commission were black, whereas the resolution is white. (*Laughter.*) Therefore, I no not think that we can close this matter without a loyal declaration on the part of the German delegation in which it would explain this contradiction. Vandervelde has even strengthened the resolution in his report, but after all he is a Frenchman from Belgium (*laughter*) and his declaration from this tribune has not the value of a declaration by accredited representatives of the German Social Democracy. If the German delegation withholds a declaration to the effect that it no longer shares the point of view of Bebel and Vollmar but adheres to the resolution, then I cannot agree to an adoption of the resolution by mere acclamation. . . . . Let us, then, have a discussion, and let us force the German Social Democracy to show its true colors and declare its whole-hearted agreement with the spirit of the resolution. (*Applause and hisses.*)

LENIN'S EVALUATION OF THE STUTTGART RESOLUTIONS

[From an article in *Proletarii,* No. 17, November 2 (October 20), 1907][76]

. . . . It is not the first time that the colonial question has occupied the attention of international congresses. Heretofore their decisions have always irrevocably condemned bourgeois colonial policy as a policy of robbery and oppression. This time the Commission [on colonial policy] of the Congress was so constituted that the opportunist elements, headed by the Dutchman, Van Kol, predominated. A phrase was inserted in the draft resolution stating that the Congress did not condemn on principle any colonial policy which, under a socialist regime, could play a civilizing role. The minority of the Commission (the German Ledebour, the Polish and the Russian Social Democrats, and many others) protested energetically against the introduction of this idea. The question was submitted to the Congress and the forces of both tendencies proved to be so nearly equal that an unprecedentedly passionate struggle flared up.

The opportunists united around Van Kol. On behalf of the majority

---

[76] Lenin, "Mezhdunarodnyi sotsialisticheskii kongress v Shtutgarte," *Sochineniia,* XII, 78–83.

of the German delegation Bernstein and David spoke in favor of recognizing the "socialist colonial policy" and attacked the radicals for their futile repudiation, for misunderstanding the significance of reforms, for lack of a practical colonial program, etc. Incidentally, Kautsky raised objections against them, and was forced to ask the Congress to declare itself *against* the majority of the German delegation. He correctly pointed out that repudiation of the struggle for reforms was out of the question; in the other passages of the resolution, which had provoked no disputes, this was stated quite definitely. It is a question of whether or not we should make concessions to the present regime of bourgeois robbery and violence. The present colonial policy is up for consideration by the Congress, and this policy is based upon a direct enslavement of savages: the bourgeoisie actually introduces slavery in the colonies, subjects the natives to unheard-of mockery and violence by civilizing them, by distributing alcohol and spreading syphilis. And under these circumstances socialists use evasive phrases about the possibility of recognizing colonial policy on principle! This would be a direct transition to the bourgeois point of view. This would signify a decisive step toward the subjugation of the proletariat to bourgeois ideology, bourgeois imperialism, which at present raises its head with special pride.

The proposal of the Commission was killed at the Congress by 128 votes against 108, with 10 abstentions (Switzerland). Let us note that during the voting at Stuttgart the nations for the first time received different numbers of votes, varying from 20 (the large nations, including Russia) to two (Luxemburg).[77] The total of small nations, which either did not pursue a colonial policy or suffered from it, outweighed the states in which even the proletariat had been somewhat contaminated with a passion for conquest.

This voting on the colonial question has tremendous significance. First, socialist opportunism which capitulated before bourgeois charm, has unmasked itself especially plainly. Secondly, there became manifest

[77] The allocation of votes arranged by the I.S.B. at and since Stuttgart was as follows: France, 20; Germany, 20; Austria-Bohemia, 20 (Germans, 9; Czechs, 7; Italians, 2; Ruthenians, 2); Great Britain, 20 (L.P., 10; S.D.P., 4; I.L.P., 4; F.S., 2); Russia, 20 (S.D., 10; S.R., 7; Trade Unions, 3); Italy, 15 (Party, 6; Trade Unions, 6; Syndicalists, 3); U.S., 14 (S.P., 9; S.L.P., 3; I.W.W. Trautmanites, 1½; I.W.W. Shermanites, ½); Belgium, 12; Sweden, 12; Denmark, 10; Poland, 10 (S.D., 4; Polish Socialist party, Austria, 2; Polish Socialist party, Prussia, 1; Polish Socialist party, revolutionary faction, 1; Polish Socialist party, Levitsa, 1; Polish Socialist party, Trade Unions, 1); Switzerland, 10; Hungary-Croatia, 8 (Hungary, 6; Croatia, 2); Finland, 8; Holland, 8; United Australia, 6; Norway, 6; Spain, 6; Turkey, 6 (Armenia, 4; Salonika, 2); Chile, 4; Japan, 4; Non-united Australia, 4; South Africa, 4; Argentine, 4; Bulgaria, 4; Rumania, 4; Serbia, 4; Luxemburg, 2. (*Bulletin périodique du Bureau Socialiste International*, No. 5, pp. 126–27.)

a negative feature of the European labor movement, which is capable of causing great harm to the proletariat and which therefore deserves serious attention. Marx had repeatedly pointed out one of Sismondi's aphorisms of tremendous significance. The proletarians of the ancient world—it was stated in this aphorism—lived at the expense of society. Contemporary society lives at the expense of the proletarians.

The class of propertyless but toiling elements is incapable of overthrowing the exploiters. Only the class of proletarians which supports the whole of society has the strength to carry out a social revolution. And now, the extensive colonial policy has led toward a situation in which the European proletariat has to a certain extent attained this position, namely, that in which all of society is *not* supported by the labor of the proletariat, but by the labor of nearly enslaved colonial natives. The English bourgeoisie, for example, derives more profits from tens and hundreds of millions of the inhabitants of India and of her other colonies than from the English workers. Under these circumstances there is formed in certain countries a material and economic basis for contaminating the proletariat of those countries with colonial chauvinism. This of course can be only a transitional phenomenon, but nevertheless the evil must be clearly recognized and its reasons understood in order to know how to consolidate the proletariat of all countries for struggle against this opportunism. This struggle will inevitably lead to victory, for the "privileged" nations constitute an ever diminishing portion of the total of capitalist nations. . . . .

The R.S.D.L. party's London resolution [1907] on trade unions has now acquired a firm fundamental support in the form of the Stuttgart resolution.[78] The Stuttgart resolution [on the trade unions] establishes, in general and for all the countries, the necessity of stable and close connections between the unions and the socialist parties. The London resolution points out that, for Russia, the form of this connection should be, under favorable conditions, the affiliation of the unions with the party and that the activity of the members of the party must be directed to this end.

Let us note that the principle of neutrality manifested its harmful characteristics at Stuttgart because half of the German delegation, representatives of trade unions, adhered more resolutely than anyone else

---

[78] The International Socialist Congress at Stuttgart (1907) adopted a resolution on the "relations between the political parties and the trade unions" which said that "the laboring class must strive to bring about that intimate relations shall prevail and be lastingly maintained between the party and the trade unions in all countries" (*Internationaler Sozialisten-Kongress zu Stuttgart, 1907*, p. 50). This resolution was adopted by 212½ votes against 18½ votes cast by the French, the Italians, and the Americans in favor of a resolution which advocated party independence in relations with trade unions (*ibid.*, p. 57).

to the opportunist point of view. Therefore, in Essen[79] for example, the Germans were against Van Kol (there was only a party congress at Essen without the trade unions) whereas at Stuttgart they were in favor of Van Kol. The advocacy of neutrality *actually* had harmful results in Germany; it promoted opportunism within social democracy. From now on, and especially in Russia, where the bourgeois democratic advisers of the proletariat are so numerous—advisers who recommend the "neutrality" of the trade union movement to the proletariat—it is impossible to escape reckoning with this fact.

We pass on to the last and possibly the most important resolution of the Congress: the resolution against militarism. The "famous" Hervé, who had made much commotion in France and Europe, defended, in connection with this question, a semianarchist point of view, naïvely proposing "to answer" each war with a strike and a revolt. He did not understand on the one hand that war is an inevitable product of capitalism and that the proletariat cannot pledge abstention from revolutionary war, for these wars are possible and have taken place in capitalist society. On the other hand, he did not understand that the possibility of "answering" a war depends on the character of the crisis which the war provokes. The choice of the means of struggle is made on the basis of these conditions. Furthermore, this struggle must consist (this is the third point of misunderstanding and lack of insight of Hervéism) in substituting not merely peace for war, but socialism for capitalism. It is not a matter of preventing the outbreak of war, but a matter of utilizing the crisis resulting from the war to hasten the overthrow of the bourgeoisie. But behind all the semianarchist absurdities of Hervéism there is one practical and correct foundation: without being restricted only to parliamentary methods of struggle, to develop in the masses the recognition of the necessity of revolutionary methods of action in connection with the crises which the war inevitably brings; finally, to propagate among the masses a more lively recognition of international solidarity of workers and the falseness of bourgeois patriotism, and in this way to give a stimulus to socialism.

Bebel's resolution, which the Germans proposed and which in all the essentials coincided with the resolution proposed by Guesde, was inadequate precisely because it failed to indicate the actual tasks of the proletariat. This made it possible to read the orthodox postulates of Bebel through opportunist glasses. Vollmar immediately turned this possibility into reality.

Therefore, Rosa Luxemburg and the Russian Social Democratic delegates introduced their amendments to Bebel's resolution. In these

[79] A congress of the German Social Democratic party was held at Essen from September 15 to 21, 1907.

amendments it said, first, that militarism was the chief weapon of class oppression; second, the task of agitation among the youth was pointed out; and, third, it was emphasized that the task of Social Democrats was not only to struggle against the outbreak of war or for an early termination of a war which had already broken out but also to utilize the crisis caused by the war to hasten the downfall of the bourgeoisie.

The Subcommission (which was elected by the Commission on the question of antimilitarism) included all these amendments in Bebel's resolution. Furthermore, Jaurès proposed a plan which proved to be successful: instead of pointing out the means of struggle (strikes, revolts), to point out historic examples of the proletarian struggle against the war, beginning with the demonstrations in Europe and ending with the revolution in Russia. All these efforts resulted in the working out of a resolution which was extremely lengthy to be sure but which was rich in real thought and which pointed out exactly the tasks of the proletariat. In this resolution the rigidity of orthodox, i.e., the only scientific Marxian analysis, was combined with a recommendation to the labor parties of the most resolute and revolutionary means of struggle. It is just as impossible to interpret this resolution according to Vollmar's views as it is to fit it into the narrow confines of naïve Hervéism.

On the whole, the Stuttgart Congress placed in striking contrast the positions of the opportunist and the revolutionary wing of international Social Democracy on a number of important questions and acted on these questions in the spirit of revolutionary Marxism. The resolutions of this Congress as illuminated in the debates must become a constant companion of every propagandist and agitator. Unity of tactics and unity of revolutionary struggle of the proletarians of all countries will push forward vigorously the accomplishments of Stuttgart.

The Russian delegation at Stuttgart was headed by Lenin, as a result of the fact already noted that at the Fifth Congress of the R.S.D.L. party at London the Bolsheviks had again gained a majority in the Central Committee. This majority, as Zinoviev admits in his recollections, was "a weak majority to be sure," but it enabled the Bolsheviks to form the delegation to the Stuttgart Congress; and, he adds, "we formed it so that Lenin would head it." Zinoviev tells about the attempt made by Lenin at this time to bring together the Left group within the International: "Vladimir Ilich and the late Rosa Luxemburg headed this group. In his reports and informal talks Comrade Lenin told us how, during the Stuttgart Congress, he and Rosa Luxemburg made the first attempt to assemble an illegal (not in the police sense, but with respect to the leaders of the Second International) conference of Marxists who were inclined to share his and Rosa Luxemburg's point of view. There proved to be only a few of that kind within the Second International, but nevertheless the first basis for the group was laid at that time."[80]

INFLAMMABLE MATERIAL IN WORLD POLITICS

[From an article by Lenin in *Proletarii*, No. 33, August 5 (July 23), 1908][81]

The revolutionary movement in various states of Europe and Asia has manifested itself recently with such persistence that a new and incomparably higher stage of international proletarian struggle has become quite clearly outlined. . . . .

The international revolutionary movement of the proletariat does not proceed and cannot proceed uniformly and proportionately in different countries. A complete and thorough utilization of all possibilities in all realms of activity can result only from the workers' class struggle in various countries. Every country contributes its valuable, original traits to the general stream, but in each country the movement suffers from one or another peculiarity, from some theoretical or practical deficiency of the particular socialist party. On the whole, and in general, we see a tremendous forward step of international socialism: the consolidation of proletarian armies millions strong, in a number of definite clashes with the enemy, the approach of a decisive struggle against the bourgeoisie, a struggle for which the working class is much better *prepared* than it was at the time of the Commune—that last great insurrection of the proletarians.

This forward step of international socialism as a whole along with the accentuation of revolutionary democratic struggle in Asia, places the Russian revolution in a specific and exceptionally difficult situation. The Russian revolution has a powerful international ally both in Europe and Asia, but at the same time and as *a consequence thereof* the Russian revolution has not merely a national, not merely a Russian, but also an *international* foe. A reaction against the growing struggle of the proletariat is inevitable in all capitalist countries and this reaction consolidates the bourgeois governments of the entire world in opposition to any popu-

---

[80] Zinoviev, "Lenin i Komintern," *Sochineniia*, XV, 252. Report at a solemn meeting of the Executive Committee of the Communist International and the Plenum of the Moscow Soviet devoted to the fifth anniversary of the Communist International, March 5, 1924. First published in *Pravda*, No. 54, March 6, 1924, p. 3.

[81] Lenin, "Goriuchii material v mirovoi politike," *Sochineniia*, XII, 304–309.

lar movement, to any revolution in Asia, and especially in Europe. The opportunists in our party, like the majority of the Russian liberal intelligentsia, are still dreaming of a bourgeois revolution in Russia which would not "repel" the bourgeoisie, would not terrorize it; would not rouse an "extreme" reaction, would not lead to the seizure of power by the revolutionary classes. Vain hopes! Philistine utopia! The combustibles are increasing so rapidly in all the advanced states of the world, the conflagration spreads so obviously to the majority of the Asiatic states, which only yesterday were sound asleep, that the strengthening of international bourgeois reaction and the accentuation of every single national revolution are absolutely inevitable.

The counter-revolution in Russia does not fulfill and cannot fulfill the historic tasks of our revolution. The Russian bourgeoisie inevitably tends toward international antiproletarian and antidemocratic tendencies. The Russian proletariat should not count on liberal allies. It should proceed independently along its own path toward complete victory, by basing itself upon the necessity of a forcible solution of the agrarian question in Russia, by the peasant masses themselves, by aiding them to overthrow the dominance of the Black Hundred landlords and the Black Hundred autocracy; by setting itself the task of a democratic dictatorship of the proletariat and the peasantry in Russia and bearing in mind that its struggle and its victory are unbreakably connected with the international revolutionary movement. Let us have fewer illusions about the liberalism of the counter-revolutionary bourgeoisie (in Russia, as well as all over the world) and pay more attention to the growth of the international revolutionary proletariat!

C. The Bolsheviks and the International Socialist Bureau, 1907–1910

After the Stuttgart International Socialist Congress, Lenin, as the representative of the R.S.D.L. party took part in the meetings of the International Socialist Bureau. According to Zinoviev, Lenin "went to the meetings of this Bureau with a heavy heart and always returned from there practically ill. It was possible to sense from his accounts that he witnessed disgraceful scenes there, witnessed how the greatest international organization which united twenty million workers was beginning to rot."[82] This is post factum testimony, but no doubt Lenin had reason to feel discouraged.

[82] Zinoviev, "Lenin i Komintern," *Sochineniia*, XV, 254.

He was a newcomer in the International, a newcomer who never missed an occasion to expose what he regarded as the opportunism of the majority of that body. Moreover, he was regarded by many of the leaders of the International as chiefly responsible for the disruption of the Russian Social Democratic Labor party. The result was that his proposals were seldom accepted. There were two matters which came before the International Socialist Bureau between the Stuttgart and the Copenhagen congresses which are interesting examples of Lenin's relations with the Bureau.

On October 11, 1908, the I.S.B. had before it the application of the British Labour party for admission to the International. The British Independent Labour party supported this application, and Kautsky introduced a resolution that "the International Socialist Bureau declares that it will admit the Labour party of Great Britain to the international socialist congresses, because although it does not explicitly accept the proletarian class struggle, nevertheless it carries it on in practice, and by its organization, which is independent of bourgeois parties, bases itself on the foundations, the principles of international socialism."[83] Lenin agreed that the British Labour party should be admitted, since all trade unions in general had been admitted to previous congresses. But the second part of Kautsky's resolution, Lenin maintained, was incorrect, since the Labour party was not really independent of the Liberals and did not pursue an independent class policy. He therefore proposed to amend the last part of Kautsky's resolution to read "because it [the Labour party] represents the first step of the truly proletarian organizations of England toward a conscious class policy and toward a *socialist* labor party."[84] Kautsky opposed the amendment on the ground that the I.S.B. could not adopt resolutions on the basis of expectations. He was supported by the Austrians and the delegates of a majority of the small

[83] *Bulletin périodique du Bureau Socialiste International*, No. 5, p. 182.

[84] Lenin, "Zasedanie Mezhdunarodnogo Sotsialisticheskogo Biuro," *Sochineniia*, XII, 346–47.

states, and his resolution was adopted. Avramov, the Bulgarian delegate, opposed the entire resolution as a concession to opportunism. Lenin disagreed. "The International," he wrote, "would have acted absolutely wrongly if it had not expressed directly and decidedly its complete sympathy with this tremendous step forward of the mass labor movement in England, its encouragement of the tremendous change which has begun in the cradle of capitalism. But this does not imply that the 'Labour party' should be recognized as being already a party which is independent of the bourgeoisie, a party which leads a class struggle, a socialist party, etc."[85]

The second incident concerned the conflict in the Dutch Social Democratic Labor party between the Left-wing minority led by Roland-Holst, Gorter, and Pannekoek and the more conservative majority led by Troelstra and Van Kol. When the Lefts were expelled they took the name "Social Democratic party" and applied for membership in the International. The Executive Committee of the International Socialist Bureau, after attempting without success to heal the breach, rejected this application and placed the matter on the agenda of the plenary session of the Bureau which met on November 7, 1909. In the debate Singer, a German delegate, moved for the admission of the new party "since it meets the conditions stipulated in the constitution of the International." He suggested that the matter of the new party's participation in the Bureau and the number of its votes in the Congress be left to the decision of the forthcoming Copenhagen Congress. The Austrian, Victor Adler, then offered a substitute motion that the application be referred to the Dutch section and if no agreement was made within the section, the new party should be given the right to appeal to the Bureau.[86] Lenin criticized this motion as sympathetic to opportunism and prejudicial to the Dutch orthodox Marxists and for its failure to recognize acknowledged Marxists as members of the Inter-

---

[85] Lenin, "Zasedanie Mezhdunarodnogo Sotsialisticheskogo Biuro," *Sochineniia,* XII, 349.

[86] *Bulletin périodique du Bureau Socialiste International,* No. 5, p. 183.

national.[87] Adler's motion, however, carried by a narrow majority. In commenting on this action the *Leipziger Volkszeitung* (No. 259) called it "regrettable," and the *Bremer Bürgerzeitung,* November 11, 1909, observed that "Comrade Adler comes forth as an advocate of international opportunism glittering in all its colors." "To these just words," Lenin wrote, "we Russian Social Democrats can merely add that of course our Socialist-Revolutionists along with the Polish Socialist party have hurried to take their places among the opportunist company."[88]

D. The International Congress at Copenhagen, 1910

When the Eighth Congress of the International met at Copenhagen in the autumn of 1910 imperialist rivalries had not abated, the armaments race on both land and sea was gathering speed, and revolutionary movements and social unrest were challenging with varying degrees of success the existing regimes in Turkey, Persia, India, and China. Within the international labor movement the revisionists, the Center, and the Left disagreed and compromised as before with the center of gravity to the right rather than to the left of the Center group. The Russian delegation at Stuttgart had numbered 63; at Copenhagen it was only 39, but the number of Social Democrats, especially of Lenin's followers, was larger than at Stuttgart.[89]

Five commissions were set up by the Congress to draft resolutions on the various points on the agenda. Of particular interest are the resolutions against militarism and on co-operatives. With respect to the first of these questions, the

[87] Lenin, "Rech na zasedanii M.S.B. po voprosu o raskole v gollandskoi s.d. rabochei partii," *Sochineniia,* XIV, 240, first published in *Bulletin périodique du Bureau Socialiste International,* No. 2, November 7, 1909.

[88] Lenin, "Odinadtsataia sessiia Mezhdunarodnogo Sotsialisticheskogo Biuro," *Sochineniia,* XIV, 244.

[89] S. Bantke, "V. I. Lenin i bolshevizm na mezhdunarodnoi arene v dovoennyi period." *Proletarskaia Revoliutsiia,* Nos. 2–3 (85–86), 1929, p. 28. The complete list of the Russian delegation is given in *Huitième Congrès socialiste international tenu à Copenhague du 28 août au 3 Septembre 1910. Compte Rendu Analytique publié par le Secrétariat du Bureau Socialiste International,* pp. 28–29.

Congress did not go beyond what had been done at Stuttgart. Keir Hardie and Vaillant made an attempt to have the general strike mentioned as a means of preventing wars, and introduced this amendment: "The Congress considers the general strike of workers—especially in the industries which provide war supplies (weapons, munitions, transport, etc.) and also active agitation among the people when conducted by extreme methods, to be the most effective of all means which should be used to prevent wars."[90] The amendment was voted down in the Commission by 119 votes to 58.[91] There was a general atmosphere of pacifism, and the resolution which was unanimously adopted spoke of compulsory courts of arbitration, general disarmament, and abolition of secret diplomacy, measures which Radek derided as "useless." At the plenum, Vandervelde's proposal "to submit the Hardie-Vaillant resolution to the International Socialist Bureau for further examination," and to have the Bureau report on it to the following International Socialist Congress, was adopted.[92]

Perhaps the most important commission at the Congress was that on the co-operatives. Resolutions on this question were introduced by the Belgians, the French majority, the Germans, and the Russian Social Democratic Labor party. But the Commission failed to come to a definite conclusion and the matter was referred to a subcommission under the chairmanship of Anseele. The resolution worked out by this Subcommission called forth heated debates in the Commission between Modráček, the Czech representative, on the one hand, and Seliger and Karpeles, the German and Austrian representatives, respectively, on the other. Modráček championed the consolidation of co-operatives by nationality rather than by countries. Lenin suggested that the co-operatives could have a socializing effect only after the expropriation of

90 *Internationaler Sozialisten-Kongress zu Kopenhagen, 1910*, pp. 104–105.

91 *Internationaler Sozialisten-Kongress zu Kopenhagen, 1910*, p. 105. According to *Huitième Congrès socialiste international* . . . ., pp. 211–12, the Keir Hardie–Vaillant amendment was rejected by 131 votes to 51, with 2 abstentions.

92 *Internationaler Sozialisten-Kongress zu Kopenhagen, 1910*, p. 43.

the bourgeoisie. Both of these suggestions were rejected by an overwhelming majority of the Commission. The only amendment adopted was Wurm's proposal that the phrase "it is their duty" be replaced by "invites them urgently." The resolution given below was adopted by the Commission against the votes of Modráček and Lenin.[93]

It was apparently during the work of the Commission on Co-operatives that Lenin made another attempt to organize the Left-wing members of the Congress. The introduction of the two amendments which Lenin mentions in his report on the Copenhagen International Socialist Congress (included in this chapter) were apparently discussed at that meeting. These amendments received only about 15 votes and were rejected by the Commission.

From personal notes made by Lenin at this Left-wing gathering and preserved in the archives of the Marx-Engels-Lenin Institute in Moscow, it appears that the conference was attended by Jules Guesde, Charles Rappoport, Rosa Luxemburg, J. Marchlewski, A. Braun (Austria), Lenin, Plekhanov, Riazanov, de Brouckère, P. Iglesias, and others.[94] Zinoviev also writes of this private conference in his recollections: "At this Congress, Comrade Lenin made another attempt to form the Left wing. He tried to organize an international conference of revolutionary Marxists, but the whole matter was conducted in a bungling fashion. In all ten persons met, but even half of these had cold feet. Comrade Lenin was regarded with a great degree of mistrust. He was but little known, and the most outstanding members of the Second International who were trying to effect the unification of the Russian Social Democracy spoke against him. The Copenhagen attempt to form a Left wing within the International was a fiasco."[95]

[93] *Internationaler Sozialisten-Kongress zu Kopenhagen, 1910,* pp. 80–81.

[94] S. Bantke, "V. I. Lenin i bolshevizm na mezhdunarodnoi arene v dovoennyi period," *Proletarskia Revoliutsiia,* Nos. 2–3 (85–86), 1929, p. 34.

[95] Zinoviev, "Lenin i Komintern," *Sochineniia,* XV, 253. There is still other evidence of Lenin's attempt to consolidate the Left wing of the Second International. Lenin mentions this private gathering at the Copenhagen Congress in the outline

At Copenhagen Lenin carried out the decision of the plenum of the Central Committee of the R.S.D.L. party held in January 1910. This plenum, in an effort to reconcile all groups of Russian Social Democrats, resolved to request the International Socialist Bureau to accept a second representative from the R.S.D.L. party. From that time on Plekhanov was given the right of a consulting vote in the International Socialist Bureau in addition to Lenin's regular vote.[96]

RESOLUTION AGAINST MILITARISM

[Adopted by the International Socialist Congress at Copenhagen, 1910][97]

The Congress records that, within the last few years, military armaments have shown a tremendous increase, in spite of the peace congresses and the pacific assertions of the governments. Especially competitive naval armament with its latest phase—the construction of dreadnaughts —signifies not merely a mad wasting of public funds for unproductive purposes and consequently a shortage and lack of funds for the tasks of social politics and workers' relief, but it also threatens all nations with material exhaustion through intolerable indirect burdens of taxation and all states with financial ruin. Only recently world peace was endangered by these armaments as it always will inevitably be endangered. In the face of this development [of armaments] which threatens human culture, the well-being of the peoples, and the lives of the masses, the Congress confirms the resolution of the former congresses, and in particular that of the Stuttgart Congress, and reiterates that:

The workers of all countries have neither differences nor discords among themselves which are likely to lead to war. The wars nowadays are the result of capitalism, especially the external, competitive fight of capitalist states for world markets, and of militarism which is the chief instrument of bourgeois class domination in the domestic affairs and of the economic and political repression of the working class. War will cease completely only when the capitalist economic order is abolished. The working class, which carries the greater part of the burdens of war and which is hit hardest by its consequences, is most of all interested in abolishing war. The organized socialist proletariat of all countries

of his pamphlet, *Evropeiskaia voina i evropeiskii sotsializm,* which was written in 1914 and published in *Leninskii Sbornik,* XIV, 14–23. The private meeting at Copenhagen is mentioned on pp. 19 and 22.

[96] Lenin's letter to the I.S.B. on this subject is given in his *Sochineniia,* XIV, 345.

[97] *Internationaler Sozialisten-Kongress zu Kopenhagen, 1910,* pp. 34–35.

is therefore the sole reliable guaranty of world peace. Therefore the Congress again urges the workers' parties of all countries to carry on energetically the work of exposing the causes of war among the entire proletariat, and above all among the adolescent youth, and of educating them in the spirit of the brotherhood of peoples.

By adhering to the repeatedly expressed duty of the socialist parliamentary representatives to combat armaments with all their strength and to refuse funds for them, the Congress expects these representatives:

a) Continually to reiterate the demand for compulsory international courts of arbitration in all conflicts between states.

b) Continuously to renew proposals the ultimate aim of which is a general disarmament and, first and foremost, the convocation of a conference which would limit naval armaments and abolish the right of seizure at sea.

c) To demand the abolition of secret diplomacy and the publication of all the existing and future treaties and agreements between the governments.

d) To intervene in favor of the peoples' right of self-determination and their defense against armed attack and forcible repression.

The International Socialist Bureau will support materially all socialist representatives in the struggle against militarism and, should an opportunity present itself, will guide their common action. In case of military conflicts, the Congress confirms the Stuttgart resolution, which reads: . . . . [There follow the last two paragraphs of the Stuttgart resolution against militarism already given.]

In order to initiate these measures the Congress commissions the Bureau, in case of a threat of war, to take at once the steps necessary to bring about an understanding between the workers' parties of the countries concerned, and an understanding about common action for the prevention of war.

RESOLUTION ON CO-OPERATIVES

[Drafted by a Subcommission and Adopted by the International Socialist Congress at Copenhagen, 1910][98]

Considering the fact that the co-operatives are able to offer their members not merely material advantages, but that they are qualified to strengthen the working class economically by eliminating the trade of middlemen and, by their own production for organized consumption, to improve the living conditions of the working class, to educate the workers for an independent management of their own affairs and thereby to aid the preparation for democracy and socialism, the Congress declares that the co-operative movement, though by itself it can never bring about

[98] *Internationaler Sozialisten-Kongress zu Kopenhagen, 1910,* pp. 79–80.

the liberation of the workers, can still be an effective weapon in the class struggle, which is conducted by the workers for the achievement of their immediate aim—the seizure of political and economic power for the purpose of socializing all means of production and distribution—and that the working class is very much interested in making use of this weapon. The Congress therefore invites all party comrades and all workers organized in unions to become and continue to be active members of the co-operative movement, to act in the consumers' associations in a socialist spirit in order that the consumers' associations instead of weakening the spirit of socialist solidarity and discipline, shall become valuable means of organization and education of the working class. The Congress declares it to be the duty of party comrades to exercise their influence within the consumers' associations in order that the surpluses will not be used entirely for the reimbursement of the members but will be used also for the accumulation of funds which would enable the consumers' associations themselves, or through their societies and wholesale co-operatives, to proceed with co-operative production and provide for the education, enlightenment, and support of their members to the end that the wages and the labor conditions of their employees may conform with the trade union regulations, that their own concerns be so organized as to serve as examples, and that proper consideration be given to the conditions under which commodities are produced. Whether and to what degree the co-operatives shall support the political and trade union movement directly from their own funds is to be decided by the co-operative organizations of each country. In consideration of the fact that the services which the co-operative movement can render to the working class will grow in proportion to the strength and consolidation of the working class itself, the Congress declares that the co-operatives of every country must form a unified society. Finally, the Congress declares that, in the interest of the working class in its struggle against capitalism, it is necessary that the relations between the political, trade union, and co-operative organizations become ever more intimate, without impairing their individual independence.

DRAFT RESOLUTION ON CO-OPERATIVES

[Introduced by the Russian Social Democratic Labor Party Delegation at Copenhagen but Not Adopted by the Congress][99]

The Congress believes:

1. that the proletarian consumers' associations improve the condition of the working class in that they restrict the extent of exploitation

---

[99] Lenin, "Vopros o kooperativakh na mezhdunarodnom sotsialisticheskom kongresse v Kopengagene," *Sochineniia*, XIV, 359–60. First published in *Sotsial Demokrat*, No. 17, October 8 (September 25), 1910, pp. 3–4.

by all kinds of commercial middlemen; in that they influence labor conditions of workers engaged in distributors' concerns and improve the condition of their own employees.

2. that these associations can acquire great significance for the economic and the political mass struggle of the proletariat by supporting the workers during strikes, lockouts, political persecutions, and so forth.

On the other hand, the Congress points out:

1. that improvements which can be attained with the aid of the consumers' associations can be only very insignificant so long as the means of production are in the hands of that class, the expropriation of which alone can bring about the realization of socialism.

2. that the consumers' associations are not organizations of a direct struggle against capital, and that they exist along with similar organizations of other classes, organizations which may give rise to illusions that they constitute the means through which social problems may be settled without class struggle and without the expropriation of the bourgeoisie.

The Congress invites the workers of all countries:

a) to join the proletarian consumers' associations and to aid their development in every way, defending at the same time the democratic character of these organizations.

b) by means of an incessant socialist propaganda among the consumers' associations to aid the propagation among the workers of ideas of class struggle and of socialism.

c) to strive at the same time to achieve as close a rapprochement of all forms of labor movement as is possible.

The Congress also notes that the producers' associations are important for the struggle of the working class only if they are an integral part of the consumers' associations.

THE DEBATE ON CO-OPERATIVES

[From Lenin's Account in *Sotsial-Demokrat,* No. 17, October 8 (September 25), 1910][100]

. . . . The text which was adopted by the Congress with very slight stylistic corrections is the one which was worked out by the Subcommission. . . . . The struggle within the Subcommission, in distinction to the struggle within the Commission, did not center on the question of the relations of the co-operative to the party but on a more fundamental question, namely, the significance and the role of the co-operatives. The Belgians tended toward a definition, correct in principle, of the role of co-operatives, as one of the possible (under certain condi-

[100] Lenin, "Vopros o kooperativakh na mezhdunarodnom sotsialisticheskom kongresse v Kopengagene." *Sochineniia,* XIV, 360–63.

tions) secondary weapons of the proletarian class struggle for "complete expropriation" (*expropriation intégrale*) of the capitalist class. Elm, supported by Jaurès, resolutely rebelled and completely exposed his opportunism. He said that it is uncertain whether matters will go as far as expropriation, and personally he considers it entirely improbable; that for the majority (!) this is a disputed question; that in the program of the German Social Democratic party there is no expropriation; that it should be said: "*Überwindung des Kapitalismus,*" "the overcoming of capitalism." The famous words of Bebel at Hanover spoken in concluding the debate with Bernstein—"*es bleibt bei der Expropriation,*" "we are as before for expropriation"—were forgotten by one of the members of German opportunism.[101]

In connection with these disputes the "question of socialization" came up. Jaurès made an ultimatum that the definition of the significance of co-operatives should be: "They aid the workers (as it stands in the text of the resolution, adopted by the Congress) to prepare democratization and socialization of the means of production and distribution."

This is one of those diffuse, indefinite phrases, which are fully acceptable to the ideologists of small businessmen and the theoreticians of bourgeois reformism in the composition of which Jaurès is a master and which he likes so well. What is "democratization of the means of production and distribution?" (In the Commission, after the draft resolution has been returned from the Subcommission, the French substituted *forces* for the word *moyens,* but this did not alter the matter.) Peasant production (I said in the Commission) is "more democratic" than large capitalist production. Does this mean that we socialists wish to create small production? What is "socialization"? This can be understood as the transformation into public property, but it can also be understood as any partial measures, any reforms within the limits of capitalism, beginning with peasant associations, and ending with municipal bathhouses and toilets. As a matter of fact in the Subcommission Jaurès had referred to the Danish agricultural associations, apparently assuming, in harmony with bourgeois economists, that these are not capitalist enterprises.

In organizing an opposition to this opportunism, we (Russian and Polish Social Democrats) attempted to appeal from Elm to Wurm, co-

---

[101] "It is needless to recommend that we use only 'ethical' means. Party comrades, I tell you that on the day when we are able to begin a large expropriation in Germany . . . . I shall deliver a beautiful speech and prove to you how it is our duty for 'ethical' reasons, for reasons of general welfare, to proceed with the expropriation. (*Laughter and applause.*) Hence, we are as before for expropriation. We do not renounce it." (*Protokoll über die Verhandlungen des Parteitages der sozialdemokratischen Partei Deutschlands. Abgehalten zu Hannover vom 9. bis 14. Oktober 1899,* p. 121.)

editor of *Neue Zeit,* who also represented the Germans in the Commission on Co-operatives. Wurm did not approve of the phrase about "democratization and socialization," proposed (privately) a number of corrections, and acted as a parlementaire between Elm and the Marxists, but Elm showed such "iron firmness" that Wurm achieved nothing. After the Congress I read in the *Leipziger Volkszeitung* (No. 201, August 31, 1910, 3 *Beilage*) that within the German delegation the question of co-operatives was raised even as early as Tuesday. "R. Fischer asked," the correspondent of this newspaper wrote, "whether there are dissensions on the question of co-operatives among the German delegates." *Elm* answered: "There are. It is impossible to eliminate them overnight. The decisions of congresses are always compromises, and probably in this question also the matter will end in a compromise." *Wurm:* "My point of view on co-operatives is entirely different *(durchaus andere)* from the point of view of von Elm, but we shall still agree most probably on a common resolution."[102] . . . .

When the draft resolution of the Subcommission was returned to the Commission for final approval we turned all our attention to these two points. Together with Guesde we introduced two (chief) amendments: first, to replace the words "Co-operatives assist the workers to prepare democratization and socialization of production and of distribution" by the words "Co-operatives assist to a certain extent to prepare the functioning of production and of distribution after the expropriation of the capitalist class." The meaning of this amendment, which from the point of view of style was not very successfully formulated, was not that the co-operative *cannot* at present assist the workers, but that the functioning of the future production and distribution which *is* being *prepared* now by the co-operatives can take place only *after* the expropriation of the capitalists. The second amendment concerned the point which speaks of the relation of the co-operatives to the party. We proposed either to add: "that (i.e., assistance to the workers' struggle) is in any case desirable from the viewpoint of socialism," or to replace this entire point by another which would recommend openly to the *socialists* within the co-operatives that they advocate and defend the necessity for rendering direct assistance to the class struggle of the proletariat.

Both amendments, which received only about fifteen votes, were rejected by the Commission. The Socialist-Revolutionists voted, as they usually did at the international congresses, in favor of Jaurès. . . . .

---

[102] These statements were made at the meeting of the German delegation on August 30, 1910. Wurm's statement as reproduced in *Internationaler Sozialisten-Kongress zu Kopenhagen, 1910,* p. 119, reads as follows: "So far my point of view on co-operatives and their relation to the party has not exactly harmonized with Elm's."

We discussed with Guesde the question of tactics at the plenum of the Congress. Guesde believed—and his opinion was shared by the German Revolutionary Social Democrats—that no war should be waged over any particular corrections at the plenum of the Congress. That, on the whole, it was necessary to vote in *favor* of the resolution. Its defects consist in that it *permits* the use of one revisionist phrase which phrase does not take the place of the definition of the aim of socialism but merely stands next to such a definition; and in that it contains one *insufficiently strong* expression of the idea that the workers' co-operatives must aid the workers' class struggle. An endeavor should be made to correct these defects but there was no reason to open a struggle at the plenum. We agreed with this opinion of Guesde and the resolution was adopted unanimously at the plenum of the Congress.

In estimating the total work of the Congress on the question of co-operatives, we must say, without concealing from ourselves or the workers the defects of the resolution, that the International has given in the main a correct definition of the tasks of proletarian co-operatives. Any party member, any social democratic worker, any class-conscious worker—co-operator must be guided by the adopted resolution and pursue his activity in the spirit of that resolution.

The Copenhagen Congress marks the stage of development of the labor movement, when it is chiefly expanding, so to speak, and *is beginning* to draw the proletarian co-operatives into channels of class struggle. The dissensions with the revisionists were indicated, but it is still far from the time when the revisionists will come forth with an independent program. The struggle against revisionism was postponed, but this struggle will come inevitably.

E. THE INTERNATIONAL CONGRESS AT BASEL, 1912

In October 1912 Montenegro declared war on Turkey and shortly afterward all the Balkans were ablaze. The danger that the European powder magazine would be set off by sparks from this conflict was obvious, and the International Socialist Bureau organized antiwar meetings in most European states and prepared for an Extraordinary International Socialist Congress which met in Basel on November 24–25.

The Basel Congress differed from the preceding congresses of the Second International in that there were no debates of any kind nor was there any work done in commissions. It was a solemn political demonstration against war rather than a meeting for the discussion of definite international problems. This character of the Congress was clearly stated by Greulich in his opening speech on November 24: ".... We have assembled today in order to define our attitude toward the war. The Bureau and the preparatory commissions have worked hard in elaborating an exhaustive proposal. I hope that this Extraordinary Congress will not become a debating club. The Congress can have significance only if it unanimously manifests its strong will. We ask you, on behalf of the Socialist International, to subordinate differences of opinion to great principles. Our resolution will not violate the freedom of any nation, nor will it force any nation to adopt definite measures."[103]

In the preliminary meeting there had, apparently, been a discussion during which the French demanded that a statement in favor of insurrection against war and of a general strike be included in the manifesto. But the manifesto made no mention of such tactics. Haase, who spoke on behalf of the German delegation, gave the following interpretation of the manifesto: "By applying the ,methods which our conditions and our political and trade union organizations permit, we shall use our maximum strength to assure that which all of us desire to assure—universal peace and our future."[104]

The Basel Congress was the last general session of the Second International before the World War, and it is significant that, in contrast to the previous resolutions of the International on militarism and international conflicts, this Congress declared for the first time that national wars in Europe had ceased and that a period of imperialist wars had begun.

For Lenin, the ideologist of Bolshevism, the Basel manifesto of the Second International was an important document. According to Zinoviev, Lenin made the following remark when he read the manifesto: "They have given us a large promissory note; let us see how they will meet it!"[105]

[103] *Ausserordentlicher Internationaler Sozialisten-Kongress zu Basel, 1912*, p. 22.
[104] *Ibid.*, p. 30.
[105] Zinoviev, "Lenin i Komintern," *Sochineniia*, XV, 253.

The Russian delegation at Basel numbered thirty-six, of whom six were Bolsheviks holding mandates of the R.S.D.L. party Central Committee which the Bolsheviks then controlled. At this time Kamenev was the Bolshevik representative on the International Socialist Bureau.

Kamenev reports that dissensions broke out in the Social Democratic subsection of the Russian delegation to the Congress in connection with the distribution of the votes and the sanctioning of Gorbunov's mandate which he held from the Petersburg Initiative group.[106] These dissensions led to a split within this subsection. The representative of the Petersburg Initiative group was admitted into the delegation against the votes of the representatives of the Central Committee of the R.S.D.L. party and of the Plekhanovists. The Central Committee members withdrew from the meeting and formed their own subsection.

Judging by Lenin's letter to Shklovsky of December 1912, only Kamenev had reported to the Central Committee of the R.S.D.L. party on the activity of the Bolsheviks at the Congress. Lenin writes: ". . . . I am extremely pleased with the *outcome* of the Basel Congress, for the liquidator idiots have permitted themselves to be caught in connection with the Initiative group. This scum could not be hooked any better. But the inaction of our delegates and their 'pursing of lips' which I do not understand, distresses me. Have they spoken with the German delegates? . . . . With whom? How? About what? . . . . Agitation among the Germans is *very* important."[107]

---

106 Toward the end of 1910 the Mensheviks endeavored to organize Initiative groups of Social Democrats all over Russia, but with only moderate success. It was intended that these groups should adjust their activities to Stolypin's regulations, the so-called June 3, 1907 regime, and thus represent cells of the open labor movement. The first Initiative group was formed in St. Petersburg. Here it was possible for the group to carry on its activities openly, whereas in many of the provincial towns the groups were soon forced underground. The Petersburg Initiative group was composed largely of Right Mensheviks and was guided from abroad by the Collegium of the *Golos Sotsial-Demokrata*.

107 Lenin, *Sochineniia*, XXIX, 55.

ON THE INTERNATIONAL SITUATION

[Manifesto of the Extraordinary International Socialist Congress
Basel, November 24–25, 1912][108]

The International, at its congresses in Stuttgart and Copenhagen, set up the following principles to guide the proletarians of all countries in their struggle against war:

[The manifesto then quotes the last two paragraphs of the Stuttgart resolution on militarism which have been given above, p. 59. These paragraphs are omitted here.]

Recent events have imposed upon the proletariat more than ever the duty of devoting all its forces and energy to planned and concerted action. On the one hand, the universal craze for armaments has aggravated the high cost of living, thereby intensifying class antagonisms and arousing in the working class an invincible spirit of revolt; the workers desire to put a stop to this system of panic and waste. On the other hand, the incessantly recurring menace of war is becoming more and more provocative. The great European peoples are constantly on the verge of being driven against one another; these attempts against humanity and reason cannot be justified by even the slightest pretext of serving the people's interests.

The Balkan crisis, which has already caused such horrors, would become the most terrible danger to civilization and the proletariat if it should spread further. At the same time it would be the greatest outrage in all history because of the crying disparity between the magnitude of the catastrophe and the triviality of the interests involved.

It is with satisfaction, therefore, the Congress notes that there is complete unanimity among the socialist parties and the trade unions of all countries in the war against war.

Because the proletarians of all countries have risen simultaneously in a struggle against imperialism, and because each section of the International has opposed to the government of its own country the resistance of the proletariat and has mobilized the public opinion of its nation against all bellicose desires, there has resulted a splendid co-operation among the workers of all countries which has so far contributed a great deal toward saving the threatened peace of the world. The fear of the ruling classes that a world war might be followed by a proletarian revolution has proved to be an essential guaranty of peace.

The Congress therefore calls upon the social democratic parties to continue their action by the use of all means which seem to be expedient. In this joint action it assigns a particular task to each socialist party.

[108] *Ausserordentlicher Internationaler Sozialisten-Kongress zu Basel, 1912*, pp. 23–27.

The Social Democratic parties of the Balkan peninsula have a difficult task to perform. The great European powers, by systematically frustrating all reforms, have contributed to the creation of intolerable economic, national, and political conditions in Turkey which necessarily led to revolt and war. As against the exploitation of these conditions in the interest of the dynasties and the bourgeoisie the social democratic parties of the Balkans have heroically advanced the demand for a democratic federation. The Congress calls upon them to maintain their commendable attitude; it expects that after the war the Social Democracy of the Balkans will make every effort to prevent the results of the Balkan War, achieved at the price of such terrific sacrifices, from being misused for their own purposes by dynasties, by militarism, and by the bourgeoisie of the Balkan states which is greedy for expansion. The Congress particularly urges the Balkan socialists not merely to oppose the renewal of the old hostilities between Serbs, Bulgarians, Rumanians, and Greeks but also to offer resistance to every infringement of the rights of the Balkan peoples—the Turks and the Albanians—who are now in the opposite camp. It is the duty of the Balkan socialists therefore to fight against every disfranchisement of these peoples and to proclaim the fraternity of all Balkan peoples, including the Albanians, the Turks, and the Rumanians, against unchained national chauvinism.

It is the duty of the social democratic parties of Austria, Hungary, Croatia, Slavonia, Bosnia, and Herzegovina to continue with all their power their effective work for the prevention of an attack upon Serbia by the Danubian monarchy. It is their task to continue as in the past to oppose the plan of robbing Serbia by armed force of the results of the war, of transforming her into an Austrian colony, and of involving the peoples of Austria-Hungary proper and together with them all nations of Europe in the greatest dangers for the sake of dynastic interests. The Social Democratic parties of Austria-Hungary also will continue their fight in order that those elements of the South-Slavic people ruled by the House of Habsburg may gain within the boundaries of the Austro-Hungarian Empire the right of democratic self-government.

The Social Democratic parties of Austria-Hungary as well as the socialists of Italy must pay special attention to the Albanian question. The Congress recognizes the right of the Albanian people to autonomy; but it protests against making Albania a victim of Austro-Hungarian and Italian ambitions for domination under the pretext of autonomy. The Congress sees in this not merely a peril for Albania but also in the near future a menace to the peace between Austria-Hungary and Italy. Albania can lead a truly independent life only as an autonomous member of a democratic Balkan federation. The Congress therefore urges the social democrats of Austria-Hungary and Italy to combat every attempt of their governments to draw Albania within their spheres of influence, and to continue their efforts to strengthen the peaceful relations between Austria-Hungary and Italy.

It is with great joy that the Congress greets the Russian workers' strikes of protest as a guaranty that the proletariat of Russia and of Poland is beginning to recover from the blows dealt it by the Tsarist counter-revolution. The Congress sees in this the strongest guaranty against the criminal intrigues of Tsarism, which, after drowning in blood the peoples of its own country and after many times betraying the Balkan peoples themselves and delivering them to their enemies, now vacillates between fear of the pressure of the nationalist movement which it itself has created and fear that the results of the war might not be favorable for it. However, if Tsarism should try again to act as the liberator of the Balkan nations, it will do so under this hypocritical pretext only to reconquer its hegemony in the Balkans by a bloody war. The Congress expects that the Russian, Finnish, and Polish urban and rural proletariat, whose strength is increasing, will destroy this web of lies, will offer resistance to all bellicose adventures of Tsarism, will combat every design of Tsarism whether upon Armenia or upon Constantinople, and will concentrate its whole force upon the resumption of the revolutionary struggle for liberation from Tsarism. For Tsarism is the hope of all the reactionary powers of Europe and the bitterest foe of the democracy of the peoples whom it dominates; to bring about the destruction of Tsarism must, therefore, be viewed by the entire International as one of its foremost tasks.

But the most important task in the International's activities devolves upon the working class of Germany, France, and England. At this moment, it is the task of the workers of these countries to demand that their respective governments withhold all support to both Austria-Hungary and Russia, that they abstain from any intervention in the Balkan troubles and maintain absolute neutrality. A war between the three great leading civilized peoples because of the Serbo-Austrian dispute over a port would be criminal madness. The workers of Germany and France cannot concede that any obligation whatever to intervene in the Balkan conflict exists because of secret treaties.

But should the military collapse of Turkey, on further development, lead to the downfall of the Ottoman rule in Asia Minor, then it would be the task of the socialists of England, France, and Germany to oppose with all their might the policy of conquest in Asia Minor, a policy which would inevitably lead directly to a world war. The Congress considers the greatest danger to European peace to be the artificially cultivated antagonism between Great Britain and the German Empire. The Congress therefore greets the efforts of the working class of each country to bridge this antagonism. It believes that the best means to this end is to conclude an agreement between Germany and England on the limitation of naval armaments and the abolition of the right of capture at sea. The Congress urges the socialists of England and Germany to continue their agitation for such an agreement.

The overcoming of the antagonism between Germany on the one hand and France and England on the other would eliminate the greatest menace to universal peace, undermine the powerful position of Tsarism which exploits this antagonism, render an attack of Austria-Hungary upon Serbia impossible, and assure peace to the world. All the endeavors of the International, therefore, are to be directed primarily toward this goal.

The Congress notes that the entire Socialist International is at one on these principles of foreign policy. It invites the workers of all countries to oppose the power of the international solidarity of the proletariat to capitalist imperialism. It warns the ruling classes of all states not to increase by bellicose actions the misery of the masses which has been caused by the capitalist method of production. It emphatically demands peace. Let the governments be mindful of the fact that, with European conditions and the attitude of the working class as they are, they cannot let loose a war without causing danger to themselves. Let them recall that the Franco-German War was followed by the revolutionary outbreak of the Commune, that the Russo-Japanese War set in motion the revolutionary forces of the peoples in the Russian Empire, and that competitive military and naval armaments have accentuated in an unprecedented fashion the class antagonisms in England and on the continent and have unchained vast strikes. It would be sheer madness for the governments not to realize that the very thought of the monstrosity of a world war would inevitably call forth the indignation and the revolt of the working class. The proletarians consider it a crime to fire at each other for the benefit of the capitalist profits, the ambitions of dynasties, or the greater glory of secret diplomatic treaties.

If the government authorities cut off all possibility of normal progress and thereby drive the proletariat to desperate moves, they themselves must bear the entire responsibility for the consequences of the crisis which they themselves have brought about.

The International will double its efforts in order to prevent this crisis; it will raise its protest with increasing emphasis and make its propaganda more energetic and comprehensive. The Congress therefore commissions the International Socialist Bureau to follow events with increased attentiveness, and, regardless of what may happen, to maintain and strengthen the contacts between the proletarian parties.

The proletariat is aware of the fact that at this moment it is the bearer of the entire future of mankind. The proletariat will make use of all its forces to prevent the destruction of the flower of all peoples, threatened with all the horrors of mass murder, starvation, and pestilence.

The Congress therefore appeals to you, proletarians and socialists of all countries, to make your voices heard in this decisive hour! Proclaim your will in every form and in all localities; protest in the parliaments with all your force; unite in large mass demonstrations; make use of all the means which the organization and the strength of the proletariat place at your disposal! See to it that the governments are constantly kept aware of the proletariat's vigilant and passionate will for peace! Oppose the capitalist world of exploitation and mass murder with the proletarian world of peace and brotherhood of the peoples!

THE RUSSIAN REVOLUTION AND THE INTERNATIONAL SITUATION

[From Kamenev's Report on the Basel Congress][109]

. . . . Comrades will find above in full the passage which the Basel Congress devoted in its manifesto to Russian Tsarism and the tasks of the Russian workers. The existence of the Romanov monarchy is one of the chief obstacles in the solution of the   problem which confronts the socialist proletariat of Europe. The overthrow of this monarchy, which is pressing equally upon the free development of both Europe and Asia, is a vital [literally, "blood"] task not merely of the Russian Social Democracy and the Russian proletariat but also of the proletariat of the entire civilized world. Seven years after the great Russian revolution, the Basel Congress recalled that the overthrow of the regime of "renovated Russia," the regime of June 3, is essentially an *international* task. Not "improvement" of the regime of June 3, not "expansion" of the June 3 "Constitution," but the overthrow of the monarchy—this is how the question has been posed not merely by conditions within Russia but by the entire international situation. First of all this stone must be removed from the path in order that the European proletariat can assure itself free development toward socialism. In greeting the new tide of the Russian proletarian movement, the Socialist International at the same time declares that the task which falls to the share of the Russian proletariat is one of the most responsible tasks at this moment. The conditions which have developed in Europe and Asia by the second decade of the twentieth century are such that the Russian proletariat happens to be in the center of international events. Much depends on the voice of the Russian proletariat. Proletarian Europe and Asia, which is becoming revolutionary, listen attentively to its voice and its voice must

[109] Yu Kamenev, "Na bazelskom kongresse," *Sotsial-Demokrat*, No. 30, January 25, 1913, pp. 3–4.

resound ever louder in the struggle against the Romanov monarchy. Only people who do not see the forest for the trees can fail to notice that the revolution and republican preaching are the most urgent, the most vital demands of the moment, demands which have been evoked by all the circumstances under which the new revival of the Russian laboring class is proceeding. Only under this slogan can the socialist proletariat of Russia fulfill the tasks with which it has been brought face to face by history and which were emphasized by the Basel Congress. *Revolution in Russia*—this is the Achilles' heel of the entire system of relations in Europe and Asia. Only a new revolution in Russia can open a new period of successes of the proletarian cause in Europe and of the democratic cause in Asia. Without this revolution the solution of all questions will be postponed for a long time; among these questions there will also be the one which has caused the representatives of the proletariat of all countries to assemble at Basel. The Basel Congress could not conceal from itself the fact that the matter of assuring peace in Europe demands at least one *war:* a victorious war of all the peoples of Russia against the Romanov monarchy.

But it was also clear to the Congress that if this war is inevitable as a preliminary condition for solving the problem of stable peace, a number of similar "wars" might be required for the actual solution of this problem. The French section of the International, as is known, has passed a resolution at its Extraordinary Congress, previous to the Basel Congress. In this resolution[110] it pointed directly to the general strike

[110] The following resolution was adopted at the Extraordinary Congress of the French Socialist party on November 21, 1912, against the votes of the Guesdists: "There can be no agreements, stipulations, nor secret treaties which would bind Republican France to Russian Tsarism.

"By no motives, nor under any pretext must France, which has no other than peaceful interests, intervene in the Balkans and in the conflict between Austrian and Russian imperialism.

"Should our government involve us, through its criminal policy, in these conflicts and conjure up the danger of war, the Congress recalls to all party members the decisions of the International Congresses of Stuttgart and Copenhagen. It also recalls the decisions of the National Congresses of Limoges and Nancy.

"In case of a war they must make use of the entire energy and efforts of the laboring class and the Socialist party to prevent the war by every means, including parliamentary intervention, open agitation, manifestoes, as well as a general strike and insurrection.

"The Congress counts upon you, the federations and sections of the party, to carry out these decisions of the International and of the party.

"In recognition of the fact that the action of the International will be the more effective the more unanimous this action becomes,

"The Congress requests its delegates to Basel to see to it that mutual and joint action of the national sections prevails so as to assure the greatest possible efficiency on the part of the International." ("Französischer Parteitag," *1. Beilage des Vorwärts,* No. 275, November 24, 1912, p. 1.)

and insurrection as the extreme weapons of struggle against the European war. These words, "general strike and insurrection," were not included in the manifesto adopted by the [Basel] Congress because of the same theoretical and practical considerations which determined the resolutions of the Stuttgart and Copenhagen congresses. However, this does not minimize the fact that the Congress was imbued with the understanding that the proletariat, in struggling against war, would have to develop its energy to the utmost, even to an open civil war. The references made in the manifesto to the Commune which followed the Franco-Prussian War of 1870–1871 and to the Russian Revolution of 1905 point this out unequivocally. The resolutions of the Stuttgart and Copenhagen congresses on war, which speak of struggling against war with every effort and in every way and of taking advantage of the crisis brought about by war to hasten the downfall of the entire capitalist regime— these resolutions have been reproduced wholly in the Basel manifesto. At the Congress the manifesto provoked no objections and was unanimously adopted *par acclamation.* This was achieved, thanks to a special commission of five members, who worked hard on the elaboration of the manifesto and also, thanks to the International Socialist Bureau, which had devoted. several of its meetings to this subject. In the Bureau none of its members proposed to include the mentioned passages of the French resolution. I, who represented the Central Committee of the R.S.D.L. party in the International Socialist Bureau, considered that reference to the methods of struggle as stated in the manifesto was entirely sufficient. It is true that in the present state of affairs in Russia a military adventure of the Tsarist government would become, sooner than in any other country, the starting point of an extreme revolutionary movement. The Russian delegates could have spoken with reason about general strike and insurrection by basing themselves on the experience of the Russo-Japanese War, the 900,000 political strikers, and the disturbance in the fleet in 1912. But in Russia, too, these methods of struggle against war would not merely be methods of struggle against war; they would be results of the specific social-political conditions in which Russia at present finds herself: conditions of an incomplete bourgeois revolution and a new rising tide against Tsarism. These specific revolutionary conditions of Russia have been specially designated in the Basel Manifesto. It would be strange if the Russian delegates were to attempt further to make the specific revolutionary conditions of Russia a criterion in working out methods of struggle for the entire European proletariat against war. Of course a resolution of the International, which would bind the Russian proletariat in any degree in the application of a general strike and insurrection, would be entirely unacceptable to us. *But this was entirely out of the question.* And since this was so, I thought it unnecessary to change the text of the manifesto in the spirit, let us say, of the French resolution and unnecessary to repudiate in any way the fundamental position adopted by our delegation—in addition to the German delegates—at the Stuttgart and the Copenhagen congresses.

I wish to add that, on the whole, in working out the manifesto strong unanimity prevailed in the Bureau, and, after some corrections which in turn were unanimously adopted and which were designed to make the manifesto more expressive so to speak, the text of the latter was adopted unanimously. . . . .

F. The Last Attempt at Unification of the Russian Social Democratic Labor Party, 1913–1914

The last attempt to assemble a unification conference of all Russian Social Democratic groups originated in connection with the election campaign for the Fourth State Duma in the spring of 1912. The Presidium of the German Social Democratic party had assigned 80,000 marks for the Russian election campaign on condition that the money be used only in constituencies where but one Social Democratic candidate was nominated. On April 29, 1912, the Presidium notified the Committee of the Lettish Social Democratic Party Abroad of its desire to have all Russian Social Democratic organizations come to an understanding with regard to the election campaign and select a committee which would be responsible to the German S.D. Presidium for the use of the money. The Letts undertook to call a conference of four Russian groups at Brussels on May 18, but the conference did not meet because of disagreement among the Mensheviks.

The Lettish Committee Abroad thereupon advanced a different plan in a letter to the Presidium on June 24, proposing a conference of eleven Russian Social Democratic groups. On July 22 the German Presidium forwarded copies of this letter to the eleven Russian organizations named, asking these organizations to send their representatives to Berlin for a meeting on September 5.[111] On July 29–30, in

---

[111] Lenin, *Sochineniia,* XVI, 705–706, note 31.

reply to this invitation, Lenin, on behalf of the Central Committee of the R.S.D.L. party, wrote to the German Presidium as follows: ". . . . We considered it superfluous to explain to you how odd the plan of those Letts is, for we were certain that no well-informed person could take this plan seriously. But we were surprised to learn from your letter of July 22 that you intend to adopt this plan. This compels us to voice a resolute protest, which we now forward to you. Objectively, the intention of the Presidium is merely an attempt to promote the split in our party (the R.S.D.L. party) and the formation of a new hostile party. This, so far, is without precedent in the entire International. We shall explain this in detail to the German comrades."[112]

When all efforts to convene the conference of Russian Social Democratic organizations failed, the German Presidium canceled its invitations and later granted some of the money to the national Social Democratic organizations of the R.S.D.L. party and also to the Menshevik Organization Committee elected at the "August" Conference of 1912.[113]

The withdrawal of the Bolshevik deputies from the Russian Social Democratic group in the Duma widened the breach in the party ranks and invited another attempt by the International to bring about unification. On November 13, 1913, Rosa Luxemburg proposed to the International Socialist Bureau that it include the question of restoring unity in the R.S.D.L. party on the agenda of its forthcoming meeting in London. In supporting her proposal she referred to the split in the Duma group which had been caused in "a frivolous manner" in "this last organ of social democratic unity in Russia"; to "the systematic incitement by Lenin's group of

[112] Lenin's letter is quoted in "K sovremennomu polozheniiu v R.S.-D.R.P.," Lenin, *Sochineniia*, XVI, 59. On August 13, 1912, Martov wrote to Axelrod that, although Plekhanov had at first agreed to attend this conference, he had changed his mind because refusals were received from the Bolsheviks and from the Main Presidium of the Social Democracy of Poland and Lithuania (*Pisma P. B. Akselroda i Yu. O. Martova*, I, 250). The correspondence relating to the preparations of this conference was published by the Viennese *Pravda* in No. 3 of its mimeographed bulletin (*Pisma P. B. Akselroda i Yu. O. Martova*, I, 242, note).

[113] Lenin, *Sochineniia*, XVI, 706–707, note 31.

the split among the ranks of other social democratic organizations, as well as among the Social Democracies of Russia, Poland, and Lithuania";[114] and to the irregularity of the Russian representation in the International Socialist Bureau, where "one of the representatives actually represents only one separate organization which he himself has called into being."[115]

The International Socialist Bureau met in London December 13–14, 1913, and took up the Russian question along with that of the unity of British socialists.[116] In introducing a resolution endorsed by Ebert, Molkenbuhr, and himself, Kautsky said that never in any country had party disputes caused so much hatred and mistrust as had been brought about by the violent disputes of the Russian comrades during the past ten years. Unity must come from within Russia by a strong demand on the part of working-class opinion. Since in fact the old Social Democratic party was dead, those who considered themselves Social Democrats should be asked to appear before an impartial collegium which would establish either that the differences between the Russians were important or that they were insignificant, as Kautsky himself believed. In either case the International could then act. It might be shown that the causes of the trouble were purely personal, in which case the indignant Russian proletariat would pass a resolution over the heads of the persons responsible.

Rosa Luxemburg offered an amendment to Kautsky's resolution which the Bolsheviks believed was for the purpose of excluding the Rozlomovists, that is, the opposition within the Social Democracy of Poland and Lithuania, from the

---

[114] The split within the ranks of the Social Democracy of Poland and Lithuania is discussed below in chapter vi, p. 505.

[115] "Zur Spaltung in der sozialdemokratischen Dumafraktion," *1. Beilage des Vorwärts,* No. 306, November 21, 1913, p. 2.

[116] On the eve of the meeting Plekhanov resigned from the Bureau, on which he had a consulting vote, and was succeeded by P. B. Axelrod, representative of the Organization Committee of the Mensheviks. Litvinov attended in place of Kamenev as the representative of the Bolsheviks.

unification conference. Luxemburg later withdrew her amendment, and after some further debate the resolution was unanimously adopted.

The Bolshevik newspaper *Proletarskaia Pravda* published this resolution on December 21 (8), 1913, together with a letter addressed to the workers stating the editors' opinion of the resolution and giving conditions which would make unification possible. The Mensheviks replied to this letter in a number of articles, criticizing the conditions advanced by the Bolsheviks, which, they declared, made unification impossible. The Bolsheviks, thereupon, published their conditions for party unity over the signature of " a group of organized Marxists."[117]

It was apparently during January or February, 1914, that Huysmans wrote to Lenin asking for his views on the dissensions in the Russian Social Democracy. In reply, Lenin in his own name made a brief report in which he repeated the data on the correlation of forces of the two dissenting groups which Litvinov had distributed to the delegates of the International.[118] In his report Lenin said, among other things: "The dissensions which separate us from the liquidators are identical with those which divide reformists and revolutionaries almost everywhere."[119]

On April 28 (15), 1914, *Put Pravdy* published a reply of a group of organized Marxists to the International Socialist Bureau's proposal of mediation. Lenin was the author of this reply, which concluded with a request that the International Socialist Bureau should, on the basis of the resolution of the December session, promote in every possible way "the exchange of opinions between the groups of social democrats

---

[117] Lenin, *Sochineniia*, XVII, 733, note 131. In writing of the London meeting, in the *Proletarskaia Pravda*, No. 6, December 26 (13), 1913, Lenin said that Kautsky's resolution for a general exchange of opinion was preferable to Rosa Luxemburg's plan for a "unification conference." But he strongly criticized Kautsky for saying that the old R.S.D.L. party was dead (*ibid.*, 110–12).

[118] Bantke, "V. I. Lenin i bolshevizm na mezhdunarodnoi arene v dovoennyi period," *Proletarskaia Revoliutsiia*, Nos. 2–3 (85–86), 1929, p. 47, citing Litvinov, "Russkie dela v M.S.B.," *Proletarskaia Pravda*, No. 2, December 8, 1912.

[119] Lenin, "Tov. Guismansu," *Sochineniia*, XVII, 190.

concerning the disputed questions . . . . so as to expose in an unbiased collegium and before the International, the fictitiousness of the 'August bloc' and of the Organization Committee of the liquidators and the whole of their disorganizing activity with respect to the consolidated majority of social democratic workers of Russia."[120]

PLEKHANOV'S RESIGNATION AS REPRESENTATIVE OF THE RUSSIAN SOCIAL DEMOCRATIC LABOR PARTY ON THE INTERNATIONAL SOCIALIST BUREAU

[Letter to the Secretary of the International Socialist Bureau at the London Conference][121]

SAN REMO, December 9, 1913

DEAR COMRADE!

On this occasion the International Socialist Bureau is meeting in London in order to facilitate by its action the final unification of the English socialists.[122]

I regret to diminish, by the following communication, the feeling of satisfaction which you will experience from effecting the unity of the English socialists.

The dissensions which have existed during recent years in the Russian Social Democratic Labor party have split our Duma group into two rival groups.

This division of our Duma group has occurred as a result of certain regrettable decisions adopted by our comrades—"the liquidators"—who were in the majority (seven against six).[123]

In any event this is the final blow to our unity, and I, who represent the *party* among you, can do nothing but resign.

---

[120] Lenin, "Organizovannye marksisty o vmeshatelstve mezhdunarodnogo biuro," *Sochineniia*, XVII, 317.

[121] "Réunion du Bureau Socialiste International à Londres (13 et 14 décembre 1913)," *Supplément au Bulletin périodique du Bureau Socialiste International*, No. 11, p. 6.

[122] At a meeting on December 13 and the morning session of December 14 the International Socialist Bureau considered the question of unification of the three British parties, the Independent Labour party, the Fabian Society, and the British Socialist party.

[123] Deputy Jagiello, member of the Polish Socialist party (Levitsa) represented Polish workers in the Duma. He had only a consulting vote in intra-party matters. The Menshevik group in the State Duma was therefore usually referred to as consisting of seven members. For some unknown reason this paragraph is omitted from the Russian text of this letter published in G. V. Plekhanov, *Sochineniia,* XIX, 560–61. It is quoted in other Russian sources.

I do this by means of this letter.

Allow me, however, to say that the socialist proletariat of Russia stands firmly for party unity and will support with great sympathy every attempt of the representatives of the international proletariat to help to reunite our forces.

Every action on your part to this end will be further facilitated by the fact that among our organized comrades there exists a tendency called "Party Men"[124] (whose organ is *Za Partiiu* [For the Party], a newspaper issued in Paris), which has always protested against any attempts at a split, regardless of the group from which they come— whether the "Bolsheviks" of Lenin's coloring or the "liquidators."

To this tendency belong both "Bolsheviks" and "Mensheviks" who are equally convinced that at the present time unity is our principal practical task.

I call your attention to the existence of this tendency in order that you may know about it at the moment when you have to settle the question as to how the Russian Social Democratic forces should now be represented in the International Socialist Bureau.

Very truly yours,
PLEKHANOV

P.S. My letter was already written when I received a copy of the proposal of the Central Committee of the Social Democracy of Poland and Lithuania. I believe that you will render great service by placing on the agenda of the Vienna Congress the question of the unification of the Russian Social Democratic Labor party.

G. P.

RESOLUTION ON UNIFICATION AND STATEMENTS AT THE LONDON CONFERENCE OF THE INTERNATIONAL SOCIALIST BUREAU, DECEMBER 14, 1913

[Resolution Proposed by the German Delegation and Adopted by the Conference][125]

.... The International [Socialist] Bureau recalls the resolution of the Amsterdam International Congress which states:

[124] This name was adopted by a nonfactional group composed of both the Menshevik "Party-Men" and certain Bolsheviks, who favored conciliation with the opposition groups for the sake of preserving party unity; this group was officially established in April 1912.

[125] "Das Internationale Bureau," *Vorwärts*, No. 333, December 18, 1913, p. 3. This is the final text and differs slightly from the text as introduced by the German delegation. The Russian text published in *Proletarskaia Pravda*, No. 2, December 21 (8), 1913, was accompanied by an editorial giving the editors' views on unification. Bolshevik conditions were further elaborated in resolutions signed by "a group of organized Marxists."

"In order that the working class may put forth all its strength in the struggle against capitalism, it is necessary that in every country there exist, *vis à vis* the bourgeois parties, only *one* socialist party, as there exists only *one* proletariat. Therefore, it is the imperative duty of all comrades and socialist organizations to make every effort to bring about this unity on the basis of principles established by the international congresses, a unity necessary in the interests of the proletariat before which they are responsible for all fatal consequences of a continued breach.

"In order to assist the attainment of this aim, the International Socialist Bureau as well as the parties of all countries in which such unity exists are ready to offer their services."

The realization of this resolution of the International wherever there is still no party unity becomes more and more important in proportion as our opponents unite for the suppression of the proletariat. However, the unification of social democratic forces is nowhere as necessary as in the country where the regime of bloody Tsarism is raging. Nowhere is the proletariat experiencing such cruel and violent abuses, nowhere is it deprived to such an extent of every possibility of existence—and, on the other hand, this proletariat is weakened at the same time by ever-changing internal discord which absorbs and paralyzes its best forces. This sad state of affairs has attained its climax as a result of the split in the Duma group.

Therefore, the International [Socialist] Bureau considers it the urgent duty of all social democratic groups in Russia to make a serious and loyal attempt to agree to the restoration of a single party organization and to put an end to the present harmful and discouraging state of disunion. The International [Socialist] Bureau, in conformity with the Amsterdam resolution, offers to the Russian comrades its services in the capacity of a mediator and commissions its Executive Committee to communicate without delay with all the groups of the labor movement within the Russian Empire, Russian Poland included, which recognize the program of Russian Social Democracy—to communicate with them in order to bring about a general exchange of opinion concerning the points of divergence.

The International [Socialist] Bureau refuses to investigate and to discuss the past differences of Russian Social Democracy. Russian Social Democracy can draw the strength and solidarity which it needs to fulfill its difficult and historic tasks, not from a condemnation of past mistakes, but from an agreement regarding its present and future tasks.

K. KAUTSKY, EBERT, MOLKENBUHR

[Statement by Rubanovich for the Socialist-Revolutionist
Central Committee][126]

I wish to make a brief statement in order to explain my vote. The
resolution proposed by Kautsky and amended by Rosa Luxemburg undoubtedly considers only the various groups of the Russian Social Democratic [Labor] party. But since Citizen Kautsky submits a draft resolution which is based on the resolution which was adopted at Amsterdam
concerning the *unity of all socialist parties in every country,* and, furthermore, since Citizen Vandervelde, in welcoming unity in England yesterday, appealed to all the other countries, including Russia, to establish
unity, and, finally, since at the preceding session of the Bureau, Citizen
Plekhanov, the founder of the Social Democratic [Labor] party and the
most authoritative theoretician of Russian Social Democracy, with whom
we were at variance at Amsterdam, has declared that the hour has
sounded not merely for the restoration of Russian Social Democratic
unity but even for the rapprochement of the Social Democracy with
the Socialist-Revolutionist party in Russia, I must say, in accord with
the Central Organ of my party, that we are ready to do all we can to
abolish the causes of divergence between the two parties. Certainly profound changes must occur in the general political conditions of Russia
in order that the two parties may loyally submit their controversies to
the proletariat and to the organized toiling peasants. But our party declares in advance that as soon as this consultation becomes possible it will
be inspired with the wishes of the organized masses, the only arbitrators
of unity—unity which cannot be decreed by a vote of the International
Socialist Bureau, the authority of which, however, is now great enough
to obtain from hostile affiliated parties more consideration and mutual
respect in common struggles. It is with the reservation of these remarks, which are necessarily brief, that I vote in favor of Kautsky's
proposal.

[Statement by Lapinski for the Polish Socialist Party (Levitsa)][127]

The laboring class in Poland is just as painfully affected by the split
in the parliamentary socialist group of the Duma as is the proletariat of
all Russia.

This split constitutes the last phase of the discord which has gradually seized the entire labor movement in Russia.

[126] "Réunion du Bureau Socialiste International à Londres (13 et 14 Décembre,
1913)," *Supplément au Bulletin périodique du Bureau Socialiste International,* No.
11, p. 5.

[127] *Ibid.,* p. 5. As is noted below, p. 504, a split had occurred in the Polish
Socialist party in 1906. The Right wing adopted the name Polish Socialist
party, Revolutionary Faction; the Left wing was known as the Polish Socialist
party (Levitsa). Lapinski actually represented the latter group.

This profound discord between the two groups of the Social Democratic party in Russia has a strong repercussion on the labor movement in Poland, where it sustains and accentuates the existent split between the Social Democratic parties in Poland.

Moreover, this split is regrettable since the divergences of points of view which actually separate the Polish Socialist party and the Social Democracy of Poland and Lithuania are reduced, especially today, to verbal differences, to gradations of color which are often imperceptible for the large majority of the working class, which ardently desires the coming of unity.

Furthermore, this party war hinders fatally the development of the labor movement in Poland at a moment when unity is imperative, in view of the exceptional violence committed at present in Poland by the nationalist reaction.

All efforts toward unity which would exclude one Social Democratic group would necessarily fail, would be unjust as well as incomplete. For six years the Polish Socialist party has been proclaiming repeatedly at all congresses and conferences the necessity of unity within the social democratic labor movement in Poland. This spirit of unity inspires the entire party policy, and recently its Congress, held in 1913, voted a resolution which declared the party's willingness to become affiliated with the Social Democratic Labor party of all Russia.

During the last election campaign the Polish Socialist party formed a bloc with the Bund and affiliated with the Russian party; likewise the struggle provoked by the new social insurance laws has brought about a common action between the Polish Socialist party, the Bund, and a group of the Social Democracy of Poland and Lithuania.

But it is especially the election of Comrade Sagiello [Jagiello], candidate of the Polish Socialist party and of the Bund to the Duma, and his entrance into the parliamentary Social Democratic group which have given an urgent character to the question of unity.

That is why on behalf of the Polish Socialist party I propose to the International Socialist Bureau that it make proper moves in order to establish social democratic unity in Russia and in Poland.

For the Polish Socialist party.

Stanislav Lapinski

[Statement by Chkheidze for the Menshevik Social Democrats in the State Duma][128]

Since the revolution of 1905 the Russian proletariat has been represented in the State Duma. In the first three Dumas there was a socialist group, and this is also the case now in the Fourth Duma.

---

[128] *Supplement au Bulletin periodique du Bureau Socialiste International,* No. 11, p. 5.

On account of the political situation in Russia this socialist group in the parliament is of very great importance. It constitutes the only existing and possible organ which greatly favors the unity of the polyglot proletariat of Russia.

The activity of the Social Democratic groups of the first three Dumas met with the general approval of the organized Social Democrats and the general mass of the social democratic proletariat.

In spite of the violent government repressions the group of the Fourth Duma was elected in a period of revival of the proletariat and of the democratic movement generally. A member of the Third Duma group, Citizen Chkheidze, was re-elected. The other thirteen delegates of the social democratic proletariat were newcomers in the Fourth Duma.

During the first session the activity of the Social Democratic group was well received among the ranks of Russian Social Democracy. It also had the approval of the entire press of Lenin's group. But at the beginning of the present session of the Duma the six deputies of the Leninist group[129] unexpectedly sent an ultimatum to the Duma group. They, the six [deputies], wished to have equality in the final vote with the eight other deputies.[130] But the majority rejected this demand, because otherwise, as a matter of fact, there would be a separation of the united Duma group into two independent and merely federated parts. Immediately upon this refusal the six deputies tendered their resignations to the Duma group. In our declaration concerning this division within the Duma group we have sufficiently well proved how entirely groundless were the accusations against the Duma majority, accusations made by the withdrawing members in order to excuse their manner of acting.

The blow dealt to the Social Democratic Duma group by the withdrawal of the six deputies was at the same time a hard blow to the Russian labor movement as a whole. The consequences of this blow are so much more fatal because just now a strong revival of the proletarian struggle is manifesting itself all over the country.

We believe that it is in the interests of the social democratic movement in Russia as well as of the International not to neglect any possible effort toward establishing the unity of the social democratic forces in our country which is so necessary.

For that reason we appeal to the International Socialist Bureau, asking it to act resolutely on this matter.

---

[129] R. V. Malinovsky, G. I. Petrovsky, A. E. Badaev, F. N. Samoilov, N. R. Shagov, M. K. Muranov.

[130] A. F. Burianov, I. N. Mankov, M. I. Skobelev, I. N. Tuliakov, V. I. Khaustov, N. S. Chkheidze, A. I. Chkhenkeli, E. I. Jagiello.

[Statement by the Organization Committee, the Bund, and the
Lettish Social Democracy][131]

The revival of the labor movement in Russia poses the acute question
of the re-establishment of unity within the Social Democratic Labor
party of Russia.

The real differences in tactics, which have existed among us for
several years, have since that time diminished significantly and today
are much less than the differences which exist among other fraternal
social democratic parties. Nevertheless, the cleft between the various
party groups, which is the necessary consequence of the barbarous political situation in Russia, grows daily. Every small difference of opinion,
even minute ones, are inflated artificially and form new objects of
struggle in the harmful struggle between the groups. In this manner the
so-called Leninist group has caused a split in the legal press, the trade
unions, and the educational societies, and in the struggle for the co-
operatives and, finally, in the last stronghold of social democratic unity—
the Duma group. A point has now been reached when reciprocal suspicions and hatred manifest themselves openly in every factory and every
shop.

These conditions within the party, which decrease the influence of
the Social Democracy in the eyes of the masses and which threaten to
destroy the collective action of the proletariat, have compelled several
tendencies and organizations of the party which met in August of last
year to join in a struggle for party unity.

The reverberations caused by the withdrawal of the six Leninist
members of the Duma who left the Social Democratic Duma group have
proved that the majority of party organizations are hostile to the division.
This also proves that unity is the desire of the class-conscious proletarian
majority. But the restoration of unity is a difficult and slow process on
account of the political situation in Russia. In our opinion this process
can develop more quickly with the mediation of the International, which
enjoys great authority in our young labor movement.

It is for this reason that we propose to the International Socialist
Bureau that it exercise its authority in favor of a movement toward
unity. Thus the International will forge a powerful weapon for future
revolutionary struggle.

1. The Organization Committee of the Russian Social Democratic
Labor party. DNEPROV

2. Bund (The All-Jewish Workers League of Poland, Lithuania, and
Russia). S. KURSKY

3. Lettish Social Democracy. MERKEL

[131] *Supplement au Bulletin periodique du Bureau Socialiste International*, No.
11, pp. 5–6.

BOLSHEVIK CONDITIONS OF UNIFICATION

[Resolution of a "Group of Organized Marxists" in *Proletarskaia Pravda*, No. 9, December 30 (17), 1913][132]

We welcome heartily the decision of the Workers' International on the necessity of ascertaining fully and completely the essential and fundamental dissensions which exist in Russia between political tendencies in the labor movement.

In responding to the proposal of the International we consider it necessary to indicate those fundamental dissensions which in our opinion divide the Marxists and the liquidators into two irreconcilable camps.

We declare first of all that for every class-conscious worker it is a matter not of creating some new integrity but only of fortifying and fully restoring the old organization as it was formed more than fifteen years ago—with its old program and its most important tactical decisions. From this Marxist organization the liquidators have broken away. To restore unity with them in the realm of activity *outside the Duma* the following conditions are necessary:

1. A full and unreserved recognition (in practice) of "the underground organization," an absolute submission to the decisions of its cells, and a pledge in no case to permit any unprovoked attacks whatever against it in the press.

2. A full and unreserved recognition of the fact that the true fundamental demands advanced by the working class of Russia, the realization of activity in that spirit, and a renunciation of liberal-reformist preaching, appealing for a repudiation of old tasks, constitute the chief task of this epoch.

3. The retracting of all attempts to change the program of the Marxists (the cultural national autonomy) and an absolute recognition of the program worked out in 1903.

4. In questions connected with the strike movement, full submission to the decisions of workers organized in a Marxian manner and the renunciation of struggle against the so-called "strike hazard."

5. The recognition in practice of an *independent* tactic of the proletariat and a renunciation of the belittling of the tasks of the laboring class in order to establish blocs with the liberals.

6. The recognition that in the question of activity in trade unions it is necessary to be guided by the decisions of the International Socialist Congress at Stuttgart and of the London Congress of the Russian Marxists.

7. A renunciation of the principle of constructing labor organiza-

---

[132] "Rezoliutsiia o reshenii Mezhdunaradnogo Sotsialisticheskogo Biuro." Lenin, *Sochineniia*, XVII, 681–82.

tions on the principle of nationality. The creation of *united* organizations in Poland and the northwestern area. The fulfillment by the Bund, as a whole, of the decision concerning fusion in the locality of the group's activity, which decision has been repeatedly reiterated by the Russian Marxists.

In the realm of *Duma* activity, the conditions of unity are as follows:

1. The recognition of the Duma group as an organ in absolute submission to the organized will of the Marxist whole.

2. The retracting of all violations of program (of cultural national autonomy, of the admittance of Jagiello, etc.).

3. The condemnation of the schismatic actions of the "seven," who were also condemned by G. V. Plekhanov in his letter to the International Socialist Bureau.[133]

As regards the party groups with which it would be advisable for the International Socialist Bureau to communicate in order to arrange for a general exchange of opinions, we demand first of all that *only and exclusively* those representatives of workers' organizations existing in Russia, and in no case circles abroad not connected with the Russian activity, take part in it.

And we further believe that: (1) either *only* representatives of *two* fundamental currents, struggling in Russia, i.e., of the Marxists and the liquidators, should be invited, or (2) if all dissensions in general between Russian Social Democrats and those that consider themselves Social Democrats are to be examined, then all labor organizations without exception which are active in Russia and which consider themselves close to Social Democracy should be invited. In this case there is no reason for excluding a few left Narodniks also, and also the Jewish groups which are competing with the Bund and which consider themselves socialist, etc.

Finally, we are certain that for a correct illumination of the dissensions in the ranks of Russian Social Democrats the foreign socialist press should open its pages to responsible representatives of the Russian organizations who—in contrast to the emigrant circles and irresponsible persons—could give to the foreign comrades an exact conception of the ideological-political foundation of dissensions in the Russian labor movement.

A GROUP OF ORGANIZED MARXISTS

In the spring of 1914 the International Socialist Bureau decided to investigate for itself the possibilities of unification of the Russian Social Democracy. On his way back from

---

[133] See above, p. 92.

Finland, Emil Vandervelde, chairman of the I.S.B., stopped for three days in St. Petersburg. There, according to his own account, he met some of the prominent Duma members, including the chairman, Rodzianko. He also had interviews with members of the two major groups of the R.S.D.L. party and gathered data on the correlation of the forces of the rival social democratic groups, which he published.[134]

VANDERVELDE AND THE PETERSBURG BOLSHEVIKS AND MENSHEVIKS

[A Letter from Martov to Axelrod, June 15 (2), 1914][135]

Dear Pavel Borisovich!

I hasten to write you our local news. You may learn of it partly from newspapers. Vandervelde visited here three days. He came here as a tourist on his return trip from Finland. We have made use of his stay here as profitably as we were able in the three days. At a small banquet arranged by the [Duma] deputies, with our opponents present, and later at a private conference we brought up as well as we could the question of dissensions. The Pravdists proved to be of great assistance to us by showing themselves to Vandervelde in their entire "Asiatic" splendor (this we shall state in our report on the banquet which is due to come out in three days from now).[136] Vandervelde, of course adhered strictly to the role of "impartiality," thinking that he has no right even to suggest sympathy with one or the other tendency. Nevertheless, in a private conversation with me (on the whole he conversed chiefly with us) he said: "You can guess of course that my sympathies are with your tendency, but I cannot express this." More than once while we were telling him about the platform of the "consistent" group he interrupted us by remarking, "just like the syndicalists in France." On the whole, we received the impression that during his stay here he learned to distinguish between the "Asiatic" and the "European" orientations. He remarked ironically, that "revolutionism" does not seem to prevent the Leninists from concerning themselves with such a "miserable" activity as the sick-benefit funds; he observed with amazement that the "six" had not voted at variance with the "eight"; he listened to us with apparent

---

[134] "Emile Vandervelde en Russie," *Le Peuple*, June 21, 1914, p. 1; E. Vandervelde, *Three Aspects of the Russian Revolution*, p. 19.

[135] *Pisma P. B. Akselroda i Yu. O. Martova*, I, 290–92.

[136] This report was published in *Nasha Rabochaia Gazeta*, June 5 and 6, 1913. (*Pisma P. B. Akselroda i Yu. O. Martova*, I, 292, note 1.)

understanding when we explained to him that the success of "Pravdism" in Petersburg was due to the influx of new but yet weak strata (later in his conversation with me, he applied this explanation to particular cases, as for instance the success of the Bolsheviks' hooligan campaigns in the trade unions). The following is characteristic: he asked. me how large a circulation our newspaper had. I replied by pointing out the exact (average) figure for the recent period: 16,500. Somewhat later he said: "You see, you have given me a sufficiently definite figure so that I can judge that you supplied me with an average figure, whereas in *Pravda* I was given a round figure of 40,000. I think," he added looking searchingly at me, "that they have given me the exact figure." The insinuation was plain; apparently he did not believe that this figure was accurate. I told him that we also had information about *Pravda's* circulation and presumed that 40,000 is the maximum figure, whereas most probably the average figure is 30,000. I pointed out that all the readers of *Zait* and of the Caucasian organ,[137] should be added to our figure. This would increase our *minimum* total to 25,000. Therefore, the predominance of the Pravdists over us can at the most be expressed by the proportion of 3:2. The crux on which I endeavored to concentrate his attentions consists—he could readily convince himself that this was so—in that we and the Pravdists are not working in caves and with masks on, but in a great many respects we are working under practically European conditions and that—as I put it to him—the *external* conditions of the movement differ but slightly as regards principles from, let us say, the Hungarian conditions (to this he agreed); that therefore, the Europeans should not be permitted to knock one down by phrases to the effect that the conditions in Russia, which are so different from the European, justify plans of construction upon the "old basis." I think that after seeing for himself plainly enough that the Pravdists received him pompously in the editorial office, posed for pictures with him, made appointments with him by telephone, he will no longer take seriously the talks about our "liquidationism" and will understand the charlatan character of the talks about the "underground organization."

Once, when this was convenient, he posed us an official question: would our side consent to accept not merely mediation by the International [Socialist] Bureau but also its arbitration in the disputes, arbitration which would bind us to accept principles elaborated by the Bureau. I said purposely that I could not answer this myself and translated the question to some of our people who were gathered around in a group (some thirty of them). With their approval and

---

[137] A legal social democratic newspaper, *Pikri* (Thought), in Georgian. (*Pisma P. B. Akselroda i Yu. O. Martova*, I, 292, note 2.)

on behalf of all of us I formulated the following reply: if the Bureau, or a special commission, upon acquainting itself with the essence of the dispute will point out a platform and a basis for unification, we pledge *a priori* to adopt them and cannot even imagine doing otherwise. We, in turn, asked whether this question had been posed to our opponents. It was here that Vandervelde said—as I have already mentioned—that he was in greater sympathy with our tendency and therefore had decided to ask us such a straightforward question. He also said that he was afraid to pose this question to them [the Bolsheviks] fearing that they might sense or suspect his wish to corner them (*les faire boucler*). This would have to be postponed until an official conversation.

With this I shall conclude for the time being. I think that we have accomplished a great deal in the sense of the psychological preparation of the "Latins," for whom, of course, Vandervelde's impressions will have great significance. It has turned out well: the workers' attitude toward Vandervelde's arrival was, I should say, extremely enthusiastic and sympathetic, and they themselves grasped the basic significance of the appearance of a representative of the International upon Russian soil. All their resolutions are imbued with an understanding of this significance. . . . .

With a handshake,

Yu. Tsederbaum [Martov]

[From Shliapnikov's Recollections][138]

On a June night the comrades of the Vyborg district of our party sent a messenger to fetch the "Frenchman" [i.e., Shliapnikov, who had a French passport] and have him attend a solemn banquet given by the Bolshevik and Menshevik Duma groups in honor of Vandervelde, who had come to Russia. The banquet was arranged semilegally in Palkin's restaurant, where I was shown in by other than the main entrance. There were quite a few guests in the room, but exceptionally few Bolsheviks. Among these were Comrades Petrovsky and Badaev. The Mensheviks were represented by Chkheidze, Dan, Potresov, and other stars of *Luch*. The speeches of the liquidators showed diplomatic sorrow with respect to the split in the ranks of the laboring class. I did the translating for Petrovsky and then, being authorized by our deputies, I took the floor to reply to the Menshevik lamentation concerning the split. With the facts at hand I proved that the Petersburg proletariat is united in its struggle. "In its day-to-day struggle," said I, "the working class proceeds under the banner of the Petersburg Committee of our party in spite of the intrigues of the minority which is able to pretend to be a

[138] A. Shliapnikov, *Kanun semnadtsatogo goda*, I (3d ed.), 6–7.

majority only at banquets. The practice of the labor struggle in Petersburg, even if examined superficially—you, Comrade Vandervelde, were
able to examine it only in this way, for you could not go to our shops
nor see our strikes and mass meetings—proves that the majority is in
our favor and you, the advocate of unity of the working organizations,
should propose to the minority, to the intelligentsia which sits here, to
submit to the majority. Take any form of the labor movement: the trade
unions, they are for us; the insurance work—it is our work, we have a
majority there also. Unity among us can be easily established; it is only
necessary to bind the minority to submit to the will of the majority.
Declare this, here on behalf of the International Socialist Bureau, as its
chairman, and make it obligatory for those who cry about unity to follow
your proposition—then we shall not force any of them [minority mem-
bers] out of the organization and there will be no split among us."

My speech in French aroused the Mensheviks. In spite of the presence of the distinguished foreigner I was interrupted, and I succeeded
in concluding my speech after the guest himself, i.e., Vandervelde, had
intervened—who listened and observed the gathering with much attention. After I had finished he felt that it was imperative to answer those
straightforward questions. In his speech concerning unity, tolerance,
and similar things he declared that the minority must submit to the
majority.

We all adjourned when the milky morning had taken the place of the
light northern night. That morning I was again at my bench, but I told
none of the proletarians in the shop about my night's excursion to the
banquet in honor of Vandervelde. It was known only to a limited circle
of organized comrades, party workers. . . . .

According to the files of the Russian Secret Police, plans
for the much-discussed unification conference were well under
way early in the spring of 1914. The Conference met at Brussels on July 16–17, 1914, with eleven Russian groups represented as follows: The Central Committee of the R.S.D.L.
party by I. F. Armand (Petrova), M. F. Vladimirsky, and
I. F. Popov; the Organization Committee of the R.S.D.L.
party, with the Caucasian Regional Committee and the *Borba*
group, by Yu. O. Martov, S. Yu. Semkovsky, A. B. Romanov,
L. D. Trotsky, P. B. Axelrod, V. D. Mgeladze, and A.
Zurabov; the Social Democratic Menshevik group of the
State Duma by A. I. Chkhenkeli; the *Edinstvo* group by G. V.
Plekhanov; the *Vpered* group by G. A. Aleksinsky; the Bund

by Yonov and Borisov; the Lettish Social Democracy by J. Berzin; the Social Democracy of Lithuania by Mickiewicz-Kapsukas; the Main Presidium [Zarząd Glóvny] of the Social Democracy of Poland and Lithuania by R. Luxemburg; the Regional Presidium of the Social Democracy of Poland and Lithuania by J. Hanecki, A. Malecki, and Dolecki; and the Polish Socialist party (Levitsa) by S. Lapinski. The Executive Committee of the International Socialist Bureau was represented by Kautsky, Vandervelde, Huysmans, Anseele, Němec, and Rubanovich.[139] Lenin did not go to the Brussels Unification Conference but selected Inessa Armand to read the report there on behalf of the Central Committee of the R.S.D.L. party, a report which he himself had written and which is given below. Krupskaia writes that Armand was selected because it was necessary to have as the Bolshevik representative a firm person who could "resist a storm of indignation" and who, furthermore, had a perfect command of foreign languages.[140]

The unification of the Russian Social Democratic groups was naturally a matter of interest to the Tsarist police, and the Brussels Conference was the subject of several secret reports. One agent noted that the failure of the Conference to secure definite results was due to the irreconcilable attitude of the Bolsheviks. Another agent observed (Secret Police Agent's note, No. 261, 1914) that "it is characteristic that Lenin evaded participation in this Conference although he was invited to attend" and that "the majority of the members of the Conference were greatly disgusted with Petrova's report and speech, as no one expected that the impudence of the 'Leninists' would reach such dimensions. Vandervelde, Rosa Luxemburg, Plekhanov, and Kautsky came forward with criticisms of this report. . . . Plekhanov pointed out that the entire irreconcilability of Lenin's policy was due to his desire

---

[139] G. Shklovsky, "Briusselskii blok" *Bolshaia Sovetskaia Entsiklopediia*, Vol. 7, pp. 712–13; Lenin, *Sochineniia*, XVII, 745, note 177.

[140] N. K. Krupskaia [ed.], *Pamiati Inessy Armand*, p. 15; hereafter cited as *Pamiati Inessy Armand*.

not to give up the control over the party funds, part of which he had seized by purely burglar methods. For this last statement Plekhanov was called to order by the chairman and deprived of his right to speak. The speeches of all the orators were rather passionate but did not help the situation, so that the members of the Conference, without coming to any decision, declined to participate further in the Conference."

Despite the failure at Brussels to accomplish anything the Department of Police feared that some degree of unification might be achieved and therefore instructed its agents participating in all sorts of party conferences to "steadfastly and persistently defend the idea of the complete impossibility of any organizational fusion whatsoever, of these tendencies, and especially the union of the Bolsheviks with the Mensheviks."[141]

As originally proposed, the Brussels Conference was to adopt no binding resolution; but a resolution drafted by Kautsky was offered by the chairman. Representatives of nine of the eleven Russian groups supported the resolution; the Lettish Central Committee and the Central Committee of the R.S.D.L. party, i.e., the Bolsheviks, refused to vote. According to a letter written by Borisov and preserved in the archives of the Bund, Huysmans warned the Bolsheviks that "whoever does not vote on the resolution is responsible before the entire International for the disruption of the effort to effect unity and it will be so reported to the Congress at Vienna."[142]

The Conference adopted unanimously a resolution on the unification of the Polish groups and decided to issue a general manifesto against separatism and on the necessity of unification. Three persons were commissioned to draft this manifesto, but it was never issued. In general the principal accomplishment of the Brussels Conference was not unifica-

141 M. A. Tsiavlovsky [ed.], *Bolsheviki. Dokumenty po istorii bolshevizma s 1903 po 1916 god byvsh. Moskovsk. Okhrannago Otdeleniia*, pp. 146–48. See also *Obzor deiatelnosti rossiiskoi sotsial-demokraticheskoi rabochei partii za vremia s nachala voiny Rossii s Avstro-Vengriei i Germaniei po iiul 1916 goda*, pp. 3–4.

142 Quoted in Lenin, *Sochineniia*, XVII, 745, note 177.

tion but confirmation of the split signalized by the revival of the disintegrated August bloc which now became known as the "Brussels" or "July 3rd" bloc. The organizations constituting this bloc drew up an appeal to the Russian workers, calling attention to the refusal of the Bolsheviks and the Letts to vote on Kautsky's resolution and urging the workers to support the efforts of the International to bring unity to Russian Social Democracy.[143] It was expected that the Executive Committee of the I.S.B. would report on the Brussels Conference to the International Socialist Congress which was to meet in Vienna in August 1914 and which would make a definite pronouncement on the question of Russian unity. In anticipation of this action at Vienna the Social Democrats conducted intensive agitation in Russia for workers' support of the rival groups.[144] But the war came, the Vienna Congress did not meet, the International was disrupted, and the Russian groups became even more widely separated by the issues of the succeeding years.

THE BOLSHEVIK VERSION OF THE SITUATION IN THE RUSSIAN SOCIAL DEMOCRATIC LABOR PARTY

[Report of Its Central Committee to the Brussels Unification Conference, July 16–17, 1914, and Instructions to the Delegation of the Central Committee][145]

In beginning the report on behalf of the Central Committee of the Russian Social Democratic Labor party, I wish first of all to make use of the occasion to fulfill a pleasant duty and to express on behalf of this institution my deep gratitude to Comrade Vandervelde, Chairman of the Executive Committee of the International Socialist Bureau, for his visit to our country in order to make the personal acquaintance of the leaders of the labor movement in Petersburg. We are all the more grateful to Comrade Vandervelde for having been the first to establish the direct

[143] Because of the suppression of the legal labor newspapers in Russia this appeal was not published until 1915 when it appeared in *Informatsionnyi listok zagranichnoi organizatsii Bunda*, No. 7, January 1915, pp. 14–16, and was reprinted in "Vozzvanie Briusselskoi sotsial-demokraticheskoi obedinitelnoi konferentsii" in *Pamiatniki agitatsionnoi literatury ross. sots.-demokr. rab. partii* (hereafter cited as *Pamiatniki agitatsionnoi literatury* . . . .), pp. 25–28.

[144] A. Badaev, *The Bolsheviks in the Tsarist Duma*, pp. 187–89.

[145] Lenin, *Sochineniia*, XVII, 543–71.

acquaintance of prominent members of the International with the leading and class-conscious workers of Russia and, also, for the publication in the foreign socialist press (we have in mind *Le Peuple* and *L'Humanité*) of the objective data concerning the labor movement in Russia, data obtained on the spot from the editorial boards of newspapers representing three different tendencies: those of the Pravdists (i.e., of our party), the liquidators, and the Socialist-Revolutionists.

My report on the question of the unity of Russian Social Democracy shall consist of four parts as follows: (1) first I shall state the *substance* of the chief dissensions among Social Democrats; (2) then I shall give data concerning the mass labor movement in Russia, which represents a *verification* of our party policy in terms of *the experience of this movement;* and (3) I shall give a verification of the policy and position of our opponents in terms of the same experiences. Finally, (4) I shall formulate on behalf of the Central Committee of the Russian Social Democratic Labor party concrete, positive, and *practical* proposals concerning unity.

I

Two fundamental points of view exist on what is taking place at present within Russian Social Democracy.

One point of view, expounded by Rosa Luxemburg in her proposal of last year (December 1913) to the International Socialist Bureau and shared both by the liquidators and by the groups which defend them, is as follows: there reigns in Russia a "chaos" of factional struggle between a large number of party groups, the worst of which—that of "Lenin"— is doing the most to produce a breach. As a matter of fact the dissensions do not at all exclude the possibility of joint activity. The road toward unity lies through an agreement or compromise of all tendencies and party groups.

The other point of view, shared by us, maintains that there is nothing like "a chaos of factional struggle" taking place in Russia. There is *only* a struggle against the liquidators and *only* in this struggle is there being formed the *real* workers' social democratic party which has already united an *overwhelming majority*—four-fifths—of the class-conscious workers of Russia. The illegal party, with which most of the Russian workers have united, has been represented by formal and informal conferences: January 1912, February 1913, and the summer of 1913.[146] The legal organ is the newspaper *Pravda* (*Vérité*), hence the name "Prav-

---

[146] On January 18 (5)—30 (17), 1912, the Sixth All-Russian Conference of the R.S.D.L. party met at Prague. This Conference, attended largely by Bolsheviks, adopted a resolution expelling the "liquidators" from the party. The "February" Conference, so-called for conspirative reasons, actually met in Cracow January 10 (December 28)—January 14 (1), 1913, and was attended by members of the Central Committee and certain others. It discussed the signs of rising revolutionary

dists." Incidentally, this point of view was expressed by the Petersburg worker who spoke at the banquet attended by Comrade Vandervelde in St. Petersburg;[147] it held that the workers in the factories and mills of St. Petersburg are united and that only "the General Staffs without the army" are outside this unity of workers.

In the second part of my report I shall discuss the objective data which prove the correctness of our point of view; but, at present, I shall dwell on the substance of liquidationism.

The formal exclusion of liquidators from the party took place at the January 1912 Conference of the R.S.D.L. party. However, our party raised the question concerning liquidationism much earlier. The All-Russian Conference of the R.S.D.L. party held in December 1908 had already accepted a precise and formal resolution binding for the entire party and absolutely condemning liquidationism. This resolution gives the following definition of liquidationism: (Liquidationism constitutes) "attempts of a certain group of party intelligentsia to liquidate the existing organization of the R.S.D.L. party and to replace it at any price by shapeless association within the limits of legality even if this legality be bought at the cost of an obvious repudiation of the program, tactics, and traditions of the party."[148]

This shows that as early as in 1908 liquidationism was formally declared and recognized as an *intelligentsia* tendency and that in substance it was a *renunciation* of the illegal party and the *replacing* of it, or the preaching of its replacement, by a legal party.

The plenary meeting of the Central Committee in January 1910 once more *unanimously* condemned liquidationism as *"a manifestation of bourgeois influence upon the proletariat."*[149]

This shows how erroneous is the opinion that our dissensions with the liquidators are not more profound but on the contrary are less significant than the dissensions between the so-called radicals and the mod-

temper, illegal organizations, tasks of the party, etc., and passed resolutions similar to those of the Prague Conference. On October 5 (September 22)—October 14 (1), 1913, the Central Committee and a few party members met at Poronino and adopted a resolution on the national question. This Conference in Russian party literature is usually referred to as the "Summer" or "August" conference.

[147] The reference is to Shliapnikov's speech; see above, pp. 103-4.

[148] The Fifth All-Russian Conference of the R.S.D.L. party was held in Paris, January 3-9, 1909 (December 21-27, 1908). This quotation appears in *Vsesoiuznaia kommunisticheskaia partiia (b) v rezoliutsiiakh i resheniiakh sezdov, konferentsii i plenumov TsK.*, I, 1898-1925 (5th ed.), p. 128.

[149] The plenum of the Central Committee of the R.S.D.L. party was held in Paris from January 15 to February 5 (January 2-23), 1910. At this plenum another attempt was made to unite all the groups of Russian Social Democracy. This quotation appears in *Vsesoiuznaia kommunisticheskaia partiia (b) v rezoliutsiiakh i resheniiakh sezdov, konferentsii i plenumov TsK.*, I, 1898-1925 (5th ed.), p. 158.

erates in Western Europe. Literally in not one of the Western European parties can there be found a single all-party resolution against those who wish to *dissolve* the party and to replace it by a new one!!

Nowhere in Western Europe has there even been raised, is there being raised at present, or can there be raised, the question of whether or not it is permissible to enjoy membership in a party *and at the same time* preach its dissolution, its inadequacy, its uselessness, and its replacement by a different party. Nowhere in Western Europe is the question placed in the way it is placed in our case, namely, as a question of the very *existence* of the party, the *being* of the party.

This controversy is not organizational, does not deal with the question of *how* to construct the party; it consists in a difference of opinion on the question of the party's *existence*. Any reconciliation, agreement, or compromise is in this case out of the question.

We could not have built our party (on four-fifths) and cannot continue to build it except by struggling resolutely against literary men who, in the legal press, fight against the "underground organization" (i.e., the illegal party), pronounce it an *"evil,"* justify and acclaim desertion of it, and preach an "open party."

Our party in contemporary Russia, in which even the party of moderate liberals has not been legalized, can exist only as an illegal party. The originality, the peculiarity of our position—which recalls somewhat the position of the German Social Democrats under the exemption law (although even at that time the Germans had a hundred times more legality than exists in Russia)—is this: our illegal Social Democratic Labor party consists of *illegal* workers' organizations (which are frequently called "cells") which are surrounded by a more or less dense net of *legal* workers' societies (insurance funds, trade unions, educational societies, societies for sports, for temperance, etc.). The legal societies are more numerous in the cities, while they are frequently absent in the provinces.

Sometimes the illegal organizations are rather extensive; sometimes they are quite restricted and may consist only of "proxies."

By means of legal societies a certain *covering up* of illegal organizations and a widespread legal preaching of workers' consolidation within the masses is assured. An all-Russian unification of the leading organizations of the laboring class, the creation of a center (the Central Committee), the passing of precise party resolutions on all questions—all this, it stands to reason, is entirely illegal and requires far-reaching conspirative methods and the confidence of well-tried, advanced workers.

Whoever writes in the legal press *against* the "underground organizations" or in favor of an open party merely *disorganizes* our party, and we cannot consider them other than as *irreconcilable enemies* of our party.

Naturally, a repudiation of the "underground organization" is connected with the repudiation of revolutionary tactics and with a defense of reformism. Russia is passing through an epoch of bourgeois revolutions. In Russia at present a decided discontent with the government prevails even on the part of the most moderate bourgeoisie, the Constitutional Democrats and the Octobrists. But they are all enemies of the revolution; they despise us for our "demagogy," for our endeavor to lead the masses again to the barricades as in 1905. They are all bourgeois, preach only "reforms," and disseminate among the masses convictions which profoundly corrupt them—that is, convictions of the *compatibility* of reforms with the present Tsarist monarchy.

Our tactics are different. We advocate any kind of reform (for instance, that of insurance) and all kinds of legal societies. But we advocate them in order to develop the revolutionary consciousness of the masses and revolutionary mass struggle. And in Russia, where there has been no political freedom so far, these words have for us a greater direct meaning at present than they have in Europe. Our party conducts *revolutionary strikes* which increase in Russia as nowhere else in the world. For example let us take one month, the month of May. In May 1912, 64,000 and in May 1914, 99,000 were engaged in economic strikes. And in 1912, 364,000, in 1914, 647,000 took part in political strikes. The fusion of political and economic struggles forms a revolutionary strike which, in shaking up the millions of peasants, educates them for a revolution. Our party leads a campaign of *revolutionary meetings and revolutionary street demonstrations*. For that purpose our party distributes *revolutionary proclamations* and the *illegal newspaper* of the Central Committee of the party. For an ideological unification of this entire activity of propaganda and agitation in the masses we use slogans accepted by the higher organs of our party: (1) an eight-hour working day; (2) the confiscation of landlords' estates; and (3) a democratic republic. Under present-day conditions in Russia, under complete lawlessness and arbitrariness, under the suppression of all laws by the Tsarist monarchy, *only* these slogans can really unite and direct the entire propaganda and agitation of the party in the spirit of an actual support of a revolutionary movement of the laboring class.

The liquidators' statement, for instance, that we are against "freedom of organization" seems ridiculous to us because we have not only stressed the importance of this paragrah of our program in a special resolution at the January Conference of 1912,[150] but also have utilized in practice

[150] This resolution reads as follows: "The Conference .... urges all Social Democrats to explain to the workers how very important the demand for freedom of organization is for the proletariat. At the same time it is necessary to connect this demand always and insolubly with our general political demands and with revolutionary mass agitation."—*Vsesoiuznaia kommunisticheskaia partiia (b) v*

the curtailed rights of organization (for instance, of insurance funds) ten times more successfully than have the liquidators. But when people write in the legal press that the slogans of confiscation of lands and of a republic cannot serve for agitation among the masses, then we declare that the unity of *these* people and this group of writers with our party is out of the question.

Since I have set myself the task of expounding in the first part of my report the *substance* of dissensions, I shall therefore confine myself to what I have already stated above and shall recall that, in the fourth part of my report, in the text of practical proposals, the digressions of the liquidators from the program and the resolutions of the party will be enumerated.

I shall not enter in detail into the history of the *separation* of the liquidators from our illegal party, the R.S.D.L. party, but shall only point out the *three* chief periods of this history.

First period: from the autumn of 1908 to January 1910. The party struggled against liquidationism by means of precise formal party resolutions condemning liquidationism.

Second period: from January 1910 to January 1912. The liquidators interfered with the restoration of the Central Committee of the party, they destroyed the Central Committee and *dissolved* its last remnants— the technical commission of the *Bureau* of the Central Committee Abroad. Then the committees of the party *in Russia* formed (in the autumn of 1911) a Russian Organization Committee for the purpose of restoring the party. This Committee called the January Conference of 1912. This Conference restored the party, elected a Central Committee, and excluded the group of liquidators from the party.

Third period: from January 1912 to date. The main event of that period was the rallying of the majority—four-fifths—of the class-conscious workers of Russia around the resolutions and institutions formed by the January Conference of 1912.

I pass on now to the second part of my report in which I will characterize the present-day position of our party and of the liquidators from the point of view of a mass labor movement in Russia. I shall endeavor to elucidate the question as to what extent the *experience* of *mass struggle* confirms our party line or that of the liquidators.

II

On April 22, 1912, old style, there began to appear a workers' daily newspaper, *Pravda,* which had been established *as the result* of the

---

rezoliutsiiakh i resheniiakh sezdov, konferentsii i plenumov TsK., I, 1898–1925, (5th ed.), p. 193.

restoration of the party by the January Conference in 1912, which paper is carrying out (often by inferences and always in curtailed form) the resolutions of this Conference. It is clear that we never speak *in any publication whatever* about illegal connections which exist between the illegal party Conference of January 1912, the Central Committee, which the latter established, and the legal newspaper *Pravda.* In September 1912 *Luch,* which has now become *Nasha Rabochaia Gazeta,* a liquidators' rival newspaper, began to appear. Then, in the autumn of 1912, elections were held to the Fourth State Duma. A new insurance law was introduced in 1913 in Russia, a law by which workers' hospital funds were established. Finally, legal trade unions, despite severe persecution by the government and frequent suppression, arose anew.

It is not difficult to understand that all the enumerated manifestations of *mass* labor movements—especially in the daily newspapers of *both* tendencies, give a tremendous amount of open and *objective* data which can be verified. We consider it our duty to protest resolutely to the Executive Committee of the International Socialist Bureau against the usual methods of the liquidators and their foreign defenders, of making unfounded assertions, statements, and declamations, *ignoring* the objective facts of the mass labor movement in Russia.

It is precisely these facts that have strengthened our conviction that our policy is correct.

In January 1912 the Conference of the R.S.D.L. party was held. This restored the illegal party. The liquidators and the small foreign groups (including Plekhanov) greeted this Conference with abuse. And what about the workers in Russia? The elections to the Fourth State Duma have furnished the reply to this.

These elections were held in the autumn of 1912. Whereas in the Third Duma *50 per cent* (four out of eight) of the deputies from the workers' curia adhered to our orientation, in the Fourth State Duma six of the nine deputies from the workers' curia were on the side of the party, i.e., *67 per cent.* This proves that the working masses are for the party and have renounced liquidationism. If now those six members of the Duma who tend toward liquidationism really wish unity with the *party* Duma group, with the Russian Social Democratic Labor group, then we are obliged to point out that unity is conditioned upon a recognition of the fact that the deputies carry out the will of the majority of the workers.

Further, the daily newspapers serve as important instruments in *organizing* the working class. Newspapers contain voluminous material which indicates this—for instance, the data *on the number of contributions from workers' groups.* Both the Pravdist (i.e., of our party) and the liquidators' newspapers publish reports on the money paid by the workers' groups. These reports serve for Russia as the best imaginable index, both open and legal, of the real state of *organization* of the working masses.

In Western Europe, where socialist parties are legal, the number of party members is known and is usually taken as a basis in any argument concerning an organized labor movement. In Russia there is no open legal party. The party organizations are illegal, secret—"underground," as we usually call them—but the *number of contributions* from *the workers' groups* serve as an *indirect* and infallible indication of the state of these organizations.

Since data such as these were published by us openly and regularly in both newspapers for more than two years, and for more than a year and a half by the liquidators, and furthermore, since any untruth or error would have immediately provoked a protest on the part of the workers themselves, these data are *absolutely reliable* and are the very best of the open and legal indications of organization among the laboring masses.

If our liquidators and the small groups abroad which defend them stubbornly ignore these data and are silent about them in their press, then our workers regard that conduct merely as a manifestation of a desire to *disrupt the will of the majority of workers;* they regard it as a lack of conscientiousness.

Here are the data for the *entire* year of 1913. The number of contributions by the Pravdist workers' groups was 2,181 and by the liquidators' workers' groups 661; in 1914 (to May 13) 2,873 Pravdists' workers' groups and 671 liquidators' groups had paid. This means that 77 per cent of all workers' groups organized in 1913 and 81 per cent in 1914 were organized by the Pravdists.

Beginning with 1912 the Pravdists published systematically these data, inviting a verification of them, pointing out the objectivity of the data and appealing to the *real* (and not hypocritical) friends of "unity" to recognize straightforwardly and honestly the will of the majority of the workers. Without this recognition all talk about unity is mere hypocrisy.

After the liquidators had struggled against the party for a year and a half, four-fifths of the class-conscious workers of Russia had *approved* the "Pravdist" policy, the *adherence* to "underground organizations," and revolutionary tactics. And we expect from the liquidators and their friends not phrases concerning "unity" *against* the will of the party but a definite statement: do they or do they not wish to recognize at last the will of a large majority of the class-conscious workers of Russia?

It is easy to make empty statements, but it is very difficult to organize a real workers' newspaper which would be actually maintained by the workers. All the foreign comrades, who have had more experience than we, know this. A newspaper which is pursuing the party policy and which is actually a labor newspaper, i.e., which is actually maintained by workers' money, is a tremendous organizational instrument.

And what do the data tell us? The objective data tell us that *Pravda* is really a workers' newspaper, while the newspaper of the liquidators which repudiates "the underground organization," i.e., the party, is *in practice* a *bourgeois* newspaper, both according to its ideas and according to the source of its means of existence.

From January 1 to May 13, 1914, both newspapers published as usual the financial reports on collections and these reports were summarized in our newspaper. Here are the results: *Pravda* has taken in 21,584 rubles, 53 kopeks, of which 18,934 rubles, 10 kopeks came from workers' groups; i.e., 87 per cent are collections from organized workers and only 13 per cent are collections from the bourgeoisie.

As for the liquidators, they collected 12,055 rubles, 89 kopeks, of which only 5,296 rubles, 12 kopeks, i.e., *less than one-half,* or 44 per cent, came from the workers' groups. The bourgeoisie contributed *more than one-half* of the money the liquidators received.

Furthermore, the entire liberal-bourgeois press praises the liquidators day after day, thus *helping* them to disrupt the will of the majority of workers, *encouraging* the reformism of the liquidators and their renunciation of the underground organization.

As an example of the activity of groups abroad I shall quote the newspaper *Edinstvo* of Comrade Plekhanov, Deputy Burianov, and others. I have before me three numbers of this newspaper, the first number dated May 18 and the third dated June 15 of this year. According to their reports, 1,000 rubles were contributed by someone through Olgin (a comrade living abroad) and, in addition, 207 rubles, 52 kopeks were received from collections abroad. *Six* (six!) groups of workers gave 60 rubles.

And this newspaper supported by six workers' groups in Russia, invites the workers not to obey the resolutions of the party and declares this party to be "schismatic"!! The party which in the last two and a half years has rallied *5,600* groups of workers around the definite resolutions of *three* illegal conferences in 1912 and 1913 is a "schismatic" party, while Plekhanov's group, which has rallied six workers' groups in Russia and which has collected 1,200 rubles abroad for *the disruption* of the will of the Russian workers, is a "unifying" group; don't you see!!

Plekhanov accuses others of factionalism—as though a special collection of money for a special group and the appeal to the workers not to carry out the decisions of a majority of four-fifths *was not* factionalism.

As for us, we openly declare that we regard the conduct of Plekhanov's group as an example of *disorganization*. Plekhanov's conduct amounts to the same as if Mehring in Germany had gathered six workers' groups and had appealed in a special newspaper to the German Social Democrats not to obey the party which had broken away, let us say, from the Poles.

We speak a different language than Plekhanov. We call the union of four-fifths of the workers in Russia unity in practice and not merely in words; we call the struggle of foreign groups, supported by money collected abroad, against the majority of Russian workers, *disorganization*.

Pravda is published in 40,000 copies, according to data which Comrade Vandervelde obtained in St. Petersburg and has published, while the newspaper of the liquidators comes out in 16,000 copies. *Pravda* is paid for and maintained by the workers, while the liquidators' newspaper is maintained by those whom our newspaper calls *rich bourgeois friends*.

We submit to the Executive Committee of the International Socialist Bureau the financial reports published in both newspapers for the benefit of the comrades abroad who know what a serious affair a workers' newspaper is. An acquaintance with these reports will be somewhat better than assurances, promises, statements, and railing at the "Leninists."

We ask the liquidators: do they choose to reckon no further on the *objective fact* that the newspaper of their groups is *in practice* a bourgeois enterprise for the preaching of a renunciation of the underground organization and for *the disruption* of the will of the majority of the class-conscious workers of Russia?

If the answer is yes, then all their talk about "unity" will, as before, evoke bitter sneers from our workers.

Whosoever seriously wishes unity, let him loyally recognize the complete fallibility of the entire liquidationist policy, a fallibility confirmed by the party resolutions beginning with 1908 and by *the experience* of two and one-half years' struggle of the *working masses*.

Further, here are the objective data concerning the elections of the workers to the insurance institutions. We abjure as liberal all talk about political, constitutional reforms in present-day Tsarist Russia; but we shall utilize *in practice* and not merely nominally, such *real* reforms as the insurance reform. The entire group of workers of the all-Russian insurance institution consists of Pravdists, i.e., of workers who have condemned and renounced liquidationism. At the elections to this all-Russian insurance institution forty-seven authorized representatives out of fifty-seven, i.e., 82 per cent, were Pravdists. At the elections to the city of St. Petersburg insurance institution, there were thirty-seven authorized Pravdist representatives and seven liquidators; i.e., Pravdists constituted 84 per cent.

It is the same with the trade unions. Perhaps the comrades abroad, from listening to what the Russian Social Democrats abroad say about "the chaos of the factional struggle" in Russia (that is what Luxemburg, Plekhanov, Trotsky, and others say), believe that there is a split in the Russian trade union movement.

Nothing of the kind.

In Russia there are no parallel unions. In St. Petersburg and in Moscow the trade unions are *united*. The truth is that in these unions there is a *most complete* predominance of Pravdists.

Of thirteen trade unions in Moscow there is not one liquidationist union.

Out of twenty trade unions in St. Petersburg enumerated in our labor calendar, which also gives a record of their membership, only the draftsmen, pharmacists, office clerks, and one-half of the printers are liquidators. In all other unions, and among metal workers, textile workers, tailors, wood industry workers, store clerks, etc., there is a *complete* predominance of Pravdists.[151]

And we declare openly: it is useless for the liquidators to speak of "unity" if they do not wish most resolutely to change their tactics and discontinue the disorganizing struggle against the organized majority of class-conscious workers of Russia.

Pravda acclaims the *underground organization* every day, at least by inferences, and disapproves of those who renounce it. And the workers follow *their Pravda*.

These are the summarized data of the illegal press abroad. *After* the Conference of the liquidators in August 1912,[152] our party issued

[151] The following sentence was crossed out in Lenin's report: "By struggling against this long-established indisputable majority of the workers the liquidators *disorganize* our workers' unions." (Lenin, *Sochineniia*, XVII, 551, note.)

[152] This "August" Conference, as has been noted, was held in Vienna from August 25 (12) to September 2 (August 20), 1912. It was attended by Mensheviks and the following national organizations: the Committee of "Spilka" Abroad, the Bund, the Lithuanian Social Democrats, the Georgian Mensheviks, the Lettish Social Democrats, the Polish Socialist party (Levitsa), and the *Vpered* group. Aleksinsky, representative of the latter, withdrew from the Conference before its adjournment. Plekhanov's group and the Social Democracy of Poland and Lithuania refused to attend the Conference. Several changes were made in the election platform to the Fourth State Duma: the demand for a democratic republic ceased to be one of the immediate demands; it was replaced by the slogan of a general suffrage and of a plenipotentiary Duma. The slogan of confiscation of landed estates was replaced by the demand "to re-examine the agrarian legislation of the Third Duma." The Conference elected a permanent Organization Committee, the Menshevik rival of the Central Committee of the R.S.D.L. party. This Conference gave birth to the anti-Bolshevik "August bloc."

up to June 1914 *five* numbers of a leading political illegal newspaper, the liquidators issued *none,* and the Socialist-Revolutionists issued *nine* numbers. Proclamations in Russia serving the revolutionary agitation during strikes, meetings, demonstrations are not included in this summary.

These five numbers show that our party has *44* illegal organizations, the liquidators *none,* and the Socialist-Revolutionists *21* (chiefly students and peasants).

Finally, in October 1913, when an independent Russian Social Democratic Labor group was formed in the Duma, which, in distinction from the liquidators, wished to *carry out* the will of the majority of class-conscious workers in Russia and not to violate this will, *resolutions* of workers from all parts of Russia in favor of one or the other group, namely, in favor of the party group or of the liquidationist group, were published in *both* newspapers. There were published *6,722 signatures* for the Pravdist, i.e., the party group in the Duma, and *2,985* for the liquidationist group (including 1,086 signatures of Bundist workers, and 719 from the Caucasus). Consequently, the liquidators with all their allies were able to gather *less than one-third.*

These, in short, are the objective data which we oppose to the unfounded assurances of the liquidators. These objective data relating to two and one-half years of the *mass* movement of the working class in Russia, prove finally, by the experience of the class-conscious workers, the correctness of our party policy. . . . .

[The report then states that when the employers replied to a strike with a lockout in March 1914, the illegal party organization, "the Petersburg Committee of the R.S.D.L. party" issued an illegal proclamation for a street demonstration under the slogans of a republic and confiscation of the estates. The demonstrations occurred and were reported by the bourgeois press, whose reports referring to the proclamation of the Petersburg Committee were copied by the Bolshevik *Put Pravdy,* thus giving public support to illegal party work. The liquidators' legal paper did not report the news given in the bourgeois press of the work of the Petersburg Committee but later ridiculed the tactics advocated by the Bolshevik paper.]

III

I shall pass on to the third part of my report. After having examined the *experience* of the mass labor movement in Russia, which has confirmed our policy, I wish to examine the *experience* of our opponents.

Our opponents, the liquidators, as well as small groups abroad, such as Plekhanov's group, enjoy berating us by calling us "usurpers." On the pages of *Vorwärts,* in March 1912 they reiterated this abuse, while

Vorwärts did not permit us to answer them!![153] Let us examine now the political meaning of this accusation of "usurpation."

I have already said that the Conference of 1912 was called by the Russian Organization Committee which was established by the party committee after the destruction of the old Central Committee by the liquidators. We claim the credit for restoring the illegal party, and the majority of the workers in Russia recognized this.

But let us assume for a moment that (from the point of view of those abroad and of the small intellectual groups) the opponents, who are so numerous, are right. Let us assume that we are guilty of "usurpationism," "schismaticism," etc. Is it not natural to expect in this case that our opponents would refute us, not by *mere words but through the experience* of their activity and of their own unification?

If we are wrong in asserting that a party cannot be built otherwise than in opposition to the group of liquidators, then should it not be expected that groups and organizations which differ from us would *prove* through the *experience of their own* activity that unity with the liquidators is possible?

Meanwhile, here is what the experience of our opponents tells us. In January 1912 the illegal party was restored by our Conference, at which the majority of the organizations in Russia was represented.

In March 1912[154] the following united in the pages of *Vorwärts,* in berating us: . . . .

[The report then describes how the various groups that had united in condemning the action of the Prague Conference were unable to establish unity among themselves either by membership in the "August bloc" or otherwise.]

Unity is possible only if the liquidators are ready to break resolutely with their entire tactics and stop being liquidators.

[153] At an informal conference in Paris on March 12, 1912, the representatives of the Committee of Bund Abroad, of Plekhanov's group, of *Vpered,* of the Party Bolsheviks (a group which opposed the Leninists), of the *Golos Sotsial-Demokrata,* and of the Viennese *Pravda* adopted a resolution denouncing the decisions of the Prague Conference. This resolution also contained the following passage: "Whereas the [Prague] Conference . . . . has dared in a high-handed fashion to call itself an 'All Russian' Conference, has dared to declare itself the highest party institution and to elect a Central Committee, this informal gathering pronounces that conference to be an open attempt on the part of a group of persons who have guided the party consciously toward a split to usurp the party banner. This gathering expresses its profound regret that some party organizations and comrades have succumbed to that *deception* and have thereby promoted the policy of splitting and of usurpation on the part of Lenin's gang." *Informatsionnyi listok zagranichnoi organizatsii Bunda,* No. 4, May 1912, p. 5. *1. Beilage des Vorwärts,* No. 72, March 26, 1912, p. 1. This resolution was later on subscribed to by the Committee of the Lettish Social Democrats Abroad.

[154] See note 153, above.

I now pass on to the exposition of precise and formal conditions for such a "unity."

IV

Here is our Central Committee's formulation of the practical, concrete conditions which could make "unity" of our party with the liquidators possible.

The first condition:

1. All-party resolutions of December 1908 and January 1910 on liquidationism are confirmed in a very resolute and unreserved manner precisely in their application to liquidationism.

In order that this confirmation may be accepted by all class-conscious workers of Russia as something really serious and final, and also in order that there may be no place for equivocation, it is recognized that one who writes (especially in the legal press) against the "underground organization," i.e., the illegal organization, who declares that it is a "corpse," that it does not exist, that its restoration is a reactionary utopia, etc., and in general deprecates in one way or another the role and significance of the underground organization, deserves condemnation and cannot be tolerated in the ranks of the illegal R.S.D.L. party.

It is recognized that anyone who writes (especially in the legal press) against "commending the illegal press" deserves condemnation and cannot be tolerated in the ranks of the illegal party. Only one who sincerely and with all his strength helps the development of the illegal press, of illegal proclamations and so forth, can become a member of the illegal party.

It is recognized that anyone who in any form whatsoever preaches in present-day Russia an "open" (i.e., legal) labor party, which signifies objectively a Tsarist-monarchist labor party—anyone who launches the slogan of an "open party" or of "struggle" for such a party—deserves condemnation and cannot be tolerated in the ranks of the illegal party.

It is recognized that anyone who in any form whatsoever writes (especially in the legal press) against revolutionary mass strikes (i.e., strikes which unite economic and political struggles with revolutionary agitation) against revolutionary meetings and street demonstrations deserves condemnation and cannot be tolerated in the ranks of the illegal party. To the number of these impermissible attacks upon the revolutionary activity of the party which conducts strikes and demonstrations belongs, for instance, the condemnation in the legal press of the workers' "strike venture" or of the "most intense methods of struggle" (= legal term for demonstrations).

It is recognized that the indicated digressions from the social democratic line toward "bourgeois influence" are precisely those committed by the periodical *Nasha Zaria* and the newspaper *Nasha Rabochaia Gazeta.*[155]

2. It is recognized that anyone who in any form whatsoever (especially in the legal press) declares the slogans of a democratic republic and of the confiscation of landlords' estates to be of no use or of little use for agitation among the masses—these slogans which were accepted in the program of our party and are especially urgent in present-day Russia, where the formal recognition of the constitution by the Tsar has been turned by the Tsarist monarchy into mockery of the people—deserves condemnation and cannot be a member of the illegal party.

In view of the mass propagation by the liberal press of reformist ideas which reconcile political liberties with the Tsarist monarchy and imply that the revolutionary overthrow of Tsarism is useless, harmful, and sinful, it is recognized that agitation for such constitutional reform as the freedom of organization must be conducted on a very broad scale and with a definite feeling of hostility by the working class toward the preaching of the liberal reformists. In the propagation of the slogan for a republic it must be made clear that this slogan is indissolubly connected with the slogan of the revolutionary attack of the masses on the Tsarist monarchy.

3. It is recognized that the entry of any group of the Russian Social Democratic Labor party into a bloc or union with *another* party is absolutely not permissible and incompatible with party membership.

The bloc of the Bund and the liquidators with a *non*-social democratic party, the Polish Socialist party (Levitsa) *against* the will and consent of the *Polish* Social Democracy, and without the approval of the Congress of the R.S.D.L. party, is considered a bloc which is not permitted.

Deputy Jagiello, as a member of a *non*-social democratic party, can be affiliated only with the Duma group of our party, but can by no means be a member of that Duma group.

4. It is recognized that in every town and in every locality there must be only one united Social Democratic organization, which includes all nationalities and which conducts its activities in all tongues of the local proletariat.

The national-Jewish separatism of the Bund deserves condemnation. The Bund, in spite of the decision of the Stockholm Congress of the R.S.D.L. party in 1906 and in spite of the confirmation of these resolu-

[155] "This paragraph in the manuscript of Vl. Ilich [Lenin] was given in place of the following paragraph, which he had crossed out: 'It is recognized that the tendency expressed at present in the magazine *Nasha Zaria* and *Nasha Rabochaia Gazeta,* being a liquidationist tendency, is incompatible with the illegal party membership, and that the group in charge of these publications may enter the party only after a complete and radical renunciation of their present tendency.'" (Lenin, *Sochineniia,* XVII, 558, note.)

tions by the Conference in December 1908, has refused to carry into practice locally the principle of international unity of social democratic workers, a principle which has been tested so splendidly in the Caucasus since 1898.

5. It is recognized that the demand for "national cultural autonomy" (like its equivalent, the so-called "creation of institutions which guarantee freedom of national development"), which separates the workers according to nationalities and which preaches refined nationalism, a demand rejected by a formal resolution at the Second (1903) Congress of the R.S.D.L. party, contradicts the program of the party.

All the decisions of the local, national, or special organizations of our party (including the Duma group), which admit the principle of cultural national autonomy, are revoked and their resumption without the approval of the Congress of the R.S.D.L. party is recognized to be incompatible with party membership.

6. The social democratic workers of all shades are invited by all organizations of the party and by all its publications in all languages to bring about immediately a *unity from below,* i.e., the formation locally of illegal social democratic cells, organizations, and groups, or the entry into such organizations wherever they already exist.

Furthermore, the principle of the federation or the equality of rights of all "currents" is absolutely rejected, and only the principle of the loyal subordination of the minority to the majority is recognized. The number of contributions from the workers' groups to the newspapers of various tendencies since 1913 is taken in the legal press as the most exact, although approximate, indication of the co-ordination of forces of various tendencies in the labor movement! Therefore, these data are published in all party publications and all publications recommended to the local Social Democrats, that they be guided by these data in all practical moves until the next Congress of the R.S.D.L. party.

As for the question of determining party membership, it is recognized that only entrance into an illegal cell, group, or other organization (it makes no difference whether it is a local, a factory, a district organization, or a social democratic group within legal societies) and that illegal activity in organizing meetings, discussing party resolutions, and propagating illegal literature, *only* these are to be taken into account in determining party membership.

All groups and "currents" are obliged immediately to issue clear and precise illegal proclamations to that effect.

7. The existence of two rival newspapers in one and the same town or locality is recognized as absolutely not permissible. The minority has the right to discuss disagreement over program, tactics, and organization before the entire party in a polemical journal which must be specially

established; but this minority must not write in a rival newspaper, disorganizing thereby the activities and resolutions of the majority.

The fact that the liquidationist newspaper in St. Petersburg is maintained chiefly by bourgeois and not by proletarian money, is published in spite of the will of a known and indisputable majority[156] of class-conscious social democratic workers of St. Petersburg, and introduces extreme disorganization by advocating that the will of the majority should be ignored, makes necessary immediate suppression of that newspaper and the simultaneous establishment of a polemical magazine.

8. Both the resolution of the Second Congress of 1903 and the resolution of the London Congress of 1907 on the bourgeois-democratic nature of the tendency of Narodniks in general, including the Socialist-Revolutionist party, are confirmed very definitely, and with no reservations.

Any kind of blocs or unions or temporary agreements of one group of Social Democrats with Socialist-Revolutionists (and the Narodniks in general) in opposition to the other group of Social Democrats is recognized as absolutely not permissible.

The St. Petersburg liquidators, who, even without having proclaimed at their own "August Conference" any new policy of the Social Democrats with regard to the Socialist-Revolutionists, resorted and, in the elections to insurance institutions, are now resorting to blocs and to agreements with Socialist-Revolutionists against the overwhelming majority of Social Democratic workers in St. Petersburg—these liquidators are openly and unreservedly condemned.

A literary bloc of most prominent liquidators and prominent Social Democrats from small groups which defend liquidationism (Plekhanov, Trotsky, etc.) with the Socialist-Revolutionists, who preach in the St. Petersburg journal *Sovremennik* that "at any rate the old groupings are abolished" and that "it is impossible to ascertain where Marxism ends and where populism begins" (*Sovremennik*, No. 7, p. 76), is recognized as not permissible.

Those literary men who wish to be members of the Social Democratic party and who contribute to that organ [*Sovremennik*] only because they have to make an income from bourgeois publications are invited to withdraw from the ranks of contributors to that journal and to make their withdrawal public.

[156] The liquidators in their newspaper (*Novaia Rabochaia Gazeta*, No. 34, June 13, 1914) estimate 72 per cent Pravdists and 28 per cent liquidators in St. Petersburg. This strange estimate is based not on the number of the workers' groups but on the total of rubles collected, both from workers and from the bourgeoisie, so that 10,000 workers, if they had given 10 kopeks per person, are comparable to one bourgeois who gave 1,000 rubles. As a matter of fact, from January 1 to May 13, 1914, the number of contributions from the workers' groups in St. Petersburg was 2,024 from Pravdists, and 308 from liquidators, i.e., 86 per cent and 14 per cent respectively. (Note on the original report.)

9. On account of the extreme disorganization introduced into the labor movement in Russia by separate isolated groups abroad which act without mandates from or any agreement with any party organization in Russia, it is recognized as necessary to resolve and see to it that all groups abroad without exception communicate with organizations in Russia only through the Central Committee of the party.

The groups abroad, which are not subordinated to the Russian center of Social Democratic activity, i.e., to the Central Committee, and which introduce disorganization by their separate communication with Russia without the knowledge of the Central Committee, cannot use the name of the R.S.D.L. party.

A social democratic polemical journal for a broad uncensored discussion of questions of program, tactics, and organization should be established abroad with money collected outside of Russia.

The dictum of the party constitution (paragraph 3), namely, that only "approved party organizations have the right to publish party literature," must be confirmed and be absolutely carried into practice.

These are the conditions upon which the Central Committee of our party considers it possible to realize unity and takes upon itself the initiation of a campaign in favor of unity. We consider any negotiations and communications with the group of liquidators which issues *Nasha Zaria* and *Nasha Rabochaia Gazeta* under the *present* tactics of this group impossible; and all other groups, currents, "factions," and institutions which defend the liquidators or preach unity or compromise with them are considered fictitious from the point of view of the political reality of the labor movement in Russia.

We declare that to sustain the laboring class of Russia with verbal assurances and promises concerning the possibility and easy attainment of unity with the group of liquidators is to do ill service to the cause and merely to substitute phrases for reality.

Therefore, we make the following practical proposal:

As early as a year ago the question of a party congress was raised in our party. It was also included in the resolutions of the summer conference of 1913 which was held in connection with the Central Committee of the R.S.D.L. party. At present the plan of calling a congress is almost realized. Probably in the near future, immediately after the Vienna Congress or perhaps even during that Congress, the congress of our party will be held.[157] It stands to reason that we request the comrades not to write and not to speak about it. If the arrests are very extensive, then a conference instead of a congress may be held.

[157] No Congress of the R.S.D.L. party was held until August 1917.

And thus refusing to take any steps toward unity with the group of liquidators or their defenders *so long as the above enumerated conditions are not fulfilled,* we propose to all groups, currents, and "factions" which consider possible—in contrast to us—unity, peace, or compromise with the present-day group of liquidators under its present-day tactics that they use the Vienna Congress and organize a formal discussion according to the conditions advanced by us.

Let those who preach peace or compromise with the liquidators not confine themselves to preaching, but let them prove *in practice* that unity with the present-day liquidators is possible.

We, on our part, shall be glad to be able to inform the representatives of four-fifths of the workers of Russia at the congress or conference of our party of the results of the deliberations between the group of the liquidators and all the groups which defend them.

10. The resolution unanimously adopted by the London Central Committee[158] (in the beginning of January 1908) is recognized as absolutely binding upon all Social Democrats. This resolution reads as follows:

"Intense activity of the Social Democrats in the trade union movement dictated by the present state of affairs must be conducted in the spirit of the London and Stuttgart[159] resolutions, i.e., by no means in the spirit of recognizing the principle that trade unions should be neutral or not affiliated with any party, but on the contrary in the spirit of steady endeavor for as close a rapprochement as possible between the unions and the Social Democratic party."

It is recognized that attempts to introduce into the unions agitation against the illegal R.S.D.L. party are incompatible with party membership.

The liquidators must pledge themselves not to encourage the workers to disregard the union executives, but to submit loyally to the Marxist majority within the unions, and in any case not to establish schismatic parallel unions.

This holds with regard to activity in workers' societies of all kinds, clubs, etc.

All Social Democrats are obliged to enter illegal Social Democratic cells in every union, in cultural, educational societies, etc. The decisions of the illegal party are binding upon these cells.

The struggle of all Social Democrats *against* a division of trade unions according to nationality is recognized as imperative.

11. It is recognized that newspaper attacks on the group of rep-

[158] The Central Committee of the R.S.D.L. party elected at the London Congress in 1907.

[159] The London Congress of the R.S.D.L. party in 1907, and the Stuttgart International Socialist Congress of 1907. (Lenin, *Sochineniia,* XVII, 563, notes.)

resentatives elected by the St. Petersburg workers to the insurance institutions (the All-Russian Insurance Council, the Metropolitan Council,
etc.) and appeals not to obey the instructions of this elected body, and
so forth, *cannot be permitted*. It is recognized that the insurance program
approved by this group of workers' representatives is *obligatory*.

The periodical, *Strakhovanie Rabochikh,* which competes with the
official organ of the Workers' Insurance Representation (*Voprosy
Strakhovaniia*) is to be discontinued.

12. The Caucasian Social Democrats must recognize that it is not
permissible to agitate in favor of cultural national autonomy, a slogan
rejected by the program of the R.S.D.L. party.

The Caucasian Social Democrats must pledge themselves not to
violate the principle of a united international organization in any town
and in no case to introduce in either the political or the trade union organization a division of workers according to nationalities.

13. The six deputies of the State Duma (Chkheidze's Duma group),
and also Deputy Burianov, must recognize all the conditions stated above.

Chkheidze's group must declare from the Duma tribune that, in conformity with the program of the Russian Social Democrats, it *retracts*
the proclamation of "cultural national autonomy" (and of its equivalent
[cultural-national] "institutions," etc.).

Chkheidze's group must recognize the leadership of the Central Committee of the party elected at the January Conference of 1912, the binding
nature of the party decisions, and also the *veto* power of the Central
Committee.

14. In concluding, I must touch upon a very unpleasant point but
one which cannot be avoided in a loyal and open exchange of opinions
on the question of social democratic unity in Russia. .... [The report
then charges the liquidators with conducting a campaign of personal
vilification against individual Bolsheviks: (1) charges against Lenin of
dishonest and criminal acts in Martov's pamphlet *Spasiteli ili uprazdniteli,* charges which Kautsky and Plekhanov described as "loathsome";
(2) charges of dishonesty against Dansky which the Bolshevik Central
Committee investigated and found absolutely unfounded; (3) rumors
published by the liquidators' press that Malinovsky was an *agent provocateur,* a rumor which the Central Committee had investigated and
found to be false and therefore vouched for Malinovsky; (4) publication
in the liquidators' paper of Aleksinsky's charges of treason against
Antonov [Brittman], who was in penal servitude and who had been
cleared by a commission of his fellow prisoners.]

In the name of the majority of the class-conscious workers of Russia
we shall defend the organization of our party from disorganizers and
we do not recognize any other defense than the one exercised by us and

indicated above (not to mention the bourgeois court, to the use of which we shall resort at the first opportunity).

I have finished the report which I was commissioned to make on behalf of the Central Committee of the Russian Social Democratic Labor party. I shall allow myself to summarize it in two brief theses:

The formal situation is as follows: our party, restored at the Conference of January 1912 in spite of the resistance of the group of liquidators, has excluded them from the party. The overwhelming majority of the class-conscious workers of Russia has *subsequently, after* two and a half years of labor movement, approved our party policy. Therefore, we have reason to be convinced more firmly than ever of the correctness of our policy, *and we shall not retreat from it.*

If the liquidators and the groups which defend them want us to revoke the resolution excluding the liquidators from the party, then our Central Committee is willing to submit to the Congress of the party a proposal to that effect, and to defend it, but *only* on the conditions I have enumerated.

Materially, i.e., substantially, the situation is as follows: Russia is passing through an epoch of bourgeois revolutions when small, unsteady groups of intellectuals are sometimes inclined to consider themselves Social Democrats or are inclined to support the opportunist tendency within Social Democracy against which our party has been struggling for twenty years ("Economism," 1895–1902; "Menshevism," 1903–1908; and "Liquidationism," 1908–1914). The experience of the August bloc (1912) of the liquidators and its disintegration has shown that the liquidators and their defenders are entirely incapable of creating either a party or an organization. Only in a struggle against these groups can there be formed, and is being formed, a real workers' social democratic party of Russia. Regardless of gigantic difficulties the number of class-conscious workers which has already rallied to this party constitutes eight-tenths of the social democratic class-conscious workers, or seven-tenths of the class-conscious workers in the group of Social Democrats plus Socialist-Revolutionists.

Enclosures:

INSTRUCTIONS

I. Notes privés

In connection with the question as to how the data on the majority or the minority of workers in Russia which follow the Pravdists, or more truly, who are Pravdists, relate to "unity," the following must be pointed out:

1. If a certain party or group advances definitely and precisely a program and tactics with which our party cannot agree on principle, then

of course the question of majority has no significance. For example, if the Socialist-Revolutionist party (the Left Narodniks), which differs from our party in program as well as in tactics, should draw to its side the majority of workers in Russia, this would by no means compel us to digress from our policy. This also concerns the open and decided repudiators of "underground organization" (= illegal party) in present-day Russia.

But certain groups of Social Democrats and some of the liquidators assert that they have no irreconcilable dissensions with us over principles. We are compelled to point out to these groups that they will be inconsistent if they refuse to submit to the majority.

2. We were first of all convinced of the correctness of our tactical and organizational policy through years of acquaintance with the Social Democratic labor movement in Russia and through our participation in it, as well as through our theoretical, Marxist convictions. But we adhere to the opinion that the practice of *mass* labor movement is not less important than theory and that only this practice is able to give a serious *verification* of our principles. "Theory, my friend, is dull, but green is the eternal tree of life" (Faust). Therefore, the fact that after two and one-half years of struggle against liquidationism and its allies, four-fifths of the class-conscious workers pronounce themselves in favor of Pravdism—this fact strengthens our conviction in the correctness of our policy and makes this conviction firm.

3. In Russia almost all groups or "factions" (according to the old name) accuse one another of being *not* laborite groups but bourgeois intellectual groups. We consider this accusation, or more truly this idea, this indication as to the social meaning of one or the other group, *extremely important in principle*. But just because we think it extremely important, we consider it our duty not to launch without proofs *our* interpretation of the social significance of other groups but to confirm our interpretation by means of *objective* facts; for objective facts prove irrevocably and irrefutably that *only* Pravdism is a *laborite* orientation in Russia, while liquidationism and Socialist-Revolutionism are in *practice* bourgeois intellectual orientations.

II. Notes privés

Should an attempt be made (it does not matter who makes it, whether it is the International Socialist Bureau or our adversaries) to "challenge" or *put aside* the data concerning our majority, i.e., the objective data, then it will be absolutely necessary to request permission to speak in order to present a formal protest of the following content on behalf of the entire delegation.

We categorically protest against the statement (or attempt, indication, etc.) that our objective data, regarding the question as to whom the large majority of class-conscious workers of Russia is following, are not subject to examination by the Executive Committee, because it has not yet verified these data (or because these do not relate to the question of unity). We consider, on the contrary, that the undoubted interest of the entire International and the will of the International Socialist Bureau expressed clearly in the resolution of the International Socialist Bureau (December 1913) consists without doubt in obtaining most complete, exact, and documented information on the real situation of the labor movement in Russia.

We consider that our adversaries who knew about the December resolution of the International Socialist Bureau have not fulfilled their duty, since they have not yet gathered any objective data concerning the labor movement in Russia.

We state that after Comrade Vandervelde's successful trip to Russia no doubt prevails that the Executive Committee of the International Socialist Bureau could quite legally address an open letter through Comrade Vandervelde to all the editorial boards of all workers' newspapers (or those wishing to become workers' newspapers) in Russia and to all members of the presidiums of the legal workers' societies in Russia, so as to obtain first-hand data on the question of how the class-conscious workers of Russia are divided between Pravdists, liquidators, and Socialist-Revolutionists (Left Narodniks) and other tendencies.

Without these objective data, subjective statements of representatives of various "groups" are of absolutely no value.

III. Not to be Included in the Report

Judging by certain fragmentary statements of the liquidators at the Lettish Congress and by insinuations in the press, one of the liquidators' schemes for "unification" is a proposal for a "general congress."

This proposal, which is obviously designed to catch gullible foreigners, is approximately as follows : either the formation of a "federative" organizational committee for the calling of a general congress, or else the "supplementing" of the Central Committee of our party by representatives from the liquidationist organizations for the calling of a general congress.

This plan, in whatever form, absolutely cannot be accepted by us and should it somehow or other be brought up at the "Conference" in Brussels then the delegate of the Central Committee must declare :

We absolutely cannot consent to any moves in the direction of a general congress, a federation, or a rapprochement, even in the slightest degree, so long as the group of liquidators does not satisfy the conditions which we submit. This is because we cannot show except *after* they have fulfilled these conditions, *even the slightest* confidence in the group of liquidators which was excluded from the party and which continues its daily disorganizational activity in its newspaper.

To show confidence in this group would mean *to encourage* it to continue its disorganizational activity. And we demand, on the basis of decisions of our congresses and deliberations and those of the Central Committee, *discontinuance* of this activity of the liquidators as a *conditio sine qua non* of "peace."

The protection of the liquidators by groups or organizations not formally excluded from the party (for instance, by the Bund or by the "six" deputies, etc.) absolutely does not alter the matter. *Only* one thing is essential and real in Russia from the point of view of Russian activity, namely: the group of the liquidators with their newspaper, which appeals for a violation of the will of the majority.

Let the Bund, the "six" deputies (Chkheidze, etc.), or the Caucasian Regional Committee, or Trotsky, or the Organization Committee, or anyone else, if they wish a rapprochement with us first *obtain* the acceptance of our conditions by the liquidators or else resolutely condemn that group and break with it. Without this, even the *slightest* move expressing our confidence in the group of liquidators is out of the question.

Let those who actually desire the unity of the Russian Social Democracy, not delude themselves and not give way to subjective assurances, promises, etc. There is only one way toward unity: to prevail upon the minority, which withdrew from the illegal party and which disorganizes it and disrupts its activity and the will of the majority, to break with its practice and *prove by deeds* that it wishes to respect the will of the majority.

Any direct or indirect encouragement of the group of the liquidators in its *present* conduct, or any inspiring of the hope that a "federation" or "reconciliation" or a "general congress" or a "rapprochement" with this group *so long as* it does not stop its present activity and does not *in practice* submit to the majority, will lead to nothing. The party of the social democratic workers of Russia, which has rallied four-fifths of the class-conscious workers, *will not permit* the disruption of its will.

Let the groups and institutions which "assure" themselves and others that the liquidators are not so bad (the Bund, the Organization Committee, and the Caucasian Regional Committee) understand that we require deeds and not words. Let *them,* if they have confidence in the liquidators, organize *their own* congress with the liquidators, propose to this congress *our* conditions, obtain from the liquidators a favorable answer and the practical fulfillment of these conditions. We shall see what the results are; we shall wait for *deeds,* for we do not trust promises.

Only after our conditions are fulfilled in practice, and only then, are a general congress and moves in the direction of such a congress possible.

The foreign socialist-comrades are sometimes mistaken, especially when they think of helping unity, and they inspire hope in the liquidators that we shall act in common with them, *without* a complete and radical change in their conduct, without their submitting to the will of the majority. Not assistance to unity but assistance to the dissenters—that is what these tactics objectively lead to.

Our conditions represent our proposal of a *pacte d'unité,* and until the liquidators sign this treaty, until they fulfill it in practice, any moves toward a rapprochement are out of the question.

RESOLUTION ON RUSSIAN UNIFICATION

[Introduced by the International Socialists Bureau at Brussels, July 16–17, 1914][160]

After having listened attentively to reports of various groups invited to the Conference on July 16 (3), the Executive Committee of the International Socialist Bureau reached the conclusion that at the present time there are no tactical disagreements between them which are sufficiently important to justify the split.

Conditions for unification should be:

1. All groups accept the present program of the Russian Social Democracy and consequently also the Social Democracy *per se.*

2. All groups recognize it as absolutely necessary that the minority within the unified party should always accept the decisions of the majority as binding for party activity.

3. The organization of the party must be secret at present; it is compelled to be.

The activity of all party members in legal institutions also should be under the leadership and control of the leading party institutions.

4. All groups renounce any bloc with the bourgeois parties.

5. All groups declare that they agree to participate in the general congress which must solve all questions now under dispute concerning the interpretation of the program and the question of national cultural autonomy and which must establish the details of the general party organization. This congress should be called as soon as conditions permit.

Until that time, party members should be guided in their activity by

---

[160] "Rezoliutsiia Ispolnitelnogo Komiteta Mezhdunarodnogo Sotsialisticheskogo Biuro" Lenin, *Sochineniia,* XVII, 682–83. First published as "Briusselskaia s.d. obedinitelnaia konferentsiia," in *Informatsionnyi listok zagranichnoi organizatsii Bunda,* No. 7, January 1915, p. 15.

the resolutions of the congresses and conferences of the entire party held before the split, of the plenum of 1910, and of the international congresses.

The International [Socialist] Bureau invites separate labor organizations belonging to different groups in Russia immediately to take up common activity and not to permit the voices of the hidden enemies of unification to interfere with their activity.

Common mass activities against the common enemies of the proletariat will be the best way to overcome separatist inclinations.

The International [Socialist] Bureau refuses to investigate the accusation relating to the past history of the various groups in Russia. On the basis of the London resolution it considers itself incompetent to do so; but it declares that such investigations of past events are unproductive and even harmful, because they are a means by which those elements which should be united by their points of view on the present and their aims for the future, are divided.

The present situation makes it possible to accomplish great deeds in Russia if the class-conscious proletariat comes forward unitedly and concertedly. There is no absolute necessity for a split within Revolutionary Marxism in Russia at the present time. On the contrary, when united it will be able to develop more profitably. No greater crime can be committed against the proletariat of Russia than to interfere with and to hinder the rallying of its various groups into one single organism.

Proletarians of Russia, unite!

CHAPTER II

THE ACTIVITIES OF THE BOLSHEVIKS ABROAD, 1914–1916

During the tense days preceding the commencement of hostilities the International Socialist Bureau and the constituent parties of the International carried out that part of the Stuttgart resolution which required them to exert every effort to prevent war. The real test came when war had been declared. Then the socialists had to decide if and by what means they should carry out the second Stuttgart injunction "to do all in their power to utilize the economic and political crisis caused by the war to rouse the peoples and thereby to hasten the abolition of capitalist class rule."

As is well known, a majority of the parliamentary representatives of all but two of the belligerent countries voted to support their governments' war measures on the general ground of self-defense. Against the opposition of the Center and Left-wing leaders, the German Social Democrat delegation in the Reichstag voted to give the unanimous vote of the delegation for war credits. The news of this vote by the most influential party in the International was a stunning blow to socialists everywhere, who were for some weeks unaware of the amount of opposition within the German party. The French Socialist party accepted the theory that France was the victim of aggression and the party's deputies voted unanimously for war credits. Presently Guesde and Sembat became ministers in the government of national defense. The Belgian Labor party followed the same line, and Vandervelde joined the ministry. In the Habsburg monarchy the Social Democratic party surrendered to the government's war measures against the opposition of a minority led by Friedrich Adler. The Czech and Hungarian Social Democrats took similar action. The Polish socialists were divided not only by internal disagreements but by the fact that the Polish workers were citizens of not one country but three. The deputies of the Polish Socialist party in the Austrian Reichsrat supported the war as a means of Polish liberation. On the other side of the frontier the Polish Socialist party (Levitsa) had one deputy in the Russian State Duma and he recorded his opposition to the war. The other group, the Social Democracy of Poland and Lithuania, had no representative in any parliament and so was unable to show by parliamentary action its antiwar attitude.

In Great Britain, the last of the Great Powers to be drawn into the war in 1914, the socialist and labor opposition to British involvement continued as late as August 5, but on this day when it came to a vote a majority of the Parliamentary Labour party stood by the government. MacDonald resigned as chairman of the Parliamentary group and with several other leaders of the Independent Labour party continued to criticize the government's action. The British Socialist party, which had no representative in Parliament, also took an antiwar position, but later split when H. M. Hyndman and a minority of the party joined the supporters of the government.

Only in Russia and Serbia did a majority of the social democratic deputies refuse to vote war credits. In the State Duma five Bolshevik deputies and six Mensheviks, including one deputy of the Polish Socialist party (Levitsa), left the session, refusing to vote for war credits. The deputies of the Trudovik group, Socialist-Revolutionist rather than Social Democrat in their views, likewise refused to vote. This attitude of the Duma deputies was by no means shared by all the leading personalities among the factions of the Russian Social Democrats and Socialist-Revolutionists. Many of them, like the socialists of other countries, became "defensists" and supporters of civil truce. The Social Democratic parties of the Russian national minorities such as the Latvian and Ukrainian groups and the Bund had no representatives in the Duma.

The Finnish Social Democrats, a well-organized and active party, likewise were represented not in the Duma but in the Finnish Diet. In Serbia the Austro-Hungarian invasion made it particularly difficult to refuse to accept the theory of self-defense. But the Serbian Social Democrats, unlike their French and Belgian comrades, did not consider the invasion, which they denounced, a valid excuse for the abandonment of their socialist position. They therefore refused to support their government.

The socialists of the states not immediately involved in the war were not faced with the necessity of deciding whether they would or would not support their governments. Without endangering the continued existence of their party organization, they could denounce war in general and this war in particular and demand that their own governments remain neutral. This was done with virtuous enthusiasm by socialist parties of Italy, the United States, and Portugal, and the social democratic parties of the Scandinavian countries, Holland, and Switzerland.[1]

The war itself, the action of the socialist parties, and the war regulations of the belligerent governments obviously made it impossible for the Second International to continue its functions. There was, of course, no formal dissolution of the organization, and the neutral members of the International Socialist Bureau continued as best they could to preserve in that body the rather pitiful remnant of international solidarity on which the socialists of all lands had put such great hopes. The attempts of the I.S.B. and the socialists of neutral and belligerent countries to maintain a vestige of socialist internationalism are discussed in later chapters. The present chapter is concerned with one section of the International, the Bolsheviks, who believed that the Second International had met the fate to which its opportunist leadership

---

[1] There are many accounts of these events, among them: C. Grünberg, *Die Internationale und der Weltkrieg;* W. E. Walling, *The Socialists and the War*, pp. 125–213; M. Fainsod, *International Socialism and the World War*, Ch. II; L. L. Lorwin, *Labor and Internationalism*, pp. 134–46; and J. Lenz, *The Rise and Fall of the Second International*, pp. 127–38.

had foredoomed it and that the task of the truly revolutionary Marxists was to establish a new International purged of those who had betrayed the workers.

The outbreak of the war, the sentiments it promoted, and the regulations it imposed inevitably affected the status and activities of the Bolsheviks living abroad. Those party leaders who were living in Germany or Austria-Hungary became enemy aliens subject to internment or at best close police supervision. Some like Trotsky, who was in Vienna, succeeded, before the frontiers were closed, in escaping to Switzerland, the haven of Russian political refugees for more than half a century. Others, like Lenin, who was living near Cracow, were interned, but later, under circumstances mentioned below, were allowed or managed to cross the frontier. Those Bolsheviks and revolutionists of other camps who were living in countries allied to Russia, particularly those in France, found their sphere of activity greatly circumscribed through the attentions of the police and the watchfulness of the censor. The French government, while recognizing that these Russian guests were not enemy aliens, was quite aware that they were by no means friends of the government of France's eastern ally. Quite naturally the government tried to see to it that exiles from Russia should have as little opportunity as possible to propagate their doctrines, which were opposed to the official interpretation of the causes and objectives of the war. Later, certain neutral states, under pressure from the belligerents and for their own reasons, began to increase their watchfulness over the activities of the Russian exiles.

The events of July and August had a very disastrous effect on the Bolshevik organization. The small groups constituting Bolshevik sections in Switzerland and other countries temporarily lost contact with each other and with Russia. The party had no central organ. *Pravda* had been suppressed in Russia, and most of the Bolshevik workers' organizations there had been broken up after the July strikes. The Committee of Organizations Abroad, which at Paris had served as a center for the Bolshevik sections outside Russia, had disintegrated; two of its members had enlisted in the French army and another had withdrawn, leaving only two active members. The tenuous connection was broken between that part of the Central Committee of the R.S.D.L. party which was in Russia and Lenin and Zinoviev, members of the Bureau of the Central Committee Abroad. Thus, when Lenin and Zinoviev went from Galicia to Switzerland, they carried with them about all that was left of the Bolshevik central organization abroad.[2]

On his arrival in Switzerland on September 5 Lenin at once set to work. He was eager to put before his party comrades abroad and in Russia his ideas on the causes and nature of the war and the tactics which social democrats true to the faith of Marx should employ. To do this he had first of all to re-establish contacts among the Bolshevik sections abroad; to revive *Sotsial-Demokrat,* the central organ of the party, which had suspended publication; and to arrange ways to smuggle party literature into Russia and bring news out. At the same time Lenin was determined to carry on his fight against those Russian and other social democrats whom he considered traitors to socialism and to rally those who shared his views to break with the official party majorities. During the next two and a half years Lenin wrote innumerable letters and many articles, made speeches whenever he got the chance, and prompted his friends to expound his ideas at such meetings as they were able to attend.

Despite the shortage of funds and the difficulties of communication the Bolsheviks succeeded in issuing, in the period from the outbreak of the war to the spring of 1917, twenty-four numbers of *Sotsial-Demokrat,* including two double

[2] M. Kharitonov, "Iz vospominanii," *Zapiski Instituta Lenina,* II, 119; 'V. Karpinsky, "Vladimir Ilich za granitsei v 1914–1917 g.g. po pismam i vospominaniiam," *Zapiski Instituta Lenina,* II, 72–73; I. P. Khoniavko, "V podpolie i v emigratsii (1911–1917 g.g.)," *Proletarskaia Revoliutsiia,* No. 4 (16), 1923, p. 168; see also A. Rosmer, *Le Mouvement ouvrier pendant la guerre. De l'union sacrée à Zimmerwald,* pp. 466–69; hereafter cited A. Rosmer, *Le Mouvement ouvrier pendant la guerre.* Khoniavko tells that at a meeting of the Paris Bolshevik section held early in August 1914, 11 members out of 94 favored defensism.

numbers and a supplement, two numbers of *Sbornik Sotsial-Demokrata,* one double number of *Kommunist,* and several pamphlets, among them *Sotsializm i voina* [Socialism and the War] by Lenin and Zinoviev, *Komu Nuzhna Voina* [Who Wants War] by A. M. Kollontai, *Voina i Dorogovizna* [War and High Cost of Living], *Voina i Rabochii Klass* [War and the Working Class], and *Imperializm, kak noveishii etap kapitalizma* [Imperialism, the Highest Stage of Capitalism] by Lenin.

Lenin and Zinoviev composing along with Krupskaia as secretary the Bureau of the Central Committee Abroad with great difficulty maintained contacts with Russia through A. Shliapnikov, who came to Sweden soon after the outbreak of the war and returned to Russia early in November 1915. After four months in Russia he again came to Scandinavia in February 1916, after which he went to the United States for a short time, returning to Russia late in October 1916. Letters[3] written by A. Elizarova for the Bureau of the Central Committee in Russia indicate that the transportation of illegal literature was fairly successful. When in the autumn of 1915 Lenin received from Russia news of widespread strikes and rising revolutionary sentiment, he drafted "a few theses," given below, outlining definite tactics and instructions for the party members in Russia and defining the position of the party center abroad in the anticipated revolution.[4]

Throughout the years 1914 to 1916 Lenin bitterly attacked Kautsky and other Centrists, whom he regarded as worse enemies of revolutionary Social Democracy than the avowed "social patriots." He attacked the Mensheviks, who published *Nashe Slovo,* because they would not break with the Russian majority group headed by Chkheidze, though they criticized

---

[3] These eight letters are published in *Proletarskaia Revoliutsiia,* Nos. 7–8 (102–103), 1930, p. 177–95.

[4] D. Baevsky, "Partiia v gody imperialisticheskoi voiny," in M. N. Pokrovsky (ed.), *Ocherki po istorii oktiabrskoi revoliutsii,* I, 421; hereafter cited as Baevsky, *Ocherki po istorii oktiabrskoi revoliutsii.*

its policies and upheld an internationalist point of view. Although he considered the Zimmerwald movement a step in the right direction, Lenin condemned the Zimmerwald majority as vacillating and semi-Kautskyist. Even within the Zimmerwald Left, whose members shared many of Lenin's opinions, there were sharp differences and Lenin found several of his Bolshevik followers in the opposition.

A. Bolshevik Activities Abroad, 1914

In 1914 Lenin and N. K. Krupskaia were living in the village of Poronino near Cracow. A few days after the outbreak of the war Lenin was arrested on suspicion of espionage. Through the efforts of Hanecki in Cracow and of Victor Adler and the Polish deputy, Diamand, in Vienna, Lenin was released. He secured permission to leave Austria-Hungary, and with Krupskaia arrived in Berne on September 5.[5] Zinoviev and Lilina, who were also in Galicia, came to Switzerland two weeks later. In addition to these four there were several other Bolsheviks who had been living in Switzerland or had recently come there, among them being D. B. Riazanov, Inessa Armand, Shklovsky, the two Safarovs, Samoilov (then a deputy in the Duma), Bukharin, G. Piatakov, Evgeniia Bosh, Krylenko, E. F. Rozmirovich, Troianovsky, Karpinsky, Olga Ravich, and Sokolnikov. Karl Radek arrived from Germany at the end of 1914, and later Manuilsky came from Paris.[6]

Immediately on his arrival in Switzerland Lenin wrote the theses given below and began to inquire of party comrades in Geneva about arrangements for publishing a leaflet in Russian.[7] The theses were discussed and adopted, with slight

[5] The story of Lenin's arrest and release is told by Hanecki, "Arest V. I. Lenina v Avstrii v 1914 g. po dokumentam," *Leninskii Sbornik*, II, 173–87, and in N. K. Krupskaya, *Memories of Lenin*, II, 134–40.

[6] M. Bronsky, "Uchastie Lenina v Shveitsarskom rabochem dvizhenii," *Proletarskaia Revoliutsiia*, No. 4 (27), 1924, pp. 30–31; Kharitonov, *Zapiski Instituta Lenina*, II, 115.

[7] Letter to Karpinsky, September 6, 1914, *Leninskii Sbornik*, XI, 99–100; English translation in *The Letters of Lenin*, pp. 333–34.

changes, at a meeting of a few Bolsheviks at Berne, September 6–7.

Under the title, "The Tasks of the Revolutionary Social Democracy in the European War," and over the signature, "A Group of Social Democrats, Members of the R.S.D.L. party," the theses were circulated among the Bolshevik sections abroad and were smuggled into Russia, where indirectly they were the cause of the arrest of the five Bolshevik members of the Duma—Badaev, Muranov, Samoilov, Petrovsky, and Shagov, and also certain other party members, including Kamenev. The meeting of party members held at Ozerki near Petrograd to discuss the theses was raided by the police on the night of November 16–17 (3–4), 1914, and those caught were tried and sentenced to prison or to Siberia.[8] Copies of the document were sent also to the conference of Swiss and Italian socialists at Lugano in September 1914, and most of the points were embodied in the manifesto of the Central Committee of the R.S.D.L. party which was published in *Sotsial-Demokrat* and is given below.

LENIN'S THESES ON THE WAR

[First Text, Berne, September 5 or 6, 1914][9]

1. The European and World War has the sharp and definite character of a bourgeois, imperialist, and dynastic war. The struggle for markets and the looting of countries, the intention to deceive, disunite, and kill off the proletarians of all countries, by instigating the hired slaves of one nation against the hired slaves of the other for the benefit of the bourgeoisie—such is the only real meaning and purpose of the war.

2. The conduct of the leaders of the German Social Democratic party of the Second International (1889–1914)—who have voted the

---

[8] Baevsky, *Ocherki po istorii oktiabrskoi revoliutsii*, I, 354–60; Badaev, *The Bolsheviks in the Tsarist Duma*, p. 208 ff.; F. N. Samoilov, *Vospominaniia*, IV, *Protsess bolshevistskoi fraktsii IV Gosudarstvennoi Dumy*, pp. 8 ff.; Krupskaya, *Memories of Lenin*, II, 141–42. After the revolution, copies of the theses were found in various branch offices of the Secret Police Department in Russia. *Pamiatniki agitatsionnoi literatury. ...*, pp. 256–57.

[9] *Leninskii Sbornik*, XIV, 10–12. The most significant changes in the revised version signed by the "group of Social Democrats" are noted below. The revised version is given in full in Lenin, *Sochineniia*, XVIII, 44–46, and *The Imperialist War (Collected Works*, XVIII), pp. 61–64.

war budget and who repeat the bourgeois chauvinist phrases of the Prussian Junkers and of the bourgeoisie—is a direct betrayal of socialism. In no case, even assuming an absolute weakness of that party and the necessity of submitting to the will of the bourgeois majority of the nation, can the conduct of the leaders of the German Social Democratic party be justified. In fact, this party leads at present a national liberal policy.

3. The conduct of the leaders of the Belgian and French Social Democratic parties, who have betrayed socialism by entering bourgeois cabinets, deserves the same condemnation.

4. The betrayal of socialism by the majority of the leaders of the Second International (1889–1914) means an ideological collapse of that International. The fundamental cause of this collapse is the actual predominance in it of petty-bourgeois opportunism, the bourgeois nature and danger of which has long been pointed out by the best representatives of the proletariat of all countries. Opportunists have long been preparing the collapse of the Second International by renouncing the socialist revolution and substituting bourgeois reformism for it; by renouncing class struggle, with its transformation into civil war, which is necessary at certain moments; by preaching bourgeois chauvinism under the guise of patriotism and defense of the fatherland and by ignoring or renouncing the ABC truth of socialism, expressed long ago in the "Communist manifesto," that workers have no fatherland; by confining themselves in the struggle against militarism to a sentimental Philistine point of view instead of recognizing the necessity of a revolutionary war of the proletarians of all countries against the bourgeoisie of all countries; by turning the necessity to utilize bourgeois parliamentarism and bourgeois legality into a fetish and forgetting that illegal forms of organization and agitation are imperative during epochs of crises. One of the organs of international opportunism, the *Socialist Monthly*,[10] which has long taken the national-liberal stand, is right in celebrating its victory over European socialism.[11]

5. Of the bourgeois and chauvinist sophisms by which the bourgeois parties and governments of the two chief rival nations of the continent, Germany and France, are especially fooling the masses, and which are being slavishly repeated by the socialist opportunists trailing behind the bourgeoisie (the open as well as the covert opportunists), the following

[10] *Sozialistische Monatshefte.*

[11] In the revised version, the following sentences are added here: "The so-called 'center' of the German Social Democratic party and of other social democratic parties has in reality cravenly capitulated before the opportunists. The task of the future International should consist in a resolute and irrevocable uprooting of their bourgeois trend in socialism."

should be especially noted and branded: when the German bourgeoisie refers to the defense of the fatherland, to the struggle against Tsarism, to the protection of the freedom of cultural and national development, they lie; for the Prussian Junkerdom, headed by Wilhelm II, and also the big bourgeoisie, have always pursued the policy of defending the Tsarist monarchy, and whatever the outcome of the war, they will not fail to direct their efforts toward supporting that monarchy; they lie, for, in fact, the Austrian bourgeoisie has undertaken a plunder march against Serbia, the German bourgeoisie oppresses the Danes, the Poles and the French (in Alsace-Lorraine) by waging an aggressive war against Belgium and France for the sake of robbing the richer and freer countries, by organizing the onslaught at the moment considered by them to be the most convenient for utilizing their latest improvements of military technique, and on the eve of the introduction of the so-called big military program by Russia. Similarly, when the French bourgeoisie refer to the defense of the fatherland, etc., they also lie; for in reality they defend countries which are backward in their capitalist technique and which develop more slowly, by hiring with their billions the Black Hundred gangs of Russian Tsarism to wage war for the purpose of plundering Austrian and German territories. Neither of the two belligerent groups of nations is behind the other in the cruelty and barbarism of waging war.

6. The task of Social Democracy in Russia consists in the first place in a merciless and ruthless struggle against the Great Russian and Tsarist-monarchist chauvinism, and against the sophistic defense of this chauvinism by Russian liberals, Constitutional Democrats, and others and by some of the Narodniks. From the point of view of the laboring class and the toiling masses of all the peoples of Russia, the lesser evil would be the defeat of the Tsarist monarchy and its army which oppresses Poland, the Ukraine, and a number of other peoples of Russia and which inflames national hatred for the purpose of strengthening the oppression of other nationalities by the Great Russians and for the stabilization of the reaction and the barbarous government of the Tsarist monarchy.

7. The slogans of Social Democracy at the present time should be: First, a thorough propaganda (to be spread also in the army and the area of military activity) for a socialist revolution and for the necessity of turning the weapons not against brothers, hired slaves of other countries, but against the reaction of the bourgeois governments and parties of all countries—to carry on such propaganda in all languages it is absolutely necessary to organize illegal cells and groups in the armies of all nations—a merciless struggle against chauvinism and the "patriotism" of petty townsmen and against the bourgeoisie of all countries without

exception. It is imperative to appeal to the revolutionary conscience of the working masses, which carry the heavy burden of the war and which[12] are hostile to chauvinism and opportunism, against the leaders of the contemporary International, who have betrayed socialism. Second —as one of the immediate slogans—agitation in favor of German, Polish, Russian, and other republics, along with the transformation of all the separate states of Europe into a republican united states.[13]

LENIN'S ACTIVITIES IN SWITZERLAND IN THE FIRST WEEKS OF THE WAR

[From G. L. Shklovsky's Recollections][14]

.... I may testify that the fundamental slogans of Lenin's tactic in the imperialist war had been formulated by him in Austria during the first few days of the war, for he brought them to Berne completely formulated. And further! I have every reason for stating that this tactic had matured in Lenin's head probably on the first day of the war. My arrest on the third or fourth day of the war may serve as a proof of this statement. .... My arrest was caused by a telegram from Vladimir Ilich [Lenin] addressed to me, which was intercepted by the Swiss military authorities. In this telegram Lenin suggested that I should get in touch with our comrades in Paris for the purpose of organizing the issue of war leaflets and proclamations. This indicates that there was not a moment of doubt or vacillation on the part of Vladimir Ilich and that on the first day of the war he was already thinking of a war against war, i.e., of turning the imperialist war into a civil war.

.... On about the second day [after Lenin's arrival in Berne] a meeting was held in the forest .... where Ilich spoke on the attitude toward the war, this being the only possible subject of discussion for us at that time.

.... A few days later, i.e., on September 6 or 7 [new style], a more intimate meeting was held in my apartment; at this meeting Ilich presented his theses on the war. In addition to Ilich, Zinoviev, and Nadezhda Konstantinovna Krupskaia, the following comrades were present: Samoilov, Safarov, and Lilina, and possibly Inessa. At this meeting Ilich's theses met with no objection whatsoever and were ac-

---

[12] The revised version adds: "in most cases."

[13] The revised version adds: "Thirdly and particularly, a struggle against the Tsarist monarchy and the Great Russian, Pan-Slavist chauvinism, and the preaching of a revolution in Russia, the liberation and self-determination of the nationalities oppressed by Russia on the basis of the immediate slogans: a democratic republic, the confiscation of the landowners' lands, and the eight-hour working day."

[14] "Bernskaia konferentsiia, 1915 g.," *Proletarskaia Revoliutsiia*, 5 (40), 1925, pp. 134–49.

cepted in full.[15] In a few days, Comrade F. N. Samoilov departed with these theses for Russia via Italy and the Balkans. Furthermore, I had handed several copies of these theses to a student, Shenkman, who was at that time in sympathy with us and was leaving for Russia on the same boat. . . . .

It is known that, later on, these theses became the chief evidence for the indictment of our Duma group and were referred to under the official name of the "Resolution of the Seven Points."[16]

However, the theses rendered more service than just that. Our Russian comrades—members of the Central Committee and of the Duma group—became acquainted with the theses and adopted them. From Deputy Petrovsky's testimony at the trial it was revealed that these theses were also adopted by seven of the largest concerns[17] in Petrograd. Through Comrade Shliapnikov, who arrived at Stockholm in the middle of October for the purpose of re-establishing contact with Vladimir Ilich, we were informed that the Russian section of the Central Committee had accepted these theses. Thereafter the theses were elaborated into a manifesto of the Central Committee and issued as an editorial in No. 33 of *Sotsial-Demokrat,* the first number after publication had been resumed on November 1, 1914.

The first care of Vladimir Ilich on his arrival in Switzerland was to resume the publication of the Central Organ. I remember how angry Ilich was and how he grumbled that none of us (including himself) could recall the number of the last issue after which *Sotsial-Demokrat* had been discontinued. I had to dig up my entire library in order to establish the fact that the last number of *Sotsial-Demokrat* which had appeared in Paris approximately a year before was No. 32. Furthermore, I recall

---

[15] This resolution of a "group of Social Democrats" contained, as noted above, a few additions to Lenin's draft.

[16] The reference is to the arrest of the Bolshevik deputies, Kamenev and others, on November 16–17 (3–4), 1914.

[17] In Russia these theses were mimeographed and sent to various large party organizations. Apparently they were discussed and adopted by the workers of a number of factories in Petersburg; during the second half of September 1914 they were sent to Kamenev; in October they were discussed in Moscow, according to police records. They were discovered also in Baku (Baevsky, *Ocherki po istorii oktiabrskoi revoliutsii,* I, 364, citing *Pamiatniki agitatsionnoi literatury* . . . ., p. 257, and *Den,* No. 40, which gives a report of Deputy Petrovsky's testimony at the trial). Samoilov recalls that in the middle of September 1914, immediately on his return from abroad, he presented the point of view of the Bureau of the Central Committee Abroad at a meeting of party members in Ivanovo-Voznesensk. No objections were raised and complete harmony prevailed (F. N. Samoilov, *Vospominaniia,* IV, *Protsess bolshevistskoi fraktsii IV Gosudarstvennoi Dumy,* p. 5). The theses were discussed at the conference of the Bolshevik deputies and party members on November 17 (4), 1914. A. Badaev, *The Bolsheviks in the Tsarist Duma,* p. 212.

that Ilich used to scold himself by saying that while reprimanding the liquidators we ourselves had completely given up the illegal press at the slightest possibility of securing a legal one ——. However, we had to overcome a number of technical and financial obstacles ere, on November 1, after a period of almost two months, No. 33 of *Sotsial-Demokrat* appeared, the first issue after a long interruption.[18]

.... We were entirely cut off from Russia. Only in the middle of October did we succeed, through Comrade Aleksandr (Shliapnikov), who had come to Stockholm for that purpose, in establishing the first contact with Russia.[19] Vladimir Ilich held on to that link with all his strength, fearing that it might break, especially since about November 20 news was received of the arrest of the Duma group and of the members of the Central Committee in Russia; .... Vladimir Ilich decided to call a conference of the sections of the party abroad.

But even the convoking of such a conference was far from an easy task. Communication with other countries, even from neutral Switzerland, was extremely difficult, while the arrival of delegates from belligerent countries or their passage through these countries was even more difficult. ....

.... Still, we succeeded in calling this Conference, although it was not as well represented as we had wished it. Our Scandinavian sections were not represented at the Conference, and not a single representative was present from our comrades in Germany and Austria. Nor was there a representative from the London section, which, however, had taken

[18] In his memoirs Karpinsky tells how he called on Jean Sigg in order to obtain his consent to act as patron for the *Sotsial-Demokrat*. Sigg gave his consent willingly and promised to assist the publication in every way. Since, according to the Swiss police laws, a responsible editor was required, Emil Nicolet, socialist deputy of the Geneva Council, agreed to fill this position, though at that time both he and Sigg were social patriots. The Bolsheviks had no printing shop of their own, and this naturally caused many difficulties. It was necessary to rely on a Russian printer, Kuzma, an old Russian émigré, whose service was usually very slow and irregular. This fact, along with the Central Committee's continual shortage of funds, made the appearance of *Sotsial-Demokrat* very irregular. Karpinsky, in *Zapiski Instituta Lenina*, II, 75–78; see also Lenin's correspondence with Karpinsky in *Leninskii Sbornik*, XI.

[19] Shliapnikov writes: "Immediately on arriving in Sweden I began to carry out the mission with which I was entrusted. I established contacts with the Section of the Central Committee Abroad, forwarded to the Central Organ, *Sotsial-Demokrat*, the letter-reply to Vandervelde's telegram, opened correspondence with V. I. Ulianov and G. Zinoviev informing them of the state of affairs in Russia, and wrote several reports, which were later published in our *Sotsial-Demokrat* as well as in other newspapers abroad. From the Central Committee I received information and instructions to be reforwarded to Russia." A. Shliapnikov, *Kanun semnadtsatogo goda*, I, 34; see in this connection Lenin's letters to Shliapnikov in October and November, 1914, given below, pp. 193–200.

part in the Conference by transferring its vote, if my memory does not betray me, to Comrade N. K. Krupskaia.

Meanwhile Vladimir Ilich missed no occasion of getting in touch with those individual foreigners, who in some way or other protested against the war, in the majority of cases rather diffidently and with lack of confidence. Needless to say, he paid special interest to the parties and groups which had taken a more or less internationalist position (the Italian and Swiss parties, the German Left tendency, the Left tendency among the youth organizations).

In his relations with them, he directed all the strength of his revolutionary passion and of his iron logic not so much against the open opportunists, the struggle against whom he considered to be relatively easy, but against the covert defensists, the "Centrists," with Kautsky at the head. He missed no occasion, by word of mouth, in the press, in private letters, at meetings and wherever possible, to expose and to brand them as the meanest and most dangerous traitors. . . . .

THE GENEVA SECTION OF THE BOLSHEVIKS AND LENIN'S THESES

[Letter Karpinsky to Lenin, September 27, 1914][20]

[GENEVA]

DEAR VLADIMIR ILICH:

You did not answer my letter, but one of the comrades has sent here a draft leaflet on the tasks of the Social Democrats in the present war, with a request that it be published. This puzzled us. If this is merely a draft, then obviously it cannot be published; but if this is the final text, why is it that our section, which has no men and no funds, is called upon to publish it?

We have, however, read the leaflet and consider it our duty to share our unanimous opinion with the "group of Social-Democrats." Our section commissioned me to say in general as follows:

We agree with the qualification of the war, the conduct of the leaders, the slogans, and the exposure of sophisms (paragraphs 1, 2, 5, 6, 7).[21]

Concerning paragraph 3, we believe that this draft justifies the assumption that the authors of the leaflet renounce completely the participation of Social Democrats in bourgeois cabinets, which, of course, is contrary to the resolutions of the International Congress of 1900 as well as to the opinion of Social Democracy in general and, furthermore, of its revolutionary representatives. It is imperative to point out that participation in this given case cannot be justified by the circumstances.

[20] *Leninskii Sbornik*, XI, 255–57.
[21] Paragraphs of Lenin's theses, given above, pp. 140–43.

Concerning paragraph 4, we believe that it would be an exaggeration to define all that happened within the International as its "ideological-political collapse [*sic*]."[22] Neither by volume nor by content would this definition correspond to the real happenings. The International is undergoing a difficult crisis, it has suffered an ideological-political collapse, if you like, but on one question only, the military question. With regard to the rest there is no reason to consider that the ideological-political position of the International has wavered or, moreover, that it has been completely destroyed. This would mean that after losing only one redoubt we are unnecessarily surrendering all forts.

Further, we consider as incorrect the statement concerning the "actual predominance" within the International of "petty bourgeois opportunism." So far no one, anywhere or at any time, has declared the "fatherland to be in danger" to that extent. On the contrary, we all believed that the struggle which so far has been going on within the International between opportunists and revolutionaries has ended in a defeat of the opportunists, that in the decisions and the practice of the International a revolutionary socialist tendency so far has manifested itself everywhere. We dare to think that this is not merely our modest opinion but that this is the general conviction of Social Democracy in all countries, a conviction for which a thousand proofs can be produced including those of all revolutionary representatives of Social Democracy. (Don't the anarcho-syndicalists on the other hand repeat over and over again that social democratic parties are petty bourgeois and are throughout permeated with opportunism?)

Apart from this it is entirely unclear why the authors of the leaflet consider this collapse to be a manifestation of opportunism and precisely of petty bourgeois opportunism. And doesn't this remind one too much of the (bad) custom, so widespread, within our ranks, of shifting every misfortune in the party *tout court* upon "petty bourgeois habits"?

We are inclined to consider the events as a temporary capitulation before opportunism in this question, a capitulation which can be explained by an exceptional intricacy, confusion, acuteness, and enormity of circumstances, a temporary repossessing, let us say, an atavistic belch-

---

[22] N. K. Krupskaia observes that this and other letters of Karpinsky reveal the "confusion and lack of clear thinking" among the Bolsheviks in Switzerland, a condition which cost Lenin great effort to correct (*Leninskii Sbornik*, XI, 95–96). Karpinsky, on the other hand, while conceding that he and others of the "rank and file" misjudged the state of affairs in the foreign Social Democracy and underestimated the strength of opportunism, believes that Lenin took into consideration the points raised by the Geneva section when he wrote the manifesto subsequently issued. Karpinsky admits that Lenin might have heard similar objections from others and might also have been influenced by directions from Russia. (Karpinsky, in *Zapiski Instituta Lenina*, II, 85–87.)

ing of bourgeois ideology in general. We consider correct and fine the fact that the work of the opportunists (as such) who aided the collapse has been mentioned.

We consider it necessary to add a statement to paragraph 5 about the true meaning of the role of Russia, as "defender of the Slavs," and if possible a statement concerning the falseness of the nobleness of the English. The sophism about the French ought to be expressed more exactly.

We draw your attention to the inconvenience of contrasting in this leaflet the words "Russian troops" and the "Black Hundred gangs," "troops which exert oppression, kindle enmity, and increase the yoke," etc. (paragraphs 5 and 6). It is impractical, bad tactics, and undiplomatic to mention this in a leaflet which speaks of work among these troops. Does the entire army as a whole really consist of "Black Hundred gangs"? Does it not consist largely of the best elements of the proletariat? Essentially we welcome the mention made of the role of the army as a weapon of Tsarism.

The text of paragraph 6 should be changed in order not to give rise to a misinterpretation of this passage: that the Russian Social Democrats wish for the victory of the Germans and the defeat of the Russians. Note here the possible connection: the German Social Democrats struggle against Russian Tsarism and the Russian Social Democrats greet the victory of German arms. This idea should be formulated so as to explain what would be the meaning of the victory of the Russian troops and what would be the meaning of their defeat (objectively).

In the last passage of paragraph 4 we would be in favor of more parliamentary expressions with regard to capitulation, inasmuch as this has already been said sufficiently sharply and fundamentally in paragraph 2.

By request of one of us I add that he did not insist upon the remark concerning the troops.

Personally, I attribute great significance, in explaining capitulation on the military question, to a very weak elaboration of our ideology on this point. As a matter of fact in any question of international socialism you can easily name tens and hundreds of substantial works. But can one point out anything that deserves serious mention, let us say, on the question of the attitude of Social Democrats toward the fatherland, toward the defensive war, toward the defense of the fatherland, national independence, and political liberties from barbarian incursions? Is it not possible to find in the resolutions of the international congresses passages upon the basis of which the conduct of the Germans can be easily justified? And haven't many of the statements of the leaders of German Social Democracy—statements which have been made completely in the spirit of their present-day tactics—remained without any objections whatsoever on the part of the "best representatives of the revolutionary proletariat"? Nonsense. Didn't Bebel say at the Congress that he would shoulder a rifle and go out to kill Russians in case the fatherland had to be defended? We reap now the fruits not merely of the work of opportunists but also of our own carefree attitude toward the military question in its basic point. Our work here consisted merely in solemnly proclaiming resolutions which nobody (including us revolutionarists) thought of putting into practice. It seems to me that even in our sharply negative attitude toward anarcho-syndicalists, with their extremes in their attitude toward the fatherland, toward patriotism, and toward militarism, we, without the proper foundation and criticism, patted the Social Democrats on the head for their proper way of bringing up the question. It is past discussion that the anarchists at present find themselves in the worst position yet, and that we were right in criticizing them, but have we been producing anything positive and adequate on the same questions?

The weak elaboration of the question, the helplessness of the parties to prevent the war, the disbelief that this frenzy is possible—how many proofs of this mistrust and disbelief in the nearness of war could be produced from literature!—and, consequently, the unexpectedness of war: these are the cause of the psychological unsoundness of the Social Democrats before the bacchanalia of patriotic sentiments. The sobering must soon start. The International has not perished, and cannot perish. There is no treason in the base sense of the word, merely a temporary preponderance of opportunism.

PLANS AND FUNDS FOR PUBLICATIONS

[Lenin to Karpinsky, Geneva, prior to October 11, 1914][23]

[BERNE]

DEAR KARPINSKY!

I make use of this occasion to talk to you freely.

There is *every* reason to expect that the Swiss police and the military authorities (at the first gesture of the Russian and French ambassadors, etc.) will institute court-martial and deportation for violating neutrality, etc. Therefore, write nothing openly in letters. If anything has to be communicated, write by chemistry[24] (the symbol of chemistry should be the underscored date in the letter).

We decided to publish the attached manifesto [25] instead of the theses,

[23] *Leninskii Sbornik*, XI, 102–103. Another English translation is given in *The Letters of Lenin*, pp. 335–36.   [24] I.e., by code.

[25] The manifesto is the revision of Lenin's original theses issued under the title, "The Tasks of the Revolutionary Social Democracy in the European War."

which are not very readable. Please acknowledge receipt by calling the manifesto "Development of Capitalism."

It ought to be published; but we advise you to do this on condition that you take (and can take) maximum precautions!!

Nobody should know who published it and *where* it was published. All rough drafts should be burned!! The edition should be kept *only* at the home of an influential Swiss citizen, deputy, etc.

If this is impossible, *do not* publish.

If it is impossible to print it, mimeograph it (also with maximum precautions). Reply: I have received (*so many*) copies of the "Development of Capitalism"; shall republish (*so many*) copies.

If it is possible neither to print it nor mimeograph it, then write us at once. We shall think of something else. Answer in great detail.

If you succeed in publishing, send it here *with someone who is coming this way* (the entire edition or three-fourths of it). We shall find a place to store it.

I await a reply!

Yours,
LENIN

["N.B.," in margin.] P.S. We shall find money for publication. Only write us in advance how much is required, for we have *very little* money. Could 170 francs from the Committee of Organizations Abroad be used for this matter?

THE WAR AND THE RUSSIAN SOCIAL DEMOCRACY

[Manifesto of the Central Committee of the Russian Social Democratic Labor Party, November 1, 1914][26]

The European war, prepared for decades by governments and bourgeois parties of all countries, has broken out. Growth of armaments, extreme sharpening of the struggle for markets in the latest, the imperial-

[26] *Sotsial-Demokrat,* No. 33, November 1, 1914, p. 1. A summary was published in *La Sentinelle,* No. 265, November 13, 1914, p. 1. An English translation is given in Lenin, *The Imperialist War,* pp. 76–83. The manifesto was not issued as a separate leaflet but appeared in *Sotsial-Demokrat* only after it had been approved by the party leaders in Russia and after the reply of the Russian Social Democrats to Vandervelde's telegram (see below, p. 157) had been published abroad. Karpinsky observes that it would be interesting to know what changes were made by Lenin in the manifesto as a result of suggestions from Russia. The original draft, however, does not exist. Karpinsky points out that in Lenin's theses the demand for a Russian democratic republic is made only *en passant,* while the chief task is declared to be propaganda for socialist revolution and civil war against the bourgeois governments of all countries. In the manifesto the slogan of a socialist revolution is advocated only for advanced countries, whereas the task in Russia is a gradual

ist, stage of development of capitalism in the leading countries; dynastic interests of the most backward East European monarchies—these inevitably had to lead to war and did lead to it. Seizure of territories, subjugation of foreign nations, ruining of the competing nation, robbery of its wealth, diversion of the attention of the laboring masses from internal political crises in Russia, Germany, England, and other countries, the separate and nationalist deception of workers and destruction of their vanguard with the aim of weakening the revolutionary movement of the proletariat—this is the sole, real essence, significance, and meaning of the present war.

Upon the Social Democracy in the first place falls the duty to reveal this true significance of the war, to unmask without mercy the lies, sophisms, and "patriotic" phrases spread by the dominant classes, landowners, and bourgeoisie in defense of the war.

The German bourgeoisie stands at the head of one of the fighting nations. It fools the working classes and the laboring masses by asserting that it fights in defense of its own country, of freedom and of culture for the sake of liberating the peoples oppressed by Tsarism, and for the destruction of reactionary Tsarism. In fact, this same bourgeoisie is the lackey of the Prussian Junkers, with Wilhelm II at the head, and has always been the most faithful ally of Tsarism and an enemy of the revolutionary movement of the Russian workers and peasants. In reality this bourgeoisie, together with the Junkers, will direct all its efforts, whatever the outcome of the war may be, to supporting the Tsarist monarchy against the revolution in Russia.

As a matter of fact, the German bourgeoisie has undertaken a plundering march against Serbia, with the desire to subdue her and to strangle the national revolution of the Southern Slavs, and is simultaneously directing the greater part of its military forces against the freer countries, such as Belgium and France, in order to plunder a richer

democratic transformation to a democratic republic with equality and self-determination for all nationalities, confiscation of landlords' estates, and the eight-hour day (Karpinsky, in *Zapiski Instituta Lenina*, II, 87). Baevsky notes (*Ocherki po istorii oktiabrskoi revoliutsii*, I, 379) that the slogan of defeat of one's own government raised objections in Russia and there was a tendency to eliminate the word defeat "as a very odious one." Shliapnikov also recalls (*Kanun semnadtsatogo goda*, I, 29) that, while the theses reflected the state of mind of party workers, the question of "'defeat' provoked perplexity." *Sotsial-Demokrat* (No. 51, February 29, 1916, p. 2) noted that the Bolshevik organization in Moscow adopted the manifesto with the exception of the paragraph dealing with the defeat of one's own country. There is other evidence of reluctance to adopt the defeatist point of view by party workers in Russia and outside, not only at the beginning of the war but even up to the revolution of 1917 (*Revoliutsionnoe Byloe*, No. 3, 1924, p. 6, quoted by Baevsky, *op. cit.*, p. 384). Baevsky asserts, however, that "it is impossible to speak of 'anti-defeatism' during the war as a tendency within the party."

competitor. The German bourgeoisie, by spreading fairy tales about a defensive war on its part, has in reality chosen the moment most convenient, from its point of view, to make war by utilizing its latest improvements in military technique and forestalling the new armaments already planned and decided upon by France and Russia.

The English and French bourgeoisie stand at the head of the other group of fighting nations; they deceive the working class and the toiling masses by asserting that they fight in defense of their countries, for freedom and culture against the militarism and despotism of Germany. In reality this bourgeoisie for a long time has been hiring and preparing with its billions the troops of Russian Tsarism, the most reactionary and barbarous monarchy of Europe, for an attack on Germany.

In reality the aim of the struggle of the English and French bourgeoisie is to seize the German colonies and to destroy a rival nation which is distinguished by a more rapid economic development. For this "noble" purpose the "advanced" democratic nations assist the wild Tsarism to strangle still further Poland, the Ukraine, etc., and to repress still more the revolution in Russia.

Neither of the two groups of the fighting countries is behind the other in robberies, bestialities, and the countless cruelties of war; but in order to fool the proletariat and to divert its attention from the only really liberating war—the civil war against the bourgeoisie of "their own" as well as of "foreign" countries—for this noble purpose the bourgeoisie of every country by means of false phrases on patriotism attempts to exalt the significance of "its own" national war and to assert that it strives to conquer the enemy not for the sake of robbery and seizure of territory but for the sake of "liberating" all other peoples except its own.

But the greater the efforts of the governments and of the bourgeoisie of all countries to disunite the workers and to direct them against each other, and the more violent the system of martial law and of censorship (which even now in time of war pursues the "internal" enemy more than the external one) that is used for this lofty purpose, the more urgent becomes the duty of the class-conscious proletariat to defend its unity, its internationalism, its socialist beliefs against the debauch of chauvinism of the "patriotic" bourgeois cliques of all countries. To repudiate this task on the part of class-conscious workers would mean to repudiate all their democratic, not to speak of their socialist, aspirations for liberation.

With a feeling of deepest chagrin we have to state that the socialist parties of the chief European countries did not fulfill this duty of theirs, while the behavior of the leaders of these parties, especially of those of the German party, verges on direct treason against the cause of socialism. At the moment of greatest universal-historical significance the majority of leaders of the contemporary Second (1889–1914) Socialist

International attempts to substitute nationalism for socialism. Thanks to their behavior the workers' parties of those countries did not range themselves against the criminal conduct of their governments but appealed to the laboring class to merge its position with that of imperialist governments. The leaders of the International have committed treason against socialism by voting the war credits, by repeating the chauvinist ("patriotic") slogans of the bourgeoisie of "their own" countries in justification and defense of war, and by entering the bourgeois cabinets of the belligerent countries, and so on, and so on. The most influential socialist leaders and the most influential organs of the socialist press of contemporary Europe take a chauvinist, bourgeois, liberal, and not at all a socialist position. The responsibility for thus disgracing socialism rests in the first place upon the German Social Democrats, who constitute the strongest and most influential party of the Second International. But even the French socialists cannot be pronounced guiltless, for they accepted ministerial posts in the government of the same bourgeoisie which betrayed its country and allied itself with Bismarck to repress the Commune.

The German and Austrian Social Democrats attempt to justify their support of the war by saying that thereby they struggle against Russian Tsarism. We, Russian Social Democrats, declare that such a justification is a simple sophism. The revolutionary movement against Tsarism in our country has once again grown to great dimensions during the last few years. All this time the Russian laboring class stood at the head of the movement. During the last few years strikes, with millions of participants, were conducted under the slogan of the overthrow of Tsarism and the demand for a democratic republic. Not longer ago than on the eve of the war, the President of the French Republic, Poincaré, during his visit to Nicholas II, could observe for himself barricades erected by Russian workers in the streets of Petersburg. The Russian proletariat did not stop before any sacrifice to free humanity from the disgrace of the Tsarist monarchy. But we must say that if there is anything that can, under certain conditions, delay the fall of Tsarism and assist it in the fight against the whole Russian democracy, it is the present war, a war which has placed at the disposal of the reactionary aims of Tsarism the purse of the English, French, and Russian bourgeoisie. If there is anything to obstruct the revolutionary struggle of the Russian laboring class against Tsarism it is the conduct of the leaders of German and Austrian Social Democracy, a conduct continually held up as an example for us by the Russian chauvinist press.

Even assuming that German Social Democracy was so weak as to compel it to renounce all revolutionary activities, even in a case like that, it was not permissible for it to join the chauvinist camp; it was not permissible for it to take steps which led the Italian socialists to declare with justice that the leaders of the German Social Democracy were disgracing the banner of the proletarian International.

Our party, the Russian Social Democratic Labor party, has already suffered and will suffer great sacrifices in connection with the war. Our entire open labor press has been annihilated; the majority of unions have been closed; numerous comrades have been arrested and exiled. But our parliamentary representation, the Russian Social Democratic Labor group of the State Duma, still considered it its ruthless socialist duty not to vote the war credits and even left the session hall of the Duma, thereby expressing its protest more effectively; it has considered it its duty to brand the policy of the European governments as imperialist and in spite of the tenfold oppression of the Tsarist government, the Russian worker-comrades are already publishing their first illegal proclamations against the war, thus fulfilling their duty before democracy and the International.

If representatives of the revolutionary social democracy—the minority of German Social Democrats and the best Social Democrats of neutral countries—at present experience an intense feeling of shame over this collapse of the Second International; if voices of socialists against the chauvinism of the majority of Social Democratic parties become audible in England and France; if the opportunists, as represented by the German *Socialist Monthly* (*Sozialistische Monatshefte*), who have long occupied a national-liberal position, justly celebrate their victory over European socialism—then the worst service is rendered to the proletariat by those who vacillate between opportunism and revolutionary Social Democracy (like the "center" of the German Social Democratic party) and who try to ignore or even to conceal, by means of diplomatic phrases, the collapse of the Second International.

On the contrary this collapse must be acknowledged openly and its causes understood, so that it will be possible to construct a new and firmer socialist coalition of the workers of all countries.

The opportunists have set at naught the decisions of the Stuttgart, Copenhagen, and Basel congresses which made it the duty of the socialists of all countries to fight against chauvinism under every possible condition and to respond to any war declared by the bourgeoisie and governments with an increased propaganda of civil war and of social revolution. The collapse of the Second International is the collapse of opportunism which was bred upon the soil of the peculiarities of the past (so-called "peaceful") historical epoch and which actually dominated the International in recent years. The opportunists have long been preparing this collapse by denouncing the socialist revolution and by substituting for it bourgeois reformism; by denouncing the class struggle which at times inevitably turns into civil war; by preaching the co-operation of classes;

by preaching bourgeois chauvinism under the name of patriotism and of defense of the fatherland, and by ignoring or denouncing the basic truth of socialism—stated long ago in the Communist manifesto—that the workers have no fatherland; by confining themselves in the struggle against militarism to a sentimental Philistine viewpoint instead of admitting the necessity of a revolutionary war of the proletarians of all countries against the bourgeoisie of all countries; by turning the necessary utilization of bourgeois parliamentarism and of bourgeois legality into a fetish, forgetting the necessity of illegal organizations and of agitation in times of crises. The anarcho-syndicalist tendency, a natural "supplement" of opportunism, equally bourgeois and antagonistic to the proletarian—i.e., to the Marxist point of view—distinguished itself no less disgracefully by repeating in an arrogant manner the slogans of chauvinism during the contemporary crisis.

The task of socialism cannot be fulfilled and the true international coalition of workers cannot be realized at present without a ruthless break with opportunism and without explaining to the masses the inevitability of its fiasco.

The duty of the Social Democracy of every country should be, in the first place, the fight against chauvinism in that country. In Russia this chauvinism has completely embraced bourgeois liberalism (the Constitutional Democrats) and in part, the Narodniks down to Socialist-Revolutionists and the "Right" Social Democrats. (The chauvinist declarations of E. Smirnov, P. Maslov, and G. Plekhanov, which are seized upon and spread far and wide by the bourgeois "patriotic" press, should be especially stigmatized.)

Under the present conditions it is impossible from the point of view of the international proletariat to determine which is the lesser evil for socialism, the defeat of the one group of belligerent nations or the defeat of the other. But for us, the Russian Social Democrats, not the least doubt exists from the standpoint of the working class and of the toiling masses of all the peoples of Russia that the lesser evil would be the defeat of the Tsarist monarchy, of the most reactionary and barbarous government which oppresses the largest number of nationalities and the largest mass of the population of Europe and Asia.

The immediate political slogan of the Social Democrats of Europe should be the formation of the republican united states of Europe; but in contrast to the bourgeoisie, which is ready to "promise" anything in order to draw the proletariat into the common stream of chauvinism, the Social Democrats will explain the falsehood and the absurdity of this slogan without the overthrow of the German, Austrian, and Russian monarchies.

In Russia, because of the greater backwardness of this country which has not yet completed its bourgeois revolution, the tasks of the Social Democrats should consist, as before, in the establishment of the three fundamental conditions of a consistent democratic reconstruction: a democratic republic (with complete equality of rights and with self-determination of all nations) ; confiscation of landowners' lands ; and an eight-hour working day. But in all advanced countries the war puts forward the slogan of a socialist revolution, which becomes the more urgent the more heavily the burdens of war press on the shoulders of the proletariat ; and the more active shall the role of the proletariat be in the reconstruction of Europe after the horrors of contemporary "patriotic" barbarism in the midst of gigantic technical successes of capitalism. The utilization by the bourgeoisie of martial law to close the mouths of the proletariat raises for the latter the definite problem of establishing illegal forms of agitation and illegal organizations. Let the opportunists "preserve" the legal organizations at the expense of betraying their own convictions ; the revolutionary Social Democrats will make use of the organizational experience and of the contacts of the laboring class to create illegal methods of struggle for socialism—methods which are adequate in an epoch of crises—and to establish the coalition of workers, not with the chauvinist bourgeoisie of their own country, but with the workers of all countries. The proletarian International did not perish and shall not perish. The working masses will create a new International in spite of all obstacles. The present triumph of opportunism is short-lived. The greater the number of war victims the clearer it will become to the laboring masses that the opportunists have betrayed the workers' cause and that it is necessary to turn their weapons against the governments and the bourgeoisie of every country.

The transformation of the contemporary imperialist war into a civil war is the only correct proletarian slogan, pointed out by the experience of the Commune, outlined in the Basel (1912) resolution, and derived from all the conditions of an imperialist war between highly developed bourgeois countries. No matter how great the difficulties of such a transformation, socialists will never renounce a systematic, persistent, and unfailing preparatory work in this direction, since the war has become a fact.

Only in this way may the proletariat free itself from the influence of the chauvinist bourgeoisie and in one way or another take decided steps on the road to real freedom of the peoples and on the road to socialism.

Hail! International brotherhood of the workers against the chauvinism and the patriotism of the bourgeoisie of all countries!

Hail! Proletarian International freed of opportunism!

THE CENTRAL COMMITTEE OF THE RUSSIAN
SOCIAL DEMOCRATIC LABOR PARTY

On October 17 Lenin wrote Karpinsky that it had been decided not to publish the manifesto referred to above but to bring out an issue of the Central Organ, *Sotsial-Demokrat*.[27] One of the reasons for this change of plan was the receipt of the reply of the Russian Social Democrats to Vandervelde. Vandervelde's message, to which this reply was made, was an appeal to Russian socialists to support the struggle against "Prussian militarism." It had been sent through the Russian Minister at Brussels, Prince Kudashev, at the request of the Belgian Minister of War and had been delivered to Chkheidze by the Russian Ministry of Foreign Affairs. The message was released to bourgeois newspapers before it was actually delivered. The Chkheidze group did not reply. Some of the Mensheviks said "we do not in our activities in Russia oppose the war." Four Bolshevik members of the Duma and some of the party leaders met at the home of L. B. Kamenev on October 13–14 near Mustamiaki, Finland, and drafted a reply refusing to support Vandervelde's position. This draft, somewhat modified, was published in *Sotsial-Demokrat, No. 33*, over the signature of the Central Committee of the R.S.D.L. party. The liquidators' reply was published in No. 34 of the same periodical.[28]

On October 17 Lenin also wrote to Shliapnikov that he considered "the most important thing at present is a persistent and organized struggle against chauvinism, which has taken hold of all the bourgeoisie and a majority of opportunist socialists (and those who make peace with opportunism—such as Mr. Kautsky) .... One must exert every effort to uphold the just hatred of the class-conscious workers for the hideous conduct of the Germans [i.e., the Social Democrats who voted for war credits]; one must draw from this hatred political conclusions *against* opportunism and against every concession to opportunism. This is an interna-

[27] *Leninskii Sbornik*, XI, 107–108; English translation in *The Letters of Lenin*, pp. 338–39.

[28] Lenin, *The Imperialist War*, pp. 412–13, note 24; Samoilov, *Vospominaniia*, IV, *Protsess bolshevistskoi fraktsii IV Gosudarstvennoi Dumy*, p. 6. The text of Vandervelde's message is given in E. Vandervelde's memoirs, *Souvenirs d'un militant socialiste*, pp. 185–86.

tional task. It devolves upon us; there is nobody else. One cannot shirk it. The slogan of 'simply' re-establishing the International is incorrect (because the danger of a spineless conciliatory resolution along the line of Kautsky and Vandervelde is very, very great!). The slogan of 'peace' is incorrect as the slogan must be: changing the national war into a civil war .... In order that the struggle may proceed along a definite and clear line, one must have a slogan that summarizes it. This slogan is: For us *Russians,* from the point of view of the interests of the laboring masses and the working class of *Russia,* there cannot be the slightest doubt, absolutely no doubt whatever, that the *lesser* evil would be here and now, the defeat of Tsarism in the present war .... As to ourselves, we must prepare a mass (at least a collective) action in the army not of one nation alone, and conduct *all* the work of propaganda and agitation in this direction. To direct the work (stubborn, systematic work that may require a long time) in the spirit of transforming the national war into civil war—this is the whole issue. The moment for such a transformation is a different question; at present it is not clear as yet. We must allow this moment to ripen, we must systematically 'force it to ripen.' ...."[29]

THE RUSSIAN WORKERS AND THE WAR

[Shliapnikov's Speech at the Congress of Swedish Social Democrats, November 24, 1914][30]

RESPECTED COMRADES!

I bring you the greetings of the organized Russian proletariat, the greetings of its class organization, the Russian Social Democratic Labor party. I wish the Swedish Social Democratic Labor party success in its work. At the present moment of general collapse, when the bourgeoisie of almost the whole of Europe, Western and Eastern, is pursuing an armed imperialist policy under the cloak of "national self-defense," we socialists must raise high our international revolutionary red banner and must not allow the waves of reformism to swallow us, the reformism

---

[29] Full text in Lenin, *The Imperialist War,* pp. 73–75.

[30] Shliapnikov, *Kanun semnadtsatogo goda,* I, 43–45. First published under the title, "Na shvedskom s.d. sezde," in *Sotsial-Demokrat,* No. 36, December 12, 1914, p. 2.

which in this criminal war puts into practice its theory of the "unification of classes."

We Russian workers, and especially the Petersburg workers, have observed with pleasure your struggle against the tendency which endeavored to draw the Swedish people into the World War, and we are extremely glad that all efforts in this direction on the part of the agents of militarism have resulted in a complete fiasco in your friendly country.

Please allow me to say a few words about our labor movement which, beginning with 1912, has experienced a rise, and has manifested itself in an unusually intense growth of the strike movement and especially in the growth of the so-called political mass strikes. In order to illustrate my thought I shall mention certain figures concerning our struggle.

In 1911 the number of strikers in our vast country amounted to 105,000; one year later (1912) the number of strikers reached 1,070,000, of whom 855,000 were engaged in political strikes. In 1913 the strike movement was no less extensive; during that year 1,185,000 workers took part in strikes, and of those 821,000 were engaged in political movements, though official statistics of factory inspection are not complete, as they do not include small industrial and state concerns.

Cruelties and persecutions of the government and of organized capital could not break up the solidarity of the Russian laboring class. The current year may serve as a clear example. During this year the struggle of the workers has reached extreme intensity. Thanks to governmental repressions, all economic clashes between labor and capital have been turning rapidly into political movements. The working class declared once more its readiness to fight for a republic, a Constituent Assembly, and an eight-hour working day.

In July the political struggle flared up with unusual strength. The bloody provocation by the government was answered with a general strike by the laboring class of Petersburg, a strike which included 250,000 workers in Petersburg alone. In many places the streets of the city were covered with barricades and the blood of workers was shed. The movement has already spread to the provinces and has embraced the Baltic provinces, Poland, the Caucasus, Moscow, and the South.

At this particular moment, when our struggle had reached this point, the monster of war advanced upon us. The bourgeoisie started to sound the alarm—its fatherland, the fatherland of the money bag, was in danger! Soldiers—sons of peasants and of workers—began to move to the front in gray uniforms.

In the days of mobilization the workers of Petersburg left their work and protested loudly against the war. To the sounds of revolutionary songs, with red banners and badges the workers accompanied their mobilized comrades to the places where they were to report.

We class-conscious workers did not believe in the possibility of a world war. We turned our eyes full of hope toward the West, toward our organized brothers: Germans, French, Austrians. There we expected to find support and to hear a powerful appeal for struggle against the devilish plot of the bourgeoisie. But bitter reality brought us something else. The governmental press and the bourgeois newspapers, as well as our countrymen who fled from abroad, informed us of the treason of the leaders of the powerful German Social Democracy and, thereafter, of many others who considered the situation from the "point of view of national self-defense."

But our Social Democratic Labor party did not succumb to the general conflagration; it did not forget the true causes of the present war—the result of the imperialist policy pursued by the bourgeois governments of all countries. The Duma group has correctly expressed the will of the organized proletariat by refusing to vote war budgets and by stressing its opposition to war by leaving the meeting hall. Many local organizations issued illegal leaflets on war (Petersburg, Moscow, Riga, Warsaw, Caucasus, and others).

The Central Committee of the party and its central organ, *Sotsial-Demokrat,* entered the struggle against international opportunism and appealed to all revolutionary proletarian elements of all countries to support this struggle in the name of the common interests of the world proletariat.

In concluding my speech, I wish success to our fraternal party in the work of the Congress. Hail! Swedish proletariat and its class party, the Social Democracy! Hail! the International!

[Larin's Speech][31]

DEAR COMRADES!

We greet you on behalf of the Organization Committee of the Russian Social Democratic Labor party which unites the Jewish Social Democratic Workers' League, the League of Ukrainian Social Democrats, and the Caucasian Social Democracy with the Russian organizations led by Plekhanov, Axelrod, and Trotsky[32] and which maintains organization

---

[31] Shliapnikov, *Kanun semnadtsatogo goda,* I, 45–46.

[32] Trotsky later disclaimed any responsibility for the policy of the Organization Committee and said that his name had been used by Larin without justification or authorization. The Secretariat of the Organization Committee Abroad also explained that the use of Plekhanov's name did not imply the Committee's agreement with Plekhanov's position, and further, that the reference to Trotsky was a mistake which "may have been caused by the uncertainty of Trotsky's position," as he had not officially withdrawn from the August bloc. Both letters are in *Nashe Slovo,* No. 14, February 13, 1915, p. 1.

relations with the combined Polish and Lithuanian social democracies. Though tremendous material and moral losses may be caused by the war that has broken out in Europe, we face the future with hope. Life ends neither today nor this year, and the great cause of the laboring class will undoubtedly overcome in the end all internal and external obstacles upon its road. It is very possible also that during this war and its further development there will appear some sources of a strong rise of energy and solidarity within the ranks of the international laboring class.

The present serious and responsible movement demands from the laboring class of every country especially strong energy and resolution in the face of future exigencies and events. We Russian Social Democrats, who know by personal experience the bitter fruits of a party split, wish that our fraternal Swedish party will be victorious and will prosper. We hope that in the future it will also hold high its banner of solidarity and proletarian activity and its organizational banner, which constitutes the party's greatest blessing and which serves its further development and final victory.

Hail, Swedish Social Democracy!

Hail, International Social Democracy!

Authorized by the Organization Committee of the Russian Social Democratic Labor Party.

LARIN

[Lenin's Comments][33]

.... For the first time after the beginning of the war a representative of our party, of its Central Committee, and a representative of the liquidationist Organization Committee, met at a congress of socialists of a neutral country. How did their speeches differ? Belenin [Shliapnikov] took a most definite stand regarding the grave and painful yet momentous questions of the present-day socialist movement; referring to the Central Organ of the party, *Sotsial-Demokrat*, he resolutely declared war against opportunism, branding the behavior of the German social democratic leaders (and "many others") as *treason*. Larin took no position at all; he passed over the essence of the question in silence, confining himself to those hackneyed, hollow, and foul phrases which do not fail to be rewarded with applause by the opportunists and social chauvinists of all countries. Belenin kept complete silence concerning our attitude towards the other Social Democratic parties and groups in Russia as if saying: "This is our position, and as to others we shall not express ourselves as yet, we shall wait to see which course they will take." On the other hand, Larin unfurled the banner of "unity," shed-

---

[33] Excerpts from Lenin, "And Now What?" *The Imperialist War*, pp. 104–10, first published in *Sotsial-Demokrat*, No. 36, December 12, 1914, p. 1.

ding a tear over the "bitter fruits of disunity in Russia," painting with gorgeous colors the "unity work" of the O.C., which, he said, had united Plekhanov and the Caucasians, the Bundists and the Poles, and so forth. . . . .

The policy of the Organization Committee which, in faraway Sweden, on November 23, declares its unity with Plekhanov and delivers speeches sweet to the hearts of all social chauvinists, while in Paris and in Switzerland it does not make its existence known either on September 13 (when the *Golos* appeared) nor on November 23, nor after this to the present time (December 23), is very much like the worst kind of political manoeuvering.

. . . . Some Russian socialists seem to think that internationalism consists in readiness to embrace a resolution containing an international vindication of social chauvinism of all countries, such as is about to be composed by Plekhanov and Südekum, Kautsky and Hervé, Guesde and Hyndman, Vandervelde and Bissolati, etc. We allow ourselves to think that internationalism consists only in an unequivocal internationalist policy pursued inside the party itself. In company with opportunists and social chauvinists it is impossible to pursue the true international policy of the proletariat. . . . .

B. The Attempt to Call a Conference of Russian Internationalists

A few months after Shliapnikov's appearance at the Congress of the Swedish Social Democrats, the Bolsheviks made their second appearance during the World War in the international arena at the Inter-Allied Socialist Conference which met in London on February 14, 1915.[34] This Conference is taken up in the following chapter. A few days before this, on February 6, the *Nashe Slovo* group in Paris, made up of Menshevik-Internationalists and certain Bolsheviks whose position was similar to Trotsky's,[35] sent a letter to the Central Committee of the R.S.D.L. party (Bolshevik) and the Organization Committee of the R.S.D.L. party (Menshevik), proposing a joint demonstration of internationalists at the

[34] The Bolsheviks sent a copy of their manifesto to the Copenhagen Conference, January 17–18, 1915, but were not represented.

[35] Among the members of the *Nashe Slovo* group were: Martov, Ber, Rakovsky, Semkovsky, Weltmann, Kollontai, Uritsky, from the Mensheviks; and Sokolnikov, Lozovsky, Lunacharsky, and Pokrovsky, from the Bolsheviks.

London Conference against social patriotism. Lenin replied for the Central Committee on February 9, agreeing to the desirability of such action and including a draft declaration which contained the following points: A characterization of the war as imperialist not only on the part of Germany and Austria-Hungary but also on the part of England, France, and Russia, i.e., "a war of the epoch of the last stage of capitalist development," wherefore, it was the duty of socialists to fulfill the Basel resolutions by (1) breaking with national blocs and *Burgfrieden* in all countries; (2) appealing to all workers for an energetic class struggle against their own bourgeoisie; (3) condemning any voting for war credits; (4) condemning as treason the entry into bourgeois cabinets as in Belgium and France; (5) forming an international committee, including Germans, to agitate for ending the war "not in the spirit of pacifists, Christians, and of petty bourgeois democrats, but in an unbreakable connection with preaching and organizing mass revolutionary activities of the proletarians in every country against the governments and the bourgeoisie of their own country"; (6) encouraging fraternization in the trenches between socialists of the belligerents; (7) appealing to the women socialists to agitate along the lines suggested; (8) appealing to the entire international proletariat for support in the struggle against Tsarism; and, finally, a repudiation of the defense of official social patriotism as expressed by Plekhanov, Aleksinsky, Maslov, and others. In concluding his letter Lenin expressed his suspicion that the Organization Committee and the Bund would be found on the side of "official social patriotism."[36]

The reply to *Nashe Slovo* from P. B. Axelrod for the Organization Committee has not been found, but it appears from an editorial in that paper, No. 32, March 6, 1915, that he agreed to co-operate. The *Nashe Slovo* group thereupon drew up its own declaration, which advocated many of the

---

[36] Full text of the letter is in Lenin, *Sochineniia*, XXIX, 318–25; English translation in *The Letters of Lenin*, pp. 358–61. The editors of *Sochineniia* state that the letter from *Nashe Slovo* to which Lenin replied has not been found.

tactics which were contained in the eight points of Lenin's draft. This declaration was less outspoken in the matter of defeatism and in place of the characterization of the war there was a criticism of the project of a conference of "Allied" socialists as contradictory to international policy and a condemnation of the endeavors of government socialists to use the conference to gain moral support for the policies of the Entente against the Central Powers.[37]

No joint declaration was made at the London Conference nor did any success attend the later attempts of the *Nashe Slovo* group to bring together the Russian social democratic internationalists for the purpose of formulating a definite statement of their attitude toward the war. The Menshevik Organization Committee wished a larger conference than *Nashe Slovo* proposed; the Bolsheviks wished to test those invited and exclude all but the simon-pure internationalists. The conference did not take place and, as on earlier occasions, no unity was achieved.[38]

WHO SHOULD BE REPRESENTED IN A CONFERENCE OF REAL INTERNATIONALISTS?

[Letter of the Central Committee of the Russian Socialist Democratic Labor Party to the Editorial Board of *Nashe Slovo,* March 23, 1915][39]

Respected Comrades! We quite agree with you that a unification of all real Social Democrat internationalists is one of the most urgent matters to be considered at the present moment ——. Before giving a reply to your practical proposal, we consider it necessary to clear up certain preliminary questions so as to know whether a true solidarity exists between us with respect to fundamentals. You are quite justly indignant over the fact that Aleksinsky, Plekhanov, and the like are writing in the foreign press and are representing their voices to be "the voice of the Russian proletariat or of its influential groups." *It is neces-*

---

[37] Considerable portions of the declaration were deleted by the censor when it was first published in *Nashe Slovo,* No. 26, February 27, 1915, p. 1. The full text in German was published in the *Berner Tagwacht,* No. 42, February 20, 1915, p. 1. This declaration appears also in *Leninskii Sbornik,* XVII, 199–200.

[38] *Pisma Akselroda i Yu. O. Martova,* p. 336, note 2; *Leninskii Sbornik,* XVII, 191–94.

[39] *Leninskii Sbornik,* XVII, 201–203. Taken from a letter of Krupskaia to Shliapnikov dated March 30 (17), 1915 (*ibid.,* p. 193).

sary to struggle against that. But in order to struggle, it is necessary to get at the root of the evil. It cannot be doubted that there has never been, nor is there now, a greater corruption than the so-called system of representation of the "famous currents" abroad, but we scarcely have the right to blame the foreigners for this. Let us recall the recent past. Was it not permitted to Aleksinsky and Plekhanov (and not only to them) at the Brussels Conference (August 3, 1914)[40] to personify the "currents"? Is it possible after that to be surprised if the foreigners still take them for the representatives of the "currents"? Nothing can be done about that evil by any sort of declaration. A protracted struggle is imperative. In order that it may be successful, we should say to ourselves once and for all that we will recognize only those *organizations* which for years have been connected with the working masses, organizations authorized by concerted committees, etc., and that we will brand as a deception of the workers the system under which half a dozen intellectuals—after they have issued two or three numbers of a paper or a magazine—proclaim themselves as a "current" and claim "equal rights" with the party.

Do we agree on this, respected comrades?

Further, about the internationalists: in one of the recent editorials of your paper you have enumerated all of the organizations which in your opinion share the internationalist viewpoint.[41] The Bund is named as among the first. We should like to know your reasons for counting the Bund among the internationalists. The resolution of its Central Committee contains not one definite word with regard to the sore problems of socialism. It breathes an unideological eclecticism.[42] The organ of Bund (*Informatsionnyi Listok*) undoubtedly adheres to the Germanophile chauvinist point of view, or at best gives a "synthesis" of French and German chauvinisms. Not without reason has Kosovsky's article embellished the pages of *Neue Zeit*—a magazine which (let us hope that you agree with us on that) is now one of the most indecent of the so-called "socialist" organs of the press.[43]

[40] The correct date of this conference is July 16–17 (3–4), 1914.

[41] This refers to the editorial "Gde bolshinstvo?" in *Nashe Slovo*, No. 42, March 18, 1915, p. 1. (*Leninskii Sbornik*, XVII, 203, note 3.)

[42] The resolution on the war adopted at a conference called by the Central Committee of the Bund in November 1914 was published under "Tsentralnyi Komitet Bunda o voine," in *Informatsionnyi Listok Zagranichnoi Organizatsii Bunda*, No. 7, January 1915, p. 3.

[43] V. Kosovsky's article, "Osvoboditelnaia legenda," was published in *Informatsionnyi Listok Zagranichnoi Organizatsii Bunda*, No. 7, January 1915, pp. 3–7. This article appeared later in an abbreviated form in *Neue Zeit*: See Kossowsky, "Befreiungslegenden," *Neue Zeit*, No. 19, February 12, 1915, pp. 577–83, and Lenin, *Sochineniia*, XXIX, 324, note.

We are with all our heart in favor of a unification of the internationalists. We should like it very much if there were more of them. But it is impossible to include persons and organizations in the ranks of internationalists, which as far as internationalism is concerned are known for certain to be "dead souls."

What should be understood by internationalism? Can, for example, the advocates of a restoration of the International upon the principle of a mutual "amnesty" be counted as internationalists? The most notable representative of the theory of "amnesty," as you know, is Kautsky. Victor Adler also writes in the same spirit. We consider that the defenders of amnesty are the most dangerous opponents of internationalism. The International, restored upon the principle of "amnesty," would make socialism shorter by a whole head. Any concession whatever, any agreements with Kautsky and Co., are absolutely inadmissible. The most resolute struggle against the theory of "amnesty" is the *conditio sine qua non* of internationalism. It is useless to speak about internationalism, for there is neither desire nor readiness to go to the extent of breaking with the defenders of "amnesty." And here, it should be asked, do we agree on this basic question? In your newspaper a negative attitude toward the policy of "amnesty" has flared up; but you will agree that before taking any practical steps we have the right to ask you to give us in detail your point of view on that question.

The question of attitude toward the Organization Committee is tied up with the above. We considered it necessary in our first letter to tell you frankly that there were serious reasons to doubt the internationalism of that institution. You have not attempted to dispel that opinion. We ask you again, what are your evidences for considering that the Organization Committee adheres to the internationalist point of view? It is, of course, impossible to deny that P. B. Axelrod's position as expounded in several of his published articles is an obviously chauvinist (almost Plekhanovist) position. At the same time Axelrod is undoubtedly the most noted representative of the Organization Committee. Take, furthermore, the official demonstrations of the Organization Committee. Its report to the Copenhagen Conference[44] was written in such a tone that it was reprinted by the most extreme German chauvinists. The writings of the Secretariat of the Organization Committee Abroad are of the same sort. At their best they do not say anything. On the other hand, Larin has made statements officially on behalf of the Organization Committee, and not in the name of some secretariat abroad, statements in defense of chauvinism.[45] Where is the internationalism here? Is it

---

[44] See below, pp. 267–71.

[45] See Larin's speech at the Congress of the Swedish Social Democrats above, pp. 160–61.

not clear that the Organization Committee completely adheres to the point of view of a mutual "amnesty"?

Further, what guaranties exist that the Organization Committee represents a force in Russia? Now after the articles of *Nasha Zaria*[46] this question is particularly pertinent. The *Nasha Zaria* group has pursued its own policy for years. It has created its own daily paper; it has conducted a mass agitation in its own spirit. But what about the Organization Committee?

We all recognize that the matter will be settled not through the co-ordination of the forces of the groups abroad, at Zürich, Paris, etc., but will be settled through the influence of the Petrograd workers, of the workers of the whole of Russia. We should keep this in mind in all our moves.

Such are our considerations, and we wished to communicate them to you. We shall be very glad to receive from you detailed and clear answers to all these questions. Then it might be possible to consider further developments.

NASHE SLOVO'S REPLY

[Letter of the Editorial Board to the Central Committee of the Russian Social Democratic Labor Party after March 25, 1915][47]

RESPECTED COMRADES!

In your letter of March 23 you recognized in principle the usefulness of co-ordinating the activities of those organizations of Russian Social Democracy which have taken an internationalist position in the present crisis. This agreement in principle gives us reason to hope that we shall succeed in disposing of your doubts, which were raised by our practical proposal.

That proposal consisted essentially in the calling of a conference of those organized elements of Russian Social Democracy which must represent before the International the true position taken by our party— the position which is being distorted by the social patriots—and in doing this without touching at all upon the questions of party construction and organizational unification. In order to simplify and facilitate this process of co-ordination we proposed to begin with the Russian groups in the narrow sense of the word "Russian," believing that in case of success of that first attempt the widening of agreement among the national groups would then present no difficulties. As you see from the

---

[46] V. Leonov's article, "Voina i ee prichiny," and N. Cherevanin's article, "Germaniia pered vnutrennim krizisom," in *Nasha Zaria*, Nos. 7, 8, 9, published in October 1914. (Lenin, *Sochineniia*, XXIX, 325, note.)

[47] *Leninskii Sbornik*, XVII, 204–206.

attached letter of the Secretariat of the Organization Committee Abroad, the latter has expressed itself resolutely against such a limitation. We continue to maintain our first point of view; but of course we do not attribute fundamental significance to this difference.

You put the question of our attitude toward the established mode of representation of the various "currents," a mode which was a result of disturbances within our party life and is of course abnormal. It stands to reason that this mode has been used for so long that it has been made easy at present for separate irresponsible individuals to speak before the outside world in the name of the social democratic proletariat of Russia, distorting its actual position. For the very reason of preventing this abuse we have placed on the order of the day the question of a common action which would oppose to the statements of separate individuals that which is unifying and mutual, which in spite of the existing tendencies and the persisting reciprocal alienation has consolidated the majority of the Russian organizations in their attitude toward war and toward social patriotism.

You express doubt as to whether those organizations (the Organization Committee and the Bund), the activities of which we propose to co-ordinate, stand on the basis of revolutionary internationalism. We proceed from the belief that the possibility for such a co-ordination lies in the existence of a fundamental agreement concerning general and basic factors that have been placed before Social Democracy by current events. We see this general and basic factor in a resolute and unequivocal war against the war and in just as resolute a renunciation of "civil peace" in the name of the so-called "national defense," and also in the recognition of the Stuttgart resolution on a revolutionary utilization of war and of the crisis which it has called forth. The organizations which we have approached satisfy these demands, and have proved it by their activity in Russia as well as by their definite demonstrations before the International.

If the Organization Committee gave an entirely incorrect evaluation from our point of view of the position of the *Nasha Zaria* group in the report of its Secretariat Abroad to the Copenhagen Conference—an evaluation which showed that the group was not moving inevitably toward a weakening of the revolutionary struggle against Tsarism— then, on the other hand, we consider extremely incorrect the tendency expressed in *Sotsial-Demokrat*—a tendency which is ready to turn a partial disagreement in viewpoints into a reason for counting Social Democrats among social chauvinists. This, for example, has been done with respect to the Duma group, which, however, has not hesitated to exclude Mankov from its ranks for his militarist demonstration, when this was demanded by the interests of political action.

There is no doubt that with regard to the Russian Social Democracy, as well as with regard to all socialist parties which have withstood the chauvinist wave, a certain inadequacy in the formulation in viewpoints can frequently be noticed—an insufficient precision in their answers to a number of questions raised by the situation. This is so much the more natural since among quite definite internationalists there are also essential differences (for example on the question of the significance of Russia's defeat), and absence of a definitely ascertained position (in the same *Sotsial-Demokrat*) with regard to the slogan of struggle for peace, under the banner of which all active demonstrations of internationalists are being carried on at present. But, precisely from the viewpoint of our struggle for the internationalist policy, it would be inexpedient to apply the same methods for exerting influence upon unformulated internationalism and upon fully formulated social patriotism.

It remains for us to answer the question of our attitude toward those who already speak of a "general amnesty" after the war. You must not have the least doubt that from the point of view of *Nashe Slovo* the revival of the International cannot consist in an international unification of nationalist parties which have mutually recognized each other's rights to furl the revolutionary banner in the name of "national defense," for our newspaper, as you yourselves indicate, has already expressed itself to that effect. However, we assume that any extreme Left group, which from the outbreak of the crisis has taken a definite stand, must—in the interests of the cause which it serves—not hurry at this early moment to fix organizationally those interrelations from which by the logic of events and under the influence of its activity the group will inevitably benefit. Thus we believe that we would have made a mistake, had we—at the beginning of the war, when Liebknecht and Rühle were working with the majority of the German Social Democracy—recognized as decisive the gulf between them and ourselves, and had we erected our party tactic upon such recognition. From this point of view we cannot at the present moment make a question of principle out of questions of attitude toward future "amnesty" of present nationalist elements, and thereby give occasion for the splitting with elements which both on principle and in practice struggle against social patriotism. Defending the most consistent and *ideological* severance of revolutionary socialism from nationalist and seminationalist tendencies, and assuming that revolutionary practice at the present moment must not be weakened by considerations of organizational unity and of party discipline, we believe that the revolutionary minority group—which we internationalists represent at present—must solve the question of maintaining or sacrificing unity, in every case from the point of view of expediency, i.e., with respect to the type of organizational development which would assure to it, in every single case, the maximum revolutionary influence upon the progress of class movement.

We should like to think that the explanations given by us will remove those doubts which have arisen in you and to which you have subjected our proposal—the successful realization of which, as we picture it, could be nothing but beneficial to our common cause of struggle for the victory of internationalist principles within the labor movement.

TROTSKY ON THE RUSSIAN INTERNATIONALISTS

[An Open Letter to the Editorial Board of *Kommunist,* June 4, 1915][48]

RESPECTED COMRADES!

You invite me to contribute to the periodical *Kommunist* which you are establishing. I regret very much that I have to decline your invitation; I regret so much more to have to do this, because I regard the theoretical formulation of the new problems relating to the war and the crisis of the International as extremely important and urgent; at the same time I am deeply convinced that we, Russian internationalists, possess a general theoretical and political basis which is entirely adequate for joint activity and especially for combating social patriotism in both the Russian labor movement and the International. In saying this I have no desire whatever to close my eyes to the serious differences which divide us. For instance, I cannot reconcile myself with the vagueness and evasiveness of your position on the question of mobilizing the proletariat under the slogan of *struggle for peace,* the slogan under which, as a matter of fact, the laboring masses are now recovering their political senses and the revolutionary elements of socialism are being united in all countries; the slogan under which an attempt is being made now to restore the international contacts among the socialist proletariat. Furthermore, under no condition can I agree with your opinion, which is emphasized by a resolution, that Russia's defeat would be a "lesser evil." This opinion represents a fundamental connivance with the political methodology of social patriotism, a connivance for which there is no reason or justification and which substitutes an orientation (extremely arbitrary under present conditions) along the line of a "lesser evil" for the revolutionary struggle against war and the conditions which generated this war. Furthermore, I cannot accept your organizational setting of the question of social patriotism; a setting which in my opinion is completely diffuse and shapeless and appears exact and definite only

[48] "Otkrytoe pismo v redaktsiiu zhurnala *'Kommunist,'*" *Nashe Slovo,* No. 105, June 4, 1915, pp. 1–2.

because it evades all practical issues which arise before the internationalists in their struggle against the social patriots and for influence over the laboring masses. However, these very serious differences, as well as other differences which I do not mention here, would by no means prevent me from collaborating with you in a general theoretical organ—on the contrary, I think that this organ, being a foremost organ along the united front of struggle against social patriotism, should be polemical as to questions concerning which the internationalists have no uniform opinion or over which they disagree. But such collaboration presupposes, from my point of view, a general interest on our part in actually rallying all internationalists, regardless of their group affiliation or of the tinge of their internationalism. It would seem that a policy of this kind precludes in advance every attempt to exploit the crisis in the labor movement for factional or group ends which do not derive from the requirements of this movement or from the need of exerting upon it the influence of revolutionary internationalism. Meanwhile your printed announcement concerning the publication of the periodical *Kommunist* is to me the saddest evidence of the fact that you subordinate your struggle against social patriotism to considerations and objectives, the responsibility for which I by no means have the right to take upon myself.

You declare that in launching a struggle against social patriotism you are not alone and you point to the periodicals *Lichtstrahlen* and *Internationale* in Germany, Comrades Nicod, Monatte, and Merrheim in France, the minority of the British Socialist party, the majority of the Independent Labour party in England, etc., as your allies; whereas, passing over to Russia, you refer only to the manifesto of the Central Committee and to the conduct of the five indicted deputies. Beyond these boundaries you discern only "an incipient opposition which expresses sympathy for internationalism and therefore merits a salute." But both this list and this characterization constitute a decided distortion of the real state of affairs because of the limitations of the factional perspective. The declaration was signed and defended by the five indicted deputies together with the other social democratic deputies of the State Duma. In no way did the conduct of the five deputies differ in principle from the conduct of the other half of the Duma group, and it is clear that in their statements at the trial nobody can perceive a fundamental step beyond the general declaration of the Social Democratic group in the Duma. I agree, however, that this first declaration, being a case of truly political bravery, did not possess the necessary precision. But the responsibility for this—if responsibility is spoken of at all—devolves upon both halves of the Duma group. Meanwhile the last speeches of our deputies (the speeches of Chkheidze, Chkhenkeli, and Tuliakov) and their voting undoubtedly represent steps forward toward political precision and revolutionary irreconcilability. After Plekhanov's articles and those of *Nasha Zaria* the voice of the Duma group sounded as a voice of powerful resistance to all attempts to introduce patriotic corruption into the ranks of the workers. A protest can and must be raised against the fact that the Organization Committee did not find it necessary and possible to fence itself off from its influential social patriots, who had addressed their declarations to Vandervelde and the Copenhagen Conference over the heads of the Organization Committee.[49] A still more resolute protest can and must be raised against the fact that the Secretariat of the Organization Committee Abroad has taken it upon itself to rehabilitate the aforesaid social patriotic group before the International. But we should not close our eyes to the fact that the Duma group has excluded from its ranks a deputy who drew a practical conclusion from the position of Plekhanov and of *Nasha Zaria*.[50] Along with all the revolutionary elements of the International, I am proud of the conduct of our deputies; I regard them at present as the most important channel of internationalist education of the proletariat of Russia and for that very reason consider it to be the duty of every revolutionary Social Democrat to lend them every support and strengthen their authority in the International. While you at best ignore them as if they did not exist in Russia's political life; as if upon the arrest of the five deputies of your shading—I regard them as *our* deputies—no true and deserving representatives of the laboring class of Russia were left in the State Duma. While naming and saluting Nicod, Monatte, and the Independent British Socialists as your allies, you evade, you pass in silence, you ignore Chkheidze, Tuliakov, and their comrades. Since such action cannot be caused either by the need of political precision or by the desire to benefit internationalism, I cannot support those interests by which it was guided. It is not surprising that you include neither *Golos* nor *Nashe Slovo* in the list of your allies along with *Lichtstrahlen,* Nicod, Monatte, Merrheim, and the Independent British Socialists. The *Sotsial-Demokrat,* with which you declare complete solidarity, has already made note of the "bankruptcy" of *Nashe Slovo*. Within the limits of this letter I cannot go into a lengthy appraisal of considerations which permit you to say that our newspaper has "failed." However, it will suffice to say that on questions which separate *Nashe Slovo* from your position, all the groups in the International which you have enumerated stand incomparably farther from you than we do. Hence one of the following two conclusions must be

[49] See below, chapter iii, p. 269.

[50] In January 1915 Deputy Mankov voted in favor of war credits contrary to the decision of the S.D. Duma group, for which action he was expelled from the group.

drawn: either the British Independent Socialists, Nicod, and Merrheim are your allies and so is *Nashe Slovo* (yet you pass over it in silence; for considerations which are not of a fundamental nature), or you have no allies at all in the International. For the very reason that I wholly agree with the position of *Nashe Slovo* I cannot give my name to an enterprise which appraises our paper as one which has scarcely begun "to express sympathy for internationalism" and which has already "failed."

In concluding let me express my firm belief that close contact with the revolutionary elements of the International—and we are proceeding toward the creation of such contacts—will inspire you or even compel you to broaden your criteria and change many of your standards of value. Upon this new basis collaboration within the confines of general literary establishments as well as of general political organizations will be possible and productive.

With comradely greeting,
N [L]. Trotsky

C. The Berne Conference of the Russian Bolshevik Sections of the Russian Social Democratic Labor Party Abroad

The Berne Conference of the Bolshevik sections was called to straighten out a number of difficulties that had arisen among the different sections during the first months of the war. There was the question of the composition and location of the Committee of Organizations Abroad which had lost some of its members as volunteers to the French army. Then there was the problem of the party organ. Lack of funds and of competent contributors caused the *Sotsial-Demokrat* to appear but seldom, yet the Paris and Baugy-en-Clarens sections both wanted to publish their own papers. The Paris group, having no funds, reluctantly gave up the scheme; but the Baugy group, having got some money, announced the forthcoming publication of a new paper, *Zvezda,* under the editorship of Bukharin, N. V. Krylenko, and Elena Fedorovna Rozmirovich, and did this without officially notifying the editors of the Central Organ. There were also evidences of deviation from Lenin's position by Krylenko and others.[51]

[51] Krupskaia to Karpinsky and S. N. Ravich, January 10, 1915, *Leninskii Sbornik,* XI, 134-37; also Krupskaya, *Memories of Lenin,* II, 155-57.

The Conference, which was in session from February 27 to March 4, 1915, easily disposed of the organizational questions relating to the party periodicals and the election of members to the Committee of Organizations Abroad. There were, however, some rather serious differences on matters of tactics and slogans. Bukharin disagreed with Lenin on the slogans "defeat of one's own country" and "the right of nations to self-determination" and on the minimum program in general. Bukharin also presented certain theses of his own and a resolution on the tasks of the party in the imperialist war which was submitted in behalf of the Baugy section composed of himself, Krylenko, and Rozmirovich, and which was highly critical of the position taken by Lenin in the Central Organ. He also objected to the policy of the Central Organ regarding the petty bourgeoisie and denied the possibility of the proletariat's being supported by democratic elements. In this he was not supported by other members of the Baugy group. With regard to Lenin's slogan "the United States of Europe," which others strongly attacked, Bukharin supported Lenin. Lenin proposed to eliminate this slogan, but it was adopted by the Conference.

In order to smooth over these dissensions Bukharin was elected to the Commission to draft the resolutions of the Conference. A temporary understanding was reached and a platform was worked out which became the rallying point for the Left internationalist elements during the war. Bukharin's differences with Lenin were not, however, finally compromised. They reappeared at various times during the war and in somewhat different form in Left-wing communism in 1918.[52]

[52] Kharitonov, *Zapiski Instituta Lenina*, II, 119–20; *Bolshevik*, No. 15, August 15, 1929, 86–87; Baevsky, *Ocherki po istorii oktiabrskoi revoliutsii*, I, 365–66, 444; Baevsky, "Borba Lenina protiv Bukharinskikh 'shatanii mysli,'" *Proletarskaia Revoliutsiia*, No. 1 (96), 1930, 25–29.

RECOLLECTIONS OF THE BERNE CONFERENCE

[From Syromiatnikova's Memoirs][53]

. . . . The Berne Conference was a conference only of representa- tives of the Russian Bolshevik sections abroad; Comrades E. Bosh and Piatakov, the only representatives from Russia, were not present at the Conference as official delegates of any organization.

However, against the background of that historic moment, in the period of universal militarist reaction, of ideological disintegration, and of treason among the socialists themselves, the Berne Conference be- came a fact of great significance not only in the history of the Russian Social Democratic Labor party but in the history of the international revolutionary movement.

The World War called forth a great crisis in European socialism,. a crisis which at first produced great confusion but which led to the formation of new groups among the representatives of various tend- encies in socialism and raised with great persistency the question of a new policy of socialist parties. . . . .

Only an insignificant section of the Left wing of Social Democracy, and not even that in all countries, remained faithful to the fundamental principles of the International, had not succumbed to the general feelings.

The behavior of the "Europeans" could not but have a strong reac- tion on the attitude of the Russian socialist émigrés. The war made itself felt also in the Bolshevik sections. . . . .

. . . . The confusion and lack of co-ordination which existed among the sections stimulated the idea that a party conference was necessary, and from various comrades statements began to come in to the effect that a conference of organizations abroad would be desirable. . . . .

It was even more evident to the Central Committee that a joint dis- cussion of the current questions was necessary.

The desire to introduce clarity and precision in the points of view in connection with questions of war in place of vacillation and uncer- tainty which could be noticed among the émigré circles, the desire to propagate the idea of the Central Committee concerning the "trans- formation of the imperialist war into a civil war" and to rally round this slogan all who in these difficult days had remained faithful to the socialist banner, were the reasons for calling a conference.

The Bureau of the Central Committee Abroad scheduled the con- ference for January 23, 1915; but certain organizations objected to this.

[53] "Bernskaia Konferentsiia 1915 g." *Proletarskaia Revoliutsiia*, No. 5 (40),. 1925, pp. 150–67.

date either on account of having received the notice late or because of other considerations. . . . .

The Conference opened on February 27, 1915.

The following organizations were represented at the Conference: those of Paris, Zürich, London,[54] Geneva, Berne, Lausanne, and Baugy. The delegate from Baugy arrived near the end of the Conférence. Organizations of Toulouse and Montpellier had no delegates at the Conference but sent resolutions which had been adopted by them with regard to all the questions on the agenda. Representatives of the Central Committee, the Central Organ, and the women's organization (one delegate from each) had also the right to a decisive vote. All members of the Berne section were present with a consulting vote. Certain members of the Baugy section and two comrades who had come from Russia ("the Japanese")[55] arrived toward the end of the Conference; they all had the right of a consulting vote.

The following comrades were present at the Conference: V. I. Lenin, G. Zinoviev, N. K. Krupskaia, Inessa Armand, Lilina, Kasparov, Kornblum, Ilin; G. Belenky from the Paris section, Kharitonov from the Zürich section, Shklovsky from the Berne section, Movshovich (Vladimir) from the Lausanne section, S. N. Ravich from the Geneva section; Bukharin, Krylenko, Rozmirovich, Troianovsky, from the Baugy section; E. B. Bosh and G. Piatakov (from Russia).

Comrade Shklovsky was elected chairman of the Conference, and Comrade Kornblum secretary.

The following agenda was accepted: (1) local reports, (2) war and the tasks of the party (attitude toward other political groups), (3) tasks of organizations abroad (attitude toward common activities and undertakings of various groups), (4) Central Organ and the new newspaper, (5) attitude toward colonial affairs, (6) election of Committee of Organization Abroad, (7) miscellaneous.

The first meeting of the Conference was taken up with local reports. Comrade Lenin made a report "on the most complicated and confused question of that time," upon which the attention of all those present at the Conference was centered—the question of war and other questions which the war raised.

The theses and the manifesto on the war of the Central Committee

---

[54] "The London section did not send a delegate to the Conference because of war-time conditions but transferred its mandate, if I am not mistaken, to N. K. Krupskaia." "Bernskaia Konferentsiia 1915 g.," *Proletarskaia Revoliutsiia*, No. 5 (40), 1925, p. 157, note 3, by G. L. Shklovsky.

[55] E. B. Bosh and G. Piatakov had escaped from exile in Russia through Japan and America. Their first letter which was received in Switzerland came from Japan; therefore, they were called "Japanese." ("Bernskaia Konferentsiia 1915 g.," *Proletarskaia Revoliutsiia*, No. 5 [40], 1925, p. 158, note 2.)

constituted the basis of this report and the following resolution on point two of the agenda (the war and the tasks of the party) was entered in the protocol:

"In full solidarity with the manifesto of the Central Committee, the Conference commissions three persons to elaborate theses for a resolution[56] within the limits set by the manifesto."

Only one vote opposed this decision.

Comrades Zinoviev, Lenin, and Inessa Armand were elected to the Commission. . . . .

After having disposed of the chief point on the agenda, the point connected with the war, the Conference passed on to questions of secondary importance.

In the resolution on the question of the tasks of organizations abroad[57] the Conference, in addition to the previous tasks (co-operation with the central institutions of the party, the unification of all those who shared the point of view of the Central Organ, the securing of information and financial support, and the spreading of the propaganda of Marxism), laid down new tasks connected with current events: the struggle against the chauvinists, and the work among the war prisoners.

With regard to point 4 of the agenda (the Central Organ and the new newspaper), the Conference expressed itself in favor of increased financial and literary support of the Central Organ in order to assure a regular and more frequent issue of it ("at least once a week").[58] . . . .

. . . . The Conference did not favor the issue of any other newspaper besides the Central Organ. The publication of a new paper was considered undesirable because this might divide the forces and the funds which were insufficient anyhow.

This resolution of the Conference had a special significance, since certain groups (in Baugy and Paris) during the period which preceded the conference had been planning to publish their own local paper. The conference put a stop to these attempts, at least for the time being.

At the same time the Conference adopted a resolution on the publication of pamphlets which would clarify and elaborate questions connected with the war.

In discussing the questions connected with the émigré "colonial" life, the Conference found that communications of groups and of individuals with official representatives of the Tsarist government abroad were undesirable and impermissible and that the entrance of members of the sections into those colonial institutions which had governmental

---

[56] Given below, pp. 182–86.   [57] Given below, pp. 186–87.

[58] Full text given in "Bernskaia Konferentsiia 1915 g.," *Proletarskaia Revoliutsiia,* No. 5 (40), 1925, p. 177.

connections was even more impermissible. (A report on this question was made by the delegate of the Geneva section, Comrade Olga—S. N. Ravich.)

The Committee of Organizations Abroad, the activity of which had acquired great significance in connection with the crisis, was re-elected at the Conference. Its duties were to unify all groups abroad, keep them informed, and provide them with leadership.

The following comrades were elected to the new committee: Comrades N. K. Krupskaia, Inessa Armand, Shklovsky, Kasparov, and Zina (Lilina). At the end of the Conference the report of the Commission on Circulation of the Central Organ was confirmed and the members of the Commission were thanked. The Revisory Commission consisted of Comrades G. Belenky, Ilin, and Movshovich.

The Conference closed on March 4.

. . . . In evaluating the significance of the Conference, one may say that it first of all put an end to the ideological deterioration within the ranks of revolutionary Social Democracy which had resulted from the collapse of the Second International. Here at the Conference other principles were elaborated which formed the platform of the Zimmerwald Left and which later on became the basis of the Third International.

[From Shklovsky's Memoirs][59]

. . . . As to the course of the Conference, only one question—the United States of Europe—caused long debate.

This point, as you know, appeared in the manifesto of the Central Committee.[60] It also had some importance in the theses[61] which were presented at the Conference. However, it met with certain opposition among us. The late Comrade Kasparov (party name "Slava") and I spoke against this point. We were supported by one of the comrades who had a consulting vote. Inessa vacillated. At the end of the discussion she proposed a compromise correction: "In advancing along with other demands that for a United States of Europe, *as a possible stage in the advance toward a socialist revolution* (author's italics) the Social Democracy must . . . ." When it came to voting, the resolution as a whole was unanimously adopted. Only one vote was cast in favor of Comrade Inessa's correction, whereas for Comrade Kasparov's correction (unfortunately as it says in the protocol: "the correction had not been submitted to the secretary") which repudiated the slogan of the

---

[59] "Bernskaia Konferentsiia 1915 g.," *Proletarskaia Revoliutsiia*, No. 5 (40), 1925, pp. 182–93.

[60] Given above, p. 155.

[61] See paragraph 6 in Bukharin's theses, below, p. 188.

United States of Europe, one vote was also cast. This vote belonged to the author of this article [G. L. Shklovsky].

Our objections to the slogan of a United States of Europe can be summarized as follows: (1) Under imperialism a true democracy is impossible, therefore, a United States of Europe is also impossible. (2) Furthermore, it is impossible in view of the conflict of interests of European capitalist countries. (3) If it is formed at all, it will be formed only for the purpose of attacking the more advanced United States of America.

During the discussion Ilich answered us that on the basis of our assumptions it would be necessary to discard a number of points from our minimum program as being impossible under imperialism; but although true democracy can be realized only under socialism, we do not discard these points. Further, he reproached us for not touching the economic side of the question. We answered him that the formation of a United States of Europe under imperialism would not be the highest form of democracy but a reactionary union of the belligerent countries—which were unable to conquer each other in the war—for the struggle against America. . . . .

. . . . Although Vladimir Ilich had completely convinced the Conference and although the latter unanimously voted for the theses, he did not succeed in convincing himself. On that same evening he saw Comrade Radek, who was living in Berne at that time but who did not belong to our group, and questioned him in detail about the opinion of different European comrades with regard to the question of a United States of Europe.

On the following morning, at the opening of the Conference, Vladimir Ilich took the floor and made a statement. "Although," he said, "we decided yesterday on the question of a United States of Europe, in view of the fact that this question has called forth differences of opinion within our ranks and, furthermore, in view of the fact that the discussion was one-sided and did not touch upon the economic side of the question, which remained unclear, therefore, this question must not be considered as solved." He also mentioned his meeting with Radek, who had told him that Rosa Luxemburg also was opposed to a United States of Europe. He therefore proposed to have the point concerning a United States of Europe crossed out of the theses for the time being and to open a discussion on that question in the Central Organ, devoting special attention to the economic side of the question.

The Conference agreed with Vladimir Ilich's point of view. No discussion has appeared, however, and the only article on that subject that appeared in the Central Organ was the article of Vladimir Ilich (see No. 44 of *Sotsial-Demokrat* of August 23, 1915, "O lozunge Soedinennykh Shtatov Evropy," ["The slogan of a United States of Europe"]) ;[62] this article for reasons not purely economic was directed against the slogan.

[From E. Bosh's Memoirs][63]

. . . . At the end of January 1915 I received in New York[64] a telegram, signed "Lenin," informing us of the calling of a conference and urging us to come by all means. Almost simultaneously there arrived a letter from my sister, Comrade Rozmirovich, in which she informed us that Vladimir Ilich was very much displeased by my delay in America, for he considered my presence at the conference imperative, a conference at which the most important question of the attitude of our party toward the war was going to be discussed. I replied that I would try to leave on the next boat, and began to prepare hastily for departure. But the securing of visa, tickets, and so forth detained me for at least another week. . . . . [Upon arriving in Clarens, Switzerland] I learned from Comrade Rozmirovich that Vladimir Ilich had postponed the conference pending our arrival and that now the conference had not yet adjourned; that they [the Clarens group] did not go to the conference but sent their theses, and that they did not wish to go. Here we learned that there were dissensions between Bukharin, Rozmirovich, and Krylenko, on one hand, and Vladimir Ilich on the other; that they, constituting a group of three, were preparing to publish a newspaper for discussion,

---

[62] In this article, which is translated in Lenin, *The Imperialist War*, pp. 269–72, Lenin wrote that "to argue that this slogan obstructs or weakens the slogan of a socialist revolution, is entirely erroneous. . . . . But if the United States of Europe slogan, conceived in connection with a revolutionary overthrow of the three most reactionary monarchies of Europe, headed by Russia, is entirely impregnable as a political slogan, there still remains the most important question of its economic content and meaning. From the point of view of the economic conditions of imperialism, i.e., capital export and a division of the world between the 'progressive' and 'civilized' colonial powers, the United States of Europe under capitalism is either impossible or reactionary." Lenin said further that "the United States of the World" as a separate slogan would hardly be correct, since it coincides with socialism and since it "could be erroneously interpreted to mean that the victory of socialism in one country is impossible . . . . " The victorious proletariat, "having expropriated the capitalists and organized socialist production at home, would rise against the rest of the capitalist world attracting the oppressed classes of other countries, raising among them revolts against the capitalists, launching, in case of necessity, armed forces against the exploiting classes and their states." The article ends with the editors of the Central Organ concluding that the United States of Europe slogan was incorrect.

[63] "Bernskaia Konferentsiia 1915 g.," *Proletarskaia Revoliutsiia,* No. 5 (40), 1925, pp. 179–82.

[64] I was in New York en route [to Russia] after escaping through Japan from [Siberian] exile at the end of 1914. [Author's note.]

since they were unable to clear up the dissensions in the Central Organ. I do not remember what the dissensions were, but I know very well that I had the impression that the relations with Vladimir Ilich had become acute in connection with the Malinovsky affair.

On the next day Zinoviev called us up on the telephone from Berne and informed us that it was impossible to postpone the conference any longer, and that we were expected on the next train. I promised him that I would leave at once. Comrades Krylenko, Rozmirovich, and A. A. Troianovsky,[65] after discussing the matter among themselves, decided to go also and at once sent a telegram to Comrade Bukharin, who at that time was not yet living at Clarens. We left on the first train the following morning and Comrade Bukharin joined us en route.

I consider Shklovsky's statement to be incorrect, namely: "Neither did the Clarens group come to the Conference: Comrade Rozmirovich, Krylenko, and Bukharin . . . . for they did not wish to take part in the Conference without the 'Japanese' and were strongly urging us to wait one more day." [I consider this incorrect] because neither I nor Piatakov had any relations whatsoever with the Clarens group as a group. I had personal contact with my sister; we made the acquaintance of Comrade Krylenko for the first time at Clarens, and became acquainted with Comrade Bukharin en route to Berne. We could by no means join their group in a period of one and a half days for the very reason that we were extremely tired after seventeen or eighteen days of travel. . . . .

Apparently, the fact that we arrived together with the others and stopped at the same place caused Comrade Shklovsky to count me and Comrade Piatakov with the Clarens group and to baptize all of us as "oppositionists."

. . . . Bukharin, Krylenko, and Rozmirovich formed really an "opposition"; but there was no unity among the "three." En route and in the People's House it became clear that the three had no common point of view and Comrade Bukharin was very disappointed that nobody wished to support him.

We all stopped at the People's House in Berne and went immediately to see Comrade Zinoviev. We learned from Comrade Zinoviev that all questions except the fundamental question—the attitude toward the war —had been considered by the Conference, that they had had a preliminary exchange of opinions on this question also [i.e., the war], but that the final decision, as Vladimir Ilich insisted, was postponed pending our arrival. As I remember it, we went to the meeting directly from Comrade Zinoviev's residence. . . . . Soon Vladimir Ilich and Nadezhda Konstantinovna arrived. The sitting of the Conference was opened and

[65] At this time, A. A. Troianovsky sharply diverged in his attitude toward the war, from the position of our Central Organ. [Author's note.]

Vladimir Ilich took the floor in order to make a report on the chief topic of the day. Comrade Bukharin took the floor after him in order to answer Lenin, not on behalf of the group, but personally. Comrade Rozmirovich did not speak; her point of view was developed by Comrade Krylenko. Troianovsky, a member of the Clarens group, also spoke, but his speech was so alien to our party that nobody answered him. Nadezhda Konstantinovna did not speak. . . . .

. . . . After the discussion, which lasted until midnight, Vladimir Ilich's proposal was adopted, namely, to form a commission to draw up a resolution, a commission consisting of Comrades Lenin, Zinoviev, and Bukharin. . . . .

The elaboration of the resolution, as I recall it, took two days. Heated disputes took place with Comrade Bukharin. I know this from conversations with Comrade Bukharin. Vladimir Ilich strove to come to an understanding with him, and finally the resolution of the Commission was adopted unanimously. . . . .

RESOLUTION ON THE CHARACTER OF THE WAR, "DEFENSE OF THE FATHERLAND," THE COLLAPSE OF THE SECOND INTERNATIONAL, THE THIRD INTERNATIONAL, ETC.

[Adopted at the Berne Conference][66]

On the basis of the manifesto[67] of the Central Committee published in No. 33 [*Sotsial-Demokrat*] for a better co-ordination of propaganda, the Conference lays down the following points:

ON THE CHARACTER OF THE WAR

The present war is imperialist in character. This war has been brought about by the conditions of this epoch, when capitalism has attained the highest stage of development; when not only the export of goods but also the export of capital is vitally important; when the trustification and the internationalization of economic life has reached considerable dimension; when the colonial policy has led to a division of almost the entire globe; when the productive forces of world capitalism have outgrown the limited boundaries of the national state divisions; and when objective conditions for the realization of socialism have completely ripened.

---

[66] "Konferentsiia zagranichnykh sektsii R.S.D.R.P.," *Sotsial-Demokrat*, No. 40, March 29, 1915, p. 2. "The resolution of the Conference written by Lenin represents another step in the development and a more detailed elaboration of the Bolshevik position toward the war." (Baevsky, *Ocherki po istorii oktiabrskoi revoliutsii*, I, 366.)

[67] See above, pp. 150–56.

The Slogan of the "Defense of the Fatherland"

The real essence of the present war consists in the struggle between England, France, and Germany for the division of colonies, in robbing competing countries, and in the desire of Tsarism and of the ruling classes in Russia to seize Persia, Mongolia, Asiatic Turkey, Constantinople, Galicia, etc. The national element in the Austro-Serbian war is of an entirely subordinate significance not affecting the general imperialist character of the war.

The entire economic and diplomatic history of the last decades has shown that both groups of the belligerent nations have been systematically preparing for precisely this kind of a war. The question as to which group gave the first blow or which was the first in declaring war is of no significance in defining the tactics of socialists. The phrases about the defense of the fatherland, about resisting an invasion by the enemy, about a defensive war, etc., are, in any case, means of deceiving the people.

At the bottom of real nationalist wars such as took place especially in the period between 1789 and 1871 lay a slow and long process of nationalist mass movements, of struggle against absolutism and feudalism, of overthrow of national oppression, and of the creation of states upon a national foundation as prerequisites for capitalist development.

The national ideology created by this epoch left deep traces upon the masses of petty bourgeoisie and upon a section of the proletariat. The bourgeois sophists and the betrayers of socialism, who trail behind these sophists, are making use of this at present, in an entirely different, an imperialist epoch, to divide the workers and to divert them from their class problems and the revolutionary struggle against the bourgeoisie.

The words of the Communist manifesto that "workers have no fatherland" are now truer than ever. Only the international struggle of the proletariat against the bourgeoisie can open to the oppressed masses the road to a better future.

Slogans of the Revolutionary Social Democracy

The transformation of the present imperialist war into civil war is the only correct proletarian slogan pointed out by the experience of the Commune and indicated in the Basel (1912) resolution and which follows from the conditions of an imperialist war between highly developed bourgeois countries.

The civil war, to which revolutionary Social Democracy calls in the present epoch, is a struggle of the proletariat with arms in hand against the bourgeoisie for the expropriation of the capitalist class in the advanced capitalist countries; for a democratic revolution in Russia (a democratic republic, an eight-hour working day, and the confiscation of lands from landlords); for a republic in backward monarchistic countries in general, etc.

The extreme misery of the masses created by the war cannot but produce revolutionary feelings and movements, for which the slogan of civil war must furnish the generalization and direction.

At the present moment the organization of the laboring class is badly shattered. But the revolutionary crisis ripens nevertheless. After the war the ruling classes of all countries will make a still greater effort to set back for decades the liberating movement of the proletariat. The task of the revolutionary Social Democracy, in case of a rapid tempo of revolutionary development, as well as in the case of a drawn-out crisis, will be not to repudiate long days of labor, not to scorn any of the old methods of class struggle. The task of revolutionary Social Democracy will be to direct parliamentarism as well as the economic struggle against opportunism in the sense of a revolutionary struggle of the masses.

As the first steps on the road of turning the present imperialist war into a civil war we must point out: (1) an unconditional refusal to vote war credits and the withdrawal from bourgeois cabinets; (2) a complete break with the policy of the "national peace" (*bloc national, Burgfrieden*); (3) formation of illegal organizations wherever governments and the bourgeoisie, by introducing martial law, abolish constitutional liberties; (4) support of "fraternizing" between soldiers of the belligerent nations in trenches and on the battlefields in general; (5) the support of all kinds of revolutionary mass activities of the proletariat in general.

OPPORTUNISM AND THE COLLAPSE OF THE SECOND INTERNATIONAL

The collapse of the Second International is the collapse of socialist opportunism. The latter has grown as a product of the preceding "peaceful" epoch of development of the labor movement. This epoch has taught the laboring class such important methods of struggle as the utilization of parliamentarism and of all legal possibilities, the creation of economic political organizations of the masses, of a widespread labor press, etc. On the other hand, this epoch gave birth to the tendency to repudiate class struggle and to preach social peace, to repudiate socialist revolution and the principle of illegal organizations, to accept bourgeois patriotism, etc. Certain strata of the laboring class (the bureaucracy within the labor movement and labor aristocracy, which received crumbs of the profit from the exploitation of colonies and from the privileged position of their fatherland on the world market) and also petty bourgeois associates within the socialist parties have become the chief social support of these tendencies and the conductors of bourgeois influence upon the proletariat.

The detrimental influence of opportunism has manifested itself most glaringly in the policy of the majority of official social democratic parties of the Second International in time of war. The voting of credits, the entering of cabinets, the policy of "civil peace," the repudiation of an illegal organization at the time when legality is denied signify a violation of the most important decisions of the International and a direct betrayal of socialism.

The Third International

The crisis created by the war has revealed the real essence of opportunism by showing it in the role of a direct supporter of the bourgeoisie against the proletariat. The so-called Social Democratic "Center," headed by Kautsky, has as a matter of fact completely fallen into opportunism, covering it up with particularly harmful, hypocritical phrases and by a falsification of Marxism that turns it into imperialism. Experience shows that in Germany, for example, only by a definite violation of the will of the majority of the party leadership was it possible to defend the socialist point of view. It would be a harmful illusion to hope to restore a real Socialist International without a complete organizational separation from opportunists.

The Russian Social Democratic Labor party must support every international and mass revolutionary activity of the proletariat, while striving to bring together all antichauvinist elements of the International.

Pacifism and the Slogan of Peace

Pacifism and an abstract preaching of peace are some of the ways to fool the working class. Under capitalism, particularly in its imperialist stage, wars become inevitable. On the other hand, Social Democrats cannot deny the positive value of revolutionary wars, i.e., not imperialist wars, but such as have been waged between 1789 and 1871 for the overthrow of the national oppression and in order to create national capitalist states in place of feudal multipartite states, or wars which are possible as a means of protecting the conquests of the proletariat, victorious in its struggle against the bourgeosie.

At present, the peace propaganda, which is not accompanied by an appeal to revolutionary activities of the masses, is only apt to disseminate illusions, to demoralize the proletariat by an insinuation of confidence in the humanitarianism of the bourgeoisie, and by making it a toy in the hands of the secret diplomacy of the belligerent countries. In particular, the thought that a democratic peace is possible without a number of revolutions is profoundly erroneous.

Defeat of the Tsarist Monarchy

In every country the struggle against the government that conducts an imperialist war must not stop at the possibility of a defeat of that country as a result of revolutionary agitation. The defeat of the governmental army weakens the said government, helps to free the enslaved peoples, and makes the civil war against the ruling classes easier.

This statement is especially true when applied to Russia. Russian victory will bring with it a strengthening of the worldwide reaction and of a reaction within the country and will be accompanied by a complete enslavement of the peoples in the areas already seized. For this reason the defeat of Russia under all conditions appears to be the lesser evil.

The Attitude toward Other Parties and Groups

The war by calling forth an orgy of chauvinism has revealed the fact that the democratic (Narodnik) intelligentsia, the party of Socialist-Revolutionists—with their unstable opposition tendency in the *Mysl*—and the main nucleus of the liquidators (the *Nasha Zaria*), which Plekhanov supports, have succumbed to chauvinism. Actually, the Organization Committee, from the disguised support of the war by Larin and Martov to the fundamental defense of the ideas of patriotism by Axelrod and the Bund in which Germanophile chauvinism prevails, are all on the side of chauvinism. The Brussels bloc (August 3, 1914)[68] has disintegrated, while the elements that are grouped around the *Nashe Slovo* vacillate between complete platonic sympathy with internationalism and the tendency to unite at any price with *Nasha Zaria* and the Organization Committee. The Social Democratic group of Chkheidze vacillates also, the group which on one hand has expelled Mankov, an adherent of Plekhanov—that is, a chauvinist—and which, on the other hand, wants at any price to cover up the chauvinism of Plekhanov, of *Nasha Zaria,* of Axelrod, of Bund, etc.

The task of the Social Democratic Labor party in Russia consists in a further strengthening of the proletarian unity created in 1912–1914, chiefly by the *Pravda,* in a restoration of the Social Democratic party organization of the laboring class on the basis of a decisive break with social chauvinists. Temporary agreements are permissible only with those Social Democrats who stand for a decisive organizational break with the Organization Committee, *Nasha Zaria,* and the Bund.

TASKS OF THE ORGANIZATIONS OF THE RUSSIAN SOCIAL DEMOCRATIC LABOR PARTY ABROAD

[Resolution of the Berne Conference][69]

The outbreak of the war and the resulting greater separation from Russia of the organizations of the Russian Social Democratic Labor

[68] July 16 (3), 1914; see above, chapter i, pp. 106–7.

[69] "Bernskaia Konferentsiia 1915 g.," *Proletarskaia Revoliutsiia,* No. 5 (40), 1925, pp. 176–77.

party abroad has not only raised more acutely the problems with which they were confronted before the war but has also produced a number of new, serious problems.

Therefore, in applying every effort to aid the central party institutions in the matter of effecting a unification abroad of all those who share the point of view of the Central Organ; in supplying these institutions with all sorts of information concerning the attitudes of the Russian workers as well as the workers of all countries in which there are sections of the organization abroad and in establishing contacts with Russia; in assisting the central institutions with contributions and in organizing for that purpose entertainments, lectures, special collections, etc.; in distributing party literature, in continuing the work among the students, in propagating among them the ideas of Marxism, in making use for this purpose of the democratic colonial [i.e., of "colonies" of Russians in foreign countries] institutions, the organizations abroad must at the same time pay special attention to the struggle against the social chauvinists and endeavor to lead all those who have remained faithful to Marxism and who have not succumbed to social patriotism in the direction which was pointed out by the Central Organ.

Further, a new, difficult, and responsible task of the organization abroad is the work among the war prisoners.

Finally, the Conference recommends that the sections abroad keep the comrades of foreign socialist parties informed of the feeling of the Russian workers, of the state of affairs in the Russian Social Democratic Labor party, etc., for which purpose the members of the sections must enter local socialist groups.

The Conference commissions the Committee of Organizations Abroad to establish closer contacts between the sections by keeping them informed, in as great detail as possible, of its own activity and of the party affairs in general. (*Adopted unanimously.*)

With regard to the question of common activities with other groups[70] it has been decided not to pass any resolution but to adhere to the old tactic: maximum caution.

BUKHARIN'S THESES ON THE TASKS AND TACTICS
OF THE PROLETARIAT

[Presented at the Berne Conference][71]

1. The contemporaneous epoch of imperialist wars sets before the proletariat of the advanced countries the task of realizing its ultimate

---

[70] Of Russian Social Democrats.

[71] "Tezisy Bukharina predlozhennye im na bernskoi konferentsii zagranichnykh sektsii R.S.D.R.P. 27 fevralia 1915 g.," *Proletarskaia Revoliutsiia*, No. 1 (96),

aim—the transformation of the capitalist society into a socialist society through seizure of political power.

2. Therefore the center of gravity of the proletarian struggle must shift from the sphere of struggle in favor of general democratic demands to the sphere of socialist demands of the proletariat—socialist in the narrow sense of the word.

3. In view of the fact that the *maturing* of a socialist overturn is a more or less lengthy historic process, the proletariat by no means repudiates the struggle for partial reforms and their utilization. But these partial slogans must be considered at this historic moment as a tactical approach to the slogan of seizure of power and as a method of increasing the revolutionary energy of the proletariat up to a resolute clash between classes [civil war].

4. It is the binding task of Social Democracy to oppose [resolutely] the slogan of civil peace with the slogan of civil war—breaking up of blocs, withdrawal from cabinets, voting against budgets [the establishment . . . .],[72] the slogan "war against war," etc.

5. On the other hand, social democratic slogans which ensue from the concrete state of affairs must develop the material content of the socialist revolution and represent an expression of the growing attempts on the part of the proletariat to "encroach arbitrarily on private ownership" (for instance, the transfer of bourgeois military organizations, of the economic life—the bread monopoly, the distribution of labor, etc.—into the hands of the workers; the transfer of closed enterprises [into the hands] of the unemployed; the organization of public works, the confiscation of food products and the organization of their distribution by the labor organizations, the abolition of rent payments for workers, etc.).

At the same time it is necessary to expand these slogans to their fullest extent, i.e., the slogan of seizure of power, as *a means for their realization*.

6. In reply to the imperialist unification of the countries from above, the proletariat must advance the slogan of a socialist unification of countries from below—republican socialist states of Europe—as a political-juridical formulation of the socialist overturn.

7. The methods of the proletarian class struggle [of the proletariat] which tends to develop into civil war against the bourgeoisie must change by all means in the direction of mass actions outside of the parliaments,

---

1930, p. 44. Originally printed from a manuscript preserved in the Marx-Engels-Lenin Institute, Moscow. The words given in brackets have apparently been crossed out in the manuscript by the author. Lenin refers to these theses in his letters to Shliapnikov of the spring of 1916 and June 1916 concerning the *Kommunist*. See below, pp. 241, 245.

[72] One illegible word was crossed out. [Soviet Editor's note.]

actions which end in an open clash between the working masses and their class enemies.

ON THE TASKS OF THE PARTY

[Resolution of the Baugy Group at the Berne Conference][73]

I. Fully agreeing with the slogan of "civil war" as being the only correct proletarian slogan suitable to the conditions of the approaching new epoch of imperialist wars, the *Baugy group,* however, considers it vitally important to determine the limits within which this slogan, as a slogan for agitation and as a slogan of today, may be advanced and defended at present, namely:

1. By no means does the group agree with a conception of this slogan which would turn its entire meaning into a simple demand to replace the prevailing policy of "national blocs" by the policy of "class struggle" in general. Considering that in a revolutionary epoch the class struggle must also take on revolutionary forms, any other conception of this slogan and any attempt to interpret it differently is and will be considered by the group as a direct repudiation of this slogan, and the group will protest against it in a most decisive manner.

2. At the same time the group cannot agree with an interpretation of this slogan which would advance it as the only one possible and which would *exclude all other slogans.*

Therefore, fully agreeing with the interpretation of the slogan as given in No. 33 of the Central Organ in the article on "The Position and Tasks of the Socialist International"[74] in the following words: "If not today then certainly tomorrow, if not during the present war then after it, if not in this war then in the following one, the proletarian banner of civil war will rally not only hundreds of thousands of enlightened workers" ——, etc., the group considers it absolutely impossible to agree with the following words of the same article: "Down with the clerical-sentimental and foolish preacher's yearnings for a peace at any price. Let us raise the banner of 'civil war'!" The formulation of the tasks of Social Democracy mentioned in the first quotation, and later on developed in a number of other articles in the Central Organ, as *a line of work preparatory to a civil war* "for political power and for the victory of socialism" (the concluding words of the same article)—does not exclude *but on the contrary embraces* other revolutionary slogans, such as, for

---

[73] "Bernskaia Konferentsiia 1915 g.," *Proletarskaia Revoliutsiia,* No. 5 (40), 1925, pp. 170–72.

[74] [V. I. Lenin,] "Polozhenie i zadachi Sotsialisticheskago Internatsionala," *Sotsial-Demokrat,* No. 33, November 1, 1914, p. 2; English translation, Lenin, *The Imperialist War,* pp. 84–89.

instance, the slogan of "peace" and the slogan of a "United States of Europe."

The two last slogans, in the judgment of the group, have a great agitational and revolutionary significance in so far as, first, they are advanced not in abstract form, but in connection with the slogan of "civil war" as its first aim and stage, and, secondly, in so far as both of them and especially the slogan of "peace" at the *present moment* when *none of the governments desire peace* may become the slogan directed *against the governments,* the slogan which destroys the "civil peace" and which transfers the existing struggle of the proletarians from the realm of mutual hatred and national enmity to the *realm of clashes of the classes with their own governments in each country and to civil war with the governments* (compare the Stuttgart resolution which also advances the struggle for "peace" as the first form of the revolutionary intervention of the proletariat in the war).

The group welcomes, therefore, as a correct step in this direction, the combining of both slogans, which combination has already been accomplished by the Central Committee in its declaration forwarded to the London Conference[75] and which protests ruthlessly against simply replacing one slogan by the other as occurred in the statement on the same Conference, published in the *Berner Tagwacht* of February 20, a statement which has caused some perplexity in the group.[76]

With respect to Russia in the judgment of the group the slogan of "civil war" cannot be combined with any other slogan except with the old fighting slogans of the revolution of 1905.

II. The group renounces positively any advancing of the so-called slogan "the defeat of Russia," particularly in the manner in which it has been advanced in No. 38 of the Central Organ.[77]

In the manifesto of the Central Committee as well as in the reply to Vandervelde, the defeat of Russia is described as being the "lesser evil," after an objective evaluation of the other issues of the war. The editorial of No. 38, on the other hand, says that every revolutionary is obliged to *desire* "the defeat of Russia."

Such a consideration of the question, in the judgment of the group, is not only devoid of practical sense but also introduces into the question an undesirable confusion. If a revolutionary is obliged merely to "desire" the defeat, then there is no use in writing leading articles about it in the

---

[75] See below, chapter iii, pp. 282–84.

[76] See chapter iii, pp. 280–82. This statement was· published by *Berner Tagwacht* as one which had resulted from an agreement between the Axelrod-Martov and the Lenin tendencies.

[77] "Voina i sudby nashego osvobozhdeniia," *Sotsial-Demokrat,* No. 38, February 12, 1915, p. 1.

Central Organ of the political party; but if he is obliged to do more than merely "to desire," then this would be not simply an objective evaluation but the preaching of an active participation in the war, which participation would hardly be approved by the editorial board of the Central Organ. Still more unsatisfactory, according to the opinion of the group, is the consideration of the same question in the third and concluding paragraph of the article, where the desirability of the defeat is explained by the revolutionary uprisings which may follow. The absolute impossibility of practical agitation in this sense compels the rejection *a limite* of such agitation for the defeat. We record that in the article referred to, the boundary line between the objective, fully admissible, and correct evaluation of the situation and the *agitation for the defeat* has not been traced at all; the group believes that it is an urgent necessity to have all confusion and obscurity in this question removed in a most decisive manner.

III. In the realm of organizational work, the group considers that the urgent task of the moment is the utmost strengthening of contacts with Russia and the beginning of this work immediately and not after the war; while in the sphere of *international policy* the urgent task is to begin immediately a similar work of restoration, to create the Third International, and to make contacts with the Left elements of socialist organizations. At the same time the group considers this last task of such importance that it fully admits and welcomes agreements with other sections of the Russian Social Democracy which share the international point of view, agreements similar to the one which has already been attempted with the group which issues the newspaper *Nashe Slovo*.

D. The Activities of the Bolsheviks Abroad in 1915

Three weeks after the Conference of the Russian Bolshevik sections abroad a conference of women socialists met at Berne (March 26–28). This Conference was called by Klara Zetkin, Secretary of the International Women's Bureau, with the co-operation of women members of the Central Committee of the R.S.D.L. party, among whom were N. K. Krupskaia, Inessa Armand, Zinaida Lilina, and Olga Ravich. Despite the fact that invitations were sent only to those women's organizations which were internationalist and anti-chauvinist, the Conference refused by a large majority to accept the declaration drawn up by Lenin and submitted by the delegation of the Central Committee of the R.S.D.L.

party. But, even so, the Leninists succeeded in putting their case before a group with which they desired to strengthen their contacts.[78]

The Bolsheviks were also active in calling the Conference of International Socialist Youth which met in Berne, April 5–7. Inessa Armand and Safarov attended the Conference as representatives of the Central Committee of the R.S.D.L. party, but the declaration which they presented and which the Conference declined to adopt is not available. The Conference set up an International Bureau of Socialist Youth which published *Die Jugend-Internationale* to which Lenin and Zinoviev, among others, contributed. Documents relating to these conferences are given in chapter iii.

Lenin and Krupskaia spent the summer of 1915 at Sörenberg at the foot of the Rothorn. Here Lenin wrote a long article, "The Collapse of the Second International," for the *Kommunist* (a new magazine founded by Piatakov and Evgeniia Bosh, of which more later) and with Zinoviev completed the pamphlet *Socialism and the War: Attitude of the Russian Social Democratic Labor Party towards the War.*[79] Lenin did not attend the preliminary meeting for the Zimmerwald Conference, which was held in Berne on July 11 where Zinoviev represented the Central Committee of the R.S.D.L. party. But during July and August Lenin was energetically working to secure as large and united a Left-wing representation as possible at the coming conference. Materials relating to these preliminaries and to the Zimmerwald Conference itself which met on September 5–8, 1915, are given in chapter iv. Here it is sufficient to note that the Conference refused to accept the manifesto of the Leninists, and that the Left-wingers formed their own organization, the

[78] O. Ravich, "Mezhdunarodnaia zhenskaia sotsialisticheskaia konferentsiia, 1915 g." *Proletarskaia Revoliutsiia,* No. 10 (45), 1925, pp. 167–68; Krupskaya, *Memories of Lenin,* II, 158–62; Lenin, *The Imperialist War,* pp. 192–96, 472–73; see also A. Balabanoff, *My Life as a Rebel,* pp. 131–33, and Rosmer, *Le Mouvement ouvrier pendant la guerre,* pp. 305–10.

[79] Both articles are translated in Lenin, *The Imperialist War,* the former on pp. 273–322 and the latter on pp. 215–58.

Zimmerwald Left, thus taking another important step toward the establishment of a Third International.

After Zimmerwald, Lenin and Krupskaia returned to Sörenberg for a few days and then went to Berne. Through Aleksandra Kollontai, who went to America in September 1915, through Inessa Armand, who went to Paris on some-one else's passport, and through Sapozhkov Lenin attempted to get in touch with Left internationalists in the United States and France. In the main, however, as Krupskaia records, Lenin could do little during the latter part of 1915 toward making direct contacts with the Lefts in the bellig-erent and the northern neutral countries. Lenin was engaged largely in theoretical work, the writing of polemical articles for the *Sotsial-Demokrat* and the *Kommunist,* and in cor-respondence with persons who shared his views. Late in 1915 he began the collection of data for his *Imperialism: the Highest Stage of Capitalism,* published the following year. Meanwhile news came from Russia that in October electors from Petrograd shops and factories had voted 95 to 81 for the resolution proposed by the Petersburg Committee of the R.S.D.L. party advocating the boycott of institutions set up to increase industrial production for war purposes.

Many of the matters which have been mentioned above and others arising out of the conditions under which Lenin and his co-workers labored are referred to in the letters which are included below. Following these letters is a docu-ment on Bolshevik tactics which, in view of later events, is of special interest.

THE PARTY, PERSONALITIES, AND ISSUES: EXCERPTS FROM
LENIN'S CORRESPONDENCE, 1914–1915

[To Shliapnikov, Stockholm, October 17, 1914][80]

DEAR FRIEND: [BERNE]

I have read the reply to Vandervelde and enclose my ideas regarding it.[81]

[80] *Leninskii Sbornik,* II, 198–99; another translation is in *The Letters of Lenin,* pp. 339–40.

[81] The editors of *Leninskii Sbornik* state that Lenin's comments on the Bolshevik reply are not in the Marx-Engels-Lenin Institute.

It would be extremely desirable in case the Duma is convoked (*is it true* that it will be called in one month?) for our Duma group to come forward, this time without the bloc, and declare a *consistent* point of view. Answer without delay: (1) will the Duma be convoked; (2) whether or not your communication with the Duma group is good, and how many days are required for it.

October 21, 1914.

I continue the interrupted letter. My criticism of the reply, of course, is a private matter, destined *exclusively for friends* for the purpose of establishing complete mutual understanding. Within the next few days the Central Organ will appear and we shall send it to you.

With respect to the International, don't be an optimist, beware of the intrigues of liquidators and opportunists. Although at present Martov is shifting leftward, it is only because he is alone; but what will happen tomorrow? Tomorrow he will roll down to the general plan: to shut the mouths of the workers (and their minds and consciences too) by means of an elastic resolution à la Kautsky, who is justifying everybody and everything. Kautsky is more hypocritical, more revolting, and more harmful than anyone else! Internationalism, don't you see, consists in having the worker of one country shoot at the worker of another country under the cloak of "defense of the fatherland"!!!

Let them intrigue, for to think of diplomatising with opportunism and of creating a "German" International Socialist Bureau now, at a moment of universal-historical significance, is nothing but a petty intrigue! A fundamental line must be pursued now. The Petersburg workers are in a better frame of mind—they hate the traitors of the German Social Democracy. It is necessary to support and strengthen with all our efforts this sentiment and this understanding by turning it into a firm decision to struggle against international opportunism. Up to now German Social Democracy has been the authority—now *it is an example of what must not be done!*

You are needed at Stockholm. Improve the organization of correspondence with Russia. Reforward my letters to the one who gave you the note in pencil (is this possible?). We must attain greater harmony with him with regard to details.[82] This is doubly important. We are beginning to publish the Central Organ.

Write more frequently!

Yours,

LENIN

[82] Lenin refers to L. B. Kamenev. When in the first days of the war, Shliapnikov was leaving St. Petersburg to go abroad, Kamenev transmitted through him to Lenin a note in pencil describing the situation in St. Petersburg at that time. (*Leninskii Sbornik,* II, 199, note 2.)

[To Shliapnikov, Stockholm, October 27, 1914][83]

[BERNE]

DEAR FRIEND:

I have just received your second letter and sit down to talk to you. Many thanks for the letter about the St. Petersburg events.[84] It will make a fine letter to the Central Organ. The issue of the Central Organ will appear within the next few days and we shall send it to you. Wait. Wait also for the following issue. You must stay at Stockholm until a means has been fully established for transporting (1) personal letters, (2) men, (3) literature, *through* Stockholm. For this purpose it is necessary to prepare systematically and to *try out* some reliable person in Stockholm as intermediary. Is Comrade Skovno adequate for the task? She is good because she is a Bolshevik. She will not swing over. But is she efficient, quick, and accurate?

I rejoice with all my heart that Comrade Kollontai has taken our stand, and I am also glad of Martov's wonderful (in the main) management of the *Golos* in Paris. But I am deathly afraid that Martov (and those with him) will swing over to the position of Kautsky-Troelstra. At present I hate and scorn Kautsky more than anyone else. What vile, cheap, self-conceited hypocrisy; nothing has happened, he says, principles have not been violated, everyone has a right to defend his fatherland; internationalism, don't you see, consists in having the workers of all countries shoot at each other "in the name of the defense of the fatherland."

R. Luxemburg was right—she understood long ago that Kautsky revealed "the fawning of a theoretician," servility, to put it plainly, servility before the majority of the party, before opportunism. There is *nothing* in the world at present that is more harmful and dangerous to the *ideological* independence of the proletariat than this dirty self-conceit and nasty hypocrisy of Kautsky, who wishes to cover up and disguise everything, to calm down the aroused consciences of the workers by sophisms and supposed learned loquacity. If Kautsky succeeds in this he will become the chief representative of the bourgeois rot in the labor movement. Troelstra will stand by him—oh, this Troelstra—an opportunist more skillful than the "kind" old man Kautsky! How this Troel-

[83] Lenin, *Sochineniia*, XXIX, 143–45; another translation is in *The Letters of Lenin*, pp. 341–44.

[84] The St. Petersburg events—the demonstrations which took place on the Viborg quarter during the first days of mobilization in 1914—are described in Shliapnikov's *Kanun semnadtsatogo goda,* I, 11–15. His report describing these demonstrations was published in *Kommunist*, Nos. 1–2, 1915, pp. 161–67, under the title, "Rabochii Peterburg i voina (Nabliudeniia peterburgskogo rabochego v nachale voiny)."

stra maneuvered in order to expel honest men and Marxists (Gorter, Pannekoek, Wijnkoop), from the Dutch party!! I shall never forget what Roland-Holst, who visited me once in Paris, said about Troelstra: *"ein hundsgemeiner Kerl"* (*gredin,* in French) ——— I am sorry that you have been casting pearls before him ———[85] Troelstra + the scum of opportunists in the *Vorstand* of the German Social Democracy are carrying on at present a disgusting intrigue in order to smooth over everything. Watch out with both eyes so as not to become an involuntary victim of this intrigue!! Look out that you do not inadvertently help these worst enemies of the labor movement, who in time of crisis defend chauvinism "theoretically" and who engage in a pitiful, disgusting diplomacy. The only one to tell the truth to the workers—even then not with a full voice and sometimes not very skillfully—was Pannekoek, whose articles we have sent you (forward the translation to the Russians).[86] His words to the effect that if the "leaders" of the International, which was killed by the opportunists and Kautsky, now gather and attempt to "mend" the cracks their efforts "will have no significance whatever"—these words are the *only* socialist words. *This is the truth.* Bitter truth, but truth. At present the workers need more than ever to know the truth, the whole truth and not vile diplomatizing, not the game of "mending," not glossing over the evil with elastic resolutions.

It is clear to me that Kautsky, Troelstra + Vandervelde (perhaps plus X + Y, plus or minus X, Y—it does not matter) are now busy intriguing to that end. The transfer of the International [Socialist] Bureau to Holland is a similar intrigue of the same scoundrels.

I shall keep at a distance from them and from the intrigue, shall advise our representative in the International [Socialist] Bureau (Litvinoff, 76 High Street, Hampstead, London, N.W.S.) to do the same, and you also.

"Do not go to the meeting of the wicked,"[87] do not trust Troelstra, etc., but submit a brief ultimatum: there you have the manifesto (the elaboration of the theses; we shall send them to you in printed form with-

[85] Lenin refers to Shliapnikov's conference with Troelstra in Stockholm on October 23, 1914. According to Shliapnikov, Troelstra had come to Stockholm at the end of October 1914 for the purpose of obtaining the consent of local socialists to transfer the International Socialist Bureau from Brussels to Amsterdam. The meeting between Troelstra and Shliapnikov took place in the presence of Yu. Larin, Dalin, Kollontai, and others. Shliapnikov related some news concerning Russia and transmitted to Troelstra the manifesto of the Central Committee and the letter in reply to Vandervelde. (Shliapnikov, *Kanun semnadtsatogo goda,* I, 40.)

[86] A. Pannekoek's article, "Der Zusammenbruch der Internationale," published in the *Berner Tagwacht,* Nos. 245, 246, and 247, October 20, 21, and 22, 1914. (Lenin, *Sochineniia,* XXIX, 145, note 3.)

[87] The reference is to the Copenhagen Conference, January 1915.

in the next few days) of our Central Committee on the war; would you care to publish it in your own language? No? Well then, adieu, we do not travel the same road!

If Kollontai is on our side, let her help us to "push forward" this manifesto in other languages. Get acquainted with Höglund, a young Swedish Social Democrat, the leader of the "opposition." Read our manifesto to him (refer to me: we got acquainted in Copenhagen). Try to see whether there is any *ideological proximity* (he is only a naïve, sentimental antimilitarist; these people should be told: either accept the slogan of civil war, or stay with the opportunists and the chauvinists).

The crux of the problem in Russia at present is to organize an ideological opposition to the opportunists of the International and to Kautsky. The whole crux lies there. At that, would Martov swing over?? —— I am afraid so! ——

With a firm handshake,

Yours,

LENIN[88]

[To Shliapnikov, Stockholm, November 14, 1914][89]

[BERNE]

DEAR FRIEND:

I was very glad to have the news from you that the Central Organ had been received and will be passed on to its destination.[90] With regard to your speech at the Congress of Swedish Social Democrats I can advise one thing: either do not speak at all, or else say that you greet the fraternal party of the Swedish workers and wish it every success *in the spirit of revolutionary international Social Democracy*. If it is impossible to say *this,* then there is no use of speaking at all. But if it is possible, then of course it would be better to add (1) that the Russian workers have expressed their viewpoint through the Social Democratic Duma

---

[88] A few days later Lenin again wrote Shliapnikov in a similar vein, warning him against Troelstra and Yu. Larin, criticizing Gorky for signing a protest of writers and artists against German atrocities, and expressing his opinions of Kautsky. The letter concludes: "The slogan of peace is now absurd and wrong (especially after the *treason* of practically all the leaders down to Guesde, Plekhanov, Vandervelde, Kautsky). It would in fact signify Philistine wailing. *Moreover, on military grounds* as well, we must remain revolutionaries and preach *class struggle* in the army also." (*Leninskii Sbornik,* II, 203–205; *The Letters of Lenin,* pp. 344–46.)

[89] Lenin, *Sochineniia,* XXIX, 149–51; another translation is in *The Letters of Lenin,* pp. 347–50.

[90] Apparently to Russia.

group which has *refused* to vote war credits; (2) that they are issuing *illegal* proclamations in St. Petersburg, Riga, Moscow, and in the Caucasus; (3) that their party organ, the Central Committee and the Central Organ have come forward against international opportunism.

Can that be "accepted?" Hm —— Of course Branting will not like that; but it is not our task "to please" the opportunists. If you are given ten to twelve minutes and *freedom* of speech, then you really should speak *against German* (and other) opportunism, not touching, of course, even by a single word either the Swedish Social Democrats or their "Young," etc. I should advise you *not* to speak either directly or indirectly of the restoration of the International. I am sending you an article (a very good one!) on this subject (translate it and forward it to Russia).[91] We shall be silent on the question of restoring the International and shall keep ourselves at a distance. It is necessary to wait. The *Lefts* among the Germans are beginning to stir;[92] *if* there is a split among them, *then,* perhaps, the International will be saved from rotting ——.

You are mistaken in thinking that the bourgeoisie does not wish to hear of it—the slogan of "peace"! Today I have read the English *Economist.* The *wise* bourgeoisie of that foremost country are *for* peace (of course, in order to *strengthen* capitalism).[93] And we must not permit ourselves to be mistaken for petty bourgeoisie, sentimental liberals, etc. The epoch of the *bayonet* has come. This is a fact, and, consequently, one must fight *with that kind of a weapon.*

Either tomorrow or the day after tomorrow the slogan of peace will be taken up by the *German* bourgeoisie and especially by *opportunists.* We must stand for the slogan of the *revolutionary proletariat* which is capable of *struggling* for *its own* aims; and this means nothing but civil war. It is also a *very* concrete slogan which *alone* can unmistakably reveal the basic orientations: for the proletarian cause or for the bourgeois cause.

Neither I nor Nadezhda Konstantinovna remembers anything about the debt to the Swedes.[94] But it is *quite possible* that I never did know

[91] Pannekoek's article, "Der Zusammenbruch der Internationale," referred to above.

[92] Lenin refers to the *Internationale* group, the nucleus of the future Spartakus group headed by Karl Liebknecht and Rosa Luxemburg.

[93] Apparently this refers to the article, "The Opening of Parliament," *The Economist,* No. 3716, November 14, 1914, pp. 863–65. (Lenin, *Sochineniia,* XXIX, 151, note 4.)

[94] This refers to a loan of 3,000 kroner received by the R.S.D.L. party from the Swedish Social Democratic Labor party in 1907 during the Fifth Congress of the R.S.D.L. party in London. (Lenin, *Sochineniia,* XXIX, 151, note 5.)

or else have forgotten. Therefore, some sort of cordial letter expressing our thanks, and at the same time suggesting this debt be considered as a "donation" would be very desirable. I think that you can do it very well yourself—for instance, in the name of the Petersburg Committee plus *several* Social Democratic deputies who have given authority to you in Petersburg. This would be the best form, I think. I think that it is for you also to arrange about the loan. I should advise you not to make use of my letter (it may start *"factional"* bickering!!!). If you insist I shall send a letter, but my advice is: don't. They will give to you *more willingly without me,* I assure you! Refer to Petrovsky and if necessary get a letter from him; this is better, indeed!

With a very firm handshake and my best wishes to you!

Yours,

N. LENIN

P.S. Should Kollontai translate into German the manifesto of the Central Committee (from No. 33 of the Central Organ), then perhaps you could send us a copy?

P.S. As to the question of the "peace" slogan, an interesting article by Bernstein in the last number of *Neue Zeit*[95] shows that in England, where the bourgeoisie is the most clever, the freest, etc., there is a tendency *for peace* from the standpoint of superopportunism. That is to say, peace gives better assurance of "social peace," i.e., the *subjugation* of the proletariat by the bourgeoisie, the pacifying of the proletariat, the *continuance* of the existence of capitalism. This has not been elaborated by Bernstein. But obviously there are many *such* peacemakers among the liberal and radical *bourgeoisie* of all countries. Add to this the facts (1) that *all* chauvinists are also for peace (but on *what* conditions), and in the censored press *we shall not be allowed* to speak of our conditions!!! (2) that the German and Russian *imperial courts* (today secretly and tomorrow semiopenly) are for a separate peace with each other; (3) that all sentimental bourgeoisie and citizens are "for peace," from the "antirevolutionary," common, slavish, etc., viewpoint.

Let us ask *objectively* what will derive the most benefit from the "peace slogan": at any rate not the propaganda of the ideas of the *revolutionary* proletariat! Not the idea of *utilizing* the war for the *promotion* of the collapse of capitalism!

Add to this the victory of opportunist-chauvinists in practically all countries: these people are the only ones whom the peace slogan *will help to clear themselves!*

[95] E. Bernstein, "Der englische Radikalismus und der Krieg," *Neue Zeit,* No. 6, November 13, 1914, pp. 161–69. (Lenin, *Sochineniia,* XXIX, 151 note.)

[To Shliapnikov, Stockholm, November 28, 1914][96]

Dear Friend: [Berne]

Today I received a telegram from Branting, saying that "newspapers *confirm* the arrest of the five deputies." I fear that it is impossible to doubt any longer the fact of their arrest!

A horrible thing. The government has decided, apparently, to have revenge upon the Russian Social Democratic Labor group in the Duma and will not stop at anything. The worst can be expected: falsification of documents, fraud, planting material evidence, false testimony, a trial behind closed doors, etc.

I think that without such methods the government could not have obtained a conviction.

Is it possible to do something to find out the names of the six persons arrested?

Is Kamenev safe?

In any case the work of our party has become a hundred times more difficult, and yet we shall carry it on! *Pravda* has brought up thousands of class-conscious workers from whom, despite all difficulties, a new group of leaders will again gather—the Russian Central Committee of the party. Now it is especially important that you remain at Stockholm (or *near* Stockholm) and make every effort to establish contacts with Petersburg. (Write us whether you have obtained the loan; in my preceding letter I enclosed a note about it for you. If you have not obtained it and if there is no place to obtain it, we shall probably be able to send you something; write us in greater detail.)

At Zürich it has been announced that the newspaper *Otkliki*[97] will appear beginning in December (liquidators + probably, Trotsky). In Paris, *Mysl,* the daily of the Socialist-Revolutionists, has begun to appear (*supertrivial* phrasemaking playing with the "left tendency").

What an abundance of newspapers, what phrases of intellectuals who are r-r-revolutionary today—and tomorrow ——? (Tomorrow they will *make peace* with Kautsky, with Plekhanov, and with the liquidationist "patriotic-chauvinist-opportunist intelligentsia" in Russia ——.

They had nothing and have nothing in common with the *laboring* class of Russia. It is impossible to trust them even for a penny.

I firmly shake your hand and wish you *courage.* The times are hard, but —— we'll pull through!   Yours,

                                                    Lenin

---

[96] Lenin, *Sochineniia,* XXIX, 154–55; another translation is in *The Letters of Lenin,* pp. 351–52.

[97] Apparently this refers to the resumption of the Bund periodical *Otkliki,* published in Switzerland. (Lenin, *Sochineniia,* XXIX, 155, note 2.)

[To Shliapnikov, Copenhagen, January 3, 1915][98]

[BERNE]

DEAR FRIEND!

I received your two letters with the news of your departure.

The reasons which you gave against my assumption (of the possibility of not going to Copenhagen, of not leaving Stockholm) have completely convinced me. I see that I have not taken into consideration something really very important. If you feel offended, I am ready to apologize in every way and ask you, please do not feel offended.

As a matter of fact, the village is, at present, much more dangerous (and more inconvenient for *the work*) than is the town.

On the whole, the situation is such that at present the struggle against Tsarism requires double caution—especially in the way of preserving the reserves. To spend at once still greater forces (after our *immeasurable* losses) would mean to weaken ourselves completely for the moment of more decisive activities against Tsarism. Therefore, I beg you earnestly to double and triple the conspiracy [i.e., conspirational methods] and *either* (1) to go no further than to write for someone to come to Sweden or (2) to limit yourself to a very short visit. I beg you, most earnestly, to confine yourself to the first and not to do the second (if such is at all possible).

It is better not to go to the conference (January 16) of the Scandinavians.[99] We have now discussed it thoroughly with Grimm. The Swiss did not go. Consequently this is obviously an intrigue of the Germans and Troelstra + Branting. They will make every effort to create confusion and will *prevent you from delivering your Swedish speech.* If there is no *absolute* guaranty that you will be permitted to make such a speech, better not go at all. Then we should forward (through Litvinov) : (*a*) a full translation of our manifesto; (*b*) a translation of the official announcement of the arrest of the R.S.D.L. Duma group—and all this should be sent not as a *report* (for that would mean that we *recognize* the conference) but as a *communication.*

I shake your hand firmly and send you my best wishes. Be *more careful* and *sans rancune, n'est-ce pas?*

Yours,

LENIN

[98] *Leninskii Sbornik,* II, 214–15.
[99] A conference of socialists of neutral countries in Copenhagen, January 17–18, 1915. See below, chapter iii, pp. 263–73.

[To Kollontai, Christiania, end of December 1914][100]

[BERNE]

RESPECTED COMRADE!

I received your letter and the English enclosure.[101]
I am sending you both of the items about which you wrote. Let me know about their fate, if you should translate and reforward them.

I am told that an editorial, "Über unseren Verrat an die Internationale," which appeared in the *Hamburger Echo*, states that the Germans (i.e., the German opportunist scum) are everything and that Plekhanov, Maslov, and Chkheidze are *for them*.[102]

Is it true? And what do you think about it?

Greetings and best wishes.

V. ILIN

P.S.—Ask Aleksandr to get acquainted with Kobetsky (Kobezky, Kapelveg 51, Kjobenhavn VI) and to secure from him my letter to him (to Aleksandr).

It is useless to advance a goody-goody program of devout wishes for peace if at the same time and in the first place illegal organizations and civil war of the proletariat against the bourgeoisie are not advocated.

N. LENIN

The European war has done much good to international socialism in that it has disclosed the whole extent of the rottenness, vileness, and meanness in opportunism, and thereby has given a wonderful stimulus for purging the labor movement of the dung which had accumulated during the decades of the peaceful epoch.

N. LENIN

---

[100] Lenin, *Sochineniia*, XXIX, 164–65; another translation is in *The Letters of Lenin*, pp. 354–55.

[101] Apparently this refers to A. M. Kollontai's letter to Lenin, December 5, 1914. Attached to this letter, which is preserved in the Marx-Engels-Lenin Institute, was a questionnaire on the attitude of socialists toward the war sent by the British Independent Labour party to other socialist parties. Kollontai wrote that it was desirable to publish Lenin's opinion on the war in the Christmas issue of the *Labour Leader*. (Lenin, *Sochineniia*, XXIX, 165, note 2.) The Lenin article was not published.

[102] Apparently Lenin refers to Konrad Haenisch's article, "Der deutsche Verrat an der Internationale," *Hamburger Echo*, No. 286, December 8, 1914. (Lenin, *Sochineniia*, XXIX, 165, note 3.)

[To Shliapnikov, Stockholm, end of January 1915][103]

[BERNE]

DEAR FRIEND!

Your plan concerning the April trip and the preparation for it seem to me quite right.[104] Really we should stick to this plan and prepare for it as systematically and as thoroughly as possible.

Thanks for the letters. We have written you several times already and have also sent stamped sheets. I hope you have received everything.

Today we received a number of *Nashe Slovo* which has begun to appear in Paris in place of the suppressed *Golos*. This number of *Nashe Slovo* contains Martov's (and Dan's) declaration of disagreement with *Nasha Zaria*.[105]

Evidently there is great disorganization among them (the liquidators) and nobody knows what will come of it. Axelrod obviously "reconciles" the German (and the Bundist) chauvinists with the Francophiles (and with Plekhanov).

After Zürich Martov got in tune with Axelrod, but at present he has turned "left," for how long we don't know.

We are issuing within the next few days No. 37 of *Sotsial-Demokrat*. With a firm handshake and wishing you every success.

Yours,

LENIN

We shall make an effort (together with you) to establish before April the exchange of letters and some contacts. And you also must make arrangements *beforehand*.

[To Shliapnikov, Stockholm, February 11, 1915][106]

[BERNE]

DEAR FRIEND:

I have received your two letters of February 4 and 5. Many thanks. As to the sending of *Sotsial-Demokrat* we have given your letter to

---

[103] Lenin, *Sochineniia*, XXIX, 171; another translation is in *The Letters of Lenin*, pp. 356–57.

[104] This refers to A. G. Shliapnikov's proposed trip to Russia. In accordance with his plan he went first to England to secure identification papers from some one of the Belgian refugees. From England he went in October 1915 by way of Norway and Sweden to Russia, where he lived in the status of a foreigner. (Lenin, *Sochineniia*, XXIX, 171–72, note 2.)

[105] "Zaiavlenie," *Nashe Slovo*, No. 1, January 29, 1915, p. 1. .

[106] Lenin, *Sochineniia*, XXIX, 173–75; another translation is in *The Letters of Lenin*, pp. 361–63.

the secretary of the Commission for Circulation. Tomorrow I shall remind him in person and hope that everything will be done.

The Paris people had promised to send you Plekhanov's pamphlet[107] and we are very much surprised that you have not received it. We'll order it once more and secure it for ourselves, so that we may send it to you.

Two of Plekhanov's adherents,[108] of whom you wrote, have been here. Had a chat with them. Pay attention to the white one (they are going back by the same route). Apparently Plekhanov has repulsed him more than the black one. The latter, it seems, is a hopeless chatterer, while the former is always silent and it is impossible to find out what is on his mind.

Today we received a letter from *Nashe Slovo* (which is appearing in Paris in place of *Golos*) containing a plan for a joint protest against "official social-patriotism" (in connection with the plans for a London conference *de la Triple Entente*. Whether or not this conference will take place, we do not know; recently we received a letter from Huysmans (reforwarded by Litvinov), who is up to something by convening the Executive Committee of the International Socialist Bureau at The Hague on February 20 and by organizing there on February 20 to 25, personal conferences (!!) with delegates from England, France, and Russia!! Wonderful!! It looks like some kind of preparation for something Francophile-patriotic. (By the way, you are quite right that at present there are many "philes" and few socialists. For us, Francophiles and Germanophiles are equally patriots, bourgeoisie or their lackeys, and not socialists. The majority of the Bundists, for instance, are Germano-

---

[107] This refers to G. V. Plekhanov's pamphlet, *O Voine*, published in Paris in 1914. (Lenin, *Sochineniia*, XXIX, 174, note 1.)

[108] A. Popov (N. Vorobiev), the "white one" and N. Stoinov, the "black one." Popov was a member of the Petersburg "Mezhraionka" Committee. This group was formed in November 1913 of Non-factional Social Democrats, followers of Trotsky, some Left Menshevik workers, and Bolshevik conciliators. Among the members of the "Mezhraionka" were Yu. Krotovsky, L. Karakhan, I. Flerovsky, N. Stoinov, N. M. Egorov, and A. F. Burianov. *Edinstvo*, a paper published by the "Mezhraionka" in 1914, to which Plekhanov contributed, was suppressed at the outbreak of the war. During the war the Petersburg "Mezhraionka" was close to the Bolshevik Petersburg Committee. In the spring of 1914 Stoinov had come to Russia to establish contact between Plekhanov's group and the Petersburg "Mezhraionka." Later, accompanied by Popov, he returned to Switzerland, where they called on Lenin at Berne. See A. Popov, "Stranichka vospominanii o rabote v 'Mezhduraionke'," *Proletarskaia Revoliutsiia*, No. 10 (22), 1923, pp. 96–97 and pp. 105–107. Plekhanov and other defensists resumed the publication of *Edinstvo* in 1917 and opposed the Bolsheviks. Trotsky and the "Mezhraionka" organization supported the Bolsheviks and united with them in August 1917. Cf. also I. Yurenev, " 'Mezhraionka' (1911–1917 g. g.)," *Proletarskaia Revoliutsiia*, No. 1 (24), 1924, pp. 109–39, and No. 2 (25), 1924, pp. 114–43.

philes and are glad of Russia's defeat. But what makes them any better than Plekhanov? Both are opportunists, social chauvinists, only of different colors. And Axelrod also.)

We have replied to *Nashe Slovo* that we were glad of their proposal, and have sent our draft declaration. There is little hope for an agreement with them because Axelrod, they say, is in Paris and Axelrod (see No. 86 and No. 87 of *Golos* and No. 37 of *Sotsial-Demokrat*)[109] is a social chauvinist who wishes to reconcile the Francophiles and the Germanophiles on the basis of social chauvinism. Let us see what will be dearer to *Nashe Slovo*—antichauvinism or Axelrod's benevolence.

I think that among us also, in Russia, and in the whole world, a new fundamental regrouping within Social Democracy has become manifest: chauvinists ("social patriots"), their friends and protectors, and antichauvinists. In the main, this division corresponds to the division into opportunists and revolutionary Social Democrats, but it is *plus précis,* and represents a superior, so to speak, stage of development, which is closer to a socialist revolution. And among us the old grouping (liquidators and Pravdists) becomes obsolete, being replaced by a new and wiser one: social-patriots and antipatriots. By the way, they say that Dan is a *German* "social patriot," i.e., a Germanophile, i.e., he is *for Kautsky.* Is that true? It looks very much like truth. It is amusing that the split in the Organization Committee occurred along a *bourgeois* line; Francophile (Plekhanov + Aleksinsky + Maevsky + *Nasha Zaria*) and Germanophile (Bund + Axelrod + Dan ? ? etc.).

If you do not obtain money from the Swedes, write us: we shall send you 100 francs. Consider carefully which is better (i.e., more favorable to the cause and safer for yourself—this is very important. You must safeguard yourself!!) : to wait in London or in Norway, etc. It is superimportant to organize the transport of illegal literature at least little by little. You should arrange a meeting with Plekhanov's adherents,[110] who in two or three weeks will be at your place and you should agree about all these things.

With a firm handshake and wishing you courage and everything best,

Yours,

LENIN

[109] Article by Raf. Grigorev, "P. B. Akselrod ob Internationale i voine," published in *Golos,* Nos. 86 and 87, December 22 and 23, 1914, and Lenin's article, "Russkie Ziudekumy," in *Sotsial-Demokrat,* No. 37, February 1, 1915, p. 1. (Lenin, *Sochineniia,* XXIX, 175, note 6.)

[110] A. Popov [Vorobiev] and N. Stoinov.

[To Shliapnikov, Stockholm, August 23, 1915][111]

[SÖRENBERG]

DEAR ALEKSANDR:

It is difficult for me to give you from afar definite advice with regard to the plan for your trip.[112] Our financial affairs are known to you. Nadezhda Konstantinovna [Krupskaia] has written in detail (in addition to the money which has been forwarded, 600 francs have been promised before October 10, plus 400 francs more in one month, a total of 1,000 francs. *For the time being* there is no hope of more).

On the one hand super-caution is required. Have you fully reliable papers, etc.?

On the other hand, this is the time when it would be of a decided advantage to the work if a person fully informed and independent were to visit two or three centers, make connections, establish communications, and return *immediately* to Sweden in order to transmit to us all the contacts and to discuss the further situation. This would be super-important.

No. 1 of the *Kommunist* will appear in eight or ten days; then after as many days No. 2 (or No. 1–2 together). No. 44 of the Central Organ will appear in one or two days. The pamphlet on war *with all the documents* will come out in about two weeks. It is already in the process of composition.[113]

The events in Russia have completely confirmed our position which the blockheads, social patriots (from Aleksinsky to Chkheidze), have christened defeatism. Facts have proved that we were right!! Military failures are helping to shake Tsarism and are facilitating the union of revolutionary workers of Russia and the other countries. They say, what will "you" do, if "you," revolutionaries, defeat Tsarism? I reply: (1) our victory will cause the movement of the "Lefts" in Germany to flare up a hundred times more strongly; (2) should we overcome Tsarism completely, then we would propose peace on democratic conditions to all the belligerents, and in case of a refusal would wage a *revolutionary* war.

It is clear that the advanced stratum of the Pravdist workers, the bulwark of our party, is safe in spite of the terrific devastation within its ranks. It would be extremely important if the leading groups could coalesce into two or three centers (in a *super-conspirative* manner), connect up with us and restore the Bureau of the Central Committee (it

---

[111] Lenin, *Sochineniia*, XXIX, 186–87; another translation is in *The Letters of Lenin*, pp. 372–74.

[112] This refers to A. G. Shliapnikov's trip to Russia mentioned above.

[113] Lenin and Zinoviev's pamphlet, *Socialism and War*.

seems that there is already one in Petersburg) and the Central Committee as such in Russia,[114] that they establish firm connections with us (*if necessary*, one or two persons must be brought over to Sweden); we would send leaflets and proclamations, etc. The most important thing is—to have firm and constant communication.

It is obvious that Chkheidze and Co. vacillate. They are faithful friends of *Nashe Delo*, Aleksinsky is pleased with them. (I hope you have seen the *Voina*[115] ["War"] of Plekhanov + Aleksinsky + Co.? What a disgrace!!) It is they who with Trotsky's assistance "play" at being "left"!! I think that they will not deceive the class-conscious Pravdists!

Write as soon as you decide! Greetings.

Yours,

Lenin

P.S. Would Kollontai agree to help us arrange for the publication of our pamphlet[116] in English in America?

[To Kollontai, Christiania, between September 8–13, 1915][117]

[Sörenberg]

Dear Aleksandra Mikhailovna!

It will be very sad if your trip to America is completely disarranged. We have built not a few of our hopes on that trip, among them the hope of publishing in America our pamphlet, *Sotsializm i voina*, which you will receive within the next few days—of establishing in general contacts with the publisher Charles Kerr in Chicago, and of bringing together the internationalists and finally of securing financial help which is so extremely important to us for all those urgent matters in *Russia* about

---

[114] Early in September Lenin wrote to Shliapnikov that he had been co-opted as a member of the Central Committee and again urged him to organize groups of Pravdist workers "who have *fully* analyzed the question of war" (Lenin, *Sochineniia,* XXIX, 193–94). On his return to Russia in November 1915 and after acquainting himself with the state of affairs in the Petersburg Committee of the R.S.D.L. party, Shliapnikov organized the Bureau of the Central Committee in Russia. This Bureau was also in charge of the transport of illegal literature from Finland. The Bureau consisted of : I. Fokin, V. Zalezhsky, G. I. Osipov, and K. M. Shvedchikov. During 1916 most of the members of this Bureau were arrested, and on his second visit to Russia late in October 1916 Shliapnikov found only K. M. Shyedchikov, who was to be deported from Petrograd. The Bureau of the Central Committee had to be organized again. The new Bureau consisted of A. Shliapnikov, P. Zalutsky, and V. Molotov. (Shliapnikov, *Kanun Semnadtsatogo goda,* I, 137–38, 187.)

[115] *Voina,* a miscellany by Plekhanov, Aleksinsky, Axelrod, and several other authors.

[116] I.e., *Socialism and War.*   [117] Lenin, *Sochineniia,* XXIX, 195–96.

which you wrote (and the urgency of which you have justly emphasized in connection with the desirability of our being nearer to Russia; the obstacles are in the *first* place of a financial, and in the second place, of a police nature: is it possible to reach the destination safely? ——).

If the question of the trip has been finally solved in the negative, then try to consider whether or not it is possible for you (through contact with Charles Kerr, etc.) to help us publish our pamphlet in English. This would be possible *only* in America. We *are sending* you the German edition of our pamphlet. Do everything possible to sell it in the Scandinavian countries (it is *deucedly* important for us to make at least a part of the expenses for it, as otherwise we *will be unable* to publish it in French!)

Write more details, more concretely and more frequently (in case you do not go to America), as to what kind of concrete questions come up in Russia, who raises them, how, in what instances, in what surroundings. All this would be of extreme importance for the publication of leaflets—which, you are right, is an *urgent* matter. The delegate[118] whom *you* sent will tell you about the conference of the Lefts (during which we became united well in an opposition, although we signed the manifesto) and we, too, shall write to you about it.

(No money, no money!! This is the chief trouble!)

Best greetings,

Yours,

Lenin

[To Shliapnikov, Stockholm, September 19, 1915][119]

[Sörenberg]

Dear Aleksander:

We have received your letters with the news about the good progress of transportation and are extremely glad to have them. Concerning the literature in Vardö,[120] try to save and preserve *everything*—send us the files of *Proletarii* and of *Vpered,* the pamphlets (old, 1905) we shall use also; it would pay to send them to Russia so long as there is any possibility of transport.

---

[118] This apparently refers to Nerman, who attended the Zimmerwald Conference as delegate of the Norwegian Labor Youth Organization. (Lenin, *Sochineniia,* XXIX, 196, note 5.)

[119] Lenin, *Sochineniia,* XXIX, 205–206; another translation is in *The Letters of Lenin,* pp. 376–77.

[120] The literature in Vardö (a port at the extreme north of Norway) had been discovered by Shliapnikov when he was organizing the illegal transport through this point. Large stocks of literature used in 1906–1907 were found there, part of which was used and forwarded to Russia. (Lenin, *Sochineniia,* XXIX, 206, note 1.)

I read yesterday in foreign newspapers about the dissolution of the Duma. It is obvious that the reaction has either been frightened by the bloc of the Lefts, or is speculating on some kind of "military" possibilities (or on a separate peace?). Our attitude toward the chauvinists-revolutionists (similar to Kerensky and a section of the social democrat liquidators or patriots) in my judgment, cannot be expressed by the formula: "support." Between the chauvinists-revolutionists (a revolution for the victory over Germany) and the proletarian internationalist-revolutionaries (a revolution for the awakening of the proletariat of other countries, for its unification into a general proletarian revolution) —the abyss is too great for one to speak of support. We must *utilize* every protest (even the timid and confused à la Gorky); we shall also *utilize* the revolutionary work of the chauvinists, as the opportunities present themselves; we shall not renounce "joint action" (in accord with the resolutions of our party of 1907 at the London Congress; and in 1913 at our Conference);[121] but we shall concede no further. In practice now we shall not issue joint appeals and manifestoes together with revolutionary patriots, we shall *avoid* forming Duma "blocs" with them, avoid "unification" with them when speaking at congresses, in demonstrations, etc. But *technical,* mutual services, so long as the patriots agree to them, will probably be possible (as in 1905 with the liberals), and we will not reject them. The relation should be *direct, clear:* You wish to overthrow Tsarism, for a victory over Germany; we for an international revolution of the proletariat.

We have incredibly little news from Russia. It is simply a pity that such a comparatively easy task as conspirative correspondence with Russia (*fully* possible even in war time), proves to be so utterly *poorly* organized. To do this is one of the most immediate tasks (I hope that you and *Nadezhda Konstantinovna* [Krupskaia] have discussed all this *in detail* by letter, and will do so again and as thoroughly as possible). To establish regular communication, to write for two or three leading workers to come at least to Sweden, for a detailed discussion and to establish a correspondence, in order to reach complete "harmony," this is the most urgent task. I hope that Belenin's [Shliapnikov's] trip will introduce radical improvement in this sphere. To get about quickly, to pick up contacts, to gather news—this is the crux of the whole work at present; without this it is useless to think of further developments.

[121] This refers to the resolution on the attitude toward nonproletarian parties which was adopted at the London Congress of the R.S.D.L. party in 1907 (*Londonskii sezd rossiiskoi sots. demokr. rab. partii sostoiavshiisia v 1907 g. Polnyi tekst protokolov,* pp. 454–55) and the resolution on the Narodniks, which was adopted at the summer 1913 conference of the Central Committee of the R.S.D.L. party with party workers. (Lenin, *Sochineniia,* XVII, 13–14.)

We are cogitating a plan for issuing proclamations and leaflets for transport to Russia. (We have not yet decided where to publish them, here or in the Scandinavian countries. The cheapest way must be chosen, since distance is unimportant.)[122]

I firmly shake your hand and wish you all that is best.

Yours,

LENIN

[To Shliapnikov, Stockholm, late September or early October, 1915][123]

[SÖRENBERG]

DEAR ALEKSANDR!

With respect to the leaflets, it is very, very good that you are willing to undertake this.[124] We are preparing a detailed plan for them and shall soon forward it to you and N. I-ch [Bukharin]. You know, it is nevertheless absolutely desirable that N. I. write the leaflets in duplicate (with a copying pencil and black carbon paper) and that the second copy be sent by you (or by him) immediately to us. Because the leaflets are a matter of *great* responsibility and of all types of literature the *most* difficult, it is therefore necessary to think it over more thoroughly and to confer collectively. Compared with the slowness of composition, of printing, and of transport, the loss of time in sending the material here is small and at any rate has no significance in comparison with the importance of having well-thought-out appeals.

How do you intend to sign the leaflets? You forgot to write about that.

Kollontai's pamphlet[125] is good as to its purpose, but the topic is super-difficult; to write with such a degree of popularity is super-difficult. In my judgment corrections are required. I have already written her about it and have asked for her consent to make the corrections. If she gives her consent, then the work will move on quickly, as I have already prepared a draft of all the corrections.

---

[122] The portions placed in parentheses were actually crossed out in this letter. (Lenin, *Sochineniia*, XXIX, 206, note.)

[123] Lenin, *Sochineniia*, XXIX, 207–208; another translation is in *The Letters of Lenin*, pp. 378–79.

[124] Lenin had in mind the publication of leaflets for distribution in Russia. In this connection A. G. Shliapnikov wrote to Lenin on September 26, 1915, from Christiania: "Demands for popular literature, leaflets, and sheets are coming from Russia. We would like to publish something here also." (Lenin, *Sochineniia*, XXIX, 208, note 2.)

[125] A. Kollontai's pamphlet, *Komu nuzhna voina?* published in 1916 by the Central Committee of the R.S.D.L. party. Lenin's corrections to this pamphlet are published in *Leninskii Sbornik*, XVII, 324–30. (Lenin, *Sochineniia*, XXIX, 208, note 3.)

As to the trip to your country,[126] the matter has been delayed, first, owing to lack of finances (the trip and life there are expensive), second, owing to police uncertainty. Probably we shall wait for Belenin's [Shliapnikov's] return and for his news from the native land. With firm handshake.

Yours,
LENIN

BOLSHEVIK TACTICS IN THE COMING REVOLUTION

[From "A Few Theses," by the Editors of *Sotsial-Demokrat*][127]

.... Taking into account the advice of our comrades in Russia, we formulate a few theses on some questions of the day relative to the social democratic work. (1) The slogan "Constituent Assembly" as an independent slogan is incorrect, since the question *at present* is, who is to call it. The liberals advocated this slogan in 1905, for it *could* have been interpreted as one called by the Tsar and as an assembly in agreement with the Tsar. Most correct are the slogans of the "three whales" (the democratic republic, the confiscation of landlords' estates, and an eight-hour working day) with the addition (compare No. 9 [below]) of an appeal for international solidarity of workers in their struggle for socialism, for a revolutionary overthrow of the belligerent governments and against the war. (2) We are against the participation in the war industry committees which help to wage the reactionary imperialist war. We are in favor of making use of the election campaign, i.e., of participation in the first stage of the elections for agitational and organizational purposes only. A boycott of the State Duma is out of the question. The participation in by-elections is *absolutely imperative;* so long as there are no deputies of our party in the State Duma, we must utilize from the

[126] This refers to Lenin's intention to move from Switzerland to one of the Scandinavian countries. A. G. Shliapnikov was commissioned to make preparations for this change of residence. Branting, whom Shliapnikov approached, guaranteed Lenin's safety in Sweden on the condition that Lenin would not meddle in the affairs of the Swedish Social Democratic Labor party. Lenin did not move to Sweden for reasons mentioned in the text of this letter. (Lenin, *Sochineniia*, XXIX, 208, note 4.)

[127] "Neskolko tezisov," *Sotsial-Demokrat*, No. 47, October 13, 1915, p. 2. In a letter to Shliapnikov, October 10, 1915, Lenin wrote: "These theses contain in part the answers to the questions which we touch upon in our correspondence and you in your talks with Nikolai Ivanovich [Bukharin], etc. I'll await your comments . . . . Pay special attention to the thesis about the Soviet of Workers' deputies. It is necessary to be careful with this thing; two or three hundred workers might be arrested!! Without connection with an insurrection the 'force' of the Soviet of Workers' deputies is but an *illusion*. One should not succumb to it. . . ." (*Leninskii Sbornik*, II, 249–50. Reprinted in Lenin, *Sochineniia*, XXIX, 212–13. Full text of the theses is translated in Lenin, *The Imperialist War*, pp. 356–58.)

point of view of revolutionary social democracy everything that goes on in the Duma. (3) We consider the most timely and urgent tasks to be the strengthening and widening of social democratic work among the proletariat, and then the spreading of it to the rural proletariat and the village poor and to the army. The most important task of revolutionary Social Democracy consists in the development of the strike·movement which has already begun, carrying it out under the slogan of the "three whales." In agitation a proper place should be devoted to the demand for an immediate cessation of the war. Among other demands the workers must not forget the demand for the immediate return of the labor deputies, the members of the R.S.D.L. group of the State Duma. (4) The Soviets of the Workers' deputies and similar institutions must be regarded as organs of insurrection, as organs of revolutionary power. Only in connection with the development of a mass political strike and in connection with a revolt, in the measure as it is prepared and is developing and is succeeding, can such institutions give stable service. (5) The social nature of the coming revolution in Russia can be only the revolutionary democratic dictatorship of the proletariat and the peasantry. Revolution cannot be victorious in Russia without overthrowing the monarchy and the serf-holding landlords. They cannot be overthrown unless the peasantry supports the proletariat. The division of the village into "farmer-landlords" and rural proletariat has not abolished the oppression of the village by Markov and Co. We have stood and stand now unconditionally for a *separate* organization of the rural *proletarians* under all circumstances. (6) The task of the proletariat in Russia is to complete the bourgeois democratic revolution in Russia, *in order* to kindle the social revolution in Europe. At present the second task has come unusually close to the first, but it remains still a special and a second task, since it is a matter of *different classes,* which collaborate with the proletariat of Russia: in the first task the collaborator is the petty bourgeois peasantry of Russia; in the second task, the proletariat of the other countries. (7) The participation of social democrats in the Provisional Revolutionary government together with the democratic petty bourgeoisie is considered as before to be admissible but *not* with the revolutionary chauvinists. (8) We consider those to be revolutionary chauvinists who desire a victory over Tsarism in order to overcome Germany, in order to rob other countries in order to strengthen the dominance of the Great Russians over the other peoples of Russia, etc. The foundation of revolutionary chauvinism is the class status of the petty bourgeoisie. It always vacillates between the bourgeoisie and the proletariat. Now it vacillates between chauvinism (which prevents it from being consistently revolutionary even in the sense of a democratic revolution) and proletarian internationalism.

The political spokesmen of this petty bourgeoisie in Russia at the present moment are the Trudoviks, the Socialist-Revolutionists, *Nasha Zaria,* the Duma group of Chkheidze, the Organization Committee, Mr. Plekhanov, and the like. (9) If the revolutionary chauvinists were victorious in Russia we would be opposed to the defense of *their* fatherland in this war. Our slogan is opposed to the chauvinists, even the revolutionary and republican, *opposed* to them *in favor* of a union of the international proletariat *for* a socialist revolution. (10) The question, whether the proletariat can assume the leading role in the bourgeois Russian revolution, we answer as follows: Yes, it is possible, *provided* the petty bourgeoisie in decisive moments will swing to the left. It is not only our propaganda that pushes it to the left, but also a number of objective factors, economic, financial (the burdens of war) military, political, etc. (11) The question as to what the proletarian party would do, should revolution place it at the helm in the present war, we answer thus: We would propose peace to all the belligerents on condition of liberating colonies and *all* the dependent, oppressed peoples without legal rights. Neither Germany nor England with France under their present governments would accept these conditions. If so we would have to prepare and lead a revolutionary war, i.e., we would not only carry out in full and by the most drastic means the whole of our minimum program but would systematically arouse to insurrection all the peoples oppressed at present by the Great Russians, all the colonies and the dependent countries of Asia (India, China, Persia, etc.) and likewise and first of all—would arouse to insurrection the socialist proletariat of Europe against its governments and in spite of its social chauvinists. There is not a shadow of doubt that the victory of the proletariat in Russia would give unusually favorable conditions for the development of a revolution in Asia and in Europe. *Even* 1905 proved this. International solidarity of the revolutionary proletariat is a *fact* in spite of the filthy scum of opportunism and social chauvinism. . . . .

E. Dissensions among the Bolsheviks Abroad, 1915–1916

During the latter part of 1915 and throughout 1916 the Bolsheviks abroad were involved in dissensions over theoretical and practical matters which nearly caused another organizational split in their slender forces. But along with these hotly waged controversies there were encouraging signs. Reports from Russia seemed to indicate a growing disaffection among the workers as a result of war weariness and economic difficulties. The Bolsheviks were also making some progress with their propaganda among the Russian prisoners of war in Germany and Austria through the work of a Commission for Intellectual Relief to Prisoners of War which had been organized under the Committee of Organizations Abroad early in 1915. This Commission circulated among the war prisoners 4,000 copies of Kollontai's *Who Wants War* and Gorky's leaflet, *Black Hundred Pogrom Instigators and the Jews.* During the year 1916 the Commission sent to the war-prisoner camps 2,200 kilos of books, pamphlets, periodicals, and newspapers, including the *Sbornik Sotsial-Demokrata, Kommunist,* and other Bolshevik publications.[128]

Aside from their activities among Russian workers and soldiers the Bolsheviks derived some satisfaction from the evidences of growth of a radical internationalist sentiment among socialists of other countries.

At the so-called second Zimmerwald Conference held at Kienthal, April 24–30, 1916, there were twelve delegates supporting the Zimmerwald Left program instead of eight. Moreover, the resolutions at Kienthal, which are given in chapter v below, were nearer to the line taken by Lenin and his friends than the Zimmerwald resolution. "Gregory [Zinoviev] is very enthusiastic about Kienthal," wrote Krupskaia in June. "Of course, I can judge only by reports, but there seems to have been too much rhetoric and no inner unity, the kind of unity that would be a guarantee of the solidity of the thing."[129]

There was lack of unity not only between the Zimmerwaldian majority and the Left minority, but also within the Left itself. Within this group the questions of self-determination, disarmament, and arming of the people, which are discussed in chapter vi below, separated the Dutch, Swedish, Norwegian, and Polish Lefts from the Bolsheviks. Dissensions relating to these and other controversial matters developed among the Bolsheviks, and involved Lenin in a hot

[128] *Leninskii Sbornik,* XI, 215–16.   [129] Krupskaya, *Memories of Lenin,* II, 185.

debate with the Bolsheviks of the former *Vpered* group (Lunacharsky, Manuilsky, and others) on the national question and with the Bukharin-Piatakov group on defeat of one's own government, the right of self-determination, and the minimum program in general. This latter controversy, which was in a sense a revival of the differences that had cropped up at Berne, was complicated by other party matters and was so heatedly waged that it nearly produced another party split.

One aspect of this controversy had to do with the publication of the periodical, *Kommunist*. In 1915 an editorial board was formed of Lenin, Zinoviev, Bukharin, Piatakov, and Evgeniia Bosh, with a sixth member to be chosen by Lenin and Zinoviev. Pending this choice, this vote was to be shared by Lenin and Zinoviev. According to Piatakov, the group was to be entirely autonomous in the editing of *Kommunist* and other publications. The Central Committee of the party had the right to dissolve the group but had no right whatsoever to interfere with the editing. It was especially provided that with regard to any particular question the *Kommunist* would have the right to take a position which would disagree with that of the Central Committee. In this case *Kommunist* would open a discussion of that disputed question in its pages. Apparently *Kommunist* Nos. 1–2 came out in September 1915 under this editorial board, not as an organ of the Central Committee but as a publication of the Kievskys (Piatakov and Bosh). Bukharin, Radek, and Piatakov contributed to this issue, as did Lenin and Zinoviev.[130] The first installment of Radek's article, "Chetvert veka razvitiia imperializma" ("A Quarter of a Century of the Development of Imperialism"), advanced a point of view similar to that of the Bukharin-Piatakov group. Lenin regarded this as a deviation from the party line and opposed the printing of any further installment in the *Kommunist*. Differences

---

[130] Letter from N. Lialin (G. Piatakov), March 24, 1916, in Archives of Istpart, Fund of the Central Committee, No. 976, quoted by Baevsky, *Ocherki po istorii oktiabrskoi revoliutsii*, I, 446.

over theoretical questions and the control and character of the periodical flared up with greater intensity. Bukharin proposed that a discussion of the national question, which had not been discussed in the first issue, be opened "independently of *Kommunist* matters," but it was difficult to separate this discussion from the question of control of the periodical. Zinoviev charged that Piatakov and Bosh, who were supplying the funds for the publication, were making a "money ultimatum to the party" and were demanding not only two editorial seats for themselves but also the privilege of inserting in a special section of the *Kommunist* "all they please and that we (i.e., the Central Committee) should be responsible for it."[131]

In the meantime Bukharin, Piatakov, and Bosh had left Switzerland and established themselves in Stockholm. In November 1915 Piatakov wrote Lenin and Zinoviev asking that his group (Bukharin, Bosh, Bagrovsky, and himself) be appointed by the Central Committee as a "special commission" to act as a channel of information between the Central Committee and Russia, to publish and transport literature, and to maintain liaison with the Swedish Lefts.[132] The Central Committee replied amending the proposal by denying the group the right to correspond with Russia in its own name or to send any literature to Russia without first submitting it to the Central Committee at Berne. On receipt of this letter the Bukharin-Piatakov group decided that these conditions were unacceptable, notified the Central Committee that the group would dissolve, and asked that a representative of the Central Committee be sent to Stockholm to centralize the activities which the group had proposed to carry on.[133]

[131] Letter, Zinoviev to Bukharin, with Lenin's postscript, Archives of Istpart. Fund of the Central Committee, No. 973, quoted by Baevsky, *Ocherki po istorii oktiabrskoi revoliutsii*, I, 447.

[132] Letter, Piatakov to Zinoviev and Lenin, November 8, 1915, Archives of Istpart. Fund of the Central Committee, No. 945, cited by Baevsky, *Ocherki po istorii oktiabrskoi revoliutsii*, I, 445.

[133] Letter to the Central Committee, December 3, 1915. Archives of Istpart, Fund of the Central Committee, No. 954, cited by Baevsky, *Ocherki po istorii oktiabrskoi revoliutsii*, I, 445.

Dissolution of the group did not end dissensions among the Bolsheviks abroad. The eleven theses issued by Bukharin-Piatakov group late in 1915 brought this group close to Radek's position on the question of self-determination. In the spring of 1916 the German, Dutch, and Polish Lefts outlined their tactical program, which Lenin also disapproved, and the controversy among the Bolsheviks became interwoven with that within the Zimmerwald Left. In the meantime, after a lengthy correspondence on the control and content of *Kommunist,* that periodical was given up and the Central Committee established its own organ, *Sbornik Sotsial-Demokrata,* of which No. 1 appeared in October and No. 2 in December, 1916. In the pages of this publication Lenin analyzed and attacked the attitude of Radek and Luxemburg on defense of the fatherland and the right of self-determination, the attitude of the Dutch, Polish, Scandinavian, and Swiss Lefts on disarmament, and the position of Bukharin on the state.

Meanwhile, having become the objects of the attention of the Swedish police, the entire Bukharin-Piatakov group moved to Christiania. Bukharin later, in October 1916, went to the United States, where he remained until May 1917. Before sailing for America he wrote to Lenin with reference to the controversies: "At any rate I ask you one thing: If you will polemize, etc., preserve such a tone as not to force a split. It would be very painful to me, painful beyond my strength, if joint work, even in the future, should become impossible. I have the greatest respect for you and look upon you as my revolutionary teacher and love you."[134]

There is other evidence that during this last year before the revolution in Russia Lenin added something to his already considerable reputation for irreconcilability and for the sharpness with which he attacked those who presumed to differ with him. "Never, I think, was Vladimir Ilyich in a

---

[134] "Iz materialov Instituta Marksa-Engelsa-Lenina: N. I. Bukharin—V. I. Leninu," *Bolshevik,* No. 22, November 30, 1932, p. 88.

more irreconcilable mood than during the last months of 1916 and the early months of 1917," Krupskaia writes. "He was profoundly convinced that the revolution was approaching."[135]

In February 1916 Lenin and Krupskaia moved from Berne to Zürich, where Lenin worked regularly in the library, discussed current events with young revolutionary émigrés from various countries and made closer contacts with members of the Swiss Social Democratic party who had accepted the general position of the Zimmerwald Left. In June Lenin finished his pamphlet *Imperialism, the Highest Stage of Capitalism,* the purpose of which, he later said, was "to present, on the basis of the collected returns of irrefutable bourgeois statistics and the admissions of bourgeois scholars of all countries, *a general picture* of the world capitalist system and of its international relationships at the beginning of the twentieth century—on the eve of the first world imperialist war."[136] Throughout the remainder of the year Lenin lived in Zürich. "Along with his work in the realm of theory," Krupskaia writes, "Ilyich considered it of the greatest importance to work out a correct tactical line. He thought that the time was ripe for a split on an international scale, that it was necessary to break with the Second International, with the International Socialist Bureau, to break forever with Kautsky and Co., to begin with the forces of the Zimmerwald Lefts to build a Third International. . . . ."[137]

[135] Krupskaya, *Memories of Lenin,* II, 197.

[136] Preface to the French and German editions. English translations have been published in many different editions, among them those by International Publishers, New York, and by the Co-operative Publishing Society of Foreign Workers in the U.S.S.R., Moscow, and Leningrad.

[137] Krupskaya, *Memories of Lenin,* II, 196. In addition to the various works cited in this section, see also Baevsky, "Borba Lenina protiv Bukharinskikh 'Shatanii mysli,' " *Proletarskaia Revoliutsiia,* No. 1 (96), 1930, pp. 42–43, and his article, "Bolsheviki v borbe za III Internatsional," *Istorik Marksist,* No. 11, 1929, pp. 12–48.

THESES AND PROGRAM OF THE BUKHARIN-PIATAKOV GROUP, NOVEMBER 1915

[Theses on the Right of Self-Determination][138]

1. The imperialist epoch is an epoch of the absorption of small states by the large state units and of a constant reshuffling of the political map of the world toward a more uniform type of state; in the process of this absorption many nations are incorporated into the state system of the victorious nations.

2. The realm of foreign policy of contemporary capitalism is closely bound up with the dominance of finance capital, which cannot give up an imperialist policy without threatening its own existence. Therefore, it would be extremely utopian to advance anti-imperialist demands in the realm of foreign policy while preserving *capitalist* relations. The answer to the bourgeois imperialist policy must consist in a socialist revolution of the proletariat; Social Democracy *must not advance "minimum" demands in the realm of present-day foreign policy.*

3. It is therefore impossible to struggle against the enslavement of nations otherwise than by struggling against imperialism, *ergo*—by struggling against imperialism, *ergo*—by struggling against finance capital, *ergo* against *capitalism* in general. Any deviation from that road, any advancement of "partial" tasks, of the "liberation of nations" *within* the realm of capitalist civilization, means the diverting of proletarian forces from the actual solution of the problem, and their fusion with the forces of the corresponding national bourgeois groups.

4. The slogan of "self-determination of nations" is first of all *utopian* (it cannot be realized *within the limits* of capitalism) and *harmful* as a slogan which *disseminates illusions.* In this respect it does not differ at all from the slogans of the courts of arbitration, of disarmament, etc., which presuppose the possibility of so-called "peaceful capitalism."

5. While being absorbed in the agitational side of the question it is not permissible to forget its connection with other questions. If we advance the slogan of "self-determination" for struggle against "the chauvinism of the working masses," then we act in the same way as when we (like Kautsky) advance the slogan of "disarmament" as a method of struggle against militarism. In both cases the error consists in a one-sided examination of the question, in an omission of the specific gravity of a given "social evil"; in other words, it is a purely rational-utopian and not revolutionary-dialectical examination of the question.

[138] *Ocherki po istorii oktiabrskoi revoliutsii,* I, 516–18. These theses on self-determination and the fifteen-point platform of the Bukharin-Piatakov group were forwarded to the Central Committee in November 1915. They were received by the Central Committee in Switzerland on November 19, 1915. (Baevsky, *Ocherki po istorii oktiabrskoi revoliutsii,* I, 446.)

6. Two chief cases, of a concrete application of the slogan of the right of nations for self-determination (through state independence or secession) are as follows: (1) the case where in the course of the imperialist war a "foreign" territory is annexed; (2) the case of the "disintegration" of an already formed state organism. In the first case the slogan of "self-determination" is nothing but a different form of the slogan *"defense of the fatherland,"* since, unless an appeal is also made for material defense of the corresponding state boundaries, the slogan remains only an empty phrase; in the second case we have essentially the same "harmful consequences" as with the slogan "defense of the fatherland": the attention of the proletarian masses is transferred to a different level, the international character of their activities is lost, the forces of the proletariat are split, the entire line of tactics proceeds in the direction of national struggle, and not class struggle. Besides, in this case, the slogan contains *implicite* also the slogan of "defense," since *after* the secession is achieved (the slogan of right, etc., presupposes such possibility) it becomes necessary, of course, to *defend* the "independence" (otherwise, under the constant dangers of an imperialist epoch, why should one "demand" at all?).

To struggle against the chauvinism of the working masses of a Great Power by means of the recognition, of the right of nations for self-determination, is equivalent to struggling against this chauvinism by means of the recognition of the right of the oppressed "fatherland" to defend itself.

7. The deflection of the proletariat's attention toward the settling of "national problems" becomes extremely harmful, especially now, when the question of mobilizing the proletarian forces on an international scale for their international activities, and for the overthrow of capitalism has been raised in a *practical* manner. The task of Social Democracy at the present time is a *propaganda* of *indifference* with respect to the "fatherland," to the "nation," etc., which presupposes the posing of the question not at all in a "pro-state" manner (protests against a state "disintegration") but on the contrary, posing it in a sharply expressed revolutionary manner with regard to the state power and to the entire capitalist system.

8. Hence it follows that in no case, and under no circumstances, will we support the government of a Great Power which suppresses the uprising and revolt of the oppressed nation; neither will we mobilize the proletarian forces under the slogan, "the right of nations for self-determination." Our task in this case is to mobilize the forces of the proletariat of *both nations* (in common with others) under the slogan of a civil, class war for socialism and for a propaganda against a mobilization of forces under the slogan, "the right of nations for self-determination."

9. In so far as we have before us *noncapitalist countries or countries with an embryonic capitalism* (for example, the colonies), we can *support* the uprising of the popular masses as an event which weakens the dominant classes on the continent and which does not split the proletarian forces, since in this case: (*a*) it is not a question of socialism; (*b*) it is a question of the mobilization not of the international forces of the proletariat but of the forces of the national *bourgeoisie* which is objectively helping the continental proletariat.

10. Furthermore, the slogan of the "right," etc., does not answer concretely the question concerning a *given* nation.

11. From a *formal* similarity between the position expounded in these theses and that of Cunow and *Consorten*, an essential identity ("assistance to imperialism") does not follow. To start the objection with "assistance" would mean in this case the entrance upon the road paved by Kautsky.

P.S. By the way, all *extreme Lefts* who have a well-thought-out theory are *against* [the slogan of self-determination]. Are they all *"traitors"?*

YURII [PIATAKOV]
EV. BOGD [ANOVNA BOSH]
N. BUKHARIN

[A Fifteen-Point Platform][139]

1. Imperialism is the bourgeois policy of the epoch of finance capital and is inevitable so long as the bourgeoisie is at the helm.

2. Imperialism contradicts the interests of the proletariat; therefore the party which is at the head of the labor movement is obliged to lead a ruthless struggle against it, a struggle which can end either in a victory of the bourgeoisie and the consolidation of imperialist policy or in a victory of the proletariat and the overthrow of the bourgeois domination. Without going beyond the limits of capitalism it is impossible to overcome imperialism. The only means against it is the seizure of power by the laboring class.

3. The present war, on the whole, is a consequence of the imperialist policy; imperialism can lead only to military conflicts. It is therefore necessary to expand the struggle against the war into a struggle against imperialism, against capitalism, and for socialism.

4. Finance capital has fully prepared the basis for a social revolution:

a) By creating such an economic structure as *can be* consciously organized by a proletariat which has seized the power and has expropriated the expropriators.

---

[139] *Ocherki po istorii oktiabrskoi revoliutsii*, I, 514-16.

b) By continually tossing the proletariat into the arena of *world* struggle, by placing constantly before it questions of *world* policy in their entire scope, by abolishing thereby the national-state seclusion of the working class and revolutionizing the consciousness of the proletariat in an unprecedented manner.

5. Socialism, thus, out of a theoretical prognosis becomes the task of the epoch: a social revolution is placed on the order of the day of the proletariat's concerted action.

6. From this it does not follow that the daily struggle against imperialism is to be excluded, since (*a*) individual concessions are possible, and (*b*) only in such a struggle can the fighting cadres of the proletariat coalesce and become hardened.

7. In questions of international relations we do not place any positive tasks before us within the limits of the capitalist order, i.e., questions of the outlining of boundaries, customs questions, trade agreements, the settlement of international conflicts by a tribunal, etc., etc.—all such questions can either not be solved from a proletarian point of view or, if they can be solved, then they can be carried out only in case the power is in the hands of the proletariat.

8. In questions of internal policy the *minimum* program of revolutionary socialist parties remains in force.

9. The collapse of the Second International is recognized as a fact.

10. This collapse is explained not so much by the treason of the leaders as by the objective causes of chauvinist conduct of the masses, by causes which have their roots in the conditions of the proletarian struggle in the past epoch.

11. These conditions by the very development of capitalist society in an epoch of finance capital, in an epoch of wars and internal shocks, are becoming matters of history.

12. The ideological superstructure of the past epoch has played and will play an extremely harmful part in the struggle of the proletariat for power. Opportunism forms such an ideological superstructure. We do not wait until opportunism outlives itself by the mere course of events— for that would signify fatalism—but we *declare immediately a resolute war on the opportunism of all countries.*

13. We do not at all discount the blameworthy role of the leaders in the collapse of the International, especially on account of the definite character of our parties in the past epoch. Therefore *no "amnesty" whatever to the leaders!* A resolute struggle against them beginning with Monitor from the *Preussische Jahrbücher* and ending with Kautsky in *Neue Zeit,* beginning with Heine in Germany and ending with Plekhanov and Axelrod in Russia!

14. A new *orientation* of the mass struggle of the proletariat which

would be adequate to the new conditions of this struggle is necessary; a *transfer of the center of gravity* to the activities of the masses themselves, to a struggle outside of the parliaments, is necessary, which of course does not mean a rejection of all former methods of proletarian struggle.

15. Thus, the proletarian struggle must be co-ordinated internationally upon new foundations, in conformity with the new conditions of the struggle. Upon this ground a new international organization should be formed, a Third International should be constructed, which would mean not the restoration of a painted invalid—the Second International with all its negative sides—not a complete negation of the past—but the preservation of all positive gains of the Second International and a resolute renunciation of all of its manifestations that do not correspond to the new epoch.

LENIN AND THE IMPERIALIST ECONOMISM OF THE BUKHARIN-PIATAKOV GROUP

[Lenin's Reply to P. Kievsky (Piatakov)][140]

Some the war tramples upon and breaks, and others it hardens and enlightens—as does any crisis in human life or in the history of peoples.

This is true also of the social democratic reasoning about the war and in connection with the war. It is one thing to ponder over the reasons and the significance of the imperialist war—on the basis of highly developed capitalism—over the problems of the tactics of Social Democracy in connection with the war, over the causes of the crisis of the Social Democracy, and so forth; but it is an entirely different thing to permit the war to *suppress* one's thinking, or to stop reasoning and analyzing *under the effect* of the horrible impressions, the painful consequences, or the nature of the war.

The scornful attitude of "imperialist economism" toward *democracy* constitutes one of these forms of *depression,* or *suppression,* of human reasoning by the war. P. Kievsky does not notice that this depressed feeling, this intimidation, the abandonment of analysis because of the war, passes like a scarlet thread through his entire reasoning. Well, what is the use of talking about the defense of the fatherland when we are confronted with such a beastly slaughter? What is the use of talk-

---

[140] Lenin, "Otvet P. Kievskomu," *Proletarskaia Revoliutsiia,* No. 7 (90), 1929, pp. 3–14. Reprinted in Lenin, *Sochineniia,* XXX, 257–61. The editors of *Proletarskaia Revoliutsiia* state that this is the rough draft of an article written in August or September, 1916, and that it is in a sense the summary of Lenin's ideas as expressed in a number of articles on the national question and disarmament and brings the discussion from particular questions to the fundamental one of the problem of democracy in the epoch of imperialism and proletarian revolution.

ing about the rights of nations when a general strangling reigns? How can there be self-determination, "independence" of nations, when, look, what has been done to "independent" Greece? What, in general, is the use of talking and thinking about "rights" when all rights are being trodden upon everywhere in the interests of soldiery? What is the use of talking and thinking about a republic, when in this war there is no longer the slightest difference—or more truly no difference at all—between the most democratic republics and the most reactionary monarchies?

P. Kievsky becomes very angry when it is pointed out that he has permitted himself to be intimidated, to be made captive, so that he even repudiates democracy in general. He frets and retorts: I am not at all against democracy, but merely against *one* democratic demand, which I consider "bad." But, however P. Kievsky frets, however he *"tries to convince"* us (and perhaps also himself) that he is not at all "against" democracy, his *reasoning* or, more truly, his continuous *errors* in reasoning *prove* the contrary.

The defense of the fatherland is a lie in the imperialist war, but not at all a lie in a democratic and a revolutionary war. Talk about "rights" seems ridiculous in time of war, for *any* war replaces rights with direct and open violence. But this should not make us oblivious to the fact that there have been wars (democratic and revolutionary) in past history (and that most probably there will and must be some in the future) which, by replacing in war time every "right," all democracy, with force, *have served* by their peculiar social nature, by their consequences the cause of democracy and *consequently* the cause of socialism. The example of Greece seems to "refute" all self-determination of nations;[141] but this example—if one wishes to reason, to analyze, to weigh in one's mind and not to deafen oneself with the sound of words, not to let oneself be intimidated by the effect of the nightmarish impressions of the war—is not any more serious or convincing than the mockeries over the republic caused by the fact that the "democratic"— the most democratic republics, not only France but also the United States, Portugal, and Switzerland—during this war have established and are establishing the same kind of club law of soldiery as exists in Russia.

---

[141] Kievsky had written (*Proletarskaia Revoliutsiia*, No. 7 [90], 1929, p. 13, note 2): "Greece licks the English boot by agreeing not merely to change the cabinet but also to carry out new elections in parliament." In the early months of 1916 the Bulgarians had occupied a number of Greek forts which the Entente believed had been surrendered at the orders of the Greek government. In June Entente naval forces blockaded Greek ports and prepared for a naval demonstration at Athens. Premier Skouloudis resigned and his successor, Zaimis, agreed to call new elections. King Constantine agreed to the Entente demand for the demobilization of the Greek army.

It is a fact that the imperialist war erases all differences between a republic and a monarchy, but to deduce from this the repudiation of the republic, or at the very least a scornful attitude toward it, means that one permits oneself to be intimidated by the war, means that one permits the horrors of the war to *oppress* one's thought. Many adherents of the slogan of "disarmament" (Roland-Holst, the Swiss Youth, the Scandinavian "Lefts," etc.) reason in the same way: what is the use, they say, of talking about the revolutionary utilization of the army or the militia, when there is no difference between the republican militia and the monarchist permanent army in this war, when militarism *everywhere* does such horrible deeds?

This is the *same* process of thought, the *same* theoretical and practical-political error, which P. Kievsky does not notice and which he makes in his article at virtually every step. He *thinks* that he argues against self-determination only, he *wishes* to argue only against it; but curiously enough it does not come out that way in spite of his will and knowledge! It comes out that he does *not* advance *a single* argument which could not just as well have been advanced against democracy in general!

The real source of all his curious errors in logic, of the entire confusion—not only in the question of self-determination but also in the question of defense of the fatherland, the question of divorce,[142] in the question of rights in general—is that his thinking *has been depressed* by the war and because of this depression the position of Marxism toward democracy in general has been basically distorted.

Imperialism is highly developed capitalism. Imperialism is progressive. Imperialism *is* a repudiation of democracy; "hence," democracy is "impracticable" under capitalism. The imperialist war is a clamorous violation of every democracy, alike in backward monarchies and in advanced republics, "hence," there is no use talking about the "rights" (i.e., about democracy!!). "Only" socialism can be "opposed" to the imperialist war; a way out can be found "only" in socialism; "hence," it is a deception, an illusion, an obscuring, a postponement, etc., of the slogan of the socialist overturn, if we advance democratic slogans in the minimum program, i.e., under capitalism.

[142] P. Kievsky in order to explain his position with regard to the national question compares the right of nations to self-determination with the right of divorce. In point *"e"* of chapter 1, he wrote: "Let us assume that we advance the right of divorce upon the wish of one of the parties concerned; it does not follow that we recommend separation at any cost, but it follows absolutely that in cases where one party, let us say the wife, finds further life with her husband difficult, unbearable, or simply unpleasant, she can without any circumlocution say goodbye to him, discontinue being his wife, divorce him." (*Proletarskaia Revoliutsiia*, 7 [90], 1929, p. 14, note 6.) This argument of Kievsky was criticized by Lenin in the article, "O karikature i imperialisticheskom ekonomizme," *Sochineniia*, XIX, 232-33.

This is the real source of all P. Kievsky's misadventures, although he does not recognize it as such. Here lies his *basic* error in logic, which, because it is basic and is not perceived by the author, *"explodes"* at every step like a rotten bicycle tire, "springs up" either in the question of defense of the fatherland, the question of divorce, or in the phrase about "rights": "We shall *not* speak of rights, but of the destruction of secular slavery"—a phrase so superb just because of its profound disdain for "rights" and its profound lack of understanding of this matter.[143]

To repeat this phrase reveals a lack of understanding of the relationship between capitalism and democracy, between socialism and democracy.

Capitalism in general, imperialism in particular, transforms democracy into an illusion—and at the same time capitalism generates democratic tendencies among the masses, creates democratic institutions, accentuates the antagonism between imperialism, which repudiates democracy, and the masses which strive toward democracy. Capitalism and imperialism cannot be overthrown through any reforms—not even the most "ideal" democratic reforms—but only through an economic overturn. But the proletariat which has not been educated in a struggle for democracy is incapable of accomplishing an economic overturn. Capitalism cannot be defeated without a *seizure of banks,* without abolishing *private ownership* of the means of production. These revolutionary measures, however, cannot be realized without the organization by the entire people of a democratic administration of the means of production which have been confiscated from the bourgeoisie, without attracting the entire mass of the working people—the proletarians, the semiproletarians, and the petty peasants—to a democratic organization of their ranks, their forces, their participation in the state government. The imperialist war is, we may say, a threefold repudiation of democracy ([a] every war replaces "rights" with violence; [b] imperialism as such is a repudiation of democracy; [c] the imperialist war completely eradicates differences between republics and monarchies); but the awakening and the growth of the socialist insurrection against imperialism are *inseparably* bound up with the growth of democratic opposition and of revolt. Socialism leads toward the dying off of *every* state, consequently of every democracy; but socialism cannot be realized except *through* the dictatorship of the proletariat, which combines force against the bour-

---

[143] Lenin has in mind at this point one of the concluding paragraphs of Kievsky's article, which says: "It is not a matter of documents and rights, not a matter of proclaiming freedom of the people, but a matter of establishing truly free relations, of abolishing all slavery, of abolishing social oppression in general and national oppression in particular." (*Proletarskaia Revoliutsiia,* 7 [90], 1929, p. 14, note 7.)

geoisie—the minority of the population—and a *complete* development of democracy—a really general participation, with equal rights, of the *entire* mass of the population in all the *state* affairs and in all complicated problems of liquidating capitalism.

P. Kievsky became entangled in these "contradictions" by forgetting the Marxian doctrine concerning democracy. The war, speaking figuratively, has depressed his thinking to such an extent that he has replaced all reasoning with the agitational call: "get out of imperialism"—in the same manner as an economic and political analysis of the real *meaning* of "withdrawal" of civilized peoples "from the colonies" is being replaced with the call "get out of the colonies."

The Marxian solution of the question of democracy consists in the *utilization* against the bourgeoisie of *all* democratic institutions and tendencies by the entire proletariat, a proletariat which leads its class struggle with a view to preparing for its victory over the bourgeoisie and the overthrow of the latter. This utilization is not an easy task, and for the "economists," the Tolstoyans, etc., it often seems to be as unlawful a concession to the "bourgeois" and the "opportunist" elements as is, according to P. Kievsky, the defense of self-determination of nations "in the epoch of finance capital." Marxism teaches that "the struggle against opportunism" by refusing to utilize democratic institutions in a *given* capitalist society—institutions which the bourgeoisie has created and which it corrupts—is a *complete capitulation* before opportunism!

It is the slogan of *civil war* for socialism which points out both the quickest escape from the imperialist war and *the connection* between our struggle against this war and the struggle against opportunism. Only this slogan adequately covers both the war-time peculiarities—the war continues and threatens to develop into a whole "epoch" of wars!—and the character of our activity in contrast to opportunism with its pacifism, with its legality, with its adaptability to "its own" bourgeoisie. But, besides that, the civil war against the bourgeoisie is a war which is *democratically* organized and waged by the poor masses against the propertied minority. The civil war is also a war, and consequently must inevitably put "force" in the place of right. But force in the name of the interests and the rights of the majority of the population is of another nature; it treads down "the rights" of the exploiters, of the bourgeoisie; it *cannot be realized* without a democratic organization of the army and the "rear." The civil war first of all and at once expropriates banks, factories, railways, large agricultural estates, etc. But it is precisely *for this very purpose* of expropriation that it is imperative to introduce the election by the people of all the officials and the army officers; to accomplish a *complete fusion* of the army, which wages war against the bourgeoisie, with the masses of the population; to introduce complete democracy in the matter of the control of food supplies, of production and distribution, etc. The purpose of the civil war is the seizure of banks, factories, shops, etc., the abolition of all opposition on the part of the bourgeoisie, the extermination of *its* army. But this aim can be attained *neither* from a purely military *nor* economic *nor* political standpoint without a simultaneous introduction and propagation of democracy among *our* troops and at *our* rear—an introduction and propagation which will develop in the course of that war. We tell the masses now (and the masses instinctively feel that we are right in this): "They deceive you with the great slogans of democracy while leading you into war for the sake of imperialist capitalism. You must lead and you will lead a *really* democratic war *against* the bourgeoisie and for the purpose of actually carrying out democracy and socialism." The present war unites and "fuses" the people into a coalition by means of force and financial dependence. *We,* in our civil war against the bourgeoisie, will *not* unite and consolidate the people by means of the power of the ruble, by the power of a club, by violence, but by a *voluntary* consent, by the consolidation of the toilers against the exploiters. For the bourgeoisie the proclamation of the equality of all nations has become a deception; for us it will be the truth which will facilitate and hasten the attraction to our side of all nations. Without actually organizing the relations between the nations on a *democratic basis*—and hence without granting freedom of secession—there can be *no* civil war of the workers and the toiling masses of all nations against the bourgeoisie.

We must proceed toward a socialist and consistently democratic organization of the proletariat against the bourgeoisie and against opportunism through the utilization of bourgeois democracy. There is no other path. A different "way out" is *not* a way out. Marxism knows no other way out, just as real life knows none. We must include in this policy free secession and free union among nations, rather than brush them aside or fear that their inclusion might "soil" the "purely" economic tasks.

["The Nascent Tendency of 'Imperialist Economism.' "
Lenin's Reply to Bukharin][144]

The old economism of 1894–1902 argued as follows: The Narodniks have been refuted; capitalism in Russia has been victorious; hence it is impossible to think of political revolutions. The practical deduction

[144] Lenin, "O rozhdaiushchemsia napravlenii imperialisticheskogo ekonomizma," *Sochineniia,* XXX, 250–56, first published in *Bolshevik,* No. 15, August 15, 1929, pp. 81–86. This article by V. I. Lenin represents one part of the discussion between the *Sotsial-Demokrat* and the Bukharin-Piatakov group. It was written in the spring or summer of 1916, i.e., upon Lenin's receipt of Bukharin's remarks on the theses of the editorial board of *Sotsial-Demokrat* on the question of the right of

w.ould be either "economic struggle for the workers, and political struggle for liberals"—this is a curvet to the right—or a general strike for a socialist overturn, instead of a political revolution—this is a curvet to the left, represented by a forgotten pamphlet of a Russian "economist" of the late 'nineties.

Now a new "economism" is being born which operates with two analogous curvets: "the rightward"—we are against "the right of self-determination" (i.e., against the liberation of oppressed peoples, against fighting annexations; this has not yet been thought out or completely expressed)—and the "leftward"—we are against the minimum program (i.e., against struggling for reforms and democracy), for this "contradicts" the socialist revolution.

A little more than a year has passed since this arising tendency manifested itself before a few comrades, namely, at the Berne Conference in the spring of 1915. At that time, fortunately, only one comrade [N. I. Bukharin]—who met with *general* disapproval—insisted upon these ideas of "imperialist economism" to the very end of the Conference and formulated them in written form as special "theses." *Nobody* subscribed to these theses.

Later on, two more persons subscribed to this comrade's theses against self-determination (without perceiving the inseparable connection between this question and the general position of the said "theses"). Furthermore, the appearance of the "Dutch program"[145] in February 1916, published in No. 3 of the *Bulletin* of the International Socialist Committee, had disclosed *at once* this "misunderstanding" and had *again* encouraged the author of the original "theses" to *resurrect* on this occasion his "imperialist economism" in its entire scope and not as applied to one seemingly "particular" point.

It is absolutely necessary *to warn* these comrades again and again that they have *slipped into a swamp;* that their "ideas" *have nothing in common either with Marxism or revolutionary social democracy.* This matter cannot be kept "under cover" any longer, for that would mean contributing to the ideological confusion and guiding it in the *worst possible direction,* namely, toward ambiguities, "private" conflicts, perpetual "frictions," etc. On the contrary, it is our duty to insist, absolutely and

nations to self-determination and before the issue of P. Kievsky's article, "Proletariat i pravo natsii na samoopredelenie," ("The proletariat and the right of nations to self-determination"). At this time negotiations were being conducted concerning the possible issue of a periodical or collection of articles jointly by the editorial board of the Central Organ and the publishers of *Kommunist,* G. Piatakov and E. B. Bosh, partisans of N. I. Bukharin's point of view. (*Bolshevik,* No. 15, August 15, 1929, p. 86, note.) The text of Bukharin's remarks has not been preserved. Cf. also Lenin, *Selected Works,* V, 372-73, note.

[145] See below, chapter v, p. 398.

categorically, that this must be thought over and that the questions raised must be thoroughly analyzed.

The editorial board of *Sotsial-Demokrat* in the theses on self-determination (published in German, as a reprint from *Vorbote*, No. 2)[146] has brought up this matter intentionally in the press in an impersonal but most detailed form, with special emphasis on the connection between the question of self-determination and the *general* question of struggle for reforms, for democracy, of the impermissibility of ignoring the political side of this matter, etc. In his remarks on the editorial board's theses on self-determination, the author of the original theses (of "imperialist economism") *expressed his solidarity with the Dutch program* and thereby showed especially plainly that the question of self-determination was not at all a "particular" question, as the authors of the arising tendency put it, but a general and fundamental question.

The program of the Dutch was received by the Zimmerwald Left between February 5 and 8 at the Berne meeting of the International Socialist Committee. Not a single member of the Left, *not even Radek,* pronounced himself in favor of this program; for it united in a confused fashion such points as "expropriation of banks," "the abolition of commercial customs and of the first chamber, the senate," etc. With barely a word, or without saying anything, but merely by shrugging their shoulders, the representatives of the Zimmerwald Left unanimously passed up the Dutch program as a program which was obviously inadequate as a whole.

However, the author of the original theses, written in the spring of 1915, liked this program so well that he declared: "I have said (in the spring of 1915) nothing essentially different, the Dutch *have arrived at the right thought: the economic side of their program consists in the expropriation of banks and large industries"* (enterprises), *"while the political side consists in a republic, etc. Entirely correct!"*

As a matter of fact the Dutch did not "arrive at the right thought," but submitted a rather *poorly thought out* program. The sad destiny of Russia is that some of our people grasp at what is precisely the least thought out part in the latest novelty ——.

The author of the 1915 theses thinks that the editorial board of *Sotsial-Demokrat* lapsed into a contradiction when it advanced "the expropriation of banks" even with the addition of the word "immediately" (plus "dictatorial measures") in Section 8 ("The concrete tasks"). "But, how I was scolded for this very same thing at Berne!" the author of the 1915 theses exclaims indignantly, recalling the Berne disputes in the spring of 1915.

This author forgot and overlooked a "trifle," namely, that the edi-

[146] See below, chapter vi, pp. 518–30.

torial board of *Sotsial-Demokrat* in Section 8 had analyzed clearly *two* alternatives : The first—the social revolution has already *begun,* in which case "an immediate expropriation of banks" is necessary, and so forth. The second alternative—the socialist revolution has *not* begun, in which case we should postpone speaking of these nice things.

Since *at present* it is a fact that the socialist revolution in the designated sense has not yet begun, the program of the Dutch is absurd. The author of the theses, however, "deepens" this matter by returning ("every time on that very spot ——")[147] to his old error of turning the political demands (such as "the abolition of the first chamber"?) into a "political formulation of a social revolution."

After marking time for a year the author returned to his old mistake. Here is the "chief reason" of his misadventure : he cannot solve the problem *how to connect imperialism with the struggle for reforms and with the struggle for democracy*—exactly as "economism," of blessed memory, failed to connect capitalism with the struggle for democracy.

Hence there is complete confusion in the question of the "impracticability" of the democratic demands under imperialism.

Hence there is an ignoring now, as usual, of the political struggle, an ignoring which is impermissible for a Marxist (and appropriate only in the mouth of an "economist," a *Rabochaia Mysl* partisan).

Hence a persistent trait of "wandering" from the *recognition* of imperialism to an *apology* for imperialism (as the "economists," blessed be their memory, "wandered" from the recognition of capitalism to an apology for capitalism), etc., etc.

It is impossible to analyze in every detail the mistakes of the author of the 1915 theses in his remarks to the theses of the editorial board of *Sotsial-Demokrat* on self-determination, for *every phrase is incorrect!* After all, it is impossible to write whole books or pamphlets in reply to mere "remarks"—if the initiators of "imperialist economism" have been marking time for a whole year stubbornly refusing to concern themselves with what constitutes their direct duty toward the party so long as they wish to take political questions seriously, namely, giving us a well thought out and complete exposition of what they call "our dissensions."

I am compelled to confine myself to pointing out briefly how the author applies his fundamental mistake, or how he is "supplementing" it.

The author thinks that I contradict myself : in 1914 (*Prosveshchenie*)[148] I wrote that it is absurd to seek self-determination in "*programs*

---

[147] A drunken *yamshchik* (coachman) in Gorbunov's story, "Na pochtovoi stantsii" (At the Post Station), uses these words to express his annoyance over the fact that he has once more overturned the carriage after bragging to his fare about his perfect knowledge of the local roads and his faultless driving.

[148] Lenin's article, "O prave natsii na samoopredelenie," *Prosveshchenie,* Nos. 4, 5, 6, April, May, and June, 1914. Reprinted in Lenin, *Sochineniia,* XVII, 427–74.

of Western European socialists," and then in 1916 I proclaim self-determination to be especially urgent.

The author did not bear in mind (!!) that "these programs" were written in 1875, 1880, and 1890.

Further, according to sections (the theses of the editorial board of *Sotsial-Demokrat* on self-determination) :

Section 1. There is the same "economist" unwillingness to see and pose political questions. *Since* socialism will create an economic basis for the abolition of national oppression in politics, our author, therefore, does not wish to formulate our *political tasks* in this realm! This is simply laughable!

Since the victorious proletariat does not repudiate wars against the bourgeoisie of other countries, the author, *therefore,* does not wish to formulate our political tasks in the realm of national oppression!! These are all examples of direct violations of Marxism and of logic or, if you wish, the manifestation of the kind of *logic* underlying the basic errors of "imperialist economism."

Section 2. The opponents of self-determination became unmercifully involved in references to "impracticability."

The editorial board of *Sotsial-Demokrat* explained to them the *two* possible meanings of impracticability, and their error in *both* cases.

On the other hand, the author of the 1915 theses, without even attempting to define *his own* understanding of "impracticability"—i.e., *accepting* our explanation that two different things are being confused here—*continues this confusion!!*

He connects the crises with the "imperialist policy"; our political economist *forgot* that there have been crises *before* imperialism ———!

To speak of the economic unrealizability of self-determination means to confuse, explains the editorial board. The author does *not* reply, does *not* declare that he considers self-determination impracticable *economically;* he cedes the disputed position by leaping over to politics—(it is "still" impracticable) though he had been told more than clearly that, *politically,* the republic would be as "impracticable" as self-determination under imperialism.

The author who has been thus cornered "leaps" again; now he accepts the republic and the entire minimum program merely as the "political formulation of a social revolution"!!!!

The author refuses—by leaping over to politics—to defend the "economic" impracticability of self-determination. He transfers political impracticability to the question of the entire minimum program. Here again there is not a grain of Marxism, not a grain of logic, besides the *logic of "imperialist economism."*

The author wishes *without attracting notice* (without straining his own thought and without giving anything integral, without making an effort to elaborate his own program) to discard the minimum program of the Social Democratic party! No wonder he has been marking time for a whole year!!

The question of struggle against *Kautskyism* as well is not a particular but a *general* and *fundamental* question of our time. The author *did not understand* this struggle. Just as the "economists" have been turning the struggle against the Narodniks into an apology for capitalism, so the author turns the struggle against Kautskyism into an apology for imperialism (this relates also to Section 3).

The error of Kautskyism is that it presents in a reformist fashion and at an inopportune time such democratic demands as cannot be presented otherwise than in a revolutionary manner (whereas the author wanders over to the interpretation that Kautskyism is wrong even in advancing these demands at all; in similar fashion the "economists" "misunderstood" the fight against populism because they regarded populism as implying "down with autocracy").

The error of Kautskyism is that it turns *correct* democratic demands back toward peaceful capitalism and not forward toward social revolution (whereas the author wanders over into the belief that such demands are incorrect).

Section 3. See above. The question of "federation" is *also* dodged by the author. This is the same basic shortcoming of the same "economism": inability to present political questions.[149]

Section 4. "Defense of the fatherland is derived from self-determination," the author repeats stubbornly. His mistake here is that he wishes to make the repudiation of defense of the fatherland a *pattern,* to draw conclusions not from the concrete historic peculiarity of *this* war but "generally speaking." This is not Marxism.

The author has been told this and he has not refuted it: try to think of a formulation of struggle against national oppression or national inequality, a formulation which would *not* justify "defense of the fatherland." You cannot do it.

Does that mean that we are against fighting national oppression, if defense of the fatherland *can* be derived from it?

No, for we are not "generally" against "defense of the fatherland" (see resolution of our party) but only against the *embellishment* of this *imperialist* war by this deceitful slogan.

The author wishes to present the question of "defense of the father-

---

[149] "We are not afraid of disintegrations," writes the author; "we do not defend state boundaries." Try and give an exact political formulation of that!! The crux of the matter is that *you can not do that;* you are prevented by the "economist" blindness in questions of *political democracy.* [Author's note.]

land" *unhistorically* and *fundamentally* falsely (but he fails to do this; he shows here as he did for a whole year only painful efforts) ——.

The speeches about "dualism" show that the author *does not understand* what is monism and what is dualism.

If I "combine" a shoebrush with a mammal, will this be "monism"?

If I say that to reach the aim *"a"* we have to go

$$b \rightarrow a \leftarrow c$$

from *"c"* leftwards, and from *"b"* rightwards, will this be "dualism"?

Are the positions of the proletariat of oppressed and oppressing nations with respect to national oppression alike? No, they are not alike. They do not coincide *economically, politically, ideologically, spiritually, or any other way.*

Hence?

Hence from various starting points some will arrive at this *single* aim (the fusion of nations) by *one route,* and others *by another.* Repudiation of this would be "monism" and would mean combining a shoebrush with a mammal.

"The proletarians of an oppressed nation should *not* be told this" (to be *in favor* of self-determination)—that is how the author "understands" the theses of the editorial board.

This is a curious thing!! *Nothing of this kind* has been said in the theses. The author has either not read them thoroughly or has not put much strain on his mind.

Section 5. See above concerning Kautskyism.

Section 6. The author is told of three *types* of countries in the world. The author "objects" by seizing upon "special cases." This is casuistry and not politics.

You wish to know about a "special case"; and "how about Belgium?"

See the pamphlet of Lenin and Zinoviev [*Socialism and War*]. It says there that we would be *for* Belgium's defense (even by means of a war) if this war were different.

You disagree with this?

Say so!!

You *did not think out* the question of *why* Social Democracy is against "the defense of the fatherland."

We are against it but not for the reason you think—for your presentation of the question (painful efforts and not presentation) is unhistorical. This is my reply to the author.

To term as "sophistry" the fact that we, in *justifying the war waged for the overthrow of national oppression,* do not justify the present imperialist war—which is waged by *both* sides *for the sake* of strengthening national oppression—is to use a "strong" word but *not to reason in the least.*

The author *wishes* to pose the question of "defense of the fatherland" in a "more leftward" fashion, whereas there results a continuous confusion (for a whole year already).

Section 7. The author makes the following *criticism:* "the question of the 'peace terms' in general has not been touched at all."

What a criticism! A question which we have not raised here at all has not been touched!!

But after all the question of annexation in which the "imperialist economists" have become entangled—this time together with the Dutch and Radek—has been "touched" and raised here.

Either you repudiate an immediate slogan *"against old and new annexations"* (no less "impracticable" under imperialism than is self-determination—in Europe as well as in the colonies)—and then your apology for imperialism turns from a covert into an open one or you recognize this slogan (as Radek has done in the press)—and then you have recognized self-determination of nations under a different name!!!

Section 8. The author proclaims "Bolshevism on a Western European scale" ("not your position," he adds).

I do not attribute significance to the desire to hold on to the word "Bolshevism," for I know *some* "old Bolsheviks" from whom may God preserve me. I can only say that "Bolshevism on a Western European scale" which the author proclaims, according to my profound conviction is neither Bolshevism nor Marxism but rather a petty version of the same old "economism."

To my mind it is inadmissible, frivolous, and unpartisanlike in the extreme to proclaim *new Bolshevism* for a whole year and be satisfied with this. Is it not time now to *stop and think* and give to the comrades something that would expound thoroughly and coherently this "Bolshevism on a Western European scale"?

The author has not proved and will not prove (as applied to this question) the distinction between colonies and the oppressed nations in Europe.

Among the Dutch[150] and the P.S.D. [Social Democracy of Poland and Lithuania] the repudiation of self-determination *is not merely* and, even not so much, a confusion—for Gorter has actually recognized it as did the Zimmerwald declaration of the Poles[151]—as it is a result of a special state of things within their nations (small nations with *secular* traditions and claims for *Great Power status*).

---

[150] Lenin has in mind the Left Dutch Social Democrats (D. Wijnkoop, A. Pannekoek, Gorter, Roland-Holst), who in 1909 split away from the official Social Democratic Labor party and formed the Social Democratic party of Holland. (*Bolshevik,* No. 15, August 15, 1929, p. 86, note 1.)

[151] See below, chapter iv, pp. 335–37.

It is supreme lack of thought and supreme naïveté if one imitates and repeats mechanically and uncritically what in other countries has grown up for decades as a result of the struggle against the nationalist bourgeoisie which has been deceiving the people. It is *precisely* this which should not be imitated that these folks have imitated!

THE IMPERIALIST PIRATE STATE

[Bukharin's Idea of the State and the Correct Attitude of the Workers toward It][152]

I

The most important question of tactics of our time is the question of the so-called defense of the country. For that is exactly where the line of separation is drawn between the entire bourgeois and the entire proletarian world. This word itself contains a deception, for it concerns not really the country as such, i.e., its *population,* but the *state organization,* the *state.* . . . .

The state is an *historical* concept. This means that the state is not a permanent social law but a transitional social form. In other words: the state arises only at a certain stage of development and must vanish in another stage of development. It arises as an organization of the ruling class, and this is its *nature.* It is the organization of "the ruling class which is most powerful economically and which, through the medium of the state, becomes also a ruling class politically, thus acquiring new means for the suppression and the exploitation of the oppressed class." (F. Engels, *Ursprung der Familie, usw.,* p. 137.) The conception of the state presupposes, therefore, the conception of class rule. A state without classes is, therefore, just as absurd as, for example, capitalism without classes, or as dry water. *K. Marx* has expressed this in the following words: "Even the radical and revolutionary politicians," he wrote (*Kritische Randglossen, usw.,* Nachlass B., II, 50), "are seeking the cause of evil not in the nature of the state but in a definite form of state which they wish to replace by a different form of state." Entirely different are

---

[152] "Nota Bene" [N. I. Bukharin], "Der imperialistische Raubstaat" *Jugend-Internationale,* No. 6, December 1, 1916, pp. 7–9. Lenin's reply charging Bukharin with errors in respect to the difference between anarchists and socialists in their attitude toward the state was published in *Sbornik Sotsial-Demokrata,* No. 2, December 1916, pp. 76–77, reprinted in Lenin, *Sochineniia,* XIX, 294–97, and translated in Lenin, *Selected Works,* V, 241–45. Lenin promised to return to this subject and shortly before the outbreak of the revolution in the spring of 1917 began to prepare an article on the state which was to be published with Bukharin's article in No. 4 of *Sbornik Sotsial-Demokrata.* This article was not finished then, but Lenin's notes, which are preserved in the Marx-Engels-Lenin Institute, were used in writing his "State and Revolution." Cf. Lenin, *Sochineniia,* XIX, 479, note 155.

the aims of the socialists: "All socialists," asserts F. Engels (Italian article, "Dell' Autorità," published in *Neue Zeit,* 32, I, 39), "agree that the state, and with it political authority, will vanish owing to the future social revolution; this means that the public functions will lose their political expression and will become transformed into simple administrative functions for the protection of social interests." Engels likewise writes in *Anti-Dühring* (a work which, as known, was carefully read, practically revised, and partly written by Marx) that the state "dies off." He advances the same prognosis also in the *Ursprung der Familie.* The society which organizes production anew on the basis of free and equal association of producers transfers the entire state mechanism to the place where it really belongs: into museums of antiquities, along with the spinning wheel and the bronze axe (p. 140).[153] With the abolition of class relationships the political expression of this relationship—the state —is abolished also, and a socialist society is formed without classes and without a state.

The state is the most general organization of the ruling class; this means that not merely a few strata but the entire exploited class constitute the object of exploitation. The state is a tremendous, monstrous machine for extortion, which exploits the people directly and which also serves the purpose of preserving all conditions of "normal" exploitation, guarding them and propagating them. If threatened, the state comes forth against its "enemies" with its entire force, chiefly military force. Externally these offensives are wars; internally they are brutal suppressions of rebels. The power of arms and murder has thus become a brazen law of the state, of *every* form of state without exception. It is only in a matter of degree that this phenomenon differs and changes with the type of state, which, in turn, is determined by the world and the national economic development. It is precisely in our time that with the formation of *imperialist* states general militarization acquires gigantic, unprecedented dimensions.

II

The state is an all-embracing organization of the rulers. In the pre-imperialist epoch this actually *was* the organization of the state. An especially important sphere of social life—economy—was entirely in a

---

153 We wish to take this opportunity to remark that the idea is incorrect that the difference between socialists and anarchists is that the former are in favor of a state and the others are against a state. The difference, however, lies in the fact that the revolutionary Social Democracy wishes to establish a new centralized social production—i.e., which would be technically progressive—while the decentralized anarchist production would mean merely a step backward to old technique and form of enterprise. [Author's note.]

chaotic condition. The individual enterprise, the capitalist who "works" by himself and confronts only his workers, the capitalist to whom the state assures only general conditions of his "right of exploitation"— these are typical of former economy. It is different now. The individual capitalist has become an associated capitalist. The rapid vanishing of the middle class, the victorious progress of large capital have called forth some new forms of economic life, which, naturally, have originated as special forms of class life. The formation of unions of owners of enterprises, of trusts, of syndicates, and so forth, and their mutual connections through combined enterprises and the large banks have changed entirely the old forms. And if, for the pre-imperialist epoch, *individual* capital ownership was characteristic, then for present-day financial capitalist economy, a *collective* ownership by capitalists united with each other by some organization is characteristic. This same process can, however, be noticed not only in economy. It spreads over the entire realm of class life, and if the working class for its own sake establishes trade unions, political organizations, co-operatives, educational clubs, etc., the bourgeoisie does it on a larger scale. In this manner various bourgeois class organizations are formed. . . . . But this does not conclude the process of organization. *All these organizations have a tendency to fuse with one another and to become transformed into one organization of the rulers.* This is the newest step of development, and one which has become *especially* apparent *during* the *war*. . . . . *So there comes into being a single, all-embracing organization, the modern imperialist pirate state, an omnipotent organization of bourgeois dominance, with innumerable functions,* with gigantic power, with spiritual (various methods of obscurantisms: the church, the press, the school, etc.) as well as material methods (police, soldiery). . . . . In this we see the dialectics of history: *the state, which at first was the only organization of the ruling class, transforms itself into a group of organizations one beside the other, and this group by drawing in all other organizations again becomes a single organization.* This is the present-day monster, the modern Leviathan.[154]

III

The development of world economy is leading toward an extremely harsh reciprocal struggle between "national economies" organized into states. In turn, the imperialist wars have an effect upon the state structure. And if the type described above is, so to speak, an ideal picture of the imperialist state, and if only the most advanced states have at-

---

[154] By the sugar-coated phrase "war socialism" the yellow "Social Democrats" are only trying to adorn the imperialist pirate state. [Author's note.]

tained this stage, then each day, and especially each day of *war,* tends to make this fact general. This compels the proletariat to adapt itself to the new situation. It is clear that the imperialist pirate state (we call it *pirate* because externally its "cultural mission" consists of systematically robbing weak nations, colonial lands, etc.) is the highest form of the bourgeois class organization. This organization's means of power are gigantic. Recall merely present-day militarism. The workers, therefore, are confronted with the united forces of the entire bourgeoisie. They can crush this force only with a greater force, which is the *force of the masses.* Mass actions are the inevitable means of a victorious struggle. But now more than ever it is necessary for Social Democracy, which is, or should be at least, the educator of the masses, to manifest its fundamental opposition to the state. He who drives the workers into mutual destruction, as the present-day social patriots are doing, under the pretext of defense of the country (for in reality it is an onslaught against the *state,* the worst enemy of the socialist proletariat) is a betrayer of socialism.

The present war has shown how deeply the roots of statehood have penetrated into the souls of the workers. But this war has also shown that this psychology is becoming less and less effective. It is a process which has certain analogies in the previous epoch. As before, the workers, who under patriarchal conditions have lived with their masters, have considered the interests of their exploiters to be their own interests, so now the proletarians are fighting for the interests of their exploiters and plunderers. But as the factory hammer has destroyed these idyllic relations, so *imperialism* will annihilate the servility of the workers and, under the pressure of the war and of mad oppression, the proletariat will declare the only "just war" to be war against the rule of capital.

THE *KOMMUNIST* CONTROVERSY

Selections from Lenin's Letters to Shliapnikov, March–June, 1916

[To Shliapnikov, Christiania, March 1916][155]

Dear Friend!   [Zürich]

I want to talk to you in detail concerning your letter and the mention in it of the usual reproach for my "noncompliance."[156]

---

[155] Lenin, *Sochineniia,* XXIX, 228–33. Another translation is in *The Letters of Lenin,* pp. 386–90.

[156] In his letter of March 11, 1916, Shliapnikov had written, among other things, "Your misunderstandings with K-ists [G. L. Piatakov and E. B. Bosh and others] have produced an extremely bad impression upon us. All sorts of doubts

As for James, he could never find his way through politics. He always was against a breach. He is an excellent person, James, but his judgments *on these topics* are profoundly incorrect.

In Russia (and now also in the new International) the question of a breach is *fundamental*. Any compliance *here* would have been a crime. I know well how many good-natured people (James, Galerka, the Petersburg "friends" from the intellectuals) have been *against* a breach in the Duma group. They were all a thousand times wrong. The breach was absolutely necessary. A breach with *Chkheidze and Co.* also *is imperative* at present. Whoever vacillates in that respect is an *enemy* of the proletariat and the attitude toward them should be one of *noncompliance*.

Who is vacillating? Not only Trotsky and Co. but also Yurii [Piatakov] and Evg. B. [Bosh] (as early as this summer they were "making scenes" because of Chkheidze!!). Furthermore, the *Poles* (the opposition) whose *Gazeta Robotnicza*, No. 25, contains their resolution, are again *starting to vacillate* as in Brussels on August 3/16, 1914.[157]

With regard to them it is *noncompliance* that is obligatory.

Radek is the best one of them; it has been *useful* to work *with* him (incidentally, for the Zimmerwald Left also) and we have worked. But *Radek vacillates* also. Our tactic here is two-sided (Yurii + Nikolai Ivanovich [Bukharin] did not want to understand it or else they were unable to understand it): on the one hand, *to help* Radek move to the Left and to *unite* everybody whom it is possible to unite for the Zimmerwald Left; on the other hand, not to allow a bit of vacillation *in fundamentals*.

The fundamental is a split with the Organization Committee, with Chkheidze and Co.

The Poles *vacillate* and they issued the most odious resolution *after* the issue of *Kommunist,* No. 1.

What is the inference?

That we will hold on to the name of *Kommunist* and *open the doors* to *disputes* and *vacillations;* to letters (of Radek, Bronski, perhaps of

have emerged in many comrades regarding 'Lenin's' unaccommodating disposition with respect to the comrades, his tactlessness, etc. With our lack of men we should be more considerate of our partisans. We all (including James [A. I. Elizarova]) demand that you restore *Kommunist* and come to an agreement with the contributors and *Kommunist*-editors. ...." This letter is preserved in the archives of the Marx-Engels-Lenin Institute and helps to determine the date of Lenin's letter. (Lenin, *Sochineniia,* XXIX, 231, note 1.)

[157] The Conference was held on July 16–17 (3–4), 1914, and is discussed in chapter i, pp. 104–7. The Rozlomovists, a group of Polish S.D.'s, voted at this Conference with the majority and against the Bolsheviks. The *Gazeta Robotnicza,* No. 25, January 1916, contains a resolution of the editorial board favorable to the position of *Nashe Slovo.* (Lenin, *Sochineniia,* XXIX, 232–33, note 2.)

Pannekoek, etc.) addressed to the editorial board, to complaints, to whimpering, gossiping, etc.?

Not for the world!

This is harmful to the cause.

This means help for the scoundrels from the Organization Committee, for Chkheidze and Co.

Not for the world.

Kommunist was a temporary bloc for the attainment of a definite aim. The aim had been attained: the magazine came out, the rapprochement (it was possible *at that time, prior to* Zimmerwald) was attained. Now it is necessary to go along a *different* road, to go onward.

Kommunist has become *harmful.* It must be discontinued and replaced by a *different* name: "Sbornik Sotsial-Demokrata" (under the editorship of the *editorial board of Sotsial-Demokrat*).

Only thus shall we evade a dispute, evade vacillations.

In Russia there is also discord, isn't there? Oh, of course! But *it is not our task to augment it.* Let Chkheidze and Co., Trotsky and Co. concern themselves with the increase of discords (it is their "profession") while our task is to pursue our policy. The results of *such* work are visible: the Petersburg workers are a hundred times better than the Petersburg intellectuals (even than the "sympathizers" ——).

With "the three" (Yurii + Evg. Bosh + Nik. Iv.) we had to make *temporary* concessions, since *at that time* it was impossible otherwise to publish the magazine (now it can be done), and the main thing is that at that time we did not see Evg. Bosh + Yurii at *work* and could still hope that the *work* would lead them *upward.*

But they went downward.

It is imperative to dissolve the temporary alliance. Only in that way will the *cause* not suffer and only in that way can *they* be taught.

We are not at all against a *discussion.* We are against giving editorial rights to those who have manifested unpardonable vacillation (perhaps on account of their youth? Well, then, let us wait; perhaps in five years they may straighten out).

Nik. Iv. is a studious economist, and we have always supported him *in that.* But he is (1) gullible to gossip and (2) devilishly *unstable* in politics.

The war has driven him to semianarchist ideas. At the Conference at which the Berne resolutions were passed (in the spring of 1915) he presented some theses[158] (I have them) which were the height of stupidity: a shame; semianarchism.

I attacked these theses severely. Yurii and Evg. Bosh listened and were satisfied that I was not permitting any tendency toward the Left

---

[158] See above, pp. 187–89.

(they, at that time, declared their complete disagreement with Nik. Iv.). Half a year elapsed. Nik. Iv. studied economics and *did not* concern himself with politics.

And now on the question of self-determination *he* gives us *the same* nonsense, and Evg. Bosh + Yurii sign it!! (Procure their "theses"[159] from Nik. Iv. and my answer to him.[160])

But the question is important; the question is urgent and connected inextricably with the question of *annexations*—a most burning question. These people have neither meditated, read, nor studied. They have listened two or three times to Radek (he has the old "Polish" disease; he got entangled) and have *signed hastily.*

This is a scandal. This is a disgrace. They are not editors. These people must be refuted, must be exposed, must be given time to study and to meditate, and there is no need to be in a hurry to pamper them; there are your editorial rights—take your nonsense to the workers!!

If so, then they will *carry* the matter to a polemic in the press; and then I shall be *compelled* to call them "imperialist economists," to show their *complete* blankness, *complete* unseriousness, and lack of consistent meditation. A polemic in the press will repel them *for long years to come.*

But should *Kommunist* be discontinued now they would think it over and give up that nonsense; they would do some reading and convince themselves. Well, my dears, write a serious *pamphlet,* since you announce that there are "dissensions" in politics (with which you have never concerned yourselves, and which you have never studied). Let us have it! They will think it over and *won't* give us a pamphlet. And in a few months this will "blow over."

Thus it has been and thus it will be.

In the question of annexations (and of self-determination) our position (the resolution of 1913)[161] has been *fully* confirmed by the war. And this question has become a burning question; while Radek + the Dutch (Gorter and Pannekoek) obviously got mixed up.[162] In the *Sbornik Sotsial-Demokrata* we shall explain this matter over and over again.[163]

[159] See above, pp. 219–21.

[160] The editors of Lenin, *Sochineniia,* state that this letter to N. I. Bukharin in reply to the theses has not been found.   [161] See chapter vi, p. 528, n. 36.

[162] The editors of Lenin, *Sochineniia,* state that Lenin has in mind: (1) K. B. Radek's article, "Das Selbstbestimmungsrecht der Völker," *Lichtstrahlen,* No. 3, December 5, 1915, pp. 50–54; (2) Radek's theses, "Thesen über Imperialismus und nationale Unterdrückung," *Vorbote,* No. 2, April 1916, pp. 44–51 (see below, chapter vi, pp. 507–18); (3) H. Gorter's pamphlet, *Der Imperialismus, der Weltkrieg und die Sozialdemokratie.*

[163] See Lenin's article, "Itogi diskussii o samoopredelenii," published in *Sbornik Sotsial-Demokrata,* No. 1, October 1916, pp. 11–28 (and below, pp. 531–32).

The matter must be conducted so as:

(1) to discontinue *Kommunist.*

(2) to give *as many* indulgences, rights, and privileges as possible to Yurii + Evg. Bosh in the publication of a miscellany about the Jews (*here* it would be harmless to the *cause*). Detailed conditions could be furnished in a written agreement.

(3) the same with regard to their transport group (procure from them their statutes and our corrections to them).

(4) We shall issue *Sbornik Sotsial-Demokrata* under the editorship of "the editorial board of *Sotsial-Demokrat.*"

We shall invite them as contributors. We shall tell them: if there are dissensions, then prepare a serious pamphlet! *We shall pledge ourselves to publish it* (they will not write it, they have not even started to think seriously about that question, have not even concerned themselves with it!!).

This would be a *practical* policy.

Evg. Bosh has been intending all the time to go to Russia; she could be of use there; *there is no work for her here;* she'll be inventing work.

Are you familiar with this foreign *calamity:* "the invention" of work for those who sit abroad? An awful calamity.

Well, I conclude for the present. Gather up all documents and inform yourself. We shall talk again and again.

Yours,

Lenin

P.S. I enclose a copy of my reply to N. I. Bukharin on the topic of the significance of the new "dissensions."

[To Shliapnikov, Christiania, March–April, 1916][164]

[Zürich]

Dear Aleksandr:

I wrote to you briefly yesterday.[165] I would like to talk some more today.

The "conditions" offered by the "Japanese"[166] have roused me to the depths of my soul. To give to two editors the right to insert a con-

---

[164] Lenin, *Sochineniia,* XXIX, 239–41.

[165] The editors of Lenin, *Sochineniia,* state that this letter has not been found.

[166] A draft agreement drawn up by Piatakov and sent by Shliapnikov to Lenin. It provided among other things that P. and N. Kievsky (Piatakov and Bosh) be recognized as founders of the publishing house and its responsible representatives; that editorial articles should conform to the party program but that a "polemical section" might include articles by members of the board who disagree with the majority on a particular question of party program or tactics and for this the consent of only two editors was required. (Lenin, *Sochineniia,* XXIX, 240, note 2.)

tributor's argument!! Not even to three editors, but to two—hence, the publishers "confide" in no one except themselves.

The meaning of this point is clear: it reveals a wish to hide behind Radek and to *promote* our dissensions with him and the P.S.D.'s [Polish Social Democrats]. This is not an argument but the height of intrigue, the height of meanness. It amounts to the same thing as the attempts that were made in Paris to force us to publish the argument of Rappoport, or Leva, or Viktorenok, or Bogdanov in 1911!!! I wrote you that the Polish *Gazeta Robotnicza* (February 1916) came out against us exactly as did those Parisians of former days.

On no account shall I enter an editorial board which practices such intriguing, such hiding behind argument. You wish to promote the disintegration of our party, Messrs. Japanese. Then do it upon *your own* responsibility. Your purse is full. Publish yourselves the "argument" of Radek and of *Gazeta Robotnicza;* then the *Russian* workers will see at once that you are intriguers and will chase you out. You wish to *carry* through this villainy under *the cloak* of a "joint editorial board." Pardon me, but I shall not accede to that and shall expose you.

This is my answer to the Japanese on that score.

Likewise, with regard to "equality of rights" (the elimination of the seventh member of the editorial board or of his vote). This is a continuation of the old "game." Partyism has nothing to do with it. Shall we give "equality of rights" to people who have proved themselves *obstructors!!* To what purpose? Equality of rights = the right to spoil the work! In the name of what? Why? To *perpetuate* quarrels?

No; if you wish to make a *new* experiment, then take a *new* periodical, or better, a *miscellany,* and let us *try* (the old confidence has been damaged) to issue one miscellany with an editorial board of seven. Let us make that *experiment.* This is the maximum concession which I might, honestly speaking, make. Should that experiment fail, the Messrs. intriguers and capitalists won't lose anything, since "the purse" can be taken away at any time. Then we shall issue our own collection of articles simply, plainly, without a brawl.

I shake your hand and beg you to have patience.

Yours,

LENIN

[To Shliapnikov, Christiania, June 1916][167]

[ZÜRICH]

DEAR ALEKSANDR!

Apparently the delay in our correspondence and *a number* of misunderstandings were due to the fact that you did not get our second letter

---

[167] Lenin, *Sochineniia,* XXIX, 263–65; another translation is in *The Letters of Lenin,* pp. 394–97.

sent to Stockholm.[168] I cannot explain, otherwise, *how* you could have written that we were not answering your inquiries. We have answered *everything* in super-detail. *You* were *not* answering us. Nadezhda Konstantinovna has written continuously. It will be necessary to store up patience and to repeat certain things so as to obtain results. It is necessary to come to an understanding by letter.

You wrote with regard to *Kommunist* that the breach with Chkheidze is not open to question. On whose part? On the part of Bukharin and Co.!

Haven't I written that it concerns *not* Bukharin and Co. but *Radek and Co.?*

Kommunist was our temporary bloc with two groups or elements: (1) Bukharin and Co., (2) Radek and Co. Up to now it has been *possible* to proceed with them; and this has been *imperative*. At present *it is impossible*. Thus it is necessary to separate, or more correctly, to draw aside *temporarily*.

The Poles passed a resolution in the *summer* of 1915 (*after* Nos. 1 and 2 of *Kommunist*) which again showed their fluctuation in the question about Chkheidze[169] but did not publish this resolution *until 1916*. Will it pay *now* to give them the *opportunity* and the *right* (they are contributors to *Kommunist!!*) to intrude in the periodical and spoil it by quarreling?

In my opinion it will not pay. It would be much more profitable for the cause to take on a different name ("Sbornik Sotsial-Demokrata") and to *wait* until the Poles complete their education (or until they pass over to Germany) or until the situation changes.

Further, concerning Bukharin and Co, I shall send you, without fail (but not very quickly, since it depends upon a trip to Berne) Bukharin's *spring* "theses" of 1915. Then you will see what the essentials are.

1. In the spring of 1915 Bukharin wrote (at the Conference!) certain theses in which he obviously rolled into a *swamp*. The "Japanese" were *against* him. Therefore, we acceded temporarily to "maximum indulgences" in *Kommunist* so as to create conditions suitable for *clearing up* the matter, namely, whether or not Bukharin's vacillations might be overcome in a "comradely manner" and whether or not E.B. [Evgeniia Bosh], who calls herself a Bolshevik, would help us to do so.

2. In the summer of 1915 (or in the autumn) Bukharin + three persons, the *"Japanese,"* signed the theses on self-determination. These theses, according to our conviction, are *super-false* and form a *repetition* of Bukharin's mistakes.

---

[168] This letter has not been found. (Lenin, *Sochineniia,* XXIX, 263, note.)
[169] See below, chapter iv, pp. 335–37.

3. In the beginning of 1916 Bukharin, on the question concerning the "Dutch program" (from No. 3 of the *Bulletin of the International Socialist Committee*)[170] *again* returned to the ideas of the spring theses of 1915!!!

What is the inference? A bloc is *also* impossible here; it is necessary to *wait* until Bukharin's vacillations cease. A magazine issued as an organ of the Polish-Bukharin vacillations *would be harmful*. It would, in this state of affairs, be harmful to hold on to the old name and not to be clever enough to choose another name (*Sbornik Sotsial-Demokrata*).

The non-partyism and the unscrupulous conduct of the "Japanese" are evident in their wish to shift the responsibility for *their own* vacillations *upon us*. Excuse me, my dears, we shall not let you do it! If you wish to be partisans, then you will help, partially with money, the publication of *Sbornik Sotsial-Demokrata* in which we (we do not vacillate) will analyze your errors in a comradely way, *without* naming you, *without giving* enemies an opportunity to triumph and rejoice.

And, furthermore, if the "Japanese" had approached seriously this super-serious question of dissensions abroad then (*il n'y a qu'un pas* to a separate group abroad!!—believe me, I have been observing this for almost twenty years!!), they would have forced themselves to work hard over the dissension, to meditate, to study (they have *neither* meditated *nor* studied, but simply *blurted out*); they would have expounded comprehensively *their* dissensions, either in a manuscript—for a close group of the leading comrades (who could have helped *not* to carry this question into the press)— or in a pamphlet, if *they* wish "to come out in print" (they have money).

Then *they themselves* would have answered for their ideas. This is imperative. If you wish to teach the workers new truths, then *answer for those truths* but do not shift the responsibility upon us, do not hide (we are nothing, so they say let Lenin and Co. answer before the party for this "argument," i.e., for the triumph of the enemies).

No, amiable ones!! This cock won't fight!! I shall not answer for *your* vacillations. We shall publish *Sbornik Sotsial-Demokrata* even without your help, Messrs. "Japanese." We shall give you a *postponement* to think it over, to analyze, to *decide* finally whether or not you wish to take upon yourselves the responsibility for the new confusion. If you wish only to *"set us against"* the Poles and the Dutch in the Russian press, we shall *not* let you do it.

This is the state of affairs. Here are my considerations; and I repeat that I shall send you, without fail, the spring theses of Bukharin, so that you may judge about the whole situation *from documents*.

---

[170] See below, chapter v, p. 398. It is not known to which of Bukharin's articles Lenin refers.

Nadezhda Konstantinovna is writing today about self-determination. We are *not* for partitioning. And what about the question of *annexations?* Bukharin and Co. (as well as Radek and Rosa Luxemburg and Pannekoek) have not thought out what it really means to be "against old and new annexations" (the formula given by Radek in the *press*)!![171] Well, it is *exactly* "self-determination of nations," but expressed in *different* words! Now then! Until next time,

Yours,

LENIN

The *Kommunist* affair was the subject of many other letters in the summer of 1916 between Shliapnikov in Christiania and Lenin, Krupskaia, and Zinoviev in Switzerland. Zinoviev wrote May 17 that while he agreed with Lenin completely in his evaluation of imperialist economism he did not agree that it was yet necessary to break with Radek and Co. Shliapnikov felt as Zinoviev did that it was unprofitable to quarrel with the Left Zimmerwaldists and he wrote Lenin that he was exaggerating the importance of the "constitution" of the *Kommunist,* for the intentions of the publishers were not malicious. But his efforts at a compromise failed and to Lenin Shliapnikov confessed that he was greatly bored by the whole business. Lenin, however, insisted that the matter was serious, that Radek and his friends were playing politics and had succeeded in turning Lenin and Zinoviev out of the editorial board of *Vorbote,* the newly established organ of the Zimmerwald Left, and that the proposal of Piatakov and Bosh would merely promote the dispute with Radek and with the Left Zimmerwaldists. "That is why I said, and am saying now," wrote Lenin, "that not for the world would I now join the *Kommunist,* nor will I accede to an equality of rights with the 'Japanese' woman [Bosh], nor *in general* participate along *with* Radek in our miscellany, for I am con-

---

171 Lenin quotes from K. Radek's article: "Annexionen und Sozialdemokratie," *Beilage zur Berner Tagwacht,* Nos. 252 and 253, October 28 and 29, 1915, p. 1. (Lenin, *Sochineniia,* XXIX, 265, note 7.)

vinced that *this* would make a quarrel with the Lefts inevitable."[172]

The attempts at compromise having failed, the *Kommunist* was discontinued and Lenin answered Bukharin, Radek, and other Left Zimmerwaldists in the pages of the *Sbornik Sotsial-Demokrata*.[173] These dissensions created so much bitterness that Shliapnikov, on his return to Russia late in 1916, laid the matter before the Bureau of the Central Committee of the R.S.D.L. party. The Bureau, in order to prevent a widening of the breach, adopted a resolution in which it stated that it (1) agreed with the fundamental policy of the Central Committee expressed in *Sotsial-Demokrat;* (2) opposed the transformation of the publications of the Central Committee into polemical publications; (3) considered that differences on separate questions between certain collaborators and the editorial board should not exclude these collaborators from participating in the publications of the Central Committee; and (4) proposed to make use of dissenting materials *published privately* by Bolsheviks in Russia and abroad in the issue of a special collection of articles of a polemical character.[174]

WITHIN THE RANKS OF THE PARTY ÉMIGRÉS

[From Shliapnikov's Recollections of the Bukharin-Piatakov Group and the *Kommunist* Controversy][175]

During the time of my stay in Russia strong dissensions developed within the group of our workers abroad. The former editorial board of *Kommunist* disintegrated on account of controversies concerning the national question. As always under the conditions of émigré life, these dissensions produced animosity between the two sides, and at the time of my arrival [abroad] the relations between our comrades in Switzerland (V. I. Lenin, G. Zinoviev, and others) on the one hand, and those who lived in Sweden (Comrades N. I. Bukharin, G. Piatakov, etc.) on

---

[172] Lenin's letter to Shliapnikov, June 17, 1916, in Lenin, *Sochineniia*, XXIX, 257–61; other letters from Lenin relating to the *Kommunist* affair are given in his *Sochineniia*, XXIX, 247–50, 254–56.

[173] See below, chapter vi, pp. 531–32.

[174] Shliapnikov, *Kanun semnadtsatago goda* (3d ed.), II, 72.

[175] Shliapnikov, *Kanun semnadtsatogo goda,* I, 153–56.

the other hand, were greatly strained. This had a bad effect primarily on the contacts and the activity for and with Russia which for me were more important than everything else. . . . .

I had to act as a "buffer" in those dissensions and attempt to reconcile the two sides by emphasizing the necessity of not hampering the publication of periodicals for Russia by these dissensions. During two whole months I pursued a policy of "reconciliation" but was forced to give it up, since both sides began to manifest pettiness. *Sbornik Sotsial-Demokrata* appeared in place of *Kommunist*.

One worker by the name of Bagrovsky, in the Stockholm group, which dealt with the transport of literature to Russia, proved to be unworthy of the confidence placed in him. He got in contact with a suspicious group of Estonians—particularly with a certain fellow, Keskula—accepted money, pretending it was "for party purposes," for the publication of pamphlets, etc., issued receipts for it on official blanks of the Central Committee of the R.S.D.L. party left by me, and made use of my French stamp of the representative of the R.S.D.L. party. This was accidentally disclosed by N. I. Bukharin. Bagrovsky was excluded from the party, and the Swedish comrades were notified to that effect. Comrade Bukharin conducted some investigations in that affair and got wind of an organization of provocateurs, which was endeavoring to trap Russian revolutionaries, the young Swedish socialists, etc. Keskula proved to be an agent of the German General Staff. A friend of his, who was in charge of one of the departments of the Russian Insurance Company in Stockholm, was likewise an agent. Apparently the investigations of our comrades—N. I. Bukharin and G. Piatakov—had annoyed the Swedish police to such an extent that Bukharin, who was living under the name of "Moisha Dolgolevsky," was arrested and deported, and the same thing happened soon after to G. Piatakov. The arrests and the deportations were explained as due to our comrades' participation in the Congress of the Swedish socialist youth; this, however, was not quite correct, since the comrades were only guests at the Congress. I was also present at that Congress, but the police made no inquiries about me. The police terror had at that time reached unprecedented dimensions in Sweden. . . . . The police were looking carefully for a connection between the young Swedish socialists and the Russian revolutionaries. This led to the destruction of a part of our literature and the confiscation of some of it. The agency of the German General Staff was active in representing us, Russian revolutionaries and opponents of war, as agents of the Russian General Staff in whose interests it was important that an antiwar policy be pursued in Sweden. The opportunist-socialists were also disgruntled by our support of and activity among the "young Social Democrats." For the government we were a dangerous element and it was trying to get rid of us by all means. After Bukharin, "Dolgo-levsky," a Bundist-worker-printer by the name of Gordon was deported. Many of us were under surveillance, while our letters were examined and perlustrated. . . . .

Soon the entire Stockholm group—Comrades Bukharin, Piatakov, and Kollontai—moved to Christiania. At first the police there were disturbed, but owing to the intervention of the Norwegian Social Democrats our comrades were left in peace. Our comrades there also were cautiously taking part in the publications of the "young socialists," but in the Russian activity despondency and grief prevailed. The letters of the editorial board of the Central Organ were becoming more and more overbearing, and all hopes for a publication with the participation of Bukharin and Piatakov had to be abandoned. . . . .

ON PARTY TACTICS AND PROBLEMS

[Lenin to Shliapnikov, Copenhagen, September–October, 1916][176]

[ZÜRICH]
DEAR FRIEND:

Apparently Belenin's decision concerning his "trip"[177] has already been made, to judge by his letter which Grigorii has reforwarded to me today. The time is very brief! Meanwhile it is doubly necessary for us to agree by letter and to get in harmony. This matter is now incredibly important. Therefore, I beg you very, very much to take every measure, so as to see Belenin *personally,* and to transmit to him the following and then write me (without fail!) *frankly* and in all detail how the matter stands, i.e., whether or not there are dissensions, disagreements, etc., between us and Belenin, what they are and how they can be eliminated.

The elimination of James[178] (about this elimination I earnestly beg you not to say a word to anyone abroad—you cannot imagine how dangerous in *every* respect is the foreign gossip on these topics, and *in connection* with such events) makes the situation critical and brings up the question of a general plan of work.

According to my conviction this plan is composed of : first, a *theoreti-*

[176] Lenin, *Sochineniia,* XIX, 273–76.

[177] Shliapnikov intended to return to Russia. At the time of this letter Shliapnikov was residing in Denmark, after a short trip to America. In his letter to Lenin of October 2, from Copenhagen, Shliapnikov said that it was necessary for him to go to Russia before October 15 and to leave Copenhagen not later than October 10 [1916]. (*Ibid.,* p. 474, note 125.)

[178] This refers to the arrest in Petrograd of A. I. Elizarova, who was at one time the connecting link between the section of the Central Committee abroad and the Russian organizations. (*Ibid.,* p. 474, note 126.)

cal policy; second, immediate *tactical* tasks; and, third, straight organizational tasks.

(1) On the first point: there is now on the order of the day not only the *continuation* of the policy (against Tsarism, etc.)—a policy which was confirmed by us in resolutions and a pamphlet (this policy has been remarkably confirmed by events: the split in England, etc.)—but also the matter of purging it of absurdities now grown ripe and of the confusion of repudiating democracy (this matter includes disarmament, repudiation of self-determination, the theoretically false "general" repudiation of the defense of the fatherland, the vacillations in the general questions of the role and significance of the state, etc.).

It will be extremely unfortunate if Belenin does not wait for my article[179] in reply to Kievsky (it was sent for copying only yesterday and will not be ready for a few days). What can be done? Do not scorn harmonizing our points of view; indeed, it is necessary for the work in these hard days. . . . .

[Lenin then discusses various means of maintaining contact with Shliapnikov through Kollontai.]

On the second point I think it is *essential* to publish popular leaflets and proclamations against Tsarism. Consider whether it is possible to do this in Spain. If not we shall prepare them here and then forward them. For this very *accurate* connections in the transport are required. You were quite right. The "Japanese" [Piatakov and Bosh] have proved to be *absolutely* useless. Best of all are foreigners with whom we could correspond in English or in another foreign language. I shall not write about the transport at great length, because you know and see it yourself. Too bad—no money, but in Petersburg they are supposed to collect.

The chief party question in Russia was and *remains* that of "unity." Trotsky in five or six hundred numbers of his newspaper has not considered or completely stated: is there unity with Chkheidze? Skobelev and Co.? or not? It seems that "unifiers"[180] have also remained in Petersburg, though they are very weak (are they the ones who published *Rabochie Vedomosti* in Petersburg?). "Makar" [V. P. Nogin] they say is in Moscow and is also conciliating. Conciliationism and unificationism are most harmful for the labor party in Russia. They are not merely idiotic but are also *detrimental* to the party; for in practice "unification" (or conciliation, etc.) with Chkheidze and Skobelev (in them lies the crux of the matter because they pretend to be "internationalists") means unity with the Organization Committee and through it with Potresov and Co., i.e., as a matter of fact *servility* before social-chauvinists.

---

[179] Lenin, "O karikature na marksizm i imperialisticheskom ekonomizme."

[180] Lenin refers to the "Mezhraionka" partisans.

If Trotsky and Co. do not understand this, so much the worse for them. No. 1 of *Delo,* and also the participation of the workers in the War Industries Committees, *prove* that this is so.

Not only during elections to the Duma on the day following the peace but also in general in *all* questions of party practice, "unity" with Chkheidze and Co. is the *crux* at present. We can rely only on those who understand the whole deception of the idea of unity and the whole necessity of a split with this brotherhood (with Chkheidze and Co.) in Russia. Belenin ought to consolidate *only* such people for the role of leaders.

By the way, the split, on an international scale, has also ripened. I consider it quite timely now that *all* conscious leading workers of Russia should understand it and adopt resolutions in favor of an organizational break with the Second International—with the International Bureau of Huysmans, Vandervelde and Co.—in favor of the construction of the Third International *but* against the Kautskyans (Chkheidze and Co., as well as Martov with Axelrod=Russian Kautskyans) of all the countries in bringing together *only* people who adhere to the position of the Zimmerwald Left.

On the third point: The sorest point now is the weakness of contact between us and the leading workers of Russia!! No correspondence whatever!! Nobody except James, and now not even him!! It can't go on that way. *No* publishing of leaflets, *no* transport, *no* harmony with respect to proclamations, *no* forwarding of their drafts, of proclamations, resolutions, etc., etc., can be organized without a *regular* conspirative correspondence. In this lies the crux!

Belenin did nothing about this on his first trip (perhaps he was unable to do so at that time). For Christ's sake, persuade him to do something on the second trip! Without fail! The immediate success of the trip must be measured by the number of contacts. By all means!! (Of course the personal influence of Belenin is still more important, but he *will be unable* to remain anywhere very long without danger to himself and without harm to the cause.) The success of the trip is to be measured by the number of contacts in each town!!

Two or three contacts as a minimum should be established with leading *workers* in each town; they themselves should *write,* should *themselves* master the conspirative method of writing letters (it doesn't take a God to bake a pot); they should prepare one or two successors for themselves in anticipation of failure. This should not be entrusted to the intelligentsia alone. By no means! The leading workers are able to and must do this themselves. Without this it is *impossible* to establish the succession and the unity of work which is so essential.

I believe that is all.

With respect to legal literature I shall add: it is important to find out whether my articles will be allowed to appear in *Letopis*[181] (in case the Okists [followers of the Organization Committee] cannot be kicked out by means of a bloc with the Machists [followers of Mach]) and if so with what limitations.

It is necessary to find out the details about "Volna."[182]

As for myself, I must say that I need an income; otherwise it simply means perishing. Truly!! The fiendishly high cost of living—there is nothing to live on. Money should be squeezed out forcibly (Belenin should speak about money to Katin and to Gorky himself, if this is *not too inconvenient*), from the publisher of *Letopis*, to whom two of my pamphlets have been sent (let him pay; *immediately* and as much as possible!). The same with Bonch[183] and with regard to the *translations*. If this is not arranged, then I shall not be able to hold out. Of this I'm sure. This is very, very serious.

With a firm handshake and thousands of best wishes to Belenin. Write *immediately* in acknowledgment, at least two words.

Yours,

LENIN

P.S. Write *frankly*, in what mood Bukharin is leaving. Will he write us or not? Will he comply with requests or not? The correspondence is possible (with America), *only* through Norway. Tell him that, and adjust.

In the autumn of 1916 leaders of the French Socialist party suggested the calling of a second conference of socialists of the Entente Powers. The Bolsheviks had thoroughly disapproved the action of the first conference which was held in 1915 and is discussed in chapter iii. As the resolution which is given below shows, the Bolsheviks held that they had nothing in common with the brand of socialists who were sponsoring the conference. In stating the reasons for their refusal the Bolsheviks suggested that the Zimmerwald group adopt a common line of action in respect to the conference

[181] None of Lenin's articles were published in *Letopis*. (Lenin, *Sochineniia*, XIX, 476, note 135.)

[182] "Volna"—a Bolshevist publishing house in Petersburg organized in 1916 by a number of Bolshevik writers (L. Stark, N. Skrypnik and others) with the participation of workers' groups of the insurance committees. It issued a number of pamphlets by Kamenev, Zinoviev [Skopin], and others. (*Leninskii Sbornik*, II, 281, note 10.)

[183] V. D. Bonch-Bruevich, who at that time owned the publishing house "Zhizn i Znanie." (Lenin, *Sochineniia*, XIX, 476, note 138.)

proposal. The action of the Zimmerwaldists, which is discussed in chapter v, amounted merely to the statement of opposition, for the proposed Entente socialist conference never met.[184]

THE CALLING OF A CONFERENCE ON THE ENTENTE SOCIALISTS

[Resolution of the Central Committee of the Russian Socialist Democratic Labor Party][185]

After discussing the proposal of the French social chauvinists to call a conference of the "Entente socialists" (of England, France, Italy, and their allies) the Central Committee of the Russian Social Democratic Labor party resolved to *repudiate participation in this conference.*

The agents of the French bourgeoisie, who act under the name of the French Socialist party, have organized recently a "congress" of trade unions of the "Allied Powers" in Leeds and a similar congress of co-operatives. Now an attempt is being made to call a similar conference of socialist parties. No honest socialist can set his hand to these undertakings, the aim of which is to deceive the working class.

Who is the initiator of the proposed conference? Do the initiators of this conference deserve political confidence? No! They are people who, together with the Südekums and the Scheidemanns, have trodden underfoot the decisions of the International. They are people who describe to the workers as "defense of the fatherland," defense of "freedom" and "culture," and so forth, the predatory desires of the Tsarist gang, which fights for Constantinople, Galicia, and Armenia, and the imperialist policy of the French bourgeoisie, which fights for the possession of the stolen colonies. They are the people whose leaders sit in reactionary imperialist cabinets. They are the people who do not refrain from the most unheard-of "measures" in order to crush the socialist opposition of their country.

The Executive Committee of the International Social Chauvinist Bureau has also joined these people. It takes part in the practical work in connection with the calling of the conference of the so-called Entente socialists. It is this same Executive Committee which recently in the person of Mr. Huysmans congratulated the "tenth socialist minister," Mr. Stauning, upon his entrance into a bourgeois cabinet! It is this same

---

[184] See below, pp. 467–68.

[185] "O sozyve konferentsii 'sotsialistov soglasiia'," *Sbornik Sotsial-Demokrata,* No. 2, December, 1916, pp. 80–82. Reprinted in Lenin, *Sochineniia,* XIX, 44–45. Excerpts from this declaration were published in *Labour Leader,* No. 5, February 1, 1917, p. 2.

committee which every day of its existence throughout the entire war has been a model in *forgetting* elementary socialist duty.

No, all these people deserve no more attention on the part of internationalist socialists than do the Eberts, the Scheidemanns, and the Müllers, who have gone so far as to steal the newspaper *Vorwärts* from the Berlin workers and place it at the disposal of German imperialists.

During the war we have witnessed a Conference of the "socialists" of the Central Powers in Vienna and the first Conference of the Entente "socialists" in London. At both Conferences many phrases were uttered about democratic peace, proletarian interests, restoration of the International. In practice each of these Conferences fulfilled the orders of "its" government and "its" imperialism. It stands to reason that the same thing will be repeated at this imminent Conference of the Entente.

The A B C of socialism and internationalism demands that we *repudiate* the dividing of socialists according to the same considerations which divide at this moment the imperialists of various countries by virtue of a number of secret and open treaties between the government cliques of those countries. We do not recognize a division into "Entente socialists" and "socialists of Central Europe"! We are internationalist-socialists. The "Germans," Karl Liebknecht and Friedrich Adler, are our brothers, whereas the Russian social chauvinist Plekhanov and the French social chauvinist Renaudel are our class opponents. The Austro-German social chauvinists assert that they are supporting the plan to form a "Central European" union of states, because from this imperialist institution they say there will develop a free democratic union of all the European states. The Anglo-French social chauvinists assert that they are organizing separate conferences of the "Entente socialists" because from this social-imperialist coalition they say there will develop a new Workers' International which will unite all socialists. There is just as little truth in one assertion as in the other.

Before Zimmerwald, it would have been possible to attend this conference in order to expose there the social chauvinists. We experimented with the Conference of the Entent Socialists in January 1915[186] and our representative, Comrade Maximovich, went there to declare the truth. But as soon as he began his speech and said that the socialists who recognize "defense of the fatherland" in this war are traitors, Chairman Vandervelde asked him to leave the floor! Naturally, these gentlemen could not bear to hear the truth. At present participation in a similar conference would mean *a step back* from Zimmerwald. Even at Kienthal there was *no majority* which would pronounce itself in favor of the Zimmerwaldists taking part in the meeting of the International Socialist Bureau if the latter were called. So much the more should the Zimmer-

[186] The Inter-Allied Socialist Conference held at London, February 14, 1915.

waldists repudiate participation in a separate conference of one of the social-chauvinist coalitions. When the Italian Federation of Labor declined to participate in the social-chauvinist Conference at Leeds, this was understood and approved by all internationalists. This makes the present decision of the Italian Socialist party, which adheres to Zimmerwald, to participate in the imminent conference of the "Entente socialists" so much the more incomprehensible. All the stipulations that the Zimmerwaldists might have a majority at this conference are built upon sand. The participation of the Zimmerwaldists in this conference can only harm the Zimmerwald union.

The plan of convening the Entente socialists originated not only with the French "majority" but also with the partisans of Longuet. The latter constitute "His Majesty's opposition," since they support Messrs. Thomas, Renaudel, and Sembat in all that is essential. By calling the Entente Conference they wish to appease the French workers, among whom the internationalist opposition is getting strong, and they wish to feed them with promises—as if this were the surest way of restoring the International. Among other things the recent pamphlet *Les Socialistes de Zimmerwald et la guerre,* published by the Committee for the Resumption of International Relations [*Comité pour la reprise des relations internationales*], proves the growth of the socialist opposition against the French social chauvinists. The authors of this pamphlet express resolutely their disagreement with the opposition of Longuet-Pressemane and declare that "defense of the fatherland" (in an imperialist war) is not a "socialist task." The duty of the internationalist socialists is to expose the tricks of social chauvinists rather than to cover them up.

International socialism is passing through a crisis of unheard-of difficulty. The international slaughter continues and this crisis is coming to its climax. At this time our duty is more than ever to go straight onward, to tell the workers clearly and openly that we cannot travel upon the same road with the traitors to socialism, that there is nothing about which we can confer with the Renaudels, the Plekhanovs, and the Vanderveldes—neither is there with the Scheidemanns, the Lensches, and the Südekums. Our allies, our friends, are Liebknecht, McLean, Höglund, and the German, French, English, Swedish, Russian, and other workers who struggle against the governments of their countries.

These are the reasons which impelled us to refuse to participate in the Conference of the "Entente socialists."

At the same time we propose to the Berne International Socialist Committee to call a special conference—at least of the Zimmerwald organizations which have been invited to the Entente Conference—in order that an attempt may be made to elaborate a *common* line of conduct with regard to the said Conference.

THE CENTRAL COMMITTEE OF THE R.S.D.L. PARTY

CHAPTER III

INTERNATIONAL SOCIALIST CONFERENCES, SEPTEMBER 1914–APRIL 1915

Shortly after the outbreak of the war, socialists of neutral countries began to exert themselves to restore some form of international socialist relations, which had been so violently disrupted by the events of August 1914. Socialists of every description agreed that the fundamental cause of the war was capitalism, with its imperialist and militarist manifestations. There was, however, even among the neutrals, disagreement as to the relative degree of guilt of the capitalists of the Entente and the Central Powers and there was even greater disagreement as to what the socialists should do to bring an end to the war and advance the cause of socialism. The socialists of the belligerent countries found concerted action toward these ends hampered by the fact that large numbers of them had adopted the point of view of defense of the fatherland and were prevented by their voluntary acceptance of the *Burgfrieden* or by the repressive measures of their governments from international activity except toward socialists of allied countries. Thus it was that during the first eight months of the war those socialist gatherings which had an international character were, with two exceptions, promoted and attended by socialists of neutral countries or by the socialists of the Entente and the Central Powers separately. Even in the case of the neutrals it proved to be impossible in these early months to summon a general conference of the representatives of the principal nonbelligerent states.

One of the first proposals for resuscitating the International came from the United States. At a meeting on September 19–20, 1914, the National Executive Committee of the American Socialist party worked out plans for an international conference and sent invitations to the socialists of France, Belgium, England, Germany, Austria, Italy, Holland, Sweden, Denmark, and Switzerland and to the International Socialist Bureau proposing that socialists meet at Washington "for the discussion of ways and means most speedily and effectively to stop the war" and offering to pay the traveling expenses of the delegates. In case it was impossible to meet in Washington, it was suggested that the conference be held at The Hague or at Copenhagen. Nothing came of this proposal.[1]

In Europe, meanwhile, something more was achieved by the socialists of neutral countries. On the initiative of the Swiss Social Democrats, representatives of the Swiss and Italian parties met at Lugano on September 27 to consider the situation created by the war. Resolutions looking toward the restoration of international socialist relations were drawn up and the Presidiums of the two parties were authorized to attempt to call a conference of socialists of neutral states.[2] Two weeks later, on October 11, representatives of the socialist parties of the northern neutral states met at Stockholm. At this meeting Hjalmar Branting, Fredrik Ström, and Hermann Lindquist were the Swedish delegates; Jakob Vidnes, Magnus Nilssen, and Ole Z. Lian, the Norwegian; and F. Borgbjerg, C. Madsen, and Th. Stauning, the Danish. Troel-

[1] M. Hillquit, *Loose Leaves from a Busy Life*, pp. 159–60; *Labour Leader*, No. 41, October 8, 1914, p. 4; Walling, *The Socialists and the War*, pp. 405–407; Shliapnikov, *Kanun semnadtsatogo goda*, I, p. 51; A. Trachtenberg (ed.), *The American Socialists and the War. A Documentary History of the Attitude of the Socialist Party toward War and Militarism Since the Outbreak of the Great War*, p. 11, hereafter cited, *The American Socialists and the War*.

[2] Conference socialiste internationale à Zimmerwald (Suisse). Rapport officiel pour la presse," *Internationale sozialistische Kommission zu Bern, Bulletin*, No. 1, September 21, 1915, p. 4. The *Bulletin* of the International Socialist Committee at Berne appeared in German, French, and English editions. The Hoover Library does not contain complete files in all three languages; our citations in the following pages, therefore, are made to the edition available. O. Boulanger, *L'Internationale socialiste a vécu*, pp. 104–105; *Berner Tagwacht*, No. 219, September 19, 1914, p. 1; No. 225, September 26, 1914, p. 1; *Golos*, No. 20, October 4, 1914, p. 1; *La Sentinelle*, No. 220, September 22, 1914, p. 3.

stra, of the Netherlands party, also attended. Aside from matters of regional interest, the Conference considered the proposal of the Dutch Social Democratic Labor party that since the state of war in Belgium made it impossible for the International Socialist Bureau to function properly at Brussels the Bureau be transferred to Amsterdam and the management of its affairs be placed in the hands of the Dutch party. The Swiss Social Democrats also offered to take over the affairs of the I.S.B. It was decided to call an international conference to settle the question.[3] Later, when the French and Belgian socialists and the Executive of the Bureau objected to the proposed removal, the matter was arranged by a temporary transfer of the I.S.B. to The Hague and the appointment of the Dutch Social Democrats, J. W. Albarda, P. J. Troelstra, and H. H. van Kol, as members and W. H. Vliegen and F. M. Wibaut as substitute members of the Executive.[4]

Meanwhile Troelstra visited various party headquarters in order to persuade them to take part in the proposed international conference which had been discussed at Stockholm and which was to include socialists of belligerent as well as of neutral countries. As a consequence of the disinclination of French and other socialist leaders to take part in such a conference, Troelstra's efforts had very small results. When the Conference met at Copenhagen on January 17–18, 1915, only the representatives of the three Scandinavian parties, the Dutch party, and the Bund were present. The Italian deputy Morgari failed to attend, according to Balabanoff "rather from accident than for any other reason." The Swiss declined because they were preparing on the basis of the Lu-

---

[3] Larin claims in a letter to Axelrod, January 21, 1915, that the suggestion of calling a conference was first raised by Uritsky at Copenhagen and by Chkhenkeli and Steklov at Stockholm. (*Pisma P. B. Akselroda i Yu. O. Martova*, p. 313, note 5; *Beilage des Vorwärts*, No. 283, October 16, 1914, p. 1; *Golos*, No. 39, October 28, 1914, pp. 1–2.)

[4] *Berner Tagwacht*, No. 10, January 14, 1915, p. 3; *The Clarion*, No. 1201, December 11, 1914, p. 10; *Golos*, No. 53, November 13, 1914, p. 2; R. W. Postgate, *The International during the War*, p. 19; Fainsod, *International Socialism and the World War*, p. 44.

gano resolutions for another conference, of which more later. The Spaniards disapproved of the agenda, and the Americans at the last moment decided not to be present. Among the socialists of the belligerent countries opinions differed as to the advisability of a general international conference at this time.[5]

A month after the Copenhagen meeting, representatives of socialist parties of the Entente countries met in London, on February 14, 1915, at the invitation of the British section of the I.S.B. and under the chairmanship of Keir Hardie. In addition to the British, French, and Belgians, representatives of the Russian Socialist-Revolutionists were present. As the organizers of the Conference intended to invite only Russian Social Democrats from Russia, neither the Central Committee (Bolshevik) nor the Organization Committee (Menshevik) was asked to take part, but both groups sent representatives and registered their objections to the Conference and its resolutions.[6]

Another socialist Conference of a similarly limited international composition was that held at Vienna by the socialists of Germany, Austria, and Hungary, April 12–13, 1915. This Conference received but little attention in the press of other European countries and only excerpts from the resolutions adopted were published in some of the party organs.[7] ·

The first international Conference after the outbreak of the war in which socialists from belligerent as well as neutral countries met was that of socialist women at Berne, March 26–28, 1915, which was attended by women from Great Britain, Germany, France, Russia, Poland, Holland, Switz-

[5] See above, p. 201, Lenin to Shliapnikov, January 1915. *Labour Leader,* No. 3, January 21, 1915, p. 4; *La Sentinelle,* No. 276, November 26, 1914, p. 2; Walling, *The Socialists and the War,* pp. 407–22.

[6] *Berner Tagwacht,* No. 42, February 20, 1915, p. 1; Walling, *The Socialists and the War,* pp. 424–27; Rosmer, *Le Mouvement ouvrier pendant la guerre,* pp. 197–202.

[7] *1. Beilage des Vorwärts,* No. 108, April 20, 1915, p. 2; *La Sentinelle,* No. 96 [98], *Quatrième feuille,* May 1, 1915, p. 1; *Nashe Slovo,* No. 73, April 24, 1915, p. 2.

erland, and Italy. The Conference, somewhat more radical in complexion than those already mentioned, declared against civil truce but refused to accept the radical tactical program advocated by the Bolsheviks.

A few days later, April 5–7, representatives of socialist youth organizations held an International Socialist Conference. This gathering, like the women's conference, met without official socialist sanction and by a large majority it rejected the resolution offered by the Bolsheviks.[8]

Meanwhile the Swiss and Italians had not given up their hope of calling an international conference in accordance with the Lugano decisions. In April the Italian socialist deputy, O. Morgari, was sent to lay the Italo-Swiss proposals before the French and British socialists and the International Socialist Bureau. The scant results of Morgari's trip and the action which the Italian Socialist party took as a result are discussed in the following chapter. Here it is necessary to note only that Morgari carried a letter from the Swiss Social Democrats supporting his proposals. On learning that the International Socialist Bureau was not impressed by the proposals and that it considered the Lugano and Copenhagen conferences as having no particular significance, the Swiss announced on April 26 their intention to arrange a meeting of neutral socialists at Zürich on May 30, 1915, for the purpose of discussing "socialist activity in neutral countries for peace." This meeting did not take place. The political situation at the moment was unfavorable; the Italians, as will appear, were also initiating a parallel move, and on May 22, the Presidium of the Swiss party approved the decision to abandon the Zürich conference.[9]

---

[8] W. Münzenberg, *Die sozialistische Jugend-Internationale*, pp. 37–44; Balabanoff, "Zwei internationale Konferenzen," *Neues Leben*, No. 4, April 1915, pp. 97–103; R. Schüller, *Geschichte der Kommunistischen Jugend-Internationale*, I, 98–107.

[9] Ernst Schenker, *Die sozialdemokratische Bewegung in der Schweiz von ihren Anfängen bis zur Gegenwart*, p. 116; *La Sentinelle*, No. 106, May 11, 1915, p. 2 and No. 118, May 26, 1915, p. 2; No. 238, October 13, 1914, p. 1.

A. The Lugano and Copenhagen Conferences

As has been mentioned in the preceding chapter, the Bolsheviks were greatly interested in the meeting of the Swiss and Italian socialists at Lugano and a copy of Lenin's theses was submitted and considered at the Conference. But as the following declaration shows, the delegates were not prepared to advocate such radical tactics as he proposed.

DECLARATION OF THE LUGANO CONFERENCE

[By the Swiss and Italian Socialists, September 27, 1914][10]

The present catastrophe is a sequel to the imperialist policy of the Great Powers, which policy, in absolute monarchies, coincides with dynastic interests. The European war is not a struggle for higher civilization and for the freedom of the peoples. It is a struggle of the capitalist classes to conquer new markets for exports in foreign lands, as well as a criminal attempt to crush the Social Democracy and the revolutionary movement of the proletariat in home lands.

The German and the Austrian bourgeoisie have no right to defend the war by saying that it is a struggle against Tsarism and for the freedom of national culture, for both Prussian feudal Junkerdom, with Wilhelm II at its head, and the great German industrialists have always pursued a policy supporting and upholding accursed Tsarism. Likewise the governments of Germany and Austria-Hungary have oppressed the national culture of their peoples and have shackled the movement for the liberation of the laboring class.

Neither have the French and English bourgeoisie the right to justify the defense of their fatherlands by saying that they are struggling against German imperialism and for the freedom of the peoples. Their aim is not the liberation of the peoples from capitalist and militarist oppression, for they have accentuated this oppression through their policy of alliance with Tsarist Russia and at the same time have hindered development of a higher culture.

The true causes and the actual character of this war are obscured by the chauvinist frenzy which the ruling classes of all countries have purposely kindled. Individual groups of the laboring class have likewise been carried away by this chauvinist current, and they believe that by participating in the war they are serving the cause of liberating the proletarians of other countries from the bloody rule of their governments.

10 "Die Konferenz in Lugano," *Berner Tagwacht*, No. 227, September 29, 1914, p. 1; English text in *Labour Leader*, No. 42, October 15, 1914, p. 4, under the title, "Swiss and Italian Socialists Unite."

But no war whatever can produce that result. The oppressed cannot secure freedom for themselves by struggling for their own oppressors against the oppressed classes of other countries.

To proclaim these old principles of the Proletarian International today when the international relations of the proletarians are disrupted is more than ever the duty of socialists of those countries which have been spared the horrors of war. Thus the undersigned representatives of the Italian and the Swiss socialist parties consider it their task to struggle with the utmost exertion to check the spread of war to other countries and to brand every attempt to involve other peoples in the war as an attempt upon the toiling populations and upon culture.

In this spirit the representatives of the Italian and the Swiss Social Democracies address the socialist parties of the other countries. While thus creating—among those peoples who are not taking part in the war, but who endure its effects—the foundation for joint action against a continuation of this horrible slaughter, the parties mentioned also urge the socialist parties of neutral countries to demand that their governments immediately open diplomatic negotiations with the governments of the belligerent countries with a view to bringing about an early cessation of the massacre of the peoples.

The Italian delegates: Armuzzi, Balabanoff, de Falco, Lazzari, Modigliani, Morgari, Musatti, Ratti, Serrati, Turati

The Swiss delegates: Albisser, Ferri, Greulich, Grimm, Naine, Pflüger, Rimathé, Schenkel

The sponsors of the Copenhagen Conference, desiring to achieve as great a degree of harmony as possible and to avoid offending the socialists of belligerent countries, made it known that the purpose of the Conference was to find a common basis of socialist action for peace. The sponsors hoped that the Conference would influence neutral opinion to support a settlement which would guarantee a lasting peace and would provide for (1) no change of frontiers without the acknowledgment of the right of the inhabitants to determine their fate; (2) compulsory international arbitration; and (3) limitation of armaments.[11]

---

[11] *Labour Leader*, No. 49, December 3, 1914, p. 4, and No. 1, January 7, 1915, p. 5.

THE COPENHAGEN CONFERENCE, JANUARY 17–18, 1915

[From a Report in *Nashe Slovo*][12]

.... The work of the Conference was conducted within the narrow limits of a previously established agenda, the fundamental point of which was the question of the restoration of peace.

Only four delegates from the three Scandinavian countries (Sweden, Denmark, and Norway) and four delegates from Holland (Troelstra, van Kol, Fliechek, and Wibaut) participated in the Conference. Besides these, de Roode, the editor of the Central Organ of Holland (*Het Volket* [*Volk*]) and the delegate from the Polish-Lithuanian "Bund" were admitted as guests. The American party refused to participate in the Conference on the ground that the Conference did not embrace *all* the neutral countries, as had been intended according to the preliminary scheme, but only *some* of the neutral countries. O. Morgari, the Italian socialist, who was expected as a guest, did not come either. There were no delegates (except the Bund representative) from the parties of the belligerent countries.

The entire work of the Conference was conducted behind closed doors in a strictly confidential manner. Not only were the representatives of the party press not admitted, but even persons who had special mandates from their parties were refused information. The Danish comrades explained that this secrecy was necessitated by the conditions of war time and by the need for guarding Denmark's neutrality.

The following socialist organizations and parties sent greetings to the Conference: the Swiss, the French, the German, and the Italian parties; the Organization Committee of the R.S.D.L. party, the Bund, and the Central Organization of the Independent Labour party of England; and separate trade unions and organizations of Sweden. A greeting was received also from Huysmans, secretary of the International [Socialist] Bureau, whose only explanation for his absence was that he had been unable to secure a passport from the German authorities.

In addition to their greetings the socialist parties of several countries submitted declarations to the Conference. These declarations are not yet ready for publication and will be sent to the International [Socialist] Bureau at The Hague together with the report on the Conference. Meanwhile they will be forwarded to the central party institutions of every country.

[12] "Kopengagenskaia konferentsiia," *Nashe Slovo*, No. 1, January 29, 1915, p. 2. Brief reports on the Copenhagen conference can be found in "The Conference Resolutions," *Labour Leader*, No. 3, January 21, 1915, p. 4; "La Conférence de Copenhague," *L'Humanité*, No. 3929, January 19, 1915, p. 1; and "Die Friedens-Konferenz in Kopenhagen," *Vorwärts*, No. 21, January 21, 1915, p. 2.

A manifesto[13] (published in *Sotsial-Demokrat, No. 33*) and the government communication concerning the arrest of the members of the State Duma were submitted by Russia. The Organization Committee submitted a report;[14] there was also a statement of the Bund and the *Nasha Zaria* group. The Conference opened its session on Sunday the 17th [of January 1915] and ended on the 18th late in the evening. On Sunday there was a grandiose peace meeting which closed with the singing of "The International." Three thousand people were present. The following persons spoke: Branting, Troelstra, Lian (the secretary of the trade unions of Norway), Stauning, and Borgbjerg from Denmark.....

[Resolutions][15]

RESOLUTION I[16]

The Conference records that capitalism in its imperialist form, which is manifest in the growth of armaments, the unscrupulous pursuit of the policy of expansion, and irresponsible secret diplomacy, has led the world to the present catastrophe which has long been foreseen and predicted by Social Democracy.

At a moment when all mankind is horrified by the devastations and massacres of this war, the Conference wishes to express a firm and strong desire for peace among the populations of the countries represented at the Conference.

The Conference considers that the chief task of this gathering is to unite and thereby strengthen the desire of the peoples of all countries to end the war by a stable peace.

Thus, basing itself upon the principles of international solidarity and on the proletariat's feeling of justice proclaimed by all the international congresses, the Conference addresses the Social Democratic workers, especially the workers of the belligerent countries. These principles have been recorded at the Copenhagen Congress of 1910 in a resolution against war which imposed upon the parliamentary representatives the duty to struggle for (*a*) the introduction of compulsory courts of arbitration between nations; (*b*) the reduction of armaments, with total disarmament as the ultimate aim; (*c*) the abolition of secret diplomacy and the establishment of parliamentary responsibility in matters of foreign policy; (*d*) the recognition of the right of free self-determination of peoples and the encouragement of efforts against military adventures and oppression by force.

[13] See above, chapter ii, pp. 150–56.   [14] Given below, pp. 267–71.

[15] "Les Textes de Copenhague," *L'Humanité*, No. 3941, January 31, 1915, p. 1.

[16] This resolution was drafted by a Commission composed of Th. Stauning (Denmark), Magnus Nilssen (Norway), Troelstra (Holland), and H. Branting (Sweden).

The Conference considers it to be the duty of all socialist parties to contribute to an early conclusion of peace and to make every effort to elaborate peace terms which do not conceal any germ of new wars and which may serve as a foundation for general disarmament and the democratization of international policy.

The Conference protests against the violation of international law by the injury caused to Belgium and expresses the hope that the Social Democracy of all belligerent countries will oppose most energetically any forced annexation which is at variance with the people's right of free self-determination.

The Conference reconfirms the principles of the International and invites the International Socialist Bureau as soon as it is deemed convenient, and later at the opening of peace negotiations, to convene a congress of Social Democratic parties in order to work out the demands which they will presumably formulate with regard to the peace terms. This measure is necessary in order to prevent the drafting of peace terms without the participation and against the will of the working masses.

Thus the Conference urges the workers of all countries to unite all their efforts to bring about an early peace.

The World War with all its horrors was possible only because the capitalists are still at the helm. Consequently, the Conference urges the laboring class to make every effort to seize political power in order that imperialism may be crushed and international Social Democracy may accomplish its mission of emancipating the peoples.

Resolution II

The Conference invites the Social Democrats of the neutral countries to ask their governments—through the media of their representatives or by any other convenient means—to consider separately or jointly whether it is possible to offer, with some chance of success, the services of these governments to the governments of the belligerent countries for mediation in restoring an early and lasting peace.

Resolution III

After learning that five members of the Russian Duma, who had assembled to draft a report to this Conference, have been arrested for doing this, the Conference expresses its sympathy with the five arrested party comrades and protests energetically against such treatment of the qualified representatives of the laboring class.

RUSSIAN SOCIAL DEMOCRATS AND THE WAR

[Report of the Organization Committee of the R.S.D.L. Party to the Copenhagen Conference][17]

The declaration of general mobilization, together with the war that broke out immediately after mobilization, took Russian Socialist Democracy by surprise. It is also necessary to bear in mind the events in St. Petersburg that preceded mobilization. The general strike in St. Petersburg early in July, a strike which was largely elemental in nature and which was accompanied by a number of clashes with armed police and troops, gave the government an excuse for making mass arrests and raiding the labor press. Thus, at the moment of the first crash of thunder —the collision between Austria and Serbia, an omen of the approaching storm of a European war—Russian Social Democracy was considerably disorganized and seemed unable to organize any movement of protest against the approaching events.

With the declaration of mobilization and of martial law the government closed all the labor organizations (unions and clubs) in St. Petersburg without exception. The prisons were constantly filled with active workers of the labor movement, and the Petersburg proletariat which played the leading role in the Russian labor movement was left without organization and without newspapers and was drained of its blood and deprived of its strength by the repressions. In addition to governmental repressions, the position of the Russian Social Democrats was made very difficult by the sentiments which took possession of the masses of the population. The tide of patriotic manifestations rose high in all towns. Although the government and the Right elements of society took the initiative and played a prominent role in these manifestations just as at the beginning of the Japanese War, there is undoubtedly a great difference. Unlike the Japanese War, the present war has come to be popular and has met with the active support, especially of bourgeois society. A struggle against German militarism, Prussian Junkerdom, and the preponderance of German capital and for the liberation of oppressed nationalities, the participation in the war as allies of democratic France and England—all these slogans, the purpose of which was to conceal the true causes of the war and the motives of those guilty of initiating it, were launched at the masses and helped to make the war popular. At the same time a slogan of unity was advanced—unity of all parties and their united support of the government; unity of all peoples in Russia in the struggle against the external enemy. In this general outburst of patriotism and chauvinism Russian Social Democracy took no part at

[17] "Doklad Organizatsionnago Komiteta R.S.D.R.P. kopengagenskoi konferentsii," *Izvestiia Zagranichnogo Sekretariata Organizatsionnago Komiteta Rossiiskoi Sotsial-Demokraticheskoi Rabochei partii,* No. 1, February 22, 1915, p. 1.

all, but was unable to oppose it by propaganda and agitation. Only gradually, and in proportion as the patriotic daze began to disperse and the masses began to show some signs of sobering and as Social Democracy began to recover from the blow inflicted upon it, did a new rise of the social democratic movement in Russia become possible.

Although Russian Social Democracy was placed in a very difficult position and was unable to function in the first months of war, we may say that on the whole it remained faithful to the banner of international socialism and to its own social democratic tasks. The first public demonstration of Social Democrats after the declaration of war was the demonstration of the Social Democratic group in the State Duma. The circumstances under which the Social Democratic Duma group came forth with their declaration must be considered before the full significance of that event and of the negative vote on the war credits can be understood. This event, in spite of the Duma's efforts to demonstrate "unity with the government," has undoubtedly lessened the demoralizing influence of the war upon the democratic and especially the laboring masses. The Duma Presidium succeeded in minimizing the significance of this demonstration by refusing to permit the declaration of the Social Democratic group to be published in the form in which it was delivered in the Duma and by perverting it in the reports that were published. For that reason we enclose the declaration in its original form.[18]

The conditions under which Russian Social Democrats have to live must be considered—particularly now that the country is ruled by martial law—in order to understand how difficult it is to speak of the attitude of the party as a whole toward the new questions which have arisen because of the war. Thus, willy-nilly, we are compelled to concentrate on the clarified sentiments and opinions of separate organizations and groups.

First of all, it can be stated with certainty that among an overwhelming majority of Russian Social Democrats the conviction prevails, with respect to the recently developed international situation, that only the re-establishment of the International and the efforts of the organized international proletariat can solve, in the interests of the proletariat and the democracy, questions raised by the war and can assure their interests at the time of the liquidation of the war. Therefore, in the ranks of Russian Social Democracy there has been warm sympathy toward the calling of an international socialist conference as the first step along that road, and only political conditions in Russia prevent the Russian Social Democrats from taking as active a part in this conference as they would wish to.

[18] Text of declaration in *Pamiatniki agitatsionnoi literatury* . . . . , pp. 82–83. An excerpt is given in *Labour Leader,* No. 40, October 1, 1914, p. 4, under the title "Bold Stand of Russian Socialists."

An overwhelming majority of Russian Social Democrats likewise support the demand for an early termination of the war and the conclusion of peace. On the question concerning the demands to be advanced by the international proletariat at the time of the liquidation of the war, in so far as it is possible to judge, two currents have formed. Whereas one current advances the slogan that the people's representatives, elected democratically, must participate in elaborating the conditions of peace—slogans of disarmament, courts of arbitration, the renunciation of seized foreign territories, and self-determination of various areas (by means of a plebiscite)—the second current, while supporting these slogans, considers that the question of the destiny of the disputed areas and the state formations of the various powers (Austria, Germany, Russia) should be settled by the International.

It is the question concerning the causes of this war and the evaluation of its possible consequences that arouses so many disputes. Whereas some advance general causes brought about by capitalist competition between various countries as being the most important—and from that point of view consider as unessential the question of the greater or smaller responsibility of separate nations for the outbreak of the war—others, without denying the general causes, consider it necessary to emphasize the specific characteristics of German militarism and Prussian Junkerdom which they believe to be chiefly responsible for the war. Accordingly, the adherents of the latter point of view—since they regard Germany's defeat as a guaranty of a democratic revolution in Germany and of the clearing of the way to further conquests of democracy and of the social democratic movement in all Europe—consider that in so far as it inflicts blows upon German militarism and Prussian Junkerdom this war contains in itself the elements of progress.[19] Meanwhile the adherents of the first point of view, among whom are the majority of the Organization Committee, consider it impossible to connect the success of democratic and socialist movements with the victory or defeat of one coalition or the other in the present war, and they point out in particular that a victory of Russia over Germany would carry in itself the danger of strengthening the Russian reaction and would be a menace to the European labor movement. It must be noted that among Russian Social Democrats there are those (they are a minority, however) who, proceeding from the second point of view, consider a victory of Germany over Russia to be desirable in the interests of progress.

In spite of these dissensions, practically complete harmony with

[19] This point of view was expressed in the report submitted by the *Nasha Zaria* group to the Copenhagen Conference. The text appears under "Kopengagenskoi konferentsii," *Izvestiia Zagranichnago Sekretariata* . . . . , No. 1, February 22, 1915, p. 2.

regard to the general tasks of Russian Social Democracy at the present moment can be recorded. With the exception of solitary voices, which pronounce themselves in favor of the idea that the Russian Social Democrats, in the interests of defeating German militarism, must place temporarily in the background their democratic tasks of struggle against the government and must vote its war credits, the overwhelming majority considers that in the interests of the Russian as well as of the international proletariat Social Democracy must actively advance as its next task the democratization of the governmental regime and must expose the hypocrisy of union of the government and the people which has been proclaimed. For in reality the government does not increase the people's rights but, on the contrary, actually takes advantage of the existing state of war and, without encountering any resistance from the public, restores the pre-constitutional absolutist regime by suppressing the freedom of speech, of assembly, of the press, and so forth, and suppressing also all public initiative, especially that of the democratic strata of the population, and first of all that of the proletariat. At the same time the government has increased the persecution of the Jews and is organizing and encouraging Jewish pogroms. Increase in the democratic movement in Russia is particularly necessary at the present moment, when the appetites of the dominant classes are whetted to seize foreign territories while the government is striving to introduce its reactionary policy in the territories which it has seized.

Thus, in advancing democratic slogans as the immediate task of internal policy, Russian Social Democracy must lead a struggle against chauvinism and especially against Germanophobia which is being disseminated by all the bourgeois parties (not to mention the reactionaries). Fortunately, it is possible to record that the Russian proletariat—especially its class-conscious element—remains alien to hurrah patriotism. In order to secure better success in combating chauvinism, a struggle in that direction should be conducted in all countries involved in the war, because only such a general increase of international tendencies among the international proletariat can create a sufficient bulwark to resist the rising turbid tide of chauvinism which threatens to drown the international solidarity of the proletariat. In that respect Russian Social Democracy places great hopes in the international conference.

In conclusion, we consider it necessary to point out that, in spite of terrific repressions, the Russian labor movement has not been smothered. The provinces have suffered even less than Petersburg. In various places legal labor organizations have been preserved, the work is being carried on in the sick benefit funds, attempts are being made to publish labor organs, and illegal organizations are being formed. We must note the attempt to form labor organizations (Riga, Rostov, Samara, the

Western Area) on the basis of struggle against the calamities of war (relief to the unemployed and to the families of men called to war). But all these organizations are persecuted by the government, which feels that an active demonstration by the laboring class is not far off.

We expect that the international conference will succeed in overcoming the estrangement and the mutual mistrust provoked by the war between the separate socialist parties and that it will succeed in restoring the International and in recovering a basis for the brotherly solidarity of the international proletariat. In this we perceive the first necessary step to put an end by joint effort to this horrible slaughter and at the time of the liquidation of war to assure peace conditions such as would facilitate the proletariat's way toward its ultimate aim, socialism.

We consider it necessary to draw the attention of the International to the lamentable manifestation of the reaction which is increasing in Russia. We have in mind the arrest of the five Social Democratic deputies. The Organization Committee has issued a special proclamation in this connection, but we consider it highly important and we are expecting that the International as a whole, and the socialists of England and France in particular, will raise their protest against such unheard-of arbitrary measures against representatives of the laboring class, who are being threatened with penal servitude.

THE ORGANIZATION COMMITTEE OF THE RUSSIAN
SOCIAL DEMOCRATIC LABOR PARTY

PETERSBURG, December 31 (January 12), 1915

DECLARATION OF THE CENTRAL COMMITTEE OF THE BUND

[Drafted at the Conference Held in Russia in November 1914 and Submitted to the Copenhagen International Socialist Conference][20]

It would be entirely useless to look for the individual culprits of this war. The causes of this war are so closely bound up with the very foundations of the present order that it is rather insignificant to what degree the so-called responsible factors of European politics are individually to blame. The present war, as well as its predecessors, is the result of the capitalist organization of the people's economy, an organization which creates competition between the most developed industrial countries for dominance on world markets.

To maintain their colonial policy the ruling classes of the present states have created tremendous militarist organizations and institutions of secret diplomacy which by their very existence menace international

---

[20] "Tsentralnyi Komitet Bunda o voine," *Informatsionnyi Listok Zagranichnoi Organizatsii Bunda*, No. 7, January 1915, p. 3. This Conference of the Central Committee of the Bund is discussed in *The Bolsheviks and World Revolution*.

peace. The immediate causes of the present war seem to indicate that there is a conflict between the aspirations of Austria and Germany, on the one hand, to expand their dominance in the Balkans, and the pan-Slavism of Russia on the other, which under the cloak of loud phrases regarding the liberation of the fraternal Slavic peoples, strives to assert its own power also in the Balkans and in a portion of the Austro-Hungarian lands.

But whatever the immediate causes of outbreak of the war might have been, its ultimate and basic causes lie in the competition between the English commercial industrial class and the industry of Germany, which had grown tremendously for the past few decades. England entered this war—and through her participation lent it a world character—not because of the prestige involved in a "scrap of paper" and not on behalf of freedom of civilization which "were menaced by Germany," but because she feared a great increase in German power. The working class, held in the throes of the militarist organization, proved to be helpless to prevent the outbreak of this war. It was forced to make countless sacrifices to the mad predatory policy against which it had fought so resolutely and relentlessly. But although the working class was unable to prevent the outbreak of the world catastrophe, it will undoubtedly be able to utilize for itself and for the benefit of the cause it advocates the military situation which has arisen.

The present war signifies the complete collapse of the chief strongholds of the social and state order. The system of armed peace, for the maintenance of which the world powers madly wasted the people's money, has not only proved to be incapable of guaranteeing peaceful development for the peoples but has even created a new and to a certain extent an independent menace to international peace. Once called to life and destined in the hands of the diplomats to serve as an instrument for the carrying out of the desires of the dynasties and those of the ruling classes, the militarist organization acquired an independent significance; it became transformed from an instrument of international policy into a new factor of this policy and as such created a situation in which the "guns could go off of their own accord," as has actually happened in the present war.

This war has revealed with unusual clearness and vividness the entire falsehood of the mercenary advocates of the principles of humaneness and justice. It has exposed the complete hypocrisy of the advocates of the "sanctity and integrity" of state boundaries and of the foundation of the present order—the private property. Never before have international treaties and obligations been trodden under foot so barefacedly; never before has the "sacred right" of private property been violated so impudently and so cynically as in the present war.

The working class will know how to utilize, in the interests of an early realization of its own ideal, the disintegration of the foundations of the present regime which the war affords us. But, above all, the present bloodshed must be ended by the efforts of international socialism. Through organized pressure upon the governments of all the belligerent countries international socialism will endeavor to achieve peace terms which in the future would serve as a guaranty against a repetition of a similar world massacre. International socialism will demand first of all complete disarmament of the war fleets and the replacement of the standing army by a people's militia.

As a matter of international policy it will raise the question of a complete democratization of the state order in the belligerent countries. It will demand in particular the removal of international policy from the jurisdiction of professional diplomats and its transfer to the jurisdiction of people's representatives.

On the national question, which has played such an outstanding role in the present war, the international proletariat will advance first of all the demand for complete freedom of cultural and national development for all nationalities within the territory of every belligerent country. Without pledging itself to defend state boundaries as they exist at present, but at the same time believing that it cannot and should not engage in the redrawing of the map of Europe, the international proletariat will advance as a regulatory principle, at the time when territorial questions are settled, the principle of self-determination of the population of the disputed territories based on a plebiscite.

The international proletariat, striving to establish at the conclusion of the war firm and normal conditions of development for European peoples, must pay particular attention to the horrible position of the Jews in Russia and in Rumania and must advance an independent demand for national and civil equality for the Jews.

THE CENTRAL COMMITTEE OF THE BUND

B. THE LONDON AND VIENNA CONFERENCES

The London Conference of February 14, 1915, was regarded by the participants as a private meeting, and the minutes were not published. About forty delegates attended, among whom were: from Great Britain, Keir Hardie, Ramsay MacDonald, Bruce Glasier, and W. C. Anderson of the Independent Labour party, as well as delegates from the Labour party, the Fabian Society, and the British Socialist party; from Belgium, Vandervelde, Senator Lafontaine, and Huysmans, secretary of the I.S.B.; from France, Sembat, Longuet, Vaillant, Compère-Morel, Thomas, Jouhaux, and others; and, as representatives of Russia, the Socialist-Revolutionists Rubanovich, Chernov, and Bobrov. As noted above, the organizations of the Russian Social Democratic Labor party abroad were not invited; but Litvinov (Maximovich), representing the Central Committee, and Maisky, representing the Organization Committee, attended and presented declarations of their groups. The declaration of the Organization Committee was signed also by the Polish Socialist party (Levitsa). Speaking later of the resolution actually adopted, Bruce Glasier said that it was a "compromise resolution" and that "it did not represent his own point of view." "At all events," he said, "the resolution that was passed was a definite advance upon the statements made by the French and Belgian Socialists at the beginning of the war. It was noteworthy that the resolution contained a strong statement in regard to Russia. . . . ."[21]

In his account of the Conference Litvinov says that he learned the place of meeting only the night before. At the meeting he took the floor to protest "against not inviting the official representative of our party at the International Socialist Bureau." This official representative was Litvinov himself, but the chairman said all had been invited whose names were known. When Litvinov began to read the declaration of his group he was again interrupted by the chairman, who said that his standing as a delegate had not yet been ascertained and that they had gathered "not to criticize the various parties." After the Credentials Committee had decided to allow him to participate, Litvinov thanked the Conference for its "courtesy" and said he wished to continue his declaration in order to find out whether or not he could remain. The chairman interrupted to say that he would not allow the speaker to make "conditions" to the Conference.

21 Independent Labour party (hereafter cited as I.L.P.), *Report of the Annual Conference, 1915*, p. 52; *Labour Leader*, No. 7, February 18, 1915, p. 4.

Then Litvinov asked permission to declare why he would *not* participate in the Conference. This also was refused, whereupon Litvinov announced that the R.S.D.L. party would not participate in this Conference and that he was leaving a written statement of the reasons with the chairman. With this parting shot he picked up his papers and left. The chairman of the Central Committee of the Lettish Social Democracy also stated that he fully agreed with the Bolshevik declaration.[22] The Bolshevik comment on the Conference was to call attention to "the utter futility of its resolutions, which only cover up social chauvinism."[23]

UNOFFICIAL REPORT OF THE LONDON CONFERENCE, FEBRUARY 14, 1915[24]

That Vandervelde was the initiator of the London Conference is now becoming apparent. He considered it necessary: first, to raise the spirit of the proletarians, who are now fighting, by a clear and precise resolution; and, second, by a solemn confirmation of the tactics of the "Allied" socialists to destroy the basis for the discontent of the growing opposition. Vandervelde thought it impossible officially to take upon himself the initiative of calling the Conference, and therefore he proposed that the British socialists send out the invitations.

The British Independent Labour party demanded that the Germans and the Austrians should participate in the Conference, but the French *flatly refused* to attend the Conference with the Germans. They declared that meeting with the Germans was impossible for them. The French socialists considered the Conference premature but finally yielded to Vandervelde's insistence.

The agenda proposed by the British section of the International contained the following points:

1. *The rights of nations:* this included all questions of European policy.

   a) Belgium.
   b) Poland.

---

[22] Lenin, *The Imperialist War*, pp. 140–41.

[23] *Sotsial-Demokrat*, No. 39, March 3, 1915, p. 2.

[24] *Nashe Slovo*, No. 21, February 21, 1915, pp. 1–2; this report was written on the basis of notes forwarded to the editors of *Nashe Slovo* by a person who was present at the Conference.

2. All questions concerning colonies.

3. The guaranty of future peace.

It was surmised that the Conference would not pass any resolutions, and Keir Hardie, in opening the assembly, proposed to exchange opinions without passing any declarations.

Vandervelde proposed to adopt a resolution if agreement could be reached. Otherwise he proposed that no resolution be adopted.

Vaillant made an ultra-patriotic speech demanding the adoption of a declaration in which the socialists' views on war should be formulated. Further, Vaillant spoke of the war having been imposed upon France, that France did not wish a war, that the French proletariat is *waging war for peace* and will continue to wage it until German militarism is completely destroyed.

Vandervelde agreed that the war had been produced by general conditions of the capitalist order but that nevertheless Germany and Austria were guilty of causing this catastrophe. Belgium must be liberated and compensated; Poland must be restored, while the other oppressed peoples and provinces should be permitted to decide their own destiny.

Rubanovich, a Socialist-Revolutionist and patriot, read a report on the situation in Russia. This report stated that the police regime continues to rage in Russia. Further, the Conference learned from E. Rubanovich [I. A. Rubanovich] that some of the responsibility for Austria's attack upon Serbia falls upon Russia, that a victory of the Allies means a victory of democracy, that the Russian people are in favor of war, and, finally, that the Russian socialist deputies share his, Rubanovich's, point of view.

This fantastic report concerning the deputies was not refuted by anyone, for the Social Democrats were not at the conference.[25]

The English socialists did not speak and thereby surprised all the delegates. A Commission was appointed to draft a resolution. Russian socialism was represented in the Commission by Comrade Chernov and by E. Rubanovich, an "acting" socialist.

A three-hour battle took place in the Commission in favor of making less harmful the resolution proposed by Vandervelde, a resolution in which the Franco-Belgian point of view on war and on the socialist tasks was expounded.

[25] With regard to the statements attributed to Rubanovich about Russia's responsibility, Chernov wrote: "This was said not by Rubanovich, but by another Socialist-Revolutionist delegate, who even introduced an amendment to that effect and Rubanovich spoke against this in the Commission." Chernov further says that Rubanovich did not make the statement about the attitude of the socialist deputies in the Duma and that though there were Social Democratic delegates present they made no refutation because there was nothing to refute. ("Pismo v redaktsiiu," *Nashe Slovo*, No. 23, February 24, 1915, p. 2.)

Finally, after a number of mutual concessions, the Commission adopted the text of the resolution with six votes in favor. MacDonald voted against, while Chernov abstained from voting.[26]

The paragraph on which the delegates of the Independent Labour party did not want to vote, ran as follows:

"But, on the other hand, it [the Conference] records that this war began with an offensive of the militant monarchies of Central Europe against two small nations, one of which agreed to resort to arbitration while the other considered it necessary to remain faithful to its international obligations."

In debates during the plenary meeting of the Conference dissensions became especially manifest.

Bruce Glasier declared that he could not agree with Vandervelde's point of view that the ultimatum to Serbia was the cause of the war. The "rainbow" books prove something entirely different.

Sembat found that the first paragraph of the resolution was unjust. This paragraph states that *all governments are equally guilty.* If, for instance, France had violated Belgium's neutrality, then we socialists would have raised the banner of insurrection. If one does not protest against the violation of Belgium's neutrality, one repudiates the very principle of international treaties and therefore cannot desire the conclusion of peace, for peace is based on agreement. We continue to be antimilitarists and hope that the union of France with England is a sufficient guaranty against the reactionary intentions of Russia.

Anderson was not convinced by the arguments of the preceding orators. The Conference should not adopt resolutions which might in one way or another obstruct the Social Democratic opposition in Germany.

Merrheim refused to vote on that resolution because it implied that the aim of the war is to crush Germany politically and economically.

MacDonald said that he would have voted on the resolution had it not contained the paragraph on Belgium and Serbia. It is impossible to construct a line of conduct on the basis of official documents and government communications. England would have implicated herself in the war even if Belgium's neutrality had not been violated. We shall continue as before our struggle for peace.

Chernov declared that he had nothing against the resolution on

---

[26] Chernov states that having been charged with obstructionism in the Commission he replied that since the general meaning of the whole last section was inacceptable to him he would introduce no further amendments and would not participate in the voting. In the general session he and Bobrov refused to vote on the resolution and a declaration explaining their position was read by the chairman. ("Pismo v redaktsiiu," *Nashe Slovo,* No. 23, February 24, 1915, p. 2.)

grounds of principle,[27] but he could not, as a Russian socialist, vote in favor of it. This resolution might be acceptable to the socialists of Western Europe but was not acceptable to the Russians, who must struggle on two fronts—against Germany and against Tsarism.

Vaillant threatened to introduce the original text of the resolution.

Vandervelde emphasized the fact that the French have made all the concessions they could make. We would not like to introduce the original text of the resolution, for that would weaken socialism in the Allied countries.

The debates became heated, but the English did not yield. Finally, Vandervelde saved the situation.

"We all agree," he said, "on the most essential thing: *namely, what should be done and what should not be done.* Our dissensions are in evaluating the causes of the World War. I propose to withdraw the paragraph on Serbia and Belgium."

The English asked for a recess in order to talk matters over. After the recess the delegates of the Independent Labour party adhered to the resolution which passed with one abstention. . . . .

Two curious incidents must be noted.

The representative of the Bolshevik Central Committee could not read his statement because Keir Hardie, the chairman, stopped him when he came to "treason against the proletarian cause," whereupon the representative of the Central Committee withdrew. Hence the conclusion is that treason should be mentioned at the end and not at the beginning of the declaration. A resolution was circulated among the members of the Conference in which approximately the following was proposed: after the conclusion of peace labor legislation must be organized on an international scale and be solved in the *socialist* spirit, i.e., that the workers should have equal social guaranties in all countries, and under these conditions the term "citizen of the world" would become a reality.

This resolution was not adopted by the Commission [on resolutions] and the "citizen of the world" did not become a reality!

RESOLUTIONS ADOPTED AT THE LONDON CONFERENCE, FEBRUARY 14, 1915[28]

This Conference cannot ignore the profound general causes of the European conflict, itself a monstrous product of the antagonisms which

---

[27] He said nothing of the kind, Chernov declares. "On the contrary, his entire speech contained a number of fundamental objections to the resolutions . . . ." Chernov adds that there are other inaccuracies in the report on which he is not at liberty to comment. ("Pismo v redaktsiiu," *Nashe Slovo*, No. 23, February 24, 1915, p. 2.)

[28] I.L.P., *Report of the Annual Conference, 1915*, p. 121. A French version is given in *L'Humanité*, No. 3957, February 16, 1915, p. 1.

tear asunder capitalist society and of the policy of colonial dependencies and aggressive imperialism, against which international socialism has never ceased to fight and in which every government has its share of responsibility.

The invasion of Belgium and France by the German armies threatens the very existence of independent nationalities, and strikes a blow at all faith in treaties. In these circumstances a victory for German imperialism would be the defeat and the destruction of democracy and liberty in Europe. The socialists of Great Britain, Belgium, France, and Russia do not pursue the political and economic crushing of Germany; they are at war not with the peoples of Germany and Austria but only with the governments of those countries by which they are oppressed. They demand that Belgium shall be liberated and compensated. They desire that the question of Poland shall be settled in accordance with the wishes of the Polish people, either in the sense of autonomy in the midst of another state, or in that of complete independence. They wish that throughout all Europe, from Alsace-Lorraine to the Balkans, those populations that have been annexed by force shall receive the right freely to dispose of themselves.

While inflexibly resolved to fight until victory is achieved to accomplish this task of liberation, the socialists are none the less resolved to resist any attempt to transform this defensive war into a war of conquest, which would only prepare fresh conflicts, create new grievances, and subject various peoples more than ever to the double plague of armaments and war.

Satisfied that they are remaining true to the principles of the International, the members of the Conference express the hope that the working classes of all the different countries will before long find themselves united again in their struggle against militarism and capitalist imperialism. The victory of the Allied Powers must be a victory for popular liberty, for unity, independence, and autonomy of the nations in the peaceful federation of the United States of Europe and the world.

On the conclusion of the war the working classes of all the industrial countries must unite in the International in order to suppress secret diplomacy, put an end to the interests of militarism and those of the armament makers, and establish some international authority to settle points of difference among the nations by compulsory conciliation and arbitration and to compel *all nations* to maintain peace.

The Conference protests against the arrest of the deputies of the Duma, against the suppression of Russian socialist papers and the condemnation of their editors, as well as against the oppression of Finns, Jews, and Russian and German Poles.

DECLARATION OF THE ORGANIZATION COMMITTEE OF THE
RUSSIAN SOCIAL DEMOCRATIC LABOR PARTY AND THE
POLISH SOCIALIST PARTY (LEVITSA) AT THE
LONDON CONFERENCE[29]

The unsatisfactory organization of this Conference made it impossible for the socialist parties of Russia and Poland to send a delegation which would represent them more or less completely. Nevertheless, we intended to go to the Conference as representatives of the Organization Committee of the R.S.D.L. party and the Polish Socialist party in order to state the point of view of our organizations. But barriers erected by the police prevented us, at the last moment, from carrying out our intention and going to London. Therefore, we are compelled to resort to a written statement of our opinions on the existing condition of international socialism. We consider the calling of that Conference, on an artificially restricted basis of representation of the parties of the "Allied" states, to be a fundamental error. We refuse to recognize the principle of grouping the proletarians according to a temporary coincidence of the imperialist interests of their class enemies. To recognize that principle would signify the sanctioning and strengthening of the disintegration which the International has undergone since the beginning of the war. The Conference can rectify this primary error only in so far as it will carry out in its decisions a definite internationalist point of view, a point of view which could be used as a foundation for general demonstrations of the restored International.

The present war, foreseen by international socialism, has already revealed its nature as a ruthless war for imperialist dominance. Neither the false phrases of "politicians" nor the sentimental illusions of struggling nations can change by one iota the nature of this war, which is such that the complete ruin of one of the opponents by the other would be equally dangerous for social and political progress and for the safeguarding of peace in the future.

Adhering to that point of view, the parties which we represent have rejected from the very beginning of the war every thought of any solidarity with the Russian government and with the governments of the allied countries. Accordingly, our deputies have refused to vote war credits in the Duma. The necessity of such an irreconcilable position was urged upon us so much the more because we are confronted by

[29] *Nashe Slovo*, No. 20, February 20, 1915, p. 1. This declaration was not read at the Conference but was presented by Maisky, who explained the reason for the absence of the signatories. In a letter to various French papers Martov and Lapinski state that they would have voted against the resolutions adopted at London. (*Ibid.*) The Committee of the Polish Socialist Party (Levitsa) Abroad also published a further statement, which was considerably censored by the authorities, in *Zhizn*, No. 10, April 1, 1915, pp. 1–2.

Tsarism, which, as has been repeatedly confirmed by the International, is not only the worst enemy of the people whom it oppresses but also the most reliable stronghold of an all-European reaction.

Inasmuch as the proletariat and the socialist parties were unable to forestall the war, we believe that it becomes their most urgent duty to repudiate all moral and political solidarity with this terrible slaughter and to place all responsibility for it upon the governments of the belligerent countries. According to the character and spirit of the resolutions of the International congresses, the socialist party, having failed in its struggle to prevent war, is obliged to continue its struggle against militarism after war has broken out.

The socialist party can accomplish this task only if it fervently maintains its political independence with regard to the propertied classes and their governments. In no case can it entrust the cause, which the party did not have strength to realize, to its class enemies and to the success of their arms.

The labor party will only paralyze its own activity by binding itself to a closer and closer collaboration with its class enemies, who pursue aims in this war which are completely opposed to the aims of the party.

The marasmus condition into which the International has fallen will not end so long as the socialist party, after tearing away the chains which bind it to the bourgeois governments, does not dare finally to say the word which the masses in all countries are anxiously awaiting.

It is time to put an end to this general slaughter; it is time to begin to talk about peace!

Only a co-ordinated demonstration of the proletariat of all countries in favor of peace can restore the unity of the international organization of the proletariat and arouse its revolutionary spirit.

Only if peace is obtained through the pressure exerted by the masses —and not through a new conspiracy of greedy diplomatists and reactionary cliques after general exhaustion—will socialism and democracy be able to assert their influence upon the conditions of peace and upon the future constitution of Europe. Only in that case will the masses be able to struggle successfully against violation of the independence and freedom of peoples and attempts at forced annexations, and be able to defend the right of peoples to dispose of their own destinies. Only in that case can our propaganda in favor of disarmament and the extensive application of arbitration and democratic organization of military forces leave the sphere of a pitiful and unproductive illusion.

We beg the parties represented at the Conference to abstain from any manifestations and decisions which our class enemies could possibly use to make more profound the split within the proletariat and to paralyze the cause of reviving the International. We appeal to all socialists to unite the scattered forces of the proletariat for struggle in favor of peace and for general demonstrations directed toward straightening the battlefront of the proletarian movement, toward the resumption of class struggle upon a political and economic basis, toward the overthrow of despotic governments, the enslavers of the peoples, and toward the struggle against imperialism and chauvinist passions.

L. MARTOV
The Organization Committee of the R.S.D.L. Party
LAPINSKI
The Polish Socialist Party

DECLARATION OF THE CENTRAL COMMITTEE OF THE RUSSIAN SOCIAL DEMOCRATIC LABOR PARTY AT THE LONDON CONFERENCE, FEBRUARY 14, 1915[30]

Citizens! Your Conference calls itself the conference of the socialist parties of the Allied belligerent countries: Belgium, England, France, and *Russia*. Permit me first of all to call your attention to the fact that the Social Democracy of Russia as an organized whole, represented by the Central Committee and affiliated with the International Socialist Bureau, received no invitation from you. Russian Social Democracy (the views of which were expressed by the members of the Russian Social Democratic group of the Duma—Petrovsky, Muranov, Samoilov, Badaev, Shagov—and the labor representatives of Petersburg, Ekaterinoslav, Kharkov, Kostroma, and Vladimir provinces), which the Tsarist government at present has under arrest, has nothing in common with your Conference. We hope that you will declare this openly, in order not to be accused of perverting truth.

Allow me now to say a few words with regard to the purpose of your Conference, i.e., to say what Russian, class-conscious, Social Democratic workers would expect of you.

We think that before entering upon a discussion of the question of restoring the International and before attempting to re-establish international contact between the socialist workers, our socialist duty compels us to demand:

1. That Vandervelde, Guesde, and Sembat immediately withdraw from the bourgeois cabinets of Belgium and France.

---

[30] *Sotsial-Demokrat,* No. 40, March 29, 1915, p. 1. The editors of Lenin's *Sochineniia,* XXX, viii–ix, state that this declaration was written by Litvinov (Maximovich) and was included in Volume XVIII of the second edition of Lenin's collected works by mistake. The Director of the Communist Academy Library says in a letter to the editors of this book that the declaration was "originally outlined" by Lenin in his letter of February 9, 1915, to *Nashe Slovo.* See chapter ii, p. 163, above.

2. That the Belgian and French Socialist parties break up the so-called "national bloc," which is a betrayal of the socialist banner and which serves to conceal the orgies of chauvinism indulged in by the bourgeoisie.

3. That all socialist parties stop their policy of ignoring the crimes of Russian Tsarism and resume their support of that fight against Tsarism, which is being carried on by Russian workers who stop at no sacrifice.

4. That in fulfillment of the resolution of the Basel Congress a declaration be made that we extend our hand to those revolutionary Social Democrats of Germany and Austria who have answered the declaration of war by preparing propaganda for revolutionary activities. The voting of war budgets must be absolutely condemned. The Social Democrats of Germany and Austria have committed a monstrous crime against socialism and the International by voting war credits and by concluding "civil peace" with the Junkers, the priests, and the bourgeoisie; but Belgian and French socialists have behaved no better. We fully understand that such circumstances are possible when socialists, being in a minority, are compelled to submit to the bourgeois majority; but under no circumstances should socialists stop being socialists and join the chorus of bourgeois chauvinists; nor should they forget the workers' cause and enter bourgeois cabinets.

German and Austrian socialists commit a great crime against socialism when, following the example of the bourgeoisie, they declare hypocritically that the Hohenzollerns and Habsburgs are waging a war for liberation "from Tsarism."

But no less a crime is committed by those who assert that Tsarism is becoming more democratic and civilized and who pass over in silence the fact that Tsarism strangles and ruins unfortunate Galicia as the German Emperor strangles and ruins Belgium, and by those who keep silent about the fact that the Tsarist gang has thrown the parliamentary representatives of the Russian laboring class into prison and quite recently has condemned several Moscow workers to six years of penal servitude, merely for belonging to the Social Democratic party; that Tsarism oppresses Finland worse than ever—the labor press and labor organizations in Russia have been closed, the billions required by the war are being threshed out of starving peasants and indigent workers by the Tsarist gang.

Russian workers stretch out a comradely hand to socialists who act like Karl Liebknecht, like the socialists of Serbia and Italy, like the British comrades of the Independent Labour party and some of the members of the British Socialist party, and like the arrested comrades of our Social Democratic Labor party.

We summon you to this road, the road of socialism. Down with chauvinism, which ruins the proletarian cause! Hail! International socialism!

In the name of the Central Committee of the Russian Social Democratic Labor party,

M. MAXIMOVICH

The *Nashe Slovo* group also sent a communication to London denouncing the Conference as basically antagonistic to the international policy of the proletariat and as "a new attempt to misuse the ideas and authority of international socialism by making it cover up the interests of Russian, English, and French imperialisms, which are hostile to socialism." To bring about an early peace it was necessary to break up national blocs in all belligerent countries, to resume the class struggle, to refuse war and military credits, to withdraw Social Democrats from the bourgeois cabinets of France and Belgium, to defeat attempts to frustrate fraternization at the front, to appeal to the socialist women of belligerent countries and to support the fight against Tsarism.[31]

Like the London Conference of Entente socialists, the Vienna Conference of the socialists of the Central Powers met under the eyes of the government authorities, and its declaration given below was undoubtedly colored by that fact. Moreover, as in London, many of the delegates were opposed to revolutionary tactics, particularly in the existing situation. In addition to members of the Austrian party who were the hosts, Haase, Ebert, Molkenbuhr, Müller, and Luise Zietz represented the German and Garami and Kunfi represented the Hungarian Social Democratic parties.[32]

REPORT OF THE SOCIALIST CONFERENCE AT VIENNA,
APRIL 12–13, 1915[33]

Representatives of the Social Democracy of Germany, Austria, and Hungary met for discussion on April 12 and 13, and during this discussion they manifested complete harmony.

[31] *Nashe Slovo*, No. 26, February 27, 1915, p. 1. The French censor deleted large portions of this statement, but it was printed in full in the *Berner Tagewacht*, No. 42, February 20, 1915, p. 1.

[32] L. Brügel, *Geschichte der österreichischen Sozialdemokratie*, V, 221.

[33] *Arbeiter-Zeitung*, No. 111, April 22, 1915, p. 1.

In spite of the long duration of the war the peoples of all countries are absolutely determined to defend their independence with all their power. But the war, in its dimension, duration, and intensity has brought terrible misery upon mankind and has destroyed millions of lives and numerous things of cultural value which had been accumulated by the labor of many generations. The predictions of our authoritative students of economy and history at all international socialist congresses that continuous competition in armaments would lead to a world catastrophe have fatefully come true. Naturally, the proletariat suffers most of all in every way and in particular from the economic consequences of the war. Thus the longing for the ending of war and for the establishment of peace must be growing everywhere, not only in the belligerent but in the neutral countries as well. Especially with the approach of May Day, the idea of solidarity between peoples is reviving more than ever in the hearts of class-conscious workers of all countries.

The Social Democratic parties, which have long been and naturally are still working toward a brotherhood of peoples, are the qualified prophets of the desire for peace. This desire originates in the will and the power of self-confidence and not in a feeling of weakness. The necessary conclusion is that only such a peace as would not humiliate any of the peoples is possible, for only such a peace could establish a lasting co-operation among all civilized peoples.

The parties represented at the Conference stand upon the platform of the resolutions of the international socialist congresses in general and of the Copenhagen Congress of 1910 in particular, and they consider the following conditions necessary in concluding peace:

The establishment of compulsory international courts of arbitration for the settling of all conflicts among the various states.

The subjection of all government treaties and agreements to the democratic control of the people's representatives.

A stipulated international limitation of armaments with disarmament as its ultimate aim.

The recognition of the right of self-determination of peoples.

Further, the representatives of the Social Democratic parties of Germany, Austria, and Hungary declare: The fact that the Social Democratic parties of the belligerent countries defend their countries and their people should not become an obstacle to maintaining international contact among all the socialist parties, as well as to continuing the activity of their international institutions.

C. The International Conference of Socialist Women
at Berne, March 26–28, 1915, and the International
Youth Conference at Berne, April 5–7, 1915

The Third International Socialist Women's Conference
had been set to meet in connection with the Vienna Congress
of the Socialist International in August 1914. After Sarajevo and the Austrian ultimatum it was proposed to hold both
the Congress and the Women's Conference in Paris on August 22. The outbreak of the war prevented the holding of
these meetings. But in November 1914 the Central Committee of the R.S.D.L. party through the editorial board of
Rabotnitsa, composed of N. K. Krupskaia, Inessa Armand,
Z. Lilina, and L. Stahl, sent a letter to Klara Zetkin suggesting the calling of an unofficial conference in order to unite
the Lefts. One month later this letter, which contained the
chief postulates of the manifesto of the Central Committee
of the R.S.D.L. party and which urged the women of all
countries "to remain faithful to socialism" and "to draw the
working women into the struggle against every kind of civil
peace and in favor of a war against war, a war closely connected with civil war and social revolution," was slightly
amended and forwarded as a circular to Left-socialist women
of Germany, Austria, England, France, Bulgaria, Holland,
and the Scandinavian countries.[34]

In January Klara Zetkin wrote Inessa Armand that she
considered that a conference of Left-socialist women[35] would

[34] The draft of the circular letter of the editorial board of Rabotnitsa is preserved in the Archive of Marx-Engels-Lenin Institute and is cited by Baevsky in
"Borba za III Internatsional do Tsimmervalda," Proletarskaia Revoliutsiia, No. 4,
1934, p. 27.

[35] Archive of Marx-Engels-Lenin Institute, Klara Zetkin's letter to I. Armand
of January 2, 1915, cited by Baevsky in "Borba za III Internatsional do Tsimmervalda," Proletarskaia Revoliutsiia, No. 4, 1934, p. 28. In a letter to N. K. Krupskaia, Therese Schlesinger wrote that "only a very small number of women permit
themselves to uphold a point of view which differs from that of the party representatives" and that "they would lose all their influence if they were to speak abroad
without the permission of their own organization"; and N. K. Krupskaia summed
up the situation as follows: "The English women protested .... they propose to
speak of inoffensive matters, removed from all problems of class struggle. The
Dutch and Austrian women prefer a general conference because they are afraid that

be of "great benefit." "But," she added, "in order to carry it out great obstacles and difficulties will have to be overcome. First of all, it will be *difficult to draw a line between the Lefts and the Rights* among the women. Many of them do not know themselves on which side they are; others will hesitate to make a decision; whereas still *others will definitely refuse to take part in a conference of 'Left' women only.*"

The Conference was finally called by Klara Zetkin as Secretary of the International Socialist Women's Bureau.[36] Zetkin promised not to invite organizations that had become chauvinist and she intended to hold the Conference in the face of the anticipated opposition of the German and Austrian party administrations. "All our friends," she wrote to Liebknecht, "understand fully that the Women's International is doing preparatory work for a joint action of the big International and that it is the foremost champion of peace. All have promised support. The prospects of our women's activity are very favorable, in spite of the German party Presidium and V. Adler." She intended to notify the German Presidium only when all arrangements had been completed and hoped that both the German and Austrian parties would agree to official participation when they found that continued opposition would be futile.[37] In the end, however, the German women were obliged to attend without the official sanction of their party, and there was no Austrian delegate present.

In addition to the German delegates, of whom there were seven including Zetkin, there were four from England repre-

by participating in a conference of Left women they may create friction within their own organizations. Zetkin, who at first was in favor of a conference of the Lefts, now, according to the Dutch women, also favors a general conference." (Archive of Marx-Engels-Lenin Institute; Th. Schlesinger's letter to N. K. Krupskaia of January 28, 1915, and N. K. Krupskaia's letter to A. M. Kollontai of March 12, 1915, cited by Baevsky in "Borba za III Internatsional do Tsimmervalda," *Proletarskaia Revoliutsiia*, No. 4, 1934, pp. 29–30.)

[36] Baevsky, "Lenin i Tsimmervaldskaia levaia," *Borba Klassov*, No. 3, March 1934, pp. 35–36; Krupskaya, *Memories of Lenin*, II, 158–62.

[37] This letter to Liebknecht, written early in 1915, is given in *Bolshevik*, Nos. 13–14, 1934, pp. 104–107. Zetkin states that funds for the Conference were provided through "the spirit of self-sacrifice of the Dutch women."

senting the Independent Labour party and certain socialist organizations in the British International Women's Council, one from France, three from Holland, two from Switzerland, one from Italy, and one from the Regional Presidium of the Social Democracy of Poland and Lithuania. Next to Germany, Russia had the largest representation, with two delegates from the Menshevik Organization Committee and four from the Bolshevik Central Committee. Two Belgian delegates sent word that they had been refused passports by their government, and letters of greeting were sent by Therese Schlesinger from Austria, by Aleksandra Kollontai from Norway, by the Central Committee of the Polish Socialist party (Levitsa), and by both sections of the Social Democracy of Poland and Lithuania.[38]

Although the women present came from the Left elements of the socialist parties of their respective countries they were not far enough to the Left to satisfy the Bolsheviks, and the resolutions adopted reflected what Krupskaia called the "goody-goody pacifism of the English and the Dutch," to which Zetkin and the Germans made concessions in order to prevent a breakdown of the Conference.

UNOFFICIAL ACCOUNT OF THE INTERNATIONAL CONFER-
ENCE OF SOCIALIST WOMEN AT BERNE, MARCH 26–28, 1915

[From an Article by Olga Ravich][39]

. . . . The Third International Women's Socialist Conference met at Berne at the end of March 1915.

There were delegations from Germany, France, Switzerland, Holland, Poland, and Russia. In all about thirty persons arrived at the Conference. The Austrian women did not come, and limited themselves merely to sending greetings. The coming of the delegates was made difficult by police-military conditions, and by the leading official organs of the socialist parties. The German delegation came to the Conference in

---

[38] I. Izolskaia, Internatsionalnaia zhenskaia sotsialisticheskaia konferentsiia," *Nashe Slovo*, No. 63, April 13, 1915, pp. 1–2. The British were represented by Dr. Marion Phillips, Mary Longman, Margaret Bondfield, and Ada Salter (I.L.P., *Report of the Annual Conference, 1915*, p. 15).

[39] O. Ravich, "Mezhdunarodnaia zhenskaia sotsialisticheskaia konferentsiia 1915 g.," *Proletarskaia Revoliutsiia*, No. 10 (45), 1925, pp. 165–77.

spite of the fact that its party centers had forbidden it to attend; it actually represened a delegation from the opposition. The French delegate from the Left section of the party also participated. The official group of the French socialist women refused to take part in the Conference. The English delegation was from the Independent Labour party. All the other delegates were from official parties.

Russia was represented by two delegations: that of the Central Committee, which consisted of five persons—Sablina (Nadezhda Konstantinovna), Inessa, Elena (Rozmirovich), Zina (Lilina), and Anna [Kaminskaia] (representative of Poland)—and that of the Menshevik Organization Committee, which consisted of two persons, Balabanoff and Irina Izolskaia.

The return trip of the delegates was made so difficult that it was decided not to mention the names of the delegates anywhere. The speakers were indicated by the countries they represented. This explains why there is no complete list of names of those who attended the Conference.

The chairman of the Conference, Klara Zetkin, opened the Conference with a brief speech on the situation then existing in all countries and on the duty of the working women to lead a movement against the war. She proposed that the Conference constitute the third regular International Women's Socialist Conference. This proposal was unanimously adopted.[40]

The Conference began with brief speeches of welcome, which were designed to establish the actual composition of the Conference, i.e., to show what the delegates had brought with them and what they expected from the Conference.

The Swiss delegation, in spite of its declaration that the Swiss women were ready for international struggle and its expression of sorrow that some of the comrades had abandoned the road of internationalism, immediately pointed out that the hour to judge these comrades had not yet come. As to its means of struggle against the war the delegation did not go farther than a demand for peace.

The English delegation, with an obvious feministic tinge, asserted that all women in England, even bourgeois women and suffragettes, were against the war and wished for peace. The delegation expressed its hope

---

[40] Balabanoff writes: "The women's conference .... was not an official conference, for reasons which can be well understood. The women comrades who took part in it acted neither as representatives of definite organizations nor of definite party presidiums, but on their own responsibility" ("Die internationale Frauenkonferenz zu Bern," *Lichtstrahlen*, No. 10, April 25, 1915, p. 192). The official report in *Beilage zur Berner Tagwacht*, No. 77, April 3, 1915, p. 1, does not mention this resolution, and the resolution quoted below refers to this as an "extraordinary" conference.

that this war would be the last war and that the soldiers would stop shooting.

The German delegation, after pointing out the great significance of the fact that representatives of various countries had succeeded in meeting and in giving each other their hands in brotherly solidarity, and that the German women, most of all, were depressed by the collapse of socialism, further expressed the hope that the masses would follow the internationalists instead of the official parties and stressed the necessity of building a new International.

The Russian delegation of the Central Committee of the Russian Social Democratic Labor party (Bolsheviks) reported on the attitude of the masses, the protests against the war, and the trial of the Duma group, and stated the party's viewpoint on current events.

The Russian delegation of the Organization Committee (Mensheviks) declared that there was no *Burgfrieden* ("civil peace") in Russia, that German Social Democracy had committed treason against socialism, and that this had affected adversely the revolutionary struggle in Russia. It concluded with a wish for a democratic peace.

The French delegation pointed out that in France there were few internationalists, that they placed all their hope in the fact that their comrades in other countries were stronger. It was difficult for them to work, not only on account of the police conditions[41] but even to a greater extent on account of the persecutions from their own party. All their hope was placed on the masses.

From all that was expressed in the welcoming speeches it was clear that the delegates who met spoke different languages. The prevailing conception was that the fundamental task was the struggle for peace. No one had the slightest idea about passing over to civil war. A break with the leaders who had betrayed socialism was not suggested by anyone. This circumstance put a definite stamp on the work of the Conference.

The following agenda of the Conference was accepted:

1. International activity of women in favor of peace (*Friedensaktion*)

2. Struggle against high cost of living

3. How women must struggle against nationalism and chauvinism

Klara Zetkin was the speaker on the first question. As the question about the *Friedensaktion* (struggle for peace) was the most fundamental question at the Conference, a written resolution on that question had been distributed among the delegates beforehand. This resolution was

---

[41] See Louise Saumoneau, "The Case of Louise Saumoneau," *The Socialist Review*, No. 76, January–March, 1916, pp. 44–50, in which she tells of her experiences with the police and her party on her return from Berne.

on behalf of the International Secretariat of the women's socialist organizations. . . . .[42]

The delegation of the Central Committee put forward its own draft resolution.[43] This draft was composed on the basis advanced earlier in the manifesto of the Central Committee (see No. 33 of *Sotsial-Demokrat*). It especially emphasized the necessity of transforming the imperialist war into a civil war, of leading a wide revolutionary activity in the masses—through illegal organizations in places where it could not be done legally—by disclosing the lies of the "defense of the fatherland" slogan, and by advancing the slogan of the Third International. This draft resolution also put plainly and simply the question of the necessity of a complete break with the official leaders of the party who had betrayed socialism.

The French delegate submitted her draft resolution, but after receiving some corrections from her group in Paris—these corrections could be summarized as follows: opposition to the voting of war credits and to having socialists enter bourgeois cabinets—with which she did not agree, she withdrew her resolution.[44]

Hence, after Zetkin's report, in which she defended on the whole her own resolution, debates on the two resolutions began.

The late Inessa Armand spoke in defense of the Russian resolution. With amazing precision and clearness she presented reasons for every postulate advanced in the draft resolution. She declared that the women who had gathered at the Conference were first of all socialists. The aim of the Conference was to co-ordinate international activity, not only in the work for peace but in socialist activity as a whole. . . . .

"We Social Democrats who adhere to the Central Committee consider," Inessa declared, "that the slogan of civil war must be advanced now and that the labor movement is now entering upon a new phase in the course of which socialism will be attained in the more advanced countries, and a democratic republic in the more backward countries." (At that time this way of putting the question was considered by our

[42] See below, pp. 297–300.

[43] English translation is given in Lenin, *The Imperialist War*, pp. 472–73.

[44] Louise Saumoneau, who represented the Comité d'Action Féminine Socialiste pour la Paix et contre le Chauvinisme, said that they should not discuss questions other than those dealt with in the resolutions of the international congresses; they should discuss peace and not the parties' conduct. She did not oppose the voting of war credits or socialist participation in bourgeois cabinets but she did oppose illegal activities. She said further that she believed that the corrections to her resolutions sent by the group she represented were "the result of the influence of the Russian comrades and I consider this influence harmful." (From Krupskaia's notes. Bantke, "Lenin i Tsimmervaldskoe dvizhenie vo Frantsii," *Proletarskaia Revoliutsiia*, No. 3, 1934, p. 118.)

party to be absolutely correct [Author's note]). "The working women should be told directly that peace can be attained through revolution and that real salvation from war lies in socialism."

The debates which followed really revolved around the resolution of the Russian delegation. In the main the speakers could not present serious arguments against this resolution. Some of them even stressed the correctness of treating the fundamental question that way but —— still felt that it should not be accepted. The objections were as follows: the peace Conference is not the place to discuss these questions; the examination of the conduct of the socialist parties is a matter for general international congresses; this Conference should not be transformed into a tribunal to pass one-sided verdicts; a discussion of these questions would call forth an unnecessary sharpening of relations and would create new obstacles to the activities for peace; the time to appeal for a revolution had not yet come; when the workers should have returned from the front, when from every family one or more persons should be missing and there would be material ruin in addition, anger would be so great that revolution would flare up inevitably.

Many of those who at that time argued in this way, now understand their error —— but at that time they were in the majority. The truly revolutionary resolution was declined by twenty-one votes. Only six hands of the Russian delegation were raised in its favor.

The resolution of the International Secretariat of the women's organizations was adopted by the same number of votes (twenty-one against six)—a resolution that was rather vague and which did not touch on any of the fundamental questions of action.

That then is how the most fundamental question was solved. Not at all as the Bolsheviks had wished.

The Russian delegation of the Central Committee submitted the following declaration:

"We vote against the resolution accepted by the Conference for the following reasons:

"International socialism as a whole is passing through a tremendous crisis.

"Our Conference has assembled at a moment when the Workers' International has fallen to pieces, when a new building of the Third International must be erected under great hardships. The first condition for this undertaking would be to look straight and fearlessly into the eyes of truth, to express openly the whole truth concerning the causes of the internal crisis of the socialist parties. 'Diplomacy' in the labor movement has already caused great harm to our cause. No further step can be taken without putting an end to it.

"The tactics of the official leaders of the socialist parties with regard to the war are not merely mistakes but are actual *treason* against the cause of socialism. Opportunism has for a long time been leading toward this fatal outcome and has finally achieved it. The opportunists have replaced socialism with imperialism. In no country can we socialists, who have remained such, take even one step forward without engaging in a sharp struggle against the opportunists and the social chauvinists. It is our duty to tell this to the men and women workers. There is no more fatal point of view than the position of the so-called 'Center' headed by Kautsky, Adler, and others, the 'Center' which disguises the basic controversies between the socialists and the opportunists who serve directly the bourgeoisie and the governments.

"Our resolution had to express this in one form or another. Our Conference could become the first nucleus of the future Third International if it would take a decisive stand against opportunism. This we wished to accomplish in our draft resolution. Almost all the delegates who spoke expressed solidarity with the basic principles of our resolution. We believe that if a solidarity in principle had actually existed we should have expressed it in a resolution which would have fully and definitely treated this question.

"At the same time we declare that we will support every practical move in the direction of the revolutionary mass struggle and a struggle against social chauvinism, in spite of the fact that the resolution which was accepted does not satisfy us."

The next question concerned a struggle against the high cost of living. . . . .

A resolution was accepted with regard to the high cost of living which appealed to the working women for a most decisive struggle against the high cost of living and speculation. This resolution was unanimously accepted.

The next question, the struggle against nationalism and chauvinism, again brought the Conference to a clash with the Russian delegation of the Central Committee.

The picture of chauvinism, of hatred of other nations, and of narrow nationalism, which rose out of the speeches of the delegates, was so vivid that there could be no doubt about the necessity of repudiating chauvinism. All the delegates unanimously asserted that chauvinism had deep roots, that as a matter of fact there had been a deficiency in socialist education. For instance, Klara Zetkin said that not all socialists clearly understood that socialism was not a simple political doctrine but a world philosophy. In order swiftly to overcome nationalism and chauvinism it would be necessary for the masses to think, feel, and act in the spirit of socialism.

There was nothing else to do but to begin immediately a widespread mass agitation in favor of socialism and against nationalism. Influence in the schools had to be attained at any price—schools in which chauvinism and nationalism were especially strong and were already bringing sad results.

The Russian delegation of the Central Committee was opposed to such vagueness and again attempted to put the question squarely. Among other things the delegation declared:

"It is absolutely necessary to struggle against *Burgfrieden* (civil peace), against the 'defense of the fatherland' slogan, against the voting of war credits, against entering bourgeois cabinets. It is necessary to promote fraternizing in the trenches ———.

"The most effective measure against any kind of nationalism is, of course, a close connection between the proletariat of all countries and, in particular, international labor action. The International has met and accepted general decisions but has not undertaken any joint actions. The future new International will have to pass over to joint revolutionary actions ———. In the struggle against the war the proletariat must persevere to the end and must not fear a defeat of the fatherland. Such a defeat would only facilitate the revolutionary struggle and civil war of the proletariat."

As a first practical step the organization of an international bulletin was recommended, or at least the collaboration in socialist periodicals of socialists of various countries.

It stands to reason that the Conference did not agree with the Russian delegation on that question either. At the very end the Conference considered it necessary to accept a resolution of sympathy and approval with respect to all attempts to re-establish peace. The resolution read:

"The Conference gladly welcomes all attempts of nonsocialists directed toward the attainment of peace, and it welcomes with special sympathy the international movement of the nonsocialist women in favor of peace, and sends its fraternal greeting to the international congress of pacifists which will take place at The Hague in the near future."

This resolution, which was introduced quite unexpectedly by the English delegation, called forth a protest on the part of the Russian delegation of the Central Committee, a protest which can easily be understood. The Russian delegation wished to call the women socialists to action and did not hope for anything from the pacifist Congress. This resolution seemed to ridicule the entire work of the Conference.

However, the resolution was accepted by the votes of all delegates except the Russian delegates of the Central Committee and the Polish delegate.

The unanimously accepted resolution of protest against the arrest and prosecution of the Russian Social Democratic Labor group in the State

Duma and against the arrest of Rosa Luxemburg in Germany could not rectify the line traced at the Conference by the majority of delegations . . . .[45]

MANIFESTO OF THE INTERNATIONAL CONFERENCE OF SOCIALIST WOMEN AT BERNE, MARCH 1915[46]

Women of the working people!
Where are your husbands?
Where are your sons?

For eight months they have been out on the battlefields. They have been torn away from their work and their homes—youths, the support and hope of their parents, men in the prime of life, and men with hair turning gray—the providers of their families. They are all clad in uniforms, live in trenches, and are ordered to destroy that which has been built up by diligent labor.

Millions of them already rest in common graves. Thousands upon thousands have been taken to hospitals with lacerated bodies, shattered limbs, blinded eyes, wrecked minds, seized by epidemic diseases or prostrated by exhaustion.

Burned villages and towns, ruined bridges, devastated fields, and destroyed forests are evidences of their deeds.

Proletarian women!

You were told that your husbands and sons departed to defend you, feeble women, your children, your houses, and your hearths.

What is the real truth?

A double burden has been imposed upon the shoulders of you "weaker" women. Defenseless, you have been delivered up to sorrow and misery. Your children starve and freeze and you are threatened with the loss of shelter; your hearth is cold and empty.

You were told of a great brotherhood and sisterhood between high and low, of civil peace between poor and rich. Now civil peace manifests itself by the *owners of enterprises reducing your wages, the merchant and the unscrupulous profiteer raising prices, and the landlord threatening to put you out into the street.* The state is parsimonious and *bourgeois philanthropy is cooking poor-man's soup and advising you to be economical.*

---

[45] The account of the Conference given more briefly in an official report corresponds with that given above ("Internationale sozialistische Frauenkonferenz in Bern. Offizieller Verhandlungsbericht," *Beilage zur Berner Tagwacht*, No. 77, April 3, 1915). Short notices are given in *Labour Leader*, No. 14, April 8, 1915, p. 7, and *L'Humanité*, No. 4006, April 6, 1915, p. 1.

[46] *Berner Tagwacht*, No. 77, April 3, 1915, p. 1. An incomplete text of this manifesto in English appeared in *Labour Leader*, No. 22, June 3, 1915, p. 8.

What is the purpose of this war which brings you such terrible suffering?

It is said that this is done for the welfare and the defense of the fatherland.

What is the welfare of the fatherland?

Should it not be the well-being of the many millions of people whom the war turns into corpses, cripples, unemployed, beggars, widows, and orphans?

Who endangers the welfare of the fatherland? Is it the men who are across the frontier in different uniforms who desired this war just as little as did your husbands or who knew just as little why they should murder their brothers? No! The fatherland *is endangered by those who derive their riches from the misery of the broad masses and base their dominance upon oppression.*

Who benefits from the war?

Only a *small minority in every nation.*

The *manufacturers* of rifles and cannon, armor plate and torpedo boats, *the owners of docks,* and the *suppliers of army needs.* In the interest of their own profits they have stirred up hatred among the peoples and have thus caused the outbreak of the war. The war benefits the *capitalists in general.* Is it not true that the labor of the disinherited and exploited masses has accumulated goods which they who have produced them are not allowed to use? Well, they are poor; they cannot pay for them! The *sweat of the workers* produced those goods, the *blood of the workers* must conquer new markets abroad to which those goods can be exported. Colonial lands must be seized where the capitalists can rob the ground of its treasure and exploit cheap labor.

Not the *defense* of the fatherland but its *expansion* is the *purpose* of this *war.* Such are the desires of the capitalist order, for without exploitation and oppression of man by man it cannot exist.

The workers have nothing to gain from this war but they are apt to lose all that is dear to them.

Working women and wives of workers!

The men of the belligerent countries have been forced to keep silent. The war has dulled their minds, broken their wills, and deformed their entire beings.

But you women who in addition to the gnawing worry for your loved ones at the front, endure misery and deprivation at home, why do *you* delay in voicing your will for peace, your protest against the war?"

What deters you?

So far you have *suffered* because of your loved ones, now you should *act* for the benefit of your husbands and your sons.

Enough of slaughter.

This call rings out in all languages. Millions of proletarian women sound this call. It echoes back from the trenches in which the consciences of the nations' sons revolt against the slaughter.

Women of the working people!

In these difficult days the socialist women of Germany, England, France, and Russia have assembled. Your miseries and your sufferings have touched their hearts. For the sake of the future of your loved ones they call upon you to act for peace. As the will of the socialist women is united across the battlefields, so you in all countries must close your ranks in order to sound the call: peace, peace!

The World War has imposed upon you the greatest sacrifice! It robs you of the sons to whom you gave birth in pain and sorrow, and whom you have reared with effort and worry; it robs you of the men who have been your companions in the difficult struggle of life. In comparison to these sacrifices all others are small and void.

All mankind looks to you, proletarian women of the belligerent countries. You must become heroines, redeemers.

Unite! One in will and one in deed!

Proclaim a millionfold what your husbands and sons cannot yet aver: the laboring people of all countries are brothers. Only the united desire of this people can command this slaughter to cease.

Only socialism means future peace among mankind.

Down with capitalism which sacrifices hundreds of people to the wealth and power of the propertied.

Down with war! Onward to socialism!

The International Socialist Women's Conference was attended by comrades from: *Germany, France, England, Russia, Poland, Italy, Holland* and *Switzerland.*

BERNE, March 1915

RESOLUTION OF THE INTERNATIONAL CONFERENCE OF SOCIALIST WOMEN AT BERNE, MARCH 1915[47]

The Extraordinary Conference of socialist women, which met at Berne on March 26, 27, and 28, and which was attended by active comrades from Germany, France, England, Russia, Poland, Italy, Holland, and Switzerland, declares that:

The present World War has its roots in capitalist imperialism. It was finally conjured up by the requirements of the exploiting and ruling

---

[47] *Beilage zur Berner Tagwacht,* No. 77, April 3, 1915, pp. 1–2. This resolution was drawn up by Klara Zetkin in consultation with the Dutch socialist women and submitted to the British section before the Conference met. (Marion Phillips, "The Women's International," *The Contemporary Review,* No. 593, May 1915, p. 650.)

classes in the different countries. In a competitive struggle against one another they endeavor to spread their exploitation and their dominance beyond the boundaries of their native states. At the same time they fortify and establish permanently their exploitation and their rule over propertyless compatriots. International financial interests—the large armament industries—are continually active among the propertied classes as a special war menace and a war danger. These exploit the nations by driving the states toward competitive armaments.

History will establish what a tremendous responsibility for the outbreak of war falls upon the governments and the diplomacy of various great powers. For eight months the World War has destroyed immeasurable and inestimable quantities of cultural values and caused countless hecatombs of human lives. It has trod upon and disgraced the highest achievements of civilization, the most sublime ideals of humanity. Since its outbreak, it has *violated international law*. This deserves condemnation, for it has been injurious to small, neutral *Belgium*. In the *end* it threatens *to bleed white the peoples which take part in the war* and to cause their complete economic exhaustion. It threatens to paralyze for a long time the socialist forces—the carriers of historic progress.

Above all, the *World War* is *irreconcilably opposed to the interests of the working classes* in both the belligerent and the neutral countries of Europe and all over the world. Under the misleading slogan of preserving the interests of the fatherland through a patriotic fulfillment of duty, it wastes the property and blood of the working people and in order to achieve the aims of capitalist imperialism it demands the energy of the working people, their willingness to sacrifice, and their fighting ability. Thus it places the best proletarian forces at the service of the exploiting and ruling classes.

Under the same slogan, the World War *unites nationally* the workers of the belligerent countries with their exploiters and masters and *separates* them *internationally* from their brothers, the proletarians across the frontier. In place of the class struggle of the workers for the improvement of their condition and for their ultimate liberation, it puts national "civil peace"; in place of international solidarity it puts international fratricidal slaughter. It separates the peoples not merely by the streams of blood which flow from the battlefields but also by filthy *streams* of hatred, conceit, slander, and outrage. A base chauvinist attitude which disgraces the fatherland rather than contributes to its honor through an unprejudiced recognition of the cultural achievements of other nations has spread. Through all this the World War paralyzes and corrupts nationally the class struggle of the workers and makes more difficult their international advance against their worst enemy, the capitalist order. *It prevents the working class from carrying out its great historic mission: the liberation of the proletariat as the accomplishment of the united proletarians of all countries.*

Proceeding from these considerations the Extraordinary Conference of socialist women declares *war on this war! It demands the immediate cessation* of this monstrous fight among peoples. It demands *a peace without annexations and without conquests,* a peace which would recognize the right of self-determination and independence of peoples and nationalities—including small ones—and which would not impose humiliating and intolerable conditions upon any of the belligerent states. This peace will be a premise for the liberation of the proletariat of the *belligerent countries* from the *yoke of nationalism.* It will aid the socialist parties and the labor organizations to regain completely their freedom of action for class struggle and as the vanguard of the working masses having a clear purpose to rally these masses around the banner of international socialism.

This Extraordinary Women's Conference is convinced *that an early cessation of the World War can be enforced only by the clear and unswerving will of the masses of the people themselves in the belligerent countries.* This will meet with the active and unanimous support of the socialists and the proletarians of the *neutral states.* It is the most sacred duty of the *socialist women,* especially of the working women, to lead the struggle for peace bravely, with willingness to sacrifice and with the desire for peace born of the profound sorrow caused by the war and proclaiming this desire as a clear and conscious will for peace.

The women's Conference thus urges the socialist and proletarian women of all countries, fearing neither obstacles nor persecutions, not to lose time nor to miss the opportunity of utilizing all the available ways and means to proclaim through mass demonstrations of all kinds their international solidarity and consciousness and their will for peace. This war points out to the *women* a *historic role* in the *struggle* for peace, which when understood and carried out will have great import for *women's suffrage* and the *success of socialism.*

The women's Conference which has met at this very troubled time, has proved that for the achievement of *one aim,* the *socialist women* of all countries, especially of the *belligerent countries,* are united in the old fraternal faithfulness and in recognition of one great solidarity and duty of unified will and action. The Conference hopes that the proletarian women of all countries will rally as unanimously in support of the *international peace action.* By so doing they would act in the spirit of the International Congresses of Stuttgart, Copenhagen, and Basel, which by unanimous decisions have laid down as the duty of the socialist parties of all countries the following:

".... In case war should break out notwithstanding, it is their duty to intervene in favor of its speedy termination and with all their powers to utilize the economic and political crisis created by the war to rouse the masses and thereby to hasten the downfall of capitalist class rule."

The women's Conference expects, therefore, *that the socialist parties of all countries will take it upon themselves, quickly, resolutely, and with clear aim, to lead the peoples in their struggle for peace.* The peace action of the socialist *women* must be the *forerunner* of a general movement of the working masses designed to terminate the fratricidal slaughter. It must mean an important forward step toward the restoration of the Workers' International.

A BOLSHEVIK EVALUATION OF THE INTERNATIONAL CONFERENCE OF SOCIALIST WOMEN

[From a Statement by the Central Committee of the Russian
Social Democratic Labor Party][48]

. . . . The Conference has not entirely fulfilled the task which had been placed before it by events. The Conference could have marked out the first guideposts for a general socialist struggle of socialists of various countries; it could have laid the cornerstone of the future International. It has not done so . . . .

Nevertheless, even within the restricted limits set by the majority of the Conference, the socialist women's Conference was of great significance. It was the first real international Conference since the beginning of the war at which Left women socialists of belligerent countries who in one way or the other went "against the current" met. They may have confirmed incompletely and quite insufficiently in their resolution their principal attitude toward contemporary events and tasks; nevertheless, something has been accomplished in this direction, and in so far as the struggle for peace takes on revolutionary forms the Conference will assist in unifying the international revolutionary struggle of the proletariat. . . . .

The "Lefts" have already raised in all countries the banner of socialism. Two world conceptions, two tactics have clashed, have entered a struggle. On the one hand, the tactic of national unity and defense of the fatherland; on the other hand, the tactic of class struggle and international unity of the proletariat, a tactic which, from the very beginning of the war, has been pursued by the Central Committee and by our Social Democratic Labor group in the Duma, the tactic of revolutionary socialism. The irreconcilability, the incompatibility, of these two tactics is being better and better comprehended by their advocates. The International, which will not betray the socialist ideal, can be restored only by uniting the proletariat around the banner of revolutionary socialism

[48] *Sotsial-Demokrat,* No. 42, May 21, 1915, supplement, p. 2.

and by means of a decisive separation from social patriotism and opportunism. Representatives of the majority at the Conference have taken only a timid, irresolute step, but life will push them ahead and will take what is due it.

One week after the adjournment of the women's Conference an international socialist youth conference opened in Berne. Like the preceding meeting, this was held without the blessing of the official socialist international organization, the Bureau of the International Socialist Youth League. This Bureau had been formed in March 1907 with Henri de Man of Belgium as secretary. The organization was closely connected with and dependent on the Second International, and its two regular conferences in 1907 and 1910 and an informal conference in 1912 were held simultaneously with the Congress of the International at Stuttgart, Copenhagen, and Basel. The Copenhagen Conference of the International Socialist Youth League elected a new bureau consisting of de Man, Höglund (Sweden), Škatula (Bohemia), Krogh (Norway), and Robert Danneberg (Austria), who also served as secretary. It had been planned to hold another conference at Vienna in the summer of 1914 in connection with the regular Congress of the International, and here questions relating to the incorporation of the Youth Bureau in the International Socialist Bureau and to the general organization of a Youth International were to be decided.[49] When it became clear not only that a meeting at Vienna was out of the question but that the secretary, Danneberg, was disinclined to call a conference on his own responsibility, some of the leaders of the national youth organizations took the initiative. The result was the meeting in Berne which opened on April 5 and which actually was a meeting of the opposition elements in the international youth movement.

There were fourteen delegates in full standing: three from Germany (members of the German Youth League, who opposed the policy of the majority), three from Russia (two

[49] Münzenberg, *Die sozialistische Jugend-Internationale,* pp. 15–36.

Bolsheviks and one Menshevik), one each from Poland, Holland, Bulgaria, Italy, and Denmark, one representing Norway and Sweden, and two from Switzerland. Platten, Grimm, and Vogel, representatives of the Swiss Social Democratic party, were also present at the meetings.

As appears from Münzenberg's account given below, the Russian delegation objected both to the procedure and to the resolutions of the majority of the Conference and temporarily withdrew. They were, however, persuaded to return; but they failed to secure the adoption of their resolution, the text of which has not been found, or to prevent the adoption of the majority resolution which they severely criticized. The young men and women at the Conference were not prepared to move as far to the left as the Bolsheviks wished, but it is interesting to note that by electing a new bureau and establishing a new secretariat in Switzerland, the socialist youth (at least that part represented at Berne) was seemingly less reluctant than the socialist elders to go ahead with the reconstruction of the socialist international organization broken and disabled by the war.[50]

THE INTERNATIONAL YOUTH CONFERENCE AT BERNE, April 5–7, 1915

[From an Account by Münzenberg][51]

BERNE CONFERENCE

Before the war we maintained a number of international connections. As a result of my trip through Germany a lively correspondence opened with all the youth groups which I had visited. The connections with the Central Committee of the Italian socialist youth organization and with all the groups with which we became acquainted during our trip through Italy in 1912 were never interrupted. In September 1914 we began to

[50] In addition to Münzenberg's account given below, a brief official report is given in *Berner Tagwacht*, No. 88, April 17, 1915, p. 1; other accounts are given in *Nashe Slovo*, No. 68, April 18, 1915, pp. 1–2, in *Lichtstrahlen*, No. 10, April 25, 1915, pp. 192–93, and by Krupskaya, *Memories of Lenin*, II, 163. See also N. K. Krupskaia's letter to A. Kollontai of May 7, 1915; Archive of the Marx-Engels-Lenin Institute, No. 18004, cited by Baevsky, "Borba za III Internatsional do Tsimmervalda," *Proletarskaia Revoliutsiia*, No. 4, 1934, p. 32.

[51] V. Miuntsenberg [W. Münzenberg], *S Libknekhtom i Leninym*, pp. 92–102.

correspond actively with the Norwegian, Swedish, Danish, and Italian socialist youth leagues for the purpose of calling a conference of socialist youth organizations which would revive the proletarian Youth International.

In agreement with the youth organizations of these countries, I as secretary of the Swiss Youth League proposed to the International Bureau in Vienna on November 10, 1914, that it should call an international conference of socialist youth organizations not later than the Pentecost of 1915. The International Bureau on a postal card, classically laconic, declared its incompetence to do so.

The card read as follows:

"Respected Comrade! It is entirely impossible at the present moment to tell whether or not we shall be able to hold a congress on the Pentecost of 1915. Therefore, for the time being, I can say nothing definite with regard to your proposal. Greetings!   "DANNEBERG"

We became convinced that it would be impossible to call a conference through the medium of the International Bureau and decided to organize it without the Bureau. Our correspondence became more active and resulted in a number of socialist youth organizations promising to send their delegates to the Conference at Berne during the Easter days of 1915. A negative reply was received only from the French socialist youth organization, which declared that it could not take part in that Conference since the French Socialist party had not yet pronounced itself on that question, whereas the point of view of the youth organization would automatically coincide with that of the party.[52] The Central Committee of the Austrian socialist youth organization welcomed by letter the calling of a conference but did not send delegates. The Central Bureau of the German Youth Committees, guided as usual by F. Ebert, brusquely declined to participate, and protested against any conference. . . . .[53]

[52] Bantke writes: "The feelings were different below, in the masses. Particularly in the provinces there was a left-minded socialist youth which wished but could not send delegates to Berne, for the government refused to issue passports. A telegram was dispatched, however, in which a section of the French youth expressed its solidarity with the socialist youth of all countries and promised to work in support of the antimilitarist resolutions adopted by the international congresses prior to the war." (Bantke, "Lenin i tsimmervaldskoe dvizhenie vo Frantsii," *Proletarskaia Revoliutsiia*, 3, 1934, p. 119.) Münzenberg gives the text of a telegram received by the Conference from an independent group of Paris students. The telegram was composed in this same spirit. (Münzenberg, *Die sozialistische Jugend-Internationale*, p. 39.)

[53] The letters exchanged in this connection by the initiators of the Berne International Socialist Youth Conference and the various national centers of the youth movement are given in Schüller, *Geschichte der Kommunistischen Jugend-Internationale*, I, pp. 81-93.

The opening meeting of the Conference was held in the hall of the Berne People's House and was an impressive demonstration of the ideas of the international revolutionary socialist youth movement. Aside from the representatives of the socialist youth organizations, the speakers were Robert Grimm from the Presidium of the Swiss Social Democratic party and Angelica Balabanoff from the Italian party.

The first business meeting was taken up with delegates' reports concerning the state and activity of their organizations. In his report on Norway, Olaussen stated that 16,000 members of the Norwegian socialist youth organization made up the nucleus of the Left wing of the Norwegian party. Together with the youth opposition, the Left wing was endeavoring to revolutionize this party. The same was true also of the trade unions.

The representative of the Swedish youth organization, which had 8,000 members, reported a still greater influence exerted upon the Swedish party.

In Denmark the socialist youth organization held a review of 7,000 members. At a recent convention it had worked out thoroughly the question of combating militarism. The Danish youth organization had resolved, in case of mobilization, to carry out a soldiers' strike.

Luteraan made a report on Holland. He stated that the Left-socialist organization, which he represented, in its struggle against the reformist youth organization always insisted on a revolutionary demonstration against war.

Comrade Inessa [Armand] made a report on the situation in Russia. She said that since under Tsarism youth organizations as such in Russia were prohibited by law, they functioned in the form of dramatic societies, literary circles, etc. Many young boys and girls paid dearly for their ruthless struggle against Tsarism. The youth organizations in Russia— said the speaker—were constructed differently from those in Western Europe. In the majority of cases the youth worked jointly with the elders. The Russian labor youth is at present just as internationalist-minded as it was before the war. There the struggle against Tsarism and capitalism and in favor of peace is being continued fearlessly.

Egorov reported on Poland. He said that the Polish laboring youth supported an irreconcilable class struggle. It is against soldiers' strikes and insists on the carrying out of a purposeful class struggle against capitalism.

Minev reported on the youth movement in Bulgaria.

He said that a union of socialist youth had formerly existed in Bulgaria. During the Balkan war it had been suppressed. It had been refounded after the war. Now the chief attention of the youth organization was directed toward the socialist education of the youth. Apart from the Marxist orientation of the Social Democratic party (to which the speaker belonged) there exists in Bulgaria a reformist orientation. This current has its own youth organization. One representative from the party and one from the trade unions are members of the Central Committee of the Marxist youth organization.

Stirner [sic][54] (Göttingen) first described the struggle of the German youth Vereine against reformism. He said that not only the bourgeois but also the socialist groups are endeavoring to poison the workers with the fumes of militarism. The newspaper of the youth organization, Arbeiter-Jugend, which at first was edited in a radical-revolutionary spirit, later inserted articles in which a defensist policy was advocated. Many local youth groups protested resolutely against this. In many instances the young people refused to distribute newspapers which contained social-patriotic articles. Police measures against the proletarian youth were made more severe.

Notz (Stuttgart) and Dietrich (Karlsruhe) spoke in the same spirit.

Representatives of France, England,[55] and especially Italy, from which place three delegates were already on their way to Berne, gave information of a similar revolutionary line and of a similar struggle of the youth against war.

The delegates who had assembled at Berne represented 33,800 members, not including Germany and Russia.

At the beginning of the second day there arose a dispute concerning the Russian delegation . . . . After the majority of the Conference adopted the proposed order, i.e., every country to be given only one vote, the Russian delegates withdrew from the meeting in protest. A critical situation resulted. It was obvious that an incomplete Conference, especially one at which the belligerent countries were represented by Germany alone, could not have the desired success. Therefore, we reopened negotiations with the Russian comrades who had left the Conference and reached an agreement which satisfied them so that they returned on the following day.

The chief subject of discussion at the Conference consisted, of course, of the question of war and of the position of the Social Democratic parties and the socialist youth organizations. The fundamental report on that question was made by the leader of the Swiss Social Democratic party, Robert Grimm, jointly with Angelica Balabanoff. They introduced a draft resolution. After lively and heated debates, especially concerning the demand for total disarmament, the resolution was unanimously adopted.[56]

[54] Elsewhere Münzenberg gives Sturm as the Göttingen representative.
[55] Delegates from France and England were not present at the Conference.
[56] Given below, pp. 307–8.

With the adoption of that resolution the Youth International entered a new phase of its development.

For the first time in the history of the proletarian youth movement representatives of the socialist youth assumed an independent position with regard to political events and expressed their point of view.

. . . . At the beginning of the third sitting a statement was read which had been written by the Russian comrades, who the day previous had withdrawn from the Conference because of the order of voting. After a lively discussion the Conference decided to prove its readiness to do everything to complete the work in full harmony and to yield to the wishes of the Russian comrades by granting each country two votes in future ballots and by regarding Poland as a separate country. This decision satisfied the Russian comrades and they returned to the Conference.

After their return new dissensions sprang up between them and the majority of the Conference. The Russian comrades had worked out their own resolution on war and, in connection with this, on the tasks of the socialist youth organizations. They defended this resolution in long speeches. They subjected to sharp criticism the resolution proposed by the Bureau and adopted by the Conference on the preceding day. They demanded that the paragraph directed against the revisionists be made still sharper. It was necessary, they said, to pronounce against not only this war, but any war of an imperialist character. The methods of tactics should be openly stated in the resolution. After a lengthy and thorough discussion the resolution of the Russian participants at the Conference was rejected by a majority of thirteen votes to three. The amendments entered by the Russian delegates to the resolution already adopted on the preceding day were likewise rejected by the same majority of thirteen votes to three.[57]

. . . . By nine votes to five the Conference adopted the proposal of the Scandinavian and Swiss delegates to advance the demand for total disarmament in all countries.[58]

[57] According to the report in *Berner Tagwacht* the draft resolution of the representatives of the Central Committee of the R.S.D.L. party and the Polish delegation was rejected by fourteen votes to four and their amendments were rejected by the same number of votes. The resolution given below was adopted by thirteen votes to three. The Dutch delegate and part of the Russian delegation [the two representatives of the Central Committee of the R.S.D.L. party] voted against the resolution; the Polish delegate abstained. ("Internationale Sozialistische Jugendkonferenz in Bern. Offizieller Verhandlungsbericht," *Berner Tagwacht,* No. 88, April 17, 1915, p. 1.)

[58] The following proposal was adopted: "The International Conference of the socialist youth organizations invites the youth organizations of all countries to exercise influence on the labor movements of their respective countries with a view to introduce in the program the demand for complete disarmament" ("Internationale

Upon the proposal of the Dutch delegation it was resolved to celebrate an international antimilitarist youth day to take place at the same time in all countries in which there were socialist youth organizations. The Conference decided to establish a "Liebknecht fund." The money of this fund was to serve to support an antimilitarist struggle and the victims of that struggle.

Of great significance for future development were the organizational resolutions of the Conference. They signified nothing less than a complete break with the Vienna Bureau. The first paragraph of the statute of the international youth secretariat unanimously adopted by the Conference read:

"The socialist youth organizations, which have joined the international association, establish a secretariat located temporarily in Switzerland."

Thus the Vienna Bureau forfeited its function and Robert Danneberg, who so far has been acting as International Secretary, was considered removed.

In the adopted statute a plan was outlined for a definite and strong international organization with an international newspaper, with regular contributions to the fund of the International Secretariat and with a number of obligations, organizational in character, assuring the transformation of the socialist youth organization into a truly competent organization.

Elections followed, which concluded the work of the Conference and as a result of which I [Münzenberg] was elected International Secretary, while the following comrades entered the International Bureau: OLAUSSEN (Norway), CHRISTIANSEN (Denmark), NOTZ (Germany), and CATANESI (Italy). . . . .

THE WAR AND THE TASKS OF THE SOCIALIST YOUTH ORGANIZATIONS

[Resolution of the International Socialist Youth Conference at Berne, April 5–7, 1915][59]

The International Socialist Youth Conference held on April 5, 6, and 7, 1915, at Berne and attended by delegates of nine countries, revives the decisions of the International Socialist Youth Conference at Stuttgart,

sozialistische Jugendkonferenz in Bern. Offizieller Verhandlungsbericht, Die Abrüstungsfrage," *Berner Tagwacht*, No. 88, April 17, 1915, p. 1). Both the Bolshevik and the Menshevik delegates voted against this resolution. (F. Weis, "Mezhdunarodnaia sotsialisticheskaia konferentsiia v Berne," *Nashe Slovo*, No. 68, April 18, 1915, pp. 1–2.)

[59] *Berner Tagwacht*, No. 88, April 17, 1915, p. 1.

Copenhagen, and Basel, which appealed to the laboring youth of all countries to struggle against the war which is destroying the people and against militarism.

The Conference notes with profound regret the fact that, like the socialist organizations of the elders, the socialist youth organizations in most of the countries at the outbreak of war were not guided by the decisions mentioned above.

The present war is a result of the imperialist policy of the ruling classes of all the capitalist countries. In cases where it is characterized by the ruling classes and their governments as a defensive war, it is likewise the result of that policy which is hostile to the people and inseparable from capitalism *The war is incompatible with the interests of the laboring class, whose vitality it endangers and destroys, whose organizations it cripples, whose activity against international exploitation it hampers.*

The civil peace policy, which wishes to reconcile the classes, is a policy of the resignation of Social Democracy as a party of proletarian class struggle and a policy of renouncing the vital interests and ideals of the proletariat.

Proceeding from these considerations, the International Socialist Youth Conference sounds the call to put an immediate end to the war. It welcomes heartily the attempts made by party groups in the belligerent countries and the resolution of the International Proletarian Women's Conference in particular to *force the ruling classes* by means of *the resumption of class struggle on the part of the workers to conclude peace.* The International Socialist Youth Conference declares it to be the duty of the young men and women comrades in the belligerent countries to support vigorously this ever-growing movement for peace. The Conference expects from the youth organizations of the neutral states an active support of this peace activity.

The Conference protests emphatically against attempts to place the socialist youth organizations at the service of the bourgeois young militarist guards [*Jugendwehr*] in order thus to divert the laboring youth from its real task: socialist education, the struggle against capitalist exploitation and against militarism.

In the face of the horrible results of the present war, which callously uses for cannon fodder young people who have scarcely passed school age, the Conference stresses the necessity of making clearer than ever to the young men and women workers of all countries the causes and the nature of the war and of militarism, the inevitable companions of a capitalist social order; of educating them in the spirit of international class struggle; and thus of rallying them more firmly and in greater numbers to the banner of revolutionary socialism.

CHAPTER IV

ZIMMERWALD

Despite the lukewarm reception with which the Lugano proposals were received and the decided opposition of the socialists of certain belligerent states, the Italian Socialist party persisted in its efforts to restore international socialist relations. In April 1915 the Italians with the concurrence of the Swiss Social Democrats sent Deputy Odino Morgari to France and England, where he proposed to Vandervelde, the Chairman of the Executive Committee of the International Socialist Bureau, and to other party leaders that an international conference of neutrals be held and that a full session of the International Socialist Bureau be called. Representatives of the party majorities, i.e., the patriotic socialists, turned down both proposals; but Morgari found considerable support for an international conference among the minority groups in both France and England.[1] On hearing Morgari's report at a meeting held at Bologna, May 15–16, the Executive of the Italian Socialist party decided to ignore the opposition of the majority groups and to take the initiative in calling an international conference to which were to be invited all parties and workers' organizations which were ready to come out against civil peace, to stand for united and simultaneous action of socialists in various countries against war on the basis of the proletarian class struggle. A month later, June 18, the Executive reconsidered the Bologna resolution and after a full debate confirmed it unanimously.[2]

---

[1] J. Maxe, *De Zimmerwald au bolshevisme* ...., p. 27; L. Trotsky, *Voina i Revoliutsiia*, II, 108; "Rebuilding of the International," *Labour Leader*, No. 32, August 12, 1915, p. 6; "Per L'Internazionale et per la pace—La 'missione all'estero' dell'on. Morgari," *Avanti*, No. 209, July 30, 1915, p. 1.

[2] "Conférence socialiste internationale à Zimmerwald (Suisse). Rapport officiel pour la presse," *Internationale sozialistische Kommission zu Bern, Bulletin*, No. 1, September 21, 1915, p. 5; *Avanti*, No. 136, May 18, 1915, p. 1; No. 168, June 19, 1915, p. 1.

As a result of the continued efforts of the Italian and Swiss socialists a preliminary Conference met at Berne, July 11, 1915, and formulated plans for the larger Conference, which met at the little village of Zimmerwald near Berne, September 5–8. The Conference, by the election of an International Socialist Committee with headquarters at Berne and by the adoption of a manifesto, established an organization and a program for what came to be known as the Zimmerwald movement. This platform was somewhat more conciliatory than that proposed by the Left minority under Lenin's leadership, but the Lefts remained within the Zimmerwald movement, working through their own informal organization for the acceptance of their more radical program.[3]

A. Preliminaries of the Conference

Seven persons attended the preliminary Conference at Berne on July 11: Robert Grimm of the Swiss Social Democratic party; G. Zinoviev of the Central Committee of the R.S.D.L. party; P. B. Axelrod of the Organization Committee of the R.S.D.L. party; Angelica Balabanoff and O. Morgari of the Italian Socialist party; A. S. Warski of the Main Presidium of the Social Democracy of Poland and Lithuania; and M. G. Walecki of the Polish Socialist party (Levitsa). Contrary to the wishes of Zinoviev, a majority of those present favored inviting to the general Conference not only those who were known to be Lefts but such moderates as Haase, Branting, and Troelstra. It was also decided that the forthcoming Conference should not attempt to form a new International but should limit its function to calling the proletariat to common action for peace.[4]

[3] The Zimmerwald movement in the chief European countries is discussed in *The Bolsheviks and World Revolution.* For the activities of the Zimmerwald Left, see chapter vi, below.

[4] *Internationale sozialistische Kommission zu Bern, Bulletin,* No. 1, September 21, 1915, p. 5; A. Malatesta, *I socialisti italiani durante la guerra,* pp. 83–84; G. Shklovsky, "Tsimmervald," *Proletarskaia Revoliutsiia,* No. 9 (44), 1925, pp. 76–79. As appears from Lenin's letters to Radek, the Bolshevik Central Committee

During the period between the preliminary Conference and the meeting at Zimmerwald, Lenin, Krupskaia recalls, "was very excited" and from his mountain resort in Sörenberg wrote to friends in different quarters urging that invitations be secured for reliable Lefts, that these Lefts be provided with documents giving the position of the Bolsheviks, and that in case these Lefts were themselves unable to attend the Conference they should assign their proxies to Lenin. By mid-August the Bolsheviks had prepared drafts of a manifesto, a resolution, and a declaration which they circulated among the Left Internationalists. Lenin went to Berne two days before the general Conference opened and held a meeting of those delegates who subsequently became members of the Zimmerwald Left.[5]

PROJECT TO CALL AN INTERNATIONAL SOCIALIST CONGRESS

[Decision of the Executive of the Italian Socialist Party, May 15–16, 1915][6]

We learn from Milan:

At its meeting in Bologna the Executive of the Italian party considered also the attempts made to restore the activity of the International. Comrade Morgari made a detailed report. The conclusions which he drew from an examination of the international situation, from his personal observations, and from communications with foreign party comrades met with the unanimous approval of the party Executive. In order to make the *protest against the war* more vital and more far-reaching a decision was made favoring participation in the *congress* of the socialists of the *neutral* countries scheduled for May 30 in Zürich.[7]

At the same time the party Executive decided, in line with Comrade

feared for a while that they would not be invited to the preliminary Conference at Berne; Lenin, apparently, suspected Grimm of deliberately trying to ignore the Bolsheviks, whereas Radek seems to have believed that Grimm was not doing this intentionally. (Lenin, *Sochineniia,* XXIX, 295–97, translated in *The Letters of Lenin,* pp. 366–68.)

[5] Krupskaya, *Memories of Lenin,* II, 169.

[6] "Die italienische Partei und die Internationale," *Berner Tagwacht,* No. 115, May 20, 1915, p. 1.

[7] This meeting, which was called in accordance with the Lugano decisions, did not meet, the Swiss Social Democrats having decided that it was inopportune. (*La Sentinelle,* No. 118, May 26, 1915, p. 2.)

Morgari's report and in harmony with the representatives of the fraternal parties, to take the initiative in calling an *international congress* as soon as possible at a place to be determined later. There were to be invited to this congress all socialist parties, *or their sections,* and all labor organizations which are *against* any *civil peace,* which adhere to *the basis of class struggle,* and which are willing, *through simultaneous international action, to struggle for immediate peace,* which knows neither forced annexations nor changes of state boundaries against the will of the peoples.

According to Morgari *some party leaderships* have *already declared* their willingness to *send representatives to this congress.*

PRELIMINARY CONFERENCE AT BERNE, JULY 11, 1915

[Report by G. Zinoviev, Delegate of the Central Committee of the R.S.D.L. Party][8]

[Prior to July 14, 1915]

RESPECTED COMRADES!

Our organization (the Central Committee of the Russian Social Democratic Labor party) considers it necessary to inform you of the following:

On Sunday, July 11, at Berne there took place a preliminary conference which was to prepare for the international conference of the Lefts. We were invited by Robert Grimm. There were present: Robert Grimm (representative of the newspaper, *Berner Tagwacht*), A. Balabanoff (?),[9] Morgari (the Italian party), Axelrod (representative of the so-called Organization Committee), Warski (representative of the so-called [Main] Presidium of the Polish party), Walecki (representative of the Polish Socialist party "Levitsa"), Zinoviev (representative of our organization).

It goes without saying that the composition of this conference seemed rather queer to me (Zinoviev). After all, where were the strictly *Lefts*

---

[8] "Otchet delegata TsK RSDRP o predvaritelnom soveshchanii sostoiavshemsia 11 iiulia 1915 g., po voprosu o sozyve mezhdunarodnoi konferentsii," *Leninskii Sbornik,* XIV, 161–64. This is ".... a Russian translation of a letter in German by G. Zinoviev—the only document which has been preserved that relates to the preliminary conference for the calling of an international conference of socialists. Other reports or any other materials on the work of this [preliminary] conference are not known to us. The fact that this letter was written in German makes us think that it had been intended especially for the information of the German Lefts, whose representative was not present at the conference. The typewritten letter stops abruptly on the evaluation of the speeches of the participants at the conference." (*Ibid.,* p. 160, note.)

[9] The question mark, which is in the original, was apparently to indicate Zinoviev's uncertainty about listing Dr. Balabanoff as a representative of the Italian Socialist party. She attended the conference in that capacity.

of the International? I asked whether, for instance, the Dutch Marxists, the Polish Social Democratic opposition, the Social Democracy of the Lettish area, the *Lichtstrahlen* group (Germany), and others had not been invited? I was answered—no; only those organizations had been invited which had official representatives in the International Socialist Bureau. I asked: why so? After all, this is not an official conference but a conference of the Lefts. I received my answer later in the course of the meeting.

Morgari reported on his trip to England and France. The report sounded rather pessimistic. He said that the members of the Independent Labour party had promised to come but they would have preferred waiting a little until the situation at the front became clearer. Furthermore, they did not want to provoke a sharp clash with the Labour party. The situation in France was no better. The representatives of the Paris and Lyon opposition groups would perhaps come to the conference; but should the situation at the front change unfavorably for France they were not likely to come. At any rate, the decision of the National Council of the French Socialist party (July 14)[10] should be awaited. Grimm's information on his recent negotiations on the present state of affairs with Klara Zetkin is of great importance. She told Grimm that the German opposition would participate in the conference but she was of the opinion that: (1) *only* the question of peace should be discussed; (2) contact with Haase and Kautsky should be established now. Our (i.e., Klara Zetkin's) theoretical position is, of course, not that of Haase and Kautsky. Nevertheless, an attempt should be made to work with them so as to push their group to the left. Moreover, Robert Grimm informed us that on his personal responsibility exclusively he had attempted to get in touch with Haase but had had no reply as yet. Thereupon it was decided to call a second preliminary conference (of those present + 1 German + 1 French + 1 English), which should solve completely the question of the conference as such. From the entire state of affairs it is clear that this second preliminary conference will play a decisive role.[11] It will determine the composition, the agenda, the drafts of the resolutions, etc., of the coming conference. Therefore, our representative, Comrade Zinoviev, introduced the following three proposals:

[10] At the meeting in Paris, July 14–15, the National Council of the French Socialist party expressed its opposition to the proposed conference in a resolution which declared that "the war, imposed upon the Allies by the rulers of Germany should be conducted to its logical conclusion, i.e., until German militarism is defeated ...." (*Pendant la Guerre. Le Parti Socialiste, la Guerre et la Paix, Toutes les résolutions et tous les documents du Parti Socialiste de Juillet 1914 à fin 1917*, pp. 123–27.)

[11] The proposed second preliminary conference was not held.

PROPOSAL I : Those present declare that in the main they agree with the resolution of the Executive of the Italian party. Those present resolve that there are to be invited only those parties or sections of parties (also syndicates and other labor organizations) which are ready : (1) to struggle most resolutely against civil peace, i.e., against ministerialism, against the voting of war credits, etc. ; (2) to lead a struggle against chauvinism ; (3) to strive to resume and continue the class struggle and to develop this class struggle into revolutionary mass demonstrations.

PROPOSAL II : To invite to the second conference one representative from each of the following : (1) Holland (Marxists), (2) Bulgaria (Blagoev), (3) Scandinavia (Höglund and somebody from the Norwegians), (4) Germany—the *Lichtstrahlen* group (besides the group of Zetkin, etc.), (5) the Polish Social Democratic party (the opposition), (6) the Social Democracy of the Lettish Region.

PROPOSAL III : To put the question of inviting Haase's group to the German Lefts (the *Internationale* group and the *Lichtstrahlen* group) for consideration. The preliminary agenda proposed by Zinoviev is as follows :

1. Reports.

2. Pacifism or revolutionary struggle of the proletariat for the cessation of the war.

3. Imperialist wars and revolutionary mass demonstrations of the proletariat.

4. Is an International in common with the social chauvinists possible (the principal basis of the Third International) ?

After a discussion which lasted many hours, the assembly accepted only the first paragraph of the first proposal, rejected the second proposal, and "postponed" the rest. The rejection of the second proposal seems to us particularly worthy of notice. In fact the Left elements of various parties are certainly not being invited to the deciding preliminary conference. On the contrary, those who have gathered have very plainly stated that they are determined to invite to the conference such people as Troelstra, Branting, and Haase. Axelrod said that if they did not wish to invite Haase, then for him, Axelrod, a question would arise as to whether or not *he* ought to attend such a conference. Walecki also stood up energetically for Haase.

The members of the assembly do not want to establish connections with the *Lichtstrahlen* group, while Warski was allowed to repeat the well-known gossip of the members of the Presidium of the party about Borchardt and Radek-Parabellum. In all probability, said Warski, Zetkin will not be willing to sit in the same room with Borchardt. Pannekoek has no influence whatsoever on the German Lefts. The speaker mentioned above did not wish even to waste words over Radek. After all that, it is clear that the so-called conference of the Lefts will in reality be a conference of "conciliators" of the "Center" with social chauvinists. It is clear that no one cares seriously about the calling of the so-called Left conference.[12]

RALLYING THE LEFTS: SELECTIONS FROM LENIN'S LETTERS

[To Kollontai, Christiania][13]

[Sörenberg, July 1915]

Dear Comrade:

The question of the conference of the Lefts is making progress. The first *Vorkonferenz* has already been held and the second, the decisive one, is drawing near. It is extremely important to draw in the Left Swedes (Höglund) and the Norwegians.

Be good enough to drop me a line: (1) Are we in harmony with you (or you with the Central Committee) and, if not, wherein do we disagree? (2) Will you undertake to draw in the Left Scandinavians?

Ad (1) Our position is known to you from the *Sotsial-Demokrat*. As far as Russian affairs are concerned, we shall *not* favor unity with Chkheidze's group (as desired by Trotsky, by the Organization Committee, and by Plekhanov and Co.; see *Voina* [The War]), for this is a covering up and a defense of *Nashe Delo*. In international matters, we shall *not* be for *rapprochment* with Haase-Bernstein-Kautsky (for in practice they favor unity with the Südekums; and wish to cover these up, to get away with Left phrases and to change nothing in the old, rotten party). We cannot stand for the slogan of peace, for we consider it to be superconfused, pacifist, Philistine, and an aid to the governments (who wish to hold out one hand for peace in order to extricate themselves) and an impediment to the revolutionary struggle.

In our opinion the Left must come forth with a general *ideological* declaration: (1) absolutely condemning the social chauvinists and opportunists; (2) containing a program of revolutionary actions (whether to say civil war or revolutionary mass action is not so important after all); (3) against the "defense of the fatherland" slogan, etc.—an ideological declaration of the Lefts on behalf of several countries would be of *tremendous* significance (of course, not in the spirit of Zetkin's platitude which she pushed through at the women's Conference in Berne; Zetkin *evaded* the question of condemning social chauvinism!!—perhaps out of a desire for "peace" with the Südekums + Kautsky??).

---

[12] Another account of this conference is given by Zinoviev in his *Sochineniia,* V, 463–65.

[13] *Leninskii Sbornik,* II, 231–32; another translation is in Lenin, *The Imperialist War,* pp. 208–209.

If you are in disagreement with such tactics let us know at once in a few words.

If you are in agreement will you undertake to translate: (1) the manifesto of the Central Committee (No. 33, *Sotsial-Demokrat*) and (2) the Berne resolutions[14] (No. 40, *Sotsial-Demokrat*) into Swedish and Norwegian and to communicate with Höglund as to whether or not they will agree to prepare a *general* declaration (or resolution) on such a basis. (Of course we won't part ways on account of details.) We must hurry *greatly* with this.

And so, I'll be waiting for your answer. With all kinds of greetings,

Yours,

LENIN

[To Kollontai, Christiania][15]

DEAR A. M.:   [SÖRENBERG, Summer, 1915]

We were very glad about the Norwegians' declaration and the trouble you took with the Swedes. A common international demonstration of the Left Marxists would be devilishly important! (A declaration of principles is the main thing, and for the time being the only possible thing!)

Roland-Holst, as well as Rakovsky (have you seen his French pamphlet?)[16] and Trotsky, too, are in my opinion *all* most harmful "Kautskyans," inasmuch as they are all, in one way or another, in favor of unity with the opportunists. In one way or another they embellish opportunism. They all (each in his own way) advance eclecticism instead of revolutionary Marxism.

Your criticism of the draft declaration[17] in my opinion (and if I am not mistaken) does not reveal serious dissent between us. To fail to distinguish between types of war I consider theoretically erroneous and practically harmful. We cannot be against national wars for liberation. You have quoted the example of Serbia. But if the Serbs *alone* were against Austria, would we not be *in favor* of the Serbs?

The crux of the matter is that at present the struggle *among* the great powers is carried on for the redivision of colonies and the subjugation of small powers.

And in case of a war in India, Persia, China, against England and Russia? Would we not be *in favor* of India against England, etc.? To call *this* a "civil war" is not accurate; it is obviously a forced assumption

[14] Both documents are given above in chapter ii, pp. 150–56 and 182–86.

[15] *Leninskii Sbornik*, II, 235–36, another translation is in Lenin, *The Imperialist War*, pp. 209–210.

[16] *Les Socialistes et la guerre*. A reply to Charles Dumas, Guesde's secretary.

[17] The draft declaration has not been found.

and it is extremely harmful to stretch the civil war concept to this extreme, since that *obscures* the crux of the matter—the fight of the wage-workers against the capitalists *of that state.*

Apparently the Scandinavians lapse into Philistine (and provincial, *kleinstaatisch*) pacifism when they reject "war" in general. This is not Marxian. This has to be combated, as does also their rejection of a militia.

Once more: greetings and congratulations upon the Norwegians' declaration.

Yours,
LENIN

[To Radek, Berne][18]

[SÖRENBERG, end of July 1915]
WERTER GENOSSE!

I am sending you the letter about the *Vorkonferenz.*

Make a copy of it for the *Lichtstrahlen* or have Wijnkoop (*if you are certain* of his accuracy) reforward it to them.

All this is *vertraulich.* Promise not to speak about it to Grimm or Balabanoff, or Trotsky, or anybody!

Read my letter to Wijnkoop[19] and send it off. I hope you have dispatched the preceding letter! Drop me a line about it.

Either the German Lefts will coalesce now (at least for an *ideological* action on behalf of the *anonymous* "Stern" group[20] or as you wish: later on the workers will join this group) or they ought to be given up.

(I understand that *Lichtstrahlen* cannot step forward directly. But why should the "Stern" group from $X + Y + Z$ not step forward with *resolutions* and a *manifesto??* and then spread this privately and stealthily?)

I cannot understand how you *could have overlooked* the *Vorkonferenz* at Berne!?! And you tried to exhort me!?[21]

Yours,
LENIN

P.S. Is it not hard for you to read Russian? Do you understand *everything?*

[18] Lenin, *Sochineniia,* XXIX, 298–99; another translation is in *The Letters of Lenin,* p. 369.

[19] Lenin's letter to Wijnkoop has not been found.

[20] The "Stern" group was not formed. The Bremen Left Radicals organized themselves under the name of "Internationale Sozialisten Deutschlands." (Lenin, *Sochineniia,* XXIX, 299, note 3.)

[21] Karl Radek did not attend the Conference. He was not invited by R. Grimm, for the organization to which Radek belonged had no representative in the International Socialist Bureau.

P.P.S. Either send the Berne resolutions directly to Wijnkoop (in translation if you have a copy) or send them here; we will make a copy.

It is extremely important for us, and you, to confer privately with some of the German Lefts. Could you arrange it? By the way, will you, perhaps, come here?

[To Kollontai, Christiania][22]

[SÖRENBERG, end of August, 1915]

DEAR A. M.

It appears that on September 5th the Conference itself, and not the *Vorkonferenz,* will take place. Hence, time presses.

You must strain all efforts to send either Höglund or the most Left and also the most firm Norwegian here, so that they may arrive for certain not later than September 3 (from Berne you should telephone me at Sörenberg, Hotel *Mariental, Kanton Lüzern, Telefon* 1, 11.—[1,11]).

If it is *absolutely impossible* for either of them to come, then let them send me at once (so that it will *be sure* to reach me on the 2d or 3d of September) by registered mail, either a transfer of their mandate to our Central Committee (a formal mandate in French or German) or, if they are not willing to give the mandate, then their declaration of solidarity with the Central Committee + their *"Prinzipienerklärung"* (by all means) and a letter to the Conference and a commission to our Central Committee to read the letter aloud (or to vote upon it if possible).

The crux of the struggle will be: whether or not to declare in the *Prinzipienerklärung* a ruthless (up-to-a-breach) struggle against *opportunism* = social chauvinism. Obtain as *great a clarity* and firmness of formulation *as possible,* especially on that point.

Drop me a postal card immediately saying whether or not you have received this letter and whether you hope (or are certain?) that any of these things will be fulfilled.

(Greeting to Aleksandr [Shliapnikov]!) Salut!

Yours,
LENIN

[To Radek, Berne][23]

[SÖRENBERG, late August, 1915]

DEAR COMRADE RADEK!

Herewith is your draft resolution.[24] It contains not a word about social chauvinism and opportunism or the struggle against them!! Why

---

[22] Lenin, *Sochineniia,* XXIX, 189.

[23] *Leninskii Sbornik,* XIV, 176. [German text.]

[24] Radek's original draft resolution is not available. However, a text of Radek's amended draft in the form of proofs is available; this document bears a note by

such an embellishment of the evil and such a covering-up before the working masses of their chief enemy within the Social Democratic parties?

Do you absolutely insist on not saying openly one word about the ruthless struggle against opportunism?

I hope to *arrive two days early* (i.e., September 2–3) if you inform me that the Germans will also come (otherwise Zinoviev will come alone).

(Your draft is much too "academic." It is not a call for battle, not a powder-and-shot manifesto.)

Are you sending your draft to Wijnkoop? Do you *demand* that they (the Dutch) should come?

Please send me immediately the translation (German) of my *draft* resolution (about which you wrote to Wijnkoop) and the translation of our 1913 resolution (the national question).[25] Hence: *two items.*

We must make *every* effort to have our pamphlet[26] appear (in German) prior to September 5. I am writing to Kasparov today.[27] He should help you to find one more translator (in Berne—Comrade Kinckel). Can you (with Kasparov) work "overtime" and translate the pamphlet in one week? And the printing? Is it possible to print it in three or four days?? We must exert *every effort* to do it!

I beg for an immediate reply.

Yours,

V. LENIN

[To Berzin, London][28]

[SÖRENBERG, August 20, 1915]

DEAR BERZIN!

Many thanks for the proxy[29] which I received! Please, don't be lazy now but send me *at once* the same proxy in French or German with a seal, etc., conforming to all formalities, and be certain to add to the text of the proxy that your party has always been (and is at present) not only affiliated with the International Socialist Bureau but also has had its

Radek to Lenin asking if Lenin would like to suggest any additional changes in the text. (Archive of the Marx-Engels-Lenin Institute, No. 20654, cited by Baevsky, "Bolsheviki v Tsimmervalde," *Proletarskaia Revoliutsiia,* No. 5, 1935, p. 32.)

[25] This refers to the resolution on the national question adopted at the Poronino Conference of the Central Committee of the R.S.D.L. party with party members held from October 5 to 14, 1913. See below, p. 528, n. 36.

[26] N. Lenin and G. Zinoviev's pamphlet, *Socialism and War.*

[27] Lenin's letter to Kasparov is in *Leninskii Sbornik,* XIV, 177–78.

[28] *Leninskii Sbornik,* XIV, 174–75.

[29] Apparently, Berzin did not intend at first to attend the Conference and had, therefore, transferred the proxy of the Lettish Social Democracy to Lenin. (*Ibid.,* p. 175, note 1.)

representative in it with a consulting vote. This is very, very urgent. Best regards!

Yours,

V. ULIANOV

P.S. Should you receive from us a handwritten draft of a brief declaration in Russian, then, please, pass it on to Litvinov as soon as possible, begging him to translate it into English and to send it to me quickly. Drop me an answer by postcard, so that I will know you have received this letter. Please.

B. The Zimmerwald Conference

Robert Grimm, who was in charge of the arrangements for the Conference, took great pains to prevent news of the meeting leaking out to the press. The delegates first assembled at the People's House in Berne, whence in four large coaches they rode to the little village of Zimmerwald about ten kilometers away. Thirty-eight delegates, some of whom were observers without votes, from eleven countries attended. There were ten Germans, among whom were Ledebour, Hoffmann, Ernst Meyer, Bertha Thalheimer, and Julian Borchardt, and others reflecting the point of view of the Center and Left of the German Social Democratic party. Representing the various Russian, Polish, and Lettish groups were Lenin and Zinoviev of the Central Committee, Axelrod and Martov of the Organization Committee, M. A. Natanson and Chernov of the Socialist-Revolutionists, J. Berzin of the Lettish Social Democracy, Trotsky of the *Nashe Slovo* group, P. Lemansky, an observer for the Bund, Warski of the Main Presidium and Radek of the Regional Presidium of the Social Democracy of Poland and Lithuania, and Lapinski of the Polish Socialist party (Levitsa). The Italian Socialist party sent Balabanoff, Lazzari, Modigliani, Morgari, and Serrati; Rakovsky represented the Rumanian S.D. party, V. Kolarov the Bulgarian "Narrow" socialists, Höglund and Ture Nerman the Swedish and Norwegian S.D. Lefts, Henrietta Roland-Holst "De Internationale" group of the Dutch Social Democrats, and A. Merrheim and A. Bourderon from the French Metal Workers and the Coopers Union, respectively.

The Swiss Social Democratic party refused to send official delegates but four members of the party, Grimm, Naine, Platten, and Graber attended as private delegates.[30] F. W. Jowett and Bruce Glasier, delegates of the Independent Labour party and members of the I.S.B., and E. C. Fairchild of the British Socialist party were unable to secure passports.

The *Internationale Korrespondenz,* a periodical of the German social democratic majority which opposed the Conference, wrote in No. 27, October 1, 1915, that "the organizers of the Conference racked their brains over the question of representation by the numerous party groups and group centers of *Russia* and *Poland* . . . . If every Russo-Polish organization and group had had an opportunity to delegate several representatives, these would have had a majority at the Conference and its outcome would have amounted chiefly to the issuing of a manifesto by the Russian émigrés." This, it is alleged, was avoided by giving one vote to each country and by keeping the Russo-Polish delegation as small as possible, with the result that this delegation amounted to about one-third of the entire number. This is approximately correct as to the number of Russo-Polish delegates, but the delegates voted individually.[31]

From the very beginning of the Conference three fairly distinct groups emerged. There were some nineteen or twenty delegates, constituting a majority of the Conference, who were primarily interested in a general demonstration for peace and opposed an open break with the patriotic socialists or the Second International. This group—the Right wing of the Conference—included most of the German delegation, the French, some of the Italians and the Poles, and the Russian Mensheviks. Those who were dissatisfied with this mod-

---

[30] On the composition of the Conference, see: Lenin *The Imperialist War,* pp. 437–38, note 186; Maxe, *De Zimmerwald au bolchevisme,* 33–34; Malatesta, *I socialisti italiani durante la guerra,* pp. 84–85; Shklovsky, "Tsimmervald," *Proletarskaia Revoliutsiia,* No. 9 (44), 1925, pp. 79–81; *Leninskii Sbornik,* XIV, 186; Kharitonov, *Zapiski Instituta Lenina,* II, 130; and E. Yaroslavsky (ed.), *Istoriia V.K.P. (B),* III, 108.

[31] *Internationale Korrespondenz,* No. 27, October 1, 1915, p. 393.

erate objective and favored a denunciation of civil peace, an organizational break with the social patriots, and a revolutionary class struggle, constituted a Left group of eight led by Lenin. Between these two was a smaller Center group of five or six, among whom were Grimm, Trotsky, Balabanoff, and Roland-Holst.

With this distribution of votes it was inevitable that the Left should fail to secure the adoption of its draft manifesto and resolution, but the pressure of the Left had a very considerable effect on the acts of the Conference.

PROCEEDINGS OF THE CONFERENCE
[From the Official Report to the Press][32]

3. THE DELIBERATIONS

From various sides greetings were received, among others from a member of the German Reichstag who, for certain reasons, could not be present at the Conference.[33] After all the formal matters were settled, the Conference listened to *reports on the situation in various countries.* The delegates of the belligerent countries gave information primarily about the condition of the parties and the labor movement since the outbreak of the war. They described the events which had caused the break in international relations and unanimously expressed the opinion that the imperialist war could not be regarded as a method of class struggle; that the struggle for peace could promise success only if it were carried on on *an international basis.* Only by the united action of the working class of all belligerent countries, actively supported by the socialists of the neutral states, can the interests of the proletariat be safeguarded in this struggle. The socialist workers of all countries welcome this Conference, especially the proletarians of the belligerent states, because up to the present all such efforts have failed, and the refusal of the Social Democratic party of one country to seek international conciliation in the midst of the war has served always to justify the extreme policy in the other country. But the interest of the laboring class demands an immediate ending of the war, which is opposed to the most vital interests of the people and in the course of which its true character as an imperialist war of conquest has been revealed with increasing clarity. A discussion in connection with the reports—the contents of which we can

32 "Conférence socialiste internationale à Zimmerwald (Suisse). Rapport officiel pour la presse. Les délibérations," *Internationale sozialistische Kommission zu Bern, Bulletin,* No. 1, September 21, 1915, pp. 5–8.

33 Karl Liebknecht. See pp. 326–28, below.

merely indicate here—did not take place. The Conference was of the opinion that at this moment it was not a question of debating in detail the tactics pursued by various parties.

Apart from the general reports on the situation

The Peace Action of the Proletariat

formed the chief topic of discussion. In this connection a *joint declaration* of the German and French delegations was introduced. Thus a worthy forward step was taken toward the success of the Conference. Any proletarian peace action would have been futile if there had been no such agreement between the delegates of Germany and France, i.e., of the two countries whose socialist parties had separated on national lines because of the antagonism of their governments. The Conference received with applause the text of the declaration....

THE MANIFESTO

A draft resolution[34] which was to determine the principal stand of the Conference was submitted by the delegation of the Polish Regional Committee, the Russian Central Committee, the Letts, the Swedes, and the Norwegians.[35] The statement supporting the resolution said that without a declaration of fundamental attitudes toward the World War and the collapse of the International a peace manifesto would hardly be possible, that it was necessary to understand clearly all the conditions and aims of this action for peace. Only after a renunciation of the bourgeois policy of "war to the end" would the struggle for peace be at all possible. This struggle would have to be revolutionary in nature as well as in methods. The action for peace should not be confined simply to peace as a goal. With the intensification of social antagonisms this action for peace would turn into a struggle for socialism. The second task of the Social Democracy is to lay down through propaganda the nature of the action for peace. Within bourgeois society it is impossible to banish the dangers of imperialism; therefore, the struggle for peace should simultaneously be a revolutionary struggle against capitalism.

Confronted by this conception many members of the Conference argued that a discussion of principles and the laying down of a general program would go beyond the aims of the Conference which were proposed by the organizers and which had served as the basis for participation by the various countries. Important as a new orientation of the international socialist policy might be, it could not be the task of this

[34] Of the Zimmerwald Left; see pp. 351–53, below.

[35] This report omits mentioning that the resolution was signed also by Fritz Platten and Julian Borchardt. See in this connection Lenin's letter to the International Socialist Committee, p. 369, below.

Conference. In no way should the suspicion be aroused that this Conference wished to bring about a breach and to form a new International. This, however, would happen if the submitted resolution were accepted. Moreover, this resolution suggested the means of a struggle, a topic which should be completely eliminated from the present discussion. The Conference should not become a tool of one tendency, but should attempt to start a peace action of the international proletariat, an action in which all elements sharing the socialist outlook on life would co-operate and combat civil peace, and which, regardless of the military situation in various countries at that time, would act for a rapid cessation of hostilities. Discord should not be disseminated; an *agreement* should be reached. No resolution would be necessary for that purpose. First of all, it was urgently necessary to issue a *manifesto to the European proletariat* clearly pointing out the facts and calling the working class to united action and to a resumption of the class struggle. In this sense a draft manifesto had already been elaborated by the same comrades who prepared the draft resolution.

The Conference tacitly resolved to issue a *manifesto*. In the course of the discussion two other draft manifestoes were introduced. All three drafts were transmitted to a commission, which then submitted a final draft manifesto to the Conference.[36] After a few insignificant changes had been made, this draft manifesto was adopted *unanimously* and with enthusiasm.[37] The authors of the draft resolution also unanimously voted for the draft manifesto of the Committee but 'declared,

[36] Three draft manifestoes (by the Right wing of the German delegation, the Zimmerwald Left group, and the *Nashe Slovo* representative) were submitted to the Conference. These drafts were transmitted to a commission of seven members, Grimm, Ledebour, Lenin, Trotsky, Merrheim, Rakovsky, and Modigliani. (*Leninskii Sbornik,* XIV, 187.) The Commission outlined some fundamental theses and requested Robert Grimm and L. Trotsky to write the final text. The manifesto which was adopted by the Conference is almost identical with Trotsky's draft manifesto. P. Lemansky remarks that though Trotsky was advocating in *Nashe Slovo* the theory of a coming social revolution and the necessity of creating a Third International, he preferred not to mention this in his draft manifesto. Lenin, who was on the Commission, repeatedly threatened that he and those with him would vote against the manifesto. But in spite of his threats it was evident that he would not dare so to isolate himself from the entire Socialist International and especially from its "internationalist" wing. Furthermore, on the categorical demand of the German delegates, the concrete parliamentary measures of class struggle (the refusal of credits, the withdrawal from the ministries, etc.), were not included in the manifesto, though in Trotsky's draft they had been pronounced imperative for all socialist organizations in time of war. (P. Lemansky, "Po puti k vozstanovleniiu Internatsionala," *Informatsionnyi Listok Zagranichnoi Organizatsii Bunda,* No. 9–10, December 1915, pp. 10–11; Trotsky, *Voina i Revoliutsiia,* II, 48–50.)

[37] According to V. Kolarov the situation was complicated by Chernov's refusal to accept the proposed manifesto, which contained no separate point about the Russian Tsar, and by Morgari's unexpected statement that he could not vote in favor

however, that they would have liked to see certain facts more sharply emphasized and the means of struggle more clearly outlined, but that so long as it was an appeal for struggle they would fight shoulder to shoulder with the other sections of the International and in this way would contribute to unity and common action.

In conformity with the wish of the French and German delegations, it was resolved that the manifesto should be *signed personally* by the delegates of every country. Those who at that time wished to fight for peace, to work for the ideals of socialism and the re-establishment of international proletarian relations, must also have courage to make themselves known personally in public by openly signing their names and by assuming responsibility for the adopted resolutions. Only then would the laboring class regain confidence and declare its readiness to resume the struggle. This proposal met with general approval.[38]

The proletarian action in favor of peace naturally does not confine itself to the mere publication of a manifesto on the part of its representatives. Only through a continuous, ever-increasing collaboration of all the proletarian forces can that influence which will force the rulers to cease this horrible massacre of the peoples be attained. The International Socialist Bureau would be the most suitable organization to promote the proletarian action for peace as well as to establish and maintain necessary relations between the socialist parties. At present, however, the Bureau is unable to carry out this task. So long as such a situation remains, another organization should be formed which would fulfill this mission. The Conference decided to elect a temporary *International Socialist Committee* and to make Berne its residence. The following members of the Committee were elected: O. Morgari, the Italian deputy, and the

of a manifesto which failed to say that France did not share the responsibility for the war. However, these two delegates finally agreed to raise their hands in favor of the manifesto and thus unanimity was attained. (V. Kolarov, "Vospominaniia o Tsimmervalde," *Pravda*, No. 203 [3134], September 6, 1925, p. 1.) Another reason why Chernov refused to sign the manifesto was that it did not speak at all of "agrarian socialism." V. Chernov's report on the Zimmerwald Conference was published in *Zhizn*, September 26, 1915.

[38] The *English* delegates, who were prevented by their government from attending the Conference, could not sign the manifesto at the time it was published; nevertheless, the manifesto was to be presented later to the I.L.P. for signature. Furthermore, it was decided to make it possible for all the socialist labor organizations, parties, trade unions, or other organized groups to declare their adherence to the manifesto. The larger the number of adherents, the wider the propagation of the manifesto in all countries, the more the force of the proletarian action for peace will grow. *Meanwhile the organizations and the individuals are asked to send their declarations of adherence eventually to the International Socialist Committee at Berne (address: Deputy Robert Grimm). The Committee will immediately inform the organizations and groups which are affiliated with it of the receipt of these declarations.* [Note in the original.]

National Councillors, Charles Naine and Robert Grimm, with Comrade Angelica Balabanoff in the capacity of interpreter. The Committee will establish *a temporary secretariat at Berne,* which would act as intermediary between the various parties and notify the affiliated organizations of the progress of the action for peace. In this purpose it should begin to publish a periodical *Bulletin.* This secretariat should in no case replace the existing International Socialist Bureau; it was to be dissolved immediately when the latter was able to fulfill its duties.

With the same unanimity which prevailed in accepting the resolutions mentioned above, the Conference accepted also the .... Declaration of Sympathy[39] formulated by the Bureau on the proposal of the French delegation. ....

The deliberations, so harmonious and so animated with the spirit of firm will and of brotherly solidarity, were completed in four days. The Conference ended on Wednesday night, after an expression of thanks to Comrades Angelica Balabanoff and Roland-Holst, who so splendidly carried out their duties as interpreter and secretary, respectively. The participants parted with a promise to promote the cause that had just been started and to work tenaciously to strengthen the bonds of international solidarity; they parted with the understanding that this Conference was the first necessary step toward restoring international relations and international socialist activity.

LIEBKNECHT'S LETTER TO THE CONFERENCE[40]

DEAR COMRADES!

Forgive me for writing only a few hurried lines. I am imprisoned and fettered by militarism;[41] therefore, I am unable to come to you. My heart, my head, my entire cause is nevertheless with you.

---

[39] For the war victims. See pp. 337–38, below.

[40] "Liebknecht und die III Internationale," *Die Rote Fahne,* No. 12, January 15, 1925, pp. 1–2. Here Ernst Meyer tells how this letter was received by the Conference: "Karl Liebknecht sent a written greeting which called forth a storm of enthusiasm from all the members of the Conference except Ledebour and Adolf Hoffmann, who felt hurt, not without reason, and whispered something about 'eccentricity.' Lenin liked especially the passage: 'Civil war and not civil peace.' He said, 'Civil war—that is excellent!' and repeated this sentence over and over again. Later on, Lenin took Liebknecht's letter home and on September 21 (date on the stamp) his wife, Comrade Krupskaia, sent this letter from Sörenberg near Lucerne to Comrade Zinoviev in Hertenstein near Vierwaldstätter Lake, where Zinoviev was living with his family in the summer of 1915.

"Liebknecht had written this letter in pencil. His wife brought the letter to Switzerland herself. The copy which I have contains two small and unimportant omissions consisting of one or two illegible words in the original. The letter is being published for the first time."

[41] On February 7, 1915, Liebknecht was called to the colors as *Armierungssoldat.* He was given a furlough but forbidden to leave Berlin.

You have two serious tasks, a hard task of grim duty and a sacred one of enthusiasm and hope.

Settlement of accounts, inexorable settlement of accounts with the deserters and turncoats of the International in Germany, England, France, and elsewhere, is imperative.

It is our duty to promote mutual understanding, encouragement, and inspiration among those who remain true to the flag, who are determined not to give way one inch before international imperialism, even if they fall victims to it, and to create order in the ranks of those who are determined to hold out—to hold out and to fight, with their feet firmly planted on the basis of international socialism.

It is necessary to make clear, briefly, the principles of our attitude toward the capitalist order of society. Briefly—so I hope! For in this we are all unanimous and we must be unanimous!

It is above all a matter of drawing tactical consequences from these principles—ruthlessly for all countries!

Civil war, not civil peace! Exercise international solidarity for the proletariat against pseudo-national, pseudo-patriotic class harmony, and for international class war for peace, for the socialist revolution. How the fight is to be fought must be decided. Only in co-operation, in the mutual working of one land with another, by mutually strengthening each other, can the greatest possible forces and thus the attainable results be achieved.

The friends of every country hold in their hands the hopes and prospects of the friends of every other country. You French and you German socialists especially, have one and the same fate. You French friends, I implore you not to allow yourselves to be caught by the phrase of national truce—to this you are really immune—or by the equally dangerous phrase of the party truce! Every protest against this, every manifestation of your rejection of the semiofficial government policy, every bold acknowledgment of the class struggle, of solidarity with us and of the proletarian will to peace, strengthens our fighting spirit, increases tenfold our force to work in Germany for the proletariat of the world, for its economic and political emancipation, for its emancipation from the fetters of capitalism, and also from the chains of Tsarism, Kaiserism, Junkerism, and militarism, which is no less international; to fight in Germany for the political and social liberation of the German people against German imperialists' power and lust for territory; to fight for a speedy peace, which would also restore unhappy Belgium to freedom and independence and give back France to the French people.

French brothers, we know the peculiar difficulties of your tragic situation and bleed with you as with the tormented and stoned masses of all peoples! Your misfortune is our misfortune, as we know that our pain is your pain. Let our fight be your fight. Help us, as we swear to help you.

The new International will arise; it can arise on the ruins of the old, on a new and firmer foundation. Today, friends, socialists from all countries, you have to lay the foundation stone for the future structure. Pass irreconcilable judgment upon the false socialists! Ruthlessly urge on those who vacillate or hesitate in all countries, those in Germany as well! The greatness of the aim will raise you above the narrowness and littleness of the day, above the misery of these terrible days!

Long live the people's peace of the future! Long live antimilitarism! Long live international, people-emancipating, revolutionary socialism! Proletarians of all countries—reunite!

Karl Liebknecht

JOINT DECLARATION OF THE FRENCH AND GERMAN DELEGATIONS[42]

After a year of carnage, the *unequivocal imperialist character* of this war has revealed itself more and more. This proves that the causes of war have their roots in the imperialist and colonial policy of *all* governments that are responsible for the outbreak of this carnage.

The masses of the people were drawn into this war through *civil peace* being proclaimed in all countries by the profiteers of capitalism who gave to the war the appearance of a racial struggle, a defense of rights and liberties. It is under the pressure of these sentiments that a considerable part of the labor forces of the opposition in each country were swept away by nationalism. And since then the press, at the command of the authorities, has unceasingly emphasized the liberating character of the war.

Today the chauvinists of every nation ascribe to this war *the aim of seizing by annexation whole provinces or territories.* These claims if realized *would cause future wars.*

In opposition to these ambitions there have been formed in all nations *determined minorities* which attempt to fulfill the tasks affirmed in the decisions of the International Socialist Congresses at Stuttgart, Copenhagen, and Basel. It is their task, today more than ever, to oppose these *annexationist claims and to hasten the ending of the war,* a war which has already caused the loss of millions of human lives, produced so many cripples, and provoked such extensive misery among the workers of all countries.

[42] "Conférence socialiste internationale à Zimmerwald (Suisse). Rapport officiel pour la presse. Déclaration commune de socialistes et syndicalistes franco-allemands," *Internationale sozialistische Kommission zu Bern, Bulletin,* No. 1, September 21, 1915, p. 6.

That is why we German and French socialists and trade unionists declare:

"This War Is Not Our War!"

That we *condemn* with all our energy the violation of Belgian neutrality, which was guaranteed by international conventions recognized by all the belligerent countries. We demand and shall not stop demanding the restoration of Belgium in its complete integrity and independence.

We declare that we desire the ending of the war through an early peace established on conditions which will not violate the rights of any nation or people; that we will never agree to the plans of conquest of our respective governments, plans which must inevitably carry the seeds of a new war; that we shall work in our respective countries for a peace which would disperse hatred among the nations and would make it possible for the peoples to labor together.

Such a peace, in our judgment, is possible only if *every thought of violating the rights and the liberties of the peoples is condemned.* The occupation of entire countries or provinces must not result in annexation.

So, we say: no open or masked annexations; no forcibly imposed economic incorporation which would be made still more intolerable by a further political disfranchisement of those involved. We say that the right of the peoples to dispose of their own destiny must be observed inviolably.

We take upon ourselves the explicit responsibility of acting unceasingly to this end in our respective countries in order that the peace movement may become strong enough to force our governments to stop this slaughter.

By repudiating the policy of civil peace and by remaining faithful to the class struggle which served as the foundation of the Socialist International we, German and French socialists and trade unionists, will have the strength to struggle among our countrymen against this horrible calamity and toward putting an end to the hostilities which have disgraced mankind.

For the French delegation: A. Merrheim, A. Bourderon

For the German delegation: Adolf Hoffmann, Georg Ledebour

THE ZIMMERWALD MANIFESTO[43]

Workers of Europe!

The war has lasted for more than a year. Millions of corpses lie upon the battlefields; millions of men have been crippled for life. Europe has become a gigantic human slaughter-house. All science, the work of many

[43] "French and German Delegates Put Forward a Joint Declaration," *Labour Leader,* No. 40, October 7, 1915, p. 9.

generations, is devoted to destruction. The most savage barbarity is celebrating its triumph over everything that was previously the pride of mankind.

Whatever may be the truth about the immediate responsibility for the outbreak of the war, one thing is certain : the war that has occasioned this chaos is the outcome of Imperialism, of the endeavors of the Capitalist classes of every nation to satisfy their greed for profit by the exploitation of human labour and of the treasures of Nature.

Those nations which are economically backward or politically feeble are threatened with subjugation by the great Powers, which are attempting by blood and iron to change the map of the world in accordance with their exploiting interests. Whole peoples and countries, such as Belgium, Poland, the Balkan States, and Armenia, either as units or in sections, are menaced by annexation as booty in the bargaining for compensations.

As the war proceeds its real driving forces become apparent in all their baseness. Piece by piece the veil which has hidden the meaning of this world catastrophe from the understanding of the peoples is falling down. In every country the Capitalists who forge the gold of war profits from the blood of the people are declaring that the war is for national defense, democracy, and the liberation of oppressed nationalities. THEY LIE!

In reality they are actually burying on the fields of devastation the liberties of their own peoples, together with the independence of other nations. New fetters, new chains, new burdens are being brought into existence, and the workers of all countries, of the victorious as well as of the vanquished, will have to bear them. To raise civilization to a higher level was the aim announced at the beginning of the war: misery and privation, unemployment and want, underfeeding and disease are the actual results. For decades and decades to come the cost of the war will devour the strength of the peoples, imperil the work of social reform and hamper every step on the path of progress.

Intellectual and moral desolation, economic disaster, political reaction —such are the blessings of this horrible struggle between the nations.

Thus does the war unveil the naked form of modern Capitalism, which has become irreconcilable, not only with the interests of the working masses, not only with the circumstances of historic development, but even with the first conditions of human communal existence.

The ruling forces of Capitalist society, in whose hands were the destinies of the nations, the monarchical and the Republican Governments, secret diplomacy, the vast employers' organizations, the middle-class parties, the Capitalist Press, the Church—all these forces must bear the full weight of responsibility for this war, which has been produced by the social order nourishing them and protecting them and which is being carried on for the sake of their interests.

Workers!

Exploited, deprived of your rights, despised—you were recognised as brothers and comrades at the outbreak of the war before you were summoned to march to the shambles, to death. And now, when militarism has crippled, lacerated, degraded, and destroyed you, the rulers are demanding from you the abandonment of your interests, of your aims, of your ideals—in a word, slavish submission to the "national truce." You are prevented from expressing your views, your feelings, your pain; you are not allowed to put forth your demands and to fight for them. The press is muzzled, political rights and liberties are trampled upon—thus is military dictatorship ruling today with the iron hand.

We cannot, we dare not, any longer remain inactive in the presence of a state of things that is menacing the whole future of Europe and of mankind. For many decades the Socialist working class has carried on the struggle against militarism. With growing anxiety its representatives at their national and international conferences have devoted themselves to the war peril, the outcome of an Imperialism which was becoming more and more menacing. At Stuttgart, Copenhagen, and Bâsle the International Socialist Congresses indicated the path that the workers should follow.

But we Socialist Parties and working-class organisations which had taken part in determining this path have since the outbreak of war disregarded the obligations that followed therefrom. Their representatives have invited the workers to suspend the working-class struggle, the only possible and effective means of working-class emancipation. They have voted the ruling classes the credits for carrying on the war. They have put themselves at the disposal of their Governments for the most varied services. They have tried through their press and their envoys to win over the neutrals to the Governmental policies of their respective countries. They have given to their Government Socialist Ministers as hostages for the observance of the national truce, and thus have taken on themselves the responsibility for this war, its aims, its methods. And just as Socialist Parties failed separately, so did the most responsible representative of the Socialists of all countries fail: the International Socialist Bureau.

These facts constitute one of the reasons why the international working-class movement, even where sections of it did not fall a victim to the national panic of the first period of the war, or where it rose above it, has failed, even now, in the second year of the butchering of nations, to take up simultaneously in all countries an active struggle for peace.

In this intolerable situation we have met together, we representatives of Socialist parties, of Trade Unions, or of minorities of them, we Germans, French, Italians, Russians, Poles, Letts, Roumanians, Bulgarians, Swedes, Norwegians, Dutch, and Swiss, we who are standing on the ground, not of national solidarity with the exploiting class, but of the international solidarity of the workers and the working-class struggle. We have met together in order to join anew the broken ties of international relations and to summon the working class to reorganise and begin the struggle for peace.

This struggle is also the struggle for liberty, for Brotherhood of nations, for Socialism. The task is to take up this fight for peace—for a peace without annexations or war indemnities. Such a peace is only possible when every thought of violating the rights and liberties of the nations is condemned. There must be no enforced incorporation either of wholly or partly occupied countries. No annexations, either open or masked, no forced economic union, made still more intolerable by the suppression of political rights. The right of nations to select their own government must be the immovable fundamental principle of international relations.

Organised Workers!

Since the outbreak of the war you have put your energies, your courage, your steadfastness at the service of the ruling classes. Now the task is to enter the lists for your own cause, for the sacred aims of Socialism, for the salvation of the oppressed nations and the enslaved classes, by means of the irreconcilable working-class struggle.

It is the task and duty of the Socialists of the belligerent countries to begin this struggle with all their power. It is the task and duty of the Socialists of the neutral countries to support their brothers by all effective means in this fight against bloody barbarity.

Never in the history of the world has there been a more urgent, a more noble, a more sublime task, the fulfilment of which must be our common work. No sacrifice is too great, no burden too heavy, to attain this end: the establishment of peace between the nations.

Working men and women! Mothers and fathers! Widows and orphans! Wounded and crippled! To all who are suffering from the war or in consequence of the war, we cry out, over the frontiers, over the smoking battlefields, over the devastated cities and hamlets.

"Workers of all countries unite!"

In the name of the International Socialist Conference:

For the German Delegation: GEORG LEDEBOUR, ADOLPH HOFFMAN [ADOLF HOFFMANN]

For the French Delegation: A. BOURDERON, A. MERRHEIM

For the Italian Delegation: G. E. MODIGLIANI, COSTANTINO LAZZARI

For the Russian Delegation: N. LENIN, PAUL AXELROD, M. BOB-ROFF [BOBROV]

For the Polish Delegation: ST. LAPINSKI, A. WARSKI, CZ. [JAKÓB] HANECKI[44]

For the Inter-Balkan Socialist Federation: (For the Roumanian Delegation) C. RACOVSKI [RAKOVSKY]; (For the Bulgarian Delegation) WASSIL KOLAROW [VASIL KOLAROV]

For the Swedish and Norwegian Delegation: Z. HÖGLUND, TURE NERMAN

For the Dutch Delegation: H. ROLAND-HOLST[45]

For the Swiss Delegation: ROBERT GRIMM

STATEMENTS SUBMITTED BY VARIOUS DELEGATIONS

[A. Two Declarations by the Zimmerwald Left][46]

The undersigned declare that:

The manifesto adopted by the Conference does not give us complete satisfaction. It contains no characterization of either open opportunism

[44] *Internationale Korrespondenz* in its report on the Conference stated that "Radek was to sign the manifesto for the Poles but the German delegates declared resolutely that they would not place their names beside Radek's for the formal reason that Radek had been expelled from the German party" ("Die Rumpf-Internationale," *Internationale Korrespondenz*, No. 27, October 1, 1915, p. 394). Hanecki's name was substituted for Radek's, although according to *Internationale Korrespondenz* (No. 30, October 12, 1915, p. 424) Hanecki was not present. Another source, which we consider reliable, states that Hanecki was present to sign the manifesto.

[45] Roland-Holst signed the manifesto for the Dutch delegation, as the only representative of the Dutch party minority; the Zimmerwald manifesto met with opposition on the part of both the Right and the Left parties in Holland; the Tribunists objected to the manifesto because of their disagreement with the idea of the right of nations to self-determination and refused to subscribe to the manifesto. A campaign in favor of the Zimmerwald manifesto had to be organized in Holland and a Propaganda Committee formed. In 1916 both the Dutch Social Democratic party and the Socialist Revolutionary League officially joined the Zimmerwald Left. (See Henriette Roland-Holst, "Der Kampf um Zimmerwald in Holland," *Vorbote*, No. 1, January 1916, pp. 64–68; also appeal of the Dutch Propaganda Committee addressed to the Dutch workers in behalf of the Zimmerwald manifesto, "Appel aux ouvriers hollandais à la suite du manifeste de la conférence de Zimmerwald," *Commission socialiste internationale à Berne, Bulletin*, No. 2, December 27, 1915, pp. 11–12.)

[46] *Sotsial-Demokrat*, No. 47, October 13, 1915, p. 2. Also in Lenin, *The Imperialist War*, pp. 480–81.

Lenin wished to include also the following paragraph in the declaration of the Zimmerwald Left: "We vote in favor [of the manifesto] also because we wish to please the two French comrades, who have advanced an important consideration. They have pointed out the extreme state of depression of the workers in France, their extreme corruption by revolutionary phrases, and the necessity of approaching decisive tactics slowly and cautiously. However, opportunism is the foe of the labor movement in all Europe." (*Leninskii Sbornik*, XIV, 185.)

or opportunism covered up by radical phrases—that opportunism which is not only the chief culprit of the collapse of the International but which strives to perpetuate that collapse. The manifesto contains no clear characterization of the means of combating the war.

We shall advocate, as we have done heretofore, in the socialist press and at the meetings of the International a decidedly Marxian position in regard to the tasks with which the proletariat has been confronted by the epoch of imperialism.

We vote for the manifesto because we regard it as a call to struggle, and in this struggle we are anxious to march side by side with the other sections of the International.

We request that our present declaration be included in the official report.

> [*Signed*] N. LENIN, G. ZINOVIEV, RADEK,
> NERMAN, HÖGLUND, WINTER

Another declaration was signed by Roland-Holst and Trotsky, in addition to the Lefts who had introduced the draft resolution. Here is the text of that declaration:

"Inasmuch as the adoption of our amendment [to the manifesto] demanding the vote against war credits might endanger to some extent the success of the Conference, we withdraw our proposal under protest. We are satisfied with Ledebour's statement in the Commission to the effect that the manifesto contains all that is implied in our proposal."

It may be added that Ledebour presented an ultimatum and refused to sign the manifesto if the amendment were included.

[B. Statement Submitted by the Secretariat of the Organization Committee Abroad, the Main Presidium of the Social Democracy of Poland and Lithuania, and the Polish Socialist Party (Levitsa)][47]

[After pointing out that the present war will not put an end to existing imperialist rivalries but will make new ones, creating an oppressive atmosphere of anxiety and suspicion which will lead to larger armaments, greater waste of the productive energies of the people, and the surrender of wider powers to the militarists, the statement continues]:

. . . . Immense productive capacities are being wasted in this World War, but at the same time great wealth is accumulating in a few hands.

---

[47] *Tsimmervaldskaia i Kintalskaia konferentsii. Offitsialnye dokumenty*, pp. 35–37. At Radek's request the signature of the Regional Presidium of the Social Democracy of Poland and Lithuania, the so-called "opposition" was added. The commission to which the statement was transmitted found it impossible to include it in the manifesto because of its length and because it raised questions that had not been discussed. It was suggested that this, with the draft resolution of the Left group, be transmitted to the International Socialist Committee for future discussion. *Ibid.*, p. 35.

The broad middle strata of the population will lose their economic independence. The masses of the people will have to pay for the insanity of the world slaughter by new burdens of taxation. The increase in the prices of all vital necessities, the disorganization of economic life, the increase in taxes, and the accelerated proletarianization of the masses will aggravate to the utmost the conditions of existence and struggle of the laboring class.

The growth of power of the financial oligarchy, which is closely welded to the military caste, carries in itself the menace of worse political reaction in all countries and promises to paralyze the progress of social reforms and to accentuate the exploitation and the disfranchisement of the proletariat.

The laboring class will face the necessity of exerting all its efforts to protect the conquests achieved by a half century of struggle, to protect its standards of living and its political position against imperialism's most powerful forces, which draw humanity down into the abyss of barbarism.

Under these conditions it will become more and more clear to the workers that in order to put an end to these intolerable conditions it is necessary to assault the foundations of the social order, that order in which such endless misery and dangers originate. Thus the laboring masses will face the alternative: *Imperialism or Socialism.*

The proletariat cannot wait in the role of passive observer until the results of the imperialist epoch manifest themselves to their fullest extent. Even now the proletariat must come forward in all the belligerent countries in the role of an independent political factor, inasmuch as what happens now offers an illustration of the fate which is impending.

[C. Declaration of the Polish Delegations][48]

[The declaration states that since the outbreak of the war all three organizations and the class-conscious workers have opposed the war by word and deed and remained faithful to international socialism. They have opposed the legends of liberation and fought against the efforts of the Tsarist, German, and Austrian imperialists and the Polish propertied classes to make use of Polish national sentiment to further imperialist aspirations and class interests, and they protest against the dismember-

[48] *Commission socialiste internationale à Berne, Bulletin,* No. 2, December 27, 1915, p. 14. This declaration was signed by the delegates of the Polish Socialist party (Levista), the Main Presidium of the Social Democracy of Poland and Lithuania, and the Regional Presidium of the Social Democracy of Poland and Lithuania. This text was adopted at a meeting of the editorial board of *Gazeta Robotnicza* on June 1–2, 1915, and was published under the title, "Rezolucja narady kolegjum redakcyjnego, odbytej 1–2 czerwca 1915 r.," in *Gazeta Robotnicza,* No. 25, January 1916. Lenin, *Sochineniia,* XXIX, 265, note 3.

ment of an entire country to serve the strategic and economic interests of the dominant imperialist cliques. The declaration continues] :

. . . . At the present moment the Polish territories, which have been turned into an immense battlefield, a bloody desert, are placed in imminent danger of new annexing operations and of partition.

Having deprived the Polish people of the possibility of deciding their own destiny, the German and Austrian governments regard the Polish territory as a stake in the game of future compensation, a stake which will have to be either divided between the Central Powers or bargained for by Russian Tsarism.

This lays bare most definitely the very nature of the capitalist regime, which sends the masses of the people to slaughter, and thus determines the destinies of the nations for whole generations to come.

The Social Democracy of Poland most resolutely and solemnly protests against the dissection and tearing to pieces of a whole country in conformity with what in the epoch of the Holy Alliance was called *"les Convenances de l'Europe"* and which at present has come to serve merely the strategic and economic advantage of the dominant imperialist cliques.

With great bitterness the Polish socialist workers learned that the majority of socialists in the countries of both the Entente and the Central monarchies have succumbed to the influence of the war and that, whereas by obeying the command of imperialism some have contributed actively to the rehabilitation of Tsarism, others have entrusted to the Hohenzollerns and the Habsburgs the liberation of oppressed peoples. At a moment when the German government prepared to dispose of Poland as of a foreign colony and revealed its intentions in an ill-concealed declaration of the Imperial Chancellor [Bethmann-Hollweg], this declaration called forth no opposition whatsoever on the part of German Social Democracy. The German social nationalists, who before the war condemned the Polish-Galician social patriots for favoring the war, now advocate their absurd and criminal militant utopias in order to justify thereby the support which they themselves lend their governments.

By demonstrating the inadequacy of capitalism to adjust interstate relations to the demands of world economy, and by imposing monstrous taxation on the masses of the people, the present war inaugurates a new era of military conflicts and social upheavals. The revolutionary struggle of the proletariat, which under such conditions must flare up with spontaneous force and on an international and European scale, will be directed against the very foundations of the capitalist order and thus will become a struggle for socialism.

The Polish Social Democracy expresses its conviction that only the participation in that struggle proclaimed by the revolutionary international proletariat—a struggle which will break the chains of national oppression and abolish all foreign domination—can assure to the Polish people free development of its capacities in the framework of the International of United Peoples possessing equal rights.

[D. A Letter from the Württemberg Opposition][49]

[The writers explain that since the military dictatorship may prevent their delegates from attending the Conference they send "their fraternal greetings and express their will in written form." They denounce the war as a bourgeois affair not waged to defend this or that national state or to liberate oppressed peoples but carried on in the interests of imperialist competition and to defeat revolutionary elements in capitalist society. The letter continues] :

. . . . In the face of such facts the proletariat at the present moment can have only *one* task, namely, to struggle for an early cessation of war at any price. This aim can be realized only through unanimous and simultaneous demonstrations in all the belligerent and neutral countries.

The former International has never been nor can be adequate to these tasks, for, having been formed under special historic conditions, it was merely the expression of the tendency by which the adhering socialist parties conducted primarily separate and independent battles within the limits of individual states.

As a result of the fact that capitalism has outgrown the national boundaries, a new and more centralized organization of the proletarian International is necessary. International capitalism can be overcome only by international demonstrations. Therefore, we demand that the Conference take urgent measures for the creation of a new International whose task it will be to carry out centrally organized general demonstrations in all states.

We consider it necessary that as the first demonstration a manifesto be prepared in which the real essence of the war will be explained to the workers of all countries and which will appeal to them to unite in a struggle for peace . . . .

> With a brotherly greeting,
> The Social Democrats of Württemberg
> Who Are Faithful to the Program

DECLARATION OF SYMPATHY FOR THE VICTIMS OF THE WAR[50]

The International Socialist Conference sends an expression of profoundest sympathy to the countless victims of the war, to the *Polish* and

[49] "Obrashchenie Viurtembergskoi oppozitsii k Tsimmervaldskoi Konferentsii," *Proletarskaia Revoliutsiia*, No. 7 (90), 1929, pp. 171–73.

[50] "Conférence socialiste internationale à Zimmerwald (Suisse). Rapport officiel pour la presse. Adresse de sympathie." *Internationale sozialistische Kom-*

Belgian, Jewish and *Armenian peoples,* to all the millions of human beings who are tormented by unheard-of sufferings, who are victims of horrors unprecedented in history, and who are sacrificed to the spirit of conquest and the rapacity of imperialists.

The Conference honors the memory of the great socialist, Jean Jaurès, the first victim of the war, who fell as a martyr in the struggle against chauvinism and for peace. It honors the memory of the socialist champions, Tutzowicz and Catanesi, who died on the bloody battlefield.

The Conference sends an expression of profound and fraternal sympathy to the *Duma members exiled to Siberia* who are continuing the glorious revolutionary tradition of Russia; to Comrades Liebknecht and Monatte, both of whom have led courageously the struggle against the civil peace policy in their countries; to Klara Zetkin and Rosa Luxemburg, who have been imprisoned for their socialist convictions; and to the comrades of all nationalities who have been persecuted or imprisoned because they have struggled against war.

The Conference solemnly vows to honor the living and dead by following the example of these brave comrades, by indefatigably endeavoring to arouse the revolutionary spirit in the masses of the international proletariat and to unite them in the struggle against the fratricidal war and against capitalist society.

THE DELEGATIONS AT THE CONFERENCE

[Zinoviev's Characterization][51]

. . . . However, the tendency of the organizers of the Conference to move toward the "Center" had an unfavorable influence on the composition of the Conference, especially on the composition of the *German* delegation. Germany was represented by ten delegates but the decidedly Left internationalist elements among them were only weakly represented. The German delegation was not homogeneous. There were three shades in it: The majority—five or six persons—was headed by Deputy Ledebour, who represented those elements of the Left which vacillated between Liebknecht and Kautsky. Ledebour and his adherents do not vote in the Reichstag against war credits—they abstain from voting; the reason they gave to the Conference was as follows: voting against war credits by a whole group of deputies would have signified a split in the parliamentary group, and such a split would have signified a split in the party, whereas only patience was necessary in order for the Lefts to

---

mission zu Bern, Bulletin, No. 1, September 21, 1915, p. 8. Another translation is given in Lenin, *The Imperialist War,* pp. 476–77.

[51] *Sotsial-Demokrat,* No. 45–46, October 11, 1915, pp. 2–3; reprinted in Zinoviev, *Sochineniia,* V, 218–25.

obtain a majority in the party. K. Liebknecht through his voting against the credits and through his open breach of discipline, so they say, has only helped the Rights. He, Ledebour, could not accept the obligation to vote against the credits. This is a question which only the Germans themselves can solve. Such was the position of the majority of the German delegation.

Another shade was represented by a group of two or three delegates (some from Württemberg, and some others with respect to certain questions only). These comrades were not pleased with the policy of a simple abstention from voting of war credits; they were closer to Liebknecht; but they had no unified theoretical evaluation of the moment; they had not decided to break completely with the official party, although the latter had excluded them from its ranks. They had not yet completely broken with the tradition of old, proved tactics.

The third shade was represented by one delegate only [Borchardt]. This comrade was the only one who had supported Liebknecht's tactics without any reservations. He alone spoke about social chauvinists and about the "Center" in the same tone in which these were spoken of by the magazines *Internationale* and *Lichtstrahlen*. In return the majority of the German delegation showed an extremely disloyal attitude to the said comrade.

It turned out that the German delegation at the Conference was incomparably worse than we had thought the German Left was, judging by the newspapers. The majority of the German delegation placed the Conference in an impossible position: a conference of internationalists could not advance the demand—elementary for every socialist—to vote in parliaments against war credits. Ledebour declared as an *ultimatum* that for him such voting was inacceptable. It seemed at times that in Ledebour and his friends we had before us the Kautskyans.

It would be unjust to judge all the German Left by Ledebour and his friends. At the Conference an official letter was read from one very noted representative of the German Left who spoke against Ledebour (though without naming him), demanded a "ruthless trial of the turncoats," insisted on the necessity of branding those who vacillate, declared that the Third International could be erected only on "the debris" of the Second International, etc. Furthermore, there was circulated among the delegates a private letter from another still more noted representative of the German Left who declared that he considered the attempt to arrive at an understanding with Kautsky-Haase-Bernstein to be a great mistake, that the conciliatory tendency of the "Center" was only apt to harm the Left wing.

It is possible that the position of the German Left inside the country —in organizations among the "lower strata"—is much better than was reflected by the oblique mirror of the Ledebour delegation. But one thing the conference has shown with certainty: the former role of German Social Democracy has been played out. The inheritance from the past still weighs too heavily on the opposition elements of the German Social Democracy to enable them to become leaders of the new International.

France was represented by only two delegates, the syndicalist Merrheim and the socialist Bourderon. In this small delegation the transitional situation through which the French labor movement is passing was pictured as in a small drop of water.

In France the labor class is suppressed as nowhere else. The enemy occupies one-sixth of the territory of France, and this fact presses upon the conscience of the broad masses. Not only has official socialism gone bankrupt but also syndicalism and anarchism. The workers believe no one any more. All loud revolutionary promises, all loud phrases about insurrection in case of war, all talk about *action directe*—all that has proved to be empty chatter. Guesde entered the Cabinet. Hervé became a bazaar chauvinist noisemonger. Jouhaux is actually an agent of the French bourgeoisie.

The opposition in the French working class is only beginning. Everything is still in a state of ferment. The best elements of the French labor movement are at the crossroads. A tremendous process of revival is beginning. Merrheim, a true son and talented representative of the French labor class, expresses in his own person the beginning of this deep process. He goes from syndicalism to socialism; but he gropes and looks around in fear, not yet wishing to listen to the Marxian theory ("theory" was simply a scarecrow for many delegates at the Conference), refuses still to speak about the formation of a Third International.

The Italian Socialist party sent four delegates. This party, as is known, broke away from its social chauvinists three years ago during the Italo-Turkish War, and it did this precisely because the opportunists (Bissolati and Co.) became chauvinists. This split made it easier for the Italian socialists to adopt an antichauvinist stand in the war of 1914–1915, especially since they had time to observe the fateful consequences of the social-chauvinist tactics, and at the same time made it more difficult for the bourgeoisie to deceive the workers with cries about "the defense of the fatherland."

However, it should not be assumed that the entire Italian party stands on the basis of Marxian theory. Half of the delegation (two out of four) belonged to the Left reformists (the Left reformists remained in the party after the Right were excluded). Among the Left reformists pacifist feelings are still alive; among them there is evident even a Francophile tinge. At any rate, they do not have the courage to go against opportunism, to build a Third International without and in spite of the opportunists. The Italians have much sincere socialist feeling, honesty, and devotion to the cause; but they are still far from a firm Marxist policy.

Two delegates came from the Balkan Federation: a Bulgarian "Narrow" socialist, Comrade Kolarov; and the delegate of the Rumanian party, Comrade Rakovsky. The Bulgarian "Narrow" socialists are Marxists. They have conducted a long-drawn-out struggle against Bulgarian "liquidators" ("Broad" socialists), who now are ardent pupils of Plekhanov. In their own country the "Narrow" socialist comrades pursue a splendid line of struggle, but in the International they do not yet act decisively. Rakovsky in his new pamphlet makes concessions to the idea of "the defense of the fatherland." At the Conference, not wishing to declare a decisive struggle to the end against the opportunists, he declared himself to be an adherent of the restoration of the old Second International.

From Sweden and Norway Comrades Höglund and Nerman were present. They are backed by large organizations. In Sweden the Lefts have three daily papers, and in the lower house Höglund's group of deputies numbers thirteen. On certain questions this group increases to thirty. For many years the Höglund group led a very successful struggle against the opportunist Branting. In Norway the support of the Lefts is the youth organization. The Swedes and Norwegians have adopted detailed resolutions on the war in the spirit of the manifesto of our Central Committee, the manifesto with which the Scandinavian comrades are in harmony.

From Holland only Comrade Roland-Holst, who occupies in her country a middle position between Marxists ("Tribunists": Gorter, Pannekoek) and opportunists (the party of Troelstra), was present.

Poland had three delegates: Radek (the Polish Social Democratic Opposition), Warski (the Main Presidium of the Polish Social Democracy), Lapinski (Polish Socialist party).

From Switzerland there were Grimm, Naine, and Platten.

Russia was represented as follows: the Central Committee, Lenin and Zinoviev; the Organization Committee, Axelrod and Martov; the editorial board of *Nashe Slovo* (which together with the Bund had for some reason been invited separately from the Organization Committee), Trotsky; the party of Socialist-Revolutionists, Bobrov (from the Central Committee) and Gardenin (from the editorial board of the newspaper *Zhizn*); the Lettish Social Democracy, Comrade Winter; the Bund (which had sent a delegate to obtain information only), Lemansky.

The Conference proved, therefore, to be rather diversified in its composition. Besides convinced Marxists there were sentimental socialists, elements which vacillated toward the center, comrades who had not settled their accounts with pacifism, adherents of reformism and syndicalism whom at present life pushes in a different direction than formerly, etc.

From the first day of the Conference a closely knit group of seven or eight Left-Marxists, whose number at times was increased to ten or eleven, formed. The following entered the group: delegates of the Central Committee of the R.S.D.L. party, the delegate of the Lettish Social Democracy, the delegates of the Polish Social Democratic Opposition, delegates of Sweden and Norway, and one Left German delegate. This Left wing of the Conference acted at all times unitedly and in close solidarity. It alone came forward with its draft of a Marxist resolution and a draft of the manifesto. It alone defended a definite and integral program. In all questions of an ideological-political character a duel between this Left wing and Ledebour's group actually took place at the Conference. . . . .

The objective course of events and the development of struggle between tendencies have led to the fact that, in spite of the desire of the organizers of the Conference, they have not yet attained a union with the "Center." This same course of events resulted in that—in spite of the desire of the representatives of the majority of the Conference—the recent Conference became the cornerstone of the new Third International.

The Marxists will work patiently toward this aim without making any ideological concessions, and at the same time they will not withdraw from practical activities. The time will come when all honest socialists will exclaim with us: *The Second International has died, riddled by opportunism. Hail the Third International purged of opportunism!*

LOCAL REPORTS AND THE IDEOLOGICAL STRUGGLE AT ZIMMERWALD

[A Bolshevik Account][52]

. . . . Some of the reports made by the delegates at the Conference deserve attention.

It became manifest that the opposition groups in Germany were showing wide illegal activity. Illegal leaflets were being distributed in large numbers, up to 30,000 copies. Even Ledebour has had to recognize that Germany was moving toward a revolution.

In their turn the French delegates pointed out that the war will end with a revolution. They pictured the attitude of the broad working

---

[52] Shklovsky, "Tsimmervald," *Proletarskaia Revoliutsiia,* No. 9 (44), 1925, pp. 73–106.

masses who at present do not believe anybody or anything. For a long time the French worker was educated on anarchist and Hervéist phrases which had sufficiently corrupted him. Furthermore, Merrheim said that in France there were comrades â la Rosmer and Monatte, who go much farther than he does.

The report of Comrade Kolarov, who took part in the Second Balkan War, was interesting. He told about the widely practiced fraternizing in the trenches between Bulgarian and Serbian soldiers during that war, about the execution of officers by the soldiers, etc. The Bulgarian and Serbian Social Democrats had shown great concern for the socialist prisoners and, therefore, there had been no enmity between the socialists of these countries either during or after the Second Balkan War.

In Bulgaria two socialist parties existed: "Narrow" socialists and "Broad" socialists. The "Broad" socialists greatly resembled our liquidators; in words they were "Marxists" and in deeds the most acknowledged opportunists. Their liquidationist nature became manifest also during the World War. From the very beginning they took a chauvinist stand with a Russophile orientation by declaring Plekhanov to be their "first teacher," but as soon as Bulgaria entered the war on the side of Germany they immediately changed their orientation to Germanophile. The Bulgarian, Serbian, Rumanian, and Greek parties formed a Balkan Federation, to which the "Broad" socialists did not belong. . . . .

The Italian delegates told how the working masses themselves were organizing the struggle against the war. There were many strikes, street demonstrations; there were slain and wounded. After the declaration of war the persecution of socialists began.

Comrade Rakovsky told how the Rumanian Ministry of Foreign Affairs had shown great concern about him. As soon as the Ministry received a telegram that on August 4, 1914, the German Social Democrats had voted for war credits, this telegram was immediately forwarded to him ——.

Comrade Roland-Holst, who does not belong to the group of the Tribunists and who pursued a "conciliating" policy, was herself compelled to admit that the party of Troelstra had behaved disgracefully and that *socialist* work is being conducted only by the Tribunists.

Of the Russian reports, those of the Socialist-Revolutionist Chernov and of the liquidator Axelrod were of interest. Among the Socialist-Revolutionists the situation at that time was as follows: almost all the Socialist-Revolutionists abroad had become patriotic. The official representative of the party in the International Socialist Bureau, Rubanovich, was one of the most important figures at the London Conference of the Allied socialists. There, too, half of the Socialist-Revolutionists' delegates voted for the chauvinists, and the other half abstained from voting.[53] In Russia the Narodnik press showed patriotic feelings. Kerensky and his Duma group were patriotic. The Conference of Socialist-Revolutionists, of the Trudoviks, and of the Populist socialists in Russia recognized that "participation in defending the country against the external enemy was inevitable" and considered it necessary to "attract" the State Duma, even in its present composition, to the "people's cause," etc.[54] But how did Chernov report this? From his report the whole world would be led to think that the Central Committee of the Socialist-Revolutionists stands firmly and solidly on the basis of internationalism (but neither before nor after the Conference has anyone heard that the firm internationalist Central Committee has recalled Rubanovich from the International Socialist Bureau or has disavowed other patriots of their own party). Further, it appeared that the local committees of all the large towns in Russia issued internationalist appeals, while the Conference of the Narodniks in Russia adopted internationalist resolutions ———. Briefly: "Praise, praise, the brave Russian Socialist-Revolutionist." As is known, the Socialist-Revolutionists were always proficient in phrases and boasting.

The report of Axelrod was also of approximately the same nature. There was not a word about the patriotism of the liquidators, about the Duma group, about the magazine *Nasha Zaria,* which "takes the side of the Allies!" According to his words it appeared that there was complete harmony in their camp but that at the beginning of the war he himself was more on the side of the Duma group, while in Russia even now some "liquidator comrades" think that way. But in general, everything is fine, since those were only small passing disagreements.

. . . . The ideological struggle at Zimmerwald[55] was extremely interesting.

We have already seen that the composition of the Conference was extremely unfavorable for the consistent Lefts. In general and as a whole the Conference could be divided into three groups: the rather numerous Right group, headed by Ledebour; the Zimmerwald Left; and the vacillating Central group to which the organizers of the Conference belonged.

Although the organizers of the Conference had come there with a complete draft manifesto and resolution, the Conference had to reckon with the well-organized Left group, which compelled attention and which morally and ideologically influenced the entire Conference.

While the large and small individual groups had brought with them

[53] See Chernov's explanation above, chapter iii, p. 277, n. 26.

[54] This Conference took place in Petrograd on July 11 (June 28), 1915.

[55] Lenin's account of the ideological struggle is available in English in Lenin, *The Imperialist War,* pp. 346–49.

their ideological confusion, while none of them had thought out completely even one idea, the Zimmerwald Left, having Comrade Lenin as its leader, put all the questions definitely and clearly and also gave just as definite answers to these questions, thereby forcing the majority of the Conference, in spite of its own will, to follow them.

The chief questions involved in the argument were as follows:

Although no one argued about the imperialist character of the war—this postulate had already been adopted at Lugano by the Italian-Swiss Conference—there were many among the delegates who accepted this as a beautiful phrase that meant nothing, like the phrases which were so abundant in the Second International. Scarcely anyone had thought out the meaning of the word "imperialism" or understood it as a definite system of capitalist economy with its own laws, causes, and consequences. On the contrary, there were delegates who said quite frankly—we are not Marxists, let the intellectual eccentrics occupy themselves with theories, we are politicians or simply workers who struggle for the workers' interests ——. Thus the postulate about the imperialist character of the war, a postulate officially recognized by these delegates, put them under no obligation whatever.

It was difficult to make many of the delegates understand that a good cause calls for as good an action; that if a given theoretical postulate is correct, then it should result in a definite tactic and strategy. If it is true that the war is imperialist, then it is impossible to speak at the same time of the defense of the fatherland; then it is not only impossible to vote in favor of war credits but it is obligatory to vote against them. Meanwhile Ledebour at the Conference developed some kind of a theory of voting for or against credits, a theory dependent on the strategic position of a given imperialist army.

The second postulate which was advanced by Comrade Lenin and his group was that under imperialism wars are inevitable and that it is possible to struggle against them only by struggling against the *system* in which the wars originated, i.e., against capitalism and for socialism. From that Comrade Lenin evolved a whole plan of struggle. It was necessary to settle once and for all concerning the policy of civil peace. Socialist ministers had to leave bourgeois cabinets, any co-operation with the government should cease, voting against war credits was obligatory, etc. Nay, more, it is necessary to make use of the difficulties of the governments in order to attack them. A class struggle must be led with new vigor. Any strike movement must be supported with all available strength. The proletariat must go out into the streets. Demonstrations must be followed by political strikes, etc., etc. Briefly, *civil peace must be transformed into civil war.*

Nor should our agitation stop at the trenches. There have already been examples of fraternizing in the trenches during the Balkan wars. These should be widely propagated and this method, incidentally, will be the best way of forcing the governments to settle the war more quickly.

How did the different groups at the Conference respond to this? Some said: that is childishness; it is like setting off explosives; dangerous nonsense! Others said: such things are done but are not talked about, and it is no use shouting to the whole world about civil war, fraternizing in the trenches, strikes, and demonstrations.

The French, in referring to the fact that the French worker has lost all confidence in his leader and "does not believe anyone or anything," said that consequently he would not believe this sermon either.

One Italian argued: "Your tactic comes either too late (for the war has already begun) or too early"—the war has not yet created revolutionary conditions. Moreover, our tactic was unacceptable to him because it signified a change in the program of the International, which always stood against violence.

It was not hard for Comrades Lenin and Zinoviev to prove that those who do not consider it necessary to shout about civil war pursue the policy of Kautsky. The Germans and the French have recognized that we are proceeding toward a revolution, whereas you do not wish to say this straight to the workers, to summon them to a revolution, to work out the concrete means of struggle.

More serious were the arguments of the French, but they only said that with our preaching one should approach the masses cautiously and skillfully. It was necessary to explain to the Italian (Morgari, if I am not mistaken) that the beginning of a revolution does not coincide with the beginning of the agitation and preparation for it. The first Russian revolution had not started prior to January 9, 1905, but the agitation for it was conducted much earlier. Incorrect also was his assertion that the International repudiates the use of violence. Not a single influential leader of the Second International had ever repudiated the use of violence and of direct revolutionary struggle in general.

Many arguments were called forth also by another question, previously advanced by the manifesto of our Central Committee and supported by the Zimmerwald Left, on the attitude toward the Second International, and toward the leaders of those parties who had caused the collapse of the International and the split within the parties.

The Lefts spoke definitely about the bankruptcy of the Second International, pointed to the opportunist leaders as the cause of its collapse, and put the question as to the necessity of creating a Third International, purged of opportunism. The majority of the Conference, even in respect to this, had not worked out its ideas completely . . . . "We have not come here to provide a formula for the Third International," declared the French delegate at the Conference. On the other hand, at one of the meetings this same Merrheim used the following expression: "The Socialist party, the Confédération générale du travail (the General Council of the trade unions), and the government are three heads under one cap." Lenin replied to that: "Quite so! But from this the conclusion should be drawn that struggle against imperialism and against the imperialist government is impossible without struggle against the opportunist leaders of the party and of the trade unions." But they feared this Bolshevist step like fire. . . . .

In discussing questions of organization the Zimmerwald Lefts demanded that the International Socialist Committee (the organ of Zimmerwald) should arrange from time to time enlarged meetings with permanent representatives of the parties adhering to Zimmerwald (similar to what the International Socialist Bureau had done); but this proposal did not pass, since the majority discerned in it, quite correctly, our desire to form our permanent organ in place of the [International] Socialist Bureau. It is true that later on the International Socialist Committee resorted to it,[56] but at Zimmerwald such a step was greatly feared . . . .

C. The Lefts at Zimmerwald

As has been said, Lenin was extremely active in the weeks before the Conference, rallying those Lefts who might be persuaded to uphold the Bolshevik point of view which he had set forth in drafts of a manifesto, a resolution, and a declaration, written and circulated during August. Lenin arrived at Berne on September 4 and talked with those delegates who might be won over to the Bolshevik position. Merrheim tells of these electioneering efforts in the course of his report to the Lyon Congress of the C.G.T.: "As soon as we arrived at Berne, we were met by the Russian comrades whom Lenin had sent to the station. They conducted us to a room in the People's Hall and there for eight hours on end Lenin and I discussed, toe to toe, the attitude which we should observe at the Conference at Zimmerwald." Merrheim was not won over. He was not sure that he would be allowed to return to France and describe what was done at Zimmerwald, and still less did he feel that he could pledge himself "to call

[56] See circular of the I.S.C., September 27, 1915, given below, pp. 358–62.

upon the people of France to rise up in rebellion against the war."[57] Lenin also called a private meeting, which was attended by the eight who made up the Left bloc at the Conference (Lenin, Zinoviev, Berzin, Radek, Höglund, Nerman, Platten, Borchardt) and some others, including Trotsky. According to Trotsky the meeting agreed to condemn the official socialist parties, to formulate principles of revolutionary class policy, and to unite all the Left elements on this basis. No mention was made of a mass struggle for peace. Lenin spoke on the nature of the war and the tasks of revolutionary Social Democracy and apparently offered a draft resolution which was not accepted. Radek's draft somewhat amended was adopted and later presented at the Conference in behalf of the Left group.[58]

When the full Conference met, the Lefts offered the draft resolution mentioned above and a draft manifesto. The Conference rejected the draft resolution when by a vote of 19 to 12 it refused to refer it to a Commission. On this issue Trotsky, Roland-Holst, Chernov, and Natanson voted with the Left. The draft manifesto was not adopted either but, as has been noted, was referred to a Commission along with drafts by the Germans and by Trotsky. The manifesto ultimately issued followed Trotsky's draft more closely than either of the others.

Despite the refusal of the Conference to adopt the pro-

---

[57] D. J. Saposs, *The Labor Movement in Post-War France*, pp. 35–36, translated from Confédération Générale du Travail, *XXe (XIVe) Congrès, Lyon, 1919*, p. 171.

[58] Trotsky, *Voina i Revoliutsiia*, II, 56; Lenin, *Sochineniia*, XIX, 485–86, note 198; Berzin, *Partiia bolshevikov v borbe za Kommunisticheskii Internatsional*, pp. 73–74. Lenin's draft followed in general the same line as Radek's but contained these sentences which are interesting in the light of later Bolshevik policy: "In an epoch when the bourgeoisie was progressive, when the overthrow of feudalism, absolutism, and foreign national oppression were placed on the historic order of the day, socialists, being always the most consistent and decided democrats, recognized the 'defense of the fatherland' in that sense and in that sense only. At present, should a war originate in the East of Europe or in the colonies—a war of oppressed nations against their oppressors, the great powers—the sympathy of the socialists would be entirely on the side of the oppressed." (Full text in *Leninskii Sbornik*, XIV, 166–69.)

nouncements offered by the Lefts, the Bolsheviks were rather pleased than otherwise by the results of their participation, as is indicated by Shklovsky's comments given above.[59] Their ideas were, they felt, making progress in the international socialist arena. To consolidate and extend these gains, the Lefts, while remaining in the Zimmerwald movement, organized their own bureau, consisting of Lenin, Zinoviev, and Radek, and presently, as appears below, began to issue their own publications. After Zimmerwald the Left was further strengthened by the official adherence of Roland-Holst and the Dutch Tribunists Gorter, Pannekoek, and Wijnkoop, and the International Socialists of Germany.

DRAFT MANIFESTO OF THE ZIMMERWALD LEFT[60]

PROLETARIANS OF EUROPE!

The war has lasted for over a year. The battlefields are covered with millions of corpses; millions of cripples are doomed to remain burdens to themselves and to others for the rest of their lives. The war has caused terrific devastation; it will bring about an unheard-of increase in taxes.

The capitalists of all countries, who in time of war accumulate huge profits at the price of the bloodshed by the proletariat, demand from the masses of the people that they make every effort to resist to the end. They say: the war is necessary for the defense of the fatherland; it is waged in the interests of democracy. They lie! In none of the countries did the capitalists begin the war because the independence of their country was endangered or because they wanted to free some enslaved people. They led the masses into the slaughter because they wished to oppress and to exploit other peoples. They were unable to reach an agreement between themselves as to how to divide up the peoples of Asia and Africa who had remained independent; they were watching one another in an attempt to snatch away the spoils previously seized.

Not for the sake of their own freedom, not for the sake of freeing other peoples do the masses of the people bleed white in all sections of that huge slaughterhouse called Europe. This war will bring to the

---

[59] Lenin's comments, translated in Lenin, *The Imperialist War*, pp. 346–49, cover very much the same ground.

[60] *Sotsial-Demokrat*, No. 45–46, October 11, 1915, p. 4; also in Lenin, *The Imperialist War*, pp. 478–80.

European proletariat and to the peoples of Asia and Africa a new burden, new chains.

Therefore there is no use carrying this fratricidal war to the end, to the last drop of blood; on the contrary, every effort must be strained to put an end to it.

The time for doing this has already come. The first thing you should demand is that your socialist deputies, whom you have sent to parliament to fight capitalism, militarism, and the exploitation of the people, should fulfill their duty. All of them except the Russians, Serbians, and Italians, and with the exception of Comrades Liebknecht and Rühle, have trod this duty into the mud and either have supported the bourgeoisie in its rapacious war or by vacillating have shirked their responsibility. You must demand that they either lay down their mandates or make use of the parliamentary tribune in order to explain to the people the character of the present war, and that outside parliament they help the laboring class to resume its struggle. Your first demand should be: *a refusal to vote any war credits, a withdrawal from the cabinets of France, Belgium, and England.*

But this is not enough! The deputies cannot save you from the wild beast, the World War, which drinks your blood. *You yourselves must act.* You must make use of all your organizations and publications in order to call forth a revolt against the war among the broad masses which groan under its burden. You must go out *into the streets* and fling in the face of the ruling classes your rallying cry: *Enough of massacre!* Let the ruling classes remain deaf to it—the discontented masses of the people will hear it and will join you in the struggle.

It is necessary to demand vigorously and without delay the cessation of the war; it is necessary to protest loudly against the exploitation of one people by another, against the partitioning of separate peoples among various states. All this will take place if any capitalist government wins and is able to dictate terms of peace to the others. If we let the capitalists conclude peace in the same way that they started the war—without the participation of the masses—then new conquests will not only strengthen reaction and arbitrary police rule in the victorious country but will also plant the seeds of new and more horrible wars.

The overthrow of the capitalist governments—this is the aim which the laboring class of all the belligerent countries must set itself, because only when capital shall have been deprived of the power of life and death over the people, only then will an end be put to the exploitation of one people by another and to wars. Only peoples freed from want and misery and from dominance of capital will be able to organize their inter-relationships, not through wars but through friendly agreements.

Great is the goal we set ourselves; great are the efforts which are necessary for its attainment; great will be the sacrifices before the aim will be attained. Long is the road to victory. Peaceful means of pressure will be insufficient to overcome the enemy. But only when you are ready to make at least a part of the innumerable sacrifices which you are now offering on the battlefield in the interests of capital serve your own liberation in the struggle against capital, only then will you be able to put an end to the war and to lay the real foundation for a lasting peace which will free you from capitalist slavery.

But if by deceitful phrases of the bourgeoisie and of socialist parties which support it you are kept from an energetic struggle and become satisfied with sighing, not wishing to take up the attack and to sacrifice your souls and bodies to the great cause, then capital will continue to waste your blood and your belongings at its own discretion. Every day in all countries the number of those who think as we do grows: we, the representatives of various countries, have gathered here at their command in order to summon you to the struggle. We shall lead it and support one another, for no separate interests divide us. The revolutionary workers of every country must consider it their duty and their honorable right to be an example to others, an example of energy and of self-sacrifice. Not timid expectation as to where the struggle of others will lead, but struggle in the front ranks—this is the road which leads to the formation of a powerful International, the International which will put an end to all wars and to capitalism.

DRAFT RESOLUTION OF THE ZIMMERWALD LEFT[61]

The World War which for the last year has been ruining Europe is an *imperialist* war, waged for the political and economic exploitation of the world, for export markets, sources of raw material, spheres of capital investment, etc. It is the product of capitalist development which, on the one hand, has united the whole world into a universal economic system and, on the other, has maintained independent national-state groups of capitalists with opposing interests.

By trying to conceal this character of the war, by asserting that it is a struggle for national *independence,* forced upon them, the bourgeoisie and the governments are misleading the *proletariat,* since the war is being waged for the oppression of foreign peoples and countries. No less deceiving are the legends about the defense of democracy in this war, since imperialism signifies the unscrupulous dominance of large capital and political reaction.

It is possible to overcome imperialism only by abolishing the contra-

---

[61] "Vsemirnaia voina i zadachi sotsialdemokratii," *Sotsial-Demokrat,* No. 45–46, October 11, 1915, pp. 3–4; also in Lenin, *The Imperialist War,* pp. 477–78.

dictions from which imperialism has originated through a socialist re-organization of the leading capitalist countries. Objective conditions have already ripened for the realization of this.

At the outbreak of the war the majority of the labor parties' leaders had not set up this only possible slogan as a counterpoise to imperialism. Possessed by nationalism and rotten with opportunism they delivered the proletariat up to imperialism at the moment of the World War by renouncing the fundamental principles of socialism and, therefore, any real struggle in the interests of *the proletariat.*

The point of view of social patriotism and social imperialism which is adhered to by the open patriotic majority of the former Social Democratic leaders in Germany as well as by the party Center rallying around Kautsky, which acts as an opposition, the party majorities in *France* and *Austria,* and some of the leaders in *England* and *Russia* (Hyndman, the Fabians, trade unionists, Plekhanov, Rubanovich, the *Nasha Zaria* group) is a more dangerous enemy of the proletariat than are the bourgeois advocates of imperialism—for by misusing the socialist banner it is apt to mislead the non-class-conscious element of the proletariat. Ruthless struggle against social imperialism is the first prerequisite for the mobilization of the proletariat and the restoration of the International.

It is the task of both the socialist parties and the socialist oppositions within the present social-imperialist parties to call the laboring masses to a revolutionary struggle against the capitalist governments and for the seizure of that political power which is necessary for a socialist organization of society.

Without ceasing in the realm of capitalism to struggle for every reform that would strengthen the proletariat, without renouncing any means of agitation for the organization and mobilization of the proletariat, the revolutionary Social Democrats must make use of every struggle and of every reform demanded by our minimum program in order to sharpen in general any social and political crisis of capitalism as well as the crisis caused by the war and to turn this struggle into an onslaught against the fundamental stronghold of capitalism. Under the slogan of socialism this struggle will make the laboring masses impervious to the slogan of the enslavement of one people by another, a slogan which is manifest in the support of the domination of one nation over another, in the cries for new annexations. This struggle will make the working masses deaf to the speeches about national solidarity, speeches which have led the workers to the battlefields.

The beginning of this struggle is the struggle against the World War and for an early ending of this human slaughter. This struggle demands a refusal to vote war credits, a withdrawal from cabinets, the exposure of the capitalist, antisocialist character of the war from the parliamentary tribune and in the columns of the legal and, where necessary, the illegal press, the sharpest struggle against social patriotism, the utilization of every movement of the people, called forth by the war (want, great losses, etc.), the organization of antigovernment demonstrations, the propaganda of international solidarity in the trenches, concurrence with economic strikes and attempts to turn them into political strikes under favorable conditions. Civil war, not civil peace, between the classes— that is our slogan.

Against all *illusions* which assume that the decision of diplomats and of governments can create a basis for lasting peace and can initiate disarmament the revolutionary Social Democrats must constantly point out to the masses that only a social revolution can bring about the realization of lasting peace and the liberation of mankind.

LENIN'S EVALUATION OF THE ZIMMERWALD MANIFESTO

[From His Article, "The First Step"][62]

. . . . The results of the Conference consist of a manifesto and of a declaration of sympathy for the arrested and persecuted . . . . The Conference, by a majority of nineteen to twelve, refused to submit to a committee the draft resolution which we and other revolutionary Marxists proposed, whereas our draft manifesto, together with the other two drafts for the working out of a general manifesto, were transmitted to the Commission . . . . A comparison of our draft manifesto and draft resolution with the adopted manifesto clearly indicates that we succeeded in introducing a number of the fundamental ideas of revolutionary Marxism.

As a matter of fact the manifesto adopted signifies a step toward an ideological and practical break with opportunism and social chauvinism. At the same time the manifesto, as an analysis of it will prove, suffers from inconsistency and is not comprehensive.

The manifesto declares the war to be imperialist and points out two characteristics of that concept: the desire of the capitalists of *every* nation for profit and exploitation; and the tendency of the Great Powers to divide the world and to "enslave" the weak nations. The most essential thing that must be said of the imperialist character of the war, and that was said in our resolution, is repeated in the manifesto. In this particular the manifesto only popularizes our resolution. Popularization is undoubtedly a useful thing. However, if we wish to make them clear to the working class, if we attach importance to systematic, tenacious propaganda, we must establish clearly and fully the principles that must

[62] *Sotsial-Demokrat,* No. 45–46, October 11, 1915, p. 2; also in Lenin, *The Imperialist War,* pp. 340–45.

be popularized. If we fail to do this we run the risk of repeating the error and sin of the Second International which caused its collapse, namely, we leave room for equivocations and misinterpretations. For instance, is it possible to deny the substantial significance of the idea, as expressed in our resolution, that objective conditions for socialism have ripened? In the "popular" exposition of the manifesto this idea was omitted. The attempt to combine an appeal with a clear and precise resolution based on principle has failed.

"The capitalists of all countries . . . . assert that the war is for the defense of the fatherland . . . . They lie . . . . ," the manifesto continues. Here again this direct declaration that the fundamental idea of opportunism in the present war, the "defense of the fatherland" idea, is a lie is a repetition of the most essential idea contained in the resolution of the revolutionary Marxists. And here again it is a pity the manifesto does not say all that should be said. It displays timorousness and is afraid to tell the whole truth. Who does not know, after a year of war, that the real calamity for socialism was the *repetition* and the *support* of the capitalist *lies* not only by the capitalist press (being a capitalist press it is its duty to repeat the lies of the capitalists), but also by the greater part of the socialist press? Everybody knows that it is not the capitalists' lies that have brought about the greatest crisis of European socialism but the *lies* of Guesde, Hyndman, Vandervelde, Plekhanov, *Kautsky*. Who does not know that the *lies* of such leaders suddenly revealed the whole strength of opportunism which carried them away at the critical moment?

See what is happening: in order to popularize the idea among the broad masses, they say in the manifesto that the "defense of the fatherland" idea in the present war is a capitalist lie. The masses of Europe, however, are not illiterate, and nearly everyone who reads the manifesto has heard and is hearing *precisely that same lie* from hundreds of socialist papers, magazines, and pamphlets, which repeat it from Plekhanov, Hyndman, Kautsky and Co. . . . .

Further, the manifesto repeats one more essential idea contained in our resolution when it says that the socialist parties and the workers' organizations of the various countries "have *trampled down* the obligations arising from the decisions of the Stuttgart, Copenhagen, and Basel congresses"; that the International Socialist Bureau also *failed to do its duty;* that its failure to do its duty lies in the fact that it voted war credits, participated in cabinets, and recognized "civil peace" (submission to which the manifesto calls *slavish;* in other words, the manifesto accuses Guesde, Plekhanov, Kautsky and Co. of substituting the preaching of *slavish* ideas for the preaching of socialism).

The question arises: Is it consistent to speak in a "popular" manifesto of the violation of duty by a number of parties—it is commonly known that this refers to the strongest parties and the workers' organizations of the most advanced countries, England, France, and Germany —without explaining this startling, unheard-of, and unprecedented fact? What is this nonfulfillment of duty by the majority of the socialist parties and the International Socialist Bureau itself? Is it an accident? Is it the bankruptcy of individuals, or is it the turning point of a whole epoch? If it is the former, if *we* admit such an idea to the masses, then this means *our* renunciation of the foundations of socialist doctrine. If it is the latter, how can we fail to say so directly? We are facing a moment of world-wide historic importance—the collapse of the entire International, the turning point of a whole epoch—and still we are *afraid* to tell the masses that we must look and search for the whole truth; that we must follow our thoughts to the very end; that it is preposterous and ridiculous to admit the supposition of the collapse of the International Socialist Bureau and a number of parties *without* connecting this phenomenon with the protracted history of the origin, the growth, the ripening and *over*-ripening of the all-European opportunist tendency which has deep economic roots—deep not in the sense that they are inseparable from the masses but in the sense that they are connected with a definite stratum of society.

Passing to the "struggle for peace," the manifesto declares: "This struggle is the struggle for liberty, for the brotherhood of peoples, for socialism"—and further it explains that in the war the workers make sacrifices in "the service of the ruling classes," whereas they must know how to make sacrifices *"for their own cause"* (twice underscored in the manifesto), "for the sacred aims of socialism." In the declaration of sympathy for the arrested and persecuted it says that "the Conference solemnly vows to honor the living and dead fighters by *following* their example" and that it sets itself the task of "arousing the revolutionary spirit in the international proletariat."

All these ideas are a repetition of the fundamental idea of our resolution that a struggle for peace *without* a revolutionary struggle is but an empty and false phrase, that the only way to put an end to the horrors of war is by a revolutionary struggle for socialism. But here again we find inconsistency, timidity, and failure to say everything that ought to be said, to call the masses *to imitate the example* of the revolutionary fighters, to declare that the five members of the Russian Social Democratic Labor group sentenced to exile in Siberia continued "the glorious revolutionary tradition of Russia," to proclaim the necessity of "arousing the revolutionary spirit" and at the same time *not to tell* directly, openly, and clearly what the revolutionary methods of struggle must be.

Was it advisable for our Central Committee to sign this manifesto which suffered from lack of consistency and from timidity? We think so. Concerning the disagreement not only of our Central Committee but of the whole Left *international* revolutionary Marxist section of the Conference, the motives of voting for a compromise manifesto have been expressed openly in a special resolution, in a special draft manifesto, and in a special statement. We did not conceal one iota of our views, slogans, tactics. The German edition of our pamphlet, *Socialism and War,* was distributed at the Conference. We have propagated, are propagating, and shall propagate our views no less than the manifesto itself will be propagated. That this manifesto is taking a *step forward* toward a real struggle against opportunism, toward breaking and splitting with it, is a fact. It would be sectarianism for us to refuse to take this step forward *together* with the minority of the Germans, French, Swedes, Norwegians, and Swiss when we retain full freedom and full possibility of criticizing inconsistency and of endeavoring to achieve greater results.[63] It would be bad military tactics to refuse to move together with the growing international movement of protest against social chauvinism because this movement is slow, it takes "only" one step forward, it is ready and willing to take a step backward tomorrow, to make peace with the old International Socialist Bureau. The readiness to make peace with the opportunists is as yet no more than a wish. Will the opportunists agree to peace? Is peace *objectively* possible between the *currents*—which diverge more and more profoundly—of social chauvinism and Kautskyism and revolutionary internationalist Marxism? We believe it impossible, and we shall continue our policy, encouraged by its *success* at the Conference of September 5–8. . . . .[64]

D. Activity of the International Socialist Committee between Zimmerwald and Kienthal

The Zimmerwald Conference created very little stir in the world. The censorship in Russia, Germany, and France pre-

[63] That the Organization Committee and the Socialist-Revolutionists signed the manifesto as diplomats, retaining at the same time their bonds with—and all their *bondage to Nasha Zaria,* Rubanovich, and the July 1915 Conference of the Populist Socialists and the Socialist-Revolutionists in Russia does not frighten us. We have plenty of opportunity to fight against rotten diplomacy and to unmask it. It unmasks itself more and more. *Nasha Zaria* and Chkheidze's Duma group, are helping us unmask Axelrod and Co. [Author's note.]

[64] Radek made his evaluation of Zimmerwald in *Lichtstrahlen,* No. 1, October 3, 1915, pp. 3–5, under the same title, "Der erste Schritt." He speaks of the Conference as "the first step toward restoring the International" but points out that the Lefts, in supporting the International Socialist Committee, "did so with the understanding that it was impossible to form at once a fighting organization from the remnants of the Second International."

vented the open and legal publication of the manifesto and the proceedings, and the organs of the patriotic socialist and labor parties, when they referred to the Conference at all, disclaimed all connection with it or denounced it as a factional move of self-appointed trouble makers. In Italy and England and in many neutral states the socialist papers published the manifesto and discussed the Conference. A good deal of this discussion was critical. Vliegen and van Kol, Right-wing members of the Dutch Social Democratic Labor party, alleged in *Het Volk* that the Conference was composed of representatives of small groups gathered at random and entirely without authority to set up an "International Socialist Committee." On September 29 the International Socialist Committee replied that the Central Committee of the Italian Socialist party had taken the initiative in calling the Conference, that official parties of seven countries had sent delegates, and the other delegates were representatives of organized minorities; further, the International Socialist Committee was not a rival of the International Socialist Bureau but a temporary body which would be dissolved as soon as the International Socialist Bureau opened a struggle against war in conformity with the resolutions of Stuttgart, Copenhagen, and Basel.[65]

But criticism was not confined to the Rights. Many Lefts thought the whole affair smacked too much of compromise, and the Dutch Tribunists objected not only because the manifesto had been signed by socialists who had failed to vote against war credits but because there was a paragraph about national self-determination. Despite this opposition and the censorship, Zimmerwald documents and Zimmerwald ideas found their way across the guarded frontiers of the belligerent states and gained an increasing number of supporters among the socialist and labor organizations during the period between the Zimmerwald and Kienthal conferences.

In attempting to carry out the Zimmerwald decisions the

[65] "Déclaration," *Commission socialiste internationale à Berne, Bulletin*, No. 2, December 27, 1915, pp. 1–2.

International Socialist Committee at Berne found that while the manifesto presupposed such joint actions as a struggle against civil peace, a resumption of the class struggle, and a struggle against war and for a peace which should not violate the rights and liberties of peoples, no details of procedure were laid down. General principles, the I.S.C. said in a confidential circular given below, were insufficient for carrying out a joint peace action. Whether the war ended soon or late, it was necessary to take a position toward current problems arising out of the war, problems which had not yet been considered by the Zimmerwald groups. The International Socialist Committee could not by itself make these decisions, and it was therefore necessary to call another conference.

To call such a conference, the I.S.C. pointed out, would take time; and since prompt action was desirable, a special body, an Enlarged Committee, should be formed to maintain contacts between organizations represented at the conference and to make urgent decisions.

These proposals of the I.S.C. were later adopted. Meanwhile the Committee attempted to strengthen its contacts with interested groups and issued the *Bulletin,* in which the progress of the Zimmerwald movement was reported in German, French, and English. Early in 1916 preparations began for the second Zimmerwald Conference. These activities are discussed in chapter v in connection with Kienthal.

TO THE ZIMMERWALD GROUPS

[Confidential Circular Letter of the International Socialist Committee, September 27, 1915][66]

Party Comrades! The Conference at Zimmerwald by a unanimous decision has issued a manifesto to the proletarians of Europe. Further-

---

[66] "Zur Zimmerwalder Konferenz," *Internationale Korrespondenz,* No. 41, November 19, 1915, pp. 508–510. This circular, which was apparently not to be published, fell into the hands of socialist opponents of Zimmerwald and was published by *Internationale Korrespondenz* with a few omissions as indicated in the text. The circular is not included in the official publications of the International Socialist Committee nor in Balabanoff's collection of documents on the Zimmerwald movement, but it is referred to in other documents given below.

more, it has recognized that the joint declaration of the German and French delegations was a manifestation of the newly established international proletarian solidarity. The appointment of the International Socialist Committee was also unanimous.

In the text of the manifesto, as well as in the other decisions of the Conference, there is apparent a resolute will to initiate joint proletarian action for peace. But the meeting of the Conference at Zimmerwald and the independent (isolated?)[67] continuation of the work by the socialists in various countries should not be the only manifestation of this will. If this were the case, then the Conference could have abstained from appointing a Committee and it would have sufficed to issue merely a report on the Conference instead of a *Bulletin* which appears irregularly. Nor would there be any sense in entrusting the Committee with the elaboration of the Commission's draft resolution which the Commission submitted to the Conference.

Hence it was the will of the Conference, based undoubtedly on the adopted resolutions, that the work should be carried on and the Conference should be regarded as *the first step of a joint action* rather than as a closed chapter.

Joint action presupposes a common basis for activity, common principles, and co-ordinated demands. The manifesto contains certain *general* points of view which are to guide our activity. Struggle against civil peace, resumption of the class struggle, struggle against war and for peace and moreover for a peace without annexation, "without violation of the rights and liberties of the peoples"—these were its slogans. The Conference avoided details and by doing so was able to outline the policy which it was to pursue and in harmony with which the conference made its first step.

But these general points of view are insufficient for the carrying out of our peace action. The spirit of this action cannot be determined only by the general viewpoints of the participants in the Conference or of the organizations and groups which are behind these participants. The external situation is also significant, especially the *military situation* and the war aims which are being pursued by the ruling classes, the military and imperialist cliques. We presuppose here two possibilities:

1. If an early suspension of hostilities and the conclusion of peace are to be expected—contrary to the now generally prevailing opinion that the war will yet continue for many months and perhaps even for another year—then our task would be to state concretely and in detail the international attitude of the proletariat toward the various peace proposals and programs. Neither the general points of view of our manifesto nor

---

[67] It is not clear whether the term in parentheses belongs to the original or has been inserted by the editors of the *Internationale Korrespondenz*.

the general resolutions of the congresses of the Second International are adequate for this task. When, for instance, the Alsace-Lorraine question, the Polish question, and the reorganization of national relations in the Balkans, in Armenia, etc., are brought up, then our Conference— if it wishes to be faithful to its task, namely, the attainment of a *unanimous* proletarian peace action—must assume a clear, unequivocal attitude toward these questions. The more so since it is improbable that all the parties affiliated with the International Socialist Bureau would, before the suspension of hostilities, arrive at a unified program which could provide the laboring class with an international orientation. To understand our doubt and to recognize its soundness, it is sufficient to recall the attitudes of the official party institutions and parliamentary representatives in Germany and France toward the Alsace-Lorraine question.

2. Should the war last for many months—as is now generally believed—then the continuation of the slaughter makes imperative our duty to carry out the decision of the Conference by inviting the working class to unite its forces and to fight actively in favor of peace. The continuation of the war will also create new situations toward which we shall have to define our attitude if we do not wish to betray or renounce our aim, namely, the carrying out of a unified action for peace. The deception which was spread at the beginning of the war, that this war is a war of national defense and protection, has now vanished. Our manifesto states that the guiding imperialist forces of the war have become increasingly more prominent as the war has gone on. The German-Austrian opposition against Serbia and the general mobilization in *Bulgaria* have brought results which cannot yet be estimated. At present we cannot predict what their future consequences will be: whether or not Greece and Rumania will be drawn into the general whirlpool; but it is true that these two countries are close to the possibility of entering the war. Swedish-Russian relations and the future attitude of America are still obscure; equally obscure are the future development of economic and social conditions in the belligerent countries and the effect of these conditions upon the militant sentiments and attitude of the proletariat. New storm signals of a revolution are being flashed from Russia and Poland, a revolution which is ready to break out again and the future development of which is of utmost significance to the Western European proletariat.

In any case—whether an early suspension of hostilities is to be expected or the war is to go on for many months—we are confronted with the necessity of adopting a new orientation and determining our attitude toward problems which may arise as the war continues and which today have not yet been included in our discussions.

Finally, the Conference has appointed a Committee which must become the centralizing factor of our joint activity. It stands to reason, however, that a committee of three or four persons, half of whom are from a small neutral country which plays no role in world politics, cannot by itself treat and solve the questions mentioned above under one and two. Neither the nature of the Committee's membership nor the means at its disposal are adequate to that end. The settling of these questions by correspondence with representatives in separate countries is impossible, for such settlement is a matter of issuing unanimous manifestoes and decisions. Hence, we have only one choice—to call a *new conference* as the only institution competent to make final decisions on such important questions as these.

Under present conditions, however, the Conference cannot assemble in an hour. Even when the Zimmerwald Conference was called, tremendous obstacles had to be overcome. Under certain circumstances, and owing to the further development of the war and its consequences, it may be necessary—if we are not to lag behind events—to act quickly, to make decisions, to advance slogans. Care must be taken that in situations like these we are not surprised by events and are not placed in the position in which the Second International found itself at the outbreak of the war.

To establish these firm organizational bonds, without which no *effective* action is imaginable, it is desirable to set up a special body between the Committee and the Conference. This body (let us call it the *Enlarged Committee*) would concern itself with maintaining contacts between the organizations which were represented at the Conference and in extraordinary, urgent cases it would make necessary decisions, in agreement with the affiliated organizations and groups and basing itself upon the principles outlined at Zimmerwald. The Enlarged Committee can by no means be a substitute for a Conference and cannot to any degree replace it.

Owing to conditions which are by no means very simple and because of the more or less improvised attendance at our first Conference, certain difficulties are arising which must be eliminated before our proposal can be realized.

In this connection we make the following observations:

The Conference at Zimmerwald was composed of:

1. Representatives of official parties which in their countries united in a single organization all the elements adhering to the principles of our manifesto—as for instance in Italy, Rumania, and Bulgaria;

2. Representatives of official parties which in their countries united in an organization only some of these elements, as for instance in Holland, Poland, and Russia;

3. Representatives of official parties, trade unions, etc., which . . . .

have only loose connections behind them, as for instance in Germany, France, etc.

This variegated composition makes it necessary to reach an understanding if our action is to be built upon an organizational basis, which it requires under any circumstances.

The matter would be simplified if there were *one* central organization in *every* country. But since this is not the case . . . . the following regulations would be adequate to overcome organizational difficulties.

1. An Enlarged Committee to be formed as indicated above.

2. Each country to have the right to appoint from one to three representatives to that Committee.

3. The appointment of these representatives to be based upon a consideration by each country of the special conditions of organization in every country. In appointing representatives care should be taken if possible to appoint persons who are themselves active in their particular country . . . . [unimportant details about the representatives from Russia and Poland follow]. . . . . It is also desirable that an agreement between the *German* party comrades be arrived at. Since every country has the right to send three delegates, the different tendencies within the German opposition can very well be represented. We take it for granted, therefore, that the opposition groups within the German party would reach an understanding and agree on the choice of their representatives to the Enlarged Committee. Now, when it is a question of mustering all the forces upon the basis outlined in the manifesto, it is extremely important to have a united organization which would not infringe in any way upon the different opinions. It stands to reason that in this connection no less than at the Conference, organizational independence on the basis of party lines, or more truly in the sense of a party split, is out of the question. The *groups in all countries should act as unitedly as' possible only with respect to the International Socialist Conference and its organs* in order that our work may be facilitated rather than weakened and destroyed by an unnecessary splitting of forces.

We address a request to the *Dutch* comrades to endeavor, if at all possible, to reach an agreement between "De Internationale" and the Tribunists with regard to representation. . . . .

The appointment of representatives from the other countries is not likely to cause any serious difficulties. . . . . With a socialist greeting.

On behalf of the International Socialist Committee at Berne,

R. GRIMM

PROGRESS OF THE ZIMMERWALD MOVEMENT

[Circular Letter of the International Socialist Committee at Berne,
November 22, 1915][68]

DEAR COMRADES!

.... In conformity with the deliberations of the International Conference at Zimmerwald the report and the manifesto were translated and published. The initial number of the *Bulletin* was forwarded first of all to the party and trade union papers of the *neutral countries*. Quite a few papers reprinted the documents mentioned above, so that party members in these neutral countries were informed of the deliberations of the Zimmerwald Conference.

As regards the *belligerent countries,* we have endeavored likewise to spread there the report and the manifesto. In so far as we can judge, these documents were published *in toto* by a part of the socialist press in *Italy, Bulgaria, England, France,* and *Russia.* The socialist press of Germany and Austria was compelled to confine itself to a rather summary indication of the object of the Conference.

In certain countries the partisans of the Zimmerwald Conference have published and distributed a special edition of the manifesto and of the report. This fact is evident from the statements published in the present number [*Bulletin* No. 2].

The International Socialist Committee has attempted further to get in touch with parties and groups of various countries in order to obtain their collaboration in the common cause.

We publish below the results of these moves: on September 24–26 the International Socialist Committee addressed a special circular to all parties affiliated with the International Socialist Bureau of Brussels, informing them of the Zimmerwald Socialist Conference and its decisions. Only the Central Committee of the *Danish* party replied, officially disapproving of our Conference and its deliberations....

The majority of the Central Committee of the Swiss party replied in an analogous manner but less rudely. The minority of the Central Committee was of an opinion contrary to that of the majority. The Congress of the Swiss party which met on November 20–21 at Aarau has pronounced itself on the declarations of the majority and the minority and by 330 votes to 51 held in favor of adherence to the International Socialist Committee, and accompanied this action with a decision to grant 300 francs to the International Socialist Committee.

The Central Committee of the *German* and *French* parties, as could

[68] "Communications de la C.S.I.," *Commission socialiste internationale à Berne, Bulletin,* No. 2, December 27, 1915, p. 1.

be foreseen, have disapproved of the Conference. In spite of the fact that these parties are actually divided by strong antagonism, their attitude toward the war and the so-called defense of the fatherland is identical. The Central Committee of the German party set forth its point of view in an intraparty circular, while the Central Committee of the French party published a declaration in *L'Humanité*. . . .

A congress of the *Rumanian* party confirmed the decisions of Zimmerwald, approving the mandate of Comrade Rakovsky. Other declarations of adherence came to us from *Italy, Bulgaria* (the Narrow socialists), and the Central Committee of the *Portuguese* party. Also the *Socialist Labor party* and the *Socialist party of America* have sent us their declarations of adherence. . . . .

Furthermore, a number of groups in various countries, especially the federations of the French Socialist party, have adhered to the International Socialist Committee. In other countries organizational work is in progress. We shall try to give a sketch of this work.

To facilitate joint action we have sent out a circular (September 27) submitting to the affiliated parties and groups a plan of organization. This plan will facilitate their collaboration. The plan was approved; some additional delegates suggested by the plan have been elected, so that our activity is developing also in that direction.

The principal task of parties and groups must naturally be that of *preparing the psychology of the laboring masses*. Without that, action is impossible. This preparatory work meets many obstacles, among which the attitude of the official parties toward the war plays no minor role. But the difficulties of a task need not impede its accomplishment. In so far as we accomplish that task the Zimmerwald Conference and its deliberations will be justified.

THE INTERNATIONAL SOCIALIST COMMITTEE
IN BERNE

ON THE PROPOSALS OF THE INTERNATIONAL SOCIALIST
COMMITTEE

[A Letter from Lenin Written toward the End of 1915][69]

RESPECTED COMRADES:

We received your letter of September 25[70] and express to you our complete sympathy with the plan of establishing a permanent interna-

---

[69] *Pravda*, No. 203 (3134), September 6, 1925, p. 1. The editor of *Pravda* notes certain suggestions and corrections made by Zinoviev. These are shown in the text in brackets.

[70] According to *Internationale Korrespondenz*, No. 41, November 19, 1915, p. 508, the letter was dated September 27.

tional "Enlarged Committee" (*erweiterte Kommission*) at Berne. Being convinced that all other organizations which have joined the I.S.C. will agree to this plan, we appoint from the Central Committee of the R.S. D. L. party, Comrade Zinoviev as member of this Enlarged Committee, and as acting members, substitutes [substitute] (*suppléant, Stellvertreter*), (1) Comrade Petrova and (2) Comrade Lenin.[71] The address for communication is: Herrn Radomyslsky (*bei Fr. Aschwanden*), Hertenstein, Canton Lucern, Switzerland (*Ks. Luzern Schweiz*). [Bern, Freiestrasse, 14, 1.]

Further, with regard to other questions raised in your letter of September 25, we are of the following opinion:

1. We completely agree with you that "the general points of view" (*allgemeine Gesichtspunkte*) established by the Conference of September 5–8 are "insufficient" (*nicht genügen*). A further, more thorough and detailed development of these principles is urgently necessary. This is imperative from the point of view of principle and from a narrow practical point of view, as well; for in order to realize *united* action on an international scale, clarity in the fundamental ideological conception is required, as well as precision in any practical method of action. There is no doubt that the great crisis which Europe in general and the European labor movement in particular is experiencing can make the masses understand the general aspects of this question but slowly. The task of the I.S.C., together with its adhering parties, is precisely to aid this understanding. Without anticipating something that is impossible—such as a quick consolidation of everybody upon a harmonious, definitely elaborated point of view—we must endeavor to achieve *an exact* formulation of the *chief tendencies and orientations* in present-day internationalist socialism and we must also see to it that the laboring masses acquaint themselves with these tendencies—they should discuss these in every detail, and verify them by the experience of their own practical movement. In our opinion the I.S.C. should consider this as its chief task [one of its chief tasks].

2. The letter of September 25 designates the tasks of the proletariat as either a struggle for peace (in case war continues) or "a concrete and detailed formulation of the proletariat's international point of view with regard to various peace proposals, and peace programs" (*den internationalen Standpunkt des Proletariats zu den verschiedenen Friendensvorschlägen u. Programmen konkret u. ins einzelne gehend zu umschreiben*). At the same time the national question (Alsace-Lorraine, Poland, Armenia, etc.), is especially emphasized.

We believe that in both of the documents adopted unanimously by

---

[71] The words "(1) Comrade Petrova and (2)" were crossed out. [Note by the editor of *Pravda*.]

the Conference of September 5–8, namely, the manifesto and "the resolution of sympathy" (*Sympathieerklärung*), the thought has been expressed that there is a *connection* between the struggle for peace and the struggle for socialism ("struggle for peace....is a struggle for socialism"—"*dieser Kampf ist der Kampf für den Sozialismus*"—the manifesto says)—an "irreconcilable proletarian class struggle" ("*unversöhnlicher proletarischer Klassenkampf*"). In the text of the resolution which the Conference voted on, not "irreconcilable" but "revolutionary" class struggle was the word used. If this substitution was made for considerations of legality the meaning is still no different. The resolution of sympathy definitely states that the Conference gives a "solemn promise" and must "arouse the revolutionary spirit in the masses of the international proletariat."

Any struggle for peace which is not connected with a revolutionary class struggle of the proletariat is really a pacifist phrase of the bourgeoisie which is either sentimental or which deceives the people.

[It stands to reason, you will agree with us that] we cannot and must not pose as "statesmen" and compose "definite" programs of peace. On the contrary we must explain to the masses that *without* developing a revolutionary class struggle any hopes for a democratic peace (*without* annexations, violence, robbery) are a deception. We told the masses definitely, clearly, and firmly at the very beginning of the manifesto that the cause of the war lies in imperialism and that imperialism signifies "the enslavement" of nations all over the world, by a handful of "great powers." We therefore must help the masses to overthrow imperialism, since without this overthrow a peace without annexations is impossible; certainly the struggle for the overthrow of imperialism is difficult, but the masses must know the *truth* about this difficult but necessary struggle. The masses must not be lulled with hopes that peace may be attained without the overthrow of imperialism.

3. Proceeding from these considerations, we propose that the following questions be included in the agenda of the next meetings of the Enlarged Committee (in order that theses or draft resolutions may be elaborated, summarized, or published) and also in the agenda of the subsequent international conference (in order that a *final resolution* may be adopted) :

a) The connection between the struggle for peace, and the proletariats' revolutionary mass actions or revolutionary class struggle.

b) The self-determination of nations.

c) The connection between social patriotism and opportunism.

We emphasize that in the manifesto which was adopted by the Conference *all* these questions were *touched* upon quite definitely, that their fundamental and practical significance is extremely urgent, that *not a single* practical step of proletarian struggle *can be imagined* where socialists and syndicalists do not encounter these questions.

It is imperative to elucidate these questions in order to aid the mass struggle for peace, for the self-determination of nations, for socialism, for opposing the "capitalists' lies" (the words of the manifesto) concerning the "defense of the fatherland" in this war.

If the guilt or the misfortune of the Second International consists of the uncertainty and lack of elaboration of important questions, as has been rightfully pointed out in the letter of September 25, then it is certainly our task to help the masses raise these questions more clearly and solve them more exactly.

4. Concerning the publication of the *Bulletin* in three languages: in our opinion experience indicates that this plan is devoid of purpose. Published once a month it will cost two to three thousand francs a year, a sum which is difficult to find, whereas two newspapers in Switzerland, *Berner Tagwacht* and *La Sentinelle,* publish almost all that is in the *Bulletin.* We propose to the I.S.C.: [I propose to omit this but to leave the statement concerning Kollontai and the agreement with English newspapers]. That it attempt to conclude an agreement with the editorial boards of the said newspapers and one of the newspapers in America by which the *Bulletin,* as well as all communications and materials of the I.S.C. will be published in these newspapers (either in the columns on behalf of the I.S.C. or in separate supplements).

This would not only be cheaper but would also provide a better means of informing the laboring class more fully and more frequently about the activity of the I.S.C. We are interested in having a larger number of workers read the communications of the I.S.C. and in having all draft resolutions published for the purpose of informing the workers and aiding them to define their own attitude toward the war.

We hope that no objections will be raised to the advisability of publishing also the draft resolution [showing the number of votes cast in its favor], (for which and in favor of adopting it as a basic principle twelve delegates voted, while nineteen opposed this, i.e., nearly 40 per cent of the entire number voted for it) and the letter of the prominent German socialist—without mentioning his name or anything which *did not* relate to tactics.

We hope that the I.S.C. will receive systematic information from various countries of the persecutions and arrests which result from struggling against the war, of the development of class struggle against the war, of fraternization in the trenches, of the suppression of newspapers, of the ban on proclamations in favor of peace, etc., and that all this information on behalf of the I.S.C. will appear periodically in the said newspapers.

Comrade Kollontai, at present contributor to *Nashe Slovo* and other social democratic newspapers, could probably conclude an agreement with one of the American daily or weekly papers. She has just now left for America on a lecture tour. We could get in touch with her or supply you with her address.

5. With regard to the method of representation of sections of parties (especially of Germany and France and probably also of England) we propose that: The I.S.C. be permitted to propose to comrades from these parties that they discuss whether or not it would be useful to form groups under various names, the appeals of which to the masses (in the form of proclamations, resolutions, etc.) would be published by the I.S.C., indicating to what groups they belong.

By this method, first, the masses would be informed of the tactics and points of view of the internationalists in spite of the war censorship, and, second, it would be possible to observe the development and the success of the propagation of internationalist points of view, gradually as workers' meetings, their organizations, etc., adopt decisions showing sympathy with one socialist group or the other; third, it would be possible to express various nuances of points of view (for example: in England, the minority of the British Socialist party and the Independent Labour party; in France, socialists like Bourderon and others and syndicalists like Merrheim and others; in Germany, the Conference has shown, there are also nuances *among* the opposition).

It stands to reason that these groups, as has been pointed out in the letter of September 25, would not form separate organizational units (except for the purpose of communication with the I.S.C. and for propaganda of struggle for peace) but would exist within the old organizations.

These groups would be represented in the "Enlarged Committee" and at conferences.

6. [Propose that it be crossed out.] Concerning the question of the number of members in the "Enlarged Committee" and the method of voting we propose: Not to restrict the number of members to a maximum of three, but to introduce for small groups fractions ($\frac{1}{2}$, $\frac{1}{3}$, and so forth) *during voting*.

This would be more convenient, for it is utterly impossible to deprive of representation the groups which have their own nuances and furthermore such deprivation would be harmful for the development and propagation, among the masses, of the principles established by the manifesto.

7. Concerning the danger of the "Russo-Polish nature" of the Enlarged Committee we believe that this concern on the part of comrades is *legitimate* (though it may seem insulting to the Russians) in so far as it is possible to have a representation of émigré groups which have no serious contacts with Russia. In our opinion only those organizations or

groups should be represented which have proved by *not less than three years' activity* their ability to represent the movement in Russia. We propose to the I.S.C. to discuss and establish a principle such as this and also to ask all of the groups to supply information and data on their activity in Russia. [The I.S.C. must once and for all gather material on the situation of the social democratic activity in Russia and deprive the "famous currents" of the opportunity of misusing the name of Russian Social Democracy.]

8. Finally, we make use of this occasion to point out an inaccuracy in No. 1 of the *Bulletin* and to ask that it be rectified in No. 2 (or in *Berner Tagwacht*) and in *La Sentinelle:* In *Bulletin* No. 1, page 7, column 1, it says at the beginning that the draft resolution was signed by the Central Committee, the Polish Social Democrats (*Landesvorstand*),[72] the Letts, Swedes, and Norwegians. This list omits one German delegate (whose name is not published for obvious reasons) and one Swiss delegate, Platten.

LIST OF PARTIES AND GROUPS SUBSCRIBING TO THE ZIMMERWALD MOVEMENT[73]

1. The Socialist party of Italy. 2. The Social Democratic party of Switzerland. 3. The British Socialist party. 4. The Independent Labour party of Great Britain. 5. The Social Democratic party of Rumania. 6. The Central Committee of the Social Democratic Labor party of Russia. 7. The Organization Committee of the Social Democratic Labor party of Russia. 8. The Socialist-Revolutionist party of Russia (the group of internationalists). 9. The All-Jewish Workers' League of Lithuania, Poland, and Russia (the so-called Bund). 10. The Main and the Regional Presidiums of the Social Democracy of Poland and Lithuania and the Polish Socialist party (Levitsa). 11. The Social Democratic Labor party of Bulgaria (the "Narrow" socialists). 12. The Social Democratic party of Portugal. 13. The Socialist Federation of Salonica. 14. The Young socialists of Sweden and Norway. 15. The Socialist Labor party of America. 16. The Socialist party of America. 17. The German group of the Socialist party of America. 18. The Lettish Social Democratic party. 19. The Young socialists of Denmark. 20. The Young socialists of Madrid. 21. The International Socialist League of South Africa. 22. Confederazione Generale del Lavoro of

---

[72] The Regional Presidium.

[73] This list is compiled from announcements published in *International Socialist Committee in Berne, Bulletin,* No. 3, February 29, 1916, p. 4, and No. 5, July 10, 1916, p. 8; *Internationale sozialistische Kommission zu Bern, Bulletin,* No. 4, April 22, 1916, p. 1.

Italy. 23. The Federation of Trade Unions of Bulgaria. 24. The Social Democratic party of Böckingen (Württemberg). 25. The Social Democratic Labor party of Bulgaria (the "Broad" socialists).[74]

[74] The list given does not include various groups of the opposition minority of the German Social Democratic party, the trade union and the socialist minorities of France, and the Socialist Revolutionary League of Holland included in the list of organizations affiliated with the International Socialist Committee and published together with the text of the Kienthal manifesto. (*International Socialist Committee in Berne, Bulletin*, No. 5, July 10, 1916, p. 2.) Neither does the official list include the group of Ukrainian Social Democrats rallying around the periodical *Borotba*, published in Lausanne. Although the antiwar slogans of this group were similar to those of the Russian Bolsheviks, it did not belong to the Zimmerwald Left, for in its agitation it favored the idea of cultural-national autonomy to which the Russian Bolsheviks were strongly opposed. This group addressed an open letter to the Kienthal Conference stating its position on the Ukrainian question and the war and appealed to the international proletariat to support the struggle for Ukraine's democratic autonomy. (*L'Ukraine et la Guerre. Lettre ouverte adressée à la 2me conférence socialiste internationale tenue en Hollande en mai 1916.*)

CHAPTER V

KIENTHAL

As has been suggested in the preceding chapter, the Zimmerwald movement made slow but by no means inconsiderable progress during the months following the meeting at Zimmerwald. There is evidence of this growth in the spread, among the rank and file of socialist and labor organizations, of dissatisfaction with the policies of the socialist party administrations. These policies varied in detail in different countries. Generally they included a truce in the class struggle— the *Burgfrieden*—on the theory that the nations were fighting for self-defense or the liberation of oppressed peoples and such specific policies as the voting of war credits (as in Germany) and the participation of socialists in bourgeois cabinets (as in Belgium and France). The growing dissatisfaction was primarily a product of the disillusionment and suffering caused by the war. There was no sign of an end to the slaughter. On the contrary, the theater of war had been extended by the entrance of Italy in May and of Bulgaria in October 1915, and military activities had spread across the world involving the Near and Middle East and the Orient. The professed war aims of the governments were suspiciously vague, while the imperialist ambitions of national groups were undisguised. The war losses in lives and property mounted enormously, and conditions of living became steadily more burdensome for the workers and for the families of the men who were in the lines or in their graves at the front.

This dissatisfaction contributed, of course, to the strengthening of the Zimmerwald minority; but it was also reflected in a growing demand for the resumption of socialist international relations. This meant, on the one hand, more support for Zimmerwald and, on the other, increased pressure on the

International Socialist Bureau. This pressure placed the I.S.B. in a difficult position. It disapproved of Zimmerwald, but it was not able to bring the old International to life. Huysmans, as Secretary of the Executive Committee of the I.S.B., made a public defense of the policy of that Committee, before and since the outbreak of the war, in a long speech before the Congress of the Dutch Social Democracy at Arnhem, January 8–9, 1916. In the course of this speech[1] he made a remark which provoked protest and criticism from both the conservative and the radical press in many European countries. He said: "The International is not dead. It cannot die . . . . If we have been silent, that does not signify we have done nothing. We have not allowed a single favorable opportunity to pass by without making the utmost use of it . . . . Not for one moment has the connection between the affiliated parties been severed." The work of the Bureau, Huysmans said, was twofold: "(1) To call together separately the Socialist Parties in the neutral countries, in countries of the Allies, in countries of the Central European Powers, and to discuss with each group the four points which are the foundation of the Socialist Peace Policy, (2) to receive special delegations at The Hague to discuss these points in closer detail. . . . Only after such separate consultations could we judge whether it was desirable to convene the full Bureau." The Belgians and Germans had sent delegates to The Hague. As reported in the *Berner Tagwacht*,[2] Ebert and Scheidemann had gone there to explain in person recent statements made in the Reichstag. The French had flatly refused an invitation to The Hague; and the English, though they had accepted, were unable to send a representative because of Henderson's appointment to the Cabinet.[3]

[1] The speech is given in *Labour Leader*, No. 6, February 10, 1916, p. 4, and also in *The Policy of the International. A Speech of and an Interview with the Secretary of the International, Camille Huysmans, Member of the Belgian Parliament and the Brussels City Council*, pp. 11–30, where the quoted passages appear in a slightly different phraseology.

[2] No. 305, December 30, 1915, p. 2—"Die Zusammenkunft im Haag."

[3] The Labour party originally agreed to send Henderson and MacDonald. On Henderson's entering the Cabinet John Hodge was appointed in his stead, but he

With regard to the demands for a meeting of the Bureau Huysmans said, these could not be complied with because it was certain some representatives would not come and to have attempted it might have meant a complete breakup. "Our aim is indeed to bring the parties together at the proper time, but not by hasty action. Our duty is to bring together the Bureau with the consent of the responsible parties of the belligerent nations .... Impatient comrades have summoned International Conferences, but you have seen that the interested principals have been conspicuous by their absence."[4]

Huysmans also spoke at socialist meetings in Rotterdam and Amsterdam on January 26 and 30, where he was sharply attacked by Wijnkoop and other representatives of the Left, who criticized his defense of the Bureau, his attitude toward the war, and his failure to follow the example of Liebknecht. To Wijnkoop's declaration of allegiance to Liebknecht, Luxemburg, and the revolutionary Russians and Serbs, Huysmans exclaimed: "Never will they side with Mr. Wijnkoop, even if theoretically their ideas are closer to his than to ours."[5]

After his speeches in Holland, Huysmans, accompanied by Vandervelde, went to Paris where they made another unsuccessful attempt to swing the French majority to their point

refused to go. There was strong opposition in the Labour party to Huysmans' proposal, and in the end the party Executive reversed its decision. Later it invited representatives of the I.S.B. to London. In response to Huysmans' appeal the Labour party, the I.L.P., and the Fabian Society, jointly made a loan to the Bureau of eight hundred pounds. (Carl F. Brand, "British Labor and the International during the Great War," *Journal of Modern History*, No. 1, March 1936, pp. 44–45. *Report of the Fifteenth Annual Conference of the Labour Party, 1916*, p. 33.) Speaking as a guest at the 1916 Conference of the Labour party, Jean Longuet said that when the German S.D. majority took the position "which had been taken with such pluck and such courage by their heroic comrade, Liebknecht," the French Socialist party would resume relations with the I.S.B. and other international socialist bodies. (*Ibid.*, p. 115.)

[4] *The Policy of the International* ...., pp. 20–21. To a correspondent of *Le Petit Parisien*, Huysmans on March 25, 1916, repeated this defense and added: "My personal action confines itself to the functions of intermediary, and nothing else .... The *moment* of peace is not our business, the *terms* of peace are what interest us. It is to this end that the working class should direct its policy." (*Ibid.*, p. 7.)

[5] *Camille Huysmans, ses discours prononcés en Hollande du 9 au 31 janvier, 1916*, pp. 50–51, and "Die nationalistische Kampagne Huysmans in Holland," *Beilage zur Berner Tagwacht*, No. 43, February 21, 1916, p. 1.

of view. From Paris they went to London where they were told by members of the Parliamentary Labour group that any consideration of possible peace terms at that time was absolutely out of the question and the only thing with which the Labour party would then concern itself was "the prosecution of the war to a victorious termination."[6] Huysmans and Vandervelde also used the occasion of their visit to urge leaders of the British Socialist party and the I.L.P. not to attend the Kienthal Conference.[7] Of these efforts Mrs. Sidney Webb wrote: "Camille Huysmans in particular warned with significant emphasis against any public congress of dissentient minorities in the Socialist movement," since such a congress would transform international socialism from a world alliance into an international sect "permanently out of sympathy with the mass of the proletariat of all countries concerned." Mrs. Webb urged British socialists to give heed to this warning.[8]

Along with these criticisms from the British Lefts, Huysmans and Vandervelde were accused by the nonsocialist press of conducting a "pacifist intrigue." Vandervelde replied in an interview in the *Morning Post* in which he said, among other things: "Camille Huysmans and I are Belgians. I take part in the government of national defense . . . . I have declared repeatedly that so long as German soldiers are in Belgium and France we would not listen to any peace talk. How can we then be suspected of lending our ear to 'pacifist intrigues'?" He went on to say that although they were Belgians they were also socialists and members of the Executive Committee of the I.S.B. and as such it was their right and duty to keep in contact with their friends and with them work toward a lasting and just peace. Italian and other socialists had demanded a plenary session of the I.S.B.; but this was

[6] *Report of the Sixteenth Annual Conference of the Labour Party, 1917*, p. 44.

[7] "Huysmans auf der Reise," *Berner Tagwacht*, No. 74, March 28, 1916, pp. 2–3.

[8] Mrs. Sidney Webb, "What Was the Message of Vandervelde and Huysmans?" *Labour Leader*, No. 17, April 27, 1916, p. 17. According to *The Call* (London), No. 7, May 18, 1916, p. 3, Huysmans "was plainly told that the I.S.B. must be called together at all costs if any unity of view was to be achieved."

impossible since the French Socialist party and the British Labour party had refused to meet delegates of the German Social Democratic majority. "Speaking personally," Vandervelde continued, "I am convinced that if the Belgian Labor party was able to confer on this matter its decision would have been similar. In France and Belgium we are fighting against invasion and exercising our legitimate right of defense. So long as the German Social Democrats do not officially acknowledge our right to defend ourselves and do not aid us in our defense, I consider resumption of relations with them impossible." In conclusion, Vandervelde, referring to the results of his trip to France and England, said: "Our French comrades while condemning with all their energy all endeavors to bring about a premature and lame peace have agreed with our point of view that such an examination [of peace terms] is useful and necessary. The deputies of the Labour party in London seemed to fear that these discussions would be premature and would generate misunderstanding. However, the party Executive agreed to the Executive Committee's proposal to discuss this matter."[9]

Shortly after the publication of Vandervelde's interview Huysmans stated in the Dutch press that the socialist majorities of France and Great Britain "do not judge the moment opportune for the meeting of the Bureau" and that there was "complete condemnation of the action of the Zimmerwald Congress, which is recognized neither by the French, the British, the Germans, nor the Austrians."[10]

The rather negative results of the negotiations with the majority socialists of France and Great Britain did not deter the Executive Committee of the I.S.B. from going ahead with plans for a conference of neutrals which met at The Hague, July 31 to August 2, 1916. Delegates from Holland, Argentina, Sweden, Denmark, and the United States, none of whom were identified with the Zimmerwald movement, approved

[9] *L'Humanité*, No. 4375, April 9, 1916, p. 1. See also E. Vandervelde, *La Belgique envahie et le socialisme international*, pp. 186–203.

[10] "Huysmans and the International," *Labour Leader*, No. 19, May 11, 1916, p. 4.

the policies of the Executive Committee of the I.S.B., as is noted below. The Conference also adopted some rather innocuous resolutions on the prewar socialist peace program, free trade, the restoration of Belgium and Serbia, and Polish autonomy.

Meanwhile, early in 1916 the International Socialist Committee had taken steps to carry out its proposals referred to in the preceding chapter to form an enlarged committee and to call a second Zimmerwald conference. The continuation of the war, Grimm explained, added new problems to those already existing; and he added, "The struggle which the nationalist parties as well as the International [Socialist] Bureau at The Hague led against the Zimmerwald action and the gradually maturing plans for imminent peace demanded an answer and an elucidation."[11] Representatives from ten nations, members of the Enlarged Committee, met at Berne February 5–8, 1916, drew up a circular letter setting forth their position on the existing situation, and decided to call a second conference. Invitations to this conference were sent out on February 10.[12]

The Second Zimmerwald Conference met at Kienthal, April 24–30, attended by forty-four delegates from seven nations. Resolutions were adopted which dealt with the question of peace, on the International Socialist Bureau, and expressed sympathy for the victims of political persecution. In general the pronouncements of this Conference showed that the Zimmerwaldists had moved somewhat to the left, though they were still considerably short of the position of the Zimmerwald Left. The Zimmerwald majority had apparently given up hope of bringing the International Socialist Bureau to see the light as they saw it, and there was greater willingness to support a separate organization and to engage more openly in struggle with the party executive bodies still con-

---

[11] Grimm, "Von Zimmerwald bis Kiental," *Neues Leben*, No. 5, May 1916, p. 133.

[12] *International Socialist Committee in Berne, Bulletin*, No. 3, February 29, 1916, p. 1.

trolled by the patriotic socialists. This majority, however, was still unwilling to take a stand for a definite split and the establishment of a Third International. As for the Left, its gains were fairly summarized by *Nashe Slovo* in its report of the Conference: "The Zimmerwald Left at the second Conference was weaker as an organization than at the first, but the ideas of revolutionary internationalism were more strongly represented than at Zimmerwald."[13]

The headquarters of the Zimmerwald movement continued to be in Berne until after the revolution in Russia in the spring of 1917, when preparations were made and later carried out to transfer the International Socialist Committee to Stockholm in order to be nearer Russian events. Previous to this removal there were two meetings of the Enlarged Committee: the first on May 2, 1916, to consider the position to be taken with respect to the conference of neutral socialists and the second on February 1, 1917, to consider the reply to be made to the proposed conference of socialists of Entente countries. The I.S.C. could not reach a decision on the first question and left it for the individual sections to decide. As for the other question, the I.S.C. recommended that invitations to the Entente socialist conference be declined.

A. The International Socialist Committee Conference at Berne, February 5–8, 1916

Not all the members of the Enlarged Committee were able to attend the Berne meeting. The existing accounts do not agree on the composition of the Conference, but apparently the following were present: Grimm, Platten, Yu. Martov, A. Martynov, D. Riazanov, P. Axelrod, F. Kon, Zinoviev, Lenin, Radek, Lapinski, Bertha Thalheimer, A. Hoffmann, Ledebour, F. Koritschoner, Henri Guilbeaux, Serrati, Modigliani, Balabanoff, Rakovsky, Edmondo Peluso, and Münzenberg, representing socialist parties and groups in Switzerland, Russia, Poland, Holland, Germany, Austria, France,

---

[13] *Nashe Slovo*, No. 129 (515), June 3, 1916, p. 1.

Italy, Rumania, and Portugal, and the Youth International.[14] Although the meeting, in the absence of many members of the Enlarged Committee, considered itself not a plenary but a consultative conference, it authorized the calling of a second general conference of the Zimmerwald movement and drew up a circular letter which went much farther than the Zimmerwald manifesto in denouncing socialists who had voted war credits or had upheld civil peace in the interests of national defense and in demanding the withdrawal of socialists from bourgeois cabinets. The circular spoke of "open economic and political struggle of the masses against the ruling classes and their governments" where the Zimmerwald manifesto had used the vaguer phrase "proletarian struggle for peace." The February Conference also condemned Huysmans' stand, thus anticipating the general denunciation of the International Socialist Bureau at Kienthal. Several declarations and resolutions were submitted to the I.S.C., some of which were considered at the February Conference. Among these were the theses adopted January 1, 1916, by the German *Internationale* group; a draft manifesto drawn up by Trotsky, Rosmer, Merrheim, and other French Zimmerwaldists in the name of the supporters of *La Vie ouvrière* and *Nashe Slovo;* and a draft appeal by the Socialist Revolutionary League and the Social Democratic party of Holland. A proposal of the Central Committee of the R.S.D.L. party was submitted later, after the receipt of the invitation to Kienthal. This letter of invitation[15] asked the affiliated groups to send delegates to a second Zimmerwald conference to be held not later than the beginning of April. For the benefit of the authorities Holland was named as the country where the meet-

---

[14] Cf. Zinoviev's account below. Also Lenin, *Sochineniia,* XIX, 470, note 102. It is not clear which of the delegates named held a mandate from the Dutch Zimmerwaldists. There is also some disagreement about the dates of the Conference. Zinoviev gives February 5–10, other Russian sources February 5–9; but the official report of the I.S.C. in its *Bulletin,* No. 3, February 29, 1916, p. 4, gives February 5–8, as does the *Berner Tagwacht,* No. 37, February 14, 1916, pp. 2–3, which says that the Conference lasted four days.

[15] The text is given in *Internationale Korrespondenz,* No. 71, March 7, 1916, p. 754.

ing was to be held. The letter also contained the provisional agenda and the conditions under which groups were eligible for representation. These are stated in Zinoviev's letter below.

ZINOVIEV'S ACCOUNT OF THE FEBRUARY CONFERENCE

[A Letter to Shliapnikov, Bukharin, Piatakov, and Others][16]

An important international Conference was held at Berne from February 5 to February 10 [1916] called by the I.S.C. Twenty-two persons were present. Only the French and the English were absent (letters came from both groups saying that they were absent owing to circumstances beyond their control). Because of their absence the meeting was constituted not as an official enlarged meeting of the I.S.C. but as a meeting of the I.S.C. *with members* of the enlarged committee.

Of all the local reports those of the German representatives were the most interesting. One very matter-of-fact worker (Ledebour's adherent) and a woman delegate of the *Internationale* group were present. The first painted a picture of important activities (a half-million illegal leaflets, a number of demonstrations) carried through by the Berlin opposition. But he is as afraid of the Third International, a split and so forth, as he is of fire. He has not the least interest in theoretical controversies. The second representative reported that the *Internationale* has had something like a conference[17] (the first representative denies the existence of the *Internationale* group as well as of Borchardt's group). She read aloud the theses of this Conference, written by Rosa Luxemburg.[18] A great deal in them is a repetition of what we said in our resolution at Zimmerwald. But they contain in addition something of purely "Polish" arguments (against the self-determination of nations). And, furthermore, they make a clear statement about the Third International, but say nothing of the split in Germany (this was done quite deliberately). An abundance of phrases. No clarity on the question of opportunism. This woman delegate came out against the I.S.D.[19] (Borchardt's group) in the same manner as did Ledebour's adherent. An impression was thus created that there was no serious organization behind the *Internationale* group.

---

[16] "Pismo tov. Zinovieva," Shklovsky, "Tsimmervald," *Proletarskaia Revoliutsiia*, No. 9 (44), 1925, pp. 94–98. Zinoviev wrote a more formal account of the Conference, which was published in *Sotsial-Demokrat*, No. 52, March 25, 1916, p. 2, and reprinted in his *Sochineniia*, V, 251–56.

[17] An all-German Conference of the adherents of the *Internationale* group was held on January 1, 1916, at Karl Liebknecht's residence in Berlin.

[18] See below, pp. 394–98.   [19] The International Socialists of Germany.

The chief question at the Conference of the I.S.C. was the issuance of a new manifesto. The I.S.C. (Grimm) submitted a typewritten draft to the delegates. To a considerable extent this draft borrowed its content from the theses of Rosa Luxemburg. It said that "the Second International is dead," that Huysmans & Co. "are consciously hypocritical"; it called for demonstrations, for throwing off the discipline of the official parties, etc. When the question of the manifesto was put before the Conference, it became clear at once that *no one desired* such a manifesto (or for that matter any manifesto at all) except our group. It became clear that such a manifesto would mean a long step in the direction of our policy. Martov came forward as the leader of those who wished to sabotage the manifesto. Reasons: too early, formal considerations, and thousands of others. Rakovsky (a diplomat, sympathizes with Martov) objected in the same spirit. The Italians (at this meeting they did *reach a decision*) vacillated and made confusion. We were decidedly *for.*

We were greatly helped by the fact that Grimm had already submitted the ready-made manifesto and was very enthusiastic about it. To his great vexation, he *had* to go along with us on that point. He insisted and hinted at the fact that for him a refusal would be equivalent to a disavowal of him, etc. After long debates through two whole meetings it was decided to change the manifesto into a simple appeal in the form of a circular letter (more modest, at any rate) and a Commission was elected for the editing.

Everyone on the Commission opposed Grimm's draft, except Grimm himself and our representative. In spite of that, Grimm's draft was taken as the basis for the appeal, as there was no other draft ready. A few more hours of work and the manifesto was accepted in a still more decisive form.[20]

[20] Shklovsky says that the fact that there was a more decisive rather than a more diplomatic formulation of Grimm's draft was due, among other things, to the presence of Martov on the Commission: "An argument over the formulation flared up immediately between Comrades Zinoviev and Martov. The other members of the Commission had scattered, after having declared that if the 'Russians' came to an agreement with each other, then they had nothing more to do; that the Russians as a rule are squabblers and quarrelsome people, is known to everyone, and if they reach an agreement with each other, then the others can sign any text, even without reading it. Alone and face to face with Comrade Zinoviev, that same thing happened to Martov which happened to him several times before—as for instance prior to the plenum of 1910, when he alone, without Dan, represented the Mensheviks on the editorial board of the *Sotsial-Demokrat*. The spirit of an old *Iskra* member rose in Martov. His thoughts took a left revolutionary trend. He and Comrade Zinoviev argued no more, but strengthened each other. The draft of the manifesto elaborated by them was transmitted to the expanded Conference as the draft *unanimously* accepted by the Commission." (Shklovsky, "Tsimmervald," *Proletarskaia Revoliutsiia,* No. 9 [44], 1925, p. 99.)

This manifesto mentions the "necessity of the revolutionary intervention" (*revolutionäre Intervention*) "of the international proletariat"; it greets one hundred thousand St. Petersburg workers who have refused to enter into War-Industries Committees; it points to the political strikes in Russia and also the street demonstrations in Germany. Further on it says, "even in the trenches the protest against the war is growing and is expressed in more frequent fraternizing between soldiers, etc." It points out that "the so-called 'defense of the fatherland' in this war is nothing less than a crude means of deception, used to bind the people to the wheels of imperialism."

With regard to the official socialist parties the manifesto says that by their conduct they "prolong the warfare, and by their tactics lead toward a voluntary subjection of the workers to the ruling classes." Further on it contains a sharp criticism of German social patriots (the interpellation comedy of Scheidemann in the Reichstag),[21] of the French (the Paris Congress),[22] of the English, of the Russians (a small [?] part of the Russian Social Democrats and Socialist Revolutionists had concluded a truce with Tsarism), and of the speeches of Huysmans (it says, he deceives—*irreführt*—the workers).

Further on, in summing up, the manifesto says, "The International cannot continue to exist if its sections grant credits for the mutual destruction of the workers"——. Phrases on peace do not alter the matter. "Any attempt at restoring the International by mutually granting amnesty to the opportunistic leaders who have compromised themselves, is in reality only a conspiracy (agreement—*Pakt,* deal) against socialism and a blow to the revival of the revolutionary labor movement.

"The duty of discipline with regard to the vital interests of the proletariat is more compulsory and stands above all forms of organizational discipline. Whoever acts against these interests is an enemy of the socialist proletariat. The national sections of the International which act thus undutifully free their members from all obligations with regard to their organizations."

Then follows the demand to vote against war credits "regardless of the strategic situation" (this hits Ledebour), the statement "against any voluntary participation of workers in organizations which serve the national defense" (this is against the liquidators and their participation in

---

[21] On December 9, 1915, Scheidemann and Landsberg, both members of the majority within German Social Democracy, spoke on the interpellation in the Reichstag, following the German Chancellor's speech during the debate on peace terms. Scheidemann claimed that the ideas expressed by the Chancellor were in agreement with the party's desire for peace and renunciation of annexations.

[22] The Congress of the French Socialist party held in Paris from December 25 to 29, 1915, at which pro-war resolutions were adopted.

War-Industries Committees). Finally, definite *strikes, demonstrations,* and in another place "mass actions" are recommended.

Such is the manifesto. You can see that this is a considerable step forward.

How could it happen that with a membership like this such a manifesto originated? The *logic of the situation* works for us. Since people wish to expose Huysmans, Scheidemann, Renaudel—nothing else can be said except what we have said, and by so doing these people incidentally hit Kautsky and Co., although (in spite of us) they issue ardent "invitations" to Kautsky and Haase, make advances to them, etc.

The participants in the meeting hazily understood that the logic of the development was in our favor. Because they were compelled to follow the road which we ("separatists") pointed out to them, they became more angry and revenged themselves in trifling matters; they arranged a hostile demonstration when we read the statement against the Organization Committee [of the R.S.D.L. party], tried without success to forbid us to tell the press of this incident, etc.

But the fact remains: the manifesto (circular letter or appeal) accepted by the meeting of our opponents is in reality a triumph for our point of view. Much of what was said is confusing, too elaborately phrased, obscure, lacks unity, but—it all follows our orientation, and their opponents will certainly tell them that.

Our comments in all countries (in press, at meetings, etc.) should consist mainly in pointing out the fact that the Zimmerwald majority, although unwilling and obstinate, was compelled by the course of events to follow the direction of the Zimmerwald Left.

Another important question concerned the next *conference of Zimmerwaldists*. It was decided to call it *openly*. This again means our victory over the "diplomats" who did not want it. The date is April 23 (Easter), 1916, at Berne. In the press a fictitious date and place will be indicated.

The following resolution was accepted with regard to the conditions of participation:

1. Only representatives of such political and professional organizations or individuals as adhere to the resolutions of the Zimmerwald Conference are admitted.

2. In countries where the *official* parties or groups are affiliated with the I.S.C. only representatives of those official organizations are admitted.

3. In countries where the official parties do not belong to the I.S.C. only delegates from those organizations and groups are admitted which:

a) Conduct oral and written agitation in the spirit of the Zimmerwald resolution.

b) Can prove their activity to the I.S.C.

4. Personal invitations can be issued only as an exception, and those invited have only a consulting vote.

5. A committee of nine members elected at the Conference will make a final decision concerning mandates in case of dispute—after both sides have been heard, etc. Four members of the I.S.C. must be included in the nine.

6. The distribution of votes is determined by the Conference itself.

Furthermore, *not for publication,* it was mentioned in the minutes, that *all* those who were present at Zimmerwald have the right to a consulting vote even if they are not official delegates.

After long arguments the following agenda was accepted:

1. Reports.
2. Struggle for the ending of the war.
3. The position of the proletariat on the question of peace.
4. Agitation and propaganda:
   a) parliamentary action
   b) mass action
5. Question of calling the International Socialist Bureau.
6. Miscellaneous.

Our proposals to place more general questions on the agenda—the tactics of the government in the struggle against imperialism, the question of self-determination of the nations, the question of international organization of the proletariat—were rejected. This was due in part to the fact that these questions were covered by point 3 (for instance, the question of self-determination of nations) and in part to the aversion to building up the "Third International."

The agenda as it stands in its abbreviated form, however, gives considerable freedom. If we prepare ourselves as we should we shall be able to force the discussion of questions which are vital to us.

There are then two months before the conference. But we must begin *this minute* to prepare ourselves politically and technically (passports). With an open calling of the conference the response may be strong and it may even result in something like a small congress. The Right Center of Zimmerwald is mobilizing its forces. We should mobilize ours.

The important thing for us is that, at any rate, this will be *our* conference, a conference of the *Lefts.* Therefore, it is *necessary* for us to gather in as large numbers as possible.

We recommend avoiding the transfer of mandates. Our opponents will only use that to start a brawl (as was the case with the mandate of the I.S.D.).[23] If you attribute significance to these international con-

---

[23] Lenin presented a mandate from the International Socialists of Germany. The mandate was rejected in spite of Radek's violent objections. This incident called

ferences (they undoubtedly are significant), *come in person*. Otherwise we shall be unable to do anything.

The Berne Committee has been placed under obligation to publish and to distribute at least at the conference, reports from various countries, drafts of resolutions. Send us whatever you have and we shall forward it.

We repeat: it is necessary to begin the discussion of the questions and the election of delegates *right away;* to prepare passports immediately, etc.; to elect delegates in as large a number as possible from organizations and groups of the same mind as ours, so as to allow us to come forward as a more impressive group. The conference may acquire great significance. And the main thing is—we ourselves will rally our own forces.

Delegates from trade unions which adhere to our point of view should also be induced to come. Rigola, from Italy, the chairman of the general trade union commission,[24] attended the present meeting. Several delegates from Italian unions will be present at the conference; delegates from our youth leagues should also be invited, even if only from the local ones. Resolutions of sympathy with the Zimmerwald Left should be passed.

The majority decided to call emphatically not only the German but also the Austrian Kautskyans. The Austrians (and Hungarians) say: we shall go, *if* Kautsky and Haase go. This further increases the necessity for the Lefts to make their *own* group more impressive.

Please inform us regularly and without delay of your decisions and moves.

It has been decided not to say a word in the press, or orally, until Grimm's notice appears. We emphatically ask and insist on this being observed. Not a single word to any outsider, only to organizations and groups adhering to Zimmerwald!

---

forth derisive comment from the German majority. The *Internationale Korrespondenz,* No. 71, March 7, 1916, pp. 753–54, in reporting on the February meeting of the Berne International Socialist Committee or, as it called it, "Sobelsohn's 'Third International,'" wrote as follows: *"Lenin—the Russian party 'leader'*—came to the conference with a mandate from the 'International Socialists of Germany.' The management of this organization suffers, it seems, from extreme feeblemindedness. By giving Lenin the mandate it became this time a laughing stock also at *Berne* .... Even Grimm should know by now that these private international gatherings can serve only, if at all, for mutual *information.* But, can an understanding be brought about or joint action initiated *unless* the situation in various countries and parties is *known?* What could a foreign comrade, the Russian émigré Lenin, tell *about Germany?* He is one of the most narrow-minded representatives of the Russian political exiles."

[24] Confederazione Generale del Lavoro.

CIRCULAR LETTER OF THE INTERNATIONAL SOCIALIST COMMITTEE, FEBRUARY 1916[25]

RESPECTED COMRADES! In September 1915 at *Zimmerwald,* representatives of socialist organizations and groups took the first practical step for the restoration of international proletarian relations on the basis of a class solidarity, which knows neither state nor national boundaries and which proves that the workers are capable of struggling for socialism in time of peace as well as in time of war.

The *Zimmerwald manifesto* has echoed loudly in the minds and hearts of the workers of the entire globe. Official parties and sections of them, associations of socialist trade unions and of socialist women and youth have declared their joyful adherence to the Zimmerwald action by resuming the class struggle and the struggle against the war.

In belligerent as well as in neutral countries a more or less pronounced *movement of protest against the war* has become manifest. Hundreds of workers' meetings in Germany, France, England, Italy, Russia, etc., official party congresses and conferences, and even public bodies in Italy have approved the principles of the Zimmerwald manifesto. Thus our appeal has served as a signal for a gathering and for a spiritual revival of the reserve forces of the international socialist proletariat.

Since the days of the Zimmerwald Conference the *international situation has become still more aggravated.* Day after day the number of human victims in the belligerent states increases, while the high cost of living and the misery promoted by an unscrupulous speculation and supported by widespread corruption threaten the vital forces of the peoples.

This gigantic accumulation of sacrifices and of burdens is accompanied by the *spreading and extension of the war area. Bulgaria* was forced into the circle of belligerents; *Greek neutrality* was violently abused, as was the neutrality of Belgium and of Luxemburg; and the fiction of the so-called international right of the peoples has been generally revealed by the belligerents of all countries. *New war dangers* are already lying in wait for us. Imperialist antagonism threatens to overwhelm *Sweden and Rumania* with catastrophe, and *American munitions capital,* while it strives to lengthen the present war by cool calculation, at the same time engages in feverish preparations which are driving the *United States* to the edge of the abyss paved with human corpses.

Under such circumstances, the idea "that modern capitalism has become incompatible not only with the working masses, not only with the requirements of historical development, but also with the elementary

[25] *Beilage zur Berner Tagwacht,* No. 54, March 4, 1916, p. 1. An English version is given in the *International Socialist Committee in Berne, Bulletin,* No. 3, February 29, 1916, pp. 2–3, and excerpts were printed in the *Labour Leader,* No. 16, April 20, 1916, p. 6.

conditions of human society," is again and with greater intensity proved to be true.

As a matter of fact events have shown that freedom and independence for the oppressed nations will not eventuate at the hands of imperialist states or from the imperialist wars. The example of the *Balkan countries* and especially the tragic fate of *Serbia* and *Armenia* prove that the small countries and oppressed nations are simply pawns in the imperialist game of the Great Powers and, like all the working masses which participate, will be used in the war as tools only to be sacrificed after the war on the altar of capitalist ambition.

Under these circumstances *the present World War signifies in its every defeat and its every victory a defeat of socialism and of democracy.* Except in case of revolutionary intervention of the international proletariat the war, whatever its issue may be, will lead to a revival of militarism and the voracious imperialist appetite, to a sharpening of international antagonisms, to an accumulation and entanglement of national problems, which were supposed to be solved by the war. The war has called forth in all countries an unheard-of, ever increasing reaction within the states, a weakening of public control, and thereby a degradation of parliaments into obedient tools of militarism.

The working masses themselves, which understand instinctively the fate which the war has allotted to them, are rising spontaneously against the originators of the war and against its consequences.

In *Germany* thousands of men and women in the capital as well as in the provinces have repeatedly demonstrated against high prices and have raised the cry for peace. In *England* the laboring masses have protested with increasing energy against conscription. More than a hundred thousand workers in *Petersburg* have declared against participating in War-Industries Committees and have thereby refused to take upon themselves any responsibility whatever for the war. Political strikes have broken out in Petersburg, Moscow, Nizhni-Novgorod, Kharkov, etc., in which many thousand proletarians participated. They demonstrated the attitude of the Russian laboring class against civil peace and in favor of continuing the struggle against Tsarism. A protest against the war finds expression even in the *trenches,* where fraternizing between the soldiers of belligerent armies is not infrequent. The peoples in the belligerent countries no longer believe in the legend of a liberating war, and they have become aware that the *so-called national defense in this war is nothing more than a crude means of deception to make the peoples tributary to imperialism.*

The higher spheres of those official socialist parties, which have taken upon themselves a part of the responsibility for the war, are forced to reckon with a growing protest and have therefore made some gestures to appease the impatience of the organized masses. But these gestures, made upon the basis of a policy of class reconciliation and civil peace, were not destined to remain without effect. They strengthen the voluntary subjection of the proletariat to the command of the ruling classes and contribute to the prolongation of the war.

In order to crush the workers' opposition to the policy of war to the finish, the socialist majority leaders in *Germany* have made an interpellation, which was also a pretext for expressing their confidence in the government—both in its war policy and in its peace aims. Indeed this was done at a moment when the government had openly shown its annexationist ambitions in Belgium and in Poland. On the other hand, the nationalist majority had nothing to offer to the working class except to advise it to be moderate, to economize; it advocates schooling in deprivation and self-denial during the war, by renouncing the proletariats' economic and political class demands.

In *France* the official Socialist party replied to the people's desire for peace with empty phrases about a "lasting peace," the realization of which, at the price of carrying on the endurance policy, was left to capitalist diplomats and imperialists of the Entente. The party Congress proclaimed the *union sacrée,* the necessity of voting in favor of war credits, approved the delivery of the socialist leaders as hostages to the bourgeois Cabinet, and opened a struggle against the socialist minority, which was bravely and courageously waging war against war.

The majority of the *Austrian* and *English socialists* similarly adhere to social patriotism; moreover, a small minority of Social Democrats and Socialist-Revolutionists of *Russia* have concluded a nationalist pact with Tsarism.

What has the *International Socialist Bureau* done meanwhile? As early as at Zimmerwald its complete failure to carry out the duties imposed upon it by the resolutions of the Stuttgart, Copenhagen, and Basel congresses had already been exposed. Its long period of inactivity and its latest declaration in connection with the congress of the Dutch Labor party prove that the Bureau does not wish to change its attitude. The secretary of the Executive Committee is attempting to create the belief that it is possible to preach the duty of so-called national defense—i.e., the support of bourgeois-capitalist governments—and simultaneously to build an International "more vital than ever." *That is not true,* and means nothing more than a *deception* of the masses.

The proletariat, by joining with the imperialist bourgeoisie to defeat the imperialism of another country, in this war, strengthens its own most bitter enemy—*its own ruling class*—and works for *its own defeat* and for *the destruction of the proletariat of other belligerent countries.* The International can*not* endure if its national sections grant credits for the murderous weapons which serve to massacre the proletariat of other countries; it cannot endure if its sections renounce the preparedness of the masses for the present and for the future; it cannot endure by addressing to the governments pious wishes for a coming peace without supporting the demands for peace by a purposeful will and action in the spirit of class struggle and of internationalism.

Every attempt to restore the International by means of a reciprocal amnesty of the compromised opportunist leaders, with a simultaneous recognition and continuation of the policy of civil peace, is in reality nothing but a pact *against* socialism and a blow *to* the reawakening of the revolutionary labor movement.

The class action of the proletariat of all countries must, in times of war and peace, be directed toward a *common struggle* against *imperialism*. The parliamentary and trade union activity as well as the entire activity of the labor movement, should serve the purpose of placing the proletariat of each country in vigorous opposition to the national bourgeoisie, should reveal on every occasion the political and the spiritual difference between the two, and at the same time should push into the foreground the international solidarity of the proletariat of all countries and promote its activity.

The main task of socialism today must be directed toward uniting the proletariat of all countries into a vital revolutionary power with a *unified conception* of the proletariat's interests and tasks, with *unified tactics,* and with capacity for action, in times of peace as well as of war, toward making the proletariat the deciding political factor to which it has been destined by history.

The duty of discipline with regard to these vital commands of the international proletariat takes precedence over all other organizational duties. Whoever acts against these commands is an enemy of the socialist proletariat. The national sections of the International, which act thus undutifully, free the members from all obligations with regard to their organizations.

In the struggle against war a decisive influence may be effected only by the *laboring masses* of all countries. Now that the consequences of the catastrophe press with all their force upon the laboring class of all countries, belligerent and neutral, and produce ever-increasing devastations, the opposition of the proletariat should be organized. Proceeding from a *unification in spirit* the proletariat should demand—without regard for the strategic situation—that war credits be refused and that the workers should not voluntarily participate in organizations which serve national defense; should demand the withdrawal of socialists from bourgeois cabinets, and a conscious break with civil peace on the part of their deputies, a break even to the extent of *open economic and political struggle of the masses against the ruling classes and their govern-ment.*

By throwing light upon the *true character of the war and of the see-it-through policy* in private conferences as well as in meetings of their trade unions and political organizations, by propagating suitable literature, and by consciously well-aimed verbal agitation in all countries, by en-deavoring to influence the nationalist workers as well as public opinion, by keeping in constant touch with the proletariat of other states which is hostile to the war, by keeping well informed of the events abroad, by making use of the moral and material forces for strikes and demonstra-tions, for mass movements against high prices, for an increase in wages, for the break with civil peace, and for the immediate opening of peace negotiations—by employing all these means the workers, conscious of their aim, act in the sense of the slogan advanced by the International at Stuttgart and unanimously confirmed at Copenhagen and Basel: that "In case of war it is the duty of the proletariat to intervene in favor of its rapid termination and to make every effort to utilize the economic and political crises created by the war, for the purpose of arousing the people and thereby hastening the overthrow of the capitalist rule."

We therefore invite all the parties, organizations, and groups affil-iated with the International Socialist Committee to unremitting work. The success of their activity will depend on the degree of their *co-operation* and upon their *constant contact with the class-conscious work-ers of all countries.* This can be accomplished by regular reports to the International Socialist Committee on the events in every single country; the Committee in its turn should keep the affiliated political and trade union organizations continually informed of the conditions of the inter-national movement against the war — a movement which originated within the limits set by the Zimmerwald resolutions—and thus endeavor to strengthen the international bonds of the proletariat's action.

In agreement with the representatives of the affiliated organizations the International Socialist Committee at Berne will, furthermore, pre-pare for a *Second International Socialist Conference,* which will con-tinue and strengthen the work begun at Zimmerwald. We are asking that the agenda of this second conference should be discussed even now by all organizations and all meetings, so that the success of the confer-ence may be assured—the conference which is entrusted with carrying the movement begun in September 1915 to the broader strata of the proletariat. With socialist greeting and handshake.

In the name of the Zimmerwald Conference:

THE INTERNATIONAL SOCIALIST COMMITTEE IN BERNE

DRAFT MANIFESTO FOR THE SECOND ZIMMERWALD CONFERENCE

[Drawn up by the Supporters of *La Vie ouvrière* and *Nashe Slovo*][26]

[As published in the *Bulletin* of the I.S.C. the manifesto is preceded by an introductory statement which makes the following points: (1) Events of the past five months have shown the justness of the Zimmerwald conception of the war and its consequences. (2) Social patriotism is stronger and more obstinate than had been believed, but social patriots are being forced by proletarian opposition to use socialist phraseology more frequently. Internationalists should not, however, be deceived into making concessions to the majority. Zimmerwaldists must go forward, and if discontent should drive the masses to revolt the social patriotic organizations should be overthrown and the movement led in a revolutionary spirit. (3) The problem of national defense should be stated in a categorical manner without relation to the existing military or diplomatic situations. (4) The aim of the internationalists is neither schism nor unity, but they place the interests of socialism and the class struggle above unity with official organizations. (5) With respect to peace terms, the problems of Poland, Belgium, Persia, Serbia, or Greece can be solved by the proletariat only by opposing militarism with revolutionary force. A just peace without annexations and indemnities, guaranteeing the right of self-determination and economic and political unity of peoples on a democratic basis, can be achieved only by a wider and more intense struggle of the proletariat against capitalism. "It is our duty to oppose the revolutionary truth to the illusions of the reformists and pacifists."]

Five months have passed since the Conference of Zimmerwald, where we, socialists of Europe, launched our call and expressed our indignation. Five more months, five long months of war, have passed over humanity, and each month has witnessed the self-extermination of peoples, their ruination in carnage, and their support of the atrocious achievements of unleashed militarism which can no longer be controlled by the bloody hands of the present rulers of the European nations. The automatic destruction of the flower of mankind has continued throughout these long months. New scores of billions extracted for war loans from the collective funds have been swallowed and have been squandered exclusively to destroy human lives and the conquests of civilization.

Whenever the human mind revolves within this infernal circle it

---

[26] *La Sentinelle*, No. 65, March 18, 1916, pp. 1–2. An English version with an introductory statement was published in *International Socialist Committee in Berne, Bulletin*, No. 3, February 29, 1916, pp. 4–6.

does so only to invent and perfect instruments of destruction. The problem which now occupies the minds of the rulers, the scientists, and inventors in all countries is to find a method to destroy whole armies by poisonous gases.

In the meantime the ruling classes, in their stupid obstinacy or sanguinary intoxication, go on repeating to the peoples that the war must be waged "to the finish," to final victory, until all problems which have provoked the war shall have been solved. But in reality the final solution recedes farther and farther: military operations spread to new fronts and new territories and the characteristic consequence of every new development is that new problems arise and new wounds are opened.

During these last five months, Bulgaria has entered the war in spite of the courageous opposition of the Bulgarian Social Democratic youth. Serbia and Montenegro have been robbed by the advancing Austro-German armies of the pitiful independence left them by their own criminal dynasties and the imperious extortions of the great belligerent powers. The neutrality of Greece was violated by those very ones who have so bombastically proclaimed themselves to be champions of justice and defenders of the weak. In Persia Tsarism plays the role of master and exercises its own tyranny there, thus compensating itself in the East for its failures in the West. We may prophesy for tomorrow the possible intervention in the war of Sweden and of other countries which have not yet participated in the slaughter but cannot and do not wish to remain on the hot coals of neutrality.

Finally, England, whose bourgeoisie has denounced militarism no less than it has promoted its own navalism, is now obliged by the logic of things to impose upon its own peoples the burden of compulsory military service.

Such is the complete news of the war, which on both sides of the trenches is still being qualified as a war of liberation.

By submitting to these crimes, and even by contributing to them and defending them, the central organizations, both socialist and syndicalist, have bound themselves to the ruling classes ever since August 1914 and during the last five months have sunk deeper and deeper in their abandonment of socialism.

Their role was exclusively to transform all political and moral achievements of socialism won at the price of the blood of martyrs, of the creative efforts of thinkers, and the heroic sacrifices of the masses into a weapon for preserving the bourgeois state, for protecting the ruling classes which are shaken to their roots by their own crimes. In the history of mankind which has already recorded the submission of Christianity, then Reformation, and finally of Democracy to the interests of the ruling classes, there could not be more glaring treason, no greater crime, no more disgraceful fall than this submission of official socialism to the bourgeoisie at the time of the latter's bloody decline.

Before the European proletariat we brand this alliance of bourgeois force and of socialist treason as a most formidable menace to the cause of socialism and the progress of humanity. We stigmatize the policy of social patriots who, by aiding, directly or indirectly, their governments to crush the revolutionary socialists in their own countries, approve and encourage the opposition in the enemy countries, and endeavor by the corruptive confusion thus created to save their own socialist reputation in the eyes of the awakening masses.

Between the camp of those who have remained faithful to the social-revolutionary banners and the camp of social patriots, mercenaries, prisoners, or voluntary slaves of imperialism there are partisans of a socialist truce without principles and foresight. They demand in the name of socialist and workers' unity that the minority disarm before the social patriots just as the latter have disarmed in the name of the *union sacrée* before our class enemy.

We cannot and do not wish such a truce as this when the destiny of socialism is at stake.

If our struggle at home endangers the unity of the socialist organizations, the entire responsibility for this calamity falls on those who, while profiting from the proletarian disorganization caused by the war, trample under foot the most important principles of socialism.

The defense of the fatherland, "national defense," which the social patriots continuously invoke, is in reality but a noose which the bourgeoisie, aided by social patriotic agents, has thrown around the neck of the working class. This rope which is being drawn tighter and tighter must be broken.

The proletariat cannot give up hope of the independence of nations. Rather it must assure this independence by revolutionary struggle against capitalist militarism and not by supporting this militarism which corrodes the proletariat. Our path leads to a revolt against the rulers and not to war side by side with them. The social patriotic guards of the bourgeoisie fear the discontent and the revolt of the proletariat and are now trying to prepare, through the mediation of the old International Bureau and behind the backs of the deceived socialist masses, the restoration of the fictitious bonds between the official socialist parties of the belligerent countries. Clinging to national militarism with one hand, the social patriots prepare to offer each other their free hands and to combine efforts to stifle the socialist consciousness of the awakening masses by means of a badly counterfeited international solidarity. We warn the workers against this hypocritical policy. A new International cannot be erected except on the firm basis of the principles of revolutionary socialism. The allies of the rulers—Ministers, tamed deputies, advocates of imperialism, agents of capitalist diplomacy, grave-diggers of the Second International—cannot take part in the creation of the new International.

Ruthless struggle against nationalism, definite refusal of war credits regardless of the strategic and diplomatic situation of the country, merciless denunciation of the lies of national defense or the *union sacrée,* the proletariat's mobilization for a revolutionary onslaught upon bourgeois society—these are the necessary conditions for the creation of a real socialist International. Only this plainly socialist and revolutionary policy can assure to the proletariat an influence on the actual outcome of the war and the international relations which will be established after the conclusion of peace.

The social patriots declare from their parliamentary tribunes that they are opposed to annexation. Some of them even add that they believe in the right of nationalities to dispose of their own destinies. But all these high-sounding phrases in no way alter the fact that the social patriots are making every effort to assure victory to their national militarism and are thus inevitably preparing ruthless annexations. It is impossible to struggle staunchly against annexations without combating their instrument—militarism. It is impossible to protect the independence of peoples by aiding capitalism to destroy this independence.

By preparing territorial annexations in Europe, by making attacks against national independence at Belgrade and Saloniki, at Brussels, and at Teheran the governments of both belligerent coalitions are endeavoring at the same time to prepare for the division of the Europe of tomorrow into two powerful economic camps separated by the barbed wire of customs tariffs. A continuous and implacable commercial struggle will break out between these two gigantic state trusts on the day after the conclusion of peace. This prospect, as well as the annexations, promise to the war-exhausted peoples of Europe a new rise in the cost of living, an increase of taxation and militarism, a dictatorship of banks and trusts, a curbing of social legislation, and a mad political reaction.

The struggle against the tariff trenches, which will accelerate the disintegration of European economy, cannot be carried on otherwise than simultaneously with the struggle against the military trenches. The struggle against political tyranny, standing armies, secret diplomacy, and in favor of the democratization of the European states is the primary condition of the economic and political unification of Europe.

Men and Women, Workers!

If this war, generated by imperialism, devastates Europe, then peace concluded by nationalists actually in power will but strengthen and increase the hostilities between the nations and will be the cause of new, even more devastating catastrophes. Since we have failed to prevent this war, it is now our duty to do all we can to impose upon the belligerents our peace. We must oppose our own force—a revolutionary consciousness and the will to fight without mercy—to the force of the rulers who feed on our passivity and our submissiveness.

We call you to fulfill this task! Enough of patience! Enough of silence! Let the call of indignation and revolt resound everywhere! Let words be followed by deeds!

Listen to us! Men and women, workers of Europe! If only a small portion of all the sacrifices, lives, and blood demanded by this war had consciously been sacrificed to the cause of socialism, Europe would soon have been freed from the ignominious regime of oppression and exploitation and we should possess the certainty of seeing our sons enter the kingdom of labor and justice. Make up your minds to give your strength, and if necessary also your freedom and your life, for the welfare of humanity.

Struggle against the absurd and countless sacrifices which war incessantly and endlessly demands; struggle against this unleashed militarism, against the barbarism and cowardice of the rulers. Struggle without hesitation, without rest, with all your strength.

Down with war! Down with annexations and war indemnities! Hail, national freedom and independence! Hail, economic unification of the peoples!

Hail! Revolution!

Hail! Socialism!

THESES SUBMITTED TO THE INTERNATIONAL SOCIALIST COMMITTEE BY THE GERMAN *INTERNATIONALE* GROUP

[Drafted by Rosa Luxemburg and Adopted at a Conference of the *Internationale* Group, January 1, 1916][27]

1. The World War has brought to naught the results of the forty years of labor of European socialism, by destroying the significance of the revolutionary labor class as a factor of political power and the moral prestige of socialism, by breaking up the proletarian International, by leading its national sections into a fratricidal slaughter, and by chaining the desires and hopes of the masses in the most important capitalist countries to the galley of imperialism.

2. The official leaders of the German, French, and English socialist parties (with the exception of the Independent Labour party), by voting war credits and approving the proclamation of civil peace, have strengthened the backbone of imperialism, have induced the masses of

---

[27] *Spartakusbriefe,* I, 83–86.

the people to bear patiently the misery and the horrors of the war, and thereby have contributed toward a dissolute unchaining of imperialist frenzy, toward a prolongation of the massacre and an increased number of victims, and have taken upon themselves the responsibility for the war and its consequences.

3. These tactics of the official party institutions in the belligerent countries, and primarily in Germany, hitherto the leading country of the International, constitute treason against the most elementary principles of international socialism, against the vital interests of the laboring class, against all the democratic interests of the peoples. The socialist policy of those countries, where the party leaders have remained faithful to their duties—in Russia, Serbia, Italy, and, with one exception, in Bulgaria— has also thereby been rendered impotent.

4. The official Social Democracy of the belligerent countries, by giving up the class struggle during the war and by postponing it until after the war, has granted to the ruling classes in all countries a respite which greatly strengthens their position economically, politically, and morally at the expense of the proletariat.

5. The World War serves neither national defense nor the economic nor the political interests of the masses of any of the people; it is merely a monstrous creation of imperialist rivalry between the capitalist classes of various countries for world power and for the monopoly in sucking dry and oppressing the territories not yet under the capitalist rule. *In an era of unchained imperialism national wars are no longer possible.*[28] National interests serve only as a means of deception, to make the laboring masses of the people subservient to their deadly enemy, imperialism.

6. Freedom and independence for any of the oppressed nations cannot grow out of the policy of imperialist states and from the imperialist war. The small nations, whose ruling classes are hangers-on and accomplices of their class comrades in the large states, are only pawns in the imperialist game of the Great Powers and are being misused as tools in the same way as their working masses have been misused during the war, only to be sacrificed after the war to the imperialist interests.

7. Under these circumstances the present World War signifies with its every victory and its every defeat the defeat of socialism and democracy. Whatever its outcome, unless there occurs the revolutionary intervention of the international proletariat, it is driving toward the strengthening of militarism, of international antagonisms, and of the rivalries in world economy. It accelerates capitalist exploitation and domestic political reaction, weakens public control, and reduces parliaments to obedient tools of militarism. Thus the present World War also develops all the premises for new wars.

[28] Italics by translator. This thesis was severely criticized by Lenin.

8. World peace cannot be guaranteed by means of utopian and fundamentally reactionary plans, such as international courts of arbitration of the capitalist diplomats, diplomatic treaties on "disarmament," "freedom of the seas," "the abolition of the right of capture at sea," "European state alliances," "Central European custom leagues," "national buffer states," etc. Imperialism, militarism, and wars are neither to be abolished nor to be dammed up so long as the capitalist classes uncontestedly exercise their class power. The only means to resist them effectively and the only security for world peace lie in the capacity of the international proletariat for political activity and in its revolutionary will to throw its power on the scales.

9. Imperialism as the latest phase of life and the highest stage of the political rule of world capital is the worst enemy of the proletariat of all countries. But it shares also with the earlier phases of capitalism the destiny of strengthening the forces of its worst enemy to the extent that it unfolds itself. Imperialism hastens the concentration of capital, the disintegration of the middle class, the increase of the proletariat; it arouses the growing opposition of the masses and thus leads toward the intensive sharpening of class antagonism. The proletarian class struggle, during war as well as in time of peace, should first of all be concentrated against imperialism. For the proletariat the struggle against imperialism is at the same time a struggle for political power in the state, the decisive controversy between socialism and capitalism. The socialist goal can be reached only by the international proletariat making a united front against imperialism and raising the slogan "war against war" with the utmost exertion and the extreme courage of self-sacrifice as the precept of its practical policy.

10. The main problem of socialism today is directed, therefore, to gathering the proletariat of all countries into a vital revolutionary force, to making it a decisive factor in political life through a strong international organization with a unanimous understanding of its interests and tasks, with united tactics and a capacity for political action in peace as in the war—all of which history has destined it to be.

11. The Second International has been broken up by the war. Its inadequacy has been proved by its inability to erect during the war an effective dam against national disintegration and to carry on the common tactics and action of the proletariat in all countries.

12. In view of the treason committed by the official representatives of the socialist parties in the leading countries against the aims and the interests of the laboring class, in view of their deviation from the basis of the proletarian International to the basis of bourgeois imperialist policy, it is a vital necessity for socialism to create a new Workers' International which would take it upon itself to lead and to unify the revolutionary class struggle against imperialism in all countries.

In order to fulfill its historical task the International should rest on the following principles:

1. The class struggle within the bourgeois states against the ruling classes, and the international solidarity of the proletariat of all countries are two inseparable, vital rules of the laboring class in its universal historical struggle for liberation. There is no socialism outside of the international solidarity of the proletariat, and there is no socialism outside class struggle. The socialist proletariat cannot give up either class struggle or international solidarity during peace or during war without committing suicide.

2. The class action of the proletariat of all countries must have as its main aim in peace as well as in war the conquering of imperialism and the prevention of wars. Parliamentary and trade union action as well as the entire activity of the labor movement must be subordinated to the aim of placing the proletariat in every country in sharp opposition to the national bourgeoisie, of emphasizing at every opportunity the political and spiritual differences between the two, and of advancing to the foreground and affirming the international solidarity of the proletarians in all countries.

3. The center of gravity of the proletarian class organization lies in the International. The International determines in peace the tactics of the national sections on questions of militarism, colonial policy, trade policy, the May celebration, and, furthermore, determines the general tactics to be observed in time of war.

4. The duty of executing the resolutions of the International takes precedence over all other duties of the organization. National sections which act at variance with the resolutions of the International thereby place themselves outside the latter.

5. In the struggle against imperialism and against the war, a definite authority can be established only by the consolidated masses of the proletariat of all countries. The national sections should bear in mind the importance of teaching political activity and resolute initiative to the broad masses, of assuring the international coherence of mass actions, of building up political and trade union organizations so as to bring about at any time through their medium quick and active co-operation among all the sections and thus turn the will of the International into the deeds of the broad working masses of all countries.

6. The next task of socialism is the spiritual liberation of the proletariat from the guardianship of the bourgeoisie, which manifests itself in the influence of nationalist ideology. The national sections, in their agitation in parliaments as well as in the press, should denounce the traditional phraseology of nationalism as the bourgeois instrument of power. The revolutionary class struggle against imperialism is today the only protection of all true national freedom. The Socialist Interna-

tional is the fatherland of the proletarians, to the defense of which everything else should be subordinated.

A PROGRAM OF ACTION

[Draft Submitted to the I.S.C. by the Socialist Revolutionary League and the Social Democratic Party of Holland][29]

The revolutionary Social Democracy in the belligerent countries must do its utmost to bring about immediate peace, whereas in the neutral countries it must act toward immediate demobilization. The revolutionary Social Democracy lays down at the same time the following general guiding principles for immediate action at the end of the war:

In inaugurating the struggle against the propertied classes the revolutionary Social Democracy must make the following demands:

A. In the economic realm: (1) annulment of all government debts; (2) expropriation of banks; (3) expropriation of large enterprises; (4) confiscation of war profits; (5) taxation of capital and income only; (6) the granting of pensions to workers who either do not earn at all or do not earn enough.

B. In the political realm: (1) democratization of all the representative bodies; (2) abolition of the first chamber, the Senate, etc.; (3) establishment of a republic; (4) introduction of an eight-hour working day; (5) abolition of all commercial duties; (6) abolition of the military system.

Workers! We propose to you to advance these demands in all countries, as principles of action, of the international action, after the war. We point out to you emphatically that these demands must be raised by the representatives of the revolutionary proletariat at plenary parliamentary sessions. But first of all they should be raised by the masses themselves, and, moreover, this should be done immediately upon the opening of peace negotiations, *before the troops have returned home*. But you can raise these demands only if your masses *rise for a mass struggle*. Furthermore, the revolutionary Social Democracy urges even today that an international conference be convened as soon as peace negotiations begin, a conference of all parties and groups which have actually fought imperialism prior to and during the war.

Between the February Conference of the Enlarged I.S.C. and Kienthal, Lenin wrote an article bearing directly on

---

[29] A. Balabanoff, "Die Zimmerwalder Bewegung 1914–1919," C. Grünberg, *Archiv für die Geschichte des Sozialismus und der Arbeiterbewegung*, XII, 339–40. This draft program was signed by H. Roland-Holst, J. Visscher, D. J. Wijnkoop, and J. Ceton.

questions then being discussed by the Zimmerwaldists. This article, "On a Peace Program," published in the *Sotsial-Demokrat*, No. 52, March 25, 1916,[30] first criticizes as "the vilest hypocrisy" a statement by Kautsky[31] that "all the peace programs that have been formulated so far within the scope of the International . . . . demand a recognition of the independence of nations and quite justly so. This demand should serve as our compass in the present war."

The article concludes with this statement of a peace program of Social Democracy:

"The 'peace program' of Social Democracy must consist first of all in exposing bourgeois hypocrisy and social-chauvinist and Kautskyan phrases on peace. This is primary and fundamental. Without this we are either involuntary or voluntary promoters of the *deception* of the masses. Our 'peace program' demands that the main postulate of democracy in this question—the repudiation of annexations—should be applied in deeds and not in words, should serve internationalist propaganda and not national hypocrisy. For this purpose it is necessary to explain to the masses that a repudiation of annexations—that is, a recognition of self-determination—is sincere only if the socialist of *every* nation demands the freedom of separation of nations oppressed by his own nation. As a positive slogan which draws the masses into a revolutionary struggle and which explains the necessity for revolutionary measures for a 'democratic peace' it is necessary to advance the slogan: refuse to pay government debts.

"Our 'peace program' should consist finally in explaining that neither the imperialist powers nor the imperialist bourgeoisie are capable of achieving a democratic peace. This peace must be sought and striven for—*ahead* of us, in the socialist revolution of the proletariat, and not *behind us* in the reactionary utopia of *non*-imperialist capitalism. Not one fundamental democratic demand can be realized in the ad-

[30] Reprinted in Lenin, *Sochineniia,* XIX, 49–54.

[31] In an article, "Nochmals unsere Illusionen," *Die Neue Zeit,* No. 8, May 21, 1915, p. 241.

vanced imperialist states to any extent of breadth and firmness, except *through* revolutionary battles under the banner of socialism. Whoever promises the peoples a 'democratic' peace and does not at the same time preach a socialist revolution, whoever denies the struggle for that revolution now—in this war—deceives the proletariat."

In the name of the Central Committee Lenin also submitted the proposal which is given below, in reply to the letter of invitation sent out by the I.S.C. on February 10, 1916. Two versions of this article exist: a preliminary draft containing fifteen points first published in *Pravda*, No. 255, November 7, 1927; and the final text given below. There is no substantial difference between these two drafts. The manuscript of the draft here given was circulated among the Bolshevik sections abroad prior to the Kienthal conference.[32]

PROPOSAL OF THE CENTRAL COMMITTEE OF THE RUSSIAN
SOCIAL DEMOCRATIC LABOR PARTY TO THE INTER-
NATIONAL SOCIALIST COMMITTEE[33]

1. As any war is only a continuation by violence of the policy pursued by belligerent governments and their ruling classes for many years—sometimes decades—prior to the war, so the peace at the end of the war may serve only as an account and record of the actual changes in the distribution of power attained in the course of, or as a result of, the war.

The imperialist war, so long as the foundations of the present order —i.e., the bourgeois social relationships—remain intact, can lead only to an imperialist peace, the reinforcement, expansion, and increase of the oppression of the weaker nations and countries by finance capital—capital which has grown enormously not only prior to but during the war. The objective nature of the policy upheld by the bourgeoisie and the governments of *both* groups of Great Powers, both before and during the war, leads to national enslavement and political reaction and the strengthening of economic oppression. Therefore, any peace which would conclude this war, whatever the issue may be, must strengthen this deterioration of economic and political conditions of the masses if the bourgeois social order persists.

[32] Lenin, *Sochineniia*, XIX, 457, note 59.

[33] *Sotsial-Demokrat*, No. 54–55, June 10, 1916, pp. 1–3; reprinted in Lenin, *Sochineniia*, XIX, 57–63. It also appeared with slight changes in the *Internationale sozialistische Kommission zu Bern, Bulletin*, No. 4, April 22, 1916, pp. 2–4.

2. To assume the possibility of a democratic peace resulting from an imperialist war is to substitute in theory a vulgar phrase for an historical study of the policy pursued before and during the war; is in practice to cheat the masses of the people, to obscure their political minds by covering up and embellishing the actual policy of the ruling classes who prepare the imminent peace and by concealing from the masses the main fact, namely, that democratic peace without a number of revolutions is impossible.

3. The socialists do not refuse to struggle for reforms. They must vote, for example, even now in parliaments for all kinds of improvements in the conditions of the masses, however small, for the increase in relief to the inhabitants of devastated areas, for the weakening of national oppression, etc. But the preaching of reforms for solving the questions raised in a revolutionary manner by history and by the actual political situation is a pure bourgeois deception. Such are precisely the problems which have been put on the order of the day by the present war. These are fundamental problems of imperialism, i.e., the existence of a capitalist society, problems concerning the postponement of the collapse of capitalism by means of a redivision of the world in conformity with the new correlations of forces between the "great" powers, which have developed in recent decades not only with extreme rapidity but—what is even more important—very unequally. Real political activity which does not merely deceive the masses with words but alters the correlation of the forces in society is possible only in one of two forms: either to assist its "own" national bourgeoisie in the robbing of foreign countries and to call this assistance "the defense of the fatherland" or "the country's salvation"; or to assist the socialist revolution of the proletariat by supporting and developing that revolt of the masses which has already begun in all the belligerent countries; by supporting the first strikes and demonstrations, etc.; by expanding and sharpening those still weak manifestations of the revolutionary mass struggle into a general proletarian assault for the overthrow of the bourgeoisie.

In the same way as all the social chauvinists deceive their peoples at present by disguising the actual issue—the imperialist policy of capitalists pursued in this war—by means of hypocritical phrases about an "honest" defense and a "dishonest" attack on the part of any of the groups of rapacious capitalists, so the phrases about "democratic peace" serve exclusively to deceive the people—as if the imminent peace already prepared by capitalists and diplomats can "simply" eliminate a "dishonest" attack and restore the "honest" relationships and is not the continuation, the development, and the confirmation of the same imperialist policy, i.e., the policy of financial robbery, of colonial brigandage, national oppression, political reaction, and the sharpening of capitalist exploitation in every way!! Capitalists and their diplomats are at present in need of such "socialist" servants of the bourgeoisie who would deafen, fool, and put the people to sleep by means of phrases about "democratic peace" and who would cover up with these phrases the actual policy of the bourgeoisie, would prevent the opening of the eyes of the masses to the nature of that policy, and would divert the attention of the masses from the revolutionary struggle.

4. Precisely such bourgeois deception and hypocrisy constitute the program of "democratic peace" which is at present being composed by the most outstanding representatives of the Second International. For example, Huysmans at the Conference at Arnhem and Kautsky in *Neue Zeit*, on February 10, 1915,[34] as the most authoritative official representatives and "theoreticians" of this International, have formulated this program: renunciation of the revolutionary struggle until the conclusion of peace by the imperialist governments; meanwhile an oral repudiation of annexations and indemnities, recognition of self-determination of nations, of democratization of foreign policy, of courts of arbitration for the solving of international conflicts between states, of disarmaments, of a United States of Europe, etc., etc. Kautsky revealed with extreme clearness the actual political significance of this "peace program" when, as a proof of the "unanimity within the International" on this question, he mentioned the fact that the London Conference on October 11, 1915, and the Vienna Conference on May 1, 1915,[35] had unanimously accepted the chief point of this program, "the independence of the nations." In this way Kautsky openly sanctioned before the whole world the conscious deception of the peoples by the social chauvinists who combine the oral, hypocritical testimony of "independence" (or self-determination) of nations with the support of the war by "their" governments, a testimony which imposes no responsibility and leads to nothing. They support this war in spite of the fact that it is waged *on both sides* with a systematic infringement of "the independence" of weak nations and *for the sake of* increasing their oppression.

The objective significance of this most popular "peace program" is the increasing of the subjugation of the laboring class by the bourgeoisie by means of "a reconciliation" of the chauvinist leaders and the workers who are in the process of developing a revolutionary struggle; this reconciliation is effected by disguising the severity of the crisis of socialism for the sake of returning to the prewar state of the socialist parties—

[34] This date is incorrect and has been omitted in the reprinted text in Lenin's *Sochineniia*, XIX. The reference is to Kautsky's article, "Nochmals unsere Illusionen," in *Neue Zeit*, No. 8, May 21, 1915, pp. 230–41.

[35] The editors of Lenin, *Sochineniia*, XIX, have omitted these incorrect dates and substituted "February 1915" and "April 1915." See chapter iii, pp. 273–85, above.

the state which made the majority of the leaders join the bourgeoisie. The danger of this "Kautskyan" policy for the proletariat is all the stronger because it is covered up by plausible phrases and is pursued not only in Germany but in all the countries; for example, in England this policy is being pursued by the majority of leaders, in France by Longuet, Pressemane, and others, in Russia by Axelrod, Martov, Chkheidze, etc. Chkheidze covers up the chauvinist idea of the "defense of the country" in the present war by such expressions as "salvation of the country" and, on the one hand, approves orally of Zimmerwald while on the other, in an official declaration of the Duma group, he praises the illustrious speech of Huysmans at Arnhem. He argues neither on the Duma tribune nor in the press against the participation of the workers in the War-Industries Committees and, furthermore, he continues to collaborate on newspapers which defend such participation. In Italy such a policy is pursued by Treves—see *Avanti,* the central organ of the Italian Socialist party, August 5, 1916.[36] It threatens to expose Treves and other "reformists-possibilists"—to expose "those who have set in motion all possible means to interfere with the activities of the party Executive and of Oddino Morgari, activities directed toward the Zimmerwald movement and the "creation of a new International," etc.

5. The chief "peace question" is at present the question of annexations. In this question the socialist hypocrisy which rules at present and the tasks of the true socialist propaganda and agitation are being most patently revealed.

It is necessary to explain what annexation means and why and how the socialists should struggle against it. Annexation means neither *every* annexation of "foreign" territory—since generally speaking the socialists are in sympathy with the abolition of boundaries between nations and the establishment of larger states—nor every infringement of the *status quo,* as this would be an extreme reaction and a mockery of basic conceptions of history; neither does it mean every military annexation, since the socialists cannot repudiate violence and wars in the interests of the majority of the population. Only the annexation of territory *in spite of the will* of the population should be considered a true annexation; in other words, the idea of annexation is bound up with the idea of the self-determination of the nations.

But on the basis of the present war—precisely because it is imperialist on the part of *both* groups of belligerent powers—this phenomenon had to appear and has appeared; the bourgeoisie and the social chauvin-

---

[36] The editors of Lenin, *Sochineniia,* XIX, have changed this date in the reprinted text to March 5, 1916, under which date *Avanti,* No. 65, published an article entitled "Polemica in casa nostra."

ists should "struggle" intensely against annexations when these are committed by the hostile states. It is clear that such a "struggle against annexations" and such "unanimity" in the question of annexations is a decided hypocrisy. It is clear that in *reality* the *annexionists* are those French socialists who defend the war because of Alsace and Lorraine, those German socialists who do not demand the freedom of separation of Alsace-Lorraine, of German Poland, etc., from Germany, and those Russian socialists who call the new enslavement of Poland by Tsarism "the country's salvation," demanding Poland's annexation by Russia in the name of "peace without annexations," etc., etc.

In order that the struggle against annexations should be neither a hypocrisy nor an empty phrase but should educate the masses in the spirit of internationalism, for this reason the question should be put in such a manner as to *open* the eyes of the masses to the lie which dominates the question of annexations and not to cover up this lie. It is insufficient for socialists of every nation to accept orally the principle of the equality of rights of nations or to recite, swear, or take an oath to the effect that they are against annexations; they should immediately demand absolute *freedom of separation* of those colonies and nations, which are being oppressed by *their own* "fatherland."

The recognition of self-determination of nations and of the principles of internationalism expressed in the Zimmerwald manifesto will remain at the very best only a dead symbol if the above conditions are not realized.

6. The "peace program" of socialists as well as their program "struggle for the cessation of war" should proceed from an exposure of the lie concerning "democratic peace," of the peaceful aspirations of the belligerents, etc., the peace program which the demagogic ministers, the bourgeois-pacifists, the social chauvinists and the Kautskyans of all countries address to the people at present. Any "peace program" is a deception of the people and a hypocrisy if it is not based first of all upon an explanation to the masses of the necessity for a revolution and of the support, co-operation, and development of the revolutionary mass struggle which is starting everywhere (revolts, protests, fraternizing in trenches, strikes, demonstrations, letters from the front to relatives advising them not to sign up for a war loan, and so forth).

The support, expansion, and deepening of any public movement for the sake of ending war is the duty of the socialists. But in reality this duty is fulfilled only by such socialists as Liebknecht who from the parliamentary tribune appeal to the soldiers urging them to lay down their weapons, who preach revolution and the turning of the imperialist war into a civil war for socialism.

The refusal to pay government debts should serve as a positive slogan which would draw the masses into a revolutionary struggle and which would explain to them the necessity of applying revolutionary measures in order to make the "democratic peace" possible.

It is not enough that the Zimmerwald manifesto hints at a revolution by saying that workers must bear sacrifices for their own cause and not for a foreign cause. It is necessary to point out the way to the masses definitely and clearly. It is necessary that the masses should know where to go and why; that they should know that revolutionary mass activities during war, if they develop successfully, can only have the result of transforming the imperialist war into a civil war for socialism—this is evident to everybody and it is harmful to conceal it from the masses. On the contrary, this aim should be pointed out clearly, no matter how hard its attainment might be when we are just starting out on this road. It is insufficient to say, as was said in the Zimmerwald manifesto, that "capitalists are lying when they speak of defending their fatherland" in this war, and that the workers in the revolutionary struggle should not take into consideration the military situation of their country; let us say clearly what has been only hinted at, namely, that not only capitalists but also social chauvinists and Kautskyans are lying when they apply the idea of "the defense of the fatherland" to this imperialist war; that revolutionary activities during the war are impossible without the threat of a defeat of their "own" government; and that any defeat of a government in a reactionary war facilitates a revolution, which alone is able to bring about a lasting and democratic peace. Finally it is necessary to explain to the masses that without establishing illegal organizations and without a press free from military censorship, i.e., an illegal press, without supporting and developing the beginning revolutionary movement, without criticizing its separate steps, without rectifying its mistakes, a systematic expansion and sharpening of revolutionary struggle is impossible.

7. In the question of the parliamentary struggle (*Aktion*) of socialists one should bear in mind that the Zimmerwald resolution not only expresses sympathy with the five Social Democratic deputies of the State Duma who belonged to our party and who were sentenced to exile in Siberia but it also expresses its solidarity with their tactics. To recognize the revolutionary struggle of the masses and to be at the same time reconciled to mere legal activity of socialists in parliaments is impossible and would lead to a legitimate discontent of the workers and to their withdrawal from Social Democracy, and their joining of antiparliamentary anarchism or syndicalism. It is necessary to state clearly, so that everybody can hear, that Social Democrats in parliaments should make use of their position not only for demonstrations within the parliaments but also for thorough co-operation with the illegal organiza-

tions and the revolutionary struggle of the workers outside the parliaments, that the masses through their illegal organizations should themselves verify the activities of their leaders.

8. The question of calling a meeting of the International Socialist Bureau leads to a question of principles—whether or not unity between the old parties and the Second International is possible. Every step forward taken by the international labor movement along the road indicated at Zimmerwald shows with increasing clearness the inconsistency of the position taken by the Zimmerwald majority. On the one hand, the policy of the old parties and of the Second International is identified with the *bourgeois* policy in the labor movement, a policy which answers the interests of the bourgeoisie and not of the proletariat (as for example in the words of the Zimmerwald manifesto: "the capitalists" are lying when they speak of "defending their fatherland" in this war; this is followed by a number of still more definite statements in the circular letter of the International Socialist Committee . . . .). On the other hand, the I.S.C. (the Berne International Socialist Committee) is afraid of a break with the International Socialist Bureau and promises officially to dissolve as soon as the Bureau is again convened.

We declare that such a statement was not only not voted upon but was not even discussed at Zimmerwald.

The six months which have passed since Zimmerwald have proved that work in the spirit of Zimmerwald—we do not speak of empty phrases, but only of work—is *actually* connected in all countries with a deepening and a widening of a split. In Germany illegal proclamations against the war are being issued in spite of the decisions of the party, i.e., schismatically. When *Otto Rühle,* the deputy and the closest comrade of K. Liebknecht, declared openly that there are already two parties—one supporting the bourgeoisie and the other struggling against the bourgeoisie—he was scolded by many, including the Kautskyans, but no one refuted his statement. In *France,* Bourderon, a member of the Socialist party and a decided opponent of a split, at the same time proposes to his party that a resolution be accepted which would disavow the Central Committee of the party and the Parliamentary group (*désapprouver Comm.-Adm. Perm. et Gr. Parl.*), a resolution which would have inevitably called forth an immediate split if it had been accepted. In England, on the pages of the moderate *Labour Leader,* T. Russell Williams, a member of the I.L.P., recognizes openly the inevitability of a split,[37] and finds support in the letters of the local workers. The example of America perhaps is more instructive because there, in a

[37] Williams' letters appeared in *Labour Leader,* Nos. 49 and 51, December 9 and 23, 1915, respectively. They were written in reply to Clifford Allen and argued in favor of the I.L.P. separating from the Labour party.

neutral country, two irreconcilably hostile tendencies within the socialist party have become manifest—on the one hand, the so-called "preparedness," i.e., war militarism and navalism; on the other hand, such socialists as Eugene Debs, former candidate of the Socialist party for President, who openly preaches civil war for socialism in connection with the imminent war.[38]

Throughout the whole world a split has actually occurred, resulting in two entirely irreconcilable policies of the laboring class in relation to war. It is impossible to shut one's eyes to this event. This will only lead to the confusion of the working masses, will obscure their minds, and will impede the revolutionary mass struggle with which all the Zimmerwaldists are officially in sympathy, will increase the influence over the masses of those leaders whom the International Socialist Committee in their circular letter of February 10, 1916, accuses directly of "leading the masses into confusion," and of preparing a "conspiracy" (*Pakt*) *against* socialism.

It is the social chauvinists and the Kautskyans of all countries who will continue to work toward the restoration of the bankrupt International Socialist Bureau. The task of socialists is to explain to the masses the inevitability of a split with those who pursue the policy of the bourgeoisie under the banner of socialism.

B. The Kienthal Conference

The Second Zimmerwald Conference was held April 24 to 30, 1916, in the small village of Kienthal at the foot of the beautiful Blümlis Alp. According to the official report of the International Socialist Committee forty-four delegates attended the Conference. A number of other delegates named by groups in England, Holland, Austria, Bulgaria, Rumania, Sweden, and Norway and by the Jewish Workers' League of Lithuania, Poland, and Russia were unable for various reasons to take part in the sessions. From Germany, where sixteen delegates had been designated, seven reached Kienthal: A. Hoffmann and H. Fleissner from the Haase-Ledebour groups; Bertha Thalheimer and Ernst Meyer from the *Inter-*

---

[38] In an article published in the *Appeal to Reason,* September 11, 1915, Debs wrote: "I am opposed to every war but one; I am for that war heart and soul, and that is the world-wide revolution. In that war, I am prepared to fight in any way the ruling class may make necessary, even to the barricades." Quoted by Floy Ruth Painter, *That Man Debs and His Life Work,* p. 112.

nationale group; P. Frölich from the Bremen Radical group; and two other delegates whose names are not known. Three deputies of the French Chamber—Pierre Brizon, Jean-Pierre Raffin-Dugens, and Alexandre Blanc—and the editor of *Demain,* Henri Guilbeaux, represented France. Italy had seven delegates: Morgari, Modigliani, Lazzari, Prampolini, Musatti, Dugoni, and Serrati. The Russians were the most numerous: Lenin, Zinoviev, and Inessa Armand from the Bolshevik Central Committee; Martov and Axelrod from the Menshevik Organization Committee; and Bobrov, Savelev, and Vlasov (the last two being pseudonyms which we have been unable to identify) from the internationalist wing of the Socialist-Revolutionist party. From the Polish groups Radek, Bronski, and Dąbrowski represented the Regional Presidium, and Warski the Main Presidium of the Social Democracy of Poland and Lithuania. Lapinski represented the Polish Socialist party (Levitsa). The Serbian deputy, T. Kaclerović, represented the Serbian Social Democrats, F. Koritschoner the Austrian, and Edmondo Peluso the Portuguese Socialist party. The Swiss delegation consisted of Fritz Platten, Ernst Nobs, Paul Graber, and Agnes Robmann. Grimm, Naine, Morgari, and Balabanoff held mandates from the International Socialist Committee and Münzenberg from the Socialist Youth International. A member of the British Independent Labour party was present as a guest.[39]

---

[39] Balabanoff, "Die Zimmerwalder Bewegung ....," Grünberg, *Archiv* ....,
XII, 340–41; *Beilage zur Berner Tagwacht,* No. 166, July 18, 1916, p. 1; *Nashe Slovo,* No. 128 (514), June 1, 1916, p. 1; Lenin, *Sochineniia,* XIX, 457–58, note 59; in addition to the four Swiss delegates mentioned above, the Swiss party Presidium had delegated Greulich and Studer to the Kienthal Conference ("Parteivorstandssitzung," *Berner Tagwacht,* No. 85, April 10, 1916, pp. 2–3), but Greulich was obliged to withdraw because the Italians insisted that he had compromised the Italian Socialist party by being involved in transmitting the offer of a wealthy American to furnish a large sum of money to finance pacifist propaganda of the Italian socialists in May 1915, when Italy was about to enter the war. The Italian and Greulich's version of this affair are given in *Avanti,* Nos. 211 and 215, August 1 and 5, 1915, pp. 5 and 1, respectively; see also Münzenberg, *S Libknekhtom i Leninym,* p. 136. Studer did not attend this Conference. According to the official report of the International Socialist Committee Austria was not represented either.

"The spacious dining room of the Hotel Bären," Edmondo Peluso writes, "was transformed into a conference chamber. The president's table was in the center and, as behooved an international conference, the Presidium consisted of a Swiss, a German, a Frenchman, an Italian, and a Serb. Two tables for the delegates were placed on either side and perpendicularly to the president's table. These were the Right and the Left, exactly as in parliaments. The Italian delegation, being very numerous, took their seats at another table in front of the president . . . . Grimm opened the debates. French and German were the official languages of the Conference . . . . Citizen Balabanoff, who possessed an excellent memory, translated [all of the speeches] . . . ."[40]

Unfortunately there is no record of the speeches and debates, but there are references and fragmentary information scattered in the published recollections of some of the participants as well as in the polemical literature of the opponents of the Zimmerwald movement. After Grimm's opening remarks Adolf Hoffmann spoke, and after him Pierre Brizon. Of this remarkable speech Guilbeaux recalls: "Everybody was dumfounded when he [Brizon] took the floor for the first time . . . . [and] declared, 'Comrades, though I am an internationalist, I am still a Frenchman; therefore, I declare to you that I shall not utter one word, nor will I make any gesture which might injure France, France the land of the Re-vo-lu-ti-on.' He said to old Adolf Hoffmann, whom he liked because of his beard, which reminded Brizon of the late Henri de Rochefort: 'Dear old friend, why don't you tell Wilhelm to hand us back Alsace-Lorraine; we will be glad to give him Madagascar in return.' At one time he became so provocative that Serrati jumped at him and seized him by the collar. He [Serrati] even left the Conference, but the Italian delegates . . . . brought him back . . . . He [Brizon] liked to repeat: 'These Russians are only learned braggarts,' or on another occasion: 'Look at Lenin's superior smile' . . . .

[40] E. Peluso, "Notes et impressions d'un délégué," *Demain,* No. 5, May 1916, p. 343.

The attitude of Deputy Brizon at Kienthal was so shocking that the Left—Lenin, Zinoviev, Radek, and Bronski—drafted a resolution which demanded Brizon's immediate expulsion. If I am right it was the Italian delegation which, supported by Robert Grimm and Balabanoff, helped Brizon to defend his case . . . ."[41]

Münzenberg records that Brizon spoke in a "highly rhetorical and showy manner . . . . He assumed all kinds of poses and repeatedly interrupted his speech, which lasted several hours, to get something to eat or have some coffee . . . . When at last he declared, 'we are also willing to refuse credits,' the entire audience broke forth in excited applause. But as soon as the ovation had subsided, Brizon continued calmly: 'But only on condition that there are no hostile troops on French territory.' Now general enthusiasm changed at once into general indignation and certain members of the Conference, Bronski and Paul Frölich, particularly, were even ready to give Brizon a good beating."[42]

When, after his extraordinary speech, Brizon offered the text of the manifesto quoted below, the delegates were speechless but also pleased, since, as Radek later remarked, "All that had been previously brought up against Brizon and the French opposition was said in the draft."[43] Although the extreme Left regarded this manifesto as the weakest document adopted by the Conference, it was the only one which urged the masses to demand that socialist members of national legislative bodies should henceforth vote against war credits.

The second pronouncement of the Conference was the resolution on the attitude of the proletariat toward questions of peace. This resolution, given below, gives the Zimmerwaldist explanation of the origin of the war, denounces the

---

[41] H. Guilbeaux, *Wladimir Iljitsch Lenin*, pp. 132–33. Later, during Guilbeaux' visits to Moscow, Lenin used to ask him, smiling: "Do you still remember Brizon at Kienthal, and Serrati also?" [42] Münzenberg, *S Libknekhtom i Leninym*, p. 137.

[43] Radek's remark is quoted by Solomon Grumbach, a vigorous opponent of the Zimmerwald movement, who merely expresses his "profound astonishment" without attempting to explain Brizon's apparent about-face. (S. Grumbach, *Der Irrtum von Zimmerwald-Kiental*, p. 51.)

bourgeois pacifist program of gradual disarmament and arbitration, proclaims that a revolutionary struggle for socialism is the only method of obtaining a lasting peace, and outlines a program of proletarian action for socialism and peace. This resolution was based on Grimm's draft somewhat amended. Two other drafts were also submitted. The draft by the Central Committee of the R.S.D.L. party, which contained a demand for the self-determination of nations according to Lenin's formula, was rejected on the ground that the Conference was not prepared to deal with this question. The draft of the Zimmerwald Left was essentially like the resolution adopted, but it criticized the Center socialists more sharply and openly called for civil war. It avoided a definite statement on the question of self-determination, which was the subject of heated argument among the Bolsheviks and within the Zimmerwald Left,[44] but advocated national equality, no annexations, liberation of colonies, and abolition of state boundaries. The resolution adopted, while avoiding the term "self-determination," advocated a struggle against all national oppression and the violation of weaker nations and for the protection of national minorities and the autonomy of peoples on the basis of real democracy.[45]

Members of the Right wing of the Conference did not attempt to defend the theory of a "democratic" peace but confined themselves to minor amendments to Grimm's draft.[46] Twelve delegates signed the draft of the Zimmerwald Left: three Bolsheviks, three Poles, a German, three Swiss, an Italian, and a Serb. The four new members of the group were Nobs, Platten, Frölich, Serrati, and Kaclerović, who joined this group with certain reservations.[47]

[44] See above, chapter ii, p. 214, and below, chapter vi, pp. 500–532.

[45] According to Zinoviev's account given below, Grimm's draft originally contained a point against the slogan of self-determination on the ground that it could not be realized under capitalism—i.e., the position of some of the Bolsheviks and Left Zimmerwaldists who opposed Lenin on this point.

[46] Cf. Yaroslavsky, *Istoriia V.K.P.(b.)*, III, 118.

[47] According to Mickiewicz-Kapsukas, the Lithuanian Social Democrats grouped about the Lithuanian paper, *Social-Democratas,* after acquainting themselves with the draft resolution of the Zimmerwald Left, a copy of which was sent to London

Even more controversial than the peace question was the attitude of the Conference toward the International Socialist Bureau. At Zimmerwald a majority had believed that the I.S.B. might resume its international activities, and a statement had been made that as soon as a plenum of the I.S.B. should meet the International Socialist Committee would be dissolved.[48] At the February meeting of the Enlarged I.S.C. and at Kienthal it was apparent that a majority neither hoped for nor greatly desired a meeting of the plenum of the I.S.B. as then constituted. But it was necessary for the Conference to define its attitude toward the Bureau, the more so since, spurred on by the demands of various socialist groups, the I.S.B. was showing renewed activity and, as has been noted, had begun to prepare for a conference of socialists of neutral countries to be held at The Hague during the summer. The Kienthal Conference did not discuss this proposed June meeting but authorized the Enlarged I.S.C. to examine the question. With regard to the I.S.B. in general, there were strong differences of opinion, and the resolution adopted was a compromise which, after criticizing the Bureau, directed the I.S.C. not to participate in the calling of a plenary meeting of the I.S.B. If, however, such a meeting were called and the Zimmerwald sections were to be permitted to attend, the Enlarged International Socialist Committee was to meet to work out a program of joint action.

In addition to the documents mentioned above, the Conference also issued a declaration of sympathy for the persecuted defenders of Zimmerwald principles. Certain other documents were also submitted to the Conference: a draft

---

prior to the Kienthal Conference, authorized Berzin to add their signature under this resolution. Berzin, however, did not attend the Kienthal Conference and passed his vote as representative of the Lettish Social Democracy to Zinoviev. The vote of the Lithuanians apparently was lost. (V. Mitskevich-Kapsukas, "Istoki i zarozhdenie Kommunisticheskoi Partii Litvy," *Proletarskaia Revoliutsiia*, No. 1 [84], 1929, p. 165.)

[48] The Bolsheviks criticized this statement as arbitrary and unsanctioned, and Grimm is said to have explained at Kienthal that such action would be taken only if the I.S.B. renounced its present policies and accepted the Zimmerwald platform. (Zinoviev, "Tsimmervald-Kintal," *Sochineniia*, V, 257.)

manifesto written by Axelrod, Lapinski, and Martov; a declaration condemning the socialist minority deputies of the French Chamber for continuing to vote for war credits, which was submitted by the Zimmerwald Left and supported by the twelve members of that group and seven other delegates,[49] and two resolutions of the German *Internationale* group given below. The rather passive attitude of the *Internationale* delegates at Kienthal may perhaps be best explained in the words of one of the declarations of that group: "The participation in the May demonstration in Berlin . . . . was more important than the 'dignified' participation in the Second Zimmerwald Conference, and Karl Liebknecht in his quiet prison cell is doing more for the restoration of the International in all countries than ten yards of the Zimmerwald manifesto."[50]

The last two documents in this section are estimates of the Zimmerwald movement as it appeared after Kienthal to a participant, Zinoviev, and to a socialist opponent, Grumbach, whose points of view were far apart.

PROCEEDINGS OF THE KIENTHAL CONFERENCE

[From the Official Report]

PROCEEDINGS

In agreement with representatives of the affiliated organizations and groups, the International Socialist Committee proposed in its letter of invitation the following provisional agenda:

1. The election of the Bureau and the Credentials Commission
2. The drafting of the order of proceedings
3. Report on the activity of the International Socialist Committee in Berne
4. Reports of the delegates

[49] The delegates of the German *Internationale* group did not sign this declaration, though they represented the Liebknecht group which had voted against war credits in the Reichstag. It is impossible to say whether or not the nineteen who voted for this declaration were identical with the nineteen who voted for Zinoviev's amendment to the resolution on the I.S.B.

[50] "Zur zweiten Zimmerwalder Konferenz," *Spartakusbriefe*, I, 133. For the attitude of the German Lefts toward the Zimmerwald movement, see *The Bolsheviks and World Revolution*.

5. Struggle to end the war

6. The attitude of the proletariat toward the questions of peace

7. Agitation and propaganda: (*a*) parliamentary action; (*b*) mass action

8. The question of calling a meeting of the International Socialist Bureau at The Hague

9. Miscellaneous

This agenda was followed with no substantial change and served as a guide for the proceedings of the Conference. It was decided that in order to save time for other topics of discussion the reports from various countries should be made as brief as possible—especially since the individual parties had already reported in detail, in the *Bulletin* of the International Socialist Committee, on the conditions of the socialist movement in their respective countries. The Conference, therefore, decided to listen to oral reports of the German and French delegations only. The representatives of both of these countries were able to supply encouraging news about the growth of the opposition. Events have led everywhere to the sharpest separation from the social patriots. In Germany a split has occurred in the Reichstag group and various organizations refuse to pay the membership fees to the party Presidium because they consider it impossible to support financially an institution which acts at variance with party principles and the decisions of the party congresses, and furthermore, because this support would merely strengthen the struggle against the internationally minded opposition. In France the meeting of the National Council of April 1916 represents substantial progress in comparison to the Congress at Christmas of 1915. At that Congress it was still possible to adopt a resolution that was approved unanimously, a resolution which demanded support of the government policy in the war—whereas in April there was a break: one-third of the representatives declared themselves in favor of immediate resumption of international relations. It stands to reason that the movement in France and Germany—and not only in these two countries —is yet in the process of clarification. This was evident from the reports and the supplements to the reports.

Points 5 and 6 of the agenda—the attitude of the proletariat toward the questions of peace and the struggle in favor of terminating the war— constituted the chief topics of discussion.

The unanimous adoption of a resolution on the attitude of the proletariat toward the questions of peace was preceded by a general exchange of views and by lengthy and strenuous labor on the part of the Commission. Three proposals were submitted at the beginning: (1) by the Zimmerwald Left group, (2) by the *Internationale* group of Germany, and (3) by one of the members of the International Socialist

Committee.[51] The general exchange of opinion showed that it would be useful to describe the attitude of the proletariat toward the peace questions in a special resolution rather than, as was proposed, to deal with these questions simultaneously with the resolution on the general tasks of international action and the principles for the restoration of the International. In connection with the drafting of the resolution it was especially emphasized that it would be necessary to be guided by events and facts and to promote the action initiated at Zimmerwald. The opinion was also expressed that an analysis of the attitude toward the peace questions was necessary for purely practical considerations. The decisions of Zimmerwald, listed but not explained in the manifesto, have been interpreted and criticized in a number of ways. For instance, the social patriots interpreted the manifesto as favoring support of the government policy of the Entente (see declaration of the International Socialist Committee of September 29, 1915, in the *Bulletin, No. 2*).[52] On the other hand, others maintained that the Zimmerwald manifesto, by demanding peace without annexations, wished to preserve the *status quo ante* of the period prior to August 1914. Finally, the opinion that the proletariat would be able to exert influence on the conditions of the imminent peace by merely confining itself to formulating more or less clearly elaborated peace proposals and renouncing an immediate and joint struggle against the war had to be opposed.

All participants of the Conference were united in a most resolute condemnation of such an unsocialist interpretation, which would only mislead the proletariat. It is not by folding its arms, and by elaborating resolutions, decisions, and proposals that the laboring class can counteract the dangers of future wars. If the laboring class does not struggle in favor of its own demands in time of peace as well as of war, the *laboring class* will prove to be helpless and will not be able to exert pressure upon the drafting of the peace conditions. All talk about lasting peace, where the realization of such peace is to be left to the policy of the capitalist governments and to their diplomacies, only serves to mislead the proletariat and results in nothing but a useless sacrificing of the proletariat's best forces upon the shambles of imperialism.

While no significant differences of opinion prevailed among the delegates with regard to all these questions, the points of view diverged with respect to the practical significance of the demands for the limitation of armaments, compulsory courts of arbitration, etc. In this connection a lengthy exchange of opinions took place in the Commission. Opinions did not differ as to the contention that such means as these would not abolish the danger of war rooted in imperialism, but a certain minority expressed a somewhat different point of view on the question as to

[51] R. Grimm.   [52] See above, p. 357.

whether or not any amelioration of the war dangers could be thus attained. Finally, it was agreed to leave this question without action and to submit it again for discussion at the plenum. However, no final exchange of opinion on this question took place at the plenum. This circumstance led to the fact that at the time of the final vote a number of declarations were introduced, some of which objected that the theses were not sufficiently far-reaching and others emphasized the fact that the formulation of certain passages of the resolution sounded too pessimistic. But since during the debates in the plenum and in the Commission a fundamental agreement had been attained, and since it was simply a matter of exhaustively discussing every single detail, the text of the resolution as we have published it was unanimously adopted.

The second question which aroused no less interest and attention was that of the calling of a meeting of the International Socialist Bureau at The Hague. In this connection fundamental unanimity also prevailed concerning the condemnation of the conduct of the International Socialist Bureau. Proceeding from sharp criticisms of the Executive Committee of the International Socialist Bureau, everyone agreed concerning the causes of its bankruptcy and the fact that this institution had become a hostage in the hands of the imperialist governments of the Entente. Differences of opinion prevailed only with regard to the definite conclusions which the adherents of Zimmerwald were to draw from these facts. Three tendencies became manifest on this question: one tendency maintained that the parties adhering to the Zimmerwald decisions should not promote the calling of the International Socialist Bureau—the international general staff of social patriotism should itself discover the internal rottenness and inadequacy of the International Socialist Bureau to carry on socialist activity. The second tendency advanced the point of view that although the adherents of Zimmerwald do not demand the calling of the International Socialist Bureau they should accept the invitation to the meeting of the Bureau in case the Executive Committee itself should undertake to call such a meeting. This would give opportunity for a sharp encounter with the social patriots and thus enable the Zimmerwaldists to establish before the world proletariat the treason committed against socialism and to expose the nature of social patriotism and its fateful activity. Finally, the third tendency, although it agreed with this latter criticism, maintained that the calling of the International Socialist Bureau should be demanded for this very reason, and that thus the Zimmerwaldists would have the opportunity to gain a majority in the International Socialist Bureau and to win the International over to the principles laid down by the Zimmerwald resolutions. Finally, after the relative strength of the three tendencies had been tested by complicated voting, a compromise agreement was reached and the resolution was unanimously adopted. . . . . The majority of the Conference members emphasized the fact that, although in the ranks of the national parties, as well as in the bosom of the Second International, there now exist irreconcilable antagonisms, to decree and create artificially a new International was out of the question. The latter must arise from the masses through the continuous and ever increasing struggle of the working class against its class foes, and through a clarifying of the socialist conception, and it could not be decreed by any conference.[53]

While it was imperative to adopt a definite attitude with regard to the two chief questions, it was no less important to address an appeal to the masses. In a unanimously adopted appeal the conditions caused by the war were characterized from the point of view of the workers in a form which coincided with the logical conclusions which could be drawn from the events by the laboring class itself. The main principles and the form of the appeal were elaborated in a Commission, and the Conference agreed with the work of the Commission without introducing any modifications worth mentioning.

In the interval between the discussions of the three questions mentioned above, the International Socialist Committee read its financial report—the reports of its activity, together with the question of parliamentary action and the final formulation of the texts of the resolutions and of the appeal, were transferred to the Enlarged International Socialist Committee.

From September 6, 1915 to April 20, 1916 the International Socialist Committee reported:

Income	5,209.73 francs
Expenses	4,517.35 francs
Balance	692.38 francs

The affiliated parties and groups had contributed a total of 3,478.30 francs. The contributions of individual local organizations and private persons amounted to 1,553.65 francs. The expenses consisted of 2,950.90 francs for the publishing of the *Bulletin,* etc., 988.50 for postage and general expenses of the Bureau, and 299.25 francs for the expenses of the first conference. In this connection we note that the members of the International Socialist Committee received no compensation for their work, or even for translating. The report was verified and approved by the Conference without objections. . . . .[54]

[53] "Zweite internationale sozialistische Zimmerwalder Konferenz abgehalten am 24 bis 30, April 1916. Offizieller Verhandlungsbericht," *Beilage zur Berner Tagwacht,* No. 168, July 20, 1916, p. 1.

[54] "Zweite internationale sozialistische Zimmerwalder Konferenz abgehalten am 24. bis 30. April 1916, Offizieller Verhandlungsbericht," *Beilage zur Berner Tagwacht,* No. 169, July 21, 1916, p. 1.

MANIFESTO OF THE KIENTHAL CONFERENCE[55]

To the Peoples Who Suffer Ruin and Death

Proletarians of all countries unite!

Two years of World War! Two years of devastation! Two years of bloody sacrifice and of the raging of reaction!

Who is responsible? Who backs those who have thrown a burning torch into the powder keg? Who has desired this war and has prepared it for so long?—*The ruling classes.*

When in September 1915 we socialists of the belligerent and the neutral countries joined hands across the bloody confusion and assembled at *Zimmerwald* amidst the unchained war passions, we said in our manifesto:

". . . . The ruling forces of capitalist society, in whose hands were the destinies of the nations, the monarchical and the republican governments, secret diplomacy, the vast employers' organizations, the middle-class parties, the capitalist press, the church—all these forces must bear the full weight of responsibility for this war, which has been produced by the social order nurturing them and protecting them and which is being carried on for the sake of their interests . . . ."

"Every nation," said Jaurès a few days before his death, "rushed with a burning torch through the streets of Europe."

After millions of men have sunk into their graves, millions of families have been made to mourn, and millions of women and children have been turned into widows and orphans, after ruins have been piled on ruins and irreplaceable cultural achievements destroyed, the war has come to an *impasse.*

In spite of hecatombs of victims on all fronts no decisive results have been attained! In order to shake these fronts even slightly the governments would require additional millions of human sacrifices.

Neither victors, nor vanquished. Rather *all vanquished;* all bleeding, all ruined, all exhausted—such will be the outcome of this gruesome war. The ruling classes will thus realize the vanity of their dreams of imperialistic world dominance.

Thus it has once more become manifest that only those socialists who, in spite of calumnies, have opposed the nationalist delusion and have demanded *immediate peace without annexations* have served the interests of their peoples.

Therefore, join us in our war cry: *"Down with the war! Hail peace!"*

[55] "Zweite internationale sozialistische Zimmerwalder Konferenz. An die Völker die man zu Grunde richtet und tötet," *Berner Tagwacht,* No. 106, May 6, 1916, p. 1. The manifesto was drafted by the French deputy, Pierre Brizon.

Workers in Towns and Fields!

The governments, the imperialist cliques, and their press tell you that it is imperative to hold out in order that the oppressed nations may be freed. Of all methods of deception which have been used in this war, this is the crudest. The true aim of this general slaughter lies, for some, in *making secure that which they have scraped together during centuries or conquered in many wars,* and for others in a *repartitioning of the world,* in order to increase their possessions; these wish to annex new territories, subdivide and tear apart whole nations, and degrade them to ordinary servants and helots.

Your governments and your press tell you that the war must be continued in order that militarism may be abolished.

Don't be misled! *A nation's militarism can be abolished only by the nation itself,* and, moreover, this must be done in *all* countries.

Furthermore, your governments and your press tell you that the war must be extended in order that it should be the last war.

This also is a deception. *Never has war done away with war.* On the contrary, it arouses desire for revenge, since violence provokes violence!

So after each sacrifice your torturers will demand further sacrifices. Even the road of the bourgeois pacifist revilers does not lead you out of this infernal circle.

There is but one effective means of preventing future wars: the seizure of political power and the abolition of capitalist property by the working class.

Lasting peace can result only from victorious socialism.

Proletarians!

Who are they who preach to you the policy of "endurance until victory"?—They are the responsible authors of the war, the mercenary press, the army purveyors, the war profiteers; the social patriots, who repeat the bourgeois war slogans; these are the reactionaries who rejoice secretly over the death on the battlefields of the socialists, of the trade unionists, of all those who planted the seed of socialism in towns and villages and who were but yesterday a menace to the privileges of the rulers.

They are the endurance politicians!

They control the government, *they* dominate the press, they are allowed to agitate in favor of continuing the war, of adding to the number of bloody sacrifices and devastations.

Whereas, you, the victims, are allowed only to starve, to keep silent and to endure the chains of the state of siege, the shackles of censorship and the close atmosphere of prisons.

You, the people, the working masses, are sacrificed in a war *which is not your war.*

You, the toilers from towns and villages, are now in the *trenches,* in the foremost lines, whereas the rich and their accomplices, the poltroons, may be seen *behind the lines* in security.

For them war means the death of others.

At the same time as they accentuate as never before *their* class struggle against you, and preach civil peace to you—as they ruthlessly exploit your misery—they endeavor to incite you to commit treason against your class duty, and they thus deprive you of your best strength —the hope for socialism.

Social injustice and class dominance are even plainer in war than in peace.

In peace the capitalist system robs the worker of the joy of living; *in war* it takes everything from him, even his life.

Enough of assassination! Enough of suffering!

Likewise, enough of devastations! For it is upon you workers that today and in the future those accumulations of ruins will fall.

Hundreds of billions are thrown today into the jaws of the war god and thus are lost to the people's welfare, to the cultural aims, and to the carrying out of such social reforms as would ameliorate their lot, promote public education, and lessen misery.

Tomorrow, new heavy taxes will descend upon your bowed shoulders.

Therefore, let us put an end to the wasting of your labor, your money, your vital strength! *Join the struggle in favor of an immediate peace without annexations!*

In all belligerent countries workingmen and women should rise against the war and its consequences, against the misery and the deprivations, against the unemployment and the high cost of living. Let them raise their voices in favor of restoring the civil liberties of which they have been deprived and in favor of social legislation and the demands of the working class in towns and villages.

Let the *proletarians of the neutral countries* aid the socialists of the belligerent states in their difficult struggle and oppose to their utmost a further expansion of this war.

Let the *socialists of all countries act according* to the decisions of the international congresses, which made it the duty of the working class to put forth every effort so as to bring about an early peace.

Exercise the maximum pressure possible upon your deputies, your parliaments, your governments.

Demand that the representatives of the socialist parties deny at once every support to the government's war policy. Demand from the social-

ist parliamentarians that they vote from now on against all war credits.

Every means at your disposal should be used to end quickly this slaughter!

Your slogan should be: immediate armistice! Rise up and fight, you people, led to ruin and death!

Courage! Behold that you are a majority, and that the power could be yours if you so wished.

The governments should be told that the hatred against the war and the will to social retaliation is growing in all countries and that the hour of peace between the peoples is inevitably approaching.

Down with the war!

Hail peace, immediate peace without annexations!

Hail international socialism!

THE SECOND INTERNATIONAL SOCIALIST
ZIMMERWALD CONFERENCE

May 1, 1916

THE ATTITUDE OF THE PROLETARIAT TOWARD THE QUESTION OF PEACE

[Resolution of the Kienthal Conference][56]

I

1. The modern development of bourgeois property relations gave rise to *imperialist antagonisms.* The present *World War* is one of the *consequences* of these antagonisms in the interest of which unsolved national problems, dynastic aspirations, and all the historical relics of feudalism are being utilized. The *aim* of this war is the repartitioning of former colonial possessions and the subjugation of economically backward countries to the power of finance capital.

2. The war eliminates neither capitalist economy nor its imperialist form; therefore, it cannot do away with the *causes* of future wars. It reinforces finance capital, leaves unsolved the old national and world power problems, complicates them, and creates new antagonisms. This leads to the increase of economic and political reaction, to new armaments, and the danger of further military complications.

3. Therefore, if the governments and their bourgeois and social-patriotic agents assert that the purpose of the war is to create a *lasting peace,* they lie or they ignore the conditions which are necessary for the realization of this purpose. Annexations, economic and political alliances of imperialist states, can contribute as little to the realization of a

---

[56] *Berner Tagwacht,* No. 107, May 8, 1916, p. 1.

lasting peace on a capitalistic basis as can the compulsory courts of arbitration, the limitation of armaments, the so-called democratization of foreign policy, etc.

4. *Annexations,* i.e., the forcible annexing of foreign nations, stirs up *national hatred* and *increases the areas of friction* between states. *The political alliances* and the *economic treaties* of the imperialist powers are a direct method of *extending the economic wars*—a method which leads to *new world conflicts.*

5. The plans to eliminate the dangers of wars through a *general limitation of armaments* and compulsory courts of arbitration are mere utopias. They presuppose a generally recognized authority and a material force which would stand above the opposed interests of the states. Such an authority, such a force, does not exist, and capitalism with its tendency to sharpen the antagonisms between the bourgeoisie of various countries or of their coalitions prevents its appearance. Democratic control over foreign policy presupposes a complete democratization of the state. This control may be *a weapon in the hands of the proletariat* in its struggle against imperialism, but cannot be a means for turning democracy into an instrument of peace.

6. Because of these considerations the laboring class must reject the *utopian demands of the bourgeois or socialist pacifism.* In place of the old illusions the pacifists evoke new ones and attempt to force the proletariat to serve these illusions, which in the end only mislead the masses and divert them from the revolutionary class struggle and favor the game of the see-it-through policy in the war.

II

7. If a capitalist society cannot provide the conditions for a lasting peace, then these conditions will be provided by socialism. By abolishing capitalist private property, together with the exploitation of the masses by the propertied classes and together with national oppression, socialism eliminates the causes of wars. *The struggle for lasting peace can, therefore, be only a struggle for the realization of socialism.*

8. Every action of the workers which renounces class struggle and subordinates proletarian aims to those of the bourgeois classes and of their governments and is in solidarity with the exploiting class of the proletariat—every such action works against the conditions necessary for a lasting peace, entrusts the capitalist classes and the bourgeois governments with a task which they cannot fulfill; moreover, it places on the shambles the best forces of the working class. The strongest and most capable elements of the proletariat, which both in time of war and in time of peace would be the first to be called upon to lead the struggle for socialism, are now destined to collapse and destruction.

III

9. As has already been stated in the resolutions of the Stuttgart, Copenhagen, and Basel International congresses, the attitude of the proletariat toward war cannot depend upon a given military and strategic situation. *Therefore, it is a vital commandment of the proletariat to raise the call for an immediate truce and an opening of peace nego-, tiations.*

10. The laboring class will succeed in hastening the end of the war and in gaining influence over the character of the imminent peace only to the extent to which this call finds a response in the ranks of the international proletariat and leads to forceful action directed toward the overthrowing of the capitalist class. Any other attitude leaves the establishment of the peace conditions to the fiat of governments, diplomacy, and the ruling classes.

11. In the revolutionary mass struggle for the aims of socialism—the liberation of mankind from the whip of militarism and of war—the proletariat should struggle against all *lust of the belligerents for annexations.* Likewise it should reject all attempts at establishing, under the pretext of liberating oppressed peoples, pseudo-independent states. The proletariat struggles against annexations not because it considers that the map of the world in its prewar condition corresponds with the peoples' interests and therefore requires no changes, but because socialism strives to eliminate all national oppression by means of an economic and political unification of the peoples on a democratic basis, something which cannot be realized within the limits of capitalist states. Annexations, in whatever form they occur, make the attainment of this aim more difficult, because a forcible partitioning of nations, the arbitrary subdividing and incorporation of them by foreign states, makes worse the conditions of the proletariat class struggle.

12. So long as socialism has not achieved the freedom and equality of rights of all nations, the proletariat's unfailing duty is to take part in the class struggle *against all national oppression,* to oppose any violation of weaker nations, to promote the *protection of national minorities* and the *autonomy of the peoples* on *the basis of real democracy.*

13. *The demand for war indemnities on behalf of the imperialist powers* is as incompatible with the interests of the proletariat as are annexations. Just as the ruling classes in every country try to put the burden of war costs upon the shoulders of the working class, so the war indemnities in the end will be borne by the laboring class of the country in question. This transfer of the burden of indemnities is harmful also to the laboring class of the *victorious* country, because the deterioration of economic and social conditions of the laboring class of one country affects the laboring class of other countries and thereby makes more

difficult the conditions for the international class struggle. Not the transfer of the economic consequences of the war from one people to the other, but *a general transfer of these consequences to the propertied classes* by means of an annulment of state debts brought about by the war—such is our demand.

14. The struggle against the war and against imperialism, originating in the misery of human slaughter, will in the future grow with increasing force out of the calamities with which the imperialist era scourges the masses of the people. The International will expand and deepen the mass movements against the high cost of living and unemployment and in favor of the agrarian demands of the rural workers, against new taxation and political reaction, until all these movements unite into one general international struggle for socialism.

SOCIAL DEMOCRACY AND THE QUESTION OF PEACE

[Draft Resolution of the Zimmerwald Left][57]

I. As time goes on, the World War, the true character of which is being concealed by slogans of defense, national independence, and democracy, reveals more and more its true nature. This war is a struggle of the capitalist Great Powers for a new division of backward countries which are doomed to become the objects of exploitation by various cliques of finance capital. The present war will not result in a final division of these countries. Finance capital, strengthened in the World War by the policy of loans and by a strong concentration of capital, will continue its robbery and will prepare for new wars to divide up the Near East, the territories of the Far East bordering on the Pacific Ocean, the colonies of weaker capitalist nations. Negotiations now in progress and existing secret treaties concerning a consolidation of economic agreements and a new division of the spheres of influence (i.e., plans for the formation of a Central European Alliance, the economic conference of the Allied powers, the Anglo-Japanese treaty, the Russo-Japanese treaty, etc.) serve these new aims.

II. While in the conflagration of the World War there is being forged a future peace—which represents merely an agreement between imperialist bandits on the division of spoils and which increases the menace of new wars—the petty bourgeoisie, the opportunists, and the social pacifists ("the center" of the German Social Democratic party, the Independent Labour party, and so forth) are endeavoring to ignore the real facts and to divert the masses from them; they pursue a mirage of "democratic peace" which would give to the peoples a United States

[57] *Sotsial-Demokrat*, No. 54–55, June 10, 1916, p. 3; reprinted in Lenin, *Sochineniia*, XIX, 436–37.

of Europe, compulsory courts of arbitration, disarmament, democratized diplomacy, etc. In reality all this deceives the masses, covers up and disguises the cruel facts of world politics. The capitalist bourgeoisie of all the large states is concerned only with its own profits. It strives with its utmost strength to increase profits, not to share them with the other weaker capitalist states. Each capitalist clique draws new income from armaments, protective tariffs, and new colonies. The present situation and the future of capitalism means not disarmament, reconciliation, and "democratic control" over predatory ambitions but increase and expansion of the dominance of the club law of the financial cliques and of their imperialist world policy. Consequently, the objective significance of the utopia of world capitalism, i.e., capitalism without wars, is that the masses of the people are being misled as to the real state of affairs. They are being diverted from the path of revolutionary struggle. Therefore, the policy of social pacifism is only water to the mill of opportunists, who must conceal their intentions to divide the booty with their bourgeoisie in the same way as the imperialist bourgeoisie must conceal *its own* evil intentions.

III. Imperialism which threatens the proletariat with great perils is digging its own grave. Its foundation is built upon the strong concentration of production, the decisive role of a small group of powerful banks, monopoly, and highly developed technology. But these premises are also the economic premises of socialism; thus the time for the realization of socialism is approaching. At the same time imperialism is mobilizing the masses under the influence of the unheard-of sufferings connected with the World War and its consequences (increased cost of living, aggravated conditions of the trade union struggle, reaction), thus placing before the proletariat the alternative—either the struggle for socialism, or degeneration and general exhaustion.

IV. This revolutionary mass struggle of the proletariat for socialism will arise out of the struggle of the masses against the misfortunes and burdens brought about by the epoch of imperialism and against increased prices, unemployment, increased burdens of taxation, colonial adventures, and national oppression. This struggle will be carried on under the slogan of abolishing all burdens of imperialism (annulment of government debts), of supporting the unemployed, of establishing a democratic republic and national equality, of repudiating annexations, of liberating colonies, of abolishing state boundaries. All these types of struggle will unite into one strong current of struggle for political power, a struggle for socialism and for the unification of the socialist peoples.

To call the proletariat to this struggle and to organize it for a resolute attack upon capitalism—this is the only peace program of Social Democracy.

Lay down your weapons. You should turn them only against the common foe—the capitalist governments—this is the peace program advanced by the International.

This draft resolution was signed by the following delegates to the Kienthal Conference:

The Central Committee of the R.S.D.L. party, Lenin, Zinoviev, Petrova; the Regional Committee of the Social Democracy of Poland and Lithuania, Radek, Bronski, Dąbrowski; the German Social Democratic Opposition, one delegate from the town X; members of the Swiss delegation, Platten, Nobs, Robmann; for the Serbian Social Democratic party, Deputy Kaclerović; member of the Italian delegation, G. M. Serrati (editor of *Avanti*).

Of those who signed, G. Zinoviev represented the Social Democracy of the Lettish Region also, whereas Radek represented the Socialist Revolutionary League of Holland (whose chairman was Comrade Roland-Holst).

ON THE INTERNATIONAL SOCIALIST BUREAU

[Resolution of the Kienthal Conference][58]

I

Whereas the Executive Committee of the International Socialist Bureau completely failed to carry out the tasks clearly and definitely assigned to it by the resolutions of the International Socialist congresses; whereas it refused obstinately to call a meeting of the Bureau in spite of repeated demands of various national sections; whereas the Executive Committee has done nothing to overcome the sharp crisis for the International which the war has caused, but, on the contrary, has sharpened this crisis by becoming an *accomplice in the policy* of the so-called "defense of the fatherland, and of civil peace," i.e., *a policy by which it has renounced the old principles* and a policy which has led the laboring class into a state of shameful weakness;

Whereas this complicity has received its most pregnant expression in the fact that the *Chairman of the Executive Committee* thought of uniting the position of a *Minister* in a belligerent country with the position of *Chairman of the International Socialist Bureau*, thus degrading the central organization of the Workers' International to the unworthy role of a servile tool and a hostage in the hands of an imperialist coalition; furthermore,

Whereas only after twenty months of war and in the face of a grow-

---

[58] "Zweite Zimmerwalder Konferenz," *Berner Tagwacht*, No. 108, May 9, 1916, p. 1.

ing indignation of the masses, which are freeing themselves from the heavy burden of chauvinism, has the Executive Committee examined the question of calling a meeting of the Bureau;

Whereas this endeavor was accompanied by a previous recognition of the fratricidal war, the justification of which was sought in so-called national defense;

Whereas the Executive Committee, at the moment it granted condonation to all those who had renounced the socialist banner made every effort *to defeat the revolutionary elements of the International*—elements which have not succumbed to this bloody confusion but have joined hands in the struggle against the imperialist war;

Whereas the attempt to resume relations between national sections took on the nature of *a separate peace between the social patriots;*

Whereas on account of relations between the governments and the social patriotic leaders—relations which are contrary to all socialist principles and which were created by the war in most of the countries—it is to be feared that the Executive Committee might call a meeting of the International Socialist Bureau under certain circumstances at a moment favorable for the political interests of one or of both of the coalitions of power,

The Second Zimmerwald International Socialist Conference *commands* all the organizations adhering to the International Socialist Committee at Berne to watch carefully all the activities of the Executive Committee of the International Socialist Bureau.

The Conference is of the opinion that the International can recover from its collapse as a definite political power only to the extent in which *the proletariat is able to liberate itself from all imperialist and chauvinist influences and re-enter the road of class struggle and of mass action.*

In case a *plenary meeting* of the Bureau should be held, the delegates of the parties and the organizations which are standing upon the basis of the Zimmerwald Conference and which will participate in this plenary meeting must pursue a special aim, i.e., must *expose the real intentions* of national socialism which attempted to divert the laboring class from its aim, and must also oppose to this coalition's attempt at deception—ruthlessly and without limitation—the *fundamental principles* on the basis of which the *international opposition has formed in all countries.*

II

Should the Executive Committee of the International Socialist Bureau decide to call a meeting of the Bureau, then the International Socialist Committee should if possible call a meeting of the *Enlarged Committee* and discuss the question of joint action by the representatives who adhere to the Zimmerwald resolutions.

III

The Conference recognizes the right of the *national sections* adhering to the International Socialist Committee to demand on their own part the calling of the International Socialist Bureau.

DRAFT RESOLUTION ON THE INTERNATIONAL SOCIALIST BUREAU

[Proposed by the Majority of the Drafting Commission][59]

Whereas the International Socialist Bureau has not met even once since the outbreak of the war for the purpose of initiating a struggle against the war and has thus gravely violated the obligations which were imposed upon it by the international congresses,

The sections belonging to Zimmerwald demand of the Executive Committee that it call a meeting of the Bureau and fulfill its duty. These sections submit the following proposal:

I. The Executive Committee which has manifested its inadequacy to defend and apply during the war the principles of the International must be replaced by another committee selected from the socialists of the neutral countries.

II. The sections which belong to the International must expel from their ranks those members who are participating in the governments of the belligerent countries.

III. The parliamentary representatives of sections of the International must vote against all war credits.

IV. "Civil peace" must be broken everywhere and class struggle must be resumed along the entire front.

V. These sections urge that all means be used to hasten a peace which would not sanction any annexations or indemnities and which would grant to all nations the right of self-determination.

Should the International Socialist Bureau refuse to meet, the adherents of the Zimmerwald principles will renounce every responsibility for the consequences of this refusal.

---

[59] *Sotsial-Demokrat,* No. 54–55, June 10, 1916, p. 3. The majority of the Commission consisted of Lazzari, Naine, Hoffmann, and Axelrod.

THE WORKING CLASS AND THE PROBLEMS OF
PEACE AND WAR

[Draft Manifesto Submitted to the Kienthal Conference by Representatives of the Organization Committee of the R.S.D.L. Party and the Polish Socialist Party (Levitsa)][60]

The Coming Peace

[After enumerating the actual effects of the war and the possible effects of "peace" as prepared by the "imperialist cliques of both coalitions of powers," the authors of the manifesto examine the state of affairs within official socialism in the European countries in its relation to the question of peace.]

While the capitalist classes are laying the foundation of a future Europe with the aid of cannon and money, socialism, which has accepted *Burgfrieden,* is by the logic of its policy condemned to be a passive and helpless spectator of this performance. In the name of the defense of the fatherland, socialism has declined to attempt to arouse the masses to a struggle against international imperialism. . . . .

Among raging passions of piracy the official socialism of Germany, France, etc., is able to utter only innocent wishes for a "democratic" peace which would not violate the rights of the peoples; it has renounced all means of actually influencing the course of events which is preparing the conditions of peace. The representatives of official socialism remind us in this case of the open advocates of bourgeois democracy, who do not perceive that the development of the capitalist society—the basis upon which they stand—is burying once and for all their humanitarian and pacifist illusions. But it is still worse when socialists who advocate war to the finish—unfortunately this is happening more and more often —disguise with democratic formulae the plans of conquest, plans to partition nations, and plans of future economic and military coalitions, invented by the rulers of Europe to the accompaniment of the roar of cannon, and thus take upon themselves the mission of bourgeois democrats who have completely capitulated before imperialism . . . .

The proletarians must watch most carefully the plans of their governments and their ruling classes, *who after preparing an ignominious war are now preparing a peace no less ignominious.* The war, by means of which the bourgeoisie is attempting to overcome the irreconcilable antagonisms of the capitalist order so as to prolong the life of capitalism, is turning against the vital interests of the proletariat. The predatory

[60] *Kriegs- und Friedensprobleme der Arbeiterklasse. Entwurf eines Manifestes vorgelegt der zweiten Zimmerwalder Konferenz.* This manifesto was submitted by P. Axelrod, L. Martov, and S. Lapinski, and was transmitted to the Commission which drafted the Kienthal resolution on the proletarian attitude toward peace.

plans of both belligerent coalitions which will be expressed in the peace terms are opposed to the most precious interests of the proletariat. The proletariat must understand the actual nature and significance of these plans in order, by basing itself on the struggle of the awakening proletarian class movement, to oppose to them its own program of struggle.

PLANS OF ALLIANCES BETWEEN STATES

The present war has proved that the world economy generated by capitalism has far outgrown its existing state boundaries. In the last analysis the war was provoked by the basic need of national economies to expand national territories. And we observe that both belligerent coalitions are taking into account this need in formulating their peace plans. Thus originated the plan for a "Mitteleuropa" on the one hand and for a close economic rapprochement of the countries of the "Quadruple Entente" on the other.

The manner in which the capitalist classes are attempting to solve new problems can be reconciled neither with the interests of the proletariat and of democracy in particular nor with the real requirements of social development in general. . . . .

[After discussing the undesirability of the formation of large economic units under capitalism, the manifesto continues] : Capitalism is incapable of solving the problem of an economic union of independent states upon the basis of national independence and free economic development . . . . Only the proletariat will be able to accomplish this great task after seizing political power and after abolishing the competitive system upon the basis of which irreconcilably hostile relations have developed between individual enterprise, industry, and economic units. The complete economic and political unification of all civilized nations will be the chief task of the socialist reconstruction of the present-day economic system. In the interest of unifying economically all civilized mankind, in the interest of abolishing state boundaries, customs barriers, and national isolation, the proletariat must resolutely reject all capitalist plans of economic coalitions, which undoubtedly conceal an intention to preserve and consolidate the present-day war alliances. This is sufficient reason why the proletariat should not regard these plans as the "lesser evil," even as compared with the prewar situation in Europe.

PLANS OF ANNEXATION AND THE LIBERATION OF PEOPLES

[After a brief survey of the European situation in the light of the annexation plans of the great European powers, the manifesto continues] :

Confronted with the violations and experiments on the living body of nations which the imperialist cliques are preparing to perform, Social

Democracy advocates the principle of the right of nations to self-determination, a nation's right to determine freely its legal state relationship with other nations. In defending this right, Social Democracy denies that the states of today, based on class division, are either able or willing to carry out this right with respect to any one nation; it hopes, however, to achieve the complete triumph of this principle through the abolition of this type of state, through the seizure of political power by the proletariat. But in the name of this principle, which like all other democratic principles was betrayed by the bourgeoisie which had championed it at one time, Social Democracy protests, today and hereafter, against all attempts in working out conditions of peace to determine the future destiny of peoples against their own will and without their consent; it protests *against all annexations by force, open or covert; against the partitioning and parceling out of national units; against all vassalage between the Great Powers and the weaker nations which are accorded a pseudo-sovereignty; against forceful retention of enslaved nations within the boundaries of the state which enslaves them.*

. . . . Social Democracy cannot admit that the German proletariat wishes to continue the war in order that the German state may keep Alsace-Lorraine which it had annexed against the will of the native population, or that the Russian proletariat wishes to continue the war in order that the Tsar may maintain his rule in Poland . . . . In conformity with the very best traditions of the Second International, Social Democracy proclaims to the proletariat: The premises of a truly national liberation can be created only by the overthrow of the imperialist regime! But since this war will not abolish the bonds which hold the oppressed and the oppressing nations within the boundaries of one state, it is your duty to struggle always and everywhere against national oppression and disfranchisement, to demand a far-reaching democratic autonomy and legal guaranties for the national minorities!

Guaranties of Lasting Peace

[After pointing out that the governments have violated the existing international treaties, the manifesto continues] : The Scheidemanns and the Legiens have sanctioned the violation of Belgium's neutrality and the disregard of the treaties on naval warfare in the same manner as Guesde and Vandervelde did the violation of the neutrality of Greece and the treaty concerning Egypt. This shows that the existing imperialist antagonisms, which have turned the struggle for world domination into a struggle for the establishment of capitalist giant states, are welding together in time of war in iron solidarity—the solidarity of robbery—all national classes that adhere to capitalism, and are thereby eliminating all barriers which are likely to oppose to sheer force any treaties and declarations based on something other than a mere correlation of physical forces. Therefore, the proletariat can perceive in the pacifist plans of developing further the so-called laws of nations neither real guaranties of a lasting peace nor any serious obstacles which might keep the imperialist cliques from pursuing that foreign policy of theirs which is generating new warlike conflicts. Only such means as would directly weaken the dictatorship of the imperialist cliques can check and curb their evil intentions. But this can be attained only through proletarian revolutionary struggle . . . . the disarming of the governments through a *radical democratization* of the military system that would abolish the standing army and establish a national militia—not in that crippled form which is adjusted so as to benefit the reciprocal struggles of capitalist states, so as to subject the militia to the dictatorship of the plutocratic cliques and preserve its nature as an army organization based on a caste system, but rather as a system of *actually arming the people,* a system based on democratic guaranties!

It stands to reason that this real democratization of the system of arming the people . . . . can be carried out only in conjunction with a fundamental democratization of the state itself . . . . , i.e., only as the immediate result of a proletarian class struggle for state power. This is the only basis . . . . upon which can be attained the real abolition of secret diplomacy and the real subordination of all treaties regulating international relations to the control of people's representatives. . . . . The proletariat can prepare real guaranties for the abolition of wars and their causes only in the measure that it fuses itself—more so than heretofore—into an international political power, frees itself from the vestiges of national restrictions, and refuses to subordinate its general interests to national solidarity and the so-called defense of the fatherland. . . . .

The revolutionary will and the revolutionary class-consciousness of the proletariat will be the real and the only possible peace guaranties. The war fury incessantly aroused by the imperialist forces can be stopped only by an internationally united proletarian class which struggles continually for power and replies to every new fratricidal command with a revolutionary mobilization of its own forces, the mobilization for the struggle proclaimed in the Stuttgart and the Basel resolutions. . . . .

STRUGGLE FOR PEACE

[Maintaining that the International can exert its influence upon the conditions of peace only if the proletariat succeeds in forcing the ruling classes to conclude peace at a moment which would be unfavorable for them, the authors of the manifesto continue]:

Therefore, the proletariat must regard as harmful and senseless the idea by which the diplomats of official socialism, headed by Huysmans and Vandervelde, are endeavoring to divert the proletariat from the revolutionary struggle against imperialism. The proletariat in every country is advised to pursue the policy of war to the finish .... and at the same time to work out jointly with the proletarians of other countries an ideal "peace program" which will surely be buried by international diplomacy in the waste-basket under all sorts of rubbish .... We, who have remained faithful to the principles of international revolutionary socialism, summon the proletariat of all countries from the road of self-renunciation and capitulation to another road—the road which was indicated by the Zimmerwald manifesto! We summon you: To the road of the resumption of common class struggle against the bourgeois society which is united also in war! To the road of an absolute break with so-called national solidarity, the *union sacrée* and the *Burgfrieden!* To the road of an irreconcilable war against all social forces which are waging this war, prolonging it, exploiting it, and taking advantage of it in order to fortify the unbearable political and social oppression which dominates all Europe, from "freedom-loving" England to Tsarist Russia! To the road of international understanding among the proletarians of all countries concerning the immediate cessation of the war! To the road which leads to the abolition of bourgeois class rule and to social revolution!

.... The new era in the history of the labor movement must open with a struggle for peace, the erection of a proletarian front against the belligerent states. Where the base forces unleashed by capitalism attempt to decide autocratically the destiny of the world, there the voice of human conscience and reason represented by revolutionary socialism—the liberator of the peoples— must cry out loudly:

Down with war! Down with annexations by force!

No indemnities! No economic war coalitions! No Chinese walls between nations! Down with the standing army! Down with secret diplomacy! Hail, peace! Hail, socialism! Hail, international, proletarian, revolutionary class struggle! Proletarians of all countries unite!

CONDEMNATION OF THE FRENCH SOCIALIST PARLIAMENTARY GROUP

[Declaration of the Zimmerwald Left at Kienthal][61]

The undersigned declare:

"As at Zimmerwald we declared it not permissible and a disgrace for German Social Democracy that the German Social Democratic Reichstag deputies of the opposition should merely have abstained from voting war credits, so now we declare the conduct of the minority of the

[61] *Sotsial-Demokrat,* No. 54–55, June 10, 1916, p. 3.

French Parliamentary group which has voted war credits to be *entirely incompatible with socialism and with the struggle against war.*

"This conduct makes all the protests of these deputies against the war and against the civil peace policy nothing but futile platonic statements. It is capable of undermining every confidence in the socialist party among the opposition groups.

"It weakens to an extreme degree the efforts of the internationalist parties to construct an international front for struggle against the World War."

Signatures: Lenin, Zinoviev, Radek, Graber, Guilbeaux, Kaclerović, Bronski, Dąbrowski, Nobs, Platten, Robmann, Münzenberg, Serrati, a German comrade from the town "X," Savelev, Vlasov, Petrova, Peluso, Bobrov.

DECLARATION OF SYMPATHY FOR THE VICTIMS OF PERSECUTION[62]

[Resolution of the Kienthal Conference]

The Second International Socialist Conference sends its greetings and its expression of solidarity and of deepest sympathy to all those faithful and brave champions who, in the midst of the bloody world catastrophe, have upheld the banner of socialism and who, in spite of the civil-peace and conciliation theories, have not recognized a truce in the struggle against capitalism.

At the same time as it greets all these brave fighters for freedom, right, and peace, the Conference gives expression to its burning indignation and its strong protest against the reactionary measures and unheard-of persecutions, the victims of which are our comrades in Germany and Russia, in England and France, and even in neutral Sweden.

The Conference draws the attention of the workers of all countries, on the one hand, to the ruthless raging of the reaction, which stands in such crass contradiction to the legends of a "war for liberation," and likewise to the exemplary and inspiring demonstration of the revolutionary Social Democrats, who struggle as determinedly against social-patriotism—its confusing teachings and their hypocritical advocates—as against the policy of the governments;

It greets the representatives of the socialist women in Germany and France who have been released from captivity and whose imprisonment has only increased their influence upon the masses;

It raises a decided protest against the persecutions of the Jews by

---

[62] "Zweite internationale sozialistische Zimmerwalder Konferenz abgehalten am 24. bis 30. April 1916. Offizieller Verhandlungsbericht," *Beilage zur Berner Tagwacht,* No. 169, July 21, 1916, p. 1.

the Russian government and its accomplice, the "liberal" bourgeoisie, which endeavors, according to its usual system, to make the Jews suffer for the discontent of the population as well as for the military defeats; and

It invites all parties, organizations, and minorities which adhere to the Zimmerwald action, by following the example of the persecuted men and women comrades, to stir up the spirit of discontent and protest in the masses, and to enlighten them in the spirit of international revolutionary Social Democracy, in order that the separate sparks and beacons of revolt may flare up into the powerful flame of a common, active protest of the masses and that the international proletariat, in accordance with its historic mission, may hasten the realization of its task of liberating the peoples and overthrowing capitalism.

RESOLUTIONS OF THE GERMAN *INTERNATIONALE* GROUP

[Adopted March 1916 and Submitted to the Kienthal Conference by the Supporters of the Spartakus Program][63]

I

The new International which must rise again after the collapse of the old one on August 4, 1914, can be born only of the revolutionary class struggle of the proletarian masses in the most important capitalist countries. The existence and activity of the International is not a question of organization, not a question of agreement between a small group of persons acting as representatives of the opposition strata of the workers; it is a question of a mass movement of the proletariat of all countries, the proletariat which is recovering its socialist principles. In distinction to the International which was dissolved on August 4, 1914— which was merely an external institution that maintained weak connections between small groups of party and trade union leaders—the new International, in order to become a real political power, must be rooted in the morale, the capacity for action, and the daily practice of the broadest proletarian masses. The rise of the International will take place from below by the same process and in the same degree as the laboring class in all the belligerent countries, having freed itself from the chains of civil peace and the poisonous influences of its official leaders, throws itself into the revolutionary class struggle. The chief slogan of the struggle must be a systematic mass action for the enforcement of peace. From this action alone the new, vital, and active International can be born.

As a symptom of the fact that the orientation of the socialist circles

[63] *Internationale sozialistische Kommission zu Bern, Bulletin,* No. 4, April 22, 1916, pp. 1–2.

of various countries in the indicated direction has already begun, and that an international unification has become an ever-present requirement for these circles, the conference of the *Internationale* tendency— i.e., the opposition within German Social Democracy which adhered to the "theses"[64] — welcomes the Second International Conference, which has originated in the Zimmerwald gathering, and expects that its manifestations will form a new impulse to hasten the birth of the International from the active will of the proletarian masses.

II

The situation which has developed in Germany after almost two years of war already signifies the bankruptcy of imperialism. The war, from the military point of view, has come to an impasse, so that a purely military settlement appears today more hopeless than at the beginning of this profligate slaughter. The growing high cost of living, which for the broad masses of the people signifies nothing less than actual starvation; the terrific number of dead and crippled, which amounts to millions; the immense financial burden, which now in the form of ever-increasing taxes is thrown upon the laboring people; the purely artificial machinery of industrial life which rests entirely upon war deliveries and which after the cessation of this slaughter will immediately break down; the growing shortage of raw materials as a result of the blockade of Germany; finally, the increasing difficulty of continuing even the extortion system of war loans—all this is a product of the two years of imperialist slaughter and reveals the grisly economic ruin of Germany, as well as of all the other belligerent states—a ruin which here and there is being scantily covered up by the official administration of the war instigators and a mendacious imperialist and servile press. The attitude of the broad strata of the people which these conditions produce both within the country and on the battlefield culminates in a passionate longing for peace and in a growing hatred of the endless slaughter.

The situation described above makes it the duty of the Social Democracy of Germany, as well as of other belligerent countries, to act in the spirit of the resolution of the Stuttgart International Congress and to leave no stone unturned in order to shape this antiwar attitude of the masses into a clear, purposeful, political understanding and into a strong will, capable of action.

For that purpose, the proletarian representatives of Social Democracy, who are serious about casting off the chains of civil peace, are bound:

1. In all belligerent countries to refuse—on the ground of socialist principles—to grant war credits regardless of the military situation.

[64] The theses given above, pp. 394–98.

2. To deny to the belligerent governments all taxes and financial means.

3. To utilize untiringly all the means of the existing political organizations and parliamentary activities, so that by persistently harassing and sharply criticizing the imperialist majorities and their governments they may arouse the masses and encourage them definitely to manifest their will against the war and in favor of the international socialist solidarity.

German Social Democracy, the collapse of which only proved its long existing weakness, must undergo a complete internal change if it is to lead the mass of proletarians on its historic mission.

Its development into an active revolutionary force cannot be attained by mere programs and manifestoes, by mechanical discipline, or by dead organizational forms, but only by the propagation of vital class consciousness and resolute initiative among the masses.

This presupposes the transformation of the bureaucratic system of party and trade union organizations, a system which stifles—in a chaos of official party institutions — the resolution and the strength of the masses; into a democratic system in which the functionaries are the instruments of the masses. In opposition to the betrayal and obstruction which today the party and trade union institutions exercise by their misuse of the slogans of "discipline" and "unity" and by their utilization of the organizational apparatus in order to subject the workers to the interests of the imperialist classes—in opposition to this the clear purposeful socialist will of the proletarian masses must be ruthlessly carried out from below at every opportunity in order to lead the organization back to its vocation—to serve as a spirited weapon of class struggle.

Great emphasis must be laid upon the activity of the youth and also the activity of the women who in war are called to play a particularly significant role in politics. The tendency of the youth movement to achieve an independent existence must be definitely supported.

Propaganda must be conducted, first of all, among the organized workers. But it must strive to go beyond these and to get hold of the unorganized element, which under the influence of the World War has become very favorable recruit material for socialism.

The elucidation of principles, the firmness of the fundamental and tactical attitude, a stubborn waging of the class struggle in the spirit of proletarian internationalism, these are the vital questions of socialism in wartime. A strict separation from all opportunist inclinations, in principle, tactics, and action, is imperative even where these sail under the flag of opposition to the policy of the official institutions.

The very fact of a world war dominates and determines the entire external and internal political and economic situation today.

The policy of the working class must everywhere orient itself according to this fact and oppose World War as the strongest and most detrimental activity of capitalist class domination. The socialist movement must evidence in this opposition its right to existence. Class struggle in wartime gives strength and historic significance to class struggle in peacetime. The former constitutes a most important revolutionary school for the latter. It is the task of the socialist movement during the World War—since it has failed to prevent that war—to utilize the war and the conditions which it has created for the arousing of the masses, in order thus to enforce peace and to hasten a socialist reconstruction of society. Every material and moral support is to be denied to the regime of a state of siege, the neglect of social duties, the usury on victuals, the deception of the people, and the disfranchisement of the masses—the regime of the imperialist war! During the war every taxation, "just" or "unjust," serves the war and its prolongation. The denial of all war taxes and the barring of all financial means is a war commandment against war, a commandment which promotes the undermining of the governmental power in every realm.

An attack must be conducted along this entire front.

The political and social effects of war upon proletarian class interests (the supply of victuals, social politics, system of taxation, the right of assembly, of unions and of the press, the right of free movement, personal freedom, justice, education, etc.) must incessantly be denounced before the masses and be answered by an intensified assertion of the demands of the socialist program. The slogan of the abolition of a standing army must be opposed to the militarism of the World War; the slogans of a republic, of democracy in domestic and foreign policy, the decision of the people as to war or peace, must be opposed to the absolutism of the state of siege.

At every opportunity, both within parliament and without, the state of siege must be broken; the civil peace, the lie about national class solidarity during the war, must be disrupted; the confusing phrase about one's duty to defend one's country must be refuted; the international identity of interests of the proletariat, which has not disappeared because of the war but which has risen to a high degree, must be proclaimed as a political maxim.

The commotions of political and social discontent and indignation must be increased by all possible means of agitation and demonstration.

The aim of all propaganda must be to develop premises for revolutionary mass activities on a large scale, to give mass actions, wherever they originate, a political nature and aim, to drive them forward and to shape them into a conscious opposition against the war and capitalist class domination.

THE KIENTHAL CONFERENCE AND ITS SIGNIFICANCE

[From an Article by Zinoviev][65]

. . . .

2. The Composition of the Conference and Its Political Character

The governments did everything they could to prevent the Conference. In order to draw the attention of the international police to false clues, the organizers of the Conference had had an announcement published that the Conference would take place in Holland, while actually it was held in Switzerland. Nevertheless many delegates were not able to come. Among these were about 10 German delegates, 1 Austrian, 2 Englishmen, 1 Lett, 2 Balkan delegates, and some of the Frenchmen, Scandinavians, etc. The Zimmerwald Left was thus weakened in number. In addition, the social patriots adopted "preventive measures." Huysmans, the secretary of the International Socialist Bureau, went to England and France in order to persuade the local opposition not to go to Zimmerwald. The official parties tried to frighten the representatives of the minority in every way.

Nevertheless the Conference took place. This alone meant considerable success.

Germany was represented by seven delegates. These were representatives of the three main tendencies in the German opposition. One— an adherent of the Zimmerwald Left and of the group which was called the "I.S.D." (International Socialists of Germany)—represented the international movement of the town X (a large center in which a great majority of the entire organization adhered to the point of view of the extreme Left). Furthermore, there were also two representatives of the *Internationale* group (the name of a magazine of which only one number was published, under the editorship of Luxemburg and Mehring). This group even at Zimmerwald had gone with the majority against us. Now these comrades had moved toward the "Left." In Germany the adherents of Haase-Ledebour-Kautsky had *expelled* these comrades from the general opposition groups, in spite of the fact that the adherents of the *Internationale* group had not been guilty of exceptional clearness in their attitude toward "Kautskyism." Before the Conference the *Internationale* group came forward with an appeal in which it proposed to the workers that they stop paying their membership fees to the social chauvinist party Presidium. Under conditions in Germany this meant a decisive step toward a split with the official party. Finally there were present four representatives of the moderate opposition con-

[65] Zinoviev, "Tsimmervald-Kintal," *Sochineniia*, V, 258–73; first published in *Sotsial-Demokrat*, No. 54–55, June 10, 1916, pp. 2–4.

nected with the names of Ledebour-Hoffmann. They called themselves an "opposition *within* the organization," as distinguished from the "schismatics." Their tactics, even now, are as confusing and opportunist as they were at Zimmerwald. They continue to speak against a split. They continue to repudiate the idea of creating a Third International. When Ledebour and Haase finally formed their own parliamentary group, with the active co-operation of Kautsky (as related by Spartakus), the declaration of principles of this group was worked out in a *semi-patriotic* spirit. "We vote against the credits, *because* the boundaries of our fatherland are assured against a foreign invasion"— the declaration[66] read. Quite recently Kautsky wrote that the new social-democratic Reichstag group must work "not against but beside" (*nicht gegeneinander, sondern nebeneinander*)[67] the old group of Südekum. In other words, Kautsky has again and again proposed to make peace with the agents of the bourgeoisie—with Scheidemann, Legien, David, and Co. Kautsky himself did not wish to come to the Conference in spite of the fact that he and Haase had been personally invited. They explained their lack of desire to attend by the fact that they were both (have been!) official representatives of the German party (i.e., of Südekum and Co.) in the International Socialist Bureau, and for that reason their participation in a conference such as this would be "improper."[68] This of course was a mere evasion, since the Italian, Russian, Rumanian, and other delegates to the Zimmerwald Conference have also been previously representatives of their parties in the International Socialist Bureau. In reality Kautsky and Haase wanted a union with the Renaudels, Hyndmans, Vandeveldes, and also with the Scheidemanns far more than with the internationalist elements which rally around Zimmerwald.

The deadening influence of Kautskyism is still pressing strongly on some members of the German opposition. The most important thing is that the attitude of the masses has changed. Discontent is growing everywhere. It is difficult to name any large city in which there has not been a considerable demonstration against the high cost of living, etc. The discontent in the trenches is immense. The masses are becoming

[66] The declaration was read by Deputy Geyer on December 21, 1915, in the Reichstag. (*1. Beilage des Vorwärts,* No. 352, December 22, 1915, p. 1.)

[67] K. Kautsky, "Die Spaltung der Fraktion," *Neue Zeit,* No. 2, April 14, 1916, p. 36.

[68] On this matter Riazanov wrote in *Nashe Slovo,* No. 137 (523), June 14, 1916, p. 1, that it was unfortunate that Zinoviev did not quote either the invitation or the reply which, perhaps, was reported on at a meeting of the I.S.C., and it is this report, presumably, rather than the actual text that Zinoviev recalls. Riazanov adds that neither Kautsky nor Haase was ever a permanent delegate to the I.S.B., nor were they ever appointed delegates by a party congress.

"radicalized." Should war continue till the autumn, great events are inevitable. This is what the representatives of all three tendencies of the German opposition said, and this is contrary to what they had said at Zimmerwald .... To the question put by one Italian delegate as to whether or not a serious mass action, a *practical action* against the war, could be expected at present in Germany, all the delegates answered unanimously and with complete conviction, *Yes*. This did not happen at Zimmerwald. It is the most significant omen of the time that the German delegates, who are all well-balanced and cautious people, spoke in that way. These declarations are among the most important events of the Conference.

Rather unexpectedly for the participants of the Conference, three members of the Chamber of Deputies—Brizon, Raffin-Dugens, and Blanc—came from France. Their arrival at this Conference of the Zimmerwald movement doubtless was an echo of the growing protest of the masses in France against the imperialist slaughter. The three named deputies at that time belonged to the most timid "opposition of His Majesty." They all adhered to the group of Longuet-Pressemane, to the group of the French Kautskyans of the *worst* type. They all, even at that time, repeated the phrases of Kautsky: that the French and the Germans were right when they voted war credits, for the former were threatened with Prussian invasion and the latter with the invasion of the Cossacks. All of them refused to see the deep reasons for the crisis and preached a mutual condonation of the bankrupt social-patriotic parties. They all repeated more or less the social chauvinist phrases about "noble France" which is defending in this war the traditions of revolution, etc. Hearing their speeches one might believe that these people came directly from the camp of the confused social chauvinists. But their conduct after the Conference, their demonstrations in France against the heads of the French "Socialist" party, have been different: these people, who—although very poorly, very inconsistently, and with great vacillation—still reflect the attitude of a considerable strata of democracy and of the workers, who were deceived at the beginning of the war, are at present striving against the war, against the social chauvinist deception. They make unbearable confusion. They have a great many prejudices against consistent internationalism. But the mass movement is pushing them toward Zimmerwald. Even in France, where the position of socialism at present is especially hard, the mass protest becomes stronger, the movement is awakening. In Paris and the provinces the first groups of French workers which consistently defend true internationalism and which adhere to the Zimmerwald Left are being organized. Their task is to take advantage of the developing disintegration among the French social chauvinists.

Italy was represented by seven comrades. This time two tendencies in the Italian parties were definitely indicated. The majority of the delegation belonged to the so-called "left reformists." Whether or not they are in a majority in the party is hard to say. Among the parliamentarians, in the "supreme party institutions," probably yes, but hardly among the socialist workers. This majority adheres to Kautskyism and social patriotism, continues to believe that the courts of arbitration, gradual disarmament, democratic control over the foreign policy, etc., must remain on the program as demands of international Social Democracy. The minority of the delegation (Comrade Serrati, editor of *Avanti*, the Central Organ of the party) approached closer to the Zimmerwald Left and thus defended other tactics.

From Switzerland five persons were present: Platten, Robmann, and Nobs acted as our partisans; the others supported Comrade Grimm.

The Serbian Social Democratic party was represented by the deputy Kaclerović, who adhered—though not in every respect—to the Zimmerwald Left.

Poland was represented by five delegates. Three (Radek, Bronski, Dąbrowski) from the Polish Social Democratic opposition (the Regional Presidium) belonged to the Zimmerwald Left. One delegate (Warski) from the Main Presidium of the Polish Social Democracy also supported the Zimmerwald Left on the question of calling the International Socialist Bureau; one delegate (Lapinski) from the "Levitsa" of the P.P.S. was guided more or less by the opinions of Martov.

The Russian delegation was as follows: from the Central Committee of our party, Lenin, Zinoviev, Petrova (the Lettish Social Democratic party commissioned Zinoviev as its representative). From the Organization Committee, Martov and Axelrod; from the "internationalist" elements of the Socialist Revolutionists, Bobrov and two other delegates.

3. THE SECOND OR THE THIRD INTERNATIONAL

The most important and the most heated question raised at the Conference was that on the attitude to be taken toward the International Socialist (?) Bureau (previously located at Brussels and now transferred to The Hague). This was the most important point on the agenda, because it was in this form, in reality, that the question of the Second or the Third International was to be solved.

The social chauvinists in Germany as well as in France, in Austria as well as in Russia, in England as well as in Belgium, are defending the same complexity of bourgeois ideas. They all stand on the same fundamental position. However, the war has temporarily led them apart in various countries. At the present moment they *still* cannot shake hands and they are hostile to each other.

The so-called Executive Committee of the International Socialist Bureau, as a matter of fact, carries out not the decisions of the international socialist congresses, not the orders of socialism, but the commands of the imperialist bourgeoisie of the Quadruple Alliance. This Executive Committee, i.e., Vandervelde, Huysmans and Co., hand in hand with two or three Dutch social chauvinists, has become an agency of the Anglo-French imperialists.

Nevertheless even at present Huysmans and Co. are attempting to create at The Hague a certain central mediating office for social chauvinists of *both* hostile camps. These two camps cannot yet meet; but even at present they are able to do something, as for instance to carry on a united struggle against the internationalists, to attack Zimmerwald, concertedly and through various general efforts. The appearance of a tacit agreement between the two trusts of chauvinists who have temporarily stopped fighting already exists. Huysmans and his Executive Committee are acting as "honest brokers" (hm! hm!) in this deal.

Look at the convincing facts! Huysmans comes forth with manifestoes and declarations which are with *equal readiness* being reprinted in the *Vienna Arbeiter-Zeitung* (*Victor Adler*), the newspapers of Südekum, the organ of Thomas and Sembat, and the paper of the Russian adherents of Gvozdev (*Nash Golos*). Huysmans has pleased them all equally well—Huysmans, who had made the correct discovery that the London Conference "of the socialists of the Alliance" and the Vienna Conference of the German Südekums defend fundamentally similar "principles." They are all ready to clap their hands for Huysmans, when he on the one hand hints at the possibility of peace with the Right Zimmerwaldists and on the other attacks Zimmerwald and the socialists of those countries in which there is as yet no democracy (a subtle dig at the Russian internationalists)——.

After the Second Zimmerwald Conference Huysmans gave a signal, and without any previous discussion the social chauvinists of France, Sweden, Germany, etc., declared their open protest against Zimmerwald. The French "socialist" Ministers sometimes make faces as if they were displeased by the too rapid "struggle" for peace which Huysmans is leading. But at the same time they fully "recognize" the Bureau at The Hague—thus Huysmans is right when he refers to the fact that he is equally recognized "in Berlin, in Vienna, in Paris and London"—i.e., by the social chauvinists of these world capitals.

They all—Südekum, Renaudel, Plekhanov, as well as Legien—*require* the Bureau at The Hague. The leaders of the entire "honorable" social-chauvinist gang cannot but think of what is going to happen *after* the war. After the war they must "restore" the International of deception, they must give condonation to each other, both trusts *must* join hands for struggle against the socialist workers. That is why the Bureau at The Hague is even now a political focus for the entire struggle between the socialists and the social chauvinists. The Bureau at The Hague is an embryo, a germ of the future "international" holding company for the purpose of deceiving the working class of all countries. Under the slogan "unity" and restoration of the *Second* International this company of augurs will lead a struggle against the internationalists.

Under such conditions to hold on to the Bureau at The Hague, to insist that it meet, means *for us* to help this gang to deceive the workers. The vacillating imperialist Bourderon in France, together with the representative of His Majesty's opposition, Longuet, humbly doff their caps before the "socialist" Ministers, begging them to assist in calling the International Socialist Bureau; but these decline, put on airs, and make it appear that this would endanger the interests of "culture and freedom" which they are supposedly guarding. Sembat, Thomas, and other lackeys of the Russian Tsar and of the French plutocracy "in order to overcharge" swear that "it costs them more," that they can in no wise agree to the calling of the Bureau. *At present* Poincaré and Briand do not allow them to consent, but after a while they will consent. And what will happen then? The same Messrs. Scheidemanns, Eberts, Adlers, Vanderveldes, Renaudels, Brantings, Troelstras, and Co. will have their seats in the International Socialist Bureau. It stands to reason that at such a meeting not a hair of the heads of the French social chauvinists will be touched. The first thing that these people will do will be to begin to strangle the same Bourderon who at present, with an effort which deserves a better fate, endeavors to bring about the calling of the social-chauvinist International Bureau.

Whoever places his hopes in the old International Bureau looks *backward* and is a captive of the international gang of social imperialists —is not capable of a serious struggle against this gang. A split is absolutely necessary, it is inevitable—a split has half become a fact. Only by calling the workers of all countries bravely and openly to break with the traitors and to create their own *Third* International can the honor of socialism be rescued. It stands to reason that the Third International can be born only in the storm and commotion of a *mass movement*. Of course no one conference at present can give more than an ideological-political *preparation* for the Third International. This is what one should prepare for; the direction should be selected definitely and irrevocably.

We had to listen to two kinds of objections to such a way of putting this question: one from the point of view of principle; the other of practice. Both objections in reality lead to the most shabby Kautskyism, i.e., the defense of unity with the social patriots, i.e., the complete delivery of the internationalist movement to the international trust of social chauvinists.

P. B. Axelrod made the most fundamental Kautskyan speech. Since he defended unity with local social chauvinists in Russia, he naturally wished to spread the benefits of this unity over the entire International. He is against a split. He recognizes that the Second International has proved to be inadequate—so have many organizations and tendencies in the present world catastrophe—but he is "against revolutionary up-heavals in the old socialist parties": the masses themselves were patriot-ically inclined at the beginning of the war; the leading organs (the offi-cial bodies of the party) must not be split but be drawn to our own side; we must deal with them as an experienced and attentive physician deals with his dear patient—not a single method of cure should remain untried when surgery is finally resorted to—it is not a matter of some kind of treason; as with an individual at the age of 18 the voice breaks, so with the Second International; the masses should be appealed to; it is neces-sary that the masses demand the calling of the International Socialist Bureau; we must prove there to our lost brothers that they are wrong. (In this spirit Axelrod submitted a sort of resolution; it was not read— the author declared that it was only in the form of an unfinished outline.)

Another group of objections came from "practical" opportunism. Its main representatives at the Conference were the Italian "Left re-formists" and Hoffmann, the representative of the moderate German opposition.

The Italians created a legend that at the meeting of the International Socialist Bureau the Zimmerwaldists would have a majority over the social patriots.

They said, there we will "kill off" Huysmans and Co. by the mere raising of our hands. According to the interpretation of the Italians, the socialists of Japan, of South Africa, of Australia, and even of —— India were to come to the assistance of the Zimmerwaldists.

It was easy for us to destroy this legend by producing some figures. Even if the calculations of the Italians were right, the way they put the question was still naïve. It is not a matter of who has the majority in the Bureau. It is not a matter of getting a majority by a vote of the South African socialist over a party of German social chauvinists a million strong. The question is whether by the mere essence of our points of view we constitute one party, one camp, one International, or whether there are *two* programs, and two irreconcilable programs.

Let it be that way!—they (Hoffmann, Serrati, and others) told us— but still we must not evade battles with social chauvinists in the Inter-national Socialist Bureau; we should go there in order to expose them. We replied to that: we do not at all exclude the possibility of going to the meeting of these people in order to tear the masks from their social chauvinist faces, but at present this question is not on the order of the day. The meeting of the Bureau has not been called by anyone. The question now is whether we should agitate, like Bourderon and Longuet, for the calling of the old International Bureau, or brand this Bureau, expose it, place it in the pillory, explain to the masses the policy of deception of the Messrs. Huysmans, prove to them the inevitability of a split with social chauvinists—and call for a struggle in favor of the Third International.

Two points of view—two tactics! Some think that the Second International has suffered a collapse and that in the fire of the World War the prerequisites of the Third International are being forged—a Third International freed from opportunism and nationalism. Others do not understand the character of the war or the character of the crisis endured by socialism. The entire present epoch seems to them merely an episode which will pass with the war. The old organization headed by the International Socialist Bureau will be restored anew. The lost brothers will regain their reason; "the misunderstandings" will be cleared up, and then "why should we not grant condonation to each other" (the words used by P. Axelrod in the committee)?

Which of these viewpoints had a majority at the Conference? It is not easy to answer this question exactly. A relative majority was more likely on our side, as the following facts show:

Without voting on the fundamentals of the question the Conference chose a Commission of seven persons to work out a resolution. The Commission, however, immediately split into two groups: the adherents of agitation for the calling of the Bureau, and the opponents of such agitation. To the former belonged Lazzari (Italian), Naine (Swiss), Hoffmann, the German delegate from the moderate group, and Axelrod. To the latter—Lenin, Warski (the Main Presidium of the Polish Social Democracy), and the German comrade of the *Internationale* group. As a result *two* draft resolutions were formulated. The draft of the majority is remarkable (it was published in full in No. 54–55 of *Sotsial-Demokrat*).[69] The authors are in favor of calling the Bureau. At the same time they advance such severe conditions, they criticize the social chauvinists so much, that a consistent Kautskyan, like P. B. Axelrod, supports this draft and at the same time does not support it (he supported it only as far as the calling of the Bureau). The authors demanded the dismissal of the Executive Committee, i.e., the expulsion of Huysmans and Co. Moreover, the authors demanded that the "socialist" Ministers, i.e., the leaders of the Second International, be excluded from the party.

[69] Quoted above, p. 428.

All that is not too logical from the point of view of attaining unity, nor is it logical on the whole. Millerand went into the Cabinet alone as a *franc tireur;* but Sembat, Guesde, Thomas, Vandervelde, and Henderson were commissioned *by their parties,* i.e., the social chauvinists. It is impossible to exclude those who were ordered to go without at the same time excluding those *who did the ordering.* This would openly proclaim a split.

What is the result? The logic of events has made everybody except Axelrod, a consistent Kautskyan, propose a practical solution, which *as a matter of fact* will lead to a split with social chauvinists. In it lies the omen of our time.

In the course of debates at the Conference it soon became manifest that the artificial majority of the Commission to which Axelrod belonged only unofficially was *not* backed by the majority of the Conference. Not only we but also Grimm and others pointed to the internal inconsistency of the draft of the majority. They began to look for a compromise. The Pole, Lapinski, proposed a resolution which contained a sharp criticism of the Bureau; but the question of participating in and agitating for a meeting of the Bureau remained open. We demanded a vote on all the resolutions. After our prolonged insistence preliminary voting was carried out. Its results (the only important vote at the Conference) are as follows:

The draft of the majority of the Commission, 10 votes; the draft of the minority of the Commission (of the Lefts) 12 votes; Hoffmann's draft (for the calling), two votes; Lapinski's draft, 15 votes; Serrati's draft (approximately the same as that of the majority of the Commission), 10 votes; Zinoviev's draft (if the International Socialist Bureau be called the Zimmerwaldists must meet for discussion), 19 votes.

After this voting the resolutions were again handed over to the Commission, to which were added two members of the Left (Zinoviev and Nobs). In the Commission we declared that in order to reach a compromise agreement we would not oppose the passing of Lapinski's resolution. As a result of this work, the resolution of Lapinski-Zinoviev-Modigliani was adopted with certain amendments (the Italians demanded, in the form of an ultimatum, the recognition of the right of separate parties to demand the calling of the International Socialist Bureau). One Italian opportunist (Dugoni) voted against this resolution, and Axelrod abstained from voting. The others were in favor.

A median decision came out—a decision which did not facilitate the tactics of Axelrod and Kautsky. *Not everything* has been fundamentally and consistently said; but something has been said. Whoever wishes unity with the social chauvinists and the restoration of the Second International by means of mutual condonation should *not* have voted for such a resolution. It is impossible to say in one breath: you have renounced socialism, you are weapons in the hands of imperialists, you are hostages of the government, you have degraded the banner of the International— and we favor unity with you. The working masses who confide in Zimmerwald will draw their *own* conclusions from such an evaluation of the activity of the main organ of the Second International.

At the Conference the resolution concerning the Bureau was jokingly called *ein Steckbrief* (a warrant for arrest with a detailed description of personal features). This characterization is not devoid of accuracy. The resolution, with all the accepted mitigations, as a matter of fact is an "ace of diamonds"[70] on the backs of all social chauvinists of all countries. It describes in such detail the "pleasant" features of the social-chauvinist capital crime, that the internationalist workers will scarcely have the desire to unite with these criminals. On the other hand, the social chauvinists will also draw their own conclusions. To the milder criticism in the letter of the Presidium of the Swiss party, Huysmans and Co. have replied by excluding the Swiss party from the International Socialist Bureau. What will they now say to the *Steckbrief?*

Had the matter depended only on the diplomats and the "leaders," the accepted resolution might have been in some way or other recalled.[71] But there are still socialist workers. Owing to them, the accepted reso-

---

[70] The allusion is to the Russian practice in former days of sewing on the back of a convict's uniform a piece of red cloth like the ace of diamonds.

[71] In the magazine, *New Life (Neues Leben)*, Comrade Grimm gives the following explanation of the fact that the Conference repudiated the demand to call the International Socialist Bureau. He writes: "Many socialists think that the realization of international action depends only on the activity of the Bureau at The Hague. This is not correct. International action must grow from the depths of the mass movement as such in various countries, and only thus will the fruitful reality of an international central organ become possible. *For that* (!) reason *(aus diesem Grunde)* the Conference has renounced the demand for an immediate calling of the Bureau." [R. Grimm, "Von Zimmerwald bis Kiental," *Neues Leben*, No. 5, May 1916, p. 137.]

This statement of Comrade Grimm does not at all correspond to the actuality. On any ground you wish—but not on "that" ground—did the Conference renounce the demand to call the Bureau. Such a reason was not suggested by *any* delegate.

That no central organ is able to do anything without a movement in the separate countries—this of course is a sacred truth, but here it is beside the point. This truth can also be applied to the central organ which is the International Socialist Committee *at Berne.*

The Conference renounced the demand for calling the International Socialist Bureau because there was no serious majority at the Conference which would dare, under the given circumstances at least, to defend openly an agreement with the International Socialist Chauvinist Bureau and at the same time there was a considerable minority which decisively struggled *against* it. Comrade Grimm would have done better if he had looked the truth straight in the eye and not resorted to diplomatic "explanations dragged in by the hair." [Author's note.]

lution may become a step toward the preparation for a *third* truly social-ist International ——.

4. Against Pacifism

A question next in importance at the Conference was that of the attitude of socialists toward the peace question. . . . .

Zimmerwald took the first step. It said that the "defense of the fatherland" is a slogan by means of which the bourgeoisie and the social chauvinists of all countries have mobilized the masses of the people for the defense of the interests of imperialism—that this slogan is the *greatest lie* of our time. Now the second step must be taken. It is necessary to come forward against pacifism. The imperialist peace concluded by slave-owning governments will tell the masses something about the true character of the present war. The social chauvinists must be prevented from again deceiving the masses.

Everywhere the masses have become tired of war, everywhere with increasing loudness the demand for peace makes itself heard. The social chauvinists reckon with it; they also begin to preach "peace." None other than Mr. Scheidemann came forward with a pamphlet entitled "Hail peace!"[72] It is necessary to explain to the workers that the present slaughter cannot be shortened by one minute except through *a revolutionary struggle*. If you wish for peace, then organize the revolutionary struggle against the imperialist cliques, against the governments of your own "fatherland."

Social pacifism, preached by Kautsky, Haase, Ledebour, and the English social pacifists objectively, is only one of the types of deception of the masses which represent chauvinism in general. The program of "courts of arbitration," gradual disarmament, "democratic peace" is a Philistine, petty-bourgeois utopia which merely diverts the workers from the revolutionary struggle, which only spreads illusions as if peaceful capitalism were possible—capitalism without war, without militarism, without imperialist brigandage.

That is what we said.

Social pacifists *were present* at the Conference. They were among the majority of the Italians; they were among the German adherents of Ledebour; they were among the French (Brizon at first thought that that section of our resolution which spoke against pacifism was a simple misunderstanding, so accustomed was he to identifying socialism with pacifism); they were among the Russian Kautskyans (Axelrod); but nevertheless they *were unable* to advance their draft resolution, were unable to produce any unity of opinion.

[72] P. Scheidemann, *Es lebe der Frieden.*

Formally, the Second International shared the point of view of the social pacifists. Even at the Copenhagen Congress (1910) this great wisdom about "compulsory courts of arbitration," etc., was again repeated. However, it was no longer possible at Kienthal for the social-pacifist elements to "observe the old customs." No more could they give serious battle to the revolutionary socialists. They were compelled to confine themselves to amendments and mitigations.

This time new elements joined the resolution submitted on that question by the Zimmerwald Left: the representative of the Italians, Serrati; the Serb, Kaclerović; the majority of the Swiss. The theses of Grimm were taken as a basis. These theses, though they were incomplete in many respects, still moved in the direction of the Zimmerwald Left resolution. They contained a point *against* the right of nations for self-determination with the usual scientific "proof"—that this demand "cannot be realized," etc. This point was removed upon our making one suggestion. The correction which we submitted to the Commission *in favor* of the right of nations for self-determination as one of the revolutionary demands (see "The proposal of the Central Committee . . . .")[73] was postponed owing to insufficient elucidation of the question.

The theses accepted by the Conference were as a whole directed *against* social pacifism, against Kautskyism. This does not at all signify that Zimmerwald has once and for all done away with the social-pacifist utopias. No; backslidings not only are possible but are inevitable. It suffices to say that though it voted "yes" the Italian majority has proposed "clauses" on all the important points.

Only the Left will conduct systematic propaganda against social pacifism. The resolution accepted by the entire Conference will render us valuable services in this propaganda. It will place these questions for discussion in all the parties as it has already done in the Italian press. This in itself is a long step forward.

The manifesto accepted by the Conference is in our opinion the weakest document of the Conference. It is the result of a compromise with the French. It lacks exactness, clearness. Its best point is the categorical condemnation of the social chauvinists whom it places alongside of the mercenary press and the servants of the governments.

5. WHAT NEXT?

The Second Zimmerwald Conference doubtless represents a *step forward*. The influence of the Left proved to be much greater than at Zimmerwald. The prejudices against the Left have decreased. However, is it possible to say that the die has been cast, that the Zimmer-

[73] Quoted above, pp. 400–407.

waldists have wholly entered upon the road toward a break with official "socialists," that Zimmerwald *has become* the embryo of the Third International? No, this cannot be said with a clear conscience. What can be said is that the *chances* for such a favorable turn of events for the revolutionary socialists are now *greater* than they were at Zimmerwald. But new vacillations, new concessions to social chauvinists—especially after the war, when their masters (the bourgeoisie) will permit them to turn Left only verbally—are very, very possible. No illusions whatever! The Zimmerwaldists have their own large Right wing. Whether or not it will continue to exist no one can guarantee. . . . .

Needless to say, not all the Zimmerwaldists of either the Right or the Left concurred in Zinoviev's opinion of the Kienthal Conference. Socialists of the defensist or patriotic orientation disapproved very thoroughly of Zinoviev's position and perhaps even more thoroughly of those more moderate Zimmerwaldists whom Zinoviev also criticized. One of the most persistent and caustic critics of Zimmerwald was Solomon Grumbach, a member of the French socialist majority and an important contributor under the pen name of "Homo" to *L'Humanité* and to various Right-wing socialist papers in Switzerland. In general Grumbach maintained that socialists were justified in joining in the defense of their fatherland, that the question of responsibility for the war had to be settled, and that the Second International should be restored. His reports on the Zimmerwald and Kienthal conferences were quoted in the German socialist majority press, particularly in *Internationale Korrespondenz;* but the Zimmerwaldists accused him of perverting facts, misrepresenting and deprecating their activities. They paid him off by contemptuous references in their papers: "This is obviously Homo's doing," or "Homo reported this, hence it may be false," and so forth. On June 3, 1916, Grumbach gave a public address in the center of the enemy's camp, in Berne, on "The Error of Zimmerwald-Kienthal." It was a long speech, frequently interrupted by angry outbursts of his opponents, in which he argued that the principles proclaimed at Zimmerwald and Kienthal would lead the proletariat along the wrong road and were contrary to the principles of the Second

International and that the Zimmerwaldists do not agree among themselves in their interpretation of their manifestoes and resolutions. Excerpts from this speech follow.

THE ERROR OF ZIMMERWALD-KIENTHAL

[From a Speech by S. Grumbach at Berne, June 3, 1916][74]

[Grumbach first takes up the question of the right of socialists to defend their fatherland, maintaining that this was sanctioned by the Stuttgart International Congress of 1907. He quotes from Vandervelde's report] : ". . . . the existence of the International is based on the existence of autonomous nationalities. Our federation is not an amorphous mass of individuals; it is a free federation of living nationalities . . . . We must deduce from this principle that *nations like individuals have the right to defend themselves against invasion and against attacks which might threaten their independence.* But with conditions as they are the right of nations to defend themselves presupposes technical organization of national defense. The Commission proposes to say, therefore, that the organization of a national militia constitutes a means of defense of nations and peoples and a real guaranty against the dangers of conquest to which we are exposed by the governments." [This statement, Grumbach maintains, called forth no objections at the Stuttgart Congress.]

[From the right of social democrats to defend their fatherland, Grumbach passes to the question of responsibility for the war, which the Zimmerwaldists refused to consider. He lays the entire blame for the outbreak of the war at the door of the Central Powers, and maintains that certain Zimmerwaldists were inconsistent in their attitude toward the question of responsibility for the war, recalling the text of a proclamation by a member of the Zimmerwald-Kienthal movement—the *Internationale* group—entitled "Who Is Responsible for This War," which was published in *Berner Tagwacht,* October 18, 1915, and which contained the following words: "The responsibility for unleashing this World War rests on the shoulders of German politicians . . . ." Grumbach continues] : Can we suppose even for a moment that the authors of these sentences wrote them without being convinced that this was true? Of course not . . . . The comrades who become so indignant today when socialists consider the question of responsibility to be important either must think that from the socialist point of view the authors of this proclamation deceived the Berlin workers and the entire German people, that they were not worthy Social Democrats . . . . or they must recognize the truth of what was said in the proclamation . . . .

[74] The speech was printed as a pamphlet, *Der Irrtum von Zimmerwald-Kiental.*

[Grumbach cites similar statements from other sources, including the *Berner Tagwacht,* which as he says was edited by a comrade who stood at the head of the Zimmerwald-Kienthal movement, R. Grimm. While agreeing entirely with the *Berner Tagwacht* of February 1, 1916, that "Germany had desired war in July 1914 and had brought it about at that moment, which was favorable for her" and that the assertion that Germany was the victim of an attack was a mere deception of the German people and the entire world, Grumbach continued after Radek's interruption: "You break in open doors"] : It may be superfluous to break in open doors, but not open minds, Comrade Radek—however, I do not mean yours. For, of course, both you and your close friends with your "only-imperialist" magic formula will remain inaccessible to sound, objective, and logical conclusions. This does not surprise me in the least. You will even generously admit: Very well, the formal responsibility— and the word "formal" will be pronounced by you in that sublimely contemptuous tone, which you have at your disposal at any time of the day— very well, the formal responsibility may lie at Germany's door; but what does the statement, that war is an imperialist war and has only imperialist causes, really mean? [Grumbach replies to this question by quoting from the *Vorwärts* of December 16, 1915,[75] and from Kautsky's letter published in *Berner Tagwacht* on April 20, 1916, in which Kautsky wrote that while imperialism was the starting point of the war it did not fully explain it since national, dynastic, and other factors also were involved.]

[After discussing the attitude of German Social Democrats to the question of war aims in general and annexations in particular, Grumbach takes up the question of responsibility of socialists in various countries for the war.]

But for us socialists there is yet *a third question of responsibility,* which has nothing to do either with the German state or with the question of the origin or aim of this war but which is relevant to something which interests us most of all: the Social Democratic party.

I consider this third question of responsibility extremely important. The reply to *this question,* as well as to each of the first two questions, shows why today we cannot measure the actions of various socialist parties by one and the same rule, as is done by Zimmerwald and Kienthal .... At any rate I am deeply convinced that all the parties affiliated with the International have already organized, though secretly, a little tribunal of their own and have already brought up the question: what did the socialist parties of France and Germany do before the war, what sacrifices were they willing to make, what means of struggle did they

---

[75] The article in *Vorwärts* to which Grumbach refers appeared in No. 347, December 17, 1915, p. 2, under the title, "Die diplomatischen Kriegsurkunden."

propose in order to prevent the war? . . . . It is important for us to re-call what road was taken by one or the other section of the International in their struggle against the war; it is important to refresh our memory as to how far their desires were unanimous and at what point deviation occurred. We shall see that the deviation occurred at the point where the French socialists preached revolutionary struggle against the dangers of war. . . . . The slogan of the Zimmerwald-Kienthal conferences can really be expressed in the following demand: "Rather a revolution than a war." This [revolution] is a wonderful word. . . . . But it is not new. We are familiar with it. We heard it *before* the war. It came from France. . . . . While the French socialists demanded that the Interna-tional should adhere openly to a revolutionary basis in struggling against the war . . . . who was it that constantly opposed this demand? The German Social Democracy. . . . .

Regardless of these three questions of responsibility . . . . regardless of the prewar difference between the actions of the socialist parties of France and Germany, regardless of the fact that the revolutionary will of the French socialists was manifest not only on paper but at great gatherings, before thousands and thousands of workers and citizens to whom Vaillant was forever saying, "Plutôt l'insurrection que la guerre!" . . . . regardless of the fact that all this proves the existence of great differences in the degree of responsibility, let it be said that, in the face of the existing facts, formulae are used in the Zimmerwald and Kienthal declarations which make no distinction whatsoever. It is my wish to prove now that many [Zimmerwaldists] did so with a bad conscience; that those who went there [to Zimmerwald and Kienthal] were chiefly concerned with the effect they could produce on the masses; that they would not shrink from resorting to sordid measures in order to attain this end; and, finally, that those who voted in favor of these declarations were by no means of one and the same opinion; that some of them said openly very bad things about each other and expressed various points of view on the most important principle—that of the defense of the fatherland—some of which even coincide completely with the point of view defended by me tonight. Let us begin with a seemingly superficial fact which borders on *falsification of signatures,* and which is very characteristic of the method used to deceive public opinion with regard to the Zimmerwald Conference. . . . . They did not shrink from deliberately printing under the manifesto published on September 18 the words: "For the German delegation," "For the French delegation," "For the Dutch delegation." There was also written in the manifesto in heavy type: "We, the repre-sentatives of the socialist parties, trade unions and their minorities, we German, French, etc." If the word "delegate" does not have the meaning which certain of our outstanding Russian comrades must give it on the basis of their own experiences, namely, that persons delegate themselves, but means what it has always meant—to be delegated legitimately by somebody, to be elected by an organization, appointed, authorized, etc. —then the organizers of the Zimmerwald Conference did not have even the slightest right to use this word in connection with the two "delegations" which they considered most important—the German and the French—and which therefore they placed at the top of the list. I shall waste no time in citing the example of Comrade Roland-Holst, who was permitted to sign "*for* the Dutch delegation," although she herself constituted this entire "delegation"; the "organization" which she actually represented comprised perhaps forty members and at that time had already split and soon thereafter disintegrated; and, finally, Roland-Holst has long since ceased to be a member of the Dutch Social Democratic [Labor] party. . . . . Were the socialist parties of Germany and France really represented? The official report of the proceedings furnished the reply to this question: No. Not one of the "delegates" had the right to call himself the delegate of German Social Democracy or of the Socialist party of France. Were even the minorities fully represented? By no means. Or perhaps the trade unions? Whoever knows the truth is astounded by the levity with which such a sentence was written and by the attempt at deception. But the innocent worker and reader, who does not weigh every word, must have received the impression, of course, ... that the parties and trade unions of Germany and France were represented at Zimmerwald.

[Grumbach then criticizes paragraph 2 of the official report on the delegations to Zimmerwald] :[76]

"Members" of the party: this is the majority. Lie No. 1. Comrade Bourderon was present. He was a member of the party, it is true, but his previous activity gave him no right whatsoever to call himself a "representative" of the party. As secretary of the Coopers' Union he could rather have claimed the right of a syndicalist. There was no other member of the Socialist party present at the Conference besides Bourderon, who came entirely on his own responsibility.

The second delegate, Merrheim, has belonged neither to the French Socialist party nor to the Socialist International. . . . . In reality [according to the statement in the report] Merrheim combined in his person a "member" of the *Confédération générale du travail*, the official delegate

---

[76] The paragraph to which Grumbach refers is as follows: "*France:* Here, too, it was necessary to refrain from inviting the official party which had been drawn into channels of governmental policy. Nevertheless some members of the party and of the C.G.T. were present. The Federation of Metal Workers sent official delegates, as did the minority of the C.G.T." (*Internationale sozialistische Kommission zu Bern, Bulletin*, No. 1, September 21, 1915, p. 5.)

of the Union of Metal Workers, and the official delegate of the minority of the C.G.T. . . . . Nor did the chairman of the Zimmerwald Conference, who was also elected as Secretary of the so-called International Socialist Committee, have any right, be it from delusions of grandeur, from enthusiasm, or from intentional denial of facts, to write in his article, which he published in *Berner Tagwacht* on September 20, 1915: "The international conference at Zimmerwald means more than the congresses of the former International. This was not a mere gathering; this was a union on the basis of identical points of view, identical ideas, and identical proletarian aims—the beginning of a new epoch in the proletarian development." He had no right to write this, for he knew that as early as the first conference fundamentally different points of view had clashed, that at certain moments the discussions had assumed a vehemence which threatened to break up the conference; he knew that there were two groups which sharply opposed each other; he knew that one "delegation" had threatened to withdraw from the conference if certain proposals made by the other side were adopted; he knew that this other side had lodged formal protest against this "ultimatum"; in brief, he was well informed about all the differences and difficulties which had arisen, although all those present were inspired by one and the same wish: to do something for peace. But in spite of all this he spoke of the "unanimous adoption" of the manifesto . . . . This I call deception of public opinion in the worst sense of the word . . . .

A more "reserved" attitude was adopted after the Kienthal Conference . . . . This time they were cautious enough to affix a simple signature to the manifesto: "The Second International Socialist Zimmerwald Conference." But immediately after this there follows a list of the *"organizations* which had adhered to the Zimmerwald action" . . . . Among the "organizations" listed there are also "various groups of the opposition minority of the German Social Democracy" . . . . but the group which in my opinion is most important for the International's future—the Haase-Bernstein-Kautsky group—was absent . . . .

[Referring to the attitude of the French minority the speaker asked]: Do I exaggerate if I say that the French minority rejects national defense just as little as does the French majority? Do I exaggerate if I add that Kienthal has no right to claim the support of this French minority, in spite of Brizon's presence at Kienthal and in spite of the struggle for peace, which the French opposition believes it must lead?[77]

. . . . If there is anything that provides a vital proof of the impropriety of the tactics proclaimed at Zimmerwald-Kienthal, it is the profound and for the time being unbridgeable differences which exist between the French opposition and you at Zimmerwald-Kienthal, in spite of the fact

---

[77] For Brizon's conduct at Kienthal, see above, pp. 409–10.

that your last manifesto was drafted by a member of this French opposition.

In reality the French party minority does not advocate a point of view different from that of the leading group of the German opposition—the minority of the Social Democratic group in the Reichstag.

[Grumbach then challenges Ledebour's right to demand, together with the other Zimmerwaldists, that the French minority socialists vote against war credits when he himself declared (as reported in the Chemnitz *Volksstimme,* September 21, 1915) that he would offer his support to the German government if the Russians approached the Oder. When the German armies had driven the Russians out of East Prussia it was easy for Ledebour and the others to oppose war credits. Then with biting sarcasm Grumbach recalls the declaration made by the "twenty" in the Reichstag on December 21, 1915, which said: "The frontiers of our country and our independence are assured; we are not threatened with an invasion of hostile armies." The speaker then emphasized his main thesis that the situation of the French Socialists is very different from that of the German Social Democrats]:

It is beyond your power, Comrades from Zimmerwald, either to overcome this difficulty or to alter it. Therefore, I reiterate: Your wish to restore the International as quickly as possible may be very ardent, your conviction that the parties of various countries are betraying the cause of socialism may be very profound and honest, but you cannot demand that socialists everywhere use one and the same method regardless of the past and the present . . . .

[The speaker then criticizes the Swiss Social Democrats for their resolution at the Aarau Congress that peace can be secured only through revolutionary action of the proletariat and for their failure to rescind the decisions of their party at Olten in 1906 which favored the establishment of a national army for defense]:

It is a very cheap and, under the existing circumstances, a criminal game to demand revolutionary action from those who are in the midst of a bloody struggle and at the same time to act according to different principles at home, in a country which fortunately has been spared the horrors of war. This was done for example by the Swiss Comrade *Grimm, the Chairman of the Zimmerwald and Kienthal conferences;* for like all his colleagues he had voted in favor of mobilization credits, which were demanded by the Swiss government; like all the rest Grimm has given his patriotic blessings to the election of General Wille . . . .

[Grumbach next calls attention to the differences of opinion among the Zimmerwaldists]:

There were comrades [at Zimmerwald and Kienthal] who would have been satisfied and happy if the old International had been resurrected and others who were concerned only with the establishment of an entirely new, third, International, completely different from the old one. There were comrades who consider today as they did yesterday such demands as courts of arbitration, disarmament, etc., to be self-evident, and others who believe that these demands are misleading and harmful utopias which should be counteracted. These "others" had a majority at Kienthal; they took immediate advantage of this situation to overthrow the entire former program of the International, at least on the battlefield of resolutions, and to replace it by an idea so exceptionally original for socialists, that only socialism can establish the premises to a lasting peace. . . . . [Grumbach adds that this discovery helps to solve this problem about as much as the well-known assumption that two times two is four helps the mathematicians to solve a complicated problem of higher algebra.]

There are comrades like *Lenin,* who in spite of his absolute hostility toward bourgeois society in general and . . . . his profound mistrust of all political reforms which might be introduced in the existing social order, still believes in the *right of nations to self-determination* within the existing states and therefore demands this right of self-determination . . . . [whereas Radek rejects this right together with the majority socialists like Lensch and Cunow].

[In reply to Radek's interruption: "But you are praising Lenin!" Grumbach says] :

How little you understand me, Comrade Radek. I praise Lenin, so you shout. How can you think that I should have the presumption to praise Lenin—the only ruler of the Russian Bolsheviks! Lenin is neither being praised nor censured! Facts about Lenin are merely established in the same manner as a well-intentioned citizen treats the actions of his Emperor or as a scientist treats the phenomena of nature. At the risk of offering you a weapon against Lenin, I shall just the same state that in this exceptional case [the question of self-determination] Lenin, it seems, has permitted sound political reasoning, which you consider to be so unsocialistic and so objectionable, to triumph. . . . .

[As further evidence of these differences the speaker calls attention to the criticism by the Dutch Tribunists of Trotsky's formulation of peace terms in his *Der Krieg und die Internationale.* He notes how in the pamphlet, *Die Krise und die Aufgaben der internationalen Sozial-demokratie*] the Zimmerwaldist Axelrod reproaches the Zimmerwaldist Lenin with trying to transplant "truly Russian methods," which cause confusion and schism in the intra-party struggles of [Western] Europe, with "branding almost all the known and proved leaders of international Social Democracy indiscriminately as traitors and turncoats of the bourgeois camp, declaring that comrades whose international feelings and conscience are beyond every suspicion are national-liberal chauvinists, Philistines, traitors, and so forth." This is written on page 21 and demonstrates to even the most ignorant reader the more or less sharp conflicts existing between the two outstanding members of the Zimmerwald-Kienthal action . . . . What is Axelrod's attitude toward the question of national defense? We read on page 7 of his pamphlet: "the 'duty' to defend the fatherland from foreign enemy attack has been declared long ago by the socialist parties as something which is self-evident." He repeats on page 8 "that the fundamental point of view of the socialist parties in the question of defense of the fatherland does not contradict in the least the previously generally accepted ideology." Comrade Axelrod has gone to Kienthal; he has approved the decisions which were adopted there, decisions which were essentially different from those of Zimmerwald. With all the profound respect which I have for Axelrod, I must say that I do not understand how he could do this.

As I have previously mentioned, Comrade Leo Trotsky adhered to Zimmerwald-Kienthal; there are few who have attacked the French party as severely as has Trotsky because of the party's position in this war and its practical application of the principle of national defense. But it was Trotsky just the same who wrote in his pamphlet on the war and the International sentences which form the best imaginable explanation for the attitude of the French socialists (*Interruption: "You pick out sentences from their general context"*) . . . . Naturally, "I am picking out" sentences. Should I, perhaps, read the entire pamphlet to you? . . . . He [Trotsky] scoffs at wars of defense, but his eye, unobscured by the realities, made him write on page 14: "Only one who shuts his eyes does not see that the policy of Junkerdom demanded the annihilation of France. France—is the enemy!" . . . . and on page 22 the sentence, which at one time was reprinted by *Berner Tagwacht* with the remark that "Comrade Trotsky is right in saying that": "The victory of Germany over France—a regrettable strategic necessity according to the estimate of German Social Democracy—would signify the victory of the feudal-monarchist regime over the democratic-republican regime rather than the defeat of a standing army in the regime of republican democracy."

Are these sentences clear? Could I have falsified their meaning by picking them out? No, no! If words are to mean anything, if they mean as much as they imply . . . . then they indicate that Comrade Trotsky, the Zimmerwaldist, who in this capacity refuses to examine the question of responsibility, to distinguish between the wars of aggression and of defense, and who pours out caustic criticism on all who do not agree with him, knows very well that the destruction of France was the aim of the Prussian Junkers, knows very well that France was attacked, that

she defends herself, ... that *now it became her task to protect her territory and her independence"* [p. 19 of Trotsky's pamphlet]. . . . .
[After analyzing Rakovsky's pamphlet, *Les Socialistes et la guerre,* and charging the author with a similar lack of logic, Grumbach continues] : Lenin and Zinoviev make it easier for themselves than does Rakovsky; both of them represented the Russian Bolsheviks at Zimmerwald and Kienthal. In speaking of them we deal with the Grand Inquisitors of the International, who fortunately lack the power of carrying out their ideas, for otherwise Europe would have known many more funeral pyres and quite a few of us would have been seared over a slow fire to the accompaniment of Leninist hymns on the "only true Leninist socialism" and would have been thrown into the hell of socialist traitors as lost filthy-bourgeois-chauvinist-nationalist-social-patriotic souls. And, with all that, Lenin is a kind-hearted person, a fact which he proved in the pamphlet dealing with socialism and the war which he and Zinoviev published in 1915. On page 4 of the chapter on wars of defense and of aggression he wrote : "If for instance tomorrow Morocco should declare war on France, India on England, Persia and China on Russia, these would be legitimate wars of defense, regardless of who began the war." Here madness turns into a method ! . . . . [After an interruption by Zinoviev, Grumbach continues] : You live in a world of arbitrary constructions and revolutionary illusions; this provides you with an external security, complete freedom from all inhibiting scruples—but in the long run this condition can only bring disillusionment, which would be most detrimental to the movement as a whole. Do you wish to have a proof of the illusions which Lenin, the uncontested leader of an important Zimmerwald-Kienthal tendency, maintains with regard to certain very important matters? Take the international Marxists' review which is called *Vorbote,* No. 1, of January 1916, and read the following statement in Lenin's article on the collapse of the Second International: "The facts, however, prove that in 1915, precisely because of the crisis created by the war, *revolutionary ferment is growing in the masses,* strikes and political demonstrations increase in Russia, strikes in Italy and England, *hunger and political demonstrations in Germany. What else can this be than the beginning of revolutionary mass struggles?"*
This question reveals the whole Lenin, together with the spectacles through which he looks at everything. The hunger demonstrations in Germany are supposed to be the beginning of revolutionary mass struggles! He actually dared to write this ! . . . . Does Lenin expect to aid the cause of international socialism, the cause of an early peace—which, as a matter of fact, does not interest him at all—by spreading these illusions ? . . . .

Lenin and his friends have played an important role at Zimmerwald and a *decisive* role at Kienthal; the significance of the decisions adopted there should be estimated accordingly.

With regard to these decisions I must say that a number of parties which have officially approved Zimmerwald do not act in its spirit. As my first example I have mentioned Switzerland, not merely out of courtesy, but because Switzerland was the cradle and the midwife of Zimmerwald-Kienthal. Now I shall give other examples which are actually even more important . . . . [Grumbach then points out that although the British I.L.P. has subscribed to Zimmerwald, MacDonald, "the most popular English socialist," has never repudiated national defense but actually wrote to the French socialists endorsing the defense of a country attacked. Neither have the American socialist parties also included in the Zimmerwald-Kienthal list ever repudiated national defense but, on the contrary, have approved it and further have advocated gradual disarmament and an international court of arbitration, policies denounced at Kienthal. He continues] : Well, then, I ask you, who took part in the adoption of these decisions and who are now present here? How are you connected with the American Socialist party which sent you a telegram of approval? (*Interruption. Radek: "By cable!"*)

Right you are, by cable, but this cable does not lead to your theoretical navel. (*Stormy cheers.*)

Who is it then that actually agrees with the Zimmerwald-Kienthal resolutions? [Grumbach enumerates sarcastically all the Russian groups] and even as far as these are concerned, scholars would question the existence of a complete agreement between them. . . . .

[The speaker then discusses in detail the differences and controversies dividing the various groups of the German opposition which adhered to Zimmerwald, and he concludes that Liebknecht's opposition to national defense was displayed, not because he was opposed to that policy in principle, but because he believed Germany was responsible for the war.]

. . . . Whoever says that the French socialists should adopt the same attitude as the German opposition, in order perhaps to facilitate the propaganda of this opposition in its country, misunderstands not only the duties of the German opposition but demands also, however unintentionally, from the French that they help imperial militarist Germany to assure to herself a most favorable outcome of the war and, moreover, *on the tomb of the principles which have so far been proclaimed by the Socialist International with regard to wars of defense and aggression.* It is really criminal under conditions as they are for *the Chairman of Zimmerwald-Kienthal* to make in *Berner Tagwacht* for February 1916 the atrocious statement that there is nothing to choose between having Vandervelde lecture in Western Switzerland or saying a mass for Wilhelm II in one of the Zürich churches . . . .

Never will you establish either now or in the future that an attacked country should not defend itself . . . .

. You, from the Zimmerwald-Kienthal Left, believe that the formula, "there can be no national defense for socialists," is the last word. But I am convinced that if governments should plan to provoke another war they would much more likely refrain from carrying out their plan if they knew that all the forces of the Socialist International as a whole would turn against them. . . . .

The [socialist] *action must have a dual aim: the highest and most sublime aim, the prevention of war by every means which is at the disposal of the proletariat;* and the aim of self-defense, which we must not forget in case war breaks out notwithstanding—*the concentration of all forces of the International against that government which has brought about the outbreak of the war.* This is the only basis upon which the International's vitality can be preserved . . . .

[Grumbach dwells on Jaurès' attitude toward national defense] : We shall remain faithful to Jaurès if we say today: *the demand for a simple repudiation of national defense cannot be carried out; it is utopian and therefore unsocialistic.* The *chief error* committed at *Zimmerwald-Kienthal* consists in this, that the manifestoes and the fundamental decisions adopted there *cannot be carried out in practice* . . . .

We do not need a new International with the sign on it : "All national defense prohibited here! No exceptions made! Traitors beware!" We do not need fundamentally new decisions on this question; quite the contrary! But the old decisions must be purged of certain obscurities; and above all, their spirit must be new, a spirit which is resolved to act, which sees all the possibilities and knows all the consequences, a supernational spirit, which provides the best guaranty for the preservation of the independence of all nations. Instead of rocking ourselves to sleep with the words, "We are alien to national defense," we should be inspired . . . . with the recognition that the outbreak of a new war will bring about once more the collapse of the International unless the rights of the socialists of the country attacked and the duties of the socialists of the attacking country are as clearly and as definitely outlined as I have outlined them tonight . . . .

. . . . As the largest political and internationally organized party, we must have slogans which will make us neither the plaything of events nor victims of continuous disillusionment but will enable us to act in conformity with our decisions and with the spirit of democratic socialism. Only then shall we be able to overcome in the future the most difficult crises!

C. Activities of the International Socialist Committee, May 1916—March 1917

As has been said, the Kienthal Conference did not discuss the attitude to be adopted toward the conference of socialists of the neutral countries planned by the International Socialist Bureau to meet at The Hague but referred this matter to the Enlarged International Socialist Committee which met on May 2 at Berne. The official announcement of this conference of neutrals was included by the International Socialist Bureau in its May Day manifesto, in which it was maintained that the affiliated parties, by their resolutions at the Copenhagen, London, and Vienna conferences of the preceding year, had proved their fidelity to the principles of the Second International. As to the Zimmerwald action the manifesto declared that "impatient comrades have not hesitated to ignore the parties, as at present constituted, and have attempted to introduce into the International those methods of dissolution which have been too characteristic of the socialist movement in certain countries where democracy has yet to be established. At first they modestly described themselves as organs of the minorities and protested that they had no wish to usurp the place of the International Socialist Bureau. Recently, however, they have become more frank. They proclaimed[78] on their own authority the end of the Second International and announced the birth of a Third International, in which, however, the parties of the great nations without which no International is possible have refused to take their places . . . ." The reply of the Executive Committee to the Zimmerwald action that the "Executive Committee is and must remain the connecting link between the various parties" was based this time on the support which it claimed it had from the French and British minorities which were opposed to a party split and were in favor of an immediate meeting of the Bureau. Further, on the basis of its interchanges with various parties

---

[78] The allusion is to the circular of the February meeting of the Enlarged International Socialist Committee given below, pp. 471–73.

the Executive Committee asked that "all affiliated parties, without exception .... examine with as little delay as possible, the whole of the political problems which in their opinion ought to find a solution in the terms of peace."[79]

Before taking up the action of the International Socialist Committee toward The Hague Conference it will be convenient to say something about the Conference itself. This Conference met July 31—August 2, with the following delegates present: Troelstra, Albarda, Van Kol, Wibaut, Vliegen, Van Zutphen, Fimmen, and Bruns from Holland; Repetto from Argentina; Branting from Sweden; Stauning from Denmark; and Algernon Lee from the United States.[80] Lenin tried unsuccessfully through Kollontai to have the Norwegians send to The Hague a delegate who would present the point of view of the Zimmerwald Left. Kollontai proposed Tranmael, editor of *Ny Tid;* but no Norwegian was able to attend. The Swedish Youth League, the Dutch Marxists, the Swiss, and the Rumanians, who might have represented the Left, were for various causes unable to be present.[81] Thus it turned out that the members of the Conference represented the majority or Right-wing elements of their parties. Under these circumstances it was quite natural that the Conference approved the policy of the Executive Committee of the I.S.B. in not attempting to call a plenary session of the Bureau so long as one or more parties refused to participate.

---

[79] "Manifesto from the International," *Labour Leader,* No. 21, May 25, 1916, p. 7. The Presidium of the Italian Socialist party discussed the 'manifesto on May 22 and in a letter reproached the I.S.B. for misrepresenting the aims of the Zimmerwald movement, for attempting to justify the attitude of the majority socialists of Germany, Austria, France, and Great Britain, for rousing false hopes that the governments would change their policies to avoid future conflicts and thus increasing the difficulties of resuming international relations. It urged that a plenary session of the I.S.B. be called instead of the proposed conference but asserted that the Italian Socialist party had the right to go to The Hague Conference, since it was immune to the nationalist hatred of the Italian ruling class. Full text in *Berner Tagwacht,* No. 136, June 13, 1916, p. 1.

[80] "A la conférence des partis socialistes des pays neutres," *L'Humanité,* No. 4499, August 11, 1916, p. 1.

[81] Lenin, *Sochineniia,* XXIX, 245, 266–67, and note 3; *Berner Tagwacht,* No. 186, August 10, 1916, pp. 1–2.

The delegates felt that Huysmans should continue to act as a center for indirect relations until the resumption of direct relations became practicable. But it was emphasized that the longer the socialist parties of the belligerent states deferred action on peace and peace terms, the less they would be able to influence the settlement when it came. Resolutions were adopted confirming the socialist peace program as set forth at the international congresses before the war and advocating that Belgium and Serbia be restored and Poland be granted autonomy, and that free trade be established as a preparatory step toward a world socialist state.[82]

The meeting of the Enlarged International Socialist Committee on May 2 was attended by one representative from each of the organizations which participated in the Kienthal Conference. They considered certain administrative matters, authenticated the Kienthal resolutions, and discussed questions of parliamentary action and the forthcoming conference at The Hague. On the latter question two points of view were very tenaciously upheld. Martov, according to Zinoviev, favored participation and thought this course should be recommended to the Zimmerwald groups in neutral countries on the ground that no opportunity should be missed to expose to the workers the causes of the failure of the I.S.B. Zinoviev, who opposed participation on the ground that nothing would be accomplished but to confuse and mislead the workers, moved that the matter of attending be left to the parties themselves. As there were five votes for each motion, the Enlarged I.S.C. made no recommendation except to declare that if delegates of affiliated parties went to The Hague, they were duty bound to act in conformity with the resolutions of the Second Zimmerwald Conference.[83]

[82] A. Lee, "The Neutral Socialist Conference," *The Call* (London), No. 22, September 7, 1916, p. 5. Cf. also *Labour Leader*, No. 34, August 24, 1916, p. 5; *The Call* (London), No. 19, August 17, 1916, p. 3; and *L'Humanité*, Nos. 4499–5002, August 11–14, 1916, where texts of the speeches and resolutions are given.

[83] Zinoviev, "Tsimmervald-Kintal," *Sochineniia*, V, 272–73; "Zweite internationale sozialistische Zimmerwalder Konferenz abgehalten am 24. bis 30. April 1916. Offizieller Verhandlungsbericht, 4. Die erweiterte I.S.K.," *Beilage zur Berner Tagwacht*, No. 169, July 21, 1916, p. 1.

During the spring and summer of 1916 several persons identified with the Zimmerwald movement were arrested and imprisoned. On May 1 the I.S.C. issued a proclamation of protest against the arrest of Höglund, Heden, and Oljelund on charges of high treason which were based on their advocacy of a general strike against Sweden's military preparations. "The struggle of our Swedish brothers," said the proclamation, "is a part of our general international struggle; their aims are none other than those stated in the resolutions of the International and those confirmed in the Zimmerwald manifesto. Therefore we urge all organizations affiliated with the International Socialist Committee to take a stand with regard to Swedish events in the press and at private and open meetings, to point out this ignominious persecution to the entire civilized world, and to express to the Swedish workers, who are ready to give their hearts' blood in the struggle for peace and the proletarian aims, the *inviolable solidarity of the socialists of all countries!*"[84]

Two months later, on July 1, 1916, the International Socialist Committee issued another proclamation of protest against the arrest of Liebknecht for his part in the May 1 demonstration on the Potsdammerplatz in Berlin, and against the imprisonment of Rakovsky by the Rumanian government. The I.S.C. urged the workers: "Come out and protest! Forward for the fight, which alone creates the International of strength and deeds!"[85]

The peace moves of December 1916 (the proposals of the Central Powers of December 12, the Entente reply, and Wilson's invitation of December 18 to the belligerents to state their peace terms) were the occasion of an appeal to the workers to turn their weapons "against the internal enemy in every country" as the only means of forcing the governments to make peace. This appeal, with its denunciation of the official peace moves, is given below.

[84] Full text in *Berner Tagwacht*, No. 110, May 10, 1916, p. 1. The Swedish arrests are discussed further in chapter vi, p. 559, below.

[85] Full text in *Berner Tagwacht*, No. 153, July 3, 1916, p. 1.

A plan to call a conference of Entente socialists led to another meeting of the Enlarged International Socialist Committee. On August 7, 1916, the National Council of the French Socialist party decided by a vote of 1,937 against 2, with 997 not voting,[86] to sponsor a meeting of Entente socialists "in order to consider the question of common action with a view to focussing opinion 'during the war and after the war' against the spirit of conquest and annexation, in favor of establishment of international agreements for the maintenance of peace, and an economic policy which should not be based on exploitation nor contain within it the germs of future conflict."[87] On the basis of this proposal, which had the assent of the Executive Committee of the International Socialist Bureau, the French Socialist party invited the socialists of Entente countries to select delegates according to the rules established by the I.S.B. for international congresses and to meet in Paris in March 1917.[88]

The Bolshevik Central Committee of the R.S.D.L. party declined the invitation and denounced the conference in a statement already quoted.[89] The Enlarged International Socialist Committee met at Olten, February 1, 1917, to consider this matter of the French proposal. Since, however, in addition to the members of the I.S.C. proper there were present at Olten only representatives of the Bolsheviks, the Mensheviks, the Socialist-Revolutionists, and the Polish Socialist party (Levitsa), and Henri Guilbeaux and Willi Münzenberg, the meeting could not act as the Enlarged Committee. Of those present a majority supported the Zimmerwald Left, which may explain the clash with Robert Grimm which enlivened the proceedings.[90] Under the circumstances the meeting, as is

[86] *Pendant la Guerre. Le Parti Socialiste, la Guerre et la Paix* ...., p. 148.

[87] I.L.P., *Report of the Annual Conference 1917*, pp. 9–10. See also *Internationale Korrespondenz*, No. 40, August 18, 1916, p. 296, and No. 55, October 10, 1916, p. 425.

[88] *Internationale Korrespondenz*, No. 61, October 31, 1916, pp. 465–66.

[89] Chapter ii, pp. 254–56, above.

[90] In an ironical account of this meeting, *Internationale Korrespondenz*, No. 91, February 16, 1917, pp. 709–10, says that Zinoviev and Radek appeared as members

shown in the letter of the International Socialist Committee of February 1917,[91] merely noted that all organizations represented had decided against participation in the proposed conference in Paris and summarized the reasons for this decision.

In the end the Paris conference did not meet. Apparently some of the majority socialists feared that the conference would get out of hand and so, with Vandervelde's consent, the French majority proposed to give part of the Italian Socialist party's vote to Mussolini's group and to give one of the four British Socialist party votes to Hyndman's patriotic National Socialist party. This proposal brought on a tempest of protests and accusations, but the final blow came when, a few days before the conference was to meet, the Executive of the British Labour party, which had previously agreed to send ten delegates, rescinded this decision by a small majority.[92]

The outbreak of the revolution in Russia in March 1917 had a tremendous effect on socialist thought and action throughout the world. The International Socialist Committee responded with particular enthusiasm to the news from Petrograd, and at once it began to prepare to move the seat of the committee to Stockholm in order to be nearer the scene of these historic events. Before leaving Berne, however, it issued the appeal to its affiliated parties given below, urging them to "rise and defend the insurrection of the Russian people," since it was "upon the development of the Russian revolution and its spread to the belligerent countries that rest the hopes of mankind."

---

of the Swiss delegation, accused Grimm of treachery to the Swiss party and urged that he be kicked out of the International Socialist Committee. Grimm is said to have replied in kind.

[91] See pp. 471–73.

[92] *Report of the Seventeenth Annual Conference of the Labour Party, 1918*, p. 3; Brand, "British Labor and the International during the Great War," *Journal of Modern History*, No. 1, March 1936, pp. 49–50; Malatesta, *I socialisti italiani durante la guerra*, pp. 132–37.

THE SHAM PEACE MOVES OF THE CAPITALIST GOVERN-MENTS AND THE DUTY OF THE WORKERS TO FIGHT THEIR CLASS ENEMIES

[An Appeal to the Working Class by the International Socialist Committee, December 1916][93]

The third year of war is now a reality. Two and a half years of uninterrupted slaughter, two and a half years of unprecedented destruction and devastation, are not enough. The beast unchained on August 1, 1914, after several years of systematic preparation on the part of all the capitalist governments, is not yet satiated. New streams of blood must still be shed. Still more refined and cruel methods must be devised to slaughter men. Still heavier sacrifices will be made until Europe is completely impoverished and exhausted.

Why? For what reason?

The causes of this self-destruction of peoples were indicated in the manifestoes of *Zimmerwald* and of *Kienthal*. They are: *greediness, desire of the capitalist classes for conquest,* their imperialist lust, and their criminal desire to augment profits in their own as well as in the conquered countries and to procure for themselves new sources of wealth.

This truth cannot be effaced either by diplomatic lies, by the prevarications of statesmen, or by the chauvinist phrases of ignoble exsocialists. This truth has been evidenced and confirmed once more by the events of recent months.

Rumania, whose national glory and esteem were supposed to be increased—in reality she is nothing but a pawn on the chessboard of the great imperialist powers—lies broken on the ground. She underwent the fate of Belgium, Serbia, Montenegro, the fate which tomorrow awaits Greece and other yet neutral states. The miserable farce of the "liberation" of Poland, a country which was not worse off even under the Tsar's whip than under the regime of the Austro-German "liberator," proves how little the military victor thinks of anything but complete robbery and pillage. *The deportation of Belgian and Polish proletarians* for the purpose of putting them at forced labor far from their native lands, the transformation of all the belligerent states into *national penitentiaries,* the ghastly terror against all those who appeal to common sense and reason in order to terminate the horrible massacre, the *prisons overflowing* with the best and most courageous of the fighters of the laboring class—*all these facts constitute so many reasons for indicting the ruling classes, so many proofs of their military lies and of the vile*

[93] *Commission socialiste internationale à Berne, Bulletin,* No. 6, February 18, 1917, pp. 1–2.

motives, greediness, and rapacity which underlie both this war and previous wars.

Today this war is passing through a crisis: *"No victors, no vanquished—or rather all vanquished, all bleeding, all ruined, all exhausted."* The statesmen of belligerent countries, caught in their own traps, dominated by the war, are now staging the *comedy of peace.* Just as in peacetime they play with the menace of war, so during the war they prostitute the idea of peace.

The *Central Powers* have offered to open peace negotiations with their adversaries. But how? By arming themselves to the teeth, by placing their last man under the yoke of organized manslaughter, by acclaiming their victories! *Really, such negotiations are utter buffoonery, conducted for the purpose of hiding the truth from the peoples.* No doubt these peace proposals will be rejected and thus the ferment of national hatred and of chauvinism will be revived.

The reply of the opposing Entente Powers is worthy of the proposition of the Central Powers. The guardians of *the bloody Tsar* feel at ease in the terrible bath of blood in their own country. The *advocates of pogroms prepare for a general European pogrom.* In order to extend their power to Constantinople, to the Straits, and to Prussian Poland, they are ready to sacrifice *to the last man the youth of Europe,* for they have never stopped even at the most disgraceful acts so long as their power could be maintained over the peoples oppressed by Russia.

The renegade Briand seeks by phrases of hatred and contempt to conceal from France the fact that in reality by continuing the war she is spilling her own blood and moving toward destruction and that she is doing this for the Allied Powers. The greatest demagogue of the century, Lloyd George, advances deliberately the false assertion that England is fighting for the complete liberation of the oppressed peoples. *Does he, like his friend Briand, forget that England and France, through their diplomacy and war policy, are bound to Russia's war aims? Do they forget what aspirations England is pursuing in the Orient, in Mesopotamia, and in Asia Minor?*

And what about *the note of the President of the United States?* It cannot lose the character, scarcely disguised, of a war note. Very well, if Wilson wishes peace, America should stop every individual, without any exception, from gaining billions on war deliveries and, with *that,* as proof, appear before the world as an apostle of peace.

Truly, even today the governments do not want peace, because the leaders of the war fear the inevitable *settling of accounts* which must follow, and others find war *profits* more attractive than the highest interests and human rights. There is only one power that can force them to conclude peace: *the awakened force of the international proletariat, the firm will to turn one's weapons not against one's own brothers but against the internal enemy in every country.*

Meanwhile this force is not yet very large. Even endless calamities and terrible blows have not yet opened the eyes of the peoples. However, something is stirring in every nation on earth. There is no country in which the energetic proletariat does not raise the banner of socialism signifying peace and liberty; there is not a state which does not ban these champions from society and persecute them, thus proving that they are feared as the only force in favor of a real and lasting peace.

This struggle of *socialist minorities* against their governments and against social patriotic hirelings must be continued without truce or delay. The duty toward *one's own class, toward the future of mankind, must stand above everything else.* To accomplish this task must be the unbreakable resolve of all workers in the belligerent states as well as in the neutral countries, the *former* by assembling all the forces in every country in order to oppose them to the dominant class, and the *latter* by supporting with all their moral and financial power the struggle of the minorities.

At an hour when the war has come to an impasse;

At an hour when the diplomats' hypocritical gestures of peace will lead only to still more atrocious massacres if the masses do not prove their will for peace at the price of the greatest sacrifices;

At an hour when the phantoms of want and famine have become realities—

Now it is imperative to act with faithfulness and complete devotion in the spirit of revolutionary international socialism in order to secure a prompt ending of war. It is necessary to fight for the Workers' International, the liberator of the peoples.

Hail the class struggle!

Hail peace!

Hail the Workers' International!

THE SOCIALIST INTERNATIONAL COMMITTEE
IN BERNE

ON THE PROPOSED CONFERENCE OF SOCIALISTS OF THE ENTENTE COUNTRIES

[Letter of the International Socialist Committee to Affiliated Groups, February 1917][94]

RESPECTED COMRADES!

The Executive of the Italian party has asked the International Socialist Committee to state its attitude toward the *Conference of the En-*

---

[94] "Die Internationale und der Krieg. Die Entente Konferenz," *Beilage zur Berner Tagwacht*, No. 44, February 21, 1917, p. 1.

tente socialists which the official socialists of France are convening in the middle of March 1917. The International Socialist Committee has recommended to its affiliated organizations that they abstain from attending this conference and has given reasons for this stand. The International Socialist Committee, however, considered it to be useful to summon to a conference the representatives of its affiliated organizations in the Entente countries in order that common conduct might be attained as far as possible. This conference was called on February 1, 1917, at Olten. Unfortunately, representatives living abroad [i.e., outside of Switzerland] were unable to attend this conference; only those delegates of the three Russian socialist parties, who were in Switzerland—the representatives of the National Executive of the Polish Socialist party (the Levitsa) and of the Bund, as well as a representative of *La Vie ouvrière* in Paris, who also resides in Switzerland—came to the conference. The conference could not be held under these circumstances; but between those present there took place a non-binding exchange of opinion, the outcome of which was recorded in the following declaration:

"The informal conference records that external obstacles have interfered with the meeting of the conference called by the International Socialist Committee. The question of taking part in the Entente Conference is settled by merely recording the fact that all organizations here present have *already* expressed themselves as being against participation and have given reasons for their decision."

The reasons offered by the Central Committee of the Russian Social Democratic Labor party have already been published in *Bulletin* No. 6,[95] and the reasons of the other organizations will be published in the following issue of the *Bulletin*.[96] In referring to these declarations we summarize here the motives which have led these organizations to refuse participation in the Entente Conference:

1. The division of the socialist labor movement according to the separation of the imperialist coalitions of powers must be definitely rejected.

2. We have absolutely no confidence in a conference convened by the social patriots, for those who call this conference are tools of bourgeois class governments.

3. Any influencing of the deliberations by the representatives of the Zimmerwald tendency in the spirit of internationalism and revolutionary

95 See above, chapter ii, pp. 254–56.

96 With the removal of the International Socialist Committee to Stockholm after the outbreak of the revolution in Russia, the *Bulletin* was discontinued and hence No. 6 was the last number. The official publication of the I.S.C. in Stockholm was called *Nachrichtendienst,* of which No. 1 appeared May 6, 1917.

class struggle is impossible, because the organizers of the conference have renounced the basis of class struggle and have recognized civil peace.

4. The agenda of the conference intentionally avoids the question of restoring an International which is capable of action and which would fulfill its duty now during the war.

5. Under these circumstances the participation in that conference would mean a step backward and the support of those who have been betraying socialism continuously since the outbreak of the war. Such support would hamper rather than promote the resumption of class struggle.

We ask you to accept this circular on behalf of your organizations.

With party greetings,

THE INTERNATIONAL SOCIALIST COMMITTEE
IN BERNE

THE RUSSIAN REVOLUTION AND THE DUTY OF THE WORLD PROLETARIAT

[Proclamation of the International Socialist Committee, March 20, 1917][97]

The revolution lives!

The revolution which was declared to be dead and buried, and which was considered to be impossible in the present-day states, armed to the teeth, has become overnight a vital reality. The insurrection of the people against the government has been victorious. In spite of being confronted by an external enemy the Russian laboring class has risen in the midst of a terrific war frenzy and at a moment when a revolution is both madness and crime from the point of view of social patriots; it has risen in a death-defying struggle against Tsarism.

The World War, which was intended to stifle the proletarian revolution, has evoked this revolution. Before the diplomats were able even to liquidate the slaughter which they had initiated, the revolutionary consequences of the war set in and the avengers and retaliators rose bravely and determinedly to fight.

The revolution, which was unchained by the war, has spoken its final word in the *Empire of Tsarism*. Above the Taurida Palace a waving red banner welcomed the regiments which had sided with the people. This was the banner of revolutionary socialism, a banner which since the outbreak of the war had been betrayed by many of its former bearers and seemed to have been lowered forever.

This alone has caused a panic among the ruling classes in all countries. With fear they followed the development of Russia's internal situation and are anticipating repercussions in other states. Every day

[97] *Berner Tagwacht,* No. 72, March 26, 1917, p. 1.

brings news which increases the confusion of the ruling classes. The movement which at first appeared to be merely a *coup d'état* of the liberal clique now appears even more clearly to be a struggle of the proletariat and the troops which have sided with the proletariat; this movement was systematically strengthened and incessantly accelerated until it developed from a parliamentary action into an open revolt. It appears now to be a true revolution by the people, and although peculiar national historical conditions have risen it still bears the symptoms of a European revolution such as the peoples of the Continent know from their own experiences.

The Russian bourgeoisie is endeavoring to rob the working class of the victory by adopting revolutionary methods. *A sharp class struggle has already flared up within the movement for freedom in Russia.* The liberal representatives of the bourgeoisie, by relying for support upon the leaders of the war armies, are striving to use the revolution for their own purposes. The people, which has barely freed itself from the bloody yoke of Tsarism, will be placed in a new straitjacket: the so-called bourgeois regime.

The bourgeois press of the Allied countries is instigating the new Russian government to kindle the flame of a bourgeois counter-revolution. Extreme resistance to the demands of the proletariat—this is the slogan which "democratic" France and England are trying to impress upon the recently emerged rulers of new Russia. But the Russian bourgeoisie does not require much coaxing. It is making every effort to check any development of the revolution, to moderate it politically, and to limit its social nature. Only under strong pressure from the laboring class and its allied army detachments, are the bourgeois leaders proceeding to carry out the necessary disarming of the defeated Tsarist reaction. Only under that pressure are they agreeing to a radical democratization of the social order and to struggle against the caste system in the army.

Thus the proletariat, which heads the masses, leads a purposeful socialist struggle against the counter-revolutionary powers and against the moderating tendencies of the new government rulers.

This struggle between the bourgeoisie and the proletariat of Russia is at the same time a struggle between war and peace.

The liberal bourgeoisie has taken over the reins of the old regime in the name of peace, which that regime was unable to provide. It rose to its position with the aid of the French and the English imperialisms. The continuation of war "until victory" means for the liberal bourgeoisie merely a postponement of the paying of its debt to the people, which it incurred during the first days of this war, and also gives it an opportunity to gain the sympathy of the military castes.

The workers and the soldiers, however, have not come out into the streets to conquer more favorable conditions for the bourgeoisie so that the latter may realize its imperialist aims. *"Bread and freedom" was the battle cry of the workers.* Since war has robbed them of both they could not be inspired with the idea of continuing the mass slaughter. War today is the chief obstacle to the realization of the political and the social demands of the peoples, though the realization of these demands was alleged to be a war aim. By its attitude toward this war and the national truce the bourgeoisie is demanding from the proletariat an unconditional recognition of a political and military dictatorship, a blind surrender to the forces which as early as tomorrow will endanger young liberty. For that very reason the socialist vanguard of the Russian proletariat, the majority of which had fought against the war since its outbreak, will transform the struggle in favor of a further development of the revolution into a decisive struggle in favor of peace. *Peace and a republic or war and a counter-revolution! These are the alternatives which reflect the present situation.*

Will revolution kill the war or will war kill the revolution?

The solution of this question depends on the conduct of the European proletariat during these days of a general upheaval.

Amidst raging reaction and the fratricidal war, which goes on in spite of everything, a national revolution runs the danger of being suppressed by the reviving forces of dethroned Tsarism, and by the bourgeoisie rent by internal antagonisms. The ruling classes of all countries are unanimous in their attitude toward the movement of liberation which has now won its first victory in Russia.

The Central Powers and the so-called democracies of the Entente will not miss an opportunity of dealing a deathblow to the Russian revolution. The *Central Powers,* by utilizing the civil war for the purpose of carrying out their plans of conquest in the East on a still larger scale, will promote in Russia the awakening of a new panic of patriotism in order to divert the Russian people from revolutionary domestic tasks and to subject them to the rule of international militarism. In turn *the governments of the Entente* will endeavor by means of diplomatic intrigues, moral pressure, and corruption to bring about a collapse of the revolutionary democracy so as to turn the liberal militarist party in Petersburg into an obedient instrument of the Entente's imperialist ambitions.

The agents of both groups of powers are already preparing a counter-revolution, each in its own way. They enjoy the support of the social patriotic leaders of the proletariat, these humble servants of the ruling classes and of their imperialist policy. The *French, English, and Italian social patriots* are endeavoring to win over the Russian proletariat to civil peace with the bourgeoisie in order thus to assure the continuation of the war. Representatives of the English labor movement demand from the Russian workers an unheard-of concession: the renunciation of class struggle and the mobilization of forces for the so-called defense against Prussian militarism.

Germany appears to be no less shameful. Fearing that revolution may inflict a destructive blow upon civil peace, the German social patriots denounce the Russian revolution. They picture the victorious insurrection of the people as a *coup d'état* desired and carried out for the purpose of continuing and accelerating the war. They terrorize the German workers by telling them that the revolution increases the power of Russian militarism and that this necessitates further endurance on their part. They warn the workers against "infatuation with street riots," against the adoption of revolutionary methods of struggle, and at the same time implore the Bethmanns to prevent the revolutionary spirit from penetrating into Germany by granting reforms such as Buchanan recommended to the Tsar in vain.

Such are the deeds of official socialist parties at a moment of worldwide significance. Some of them act as bodyguards of the Russian monarchy and others as bullies of Anglo-French imperialism; but all of them are in the first lines of the deadly foes of the Russian revolution!

By betraying the Russian revolution the social patriots betray the interests of their own peoples. The shallow hope for an early conclusion of peace through a decisive victory of one or the other coalition of powers has vanished; the anticipation that the exhaustion of one group of powers would mean victory for the other group has disappeared; the pacifist illusions concerning peace mediation by the neutral governments have been dispersed. All hopes that the war would cease early of its own accord have proved to be false. Now, after all these disappointments, the bleeding peoples for the first time behold a ray of light: *The people's revolution, which can kill the war, has raised its head.* It gives back to the broad masses that which no other power on earth has been able to restore to them: a belief in and a hope for the future. What do we experience at this moment? Now after the strongholds of Tsarism have been attacked, now when the German people should also overthrow the power of Prussian absolutism, the social patriots are telling the people that the Russian revolution will be crushed by the intervention of the German armies. It seems that the game of 1870–71 will be repeated. As at that time a republic in the West, so now a democracy in the East will serve as a pretext for the carrying out of forcible conquests and for the threatening of the achievements which a people has gained for itself in a death-defying fight. *The social-patriotic policy really amounts to a tightening of one's own chains of slavery and the endangering of revolutionary achievements in a foreign land.*

Against whom are all these ignominious acts directed? The European proletariat is now confronted with a working class which, in days of a general chauvinist delirium, has broken its shackles; a working class which, amid an insane fratricidal slaughter, has dared to shed its blood for its own cause; which has refused to mold deadly lead into shapes which would pierce the breasts of class comrades in the other war camps; a proletariat which robs the army leaders of their strongest weapons and which, inspired with a legitimate hatred of the oppressors, overthrows the Bastilles in its homeland.

The revolution in Russia has had its origins in the misery, deprivation, and slavery to which the laboring people of the belligerent and the neutral countries are likewise subjected. The Russian proletariat has risen in order to secure for itself bread and freedom. The war has deprived the peoples of all countries of bread and freedom. Neither war nor civil peace can procure these and at the same time protect the peoples from falling into the abyss of utter ruin. Hence, the historic moment has come when the proletariat of all countries is brought face to face with the alternative: to side *either with the war or with the revolution.*

Today more than ever it should be the task of the European proletariat not to side with its own oppressors, not to side with the mass slaughterers. There is only one slogan for the international working class at this historic hour: the defense of the Russian revolution, active struggle of the masses against the war.

In every country this struggle in defense of the Russian revolution is a national struggle of the workers against their own exploiters and against the policy of the latter. The moment has come when the proletarian struggle may consist only in a decisive action in all countries, and primarily in belligerent countries—an action which is directed toward the attainment of the ultimate socialist aims and which disregards all other considerations. *The moment is here when in the name of the social and political liberation of one's own country the proletarian action must become a powerful international struggle against the war.*

The spokesmen for the laboring class who have remained faithful to the International must demand repeatedly from the PARLIAMENTARY TRIBUNE THE SUSPENSION OF HOSTILITIES and the *immediate opening of peace negotiations.* But these parliamentary demonstrations cannot further our struggle by one step unless they are supported in the belligerent and neutral countries by a constant preparedness for mass movements by means of which the revolutionary will of the proletariat may exercise pressure upon the ruling classes. The *working class* of the *neutral countries* must make the Russian revolution its own. In pacifist demonstrations based upon a firm decision to wage a ruthless class struggle, the working class of the neutral countries must help to promote and develop the action of the proletariat in the belligerent countries.

By supporting the Russian revolution and its vanguard, the Russian men and women workers, the proletariat of the belligerent and of the neutral countries must, by developing its own forces to the utmost, fight every attempt of the bourgeois classes and their governments either to suppress or to exploit the revolution. Upon the development of the Russian revolution, upon its spread to the belligerent countries, rest the hopes of mankind which has been tortured and exhausted by the three years of unprecedented war of destruction. *If the world proletariat does not rise, if, above all, the German and Austrian working classes permit the germs—which have originated amidst the stench of blood—of the movement for liberation to be destroyed by the unhampered continuation of the war; if they permit the war which began under the false slogan of struggle against Tsarism, to end with a restoration of the Tsarist rule now defeated by the revolution, this would be an unheard-of sin committed by an entire class against its own destiny. This is no time for hesitation, for passive waiting, for a postponement of the struggle, for political optimism. All the revolutionary energy which the proletariat possesses and which it has kept alive must be transferred into deeds in reply to the cheers of freedom which sound from Russia. No assistance can be rendered to the Russian revolution without a revolutionary struggle.*

Therefore, rise to defend the insurrection of the Russian people! Line up against reaction, against imperialism, against the war, and in favor of immediately suspending hostilities and concluding peace between the peoples. People in towns and fields, workers clad in work shirts and in uniform! Rise in a revolutionary mass struggle to secure for yourselves bread, freedom, and peace! Down with civil peace! Down with the war!

Hail the international action of the proletariat!
Hail the Russian and the international socialist revolution!

THE INTERNATIONAL SOCIALIST COMMITTEE
IN BERNE

CHAPTER VI

TACTICS AND DISSENSIONS OF THE ZIMMERWALD LEFT

The Zimmerwald Left group formed at the Zimmerwald Conference in September 1915 began its activity, Zinoviev tells in his memoirs, with one hundred francs which had been raised by the Russian Bolsheviks. Apparently this group as such never had any considerable amount at its disposal, and its propaganda was for the most part provided for by the individuals or groups accepting the Left position. One of the few publications of the Zimmerwald Left was a leaflet, *Internationales Flugblatt*, No. 1, which contained the draft manifesto and resolution offered at Zimmerwald and a brief introductory statement under the title, "Die Zimmerwalder Linke über die Aufgaben der Arbeiterklasse. Zur Einführung." Later the Dutch Marxist group, which joined the Zimmerwald Left, proposed to issue a periodical called *Vorbote,* in the editing of which various Lefts of other nationalities were to participate. Funds for publication were provided by Roland-Holst and Pannekoek, who were therefore in a position to have the final word on editorial policy. Trotsky and Merrheim declined to serve as contributors. Lenin and Zinoviev agreed to serve on the editorial board, but later withdrew when they found themselves deprived of certain editorial rights which they believed had been promised them. Only two numbers of *Vorbote* appeared.

As has been shown in earlier chapters, Lenin took the initiative in organizing the Left Zimmerwaldists, but he was unable to bring all those who supported the Left position in general to agree with him on certain specific questions. Dissensions broke out among the Russian Bolsheviks and the Poles, Scandinavians, and Dutch on the issues of arming or disarming the people and the right of self-determination, dissensions which were further complicated by the fact that some of the Bolsheviks, the Bukharin-Piatakov group in particular, were opposed to Lenin also on the question of self-determination. By the end of 1916 and the beginning of 1917 Lenin had concluded that the differences between the Zimmerwald Right and Left had become too great for the two wings to remain in the same organization. Events of 1917 aggravated these differences, and the revolutionary internationalists in various countries, despite the controversies among themselves, gradually became organized on the platform originally adopted by the small group of eight persons at the first Zimmerwald Conference.

Matters closely connected with the activities of the Zimmerwald Left have been touched upon in chapters iv and v. The following pages deal with certain general issues confronting the Lefts, the dissensions within the movement, and the efforts of the Lefts to influence the policies and tactics of the socialist and labor movements in Switzerland, the Scandinavian countries, France, and the United States. The gradual transformation of the Zimmerwald Left during 1917–1918 into the Third International is discussed in *The Bolsheviks and World Revolution: Founding of the Third International.*

A. THE TASKS OF THE ZIMMERWALD LEFT

The documents which follow give the program of the new review founded by Roland-Holst and Pannekoek and present Lenin's objection to the revision of the agreement for editorial control. In the third document in this section Lenin shows how the discussions of peace revealed the deep and fundamental differences between the Zimmerwald Right and Left.

THE TASKS OF THE LEFTS IN THE ZIMMERWALD
MOVEMENT

[From the Introduction to *Internationales Flugblatt*, No. 1,
November 1915][1]

[The article begins with a statement of the nature and purpose of
the Zimmerwald Conference. The manifesto of that Conference criticizes the majority socialist parties; but it does not answer the question,
"Why have the majority of the socialist leaders united with capital
against the working class?" There follows an account of the development of opportunism and a labor aristocracy and its effect on the revolutionary movement. "The Zimmerwald Conference did not say with
the necessary clearness what it should have said with regard to the past,
the disgraceful present, and the future," because the majority of the
Conference either did not wish to break with the majority parties or
thought such a break would be premature. The delegates who constituted the Left presented their own drafts of a resolution and manifesto
(which are given above), but these were rejected by the majority. The
Lefts therefore voted for the manifesto which was offered by the majority of the Conference but made a separate declaration in which the Left
position was set forth]:
   . . . . The matter at issue, growing out of the Zimmerwald manifesto and lying within the international limits created at Zimmerwald
upon the basis of the parties affiliated with the Berne Committee, is one
of supporting with all our energy every revolutionary mass action and
of taking up the work of spiritual enlightenment and secret organization. To this end it is necessary first of all to see to it that the broadest
strata of class-conscious workers understand clearly the aims and means
of our struggle during and after the war. We are publishing the resolution and the draft manifesto of the Zimmerwald Left. We invite the
workers to take them as the basis of their discussions, to invite those
who think differently but who oppose social patriotism, to make a clear
presentation of their points of view. The determining of the method of
proletarian struggle cannot be the task of small conventicles of leaders.
The liberation of the working class can be achieved by itself alone!
Well, then, discuss how this can be done.
   We do not wish to make you believe that we are already a great
united force. We represent the gradually awakening section of the
international proletariat. But, despite all the obstacles of censorship,
voices are reaching us every day from the belligerent countries which
convince us that the internationalist group which thinks and acts as we
do is larger than we thought. This group will grow day by day until it

[1] *Jahrbuch der sozialdemokratischen Partei der Schweiz 1915*, pp. 54–59.

becomes a great army of fighters. For the points of view which we advocate and the means of struggle which we recommend to the proletariat are not magic remedies which we have invented; they are points of view which must gain recognition among the proletarians as a result of the effects of the consequences of the war, of the growing burdens, of the growing social antagonisms, of the growing reaction. In spite of the shouting of the social patriots that there can be no international revolutionary movement during the war, we see political strikes in Russia, demonstrations against the high cost of living in Germany, strikes in England and Italy—only beginnings, it is true, but such beginnings as might develop with the support of revolutionary elements into a mass struggle of the proletariat against the war and capitalism. Blindness toward these facts only proves that the social patriots are afraid; they shout that there can be no revolution only so that they will not have to support its beginning. But neither the treacherous phrases of the social patriots nor governmental persecutions will succeed. Proclaimed today as revolutionary illusions, tomorrow in the growing revolutionary movement our slogans will be the possession of the class-conscious proletariat, its banner carried at the head of the struggle.

TASKS OF THE NEW ORGAN OF THE ZIMMERWALD LEFT

[From "Zur Einführung," in the First Issue of *Vorbote*][2]

. . . . A tremendous number of new questions confront us. First, the question of imperialism, its economic roots, its relations to the export of capital, to the supply of raw materials, and to heavy industry, its influence on politics, parliament, and bureaucracy, its moral dominance over the bourgeoisie and the press, its significance as a new ideology of the bourgeoisie. Then come questions which concern the proletariat, the causes of its weakness, its psychology, and the phenomena of social imperialism and social patriotism. Further, the questions of proletarian fighting tactics; the significance and possibility of parliamentarism, mass action, the tactics of trade unions, reforms and partial demands, the future role of the organization, as well as questions of nationalism, militarism, and colonial policy.

. . . . Under the new conditions the proletariat can find no policies for action among the old standards and ideas of pre-imperialist times. The Social Democratic parties cannot command the proletariat to halt. In a large majority of cases they have devoted themselves to imperialism. The conscious active or passive support of the war policy by representatives of parties and of trade unions has left a mark too deep to permit

[2] *Vorbote*, No. 1, January 1916, pp. 1–4.

an easy return to the old prewar standpoint . . . . *Organizational unity between those who wish to turn Social Democracy into an instrument of imperialism and those who wish to turn it into an instrument of the revolution is no longer possible.*

The task of the elucidation of these problems, of advancing new slogans, of formulating policies for the new struggle, devolves upon those who have not allowed themselves to be fooled by the war and who have held on faithfully to internationalism and the class struggle. Marxism shall be their instrument. . . . . Now it is regaining its right as a theory of revolutionary action. . . . .

There is no task more urgent than the task of elucidating the new problems; for it is of vital importance for the proletariat and hence for the whole development of mankind that the proletariat should see clearly the way to its new ascent. Moreover, these are not questions for the future, the solution of which can be postponed until they can be discussed peacefully. These questions cannot be postponed. . . . . At the end of the war a gigantic universal economic upheaval will manifest itself with all its force, when, under a general exhaustion, unemployment, and lack of capital, industry will have to be regulated anew, when the terrific indebtedness of all states will drive them to tremendous taxation, and when state socialism—militarization of the economic life— will seem to be the only way out of financial difficulties.[3] It will be necessary to act then with or without a theory. But then lack of theoretical clearness will entail mistakes heavy with consequences and errors.

This is the great task of our review. Through treatment, discussion, and elucidation of these questions it will support the material struggle of the proletariat against imperialism. As *an organ of discussion and elucidation this review is at the same time an organ of struggle.* A common will for struggle and a common stand with regard to the chief problem of immediate tactics has brought together the publishers and the contributors of the review. First of all, struggle against imperialism, the chief enemy of the proletariat! But this struggle is possible only through an equally ruthless struggle against all elements of the former Social Democracy which bind the proletariat to the chariot of imperialism: against open imperialists who became ordinary agents of the bourgeoisie as well as social patriots of all tinges who seek to reconcile incompatible antagonisms and to keep the proletariat, by the most acute methods, from struggling against imperialism. *The formation of the Third International* will be possible only after a resolute break with social patriotism. In recognition thereof we stand upon *the same platform as the Zimmerwald Left.* . . . .

Through theoretical work our review will aid—by means of a most

[3] The term "fascism" was not, of course, in use at this time.

acute struggle against social patriotism and by a merciless analysis of the inadequacies of the old revisionist and radical socialism—the group of international social democrats to attain the aim which they have set for themselves in their practical-political debut: to prepare the new International. . . . .

ON THE CONTROL OF *VORBOTE*

[Fragment of a Letter from Lenin to Roland-Holst, early 1916][4]

RESPECTED COMRADE!

Comrade Radek has just shown us Comrade Pannekoek's letter and the introduction.

This letter and introduction decidedly change the constitution of the review[5] as previously agreed upon. Previously, it was agreed that the review was to appear as an organ of two groups, namely: (1) the group of Roland-Holst and Trotsky (possibly, Roland-Holst and her friends without Trotsky, if Trotsky does not wish to enter); (2) the group of the Zimmerwald Left (the bureau of which consists of three comrades: Radek, Lenin, and Zinoviev). Comrade Pannekoek has been designated as representative of this second group.

Now, *by virtue of* the documents mentioned above (the letter and the introduction), conditions are changed: the review becomes the organ of two comrades, Pannekoek and Roland-Holst.[6]

If Comrades Pannekoek and Roland-Holst have decided to make *this change,* then we must take notice of it. The owner of this *review* [Roland-Holst] had full right to make *this change.*

We do not repudiate joint activity under the new conditions, but we must demand certain guaranties. The review is to appear for the first time as an organ of the Zimmerwald Left or "upon the platform of the Zimmerwald Left." We have been elected representatives of this Left by all members of the Zimmerwald Left (except Platten) who were present at Zimmerwald. Therefore, we think—and all three of us agree on this point—that you will undoubtedly give this guaranty as a matter of course. The guaranty is that in cases where fundamental dissensions

---

[4] Lenin, *Sochineniia,* XXIX, 309.

[5] *Vorbote.*

[6] Lenin refers to this incident in a letter to Shliapnikov, May 23, 1916: "Most probably you do not know that Radek has turned us out of the editorial board of *Vorbote.* At first it was agreed that there would be an editorial board composed of two groups: (1) the Dutch (+ Trotsky perhaps) and (2) us (i.e., Radek, *Grigorii, and me*). This condition gave us equality on the editorial board. Radek has been intriguing for months and has obtained from the 'owner' (Roland-Holst) the cancellation of this plan. We were transferred to the position of contributors. This is a fact!" (Lenin, *Sochineniia,* XXIX, 248.)

arise between us [i.e., between the Zimmerwald Left group, represented by Radek, Lenin, and Zinoviev, and Roland-Holst's group] the revision of the article of the Central Committee of the R.S.D.L. party (representative ....) [The manuscript ends here.]

ZIMMERWALD AT THE CROSSROADS

[From Part IV of Lenin's Article, "Patsifizm burzhuaznyi i patsifizm sotsialisticheskii," January 1, 1917][7]

[After noting the fact that the comments of various socialist and labor leaders on the peace notes of the German government and President Wilson have revealed "two fundamentally different policies which, so far, have somehow gotten along well together within the Zimmerwald movement but which now have completely separated," Lenin continues] :
.... Either one or the other.

Either expose lack of content, absurdity, hypocrisy of bourgeois pacifism *or* "paraphrase" it into a "socialist" pacifism. Either struggle against Jouhaux and Renaudel, against Legien and David, as against government "hirelings" *or* unite with them on the basis of empty pacifist declarations after the French or the German patterns.

That is now the dividing line between the Zimmerwald Right, which has always protested with utmost vigor against breaking with social chauvinists, and the Zimmerwald Left, which even at Zimmerwald was not without reason concerned with publicly drawing a line between itself and the Right, with advancing a special platform at the conference and later also in the press. The approach of peace, or at least an intense discussion by some bourgeois elements of the question of peace, has called forth, not accidentally but inevitably, a particularly obvious divergence between the two policies. For the bourgeois pacifists and their socialist imitators or parrots have always drawn and continue to draw a picture of peace as something which is fundamentally distinct from war, since the idea, "war is a continuation of the policy of peace, peace is the continuation of the policy of war," has never been understood by the pacifists of both shades. Neither the bourgeois nor the social chauvinists wish or have ever wished to see that the imperialist war of 1914–1917 is a continuation of the imperialist policy of the years 1898–1914, if not of a still earlier period. Neither the bourgeois nor the socialist-pacifists realize that if the bourgeois governments are not overthrown in a revolutionary manner peace can *now* be only an imperialist peace, which would continue the imperialist war.

Just as the evaluation of this war has been approached with senseless,

[7] Lenin, *Sochineniia*, XIX, 375–78; another English translation is in V. I. Lenin, *Selected Works*, V, 260–64.

vulgar, Philistine phrases about offense and defense in general, so now the evaluation of peace is being approached with similarly general Philistine conceptions, forgetting the concrete historic situation, the concrete actuality of struggle between imperialist powers. It has been natural for the social chauvinists—those agents of governments and of the bourgeoisie within the labor parties—to seize upon the idea of an approaching peace, or even merely peace talk, in order to *gloss over* the depth of their reformism and opportunism which has been exposed by the war and in order to restore their undermined influence upon the masses. Therefore, as we have seen in Germany and in France, the social chauvinists are making intense efforts to "unite" with the spineless and unscrupulous pacifist section of the "opposition."

It is also most probable that within the Zimmerwald movement attempts will be made to gloss over the divergence between two irreconcilable lines of policy. Two kinds of these attempts might be foreseen. A "business deal" reconciliation will mean merely that loud revolutionary phrases (like the phrases in the appeal of the International Socialist Committee) will be automatically combined with opportunist and pacifist practice. Thus it has been in the Second International. Super-revolutionary phrases in the appeals of Huysmans and Vandervelde and in certain resolutions of the congresses served merely to cover up a super-opportunist practice of the majority of the European parties, without altering or undermining it and without struggling against it. It is doubtful if this tactic will again succeed within the Zimmerwald movement.

The "conciliators in principle" will attempt to offer a falsification of Marxism; for instance, they might argue something like this: reforms do not exclude revolution; an imperialist peace with certain "improvements" in boundary lines between nationalities, with improvements in international law, or in the budget of expenditures for armaments, etc., is possible along with a revolutionary movement—as "one of the moments in the unfolding" of this movement—and so forth and so on.

This would be falsifying Marxism. Certainly reforms do not exclude revolution. But at present the issue is not this but rather that the revolutionaries shall not efface *themselves* before the reformists—that is, that the socialists shall not exchange their revolutionary activity for a reformist one. Europe is passing through a revolutionary situation. War and high cost of living accentuate this situation. The transition from war to peace will not necessarily abolish it, for it does not at all follow that millions of workers who have now excellent arms in their hands would absolutely and without fail permit themselves to be "disarmed peacefully" by the bourgeoisie instead of carrying out K. Liebknecht's advice, i.e., to turn their arms against *their own* bourgeoisie.

The question as the pacifists and Kautskyans pose it—either a reformist political campaign or a repudiation of reforms—does not confront us, since this is a bourgeois presentation of the question. Actually the question which confronts us is: either a revolutionary struggle, in which reforms are side issues if success is incomplete (that they are has been proved by the entire history of revolutions all over the world), or nothing except talk about reforms and promises of reforms.

The reformism of Kautsky, Turati, and Bourderon, which is now coming forth in the form of pacifism, does not merely leave aside the question of revolution—(this is *already* a betrayal of socialism); does not merely repudiate in practice every systematic and persistent revolutionary activity—but also goes so far as to declare that street demonstrations are merely adventures (Kautsky in *Neue Zeit*, November 26, 1915)[8] and goes so far as to defend and achieve unity with the Südekums, Legiens, Renaudels, Thomases, and so forth, the open and decided opponents of revolutionary struggle.

This reformism is absolutely irreconcilable with revolutionary Marxism, which must make complete use of the present revolutionary situation in Europe for the direct advocacy of a revolution, the overthrow of bourgeois government, and the seizure of power by the armed proletariat—all this without repudiating or making a pledge against the use of reforms as a method of developing the struggle for the revolution as well as during that struggle.

The near future will reveal the course of events in Europe in general and of the struggle between reformist-pacifism and revolutionary Marxism in particular, including the struggle between the two parts of the Zimmerwald movement.

B. Dissensions in the Zimmerwald Left

Socialists were in general united in their desire to abolish militarism and achieve total disarmament. They agreed that militarism was an attribute of capitalism, but they were not agreed as to whether arming or disarming the people was the correct policy under existing conditions. The documents which follow illustrate the arguments advanced by the adherents of the Zimmerwald Left on these issues.

[8] This refers to K. Kautsky's article, "Fraktion und Partei," in *Neue Zeit*, No. 9, November 26, 1915, pp. 269–76; Lenin, *Sochineniia*, XIX, 484, note 190.

THE DUTCH SOCIAL DEMOCRATS AND THE SLOGAN "ARMING THE PEOPLE"

[From an Article by D. J. Wijnkoop][9]

I

One of the demands which is advanced by the Social Democratic party (S.D.P.) of Holland in their program of action is that of arming the people.

The Social Democratic party's program of action indicates the means which the revolutionary proletariat must use in struggling against the capitalist state in order to seize political power. Only if the struggle is viewed in the form it will actually assume internationally is it possible to understand that the proletariat requires the arming of the people in its revolutionary revolt against capitalism and all that this arming implies.

.... And if we are now to discuss the postulate of the arming of the people, then certainly we are to adopt not the logically possible standpoint of an armistice but that of the mass struggle which is actually coming, a struggle with one general aim, namely, to abolish the misery of the proletariat—a struggle which in the twentieth century has already had its forerunner in mass movements in practically all large capitalist countries. If there were to be an armistice and not a conflict, then not merely the arming of the people but the entire program of action would be devoid of sense as a means of struggle against capitalism. But if mass struggles are to come, then the demand for the arming of the people has just as much sense as the demand for complete democracy or the demand for a strongly progressive income tax. In struggle all these become necessary means of defense and attack.

Since the Russian revolution [of 1905], and even prior to it, much has been said about mass struggle as the revolutionary proletariat's proper method of struggle. However, this method should be examined more closely in actual process.

Mass movements of the proletariat lead necessarily toward mass strikes. Nobody will deny this. But to what do mass strikes lead when the proletariat is no longer in a joking mood? Will anyone deceive himself that capital will peacefully give the masses the opportunity—i.e., an increasing opportunity—to win these strikes? If in its struggle for power the proletariat suffers a partial defeat, as has happened so often and as will often happen in the future, it will be temporarily exhausted; then hard reality must come striding in to arouse it from its inertness and to new resistance. But if in its mass struggle for power the proletariat wins a partial victory, then it cannot stand still and be satisfied with this

[9] D. J. Wijnkoop, "Volksbewaffnung," *Vorbote*, No. 2, April 1916, pp. 27–36.

partial victory; it must go forward to complete victory. But capital will not permit this. Never yet has a privileged class surrendered its privileges without a struggle to the bitter end, and the present World War is proving that capital will unchain unprecedented bloody battles rather than give up its capitalism, its "privilege" of exploitation.

II

.... By this we wish to say merely that as both the masses and militarism become stronger, the first in the service of human liberation, the second in the service of human oppression, both, though formed from the same human material, must at some time or other come to grips with each other, provided, naturally, that the masses do not stop struggling to liberate themselves from misery and provided, likewise, that the rulers do not stop attempting to preserve their class privileges and to expand them ....

If we look at things thus, naturally it does not matter whether the military system and the standing army are formed after the German-French manner on the basis of a national guard, or, according to the Anglo-Saxon manner, of "trained wage soldiers"; this has already been pointed out in the Dutch Social Democratic organ *De Tribune*, April 10, 1915. What really matters is that the military system is being used to hold the proletariat "in check," that in a revolutionary struggle (which, as we have seen, is the only possible struggle to achieve economic as well as political reforms—the lever of socialism—and to rid oneself of capitalism) the proletariat encounters violence—the military system—which the capitalist will by no means "abolish" but on the contrary will make greater use of; and that the proletariat will oppose this system with another *principle of armament* under the threat of being massacred to the last man, a penalty far worse than that at Jerusalem in the year 70, or in 1535 when the cathedrals were destroyed, or in 1871 at the slaughtering of the Commune, or in 1905 in the Moscow massacre.

III

.... As a revolutionary party's means of struggle the arming of the people can be "realized" just as much or just as little as any other means, and is just as much or just as little utopian. In other words, only in the revolutionary struggle does this arming of the people become desirable and possible and at the same time necessary. The fact that radical and reformist bourgeoisie, and perhaps individualists and anarchists also, are stupidly misusing the words "arming of the people" by representing revolutionaries as militarists—this fact can serve as a reason for discarding the arming of the people just as little as an error on the opposite side has served us as a reason for discarding the demand for general suffrage.

The arming of the people can be a means of keeping war at a distance just as little as our program of action can prescribe a remedy for some capitalist calamity. But the arming of the people becomes a means of struggle against capitalism in the same degree as the working people in its struggle is more nearly able to carry out this means, in other words, in the same degree as the class struggle increases tangibly and becomes more accentuated; also from the proletarian standpoint, the capitalist will hesitate before he would light-mindedly force the masses to fight again in a war, fearing that the workers might present a common front against foreign and internal war, not merely through a mass refusal to serve but also through active and organized armed resistance which will herald the end of capitalism. In other words, the workers would answer the appeal for a foreign war with "civil war" . . . .

THE NORWEGIANS AND THE SLOGAN "DISARMAMENT"

[From an Article by Arvid Hansen Especially Written for the *Sbornik Sotsial-Demokrata*][10]

. . . . Antimilitarism is deeply rooted in the Norwegian laboring class, whose hatred of soldiery is as intense as the cold of a Russian winter night. Many a time the question of the *arming of the proletariat* has been officially discussed; but it is *disarming* that has become the official slogan of the party. The Norwegian Social Democracy attained the clearest expression of its antimilitarist point of view at the party congress in May 1915, at which the following demands were advanced as a program: disarmament, permanent neutrality, and compulsory international courts of arbitration. The chief official motifs of the program were as follows:

"The system of militarism is, for Social Democracy, a vivid expression of a social regime based on private capital. In all countries militarism is being concealed under the name of 'armed defense.' But we have seen that precisely this armed defense can contribute to drawing a country into war. Thus our struggle against militarism must inevitably lead toward disarmament. We are *opponents of armed defense,* for it is accompanied by such unbelievable burdens, and demands such big sacrifices from those who are conscripted as to destroy the welfare both of the state and of individual citizens. These expenses are met by the direct and indirect exploitation of productive labor, i.e., by means of depriving the workers of the results of their labor. Furthermore, this exploitation

---

[10] Arvid Gansen [Hansen], "Nekotorye momenty sovremennago rabochago dvizheniia v Norvegii," *Sbornik Sotsial-Demokrata,* No. 2, December 1916, pp. 40–44. Another article by Hansen on the same subject was published in *Die Jugend-Internationale,* No. 5, September 1, 1916, pp. 8–9. Eugène Olaussen also discussed this matter in an article in the same publication, No. 3, March 1, 1916, pp. 8–10.

slows down the movement of the laboring class toward social liberation and the conquest of society. Since the greater part of ordinary state profits is used for military expenditures, the state is forced to pursue a policy of borrowing which makes the state highly dependent on local and foreign capital. If the millions which are now being spent on defense could be used to realize the cultural and material program of our party, it would have a tremendous influence on the welfare and happiness of the entire people.

"We are opponents of militarism because in the hands of the ruling class it is a dangerous weapon against the demonstrations made by the laboring class to improve its position.

"We are opponents of armed defense because we are convinced that the military strength which our country can organize cannot really protect it, on the contrary that it is a menace to the country's independence and neutrality.

". . . . It stands to reason that our party will exert its utmost effort in order that our neutrality and independence may be regulated by international agreements on the basis of disarmament. Likewise there is no reason to presume that this agreement will encounter insurmountable difficulties. But disarmament must not be bound by the condition of simultaneous agreements. These agreements might be attained sooner if our country would carry out the program of disarmament in complete earnestness."

It would be incorrect to deny that there are some pacifist elements in Norwegian antimilitarism. The fact that there is a desire to abolish militarism by parliamentary procedure is only a logical consequence of the conviction that capitalism itself may be abolished in that same way.

The interest in international relations and contacts in Norway has increased considerably. On the one hand, this is the natural result of the great European nationalist frenzy; and, on the other, it is the result of the internationalist propaganda being carried on by the Socialist Youth League. The reception accorded the pamphlet on the "Third International" (translated from Swedish) bears witness to this interest. Our League worked systematically for the ideas and the principles of Zimmerwald, chiefly in the League's organ *Klassekampen* (Class Struggle). Therefore, we think that the party owes us [members of the Youth League] something for the decision of the party's Central Committee on June 3 {1916] concerning the International. This decision, which truly does not at all signify—as we demanded—an organizational adherence to the Berne Committee, is nevertheless in comparison with the conduct of the Swedish and Danish party presidiums a resolute step leftward. It reads:

"The party presidium welcomes the energetic struggle of the Italian comrades against their country's participation in the World War and expresses complete recognition of the endeavors of the socialist parties in various neutral and belligerent countries to unite the world proletariat in an energetic struggle against war and for peace, and it demands insistently that the Executive Committee of the International Socialist Bureau utilize every means at its disposal in order to gather again into the International parties of all countries for the resumption of the struggle in favor of terminating the war and in favor of disarmament. It also expresses the hope that this struggle will be led in the future on the basis of class struggle and in agreement with the decisions of the congresses of Stuttgart, Copenhagen, and Basel.

"The party presidium further declares that it *recognizes the principles which underlie the Zimmerwald Conference,* and the attempts made to re-erect the International of 1889 on the basis of class solidarity and class struggle, but that it does not join Zimmerwald organizationally. The party presidium authorizes the Executive Committee of the party to open communication with the Zimmerwald Conference."[11] ....

The attitude of the Norwegian laboring class toward extra-parliamentary demonstrations against militarism—demonstrations which for many years have been advocated by our League—is revealed in the fact that the party and the trade unions have elected a joint committee in which our League also has one vote, a committee which must examine the questions of an organized repudiation of military service and of mass strike against militarism. The findings of this committee must be sent out to party and trade union organizations as materials for discussion, and decisions binding upon everybody must be adopted at the next congress. *Klassekampen* circulated a questionnaire in connection with these questions. The results of this questionnaire revealed that the general strike against the war has found general recognition and that the struggle against militarism in times of *peace* was also spoken of very forcefully. This questionnaire appeared later in the form of a pamphlet published by the League. The present-day Norwegian labor movement as a whole is young in comparison with the movement of the Russian proletariat which has matured in struggle. A highly necessary process of socialist education proceeds in all realms, and everywhere new policies in tactics are submitted for discussion and are being tried out. Passionate hatred of capitalism and militarism and a similarly passionate desire to overthrow the destructive forces are coupled at the same time with doubt concerning the adequacy of the existing means of struggle and with a search for new paths—all this is most characteristic of the labor movement in Norway at the present time. The Norwegian worker has good inclinations, but it is necessary for him to learn to see wider horizons, greater aims.

[11] See in this connection letter of March 5, 1917, below, pp. 579–81.

Therefore, I think that a closer and more intimate contact with the socialist fighters of Russia will inspire us with that spirit of struggle without which the victory of socialism is impossible.

LENIN ON THE SLOGAN, "DISARMAMENT"

[From an Article in *Sbornik Sotsial-Demokrata*][12]

.... Let us examine closely the position of the defenders of disarmament.

I

One of the basic arguments favoring disarmament is the not always straightforwardly expressed consideration: we are against war, against war in general; whereas it is the demand for disarmament which expresses this point of view of ours most definitely, clearly, and unequivocally.

We have dwelt on the incorrectness of this consideration in the article concerning Junius' pamphlet to which we refer the reader.[13] Socialists cannot be against any war whatsoever unless they stop being socialists. We should not permit ourselves to be blinded by the present imperialist war. It is just these wars between "great" powers that are typical of the imperialist epoch; but at the same time democratic wars and uprisings such as wars of oppressed nations against their oppressors and for their own liberation from oppression are not in the least impossible. Civil wars of the proletariat against the bourgeoisie and for socialism are inevitable. There can be wars against other bourgeois and reactionary countries waged by a socialism which has been victorious in one country only.

Disarmament is the ideal of socialism. There will be no wars in a socialist society. Consequently disarmament will be realized. But he is not a socialist who waits for the realization of socialism *without* a social revolution and a dictatorship of the proletariat. Dictatorship is a government power which leans directly on *violence*. In the epoch of the twentieth century as in any epoch of civilization generally, violence is not a fist and a club, but an *army*. If we were to introduce "disarmament" into the program, this would have the general meaning that we are against the use of arms. There is not a grain of Marxism in this, and it would be identical to our saying we are against making use of violence! We must note that the international discussion on this question has

---

[12] Lenin, "O lozunge razoruzheniia," *Sbornik Sotsial-Demokrata*, No. 2, December 1916, pp. 29–34; reprinted in *Sochineniia*, XIX, 314–22.

[13] R. Luxemburg (Junius), *Die Krise der Sozialdemokratie* (also in English), and Lenin, "O broshiure Yuniusa," *Sochineniia*, XIX, 176–90, reprinted from *Sbornik Sotsial-Demokrata*, No. 1, October 1916, pp. 28–34.

been conducted, chiefly if not exclusively, in the German language. In German two words are used, but the difference between them cannot be easily expressed in Russian. One word really means "disarmament" and is used, for instance, by Kautsky and the Kautskyans in the sense of a limitation of armaments. The other word really means "unarming" and is used primarily by the Lefts to indicate their demand for the abolition of militarism, abolition of the military system. We will speak in this article of this *second* demand, which is common to certain *revolutionary* Social Democrats.

The Kautskyan preaching of "disarmament" which is addressed precisely to the present governments of the great imperialist powers is the vilest opportunism and bourgeois pacifism, which in *practice*—notwithstanding "the good wishes" of the sugary Kautskyans—is serving to divert the workers from revolutionary struggle. For this preaching inspires the workers with the thought that the present bourgeois governments of the imperialist powers are *not* enmeshed by thousands of threads of finance capital and by tens and hundreds of corresponding (i.e., predatory, brigandish, preparatory for imperialist war) *secret treaties*.

II

The oppressed class which would not strive to learn to handle arms or to possess arms would deserve to be treated as slaves. After all we cannot forget, without turning into bourgeois pacifists or opportunists, that we are living in a class society and that there is and can be no way out except through class struggle and the overthrowing of the power of the dominant class.

In any class society—be it based on slavery, on serfdom, or, as it is now, on hired labor—the oppressing class is armed. Not merely the present standing army but also the present militia—even in the most democratic bourgeois republics, for instance, in Switzerland—is but an arming of the bourgeoisie *against* the proletariat. This is such an elementary truth that it is hardly necessary to dwell on it. It is enough to recall the use of troops (including the republican-democratic militia) against strikers—a phenomenon common to all capitalist countries without exception. The arming of the bourgeoisie against the proletariat is one of the most substantial, basic, and important facts in present-day capitalist society.

And in the face of this fact the revolutionary social democrats are being asked to advance the "demand" for "disarmament"! This is tantamount to a complete renunciation of the point of view of class struggle, a recantation of every thought of revolution. Our slogan should be: the arming of the proletariat in order to defeat, expropriate, and disarm the bourgeoisie. This is the only possible tactic of the revolutionary class.

a tactic derived from the entire *objective development* of capitalist militarism and prescribed by this development. Only *after* the proletariat has disarmed the bourgeoisie can it without betraying its universal-historical task scrap all arms in general. The proletariat will doubtless do this, but only after disarming the bourgeoisie and no earlier.

If the present war provokes *only* horror and fright on the part of reactionary Christian socialists and tearful petty bourgeois, only aversion toward any use of arms, toward blood, death, etc., then we must say: capitalist society itself has always been and is *an endless horror*. And if the present war, the most reactionary of all wars, is now preparing *a horrible end* for this society, we have no reason whatsoever to despair. But the objective meaning of the "demand" for disarmament—more truly "dreaming" of disarmament—at a time when before everyone's eyes the only lawful and revolutionary war—namely, civil war against the imperialist bourgeoisie—is being prepared by the forces of the bourgeoisie itself is nothing but a manifestation of such despair.

To whoever says that this is an abstract theory, we will recall two universal-historical facts: the role of trusts and the factory work of women, on the one hand, and the Commune of 1871 and the December uprising of 1905 in Russia, on the other.

It is the work of the bourgeoisie to develop trusts, to drive children and women into factories, to torture them there, corrupt them, and condemn them to the utmost misery. We do not "demand" such a development; we do not "support" it; we struggle against it. But *how* do we struggle? We know that trusts and the factory work of women are progressive. We do not wish to go backward to crafts, to pre-monopolist capitalism, to domestic work of women. Forward through the trusts, etc., and beyond them toward socialism!

This argument, which takes into account the *objective* course of development, can also be applied with necessary modifications to the present-day militarization of the people. Today the imperialist bourgeoisie is militarizing not merely men but also the young people. Tomorrow it will begin, perhaps, to militarize the women. We must say in this connection, so much the better! This means a quicker progress! The sooner this happens the nearer will be an armed uprising against capitalism. How can the Social Democrats permit themselves to be scared by a militarization of the youth, etc., if they remember the example of the Commune? This is not "an abstract theory"; it is not a dream, but a fact. And it would be indeed too bad if the Social Democrats, in spite of all economic and political occurrences, should begin to doubt that the imperialist epoch and the imperialist wars will inevitably lead toward a repetition of such occurrences.

One bourgeois observer of the Commune wrote in an English news--

paper in May 1871 : "If the French nation consisted only of women, what a frightful nation it would be !" During the Commune women, and children thirteen years old, struggled side by side with men. Nor can it be otherwise in the coming battles for the overthrow of the bourgeoisie. Proletarian women will not watch passively the shooting of poorly armed and unarmed workers by the well-armed bourgeoisie. They will seize arms as in 1871, and from the nations which are now intimidated—or more truly from the present labor movement which has been disorganized by the opportunists rather than by the governments—an international union of "frightful nations" of revolutionary proletarians will develop sooner or later beyond any shadow of doubt.

At present militarization completely permeates social life. Imperialism is a bitter struggle between great powers for the division and repartitioning of the world. Therefore it must inevitably lead toward further militarization in all countries, neutral and small. What will the proletarian women do to counteract this ? Will they merely condemn all wars and everything that is military ? Will they merely demand disarmament ? The women of the oppressed class which is really revolutionary will never become reconciled to this infamous role. They will tell their sons :

"You will grow up to be big men, you will be given rifles. Take them and study military science thoroughly. Proletarians require this science; not for the purpose of shooting your brothers, the workers of other countries, as is being done in the present war and as the betrayers of socialism advise you to do, but in order to struggle against the bourgeoisie of your own country, in order to put an end to exploitation, to poverty and wars ; not by means of goody-goody wishes, but by means of defeating and disarming *the bourgeoisie.*"

If in connection with the present war we are to give up this propaganda, and precisely this propaganda, then it would be better if we were not to speak big words about international revolutionary Social Democracy, about the socialist revolution, about war against war.

III

Partisans of disarmament are coming forth against that point of the program which concerns "arming the people," among other reasons because this latter demand supposedly leads more easily toward concessions to opportunism. Above we have examined the most important matter : the relation of disarmament to the class struggle and to the social revolution. Let us now examine the relation between the demand for disarmament and opportunism. One of the most important reasons why this demand is not acceptable is precisely that it and the illusions it creates inevitably weaken and enfeeble our struggle against opportunism.

There is no doubt that this struggle constitutes the chief and immediate question to be solved by the International. Unless the struggle against imperialism is bound indissolubly with the struggle against opportunism it is but an empty phrase or a deception. One of the chief defects of Zimmerwald and Kienthal, one of the basic reasons for a possible fiasco (failure or bankruptcy) of these embryos of the Third International consists precisely in that the question of struggle against opportunism has not even been posed openly, to say nothing of its not having been solved in the sense of a necessary break with the opportunists. Opportunism is for the time being victorious in the ranks of the European labor movement. In all large countries two chief shades of opportunism have formed: first, the frank and cynical and therefore less dangerous social imperialism of the Messrs. Plekhanovs, Scheidemanns, Legiens, Albert Thomases, Sembats, Vanderveldes, Hyndmans, Hendersons, and so forth. Secondly, covert Kautskyan opportunism: Kautsky-Haase and the Social Democratic *Arbeitsgemeinschaft* in Germany; Longuet, Pressemane, Mayéras, and so forth in France; Ramsay MacDonald and other leaders of the Independent Labour party in England; Martov, Chkheidze, and so forth in Russia; Treves and other so-called Left reformists in Italy.

Open opportunism, which is frankly and directly against revolution and against the beginning revolutionary movements and outbursts, is in direct alliance with the governments, regardless of the form of this alliance, be it participation in the Cabinets or participation in the War Industry Committees. Covert opportunists, the Kautskyans, are much more harmful and dangerous for the labor movement because they hide their defense of alliance with the government by means of pleasant-sounding "Marxist" words and pacifist slogans. The struggle against these two forms of prevailing opportunism must be carried out in *all* realms of proletarian politics: in parliamentary activities, trade unions, strikes, military affairs, etc.

What is the chief distinguishing characteristic of these *two* forms of prevailing opportunism?

It is that the concrete question of the *connection between the present war and revolution and also other concrete questions of revolution* are being passed over in silence, are being covered up or treated cautiously with an eye to police restrictions. And this is done in spite of the fact that on innumerable occasions before the war there was pointed out unofficially, and also officially in the Basel manifesto, a connection between *this* very war, which was anticipated at that time, and the proletarian revolution.

The chief defect of the demand for disarmament is precisely that it evades all concrete questions of revolution. Or do the partisans of disarmament advocate an entirely new type of unarmed revolution?

IV

Further, we are by no means against struggling for reforms. We do not wish to ignore the sad possibility that, at the worst, mankind will live to see a second imperialist war if in spite of numerous outbursts of mass ferment and mass discontent and in spite of all our efforts a revolution does not grow out of this war. We are partisans of a program of reform such as should be directed *also* against the opportunists. The opportunists would be only too glad if we were to let them struggle alone for reform and would retreat beyond the clouds of some utopian "disarmament," thus escaping from sad reality. "Disarmament" is precisely a flight to escape an unpleasant reality and not at all a struggle against this reality.

Incidentally, one of the great defects in treating questions, for instance, on the defense of the fatherland, among some of the Lefts, consists in the insufficient concreteness of their answer. It is much more correct theoretically and immeasurably more important practically if we say that in *this* imperialist war the defense of the fatherland is a bourgeois reactionary deception than if we advance a "general" postulate against "any" defense of the fatherland. Such a postulate would be incorrect and would not "hit" the opportunists who are the direct enemies of the workers within the ranks of the labor parties.

In working out the necessary concrete and practical reply in the question of the militia we should say: we are in favor not of a bourgeois militia but only of a proletarian militia. Therefore, "not one penny and not one man" should be given for a standing army or a bourgeois militia, even in such countries as the United States, Switzerland, Norway, or the like. Moreover, we see in the freest republican countries (for instance, in Switzerland) an ever-increasing Prussification of the militia and its prostitution for the purpose of mobilizing the troops against the strikers. We can demand: the election of army officers by the people; the abolition of every military tribunal; the equalizing of the rights of foreign and native workers (an especially important point for imperialist states which like Switzerland are exploiting an ever larger number of foreign workers and in an ever more shameless fashion, without granting them any rights). Further, we can demand the right for every, let us say, one hundred residents of a country to form a free union for the study of military affairs, the freely elected instructors to be paid by the state, etc. Only under those conditions could the proletariat actually *for its own benefit* and not for the benefit of its slave owners, study military affairs; and the interests of the proletariat absolutely demand this study. The Russian revolution has proved that every success of the revolutionary movement, even though it might be only a partial success—for instance, the capture of a certain town, of a certain factory settlement, of a certain army unit—will inevitably *force* the victorious proletariat to carry out precisely this program.

Finally, it stands to reason that it is possible to struggle against opportunism not by means of programs alone but by seeing to it persistently that these programs are actually put into effect. The greatest and most fatal mistake of the bankrupt Second International was the fact that its words did not coincide with its deeds, that it cultivated the habit of unconscientious revolutionary phrases (see the present attitude of Kautsky and Co. toward the Basel manifesto). In approaching the demand for disarmament from this angle we must first of all ask what is its *objective* significance. Disarmament, as a social idea—i.e., an idea which would be germinated by a definite social environment—can influence a definite social medium but cannot be a personal or group whim apparently germinated by the special and exceptional "peaceful" conditions of life of separate small states which have been aloof from the bloody, universal road of wars for a rather long period and which hope to remain thus aloof. In order to convince ourselves that this is so, it is enough, for instance, to think carefully about the arguments of the Norwegian adherents of disarmament: "We," they say, "are a small country; our army is small; we can do nothing to resist the Great Powers" (and therefore we are also helpless to resist being forcibly drawn into an imperialist *alliance* with one or another group of Great Powers!). "We wish to be left in peace in our faraway corner and to continue to pursue a Philistine policy, to continue the demand for disarmament, for compulsory courts of arbitration, permanent neutrality, etc." ("Permanent" presumably like Belgian neutrality?)

The narrow tendency of small states to remain aloof, their petty-bourgeois desire to be as far as possible from the great battles of world history, to utilize their comparatively monopolist position for maintaining their hardened passivity—this is the *objective* social environment which can assure a certain success for the idea of disarmament and also a certain amount of propagation of this idea in some small states. It stands to reason that this tendency is reactionary and is based entirely upon illusions, for in one way or another imperialism is drawing small states into the whirlpool of universal economy and world politics.

Let us explain this by taking Switzerland as an example. Her imperialistic environment objectively prescribes for her *two* lines of labor movement. The opportunists in alliance with the bourgeoisie are striving to turn Switzerland into a republican-democratic monopolist state for the purpose of deriving profits from the tourists of the imperialist bourgeoisie and in order to make use as profitably and as peacefully as possible of this "peaceful" monopolist condition. In practice this policy is a policy of union of a small privileged stratum of workers of a small country—which has been placed in a privileged position—with the bourgeoisie of its own country *against* the proletarian masses. The real

Social Democrats of Switzerland strive to utilize the comparative freedom of Switzerland—her "international" position (her proximity to the most highly cultured countries) and the fact that Switzerland speaks, thank God, not "her own" language but three world languages—to expand and fortify the *revolutionary* union of the revolutionary elements of the proletariat of all Europe. Let us help our own bourgeoisie to continue to monopolize the super-peaceful trade in Alpine fascinations—perhaps a penny will fall also to our share—this is the objective content of the policy of the Swiss opportunists; let us help the union of the revolutionary proletariat among the French, the Germans, and the Italians for the overthrow of the bourgeoisie—this is the objective content of the policy of the Swiss revolutionary Social Democrats. Unfortunately this policy is carried out by the "Lefts" in Switzerland in a manner which is far from satisfactory, and the splendid decision of the party Congress in Aarau in 1915 (the recognition of the revolutionary mass struggle)[14] so far stays on paper. But this does not concern us just now.

The question which interests us right now is as follows: Does the demand for disarmament correspond with the revolutionary tendency among the Swiss Social Democrats? Apparently it does not. Objectively the "demand" for disarmament corresponds to the opportunist, narrow-national policy of the labor movement, a policy which is limited by the horizon of a small state. Objectively, "disarmament" is the most national and specifically national program of small states, rather than an international program of the international revolutionary Social Democracy. ....

The issue of the right of self-determination, which was one of the controversial questions within the Zimmerwald Left, was a long-standing subject of dispute between some of the Polish socialists, who raised the issue at this time, and the Bolsheviks. This question, or rather the specific question of Polish independence, was also one of the causes of controversy within the Polish socialist movement from its early days. The earliest Polish socialist group of consequence, the "Proletarjat," was international rather than national in its point of view and worked in close relation with the Russian "People's Will" partisans. Government raids, arrests, and executions in the 1880's greatly weakened this movement, which was further disturbed by differences between the internationalists and the national or patriotic socialists led by

14 In this connection, see below, pp. 534, 549, n. 72.

Boleslaw Limanowski. Polish socialists, however, were able to issue their publications abroad, particularly at Geneva and Paris. In the latter city representatives of several Polish socialist societies met in November 1892 under Limanowski's chairmanship and organized the Polish Socialist party (P.P.S.) with national independence as an important plank of its program. The internationalists did not join the new party but on July 30, 1893, formed their own party, to be known as the Social Democracy of the Kingdom of Poland. But in 1895 this party was almost completely destroyed by the police. In 1899 it was revived, and in December of the same year at a conference in Vilna the Social Democracy of Poland united with a section of the Lithuanian party, forming the Social Democracy of the Kingdom of Poland and Lithuania.[15]

The Social Democracy of Poland stated its attitude on the demand for Polish independence in the concluding paragraph of a resolution adopted at the First Congress of the party held in Warsaw in March 1894: "The First Congress of the Polish Social Democracy, considering that a struggle against national oppression—as against any other form of oppression—is necessary and possible within the limits of its general political program, believes at the same time that under existing conditions in Poland the program's demand for Poland's restoration means a complete renunciation of a successful political struggle and a postponement of the realization of the ultimate as well as immediate task of the proletariat."[16]

This party continued to oppose the independence movement even after the Second International at the London Congress in 1896 had adopted the following resolution on self-determination:

[15] The events which led to the formation of the Social Democracy of Poland and Lithuania are discussed in *The Bolsheviks and World Revolution.*

[16] This resolution was first published in the Paris party organ, *Sprawa Robotnicza,* for 1894, and was reprinted in Mazowiecki (Kulczycki), *Historja ruchu socjalistycznego w zaborze rosyjskim,* Cracow, 1904, p. 277, cited in Leder, "Natsionalnyi vopros v polskoi i russkoi social-demokratii," *Proletarskaia Revoliutsiia,* Nos. 2–3 (61–62), 1927, p. 154.

"The Congress declares that it is completely in favor of the right of all nations to self-determination and expresses its sympathy with the workers of any country which suffers at present under the yoke of military, national, and other absolutism; the Congress invites the workers of all such countries to join the ranks of class-conscious workers of the world in order to struggle jointly to overcome international capitalism and to realize the aims of international social democracy."[17]

Then and in the following years Rosa Luxemburg expounded the point of view of her party in *Critica Sociale, Neue Zeit, Sozialistische Monatshefte,* and the party organ, *Przegląd Socjal-Demokratyczny.* The crux of the argument was that the slogan of independence was incompatible with the general struggle of Polish and Russian workers to overthrow Tsarism and carry out a social revolution. This and the opposition to the alleged bourgeois tendencies of their rivals of the P.P.S. led the Social Democracy of Poland to emphasize particularly an irreconcilable class struggle with ruthless opposition to revisionism and opportunism and thus to stand on the extreme left of the Second International.

The conflict between the Polish Social Democracy and the R.S.D.L. party on the national question dates from the time of the Second Congress of the Russian party in 1903. The R.S.D.L. party had considered the matter of Polish independence at its First Congress in 1898, and in a resolution of that time stated that "The party recognizes that each nationality has the right of self-determination."[18] When this principle appeared in the draft program of the Russian party published in *Iskra,* No. 21, June 1, 1902, it was strongly criticized by Tyszka, one of the leaders of the Social Democracy of Poland and Lithuania, and at the Fourth Congress of this

[17] *Verhandlungen und Beschlüsse. des internationalen sozialistischen Arbeiter- und Gewerkschafts-Kongresses zu London vom 27 Juli bis 1 August 1896,* p. 18; quoted in Lenin, *Sochineniia,* XVII, 455, note.

[18] B. Eidelman, *Pervyi sezd R.S.D.R.P.,* pp. 77–78, cited by Leder in "Natsionalnyi vopros v polskoi i russkoi sotsial-demokratii," *Proletarskaia Revoliutsiia,* Nos. 2–3 (61–62), 1927, p. 148.

party in 1903 a resolution on union with the Russians was adopted. As one of the conditions for unification the Poles demanded "the replacement of the paragraph on self-determination by a more precise formula, which would exclude an interpretation in a nationalist spirit." Two Polish delegates attended the Second Congress of the R.S.D.L. party, where Warski read the resolution just cited.[19]

The Second Congress of the R.S.D.L. party elected a commission to study the Polish proposal, but before any action was taken the Polish delegates, Warski and Hanecki, withdrew as a result of Lenin's reference to Polish self-determination in his article, "Natsionalnyi vopros v nashei programme," in No. 44[20] of *Iskra* of July 15, 1903, which was contrary to the position taken by all the Polish party congresses.

Between 1903 and 1907, because of the struggle between the Mensheviks and the Bolsheviks, no further action was taken on the question of the union of the Social Democracy of Poland with the R.S.D.L. party. In the meantime, during the revolution of 1905, the Polish Social Democrats had been active, especially in such industrial centers as Warsaw, Lodz, and Dobrowa, where they fought both the authorities and their rivals of the Polish Socialist party. Early in 1906 when the combined Central Committee of the R.S.D.L. party was formed, the Poles again raised the question of union, and Warski, Hanecki, and Dzierzynski took part in the Fourth, or Unification, Congress of the R.S.D.L. party at Stockholm. Here an agreement was reached on the matter of territorial autonomy.[21] Two years later, in 1908, Rosa Luxemburg again raised the issue in the press, and at the Sixth Congress of their party the Poles adopted her resolution on the subject,

---

[19] Text is given in *Vtoroi ocherednoi sezd ross. sots.-dem. rabochei partii* ...., pp. 135–36.

[20] Reprinted in Lenin, *Sochineniia*, V, 337–44. Luxemburg and Tyszka read this article while the Second Congress was in session and before its removal from Brussels to London.

[21] *Protokoly obedinitelnogo sezda rossiiskoi sotsial-demokraticheskoi rabochei partii sostoiavshegosia v Stokgolme v 1906 godu*, p. 338.

which included the following: "The Social Democracy of Poland and Lithuania in advancing its program of autonomy . . . . proceeds from the social development of Poland and Russia and the realization of the consequences of this development in the spirit of the revolutionary policy of the proletarian class. The Social Democracy of Poland and Lithuania therefore endeavors to achieve autonomy not through any joke-parliament like Stolypin's Duma, as is done by all the bourgeois parties in Poland, nor through a 'Warsaw Constituent Assembly,' but through an all-state constituent assembly convened after the overthrow of Tsarism on the basis of universal, secret, and direct suffrage of the entire population of the state."[22]

Meanwhile a split had occurred in the Polish Socialist party. After the events of 1905 the older, more conservative wing, which included Józef Pilsudski, lost control of the party machinery to the younger and more radical members who favored replacing the demand for independence with one for autonomy and advocated closer relations with the Russians. After the party's Ninth Congress at Vienna, the conservatives left the party and organized the P.P.S. Revolutionary Faction, whose members are referred to in Russian literature as "*fraki.*" The other wing of the party, thereafter known as the Left or "Levitsa," abandoned the independence program for autonomy and established close relations with the Mensheviks.[23]

This change of program did not win the approval of the Bolsheviks for the Polish Socialist party (Levitsa). Lenin

[22] *Sprawozdanie z XI Zjazdu* . . . ., cited by Leder in "Natsionalnyi vopros v polskoi i russkoi sotsial-demokratii," *Proletarskaia Revoliutsiia,* Nos. 2–3 (61–62), 1927, p. 184.

[23] Four representatives of the P.P.S. (Levitsa) attended the Menshevik Conference in August 1912, and the Organization Committee agreed that in political moves affecting the entire country agreements could be made with "Levitsa." Out of deference to the Georgian S.D. Mensheviks, who had shifted from advocacy of the right of self-determination to that of cultural-national autonomy, this Conference, without taking a position on the issue, proposed that it be on the agenda of the next congress of the R.S.D.L. party. (*Izveshchenie o konferentsii organizatsii R.S.D.R.P.,* pp. 32, 42.)

and his friends were much more interested in the differences which were developing within the Social Democracy of Poland and Lithuania between its Warsaw organization and its Main Presidium in which the old leaders of the party—Luxemburg, Tyszka, Warski, and Marchlewski—were leading personalities. These differences led to a definite break in June 1912, and in March 1914 a new party organization was set up known as the Regional Presidium of the Social Democracy of Poland and Lithuania. The sympathies of the Bolsheviks were with the new group, known also as "Rozlomovists," and Lenin defended it against the charges of the Main Presidium before the International Socialist Bureau.[24] In return the "Rozlomovists" supported the six Bolshevik deputies at the time of the split in the Russian S.D. Duma group in 1913.

During the years 1912–1914 the question of cultural-national autonomy and Rosa Luxemburg's repudiation of self-determination were hotly debated in the socialist press of the Russian and national minority parties, with Lenin, Zinoviev, and Stalin upholding the Bolshevik point of view against Semkovsky, Kosovsky, Medem, Libman, Yurkevich, Zhordania, and others speaking for the Mensheviks, the Bund, and the Ukrainian and Georgian Social Democrats. But even the "Rozlomovists" were unwilling to accept Lenin's definition of self-determination. Their four delegates—Hanecki, Domski, Lenski, and Wenckowski—who attended the Poronino Conference of the Central Committee of the R.S.D.L. party in September 1913, fought against the resolution which defined the right of self-determination as the right to separate. The World War naturally gave new impetus to the discussion of the national question, especially in its relation to the program of socialist revolution. Thus it became one of the controversial issues within the Zimmerwald Left. The documents which follow present the points of view of the Regional Committee of the Social Democracy of Poland and Lithuania and the Bolsheviks.

[24] Lenin's letter to the I.S.B., August 31, 1912, in Lenin, *Sochineniia*, XVI, 109–10.

Even after the establishment of the Soviet government in Russia and the adoption of its nationality policy, Polish Communists clung to the traditional point of view on this question, and only at the Second Congress of the Polish Communist Labor party in September 1923 was the Bolshevik position accepted, and then neither readily nor unanimously. In this connection Warski quotes a passage from Dzierzynski's letter to the workers of Dolbyt, written in November 1925: "Our mistake [i.e., that of the former Social Democracy of Poland and Lithuania] was in repudiating Poland's independence, for which Lenin always rebuked us. We believed that there could be no transitional period between capitalism and socialism and consequently that there was no need of independent states, since there could be no state organization under socialism. We did not understand that there would be a rather long transitional period between capitalism and socialism, during which, under the dictatorship of the proletariat, classes and a proletarian state supported by the peasantry will exist side by side . . . . As a result of repudiating every independence, we did not understand this truth and lost our struggle for an independent Soviet Poland. . . . ."[25]

[25] In addition to the works cited in this section, see also: A. Warski, "Sotsial-demokratiia Polshi i Litvy i II sezd R.S.D.R.P.," *Kommunisticheskii Internatsional*, No. 14 (192), April 5, 1929, pp. 30–41, and No. 16–17 (194–95), April 26, 1929, pp. 24–39; N. Popov, *Outline History of the Communist Party of the Soviet Union*, Part I, pp. 106, 184–85, 193–94, 284; D. R. Gillie [trans. and ed.], Joseph Pilsudski, *The Memories of a Polish Revolutionary and Soldier*, pp. 9, 14–16, 151, 162; Jan Alfred Regula, *Historja Komunistycznej Partji Polski w świetle faktów i dokumentów* [2d ed.], pp. 9–31; S. Krzhizhanovsky, "Polskaia sotsial-demokratiia na II sezde R.S.D.R.P.," *Borba Klassov*, Nos. 8–9, August–September, 1933, pp. 113–21; S. Krzhizhanovsky, "Polskaia sotsial-demokratiia i II sezd RSDRP," *Proletarskaia Revoliutsiia*, No. 2, 1933, pp. 104–135; Ya. Ganetsky, "Delegatsiia SDP i L. na II sezde RSDRP," in *Proletarskaia Revoliutsiia*, No. 2, 1933, pp. 187–200.

THE POLISH SOCIAL DEMOCRATS AND THE RIGHT OF SELF-DETERMINATION

[Theses and Resolution of the Editorial Board of *Gazeta Robotnicza,*
Organ of the Regional Presidium of the Social Democracy of
Poland and Lithuania][26]

I. National Oppression and International Social Democracy

1. Imperialism represents the tendency of finance capital *to outgrow the limits of national states,* to seize for national capital transoceanic sources of raw material and of food supplies, spheres for investment, and markets, and to form, *in Europe also, larger state units* by combining adjacent territories that complement each other economically, regardless of the nationality of the inhabitants. This latter tendency is based also on military reasons, since imperialism, by sharpening the antagonisms between the states, engenders the necessity of both attack and self-defense.

The tendencies of imperialism toward colonial and continental annexations signify an *increase and general extension of national oppression,* which hitherto has existed only in certain states with a heterogeneous population (i.e., with national minorities) where by virtue of historic and geographic reasons one nationality ruled over several.

2. This national oppression *contradicts the interests of the working class.* The same imperialist bureaucracy, which is the organ of national oppression, becomes also the executor of *class oppression of the proletariat of its own nationality;* it turns all the *means* used in the struggle against the oppressed peoples against the fighting proletariat of the oppressing nation. *As for the working class of the oppressed nation,* national oppression *checks its class struggle* not only by restricting its *freedom to organize,* by pressing down its cultural level, but also by arousing in it *feelings of solidarity with its national bourgeoisie.* Tied hand and foot, corrupted politically by nationalism, the proletariat of the oppressed nation becomes a *helpless object of exploitation* and hence a dangerous rival (wage-cutter, strikebreaker) of the workers of the oppressing nation.

The forcing of nationally alien parts into the boundaries of a victorious state creates new causes for war, since the vanquished state will endeavor to regain these parts because it needs them economically and militarily or because a national revenge slogan can best cover up the imperialist policy of the vanquished state.

3. The Social Democratic party, therefore, must *fight* most energeti-

[26] [K. Radek], "Thesen über Imperialismus und nationale Unterdrückung," *Vorbote,* No. 2, April 1916, pp. 44–51.

cally *against imperialism's policy of annexation,* as well as against the *policy* of national *oppression* that follows it. To the assertion of imperialists that the acquisition of colonies is necessary for the development of capitalism, the Social Democratic party opposes the fact that in Central and Western Europe, as well as in the United States of North America, the time has already come for transforming capitalism into socialism, which requires no colonies, for it renders to backward people so much unselfish cultural support that it will be able to obtain from them, in free exchange and without dominating them, all that the peoples under its regime are themselves unable, because of geographic reasons, to produce.

Not expansion and extension, but the overcoming of capitalism, forms the historic task of the proletariat; a task which can be fulfilled even now. To the assertion that annexations in Europe are necessary for the military security of a victorious imperialist state, and hence for the assurance of peace, Social Democracy opposes the fact that annexations only sharpen antagonisms, thereby increasing the danger of war. But, even if this were not true. Social Democracy could not lend its hand to the establishment of a peace based on the oppression of peoples. Should it approve of such a peace, it would thereby open *an abyss between the proletariat of the ruling and of the oppressed nations.* While the proletariat of the ruling nation, by approving annexations, would become responsible for the imperialist policy, would also have to support further the policy and hence would become a *slave of imperialism,* the proletariat of the oppressed nations would unite with *its bourgeoisie, and would see an enemy in the proletariat of the ruling nation.* Instead of the *international class struggle of the proletariat against international bourgeoisie, there would occur the splitting of the proletariat and its spiritual corruption.* Both in the struggle for its daily interests and in the struggle for socialism and against imperialism, the proletariat would be completely paralyzed.

4. The starting point of the struggle of Social Democracy against annexations, against a forcible detention of oppressed nations within the boundaries of the annexing state, is *the renunciation of any defense of the fatherland,* which in the era of imperialism is but a defense of the rights of one's own bourgeoisie to oppress and plunder foreign peoples. It consists in *denouncing national oppression* as a blow directed against the interests of the proletariat of the dominant nation, and in demanding for the oppressed *all democratic rights,* including freedom of agitation for political separation—for democratic principles demand that agitation, whatever it may be, should be overcome only through intellectual methods and not through violence. While declining in this way every responsibility for the consequences of the imperialist policy of oppression and while

strongly fighting against it, *Social Democracy does not advocate either an erection of new boundary posts in Europe or the re-erection of those which have been torn down by imperialism.* Wherever capitalism has developed unprotected by its own state, there historical development has shown that an independent state was by no means an absolute prerequisite for the unfolding of the productive forces and for the introduction of socialism. Wherever the crushing wheel of imperialism passed over an already existing capitalist state, there through the brutal means of imperialist oppression a political and economic concentration of the capitalist world takes place which prepares for socialism. Basing itself on the consequences of this political and economic concentration that arouse the masses through national and economic oppression, Social Democracy has to educate the masses of the people of the oppressed as well as of the oppressing nations for a united struggle, which alone is capable of abolishing national oppression and economic exploitation, by leading mankind *beyond imperialism toward socialism.*

When in developed capitalist countries, Social Democracy will be able to see that defeat of imperialism is not brought about by the return to old forms, by the organization of new and in the restoration of old national states, but rather by clearing the road for *socialism*—for which the economic conditions here are already ripe—with the cry, *away with boundaries!* then from that task of Social Democracy there also ensues the demand, *away with the colonies!* which demand drowns out our struggle against imperialist national oppression. The colonies are sources of a new stream of profits for capital which prolong its life. Nay, capitalism seeks to draw physical strength from the colonies by forming native troops, which some day it will use against the revolutionary proletariat also as it now uses them in the World War against its rivals. This international renunciation of colonial expansion, which may be achieved by the proletariat only in a revolutionary struggle, would in no case mean the relapse of undeveloped capitalist countries into barbarism, as social imperialists assert. In the most important countries of the Orient (Turkey, China, India) for years there was noticeable a growth of bourgeois elements which were capable of themselves fulfilling the task of developing productive forces, a task still imminent there for capitalism. While demanding of European capitalism the renunciation of colonial expansion and *making use* of the struggle of the young colonial bourgeoisie against European imperialism *for the sharpening of the revolutionary crisis in Europe,* Social Democracy in order to hasten the approach of the moment when the hour will strike also for socialism outside Europe, will support the proletarian struggles in the colonial countries against European and native capital, and will also attempt to spread among the colonial proletariat the understanding that its own lasting interest demands its solidarity, not with its national bourgeoisie, but with the European proletariat which fights for socialism.

5. Just as under capitalism it is impossible to alter imperialism in accordance with the interests of the laboring class, or to put an end to its armaments, *so imperialism cannot be stripped of its tendency to national oppression or made to recognize the right of the peoples to self-determination.* Therefore *it is a question of conducting the struggle against national oppression as a struggle against imperialism and for socialism.*

In order to aim at liberating nationally oppressed masses, the struggle of Social Democracy *must be of a social-revolutionary nature* and must strive to extirpate the rule of capitalism. For only by eliminating capitalist private property can the working class abolish the desire for national oppression, which is only a part of class dominance. A socialist society will know no oppression; it will grant to all peoples the right of deciding in common all their needs, to every citizen *the freedom to have a part in deciding upon* the common task which he will help to accomplish.

The guidance of the struggle against national oppression into the wide stream of revolutionary mass struggle for socialism does not signify a postponement of that struggle for an indefinite period, nor does it signify empty promises to the oppressed peoples for the future; for the striking revolutionizing consequences of the imperialist epoch make it at the same time an era of socialist revolutions in the course of which the proletariat will break all chains.

II. THE SO-CALLED RIGHT OF NATIONS TO SELF-DETERMINATION

As an inheritance from the Second International there has persisted the formula of the right of self-determination. It has played an equivocal role in the Second International: it had to express, on the one hand, a protest against every national subjugation and, on the other, the readiness of Social Democracy to "defend the fatherland." It was applied to separate national questions solely in order to avoid an analysis of their actual content and the tendency of their development. While the consequences of the policy of the defense of the fatherland in the World War have shown very plainly the counter-revolutionary character of this formula in an era of imperialism, its deceptive character as a formula which must embrace our struggle against national oppression still remains obscure for many. Since it states sharply the antagonism toward the imperialist tendencies of oppression, revolutionary Social Democrats (for example, those of Russia) also see in it a necessary attribute of our revolutionary agitation. While we value fully the proletarian revolutionary aims which the proletariat pursues by spreading the slogan of the right of self-determination, we cannot, however, recognize this formula as a correct expression of our struggle against imperialism. Here are our reasons:

1. *The Right of Self-Determination Is Impracticable in Capitalist Society.*—Modern nations represent the political-cultural form of the bourgeois rule over the masses of the people of the same language. The nations, split into classes, have no common interests and no common will. The "national" policy is one that corresponds to the interests of the ruling classes. This is not contradicted by the existence of political democracy in different capitalist countries. The influence of the economic rule of capital upon the masses of the people, the continuous systematic conditioning of them by all the organs of the capitalist state (the church, the school, and the press) allows the bourgeoisie to force the capitalist will upon the majority of the people indirectly and thus makes the will of capitalism appear to be the will of the people. This is modern democracy! The interest of the strongest bourgeoisie, or that of an alliance of several of its national groups, determines the relations between nations. Since capital with its expansion cannot wait until it can, through economic and cultural influences, impose its will on the masses of the people in the territories of that expansion—a peaceful expansion which would require decades and, which frequently encounters an opposite desire of other capitalist groups and makes such expansion impossible—*the forms of political democracy are cast aside, and open violence settles the questions concerning the incorporation of foreign territories.* A plebiscite can here be used only as an open deception for sanctioning the deeds of violence. Therefore, on the basis of capitalist society it is totally impossible to make the will of nations a deciding factor in questions concerning the changing of boundaries as the so-called right of self-determination demands.

In so far as this demand is interpreted—that a single section of a nation should decide whether it wishes to belong to one or the other state—it is not only utopian—because capital will never permit the people to determine state boundaries—it is also particularistic and undemocratic. Had the masses of the people of a country been empowered to determine their boundaries, then such an issue would have to be passed throughout the entire state and not in one province; nay, in questions of dispute between two countries, democracy would request an "understanding" between their democratically elected representations. For example, should France's incorporation of Alsace-Lorraine raise a national question there—the aspirations of that section of the population which longs to be again in the German empire—should this incorporation call forth the danger of revenge in Germany and thus threaten France with new wars, then it is clear that it would be by no means democratic to thrust upon the French people all these consequences on the basis of the Alsatians' desire alone and without letting the French people decide for themselves.

2. *The Right of Self-Determination Is Not Applicable to a Socialist Society.*—The so-called right of self-determination is also used with the remark that it can first be realized under socialism, and consequently expresses our desire for socialism. The following objection can be raised against this. We know that socialism will abolish all national oppression, because it abolishes all class interests which drive toward this oppression. Nor have we any reason to assume that in a socialist society a nation would acquire the character of an economic-political unit. In all probability it would possess only the character of a cultural and linguistic unit, since the territorial subdivision of the socialist cultural sphere, in so far as the latter might exist, can result only by virtue of the demands of production, and then, of course, instead of individual nations having to decide separately about subdivision on the basis of their own supremacy (as *"the right of self-determination"* demands) all citizens concerned would *participate in that decision.* The assigning of the formula of the "right of self-determination" to socialism is due to the complete misunderstanding of the character of a socialist community.

3. *The Tactical Consequences of Applying the Formula of the Right of Self-Determination.*—Like every utopian slogan, this slogan also spreads false conceptions regarding the character of both a capitalist and a socialist society, and misleads the proletariat which is struggling against national oppression. Instead of telling the proletariat openly that *unless it does away with capitalism* it is just as little able to free itself from the danger of having its destinies arbitrarily determined in accordance with the military and economic interests of a capitalism torn by antagonisms as it is to free itself from the danger of wars, this slogan arouses *hopes which cannot be fulfilled,* the hope that capitalism is capable of adjusting itself to the national interests of the weak peoples. Thus, independently and even against the will of its prophets, this slogan replaces *the social revolutionary view,* which has been the most important result of the World War, with the national reformist view. In the program of the proletariat of the *oppressed nations* the slogan of the right of self-determination may serve as a bridge to social patriotism. As the experience of the Polish, Ruthenian, and Alsatian labor movements indicates, this slogan serves as an argument for the nationalist movement within the laboring class and as an argument for the hopes built on the success of one of the belligerent countries, thus disrupting the international front of the proletariat.

Incorporated in the program of the proletariat of the oppressing nations, in the guise of a solution of national questions, this slogan makes it possible for social imperialists to prove its illusory character and thus depict our struggle against national oppression as an historically unwarranted sentimentality—and thus to undermine the confidence of the proletariat in the scientific foundation of the Social Democratic program. Nay more, this slogan could arouse in the proletariat of the oppressing nation the illusion that—in contrast to the proletariat of the oppressed nations—it is already able to determine its own destinies and is, therefore, obliged to protect, together with the other parts of the nation, their "common" interests and their will. In a socialist society it is impossible for an isolated national group to exercise the right of self-determination on questions which concern all citizens; but even regardless of this fact, if, for agitation purposes, the slogan of the right of self-determination is used as one which can be realized for the first time only by a social revolution, thus leading us into the struggle for socialism, even then it is insufficient for our purposes; for in a period of transition when socialism is already possible economically but when the social revolutionary class struggles have not yet begun, our *tactical interest* requires that *sharp emphasis be placed on a clear and naked slogan of socialism and upon the socialist revolution as the central idea that sharpens and expands our separate struggles.*

4. *Historic Material for Judging That Question.*—Any references to Marx's position with regard to the national questions in the period 1848–1871 have not the slightest value, for when Marx stood up for the liberation of Ireland and for Poland's independence he was, at the same time, against movements toward independence on the part of the Czechs, South Slavs, and so forth. Furthermore, Marx's position shows exactly that it is not the task of Marxism to formulate an attitude toward concrete questions in terms of abstract "rights." The negative attitude of Social Democracy toward every national oppression is, as we have proved in the first section of our theses, the result of the incompatibility of the proletariat's class interests with the support of the ruling classes. The positive attitude toward every national problem (the Alsace-Lorraine, the Polish, and the Balkan questions) can be achieved only on the basis of the concrete development of the tendencies of this question within the limits of the entire imperialist epoch.

The characterization of the Marxist position, which is directed against the formula of the right of self-determination, as a Proudhonist position is nonsensical. Proudhonism denied the national question and wished to solve all social questions not through class struggle but through petty bourgeois associations. The Marxist opponents of the so-called right of self-determination do not deny the national question; they do not postpone the struggle against national oppression until socialism is victorious. While they cannot be hurt by being reproached for their Proudhonism, it is, however, possible to designate the method of those who adhere to the right of self-determination as a stereotyped application of democratic conceptions.

5. *Polish Social Democracy and the Question of the So-called Right of Self-Determination.*—In 1893 the Social Democracy of Russian Poland formulated its position on the Polish question, on an analysis of the tendencies of the economic development of Poland. The following twenty years of Polish history have fully confirmed this analysis, especially since neither in the revolution of 1905–1906 nor in the World War have any *earnest* social strata in *Poland* manifested *their strivings toward independence*. The Polish Social Democracy rejected the slogan of the right of self-determination when the London International Congress proposed it in 1896, in order to avoid adopting toward this slogan the attitude of the Polish social patriots, who had placed the struggle for Poland's independence on their banner. After the phrase about self-determination had become a cloak of social patriotism, the representatives of the Polish Social Democracy fought against its acceptance in the program of the Russian Social Democracy in 1903. Although this phrase had been accepted, the Social Democracy of Russian Poland entered the general party in 1906, since, on the one hand, our complete victory over social patriotism had decreased the danger of having social patriots refer to that paragraph of the Russian Social Democratic program, and since the revolutionary mass struggle demanded imperatively, in spite of all differences of opinion, the closing of the ranks. The Social Democracy of Russian Poland could join the Russian Social Democratic party so much the more easily since this paragraph of the program had not played even the smallest part in the agitation of the Russian Social Democracy during the revolution [of 1905] and since we had our own representatives in the central organs of the party and enjoyed the widest autonomy in agitation. When, in the era of counter-revolution, the national question acquired great political importance in Russia, and a discussion in that connection began on the attitude of Social Democracy toward this question, the Social Democrats of Russian Poland stated in detail their stand on this question.

This stand we have expounded and confirmed in general in these theses. Their application to the Polish question we have given in a special resolution of *September 1915,* which we quote herewith in order to show concretely how, in our opinion, the agitation among the workers of the oppressed nations should be conducted from the social revolutionary standpoint.

III. The Polish Question and Social Democracy[27]

1. The position taken by the propertied classes during the World War has proved quite plainly the correctness of the assertion of the Social Democracy of Russian Poland that capitalist development has split the interests of Polish capitalism into antagonistic parts and has bound them up with the interests of the annexing powers [Russia, Germany, and Austria-Hungary]. This *internment of the desire for independence* found its expression in a conscious renunciation of the slogan of independence on the part of the Polish bourgeoisie: all its war programs are to be realized not only by the force of weapons of one or the other imperialist camp but also by the bourgeoisie's endeavors to strengthen one of these camps by uniting the Polish regions with it. All war programs of the Polish bourgeoisie are directed against Poland's independence.

The World War has proved that the period of the formation of national states in Europe has passed. In the imperialist period of capitalism every state strives to expand its boundaries by annexations and the oppression of foreign countries. The position of the Polish bourgeoisie in all the three annexing states has bluntly shown that the ideal of a national state in the imperialist period is an anachronism, and it has confirmed the correctness of the position taken by the Social Democrats of Russian Poland with respect to a desire for independence.

The Polish proletariat has never made national independence one of its aims. The Polish proletariat originated by virtue of capitalist unification of the three parts of Poland with the respective annexing powers, and it has conducted its struggle for democracy, for the improvement of its economic state, and for socialism *together with the proletarians of all other nations, within the limits of the historically existing states.* It has sought *to destroy not the existing state boundaries but the character of the state as an organ of class and national oppression. Today,* in the face of the experiences of the World War, the advancement of the *slogan of independence* as a means of struggle against national oppression would be not only a *harmful* utopianism but a *repudiation of the simplest principles of socialism.* This slogan would signify an endeavor to form a new imperialist power, a power which would strive also to subjugate and oppress foreign peoples. The only result of such a program would be the weakening of class-consciousness, the sharpening of national antagonisms, the splitting of the forces of the proletariat, and the strengthening of new war dangers.

[27] Resolution of the editorial board of *Gazeta Robotnicza* adopted on September 9–10, 1915; first published in *Gazeta Robotnicza*, No. 25, January 1916. (V. Leder, "Natsionalnyi vopros v polskoi i russkoi sotsial-demokratii, *Proletarskaia Revoliutsiia*, Nos. 2–3 (61–62), 1927, pp. 200–201.)

2. The programs of uniting Polish territories under the rule of one of the imperialist states or a coalition of them—as for example the program which was advanced by the Polish *Austrophiles* and *Russophiles*—originate with the desire of the Polish bourgeoisie to strengthen its own position as compared with that of the bourgeoisie of the annexing powers, so as to assure for itself a larger share of the state's imperialist spoils.

The tendency of the annexing powers [Russia, Germany, and Austria-Hungary] to annex Polish territories originated from strategic as well as from general imperialist interests, which demanded an increase of the state territory. Born of the imperialist interests of the Polish bourgeoisie and of the interests of ruling bourgeoisie of the annexing powers, the unification of Polish territories under the rule of one Great Power or of a coalition of Great Powers could be only *an instrument of imperialist policy.* Since these imperialist interests, both the general interests and especially the economic interests, demand that the Polish territories should be maintained in complete subjugation, they permit no democratic system in these territories. Needless to say, such a unification would give only the minimum guaranties for a free cultural development of that aspect of the national question which concerns the proletariat's interests.

Whether or not the war leads to a unification of the Polish territories into one whole organism connected with the victorious state will depend on the military results of the war and on the diplomatic situation brought about by the war. The war can also end with a *breaking up* of the *Polish territories* through new annexations, with a new cutting up of the map of Poland. However, all fears that this new partitioning and the changes in market, custom, and law conditions which it would cause would strangle Poland's capitalist development—and thus also the socialist movement in Russian Poland—are exaggerated; the comparatively high degree of Poland's economic development has already generated productive forces which can adjust themselves to new conditions, and the weakening of the socialist movement in one section of Poland would be compensated by its increased strength in another section. Nevertheless the necessity for such an adjustment would cause a long economic *crisis* which would press heavily on the backs of the proletariat.

The facts mentioned above refer also to the idea of an independent *buffer state,* which incidentally would be an empty utopia of small, weak groups. If realized, this idea would signify the creation of a small Polish *Rumpfstaat,* which would become a military colony of one or the other group of Great Powers, a toy for their military and economic interests, a region exploited by foreign capital, a battlefield of future wars.

3. It follows, therefore, that the interests of the proletariat—eco-

nomic, cultural, and political—exclude *every support of the war programs of the Polish bourgeoisie.* The old proletarian policy, which was determined by the class interest of the proletariat, must remain unaltered and the laboring class has not the slightest reason to give it up for the sake of the bourgeois war programs. Founded on no real advantage, the support of these programs would signify a renunciation of independent class action, an agreement to an alliance with the bourgeoisie for the entire war period, and, finally, would divert for many long years the tactics of the proletariat from the correct course. On the other hand, the proletariat cannot undertake *to defend the boundaries of the annexing powers,* because in the present epoch every capitalist state would thus become a drag on progress, to say nothing of the fact that the annexing powers have been for the Polish proletariat organs not only of class but also of national oppression.

Without being blind to all the dangers indicated above, dangers which the Polish proletariat will have to face if Poland is broken up again, the proletariat must understand that just as it is impossible to eliminate all other dangers of imperialism without a victory of socialism, so these dangers *cannot be eliminated within the limits of an imperialist epoch.*

4. The impossibility of solving the general questions brought up by the war, as well as the impossibility of profitably protecting the national cultural interests of the Polish proletariat in the epoch of imperialism, naturally does not signify that the proletariat must "wait" with arms crossed until socialism frees it from the new dangers and burdens of the war as well as from new dangers of national oppression. Imperialism is a policy of capitalism in that stage of development which makes a socialist organization of production possible. The sacrifices of the proletariat for the war, the increased pressure of taxation, the political reaction, the deterioration of labor conditions—all the consequences of the war will drive the proletariat toward revolutionary struggles for socialism, which will fill the next historical epoch. The struggle against war opens up this new epoch. By showing the proletariat how capitalism, which in the name of its own interests leads the peoples to the shambles, tears the nations to pieces, suppresses national requirements, treats the masses of the people as though they were dumb animals, and by protesting against this wasting of people's blood, this arbitrary tearing to pieces of nations by the Great Powers, this double increase of national oppression, we prepare the proletariat for the revolutionary struggle.

Regardless of whether the sharpening of the political crisis will permit the proletariat to play an active part even during the war or whether these struggles will take place only later, the proletariat will *not* lead a *separatist policy* (the defense of the *status quo,* the struggle for the unification under one rule), nor will it pursue a vision of Poland's independence; *it will transform its protest against the consequences of war* (the bloody sacrifices, the economic damages, annexations, national oppression) *into a struggle against the causes of imperialism.* This consolidated struggle, in the sense of a conscious *striving toward a social revolution,* the Polish proletariat will *lead in solidarity with the international proletariat in general and that of the annexing powers in particular.* This social revolutionary struggle *does not exclude the tendency toward a democratization of the political conditions* under capitalism—for example, the overthrow of Tsarism in Russia—nor does it exclude the conquest of national liberties—for example, the expansion of local, provincial, and state autonomy. On the contrary, the revolutionary prospects must strengthen the enthusiasm of the proletariat in its struggle for immediate achievements, since the understanding that social revolution alone forms the road to a complete abolition of class and national oppression will arm the proletariat against any policy of compromise which decreases the strength of the class struggle.

EDITORIAL BOARD OF "GAZETA ROBOTNICZA"
Organ of the Regional Presidium of the Social Democracy
of Russian Roland

THE SOCIALIST REVOLUTION AND THE RIGHT OF SELF-DETERMINATION

[Theses of the Central Committee of the R.S.D.L. Party][28]

1. IMPERIALISM, SOCIALISM, AND THE LIBERATION OF THE OPPRESSED NATIONS

Imperialism is the highest stage in the development of capitalism. Capital in the advanced countries outgrew the limits of national states, established monopoly in place of competition, and thus created all objective premises for the realization of socialism. Therefore the revolutionary struggle of the proletariat for the overthrow of the capitalist governments, for the expropriation of the bourgeoisie, stands on the order of the day in Western Europe and in the United States. Imperialism pushes the masses toward such a struggle by tremendously sharpening class antagonisms, by making the life of the masses worse economically—through trusts and the high cost of living—and, politically, through the growth of militarism, more frequent wars, the strengthening

---

[28] Lenin, "Sotsialisticheskaia revoliutsiia i pravo natsii na samoopredelenie," *Sochineniia*, XIX, 37–48; first published in German in *Vorbote*, No. 2, April 1916, pp. 36–44, and in Russian in *Sbornik Sotsial-Demokrata*, No. 1, October 1916, pp. 1–6. Another, English version, is given in Lenin, *Selected Works*, V, 267–81.

of reaction, and the consolidation and expansion of national oppression and colonial robbery. Victorious socialism must necessarily bring about complete democracy and, consequently, not only effect the complete equality of the rights of nations but also introduce the right of self-determination of the oppressed nations, i.e., the right of free political secession. Such socialist parties as do not prove by their entire activity both now, during a revolution, and after its victory that they will free the oppressed nations and will build up relations with them on the basis of a free union (while a free union without the freedom of secession would be only a deceitful phrase) would be committing treason against socialism.

Democracy, to be sure, is a form of state organization which must also vanish when the state as such vanishes; but this will happen only with the passage from a completely victorious and consolidated socialism to complete communism.

2. A Socialist Revolution and the Struggle for Democracy

A socialist revolution is not only a single act, not only a single battle on a single front, but a whole epoch of accentuated class conflicts, a long series of battles on all fronts, i.e., on all questions of economy and politics, of battles which can only end with the expropriation of the bourgeoisie. It would be a fundamental error to think that a struggle for democracy would be capable of diverting the proletariat from a socialist revolution or of obscuring, overshadowing, etc., such revolution. On the contrary, just as victorious socialism is impossible unless it achieves complete democracy, so the proletariat cannot prepare for a victory over the bourgeoisie if it does not lead a broad, consistent, and revolutionary struggle for democracy.

The elimination of one of the paragraphs of the democratic program —for example, the paragraph about self-determination of nations—supposedly for the reason of its "impracticability" or "illusiveness" under imperialism, would be no less an error. The assertion that the nations' right of self-determination is impracticable within the realm of capitalism can be interpreted either in an absolute, economic sense or in a conditional, political sense.

In the first case the assertion is fundamentally false in theory. First, in this sense the introduction of labor money, and the abolition of crises, etc., are impracticable under capitalism. It is completely wrong to say that the self-determination of nations is *likewise* impracticable. Secondly, even the single example of the separation of Norway from Sweden in 1905 is sufficient to refute the idea of "impracticability" in this sense. Thirdly, it would be ridiculous to deny that with a slight change in political and strategic relations between Germany and England, for example, the formation of such new states as Poland, India, etc., could be well "realized" today or tomorrow. Fourthly, finance capital in its endeavors to expand will "freely" buy and bribe even the freest of democratic and republican governments and the elective officials of any country, even of an "independent" one. The domination of finance capital, as of capital in general, can be abolished by *no* reforms *whatsoever* in the realm of political democracy; while self-determination belongs wholly and exclusively to that realm. But this domination of finance capital will by no means abolish the significance of political democracy as a freer, broader, and clearer *form* of class oppression and thus of class struggle. Therefore, all arguments about the "impracticability" in the economic sense of one of the demands of political democracy under capitalism lead to a theoretically false definition of the general and fundamental relations of capitalism and of political democracy in general.

The assertion in the second case is incomplete and inexact, since not only the nations' right of self-determination but *all* fundamental demands of political democracy "can be realized" under imperialism only incompletely, distortedly, and as a rare exception (for example, the secession of Norway from Sweden in 1905). The demand advanced by all revolutionary Social Democrats for the immediate liberation of colonies is also "impracticable" under capitalism without a number of revolutions. It does not follow that Social Democracy is repudiating an immediate and a most resolute struggle for *all* these demands—since such a repudiation would only play into the hands of the bourgeoisie and of the reaction—but, on the contrary, there follows the necessity on the part of Social Democrats to formulate and carry out all these demands not in a reformist but in a revolutionary manner, without confining themselves to the limits of bourgeois legality but by breaking these limits; without becoming satisfied with parliamentary speeches and verbal protests but by drawing the masses into active demonstrations; by expanding and firing the struggle for every fundamental democratic demand as far as a direct onslaught of the proletariat against the bourgeoisie, i.e., a socialist revolution which would expropriate the bourgeoisie. A socialist revolution can flare up not only from an extensive strike or a street demonstration, or a hunger riot, or a military rebellion, or a colonial mutiny, but also from any political crisis, such as the Dreyfus affair or the Zabern incident,[29] or in connection with a referendum on the secession of an oppressed nation, etc.

[29] In November 1913, Zabern, a French town then under German rule, was the scene of an affair which caused great bitterness in France and assumed the proportions of an international incident. A German lieutenant named Forstner insulted Alsatian recruits, and a street riot followed. Twenty-nine persons were arrested.

The intensification of national oppression under imperialism implies for Social Democracy, not a renouncing of an "utopian"—as the bourgeoisie calls it—struggle for the nations' freedom of secession, but on the contrary a more thorough utilizing of conflicts caused by this intensification as incentives for mass action and for revolutionary demonstrations against the bourgeoisie.

3. The Significance of the Right of Self-Determination and Its Relation to Federation

The right of nations to self-determination signifies exclusively a right to independence in the political sense, to a free political secession from the nation that oppresses. Concretely, this demand of political democracy signifies complete freedom of agitation in favor of secession and of settling the question of secession by means of a referendum of the nation that secedes. Thus this demand is not at all identical with the demand for secession, for partitioning, for forming small states. It signifies only a consistent expression of the struggle against any national oppression. The closer the democratic state order is to a complete freedom of secession, the less frequent and the weaker will be the endeavors to separate in practice, since the advantages of large states from the point of view of both economic progress and the interests of the masses are assured, and, furthermore, they increase with the growth of capitalism. The recognition of self-determination is not equivalent to the recognition of federation as a principle. It is possible to be a resolute opponent of this principle and an adherent of democratic centralism, and yet to prefer federation—which is the only road to complete democratic centralism—to national inequality. Exactly from that viewpoint Marx, being himself a centralist, preferred a federation of Ireland with England to a forced subjugation of Ireland by the English.[30]

Socialism aims not only to abolish the existing subdivision of mankind into small states as well as all national isolation but also to bring about a rapprochement between nations and even their fusion. And precisely in order to attain that aim we must, on the one hand, explain to the masses the reactionary nature of the ideas of Renner and O. Bauer about the so-called "cultural-national autonomy," while, on the other hand, we must demand the liberation of the oppressed nations, not in general, deliquescent phrases, not in senseless declamations,

On December 2 Forstner caused the arrest of a boy at Zettweiler and struck him with his saber. The affair led to a vote of censure of Bethmann-Hollweg in the Reichstag; but the military party secured the acquittal of Forstner by an appeal to the war council.

[30] This refers to Marx's letters to Engels on the question of Ireland's indépendence, written in the period from 1867 to 1869.

not by "postponing" the question until the advent of socialism—but in a clearly and precisely formulated political program which takes specifically into account the hypocrisy and cowardice of the socialists of the oppressing nations. Just as mankind may come to the abolition of classes only through a transitional period of the dictatorship of the oppressed class, so mankind can come to an inevitable fusion of nations only through a transitional period of the complete liberation of all oppressed nations, i.e., their right to secede.

4. The Proletarian Revolutionary Presentation of the Question of the Self-Determination of Nations

Not only the demand for the self-determination of nations but *all* paragraphs of our democratic minimum program have been advanced *previously,* as early as the seventeenth and eighteenth centuries, by the petty bourgeoisie. The petty bourgeoisie to this day advance *all* these demands in a utopian fashion without perceiving the class struggle and its intensification under democracy and while believing in "peaceful" capitalism. Such is exactly the utopia of a peaceful union of nations with equal rights under imperialism, a utopia deceiving the people and defended by the Kautskyans. As against this Philistine, opportunist utopia, the program of Social Democracy must advance division of nations into oppressed and oppressing, a division which is most essential, basic, and inevitable under imperialism.

The proletariat of the oppressing nations cannot confine itself to general, trite phrases repeated by any pacifist bourgeois—phrases against annexations and for national equality in general. The proletariat cannot pass over in silence the question of the state *boundaries* based on national oppression, which is most "unpleasant" for the imperialist bourgeoisie. The proletariat cannot do otherwise than struggle against a forcible retention of the oppressed nations within the boundaries of a given state, and this actually means to struggle for the right of self-determination. The proletariat must demand freedom of political secession for colonies and nations oppressed by "its own" nation. Otherwise proletarian internationalism will remain an empty phrase, and neither confidence nor class solidarity between the workers of the oppressed and of the oppressing nations will be possible. The hypocrisy of the reformist and Kautskyan defenders of self-determination, who do not talk about the nations oppressed by "their own" nation and forcibly retained in "their own" state, is left unrevealed.

On the other hand, the socialists of oppressed nations in particular must advocate and carry out a complete, absolute, and organized unification of the workers of the oppressed nation with the workers of the oppressing nation. Without this unification it is impossible to protect an independent policy of the proletariat of the oppressed nation and its class solidarity with the proletariat of other countries from any and every kind of trick, betrayal, and fraud of the bourgeoisie; for the bourgeoisie of the oppressed nations is continually using the slogans of national liberation to deceive the workers; in internal politics it utilizes these slogans to conclude reactionary agreements with the bourgeoisie of the dominant nation (for example, the Poles in Austria and Russia, who conclude deals with the reactionary elements for the oppression of the Jews and the Ukrainians); in foreign politics it endeavors to conclude deals with one of the rival imperialist powers in order to attain its own predatory aims (the policy of small Balkan states, etc.).

The fact that the struggle for national freedom against one imperialist power can under certain conditions be utilized by another "Great" Power for its equally imperialist aims, can as little force Social Democracy to renounce the recognition of the right of nations for self-determination as can the multiple cases of the bourgeoisie utilizing republican slogans for political deception and financial robbery—for example, the Latin countries—force the Social Democrats to renounce their republicanism.[31]

5. Marxism and Proudhonism in the National Question

In contrast to the petty-bourgeois democrats, Marx regarded all democratic demands without exception, not as an absolute, but as an historic expression of struggle of the masses, guided by the bourgeoisie, against feudalism. Every one of these demands might have served and has served the bourgeoisie under certain circumstances as an instrument for deceiving the workers. To single out in that respect one of the demands of political democracy—namely, the demand for the self-determination of nations—and to oppose it to the rest is fundamentally wrong in theory. In practice the proletariat can maintain its independence only by subordinating its struggle for all democratic demands —not excluding the demand for a republic—to its revolutionary struggle for the overthrow of the bourgeoisie.

[31] Needless to say, a renunciation of the right of self-determination, on the ground that it seemingly implies the "defense of the fatherland," would be ridiculous. With the same right, i.e., with equal shallowness, the social chauvinists referred in 1914–1916 to any demand of democracy (for example, to its republicanism), and to any formulation of struggle against national oppression, in order to justify the "defense of the fatherland." Marxism derives both the recognition of the defense of the fatherland in the war—for example, during the great French revolution, or the wars of Garibaldi in Europe—and the renunciation of the defense of the fatherland in the imperialist war of 1914–1916, from the analysis of the concrete-historic peculiarities of every single war and not at all from some "general principle," or from some separate paragraph of the program. [Author's note.]

On the other hand, in contrast to the Proudhonists, who "negate" the national question "in the name of a social revolution," and by keeping in view above all the interests of the proletarian class struggle in the advanced countries—Marx advanced to the foreground the fundamental principle of internationalism and socialism: a people which oppresses other peoples cannot be free. It was precisely from the point of view of the interests of the revolutionary movement of the German workers that Marx demanded in 1848 that the victorious democracy of Germany should proclaim and give freedom to the peoples oppressed by the Germans. It is precisely from the point of view of the revolutionary struggle of the English workers that Marx demanded in 1869 the separation of Ireland from England and added, "even if after the separation a federation should result." Only by advancing such demands was Marx really educating the English workers in an internationalist spirit. Only thus could he oppose to the opportunists and to bourgeois reformism—which even now, half a century later, has not materialized the Irish "reform"—the revolutionary solution of that historic problem. Only in that way could Marx in contrast to the apologists of capital—who shout about the utopian nature and impracticability of small nations' freedom of secession and about the progressive nature not only of economic but also of political concentration—argue that this concentration was progressing in a *non*-imperialist manner or argue in favor of a rapprochement between the nations, based not on violence but on a free union of the proletarians of all countries. Only in that way could Marx oppose the revolutionary action of the masses—*also* in the realm of national questions—to the verbal and frequently hypocritical recognition of the national equality and of the self-determination of nations. The imperialist war of 1914–1916 and the opportunists' and the Kautskyans' Augean stables of hypocrisy which it revealed have plainly confirmed the correctness of Marx's policy, which should become an example for all advanced countries, for every one of them now oppresses foreign nations.[32]

---

[32] Reference is frequently made—for instance, recently by the German chauvinist Lensch in Nos. 8 and 9 of *Die Glocke* [Paul Lensch, "Die Selbstbestimmungsflause," *Die Glocke*, No. 8, December 15, 1915, pp. 465–76, and "Sozialismus und Annexionen in der Vergangenheit," *ibid.*, No. 9, January 1, 1916, pp. 493–500.]—to the fact that Marx's negative attitude toward the national movements of certain peoples, for instance, of the Czechs in 1848, refutes the necessity of recognizing the self-determination of nations from the point of view of Marxism. But this is not correct, since in 1848 there were historic and political reasons for distinguishing between "reactionary" and revolutionary democratic nations. Marx was right in condemning the former and defending the latter. The right to self-determination is one of democracy's demands which naturally should be subordinated to the general interests of democracy. In 1848 and the following years these general interests dealt primarily with the struggle against Tsarism. [Author's note.]

6. THREE TYPES OF COUNTRIES WITH RESPECT TO THE SELF-DETERMINATION OF NATIONS

In this respect three main types of countries must be distinguished: first, the advanced capitalist countries of Western Europe and the United States. The bourgeois progressive national movements have long been completed there. Each of these "great" nations oppresses foreign nations both in colonies and within its own country. There the problems of the proletariat of the dominant nations are exactly what the problems of the proletariat were in England in the nineteenth century with respect to Ireland.[33]

Secondly, Eastern Europe: Austria, the Balkans, and especially Russia. There the twentieth century has especially developed the bourgeois-democratic national movements and has sharpened the national struggle. The tasks of the proletariat of these countries both in the matter of completing their bourgeois democratic reforms and in the matter of assisting the socialist revolution of other countries cannot be accomplished without defending the right of nations to self-determination. Particularly difficult and important in this case is the task of merging the class struggle of the workers of both the oppressing and the oppressed nations.

Thirdly, semi-colonial countries, such as China, Persia, Turkey, and all colonies, totaling a billion population. There the bourgeois-democratic movements are either barely beginning or are still far from complete. Socialists must not only demand the absolute and immediate liberation of colonies—without compensation—and this demand in its political expression signifies nothing else but the recognition of the right of self-determination—but they must render resolute support to the most revolutionary elements of bourgeois-democratic national movements for liberation in these countries, and assist their revolts, and occasionally also their revolutionary war *against* their oppressors the imperialist powers.

[33] In certain small states which have remained aloof from the war of 1914–1916, for example, Holland and Switzerland, the bourgeoisie uses extensively the slogan of "self-determination of nations" to justify participation in the imperialist war. This is one of the motives which drive the Social Democracy of these countries to negate self-determination. The correct proletarian policy, namely, the repudiation of "defense of the fatherland" in the *imperialist* war is defended by incorrect arguments. There results, in theory, a distortion of Marxism, and in practice a sort of petty national narrowness, oblivious to *hundreds of millions* belonging to nations enslaved by the "Great Power" nations. Comrade Gorter in his excellent pamphlet "Imperialism, War, and Social-Democracy" [Gorter, *Der Imperialismus, der Weltkrieg, und die Sozialdemokratie*] repudiates wrongly the principle of self-determination of nations but applies it correctly when he demands *immediate* "political and *national* independence" for the Dutch Indies and exposes the Dutch opportunists who refuse to advance such a demand and to fight for it. [Author's note.]

7. Social Chauvinism and the Self-Determination of Nations

The imperialist epoch and the war of 1914–1916 have especially brought forward the task of struggling against chauvinism and nationalism in the advanced countries. On the question of the self-determination of nations there are two main shades among social chauvinists, i.e., the opportunists and the Kautskyans, who embellish the reactionary imperialist war by applying to it the "defense of the fatherland" idea.

On the one hand, we see rather outspoken servants of the bourgeoisie defend annexations because they believe that imperialism and political concentration are progressive and deny, as it were, the utopian, illusory, and petty bourgeois, etc., right of self-determination. To these belong: Cunow, Parvus, and the extreme opportunists of Germany, certain Fabians, and the trade union leaders in England, the opportunists in Russia—Semkovsky, Libman, Yurkevich, etc.

On the other hand, we see the Kautskyans, including also Vandervelde, Renaudel, and many of the pacifists of England and France, etc. They are for unity with the former and in practice coincide with them entirely by defending the right of self-determination in a purely verbal and hypocritical fashion. They consider the demand for freedom of political secession "exorbitant" ("zu viel verlangt": Kautsky, in *Neue Zeit*, May 21, 1915) ;[34] they do not regard revolutionary tactics as especially imperative for socialists of the oppressing nations; but on the contrary they disguise their revolutionary duties, justify their opportunism, aid them to deceive the people, evade the very question of the *boundaries* of a state which forcibly retains within these boundaries nations deprived of national equality, etc.

Both the former and the latter group are equally opportunists who prostitute Marxism, having lost every ability to understand the theoretical significance and practical urgency of Marx's tactics, explained by him with the example of Ireland.

As to annexations in particular, this question has acquired special significance in connection with the war. But what is annexation? It is easy to convince oneself either that the protest against annexations amounts to a recognition of self-determination of nations or that it is based on a pacifist phrase which defends the *status quo* and is hostile to *every* violence, even revolutionary violence. Such a phrase is fundamentally false and is irreconcilable with Marxism.

[34] Kautsky, "Nochmals unsere Illusionen. Eine Entgegnung," in *Neue Zeit,* No. 8, May 21, 1915, pp. 230–41; No. 9, May 28, 1915, pp. 264–75.

8. The Concrete Tasks of the Proletariat in the Immediate Future

A socialist revolution may begin in the very near future. The proletariat in that case would be confronted with the immediate task of seizing power, of expropriating the banks, and of adopting other dictatorial measures. At a moment like this the bourgeoisie—and especially the intelligentsia of the Fabian and the Kautskyan types—will endeavor to split and to hinder the revolution by forcing upon it restricted democratic aims. Whereas *all* purely democratic demands, assuming that an onslaught against the foundations of bourgeois power has already been started by the proletarians, may become, in a certain sense, impediments to the revolution, the necessity of proclaiming and granting freedom to *all* oppressed peoples (i.e., their right of self-determination), will be as urgent in a socialist revolution as it was urgent for the victory of the bourgeois democratic revolution, such as in Germany in 1848, or in Russia in 1905.

It is, however, possible that five, ten, or even more years may elapse before the socialist revolution begins. Revolutionary education of the masses will stand on the order of the day, education in a spirit which would make it impossible for socialist-chauvinists and opportunists to belong to the workers' party or for them to achieve a victory similar to the one in 1914–1916. Socialists will have to explain to the masses that: British socialists who do not demand freedom of secession for colonies and for Ireland; German socialists who do not demand freedom of secession for colonies, for the Alsatians, for the Danes, and the Poles, who neither spread directly their revolutionary propaganda and revolutionary mass action in the realm of struggle against national oppression nor utilize such incidents as the Zabern incident for spreading illegal propaganda among the proletariat of the oppressing nations in favor of street and revolutionary mass demonstrations; Russian socialists who do not demand freedom of secession for Finland, Poland, the Ukraine; and so forth and so on—all act as chauvinists, as lackeys of the imperialist monarchies and imperialist bourgeoisie which have disgraced themselves with mud and blood.

9. The Attitude of Russian and Polish Social Democracy and of the Second International toward Self-Determination

Disagreements between revolutionary Social Democrats of Russia and the Polish Social Democrats on the question of self-determination came up in 1903 at the Congress which had adopted the program of the R.S.D.L. party and which in spite of the protest of the Polish Social Democratic delegation had included in this program paragraph 9, which recognizes the right of nations to self-determination. Since then the Polish Social Democrats have not once in the name of their party repeated the proposal to eliminate paragraph 9[35] from the program of our party and to replace it by some other formulation.

In Russia—where not less than 57 per cent, i.e., over 100 million of the population, belong to the oppressed nations, where these nations largely inhabit the borderlands, and where some of these nations are more cultured than the Great Russians—where the political regime is distinguished by an especially barbarous and medieval character, and where the bourgeois democratic revolution has not yet been completed, the recognition of the right of the nations oppressed by Tsarism to a free secession from Russia is absolutely imperative for Social Democrats in the name of their democratic and socialist tasks. Our party, restored in January 1912, accepted a resolution in 1913[36] which confirmed the right of self-determination and explained its concrete significance precisely as has been outlined above. The debauch of Great Russian chauvinism in 1914–1916 among the bourgeoisie as well as among the opportunist-socialists (Rubanovich, Plekhanov, *Nashe Delo,* etc.) impels us still more to insist upon this demand and to recognize the fact that those who repudiate it serve in practice as supports of Great Russian chauvinism and Tsarism. Our party declares that it emphatically declines all responsibility for such opposition to the right of self-determination.

In the latest formulation of the position of Polish Social Democracy

[35] The program of the R.S.D.L. party adopted in 1903 at London states, among other things, that "The Russian Social Democratic Labor party sets itself the immediate political task of overthrowing the Tsarist autocracy and of replacing it by a democratic republic the constitution of which would assure .... (9) self-determination of all nations which enter into the composition of the state" (*Vtoroi ocherednoi sezd ross. sots. dem. rabochei partii ....*, pp. 3–4). Complete text of this program appeared in *The Masses,* No. 11, September 1917, pp. 8–9.

[36] The resolution on the national question adopted at the Poronino Conference of the Central Committee of the R.S.D.L. party included the following points: (1) National peace in capitalist society can be attained, if at all, only under a fully democratic, republican regime guaranteeing equality for all nationalities and languages, education in local languages, regional autonomy, and democratic local self-government. (2) Subdivision of school affairs according to nationalities within one state is harmful for democracy and the class struggle. (3) The interests of the working class demand the fusion of workers of all nationalities of a given state into united proletarian organizations, political, educational, etc. (4) The S.D. party must defend the right of the nations oppressed by Tsarism to separate and form independent states. (5) This question of the right of self-determination must not be confused with the expediency of such a separation, which must be solved independently in each case and in the interests of general social development and the class struggle. (Included in *Izveshchenie i rezoliutsii letniago 1913 goda soveshchaniia Tsentralnago Komiteta R.S.D.R.P. s partiinymi rabotnikami;* published by the Central Committee, 1913, and reprinted in Lenin, *Sochineniia,* XVII, 11–13.)

on the national question (the declaration of the Polish Social Democracy at the Zimmerwald Conference) the following thoughts are included:
This declaration condemns the German and other governments, which regard the "Polish regions" as hostages in the imminent game of compensations, *"by depriving the Polish people of the possibility to decide its own destiny."* "Polish Social Democracy resolutely and solemnly protests against the *repartitioning and cutting up* into sections of a *whole country"* .... It lashes the socialists who have left to the Hohenzollerns .... the "task of *liberating the oppressed peoples."* It expresses the conviction that only participation of the revolutionary international proletariat in the approaching struggle—a struggle for socialism—*"will break the chains of national oppression,* and destroy *all forms of foreign* domination and assure to the *Polish people* the possibility of a broad and free development in the capacity of a member *with full rights* in a union of nations." The declaration recognizes the war *"for the Poles"* as *"doubly* fratricidal" (*Bulletin of the International Socialist Committee,* No. 2, September [December] 27, 1915, p. 15 [14]. A Russian translation is to be found in the collection *Internatsional i voina,* p. 97).[37]

These postulates do not differ essentially from the recognition of the right of nations to self-determination; they are merely afflicted with a greater deliquescence and vagueness of political formulation than are the majority of programs and resolutions of the Second International. Any attempt at expressing these ideas in exact, political terms and at determining whether or not they can be applied to the capitalist order or rather to the socialist order, will only show more obviously the fallibility of the renunciation by the Polish Social Democrats of the self-determination of nations.

The decision of the London International Socialist Congress in 1896, which recognized the self-determination of nations, must be supplemented on the basis of the theses given above by referring to (1) the special urgency of this demand under imperialism; (2) the politically conditional and class nature of all demands of political democracy, including the demand for self-determination; (3) the necessity for distinguishing the concrete tasks of the Social Democrats of both the oppressing and the oppressed nations; (4) the inconsistent, purely verbal, and, therefore, by its political significance, hypocritical recognition of self-determination by the opportunists and the Kautskyans; (5) the actual coinciding of the chauvinists with the Social Democrats, particularly those of the Great Power nations (Great Russians, Anglo-Americans, French, Italians, Japanese, etc.) who do not advocate freedom of seces-

---

[37] See chapter iv, pp. 336–37, above.

sion for the colonies and nationalities oppressed by "their own" nations; and (6) the necessity of subordinating the struggle for that demand, like all fundamental demands of political democracy, to the direct revolutionary mass struggle for the overthrow of the bourgeois governments and for the realization of socialism.

To transfer to the International the point of view of some small nations—especially of the Polish Social Democrats, who because of their struggle against the Polish bourgeoisie, which deceived the people with nationalist slogans, were led to repudiate wrongly self-determination— would be a theoretical error, would mean a substitution of Proudhonism for Marxism, and, in practice, would signify rendering involuntary support to the most dangerous chauvinism and opportunism of the Great Power nations.

THE EDITORIAL BOARD OF "SOTSIAL-DEMOKRAT," THE
CENTRAL ORGAN OF THE R.S.D.L. PARTY

Postscriptum: In the latest issue of *Neue Zeit* of March 3, 1916, Kautsky openly extends a Christian hand of reconciliation to Austerlitz, representative of the filthiest German chauvinism, by repudiating for Habsburg Austria freedom of secession of the oppressed nations, but at the same time recognizing this freedom for *Russian* Poland in order to render a lackey's service to Hindenburg and Wilhelm II.[38] There could be no better self-exposure of Kautskyism!

As has been noted, self-determination had been for a long time a matter of controversy among the Polish Social Democrats and between them and the Russian Bolsheviks. The two theses by the *Gazeta Robotnicza* and the Central Committee of the R.S.D.L. party constituted by no means the only contribution to this controversy during the period of the World War. Shortly after the Zimmerwald Conference, where the Poles submitted a resolution[39] on this subject, Radek came out with an article, "Annexionen und Sozialdemokratie."[40] To this Lenin wrote a reply under the title, "Das revolutionäre Proletariat und das Selbstbestimmungsrecht der Nationen."

[38] This refers to K. Kautsky's article, "Noch einige Bemerkungen über nationale Triebkräfte," *Neue Zeit*, No. 23, March 3, 1916, pp. 705–13. (Lenin, *Sochineniia*, XIX, 456, note 51.)

[39] See chapter iv, pp. 336–37.

[40] *Beilage zur Berner Tagwacht*, No. 252, October 28, 1915, p. 1, and No. 253, October 29, 1915, p. 1.

This article was not published at the time but was later printed in German and Russian in *Leninskii Sbornik*.[41]

In the autumn of 1916 Lenin wrote another article[42] on the subject in which he took up the theses of the *Gazeta Robotnicza* point by point, presenting arguments and authorities in refutation of the Polish position and in support of the theses of the Central Committee, which are given above. In the article referred to, Lenin gives the following explanation of the opposition of the Dutch and Polish Marxists to self-determination:

". . . . There is not the slightest doubt that the Dutch and Polish Marxists who are against self-determination belong to the best revolutionary and internationalist elements of international Social Democracy. How *can* it be, then, that their theoretical reasoning represents, as we saw, a continuous chain of errors? It contains not even one single correct general consideration, nothing except 'imperialist-economism'!

"Not the extremely bad subjective qualifications of the Dutch-Polish comrades but the *specific* objective conditions of their countries account for that: (1) Both countries are small and helpless in the present-day 'system' of Great Powers; (2) both are geographically located between imperialist predatory powers of gigantic strength, among whom there prevails a most acute rivalry (England, Germany, and Russia); (3) in both countries the recollections and traditions of the times when they *themselves* were 'great and powerful' are extremely strong (Holland was a great colonial power, stronger than England; Poland was more cultured and was a stronger Great Power than Russia or Prussia); (4) up to now both countries have maintained the

---

[41] *Leninskii Sbornik*, VI, 6–22; an English translation is given in Lenin, *The Imperialist War*, pp. 367–73, and in Lenin, *Selected Works*, V, 282–89.

[42] "Itogi diskussii o samoopredelenii," *Sbornik Sotsial-Demokrata*, No. 1, October 1916, pp. 11–28; reprinted in Lenin, *Sochineniia*, XIX, 239–72; a portion of this article (chapter x, dealing with the Irish rebellion of 1916) has been published in English in *The Labour Monthly* (London), No. 4, April 1929, pp. 215–19, in *Lenin on Britain*, pp. 164–68, and in Lenin, *Selected Works*, V, 301–306. See also the note in the last-named volume, pp. 378–80.

privilege of oppressing foreign peoples—the Dutch bourgeoisie owns the rich Dutch Indies, the Polish landlord oppresses the Ukrainian and White Russian 'serf,' the Polish bourgeoisie oppresses the Jew, etc.

"Such a peculiarity, consisting of a combination of these four special conditions, you will not find in the situation of Ireland, Portugal (she was once Spain's possession), Alsace, Norway, Finland, the Ukraine, the Lettish and White Russian areas, or many others. And precisely this peculiarity is *the crux* of the matter! When Dutch and Polish Social Democrats reason against self-determination by means of *general* arguments, i.e., those concerning imperialism in general, national oppression in general, they make, we may truly say, one error follow on the heels of another. But if one only casts off this obviously false *cloak* of general arguments and looks at the *crux* of the matter from the point of view of the peculiarity of the *special* conditions in Holland and Poland, their peculiar position becomes *understandable* and quite legitimate. It is possible to say, without being afraid of lapsing into a paradox, that when the Dutch and Polish Marxists foam at the mouth in opposing self-determination they say not quite what they mean to say, or, in other words, what they mean to say is not just what they do say."[43]

C. The Zimmerwald Left and the Swiss Labor Movement

During the years 1914–1917 the Swiss Social Democratic party passed through a series of internal conflicts in which the Left Zimmerwaldists and the Bolsheviks in particular had a hand. The outbreak of the World War naturally had a profound effect on the Swiss party, which had been strongly influenced by German Social Democracy and also had had close connections with the French socialists. The declaration of a *Burgfrieden* policy by the majority socialists of these countries produced a critical reaction among the Swiss S.D.'s

[43] Lenin, *Sochineniia,* XIX, 263.

and contributed to the split which almost at once began to separate the Lefts from the Rights. Although the Swiss party acted unanimously at the Lugano Conference in September 1914, the campaign against social patriotism had already been begun by Robert Grimm in the pages of the *Berner Tagwacht.*

After the Presidium of the Swiss party had failed to arouse the International Socialist Bureau at The Hague to action and had been obliged to give up the idea of calling independently a conference of socialists of the neutral countries in the spring of 1915, the Left (internationally minded) group led by Grimm proposed at a meeting of this party Presidium, on May 22, 1915, to call a conference of minority socialists. But at that time a majority of the Presidium was unwilling to take such radical action and, therefore, refused officially to participate in Grimm's undertaking, leaving the attendance at that conference entirely to the discretion of the individual party members.[44] Thus the Zimmerwald Conference in September 1915 was attended by Grimm, Naine, and Platten without the authorization of the Swiss Social Democratic party. This Conference and its principles formed the demarcation line between the Right and the Left wings of the Swiss party. Later, after the formation of the Zimmerwald Left group at the Zimmerwald Conference, there began to appear in the party a center tendency which was within the Zimmerwald movement but was more conciliatory than the Left.

The split within the party leadership came definitely into the open after a meeting of the party Presidium in Zürich on October 15, 1915, where a resolution was adopted against recognition of the principles recently formulated at the Zimmerwald Conference. Two members of the minority of the Presidium, Fritz Platten, who had joined the Lefts at Zimmerwald, and Hans Vogel, thereupon issued a declaration ex-

---

[44] "Parteinachrichten. Sozialdemokratische Partei der Schweiz," *Berner Tagwacht,* No. 118, May 25, 1915, p. 3; *Jahrbuch der sozialdemokr. Partei der Schweiz, 1915,* p. 63.

pressing complete agreement with Zimmerwald; and a resolution of the same tenor was carried by 229 votes to 44 in the Zürich municipal socialist organization.[45] The struggle thus begun resulted in a test of strength at the general party Congress at Aarau, November 20–21, 1915, where three resolutions were introduced: the first by the Zürich delegation (Grimm, Nobs, Platten, and others), recognizing the Zimmerwald pronouncements; the second by the Neuchâtel delegation headed by Graber, approving the Zimmerwald principles, with the amendment that they could be realized only by the revolutionary mass action of the proletariat; and the third by the majority of the party Presidium, rejecting both of the above. After a stormy debate the Congress adopted Graber's amendment by 258 to 141, and then the Zürich delegation's resolution with the amendment by 330 to 51.[46] The Lefts won a further victory at this Congress by electing a majority of the party Presidium. The general leftward trend of the Swiss party found its expression also in the adoption of a resolution by which the Grütli-Verein was deprived of its right of autonomy within the party organization. No Grütli members were elected to the new Presidium.[47]

The Kienthal Conference, which had proclaimed a definite

[45] *Beilage zur Berner Tagwacht,* No. 243, October 18, 1915, p. 1; *La Sentinelle,* 1915, Nos. 244, 245, 246, October 20, 21, 22, p. 1; *Berner Tagwacht,* No. 244, October 19, 1915, p. 1; *Jahrbuch der sozialdemokr. Partei der Schweiz 1915,* pp. 64–66.

[46] Kharitonov, a Russian Bolshevik, who attended the Congress as a member of the Swiss S.D. party, relates that when the Lefts, at Grimm's insistence, permitted Graber to withdraw his amendment, Kharitonov took the floor and offered the amendment in his own name. Grimm, according to this account, seeing the disadvantage of being identified with the Right, supported the amendment in a brilliant speech, which was enthusiastically applauded, as was Platten's in support of the same cause. (Kharitonov, "Iz vospominanii," *Zapiski Instituta Lenina,* II, 133–34. The reports of the Aarau Congress are given in *Berner Tagwacht* and *Beilage zur Berner Tagwacht,* No. 273, November 22, 1915, pp. 1 and 2–3, respectively; *Beilage zur Berner Tagwacht,* No. 274, November 23, 1915, pp. 1–2; *Jahrbuch der sozialdemokr. Partei der Schweiz 1915,* pp. 27–33.)

[47] The Grütli-Verein had been formed in Geneva, May 20, 1838, by thirty-three workmen, commercial employees, and students. It took its name from Grütli, on the Lake of the Four Cantons, where, according to tradition, three Swiss cantons formed a secret alliance against the rule of Rudolph of Habsburg-Laufenburg. Grütli associations were formed in the larger Swiss cities with a central committee in Geneva. The first slogan of the association was "through education to freedom,"

break with social patriotism and which was officially attended by Platten, Nobs, Graber, and Agnes Robmann from the Swiss party and by Münzenberg from the Youth International, signified the victory of the Left and gave impetus to its antimilitarist propaganda.

The Zimmerwald Left, as already mentioned, had gained the co-operation of Fritz Platten, the most popular leader of the Zürich party organization; it also won Willi Münzenberg's support, and with him that of the Swiss and the international youth organizations. But in its antimilitarist campaign the Zimmerwald Left had some independent allies—Naine and Graber of western Switzerland, who even before the World War had not shared the party's point of view on wars of defense. Antiwar demonstrations and assaults against military officers occurred more and more frequently in western Switzerland.[48]

Since the military question was steadily growing in importance, owing to the increasing possibility of the country's being drawn into the war, the party Presidium decided in April 1916 to work out theses on the questions of war and militarism, and under the influence of the Zimmerwald Left the further decision was taken on August 5 that there should be an extraordinary party congress on February 10–11, 1917, to discuss these matters.[49] Meanwhile, during August 1916, Grimm, Müller, Naine, Pflüger, Schenkel, and Scherrer at

and its program was primarily national. Some sections, however, joined the First International; later the entire association joined the Second International and played an important role in the Swiss labor movement. After the Zürich Congress, November 4–5, 1916, the Grütli-Verein was expelled from the Swiss Social Democratic party of which it was an autonomous member. During the war it upheld a nationalist point of view and the "defense of the fatherland" slogan.

The relation of the Grütli-Verein to the Swiss Social Democratic party is discussed in Ernst Schenker, *Die sozialdemokratische Bewegung in der Schweiz von ihren Anfängen bis zur Gegenwart*, pp. 104–108, 129–37; W. Bretscher and E. Steinmann [eds.], *Die sozialistische Bewegung in der Schweiz, 1848–1920*, pp. 54–61; hereafter cited as Bretscher, *Die sozialistische Bewegung*.

[48] Schenker, *Die sozialdemokratische Bewegung in der Schweiz von ihren Anfängen bis zur Gegenwart*, p. 138.

[49] *Berner Tagwacht*, No. 85, April 10, 1916, pp. 2–3, and No. 183, August 7, 1916, p. 3.

the request of the party published their opinions on these questions in the principal Swiss socialist papers, and the Zürich party Congress, November 4–5, 1916, decided to appoint a commission to draft a resolution on the same topics for discussion at the forthcoming extraordinary sessions in February. This Congress also adopted the resolution proposed by the Basel party organization by which the Grütli-Verein was expelled from the party. The new elections gave Münzenberg a seat in the party Presidium. But in spite of a predominance of the Lefts at the Congress the Center still was victorious, owing to the adoption of the Huber-Grimm resolution (given below) on the national finance reform.[50]

For the reasons which have already been mentioned, the Russian Bolsheviks in Switzerland became increasingly interested as these discussions developed. In February 1916 Lenin moved from Berne to Zürich where, Krupskaia explains, "there was a considerable number of young foreigners imbued with revolutionary sentiments, there were a lot of workers there, the Social Democratic party there was inclined more to the left, and there seemed to be less of the petty-bourgeois spirit about the place."[51] There Lenin worked in the library, maintained contact with revolutionary-minded foreigners, many of whom worked in local factories, and occasionally lectured to audiences of Swiss workers. Apparently the medicine Lenin prescribed sometimes seemed a little too strong for even the more radical Swiss. Krupskaia tells of the efforts of the Russians and Poles to hold joint meetings with the Swiss workers. "The first meeting," she writes, "was attended by about forty persons. Ilyich spoke on current events and posed the problems very sharply. Though the gathering consisted of internationalists, the Swiss were quite embarrassed by the sharpness with which Ilyich made his

---

[50] "Der Zürcher Parteitag," *Berner Tagwacht*, No. 261, November 6, 1916, pp. 1–3; *Jahrbuch der sozialdemokr. Partei der Schweiz, 1916*, pp. 30–34.

[51] *Memories of Lenin*, II, 176. Krupskaia denies that Lenin had "any particular hopes of the Swiss movement" or thought that it might "become almost the center of the coming social revolution." *Ibid.*, p. 182.

points. I remember the speech of a representative of the Swiss youth to the effect that one cannot break through a stone wall with one's forehead. The fact remains that our meetings began to melt away, and to the fourth meeting only the Russians and the Poles came, and after exchanging some banter they went home."[52]

Of more significance than these direct efforts to influence the Swiss workers were the discussions and decisions of a group of Russian, Polish, German, and Swiss supporters of the Zimmerwald Left who met regularly each week, and who called their organization the "Kegelklub." "This club," says Münzenberg, who was a member, "became, especially after Lenin's arrival in Zürich, the chief nucleus of revolutionary agitation and propaganda in Switzerland. All political and tactical questions were discussed there and resolutions and theses were worked out which later on were submitted, particularly by the youth group, to party meetings and congresses."[53] Leaflets and pamphlets were also issued by the club for the enlightenment of Swiss workers.

After the Swiss S.D. party congress of November 4–5, 1916, at which he spoke,[54] Lenin became absorbed in the questions which the Swiss were discussing. These included not only that of war and militarism but the struggle against the high cost of living and proposals of fiscal reforms arising out of the failure of the government to balance its budget. In connection with these questions Lenin wrote his theses on "The Tasks of the Left Zimmerwaldists within the Swiss Social Democratic Party"[55] and "Theses on the Attitude of the Swiss Social Democratic Party toward the Question of War," given below. By these theses and through consultations with Platten he attempted to influence the content of the draft resolution on war and militarism which was being worked out by a commission for submission to the extraordi-

[52] *Memories of Lenin,* II, 182–83.
[53] W. Münzenberg, *S Libknekhtom i Leninym,* pp. 134–35.
[54] Lenin's speech is given in Lenin, *Sochineniia,* XIX, 277–79.
[55] Lenin, *Sochineniia,* XIX, 333–42.

nary party congress in February 1917. In this he was not very successful, for the draft of the majority of the Commission, though it included some of Platten's suggestions, was in the main based on Grimm's theses, which Lenin opposed. The minority resolution was patriotic and supported national defense in case of attack.[56]

The Swiss Social Democrats did not have an opportunity to vote on these resolutions in February, for on January 7, 1917, on Grimm's motion, the party Presidium voted to postpone the congress.[57] This brought down on Grimm's head the wrath of Lenin and the other Left Zimmerwaldists, who now no longer doubted that the chairman of the International Socialist Committee was conciliatory toward the Right. Münzenberg writes: "At a conference early in February 1917 it was decided to break with Robert Grimm openly. This conference was held in my home and was attended by Lenin, Zinoviev, Radek, Krupskaia, Paul Levi, Fritz Platten, Mimiola, a member of the Swiss Executive, and myself. Lenin presented his point of view on the state of affairs in the Swiss labor movement and gave reasons for breaking immediately and irrevocably with Grimm's group. Fritz Platten tried to obtain something like a probation period for Grimm and proposed postponing the break, but Lenin could not be dissuaded . . . . [of all those present] only Platten asked that a few days be given him to think the matter over."[58] Lenin tried without success to get the Swiss Lefts to wage an open fight on Grimm and the majority of the Presidium by means of a party referendum. Of the several articles which Lenin wrote in this connection only his thesis on Greulich's stand on the "defense of the fatherland" slogan was published.[59]

[56] *Beilage zur Berner Tagwacht*, No. 8, January 10, 1917, p. 1. Grimm's theses appeared in *Berner Tagwacht*, No. 163, July 14, 1916, pp. 1–2, and were expounded by him in *Neues Leben*, Nos. 7–8, July–August 1916, pp. 193–222.

[57] *Berner Tagwacht*, No. 7, January 9, 1917, p. 1; *Jahrbuch der sozialdemokr. Partei der Schweiz, 1916*, pp. 18–19.

[58] W. Münzenberg, *S Libknekhtom i Leninym*, p. 139.

[59] *Volksrecht*, Nos. 26 and 27, January 31 and February 1, 1917; reprinted in *Leninskii Sbornik*, XVII, 126–38.

Perhaps these articles and Lenin's open letter to Naine had some effect, for when a further postponement of the congress was suggested, Grimm opposed it, though at the same time he drew a clear line between himself and the Zimmerwald Left. When the Extraordinary Congress met in Berne on June 9–10, 1917, Grimm was in Russia. In his absence the Congress adopted, by the vote of 222 to 77, the antimilitarist resolution of the majority of the drafting commission. Actually the military question was not settled, since in order to avoid a party split at that time the majority resolution was attenuated by the addition of a paragraph proposed by Jacques Schmid which read as follows: "The Social Democratic party of Switzerland declares that it is ready to give up together with the socialists of all countries the defense of the bourgeois fatherland and to open a struggle for peace and the union of the peoples upon a democratic basis."

This Congress dealt also with the resolutions of the Kienthal Conference. Three proposals introduced by the party Presidium, by Nobs, and by the Zürich party assembly provoked heated debates, in spite of the fact that all three proposals were in favor of approving the Kienthal decisions. In the end the most outspoken revolutionary resolution of the Zürich group was adopted by 151 to 89 votes. This resolution contained the following paragraph: "The party congress declares its solidarity with the internationalists of all countries who, by organizing and continuing the class struggle, are endeavoring to undermine their respective governments and, by kindling a revolution, are striving to bring about the conclusion of the war and are clearing the road for a socialist peace. The party congress regards as renegades those socialists who support their governments' war policy and calls upon the workers of all countries to act in the spirit of the decisions of Zimmerwald and Kienthal."[60] Further-

[60] *Beilage zur Berner Tagwacht*, No. 89, April 17, 1917, p. 1; No. 135, June 12, 1917, p. 1; *Berner Tagwacht*, No. 134, June 11, 1917, pp. 1–2; No. 135, June 12, 1917, p. 1; Ernst Schenker, *Die sozialdemokratische Bewegung in der Schweiz von*

more, the Swiss Social Democratic party approved the criticism at the Kienthal Conference of the International Socialist Bureau's attitude and decided by 140 votes against 119 to send delegates to the Stockholm Conference only in case the Third Zimmerwald Conference recommended attendance.[61] By this time, however, the Russian members of the Zimmerwald Left were no longer taking part in Swiss Social Democratic affairs, as most of them had returned to Russia where their program and tactics were meeting with greater immediate success than they had achieved in Switzerland. But the seeds of their propaganda and the few written instructions left by Lenin and his group had not fallen on barren soil. They soon began to sprout first in Chaux-de-Fonds and then in Zürich, where the youth organization was permeated with revolutionary ideas and where the foreign element was most numerous. An illegal organization, Die Forderung, was formed by an able member of the youth organization, Jakob Herzog, and the German anarchist, Anton Waibel. In October 1917 this organization began to publish a newspaper by the same name, advocating revolutionary action, demonstrations, propaganda in the army, the formation of labor councils, an eight-hour working day, nationalization of banks, expropriation, etc. When the news of the Bolshevik victory and their peace decree became known in Switzerland, Max Dättwyler and Max Rotter, both pacifist Social Democrats, without either the authorization or the co-operation of the party organization, called upon the masses to close the munition factories in Zürich. This led to riots on November 15–17 in which the *Forderung* group and the youth organizations had a hand, although Platten and Münzenberg, who did not approve of Dättwyler's undertaking, remained aloof from the

ihren Anfängen bis zur Gegenwart, pp. 126, 139–40; Bretscher, *Die sozialistische Bewegung,* pp. 103–105. Bretscher bases his account of the 1915–1917 period largely on information contained in *Bericht des 1. Staatsanwaltes A. Brunner an den Regierungsrat des Kantons Zürich über die Strafuntersuchung des Aufruhrs in Zürich im November 1917,* Zürich, 1919.

[61] Text of the resolution is included in chapter vii, pp. 650–51, below.

events. These November strikes and riots were the first repercussions of the Bolshevik revolution in Switzerland.[62]

From that time on the Swiss party moved rapidly along the revolutionary path, which led on February 4, 1918, to the formation of the Olten Action Committee in which Robert Grimm, who had meanwhile regained his former standing in the party, played an important part, and to the organization of the general strike in November 1918. Since the disturbances of November 1917 the strike movement and the political demonstrations in Switzerland had been steadily growing, aggravated by the economic situation. The Swiss government adopted various retaliatory measures, such as the deportation of undesirable aliens, of whom Willi Münzenberg was the first. In the summer of 1918 Berzin, the unofficial representative of the Soviet government, with his staff was permitted to enter Switzerland on condition that the Russians should not carry on propaganda. But, as Berzin later admitted, they engaged in revolutionary activity until November 8, when they were asked to leave Switzerland within twenty-four hours.[63]

Meanwhile, in view of the S.D. Presidium's decision to celebrate the anniversary of the Bolshevik revolution, the Swiss government took precautionary measures by ordering troops to Zürich. This measure, which was regarded as an insult by the S.D.'s, led the Olten Action Committee to call a one-day strike on November 9 in the largest industrial centers. The strike was general and peaceful, but the government did not remove the troops. In Zürich the workers voted to continue the strike in spite of the orders of the Action Committee, which again presented its demands to the Federal Council. But not one of the three demands—the removal of

---

[62] "Der neueste Zürcher Kosakenstreich," *Berner Tagwacht*, No. 270, November 17, 1917, p. 3; "Über die Zürcher Demonstration am Donnerstag abend," *Beilage zur Berner Tagwacht*, No. 270, November 17, 1917, p. 1; "Die Vorgänge in Zürich," *Berner Tagwacht*, No. 271, November 19, 1917, pp. 1–2; Ernst Schenker, *Die sozialdemokratische Bewegung in der Schweiz von ihren Anfängen bis zur Gegenwart*, pp. 141–43; Bretscher, *Die sozialistische Bewegung*, pp. 109–12.

[63] See, in this connection, *The Bolsheviks and World Revolution*.

troops, the recall of the expulsion order of the Soviet delegation, and the release of Münzenberg—was granted. On November 11 the Action Committee called a general strike,
which had been provisionally approved as early as at the
general labor congress in Basel, July 27–28, 1918, but which
had not been carried out at the time because of certain concessions granted by the government. In connection with the
November strike the Olten Action Committee addressed an
appeal "to the working people of Switzerland" which contained a number of demands, including immediate re-election
of the National Council, woman suffrage, reorganization of
the army, old-age and invalid pensions, state monopoly on
import and export, etc. The intensity of the strike surprised
even its leaders; many of the railroads ceased operations and
no bourgeois newspapers were printed. The government replied by making use of military force and closing the *Berner
Tagwacht.* The latter, however, was replaced by *Die Rote
Fahne,* a bulletin containing news of the strikes. Whereas in
certain localities, especially in western Switzerland, the strike
began to subside on the second day, owing either to the measures of the government or to lack of enthusiasm of the workers, in other regions it was on the verge of turning into a civil
war. Unable to cope with the situation and fearing that it
might lose control of the strike movement, the Olten Action
Committee called off the general strike on November 14, before any of its demands had been met by the government.
The Action Committee gave as reasons for its action the lack
of unanimity in the attitude of the railroad workers and of
the mobilized troops. The Left-wingers blamed the failure of
the strike on the inadequate leadership of the Olten Committee. Thus the party emerged from the November events more
divided than ever, and in view of recent events at home and
the revolutions in Germany and Austria-Hungary it faced the
necessity of deciding its future tactics. The party Presidium
resigned on November 25, thus giving the party Congress of
December 21, 1918, a carte blanche. This Congress, which
was followed immediately by a general labor congress, dis-

cussed the November strike and, without altogether repudiating mass action, the party condemned the Bolshevik tactics of the Zürich Social Democrats and approved the action of the Olten Action Committee by a vote of 262 to 68.[64]

During the November 1918 strikes Switzerland had already its own Communist group. Expelled from the Swiss Social Democratic party for breach of discipline, Jakob Herzog early in October 1918 formed the first group of Swiss Communists, the so-called "Old-Communists." When on November 6, 1918, the government ordered troops to Zürich the Communists distributed a proclamation devoted to the anniversary of the Zürich events of 1917 demanding the release of all political prisoners, the discontinuance of all military and civil lawsuits, the lifting of the ban from *Die Forderung, Die Freie Jugend,* and *Die Jugend-Internationale,* which had been suppressed by the government, and the restoration of the rights of asylum and assembly. During the November 1918 events this group of Communists worked in contact with the anarchists.[65]

After the failure of the November strike the Communists and the Left wing of the Social Democratic party continued their revolutionary activity, chiefly in Basel and Zürich. They attempted to organize another general strike in August 1919 but failed. In March 1921 the Swiss Communists and the Left wing of the S.D. party merged into the Communist party of Switzerland.

[64] "Nach der Konferenz," *Berner Tagwacht,* No. 29, February 5, 1918, p. 1; "Das Oltener Aktionskomitee zur Lage," *Berner Tagwacht,* No. 262, November 8, 1918, p. 1, and "An das arbeitende Volk der Schweiz," *Berner Tagwacht,* No. 263, November 11, 1918, p. 1; "Zur Ausweisung der Sovietgesandschaft," *Berner Tagwacht,* No. 263, November 11, 1918, p. 3; "Die Motive der Zürcher Regierung," *Berner Tagwacht,* No. 263, November 11, 1918, p. 3; "An die Arbeiterschaft der Schweiz," *Berner Tagwacht,* No. 265, November 15, 1918, p. 1; "Zu neuem Kampf," *Berner Tagwacht,* No. 265, November 15, 1918, p. 1; "Parteitag und Arbeiterkongress," *Berner Tagwacht,* No. 297, December 23, 1918, pp. 1–3; "Schweiz. Arbeiterkongress," *Beilage zur Berner Tagwacht,* No. 298, December 24, 1918, p. 1; W. Münzenberg, *S Libknekhtom i Leninym,* pp. 152–55; Ernst Schenker, *Die sozialdemokratische Bewegung in der Schweiz von ihren Anfängen bis zur Gegenwart,* pp. 159–73; Bretscher, *Die sozialistische Bewegung,* pp. 130–37.

[65] Bretscher, *Die sozialistische Bewegung,* pp. 132–33.

Early in 1919 the Left prevailed upon the Swiss party not to participate in the Berne Conference of the Second International but failed to obtain its adherence to the Third International. Consequently, at the First Congress of the Comintern held in Moscow in March 1919, Switzerland was represented only by a delegate of Jakob Herzog's group and by Platten, who took part in the Congress without a party mandate.[66]

The documents which follow consist principally of articles and letters of Lenin bearing on the events mentioned above. It is significant that in the concluding paragraph of his article addressed to the "workers who struggle against the war" he charged that Grimm, like Merrheim and Raffin-Dugens, had gone over to fusion with the social chauvinists and therefore "that any support of illusions concerning unity within Zimmerwald and of its struggle in favor of building the Third International causes, under these conditions, tremendous harm to the labor movement . . . . we declare that if this situation continues we shall not remain members of the Zimmerwald movement." Thus in January 1917 the two wings of the Zimmerwald movement had moved so far apart that Lenin was contemplating withdrawal.

THE TASKS OF THE LEFT ZIMMERWALDISTS WITHIN THE SWISS SOCIAL DEMOCRATIC PARTY

[Extract from Theses Written and Submitted by Lenin to the Swiss Lefts in December 1916][67]

[Theses 1–8 relate to the attitude the Swiss Left Zimmerwaldists should take toward war and the bourgeois government; theses 9–15 discuss the high cost of living and the economic condition of the masses and the duty to advocate high income and property taxes; theses 16–19 deal with urgent democratic reforms and the utilization of the election campaign for political propaganda; and theses 20–23 advocate intensive agitation, propaganda, and organization among the masses, particularly among the workers and soldiers.]

[66] See, in this connection, *The Bolsheviks and World Revolution.*

[67] Lenin, "Zadachi levykh Tsimmervaldistov v shveitsarskoi s.d. partii," *Sochineniia,* XIX, 333–42.

. . . . 24. The explaining to the masses of the unbreakable connection between the practical work in a consistent revolutionary social democratic direction, expounded above, and the systematic struggle *on principle* between the *three chief* tendencies within the present-day labor movement, which have formed in *all* civilized countries and which have become completely outlined also in Switzerland (especially at the Zürich Congress of 1916). These three tendencies are as follows: (1) social patriots, i.e., those who openly recognize "defense of the fatherland" in this imperialist war of 1914–1916. This is the opportunist tendency of agents of the bourgeoisie within the labor movement. (2) The Left Zimmerwaldists, who renounce the defense of the fatherland in the imperialist war on principle and who are in favor of a split with the social patriots as agents of the bourgeoisie and are for revolutionary mass struggle which is bound up with a *complete* reorganization of the social democratic tactics as applied to propaganda and to preparation of this struggle. (3) The so-called "center" (Kautsky-Haase "*Arbeitsgemeinschaft*" in Germany; *Longuet-Pressemane* in France),[68] which is in favor of unity between the first and the second tendencies. Such a "unity" only ties the hands of revolutionary Social Democracy by preventing it from developing its activity and by corrupting the masses through lack of a complete and unbreakable bond between party principles and party practice.

(Explaining to the masses the significance of the speeches, at the Zürich Congress of 1916, of Greulich, Naine, and Platten, who admitted that there were two chief tendencies but who approached their evaluation from different angles and who did not draw final conclusions.)

At the Congress of the Swiss Social Democratic party at Zürich in 1916, in three speeches concerning the *Nationalratsfraktion,* namely, the speeches of Platten, Naine, and Greulich,[69] it was stated especially plainly that the struggle between various tendencies of social democratic policy within the Social Democratic party of Switzerland *had long been a fact.* The sympathy of the majority of delegates was obviously on Platten's side when he spoke of the necessity to support consistently the work in the spirit of revolutionary Social Democracy. Naine declared openly, plainly, and definitely that there are within the *Nationalratsfraktion* two tendencies which are continuously struggling, and that the labor organizations should concern themselves with sending to the *Nationalrat* adherents of the revolutionary tendency who would truly agree among themselves. When Greulich said that the party has forsaken its old

---

[68] This center is sometimes identified in the German Social Democratic press, and justly so, with the *Right* wing of the "Zimmerwaldists." [Author's note.]

[69] These speeches are given in *Berner Tagwacht,* No. 261, November 6, 1916, p. 1.

"darlings" (*Lieblinge*) and has found new "darlings," he recognized the same fact—that various tendencies existed and struggled. But not a single thinking and class-conscious worker will agree to the "theory of darlings." It is precisely in order that the inevitable and necessary struggle between the tendencies should not degenerate into a rivalry between "darlings"—into personal conflicts, into petty suspicions and petty scandals—precisely for that reason it is the duty of all members of the Social Democratic party to engage in an *open* struggle on principle between the various tendencies of the Social Democratic policy.

25. Intense struggle against the *Grütli-Verein* from the point of view of *principle*, as against a visible manifestation on Swiss territory of *bourgeois* labor political tendencies, namely: opportunism, reformism, social patriotism, and corruption of the masses by bourgeois-democratic illusions. The explaining to the masses, by using the example of the actual activity of the *Grütli-Verein*, that the policy of social patriotism and of the "center" is entirely erroneous and very harmful.

26. It is necessary to start at once to prepare for the elections to the February (1917) Congress at Berne[70] in order that these elections may proceed not otherwise than on the basis of discussion of the fundamental concrete-political platforms by every party organization—the platform which is being outlined here should be the platform for the consistent revolutionary internationalist Social Democrats. The election of officials to all the leading party posts, to the *Presskommission*, to all representative institutions, to all presidiums, etc., should proceed not otherwise than on the basis of a similar discussion of the platform.

Careful control over the local party press by every local organization, for the purpose of introducing the points of view and the tactics of an *absolutely definite* Social Democratic *platform* rather than those of Social Democracy in general.

V. International Tasks of the Swiss Social Democrats

27. In order that the recognition of internationalism by the Swiss Social Democrats may be not merely an empty phrase which carries no obligation—an empty phrase to which the adherents of the "Center" and Social Democrats of the epoch of the Second International in general usually confine themselves—it is necessary, first, to struggle consistently and steadfastly for an organizational rapprochement and fusion within the unions and for a complete (civil and political) equalization of the foreign and the Swiss workers. The specific peculiarity of Swiss imperialism consists precisely in a growing exploitation of the disfran-

[70] The Swiss party congress at Berne was supposed to meet on February 10–11, 1917, to discuss the question of the party's attitude toward the war and militarism.

chised foreign workers by the Swiss bourgeoisie, which is building its hopes upon the alienation of these two ranks of workers.

Secondly, every effort should be made to create among the German, French, and Italian workers in Switzerland a *united internationalist* tendency, really united, applying to all the *activities* of the labor movement and struggling just as resolutely and consistently in principle against the French (Latin Switzerland) social patriotism as against the German and the Italian. This platform should become the foundation of a general and united platform of the workers of the *three* chief nationalities or tongues, which live in Switzerland. Unless the workers of all nationalities in Switzerland who are on the side of revolutionary Social Democracy fuse, internationalism is an empty word.

In order to facilitate this fusion it is imperative to obtain the publication of supplements (at least weekly—or monthly—and at the beginning consisting of only two pages) to all the Swiss Social Democratic newspapers (and to all organs of economic labor unions, of employees, etc.) reprinted *in the three languages* and expounding this platform in connection with the politics of the day.

28. The Swiss Social Democrats must support *only* the revolutionary internationalist elements of all the other socialist parties, elements which adhere to the Zimmerwald Left. This support, furthermore, should not be merely Platonic. Especially important is the reprinting in Switzerland of the anti-government appeals, published secretly in France, Germany, and Italy, their translation into the three languages, and their distribution among the Swiss proletariat and among the proletariat of all the neighboring countries.

29. The Social Democratic party of Switzerland must not only sanction at the Congress in Berne (in February 1917) its adherence and, moreover, its unreserved adherence to the decisions of the Kienthal Conference but must also demand an immediate, complete, and organizational break with the International Socialist Bureau at The Hague— the bulwark of opportunism and social patriotism, which are irreconcilably hostile to the interests of socialism.

30. The Social Democratic party of Switzerland, which possesses unique opportunities to acquaint itself with events within the labor movements of the advanced European countries, and to unite the revolutionary elements of this labor movement, must not await passively the development of an internal struggle within that movement but should *lead* that struggle. It is the Social Democratic party of Switzerland which must proceed along the road of the Zimmerwald Left, whose correctness is increasingly revealed every day by events within socialism in Germany, France, England, the United States, and all civilized countries in general.

THESES ON THE ATTITUDE AND TACTICS OF THE SWISS SOCIAL DEMOCRATIC PARTY TOWARD THE QUESTION OF WAR

[Written by Lenin in December 1916][71]

1. The present World War is an imperialist war, which is waged for the purpose of exploiting the world politically and economically, of securing markets for export, sources of raw material and new regions for the investment of capital, and of oppressing weak peoples, etc.

The claptrap of both belligerent coalitions about "defense of the fatherland" is nothing but bourgeois deception of the peoples.

2. The Swiss government is manager of affairs for the Swiss bourgeoisie, which is completely dependent on international finance capital and is most closely bound up with the imperialist bourgeoisie of the Great Powers.

Therefore, it is the inevitable result of these economic facts, rather than an accident, that the Swiss government engages in secret diplomacy and pursues a policy which becomes daily more and more reactionary— and this has been going on for decades—suppressing and violating the democratic rights and liberties of the people; that it cringes before the military clique and systematically sacrifices without shame the interests of the broad masses of the population to the interests of a handful of finance magnates.

Now, thanks to the dependence of the Swiss bourgeois government on the interests of the financial oligarchy and by virtue of strong pressure exerted by one or the other coalition of imperialist powers, Switzerland may become at any moment involved in the present war.

3. Therefore, "defense of the fatherland" when applied also to Switzerland is at present nothing but a hypocritical phrase, for in reality it implies not defense of democracy, of the independence and the interests of the broad popular masses, etc., but, on the contrary, the strengthening of capitalist dominance and of political reaction, preparation for the slaughtering of workers and petty peasants with a view to preserving bourgeois monopolies and privileges.

4. Proceeding from these facts, the Swiss Social Democratic party repudiates on principle the "defense of the fatherland," demands imme-

71 V. I. Lenin, *Sochineniia*, XXX, 268–72. At the Zürich party congress it was decided to form a commission which should draft a resolution on the party's attitude toward war. This resolution was to be submitted to the February 1917 congress of the party. This Commission consisted of E. Klöti (chairman), G. Affolter, P. Graber, J. Huber, G. Müller, C. Naine, P. Pflüger, E. Nobs, and J. Schmid. The party secretaries, F. Platten and M. Fähndrich, attended the Commission with consulting votes. (*Leninskii Sbornik*, XVII, 43; Lenin, *Sochineniia*, XXX, 458, note 177.)

diate demobilization, and invites the laboring class to reply to the military preparedness of the Swiss bourgeoisie as well as to the war, if it breaks out, with the sharpest means of proletarian class struggle.

Let us especially point out some of these means:

a) No civil peace; the accentuation of class struggle against all bourgeois parties, against the *Grütli-Verein,* which is an agent of the bourgeoisie within the labor movement, and against the Grütlian tendencies within the socialist party.

b) The denial of all military credits in time of peace as well as of war, regardless of the pretext under which they are demanded.

c) The support of all revolutionary movements and of every struggle of the laboring class in the belligerent countries waged against the war and against one's own government.

d) The rendering of assistance to revolutionary mass struggle in Switzerland, to strikes, demonstrations, and armed insurrections against the bourgeoisie.

e) A systematic propaganda in the army, and the creation for this purpose of special social democratic groups in the army as well as among the youth undergoing preparatory military drill.

f) The creation by the laboring class of illegal organizations in answer to every curtailment and abolition of political liberties by the government.

g) An organized preparation of the workers through the systematic expounding of the situation whereby the leadership of all labor and employees' organizations without exception would pass into the hands of persons who recognize and are able to carry on the struggle mentioned above against the war.

5. As the goal of revolutionary mass struggle already recognized at the Aarau party congress in 1915, the party advances a socialist overturn in Switzerland.[72] Economically this overturn can be realized immediately. It represents the only real means by which the masses can be liberated from the horrors of the high cost of living and famine. This overturn is approaching as the result of a crisis which all Europe now endures; it is absolutely imperative for the complete abolition of militarism and of all wars.

[72] Lenin refers to the proposal which was introduced by the Neuchâtel party group at the Congress in Aarau on November 20–21, 1915, and which was included in the resolution of the Congress (*La Sentinelle,* No. 272, November 22, 1915, p. 2):

"The Congress expresses its sympathy with all the comrades who in belligerent countries have remained faithful to the principles of the International and of the class struggle.

"It demands a peace based on the principles of the Zimmerwald resolution, but considers that this peace must not be brought about by a continuation of the war but rather by a social revolution."

The party declares that unless this goal and the revolutionary paths which lead toward it are recognized, all bourgeois pacifist and socialist pacifist phrases against militarism and wars represent illusions and lies, which merely serve to divert the laboring class from all serious fighting against the foundations of capitalism.

Without discontinuing the struggle favoring improvement of the condition of the hired slaves, the party calls the laboring class and its representatives to place on the order of the day the propaganda for an immediate socialist overturn in Switzerland, through mass agitation, through parliamentary speeches, proposals for initiative, etc., and by proving the necessity of replacing the bourgeois governments with a proletarian government, which would rest upon the masses of the propertyless population, and by explaining the urgency of adopting measures such as the expropriation of banks and large enterprises, the abolition of all indirect taxes,[73] the introduction of one direct tax with high revolutionary rates for large incomes, etc.

---

[73] This would imply the annulment of the decision of the Aarau party congress of 1915 and of the Huber-Grimm resolution which was adopted at the Zürich party congress of 1916 and which read as follows (*Berner Tagwacht*, No. 261, November 6, 1916, p. 2):

"The Social Democratic party of Switzerland declares its readiness to take active part in the introduction of the government financial reform. It declares that the means of effecting this reform are: the introduction of a direct government tax, the introduction of a tobacco monopoly the revenue from which is to be used entirely or to a large degree for social purposes; the introduction of a stamp duty in so far as it is of a property-tax nature; the extension of the alcohol monopoly; and, finally, the revision of the law on the payment of the military-exemption fee. The party congress agrees to the draft, presented by the party Presidium, of a people's inquiry concerning the introduction of the direct government tax. The party congress commissions the party's Executive Committee to begin to collect at a convenient time signatures for this initiative and authorizes it to take the necessary steps of its own accord toward carrying out the other proposals or to submit to the next party congress corresponding proposals.

"The co-operation in the carrying out of the finance reform proceeds according to the premise laid down by the Aarau party congress in 1915, namely, that first of all the direct progressive government tax on property and income is to be assured, the introduction of which will determine the party's attitude toward the other proposals for reform."

This resolution was adopted against the votes of a significant minority.

FOR A REFERENDUM ON MILITARISM AND THE EXPROPRIATION OF CAPITALIST ENTERPRISES

[Lenin to A. Schmid][74]

[ZÜRICH, December 1, 1916]

RESPECTED COMRADE:

Would you allow me to make one proposal?

I must confess that I paid insufficient attention yesterday to one very important point of your explanation,[75] namely, to the thought that one of Switzerland's peculiarities is that it has attained a high degree of democracy (voting by the entire people) and that this peculiarity must be used *also* for propaganda. This thought is very important and in my opinion entirely correct.

Could this idea be used perhaps so as to eliminate our dissensions (most probably very insignificant ones)? For instance:

If we were to submit the question to a referendum *only* as follows: in favor of abolition [of militarism] or against it?—then we shall obtain a medley of pacifist (bourgeois pacifist, etc.) and socialist votes, i.e., we shall attain not a clarifying of the socialist consciousness but rather an obscuring of the consciousness; we shall succeed in applying not the idea and the policy of *class struggle* to this specific question (the question of militarism) but rather a repudiation of the viewpoint of class struggle with regard to the question of militarism.

But if we were to submit to a referendum the question as follows: in favor of the expropriation of large capitalist industrial and rural enterprises, *as the only means* to abolish completely militarism, or against such expropriations, then we in our practical policy would be saying precisely that which we all recognize theoretically, namely, that complete abolition of militarism may be conceived and accomplished only in connection with the abolition of capitalism.

Consequently something like the following formula should be adopted:

1. Demand *immediate* expropriation of large enterprises—perhaps by means of a direct national property and income tax with such high and revolutionary high rates with respect to large fortunes as would actually expropriate the capitalists.

2. We declare that now this socialist reconstruction of Switzerland is possible economically, and because of the intolerably high cost of

[74] *Leninskii Sbornik*, XVII, 39–41; another translation is in *The Letters of Lenin*, pp. 403–404.

[75] Apparently on November 30 there had been a meeting of Left Social Democrats, which Lenin also attended, to discuss the theses on the attitude toward war. (*Leninskii Sbornik*, XVII, 40–41, note.)

living it is also urgently necessary. In order to carry out this reconstruction politically Switzerland requires a proletarian rather than a bourgeois government, a proletarian government which would be supported not by the bourgeoisie but by the broad masses of hired workers and the poorest strata. The revolutionary mass struggle, the beginning of which we observe for instance in the Zürich mass strikes and street demonstrations and which has been recognized by the Aarau decision, pursues *precisely* the task of *really* putting an end to this intolerable condition of the masses.

3. We declare that this reconstruction of Switzerland will inevitably be imitated and resolutely and enthusiastically supported by the laboring class and the exploited masses in *all* civilized countries and that through this reconstruction alone the *complete abolition of militarism* toward which we strive and for which the broad European masses hunger instinctively will no longer be an empty phrase, a goody-goody wish, but a really practicable and politically comprehensible measure.

What do you think about this?

Don't you think that in thus presenting the question (in practical agitation as well as in parliamentary speeches, and in proposals for the initiative and the referendum) we shall escape the danger of having the bourgeois and the "socialist" pacifists misunderstand and misinterpret our antimilitant slogans in a sense that we consider a complete abolition of militarism in *bourgeois Switzerland,* in her *imperialist* surroundings, possible *without* a socialist revolution (this, of course, would be nonsense and we unanimously reject it).

With party greetings,
N. Lenin

AGAINST GRIMM AND THE POSTPONEMENT OF THE EXTRAORDINARY PARTY CONGRESS

[Lenin to the Karpinskys, Geneva][76]

[Zürich, January 8, 1917]

Dear Comrades!

I am sending you a *most important* communication.

Consider it yourself and then transmit it to Brilliant and Guilbeaux. That is where the question will be solved: *for* whom they are and *who* they are: whether they are cowards or are capable of struggling.

The *entire* struggle will now be transferred here.

Drop me a line as to what their reaction has been and whether or not there are any chances of publishing a protest or an open letter.

---

[76] *Leninskii Sbornik,* XI, 239–41; another translation is in *The Letters of Lenin,* pp. 405–407.

The fact that *Naine* is an incontrovertible authority in French Switzerland should be made use of.

Best greetings,

Yours,

[Enclosure[77]]

On Sunday, January 7, 1917, a meeting of the Presidium (*Parteivorstand*) of the Swiss Socialist party was held at Zürich.

A disgraceful decision was adopted: to postpone indefinitely the party congress which had been set for February 10, 1917, in Berne and which had been called specially to discuss the question of militarism. The motives for this decision were: the high cost of living must be combated; the workers are not yet ready; no unanimity was attained in the Commission and so forth—motives which simply make the party look foolish. Two draft proposals have already been elaborated by the Commission and have been *confidentially published:* that of Affolter, [Platten,] Nobs, Schmid, Naine, and Graber *against* defense of the fatherland; and that of G. Müller, Pflüger, *Huber,* and *Klöti for* defense of the fatherland.[78]

The meeting of January 7 was very stormy. Grimm, who headed the Rights—i.e., the opportunists, i.e., the nationalists—shouted the meanest phrases against "foreigners," against *the young,* and accused them of "splitting" (!!!) the party, etc. Naine, Platten, Nobs, and Münzenberg spoke *firmly* against postponing the congress. Naine openly declared to Grimm that he, Grimm, "an international secretary," was cutting his own throat!

The adopted decision signifies Grimm's complete treason, and a *mocking of the party* by the opportunist leaders, the social nationalists. The *entire* Zimmerwald-Kienthal movement has *actually* been transformed into a mere phrase by a handful of leaders (including Grimm) who are threatening to give up their mandates (*Sic!!*)—if the defense of the fatherland should be repudiated—and who have decided *not to permit* this question to be discussed by the party "rabble" until the end of the war. *Grütlianer* (of January 4 and January 8) speaks *the truth* and at the same time slaps *such* a party as this in the face.[79]

[77] The enclosure was a carbon copy in Lenin's own handwriting (*Leninskii Sbornik*, XI, 239, note).

[78] Both draft proposals were published in *Beilage zur Berner Tagwacht*, No. 8, January 10, 1917, p. 1, under the common title, "Sozialdemokratische Partei der Schweiz. Anträge der Militärkommission." One proposal, "Antrag der Mehrheit," was signed by H. Affolter, P. Graber, Ch. Naine, E. Nobs, J. Schmid; and the other, "Antrag der Minderheit," was signed by J. Huber, E. Klöti, G. Müller, and P. Pflüger.

[79] Reference is made to unsigned articles, "Von unsern 'linken' Genossen," in No. 2 of *Grütlianer*, January 4, 1917, and "Der Streit um den Parteitag," in No. 5, January 8, 1917. (*Leninskii Sbornik*, XI, 241, note 2.)

The entire struggle of the Lefts *for* Zimmerwald and Kienthal has now been transferred to different ground: the struggle against this gang of leaders who have spat upon the party. It is imperative to rally the Lefts everywhere and to consider the methods of struggle. Hurry!

Would it not be a better method of struggle (not a minute can be lost) if we were to pass at once in La Chaux-de-Fonds and in Geneva resolutions of protest plus the open letter to Naine and publish them at once. There is no doubt that the "leaders" will put all machinery in motion so as to prevent the protest from appearing in the newspapers.

We could state directly in the open letter all that has been said here and pose our questions point-blank: (1) Does Naine refute these facts? (2) Does he consider that the annulment of a decision of the Congress by a decision of the party Presidium can be *tolerated* within a socialist democratic party? (3) Can the concealment from the party of the voting and the *speeches* of the betrayers of socialism at the meeting of January 7, 1917, be tolerated? (4) Can a reconciliation be tolerated with such a chairman of the *Internationale Sozialistische Kommission* as this (Grimm), a chairman who combines Left phrases *with the aiding* of Swiss nationalists, opponents of Zimmerwald, "defenders of the fatherland," Pflüger, *Huber* and Co., in the matter of an actual *disruption* of the Zimmerwald decisions? (5) Can the berating in *Berner Tagwacht* of German social patriots be tolerated while the Swiss social patriots are aided surreptitiously?

I repeat: It is clear that this will not be allowed to appear in newspapers. The best way would be to print an open letter written to Naine himself on behalf of some group. If this is possible, then hurry and answer without delay.[80]

TO THE WORKERS WHO SUPPORT THE STRUGGLE AGAINST WAR

[Excerpt from the Draft of an Article by Lenin Written in January 1917][81]

. . . . This complete fiasco of the Zimmerwald Right has manifested itself with still greater force in Switzerland, the only country of Europe in which the Zimmerwaldists could meet freely and in which they have established their base. The Socialist party of Switzerland, which has held its congresses during the war without any interference by the gov-

[80] See "Otkrytoe pismo k Sharliu Nenu, chlenu Mezhdunarodnoi Sotsialisticheskoi Komissii v Berne," Lenin, *Sochineniia*, XIX, pp. 393–400, which embraces all the points mentioned here. (*Leninskii Sbornik*, XI, 241, note 3.)

[81] Lenin, "K rabochim podderzhivaiushchim borbu protiv voiny i protiv sotsialistov pereshedshikh na storonu svoikh pravitelstv," *Sochineniia*, XIX, 387–92. This draft appeal was addressed to the International Socialist Committee but was never forwarded.

ernment and which had the greatest opportunity of all to aid in the international consolidation of the workers of Germany, France, and Italy in their hostile attitude toward the war, has officially adhered to Zimmerwald.

One of the leaders of this party, the chairman of the Zimmerwald and the Kienthal conferences, the most prominent member and representative of the Berne International Socialist Committee, the National Councilor R. Grimm, *has gone over to the side* of social patriots of *his country* on a question which was decisive for the proletarian party: at the meeting of the *Parteivorstand* of the Swiss Socialist party on January 7, 1917, he carried through the decision[82] of *postponing* for an indefinite time the party congress which was specially called to solve the questions of defense of the fatherland and of the attitude to be adopted toward the Kienthal resolutions condemning social pacifism!

In the appeal signed *"Internationale Sozialistische Kommission"* and dated December 1916[83] Grimm calls the pacifist phrases of the governments hypocritical but does not even mention socialist pacifism, which has united Merrheim and Jouhaux, Raffin-Dugens, and Renaudel. In this appeal Grimm invites the socialist minorities to struggle against the governments and their social-patriotic hirelings, and at the same time he *buries,* jointly with the "social-patriotic hirelings" within the Swiss party, the party congress, a fact which arouses so justly the indignation of all class-conscious and sincere internationalist workers of Switzerland.

No lame excuses can conceal the fact that the decision of the *Parteivorstand,* January 7, 1917, signifies precisely the complete victory of the Swiss social patriots *over* the Swiss socialist workers, the victory of the Swiss opponents of Zimmerwald *over* Zimmerwald.

. . . . Let the Swiss social patriots, those "Grütlians"—who wish to introduce from within the party the policy of Grütli, i.e., the policy of their national bourgeoisie—let them berate the foreigners, let them defend the "inviolability" of the Swiss party from criticism by other parties, let them advocate the old, bourgeois-reformist policy, which led to the collapse of the German and other parties on August 4, 1914—we

---

[82] The resolution adopted by the party Presidium stated that the reasons for postponement were: that there had been no adequate discussion in the party groups or press; that differences on principles and tactics had developed in the drafting commission; that under these circumstances the time remaining before February was insufficient for discussion and to prepare the minds of the party members; and that the energies of the party were wholly taken up with the struggle for a national tax, against the high cost of living, and with efforts to secure party unity. The resolution was adopted by a vote of 25 to 8. (*Berner Tagwacht,* No. 6, January 8, 1917, p. 1, and No. 7, January 9, 1917, p. 1.)

[83] See above, pp. 469–71.

the partisans of Zimmerwald, not in words but in practice, understand internationalism to be something entirely different.

We refuse to observe silently the tendencies which have been completely revealed and which were elucidated by the chairman of the Zimmerwald and the Kienthal conferences himself, tendencies to preserve everything as it used to be within the corrupt European socialism and by means of a hypocritical agreement with K. Liebknecht to *evade* the real slogan of this leader of international workers, his call to effect a "regeneration" of the old parties "from the top to the bottom." We are certain that we have on our side all the class-conscious workers of the entire world, who have enthusiastically greeted K. Liebknecht and his tactics.

We come forth openly with an exposure of the Zimmerwald Right, which has deserted to bourgeois-reformist pacifism.

We come forth openly with a disclosure of the treason to Zimmerwald on the part of R. Grimm and demand the calling of a conference for his recall as a member of the *Internationale Sozialistische Kommission*.

The word "Zimmerwald" is a slogan of international socialism and of revolutionary struggle. This word should not serve as a cloak for social patriotism and bourgeois-reformism.

For true internationalism, which demands a struggle against the social patriots and, *first of all,* those of one's own country! For a true revolutionary tactic which cannot be achieved if agreements are concluded with the social patriots and *against* the social revolutionary workers![84]

---

[84] The original draft of this appeal (published in Lenin, *Sochineniia*, XXX, 294–303) ends with the following paragraph: "We are deeply convinced that at present it has become completely manifest that the Zimmerwald majority or the Right instead of struggling against social chauvinism has turned *entirely* toward surrendering all its forts and in favor of fusing with social chauvinism upon the platform of empty pacifist phrases. Therefore, we consider it to be our duty to declare openly that any support of illusions concerning unity within Zimmerwald and of its struggle in favor of building the Third International causes, under these conditions, tremendous harm to the labor movement. Not as a 'threat' and not as an 'ultimatum,' but merely as an open communication of our decision we declare that if this situation continues we shall not remain members of the Zimmerwald movement."

ON BOLSHEVIK ACTIVITIES IN THE SWISS SOCIAL
DEMOCRATIC PARTY

[Lenin to S. N. Ravich, Geneva][85]

[ZÜRICH, about February 15, 1917]

DEAR COMRADE OLGA!

Many thanks for your letter about the affairs in your local party. To tell the truth, "pessimism" frequently takes hold of others besides yourself.[86]

The party here is opportunist to the core; it is a philanthropic institution for Philistine bureaucrats.

Even leaders who are seemingly Left-minded (like Nobs and Platten)[87] are *good for nothing,* especially the two mentioned. Without access to the masses nothing can be done. But though we do not deceive ourselves with excessive hopes, it is useless for us to lapse into pessimism: this is an important moment and if we help only a *little* (a couple of leaflets, etc.) it will be *something* at least and *will not vanish* without leaving some trace.

I am very glad that you intend to aid in the distribution of the leaflet in every way.[88] Please do not forget to destroy our *entire* correspondence.

When will your cantonal congress of the Socialist party be held?

[85] *Leninskii Sbornik,* XI, 250–52; another translation is in *The Letters of Lenin,* pp. 409–10.

[86] At that time, according to Olga Ravich: "The entire Geneva organization of [Swiss] Social Democrats headed by the noted Jean Sigg, who was an opportunist to the marrow, was super-chauvinistically minded. The task of Russian internationalists consisted in creating, together with a small group of Geneva workers such as Brunner, the working woman Schleifer, and others, a consolidated internationalist wing in that organization [of Swiss Social Democrats]. Our activity was rather animated and enjoyed strong support on the part of Vladimir Ilich. He reminded us frequently of the importance of our work, gave instructions, advised us how and what resolution we should carry through. At times when we were in doubt or in low spirits Vladimir Ilich endeavored to emphasize the importance of the work." (Olga Ravich, "Fevralskie dni 1917 goda v Shveitsarii," *Katorga i Ssylka,* No. 1 [30], 1927, p. 181.)

[87] This refers to the conduct of S. Nobs and F. Platten, during the accentuation of the struggle within the Swiss Social Democratic party in connection with the questions of militarism, and the conduct of the Social Democrats in parliament on the question of war credits. Thus, for instance, Nobs was against giving reasons for the referendum undertaken by the Lefts on the question of an urgent calling of the party congress. Both (Nobs and Platten) took part in the informal conference of the partisans of the center, held on February 3, 1917. (*Leninskii Sbornik,* XI, 251, note 3.)

[88] Lenin refers to a leaflet published and distributed by the group of Left Zimmerwaldists in Switzerland.

I have sent the draft resolution to Abramovich. Has he reforwarded it to you? Do you know anything (in addition to *Volksrecht*) about the congress of the Zürich party in *Töss?*[89]

Who reported on the meeting of February 1 at Olten?[90] Only Guilbeaux & Co.?

They got cold feet!! They did not understand the task and got scared!

I cannot read French.

I shake your hand and wish you all kinds of success. Greetings to Viacheslav Alekseevich [Karpinsky]!

> Yours,
> LENIN

And how do matters stand with the referendum? How many signatures? Are they still being collected?[91]

D. ACTIVITIES OF THE ZIMMERWALD LEFT IN SCANDINAVIA, FRANCE, AND THE UNITED STATES

In addition to the efforts which Lenin and his associates were making in Switzerland to build up an organized revolutionary group within the ranks of the Social Democrats, Lenin was attempting through contacts with Left groups in the Scandinavian countries, France, and the United States to spread the ideas of the Zimmerwald Left and to draw a very definite line of distinction between the Zimmerwald Left and both the patriotic socialists and the Zimmerwald Right.

[89] The cantonal congress of the Zürich Social Democratic organization opened in Töss on February 11, 1917. *Volksrecht*, No. 36, February 12, 1917, devoted an editorial to it. ("Der Parteitag in Töss," *Leninskii Sbornik*, XI, 252, note 5.)

[90] A conference called by the International Socialist Committee was held on February 1, 1917, at Olten to discuss the question of attending the Entente Socialist Conference.

[91] An "initiative committee" (*Initiativkomitee*) was formed by the Swiss Left Zimmerwaldists for the purpose of organizing a referendum in favor of calling the party congress at Easter of 1917 (*Berner Tagwacht*, No. 18, January 22, 1917, p. 2). The text of the referendum was published in *Volksrecht*, No. 19, January 23, 1917, p. 2, under the title "Das Referendum gegen den Parteivorstandsbeschluss ergriffen." This referendum found some response among the workers of German and French Switzerland, but the congress did not meet until June 1917, as had been decided on January 31, 1917, by the party Presidium. ("Parteinachrichten," *Berner Tagwacht*, No. 28, February 2, 1917, p. 2.)

The Swedish and Norwegian opposition groups seemed to offer an especially promising field for the spread of Zimmerwald Left ideas. Z. Höglund, representing the Swedish Socialist Youth League, and Ture Nerman, who held a mandate of the Socialist Youth League of Norway, had signed the declaration of the Lefts at the Zimmerwald Conference; but neither of these organizations had officially joined the Zimmerwald Left, despite the fact that during the years 1915–1916 both opposition groups moved toward the left and grew in numbers and influence.

The first victory of the Swedish Lefts was when they succeeded in having three members expelled from the Social Democratic Labor party for favoring Sweden's participation in the war. They won a second victory when the Youth League succeeded in holding a labor congress at Stockholm, March 18–19, 1916, in spite of the opposition of the Social Democratic majority. This Congress adopted an anti-government manifesto, whereupon the authorities confiscated the issue of the Youth League organ, *Stormklockan,* containing the manifesto and arrested Z. Höglund, E. Heden, and L. Oljelund, who were tried for high treason and sentenced to hard labor. The entire opposition and especially the Youth League carried on an energetic campaign for the release of the three, who were finally freed.[92]

In connection with this campaign and the Left propaganda against the majority the opposition established late in April 1916 a new paper, the *Politiken,* edited by Ture Nerman.

These activities aroused the party majority. The Presidium issued a manifesto denouncing the opposition for breach of party discipline and at the party congress in February 1917 put through a resolution which ordered the Youth League under threat of expulsion to submit to the will of the party majority. The opposition, including the Social Demo-

[92] K. Chilbum [Kilbom], "Shvedskaia sotsial-demokratiia i mirovaia voina," *Sbornik Sotsial-Demokrata,* No. 2, December 1916, pp. 36–40; *Berner Tagwacht,* No. 73, March 27, 1916, p. 3; *Internationale sozialistische Kommission. Nachrichtendienst,* No. 2, May 10, 1917, p. 6. The last named will hereafter be cited as *I.S.K. Nachrichtendienst.*

cratic minority deputies in the Riksdag and the Youth League, replied by calling a congress in May of that year to form a new socialist party on Zimmerwald principles. This Congress laid the foundations of the Left Social Democratic Labor party of Sweden, which at the later Congress of June 12–16, 1919, adhered to the Third International and advocated the establishment of the Soviet system in Sweden. In spite of this leftward swing the new party held tenaciously to its old demand for complete disarmament to which Lenin was so decidedly opposed.[93]

Lenin's letters given below show his deep interest in the split in the Swedish party and his desire to have the new party accept what he considered the truly revolutionary program. When, however, the new party actually came into being, Lenin was too deeply involved in affairs in Russia to follow or directly influence its course.

In Norway the Left tendency was even stronger than in Sweden. An opposition group in the labor movement had been gaining in numbers and influence since 1911, as had an energetic Socialist Youth League led by Arvid Hansen. During the early years of the war the Norwegian Lefts took an internationalist position, and in April 1916 the Youth League voted to join the Zimmerwald movement. This organization also published Lenin's and Zinoviev's *Socialism and War* in their organ *Klassekampen*. On June 3 of this year, under pressure from the Left, the Social Democratic party Presidium adopted a resolution recognizing the Zimmerwald principles, but did not join the Zimmerwald movement. As elsewhere, the Russian revolution strengthened the Lefts, who

---

[93] "Ein schwedisches Manifest," *Berner Tagwacht,* No. 86, April 11, 1916, p. 1; "Nach dem Hochverratsprozess," *Berner Tagwacht,* No. 116, May 18, 1916, p. 1; "Der schwedische Parteitag gegen die 'Jungen,'" *Beilage des Vorwärts,* No. 50, February 20, 1917, pp. 1–2; "Spaltung der schwedischen Partei durch die Zimmerwalder," *Vorwärts,* No. 57, February 27, 1917, p. 4; Kollontai, "La Vie politique et sociale. Suède," *Demain,* No. 13, May 1917, pp. 46–48; Wilhelm Jansson, "Die Spaltung in der schwedischen Sozialdemokratie," *Internationale Korrespondenz,* No. 16, June 1, 1917, pp. 110–12; "Rezoliutsiia shvedskoi levoi sotsial-demokraticheskoi partii," *Kommunisticheskii Internatsional,* No. 5, September 1919, pp. 697–98; *Social-Demokraten,* Nos. 111–14, May 14 to 18, 1917.

became in 1918 the majority within the party. At its congress held in Christiania, March 29 to April 2, 1918, the Norwegian party officially joined the Zimmerwald movement by 150 votes to 127.[94] On June 8, 1919, the Norwegian Social Democratic party voted to withdraw from the Second International and join the Third, and a telegram to this effect was sent to Lenin.[95]

Because of the situation in the French labor and socialist movements, the Zimmerwald Left achieved relatively small results from its activities in France. The majority of the Socialist party took a defensist and patriotic position. The minority took a position which in general corresponded to that of the Zimmerwald Right, a position which Lenin very roundly denounced in the letters which follow. A few individuals well known in the labor movement and certain rather small groups were won over to the position of the Zimmerwald Left, but their propaganda and organizational activities were very severely restricted by the activities of the police and the disapproval of the socialist and syndicalist majorities.

Lenin's principal contacts with developments in France were through those members of the Bolshevik Paris section who had not been swept away from their party moorings by the wave of patriotic sentiment of the first days of the war. These Bolsheviks, who had previously taken no part in the French socialist movement, joined the French Socialist party after the outbreak of the war and endeavored to spread Bolshevik ideas by speeches and by translations of articles from the *Sotsial-Demokrat*. The results of these efforts, according to one of Lenin's correspondents, were "microscopic."

In January 1916 Lenin sent Inessa Armand to Paris to

[94] *Social-Demokraten*, No. 74, March 30, 1918, p. 1, gives 150 votes against 117.

[95] "Pismo Ts.K. norvezhskoi rabochei partii," *Kommunisticheskii Internatsional*, No. 5, September 1919, pp. 695–96; "Die norwegische Partei für Zimmerwald," *Berner Tagwacht*, No. 136, June 13, 1916, p. 2; "La Vie politique et sociale. Norvège," *Demain*, No. 24, April 1918, p. 386; Arvid G. Hansen, "Norwegen," *Jugend-Internationale*, No. 5, September 1, 1916, pp. 15–16; *Social-Demokraten*, No. 74, March 30, 1918, p. 1; No. 75, April 2, 1918, p. 1; and No. 76, April 3, 1918, pp. 1, 3; Lenin, *Sochineniia*, XIX, 489, note 216.

help spread Zimmerwald Left propaganda. A thousand copies of the Zimmerwald Left manifesto were published in January 1916, and through the Secretary of the Syndicalist Youth Section Inessa Armand was admitted to the International Action Committee (Comité d'action internationale), established in December 1915 by the French syndicalists-Zimmerwaldists. In a letter written early in January she tells Lenin of her activities:

".... I have succeeded in seeing a tremendous number of people .... For the last two or three days I have done nothing but go from one rendezvous to another .... I have, by the way, seen N. V. [Sapozhkov] .... ; he was wounded in the leg and is still limping—he looks very thin, pale, and tired, but tries to keep up his spirits. He told me many interesting things..... N. V. shares completely the point of view of the Central Organ. I am sending you his paragraph for the newspaper. It would be possible to carry on propaganda in the army on a fairly large scale, to distribute leaflets and so forth. But if we are to publish especially for soldiers, then we should have to have a name, and we are at a loss to find one. If you think it advisable, then perhaps the Left can give its own name. This is undoubtedly a risky game and should be carried on simultaneously in the German army. Write us your opinion....."[96]

The fusion of the Socialist Minority Committee and the International Action Committee to form the Committee for the Resumption of International Relations (Comité pour la réprise des rélations internationales), led to some very warm debates which revealed the reluctance of many of the French Zimmerwaldists to follow the Left line. A manifesto proposed by Bourderon and supported by Louise Saumoneau stated that the new committee would continue to function "until the party majority and the International Socialist Bureau resume international relations." Loriot and Merrheim

[96] N. K. Krupskaia [ed.], *Pamiati Inessy Armand*, p. 19; hereafter cited *Pamiati Inessy Armand*.

objected, and Merrheim offered an amendment, which was adopted, stating that as Zimmerwaldists they were bound by Zimmerwald decisions and therefore the new committee should continue as long as the Zimmerwald Committee existed.[97] Of subsequent discussions of the attitude of the new committee Inessa Armand wrote:

"Dear friends, I am sending you only a few words, for I am very busy. Since I last wrote two meetings of the Action Committee have been held. The appeal[98] (which states that the French party minority agrees with the German 'minority' rather than the 'majority,' and which speaks about the restoration of the International) was discussed at one of these meetings. Trotsky's draft was rejected and replaced by that of Merrheim, *which does not speak* about restoration but merely says that 'the International must be based on class struggle, struggle against imperialism and struggle for peace. This is the International which we shall join.' Then it says that an international which does not rest on this basis would be a deception of the proletariat. I proposed a few amendments—about the struggle against the social chauvinists (I was told that this would be added at the end of the appeal), about the fact that the International struggles against imperialism (this was adopted); and finally I expressed myself as being against the following sentence: 'This is the International which we shall join,' and proposed instead, 'We shall reconstruct the International on this basis, etc.' For this word 'reconstruct' both Merrheim and Bourderon fell upon me. Merrheim told me that we were Guesdists (old methods), that our thinking was detached from reality, that we did not reckon with circumstances, that in France the socialists did not even wish to hear of a split and so forth. I replied that a Guesdist of the old type was not at all bad, that at present our tactics were vital and true to life, for the proletarian forces could be rallied only by vividly and definitely distin-

---

[97] S. Bantke, "Lenin i Tsimmervaldskoe dvizhenie vo Frantsii," *Proletarskaia Revoliutsiia*, No. 3, 1934, pp. 129–30.

[98] For details, see *The Bolsheviks and World Revolution*.

guishing one's own point of view from that of the chauvinists; that the treason of the leaders had called forth mistrust and disappointment; that many a factory worker who read our pamphlet had said: 'All this is fine, but there are no socialists any more'; we must carry into the masses the happy news that there are socialists, and we can do this only after having completely broken with the chauvinists."[99]

In one of her early letters from Paris to Lenin, Inessa Armand said: "I think that by acting from above—i.e., through Merrheim's Committee—hardly anything can be accomplished in a short time. Therefore, we shall attend the meetings of this Committee regularly and shall do all we can there; but it is imperative to look for other channels—to endeavor to act from below."[100] In carrying out this plan she worked with the socialist youth organization of the Seine Department, which joined Zimmerwald, and with a small group within this organization which adopted a Zimmerwald Left resolution. A group of members of one of the Paris sections of the syndicate of mechanics also adopted a resolution drafted by Armand, criticizing the Zimmerwald Right and approving the manifesto of the Left. Contacts were likewise established with French and Russian soldiers in the French army and through them illegal publications received some circulation among the troops. At St. Nazaire, where Safarov was employed on the docks, Zimmerwald Left publications were distributed and a circle of dock workers was formed which decided to establish contact with the International Socialist Committee in the belief that the I.S.C. was a committee of the Third International. Later a similar group was formed among the longshoremen at Brest.[101] Lenin's letter to Safarov, given below, criticizing the tactics of Merrheim and Bourderon was written at the request of the organizers of these Left groups. Other activities of the Russian Bolsheviks

[99] *Pamiati Inessy Armand,* pp. 21–22.

[100] *Ibid.,* p. 18.

[101] S. Bantke, "Lenin i Tsimmervaldskoe dvizhenie vo Frantsii," *Proletarskaia Revoliutsiia,* No. 3, 1934, pp. 133–35, 145.

and the French Left-Zimmerwaldists included the establishment of a secret printing plant which issued and distributed illegal appeals and manifestoes. Three Bolsheviks were selected to form the editorial board of the establishment and were given their instructions by Lenin. *Socialism and War* was translated and sold to the workers in the autumn of 1916; this French translation of the pamphlet contained also certain materials dealing chiefly with the Zimmerwald movement. At this time the Committee for the Resumption of International Relations adopted the Left-Zimmerwaldist program set forth by Loriot in his pamphlet, *Les Socialistes de Zimmerwald et la guerre.*[102]

Demain, edited by Guilbeaux and published in Switzerland, became a medium for the dissemination of Left views, and in May 1917, *La Nouvelle Internationale,* edited by Loriot, made its appearance. Thus, early in 1917, the French Left Zimmerwaldists had moved from a position reflected by the slogans, "struggle for peace" and "resumption of international relations," to a more radical stand expressed in the slogans, "the masses must utilize the war for a revolution" and "for a Third International."[103]

As in the case of France, the contact of the Zimmerwald Left with American socialists was largely through certain Russian Bolsheviks who happened to be in the United States during the war. Lenin hoped that individuals or groups within the American Socialist and Socialist Labor parties

[102] S. Bantke, "Lenin i Tsimmervaldskoe dvizhenie vo Frantsii," *Proletarskaia Revoliutsiia,* No. 3, 1934, p. 145; Baevsky, "Bolsheviki v Tsimmervalde," *ibid.,* No. 5, 1935, p. 38. For excerpts from Loriot's pamphlet, see *The Bolsheviks and World Revolution.*

[103] F. Loriot, "Vers la Troisième Internationale," *La Nouvelle Internationale,* No. 1, May 1, 1917, p. 1.

Alfred Rosmer, however, is of the opinion that no Zimmerwald Left really existed in France. He says that he and the other leaders of the syndicalist minority were not aware of the activity of the members of the Bolshevik section in Paris; that, in fact, they were not even acquainted with any of the persons who, as the Bolshevik historians claim now, were spreading the Zimmerwald Left ideas in France, and that the pamphlet, *Les Socialistes de Zimmerwald et la guerre,* was written by F. Loriot in collaboration with L. Trotsky. (A. Rosmer, *Le Mouvement ouvrier pendant la guerre,* pp. 456–64.)

might be brought around to the internationalist revolutionary point of view and that with the aid of such converts Bolshevik and Zimmerwald Left literature could be published in English for distribution not only in America but in England.

Kollontai made two trips to the United States in 1915–1917 and during her visits tried to persuade the American parties to join the Zimmerwald movement. On October 18, 1915, she wrote to Lenin from Milwaukee that at a meeting of the German group of the American Socialist party Lore proposed a resolution in favor of joining Zimmerwald: "But," Kollontai said, "after heated debates Hillquit and Romm defeated our proposal."[104]

In November 1915 Lenin received a leaflet of the Socialist Propaganda League, and since the leaflet seemed to show an internationalist trend, he sent to the League the pamphlet, *Socialism and War,* and the *Internationales Flugblatt* of the Zimmerwald Left along with a letter in which he urged the American group to join with the Bolsheviks in their struggle "against the conciliators and for true internationalism."[105] The Socialist Propaganda League, which was one of several opposition groups in the American socialist movement, did not apparently need much urging to take this position. The League had been formed early in 1915 by two émigré socialists, F. Rozin, Secretary of the Lettish Group No. 1 in Boston, and S. J. Rutgers, who had established contact with Rozin through the Dutch *De Tribune* group. The members of the League were chiefly workers of foreign birth or descent; they were critical of the Second International and were advocates of industrial unionism and mass action by the

---

[104] Archive of Marx-Engels-Lenin Institute, No. 20618, A. Kollontai's letter to V. I. Lenin, October 18, 1915, cited by Baevsky in "Bolsheviki v Tsimmervalde," *Proletarskaia Revoliutsiia,* No. 5, 1935, pp. 38–39. On November 23, 1915, the International Socialist Committee at Berne received an official telegram from the Executive of the American Socialist party stating that the party, including all its foreign groups, joined the Zimmerwald movement. ("Le Socialist Party de l'Amérique et la C.S.I.," *Commission socialiste internationale à Berne, Bulletin,* No. 2, December 27, 1915, p. 13.)

[105] A translation of Lenin's letter is given in Lenin, *The Imperialist War,* pp. 374–76; see also *ibid.,* p. 439, note 196.

workers.[106] According to Rutgers, writing many years after the events, as soon as the news of the Zimmerwald Conference reached America the League adopted the position of the Zimmerwald Left. It distributed and explained the Left's resolutions to American workers, published a "credo" in November 1916, and in January 1917 began to publish a periodical called *The Internationalist* in Boston. Later, headquarters were moved to New York and the name of the paper changed to *The New International*. When the United States entered the war *The New International* was excluded from the mails; but with the help of Russian and other Lefts, including the Japanese socialist Katayama, the paper was published irregularly and was sold in the streets. After the Russian revolution, the League, with the help of the Russians in New York, established a Bolshevik Information Bureau and published a collection of Lenin's speeches.[107] As for American party affairs, the League, according to Kollontai's account[108] opposed militarism, both defensive and offensive, advocated mass action and the control of the legislative activity of socialists by workers' organizations, but apparently did not come out for an open break with the patriotic socialists or for taking advantage of the World War for revolutionary action.

In the same account Kollontai also describes the activities of the New York Opposition, which inclined toward the Zimmerwald Center rather than toward the Left and was made up chiefly of the internationalists of the German and Russian groups, whose "aim was to unite the American internationalists who maintain continuous contacts with the European

---

[106] The position of the Socialist Propaganda League is set forth by one of its leaders in Louis C. Fraina, *Revolutionary Socialism. A Study in Socialist Reconstruction.*

[107] S. Rutgers, "Vstrechi s Leninym," *Istorik Marksist*, Nos. 2–3 (42–43), 1935, pp. 86–87; L. Zubok, "U istokov kommunisticheskogo dvizheniia v S.Sh.A.," *ibid.*, Nos. 5–6 (45–46), 1935, pp. 42–43.

[108] "La Vie politique et sociale. Amérique," *Demain*, No. 13, May 1917, pp. 34–39; "Die Opposition in der 'American Socialist Party,'" *Arbeiterpolitik*, No. 14, April 7, 1917, pp. 108–10.

Zimmerwaldists and to force the [Socialist] party to choose definitely between the chauvinists of The Hague and the internationalists of Berne." Kollontai reported further that the New York Opposition encouraged mass protests against the high cost of living, initiated a movement under the slogans, "Down with the World War! Down with the hypocritical policy of Wilson and the Kings of Wall Street." The Opposition also drafted a manifesto attacking Wilson's peace efforts, exposing the true character of the war, and calling on the workers to struggle against militarism in the United States and for immediate peace. The manifesto was adopted by the German, Russian, Lettish, and several other groups of the Socialist party.

Bukharin, Berzin, and Trotsky were also in the United States in the winter of 1916–1917. On October 14, 1916, Lenin wrote Bukharin to arrange if possible to publish in English the manifesto of the Zimmerwald Left and *Socialism and War,* and to send to him "without cost to the Central Committee" publications of the Socialist party and the Socialist Labor party along with official economic statistical publications of the United States. He urged that a small group of Russian Bolsheviks and Lefts be organized to send interesting literature to Lenin and translate and publish material sent from Europe and to push forward various questions concerning the Third International and the Left movement. "There must be," Lenin wrote, "a base in the United States for struggle against the English bourgeoisie which has carried the censorship to absurdity." Lenin further urged Bukharin to try to get in touch with the Propaganda League and to pay special attention to the Letts in America.[109]

No very great progress had been made in America in the organization of supporters of the Zimmerwald Left when the first Russian Revolution of 1917 turned the attention of the Bolshevik émigrés to affairs in their own country to which

---

[109] "Iz materialov Instituta Marksa-Engelsa-Lenina. Lenin–N. I. Bukharinu," *Bolshevik,* No. 22, November 30, 1932, p. 91.

most of them presently returned. Likewise the breaking of diplomatic relations with Germany and the declaration of war by the United States focused the attention of American socialists on the issues which those events raised. An emergency convention of the American Socialist party held in St. Louis in April 1917 adopted by a large majority a manifesto characterizing the declaration of war as "a crime against the people of the United States and against the nations of the world." The manifesto called for opposition to conscription, military training, and censorship, and advocated propaganda to enlighten the masses regarding capitalism and the war, restriction of food exports, socialization and democratic control of great industries, land, and other natural resources held out of use for speculative purposes. Some of the leaders of the Socialist party rejected the manifesto and took a patriotic stand; many of those who attempted to carry out the recommendations of the manifesto were arrested under the Espionage Act of June 15, 1917, tried, and given long sentences. Socialist periodicals were denied mailing privileges, and the radical wing of the movement was driven under ground.[110]

THE SWEDISH AND NORWEGIAN SOCIAL DEMOCRATS AND THE ARMING OF THE PEOPLE

[Lenin to Kollontai, Christiania][111]

[BERNE, spring 1915]

DEAR COMRADE!

Many thanks for all your efforts and for your help of which you wrote in your last letter.

Your articles in *Nashe Slovo* and for the *Kommunist*[112] about Scandinavian affairs have raised in my mind this question:

[110] Cf. *The American Socialists and the War*, pp. 33–45; James Oneal, *American Communism*, pp. 32–40; *The New York Call* for April 1917.

[111] Lenin, *Sochineniia*, XXIX, 176–77; another translation is in *The Letters of Lenin*, pp. 364–65.

[112] A. M. Kollontai published in *Nashe Slovo* the following articles: (1) "Kopengagenskaia konferentsiia," *ibid.*, No. 1, January 29, 1915, p. 2, and No. 4, February 2, 1915, p. 1; (2) "Chto delat? Otvet sotsialistkam," *ibid.*, No. 19, February 19, 1915, p. 1; and (3) "Zhenskii sotsialisticheskii Internatsional i

Is it possible to praise and to consider correct the stand of the Left Scandinavian Social Democrats, who renounce the arming of the people? I argued this with Höglund in 1910 and tried to prove to him that this is not radicalism, not a revolutionary attitude, but simply the Philistinism of provincial Philistines. These Scandinavian Philistines in their small states have climbed almost to the North Pole and are proud of the fact that one may gallop for three years and still not get there! How is it possible to admit that on the eve of a socialist revolution the revolutionary class should be *against* arming the people? This is not a struggle against militarism, but a cowardly desire to dodge the major questions of the capitalist world. How is it possible to "recognize" the class struggle without understanding the inevitability of its transformation at certain moments into civil war?

It seems to me that it would be advisable to collect material on that question and to come forward decisively *against* it in the *Kommunist,* and for the enlightenment of the Scandinavians you could later print it in Swedish, and so forth.

I should like to know in great detail your opinion about it.

Bruce Glasier in my judgment is a bad collaborator; although he has a proletarian strain, he is nevertheless an unbearable opportunist. It is hardly possible to work with him; he will start crying in two days and will say that he was "inveigled," that he neither desired nor recognized anything of the kind.

Have you seen David's book and his opinion of our manifesto?[113]

Is there any material in the Scandinavian countries on the struggle of the *two currents* with regard to the question of attitude toward the war? Is it possible to gather exact material (opinions, evaluations, resolutions) with an exact comparison of *facts* concerning the tendencies of both currents? Do facts confirm (in my judgment they do) that opportunists taken as a *current* in general are more chauvinist than are the revolutionary Social Democrats? What do you think of the possibility of gathering and elaborating such material for the *Kommunist?*

With a firm handshake and wishing you all blessings.

N. Lenin

P.S. Who is this Shaw Desmond that lectured in the Scandinavian countries? Can his lecture be found in English? Is he a thorough revolutionary or à la Hervé?

---

voina," *Nashe Slovo,* No. 33, March 7, 1915, pp. 3–4. *Kommunist,* No. 1–2, 1915, pp. 159–61, published Kollontai's article, "Pochemu molchal proletariat Germanii v iiulskie dni?" (Lenin, *Sochineniia,* XXIX, 177, note 2.)

[113] In his book, *Die Sozialdemokratie im Weltkrieg,* pp. 166–72, Eduard David criticized the Bolshevik manifesto of November 1914 and called the desire to transform the World War into a civil war "insanity."

ON THE LEFTS IN THE UNITED STATES

[Lenin to Kollontai, Milwaukee (?)][114]

[BERNE, November 9, 1915]

DEAR ALEKSANDRA MIKHAILOVNA!

Only yesterday we received your letter of October 18 from Milwaukee. Letters take a terrifically long time! You have not yet received my letter (and Nos. 45–46 and 47 of *Sotsial-Demokrat*) about Zimmerwald and containing all the answers to your questions, though I wrote that letter more than a month ago.[115] Try to figure out, at least, where you will be (let us say in a month and a half) and give me such addresses (for letters to you) as would be the closest possible to your whereabouts.

With respect to the New York *Volkszeitung*, Grimm has assured me today that these people are entirely Kautskyans! Is that so? I think that our *German* pamphlet could help you to determine "the strength" of in- ternationalism. Do you have it (500 copies were sent to you)?

Within the next few days we shall publish here (in German and later we *hope* in French and even in Italian, if we succeed in squeezing out the money) a small pamphlet on behalf of the *Zimmerwald Left*. Under this name we should like to launch internationally and as extensively as possible our Left group at Zimmerwald (the Central Committee + the P.S.D. [the Regional Presidium of the Social Democracy of Poland and Lithuania] + Letts + Swedes + Norwegians + 1 German + 1 Swiss) with its *draft resolution* and *draft manifesto*[116] (published in No. 45–46 of *Sotsial-Demokrat*). A small pamphlet (20–30–35 thousand letters)[117] will contain those two documents and a short introduction. We trust that you will publish it in America *in English* (since it is hopeless to do so in England; it will have to be imported there *from* America) and, if pos- sible, in other languages. This must be the first demonstration of the *nucleus of the Left* Social Democrats of *all* countries who have a clear, exact and full *answer* to the question what to do and where to go. If we succeed in publishing it in America, it would be super-important to spread it as widely as possible and *to establish firm contacts with pub- lishers (Charles Kerr* [N.B.] in Chicago, *Appeal to Reason* in Kansas, etc.), because in general it is super-important for us to come forth in various languages (you could do *a great deal* in that respect).

[114] Lenin, *Sochineniia*, XXIX, 214–15; another translation is in *The Letters of Lenin*, pp. 380–82.

[115] This letter has not been found. (Lenin, *Sochineniia*, XXIX, p. 214, note.)

[116] See chapter iv, pp. 349–53.

[117] The Russian method of estimating the size of a manuscript for publication consists in counting the letters, instead of words as is usual in the United States. This pamphlet came out under the title *Internationales Flugblatt*, No. 1 ("Die Zim- merwalder Linke über die Aufgaben der Arbeiterklasse"), November 1915.

Try to establish contacts with them at least by correspondence, if you are not going to be in Kansas. Sometimes their little newspaper is *not bad*. By all means test them out with our resolution of the "Zimmerwald Left." And what is *Eugene Debs?* Occasionally he writes in a revolutionary manner. Or is he another milksop, à la Kautsky? Write *when* will you *again* be in New York and for *how many* days? Endeavor to see (for five minutes at least) the local *Bolsheviks everywhere;* "freshen" them up and *connect them with us.*

Concerning money, I saw with regret from your letter that so far you have not succeeded in collecting anything for the Central Committee. Let us hope this "manifesto of the Lefts" will help ——.

That Hillquit would stand for Kautsky and would be even *more to the right* than Kautsky, I do not doubt, for I saw him at Stuttgart (1907) and *heard* how he *later* defended the exclusion of the yellow races from America ("an internationalist") ——.

The Zimmerwald manifesto as such is *insufficient.* Kautsky and Co. are ready to be reconciled to it on one *condition:* "not a step farther." We do *not* accede to this, for it is *pure hypocrisy.* Hence, if in America there are people who are afraid *even* of the Zimmerwald manifesto, disregard them and select only those who are *to the left of the Zimmerwald manifesto.*

With a firm handshake and wishing you all kinds of success!

Yours,
LENIN

(Uljanow, Seidenweg, 4-a III, Bern)

ON THE TASKS OF THE OPPOSITION IN FRANCE

[Lenin to Safarov][118]

[BERNE, February 10, 1916]

DEAR COMRADE!

Your deportation from France—which by the way has been marked by a protest even in the chauvinist newspaper *La Bataille,*[119] which, however, did not wish to tell the truth: that you have been deported for sympathizing with the opposition—has recalled to me once more the sore question of the position and tasks of the opposition in France.

I saw Bourderon and Merrheim at Zimmerwald. I heard their reports and read in the papers of their activity. I cannot permit myself to entertain even the slightest doubt with regard to their sincerity and devo-

[118] Lenin, *Sochineniia,* XIX, 21–24.

[119] The report that Safarov had been deported from France because he was accused of being a spy was published in *La Bataille,* No. 87, January 28, 1916, in a paragraph entitled: "Une Expulsion," and signed Ch. Marck. The paragraph was written in a sympathetic tone. Safarov was deported on January 25, 1916. (Lenin, *Sochineniia,* XIX, 449, note 21.)

tion to the proletarian cause. But nevertheless it is plain that their tactics are wrong. Both of them are most of all afraid of a split. Not one step, not one word which might lead to a split within the Socialist party or the labor unions in France, or a split within the Second International, or the creation of a Third International!—such is the slogan of Bourderon and Merrheim.

Meanwhile the world-wide split within the labor movement and socialism has become a fact. We are confronted with two irreconcilable tactics and policies of the laboring class with regard to the war. It would be ridiculous if we were to shut our eyes to this. To attempt to reconcile something which cannot be reconciled would be to condemn one's entire work to futility. Even deputy Otto Rühle, Liebknecht's comrade in Germany, has openly recognized the inevitability of a party split, for the present party majority, the official "high spheres" of the German party, have taken the side of the bourgeoisie.[120] The objections against Rühle and against the split raised by the so-called representatives of the "center" or "the swamp" (le marais)—Kautsky and Vorwärts—are only lies and hypocrisy, however "well-intentioned." Kautsky and Vorwärts cannot and do not even try to refute the fact that, in practice, the majority of the German party is pursuing the policy of the bourgeoisie. Unity with such a majority as this is harmful for the laboring class. Such unity means subjecting the laboring class to the bourgeoisie of "one's own" nation, means a split within the international laboring class. And as a matter of fact Rühle is right when he says that there are two parties in Germany. One is the official party and pursues the policy of the bourgeoisie. The other party, the minority, publishes illegal appeals—and organizes demonstrations, etc. We can see the same picture all over the world. The helpless diplomats, or the "swamp," like Kautsky in Germany, Longuet in France, Martov and Trotsky in Russia, are doing tremendous harm to the labor movement, by defending the fiction of unity and thereby interfering with the fully matured and urgent unification of the oppositions in all countries and with the creation of the Third International. Even such a moderate newspaper as the Labour Leader in England is publishing the letters of Russell Williams on the necessity to split away from the "leaders" of the labor unions and of the Labour party, who "have sold out" the interests of the working class. A number of members of the Independent Labour party declare in the press that they are in sympathy with Russell Williams. Even in Russia the reconciler, Trotsky, is now compelled to recognize the inevitability of a break with the "patriots"—i.e., the party of the "Organization Committee," the O.C.—who are justifying the en-

---

[120] Otto Rühle's statement under the title, "Zur Parteispaltung," was published in Beilage des Vorwärts, No. 11, January 12, 1916, pp. 2–3.

trance of the workers into War Industries Committees. And out of sheer false pride, Trotsky continues to defend "unity" with Chkheidze's Duma group, which is a very faithful friend, a cover and a defense for the "patriots" and the "O.C."

As a matter of fact there is a complete split even in the United States, for some of the socialists there are in favor of having an army, in favor of "preparedness" and war. Others, including the very popular labor leader, Eugene Debs, candidate of the Socialist party for the post of President of the Republic, are preaching civil war against the war between the peoples!

And look at the *accomplishments* of Bourderon and Merrheim themselves! Verbally they are against a split. But read the resolution which Bourderon introduced at the congress of the French Socialist party.[121]

In this resolution the withdrawal of socialists from cabinets is demanded!! The resolution utterly *"désapprouve"* of the C.A.P. and G.P. (C.A.P.—Commission Administrative Permanente; G.P.—Groupe Parlementaire)!!! It is as clear as daylight that, if this resolution were adopted, it would mean a split in the Socialist party *as well as* in the labor unions, for the Messrs. Renaudels, Sembats, Jouhaux et Cie., would never be able to reconcile themselves to this.

Bourderon and Merrheim both share the mistake, the weakness and the faint-heartedness of the *majority* at the Zimmerwald Conference. On the one hand, this majority appeals *indirectly* in its manifesto for *revolutionary* struggle but is afraid to say so openly. On the one hand it writes, capitalists of *all* countries *lie* when they speak of the "defense of the fatherland" in this war. On the other hand, the majority has been afraid to add the obvious truth, which, however, will be added by any thinking workman, namely, that "not only the capitalists but also Renaudel, Sembat, Longuet, *Hyndman, Kautsky, Plekhanov et Cie., are lying!!"* The majority of the Zimmerwald Conference *wishes* to become reconciled again with Vandervelde, Huysmans, Renaudel and Co. This is *harmful* for the laboring class, and the "Zimmerwald Left" acted correctly when it *openly* stated the truth to the workers.

Look, how *les socialistes-chauvins* are dissimulating: in France they

121 The *Labour Leader,* in reporting on the Congress of the French Socialist party held on December 25–29, 1915, says: "Bourderon, who proposed the resolution of Zimmerwald, reproached the chiefs of the party for having abandoned the class struggle in favour of the 'sacred union' of which the working classes were the victims. He demanded a return to internationalist traditions and the withdrawal of the Socialist Ministers from the government and said that whatever happened he himself would continue to work for peace" ("What happened at the French Socialist Congress," *ibid.,* No. 4, January 27, 1916, p. 8). Bourderon's resolution was voted down by 2,736 votes to 76 and 102 abstentions ("Au Congrès national du parti socialiste," *L'Humanité,* No. 4274, December 30, 1915, p. 1; translated text of the resolution in *The Bolsheviks and World Revolution.*

are praising the German *"minorité,"* whereas in Germany they are praising the *French* minority!!

How tremendously significant it would be if the French opposition were to come forth directly and declare openly and without fear before the entire world: We identify ourselves *only with the German* opposition, *only with Rühle* and his partisans, only with those who are breaking fearlessly with open as well as covert social-chauvinism, *socialisme chauvin,* i.e., with all the "defenders of the fatherland" in this war!! We ourselves are not afraid of a break with French "patriots," who are calling the defense of colonies a "defense of the fatherland"; we are calling for a *similar break* with the socialists and the syndicalists of all countries; we are stretching out our hands to Otto Rühle and to Liebknecht, and *only* to them and their partisans; we condemn the French and the German *majorité* and *"le marais";* we proclaim a great international alliance of all socialists all over the world who in this war have broken with the false phrase about "the defense of the fatherland" and who are preaching and preparing for a universal proletarian revolution!!

Such an appeal would have gigantic significance. It would disperse the hypocrites, expose and unmask international deception, and give a tremendous stimulus to the rapprochement of the workers all over the world who have remained *really* faithful to internationalism.

The anarchistic phraseology has always done much harm in France. But now the anarchist-patriots, the anarchists-*chauvins,* like Kropotkin, Grave, Cornelissen, and other knights *de la Bataille chauviniste,* will help to cure a great many workers of the anarchistic phraseology. Down with the socialist-patriots and the socialist-*chauvins* and "down with the anarchist-patriots" and the anarchists-*chauvins!* This call *will* find response in the hearts of the French workers. Not anarchist phrases about revolution are required, but long, serious, obstinate, persistent, and systematic work for the creation *everywhere* of illegal organizations among the *workers,* for the distribution of *free,* i.e., illegal literature, for preparing the movement of the *masses* against one's own government—that is what the working class in all countries requires!

It is not true that "the French are incapable" of carrying on systematic illegal work. It is not true! The French have learned quickly to keep out of sight in the trenches. They will also learn quickly the *new* conditions of illegal activity and systematic preparation of the *revolutionary* movement of the *masses.* I believe in the French revolutionary proletariat. It will also push forward the French opposition.

Best wishes.

Yours, LENIN

P.S. I propose to the French comrades that they publish a translation (a complete translation) of my letter, as a *separate leaflet.*[122]

[122] This letter to Safarov was published in French as a leaflet under the title

PROGRESS OF THE LEFTS IN THE UNITED STATES AND THE DECLINE OF THE ZIMMERWALD MOVEMENT

[Lenin to Kollontai, Christiania][123]

[ZÜRICH, February 17, 1917]

DEAR A. M.!

Today we received your letter and were very glad to have it. For a long time we did not know that you were in America and have had no letters from you except one with the news of your departure from America.

I wrote you on January 7 or 8 (the date the letter was dispatched from Stockholm: the French intercept everything that is mailed directly from here to America!), but this letter (with the article for *Novyi Mir*) obviously missed you in New York.[124]

In the same degree that I was pleased to hear from you about the victory of Nikolai Ivanovich [Bukharin] and Pavlov [P. V. Berzin] in *Novyi Mir* (I am getting this newspaper with devilish irregularity, obviously as a fault of the mail and not of the newspaper office itself), I was sorry about the news of Trotsky's bloc with the "Rights" for a struggle against Nikolai Ivanovich. What a swine that Trotsky—Left phrases yet a bloc with the Rights against the aim of the "Lefts"!! He should be exposed (by you) at least in a brief letter to *Sotsial-Demokrat!*[125]

N. Lenine, Sur la tâche de l'opposition en France (Lettre au Camarade Safarof), Genève, Bibliothèque russe, probably in 1916, and by the Central Committee of the R.S.D.L. party (Lenin, *Sochineniia,* XIX, 451, note).

[123] Lenin, *Sochineniia,* XXIX, 290–93; another translation is in *The Letters of Lenin,* pp. 410–12.

[124] The editors of the *Sochineniia* were unable to find the letter or identify the article to which Lenin refers (*ibid.,* XXIX, 290, 292, notes).

[125] In a letter to Lenin of January 11, 1917, A. Kollontai wrote about Trotsky's influence as follows: "The Dutch Comrade Rutgers (a Tribunist), Katayama, and our group have taken a step toward the 'Zimmerwald Left.' However, Trotsky's arrival strengthened the Right wing at our meetings and by the time of my departure the platform [of the Zimmerwald Left] had not yet been adopted" (Archive of Marx-Engels-Lenin Institute, A. Kollontai's letter to V. I. Lenin, January 11, 1917, cited by D. Baevsky, "Bolsheviki v Tsimmervalde," *Proletarskaia Revoliutsiia,* No. 5, 1935, p. 39). Trotsky, after drawing unflattering portraits of Bukharin and Kollontai, accuses Kollontai of sending to Lenin "utterly worthless information" on the basis of which Lenin made "mistaken utterances" about Trotsky which Lenin later recanted "both by word and deed." Trotsky maintains that while he was in New York he was doing precisely what Kollontai says he was not doing—at-

I have already received No. 1 of *The Internationalist* and was very glad to get it. I have incomplete information about the conference of the Socialist Labor party and the Socialist party on January 6–7, 1917. It seems that the Socialist Labor party discards the whole minimum program (that is a temptation and danger for Bukharin who has been stumbling on "that very spot" ever since 1915!!). It is too bad that I cannot gather all the documents of the Socialist Labor party. (I have begged Bukharin to do so, but apparently the letters get lost.)

Have you any materials? I can return them after reading them through. I am preparing (have practically completed) an article on the question of the relation of Marxism to the state.[126] I have come to conclusions that are much sharper against Kautsky than against Bukharin (have you seen his "Nota Bene" in No. 6 of *Jugend-Internationale?* and *Sbornik Sotsial-Demokrata,* No. 2?).[127] The question is super-important; Bukharin is much better than Kautsky, but Bukharin's mistakes *may destroy* the "just cause" in the struggle against Kautskyism.

I shall send you my article on self-determination directed against P. Kievsky.[128]

How sad—we have no money! We would publish *Sbornik Sotsial-Demokrata,* No. 3 (all material is *on hand* and waiting) and No. 4 (Bukharin's article on the state[129] which we declined at first, and my article on the state)!

In my opinion the Zimmerwald Right has ideologically buried Zimmerwald; Bourderon + Merrheim in Paris have voted for *pacifism;* also Kautsky in Berlin, on January 7, 1917, Turati (December 17,

---

tempting to spread internationalist revolutionary propaganda among American socialists. Cf. Trotsky, *My Life,* pp. 270–77.

[126] Lenin refers to the notebooks, "Marksizm o gosudarstve," which later on formed the basis of his book, *Gosudarstvo i revoliutsiia,* published for the first time in 1918 and reprinted in Lenin, *Sochineniia,* XXI, 365–455.

[127] Lenin has in mind N. I. Bukharin's article, "Der imperialistische Raubstaat"; see pp. 236–39, above, and his own article, "Internatsional Molodezhi," p. 236, n. 152, above.

[128] Lenin's article, "O karikature na marksizm i ob imperialisticheskom ekonomizme," Lenin, *Sochineniia,* XIX, 191–235. See, in this connection, chapter ii, pp. 223–36, above.

[129] This refers to N. I. Bukharin's article, "K teorii imperialisticheskogo gosudarstva," written in 1916 for *Sbornik Sotsial-Demokrata.* A section of the manuscript which had been preserved was for the first time published in *Revoliutsiia Prava,* No. 1, 1925, pp. 5–32. In a letter written either at the end of September or the beginning of October 1916, published in *Bolshevik,* No. 22, November 30, 1932, pp. 85–86, the editorial board of *Sbornik Sotsial-Demokrata* refused to publish Bukharin's article and gave its reasons for so doing.

1916!!)[130] and the whole Italian party. This is the death of Zimmerwald!! They have *condemned* "social pacifism" verbally (see the Kienthal resolution) but in practice have turned toward it!!

Grimm has basely switched toward the social patriots within the Swiss party (our friend at Stockholm will send you material about it), by concluding a bloc with them on January 7, 1917, at the *Parteivorstandssitzung against the Lefts* in favor of postponing the congress!! And now he has attacked the Lefts more basely than ever for the *Begründung des Referendums* (we'll send you this), and composed a "median," "centrist" resolution. Have you or can you obtain the Zürich *Volksrecht?* If not, we shall send you something in this connection, or shall attempt to.

Tomorrow (February 18) [*sic*] will be the Congress of the Swedish party. Probably a split? It seems that among the "Young Socialists" there is a *devilish* discord and confusion. Do you know Swedish? Can you arrange (for me and for the other Lefts) to collaborate on the newspaper of the Swedish youth?[131]

Please reply at least briefly, but *quickly* and accurately, since it is terribly important for us to establish a *good* correspondence with you.

Best regards!

Yours,

Lenin

[130] On January 7, 1917, the *Arbeitsgemeinschaft* group held a Conference in Berlin, in which the Spartakus and the International Socialists' groups took part, to discuss the tactics of the opposition in the Reichstag and toward the party Presidium. Kautsky drafted a manifesto which was unanimously adopted. Later, however, Borchardt said that he had been absent when the vote was taken but had he been present he would have voted against the manifesto, which he described as "decidedly bourgeois pacifist and not at all social democratic." The text is given in *Beilage des Vorwärts*, No. 8, January 9, 1917, pp. 1–2, and Borchardt's statement in *ibid.*, No. 11, January 12, 1917, p. 1.

Turati, in the speech to which Lenin refers, spoke of the official peace moves of December 1916 and said among other things that "the arguments advanced in favor of arbitration prove above all that arbitration may be applied during the war instead of waging war." He spoke of the various territorial questions that might be solved in this way, including "rectification of the Italian frontier, according to what is indisputably Italian and corresponds to guaranties of a strategic nature." This evoked tremendous applause from all sections of the Chamber, and Turati added hastily: "It is one thing to admit the opportunity and the right of national unity which we have always advocated and another to invoke or justify war on that account" (*Avanti*, No. 345, December 18, 1916, p. 1).

[131] This was a reply to Kollontai's letter in which she wrote as follows: "Would it not be possible to do something from Berne so as to support the Swedish youth? It is necessary to give them courage. Their position right now is very difficult. Think this over." (Archive of Marx-Engels-Lenin Institute, No. 20626, A. Kollontai's letter to V. I. Lenin, quoted by Baevsky, "Lenin i Tsimmervaldskaia Levaia," *Borba Klassov*, No. 3, March 1934, p. 44.)

THE BANKRUPTCY OF ZIMMERWALD AND PLANS FOR PROPAGANDA IN THE SCANDINAVIAN COUNTRIES

[Lenin to Kollontai, Christiania (?)][132]

DEAR A. M.!   [ZÜRICH, March 5, 1917]

Newspaper reports speak of the calling of the Congress of the Young Socialists in Sweden on May 12 to found a new party "upon Zimmerwald principles."

I must admit that this news especially disturbs and arouses me, because "Zimmerwald" has obviously become bankrupt and a good name again serves to cover up rot! The *whole* Zimmerwald majority, which is composed of Turati and Co., Kautsky with Ledebour and Merrheim, has passed over to the position of social pacifism which was so solemnly (and so fruitlessly!) condemned at Kienthal. The manifesto of Kautsky and Co., of January 7, 1917, a number of resolutions of the Italian Socialist party, resolutions of Merrheim, Jouhaux, and Longuet, Bourderon (Raffin-Dugens in *unanimity* with Renaudel)—do these not mean the bankruptcy of Zimmerwald? And the Zimmerwald "Center," R. Grimm, who, on January 7, 1917, entered a union with the social patriots of Switzerland for struggle against the Lefts!! Grimm, who rails at social patriots of *all* countries, *except* the Swiss whom he *covers up!* *C'est dégoutant!* I am beside myself with rage against these scoundrels. It is disgusting to hear them and about them and still more disgusting to think of working with them. Farcicality!

We intend to gather material for you about this collapse of R. Grimm. Reply whether you can obtain the Zürich *Volksrecht.* There, in the *motives* of the referendum and in the resolution of the *Lefts* in Töss[133] (February 11, 1917) and so forth, you will find the *chief* material.

But the majority of the Swedish Lefts are *certainly* sincere. This is clear; and it is necessary to help them at any cost to understand *beforehand,* before May 12, all the vileness of social pacifism and Kautskyism, to help them to understand the hideousness of the Zimmerwald majority, to help them to work out for themselves a good program and tactic for the new party.

Indeed we must (all of us, both the Lefts in Sweden and those who

[132] Lenin, *Sochineniia,* XIX, pp. 401–403.

[133] This refers to the Congress of the social democratic organizations of the Zürich canton in Töss on February 11, 1917. The war question was the chief item on the agenda. Two resolutions were introduced: the resolution of the Rights (Greulich, Pflüger, Otto Lang, and others) in support of the "defense of the fatherland," and the resolution of the Lefts (Platten, Nobs, and others) repudiating the "defense of the fatherland." The Congress adopted the resolution of the Lefts by 93 votes to 65. (Lenin, *Sochineniia,* XIX, 488, note 212.)

can get in touch with them) unite, strain all our efforts in order to give aid, as this moment is *decisive* in the life of the Swedish party and of the Swedish and *Scandinavian* labor movement.

Since you read Swedish (and also speak it)—and if we are to understand "internationalism" not in the sense "I know nothing and I meddle not"—a large share of responsibility devolves upon you.

I am certain that you are doing a great deal. It is desirable to consolidate and unify the Lefts in order to help the Swedes in this difficult moment of their life. Is it possible to organize for that purpose in Christiania, Copenhagen, and Stockholm a group of Russian Bolsheviks and Lefts who know Swedish and who can help? Is it possible to divide the work: to gather the chief documents and articles (I was sent the polemics between Nerman and Mauritz Västberg in *Politiken,* November 28, 1916,[134] on the topic "At First a Program Then a New Party," but I was unable to understand), to work out our theses in order to help them, to publish for their sake a number of articles? The Swedes who *can write* German, French, or English could also enter this group.

In your opinion, is it or is it not possible? It is worth the trouble!

In my judgment it is worth while, but from afar and from the outside I, of course, am unable to judge. I only see and *know* quite definitely that the question of the program and tactics of *new* socialism, of really revolutionary Marxism, and not dirty Kautskyism, *stands everywhere* on the order of the day. This can be seen also in the Socialist Labor party and the *Internationalist* in America, and in the data concerning Germany (the resolutions of the Lefts on January 7, 1917)[135] and France (the pamphlet, *Les Socialistes de Zimmerwald et la guerre*), of the Lefts in Paris, etc.

In Denmark Trier and others would most certainly join the cause of creating a Left Marxist party in Scandinavia;[136] a section of the Nor-

[134] This refers to M. Västberg's and T. Nerman's letters published in *Politiken* No. 92 of November 28, 1916, under the title "Mauritz Västberg vill ha klarhet. En interpellation om oppositionen." (Lenin, *Sochineniia,* XIX, 488, note 213.)

[135] Lenin apparently had in mind the resolutions submitted to the All-German Conference of the opposition, held on January 7, 1917, at Berlin, by the Spartakus group and by Borchardt's group of the International Socialists of Germany. Both resolutions expressed their reluctance in co-operating with the *Arbeitsgemeinschaft* except in the question of opposing the policy of the Presidium and criticized the *Arbeitsgemeinschaft*'s inactivity. ("Die Reichskonferenz der Partei—Opposition," *Beilage des Vorwärts,* No. 8, January 9, 1917, pp. 1–2.)

[136] As early as in February 1915, A. Kollontai wrote as follows about the situation in Denmark: "There is a fine 'Left' wing here and the whole party is more radically minded than in the other Scandinavian countries. In one month from now they expect to launch a campaign against militarism throughout the country and it seems to me that it is our duty to help all we can; *their intentions are fine, the spirit is radical, but often they lack foundation and clarity of policy.*" (Archive of Marx-Engels-Lenin Institute, No. 27243, A. Kollontai's letter to N. K. Krupskaia,

wegian Lefts would join also. The struggle against Branting and Co. is a serious task; necessity will compel a more serious attitude toward questions of the theory and tactics of revolutionary Marxism.

In my opinion one ought *immediately* to set in motion, simultaneously from *three* sides, preparatory work for May 12: (1) The group to give aid which was mentioned above; (2) the group of the Scandinavian Lefts—write an article (in Swedish newspapers) on the necessity of forming *at once* such groups to prepare the program and tactics for May 12; (3) the third interests me especially, *not* because it is the most important thing (the initiative from within is more important), but because *we* can help here—could you for instance *immediately* after reviewing the chief literature of the Lefts and Rights in Sweden, outline on the basis of it a few theses like this: theoretical (pertaining to program), and practical (pertaining to tactics) dissensions: defense of the fatherland; conception of imperialism; character of war; disarmament; social pacifism, the national question, revolution; "mass action"; dictatorship of the proletariat; civil war; the attitude toward trade unions; opportunism and struggle against it; etc.

Each thesis should include: (*a*) what the Lefts have said (the *"essence"*) about this in Sweden, (*b*) and what the Rights there have said.

On this basis, and taking into account the position of the Lefts in Russia, Germany, America (the chief countries in this connection), we could work out our own theses and, by publishing them in Swedish, could *help* the Swedes to carry on the preparation for May 12.

Certain of the *chief* passages from the *principal* resolutions and articles of the Right and Left wings of Sweden should be translated for that purpose into Russian, German, French, or English.

As a matter of fact, morally and politically we are all responsible for the "young" Swedish socialists and must help them.[137]

Your position is super-favorable to render such assistance. Write at once what you think about it. It might be useful to forward this letter to Liudmila [Stahl], together with your thoughts.

What sort of a person is Lindhagen? S.-R.? "Narodnik"? Radical-socialist? Hervé?

With a firm handshake and wishing you all kinds of success.

Yours,

LENIN

February 10, 1915, cited by Baevsky in "Borba za III Internatsional do Tsimmervalda," *Proletarskaia Revoliutsiia,* No. 4, 1934, pp. 21–22.)

[137] In March 1917, A. Kollontai wrote Lenin that the "young" Norwegian and Swedish socialists, while adhering to Zimmerwald, "have in mind none other but the Left Zimmerwald" (Archive of Marx-Engels-Lenin Institute, No. 20616, A. Kollontai's letter to V. I. Lenin, cited by D. Baevsky, in "Bolsheviki v Tsimmervalde," *Proletarskaia Revoliutsiia,* No. 5, 1935, p. 41).

CHAPTER VII

STOCKHOLM: THE THIRD ZIMMERWALD CONFERENCE

The Third Zimmerwald Conference, held at Stockholm in September 1917, is considerably less important in the history of the origin of the Third International than the earlier conferences at Zimmerwald and Kienthal. Events in Russia moving swiftly toward the Bolshevik overturn shifted the center of gravity of the Left socialist movement from Switzerland to Russia. Further, these Russian events and the deepening war weariness which affected all belligerents stimulated the peace movement generally, and especially among the Left socialists, who now pressed more insistently for the resumption of socialist international relations. As a result of the pressure of these developments, three proposals for an international socialist conference were put forward: by neutral socialists affiliated with the International Socialist Bureau, by the Petrograd Soviet, and by the Zimmerwaldist International Socialist Committee. The projects of the I.S.B. and the Petrograd Soviet were merged with the formation, on July 11, 1917, of a joint Russian-Dutch-Scandinavian Committee. Although the Dutch-Scandinavian Committee held separate conferences with representatives of socialist and labor groups of several belligerent states, no general conference met because of the opposition of the Entente governments and of certain labor and socialist organizations which were still opposed to conferring with socialists of enemy states. Despite official and other opposition the International Socialist Committee went forward with its plans for a Third Zimmerwald Conference, which, after many postponements, met on September 5–12, 1917. The Conference, owing to the absence of delegates from France, England, and Italy, was less representative than the earlier ones; it received less attention, and in its resolutions merely reaffirmed the theses adopted at Zimmerwald and Kienthal.

In this chapter we are primarily concerned with the Third Zimmerwald Conference and the documents which follow relate primarily to it. Since the action of the Zimmerwaldists was considerably involved in the other two projects, it is desirable to say something of the origin and outcome of the other plans for a socialist conference at Stockholm.

Stockholm

Early in January 1917 there were renewed demands for the resumption of socialist international relations when the Presidium of the Dutch Social Democratic Labor party and the Dutch members of the Executive Committee of the International Socialist Bureau in a joint meeting decided to make another attempt through Vandervelde to get the British and French socialists to attend a plenary session of the Executive Committee of the I.S.B. for the purpose of considering a general session of the International Socialist Bureau.[1] This, like earlier attempts in the same direction, failed. The Commission Administrative Permanente of the French Socialist party voted 13 to 11 against attending a meeting of the I.S.B., and on January 25 the British Labour party not only voted down Bruce Glasier's motion in favor of calling a meeting of the I.S.B. but adopted by 1,036,000 to 464,000 Will Thorne's motion "that the fight should continue until victory is achieved and that the Socialist and Trade Union organizations of the Allied Powers should meet simultaneously with the Peace Congress."[2]

At about the same time the National Executive Committee of the American Socialist party made a move in the same direction in a message addressed to the I.S.B. and the party

[1] "Der Versuch zur Einberufung des internationalen Bureaus," *Vorwärts*, No. 14, January 15, 1917, p. 1.

[2] "Franzosen und Internationale," *ibid.*, No. 27, January 28, 1917, p. 1; "Die Internationale und die französische Partei," *Internationale Korrespondenz*, No. 86, January 30, 1917, p. 673; *Report of the Sixteenth Annual Conference of the Labour Party, 1917*, pp. 126–27.

executives of Germany, Austria, Sweden, Norway, Denmark, England, France, Italy, Spain, Switzerland, Russia, Belgium, and the Argentine, urging that the time was ripe for a revival of the Socialist International and for a concerted working-class movement for peace and that an international congress be called June 3, 1917, at The Hague. Unless the I.S.B. took steps by March 1 to call such a meeting, the Americans proposed to do so on their own initiative.[3] The National Executive Committee followed up this demand by a statement to the socialists of all countries giving its reasons for the calling of such a congress and expressing the belief that by this means "the sundered strands of our international solidarity can be reunited, and that we can enlist the workers of all lands to fight side by side once more in the great struggle to overthrow the system of economic exploitation and servitude whose natural fruitage is the murder, rapine and destruction of war."[4] The International Socialist Bureau did not act on the American proposal, and the American socialists within a few weeks became too deeply involved in affairs connected with America's entrance into the war to carry out their threat to summon a conference on their own responsibility.

Thus by February 1917 the various efforts to resume international socialist relations had made no more progress toward their objectives than had been made by the official peace moves of 1916 toward bringing the war to an end. Then suddenly the situation changed. In March the Tsarist regime fell, a Provisional government was formed, and at the same time the Petrograd Soviet of Workers' and Soldiers' deputies, dominated by socialists, was established. One of the early acts of the Executive Committee of the Soviet was to issue on March 24 (11) an appeal to the international proletariat calling on the peoples of Europe to take "concerted, decisive action in favor of peace .... to take into their own

---

[3] *The New York Call*, No. 8, January 8, 1917, p. 1, reprinted in *The American Socialists and the War* ...., p. 31.

[4] *The New York Call*, No. 12, January 12, 1917, p. 1; *The American Socialists and the War* ...., pp. 31–33; Hillquit, *Loose Leaves from a Busy Life*, p. 160.

hands the decision of the question of war and peace . . . . [to] refuse to serve as an instrument of conquest and violence in the hands of kings, landowners and bankers . . . ." To the appeal for revolutionary mass action, which was in line with Zimmerwald principles, the Soviet appended a statement which was not in accord with the Zimmerwald spirit. The Soviet declared: "We will firmly defend our own liberty from all reactionary attempts from within, as well as from without. The Russian revolution will not retreat before the bayonets of conquerers, and will not allow itself to be crushed by foreign military force. . . . ."[5]

This peculiar combination of the Zimmerwald demand for revolutionary mass action with the advocacy of what came to be known as "revolutionary defensism" is attributable to the composition of the Petrograd Soviet in which the Socialist-Revolutionists and Mensheviks had the largest representation, with the Bolsheviks in third place. Some of the Socialist-Revolutionists and the Mensheviks were internationalists and as such had joined the Zimmerwald movement. Many of the leaders of these groups, however, had taken a defensist position and for them the support of revolutionary defensism was a natural and logical step.

The compromise between the Zimmerwaldists and the defensists reflected in the appeal of the Petrograd Soviet of March 27 (14) was not easily achieved. It was especially difficult for the Mensheviks, whose ranks had been badly split on the issues of internationalism and defensism but who felt it essential to reform their lines and muster all available party forces. Menshevik party conferences met on March 16 (3) and 19 (6). Internationalists and defensists agreed on the question of organization of state power, but as in the preceding three years they could not agree on their attitude toward the war or on a peace formula. The March 19 (6) conference expressed somewhat hazily its support of a general peace

[5] *Petrogradskii Sovet Rabochikh i Soldatskikh Deputatov. Protokoly zasedanii Ispolnitelnogo Komiteta i Biuro I.K.*, pp. 40, 300–301, as translated in Golder, *Documents of Russian History, 1914–1917*, pp. 325–26.

"without annexations or indemnities," its intention to put pressure on the Provisional government and other belligerent governments by appealing to the workers of all countries, and its opposition to putting an end to the war "by means of a disorganization of the technical and strategic defense." According to the report of this meeting the internationalists abstained from voting and the unification achieved was more apparent than real.[6]

The arrival on March 31 (18) from Siberia of a group of exiles known as the Siberian Zimmerwaldists, among whom was the eloquent and able I. G. Tsereteli, strengthened the party organization and leadership but did not produce unity, for the newcomers took the internationalist position in demanding an early, general, and democratic peace; but they believed that such a peace could not be secured unless revolutionary Russia possessed adequate national defense. Nor was unity achieved by the resolution adopted by the Organization Committee on April 2 (March 20). On the ground that their chief task was to struggle for a general peace without annexations or indemnities on the basis of self-determination for nations, the resolution advocated: (1) mobilization of public opinion to bring pressure on the Provisional government to take steps together with the Allied governments toward opening peace negotiations; (2) an appeal to the proletariat of all belligerent countries to put pressure on their governments to the same end; (3) support of the Provisional government but opposition to any attempts at an annexationist policy; (4) opposition to all activities "tending to a disorganization of the cause of defense."[7] When this resolution came before the United Petrograd Organization of the R.S.D.L. party (Mensheviks) it was accepted over the strong protests of the internationalist minority.[8]

[6] *Izvestiia*, No. 16, March 16, 1917, p. 4; *Rabochaia Gazeta*, No. 1, March 7, 1917, p. 3, and No. 2, March 8, 1917, p. 2.

[7] *Rabochaia Gazeta*, No. 16, March 25, 1917, p. 4.

[8] *Ibid.*, No. 18, March 28, 1917, pp. 3–4.

This resolution of the Mensheviks is significant for several reasons. It represents in general the attitude toward peace and defensism taken by the majority of the Petrograd Soviet during the period of the Stockholm negotiations. It led to the formation by the Menshevik internationalists of their own groups in the Soviet and in all party organizations. This attitude set forth in the resolution and the subsequent entrance of Mensheviks and Socialist-Revolutionists into the Provisional government deepened the differences between the Bolsheviks and the Menshevik majority and produced, as will appear, an increasing estrangement between the Zimmerwald movement and the representatives of the Soviet. These developments contributed not a little to the disintegration of the Zimmerwald movement.

Quite apart from the fact that the Soviet peace policy caused dissensions within the parties represented in the Soviet, that peace policy gave great impetus to the movement to resume socialist international relations first by bringing into personal contact with Soviet leaders and Russian conditions several Entente socialists who had opposed the resumption of such relations as premature. Secondly, the Soviet peace demands stimulated the neutral socialists, whose plans for an international socialist conference had been blocked by the I.S.B., to force the issue by taking the initiative into their own hands.

Entente socialists were sent or were permitted to go to Russia as a part of the plan to strengthen the hands of the Provisional government and prevent the initiation of negotiations for a separate or a general peace. The Entente governments desired at any cost to prevent a separate peace by Russia, and regarded general negotiations as premature, since war objectives both declared and secret had not been obtained. Foreign Minister Miliukov's statement that the Provisional government would stand by the international engagements of the fallen regime was satisfactory to the Entente but not to the Soviet. The Soviet statement of April 9 (March 27) against "seizure of the national possessions or forcible occupation of foreign territories" and for a "stable peace on the basis of self-determination of peoples,"[9] the controversy with Mili-ukov which later caused his resignation, and the appeals of the Soviet to the workers of all countries to bring pressure on their governments to take up peace negotiations, caused a good deal of uneasiness in the foreign offices of the Entente. Ribot, then Premier, writes that he "telegraphed to London and Rome to ask our Allies if they did not think it necessary to invite the Provisional government to cut short all ambiguity as soon as possible. M. Sonnino was prepared to issue instruc-tions in this sense. But the English Foreign Office thought it would be more politic to abstain from doing this. In their view we ought to leave the Socialists who had been sent to Russia from France and England the requisite time to in-fluence their political co-religionists."[10]

The British and French delegates, who were expected, according to Ribot, to try "to dissipate the extravagant dreams with which the minds of the Russian revolutionaries were haunted" and, according to Lloyd George, to persuade the Russian Socialist party "to do all in its power to bring the war to a satisfactory conclusion,"[11] arrived in Petrograd on April 13 (March 31). These delegations consisted of three labor M.P.'s—Will Thorne, James O'Grady, and Stephen Sanders—and three socialist deputies—Marcel Cachin, Ernest Lafont, and Marius Moutet. Besides these British and French there were Italian and Belgian delega-tions. In April Albert Thomas and in May Arthur Henderson went to Russia on missions for their governments; Vander-velde, the chairman of the I.S.B., reached Petrograd on May 17 (4); and on June 13 (May 31), the Root Mission, which included Charles Edward Russell and James Duncan as rep-resentatives of the American Socialist party and the Ameri-can Federation of Labor, arrived in the Russian capital. Since all these missions were under official auspices, it is not surpris-

[9] Golder, *Documents of Russian History, 1914–1917*, p. 331.
[10] A. Ribot, *Letters to a Friend*, p. 210.
[11] D. Lloyd George, *War Memoirs*, IV, 1885.

ing that there were no members of the minority groups among the men chosen to represent the socialist and labor organizations.

These missions by no means achieved all that was hoped. The Provisional government, it is true, did not attempt to start peace negotiations; but this may be attributed to other causes. As for the Soviet Executive Committee, the Entente socialists not only failed to gain a general acceptance of the position that the war must go on until the Entente's war aims could be realized but, under severe cross-examination from the Bolsheviks, the Mensheviks, and the S.R. Internationalists, were themselves obliged to make concessions. One concession was recognition that the Alsace-Lorraine question should be settled by a plebiscite. In defending himself against his ambassador's reproaches, Cachin is reported to have replied: "I said what I did because, honestly and truly, no other course was open to me. Instead of being received as friends we were put through a regular cross-examination, and in such a tone that I could see the moment coming when we should be obliged to retire."[12] The Entente delegates were confronted with statements from the Swedish Left Social Democratic labor press exposing the real purpose of their trip to Russia; they were asked to explain why there were no minority socialists in their delegations, why they were so much concerned about peoples oppressed by other nations and so little about their own colonies, and many other questions to which satisfactory answers were not easily found.[13]

Although the Entente socialists did not succeed in dissipating "the extravagant dreams" of the Russians, they learned something about the state of mind of those with whom they conferred, and many, including Albert Thomas, were won over to the idea of an international socialist conference and a restatement of war aims. In pleading the cause of the Stock-

[12] M. Paléologue, *An Ambassador's Memoirs*, III, 300.

[13] Ribot, *Letters to a Friend*, pp. 210–11; A. Shliapnikov, "Fevralskaia revoliutsiia i evropeiskie sotsialisty," *Krasnyi Arkhiv*, II (XV), 1926, pp. 63–69; see also "Bericht der französischen Delegierten über ihre russische Reise," *Internationale Korrespondenz*, No. 17, June 6, 1917, p. 118.

holm Conference before the National Council of the French Socialist party after his return from Russia, Moutet said, among other things: "No longer do the Russian revolutionaries wish to wage war for imperialist aims. They demand from their government that it should impress this upon the Allied governments. They have rejected all imperialist policy, including that of Miliukov .... [who] is just as dangerous as Lenin...."[14]

The Entente socialists were, of course, not the only ones to be moved by the currents of opinion stirred by the Russian revolution and the activities of the Soviet. Socialists of neutral countries, whose previous attempts to restore international socialist relations had been blocked, were now encouraged to renew the attempt regardless of the opposition. The first moves came from the Danes and the Dutch. Stauning, the Social Democratic member of the Danish government, wrote to the I.S.B. that "if the Executive Committee were not willing to act, or could not act, the conference would take place without them."[15] On April 15, the Dutch section of the I.S.B. met at Laren and decided to take the initiative, proposing that the seat of the I.S.B. be transferred to Stockholm, where a plenary meeting of the International should be organized "to examine the international situation." Later, without consulting the Belgian members of the Executive Committee, the Dutch decided to go to Stockholm and with the adherence of Scandinavian socialists form a committee to call the proposed international conference. The Dutch were to act as representatives of their party rather than of the I.S.B.[16] Prior to the departure of Troelstra, Van Kol, Wibaut, and Albarda, Huysmans, who went with them, issued on April 22, at the request of the Dutch delegates, a letter to all the national sec-

[14] *Internationale Korrespondenz*, No. 17, June 6, 1917, p. 118.

[15] Vandervelde, *Three Aspects of the Russian Revolution*, pp. 210–11.

[16] "Absichten und Methode des holländischen Arbeitsausschusses des I.S.B.," *Internationale Korrespondenz*, No. 16, June 1, 1917, p. 113; "Troelstra on the Rebirth of the International," *Labour Leader*, No. 20, May 17, 1917, p. 4; Comité Organisateur de la Conférence Socialiste Internationale de Stockholm, *Stockholm*, hereafter cited *Stockholm*, p. vii.

tions of the International inviting them to send representatives to a conference at Stockholm on May 15. The invitation included both majority and minority socialists of the belligerent states.[17] In promoting this plan, the Dutch, it should be noted, were acting not in the spirit of Zimmerwald but in line with certain statements by Kerensky and President Wilson regarding war aims. By moving in the direction taken by responsible statesmen, Troelstra explained, they would have a better chance of securing peace.[18]

These moves had a hostile reception in France and Great Britain. Some newspapers accused the Dutch of playing into the hands of German imperialists by promoting a separate peace with Russia, and majority socialist organs charged that the rights of the I.S.B. were being usurped. The French majority socialists refused to go to the conference on the ground that the invitation did not come from the proper source; and the British Labour party Executive also decided not to accept this invitation but to attempt to hold a meeting of Entente socialists in London.[19] In the face of these refusals a meeting on May 15 was obviously impossible. The Dutch, however, did not give up their project. On the arrival of their delegates in Stockholm they set up on May 3 a Dutch-Scandinavian Committee composed of Branting, Gustav Möller, and E. Söderberg from the Swedish, Stauning from the Danish, and Vidnes from the Norwegian Social Democratic parties, in addition to the Dutch socialists named above, with Huysmans as secretary. The new committee postponed the date of the conference to June 10, and in order to secure the approval of Vandervelde, proposed that separate conferences be held between the Dutch-Scandinavian Committee and the delegations of the different national socialist and labor parties preparatory to a plenary meeting of the International. On this basis, Vandervelde and De Brouckère, who were opposed

---

[17] Text in *Stockholm*, p. viii, and *Vorwärts*, No. 118, May 1, 1917, p. 1.

[18] Troelstra's statement given to *Het Volk* was reprinted in *Internationale Korrespondenz*, No. 7, April 27, 1917, p. 46.

[19] *Report of the Seventeenth Annual Conference of the Labour Party, 1918*, p. 3.

to a meeting with the German majority Social Democrats, agreed to urge the Entente socialists to attend the conference.[20] On May 10 the Committee constituted itself a permanent body with the addition of H. Lindquist, Sweden, Magnus Nilssen and Ole Lian, Norway, and Madsen, Denmark. Dates were set for the first series of separate conferences, a questionnaire was drafted, and a manifesto was drawn up which defined the purpose of the preliminary conferences as an attempt "to formulate if possible a common program inspired by socialist conceptions and finally to examine the possibility of calling a general conference."[21]

Under these not very favorable circumstances the movement for the Stockholm conference was launched. The promoters of the plan recognized, from the very first, the importance of gaining Russian socialist support both for its own sake and as an aid in winning over British and French majority groups. There was another reason for establishing contact with the Russians. Since the very first days of the revolution Mensheviks in Russia and abroad had discussed and advocated the calling of an international socialist congress as a means of ending the war. P. Axelrod from abroad urged the Soviet to propose that all proletarian parties begin preparations for such a conference, and on April 12 (March 30), Lieber, speaking for the Mensheviks at the All-Russian Conference of Soviets, said that his party would support the resolution of the Executive Committee on mobilizing "all vital forces of the country .... for the strengthening of the front or the rear" if the resolution also invited the Russian socialists to take an initiative in calling an international socialist congress to work out conditions of peace and ways of bringing it about.[22] Thus the matter was already before the

[20] *Stockholm*, pp. viii-ix; *Vorwärts*, No. 122, May 5, 1917, p. 1; *Internationale Korrespondenz*, No. 15, May 26, 1917, p. 101; Vandervelde, *Three Aspects of the Russian Revolution*, p. 212.

[21] *Stockholm*, p. x; *Internationale Korrespondenz*, No. 11, May 11, 1917, p. 71, and No. 12, May 15, 1917, p. 79; full text of the manifesto, dated May 18, 1917, is given in *Stockholm*, pp. 481–83.

[22] *Rabochaia Gazeta*, No. 18, March 28, 1917, p. 2; No. 21, March 31, 1917,

Soviet when Borgbjerg, a Danish Social Democrat, arrived in Petrograd, April 27 (14), with an invitation to the Russian socialists to attend the Stockholm Conference.

Borgbjerg talked with Kerensky, Chkheidze, Skobelev, and other leaders in the Soviet, explained about the proposed conference, and gave them a message from the German Social Democrats on peace terms with the promise that the Germans would make no offensive against Russia.[23] On May 6 (April 23), he urged the Soviet Executive Committee to attend the conference at Stockholm, arguing that the German peace terms offered a basis and guaranty of success. Like the Entente socialists, Borgbjerg was closely questioned. How did the Germans reconcile their support of self-determination with their attitude toward Alsace-Lorraine? What were the prospects of a revolution in Germany? Was Borgbjerg in touch with the Berne International Socialist Committee? And so forth.[24] Borgbjerg answered as best he could, and two days later the Soviet Executive Committee voted on the Stockholm invitation.

The Bolsheviks, on the ground that Borgbjerg was "directly or indirectly" an agent of the German imperialist government, were against accepting his invitation, as were the Petrograd group of the Polish Social Democracy and the Central Committee of the Lettish Social Democrats. The Menshevik Organization Committee telegraphed an acceptance to the Dutch-Scandinavian Committee and appealed to both majority and minority parties of other countries to co-operate.[25] The Organization Committee was ready, how-

---

p. 2, and No. 25, April 7, 1917, p. 1; *Revoliutsiia 1917 goda (Khronika sobytii),* I, 148–49.

[23] P. Scheidemann, *The Making of New Germany,* I, 362–63. With the approval of the German Foreign Office Ebert and Scheidemann had talked with Borgbjerg in Copenhagen before his departure.

[24] "Borgbjerg's Friedensmission in Petersburg," *Internationale Korrespondenz,* No. 12, May 15, 1917, p. 78; *Petrogradskii Sovet Rabochikh i Soldatskikh Deputatov. Protokoly zasedanii Ispolnitelnogo Komiteta i Biuro I.K.,* pp. 123–26; Scheidemann, *The Making of New Germany,* I, 367–68.

[25] *Rabochaia Gazeta,* No. 40, April 26, 1917, p. 1; *Stockholm,* p. xvi. The resolution of the All-Russian Conference of Bolsheviks, April 1917, rejecting

ever, to attend a conference of minority socialists only. The Trudoviks favored a conference if the British and French majority socialists would attend; the Bund was for the conference unconditionally. When the question came to a vote, those who favored a conference of only those minority socialists who had fought against the imperialist and annexationist ambitions of their governments were beaten. An overwhelming majority of the Soviet Executive Committee voted on May 8 (April 25) for Dan's motion to the effect that the Soviet should take the initiative in calling in a neutral country an international socialist congress to which should be invited all parties and groups in the International which were ready to accept the platform outlined in the Soviet's appeal to the peoples of the world adopted on March 24 (11), 1917.[26] The Soviet followed up the adoption of this resolution by an appeal "To the Socialists of All Countries," dated May 15 (2), in which it was explained that the Russian revolution was a revolt not only against Tsarism but against "the horrors of the world butchery," that it was not merely a national revolution but "the first stage of the world revolution which will end the baseness of war and bring peace to mankind," that the Russian democracy did not want a separate peace but a general peace acceptable to the workers of all countries, and that the Soviet had taken the initiative in calling a conference of all socialist parties and factions of all countries in order that the "work for peace started by the Russian revolution be brought to a conclusion by the efforts of the international proletariat."[27]

In addition to this general invitation to a formal conference the Department of International Relations of the Soviet

Borgbjerg's invitation, is given in Lenin, *The Revolution of 1917* (Collected Works, Vol. XX), II, 401–403. The Bolshevik attitude toward the various Stockholm conference proposals is discussed in *The Bolsheviks and World Revolution*.

[26] *Petrogradskii Sovet Rabochikh i Soldatskikh Deputatov. Protokoly* ...., p. 128; text of Dan's resolution on pp. 322–23; translated in Golder, *Documents of Russian History, 1914–1917*, pp. 339–40.

[27] Full text in Golder, *Documents of Russian History, 1914–1917*, pp. 340–43, from *Izvestiia*, No. 55, May [2], 1917, pp. 1–2.

Executive Committee had telegraphed on May 7 (April 24) invitations to minority socialists in Great Britain, France, Italy, Switzerland, and Sweden to send delegates to Petrograd to confer informally with the Soviet.[28] The situation was further complicated when the Berne International Socialist Committee sent out on May 10 an invitation to the members of the Zimmerwald movement to send delegates to Stockholm for a Third Zimmerwald Conference on May 31. Thus by the middle of May three projects for a socialist congress had been launched. Although these projects had originated in groups of somewhat different orientation, they were not mutually exclusive. The Dutch-Scandinavian Committee at its inaugural meeting on May 10 had welcomed the Russian initiative; some of the Zimmerwald parties had offered to cooperate in the projects of both the Dutch-Scandinavian Committee and the Soviet; and Grimm, the chairman of the International Socialist Committee, after his arrival in Russia took part in the discussions of the Conference in the Soviet Executive Committee.[29]

These discussions resulted in decisions which led in the end to the amalgamation of the Russian and Dutch-Scandinavian projects. First, on May 28 (15) the Soviet Executive Committee appointed a commission for calling an international conference, the conference to be held between July 1 (June 18) and July 15 (2) in Stockholm. Three days later the Soviet Executive Committee approved an appeal to socialist and trade union organizations in which the chief task of the proposed international socialist conference was said to

---

[28] *Izvestiia*, No. 52, April 28, 1917, p. 3.

[29] The All-City Petrograd Conference of the Mensheviks voted on May 18 (5) to take part in the Third Zimmerwald Conference and proposed that later the Zimmerwaldists should participate in the general socialist conference (*Rabochaia Gazeta*, No. 49, May 6, 1917, p. 4). On May 24 (11), the All-Russian Menshevik Conference authorized the Organization Committee to take part in the Third Zimmerwald and such other preparatory conferences as might be necessary for the meeting of the international conference (*ibid.*, No. 54, May 12, 1917, p. 3). The Bolsheviks opposed both the Dutch-Scandinavian and the Soviet conference projects but voted, over Lenin's objections, to send delegates to the Third Zimmerwald Conference (this is discussed in *The Bolsheviks and World Revolution*).

be an agreement to abolish "national alliances" with those imperialist governments and classes which repudiated the struggle for peace. All parties and groups accepting this point of view were invited to take part in the conference.[30] At this same meeting the Soviet Executive Committee learned from a telegram from Cachin and Moutet that the National Council of the French Socialist party had accepted the invitation to Stockholm on the basis of the Soviet platform. This acceptance was coupled with the hope, expressed in the language of revolutionary defensism, that the French Socialists would advance with the Russians "against the imperialist armies for the restoration of the International and in defense of the rights of peoples to national freedom."[31]

After the publication of this appeal on June 2 (May 20), internal affairs absorbed so much of the attention of the Soviet that there was a delay in pushing forward the conference project. The matter came up during the heated discussions of war and peace at the First All-Russian Congress of Soviets, in June, and Rozanov explained that the Soviet Executive Committee had issued its invitation because the Dutch-Scandinavian Committee and the International Socialist Committee represented only segments of international socialism. Furthermore, the Soviet Executive Committee, believing that the plan of separate interviews adopted by the Dutch-Scandinavian group would not lead to any real action, aimed to secure unification of the socialists on the principle that "in order to put an end to the war it was necessary to lead an energetic struggle against the militarist aims in the foreign policy of all countries."[32] The Congress, over the opposition of the Bolsheviks, approved the action taken by the Executive Committee. The Congress also authorized the sending of a delegation to allied and neutral countries and invited social-

[30] *Izvestiia,* No. 72, May 21, 1917, p. 3; Shliapnikov, "Fevralskaia revoliutsiia i evropeiskie sotsialisty," *Krasnyi Arkhiv,* II (XV), 1926, pp. 79–81.

[31] *Petrogradskii Sovet Rabochikh i Soldatskikh Deputatov. Protokoly ....,* pp. 156–57.

[32] *Pervyi Vserossiiskii Sezd Sovetov R. i S.D.,* I, 428–34.

ist groups of all complexions to send delegates to Russia. The resolution included a protest against Allied action in preventing such delegates from visiting Russia.[33]

Despite their doubts about the procedure adopted by the Dutch-Scandinavian Committee, the Soviet delegates, who arrived in Stockholm in the first days of July, met with this Committee on the 4th, and on the 11th set up a Russian-Dutch-Scandinavian Committee composed of the following: for the Netherlands, Troelstra, Van Kol, and Albarda, with Vliegen and Wibaut as alternates; for Sweden, Branting, Möller, and Söderberg; for Norway, Vidnes; for Denmark, Borgbjerg, with Nina Bang as alternate; for Russia, Ehrlich, Goldenberg, Rusanov, Smirnov, and Rozanov, who was later replaced by Panin.[34] The establishment of the joint committee was announced in a manifesto inviting parties affiliated with the International Socialist Bureau, the International Socialist Committee, and the Trade Union International to a conference at Stockholm on August 15 to consider the following matters: (1) the World War and the International; (2) peace proposals of the International; and (3) ways and means of putting the program into effect and of bringing the war to an early end.[35]

While the Russians and the Dutch-Scandinavian Committee were getting together on a project for a general conference, the latter committee had been holding separate conferences with socialist representatives of Germany (of both the majority and the minority), Austria, Bohemia, Finland, Hungary, and other countries. These conferences with socialists of the Central Powers plus a suspicion of the revolutionary exuberance of the Russians created opposition in official circles and among majority socialist and labor groups in the Entente countries and America. The United States government refused passports to Morris Hillquit, Victor L.

---

[33] *Pervyi Vserossiiskii Sezd Sovetov R. i S.D.*, II, 12. The Congress also dealt with the Grimm affair discussed below, pp. 613–29.

[34] *Stockholm*, p. xix; see also *Vorwärts*, No. 182, July 6, 1917, p. 1.

[35] Complete text in *Stockholm*, pp. 484–86, and *Report of the Seventeenth Annual Conference of the Labour Party, 1918*, pp. 43–44.

Berger, and Algernon Lee, who had been named as delegates of the American Socialist party to Stockholm. Samuel Gompers in the name of the American Federation of Labor said that the time was inopportune for such a conference. Despite governmental opposition, M. Goldfarb, Boris Reinstein, and D. Davidovich, either without passports or as Russian subjects, succeeded in getting to Stockholm and conferring with the Dutch-Scandinavian Committee on June 20–21.[36] The French government likewise refused passports to Brizon and Longuet,[37] and both these governments urged the British to adopt a similar policy.

The British Cabinet acted less arbitrarily but to the same end. Passports were granted to MacDonald and Jowett of the I.L.P. and to Inkpin of the B.S.P., who intended to go to Russia and stop off at Stockholm, but with the provision, as Lord Robert Cecil explained in Parliament, that the holders should not be permitted to attend or take part in any international conference at Stockholm, and still less to communicate directly or indirectly with enemy subjects at Stockholm or elsewhere. In the end these precautions proved to be unnecessary, for the British Sailors' and Firemen's Union refused to allow MacDonald and his companions to sail.[38]

Other difficulties, some of them internal, troubled the Russian-Dutch-Scandinavian Committee. The Russian delegates complained that the Soviet paid no attention to their reports,

[36] United States Department of State, *Papers Relating to the Foreign Relations of the United States, 1917, Supplement 2, The World War,* I, 739, 744 45; Hillquit, *Loose Leaves from a Busy Life,* pp. 155–56; *Stockholm,* xiii–xv; *The New York Call,* No. 129, May 9, 1917, p. 1. The American refusal of passports was based on the Logan Act. The Dutch-Scandinavian Committee protested in vain to President Wilson that the conference was being called on the basis of his principles and that the action of the American Republic would be misunderstood. The American government consistently opposed the Stockholm Conference throughout 1917 and contributed to its failure to meet.

[37] Ribot, *Letters to a Friend,* p. 232. Renaudel and Longuet had been officially delegated May 31, 1917, by the Commission Administrative Permanente to go to Russia and to stop en route at Stockholm (*Pendant la Guerre. Le Parti Socialiste, la Guerre et la Paix* ...., p. 169).

[38] Lloyd George, *War Memoirs,* IV, 1890–96; *The Parliamentary Debates, House of Commons* [hereafter cited: *P.D. Commons*], Fifth Series, XCIV, 494–95.

sent no directions, and furnished no funds for the *Bulletin du Département des Rélations Internationales,* being issued at Stockholm under Weinberg's editorship.[39] There were indications, also, that the Dutch and Scandinavians, despite their acceptance of Russian collaboration, distrusted the Soviet initiative and were considerably less than enthusiastic about the participation of the Zimmerwald parties, which the Russians were anxious to bring about.[40] For quite different reasons the Zimmerwald Left denounced the Stockholm project and in a statement issued on July 20, in behalf of the Central Committee of the R.S.D.L. party (Bolsheviks), the Main Presidium of the Social Democracy of Poland and Lithuania,[41] the Bulgarian S.D.L. party ("Narrow" socialists), the Left wing of the Swedish S.D.L. party and the Swedish Youth League, analyzed the conference proposal and refused to have anything to do with it.[42]

Despite these objections from socialist groups and despite the strong official opposition of the Entente and American governments and the efforts of certain correspondents to kill the whole project,[43] the invitation of the Russian-Dutch-

[39] Shliapnikov gives the text of Rozanov's letter of complaint in "Fevralskaia revoliutsiia i evropeiskie sotsialisty," *Krasnyi Arkhiv,* III (XVI), 1926, 25–27.

[40] See Rozanov's speech before the Soviet Central Executive Committee, August 2 (July 20), 1917, in *Revoliutsiia 1917 goda (Khronika sobytii),* III, 198, and Ehrlich's letter of July 17 to Rozanov, given by Shliapnikov in "Fevralskaia revoliutsiia i evropeiskie sotsialisty," *Krasnyi Arkhiv,* III (XVI), 1926, 33–34. Louis Dubreuilh, for the French Socialist party, protested against either inviting or consulting the Berne International Socialist Committee in connection with the proposed conference (*Pendant la Guerre. Le Parti Socialiste, la Guerre et la Paix ....,* p. 178).

[41] At the unification conference in Warsaw held from October 30 to November 4, 1916, the two sections of the Social Democracy of Poland and Lithuania represented by the Main and the Regional Presidiums, respectively, agreed on a common program, pledged themselves to support the extreme Left of the International, the so-called Zimmerwald Left, and elected a new Main Presidium on a parity basis. This new Presidium was commissioned to appoint a representative and an alternate to the International Socialist Committee. (B. Szmidt, *Socjaldemokracja Królestwa polskiego i Litwy. Materjaly i dokumenty 1914–1918,* pp. 169–71.)

[42] See below, pp. 656–63. The German *Internationale* group had already, in April, refused to attend a conference with majority socialists (see below, pp. 648–49).

[43] "One representative important foreign news service remarked half a dozen times last fortnight *à propos* tenor his dispatches on conference: 'I think I have killed it!'" (Editor of the Chicago *Tribune* to the Secretary of State, June 12, 1917,

Scandinavian Committee had been accepted by the end of July by the majority and Independent Social Democrats of Germany, the Social Democratic parties of Austria, Hungary, and the Scandinavian countries, the French and Italian Socialist parties, and the British minority groups.[44] In order to follow up the conference invitation the Russian representatives—Ehrlich, Goldenberg, Rusanov, and Smirnov—left Stockholm in July to confer with labor and socialist leaders in England, France, and Italy. In London, while urging the Labour party leaders to send delegates, the Russians made it clear that they intended to hold an international conference whether the British decided to go or not. On Henderson's recommendation the Labour party Executive voted to call a special party conference to act on the Stockholm invitation and to recommend acceptance of the invitation on condition that no binding resolutions should be adopted.[45]

From London the Russians went to Paris, accompanied by Henderson, Wardle, and MacDonald, who had been invited by the French Socialist party to take part in the discussions.[46] In the conferences, which took place on July 29–31 with the Commission Administrative Permanente, differences arose on whether the resolutions at Stockholm should be binding. Apparently the Russians had misunderstood the attitude of Henderson and the Labour party, for in a telegram from Paris they expressed their surprise at Henderson's "about face" in insisting that the resolution should not be binding.

enclosing telegram from *Tribune* correspondent in Stockholm of same date, United States Department of State, *Papers Relating to the Foreign Relations of the United States, 1917, Supplement 2, The World War,* I, 743.)

[44] The Italians had voted on July 23–27 to attend the Third Zimmerwald Conference August 10, and there to urge attendance at the Congress called by the Russians. (Malatesta, *I socialisti italiani durante la guerra,* p. 150; "L'ordine del giorno per Stoccolma," *Avanti,* No. 207, July 28, 1917, p. 1.)

[45] See Henderson's speech in the House of Commons, August 13, 1917, *P.D. Commons, 5th Series,* XCVII, 911, 913; Mary Agnes Hamilton, *Arthur Henderson,* pp. 135–36.

[46] *Pendant la Guerre. Le Parti Socialiste, la Guerre et la Paix* ...., p. 177. *Report of the Seventeenth Annual Conference of the Labour Party, 1918,* p. 4. Henderson defended his participation in the Paris discussions in the Commons. *P.D. Commons, 5th Series,* XCVI, 2193, 2195.

This question was not settled at this time, but it was agreed to postpone the Stockholm meeting until September 9 and to hold an Inter-Allied Socialist Conference in London on August 28–29.[47]

From Paris the Russian delegates went to Rome, where on August 7, 1917, they reached an understanding with the Italian Socialist party regarding the program and scope of the Stockholm Conference, the Italians agreeing "to accept and apply the decisions [of the Stockholm Conference] in the spirit of socialism and internationalism in order to achieve union of the workers by joint action directed toward the hastening of the conclusion of the war."[48]

In the meantime Henderson had returned to England to recommend to the Labour party conference the acceptance of the Stockholm invitation. By the decisive vote of 1,846,000 to 550,000 the Conference accepted the invitation; but an amendment of the Miners' Federation excluded the appointment of separate socialist delegates by limiting the British representatives to twenty-four, to be selected by the party Executive, the Parliamentary Committee of the Trade Union Congress, and the party conference. This action contravened both the text and the spirit of the Stockholm invitation and raised other questions which were held over for action at a subsequent conference on August 21. At this meeting a resolution accepting the Stockholm invitation and permitting minority representation on the British delegation passed by the close vote of 1,234,000 to 1,231,000, but a resolution including the miners' restriction on the composition of the delegation passed by 2,124,000 to 175,000.[49] British labor

[47] Shliapnikov, "Fevralskaia revoliutsiia i evropeiskie sotsialisty," *Krasnyi Arkhiv*, III (XVI), 1926, p. 36; *Stockholm*, pp. xxi–xxii; *Report of the Seventeenth Annual Conference of the Labour Party, 1918*, pp. 45–46.

[48] Malatesta, *I socialisti italiani durante la guerra*, pp. 153–54; "La riunione alla Direzione del Partito. Le dichirazioni dei Delegati per una azione internazionale per la pace," *Avanti*, No. 218, August 8, 1917, p. 1.

[49] *Report of the Seventeenth Annual Conference of the Labour Party, 1918*, pp. 5–8; Brand, "British Labor and the International during the Great War," *Journal of Modern History*, No. 1, March 1936, pp. 54–56.

was apparently strongly in favor of going to Stockholm but doubtful about allowing the Left minority to take part.

Between the Labour party conferences of August 10 and 21 two things of importance had taken place. Henderson's trip to Paris, his speech recommending acceptance of the Stockholm invitation, and the vote of the Labour party conference raised a great hue and cry in the conservative press and in Parliament, and Henderson was forced out of the government.[50] The second event bearing more directly on Stockholm was Bonar Law's announcement in Parliament, August 13, 1917, that the government had been advised by its law officers that "it is not legal for any persons resident in His Majesty's Dominions to engage in a conference with enemy subjects without the license of the Crown duly given. The Government have decided that permission to attend the Conference will not be granted."[51]

Stockholm was again an issue at the Inter-Allied Socialist Conference in London, August 28–29. French, Belgian, Russian, Portuguese, South African, Greek, and Italian delegates attended, along with representatives of the Labour party, the Independent Labour party, and the British Socialist party; all together sixty-eight attended. Seven different statements on war aims were presented; but no single inclusive statement was adopted, this question being left open for further discussion. As for Stockholm, the Conference voted 48 to 13, with the French majority socialists and the delegates of the British Trade Union Congress not voting, to accept the following resolution: "The Conference therefore welcomes the invitation to the Stockholm Congress issued by the Soviet in accord with the Dutch-Scandinavian Committee, and supports particularly the provision that minorities as well as majorities ought to be represented in order that the Congress may be fully representative and therefore be in a

---

[50] Hamilton, *Arthur Henderson*, pp. 138–62; Lloyd George gives his version of this affair in Lloyd George, *War Memoirs*, IV, 1900–1924; see also *P.D. Commons, 5th Series,* XCVII, 909–34.

[51] *P.D. Commons, 5th Series,* XCVII, 865.

position to judge the problems from every point of view." The Belgian, South African, and Greek delegates voted against this resolution. Thus there was no agreement on either of the main issues before the Conference. This was emphasized in a statement signed by the French, Belgian, British, and Italian majority sections and deposited with the chairman, to the effect that they could not attribute any importance to the majority vote on questions of principle or consider this vote as representing the opinion of the Conference. They also asked that the votes should not be made public.[52] The only positive action of this London Conference was to protest against the refusal of passports, to demand that passports be granted to both majority and minority socialists, and to recommend the appointment of a Standing Orders Committee representing the Allied national sections to discuss peace and take charge of another Inter-Allied Socialist Conference.

Convinced that the Stockholm project had failed, the International Socialist Committee decided to hold the repeatedly postponed Third Zimmerwald Conference in spite of the refusal of passports to Zimmerwaldists of the Entente states. This Conference, which is described below, met in Stockholm September 5–12, adopted resolutions reaffirming Zimmerwald principles, and adjourned without attracting much attention in either the socialist or bourgeois press.

By the action of the governments in refusing passports and by the failure of the London Conference there was no longer any hope that socialists of the Allied states would be represented at a general socialist conference at Stockholm. But the project received still another blow when the British

---

[52] *Labour Leader*, No. 35, August 30, 1917, p. 1; No. 36, September 6, 1917, p. 5; *Report of the Seventeenth Annual Conference of the Labour Party, 1918*, pp. 8–11. The signers of this statement issued a manifesto on September 2, 1917, declaring the Allies must continue their military efforts in order to crush German imperialism and that the Russian peace formula must be clarified and extended to provide for reparation for damages, liberation of territories conquered by force, and plebiscites guaranteed by a league of nations; full text is given in *Pendant la Guerre. Le Parti Socialiste, la Guerre et la Paix* . . . ., pp. 183–87.

Trade Union Congress at Blackpool, September 3–8, 1917, voted by 2,849,000 to 91,000 to endorse the resolution of its Parliamentary Committee that "a conference at Stockholm at the present moment could not be successful" but that a further attempt should be made by the workers of the Allied states to reach a general agreement regarding the conditions of peace and as the basis of a successful International.[53]

Disappointed with the results of their visits to London and Paris and by the action of the Blackpool Conference, the Russian delegates returned to Stockholm early in September and shortly afterward to Petrograd. Before the Russians left Sweden the Russian-Dutch-Scandinavian Committee issued a manifesto dated September 15, 1917, announcing that the Stockholm Conference had been again postponed but by no means abandoned. The workers were told that the refusal of passports by the French and British governments was responsible for this postponement but that "If you were only to wish so, the international conference would shortly take place. In order to attain this goal the parties must merely recognize the great responsibility that rests on them." The manifesto recorded that despite the opposition of the adversaries of socialism, the Stockholm project had won the widest support among workers and socialists, and that the Committee would continue its activity and would publish the memoranda on peace issues submitted by the various socialist parties along with a general report in which the delegates of the neutral states would make an objective summary of the memoranda.[54]

The document drawn up by the delegates of the neutral countries entitled "A Draft Program of Peace" was published on October 10, 1917, after lengthy and heated debates in the Committee. Part One of this document was a general manifesto upholding the formula, "no victors, no van-

[53] *Report of Proceedings at the Forty-ninth Annual Trades Union Congress, 1917*, pp. 70, 90.

[54] In *Stockholm* the memoranda on peace issues are given on pp. 1–409 and the manifesto of September 15, 1917, on pp. 487–90.

quished," and advocating international arbitration through a league of nations as a means of maintaining peace. The second part, an explanatory memorandum, dealt with general and specific conditions of peace and offered a minimum program as merely a basis of discussion at a future conference. Despite the modest aims of the Committee, the program did not, of course, reconcile the irreconcilables, and was severely criticized.[55]

The publication of this draft peace program was the last independent pronouncement of the Dutch-Scandinavian Committee. The Stockholm Conference as planned by the Committee never met and the leadership in the drafting of a program for peace passed to the Executive Committee of the British Labour party and the Parliamentary Committee of the Trades Union Congress. These Committees appointed a Joint International Subcommittee which redrafted a Memorandum on War Aims for submission to a conference of societies affiliated with the Labour party and the T.U.C. This Conference accepted the Memorandum on December 28, 1917, and plans were made to call another conference of socialists of Allied states.[56] Meanwhile the Bolsheviks, having taken power in Petrograd, were causing great consternation among the Entente states by their armistice with the Central Powers and their declared intention to negotiate a separate peace if the Entente Allies would not join general peace negotiations. Voices were raised, particularly by Danish and Hungarian Social Democrats, for an international socialist conference to do something to prevent the signing of a separate peace. Nothing came of this, however, though Huysmans sent to the Bolshevik authorities the protest of British laborites against a separate peace. In this connection the Russian-Dutch-Scandinavian Committee met, apparently for the last time, on January 7–8, 1918, to draft instructions for Huysmans, who had been invited to attend the Labour party conference at Nottingham. In the instructions adopted

[55] The text of this document is in *Stockholm*, pp. 493–521.
[56] Hamilton, *Arthur Henderson*, pp. 170–72.

at this time there is an implied abdication in favor of the British Joint International Subcommittee.[57]

The British Memorandum on War Aims was placed before the socialists of France, Italy, Belgium, and Serbia at the Third Inter-Allied Socialist Conference in London, February 20–24, 1918, and was adopted with certain amendments relating to colonial policy, Alsace-Lorraine, and Italy's territorial claims. In organizing this Conference, the British discarded the method of representation usually employed by the International Socialist Bureau in international congresses, with the result that the British Socialist party and the Independent Labour party were denied separate representation and the Conference was in the control of the conservative wing of the labor movement. Delegates from the American Federation of Labor were invited but were unable to reach London in time for the meetings. Later, when the Americans had arrived in England, a British-American Conference was held in which the British Memorandum on War Aims and a draft of "War Aims of the American Federation of Labor" were discussed and found "to be inspired with similar principles." In the meantime copies of the British Memorandum as amended at the London Conference had been sent to socialist parties of the enemy states. Encouraging replies came, despite the censorship of both sides, from Bulgaria, Hungary, and Austria. The German majority Social Democrats agreed with the general principles but did not accept the territorial clauses.[58]

During the summer of 1918 the last great German drives on the Western front held the attention of the socialists and workers of the Entente states. But with the turn of the tide in August the Allied socialist and labor leaders resumed their efforts to work out a statement of labor's war aims for which general agreement could be secured. The British and Amer-

[57] *Stockholm*, pp. xxviii–xxx.

[58] *Report of the Eighteenth Annual Conference of the Labour Party, 1918*, pp. 7–9; I.L.P., *Report of the Twenty-sixth Annual Conference, 1918*, pp. 14–15; *Labour Leader* for 1918, No. 8, February 21, pp. 1, 2, No. 9, February 28, p. 1, and No. 29, July 18, pp. 1, 3.

ican memoranda on war aims were again discussed at another Inter-Allied Conference in London on September 17–
20, 1918, attended by delegates from Great Britain, France,
Italy, Belgium, the United States, Canada, Greece, Serbia,
and Rumania. Five Russians who planned to attend as consultative delegates were refused passports by the Bolshevik
authorities. The Conference adopted a resolution on the Russian situation in which it referred to Allied intervention as
an effort "to assist the Russian people" which "must be influenced only by a genuine desire to preserve liberty and
democracy in an ordered and durable world peace in which
the beneficent fruits of the Revolution shall be made permanently secure." After two days of debate the Conference
adopted by 57 to 10 votes, with Canada and the United States
not voting, a compromise memorandum based on the British
and American proposals and on certain other resolutions on
specific territorial and national problems. The Conference
also elected Gompers to the Committee (Henderson, Albert
Thomas, and Vandervelde) appointed at the February Conference to organize a world labor congress to meet concur-
rently with the official peace conference.[59]

Because of the war attitude of the American Federation
of Labor and its President, the British Left and Center groups
which were not represented at the Conference protested
against Gompers' presence as "an insult to the international
socialist movement." There were also protests from the
former French minority, which had become the majority, and
from Italian, Serbian, American, and Belgian socialists, as
well as from socialists of neutral states, that the compromise
memorandum on war aims "misrepresented the real character
of the war." This dissatisfaction stimulated a demand on the
part of many socialists for the reconstruction of the International.[60]

During 1919 and 1920 the Second International was re-

[59] *Report of the Nineteenth Annual Conference of the Labour Party, 1919,*
pp. 3–10.

[60] *Labour Leader,* No. 39, September 26, 1918, p. 1.

established under a new constitution. It did not, however, include in its membership all the parties that had participated in the prewar organization. Some of these parties united with the Third International in 1919 and others with the so-called Two-and-a-Half International formed in 1921. These developments are discussed in *The Bolsheviks and World Revolution*.

INVITATION TO THE THIRD ZIMMERWALD CONFERENCE

[Circular Letter of the International Socialist Committee to All Affiliated Organizations and Groups, May 10, 1917][61]

Dear Comrades! The Dutch delegation to the International Socialist Bureau called a general international conference for May 15, and the days following, at Stockholm. Later, however, this conference was postponed until June 10, 1917. The Secretariat of the International Socialist Bureau[62] is also taking part in the preliminary work of this conference; the conference is to be held in accordance with the organizational provisions made by previous international [socialist] congresses.

The International Socialist Committee has been commissioned by the Kienthal Conference to invite all representatives of the parties that adhere to the Zimmerwald resolutions, to a conference as soon as one is called by the International Socialist Bureau, in order to attain a unified attitude. Since some parties have pronounced themselves as being fundamentally in favor of participating in this conference and have appointed their representatives, we act in the spirit of the Kienthal resolution by inviting them herewith to a Third Zimmerwald Conference to be held at Stockholm on May 31, 1917, and on the days following. We submit the following provisional agenda: the question of peace, and the attitude toward the Stockholm Conference called by the Dutch delegation.

The conditions stated in No. 3 of the *Bulletin* are valid for sending delegates to the conference.[63]

[61] "Eine dritte Zimmerwalder Konferenz," *I.S.K. Nachrichtendienst*, No. 3, May 12 [1917], pp. 1–1a.

[62] In the Russian text of this circular letter published under the title, "O mezhdunarodnoi sotsialisticheskoi konferentsii," in *Izvestiia*, No. 54, April 30, 1917, p. 5, the word "Committee" is used instead of "Bureau." This is an important error, since the International Socialist Committee did not take part in the work preliminary to the general Stockholm Conference.

[63] See invitation to the Kienthal Conference dated February 10, 1916, referred to above, p. 376.

Kindly wire the number, the names, and the time of arrival of the delegates of your organization to the National Councilor, Robert Grimm, who is staying at present at the Hotel Auditorium, Stockholm.
With a socialist greeting,

The International Socialist Committee at Berne
I.A.[64] (*Signed*) ROBERT GRIMM

. . . . Invitations to the Third Zimmerwald Conference have been forwarded to the following parties:

(1) The Workers' and Soldiers' Soviet, Petrograd, (2) The Central Committee of the Social Democratic Labor party of Russia, (3) The Organization Committee of the Social Democratic Labor party of Russia, (4) The Central Committee of the Socialist-Revolutionists of Russia, (5) The Central Committee of the All-Jewish Workers' League of Poland, Lithuania, and Russia, (6) The Independent Social Democratic party of Germany, (7) The Zimmerwald tendency of the Socialist minority of France, (8) The Social Democratic [Socialist] party of Italy, (9) The Main and the Regional Presidiums of the Social Democracy of Poland [and Lithuania],[65] (10) The Polish Socialist party (Levitsa), (11) The Social Democratic Labor party of Bulgaria, (12) The Social Democratic party of Rumania, (13) The Social Democratic party of Switzerland, (14) The Independent Labour party of England, (15) The British Socialist party, (16) The Left Social Democratic [Labor] party of Sweden, (17) The Social Democratic Youth League of Sweden and Norway, (18) The Social Democratic party of Norway, (19) The Social Democratic party of Serbia, (20) The Social Democratic Youth League of Denmark.

Furthermore, all parties and organizations which recognize the Zimmerwald resolutions but which have not been mentioned in this list have the right to attend the Conference. The invitation could not be delivered to the American Socialist parties and the International Socialist League of South Africa on account of the early date of the Conference.

THE PEACE POLICY OF THE RUSSIAN COALITION GOVERN-MENT; THE RESPONSIBILITIES OF THE SOCIALIST MINISTERS; THE STOCKHOLM CONFERENCE

[From a Speech by Robert Grimm at the All-Russian Conference of Social Democrats–Mensheviks in Petrograd, May 23, 1917][66]

. . . . An acute struggle against all capitalist and imperialist governments and against their war policy was proclaimed at Zimmerwald as the

---

[64] In absentia. [65] Should read: The Main Presidium only. See above, p. 599, n. 41. [66] Robert Grimm based his speech on the main thesis of the proclamation issued

foundation of the revolutionary action of the laboring class. The Kienthal Conference demanded the withdrawal of socialists from bourgeois governments and a break with civil peace as prerequisites of the proletarian peace action. All of us who were able to attend the Zimmerwald and Kienthal conferences were proud that the majority of Russian Socialists had not waited until these slogans were issued by the two international conferences but had waged this struggle from the very outbreak of the war. Therefore the entrance of the socialists into the Russian coalition government was so much more unexpected by us; moreover, we were puzzled by this action, since one of the members of the new government of national defense took part in the first Zimmerwald Conference.[67]   None of us could even dream that the road from the idyllic Swiss mountain village to a ministerial seat in Petrograd could be so short.

But this is not all. This fact has already found a special ideology: *the ideology of social patriotism*. This is the same state of mind as that of social patriots of other countries. I was amazed at the similarity between the arguments with which I was presented in justification of this entrance into the Coalition Cabinet and the reasons which were advanced by the social patriots of Germany and France in justification of the policy which they inaugurated on August 4, 1914.

. . . . By pointing to the acceptance of ministerial posts by the Russian Socialists, the French, English, and Belgian Socialists deceive the indifferent masses with their justification of their own policy of social patriotism. This reference to the Russian example—though in Russia this [the entrance into the Coalition government] has taken place under entirely different conditions — cripples and harms the revolutionary struggle of the minorities, strengthens social patriotism against internationalism, and in return inflicts *an international blow upon the Russian revolution.* . . . .

. . . . The three comrades have entered the Cabinet in order to save the revolution. If they really wished to do this, then they should have entered the government imbued with a resolute will for peace. There cannot be the slightest doubt that the three comrades are sincerely inspired by this will. The proclamation of the Coalition government seemed to manifest this will for peace. The positive character of the proclamation lay in the acknowledgment of the idea of peace without annexations or war indemnities, and in the assurance of the right of nations to self-determination. But the *cloven hoof* has already shown

---

by the International Socialist Committee on March 20, 1917: "Either the war will kill the revolution, or the revolution will kill the war." See above, chapter v, pp. 473–78.

[67] V. M. Chernov, Minister of Agriculture.

itself in the *camouflaged threat of the liberation offensive*, and in the course of only a few days the negative character [of the Coalition government's program], the element which was hostile to peace, prevailed.[68]

. . . . So long as Russia is bound by open or secret treaties to England, France, or any other imperialist coalition of powers, so long as its Allies do not themselves renounce the policy of conquests, the Coalition Cabinet of the Russian revolution cannot be a Cabinet of peace. . . . .[69]

. . . . *A government which seriously desires peace must first of all declare its willingness to conclude an immediate truce.* . . . .

Has the Russian government issued such a declaration as this? No. This fact not only proves that the Russian government has no right to refer in its peace policy to Zimmerwald, for one of the chief demands of Zimmerwald is the demand for the conclusion of an immediate truce for the purpose of bringing about peace negotiations. . . . .

. . . . *Either the socialist Ministers stand on the basis of Zimmerwald and hence must support the Zimmerwald peace program by demanding immediate suspension of hostilities, or, if they refuse to do so, they have renounced the Zimmerwald policy.* And, furthermore, should the Provisional government refuse to fulfill the demands of the socialist Ministers, then this government ought to be opposed in every possible way. The resignation of the socialist Ministers would then be the first prerequisite to this struggle and incumbent upon the Ministers for reasons of self-respect. . . . .[70]

. . . . By demanding the immediate cessation of hostilities the Russian revolution would provide the fighting workers of other belligerent countries with a practical slogan. . . . . If the workers in Germany and Austria can point to the fact that in Russia there has been initiated a strong and influential movement for peace, which aims to conclude an immediate truce, then the arguments of social patriots to the effect that Russia, revolutionary Russia, has likewise become a menace to peace will be refuted. Then the revolutionary socialist movement would find

---

[68] This section of the Russian Coalition government's proclamation read as follows: ". . . . we wish peace without annexations, without indemnities, and on the basis of self-determination of peoples. . . . . Believing that the defeat of Russia and her Allies would not only be the source of the greatest calamity for the people, ... the Provisional government trusts that the revolutionary army of Russia will not allow the German troops to crush our Allies in the West and then turn against us. To strengthen the democratization in our army, to organize and strengthen its fighting power for both defensive and offensive operations, is the most important task now before the Provisional government." (Golder, *Documents of Russian History, 1914–1917*, p. 354.)

[69] "Zimmerwald und die russische Revolution," *Berner Tagwacht*, No. 157, July 7, 1917, p. 1.

[70] *Ibid.*, No. 158, July 9, 1917, p. 1.

an entirely different response in the countries of the Central Powers and the socialist Ministers, given the existing war fatigue of the population, would be able to act efficiently and enforce peace. When the proletarians of France, England, Italy, etc., know that new Russia has confronted the governments with the question of immediately ceasing all hostilities, they will support their previous demands for peace with greater determination by basing themselves upon this fact and will be able to exert stronger pressure upon their respective governments. . . . .

. . . . The Soviet of Workers' and Soldiers' deputies has seized the initiative in the calling of an international peace conference of the proletariat. We have gladly welcomed this initiative as a legitimate attempt of the Russian revolution to liquidate the war as quickly as possible and to rally the workers around a policy of revolutionary struggle.

. . . . But the will to call an international conference is in itself insufficient. The conference must have a firm, solid basis; otherwise it may become a hilt without a blade.

What is this basis? In my opinion the Russian revolution, as such, has provided this basis. . . . . A brave and determined struggle against imperialism, against the capitalist society is the prerequisite of peace. There can be no peace which would answer the interests of the broad masses unless this struggle is waged. This also is true of the conference under discussion. It will have meaning and significance only if its participants are imbued with this will to struggle.

We know, however, that the official socialist parties of other countries, with only a few exceptions, have not only declined this struggle but even have attempted to suppress every endeavor to conduct this struggle . . . . If the invitations to the international conference have been sent out indiscriminately by the Soviet of Workers' and Soldiers' deputies to all parties, regardless of whether they are on the side of the governments or in the camp of the revolutionary movement, then there arises the danger that these parties through their representatives would agree to all sorts of peace resolutions in Stockholm, *but that at home they would continue their former shameful policy of civil peace, of support of the imperialist war, of granting war credits, and of struggle against the revolutionary minorities.*

Very definite guaranties are necessary here. They can be provided by advancing a clear platform which would regulate the attendance of the conference. . . . .

Since this formula (peace without annexation and indemnities, etc.) is apt to be misinterpreted or interpreted at random, the platform of the international conference must be outlined and delimited still more sharply. As the declaration of the Provisional government of Russia has shown, it has become possible to speak in one breath about peace without annexation and indemnities and about continuation of war through an offensive. . . . . the conference must declare that only those parties can take part in the conference which are willing to *combat any government with weapons which are at the disposal of the revolutionary mass action if this government does not declare its willingness to conclude peace without annexation and indemnities and to initiate the peace negotiations by their willingness immediately to cease all hostilities*. . . . .

The advance of such a platform as this for attending the conference, however, presupposes that the initiators of the conference consider themselves also bound by that platform. . . . .

. . . . The unconditional inviting of the Scheidemanns, the Renaudels, and the Hendersons to the conference would be identical to an international recognition and sanctioning of their previous policy of civil peace and social patriotism, hence of a policy against which the Russian proletariat has pronounced itself since the very beginning of the war. . . . . [Such an invitation would be] treason against the revolutionary struggle of the Russian workers and soldiers ; . . . . this would be nothing less than the deception and the sacrifice of the Zimmerwald ideas, their renunciation in favor of social patriotism. . . . .

I am deeply convinced that this digression from the principles of the Zimmerwald movement, which for two years has constituted the policy of the revolutionary laboring class of Russia, cannot be desired by the Russian proletariat. . . . . The revolution at this moment is in the throes of an internal crisis which demands solution in one way or another. All internationalists, and above all the workers who adhere to Zimmerwald and Kienthal, must, by uniting all forces, assume the task of showing the way out of this crisis. The rallying of all internationalist elements upon the platform of Zimmerwald and Kienthal, faithfulness toward international socialism and its revolutionary nature—these are the prerequisites of the further success of the revolution. Only on this condition will the Russian revolution realize its slogan—bread, peace, freedom!—and become a powerful impetus for the development of the revolutionary movement in Western Europe. . . . .[71]

A. The Stockholm Conference and the Affair of Robert Grimm

As has been said, after the overthrow of Tsarism in Russia, the Enlarged International Socialist Committee decided to transfer the headquarters of the Committee from Berne to Stockholm. Robert Grimm, the chairman, and Angelica

[71] "Zimmerwald und die russische Revolution," *Beilage zur Berner Tagwacht,* No. 159, July 10, 1917, pp. 1–2.

Balabanoff, secretary of the Committee, went to Sweden for this purpose. Grimm and Balabanoff presently went to Russia, where Grimm committed a diplomatic indiscretion which aroused a good deal of anger and suspicion inside and outside the socialist movement and confirmed the belief of the opponents of Zimmerwald that this movement was serving the interests of the Central Powers. Thus the affair undoubtedly had some influence on the attitude of the Entente governments and conservative socialists and workers toward the Stockholm project and contributed its share to the disintegration of the Zimmerwald movement.

Grimm originally undertook to go to Russia partly in the interests of the International Socialist Committee but also at the request of Russian political exiles who wished to return to their native country. The first group of Russian exiles to return from abroad, the group of which Lenin was one, reached Petrograd on April 16 (3), 1917, but by no means all of the well-known Russian Zimmerwaldists were in this party. Those who were left in Switzerland, through the Central Committee for the Return of Political Exiles to Russia, asked Grimm on April 17, 1917, to go to Russia to arrange for an exchange of Russian émigrés in Switzerland for German civil prisoners in Russia and "to transmit personally to the Soviet of Workers' deputies, the Minister of Justice Kerensky, and the Vera Figner Committee an expression of the sentiment which dominated the majority of the émigrés in Switzerland." Grimm agreed, left Switzerland on the 20th, and arrived in Stockholm on April 24. Miliukov, then Foreign Minister of the Provisional government, notified the émigrés that the proposed exchange was not possible, and, after waiting until nearly mid-May for an answer, Grimm learned that his request for permission to enter Russia had been refused, the apparent reason being, according to Martov, that Miliukov had information that Grimm was a German agent. The members of the Soviet to whom this statement was made were indignant but unable to do anything.[72]

[72] *Beilage zur Berner Tagwacht*, No. 107, May 8, 1917, pp. 1–2; *I.S.K. Nach-*

Matters were in this state when a train with over two hundred and fifty political exiles and their wives and children arrived in Stockholm after a trip through Germany. On this train were the Social Democrats Yu. Martov, Lunacharsky, Riazanov, Axelrod, Martynov, the Socialist Revolutionist Bobrov, and others, including Angelica Balabanoff and the Swiss Social Democrat Hans Vogel.[73] Grimm boarded the train to discuss Zimmerwald matters, but while en route to the Russian frontier he learned that Miliukov had resigned and that the Provisional government had been reconstructed with the inclusion of two Mensheviks, Tsereteli and Skobelev, and the Socialist-Revolutionist, Chernov, who had been at Zimmerwald. Grimm decided to try again for a visa. The Menshevik Ministers agreed to vouch for him, but permission did not reach Grimm until he had already crossed the Russian frontier with an escort from the Helsingfors Soviet, which had taken the responsibility to see that he reached Petrograd.[74]

The returning exiles and their Swiss companions arrived in Petrograd in time to take part in the All-Russian Menshevik Conference called by the Organization Committee on May 20 (7). Grimm addressed the meeting at length, advocating the acceptance of Zimmerwald principles and arguing that only by so doing and by bringing about an immediate cessation of hostilities would the Russian socialists justify their participation in the Provisional government. The Conference went on record as favoring participation in both the general Stockholm Conference and the Third Zimmerwald Conference.[75]

richtendienst, No. 3, May 12 [1917], pp. 5–6; *Internationale Korrespondenz*, No. 15, May 26, 1917, pp. 105–106; *Berner Tagwacht*, No. 112, May 14, 1917, p. 2; *Pervyi Vserossiiskii Sezd Sovetov, R. i S.D.,* I, 7.

[73] *Revoliutsiia 1917 goda (Khronika sobytii)*, II, 128; *Berner Tagwacht*, No. 112, May 14, 1917, p. 2.

[74] Balabanoff, "Die Zimmerwalder Bewegung ....," Grünberg, *Archiv* ...., XII, 364; *Berner Tagwacht*, No. 117, May 21, 1917, p. 2; *Pervyi Vserossiiskii Sezd Sovetov R. i S.D.*, I, 7; see also Balabanoff's account in her *Erinnerungen und Erlebnisse*, pp. 135–42.

[75] *Rabochaia Gazeta*, No. 52, May 10, 1917, p. 3; *Den*, No. 56, May 11, 1917, p. 2, and No. 57, May 12, 1917, p. 2.

Grimm and Balabanoff also attended meetings of the Executive Committee of the Soviet when the Stockholm question was debated, but no detailed account of these discussions is available. Balabanoff in her collection of documents gives details of only the meeting on May 28–29 of Russian Zimmerwaldists and members of the International Socialist Committee, when the following persons took part in the discussion: Balabanoff, Grimm, and Bobrov, of the S.R. internationalists; Zinoviev, Lenin, and Kamenev, of the Bolsheviks; Abramovich, of the Bund; Lapinski, of the Polish Socialist party (Levitsa); Riazanov, Trotsky, and Uritsky, of the "Mezhraionka";[76] Bienstock, Martov, Martynov, and Larin, of the Menshevik internationalists; and Rakovsky, of the Rumanian S.D. party. Balabanoff reports that Trotsky, Kamenev, Zinoviev, Riazanov, and herself favored boycotting the general conference called by the Soviet, while Rakovsky, Grimm, Martynov, and Bobrov favored the appointment of delegates, since the proposed conference was no longer under the auspices of the International Socialist Bureau but had been called by the revolutionary workers' Soviet. Decision was, however, postponed until the Third Zimmerwald Conference.

In the course of the discussion Zinoviev, Lenin, and Kamenev moved that the International Socialist Committee issue a statement disapproving the entrance of Russian socialists into the Provisional government. Practically all who expressed themselves on this matter, except Bobrov, condemned the acceptance of ministerial posts; but a large majority felt that the I.S.C. could not properly make such a statement without first consulting the affiliated groups. The I.S.C. confined its official action to issuing the invitations to the Third Zimmerwald Conference to be held three days before the general conference and to appealing to Russian workers to support the socialist minorities in the belligerent states. The same point was emphasized by Grimm and Balabanoff

---

[76] Balabanoff at the time belonged to this group (Balabanoff, *Erinnerungen und Erlebnisse*, pp. 148–49).

and the Russian Zimmerwaldists at many mass meetings in Petrograd.[77]

Grimm's campaign in Petrograd was conducted under a hostile cross fire from the Right and the Left. The Rights suspected him of being a German agent and the Lefts, as has been noted, considered him as a representative of the Zimmerwald Right and an ally of Kautsky, Haase, and their friends. Aside from theoretical differences, some of the Russian Lefts, notably Lenin and Zinoviev, who had returned from Switzerland in the first party of homecoming exiles, had had differences with Grimm because of his failure to make arrangements for their return promptly and had turned to Fritz Platten, through whom the negotiations with the Germans had been carried out.[78] Moreover, the Bolshevik All-Russian conference May 7–12 (April 24–29) had voted to stay away from the conference proposed by the Soviets and to withdraw from the Zimmerwald movement in case the announced Third Zimmerwald Conference should vote to take part in the general socialist meeting at Stockholm.

On June 16 (3) the Provisional government published the telegram from the Swiss Federal Councilor, Hoffmann, to Grimm, in which Hoffmann outlined what amounted to a German offer of a separate peace and gave assurance that the Germans would make no offensive so long as there was a chance of agreement with Russia. With the text of this telegram the Provisional government announced that, with the concurrence of Ministers Skobelev and Tsereteli, who had vouched for him, Grimm had been deported.[79] These revela-

[77] Balabanoff, "Die Zimmerwalder Bewegung ....," Grünberg, *Archiv* ...., XII, 364–65; Balabanoff, *Erinnerungen und Erlebnisse,* pp. 146–49.

[78] *Volia Naroda,* No. 31, June 4, 1917, pp. 1–2. It is interesting that on May 21, 1917, after Grimm was already in Petrograd, Prince Fürstenberg in Stockholm reported to Count Czernin that Miliukov had succeeded in keeping Grimm out of Russia so that Grimm would be unable to carry out his "secret mission," which was "to start in Petrograd a pro-German propaganda and an agitation against the Imperialism of the Western Powers. He was also to try to bring about a *rapprochement* between the radical Socialists in Petrograd and those German Socialists who were of the same opinion." (R. H. Lutz, *Fall of the German Empire,* II, 57.)

[79] *Izvestiia,* No. 82, June 3, 1917, p. 5; see also account in Balabanoff, *Erinnerungen und Erlebnisse,* pp. 157–63.

tions gave the opponents of Zimmerwald the opening they had
been waiting for and they made the most of it. The Constitutional Democratic paper, *Rech,* rejoiced that the man whom
it had repeatedly accused of being a German agent and an accomplice of Lenin had now begun "to shed the beautiful ap-
parel in which he had clad himself" and revealed that "this
symbol of Zimmerwald is a common adventurer whose actions
are subject to investigation by a court-martial." Zimmerwald,
according to *Rech,* was responsible for the slogan "without
annexations and indemnities," for the Soviet appeal to the
peoples for peace, and for the disturbances in the streets of
Petrograd on May 3–5 (April 20–22), and finally that Zimmerwald was a "bonfire kindled by Grimm . . . . so as to work
in favor of Germany through the International."[80] None of
the socialist papers tried to defend Grimm. The Right Socialist-Revolutionist *Volia Naroda* criticized him, as the Bolsheviks had done, for his advocacy of "defense of Switzerland's neutrality" in opposition to Nobs and Platten.[81] The
Rabochaia Gazeta of the Menshevik-Internationalists, when
forced by Grimm's admission to give up the hope that the
accusations might be false, denounced him as a hypocrite and
a coward but rejected the allegation that he was a German
agent.[82]

It so happened that the deportation of Grimm occurred
just a few hours before the opening of the First All-Russian
Congress of Soviets. Delegates of the various socialist groups
who had differed violently in respect to Zimmerwald principles now seized upon the Grimm affair to renew their controversy with greater vigor. Grimm's friends, who were still
in the dark about much of the affair (Grimm's admission that
Hoffmann's telegram was an answer to his own was not
known in Russia until June 30), did their best to defend him.
The socialist Ministers, under the sharp criticism of Martov,
Grimm's closest friend and warmest defender, endeavored

---

[80] *Rech,* No. 129, June 4, 1917. p. 2, and No. 130, June 6, 1917, p. 2.
[81] *Volia Naroda,* No. 20, May 21, 1917. p. 1.
[82] *Rabochaia Gazeta,* No. 83, June 17, 1917, p. 2.

to justify having given their consent to Grimm's deportation. Tsereteli explained the circumstances of Grimm's admission to Russia, the interception of Hoffmann's telegram by the Provisional government, Grimm's unsatisfactory explanation, and his refusal to charge the Swiss and German governments with attempting to use him to discredit the Zimmerwald movement. Skobelev emphasized the harm done to the general peace efforts of the Russian democracy. Kerensky declared his approval of the deportation, as did Gotz for the Socialist-Revolutionists and Lieber for the Mensheviks in the Soviet. Zinoviev for the Bolsheviks accused the socialist supporters of the Provisional government of injustice in ordering the deportation without a thorough investigation and with inconsistency since the socialist Ministers themselves openly dealt with imperialists. Abramovich of the Bund argued the injustice of the government's action since it did not clear Grimm of the charge of being a German agent, a charge which the socialist Ministers professed not to believe. Four resolutions reflecting these points of view were offered. A joint resolution of the Mensheviks and Socialist-Revolutionists approving the action of the Provisional government received an overwhelming majority.[83]

As soon as he returned to Stockholm, on June 19, Grimm resigned from the International Socialist Committee and asked that a commission be appointed to investigate his case. Apparently the Swedish Youth League and the Russian Bolsheviks in Sweden intended to ask him to withdraw from the leadership of the Zimmerwald movement until the affair was satisfactorily cleared up, but Grimm insisted at the time that his resignation was offered voluntarily.[84] In any event, the Swedish members of the I.S.C. appointed Höglund and Lindhagen (Sweden), Kirkov (Bulgaria), Moor (Switzerland), Orlovsky (Russia), Radek (Poland), and Rakovsky (Ru-

---

[83] *Pervyi Vserossiiskii Sezd Sovetov R. i S.D.*, I, 6–40.

[84] *Berner Tagwacht*, No. 145, June 23, 1917, p. 2, and No. 146, June 25, 1917, pp. 1–2; *I.S.K. Nachrichtendienst*, No. 9, June 20, 1917, pp. 4–5. Hoffmann also resigned as Federal Councilor on June 19.

mania) to a commission to investigate the affair.[85] In connection with this inquiry Grimm wrote to Mayor Lindhagen a defense of his action, in which he admitted that the Hoffmann telegram was a reply to one of his own. After examining Grimm and various witnesses the Commission on July 5 issued a report which acquitted Grimm of the charge of being a German agent but censured him for failing to make known his intention to Balabanoff or the Russian Zimmerwaldists and for not revealing his telegram to Hoffmann. In the name of the Zimmerwald movement the Commission disclaimed all responsibility for Grimm's action.

The affair naturally had repercussions in Switzerland, where, as in Russia, both the Right and the Left Social Democrats rose to the attack. The *Berner Tagwacht,* while faithfully publishing all the documents, stood by Grimm, and presented his explanations. Grimm defended himself in letters to the Presidium of the Swiss S.D. party and to the International Socialist Committee, representing himself as the victim of a plot by the Entente, whose plans he had interfered with, and attributing the consent of the Russian Socialist Ministers to his deportation to the influence of the Entente and the bourgeois members of the Provisional Government.[86] The Swiss S.D. party took official cognizance of the affair when the Presidium appointed an investigation commission which reported on September 1, 1917. The Presidium voted 18 to 15 to accept the majority report of the Commission, which coincided in the main with the report of the investigation commission in Stockholm, and proposed that as a party member Grimm be restored to his former positions. The minority report signed by Naine was far more condemnatory and denied the right of the Presidium to determine the validity of Grimm's mandates.[87]

---

[85] *I.S.K. Nachrichtendienst,* No. 10, June 22, 1917, pp. 1–2.

[86] *Berner Tagwacht,* No. 147, June 26, 1917, p. 1, and No. 149, June 28, 1917, p. 1; *I.S.K. Nachrichtendienst,* No. 9, June 20, 1917, pp. 1–4.

[87] *Beilage zur Berner Tagwacht,* No. 207, September 5, 1917, pp. 1–2.

THE GRIMM-HOFFMANN TELEGRAMS[88]

[Grimm to Hoffmann, May 26/27, 1917]

PETROGRAD

Affaires étrangères, Berne

National Councilor Grimm, who is staying at present in Petrograd, requested us to transmit to Federal Councilor Hoffmann the following telegram:

There is a general desire for peace. The conclusion of peace is urgently needed for political, economic, and military reasons. This is recognized by the authorities. France causes delay and England creates obstacles. Negotiations are in the air at present and the prospects are favorable. During the next few days the exertion of a new and increased pressure is to be expected. Only a German offensive in the east could possibly spoil the negotiations. But should this offensive not take place, the liquidation [of the war] might be carried out in a relatively short period.

An international conference called by the Soviet of Workers' deputies is a part of the peace policy of the new government. The holding of this conference is certain, so long as the governments do not present obstacles to the obtaining of passports. All countries have agreed to attend. Inform me if possible about the governments' war aims known to you, since this would facilitate the conducting of negotiations. I shall stay about another ten days in Petrograd.

Swiss Legation: ODIER

[Hoffmann to Grimm, June 3, 1917]

Légation suisse, Pétrograd
[*Cipher*]

Germany will not undertake an offensive so long as an agreement with Russia seems possible. After repeated conversations with noted persons I have become convinced that Germany is seeking a peace with Russia, honorable for both sides, a peace which will establish close commercial and economic relations and will provide for financial assistance for the restoration of Russia. She seeks no interference with Russian affairs but rather a friendly treaty concerning Poland, Lithuania, and Courland, with the recognition of national equality. She will return the occupied territories in exchange for the Austrian provinces seized by Russia.

I am convinced that if Russia's allies were willing Germany and her

---

[88] "Der Wortlaut des Depeschenwechsels Grimm-Hoffmann," *Berner Tagwacht*, No. 149, June 28, 1917, p. 3.

allies would be ready to open immediate peace negotiations. Concerning the German war aims, read the statement in the *Norddeutsche Allgemeine Zeitung* where, in agreement with Asquith on the question of annexations, it is asserted that Germany desires no territorial acquisitions for the purpose of expansion, nor does she wish economic or political exaltation.

GRIMM'S FIRST EXPLANATION

[Statement Published by the Provisional Government][89]

In connection with this document [Hoffmann's telegram] the Provisional government commissioned I. G. Tsereteli and M. I. Skobelev, members of the Provisional government, to request an explanation from the Swiss citizen, Robert Grimm. As a result of this explanation Robert Grimm handed to G. I. Tsereteli and M. I. Skobelev the following document:

1. Shortly before my departure, the Ministers Tsereteli and Skobelev informed me that the Swiss Minister in Petrograd had received a telegram from Berne in which he was commissioned to inform me of some German peace plans.

I must put on record that this communication was not delivered to me by the Swiss Minister directly or through the medium of anyone else.

2. The contents of the telegram should be considered as an attempt on the part of the German government to take advantage of my Petrograd speeches, which favored the establishing of international socialist relations and a general peace, in order to further its own interests, its diplomatic plans, and the separate peace toward which it strives. This attempt represents a crude maneuver.

3. In Berne, likewise, when I went to the German Legation to secure a visa on my passport, which was necessary for my journey, I refrained from all political conversations, and during the trip to Stockholm refrained from all contacts with representatives of the majority of the German Social Democratic party.

4. With regard to the participation of the Swiss government in this matter, I can establish the real ins and outs of it only in Switzerland.

5. As a Social Democrat I shall not permit myself to be used as a transmitter of imperialist peace plans between governments. Any such attempt I shall expose ruthlessly.

PETROGRAD, June 12 (May 31), 1917

ROBERT GRIMM

[89] "Ot Vremennago Pravitelstva," *Izvestiia*, No. 82, June 3, 1917, p. 5.

SIGNIFICANCE OF THE GRIMM CASE FOR SOCIALISM

[From a Speech by Zinoviev at the All-Russian Congress of Soviets, Petrograd, June 16 (3), 1917][90]

Zinoviev (*applause*) : Comrades, our party and the Bolshevik group [in the Soviet], which is taking part in this sitting, know only what we have today learned from newspapers and from speeches delivered here. Not one of us has had an opportunity to hear the explanations which, as we know, were presented today in a number of group gatherings; not one of us knows anything at all about the parleys that revolved around this case and which apparently have been taking place for several days prior to the publishing of this material. We form our opinions on this case, I repeat, exclusively on the basis of the material which is in our possession now. (*Applause from the Bolsheviks.*) Comrades, our orientation has never identified itself with the orientation defended by Robert Grimm. From the very beginning at Zimmerwald we constituted the Zimmerwald Left, having diverged from Grimm on a number of extremely important questions. Further, I say frankly to everybody that the explanations given by R. Grimm in the press cannot be considered by us as satisfactory. We cannot understand why Grimm has not been able to say that he considers this action on the part of "his" Minister Hoffmann as provocation (*applause*) ; we cannot understand why, with respect to his Minister Hoffmann and to his imperialists, he could not use the same language which is becoming to revolutionaries and socialists with respect to their governments (*applause*). But (*turning to Tsereteli*), Comrades, there is an English proverb: first of all you should sweep before your own house. Thus we ask the socialist Ministers : *why have they not first taken care to sweep before their own houses?*

Of what is Grimm being accused? If the socialist Ministers were to come forward now and tell us that they accuse Grimm of being a conscious agent of the German government, we would say that the case would have to be investigated by a proper committee. We know that in the course of the World War many reputations have been ruined, and many, far too many, socialist reputations. We would say that we admit everything; but, please, investigate, examine the matter. But, Comrades, there has been heard no such accusation; we have heard from Tsereteli and Skobelev only long-winded demonstrations that Grimm is a bad internationalist. I agree willingly to that. We have said as much to Grimm long since; we said in the press, at the Zimmerwald and Kienthal conferences, and at the Swiss meetings before the workers, that Grimm

[90] "Rech t. G. Zinovieva na vserossiiskom sezde sovetov rab. i sold. deputatov o dele Grimma," *Pravda*, No. 74, June 6, 1917, pp. 2–5, reprinted in *Pravda, 1917*, IV, 50–53, and also in *Pervyi Vserossiiskii sezd sovetov R. i S.D.*, I, 21–24.

belongs to the tendency which we call "Center," belongs to the tendency which desires peace with the social chauvinists, which does not wish to break with those who went over to the side of the governments. If they accuse Grimm of being a bad internationalist, of not having had the courage to speak against any imperialism, then we shall permit ourselves to ask the socialist Ministers: what is their attitude toward the *English* and *French* representatives of imperialism? (*Applause from the Bolsheviks.*)

We cannot forget the first arrival in Petrograd of the English guests headed by O'Grady; we cannot forget that our comrades fraternized with them before the entire Russian working class; we cannot forget that not an awful Bolshevik, but *Viktor Chernov,* who came here and who is at present sitting in your midst, told you that the English socialists had commissioned him to announce that this delegation of O'Grady's and of others was sent by the English *government* and was in close contact with the *English government,* i.e., English imperialists. Chernov told it all over Russia; but have you called O'Grady to order?

We cannot forget that Albert Thomas was visiting here recently and that, when he came to the Executive Committee meeting, all the members rose in his honor and did likewise when he left. Before his departure he organized a grandiose meeting in Petersburg at which he fraternized with Miliukov, whom you have ousted. Miliukov fraternized with him and declared that on the whole he agreed with his explanation.

Furthermore, we cannot forget that Henderson is also a representative of the *English imperialists.* Now, we ask the comrades—since they are so strict and cannot bear the failure of other people to separate themselves sufficiently from imperialism—have they separated from Henderson, the English imperialist, or from Albert Thomas, the French imperialist?

You are familiar with the note published by the French and English governments—the note which has nullified the entire policy of the Soviet of the Workers' and Soldiers' deputies, the note which destroyed your entire policy of agreements with French and English capitalists. We ask the Ministers if they have demanded that Thomas and Henderson say openly that they are not in agreement with that note, nor in agreement with "their" governments and "their" capitalists? They have not done so, and we consider it our duty to tell them: sweep first of all before your own house. (*Applause of a section of the gathering.*) But, Comrades, among other things, you are confronted by another and much more important question, which concerns not so much the principles of socialism as those of simple *democracy.* We say that what has been done with regard to R. Grimm is *a breach of the elementary principles of democracy;* and in this respect we agree completely with Comrade Martov.

We ask why the Ministers have not called a conference, at least of their own parties, the Socialist-Revolutionists and the Mensheviks; why have they not consulted their own Executive Committee of which they are the representatives and in which they are assured of a majority? We ask them: since when has deportation become a means of struggling against bad internationalists? (*Applause of a section of the gathering.*) We say that if this were a matter concerning R. Grimm alone, then of course it would be the duty of the Russian revolution to protect the honor of every individual, even if he is not a revolutionary—since the personal honor of everybody is dear to us;—but, Comrades, we say that [this does not concern Grimm alone], it concerns more important matters: *our own honor, the honor of the Russian revolution, the honor of the Soviet of Workers' and Soldiers' deputies.* (*Applause.*) I think, Comrades, that when this question has subsided somewhat, when our passions are not so tense, then the adherents of the Ministers, of Comrades Tsereteli and Skobelev, will tell themselves that this has not been the most glorious page of their activity. (*Voice: "A beautiful page."*)

For the first time administrative deportation has been applied in free Russia, and applied *by whom?* By your own comrades.

We consider that in this incident the entire state of present-day socialism with all its horrors and weak points has been reflected as in a drop of water. Grimm was unfortunate because he proved to be not a resolute internationalist, because he had given one finger to his capitalists and another finger to his social patriots, and this was the reason he and the movement he heads were placed in an equivocal position. Further, we say that our comrades, Russian Socialist Ministers, who, alas, have given to their capitalists not only one finger but all five fingers, have thus placed themselves in a position in which they are obliged to perform functions like that of deportation, functions which we, at any rate, cannot recognize as especially dignified.

Our party is by no means defending Grimm's declaration. We cannot understand, we refuse to understand, what prevented him from saying that Hoffmann and German or Swiss capitalists are the same kind of provocateurs, the same kind of villains as the capitalists of all countries. It was his duty, his task, to say this. But we completely refuse to understand how it was possible to deport a person without a trial, without investigation, without consulting their own comrades, without consulting the Executive Committee; how was it possible to place before you, this Congress, an already accomplished fact knowing that the Congress was going to assemble at once and that it would be possible to talk to the delegates, and that no one really accuses Grimm of being a spy and agent. We say that this entire incident reflects the whole state of affairs. Whoever wishes not only to be attracted by appearances but also to pay attention to what the newspapers will shout (the newspapers have already begun shouting that the selfish Leninists are responsible for everything, the Leninists, who, by the way, have never gone hand in hand with Grimm); whoever wishes to understand the fact that the delegates of the All-Russian Congress who had gathered from all parts of Russia were confronted by this surprise, must say: all this has its roots in the crisis of socialism. There is no salvation so long as we look for a mote in the eye of our neighbor and fail to notice the beam in our own eye, fail to notice that so long as we sustain a bloc, a union with "our own" imperialists, all our criticisms directed in defense of the International and of socialism will necessarily sound false. (*Applause of a section of the gathering.*) Let this sad incident, which has been destined to become an introduction to our work [at the Congress], prove that in order to be an internationalist, *not in words but in deeds,* it is necessary to struggle against our own imperialists, *our own* capitalists; it is necessary to dissolve the union with our own capitalists. Only then shall we have the right to speak about international socialism (*applause*).

GRIMM'S ADMISSION

[Extract from a Letter to Mayor Lindhagen of Stockholm][91]

This inquiry was made at Berne according to my desire and my commission. I described in a few words the general state of affairs and begged to be informed of the war aims of the governments which were known to Mr. Hoffmann. I expressed this wish in a general way. I spoke neither about special aims of the war nor the conditions of a separate peace. Previously there had been no agreement whatsoever to that effect between Hoffmann and me. Besides the known telegram we exchanged no telegraph messages. Hoffmann did not communicate to me any proposals or terms. The suspicion that I am an agent of Germany because I received a reply to my inquiry is absurd. I have no reason to defend myself against these suspicions.

[Further on, Grimm says as follows]:

I wish to reply immediately to two questions which I may rightfully be asked from the point of view of the Zimmerwald movement: what has impelled me to pose this question and why have I posed this question to Hoffmann? The answer to this question is that our party, in agreement with the Zimmerwald resolution, has taken upon itself the responsi-

---

[91] "Soznanie R. Grimma," *Izvestiia,* No. 94, June 17, 1917, pp. 4–5. These excerpts from Grimm's letter to Mayor Lindhagen were published first in *Politiken* and later in *Berner Tagwacht,* No. 150, June 29, 1917, p. 1, under the title, "Der Brief Grimms an Lindhagen."

bility of acting in favor of a general peace. Proceeding from this resolution our party approached the Swiss government expressing a wish that it would aid in the establishment of peace and, in particular, in all negotiations for peace. The first question, on the other hand, can find an answer only in the present internal situation of Russia. In order not to be subjected to accusations of transmitting facts which might be utilized by another belligerent government in its own interests, I must refrain from giving details. However, I shall betray no secret if I remark that every day in the chauvinist press there is a statement of the fact, which is to a certain degree being ratified by the Provisional government itself, that the present situation, from the military, economic, and social points of view, is intolerable and that reorganization is necessary, which, however, cannot be accomplished for several weeks. But whereas some persons demand reorganization in order to continue the war, others desire it in the interests of an early peace. This is not merely my own conviction but also the point of view of a large majority of socialists with whom I have had the opportunity to speak. This reorganization, which could alone prevent a final catastrophe, is a premise for an early termination of war, and only a hastening of peace may save the revolution, consolidate its results, and resist the counter-revolution.[92]

THE INTERNATIONAL SOCIALIST COMMITTEE REPORT ON THE GRIMM CASE

[Declaration of the Investigating Commission Appointed by the International Socialist Committee, July 5, 1917][93]

The Commission to investigate Comrade Grimm's case, which was appointed by the International Socialist Committee, has examined the telegrams exchanged between Grimm and Hoffmann and the accusations against Grimm, and has heard Comrade Grimm and the witnesses.

It submits to the Third Zimmerwald Conference the following findings and conclusions in this case.

[92] A. Balabanoff tells in her recollections that once when they were passing through the empty streets of Petrograd after the excitement of the March revolution had subsided, Grimm told her in a very serious tone, bordering on despair: "Do you know, Angelica, that unless peace is concluded very soon, much blood, proletarian blood especially, will flow in these streets." Balabanoff adds: "I had to remind myself and others of Grimm's words, his tone, and the expression of his face; this is the only extenuating fact which can be brought up: the fear for the destiny of the revolution drove Grimm to commit his irresponsible deed." (A. Balabanoff, *Erinnerungen und Erlebnisse*, p. 148.)

[93] "Erklärung der Untersuchungskommission in der Angelegenheit des Genossen R. Grimm," *I.S.K. Nachrichtendienst*, No. 13, July 8, 1917, pp. 1–2.

I. Comrade Grimm dispatched a telegram on May 27 from Petrograd to the Swiss Federal Councilor Hoffmann through the Swiss Minister Odier.

He took that step without having discussed it either with Comrade Angelica Balabanoff, the member of the International Socialist Committee, who was at that time present in Petrograd, or with representatives of the Russian Zimmerwald parties. Later on, when the matter appeared in the press, he also failed to notify the Russian comrades in Petrograd that he had sent that telegram to Hoffmann.

II. According to his testimony, Grimm had in view only the obtaining of information concerning the war aims of all the governments.

But Comrade Grimm did not confine himself to asking the Federal Councilor Hoffmann only that simple question about the war aims of the governments; moreover, in his telegram he spoke of the dangers which a German offensive would have for the peace negotiations and of the necessity of making out passports for the delegates to the international conference of the Soviet of Workers' deputies. These various allusions suggest that Grimm through his telegram wanted to give a stimulus to the peace negotiations.

In no way did it [the telegram] concern *a separate peace* between Germany and Russia but, on the contrary, *general* peace negotiations between all the governments.

The Commission does not consider it to be its task to investigate what aims the Federal Councilor Hoffmann had in mind in his answer. But it declares that there are no reasons to believe that Grimm acted according to a previously established understanding with Hoffmann; this stand has also been taken by Grimm himself. Owing to the personal relations which exist in Switzerland between the members of Parliament of the opposition and the state authorities, it was possible for Grimm to address Hoffmann without some previous conference.

That Grimm acted as an agent in the *interest of German imperialism is supported by no fact known to the Commission.* But Grimm's determined, three-year struggle against German imperialism, the support which he has always rendered to the German opposition, for which reason he has been attacked for three years in the German press as an *agent of the Entente,* and the contents of *Grimm's* telegram mentioned above speak against this possibility. The investigating Commission believes the most important motive of Grimm's action to be his *concern about the fate of the Russian revolution,* which Grimm considered to be threatened by a further continuation of the war and which he wanted to rescue through peace negotiations.

III. The investigating Commission regards as high-handed and as something *for which the Zimmerwald movement must decline all respon-*

sibility the fact that Grimm undertook to act without the knowledge of either the members of the International Socialist Committee present in Petrograd or the representatives of the Russian Zimmerwald parties, who doubtless would have prevented him from sending the telegram. The Commission takes this attitude not only because Grimm's action gave the enemies of Zimmerwald an opportunity to interpret the [Zimmerwald] movement, which was directed against *all* imperialist governments, as being the instrument of one government but also because it considers this action fundamentally impermissible.

The investigating Commission declares that recourse to secret diplomatic methods in order to bring about peace, as practiced by Grimm, is contrary to the nature of the Zimmerwald movement.

Signed by:

> HÖGLUND, Sweden; KIRKOV, Bulgaria; LANG, Switzerland; LINDHAGEN, Sweden; OLAUSSEN, Norway; ORLOVSKY, Russia; RADEK, Poland

B. THE ZIMMERWALD MOVEMENT UNDER NEW LEADERSHIP

On Grimm's resignation from the chairmanship of the International Socialist Committee, Höglund, on behalf of the Swedish Left S.D.L. party, stated on June 20, 1917, that the Presidium of the party and the Swedish S.D. Youth League had appointed a committee of three—Zöta Höglund, C. N. Carleson, and Ture Nerman—"to take care temporarily of the affairs of the International Socialist Committee."[94] As has been mentioned in an earlier chapter, Höglund and Nerman had taken part in the formation of the Zimmerwald Left group and they and Carleson were determined opponents of social patriotism. Standing as they did somewhat to the left of Grimm, they were less inclined than he to compromise with socialists of more moderate views. Under their guidance the I.S.C. became less well disposed toward the general conference called by the Russian Soviets. This became apparent in meetings with delegates of the Soviet Executive Committee who came to Sweden in connection with the Soviet conference project, as has been described earlier in this chapter.

The first meeting, held in the office of *Stormklockan* on

---

[94] *I.S.K. Nachrichtendienst*, No. 9, June 20, 1917, p. 5. The first act of this Committee was to recall Balabanoff from Russia (*ibid.*, p. 6).

July 3, was primarily for the purpose of an exchange of opinion on the general international situation and the prospects of the Zimmerwald movement in the various countries.[95] In addition to the Soviet delegates, Goldenberg, Rozanov, and Smirnov, there were present: Kirkov (Bulgaria); Y. Sirola (Finland); Kautsky, Haase, Louise Zietz, and Oscar Cohn (Germany); Lindström, Lindhagen, and Höglund (Sweden); Olaussen (Norway); Lang (Switzerland); Orlovsky, Radek, Hanecki (Bolsheviks); and Boris Reinstein (the Socialist Labor party of the United States). In her account of this meeting Balabanoff writes that she, Orlovsky, and Reinstein stressed the fact that the Soviet invitation was too inclusive, since it would admit the majority parties to the conference. Goldenberg replied that the Soviet had made no conditions whatever and was ready to admit the majority parties, who, in fact, had been invited along with the minorities. Most of those present then declared themselves against sending delegates to a conference so constituted, and Radek announced that the Bolsheviks had decided to withdraw from the Zimmerwald movement if it should decide to take part in the conference called by the Soviets and the Dutch-Scandinavian Committee. Haase, on the other hand, declared that the German Independent Socialists would attend, whereupon Balabanoff pointed out that the International Socialist Committee would not be bound by the declarations of either the Bolsheviks or the Independent Socialists, since only a general conference was competent to decide this matter. The discussion was continued the following day, in the absence of the Soviet representatives, and it was decided to hold the Zimmerwaldist Conference a few days before the general conference called by the Soviet; but, should the latter conference not take place, the Zimmerwaldists would meet as soon as possible.[96]

---

[95] *I.S.K. Nachrichtendienst*, No. 13, July 8, 1917, pp. 5–6.

[96] Balabanoff, "Die Zimmerwalder Bewegung .... ," in Grünberg, *Archiv* ...., XII, 372–73; *The Call* (London), No. 67, July 19, 1917, p. 3; *Berner Tagwacht*, No. 157, July 7, 1917, p. 3.

At another meeting on July 9, Rusanov and Ehrlich tried to persuade Balabanoff, Höglund, and Carleson that the I.S.C. should join the Soviet representatives and the Dutch-Scandinavian Committee in signing the invitation to the general socialist conference at Stockholm and thus inferentially endorse the platform on which the conference was to be summoned. No decision was made at this meeting; but two days later the International Socialist Committee, without flatly refusing to aid the Soviet representatives, officially declined to take part in the preparatory work for the general conference. Thus the invitation issued on July 12 for the socialist conference at Stockholm on August 15 was signed only by the joint Russian-Dutch-Scandinavian Committee.[97] On the announcement of this date, the I.S.C. put the time of meeting of the Third Zimmerwald Conference on August 10. This date was again changed at a meeting of Zimmerwaldists on August 1. Present were: Lindhagen, Lindström, and Ström (Sweden); A. Ermansky (Russia); Sirola (Finland); J. Eads How (United States); Ledebour (Germany); Radek and Hanecki (representing both the Social Democracy of Poland and Lithuania and the Russian Bolsheviks); and Balabanoff, secretary of the I.S.C. By this time the general Stockholm Conference had once more been postponed because of the refusal of passports, and the Zimmerwaldists, therefore, announced that their conference would be held on September 5, regardless of the plans of the Russian-Dutch-Scandinavian Committee.[98]

The refusal of the International Socialist Committee to identify itself with the Soviet conference project caused some criticism in Russia when the report of these negotiations by the Soviet foreign delegation was published. *Izvestiia*[99] declared that Balabanoff and Radek were doing everything possible to hinder the meeting of the international conference and

---

[97] *Vorwärts,* No. 190, July 14, 1917, pp. 1–2.

[98] Balabanoff, "Die Zimmerwalder Bewegung ....," in Grünberg, *Archiv ....,* XII, 395–96.

[99] No. 107, July 2, 1917, pp. 2–3.

questioned the right of these two with Höglund and Carleson to speak for the Zimmerwald groups, since the German, French, English, Italian, and Swedish Zimmerwald groups had already accepted the invitation of the Soviets. As will appear in later documents, by no means all these had accepted the Soviet invitation without reservations. The I.S.C. denied any intention of hindering the work of the Soviet Foreign Delegation and stated that their refusal to take part in the preparatory work was based on reasons of a fundamental nature.[100]

In various circular letters the I.S.C. expounded its point of view and called particular attention to the changes in the policy of the Russian Provisional government and of the Soviets, which had approved Kerensky's disastrous offensive. These changes of policy in Russia contributed to the defeat of the Stockholm project, as did the results of the Inter-Allied Socialist Conference at London, August 28–29, and the Blackpool Trade Union Congress—which proved, according to the I.S.C., that the general conference had failed to meet not only because of the refusal of passports but because of the attitude of the majority socialists.[101]

PEACE WITHOUT ANNEXATIONS

[Statement of the International Socialist Committee][102]

When the First Zimmerwald Conference coined the slogan, "Peace without annexations or indemnities," it was ridiculed on all sides. How ridiculous! Would anyone believe that after such fighting the boundary lines could remain unchanged? Would anyone share the childish opinion that the vanquished side should not be responsible for the damages caused by its war and should not pay for them? This was the cry of all camps of social patriots and it was explained in profound treatises how ostensibly absurd the Zimmerwald formula was.

---

[100] I.S.K. Nachrichtendienst, No. 18, August 12, 1917, pp. 5–6. In this article the accuracy of many details of the report to the Soviet is challenged.

[101] Ibid., No. 23, September 24, 1917, p. 3; see also No. 20, August 20, 1917, pp. 1–2.

[102] "Friede ohne Annexionen," ibid., No. 11, June 26, 1917, pp. 1–2.

More than a year has elapsed since that time. The end of the war is not in sight, and in the meantime the Russian revolution has taken place. In this connection, opinions on peace without annexations and indemnities have also changed. Some see that in spite of all intentions of conquest nothing will result from the war; others feel that it is impossible to conclude a pact with the Russian revolution, at least without seeming to renounce annexations and indemnities. Now, the picture has changed essentially. This change is convenient for those who have rallied round the International Socialist Bureau at The Hague and who, so far, have not moved one finger and have willingly delivered the institution of the International as hostage to Anglo-French imperialism. It is now convenient for them to attempt to restore the International, which, according to the testimony of Huysmans and others, has never been so virile as when the workers in the belligerent countries were executing each other in the interests of the propertied classes. The Zimmerwald formula suddenly was respected and now the slogan "peace without annexations and indemnities" can be heard from all social patriots.

However, it must be recognized that some caution is advisable at all times if people who so far have been extreme opponents of a slogan suddenly become enthusiastic over it and adopt it as a means of enlisting support for their policy. This is true also of peace without annexations and especially of the ardent efforts of the social patriots, who now, after three years of war, are granting mutual amnesty at an international conference and hatching out well-calculated peace formulas for the diplomacy of the governments.

Truly speaking, the formula of "peace without annexations and indemnities" has today become a phrase intended to deceive the workers once more as it has done practically every day for the last three years.

"Peace without annexations!" shout the Hendersons, the Vanderveldes, the Thomases; but without doubt this means that Alsace-Lorraine should be handed over to France, Trient and Triest to the Italians, and Transylvania to the Rumanians.

"Peace without annexations!" reply the German social patriots. But who wants to believe that, as Scheidemann said in his last interpellation in the German Reichstag, all boundary lines will be left unchanged after this abominable conflict?

"Peace without annexations!" twitter the government socialists of Bulgaria, though none of them would object to Dobrudja and Macedonia being under Bulgarian dominance.

"Peace without annexations" solemnly announces the Second Provisional government of Russia and degrades this formula to emptiness by simultaneously calling for a counter-offensive.

So it is with indemnities. No war contributions, but compensation for damages—this is a matter of course!

It is clear that under these circumstances nothing can be done with merely the formula. Peace without annexations is not a criterion of the will for peace, nor is it a peace aim, so long as all parties concerned do not wish at the start to have rated as annexations the open or covert annexations which are included in programs of their governments. And here the facts show how important it was that the Second Zimmerwald Conference continued to pursue the policies of the first manifesto and no longer confined itself to a general war cry and a general peace aim, but indicated the *means* which might lead toward this peace and which must be applied if the working class wishes to emerge from the endless war. These means were described in the Kienthal manifesto: not diplomatic negotiations to determine the best peace formula, but war on war, break with civil peace, struggle against the governments by refusing war credits regardless of the strategic situation, withdraw from bourgeois Cabinets, demand an immediate armistice in the parliaments, at public meetings, in the press, through strikes and demonstrations.

Today these demands acquire special meaning. First it must be stated plainly that every international conference carries in itself the germ of death if it does not stand on the basis of revolutionary struggle. And since the conference which is being prepared by the Scandinavian Committee does not adhere to that basis, it can have no practical meaning for peace. Therefore it is all the more necessary that the Third Zimmerwald Conference state the facts clearly and plainly.

THE ATTITUDE OF THE INTERNATIONAL SOCIALIST COMMITTEE TOWARD THE PROPOSAL OF THE RUSSIAN SOVIETS FOR A SOCIALIST CONFERENCE AT STOCKHOLM

[Letter from Balabanoff to the Representatives of the Russian Soviet of Workers' and Soldiers' Deputies, July 11, 1917][103]

To the representatives of the Russian Soviet of Workers' and Soldiers' deputies

DEAR COMRADES!

With reference to our Conference of July 9, we repeat what we have already said and what has already been published in the press. In agreement with the affiliated parties, with which we have been able to discuss this matter, we have resolved to make our participation at the Conference called by the Workers' Soviet, dependent upon the decisions

---

[103] "Die I.S.K. und die Einberufung der Arbeiterrats Konferenz," *I.S.K. Nachrichtendienst*, No. 14, July 15, 1917, pp. 3–4.

of the Third Zimmerwald Conference, which will take place five days before your conference. At the Third Zimmerwald Conference it will be decided if and on what platform the organizations adhering to the International Socialist Committee are to take part in the conference called by the Workers' Soviet.

Regarding the inquiry as to whether or not our Committee is inclined to take part together with the Dutch-Swedish delegation in the *preparatory work* for the conference of the Workers' Soviet, the International Socialist Committee is of the opinion that because of the way the circular letter of the Workers' Soviet has been supplemented or rather altered— a letter which was to serve as the basis for the forthcoming conference— through the reply to Vandervelde, and the character of the delegations mentioned above which were attracted to the preparatory work, the conference will not be able to promote the international class struggle or aid the cause of proletarian peace. Whereas it was stated in the circular letter that the agreement between the parties with respect to breaking the civil peace was an inevitable condition for the development of the peace action, the Executive Committee of the Workers' Soviet declared in their reply to Vandervelde and Thomas,[104] who protested against the aforementioned passage of the circular letter, that this was a misunderstanding, that it was out of the question to make the participation of

---

[104] In reply to a letter by Vandervelde, Thomas, and De Brouckère addressed on May 22, 1917, to the Petrograd Soviet, the Executive Committee of the latter defined the meaning of "general peace without annexations and indemnities on the basis of the right of nations to self-determination" as a "manifestation of the desire for a stable peace, the conditions for which will be formulated so as to answer exclusively the interests of the toiling people .... only if this attitude prevails among the participants of the conference, may it become a turning point in the dreadful epopee of the three years of fratricidal slaughter of civilized peoples .... By recognizing the right of the nations to self-determination the participants of the conference can easily agree upon the future fate of Alsace-Lorraine as well as of the other regions. .... Likewise .... it will not be difficult to agree concerning the methods and amounts of compensation of the population in countries which were especially badly ruined and devastated by the war, as for instance Belgium, Poland, Galicia, Serbia, etc. .... It stands to reason that such compensation should have nothing in common with war contributions imposed upon a vanquished state. Concerning your statement that you cannot break the *union sacrée,* this statement must certainly rest upon a misunderstanding .... the Soviet of Workers' and Soldiers' deputies points out that it does not demand from any of the parties, as the preliminary condition for being invited to the conference that they should renounce their previous policy .... this would only create the appearance that there exist irreconcilable antagonisms, whereas in a joint discussion the spirit of proletarian solidarity might aid to find a solution which would be equally acceptable to all. Concerning your desire to attain a preliminary agreement between socialists of the Allied Powers, a preliminary conference from our point of view is unnecessary" .... ("Otvet Ispolnitelnago Komiteta T. T. Vandervelde, Toma, De-Brukeru." *Izvestiia,* No. 81, June 2, 1917, p. 5.)

parties in the congress of the Workers' Soviet dependent on any conditions. The only condition would be the pledge of the parties to submit themselves to the decision of the conference. This interpretation allows not only the participation of those who even today support civil peace and solidarity with the governments and the ruling classes but also the possibility that precisely this tendency will have the upper hand at the conference in opposition to the tendency of the Zimmerwald minorities, which are opposing the majorities for the very reason that they consider the breaking of civil peace and the international class struggle to be the absolute premises of the proletarian struggle for peace—regard it even as a question of life and death to revolutionary socialism and have acted accordingly.

For the reasons mentioned the International Socialist Committee cannot take upon itself the responsibility for the platform and the composition of the conference called by the Workers' Soviet with the aid of the Dutch-Swedish delegation and consequently cannot take part in the preparatory work for that conference.

With party greetings for the International Socialist Committee.

ANGELICA BALABANOFF

INVITATION TO THE THIRD ZIMMERWALD CONFERENCE

[Issued by the International Socialist Committee, July 18, 1917][105]

To the affiliated parties and groups:

DEAR COMRADES!

In fulfillment of the decisions which have already been published, the International Socialist Committee invites its affiliated parties to the Third Zimmerwald Conference which will be held at Stockholm on August 10, 1917, and the days following. We designate the following provisional agenda:

Report of the International Socialist Committee.

The Zimmerwald parties and the proletarian peace movement in the belligerent countries.

Attitude toward the conference of the Workers' Soviet.

Grimm's case.

The conditions for participation in the conference as stated in *Bulletin* No. 3 are valid.

In consideration of the growing significance of the proletarian women's movement for peace and socialism and the resulting urgent necessity of co-ordinating the class demands of the feminine proletarians

---

[105] "Dritte Zimmerwalder Konferenz," *I.S.K. Nachrichtendienst*, No. 15, July 22, 1917, p. 1.

of all the countries on the basis of decisions of the International Socialist Women's Conference at Berne, 1915, we ask, in agreement with the
International Secretary of the socialist women, Comrade Klara Zetkin,
the parties and organizations affiliated with us to delegate·to the Third
Zimmerwald Conference women comrades also or to induce the socialist
women's organizations to elect delegates from their ranks to an international conference of socialist women which is to be held at Stockholm
in connection with the Third Zimmerwald Conference.

CONFERENCES WITH THE ZIMMERWALDISTS AND WITH THE DUTCH-SCANDINAVIAN COMMITTEE

[Report of the Foreign Delegation of the All-Russian Congress of Soviets][106]

On the day they reached Stockholm, Goldenberg, Rozanov, and
Smirnov were invited to the conference of Zimmerwaldists which was
attended by the Berne Committee, the German minority, the Swedish
Lefts, the Bolsheviks, and Kirkov, a "Narrow" [Bulgarian] socialist.

The agenda concerned preparations for the Zimmerwald Conference.
When asked, the delegation replied: that it would not take part in the
preparatory work of the Zimmerwald Conference; that its task was to
prepare for a general conference; and that it attended this meeting for
purposes of securing information and of explaining the platform and
tasks (the aims) of the general conference called by the Soviet of
Workers' and Soldiers' deputies (in order to gain the co-operation of the
Berne Committee). Radek's proposal to discuss the question of the
conference of the Soviet of Workers' and Soldiers' deputies was accepted.

Radek was the first to take the floor. He spoke against the platform
of the appeal and the letter-reply (of the Executive Committee) to Vandervelde, De Brouckère, and Thomas, finding that these documents were
contradictory. (The policy of the Soviet was not clear and was inconsistent.)

The delegation stated that, according to its fixed policy, a break with
civil peace should not be made a preliminary condition [of participation
in the general socialist conference] but that agreement to comply with
whatever decision the conference should make should be demanded.

In their speeches, Radek (Hanecki) and Kirkov pointed out that
class struggle has not been sufficiently emphasized in the platform of the

---

[106] "Otchet zagranichnoi delegatsii sezda sovetov," *Izvestiia*, No. 106, July 1,
1917, pp. 6–7. This is a revised text of Rozanov's telegram to the Petrograd Soviet.
Insertions given in parentheses have been supplied from the text of Rozanov's
telegram as it appears in A. Shliapnikov, "Fevralskaia revoliutsiia i evropeiskie
sotsialisty," *Krasnyi Arkhiv*, III (XVI), 1926, pp. 27–29. There are other stylistic
differences between the two texts, but the meaning conveyed in them is the same

Soviets; they considered a general conference with the participation of the majority [socialists] inacceptable and reproached the Soviet of deputies with hampering the revolutionary movement in the west.

After repeated replies by the delegation, the German minority declared that it had decided to take part in the conference of the Soviets of Workers' and Soldiers' deputies. (Radek declared: "In no case are we going to the conference.")

Balabanoff also criticized the platform of the Soviet. Other members of the Berne Committee did not express themselves.

The delegation did not obtain a final reply from the Berne Committee as to whether or not it would take part in the calling of the conference.

A few days later informal conferences with the Dutch-Scandinavian Committee began. Significant difficulties were also encountered in this Committee. The pourparlers lasted several days and were attended by the entire delegation.

The Dutch-Scandinavian Committee raised the question of definitely deciding upon a peace formula. The delegation succeeded in convincing it that this would be anticipating the decisions of the [general socialist] conference and would therefore be out of place. The Dutch-Scandinavian Committee seemed to think that these decisions should not be binding [on the participants]. Branting (Huysmans) and Vliegen said that such a condition would create difficulties for France and England.

Troelstra, who occupied a conciliatory position, said that the obligation to follow the decisions of the conference could not be realized if the decisions were not in the interests of the rank and file members of some party or other. [He said that] a party could pledge to carry out only that decision for which it had voted.

The delegation of the Soviet of Workers' and Soldiers' deputies replied that it was bound by the instructions set forth in the appeal of March 14.[107] It believed, however, that in pourparlers with individual parties it would support the idea of making the decisions of the conference binding. [It also believed that] this fact should be mentioned in the invitations [to the conference].

Branting and Vliegen insisted that the question of the origin of the war should be included on the agenda.

The delegation finally obtained the exclusion of this question.

The question of the Berne Committee's participation provoked very great disputes. The Dutch-Scandinavian Committee was inclined to oppose it, though it agreed that the representation of minorities was necessary. In spite of the absence of a reply from the Berne Committee, the delegation considered it to be its duty to defend the latter's participa-

107 Complete text in F. A. Golder, *Documents of Russian History, 1914–1917,* pp. 325–26.

tion. Acting in accordance with its own mandates the delegation obtained the consent of the Dutch-Scandinavian Committee concerning this question.

As regards the question of establishing a preparatory organization commission at Stockholm, the Dutch-Scandinavian Committee proposed that the delegation should join [this commission]. The delegation would not accept this proposal.

According to the delegation's proposal a commission of three parts should be organized, namely: the Russian delegation, the Dutch-Scandinavian Committee, and the Berne Committee, if the latter would agree.

However, since the Berne Committee did not answer, the delegation took the initiative in suggesting that the [Berne] Committee should meet on July 9. The following were present: Balabanoff, Höglund, and Carleson.

The latter two are co-opted members.

The delegation of the Soviet of Workers' and Soldiers' deputies was represented by Rusanov (Rozanov) and Ehrlich. It explained once more the position of the Soviet and replied to many questions of a fundamental nature.

Noticing that there was prejudice against it, the delegation permitted itself to point out that the majority of the parties belonging to the Zimmerwald movement had already expressed their wish to take part in the conference of the Soviets. Balabanoff replied that such decisions prior to the Zimmerwald Conference constituted rude violations of discipline.

But still our delegation received no final answer [from the Berne Committee]. It was said that the Berne Committee understood the issue and had promised to inform the delegation of its decision the next day, but on the next day no reply was forthcoming. This placed the delegation in an embarrassing position. Once more it tried to induce the Berne Committee to take part in the preparatory work.

The delegation succeeded in finding out only that the reply of the Berne Committee would be in the negative. The delegation endeavored to arrange another conference, but this was impossible on account of the departure of the (two) members of the Committee.

In the meantime an agreement was reached with the Dutch-Scandinavian Committee upon the principles mentioned above.

The delegation decided, in the event of a (final) refusal by the Berne Committee, to issue simultaneously a formal invitation to all parties, the signed agreement between the delegation and the Dutch-Scandinavian Committee, and a statement of regret that the Berne Committee had declined [the invitation to work on the preparatory commission] and for that reason the minorities could not be attracted through their center [the Berne Committee] to the preparatory work.

The delegation sets itself the task of assuring all the minority groups of representation [at the general socialist conference].

The delegation will go to the Zimmerwald Conference, which is to take place five days prior to the general [conference], in order to invite [its participants] to attend the general conference.

The delegation considers that the participation (besides a section of the Russian Zimmerwaldists) of the German minority (the Independent Social Democratic party) in our conference is assured, including even the Spartakus group, the English and the French minorities, and the Italian party. The Dutch-Scandinavian Committee, consisting of official representatives of parties of the northern neutral countries, supplies the technical apparatus which is rather necessary for the calling [of the conference].

The time of convocation is August 15, new style.

The agenda: (1) World War and the International; (2) The peace terms of the International; (3) The means of realizing these terms and an early cessation of war.

(ROZANOV)

ATTITUDE OF THE INTERNATIONAL SOCIALIST COMMITTEE TOWARD THE STOCKHOLM CONFERENCE

[Statement of the International Socialist Committee][108]

In our letter to the representatives of the Workers' and Soldiers' Soviet we have already stated the reasons why the International Socialist Committee could not come to an understanding with the Dutch-Scandinavian Committee with regard to participating in the work of calling the conference of the Workers' Soviet. Our attitude was also a logical consequence and application of the Zimmerwald decisions. It is hardly necessary, therefore, to give any further explanations to our affiliated parties. In the meantime the proclamation[109] published on behalf of the combined committees of the organizations mentioned above provides an-

108 "Die I.S.K. und die vom russischen Arbeiterrate und holländisch-skandinavischen Komité einberufene Konferenz," *I.S.K. Nachrichtendienst*, No. 15, July 22, 1917, pp. 1–3.

109 On July 12, 1917, the delegation of the Petrograd Soviet of Workers' and Soldiers' deputies and the Dutch-Scandinavian Committee issued a joint invitation to the International Socialist Conference to be held on August 15 and the following days at Stockholm. The purpose of the conference would be "to bring about an early peace without annexations and indemnities, based upon the right of nations for self-determination." The announcement was also made in the invitation concerning the formation of an Organization Bureau for the calling of the conference. "Einladung zur internationalen Sozialistenkonferenz," *Vorwärts*, No. 190, July 14, 1917, p. 1.

other proof of the fact of how few fundamental and tactical points of contact exist between these organizations and the International Socialist Committee, and that co-operative preparatory work, which presupposes a fusion of the International Socialist Committee with the Organization Bureau which had been formed, is fundamentally and practically impossible.

In the proclamation which is to be used to rally world socialism under the banner of the Russian revolution after three years of imperialist frenzy, after a complete failure of the majority of the parties affiliated with the Second International, no word is said about the basis upon which a conference which is destined for world historic action is to convene and to act. The unavoidable contradictions in which the initiators of the conference have already become entangled find their pregnant expression, either because the position of the Workers' Soviet has become highly obscure and ambiguous, especially after its advances to the majority socialists, or as a result of fusion with the Dutch-Scandinavian Committee. On the one hand, the initiators assert that the International must compel all parties and all trade union organizations to deny all co-operation with their governments, yet do not dare to consider acceptance of the idea of breaking with the civil peace to be a premise for participating in the conference. And this, in spite of the fact that an ever-growing number of socialists who belonged to the Second International consider that the preservation of civil peace hinders international class action and even consider it to be a crime and a betrayal of the proletarian cause and of peace. At the pourparlers on July 3, to which the International Socialist Committee had invited the three representatives of the Soviet of Workers' and Soldiers' deputies who were present at Stockholm, they [these representatives] declared that they would attend it purely for the purpose of securing information. They repeatedly emphasized, when the contradiction between the first proclamation and the letter to Vandervelde was discussed, that the establishment of prerequisites was out of the question, that a concession to the French majority had been necessary, and that this concession might eventually be followed by other admissions with respect to other majorities.

When on the 9th [of July] the delegates of the Workers' Soviet (in the meantime they had had no pourparlers with the International Socialist Committee, while their pourparlers with the Swedish-Dutch Committee on the day mentioned had already neared their conclusion) invited the International Socialist Committee to a conference which was held on the 9th in the quarters of the International Socialist Committee, they repeated that premises for attending the conference were out of the question. We have briefly summarized the situation once more because the Russian initiators of the general conference are emphasizing that they regret that they were unable to win over the International Socialist Committee for the preparatory work of their conference. We state in this connection that this might have been possible if, when the principles were laid down, the representatives of the Workers' and Soldiers' Soviet had indicated a possibility or a desire to adapt themselves at least to the Zimmerwald platform. If there had been such a possibility or a desire, the representatives of the Workers' Soviet should have invited the International Socialist Committee to a conference at a time when fundamental changes and decisions were yet possible and not only when the pourparlers with the Dutch-Scandinavian Committee or the fundamental policies of the program of united action had been already established.

This we note parenthetically.

Meanwhile events are developing at a furious rate. Especially in Russia the situation is becoming greatly accentuated. The parties which are serious about peace and the re-establishment of the International have no *alternative*. They confront an historic *fact* or, as our German party comrades have appropriately said, "an international understanding which actually furthers the possibility of peace among the peoples and does not obscure the plans of the governments is possible only between consistent adherents of internationalism."

The road toward peace is through Zimmerwald.

THE RUSSIAN-DUTCH-SCANDINAVIAN COMMITTEE, THE PROVISIONAL GOVERNMENT, AND THE ENTENTE

[An Article by the International Socialist Committee on the Preparations for the Stockholm Conference, August 12, 1917][110]

The changes which the preparations for the conference called by the Russian-Dutch-Scandinavian Committee are undergoing reflect all those conditions and contradictions that lend the impending conference a social-diplomatic character. After all, what has remained of the first appeal the Workers' Soviet addressed some time ago to the socialists of all countries? The concessions which the Russian organizers [of the conference] are making daily to the government socialists have gradually killed the meaning and the spirit which animated the first appeal. This, of course, is not a coincidence but a direct, inevitable reaction to the events in Russia and to the role to which the Workers' Soviet is being doomed in the internal and external policy of Russia. The statements made by Lloyd George in his letter to Henderson are extremely characteristic, for he points directly to the fact that the changes in the internal policy of

---

[110] "Die Vorbereitungen zur Stockholmer Friedenskonferenz," *I.S.K. Nachrichtendienst*, No. 18, August 12, 1917, pp. 1–2.

Russia serve as an incentive to the Allied governments to change their attitude toward the impending conference. When the Soviet was still strong and spoke a socialist anti-imperialist language in the name of the Russian people, everybody had to listen to it. But now that the iron fist of Kerensky is directing the destinies of Russia, now that the voice and the will of the people are being suppressed with increasing brutality, now that the socialist parties of Russia and the erstwhile executives of the revolutionary people are being subjected to ever-growing humiliations, nobody has to pay attention to the organizers of the conference——. Undoubtedly most significant is the fact that the Russian government has informed Lloyd George that the conference which is being convened by the Soviet is not in the least binding upon official Russia, that it concerns only a party matter. Has not Lloyd George rendered a poor service to his colleagues in Russia by publishing these cynical statements of the petty bourgeois who are at the helm of the Russian revolution! What will be the attitude of the Soviet and of its advocates abroad to this statement? Will the Soviet be simply content with such an abasement? Will it for the sake of Kerensky-Plekhanov-Miliukov's policy submit to this death sentence without further ado?

That which Lloyd George and the representatives of the Russian government declare with brutal frankness is being advocated and fought for in a more or less disguised form by the government socialists of France and England. What is signified by the demand that the question of responsibilities be discussed first of all, if not an assurance to their own governments and the ruling classes that their "honor" and interests will be defended first of all by their socialist countrymen at the international gathering? The establishment of evidence that only one imperialist coalition is guilty of the war and that the others are merely innocent victims has for its purpose not merely an argument with the Scheidemanns-Davids, but also a "settling of accounts" with all the internationalist, revolutionary elements of socialism which regard the war as a consequence of capitalist development and consider all the governments equally responsible for the peoples' slaughter. At Stockholm the social diplomats will have to settle accounts also with their minorities; they [the social diplomats] will defend their governments before the masses in their own country and thereby continue to do what the Stuttgart resolution forbade the members of the Second International to do in case of war. The way in which the English and French government socialists seek permission of their governments and ruling classes, and even that of petty bourgeois public opinion, to go to Stockholm, and the guaranties which they are ready to produce testify plainly as to the intentions by which they are animated. Their patriotic loyalty must be affirmed at all costs. The English members of the International declare, as is known, that they would go to Stockholm precisely in order to prevent a too rapid conclusion of peace, whereas French participants in the anticipated Stockholm Conference declare that they attach concrete demands to their participation in the conference; hence, everything is done with the consent of and in agreement with their own diplomatic and imperialistic circles ———. In spite of all this, passports may still be refused them. This proves, among other things, how the governments treat their faithful fellow-workers and especially the organizers of the conference, the Russian allies ———.

Those workers who still hold on to the sacred union with their governments should also learn something from this episode. In spite of the fact that in England they have already manifested millions of times their desire to be represented at Stockholm, in spite of the fact that in France party organizations and trade unions are expressing the same desire, the solution of the question of being able to attend [the conference] is still left to the arbitrary decisions of the governments ———.

As regards Italy, the party there has never entered into any relation with the government and the refusal to grant passports will only sharpen its opposition. But what about France, England, and America?

Will the workers of these countries maintain civil peace any longer?

More important events than the Stockholm semiofficial peace conference depend on the answers of the workers to these questions (also of workers of countries in which passports are not being denied at this moment) ———.

THE SIGNIFICANCE OF THE ENTENTE SOCIALIST CONFERENCE AT LONDON AND THE TRADE UNION CONGRESS AT BLACKPOOL

[Statement by the International Socialist Committee][111]

The long-desired conference of the socialists from Allied countries[112] has decided that, for the present, it is impossible for the leaders of the labor movement to make a decision concerning the Stockholm affair. The gathering at Blackpool[113] has confirmed and strengthened this "decision." Three years of imperialist frenzy have not been sufficient to open the eyes of the workers of even the most democratic country and to induce

---

[111] "Nach Zimmerwald, " *I.S.K. Nachrichtendienst*, No. 21, September 2, 1917, pp. 2–5. The material contained in this issue of *Nachrichtendienst* indicates that it must have been published several days later than the date actually given by the publishers.

[112] The Inter-Allied Socialist Conference was held on August 28–29, 1917, at London.

[113] The British Trade Union Congress met on September 3, 1917, at Blackpool.

them to take independent class action. All that mankind, the working class especially, has experienced and lived through during this long war period, together with the vision of what inevitably awaits it, has been insufficient to put an end to the war: according to the workers' representatives, only the satisfying of the imperialist lust of the world rulers can do that. War aims should first be discussed and committees elected to decide whether to send delegates to the Stockholm Conference or to repudiate it! To the organizers of that conference this was a hint of the failure of that conference to meet—a hint which was furthermore superfluous, since only those who believe that politicians are incurably optimistic could pretend in the face of recent events that the Stockholm Conference will take place. Perhaps such persons will continue even now to assert this belief, undisturbed by the fact that in politics the *why's* and *if's* sometimes coincide, i.e., circumstances provide reasons. Of course it is not impossible that somehow and at some time there will be a meeting in Stockholm; but it will not be the same as the one that was planned, since for such a conference the date and the method of its organization is of decisive significance. It is precisely on account of the resistance which the calling of the conference has encountered that its postponement is not accidental but fundamental in character.

If the London pourparlers, as far as a concrete issue is concerned, have resulted in nothing new and unexpected, nevertheless they have had a certain significance and their effect has not remained unnoticed by the workers, precisely because of the disgraceful character of these pourparlers. It is unbelievable but true that workers' representatives, who in the year 1917, after thirty-seven months of the most horrible and rapacious of all modern wars, at a time when it has become commonplace in the bourgeois press to consider the war as a war conducted for imperialist reasons, at a time when the ruling classes do not conceal the fact that the working masses are being used merely as cannon fodder—because at the same time that the worker's patriotic spirit of self-sacrifice is being acclaimed his political and social rights are being cut down, and even abolished, in a dictatorial fashion—it is unbelievable that in spite of all this the workers' representatives and the socialists have declared that the time has not yet come for conferences on the opening of negotiations which would directly or indirectly hasten the conclusion of peace! This outcome of the long deliberations which has been awaited by countless people with anxiety and hope constitutes the most disgraceful of all the disgraceful documents so abundantly produced by this war. Those organizers of the Stockholm Conference and those participants in the London conferences, including the delegates of the Russian Workers' Soviet, who really desire peace will not only become poorer by one illusion but will regard the conferences at London and at Blackpool as having made the general situation considerably worse. Of course it is not difficult to foresee that (as is being asserted by the participants in the London pourparlers) in spite of the final official fiasco [of the London Conference] some good results have been attained, namely, the socialists of Allied countries have established "closer contact" with each other—for the decision to form a committee is at least a decision. Those who consider it more important to rouse the laboring masses than to settle diplomatic questions undiplomatically realize that, while the refusal of passports and Henderson's farce may in some way help to drive the workers to rise in opposition and may inspire the hope that the entire policy of the government may itself break down civil peace, the London pourparlers actually serve to reinforce civil peace. Those who refuse to grant passports and who pose as "guardians" of the laboring class require no other reasons to justify their own attitude than those provided by the workers' representatives. With what malicious joy, with what victorious class-consciousness will they, the worst enemies of the laboring class, point to the decisions of the workers themselves! But, as we have already said, how disgraceful the issue of the pourparlers has been surprises only those who refuse to accept the truth. Was it at all possible to reconcile the outspoken imperialism of some, the social patriotism of others, and the desire for peace of yet others by a concrete solution of concrete imperialistic questions? If such an attempt proved a total failure, even among the "Allies," it can easily be imagined what would be the outcome of a similar attempt made with the representatives of "hostile powers."

Not on the basis of a diplomatic-imperialist agreement but only through international class struggle can peace among the peoples be enforced, and socialists and workers' representatives who are faithful to their governments are not called upon, nor are they willing to hasten the conclusion of peace for which the peoples are thirsting. It is not really possible to unite the interests of the governments with those of the peoples. The role which the governments assign to the government socialists who are going to Stockholm is made sufficiently clear by Henderson's farce and the declarations of the French social patriots. May we be permitted to point out a characteristic opinion of an influential French review in which it is said that we owe "the Russian offensive to the efforts of Messrs. Thomas, Henderson, Vandervelde, and Root"; and, further, it says with regard to that same offensive: "The sky is beginning to clear up in the North. And this miracle has occurred without our socialists having to go to Stockholm, although their journey to Russia may not have been wasted."

The attempt to call a conference of socialists and workers' representatives has in the end shattered itself against the attitude of the workers' representatives themselves, who for imperialist-chauvinist reasons consider such a gathering to be "for the time being, premature." This disgraceful fact represents one side of the tragedy which the laboring class has had to endure for the last three years; but it also serves as an instructive example for both the workers who have become tired of their leaders and of the war and for the masses in general; it shows them that there is only one way out of this bloody chaos, namely, that which was pointed out at Zimmerwald two years ago: a return to international class struggle, a break with civil peace, the proletarian struggle in all countries carried out by proletarian methods, without considering the strategic-diplomatic prospects and desires of the imperialist governments. The masses will be forced more and more to take this road because of the general intolerable conditions and the challenging policy of the ruling classes, because the attempts to solve the world catastrophe by means of social diplomacy have been shipwrecked—the world catastrophe has been unchained by imperialism.

Therefore the Zimmerwald pourparlers which are to be opened at Stockholm at this sorrowful time will achieve their purpose through achieving a closer understanding among the revolutionary, socialist circles of all countries, and through unanimity in words and deeds, thus proving to the proletarians—who are being bled white—that imperialism which has conquered so much and so many has not been able to kill the spirit of international socialism. The Zimmerwaldists, in spite of persecutions by law and by the social patriots, and in spite of obstacles, have always worked in agreement with each other. The fact that every Zimmerwaldist organization at the conference cannot have its own representatives will not seriously weaken the political and practical significance of that conference, for the Zimmerwaldists are not gathering to discuss problems of tactics. Therefore the refusal of the governments to grant passports can influence the importance of their decisions only externally, that is, by making it difficult for them to assemble.

In the name of all those who desire to be with us but who are prevented from so doing by the political authorities, and sincerely hoping that we may succeed in doing our duty to its full measure and that our movement will prove adequate to the hopes that have been placed in us, we heartily welcome those few of our brothers in the struggle who have safely reached Stockholm.

C. The Zimmerwald Groups and the Stockholm Conference

The preceding pages have shown something of the attitude of the International Socialist Committee and of the Swedish

Zimmerwaldists toward the Stockholm project. This attitude did not, of course, reflect the position of all the parties and groups which had accepted the Zimmerwald resolutions. Zimmerwaldists of the Right were inclined to be conciliatory toward the plans of the Russian-Dutch-Scandinavian Committee, but those of the Left denounced Stockholm as a fraud perpetrated by social patriots and a betrayal of the interests of the workers. The documents which follow illustrate these various attitudes.

THE GERMAN *INTERNATIONALE* GROUP AND THE PROPOSED CONFERENCE

[Franz Mehring to Chkheidze, April 29, 1917][114]

Owing to external obstacles we are perhaps the last to extend our best wishes and brotherly greetings, whereas we should have been the first, since our orientation in Germany, the so-called *Internationale*, is struggling under the most difficult circumstances, on the same basis, with the same methods, and by applying the same tactics as you did before the glorious revolution crowned your struggle and your efforts with victory. We refrain from giving special expression to our delight, since your victory is our victory, a victory of that group of the proletariat of all countries which has remained faithful to socialism even in the crisis of war.

Not only is the revolution in Russia one of the greatest events of world history but, what is much more important, the role and the accomplishment of the class-conscious Russian proletariat in the revolution signifies the honorable salvation and assurance of international socialism. It shows what the proletariat in the belligerent countries can accomplish if it leads unswervingly a relentless class-struggle against the power of imperialism. It guarantees in all the civilized countries the victory of socialism which only yesterday was apparently rendered completely helpless.

At present the most burning task for all of us is to attain peace, and the proposed international conference at Stockholm is to serve this purpose. As German Social Democrats we protest most sharply against the admission to the conference of the so-called Social Democratic majority, i.e., the governmental socialists who rally around the party Presidium as a matter of principles as well as of expediency. We decline any par-

---

[114] Balabanoff, "Die Zimmerwalder Bewegung ....," Grünberg, *Archiv* ...., XII, 370–72.

ticipation in the conference with these elements and, in the interests of a proletarian peace and the resurrection of a real socialist International, we urge our Russian comrades and partisans to oppose with all their strength the admission of the German majority. At the conference this majority would in fact represent not socialism and not the German proletariat but the German government and its interests. Should the international proletariat take the cause of peace into its hands, as was demanded in your appeal to the peoples, which corresponded with our conviction, it could not do it in common with the belligerent imperialist governments or, what would amount to the same thing, with their secret representatives, who are at home sworn opponents of every independent mass activity of the workers and who act with the bourgeoisie as a bulwark of its class solidarity.

Furthermore, should the International, which has collapsed on account of the war, be revived through the proletariat's international activity in the struggle for peace, then from the start the social-imperialist elements must stay away from it because a united struggle against imperialism, led on an international basis, will and must form the central axis and even the very nature of the new International. And, finally, the agreement of the Russian comrades to the admission of Messrs. Südekum, Scheidemann, Legien, etc., to the Stockholm Conference would be a hard blow for international socialist thought in Germany and for our common cause. If this action were interpreted to mean that these persons were recognized as legitimate members of international socialism, this action would have an extremely confusing effect upon the enlightenment of the German workers, which has already proceeded far.

We are firmly convinced that our Russian friends will spare the German comrades this blow. What has been said above leads us to express the hope with which the *Internationale* group in Germany is animated, and I am sure that I may speak also in the name of my friends imprisoned and confined in the penitentiary, Comrades Luxemburg and Liebknecht.

In case external obstacles should prevent my friends and me from coming to the conference, I declare that no other delegation from Germany is permitted to represent us. We extend to you our hearty wishes for success on the road to the new difficult struggles which await you. Hail, the Russian revolution! May it serve as a guide to the international proletariat.

P.S. Dear Comrade Chkheidze! I beg you to make this letter known to the Soviet of Workers and Soldiers at an open meeting and also to the press.

THE GERMAN INDEPENDENT SOCIAL DEMOCRATIC PARTY AND THE STOCKHOLM CONFERENCE[115]

1. The Independent Social Democratic party of Germany sends its representatives to the Stockholm Conference.

2. It will not take part in the work of the Conference if the Russian socialists do not take part in it.

3. It will endeavor to hold a peace conference at Stockholm with the socialists of Russia, Italy, and the minority socialists of other belligerent states and if possible with the socialists of the neutral countries.

4. If in addition to Plekhanov's adherents representatives of other groups, especially of the Workers' and Soldiers' Soviet, take part in the conference, then it is the duty of our representatives to advocate their own points of view jointly with the representatives of these groups.

5. Should they fail to put through their points of view, then the minorities will have to adopt separate resolutions.

6. Under no circumstances should our party agree to a loose and vague resolution which tries to reconcile all points of view.

7. First of all it has to propagate struggle against the war policy of the governments—class struggle.

THE ITALIAN SOCIALIST PARTY AND THE STOCKHOLM CONFERENCE[116]

Whereas all the sections of the International (but, as was just and practical, not the other groups) were invited by the International Socialist Bureau to the Conference at Stockholm, and whereas it has still been impossible for the gatherings at Zimmerwald and Kienthal to establish a Third International, the Executive Committee decides, reserving the right to change this decision later, to attend the Conference and to invite all the Zimmerwald sections also to take part in the Conference in order to define the program and action of all sections with regard to reorganizing the International.

THE SWISS SOCIAL DEMOCRATIC PARTY AND THE STOCKHOLM CONFERENCE

[Resolution of the Party Congress at Berne, June 9–10, 1917][117]

PARTICIPATION IN THE INTERNATIONAL SOCIALIST BUREAU

The party Congress agrees with the criticism and condemnation by the Kienthal Conference of the International Socialist Bureau's attitude.

[115] A. Balabanoff, "Die Zimmerwalder Bewegung ....," Grünberg, *Archiv* ...., XII, 369–70.

[116] "Stellungnahme der Italiener," *Vorwärts*, No. 132, May 15, 1917, p. 1.

[117] "Ausserordentlicher Parteitag in Bern," *Berner Tagwacht*, No. 134, June 11, 1917, p. 1.

In order to restore the Socialist Workers' International it is necessary to break with the policy of tolerating those who have given up the class struggle and have thus renounced the decisions of the Second International; it is also necessary resolutely to condemn the policy of social patriots and social imperialists and energetically to proclaim the principles of the class struggle. The future International must be erected upon the mutualism of these principles and upon the will for joint action.

In consequence of this declaration the party congress decides to accept the invitation of the International Socialist Bureau to the peace conference only if the Third Zimmerwald Conference decides to take part in it.

THE ATTITUDE OF THE ZIMMERWALD GROUP OF THE FRENCH SOCIALIST PARTY ON WAR AND PEACE AND THE DUTY OF THE SOCIALIST INTERNATIONAL[118]

In reply to the questionnaire of the Dutch-Scandinavian Committee the Zimmerwald group of the French Socialist party declares that:

"The present war is a brilliant confirmation of the theoretical and practical postulates of socialism and an indisputable proof of how right the socialists of all countries were in assuming the position which they defended before the war. As its first step the reconstituted International must assert the proved socialist principles. Those members of the International who have deviated from the tactics which were in force within the International before the war should return to them and if they do not do so they should be excluded from the International.

It is as irrevocably true as ever that wars are caused by the rivalry of the ruling classes of countries which take part in war and that wars mark the closing of a whole epoch in history.

The war that we have endured for the last three years was foreseen by the socialists; they pointed out its threatening danger at Basel and attempted to unite the international proletariat in defense against it. The causes of the war and the responsibility for it were established both in the resolutions of the international congresses and in the writings of the most prominent champions of socialism. To judge such a phenomenon as war on the basis of recent events would only contradict socialist conceptions and even modern historical methods.

Moreover, as the light of truth illuminates the immediate causes of the present conflict, the responsibility of all the governments appears more and more to be of a general and a more oppressing nature.

[118] "Die französischen Zimmerwaldienner und der Krieg," *I.S.K. Nachrichtendienst*, No. 20, August 20, 1917, pp. 4–7; also, "Réponse de la fraction du Parti socialiste (S.F.I.O.), adhérente aux conférences de Zimmerwald et de Kienthal, au questionnaire de Stockholm," *Stockholm*, pp. 339–43.

No metaphysics, no rhetorics, no hairsplitting, no political cleverness can abolish the imperialist character of the war. The war was and remains for all governments a war for the greatest possible conquests. The period of immediate responsibilities lasted to the very moment of the official breaking of the state of peace which isolated from each other the masses involved in the war; the establishment of these responsibilities—after all, a secondary matter and one which would not be fixed by the mere refusal of arbitration before a bourgeois tribunal—belongs to history.

So long as the peoples permit their destinies to be determined by class governments which are the authors of the bloody clashes between the peoples and are interested in concealing their own responsibility, it will be impossible to establish the real responsibility in every single case at the decisive hour. Our group therefore cannot share the standpoint of those who wish to make the attitude of socialists toward war dependent on the solution of the question of responsibility. Our group opposes with all its energy the attempt to make the convocation of the International dependent on a preliminary agreement of all its affiliated parties with regard to one disputed point—that in the event of war the proletariat of the attacked nation has the right to claim the help of all nations, belligerent as well as neutral.

The duty of socialists with respect to the war, the nature of which was known and asserted to be only imperialistic, has been plainly described by the international congresses. This has been stated in the following passage which was adopted at Stuttgart and has been taken up again in the resolution of the Basel Congress: "In case war should break out anyway, it is the duty of socialists to intervene in favor of its speedy termination and to utilize, with all their power, the economic and political crisis created by the war to rouse the deepest strata of the peoples and, thereby, to hasten the downfall of capitalist class rule."

The socialist parties should have maintained their independence with regard to their governments and strengthened their socialist and revolutionary propaganda against the war and capitalism. Either the re-established International will impose this duty upon the parties or it will accomplish nothing.

We subscribe to the peace formula of the Russian socialists which, by the way, had been proclaimed in Zimmerwald and Kienthal: immediate peace without annexations and without war indemnities. Our group clearly recognizes this peace formula in accordance with its spirit and its text and rejects all phrases which serve to conceal annexations and indemnities.

This signifies that the territories which have been occupied in the present war should be completely evacuated. Our group knows, of course, that the restoration of the nation inside the prewar country limits leaves certain problems unsolved; but it is of the opinion that every new partitioning resulting from the victory of one or of another belligerent coalition would be a still more fatal cause of future war.

Referring to the point of view of the French socialists, who have always asserted that they would never support a war for the return of Alsace-Lorraine to France, our group does not subordinate its desire for peace to the solution of this question by means of war, a question that may be solved only by an agreement between the nations which have to decide their own destiny.

The demand that only free peoples may decide their own political destiny should be applied to all those nationalities which before the war were attached to one of the groups of belligerent countries, for none of the capitalist governments that are struggling for world hegemony offers sufficient guaranties of sincerity and independence with regard to those classes whose privileges they uphold. The difficulties which "liberal" England is encountering with regard to Ireland show how a class government is incapable of solving the problem of nationality.

Since only by agreement with the peoples concerned can the existing conflicts be solved in a manner which would insure lasting peace, the Socialist International must, in accordance with the resolutions of the international congresses, strive with all its power to realize the transfer of power to the peoples.

Our group understands the slogan "without war indemnities" to mean an absolute rejection of any kind of contribution which might become a burden to the people either as a war indemnity or as war reparation.

Since we have always recognized the collective responsibility of the ruling classes, we can therefore find only one way of disposing of war indemnities—by apportioning them among the ruling classes as indemnities for the harm they have caused through their guilt and their desire for profits.

The duty of restoring the small countries which were unwillingly drawn into the war devolves upon those capitalists of the large states who caused the war.

The ruling classes are unable to solve the national problem which has resulted from centuries of violence and plundering; they are likewise unable to assure a "lasting peace" by periodically settling the international conflicts which are produced by economic competition within capitalist society.

If in the interior of each country legislation is inadequate to solve the conflicts between capital and labor, if the most important labor laws require the energetic pressure of the organized proletariat in order to be put into effect, how can this legislation, the existence and sanctions of which are hypothetical and whose representatives are at the same time judges and litigants, be adequate to settle international disputes?

The political democratization of individual countries, although it can promote their internal development, offers no sufficient guaranty of peace.

The example of the struggle between capital and labor and an insight into the condition of the two countries, England and Germany, which at present are standing at the head of the competing imperialist coalitions, prove that even where the interests of the ruling classes are at stake the political form of government usually called democratic is not always profitable for the laboring class.

In this question, as in all others, our group remains faithful to the standpoint which it held before the war.

Among the adherents of the Socialist International the opinion always prevailed, even when we supported the pacifist endeavors of other circles, that the best guaranty of peace lies in an international agreement within the international laboring class. Similarly it was always their opinion that the best court of arbitration is the Socialist International, which has condemned to death the capitalism of all countries and has appealed to the proletarians of all countries to unite in order to carry out this death sentence. The Socialist International was also of the opinion that the only force which is capable of attaining and guaranteeing peace is the force of the organized proletariat, of all countries, standing independently in opposition to imperialism.

Therefore, standing on the basis of the Zimmerwald resolutions, the group of French Socialists can consider a union of states composed of representatives of the ruling classes no more capable of guaranteeing peace than it would be capable of bringing about the liberation of the oppressed peoples, the victory of justice over violence, and, in general, a righteous solution of the problems which have grown out of capitalism and war. Only a society of free peoples, determining their own destiny, i.e., a socialist society, can attain this aim.

We remind you that in Amsterdam in 1914 [1904] the entire International declared that the Socialist party, revolutionary in the best meaning of the word, could not approve any measure adopted to assure the power of the ruling classes and rejected all co-operation between the party and the government during war as well as during peace.

The action of the Socialist International must be the exertion by the masses of external pressure upon the ruling classes.

On the whole, our group demands the return to the resolutions of the International and to the revolutionary tradition of the class-conscious organized proletariat of all countries.

THE INDEPENDENT LABOUR PARTY AND THE STOCKHOLM CONFERENCE

[From the Executive of the I.L.P. to the Executive of the Labour Party, August 21, 1917][119]

To the Executive of the Labour party

GENTLEMEN:

In view of the decision of the Labour Party Conference to-day to exclude the separate representation of the I.L.P. at the Stockholm Conference, I am requested to submit to you the views and decisions of the Independent Labour Party thereon.

We decline for the following reasons to accept or abide by its decisions:

1. We deny the right of the Labour Party Conference, which, like the I.L.P., is only a section of the International, to determine British representation at an International Conference, or to take away the right of any other section.

2. We are determined to hold our position in the International Socialist movement as a separate section, entitled to all the rights attached to a separate section.

3. We decline to merge our representation at the Stockholm Conference in that of the Labour Party, because if we were to do so we should have renounced our right to separate existence in the International.

4. We repudiate the suggestion that we, as a Party, should endeavour to get representation through the Labour Party, and to go to Stockholm as majority delegates voicing the views of the majority.

5. We reject the resolution of the Labour Party Conference because it is opposed to the conditions on which the Stockholm Conference has been called, which specially invites the representation of minority parties.

6. We dissociate ourselves from the decision of the Conference because if it were accepted it would put the British representation on a different footing to the Socialist representation from other countries, where minorities as well as majorities are represented.

7. Holding these views, and declining to recognize as valid the resolution of the Labour Party Conference, we beg to inform you that we shall not take part in the nomination of the Labour Party delegates, nor in the election of such delegates. We shall proceed, as we are entitled to do, both by right of our position in the International, by the terms of the invitation to the Stockholm Conference, and appoint our delegates to the Stockholm Conference.

[119] *I.L.P., Report of the Twenty-sixth Annual Conference, 1918,* p. 12.

As we have already informed you, our delegates are Messrs. Anderson, Glasier, Jowett and MacDonald.

Believe me, yours very truly,

(*Signed*) PHILIP SNOWDEN, *Chairman*

AGAINST THE STOCKHOLM CONFERENCE

[Appeal of the Zimmerwald Left, July 20, 1917][120]

To the Socialist International!

THE INTERNATIONAL SITUATION

The third year of war draws to an end but still the capitalist governments are incapable of curbing the unchained fury of war. They have wasted hundreds of billions worth of goods, so that the interest on the war loans alone has greatly exceeded the hitherto existing tax income. They have sacrificed millions of human lives, created a world of widows and orphans. A pale fright overpowers them at the thought that the day of settling accounts between the peoples will come when peace will be established and they will have to explain to the peoples of all countries why they have imposed upon them all these sacrifices. Some of them—the governments of England and France—hope that if they drag out the war for a longer time they will be able, with the help of the United States of America, to crush the Central Powers and, in the intoxication of enthusiasm of victory, in the midst of their elation, to hold back the masses of the workers from bringing up the question why they have shed their blood. They have not yet given up their plans of annexation. They are still stretching out their arms for Alsace-Lorraine, for the German colonies, for Trieste and Turkey. The Central Powers, which from the continuation of the war may only expect the worsening of their position, speak continually of peace, but they are neither able nor eager to propose a peace which would guarantee to the peoples the restoration of their economic forces, a recompensation for their losses. The government of Germany, in spite of its difficult situation, could not be made to renounce once and for all every annexation and contribution, not to mention being made willing to liberate the nations which have been previously subjected by it. Austria-Hungary has not even renounced the

[120] Balabanoff, "Die Zimmerwalder Bewegung ....," Grünberg, *Archiv* ....,
XII, 381–88. This appeal was published in *Russische Korrespondenz, "Prawda,"*
No. 14 (no date), pp. 154–63, and in the Swedish Left socialist press. The appeal
was signed by the Central Committee of the R.S.D.L. party (Bolsheviks), the Social
Democracy of Poland and Lithuania, the Bulgarian S.D.L. party ("Narrow"
socialists), the Swedish Left Social Democratic Labor party, and the Swedish Youth
League.

annexations in the Balkans, but, on the contrary, its Minister of Foreign Affairs, Count Czernin, throws down the gauntlet in a provocative manner to the peoples by declaring in the State Council that the black-yellow monarchy recognizes *no right of the peoples* but solely *the right of the Kaiser* to conclude war and peace according to his own judgment.

The Struggle of the Masses against the War

The government cannot escape the trap in which the peoples are being bled white. But the masses of the workers in all countries are satiated with the war. In all countries they have lost to a great extent all confidence in their governments; they themselves have found out that they were cheated and deceived when they were promised bread and freedom as a reward for their endurance in the war. In all countries there is an uprising among the workers; everywhere, increasing masses of the proletariat are joining the movement. Although each government tries to conceal from foreign countries what goes on in its own country, it cannot cover up any longer the fact that the foundation of *the clique's power which has called forth the war, and which for the last three years has driven the masses of the peoples to the battlefields, has now begun to totter.*

In Germany there are daily hunger revolts. In spite of the efforts of the social patriots, strikes occurred among the munition and dock workers in *Berlin, Leipzig, Bremen, Hamburg, Stettin, Essen, and Düsseldorf, in addition to the strikes of the miners in Rhine-Westphalia and Upper Silesia.* In Hungary the war instigator Tisza has had trouble with *Budapest munition strikes,* while in Austria a strike of 80,000 workers took place in Vienna, in the Ostrau and the Karvin coal region extensive strikes were organized, and in Prossnitz women and children were fired upon because they demanded bread. The press of the Entente believes that the awakening of the masses of the workers of the Central Powers will bring it victory. But it is sufficient to ask whether it has forgotten the *Russian revolution,* which was born out of the longing for peace, out of the cry for bread. Even the Russian peasants and workers who allowed themselves to be driven by the petty-town social patriotic leaders to a new offensive desire peace, and nothing is so well suited [as this offensive] to persuade them that a peace which agrees with the interests of the people is to be found not on the battlefields of the war of nations but on the battlefields of civil war, while the offensive, if its outcome is military as it probably will be, cannot bring peace but will swallow up new *thousands* of sacrifices. And what about France? It is sufficient to read the legal page of the Paris newspaper in order to follow Hervé's cry against the peace movement within the army, [or to read] the articles of the militarist writers, full of fright, in order to know that broad masses of the people have awakened in France and that the soldiers, who with the women workers are today parading in Paris in protest against capitalists and the police, will tomorrow attack the bloody regime that is turning France into a land of old men, women, and children, into a country of graveyards. In England, strikes have not stopped for a moment and even such war-instigating capitalist newspapers as the *Times* have to admit that it is a matter of general discontent of the masses and not only of economic demands.

THE SOCIAL PATRIOTS IN A PINCH

Everywhere the people are awakening, everywhere the moment for settling accounts is approaching. The social patriots of Germany, Austria, and Russia, whose consciences prick them most, feel that the awakening masses of the people will throw them, together with the leaders of capital, over the precipice because they have been working hand in hand with the capitalist governments; they are attempting to save the situation at the last moment. They are trying to induce the capitalist governments to declare a peace of understanding, of reconciliation. This is the task of the *international—and allegedly socialist—conference at Stockholm.* Its initiative came partly from the social patriotic agents of the German-Austrian government, Scheidemann and Adler, who with the help of the Dutch social patriots (Troelstra, the man of civil peace) and of the Danish social patriots (Minister Stauning) attempted to call an international conference. Later on, the leaders of the majority of the Petersburg Workers' deputies, the Russian social patriots, joined them. These men, enjoying the confidence of the people, behind its back lead the Russian people in agreement with the capitalists of Russia, England, and France toward new slaughters in order to obtain from the Entente money which they do not dare to take away from the Russian capitalists.

THE STOCKHOLM "PEACE CONFERENCE" OF THE SOCIAL PATRIOTS

What is the purpose of the Stockholm Conference? The German and the Russian social patriots hope to persuade the French and English to erect the foundation of a chaffering peace that would be acceptable for all the governments and to persuade them to influence their governments to accept such a peace. They speak bombastically about peace without annexations and indemnities on the basis of the self-determination of nations. But this is a lie and a deceit. How can the government of Germany be forced to give freedom to the Poles, the Danes, the peoples of Alsace-Lorraine without taking the power out of the hands of the German capitalists? How is it possible to force the Austrian and Hungarian Junkers and bureaucrats to give the oppressed Southern Slavs the freedom of deciding their own destiny without forcing the former to their knees? How is it possible to tear from the clutches of English world capital India and Egypt, countries from which the English capitalists squeeze out yearly billions of money, unless the red banner of the triumphant socialist revolutions flies high above the City of London? They have only recently robbed Mesopotamia in order to establish a new feudal state under the pretext of an independent Arabic state. A peace without war indemnities! What does that mean? It means that no country is to be robbed for the profit of another country! But if capitalists remain at the helm in all countries, then they will impose the burdens of the war upon the shoulders of the workers, small craftsmen, poor peasants. For decades they will have to pay taxes to the capitalists, i.e., work more, eat less, be worse clad and subject to worse living conditions.

Without the revolution in all countries, peace will mean only a temporary suspension of hostilities. First of all, the capitalists will gather all their forces against the workers and try to overthrow them with combined efforts in order to free their own hands for new armaments, for new conquests, and, finally, for new wars. This is the way the *Spartakus,* the illegal organ of the German revolutionary internationalists, the adherents of Karl Liebknecht, has written in its April number: *"Today the socialist peace policy is contained in the simple words: You workers! Either the governments will declare peace, as they have declared the war, then whatever the issue of the war may be, imperialism will remain the ruling power and then armaments, wars, and the ruin, reaction, and barbarism will continue inevitably; or you brace yourselves for mass revolts, for a struggle for the attainment of political power in order to dictate your peace within and without. There will be either imperialism and sooner or later a debacle of society, or a struggle for socialism as the only salvation. There is no middle course, no third possibility."*[121]

No Return for the Social Patriots!

The social patriots of all countries know this as well as we do: the Scheidemanns and Legiens, the Adlers and Renners, the Renaudels and the Sembats, the Hendersons and the Hyndmans, the Plekhanovs, Dans, and Tseretelis. But some of them act as though they do not know it, because they are no less afraid of the approaching revolution than are the bourgeoisie. They have been so much attached to the governments for the last three years that they are afraid, in case of a revolution, they will fall with the governments into the abyss. They were silent while the governments were filling the prisons with the vanguard of the prole-

[121] See *Spartakusbriefe,* II, 76.

tariat; they have helped them to put the workers into chains and confine them to forced labor; they were silent while the Armenians in Turkey and the Ukrainians in Galicia were being tortured by the thousand. Others of the social patriots might have wanted to withdraw from that ignominious road, but they lost all their strength serving the governments, lost all their belief in the people; they comfort themselves with the idea of a struggle after the war, although they must admit to themselves that the bourgeoisie will be able to handle them much more easily when they give up their arms than now when the workers are in possession of the government's means of oppression. The *social patriots* of all countries have already decided in favor of the *counter-revolutionary policy;* in their homelands they are suppressing both strikes and demonstrations with all their powers because they are afraid they might develop into a revolution. In the face of the political crisis which is forcing the governments to make democratic promises in Germany and Austria they do not dare to advance even the consistent democratic demands such as a republic; but, on the contrary, they try to win the friendship of the people by means of piecemeal reforms and for this purpose they conduct a servile monarchist agitation. In the international realm their true aim is to reconcile the capitalist governments and not to achieve the proletarian revolution and a peace concluded on the ruins of the capitalist governments.

The Vacillating Elements and the Stockholm Conference

The international conference summoned under the banner of the Russian revolution will be a conference against the cause of the proletariat, against the proletarian revolution. Because the social patriots of the Central Powers and of the Entente are working with their governments and are pulling at each others' hair at present, they cannot for the time being reach one another except by using the *opposition minorities as a bridge.* If Ledebour and Haase, the parliamentary leaders of the moderate German opposition, had not been present, if they were to refuse to sit at one table together with the Scheidemanns, how could Renaudel and Chkheidze then be responsible before the French and the Russian proletariat for sitting down at the same table with those betrayers of the proletariat, those guests of the executioners of Belgium, those accomplices of the jailers of Liebknecht, those silent witnesses of the martyrdom of the thirty thousand Ukrainian peasants who have been hanged, those who have been scourged by Friedrich Adler? If the Pressemanes and Longuets were to declare that they would not go to a "peace conference" with the war agents of the French government, how could the Scheidemanns then try to convince the workers that it is a socialist conference? If the *Italian Social Democracy,* which, thanks to its uninterrupted protest against the war, has gained high authority in the eyes of the peoples of Europe, had refused to negotiate with the social patriotic agents of the governments, then their game would have been revealed. *Without the help of certain of the organizations of the old International which have remained faithful to socialism, the conference of the government socialists would not have taken place, or it would have appeared from the start what it actually is: a preliminary conference of imperialist diplomacy.*

But *the game of the government agents seems to be successful.* Not only are the Longuets and Pressemanes, the representatives of the moderate French opposition who differ from the French social patriots only by their phraseology, going to take part in the conference, but also the pilgrims of Kienthal, the deputies Brizon, Blanc, and Raffin-Dugens, who, during the second year of the war, joined the Zimmerwald movement and have bravely voted against war credits in the Chamber. The *Independent Labour party of England* and the *Socialist party of Italy* which belong to the Zimmerwald movement have also decided to participate in the conference. Lately the invitation to the conference has also been accepted by the majority of Independent Social Democracy of Germany under the leadership of Ledebour and Kautsky. The illusion that the initiators of the conference, the *Russian social patriots,* are "responsible" for the Russian revolution may play a great role in directing the conduct of many of these parties—though in reality during the war these Russian social patriots either have been carrying on a fight against the revolutionary movement or have been passive toward antirevolutionary agitation. Ignorance with respect to the actual policy of the majority of the Soviet of Workers' deputies may play an important role in determining the conduct of certain parties—though the majority in the Soviet, supported by the peasant elements, does not pursue a socialist policy but by allying itself with the bourgeoisie is directly *preparing the ground for the counter-revolution,* is nothing but a toy in the hands of the Entente, and lately has been shedding the blood of the revolutionary proletarians and soldiers in Petrograd. Nevertheless the determining influence upon the decision of these parties to take part in the social-patriotic "peace conference" was exerted by the *fundamental nature* of these parties themselves. Since the beginning of the war they have not attempted to arouse a mass action against the war but were satisfied with Platonic protestations. Accordingly, their aims were not to overthrow capitalist governments or to kindle a struggle for socialism in all capitalist countries but only to exercise pressure on the governments for an early conclusion of a peace which they have been calling erroneously the peace of the peoples. They wish to reform imperialism, to force it to respect treaties, and thus to limit armaments. As the states that have bled white are now compelled to slow down temporarily the tempo of armaments, the demands of the passive internationalist parties can of course be reconciled with the aims not only of the social patriots but even of the imperialist governments. Now at the end of the third year of the war, when increasingly large masses of the workers go out in the streets and demonstrate against the governments, the social patriots will also allow themselves to use phrases against the imperialist policy. Even though the comrades belonging to the Independent German Social Democracy, as well as to the Italian Socialist party, may try to convince themselves that in their fight against the social patriots at the Stockholm Conference they will succeed in unmasking them before the eyes of the masses, today, by consenting to participate in the Conference, they have already helped them [the social patriots] to raise their prestige in the eyes of the working masses as champions of peace, *a prestige which the Scheidemanns and the Renaudels will make use of only to combat the revolutionary movement, whereas at the Conference the pacifist minority elements will become captives of the social patriots.* Because they do not dare openly to tell the masses that revolution alone can lead the working class out of the blind alley, they will have nothing to oppose to the phrases of the social patriots. Because they themselves pursue the chimera of a peaceful capitalism which will not oppress the peoples, they will accept the same peace program as the social patriots. If we, the revolutionary Social Democrats, were to take part in the conference, as the leaders of the Right wing of the Zimmerwald movement are attempting to persuade us to do, we should find ourselves there in opposition to a social patriotic pacifist bloc.

The Revolutionary Social Democrats and the Stockholm Conference

But we shall not take part in the conference of the social-patriotic agents and their accomplices, who have not freed themselves from illusions with respect to the nature of social patriotism. It was not simply phrase-making when for three long years we told the workers that *social patriots* are accomplices of the imperialist bourgeoisie, when we urged them to break away from them. For us it was not plain phrase-making when in the Kienthal resolution on peace we "refused to satisfy the utopian demand of bourgeois or socialist pacifism" and declared: "Pacifists substitute new illusions for the old ones and attempt to make the proletariat serve these illusions, which in the end *mislead the masses* and divert them from the revolutionary class struggle and favor *the game of an endurance policy in the war.*" It was not plain phrase-making when in Kienthal we said that "the relations that have been created by the war between the governments and the social-patriotic leaders are contrary to all fundamental principles." *Faithful as we have remained to the principles which we have defended throughout the entire war period, we now address the following appeal to all the revolutionary workers and social democratic organizations:*

1. *Expose* to the workers the *lie and the deceit of the social-patriotic conference at Stockholm!* Tell the workers that a peace in the interest of the proletariat cannot result from a conference of those who for three years have subjected the interests of the workers to those of capitalists but can be attained only through a *proletarian revolution,* a peace without annexations and indemnities, a peace of peoples freed from the yoke of capitalism and of any national oppression.

2. *Disavow your party leaders who belong to the Zimmerwald movement and who, contrary to its aim, seat themselves at the same table with social patriots* in order to help them to bring about their chaffering imperialistic peace! Explain, as Franz Mehring has done, that you cannot recognize such representatives as yours. Take away from them, as the *Chemnitz group of the Independent Social Democracy* has done, the right to speak in your name.

3. *Send delegates to Stockholm* to discuss with representatives of outspoken international organizations the question of a further struggle for peace, and in view of the split of the Zimmerwald movement caused by the vacillating and undecided elements to discuss also the possible unification of all the revolutionary social-democratic elements. *Demand passports from the governments, and if they are refused to your delegates notify the public accordingly.* This will serve better than anything else to open the eyes of the workers as to the nature of the Stockholm Conference, a conference of government agents and their unwitting supporters.

Print this leaflet, send us your agreement with our appeal.

D. The Third Zimmerwald Conference

After many postponements the Third Zimmerwald Conference finally met at Stockholm, September 5–12, 1917. Although there were present delegates from Germany, Russia, Rumania, Switzerland, the United States, Norway, Sweden, Austria, also a representative of the Finnish Social Democratic party which at its Congress at Helsingfors June 15–18, 1917, had resolved to join the Zimmerwald movement,[122] and the members of the International Socialist Committee, the

[122] "Finnland für Zimmerwald," *I.S.K. Nachrichtendienst,* No. 10, June 22, 1917, p. 1.

attendance was smaller than at either the Kienthal or the Zimmerwald conferences. No representatives of the press were admitted to the meetings.[123] This is one reason why practically no information about the Conference can be found in the contemporary press except the official report of the International Socialist Committee which is given below and which was published in *Nachrichtendienst* and *Berner Tagwacht*.[124]

Balabanoff supplements the official report by the following account of the proceedings:

"In the discussion as to whether or not the Zimmerwaldists should participate in the general Stockholm Conference, Radek, Duncker, Balabanoff, Ledebour (the latter expressed his personal point of view with the remark that he would submit himself to the general decision of the Independent Social Democratic party of Germany), Höglund, and Sirola pronounced themselves against participation; Haase and Stadthagen favored participation for the reason that they were planning to make use of the general conference for the purpose of settling accounts with the majority parties. Axelrod declared that his mandate permitted him to take part in the Zimmerwald Conference only if the latter decided to participate in the general Stockholm Conference. Ermansky was heart and soul for attending the general conference. . . . . Following the reports of Therese Schlesinger (Austria), Ahsis (America), Nissen (Norway), Sirola (Finland), Constantinescu (Rumania), Ahsis proposed in the name of the Socialist Propaganda League the following demands:

" '(1) An immediate cessation of hostilities in order to prepare a general peace without annexations and war indemnities on the basis of the right of peoples to self-determination. (2) The solution of the main problems of the oppressed peoples, including the colonies. A general class struggle against imperialism. (3) Financial assistance to the coun-

---

[123] "Die Internationale und der Krieg. Eröffnung des Zimmerwalder Kongresses," *Beilage zur Berner Tagwacht*, No. 210, September 8, 1917, p. 1.

[124] *I.S.K. Nachrichtendienst*, No. 23, September 24, 1917, pp. 1–8; *Berner Tagwacht*, No. 240, October 13, 1917, p. 1.

tries ruined by war from a general fund to be obtained by means of international taxation of war profits. The establishment of a Workers' and Soldiers' Council consisting of representatives of all the belligerent countries and representatives of the revolutionary socialists of the neutral countries for the purpose of controlling the activities of the capitalist peace conference.' ....

"During the meeting of September 10 additional reports were made by representatives of France, England, and Italy,[125] who had arrived at Stockholm in the meantime, as well as by Goldenberg and Ehrlich of the Russian Workers' Soviet, after which, upon the suggestion of the Swiss representative, Nobs, a commission was formed for the purpose of formulating an appeal for mass action or a mass strike. Haase, who thought a declaration would be sufficient, voted against forming a commission. The Commission consisted of Haase, Ledebour, Radek, Ermansky, Balabanoff, Schlesinger, Höglund, and Duncker. At the same time it was emphasized by the Presidium and the individual delegates that a mass action should take place only if all parties and in particular the Zimmerwald parties in belligerent countries, especially the Entente countries, would agree to the manifesto, which was to be forwarded to them without delay by the International Socialist Committee. It was also unanimously decided to keep the manifesto strictly secret pending the consent.

"The drafting of the manifesto took five meetings of the Commission. The draft was then unanimously adopted at the meeting of the Conference on July 12 [September 12], and upon the proposal of Stadthagen the title, 'PEACE MESSAGE FROM STOCKHOLM,' was chosen."[126]

Since two representatives of the Menshevik Organization

[125] As Dr. Balabanoff states in "Die Zimmerwalder Bewegung ....," Grünberg, *Archiv* ...., XII, 397, there were actually no delegates from these countries present because of the refusal of their governments to issue passports. But informal reports on the situation in France, England, and Italy were made by Goldenberg, Ehrlich, and Rusanov, who had recently visited those countries.

[126] A. Balabanoff, "Die Zimmerwalder Bewegung ....," Grünberg, *Archiv* ...., XII, 402–403; see also her account in her *Erinnerungen und Erlebnisse*, pp. 167–71.

Committee of the R.S.D.L. party were taking part in the Conference and were making reports on behalf of their organization, the Central Committee of the R.S.D.L. party and its Bureau Abroad jointly with the representatives of the Social Democracy of Poland and Lithuania introduced a declaration through Orlovsky, demanding that the Conference condemn the policy of the Mensheviks in Russia and threatening to withdraw from the Conference if this were not done. According to Balabanoff this declaration was not acted upon[127] and the Bolsheviks and their allies did not carry out their threat.

In accordance with the understanding the manifesto of the Third Zimmerwald Conference was not immediately published. In order to transmit the manifesto to the Zimmerwaldists in the Entente countries and to make sure that the text did not fall into the hands of the governments, a young Danish socialist agreed to memorize the entire appeal in English and go to England to transmit the manifesto to the antiwar socialists there. In London a French version was to be memorized and delivered in Paris by another messenger. While waiting for the consent of the Entente Zimmerwaldists, Balabanoff, as custodian of the text of the manifesto, was under pressure from one quarter to delay publication and from another to publish immediately. The German Independent Socialists were being accused of inciting mutinies in the German fleet and were in a position of considerable danger. In the circumstances the Independents sent Luise Zietz to Stockholm to ask that publication be postponed. At the same time Radek, on behalf of the Bolsheviks, demanded that the manifesto be published at once in the belief, apparently, that the appeal for an international general strike would aid the Bolsheviks in their plans to seize power in Russia.

On September 28, 1917, the Zimmerwaldists discussed Luise Zietz's request for postponement and Radek's demand for immediate publication. The International Socialist Committee rejected both proposals but adopted a resolution to

[127] A. Balabanoff, "Die Zimmerwalder Bewegung ....," Grünberg, *Archiv* ...., XII, 400–402.

the effect that while the manifesto must sooner or later be published, the I.S.C., in view of the extraordinary conditions in Germany, would postpone the publication. The date of publication would be decided after personal or telegraphic consultation with the German Independents. Should consultation be impossible, the I.S.C. would act at its own discretion. Despite this decision Radek continued to insist on publication, and when Balabanoff refused he threatened to publish the manifesto himself. From this it was apparent that Radek in some way had secured a copy, which in fact he did publish without Balabanoff's consent in a Finnish paper under Bolshevik control. But by this time—November—the Bolshevik revolution was in full swing and the manifesto was overshadowed by more momentous events.[128]

It is an interesting indication of the divergence of opinion within the Zimmerwald movement that whereas the German Independents regarded the manifesto of the Third Zimmerwald Conference as sufficiently revolutionary to threaten the existence of their party if it were published, the Bolsheviks, though seeing some advantage in its publication, were generally contemptuous of the manifesto, since instead of advocating a revolutionary uprising it merely appealed for a "general strike of the international proletariat in favor of peace."[129] That the secretary of the International Socialist Committee had no illusions about the significance of the Third Zimmerwald Conference is clear from her acknowledgment that all that needed to be said about the origin of the war and its consequences and all that could be said about the only way to stop the slaughter had been said in previous conferences and in the press. The Third Conference served only to emphasize by a new appeal how the war might be ended.[130]

[128] Balabanoff, *My Life as a Rebel,* pp. 168–70; *Erinnerungen und Erlebnisse,* pp. 172–73; "Die Zimmerwalder Bewegung ....," Grünberg, *Archiv* ...., XIII, 232–33.

[129] I. Vavilin, "Bolsheviki i Tsimmervald," *Krasnaia Letopis,* No. 2 (59), 1934, p. 22. The attitude of the Bolsheviks is discussed at greater length in *The Bolsheviks and World Revolution.*

[130] Balabanoff, "La IIIe Conférence de Zimmerwald," *Demain,* No. 20, December 1917, pp. 93–100.

Balabanoff tells also of another meeting on October 10, 1917, at Stockholm between some of the Zimmerwaldists and representatives of the Serbian S.D. party. The Serbs were one of the few social democratic parties in the belligerent states to vote against war credits. Moreover, Deputy Kaclerović had attended the Kienthal Conference and the Serbian S.D. party had adopted the Zimmerwald platform; but when the Serbian representatives arrived in Stockholm they got in touch with the Dutch-Scandinavian Committee and submitted a memorandum to it. To the Zimmerwaldists, Kaclerović explained that his actions at Kienthal were on his own personal responsibility and did not signify that the Serbian S.D. party had joined the Zimmerwald movement. Popović, another Serb, emphasized that Zimmerwald represented merely a transitional period and since the majority parties now favored a peace conference the Zimmerwald action was superfluous. All those present denied this, but nothing could be done about it.[131] This incident, like the differences manifested during the preliminary negotiations and at the Third Zimmerwald Conference, reveals the disintegration of the Zimmerwald movement.

Immediately after the Third Zimmerwald Conference the women delegates held an unofficial international conference of women socialists, September 14–15. No particulars other than the official report on that conference as published in the *Nachrichtendienst* are known to us. The conference based its discussions on the resolutions of the International Socialist Women's Conference held at Berne in March 1915 and upon some resolutions by the All-German Women's Committee of the Independent Social Democratic party of Germany.

[131] Balabanoff, "Die Zimmerwalder Bewegung ....," Grünberg, *Archiv* ...., XIII, 233–34. In addition to the Serbs the following attended this meeting: Rakovsky (Rumania); Kharlakov and Tinev (Bulgaria); Radek, Orlovsky, Hanecki (representatives of the Bolsheviks abroad); Sirola (Finland); Ahsis (U.S.A.); and the members of the I.S.C.

OFFICIAL REPORT OF THE THIRD ZIMMERWALD CONFER-
ENCE AT STOCKHOLM, SEPTEMBER 5-12, 1917[132]

. . . . When the International Socialist Committee, in agreement with its affiliated parties, called the Third Zimmerwald Conference for September 5, it knew, of course, that the Conference would be hampered by the absence of comrades to whom passports had been denied. But it also knew, as did all the adherents of the Zimmerwald movement, that this hampering would have no fundamental effect, and even no decisive political or practical significance, because among the Zimmerwaldists of all countries there were no differences of opinion with regard to the questions concerned.

Even though the starting point of the Zimmerwald movement was that the proletarians of *all belligerent countries* were to carry on a *common struggle* against their own governments and against imperialism in all countries, the Kienthal resolution still emphasized explicitly—and, moreover, with reference to the International Congresses of Stuttgart, Copenhagen, and Basel—that "the attitude of the proletariat toward the war could not depend upon the military or strategic situation." The Russian revolution and the conditions brought about in all countries by the imperialist war have produced thousands of proofs that the struggle of the working class upon this basis is the only honest struggle in favor of peace without annexations and the only one likely to be successful. Recourse to strategic diplomatic interests of this or that belligerent coalition is just the thing to doom "to complete failure the attempt of the government socialists to reach an understanding."

For the Zimmerwald parties it is at present a matter of drawing concrete conclusions from principles worked out jointly, so that present external conditions may be taken into consideration only incidentally. In basing their conclusions upon the expressed opinions and the letters of numerous organizations, the participants in the Third Zimmerwald Conference are certain of the approval and active support of their partisans in the various countries because it is necessary to maintain fundamental unity with regard to the means by which the proletarian struggle for peace must be led and, furthermore, must be led in all countries. . . . .[133]

DELIBERATIONS

The agenda read:

Report of the International Socialist Committee.

The Grimm affair.

---

[132] "Offizieller Verhandlungsbericht. Zur Vorgeschichte," *I.S.K. Nachrichtendienst*, No. 23, September 24, 1917, pp. 1–8.

[133] There follows a list of parties represented. See below, pp. 674–75.

Attitude toward the conference of the Workers' Soviet.

Struggle for peace and the Zimmerwald movement in various countries.

After the report of the International Socialist Committee was heard and approved, and the conclusions of the international commission for investigation of Grimm's affair were adopted, the Conference passed to those points on the agenda which were fundamentally and tactically of the greatest significance for the Zimmerwald movement, particularly a review of the movement in all countries, of the general situation, and of the attitude of the working class.

The discussion was preceded by detailed reports, accompanied by documented speeches, and lasted several days. There was perfect unanimity throughout the proceedings with regard to the practical attitude toward events, so that the manifesto which resulted from the discussion was *unanimously* adopted and there is every guaranty that the points of view and the practical measures to which it refers will be just as ardently agreed to by the adherents of Zimmerwald of all countries and of all groups. The fact that such unanimity with regard to the principal question could be attained without any difficulty shows how imperiously external conditions are pushing the proletariat toward the only road by which it may attain peace and the re-establishment of active international relations. A *gigantic task* awaits the workers, the task of ridding the world of the slaughter of people, particularly by the unfolding of *their own gigantic* forces that are slumbering in the proletarians of all countries. The proletariat should and can rescue itself from the curse and the disgrace that would threaten it, if, after the countless sufferings and crimes which were committed upon the laboring class of all countries by the imperialist war, the holy alliance of the Pope and the governments should succeed in "presenting" the peoples with the desired peace and thereby surrounding the reactionary powers, which in the eyes of the unconscious groups of the people are responsible for the war, with a prestige of "humanitarianism." The people's hope for peace "presented" to them by the Pope, by dynasties, or by social diplomats can only infinitely prolong the bloody massacre, while such a peace would not only contain germs of new wars and impose unheard-of war burdens on the famished and exhausted masses but would also infringe upon the class-consciousness of the masses, turn the day of reckoning between the masses and their rulers and exploiters into a day of new enslavement, a new subjugation. Not only the war but the entire labor movement also is standing at the parting of the ways: the one way leads through unanimous mass struggle toward peace on the part of the masses of all countries, through new social and political struggles toward socialism; the other way leads through subjection and endurance, through further renunciation of human rights toward further shedding of blood toward new enslavement, toward new limitations of rights, toward a stabilization of class power, of militarism, of the money-bag, and of dynastic privileges.

Since complete unanimity prevailed with regard to just this point, all other differences of opinion were completely pushed into the background. Therefore it may be said without exaggeration that the Stockholm gathering of Zimmerwaldists means a step forward as much as any congress or conference can represent progress toward action. What the peoples have unfortunately so far been unable to accomplish, what the government socialists were neither able nor eager to accomplish because they are base accomplices of their governments, should be enforced by the class-conscious proletariat under the banner of international socialism.

Where the question of the attitude toward the Workers' Soviet conference was concerned, the discussion was of a general political and tactical nature and merged into the principal topic: the proletarian struggle for peace and the Zimmerwald movement. As the Stockholm Conference was definitely shattered, there was really no necessity of discussing the question of the attitude toward it. That this question was nevertheless discussed in detail and that the proposal not to discuss it because the Conference had not taken place was not followed was due to the fact that those who were opposed to participating in the conference called by the Dutch-Russian Committee considered this question to be fundamental and a discussion of it necessary, although the practical conclusions in this particular case would not be applied. It was a matter of opening the eyes of the proletariat as to how and why the conference was shattered, whereas if it had met it could under any circumstances only have contributed to the confusion of the masses, to setting up a travesty of a separate peace between the social patriots of various countries. Those comrades who were of the opinion that participation in the general conference should not be rejected offhand considered this question to be purely tactical; the opportunity should not be missed of telling the social patriots at home, before the forum of the International, things which otherwise could not be told in one's own country because of the war censorship.

But, as was mentioned, it was not a matter of adopting a resolution. This was adequately covered by a general expression of attitude toward social patriotism, which attitude was exhaustively discussed during the consideration of the principal topic. The discussion of the principal topic was preceded by a report on the Zimmerwald, or the proletarian movement in various countries. The reports of delegates were supplemented by written reports sent to the International Socialist Committee from countries whose representatives were prevented from attending the Conference in person on account of the refusal of passports. All reports without exception showed that everywhere not only the objective conditions brought about by the war but also the subjective attitude of a large part of the working masses pointed toward a considerable unrest in all belligerent countries. Single demonstrations have already taken place in all countries; these reveal not only war weariness, famine, etc., but also the fact that the masses are coming more and more to understand that war can be stopped only by an energetic struggle of the peoples against the governments and the ruling classes of all countries. In spite of the raging reaction and censorship, the abolition of the right of organization and of social legislation in general, in spite of the fact that many government socialists and leaders of trade unions have placed themselves completely at the service of the governments and have become the most eager proponents of civil peace and of the endurance policy, the masses are proving, through economic and general strikes of protest, that they wish to be no longer in the service of the slaughter of people and capitalist slavery. However, isolated demonstrations lose significance, in spite of the courage and self-sacrifice of the workers who take part in them, because the measures of violence and censorship succeed in separating the proletarians from one another so that the demonstrations of the one are not at all known to the others or else the information about them comes too late.

If the proletarians of one country could know how decided is the feeling of the proletarians of the "hostile" country, then they would be freed from the heavy burden which up to the present has inhibited their action; at every stirring of the home proletariat the bourgeoisie and the social patriotic press points out in a demagogic manner that the labor class of the hostile country is enthusiastic over the war and would take advantage of the antiwar movement in the interest of the imperialism of its own country.

Meanwhile the delegates of the Workers' Soviet had returned from France, England, and Italy; so they were invited by the Zimmerwald Conference to report on their journey. Their reports were practically the same as the statements in the press and in the letters received by the International Socialist Committee from the corresponding countries.

Russian events aroused a lively discussion, especially because representatives of three different tendencies within the Russian Social Democracy had a chance to speak and also because it concerned events which are of very great significance to the Socialist International, and a thorough knowledge of them and their evaluation is of very great importance for the peoples of Europe. What conclusions can be drawn from the Russian revolution, what factors are responsible for its defeat, what verdict should be held about the various parties and members who, after they have joined the fight for an early peace without annexations and indemnities under the banner of Zimmerwald, have more and more submitted to the power of Entente imperialism and have taken up the reactionary and most unworthy means of struggle?

These questions were debated at great length, although it was not a question of adopting any resolutions (in the rules of the agenda it was stated in advance that resolutions should be taken only if there was absolute unanimity on any particular question). Even though some of the delegates declared that whereas they could only severely condemn the repressive measures exercised in Russia they were not sufficiently well informed to be justified in passing judgment on the responsibility of various parties and comrades in the form of a resolution, there is no doubt that a discussion of the Russian events was just the thing to help the non-Russian delegates to formulate their opinion in connection with this extremely important and vital question.

After the representatives of all countries and tendencies had pronounced themselves on the situation in the various countries, as well as on the Stockholm Conference and the proletarian struggle for peace, a Commission was formed and its resolution was unanimously adopted by the participants of the Conference.

At the opening of the deliberations, declarations of solidarity and telegrams wishing success were received from comrades and organizations which were unable to come to Stockholm on account of the denial of passports. Among these were messages from the French Zimmerwaldists, from Klara Zetkin, from Holland, and from many others. Other wishes for success were received after the adjournment of the Conference.

The men and women comrades who had come to the Third Zimmerwald Conference sent a warm fraternal greeting to the heroic and brave fighters—Friedrich Adler, Karl Liebknecht, Klara Zetkin, Rosa Luxemburg, and all the courageous vanguard of fighters of the International who have been persecuted by different governments and who are struggling in various countries for international socialism.

A telegram of solidarity was dispatched to Comrades Lenin, Trotsky, Zinoviev, Kollontai, and Rakovsky, in which the libels against these comrades were resolutely rejected.

At the conclusion of the Conference the Swedish members of the International Socialist Committee, Comrades Carleson, Höglund, and Nerman, who were temporarily elected in July, were definitely and unanimously elected as members of the International Socialist Committee. Comrade Balabanoff was named secretary of this Committee.

The participants in the Conference parted with the conviction that a significant forward step had been taken along the road of the Zimmerwald resolutions. The objective condition under which the Conference met, as well as the subjective attitudes of the participants and the character of the debates, justify the hope that the Third Zimmerwald Conference has been a conference of *action*.

If the class-conscious proletarians of all countries deem it their duty to confirm and to make their own the resolutions of the three Zimmerwald conferences, then, in spite of the collapse of the official Stockholm Conference, which has stirred up so much dust and has awakened and disappointed so many hopes, the desired proletarian peace manifesto from Stockholm has been awaited not quite in vain ——.

DELEGATES TO THE THIRD ZIMMERWALD CONFERENCE[134]

Germany, The Independent Social Democratic party: GEORG LEDEBOUR, HUGO HAASE, ARTHUR STADTHAGEN, KÄTHE DUNCKER, ADOLF HOFER, ROBERT WENGELS

Russia

The Central Committee of the R.S.D.L. party (Bolsheviks): ORLOVSKY and ALEKSANDROV [N. SEMASHKO]

The Organization Committee of the R.S.D.L. party (Mensheviks): P. AXELROD, PANIN

The Mensheviks-Internationalists: A. ERMANSKY

Poland, The Regional Presidium of the Social Democracy of Poland and Lithuania:[135] K. RADEK, HANECKI

Finland, The Social Democratic party: YRJÖ SIROLA

Rumania, The Social Democratic party: A. CONSTANTINESCU and J. C. FRIMU

Switzerland, The Social Democratic party: ROSA BLOCH and ERNST NOBS

America, The Socialist Propaganda League and the International Brotherhood: AHSIS and J. EADS HOW

Norway, Socialist Youth League: EGEDE NISSEN, ERNST CHRISTIAN, SENIOR, and JOHANNES ERWIG

Sweden, The Socialist Youth League and the Left Social Democratic [Labor] party: OSKAR SAMUELSON, STRÖM, LINDHAGEN, and JEORJ LINDSTRÖM

Austria, the opposition within the Austrian Social Democratic [Labor] party: THERESE SCHLESINGER and MRS. LUZZATO.

[134] A. Balabanoff, "Die Zimmerwalder Bewegung ....," Grünberg, *Archiv* ...., XII, 396–97.

[135] Should read: "The Main Presidium of the Social Democracy of Poland and Lithuania"; see above, p. 599, n. 41.

Finally, The International Socialist Committee: ANGELICA BALABANOFF, C. N. CARLESON, HÖGLUND, TURE NERMAN

The following statement must be made with regard to the attitude of these delegates at the Conference and toward it:

One of the two delegates of the Organization Committee of the Mensheviks [P. Axelrod], after attending one meeting of the Conference, declared in a letter that he would not take part in it because those who gave him his mandate had commissioned him to take part in the Zimmerwald Conference only if it was fully attended and if it decided to participate in the general Stockholm Conference. The second delegate, who had taken part in some of the meetings and discussions of the Conference but who was absent during the working out of the resolution, refused to give his consent to the resolution subsequently because of differences in opinion with regard to the formulation of one of its points.

Two delegates from Bulgaria arrived at the end of the Conference: the deputy Kharlakov and Katerina Tinev, representatives, respectively, of the opposition within the "Broad" party and the General Trade Union Federation. They arrived late because of some difficulties during the journey. The other two, Kolarov and Kirkov, who also had come to Stockholm to attend the Third Zimmerwald Conference and had been staying there for some time, had to depart before the opening of the Conference. All the Bulgarian delegates entirely agreed with the resolutions of the Third Zimmerwald Conference.[136]

The representatives of the Entente countries could send only a written communication saying that on account of lack of passports they could not come.

Carl Lindhagen was elected chairman of the Presidium of the Conference and Angelica Balabanoff secretary.

[136] In addition to the delegations mentioned above the *I.S.K. Nachrichtendienst*, No. 23, September 24, 1917, p. 4, mentions the Danish Socialist Youth League. Delegates of the Serbian S.D. party were also in Stockholm shortly after the Conference closed and conferred with the Zimmerwaldists. Lenin made an interesting comment on the varied composition of the Conference in an article written in October 1917 and based on a report in *Politiken*. According to Lenin, the Left, "the internationalists in practice," included the Swedish Youth and Left S.D.'s, the Bolsheviks, the American Propaganda League, the Polish Social Democracy, and the Austrian S.D. opposition. In the "Kautskyan Center" he placed the German Independents, the Swiss, Finnish, and Rumanian S.D.'s, the Menshevik Internationalists, and the Bulgarian independent trade unionists. Between the Center and the Left were the Norwegians and the Serbs and on the Right, "defensists, ministerialists, social chauvinists," were the Menshevik Organization Committee and the Danes. Lenin observes that in a gathering so constituted there could be no agreement on fundamentals and the result was bound to be quarrels and reproaches or "compromise resolutions drafted for the purpose of concealing the truth." (*Leninskii Sbornik*, VII, 331–33.)

CRITICISM OF THE POLICY OF THE MENSHEVIKS IN RUSSIA

[Joint Declaration by the Bolshevik Central Committee, Its Bureau Abroad, and the Main Presidium of the Social Democracy of Poland and Lithuania][137]

Representatives of the so-called Organization Committee of the Russian Social Democracy are taking part in the Conference. Although its representatives Axelrod and Martov participated in working out the resolutions of Zimmerwald and Kienthal, it [the Organization Committee] is now taking part, contrary to the Kienthal resolutions, in a capitalist war government; it has also helped to prepare the policy of an offensive behind the backs of the proletarians; and since the ignominious collapse of this policy it is now taking part in the most outrageous repressions against the soldiers' masses (the introduction of capital punishment in the army), and is supporting the shooting of the Petrograd workers, the suppression of their newspapers, the imprisonment of their leaders, and campaigns of most ignominious calumny against them. It is wholly responsible for the entire Kerensky regime, because it has not recalled its representatives from his government after all his infamous actions.

Inasmuch as the present Conference, on account of its incomplete plenum, has deprived itself of the right to pass any authoritative resolutions, we have given up the idea of proposing here the expulsion of the Russian social-patriotic organizations which deem it possible to lead their crusade against the Russian internationalist organizations and at the same time to belong to Zimmerwald, though the resolutions of our last party conference oblige us actually to demand this. But the formal impossibility of expelling the Organization Committee from the Zimmerwald organization at this Conference does not relieve the Conference of the duty to state clearly and simply what the parties which are present here think of the policy of delivering the Russian proletariat to the Russian and the Entente imperialists, of reintroducing capital punishment in the army, of shooting Petrograd workers by order of the Russian government and with the consent of the majority of the Soviet leaders, of suppressing the social democratic press, which is conducting a struggle for peace, of imprisoning the revolutionary leaders who, entirely at the mercy of the beadles of old Tsarism in the prisons of free Russia, have to resort—as under Tsarism—to a hunger strike in order to find out what they are being accused of. It is also the duty of the Conference to state finally what it thinks of the dishonest calumny against the Bolshevik party and against its leaders

---

[137] Balabanoff, "Die Zimmerwalder Bewegung ....," Grünberg, *Archiv* ...., XII, 401–402.

as the bribed agents of Germany. No reference to inadequate information can free the Conference of this duty. The Zimmerwald Conference *should not be in the dark* as to who is struggling in Russia for the fundamental principles of Zimmerwald, and who is helping the imperialist bourgeoisie to suppress this struggle by all possible means. If the Conference is ignorant about it, it should procure this information. At any rate it should not demand of the representatives of the proletarians who were shot down, of the representatives of the parties which were forcibly suppressed, that they should calmly take part in the Conference, *without knowing with whom they are actually negotiating:* with either the representatives of the revolutionary proletarian parties, who are bound with the Russian revolutionary social democrats by at least moral solidarity, or with politicians, who cannot make up their mind whether they are for the struggling revolutionary proletarians or for the social patriotic persecutors. Since yesterday's debate has shown that one part of the Conference is not clear about this fundamental duty, we demand that the discussions be interrupted and a resolution be adopted with regard to the situation in Russia, which [resolution] would give us a guaranty that there are *premises* for some joint activity. We are ready to present to the Conference in the presence of our adversaries the facts supported by documents, concerning the situation in Russia. Unless the Zimmerwald Conference decides unequivocally with whom it agrees—with the fighters for Zimmerwald ideas, with the revolutionary Russian internationalists, or with the accomplices of the Russian *Cavaignacs*—we shall not take part in the Conference.

PEACE PROGRAM OF THE GERMAN *INTERNATIONALE* GROUP

[Presented by Käthe Duncker][138]

1. Peace as a point of departure for further political development, and a peace which would not subject the proletariat to slavery and oppression due to the burdens created by the war, can be the result only of revolutionary activity of the laboring masses in belligerent countries.

2. A true peace action on the part of the proletariat can be carried through only internationally, as the fate of the Russian revolution signifies. The Russian proletariat, left alone in the struggle for peace because of the passive attitude of the laboring masses in other countries, is being forced to take the road of militarism and, consequently, of co-operation with the bourgeois classes; it is thus stopped in its class struggle and prevented from unfolding without hindrance its revolutionary energy.

[138] Balabanoff, "Die Zimmerwalder Bewegung ....," Grünberg, *Archiv* ...., XII, 398.

3. The self-determination of nations is and remains an empty phrase so long as the bourgeois state persists. The only true realization of the self-determination of the peoples is the revolutionary self-determination of the working people by means of struggle for the political power in the state.

4. All projects for "lasting peace," such as the international disarmament treaties, courts of arbitration, and others, are bourgeois-pacifist utopias. The only guaranty of a lasting peace is the seizure of political power by the European laboring class.

5. The peace program of the international proletariat should be:

(1) The abolition of monarchy, wherever it still exists.

(2) The abolition of militarism in all its forms.

(3) A complete democratization of the right of election and equal political rights for both sexes.

(4) Guaranties of the free political cultural development of nationalities in every state.

(5) A political and economic declaration of the independence of all colonies.

(6) An eight-hour working day.

(7) The abolition of customs duties and indirect taxation.

(8) Cancellation of all government debts resulting from the World War.

OPPOSITION TO PARTICIPATION IN THE STOCKHOLM CONFERENCE

[Declaration of the *Internationale* Group Added to the Protocol of the Third Zimmerwald Conference][139]

The struggle for the cessation of the capitalist slaughter of the peoples which has been raging unchecked for the last three years is a question of life and death to international socialism. The course of the World War to date and its continuous tension and the pitiful failure of the attempts of the belligerent powers to come to some understanding, as well as the attempts of the neutrals at peaceful mediation, have proved that the war can be ended neither by a military decision nor by bourgeois diplomacy. Hence it can be stopped only by a general and complete exhaustion, i.e., after the social collapse of the belligerent countries.

The only means that may stop the barbaric slaughter of the peoples and prevent the progressive ruin of cultural life and all the foundations of a further development of society is the revolutionary uprising of the international proletariat. Any peace settled without the powerful sanction

---

[139] Balabanoff, "Die Zimmerwalder Bewegung ....," Grünberg, *Archiv* ....,
XII, 398–400.

of the European laboring class, which has reawakened to political activity, and any understanding between the belligerent powers arrived at by way of diplomacy would help only to strengthen imperialism, to stabilize the rule of the capitalist class, and would lead to an era of raging reaction of which the first victim of the reconciled international bourgeoisie would be the revolutionary Russian proletariat.

On the other hand, international socialism can recover from its present collapse only by means of a vigorous mass action of the laboring class in belligerent countries in favor of terminating the war. Only in a revolutionary struggle for peace can socialism again become a factor of public life and transform the end of the imperialist orgy into a powerful advance along the road toward the realization of ultimate socialist aims. If peace, as well as war, consisted merely of abolishing the active policy of the proletarian masses, then the historic role of international socialism would be ended for a considerable time.

As far as the vital interests of socialism are concerned, the peace action of socialists cannot consist of attempts to induce individual governments to agree to announce their war aims, to initiate an understanding between them, to invent a peace formula that would be acceptable by all belligerent states, to work out plans for a future map of state boundaries, or to express their pious wishes for the so-called guaranties of a lasting peace in the form of utopian bourgeois pacifist proposals, such as the disarmament treaties, international courts of arbitration, and similar things.

The only actual peace action of socialists must be a pure and simple appeal to the proletarian masses of all the belligerent countries for revolutionary class struggle in favor of peace, for a struggle for political power after the example of the Russian proletariat, in order to bring to their attention the tremendous political tasks of the present historic hour, the lesson of the World War and of the Russian revolution, and the duties which follow from them.

Naturally, in the socialist activity for peace there must be at the same time a strict settling of accounts with government socialism in all countries, i.e., a stigmatizing of the prostitution of socialist ideas which it has been carrying on for the last three years, a strangulation of the class struggle, and a demoralization of the proletariat. The peace activity of international socialism can be introduced only as an action of self-assertion, of self-criticism, and of a break with the hitherto existing disgrace and corruption in the official socialist parties.

Hence it is clear that an international peace conference with the government socialists who, up to now, especially through their endurance policy, have done their best to degrade the proletariat in all countries into weak tools of imperialism and thus prolong the slaughter of the peoples would directly contradict the vital interests of international socialism.

As the inevitable result of such a conference, socialist peace activity, instead of planting strongly and visibly the banner of revolutionary class struggle, would engage in preliminary bourgeois pacifist work in the interests of the diplomacy of the belligerent states and thus aid the ruling classes. Furthermore, the tendencies toward the internal clarification of international socialism and its resurrection from its present state of decay would be lost again in the melee with the elements of corruption. Finally, the government socialists of all countries would again be considered as factors equal to the adherents of international socialism and as representatives of the laboring class, thus making it more difficult and fatal to purge the international labor movement of these elements.

On the contrary, such a peace conference at which all traitors of socialism in all countries wish to absolve each other in a grand farce of reconciliation would represent the first step toward the solution of the present crisis which all the government socialists desire.

From all these points of view a peace conference with the government socialists would not be an action of enlightenment and of progress toward the reassumption of the proletarian class struggle and the realization of peace, but would serve to create new confusion in the labor movement and to divert the proletariat from true peace action through its own revolutionary struggle.

In view of these considerations the *Internationale* group declares that it will under no circumstances take part in a conference with the government socialists.

MANIFESTO OF THE THIRD ZIMMERWALD CONFERENCE[140]

.   .   .   .[141]

Proletarians of All Countries!

The peoples are being driven helplessly into the fourth winter campaign with all its horrors! Millions of men have been murdered, millions have been crippled, and further millions are being dragged to the shambles day after day. Hunger and misery rot away those men, women, and children who have remained at home, not only in the belligerent countries but in the neutral countries as well. It is the self-destruction of the peoples as the result of capitalist competition for power and spoils.

---

[140] "Friedenskundgebung aus Stockholm," *I.S.K. Nachrichtendienst,* No. 28, November 10, 1917, pp. 1–4; text is also given in *Berner Tagwacht,* No. 271, November 19, 1917, p. 1, and in *Current History,* No. 2, February 1918, pp. 208–10.

[141] The list of delegations to the Third Zimmerwald Conference which precedes the text of the manifesto is omitted.

In the face of these horrors and afflictions the cry rises louder and louder from the suffering peoples: give us peace; end the slaughter of the peoples! And still the dawn of peace is not near. Under the pressure of the war-weary peoples the rulers in both camps acknowledge their desire for peace, but behind their solemn assertions of this desire the unsatisfied lust for smashing the adversary, for conquests, and for new opportunities of exploitation can be concealed only with difficulty.

All the capitalist governments are afraid to return from the battle-fields without spoils, burdened only with debts millions large and the curse of millions of widows and orphans. They tremble before the day of peace which will be a day of reckoning. Therefore they will not agree concerning peace so long as they have any power at all and so long as the slightest hope of overcoming the enemy tempts them.

Not less hopeless is the so-called peace and conciliation activity of the government socialists, who have promised to the proletariat definitely to promote the cause of peace at Stockholm.

No bridge can be built between the government socialists of the two coalitions of powers; they are only the accomplices of their own governments. Their hodman services for the maintenance of civil peace and for the support of the imperialist war policy have robbed them of the capacity of revolutionary struggle for proletarian interests. Only the proletarian masses in all countries are capable and are called upon to carry through this revolutionary struggle, the masses that have remained faithful to their socialist ideals or that are being won over by them anew. These internationally minded proletarians are welded together into a unity by common points of view and the recognition of common interests; they go forward irresistibly toward a common aim. The march of events forces them imperiously to a rapid realization of the great and vital task.

Only peace achieved and established by the socialist proletariat through decisive mass actions can prevent forever the resumption of the world massacre. A capitalist peace, however it might be established, would result in imposing the immeasurable war debts in every country upon the shoulders of the working masses. The proletariat has nourished the war for years with the blood of its sons, with the vital strength of all its men and women. The capitalist clique, easily getting hold of the war profits, has strengthened its vampire forces. A capitalist peace would reward the proletarians with a limitation of their rights and facilitate the capitalists in sucking out the strength of the people.[142] In order to assure a lasting peace it is necessary to democratize all states thoroughly and obliterate all the money-bag privileges. The realization

---

[142] This sentence is taken from the text of the manifesto as quoted in Balabanoff's article, Grünberg, *Archiv* ...., XII, 405, since the corresponding sentence in the *I.S.K., Nachrichtendienst* involves an omission which makes it devoid of sense.

of a socialist republic is the only protection against the return of a world war.

But the conditions in Russia are also pressing toward an acceleration of the international proletarian struggle. By a marvelous revolution and the overthrow of Tsarism the Russian fighters for freedom have taken a promising first step along the road toward enforcement of peace and toward the liberation of the peoples. But the proletariat of one country, if it is isolated, cannot attain peace in the World War. So far, the masses of the proletariat in other countries have not followed their Russian brothers on the road toward liberation. This has led to the fact that reaction in Russia has been enabled to raise its threatening head.

The international proletarian mass struggle for peace signifies at the same time the rescue of the Russian revolution.

Separate activities of the proletariat have already manifested themselves here and there. Men and women have, in spite of all persecutions, sounded in the streets the cry for bread, peace, and freedom. The masses of workers are conducting a proletarian struggle; they have refused to work in the bondage of war capitalism in order to protect their most elementary human rights. They have undertaken these strikes in spite of the fact that the government socialist leaders of trade unions and parties have renounced the right of organization. These are symptoms not only of the war weariness of the proletarians in various countries but also of their recognition that only proletarian means of struggle can bring about peace.

But such isolated struggles, of which the proletariat of other countries gets either no information at all or belated information, cannot attain the eagerly desired aim. The hour has struck when there should begin in all countries a great common struggle for the establishment of peace, for the liberation of the peoples through the socialist proletariat. The means for this lies in the general international mass strike.

Our call concerns the workers of all countries. Their personal fate is inseparably bound up with the fate of the world proletariat. The workers of one country who keep aloof from the common struggle or who attack it from the rear frustrate peace, lengthen the war and the exploitation of the peoples, and ruin their own future. They commit treason against the common cause of humanity! This must not be!

Proletarians of all peoples! A most difficult duty awaits you, but the sublime aim, the final liberation of mankind beckons you!

Men and women workers! Recruit for the international proletarian mass action in every shop where life throbs, in every hut where it groans! The struggle will be long and difficult. The ruling classes will not give way at the first stroke, let alone capitulate. The harder the struggle the more resolutely should it be conducted. It is a question of winning through struggle, because continued endurance without protest must ultimately result in the fall of the proletariat.

Hail! The international mass struggle against war! Hail! The socialist peace!

E. The International Socialist Committee after the Third Conference

The disintegration of the Zimmerwald movement and the decline in influence of the International Socialist Committee, which were apparent during the summer of 1917, were not checked by the Third Zimmerwald Conference but, on the contrary, became even more obvious after the Bolshevik seizure of power in Russia in November. When the news of this event reached Stockholm, the I.S.C. met with Rakovsky, Radek, Kharlakov, and Tinev and decided to send a telegram on behalf of all parties affiliated with the International Socialist Committee to the Petrograd Soviet of Workers' and Soldiers' deputies congratulating it on its success. This decision, however, was not unanimous, as Rakovsky urged the International Socialist Committee to wait until the situation in Russia had become entirely clear and until all Russian parties and the parties of the other countries had taken a definite stand on Russian events. He was also of the opinion that the International Socialist Committee should urge all the Russian socialist parties to unite.

It was at this Conference on November 8 that Radek submitted an appeal addressed to the workers of all countries which he had drafted according to instructions from Petrograd.[143] He asked the International Socialist Committee to sign it jointly with the representatives of the Central Committee of the R.S.D.L. party abroad. In this appeal Radek urged the proletarians of all countries to strike and to form Councils of Workers' and Soldiers' deputies everywhere in order to safeguard Russia from any counter-revolutionary movement and to enforce peace. He also invited the represen-

[143] This is given below.

tatives of all parties which approved the course of events in Russia and were willing to join the revolutionary movement to come to Stockholm at once. The International Socialist Committee signed this appeal, and it was published in *Politiken* and sent abroad by telegraph.

At another conference in the evening of the same day the International Socialist Committee moved that the manifesto of the Third Zimmerwald Conference be published at once, since the reasons brought up against its publication had been nullified by the November revolution in Russia. This decision was in line with the desires of the Bolsheviks, who were insisting on immediate publication. In spite of a contrary point of view of some of the participants in the gathering, it was decided to publish the text of the manifesto and also a special edition of the *Politiken* devoted exclusively to the November revolution in Russia and containing expressions of solidarity by some of the Zimmerwald parties as well as articles by Carleson, Nerman, Lindhagen, Balabanoff, Rakovsky, and Radek.[144]

From this time until the autumn of 1918 the International Socialist Committee devoted its efforts to defending the interests of the proletarian revolution in Russia. In a number of circular letters it denounced the German offensive against Russia and the treaty of Brest-Litovsk and urged mass action to enforce a general peace and to counteract the intervention of the Allied powers in Russia.

Lack of contact and harmony between the Zimmerwald parties in various countries made the efforts of the International Socialist Committee little more than benevolent gestures, and made them little appreciated by the Russian Bolsheviks, who at that time were already planning the formation of the Third International.

In 1917–1918 the I.S.C. established close contact with the Finnish Social Democrats, who in June 1917 had joined the

---

[144] A. Balabanoff, "Die Zimmerwalder Bewegung . . . .," Grünberg, *Archiv* . . . ., XIII, 234–37 ; see also her *Erinnerungen und Erlebnisse,* p. 175.

Zimmerwald movement and delegated Yrjö Sirola to attend the Third Zimmerwald Conference and to keep in touch with the International Socialist Committee. The Committee published in its official organ a great many resolutions and appeals by the Social Democratic party of Finland presenting that party's attitude toward the policies of the Russian Provisional government and later the Soviet government. It also gave ample space in the columns of *Nachrichtendienst* to accounts of the situation in Finland in the autumn of 1917, the general strike which was declared on November 14, and the events leading to the revolutionary uprising on January 27, 1918, which marked the beginning of civil war. This civil war went on until May and ended in the defeat of the Finnish proletariat and a period of White terror. In a special letter of February 22, 1918, the International Socialist Committee appealed to the German workers to take action against Germany's offensive in Russia, Estonia, and Finland.

When in August 1918 the Soviet government issued a call to the workers of the Entente countries to oppose Allied intervention in Russia, the International Socialist Committee published this appeal and a supporting special letter to the workers of all countries in the last issue of *Nachrichtendienst,* September 1, 1918. This issue was devoted chiefly to the question of intervention in Russia and contained besides the two documents mentioned above, which were reproduced in various languages, the appeals against the Allied intervention issued by the British Socialist party and the Independent Labour party. With this issue the written periodical propaganda of the International Socialist Committee ceased.

Of other publications of the I.S.C. Balabanoff speaks in her memoirs of the issue in March 1918 of an illustrated "Zimmerwald-Russland" review entitled *Frieden, Brot und Freiheit,* which was published in twelve languages and which contained articles by prominent Russian Bolsheviks and a number of European minority socialists. She speaks also of the publication, at the request of the Russian Bolsheviks, of a propaganda pamphlet written by Bukharin and entitled,

"Thesen über die sozialistische Revolution und die Aufgaben des Proletariats während seiner Diktatur in Russland."[145] In an effort to revive the failing influence of the I.S.C. Balabanoff made a trip in September 1918 to Russia and several other countries. She accomplished very little, a fact insufficiently appreciated by the Swiss government, which in November expelled her from that country, and by the Swedish government, which refused to readmit her to Sweden.[146]

Meanwhile the Swiss social democratic press had begun to demand another conference of Zimmerwaldists and to suggest that the seat of the International Socialist Committee be transferred back to Switzerland as a means of restoring its vitality. This imputation that the decline in the Zimmerwald movement was the fault of the I.S.C. was vigorously denied by the *Berner Tagwacht* and by Balabanoff. Both declared that the trouble was with the workers themselves. The *Tagwacht* gave a rather gloomy account of the apathy of the masses. "The masses themselves should begin to stir. This would require psychological and objective premises, which today—let us be honest about it—*are absent*. In Germany there is no visible mass action in spite of the work of the minorities and in spite of a tremendous advance in the development of the internal situation during the last few months. In Italy it was possible to indict the bravest and best Zimmerwaldists, Lazzari and Serrati, and to prohibit the party congress without any signs of protest being made. In Austria where food conditions are worse than in any of the belligerent countries and where absolutism is indulging in orgies, there is no sign of mass protest. In France there is a slight change, but along with it a new and active republican coalition between socialists, Zimmerwaldists, social patriots, and the bourgeoisie in connection with the Malvy trial. Eng-

---

[145] These theses are included by Ernst Meyer [ed.], in *Spartakus im Kriege. Die illegalen Flugblätter des Spartakusbundes im Kriege*, pp. 211–20.

[146] Balabanoff, "Die Zimmerwalder Bewegung ....," Grünberg, *Archiv ....*, XIII, 258, 275, 283; see also her account in *Erinnerungen und Erlebnisse*, pp. 190–212.

land is completely shut off so that we can perceive only vaguely what is going on within the labor movement ...." According to the *Berner Tagwacht,* even if a conference were to be held, everyone familiar with Russian conditions should know that a unification of the former Zimmerwald parties would be impossible there. The transfer of the seat of the International Socialist Committee would no more bring about a mass movement than would an international conference, since the premises for a mass movement were lacking.[147] Balabanoff stressed the point that further discussions were not only futile but actually injurious, since they might suggest that something besides mass action could save the proletariat and defeat imperialism. "After four years of mass slaughter, when the only country which had applied the correct means of terminating the war .... is ablaze and is attacked and threatened on all sides not merely by blood-intoxicated imperialism but also by militarized and terrorized proletarians of other countries, there is no time to adopt resolutions. The program and the *means* of struggle are given to the peoples through their own experience."[148]

Neither the I.S.C. nor the Swiss Social Democrats could save the Zimmerwald movement, and when the German revolution broke out the International Socialist Committee was silent. Events in the various countries—especially after the end of the war and the collapse of the Hohenzollern and Habsburg monarchies—not only absorbed the energies of the old Zimmerwaldists but widened the breach between the Right and the Left. The Rights made peace with majority socialists and found their way back into the revived Second International. The Center ultimately reached the same goal after bringing to life briefly the Two-and-a-Half International. The Left naturally looked to the Russian Bolsheviks; but the Bolsheviks, even before the Third Zimmerwald Conference, had lost their interest in the Zimmerwald movement and

[147] *Berner Tagwacht,* No. 200, August 28, 1918, p. 1.
[148] *Beilage zur Berner Tagwacht,* No. 215, September 14, 1918, p. 1.

after their triumph in Russia in November used the International Socialist Committee and its publications merely as convenient channels for communication with their friends in the West and for protests against intervention and against the support of counter-revolution. The Bolsheviks therefore did not withdraw from the Zimmerwald movement. There was, perhaps, no reason to do so, since the organization was actually dead; but at least they gave it a decent burial when it was officially dissolved at the First Congress of the Communist International in Moscow in March 1919.[149]

THE INFORMAL SOCIALIST WOMEN'S CONFERENCE AT STOCKHOLM

[Official Report of the Sessions, September 14–15, 1917][150]

In connection with the Third Zimmerwald Conference, a conference of all the women comrades who had attended the Third Zimmerwald Conference was held at Stockholm on September 14. The need for more active relations, especially among the active women socialists of all countries, and the need for conferring about the most important questions which the war had raised for women, had made themselves felt for a long time. However, it was impossible to call a regular conference because of general police restrictions and, furthermore, it would be impossible for women representatives of some countries and also for our foremost fighter and leader of the international socialist women's movement, to attend a regular conference. The Extraordinary Socialist Women's Conference held at Berne in March 1915 pointed out and cleared the road for the socialist women's movement, and perhaps not for the women's movement alone. For the first time since the outbreak of the imperialist slaughter of people, a fundamental and a tactical attitude toward it was adopted at the said [Berne] Conference. The Zimmerwald manifesto and the resolutions which have been published during the course of time in national and international publications on behalf of the social democracy which had remained faithful to internationalism have emphasized and underscored the principal lines of the first document of the awakening International and have adopted them as the policy of socialist action in all countries. The fact that from the very start the women within the socialist parties belonged to the most radical

---

[149] Details in *The Bolsheviks and World Revolution*.

[150] "Internationale sozialistische Frauenbesprechung," *I.S.K. Nachrichtendienst*, No. 23, September 24, 1917, pp. 8–10.

wing can be explained among other things by the fact that they found a good leader precisely in the resolution of that Conference [March 1915] and that the women participants in this Conference, being conscious of their principal duty, joined in an appeal which could be generally understood and which was spread throughout all countries at the time of its issue, and pointed out to the women of the working and the deprived classes, to the mournful and drudging women proletarians, the causes of the war, the rights and the social duties resulting from the fact that war has turned them into soldiers at home.

The women comrades who met at Stockholm on September 14, 1917, agreed at once and without further ado that the socialist activity among women and the struggle against the war were to be developed only upon the basis of the Berne resolution. They were just as unanimous with regard to the decision that the Stockholm gathering should be only informal in character.

Since the women internationalists of all countries have agreed on the principles guiding their agitation against the war, it stands to reason that it is highly desirable to bring about an equally unanimous action on the part of the class-conscious proletarians of all countries with regard to the concrete political and social demands. Generally speaking it is precisely upon the activity and the life of women that the war has exerted an exceptionally leveling influence or even an "internationalizing" influence. Written reports were received also by the Conference from France, England, and America, accompanied by a letter from our French women comrades, who pointed out that an understanding was especially required with the German women comrades and women organizations with regard to basic questions such as "the same wages for the same labor" and "social legislation for women and for the protection of children." The Conference approved the decision of the All-German Committee of the Independent Social Democracy[151] with regard to these questions and also demands of the French women comrades and women leaders of the trade unions, demands which agreed with the decisions of the Independent Social Democracy of Germany. The Conference was opened with a manifestation of solidarity and with sympathy for the international secretary, Klara Zetkin, whose absence was profoundly regretted. A strong protest was raised against the shameful suppression of *Gleichheit,* a blow against the Women's Socialist International. That this was not a Platonic protest could be seen from the fact that according to reports

---

[151] The complete text of the demands for the improvement of the labor conditions for women and for the protection and education of children as drafted by the All-German Women's Committee of the Independent Social Democratic party of Germany may be found in Balabanoff, "Die Zimmerwalder Bewegung ....," Grünberg, *Archiv* ...., XII, 406–408.

from various countries the women comrades have begun to raise money for a new *Gleichheit*. Now more than ever the socialist women's movement requires an international organ which will guide the women socialists in carrying out the responsible duty which the development of history has imposed upon them. Such an organ as this could be entrusted only to Klara Zetkin, and therefore the socialist women of all countries consider it to be their honorable duty to make it possible for the foremost fighter of the socialist women's movement to unfold after the war as she did before, and without interference, her incomparable and irreplaceable activity in the interest of schooling and rallying the international female proletariat. All letters addressed to the Conference begin with a personal greeting to Klara Zetkin, including the letter from the French and Finnish women comrades. The Italian *Difesa delle Lavoratrici* is devoting several articles to commenting on the suppression of *Gleichheit* and to the campaign for raising money in order to resume its issue. The campaign is being supported by the Italian party Presidium and all the socialist organizations of Italy.

The larger part of the meetings consisted in hearing reports of comrades from Germany, Austria, Finland, Bulgaria, Russia, Rumania, Sweden, and Switzerland and in reading aloud the letters of women comrades who were absent. The World War has confronted the proletarian women everywhere with the same misery and deprivation, the same too-heavy burden of hard physical labor and great worries. Everywhere the growing generations are being threatened with undernourishment and degeneration. Death, hunger, and brutalization reign everywhere and the exploiters and the war profiteers are making use of the same means everywhere. The proletarians who offer their lives for their fatherland are being rewarded by having their wives and children in the rear die a slow death from hard bondage, starvation wages, exorbitant prices for food products, the abolition of protective legislation, and so forth. Everywhere there is speculation upon the fact that among the petty bourgeoisie and the backward strata of the unorganized proletariat there are young girls and women who regard the wages which they are now earning and the freedom "which they enjoy in the absence of their husbands" as an "improvement" of their condition. This rashness and contentedness which merely point out how "happy" these unassuming creatures were before the war gives the exploiters and preachers of morals one more reason for coming forth with words and deeds against the "riots" and the "far-fetched demands" of the class-conscious workers who are fighting for peace and for an existence worthy of a human being. The social changes produced by the war, especially among women, coincide in every detail with the psychological changes: it is becoming more clearly and more irrevocably understood by the class-conscious proletarian women that they actually have nothing else to lose but their chains and thorns.

The women comrades closed the Conference, at which so many interesting communications, so much advice and so many experiences were exchanged, with a renewed and affirmed intention to draw closer and closer the proletarian women of all countries to the fulfillment of the Berne and the Zimmerwald resolutions, which were strengthened and supplemented at the Third Zimmerwald Conference. The demonstrations for peace and against hunger, organized by the women in various countries—Russia, Italy, Germany, Rumania, France—are proof that the women of the working class know that they can obtain the right to live only by fighting.

APPEAL FOR THE SUPPORT OF THE NEW SOVIET GOVERNMENT

[Joint Proclamation of the Central Committee of the R.S.D.L. Party (Bolsheviks) and the International Socialist Committee, November 8, 1917][152]

To the Proletarians of All Countries!

Men and Women Workers!

The workers and soldiers were victorious on November 7 in Petrograd over the government of capitalists and Junkers. The power is in the hands of the Workers' and Soldiers' Soviet. The same will have taken place in all the centers of the labor movement at the moment when you read this appeal. The Baltic fleet, the army in Finland, and the large majority of soldiers at the front and in the rear are certainly faithful to the banner of the Workers' and Soldiers' government.

The government has been overthrown; that government which was established by the people on the ruins of Tsarism and which trod their interests underfoot; which raised the price of bread in order to help the Junkers to snatch whatever was left untouched by the war profiteers; which gave the people martial law instead of freedom; which, as a hostage of Entente capital, drove the workers and soldiers into the war again and again without attempting even to inititate peace negotiations. The workers and soldiers of Petrograd have chased that government out, as they chased out the Tsar. Their first word is *peace.* They demand the immediate suspension of hostilities, immediate peace negotiations which will lead toward an honest peace without annexations and indemnities on the basis of the right of nations to self-determination.

Men and women workers! Red Petrograd is calling to you! You, into whose eyes the specter of the fourth winter campaign is looking, you to whose sons, fathers, and brothers it stretches out its icy hand, you

[152] *I.S.K. Nachrichtendienst,* No. 28, November 10, 1917, pp. 6–7.

have to speak now. Though the proletarians and soldiers of Russia are heroes, alone they cannot conquer bread or freedom or peace. Capital, the Junkers, and the Russian generals—all these powers of exploitation and oppression—will strain all their efforts to stifle in blood the revolution of workers and soldiers. They will attempt to cut off the food supply of the towns, to instigate the Cossacks against the revolution. If they succeed in suppressing the revolution they will continue the war. But it is not they alone who threaten with death the Russian revolution and its cause of peace. Both the governments of the Central Powers and those of the Entente are its enemies because it initiates the cause of liberation of the masses of the people. The Central Powers may take advantage of the civil war in Russia to freshen up by new victories the peoples' dying will to fight, and the Entente powers will support the Russian counter-revolution with money.

Proletarians of all countries, your vital interest, your blood is at stake. If the Russian revolution is defeated by the joint efforts of Russian and foreign capital, then the capitalists will drag you from one battlefield to another until you bleed white. Join the Russian revolution!

We call to you not for expressions of sympathy but for struggle. Rise; go into the streets; leave the factories; exert influence with every means and every strength. There shall be no fourth winter campaign. Not another shot shall be fired. Peace negotiations must be opened at once. Trust no pacifist phrases. Judge every government by whether or not it accepts immediate suspension of hostilities on all fronts, whether it recognizes immediate peace negotiations and peace without annexations and indemnities on the basis of the right of nations to self-determination. Form everywhere Workers' and Soldiers' Councils as organs of your struggle for peace!

We invite to Stockholm the representatives of all parties which wish to lead this struggle. Insistently demand passports for the delegates; demand the release of the imprisoned comrades who enjoy the confidence of the international proletariat, so that they may take part in the work for peace.

Hail! Immediate suspension of hostilities!

Not another shot must be fired!

On toward peace negotiations!

Move on to struggle for peace without annexations and indemnities!
Peace concluded by the free will of the peoples!

Hail, international solidarity of the proletariat!

Hail, socialism!

REPRESENTATIVES OF THE CENTRAL COMMITTEE OF THE
BOLSHEVIKS ABROAD

THE INTERNATIONAL SOCIALIST COMMITTEE

THE SIGNIFICANCE OF THE BREST-LITOVSK PEACE NEGOTIATIONS

[Circular Letter of the International Socialist Committee, December 27, 1917][153]

To the working class!

In this horrible war, values have long since lost all their meaning. Any single fact of the war defies portrayal in words and is utterly beyond imagination, and every attempt to describe it to those who have experienced it themselves appears childish, if not simply malicious. The situation is similar with regard to the means which the bloody experience of all these years, and especially of the last few months, seems to designate as the only means destined to put an end to all these horrors. Since the outbreak of the Russian revolution all indications that only the revolutionary power of the peoples is capable of putting an end to the war have been confirmed by facts. Whoever was alien or even hostile toward the Zimmerwald movement now understands and feels that this movement was right. Just as the proletarians tremble before the horror and the threatened continuation of the war, so they tremble before the importance and the sublimity of the events which are unfolding in Russia and at Brest-Litovsk. It is the destiny of human civilization and of millions of human beings that is being decided there, and not merely the questions of war and peace, of victory for one or the other; it is not the territorial fate of individual countries which is being decided there—a duel between the classes has opened there. It is a question not merely of the right of nations to self-determination but of THE RIGHT OF THE PEOPLE, OF THE PROLETARIAT, OF HUMAN BEINGS TO SELF-DETERMINATION. The Russian people, by means of its revolutionary power, has forced the mighty and the omnipotent members of the existing social order, who hold the life and death of whole nations in their hands, to recognize its power heretofore prohibited and scorned. It is precisely this duel that has called forth a very great commotion within the ranks of the imperialists and their accomplices, the social patriots. Everything, so they maintain, must be done to prevent the victory of the Russian revolutionary power. The imperialists of all countries have reason to fear that such a victory might upset all their calculations and force them to conclude a peace without annexations. The social patriots are also afraid that the victory of the Russian revolution might expose their tactics before the peoples more than ever before. Therefore, because of the Russian peace negotiations, a crusade is being led against the Russian revolution, a crusade which shrinks from no

[153] "Rundschreiben an die der I.S.K. angeschlossenen Parteien und Organisationen," *I.S.K. Nachrichtendienst*, No. 33, January 3, 1918, pp. 1–2.

means, threats, intrigues, etc. They seek to gain time in order to save social patriotism at the expense of anxiously awaited peace and the future of mankind. In spite of all this the Russian Workers', Peasants', and Soldiers' government has suspended peace negotiations for ten days so as to give the peoples an opportunity to exert pressure and take steps so that *the Russian people will not stand alone in its struggle against world capitalism* which is destroying mankind. Action by the Russian masses is to replace the most powerful written and verbal agitation. *Active support is urgently called for!*

The Zimmerwald parties and organizations know that it is their duty and honor to take advantage of this ten-day period.

THE INTERNATIONAL SOCIALIST COMMITTEE

WORKERS' AGITATION, THE STRUGGLE IN FINLAND, AND THE NEED OF UNITED ACTION

[Proclamation of the International Socialist Committee to the Zimmerwald Parties and the Working Class, February 6, 1918][154]

The hour has struck to open in all countries a unanimous fight for the re-establishment of peace, for the liberation of the peoples by the socialist proletariat. These words express neither a desire nor a warning nor a prophecy, but a fact which has already been inscribed on the record of contemporary history in the blood of proletarians. Through powerful pressure exerted by the Russian revolution on the rulers and the proletarians of all countries, the proletarians have finally broken their passive attitude and changed from the defensive to the offensive. At last they have grasped the weapon of class struggle, the weapon which the ruling classes never stopped using. The Zimmerwaldists, the revolutionary Social Democrats, always regarded the war as a dexterous move on the part of the rapacious ruling classes against the disfranchised proletariat, as a raid the purpose of which was not merely to accomplish imperialist conquests but to deprive the subjected classes of their physical and political strength, to strike at the ranks of the class-conscious proletarians, the workers, and the social democrats in their own country. The peace negotiations enforced by the Russian people after a difficult struggle have served to reveal completely and irrevocably the true nature of the war; even credulous people now understand that war is a raid conducted at the expense of the disinherited classes of all countries. Is there a man, woman, or child who would now believe that the rulers are defending something or that they wish to conclude a peace without annexations? The German and Austrian rulers are revealing their

[154] "An die Zimmerwalder Parteien, an die Arbeiterklasse," *I.S.K. Nachrichtendienst*, No. 35, February 6, 1918, pp. 1–3.

concrete plans of annexations. By their presumptuous conduct and their system of extortion they are complicating to the utmost any conclusion of peace, whereas the representatives of the Entente Powers declare in the same provocative fashion that they would like more than ever to continue the war with the most sanguinary methods. The governments have produced material reasons for believing that the competition of imperialist states can only be solved on the battlefields of class struggle. The powerful signal that has sounded from Russia evoked an echo in all countries. In both Germany and Austria the working masses have frequently seized the proletarian weapon, the mass strike, in spite of their leaders' protest. Let the governmental organs boast as loudly as they wish of having "suppressed the movement," a movement which was presumably purely economic in character; "the rulers" know better than anyone else what this movement signifies. The governments comprehend the political and social character of the strikes and they know that it is not a matter of single battles. England, France, Spain, and Italy are seized by the proletarian movement. The significance of this movement is clear to everybody despite the fact that the censors are concealing the character and duration of the movement and pretend victory in place of defeat. The proletarians have finally understood that the deepest trenches they have to overcome are those that are formed not by national boundaries but by class antagonisms, which have never before appeared in such a glaring bloody light as at this very time. At Brest-Litovsk the arch enemies of the Allies are in fact defending their own interests. The annexations in the East, which will be recognized in favor of Germany, will clear the way for other annexations. Hence it is a matter of enforcing the principle of an undemocratic annexationist peace in order that it may serve as a basis for a general "horse trading." Two world outlooks of two classes and not of hostile nations are fighting at Brest-Litovsk. There, as elsewhere, the issue is power, an issue which will be settled on the battlefields of class struggle. Will the support given by the proletarians of other countries to the Russian people be sufficient to assure victory in the gigantic fight against the rulers of the entire world in the interests of the peoples of all countries? The class-conscious proletariat knows what the point in question is: it will continue the struggle against the exploiters in its own country and not forsake the vanguard of the proletarian revolution. The rulers take sufficient care of this. To the proletarian manifestations in favor of immediate peace they reply with Draconic verdicts, disdain, and lead. In Germany, Italy, America, and France the prisons are being filled with fighters for peace. The majority of them have to pay for their sins with their lives at the front. In Finland, a country in which, according to the nationalist theories which have cost the proletariat of all countries so much blood, the greatest quiet should reign, in which there should be the honeymoon of a liberated people, the blood of the suppressed classes is flowing; trenches and barricades are erected against the internal enemy with a cruelty and cynicism that have nothing to learn from the war methods which are raging on various fronts. The patriotic Russian generals who a few months ago led the Russian soldiers into death in the struggle against the "German enemy," are now leading the German soldiers, the riflemen trained in Germany, in a destructive fight against the Russian proletariat.[155] The Finnish bourgeoisie is proving its patriotism by employing a mercenary army, paid with the money the bourgeoisie extorts from the people, to shoot the starving people with weapons received from abroad. The bourgeoisie of all countries—a brilliant example of it is in Sweden—declares its sympathy with the "poor" bourgeoisie whose privileges are threatened. The struggle in Finland is followed with eager interest by the ruling classes of the entire world, which are exasperated by any violence on the part of the self-defending proletariat, which of course seems to be much more terrible for the bourgeoisie than millions of proletarian corpses and of ruined lives caused by the execrable war. Switzerland, peaceful Switzerland, where the unpretentiousness of the working class has become proverbial, even she is challenged by its ruling class to open a fight. In a country in which the propertied classes have always offered the people democracy and hospitality the workers and the foreign proletarians are being treated as slaves of the lowest class, while the civil service, which is to be introduced there, is of an outspoken class character such as has never before occurred even in any monarchist militant state. Against all these violences the proletariat possesses only the weapon of class struggle, and this weapon must be used with all possible rigor and consistency. Proletarians! The bourgeoisie has surpassed you in this struggle. We remind you of the Zimmerwald manifesto:

"Our appeal is directed to the workers of every country. Their own fate is indissolubly bound to that of the world proletariat. The workers of a country who exclude themselves from the common struggle or, worse than that, who attack it from the rear, frustrate peace, lengthen war and the exploitation of the peoples, and ruin their own future. They commit treason against the common cause of mankind. This must not be !"

We invite you to express everywhere at public meetings your desire for peace, to demonstrate in favor of the sacred cause of the proletarian International from the 10th to the 17th of the month.

[155] Baron Mannerheim, the commander of the White forces in Finland, was a former Russian general. The "riflemen" are presumably the Jäger Battalion of Finns trained in Germany for service against Tsarist Russia and employed against the Finnish Reds and their revolutionary Russian allies.

Hail! Revolutionary Socialism!
Hail! Peace!

THE INTERNATIONAL SOCIALIST COMMITTEE

FOR THE FIRST OF MAY

[Proclamation of the International Socialist Committee, May 1, 1918][156]

FOR PEACE AMONG THE PEOPLES AND THE RIGHT OF THE MASSES!

Proletarians, comrades!

The bloody waves of war, which does not wish to cease, are rising ever higher. Larger and larger sacrifices are being reaped on the battlefields. The instruments and the weapons of destruction are more devastating than ever, and higher and higher grow the walls of irritation and hatred, which are being erected between the peoples by the continued war frenzy.

The only ray of *dawn* which breaks through this awful darkness and thick fog is that of the Russian Workers' and Peasants' revolution. Through an imposing *manifestation of the will* of the awakening powerful proletarian forces struggling for universal peace and for a socialist reconstruction of society as the only strong foundation of the understanding between the masses of the nations, the Russian proletarian revolution has also addressed an energetic appeal to the masses and to labor parties all over the world, urging them to force the war to end, to carry into action the idea of a mass uprising advanced at the International Socialist congresses.

The response provoked by this appeal, which came from Zimmerwald and which has manifested itself in mass demonstrations and mass strikes in several countries, has been insufficiently strong, however, to prevent the *renewal of tremendous bloodshed* on the remaining scenes of warfare. So far the socialist majorities within the world of organized labor have not made up their minds to break the bond of civil peace and to plant the banner of resumed class struggle among the downtrodden and misled masses which are caught in the shackles of war patriotism.

The hour of decision is drawing near. There is passing through the world a feeling that the forces of society and of violence, which are active in favor of prolonging this madness, are beginning to exhaust themselves. *The situation within the states is becoming ever more intolerable, the specter of universal famine is entering the gates of all countries;* the destruction of all material and ideological values has reached such a degree that even leaders and statesmen of capitalist militant states are

---

[156] "Auf zum ersten Mai!" *I.S.K. Nachrichtendienst,* No. 39, April 1–May 1, 1918, pp. 2–3.

beginning to dread the future. In the labyrinths of their criminal diplomacy they are groping for a way out of the chaos which has been caused by the bourgeois capitalist order of society based upon cannon and bayonets. They are beginning to dread the accomplishment of their own hands. At the same time the inherent laws and forces of their own society are driving them unmercifully *into the infernal abyss of this mad policy*.

In spite of the fact that peoples are afflicted with extreme sufferings, in spite of their immeasurable sacrifices and losses, seeds of new and similar wars are being planted on the battlefields. In spite of the material which is brought to light with increasing frequency and which throws light upon the responsibility of the ruling classes for the outbreak of the war, as well as on the manner in which they gamble with the destinies of the nations, nevertheless the *spirit* of the rulers *testifies* to the same arrogance, the same lust for power and profit, the same means of deception, the same will (in spite of the fact that they render lip service to the idea of peace without annexations and indemnities) to annex and exploit which in the first days of war was expressed in the announcement of the doctrines of despotism originating from bourgeois and imperialist society.

The peace treaties concluded in the East testify to this. They draw the pattern of universal peace, which, however, in the West will be made to appear as a despotic peace in order to perpetuate for an indefinite period the system of armaments, war menace, and the old irresponsible secret diplomacy.

As they are put into effect the predatory imperialistic nature of these peace treaties is being exposed; it is seen that they are incapable of restoring the balance and peace; that, on the contrary, they are being followed by fierce and bloody civil wars called forth by the imperialist efforts of the Central Powers on behalf of capitalism. In the Baltic provinces the disinherited classes of the population are being subdued; in the Ukraine and in Finland the laboring masses, which have risen in defense of their rights, are being suppressed by the local White guards and their allies, the Prussian and the Austrian troops. On the day when the fraternization of the peoples is realized the workers of all countries will recall with pain and shame that the Finnish and the Russian workers in their hard struggle for liberation received no help from workers of other countries but that, on the contrary, the German and Austrian proletarians, supported by the social patriotic leaders, engaged in stifling the freedom of their brothers with their own hands and in the interest of tyrants.

These are brilliant examples of *solidarity* among the bourgeois classes of various countries, and at the same time they constitute an omen and a signal for the laboring class all over the world to rid themselves of the hypocritical phrases of civil peace and *to unite against the only real enemy*.

Events which we have witnessed in the East and which we continue to witness confirm our point of view. Whatever the outcome of the offensive will be, this duel fought to the utmost can be settled only by an uprising of the bleeding masses on the day of settling accounts and by the necessary *internal* settling of accounts between the classes of every country.

The first of May is drawing near—the great day of the gathering of the world proletariat which, since the outbreak of war, has been covered with the blood of the tortured masses. The sounds of this day are drowned by the thundering of cannon, the death rattle of the dying, the distress of the wounded.

The first of May is here. On the fourth "May first" of this war the thoughts of hundreds of thousands, even millions of men, from trenches, hospital cots, prison camps, bereft of houses and herds, turn to the aspirations and ideals for which in the days of peace they went in processions to the places of demonstration.

May the class-conscious proletariat of all countries show all those victims of war that all the barbarism of war and all the arts of diplomacy have not been able to extinguish the flame of *international* proletarian *solidarity,* the flame which was kindled more than fifty years ago by a small group of men in the First International.

When we think of this great heroic attempt of universal fraternization and peace attained through class struggle for the benefit of mankind, the memory of one great personality, of a life of gigantic achievements devoted to the world-liberating mission of the socialist idea awakens in us. Across the hell of today there glows the memory, a hundred years old, of the day when Karl Marx was born. The same powers which he exposed and against which he fought are accomplishing in the World War their historic and sacrilegious mission, applying, in spite of their own will, the seal of truth to his prophecy.

May the red banners celebrate his memory today in a dignified manner! The May Day celebration of 1918 can be dignified only if we, inspired by the sublime examples of the history of socialism and of Marx, raise a lasting, loud, and impressive protest against the continuation of this criminal war, against the powers and the forces which make war possible, against the conspiracy of capitalism and militarism which is an irreconcilable enemy of a lasting, universal peace and of the rights and fraternization of the peoples in all countries.

Though all our sentiments and thoughts are directed toward it, and all occurrences and experiences bear the fatal stamp of these bloody events, the war with its horrors and its open imperialist character is far from driving into the background the May First demands of the revolutionary proletariat, but on the contrary emphasizes their importance and urgent character.

Men and women workers of all countries! Join the world demonstration of the proletariat. By coming forth proudly and self-assertively in favor of it, you proletarians of the neutral and the belligerent countries are approaching the day when capitalist society, charged with blood and disgrace, will collapse under the pressure of its victims: the exploited of all countries.

Hail, May First! Hail, universal peace! Down with war! Down with militarism! Hail, the active solidarity of the international proletariat! Hail, an eight-hour working day! Down with capitalism! Hail, the International of class-conscious revolutionary fighters for the emancipation of labor!

THE INTERNATIONAL SOCIALIST COMMITTEE

APPEAL OF THE ZIMMERWALD COMMITTEE TO THE WORKING MASSES OF ALL COUNTRIES

[Issued in August by the I.S.C. to Accompany the Appeal of the Soviet Government to the Workers of the Entente Countries][157]

PROLETARIANS!

The war is destroying and annihilating everything except your patience, your will to endure pain and sorrow. No tyrant, no autocrat, no slaveowner in the darkest period of the past could permit himself to destroy so many human lives and so to oppress his slaves as do the present rulers daily and hourly in the "constitutional" states, the "democracies," and the like ———. Daily, even hourly, new mockeries, new abuses and crimes are added to the innumerable sorrows and unprecedented bloody sacrifices of the popular masses. Your exploiters are becoming more and more shameless. Your submissiveness encourages them: formerly the press used to say that the fatherland was in danger, that freedom had to be defended; now this criminal, mercenary press, this murderer of the people, conscious of its mission, no longer has to resort to these demagogic tricks. The lust for conquest of the imperialist bandits is now being openly satiated by mountains of proletarian corpses, by oceans of proletarian blood. In this bloody world competition the proletariat plays the rôle of Cain—it not only destroys its own brothers instead of its enemies but it also destroys itself; it ignominiously betrays its own class, its own children, and its honor. Any workman, if he

---

[157] *I.S.K. Nachrichtendienst*, No. 44, September 1, 1918, pp. 11–13. This issue published the appeal in German, French, Swedish, Italian, and English. The version given here is a translation of the German text.

could understand the situation clearly, would prefer death ———. The capitalists and their mercenary accomplices, the bloodstained press, have known for a long time that no settlement can be made on the battlefield. The offensives and counteroffensives, with their ghastly destruction of human life, their panic, and "patriotic" frenzy, are to divert the attention and the anger of the masses of both the defeated and the "victorious" countries from a realization of their deception and the futility of their sacrifices. Why, since they recognize this, don't the rulers declare peace? Because—as the revolutionary internationalist Zimmerwaldists have perceived and explained to the masses—the rulers fear the day of reckoning. Ever since the outbreak of the triumphant revolution in Russia this reckoning has acquired a definite form for the rulers: the "Red phantom" in the distant east has become flesh and blood; it calls the exploited of all countries and by its own example it leads them onward. Therefore the foremost duty is to *fight proletarian Russia*. It does not matter to Germany that she has been fighting Russian Tsarism. To those whose wealth and parasitic existence are made possible by wage slavery, the class-conscious proletarians, the Russian revolutionary government are the real and truly *hated dangers*. Therefore, on against Red Finland, against socialist Russia! The Entente countries, which try to justify their infamous part in the slaughter by saying that they are shedding the blood of the international proletariat on behalf of the right of nations to "self-determination," and America, whose trust magnates shed crocodile tears over German imperialism, are now all aiding German imperialism and trying to impose an autocrat upon the proud Russian republic, an autocrat who will be more despotic than either Nicholas or Wilhelm. The Czechoslovaks, who would have been regarded as traitors if they were not in the service of the Entente—these hirelings of Franco-British capital—are now recognized as an independent power. Those who have whined hypocritically over the fate of neutral Belgium are now attacking a defenseless country which not only is neutral but which proved by word and deed that it does not wish to *make war*. The sons of revolution, the standard-bearers of freedom, are striking down representatives of a country, of a class, who have carried out a most glorious deed of liberation by freeing the lowliest slaves from the heaviest yoke and who have replaced the most abominable autocracy by the self-determination of an oppressed class ———. The West-Europeans are raising their swords, not against militarism, which deceives the people and destroys human beings and freedom, but against the builders of a new culture. This is the task to which the sons of the people are to devote themselves: to forge their own chains, to stain their hands forever in the blood of their brothers, with their own hands to put off for centuries socialism which liberates the peoples. Those proletarians who have justly regarded Tsarism as their worst enemy and the Russian revolutionist as a martyr and hero of the cause of liberation are now to be drowned in proletarian blood.

The Russian government, which finds itself in a most difficult position in which a government of people's representatives can be placed only by a diabolical conspiracy, turns, as it did before the conclusion of the Brest-Litovsk treaty and as on various other occasions, to you, workers of the Entente countries. But liberation is an international task. Therefore, we address *all proletarians* regardless of country: Proletarians, do not commit a bloody treason; save yourselves from suicide; do not murder a newly born child of the socialist revolution!

As the German internationalists protested before the attack upon Finland, so now the internationalist groups of England, France, and, above all, the persecuted and penalized Italian Socialist party and the martyrs of internationalism in America are raising their burning protest against the intervention in Russia, in spite of the cruelest reaction. But all these groups are minorities, helpless minorities, against whom the authorities proceed by imposing prison sentences, whose voices are being silenced, whose activity is being paralyzed as long as you, working masses, are not behind them, as long as you do not throw upon the scales your power, your class-consciousness, as long as you do not proclaim your revolutionary will. The Scheidemanns of Germany have shamelessly approved Germany's bloodshed in Finland and Russia and thus have cleared a path for all the other traitors; the Judases of French socialism have betrayed the socialist cause to the extent of supporting their government and thereby making it easier for it to attack the Russian proletarian republic; the British social imperialists surpass all others by their shameless support of the interests of the murderers of socialists; the Italian ex-socialists have become the most despicable mouthpieces of imperialism and of monarchy; the American representatives of those imperialists who personify the worst hypocrisy in this war prostitute the socialism which they formerly supported: commissioned by the trust kings they undertake trips to "persuade" the war-weary proletarians to continue to serve as cannon fodder. While the Japanese proletarians shed their blood in order not to yield to imperialism and the entire world trembles and shakes, the "socialist" representatives of the neutral countries, who are granted passports by their governments for their good services, are traveling around compromising with the governments and distracting the attention of the peoples with talk about a conference which they know can take place only as a mouthpiece of imperialism, concerned with the crowning of the imperialist orgy, and committed to the necessity of waiting for the victory of the Entente before it even can open. Precisely this kind of "agitation" is needed by the governments which are already sending young children into the hell of the World War.

When the German and Austrian workers were about to commit an irreparable crime by wishing to introduce "order" in Russia and Finland, we told them: "All the achievements of socialism and of the proletariat of all countries, the most elementary rights of the people as well as the highest and most sublime ideals of the exploited classes are at stake."

The situation is more serious than ever. Two equally tragic questions arise. First: Is it possible that this war, which has deprived the peoples of everything and which by its origin and progress, by its direct and indirect results constitutes but an increasing challenge to the popular masses, is likely to end in the victory of the instigators and profiteers? Will they plant their victorious banner on the corpses of their slaves? Will this war encourage new wars, and will war rage on for a long time to come under the rule of a terrific reaction? Along with the crushing of the Russian and the Finnish revolutions and of the proletarian republic in the Ukraine, will the very idea of a people's government, of a socialist state be crushed?

The second thought, which is no less terrifying, no less humiliating: Will the German and the Austrian peoples, following the fratricidal call of their enemies, raise their hand against the socialist republic, against a brother who does not take part in the imperialist world contest? Who compose the German troops? Are they proletarians, sons of the people, who regard the socialist land of freedom as an "enemy land"?

Now the question becomes broader, deeper, and more tragic. Fearlessly and proudly the Russian people fought against a world of enemies in order to give peace to the peoples and in order to be able to devote themselves to a reconstruction of society, to the building of a new life upon the ruins of the dying social order. The ruling classes, encouraged by the passivity of their slaves, are forcing the Russian people to take up their arms once more. Proletarians of Europe and America, think of the role which you are made to play! The spirit of socialism which will liberate the peoples will be stifled by you. You will destroy your own liberation, so that your exploiters, stepping over your bodies, can consign your wives and children to starvation and slavery in full realization that the world is theirs, that the rule of force and slavery is invincible! On the ruins of the Russian republic, on the corpses of the socialist Soviets, the imperialists of all countries wish to erect the bloodstained banner of capitalist order.

Working men and women, you won't let this happen. Proletarians of all countries unite! Rescue the banner of international socialism!

Hail, the revolutionary Socialist International!

On to struggle for the Russian workers' and peasants' republic! Hail, the Zimmerwald action in all countries! Down with imperialism!

THE INTERNATIONAL SOCIALIST COMMITTEE

CHRONOLOGY, 1848–1918

(All dates are given in the Georgian calendar; for some events dealing with Russia the Julian calendar date is given in parentheses.)

1848. The Communist Manifesto issued by Karl Marx and Friedrich Engels. Revolutions in France, the Germanies, and the Habsburg Empire.

Failure of the socialist uprising in Paris.

1861. Proclamation to the "Younger Generation" urging the revolutionary overthrow of the existing order in Russia, published in *Velikorus* by Chernyshevsky's followers.

1862. The "Land and Freedom" society organized to lead the expected peasant revolt; ceased to exist by 1864.

1863. Allgemeiner deutscher Arbeiterverein organized by Lasalle.

1864. The First International organized in London.

1866. September 3–8. First Congress of the First International at Geneva.

1867. Volume I of Marx's *Das Kapital* published. Volumes II and III published posthumously by Friedrich Engels in 1885 and 1894.

September 2–8. Second Congress of the First International at Lausanne.

1868. Publication of Petr Lavrov's *Istoricheskiia pisma* ("Historical Letters") begun.

September 6–15. Third Congress of the First International at Brussels.

1869. German Social Democratic Labor party organized by Wilhelm Liebknecht and August Bebel.

Chaikovsky's circle established in Russia.

September 6–12. Fourth Congress of the First International at Basel.

1869–71. The Nechaev affair (trial in 1871).

1870–71. The Franco-Prussian war.

1871. The Paris Commune.

1872. The first volume of Karl Marx's *Das Kapital* translated into Russian.

September 2–7. Fifth Congress of the First International at the Hague. Anarchists expelled and the General Council transferred from London to New York.

September 15–16. Anarchist Congress at Saint-Imier; Anarchist International organized.

1873. The Dolgushin circle established in Russia.

1874. Social Democratic Workingmen's party organized in the United States.

1875. The South Russian Workers' League formed in Odessa.

Portuguese Socialist party founded.

May 22–27. Union of the Lasalle and Liebknecht-Bebel groups at the Gotha Congress; the Socialist Labor party of Germany established.

1876. The Northern Revolutionary Narodnik group organized in St. Petersburg by Narodnik revolutionists who had escaped the repressive Tsarist measures of 1873–75.

The First International dissolved.

July 1. Death of Mikhail Bakunin.

1877. Mass trials of Narodniks in Russia.

Social Democratic Workingmen's party of the United States changed to the Socialist Labor party of North America.

September 9–16. The World Socialist Congress at Ghent; failure of the socialists and anarchists to agree on a common program.

1877–78. The Russo-Turkish war.

1878. The name "Land and Freedom" assumed by the Northern Revolutionary Narodnik group.

Laws adopted for the suppression of the social democratic movement in Germany.

Social Democratic League founded in Holland.

Social Democratic League founded in Denmark.

November. The North Russian Workers' League formed in St. Petersburg.

1879. Spanish Social Democratic Labor party founded.

June. The split of the "Land and Freedom" party into the "People's Will" party and the "Black Partition," headed by Plekhanov.

October 20. Opening of the French labor congress in Marseille in which the socialists had a majority; Federation of the Party of Socialist Workers of France organized.

1880. French labor congress at Havre; nonsocialist members withdraw; socialist program drafted by Jules Guesde and Paul Lafargue adopted.

1881. Emigration of Plekhanov and other leaders of the "Black Partition" group to Switzerland.

Central Revolutionary Committee (later called the Socialist Revolutionary party) formed by the Blanquists in France.

1881. The Democratic Federation founded in England.

March 13 (1). Assassination of Alexander II by order of the Executive Committee of the "People's Will" party.

October 2–12. International congress of socialists at Chur. Attempt to revive the First International failed.

1882. "People's Will" party suppressed. Its leaders sought refuge abroad. The Italian Workers' party (Partito operaio) organized.

September 25. French labor congress at Saint Étienne; the Guesdists withdrew and held their own congress at Roanne where the French Labor party was organized.

1883. Fabian Society organized in England.

Blagoev's circle organized in St. Petersburg under the name, "The party of Russian Social Democrats."

March 14. Death of Karl Marx.

September 25. The "Emancipation of Labor" group formed by Russian emigrés in Switzerland.

1884. The Democratic Federation of England renamed the Social Democratic Federation.

The first draft program of Russian Social Democrats, a mixture of Marxist and Narodnik ideas, published by the "Emancipation of Labor" group.

1885. Belgian Labor party organized.

April. Congress of the Italian Workers' party in Milan; program adopted.

October 13 (1). Last number of the publication *Narodnaia Volia* ("The People's Will"), which acknowledged the defeat of the "People's Will" party.

1886. April 25–26. Italian socialist congress at Montava; decision to cooperate with the Italian Workers' party adopted.

1887. The Blagoev group suppressed by the Russian government.

Norwegian Social Democratic Labor party founded.

1888. Swiss Social Democratic party founded.

The leadership of the Austrian labor movement captured by the socialists; the United Socialist party of Austria organized.

1889. The first strictly Marxist circles, which became active in the "self-education" movement, organized in various Russian towns.

Swedish Social Democratic Labor party founded.

July 14–20. First Congress of the Second International in Paris.

1890. October. Congress of the Federation of Socialist Workers of France at Châtellerault, at which a split occurred. The Revolutionary Socialist Workers' party formed by the Allemanists.

October 12–18. Congress of the German Socialist Labor party at Halle; party name changed to German Social Democratic party.

1891. August. Italian labor congress, with a socialist majority, at Milan; foundation for a Marxist workers' party laid.

August 16–23. Second Congress of the Second International at Brussels.

October. Former members of the "People's Will" party succeed finally in organizing the group of "People's Will" partisans.

October 14–20. The German Social Democratic party congress at Erfurt; the new program drafted by Karl Kautsky adopted.

1892. February. Program issued by the group of "People's Will" partisans. Many groups organized during the following years as groups of the "People's Will" partisans or of Socialist Revolutionists.

August 14. Italian labor congress at Genoa; the party of Italian Workers (Partito dei lavoratori Italiani) organized and program adopted.

November. Polish Socialist party organized in Paris.

1893. British Independent Labour party organized.

Bulgarian Social Democratic Labor party organized.

July 30. Polish Social Democratic party organized.

August 6–12. Third Congress of the Second International at Zürich.

September 8. Congress of the Party of Italian Workers at Reggio Emilia; intransigent policy adopted. Name changed to Socialist Party of Italian Workers.

1895. Death of Friedrich Engels.

Formation abroad of the League of Russian Social Democrats on the initiative of the "Emancipation of Labor" group.

January 13. Congress of the Socialist Party of Italian Workers at Parma; name changed to Italian Socialist party.

Autumn. The St. Petersburg League of Struggle for the Liberation of the Working Class formed.

December 20–21 (8–9). Lenin arrested and in February 1897 exiled to Siberia for three years.

1896. A program for Russian Social Democrats, advocating a centralized all-Russian party, drafted by Lenin.

July 27–31. Fourth Congress of the Second International at London. Delegates of Russian workers' organizations took part for the first time.

1896–97. Bernstein's revisionist articles "Probleme des Sozialismus" published in *Die Neue Zeit.*

1897. August. The Socialist-Revolutionist party organized at Voronezh.

September 25–27. Constituent Congress of the All-Jewish Workers' League of Lithuania, Poland, and Russia (the so-called Bund) at Vilna.

1898. Publication of a systematic exposition of economism by Kuskova under the title "The Credo."

Lenin's pamphlet *Zadachi russkikh sotsial-demokratov* ("The Tasks of Russian Social Democrats") published.

March 13–15 (1–3). First Congress of the R.S.D.L. party at Minsk; manifesto issued.

March 23–24 (11–12). Participants in the First Congress of R.S.D.L. party arrested and the organization destroyed by the Russian government.

April. Beginning of the Spanish-American war.

October 3–8. Congress of the German Social Democratic party at Stuttgart; revisionism denounced.

November. First Congress of the League of Russian Social Democrats at Zürich; the "Emancipation of Labor" group refused to take part in the League's publications because of the latters' economist tendency.

1899. Bernstein's *Die Voraussetzungen des Sozialismus und die Aufgaben der Sozialdemokratie* and Kautsky's reply, *Bernstein und das sozial-demokratische Programm: eine Antikritik,* published.

February. Student strikes in Russia.

June. Millerand entered French Cabinet; the issue of "Millerandism" raised in the socialist press by Rosa Luxemburg.

October. Beginning of the Boer war.

October 9–14. Congress of German Social Democratic party at Hannover; revisionism repudiated but the revisionists remained in the party.

December. Union of the Social Democratic parties of Poland and Lithuania at Vilna, under the name "Social Democracy of the Kingdom of Poland and Lithuania."

December 3–8. First general congress of the French socialist organizations in Paris. Participation in bourgeois cabinets condemned. Proposal for party unification adopted.

1900. Lenin, Martov, and Potresov returned from Siberian exile.

February 27. British Labour party formed.

April. Second Congress of the League of Russian Social Democrats at Geneva. Plekhanov and his followers withdrew and formed a new revolutionary organization, "the Social Democrat."

1900. May. Illegal conference of Russian Social Democrats at Pskov; plans made for the publication of a newspaper and for the establishment of contacts with the "Emancipation of Labor" group.

August. Congress of the Socialist Revolutionist party at Kharkov; party manifesto adopted.

September 23–27. Fifth Congress of the Second International in Paris; resolutions on ministerialism, colonial policy and militarism adopted; the International Socialist Bureau organized.

September 28. Second general congress of French socialist organizations in Paris; the United Socialist party split; the Guesdists withdrew.

December. *Iskra* founded.

1901. Campaign against the *Rabochee Delo* led by *Iskra*.

Formation of *Yuzhnyi Rabochii* ("the Southern Worker's") group in Russia.

Fusion of the Socialist Revolutionist League and the Socialist Revolutionist party. *Revoliutsionnaia Rossiia* transferred abroad under the control of the Central Committee as the official party organ. The slogan "In struggle shall you obtain your rights" adopted.

American Socialist party founded.

March 26. Third general congress of French socialist organizations at Lyon; the Blanquist Socialist Revolutionary party withdrew because of the Millerand issue.

November 3. Congress of the Guesdist French Labor party, the Blanquist Socialist Revolutionary party and various other federations and groups at Ivry; the Socialist party of France organized, but separate centers maintained by the Guesdists and the Blanquists.

1902. Party program drafted by editors of *Iskra* in preparation for the party congress.

January. Conference of South Russian Social-Democratic party organizations called at Elizavetgrad by the "Southern Worker's" group; agreement with *Iskra's* policy expressed.

March. Congress of French socialist reformists at Tours; the French Socialist party, headed by Jaurès organized.

April 5–10 (March 23–28). Conference of representatives of committees and organizations of the R.S.D.L. party in Belostok; committee to call a party congress elected; committee soon arrested.

November 15–16 (2–3). Conference of the R.S.D.L. party at Pskov; new committee formed for the calling of a party congress.

1903. June 10. Assassination of King Alexander and Queen Draga in the palace revolution in Belgrade.

1903. July 30—August 23 (July 17—August 10). Second Congress of the R.S.D.L. party in Brussels and London; the party splits into the so-called Bolsheviks and Mensheviks.

September. Congress of the Socialist party of France at Reims; decided to submit the question of ministerialism to the international socialist congress; complete fusion of the Blanquists and the Guesdists accomplished.

September 13–20. Congress of German Social Democratic party at Dresden; ministerialism condemned by 288 to 11, but revisionists not expelled from the party.

October 26–31. Third Congress of League of Russian Social Democrats at Geneva; disapproved of conduct of the Bolsheviks and expressed mistrust of the Central Committee under Bolshevik control.

November. After Lenin's resignation, Plekhanov coopted Axelrod, Zasulich, Potresov, Martov, and Martynov into the editorial board of *Iskra*.

1904. January. Millerand expelled from French Socialist party.

February 7. Meeting of the International Socialist Bureau at Brussels; socialists of all countries urged to try to prevent the impending Russo-Japanese war.

February 9 (January 27). Beginning of the Russo-Japanese war.

April 8. The Dual Entente between France and Great Britain.

July. The so-called "July declaration," giving a number of concessions to the Mensheviks, adopted in Lenin's absence by three Bolshevik members of the Central Committee.

August 14–20. Sixth Congress of the Second International at Amsterdam. Reports submitted by Russian Bolsheviks and Mensheviks; revisionism debated.

December. Three Mensheviks enter the Central Committee of the R.S.D.L. party.

December 26 (13). Beginning of a general strike at Baku, which lasted until January 18 (5), 1905.

1905. Trans-Siberian Railway completed.

January 4 (December 22, 1904). First issue of *Vpered* published by the Bolsheviks.

January 16 (3). Beginning of a strike at the Putilov works in St. Petersburg.

January 20 (7). General strike in St. Petersburg.

January 22 (9). Bloody Sunday in St. Petersburg.

January 23 (10). Beginning of a general strike in Moscow.

1905. February 22 (9). Arrest of all members of the Central Committee of the R.S.D.L. party in Russia, except two (A. Krasin and A. Liubimov).

March. Visit of Wilhelm II to Tangier; the first Moroccan crisis.

March 25 (12). An organization committee formed by the Bureau of the Majority Committees and the Central Committee of the R.S.D.L. party for the calling of the third party congress; draft program issued.

April 7 (March 25). Opposition to the calling of the third party congress, which was believed to be illegal, expressed by the Council of the R.S.D.L. party.

April 23–25. Unification Congress of the French Socialist party and the Socialist party of France; Socialist party, French section of the Workers' International, formed.

April 25—May 10 (April 12–27). Third Congress of the R.S.D.L. party in London; Mensheviks do not attend but gather at Geneva.

May 25 (12). Beginning of a general strike at Ivanovo-Voznesensk, which lasted until August 9 (July 27).

May 26–28 (13–15). A Soviet of Workers' Deputies organized at Ivanovo-Voznesensk.

May 27 (14). *Vpered* replaced by *Proletarii*.

June 11 (May 29). Plekhanov withdrew from the R.S.D.L. party council and from the editorial board of *Iskra*.

June 18 (5). Workers' demonstrations in Lodz develop into a general strike there.

June 26 (13). Strikes in Odessa, Warsaw, and other industrial centers of Russian Poland, in support of the striking workers of Lodz.

June 27 (14). Mutiny on the battleship "Potemkin-Tavricheskii."

August. Axelrod's proposal for a nonpartisan labor congress to lay the foundations of a legal labor party in Russia.

August 19 (6). The Tsar's manifesto on the Bulygin Duma.

September 5 (August 23). Treaty of Portsmouth signed.

October 7 (September 24). Strikes, demonstrations and street fighting in Moscow.

October 16 (3). Beginning of strikes in St. Petersburg; clashes with troops.

October 19 (6). Beginning of a railway strike, which developed into a general strike throughout Russia causing suspension of business and public services.

October 26 (13). First meeting of the Petersburg Soviet of Workers' deputies.

October 30 (17). The Tsar's "October manifesto" granting civil liberties and an elected State Duma with legislative powers.

1905. October 31 (18). Manifesto of the Central Committee of the R.S.D.L. party "To all the people."

November 3 (October 21). End of the general strike in St. Petersburg; amnesty granted political prisoners.

November 8–9 (October 26–27). Mutiny of sailors and soldiers at Kronstadt.

November 11 (October 29). Preparations for an armed uprising begun by the Petersburg Soviet of Workers' deputies.

November 15 (2). Decision to call a general strike throughout all Russia adopted by the Petersburg Soviet of Workers' deputies; beginning of this strike at St. Petersburg.

November 18 (5). Discontinuance of general strike voted by Petersburg Soviet of Workers' deputies; end of strike set for November 20 (7).

November 24–28 (11–15). Mutinies in the Black Sea fleet.

November–December. Formation of Soviets of Workers' deputies in various Russian towns. Mutinies in the army increased.

December. Spread of peasant disturbances, especially in Georgia and the Baltic provinces.

December 5 (November 22). Meeting of the Moscow Soviet of workers' deputies.

December 16 (3). Executive Committee of the Petersburg Soviet of Workers' deputies arrested.

December 19 (6). Decision to call a general strike on December 20 (7) adopted by Moscow Soviet of Workers' deputies. The general strike called jointly by the Petersburg Soviet of Workers' deputies and the socialist parties. First issue of the Bolshevik-Menshevik *Severnyi Golos* published.

December 20–21 (7–8). Beginning of the general strike in Moscow A republic proclaimed in Krasnoiarsk, with a revolutionary committee in control.

December 22 (9). Barricades and street fighting in Moscow continuing until January 1 (December 19).

December 25–30 (12–17). First Conference of the R.S.D.L. party; resolution on the unification of Social-Democratic groups and the immediate formation of a united Central Committee adopted.

December 29 (16). Decision to call off the general strike on January 1 (December 19), adopted by the Moscow Soviet of Workers' deputies and the Moscow Committee of the R.S.D.L. party.

December 30 (17). Beginning of severe suppressions by the government. Decision to call off the general strike on January 1 (December 19) adopted by the Petersburg Soviet of Workers' deputies.

1905. Late December. Fusion of the Bolshevik and Menshevik party centers; United Central Committee organized.

1906. January 1 (December 19). Moscow uprising suppressed. Other uprisings suppressed during January and February, accompanied by arrests, courts-martial, pogroms, and punitive expeditions. Agrarian disturbances.

January–February. Bolshevik Military Organization, formed late in 1905, placed under control of the Petersburg Committee of the R.S.D.L. party.

March 4. Meeting of the International Socialist Bureau at Brussels to protest against the war which threatened because of the Moroccan crisis.

March 5 (February 20). Imperial manifesto and ukase granting a State Duma and State Council with legislative powers.

May 10 (April 27). The First State Duma opened.

April 23—May 8 (April 10–25). Fourth Congress of the R.S.D.L. party, the so-called Unification Congress, at Stockholm.

July 21 (July 8). The First State Duma dissolved.

July 23 (10). The Viborg manifesto issued by the Constitutional Democrat, Trudovik, and other Left Duma deputies.

August 2 (July 20). Mutiny on the cruiser "Pamiat Azova" at Reval.

November. Ninth Congress of the Polish Socialist party in Vienna; final split between the Right and the Left. The former being known as "the Revolutionary Faction of the Polish Socialist party."

November 16–20 (3–7). Second Conference of the R.S.D.L. party at Tammerfors. It was decided to call a party congress in 1907.

1907. March 5 (February 20). The Second State Duma opened.

May 13—June 1 (April 30—May 19). Fifth Congress of the R.S.D.L. party at London; Bolshevik majority.

June 16 (3). The Second State Duma dissolved and the "June 3" electoral law promulgated. S.D. deputies arrested, later tried for high treason and sentenced to hard labor in exile.

August 3–5 (July 21–23). Third Conference of the R.S.D.L. party at Helsingfors.

August 18–24. Seventh Congress of Second International at Stuttgart; the first International Socialist Women's Conference at Stuttgart.

August 24–26. First International Socialist Youth Conference at Stuttgart.

August 31. The Anglo-Russian Entente.

November 14 (1). The Third State Duma called; ended on June 22 (9), 1912.

1907. November 18–25 (5–12). Fourth Conference of the R.S.D.L. party at Kotka, Finland.

1908. July. "Young Turk" revolution.

September. The Casablanca affair; the second Moroccan crisis.

September 6–7 (August 24–25). Plenum of the Central Committee of the R.S.D.L. party at Geneva; formation of the Bureau of the Central Committee Abroad.

October. Bosnia and Herzegovina annexed to Austro-Hungarian Empire.

1909. January 3–9 (December 21–27, 1908). Fifth Conference of the R.S.D.L. party in Paris.

January 3, 9–11 (December 21, 27–29, 1908). Plenum of the Central Committee of the R.S.D.L. party in Paris; a new editorial board of *Sotsial-Demokrat* and a new Bureau of the Central Committee Abroad elected.

May. Plekhanov resigns from the editorial board of *Golos Sotsial-Demokrata*.

June. Proclamation issued by the International Socialist Bureau opposing the trip of Nicholas II to Europe. Workers' demonstrations and meetings of protest organized in Sweden, Germany, England, and Italy.

December 28 (15). *Vpered* group formed by the ultimatists and the recall advocates of the R.S.D.L. party.

1910. January 15—February 5 (January 2–23). Plenum of the Central Committee of the R.S.D.L. party in Paris; party unification not achieved.

February, March, April. Large popular demonstrations in Berlin, Halle, Frankfort, and elsewhere in support of secret universal suffrage.

August 26–27. Second International Socialist Women's Conference at Copenhagen.

August 28—September 3. Eighth Congress of the Second International at Copenhagen.

September 4. Second International Socialist Youth Conference in Copenhagen.

October. Great railway strike in France.

1911. The Social Democratic Federation of England changed to the British Socialist party.

May 27. Withdrawal of the Bolshevik representative from the Bureau of the Central Committee of the R.S.D.L. party abroad.

June 10–17 (May 27—June 4). Private Conference of the Central Committee of the R.S.D.L. party in Paris; plans laid for the calling of an all-party conference; this effort at unification failed.

1911. July 1. Arrival of a German warship in Agadir; the third Moroccan crisis.

August–September. Peace demonstrations by socialist and labor organizations in London and Berlin in connection with the Moroccan crisis.

October. Beginning of the Chinese Revolution; the Manchu Emperor abdicated on February 12, 1912.

1912. January 18–30 (5–17). Sixth Conference of the R.S.D.L. party at Prague dominated by the Leninist Bolsheviks; the so-called "liquidators" expelled from the party and a new Central Committee of Bolsheviks elected.

Late January. A conference of the Bund and of Social Democratic organizations of minority nationalities in Russia; a Bureau of the Organization Committee elected and plans for the Menshevik Conference in August worked out.

March 12. Meeting of representatives of various R.S.D.L. party groups in Paris; resolution condemning the Bolshevik action at Prague adopted.

April 17 (4) Troops fire on workers in the Lena goldfields—the "Lena massacre."

April–May. Strikes in various Russian towns in protest against the "Lena massacre."

July 2. The Bureau of the Central Committee of the R.S.D.L. party abroad transferred to Cracow.

August 25—September 2. Conference of Menshevik groups in Vienna; the so-called "August bloc" formed.

October 8. Montenegro declares war on Turkey; beginning of the First Balkan war.

November 17 (4). Meetings of protest against the Balkan war and intervention in Balkan affairs organized in Paris, London, and Berlin on the initiative of the International Socialist Bureau.

November 24–25. Extraordinary Congress of the Second International at Basel.

November 28 (15). The Fourth State Duma called.

1913. January 10–14. The so-called "February" conference of the Central Committee of the R.S.D.L. party with certain party workers in Cracow.

June 29–30. Beginning of the Second Balkan war.

August 13. Death of August Bebel.

October 5–14 (September 22—October 1). The so-called "August" or "Summer" conference of the Central Committee of the R.S.D.L. party with certain party workers at Poronino.

1913. November 11 (October 29). Split in the Social Democratic Duma group; the Bolshevik Duma group formed.

December 13–14. Meeting of the International Socialist Bureau in London; plans made for a meeting of representatives of Russian Social Democratic groups.

1914. March. Conference of the Warsaw, Lodz, and Czestochowa Committees of the Social Democracy of Poland and Lithuania; the opposition elects its own executive, the so-called Regional Presidium.

March 4–12. Strikes of protest against persecution of the labor press, trade unions, and cultural-educational societies in St. Petersburg.

March 20 (7). Lockout declared by the St. Petersburg factory owners.

April 17 (4). Strike in St. Petersburg on the anniversary of the "Lena massacre."

June 28. The assassination of Archduke Francis Ferdinand at Sarajevo.

July 14–16. Congress of the French Socialist party in Paris favored the general strike as a means of preventing war.

July 14–28 (July 1–15). Strikes in St. Petersburg.

July 16–17. Unification conference of Russian Social Democrats, under the auspices of the International Socialist Bureau, at Brussels.

July 17–28 (July 4–5). Strikes in Moscow.

July 21 (8). *Trudovaia Pravda* suppressed in St. Petersburg.

July 23. Austrian ultimatum to Serbia.

July 25. Antiwar proclamation issued by the Presidium of the German Social Democratic party.

July 26–30. Demonstrations protesting against the impending war in Paris, Berlin, and other large European centers.

July 28. Austria declares war on Serbia.

July 29–30. Meeting of the International Socialist Bureau at Brussels followed by a demonstration and a mass meeting protesting against the war.

July 31. Assassination of Jaurès.

August 1. Serbian Social Democrats refused to vote war credits.

August 1 (July 19). War declared on Russia by Germany.

August 3. War declared on France by Germany. By a vote of 78 to 14 the Social Democratic Reichstag group favored the voting of war credits unconditionally.

August 3. Declaration of Italian neutrality.

August 4. State of war between Belgium and Germany.

1914. War declared on Germany by Great Britain.

German Social Democratic Reichstag group votes war credits.

Belgian socialists in the Chamber of Deputies expressed readiness to support their government; Vandervelde's appointment to the Cabinet sanctioned.

War credits unanimously approved in French Chamber of Deputies.

August 5. Joint conference of the Executive of the Italian Socialist party, the Confederazione Generale del Lavoro, and other workers' organizations in Milan; statement issued denouncing the imperialist war and calling upon the Italian proletariat to manifest its will for peace and for the maintenance of Italy's neutrality.

Resolutions registering labor's opposition to the policies responsible for the war adopted by the Executive of the British Labour party.

August 6 (July 24). War on Russia declared by Austria-Hungary.

August 8 (July 26). Declaration of the entire Social Democratic Duma group refusing to vote war credits read before the State Duma.

August 10. War declared on Austria by France.

August 12. Fraternal sympathy to the workers of Europe extended by the National Committee on Immediate Action of the American Socialist party. The party's opposition "to this and all wars waged upon any pretext whatsoever" reiterated.

War declared on Austria by Great Britain.

August 13. Antiwar manifesto published by the National Council of the Independent Labour party in *The Labour Leader*.

August 28. A manifesto approving the entrance of Guesde and Sembat into the government issued by the Parliamentary group of the French Socialist party, the Commission Administrative Permanente, and the Conseil d'Administration of *L'Humanité*.

September 4 (August 22). Agreement signed by Great Britain, France, and Russia not to conclude a separate peace with the Central Powers.

September 5. Arrival of Lenin and family at Berne.

September 6–7. Meeting of the local Bolsheviks at Berne; Lenin's theses on the war adopted.

September 19–20. Plan for the calling of an international socialist congress perfected by the National Executive Committee of the American Socialist party; invitations forwarded to the Executives of the various European socialist parties.

September 22. Antiwar manifesto which favored Italy's neutrality, issued by the Executive of the Italian Socialist party.

September 27. Conference of Italian and Swiss Socialists at Lugano.

1914. October 11. Conference of representatives of the Socialist parties of Norway, Sweden, and Denmark at Stockholm; the transfer of the International Socialist Bureau from Brussels to The Hague discussed.

October 13–14 (September 30—October 1). Conference of the Bolshevik Duma group near Mustamiaki, Finland; reply to Vandervelde's telegram drafted.

October 15. Manifesto issued over the signature of most of the Labour M.P.'s, the Parliamentary Committee of the Trade Union Congress, and other Labour leaders explaining the party's support of government war measures.

October 29 (16). Hostilities opened between Turkey and Russia.

November 16–17 (3–4). Conference of Bolshevik Duma deputies and party members at Ozerki; Lenin's theses on the war discussed. The participants of the conference were arrested on the following day.

1915. January 17–18. Conference of Socialists of Sweden, Norway, Holland, and Denmark at Copenhagen.

February 14. Conference of Socialists of the Allied countries in London.

February 23–26 (10–13). Trial of the Ozerki Conference participants; the five Bolshevik deputies are sentenced to penal labor and exile in Siberia.

February 27—March 4 (February 14–19). Conference of the Bolshevik section of the R.S.D.L. party at Berne.

March 26–28. Third International Socialist Women's Conference at Berne.

April 5–7. International Socialist Youth Conference at Berne.

April 12–13. Conference of Socialists of the Central Powers, at Vienna.

April 26. Intention to call a conference of socialists of the neutral countries announced by the Presidium of the Swiss Social Democratic party; the conference scheduled to meet on May 30.

April 26. Italy adhered to the Anglo-French-Russian declaration of September 5, 1914; preparations to enter the war begun.

May. A new section added to the American Socialist party's statutes stating that party members "who shall in any way vote to appropriate moneys for military or naval purposes, or war, shall be expelled from the party."

May 15–16. Decision to take the initiative in calling an International Socialist Conference adopted by the Executive of the Italian Socialist party.

May 22. Plan to call a conference of Socialists of the neutral countries abandoned by the Presidium of the Swiss Social Democratic party.

1915. May 23. War declared on Austria by Italy.

June 18. Decision to call an International Socialist Conference reiterated by the Executive of the Italian Socialist party.

July 11. Conference at Berne preparatory to the Zimmerwald Conference.

July 14–15. Meeting of the National Council of the French Socialist party in Paris; resolution approving the actions taken by the Commission Administrative Permanente and by the Parliamentary group since the outbreak of the war adopted.

September 5–8. International Socialist Conference at Zimmerwald; International Socialist Committee elected.

September 5–10. Conference of representatives of the defensist groups of the R.S.D.L. party and the Socialist Revolutionists at Geneva.

September 27. Confidential circular on the Zimmerwald Conference issued to all affiliated groups by the International Socialist Committee.

September 29. Declaration of the International Socialist Committee in reply to Vliegen's and Van Kol's criticisms of the Zimmerwald manifesto and the Zimmerwald movement.

October 10 (September 27). First elections to the Central and the Petrograd War Industries Committees; Bolshevik resolution to boycott all defense institutions adopted.

October 14. War declared on Serbia by Bulgaria.

November 20–21. Congress of the Swiss Social Democratic party at Aarau; Zimmerwald resolutions approved.

December 12 (November 29). Second elections to the Central and the Petrograd War Industries Committees; ten labor representatives elected over the protest of the Bolshevik and certain Socialist-Revolutionist representatives.

December 25–29. Congress of the French Socialist party in Paris; prowar resolutions voted by large majority.

1916. January 1. An All-German Conference of the *Internationale* group in Berlin; Rosa Luxemburg's theses adopted.

February 5–8. A meeting of the Enlarged International Socialist Committee at Berne; the matter of calling the Second Zimmerwald Conference discussed.

February 8. An open International Socialist meeting at Berne; speeches on the war and the tasks of the working class delivered by Modigliani, Lenin, Rakovsky, Balabanoff, and Grimm.

February 10. Invitation to the Kienthal Conference issued by the International Socialist Committee.

March 9. War declared on Portugal by Germany.

1916. March 18–19. Congress of the Swedish Socialist Youth League at Stockholm; antigovernment manifesto adopted.

March 24. Hugo Haase and seventeen Social Democratic deputies of the Reichstag expelled from the Social Democratic Reichstag group for voting against war credits; Sozialdemokratische Arbeitsgemeinschaft formed.

April 9. Meeting of the National Council of the French Socialist party; decided to continue to work for the defense of France and the restoration of Belgium and Serbia. Policies of the International Socialist Bureau approved and the Zimmerwald action condemned.

April 24. Beginning of the Irish Rebellion.

April 23–24. Annual conference of the British Socialist party. Party split led to the formation of the National Socialist party.

April 24–30. The Second Zimmerwald Conference at Kienthal.

May 1. May-Day manifesto, which contained a call for a Conference of Socialists of Neutral Countries, issued by the International Socialist Bureau.

Manifesto of the Kienthal Conference issued.

May 2. Meeting of the Enlarged International Socialist Committee at Berne; question of parliamentary action discussed and the invitation to attend the Conference of Socialists of the Neutral Countries considered.

May 12. Circular stating the attitude of the Zimmerwald groups toward the calling of the Conference of Socialists of Neutral Countries issued by the Enlarged International Socialist Committee.

May–June. Hunger riots in Germany.

June 27–28. Strikes in Braunschweig, chiefly in the munition shops.

July 6–7. Annual meeting of the Council of the General Federation of Trade Unions at Leeds, attended by labor delegates from France, Italy, and Belgium.

July 31—August 2. Conference of Socialists of Neutral Countries at The Hague.

August 6–7. Decision to call a Conference of Socialists of the Allied Countries adopted by the Commission Administrative Permanente of the French Socialist party.

August 27. War declared on Austria-Hungary by Rumania.

August 28. War declared on Germany by Italy.

August 28. War declared on Rumania by Germany.

August 30. War declared on Rumania by Turkey.

October 21. Assassination of Count Stürgkh by Friedrich Adler.

1916. October 30 (17). Beginning of strikes in Petrograd.

October 30—November 4. Unification Conference of the Social Democracy of Poland and Lithuania in Warsaw; new platform adopted and new Main Presidium elected on a parity basis.

November 4–5. Congress of the Swiss Social Democratic party at Zürich; financial reforms discussed; resolution expelling the Grütli Verein adopted.

November 24. Resolution favoring United States' intervention with a view to ending all hostilities introduced in the Italian Chamber of Deputies by the Socialist group.

December 1. Joseph C. Grew, American Chargé in Germany, notified the Secretary of State that the German Chancellor appeared to favor "any steps which might lead to peace."

December 11. Arthur Henderson's appointment to British War Cabinet announced.

December 12. Peace note issued by the Central Powers.

December 15 (2). Decision to reject the German peace proposals adopted by the State Duma.

December 18. President Wilson's note to the belligerent governments, suggesting that they state their terms of peace.

December 24–25. Congress of the Confédération Générale du Travail in Paris; policy of the C.G.T. Executive approved; support of President Wilson's intervention for peace promised.

December 24–30. Congress of the French Socialist party in Paris; party's participation in national defense and in the Cabinet approved; President Wilson's peace efforts favored; readiness declared to discuss the calling of a plenary meeting of the International Socialist Bureau, provided the German Social Democratic party disapproved of the Central Powers' refusal to state their peace terms.

December 26. Reply to President Wilson's peace note issued by the German government; meeting of delegates of belligerent countries on neutral ground proposed.

December 30. Joint reply by the Allies rejecting the Central Powers' peace proposal.

1917. January 6–7. Unification Conference of the Socialist Labor party and the Socialist party of the United States in New York; unification not achieved.

January 7. Conference of the German Social Democratic opposition in Berlin.

Meeting of the Presidium of the Swiss Social Democratic party at Zürich; party congress scheduled for February 10–11, 1917, postponed indefinitely.

1917. January 10. Allied reply to President Wilson's note of December 18, 1916, suggesting that the belligerent governments communicate their terms of peace.

January 23–26. Annual Conference of the British Labour party at Manchester; motion to call a meeting of the International Socialist Bureau rejected; policy of "war to the finish" approved; meeting of Socialists and trade unionists, to be held simultaneously with the peace conference, favored.

February 1. Conference of the Enlarged International Socialist Committee at Olten; matter of the Allied Socialist Conference as proposed by the French Socialist party considered.

February 12–20. Congress of the Swedish Social Democratic Labor party at Stockholm; Youth League ordered to submit to the party majority under threat of expulsion from the party.

March 8 (February 23). Strikes and demonstrations in Petrograd increase.

March 12 (February 27). Soviet of Workers and Soldiers' deputies organized in Petrograd.

March 13 (February 28). First meeting of the Petrograd Soviet.

March 14 (1). Russian Provisional Government formed.

March 15 (2). Abdication of Nicholas II.

March 24 (11). Appeal to the peoples of the entire world for a democratic peace adopted by the Executive Committee of the Petrograd Soviet.

March 27 (14). Appeal to the peoples of the entire world approved by the Plenum of the Petrograd Soviet.

April 6. War declared on Germany by the United States.

April 7–14. Emergency convention of the American Socialist party at St. Louis; "Majority report," protesting against America's participation in the war adopted.

April 9. Declaration of the Russian Provisional Government denouncing seizure or forcible occupation of foreign territory.

April 11–16 (March 29—April 3). All-Russian Conference of the Soviets of Workers' and Soldiers' deputies in Petrograd.

April 13 (March 31). Arrival of British and French labor delegates in Petrograd.

April 16 (3). Arrival in Petrograd of the first group of returning political emigrés—among them Lenin.

May 1 (April 18). Miliukov's note to the Allies confirming the Provisional Government's intentions to fulfill its treaty obligations to the Allies.

1917. May 3. The Dutch-Scandinavian Committee formed at Stockholm.

May 3–5 (April 20–22). Demonstrations in Petrograd in protest against the foreign policy of the Provisional Government.

May 7 (April 24). Invitations to minority socialists to come to Petrograd for a conference issued by the Executive Committee of the Petrograd Soviet of Workers' and Soldiers' deputies.

May 7–12 (April 24–29). Seventh Conference of the R.S.D.L. party (Bolsheviks) at Petrograd; Borgbjerg's invitation to attend the Stockholm Conference rejected.

May 8 (April 25). Decision to take the initiative in the calling of an International Socialist Congress adopted by the Executive Committee of the Petrograd Soviet.

May 10. Invitation to the Third Zimmerwald Conference issued by the International Socialist Committee.

May 13–16. Congress of the Swedish Social Democratic Labor party minority and the Swedish Socialist Youth League at Stockholm; the Left Social Democratic Labor party of Sweden established.

May 15 (2). Appeal to the "Socialists of all countries," urging them to struggle for peace, issued by the Petrograd Soviet.

May 16–18 (3–5). Decision to attend the Third Zimmerwald Conference and the general Socialist Conference adopted by the All-City Conference of Mensheviks in Petrograd.

May 17 (4). Arrival of Emile Vandervelde in Petrograd.

May 18 (5). Russian Provisional Coalition Government formed.

May 20–25 (May 7–12). All-Russian Conference of the R.S.D.L. party (Mensheviks) in Petrograd; Organization Committee authorized to send delegates to the Third Zimmerwald Conference and also to take part in conferences preparatory to the general Socialist Conference.

May 22 (9). Arrival of the second train of Russian political emigrés in Petrograd.

May 28–29. Meeting between the Russian representatives of the Zimmerwald movement and Robert Grimm and Angelica Balabanoff of the International Socialist Committee in Petrograd.

June 2 (May 20). Decision to issue an invitation to all socialist parties and central trade union organizations of the world for an International Socialist Conference at Stockholm adopted by the Executive Committee of the Petrograd Soviet.

June 3. Conference of British Labor at Leeds; Russia's declaration of foreign policy and war aims endorsed; establishment of a Workers' and Soldiers' Council approved and an immediate democratic peace favored.

June 9–10. Congress of the Swiss Social Democratic party at Berne; adherence to Kienthal resolutions reiterated; activity of the Interna-

1917. tional Socialist Bureau criticized; invitation to the Stockholm Conference accepted on condition that the Third Zimmerwald Conference approves participation.

June 10. Letter to all its affiliated organizations announcing the calling of the Third Zimmerwald Conference at Stockholm, three days prior to the meeting of the general Socialist Conference, issued by the International Socialist Committee.

June 13 (May 31). Arrival of the Root mission in Petrograd.

June 15–18. Congress of the Finnish Social Democratic party at Helsingfors; decision to join the Zimmerwald movement adopted.

June 16 (3). Robert Grimm deported from Russia.

June 16 (3). Telegram from the Swiss Federal Councilor Hoffmann published by the Provisional Coalition Government.

June 16—July 7 (June 3–24). First All-Russian Congress of Soviets of Workers' and Soldiers' deputies in Petrograd.

June 19. Robert Grimm resigned as Chairman of the International Socialist Committee.

June 20. Appointment of a provisional International Socialist Committee by the Swedish Left Social Democratic Labor party.

June 29 (June 16). Orders to launch an offensive against the Central Powers issued by Kerensky.

July 3–4. Meeting of the International Socialist Committee with other Zimmerwaldists at Stockholm; question of attending the general Socialist Conference discussed.

July 9. Conference of members of the International Socialist Committee and delegates of the Petrograd Soviet at Stockholm. Possible participation of the International Socialist Committee in preparing for the general Socialist Conference considered.

July 11. Russian-Dutch-Scandinavian Committee formed.

Participation in the preparatory work for the general Socialist Conference refused by the International Socialist Committee; assistance to the delegates of the Petrograd Soviet promised.

July 12. Invitation to the general International Socialist Conference at Stockholm issued by the Russian-Dutch-Scandinavian Committee.

July 16–19 (3–6). Strikes and demonstrations in Petrograd under the slogan "All power to the Soviets"; armed demonstrations in Moscow; order to arrest the Bolshevik leaders issued; Bolshevik newspaper plants raided.

July 18. Invitation to the Third Zimmerwald Conference issued by the International Socialist Committee.

July 20. Statement denouncing the Stockholm general Socialist Conference issued by the Zimmerwald Left group.

1917. July 23–27. Decision to attend the Third Zimmerwald Conference adopted by the Italian Socialist party; Italian delegates to that conference are urged to insist that the Zimmerwald parties attend the general Socialist Conference at Stockholm.

August 3. Decision to call the Third Zimmerwald Conference on September 3, 1917, adopted by the International Socialist Committee; affiliated parties and groups informed accordingly.

August 8–16 (July 26—August 3). Sixth Congress of the R.S.D.L. party (Bolsheviks) at Petrograd; union of "Mezhraionka" with Bolsheviks.

August 10. Conference of the British Labour party in London; invitation to the Stockholm Conference conditionally accepted.

August 13. Announcement to the effect that British delegates will not be permitted to go to Stockholm made by Bonar Law in the House of Commons.

August 21. Conference of the British Labour party in London; representation at Stockholm limited to the Executive of the Labour party, the Parliamentary Committee and the Trade Union Congress.

August 21–25. Antiwar demonstrations, strikes, and hunger riots in Turin.

August 28–29. Inter-Allied Socialist Conference in London; all statements on war aims rejected; no definite pronouncement on the Stockholm issue.

September 3–8. British Trade Union Congress at Blackpool; Stockholm Conference declared inopportune.

September 5–12. The Third Zimmerwald Conference at Stockholm.

September 8–12. The Kornilov affair.

September 14–15. Informal International Socialist Women's Conference at Stockholm.

September 15. Postponement of the Stockholm Conference announced by the Russian-Dutch-Scandinavian Committee.

September 28. Publication of the manifesto of the Third Zimmerwald Conference temporarily postponed.

October 10. A "draft program of peace" drawn up by the socialist delegates of the neutral countries at Stockholm and published by the Russian-Dutch-Scandinavian Committee.

October 10. Meeting of the International Socialist Committee jointly with the Serbian delegates and all Zimmerwaldists present at Stockholm.

November 7 (October 25). Seizure of power by the Bolsheviks in Petrograd.

1917. November 7–8 (October 25–26). Second All-Russian Congress of Soviets; decrees on peace and land issued; members of Soviet Government elected.

November 14. Beginning of general strike in Finland.

November 15–17. Street riots in Zürich.

November 23 (10). Publication of the secret treaties between Tsarist Russia and the Entente states begun by the Soviet Government.

November 26. Congress of the Hungarian Social Democratic party in Budapest; decision to organize strikes in the provinces and to intensify the antiwar propaganda adopted.

December 6. Proclamation of Finland's independence by the Finnish Diet.

December 15. Armistice signed in Brest-Litovsk.

December 22. Opening of peace negotiations at Brest-Litovsk.

December 24 (11). Decision to take part in the Brest-Litovsk peace negotiations announced by the Ukrainian General Secretariat.

December 27. Circular letter issued by the International Socialist Committee to its affiliated parties and groups; calls for protest against the enforcement of the Brest-Litovsk peace terms on Russia.

December 31 (18). Finland's independence granted by the Russian Soviet Government.

1918. January 7–8. Last meeting of the Russian-Dutch-Scandinavian Committee at Stockholm.

January 8. President Wilson's "Fourteen points" made public.

January 19 (6). Russian Constituent Assembly dissolved by the Bolsheviks.

January 23–31 (January 10–18). Third All-Russian Congress of Soviets in Petrograd; declaration on the rights of the toiling and exploited peoples issued.

January 27. Revolutionary uprising and beginning of civil war in Finland.

February 4. Formation of the Olten Action Committee by Swiss labor as a measure of enforcing economic and political demands by the working class.

February 6. Proclamation of the International Socialist Committee to its affiliated parties and groups, calling for a demonstration in favor of a democratic peace and advocating united action.

February 8 (January 26). Occupation of Kiev by Russian Soviet troops; the Ukrainian Central Rada deposed.

February 9 (January 27). Separate peace signed between the Ukraine and the Central Powers.

1918. February 18–19. Advance launched by the Central Powers on the Eastern front; Dvinsk occupied by German troops.

February 19 (6). Brest-Litovsk peace terms agreed to by the Russian Soviet Government.

February 20–24. Inter-Allied Labor and Socialist Conference in London. British Memorandum on War Aims adopted.

February 21 (8). New German peace terms received by Russian Soviet Government.

February 22. Proclamation of the International Socialist Committee appealing to the German and the world proletariat to take action against Germany's offensive in Russia, Estonia, and Finland.

February 24 (11). Pskov occupied by the Germans.

March 1–2. Kiev occupied by German troops; the Ukrainian Central Rada restored.

March 3. Brest-Litovsk treaty between Germany and Russia signed.

BIBLIOGRAPHY

This bibliography includes the primary sources used in compiling this book, the books and articles cited, and certain other titles which deal with subjects treated in this volume.

BOOKS, PAMPHLETS, AND ARTICLES

ADLER, F. W. *Die Erneuerung der Internationale. Aufsätze aus der Kriegszeit (Oktober 1914 bis Oktober 1916),* Vienna, 1918, 215 pages.
> A collection of articles covering the period from October 1914 to October 1916, with a preface by Kautsky. The articles deal chiefly with the attitude of various socialist parties toward the war and the status of the International.

Ausserordentlicher Internationaler Sozialisten-Kongress zu Basel am 24. und 25. November 1912. Berlin, 1912, 56 pages.

AXELROD, P. B. *Die russische Revolution und die sozialistische Internationale,* Jena, 1932, 205 pages.
> A collection of articles, including "Die Krise und die Aufgaben der internationalen Sozialdemokratie," written in the summer of 1915.

BADAEV, A. *The Bolsheviks in the Tsarist Duma* (with an article by Lenin on the work and trial of the Bolshevik group in the Duma, and an introduction by Em. Yaroslavsky), New York, [1932], 250 pages.
> Recollections of a Bolshevik member of the Fourth State Duma, covering Bolshevik activity in the Duma and the split of the Social Democratic Duma group.

BAEVSKY, D. "Bolsheviki v borbe za III Internatsional" ("The Bolsheviks' Struggle for the Third International"), *Istorik Marksist,* No. 11, 1929, pp. 12–48.
> This and the four following articles by the same author are based on Lenin's correspondence and on unpublished materials in the Marx-Lenin-Engels Institute. This article analyzes points at issue in Lenin's controversy with the Bukharin-Piatakov group during the World War.

BAEVSKY, D. "Bolsheviki v Tsimmervalde" ("The Bolsheviks in Zimmerwald"), *Proletarskaia Revoliutsiia,* No. 5, 1935, pp. 27–48.
> A discussion of the Bolsheviks' efforts to win socialist support for the Zimmerwald Left in 1915–1916.

BAEVSKY, D. "Borba Lenina protiv Bukharinskikh 'shatanii mysli'" ("Lenin's Struggle against Bukharin's 'Vacillations of Thought'"), *Proletarskaia Revoliutsiia,* No. 1 (96), 1930, pp. 18–46.
> Contains interesting excerpts from letters in the Marx-Engels-Lenin Institute bearing on the disagreement between the Central Committee of the R.S.D.L. party and the Bukharin-Piatakov group in 1915–1917. The author's analysis is strongly influenced by the Communist party stand on Left deviations and Trotskyism.

BAEVSKY, D. "Borba za III International do Tsimmervalda" ("The Struggle for the Third International prior to Zimmerwald"), *Proletarskaia Revoliutsiia,* No. 4, 1934, pp. 13–36.
> A study of the Bolsheviks' attempts to influence the Lefts in Western Europe.

BAEVSKY, D. "Lenin i Tsimmervaldskaia levaia" ("Lenin and the Zimmer-wald Left"), *Borba Klassov,* No. 3, March 1934, pp. 34–47.

A discussion of Lenin's part in the formation and activities of the Zimmerwald Left.

BALABANOFF, A. *Die Zimmerwalder Bewegung, 1914–1919,* Leipzig, 1928, 160 pages. Reprinted from the *Archiv für die Geschichte des Sozialismus und der Arbeiterbewegung* (C. Grünberg, editor), Vol. XII, pp. 310–413; Vol. XIII, pp. 232–84.

A very valuable collection of documents on the Zimmerwald movement compiled by the Secretary of the Zimmerwald Committee. Contains explanatory comment.

BALABANOFF, ANGELICA. *Erinnerungen und Erlebnisse,* Berlin, 1927, 299 pages.

Brilliantly written reminiscences of the author's activity in the Italian and international socialist labor movement, the anti-war and pacifist activity during the World War, the Zimmerwald movement, and the formation of the Third International. The account stops with 1920 when the author broke with the Russian Communists.

BALABANOFF, ANGELICA. *My Life as a Rebel,* New York, London, 1938, 324 pages.

The autobiography of a leader of the international socialist movement written against the background of the Communist and Fascist movements in Europe.

BALCH, EMILY GREENE. *Approaches to the Great Settlement,* New York, 1918, 351 pages.

Contains documents dealing with the attitude of the socialist parties toward the proposed Stockholm Socialist Conference of 1917.

BANTKE, S. "V. I. Lenin i bolshevizm na mezhdunarodnoi arene v dovoennyi period" ("V. I. Lenin in the International Arena in the Prewar Period"), *Proletarskaia Revoliutsiia,* Nos. 2–3 (85–86), 1929, pp. 3–57.

A study of the relations between the Second International and the Bolshevik group of the R.S.D.L. party, for the period 1904–1914.

BEER, MAX. *Krieg und die Internationale,* Vienna, 1924, 72 pages.

A study of the attitude of the leaders of the First International, of the Second International, and of the German, the French, and the Russian socialists toward war.

"Bernskaia konferentsiia 1915 g." ("The Berne Conference of 1915"), *Proletarskaia Revoliutsiia,* No. 5 (40), 1925, pp. 134–93.

Recollections of the Berne Conference of the Bolshevik sections abroad, February–March 1915, written by participants. Contains the following articles:

G. L. Shklovsky, "Vladimir Ilich nakanune konferentsii" ("Vladimir Ilich on the Eve of the Conference"). This deals with Lenin's arrival in Switzerland, the discussions among the Bolsheviks in Switzerland of the draft of Lenin's "theses of seven points," their final formulation at the Berne Conference, and the Bolshevik statements at the Congress of the Swedish Social Democratic Labor party, September 1914, and at the London Conference of the Entente Socialists, February 1915.

M. Syromiatnikova, "Bernskaia konferentsiia zagranichnykh organizatsii R.S.D.R.P. v 1915 g." ("The Berne Conference of the Organizations of the R.S.D.L. Party Abroad in 1915"). This deals with the efforts made by the Bolsheviks soon after the outbreak of the war to revive the disintegrated Committee of Organizations Abroad and to call a conference of these Bolshevik organizations. The article is based on memory and is reinforced by documentary material; valuable appendices contain complete texts of resolutions submitted to the Berne Conference and the protocols of the Conference.

"Vospominaniia uchastnikov Bernskoi konferentsii" ("Recollections of Participants in the Berne Conference"). Recollections of the Berne Conference by E. Bosh and G. Shklovsky.

BERNSTEIN, EDUARD. *Die Voraussetzungen des Sozialismus und die Aufgaben der Sozialdemokratie,* Stuttgart, 1899, 188 pages.
An interpretation of Marxian doctrine. This volume became the basis of so-called "revisionism."

BERNSTEIN, EDUARD. *Die Internationale der Arbeiterklasse und der europäische Krieg,* Tübingen, 1916, 56 pages.
A reprint from the *Archiv für Sozialwissenschaft und Sozialpolitik.* Deals with the attitude of and the conditions within the Social Democracy of belligerent and neutral countries.

BERZIN, YA. *Partiia bolshevikov v borbe za Kommunisticheskii Internatsional,* Moscow, Leningrad, 1931, 126 pages.
One of the best accounts, by a member of the Zimmerwald Left, of the origin of the Third International and its relations to the Zimmerwald movement, the decline of the movement and the liquidation of the Zimmerwald Committee at the First Congress of the Third International in 1919.

BESHKIN, G. "Borba s likvidatorstvom na mezhdunarodnoi arene v dovoennye gody" ("The Struggle against Liquidationism in the International Arena of the Prewar Years"), *Proletarskaia Revoliutsiia,* No. 9 (104), 1930, pp. 3–34.
An analysis of the Bolshevik struggle against "liquidationism" as part of their struggle against Western European reformism for the period 1908–1914.

BORKENAU, F. *The Communist International,* London, 1938, 442 pages.
A study of the origins and activity of the Communist International by a former member of the German Communist party. The author deals with the Comintern as an instrument of world revolution, as a force in the Russian factional struggle, and as an instrument of Soviet foreign policy. He sketches the party history, the Bolshevik activity during the World War, the revolutionary upheavals in Europe during 1917–1923, the formation of the Third International, and the various changes in its policy from 1919 to 1937. As here presented, the history of the Comintern is largely a record of failures.

BOSH, O. "Prazhskaia konferentsiia (Yanvar 1912 g.)" ("The Prague Conference [January 1912]"), *Proletarskaia Revoliutsiia,* No. 4 (39), 1925, pp. 179–206.
An account of the events which led to the calling of the Prague Conference of the R.S.D.L. party and the attitude of dissentient party members and groups toward this conference. The narrative is reinforced by documentary materials such as resolutions, statements, etc.

BOULANGER, O. *L'Internationale socialiste a vécu,* Paris, 1915, 312 pages.
An account of the attitude of various sections of the Second International toward the World War. The book consists of chronologically arranged documents, beginning with the anti-militarist resolutions of the Stuttgart and Basel International Congresses. It includes some speeches and articles by Jaurès, an account of the meeting of the International Socialist Bureau at Brussels preceding the outbreak of the war and documents on the anti-war attitude of various socialist groups prior to the declaration of war. The author carries his account down to July 1915 and gives the resolutions of the Lugano, Copenhagen, and London socialist peace conferences and the chief resolutions and manifestoes of the French and German parties, with some reference to the activity of the minority groups in those countries.

BRAND, CARL F. "British Labor and the International during the Great War," *Journal of Modern History*, No. 1, March 1936, pp. 40–63.

A study based on primary and secondary sources.

BRASLAVSKY, I. *Istoriia mezhdunarodnogo rabochego dvizheniia (1864–1924)* ("The History of the International Workers' Movement [1864–1924]"), Moscow, 1925, 281 pages.

The first half of the book deals with the First International. The second half deals with the policies of the Second International prior to and during the World War, the Zimmerwald and Kienthal conferences, the formation of Communist parties in various countries, the formation of the Two-and-a-Half International, and the restoration of the Second International. The last chapter gives a chronological account of the formation of the Comintern and its activity up to and including the Fifth Congress.

BRETSCHER, W., AND E. STEINMANN (editors). *Die sozialistische Bewegung in der Schweiz 1848–1920*, Bern, 1923, 160 pages.

An objective account of the events within the social democratic labor movement in Switzerland from 1848 to 1920. Part II, "Wandlungen der schweizerischen Sozialdemokratie 1914–1920," by W. Bretscher, a well-known Swiss journalist, deals with the war period, the Leftist tendencies within the party ranks, the influence of the Russian Bolsheviks upon the Swiss labor movement, the strikes in 1917–1918, and the party split.

BRONSKY, M. "Uchastie Lenina v shveitsarskom rabochem dvizhenii" ("Lenin's Participation in the Swiss Labor Movement"), *Proletarskaia Revoliutsiia*, No. 4 (27), 1924, pp. 30–39.

An account of Russian Bolshevik participation in the Swiss socialist labor movement for the period 1915–1917, written exclusively from memory.

BRÜGEL, LUDWIG. *Geschichte der österreichischen Sozialdemokratie*, Vienna, 1922–25, 5 volumes in 6. Vol. V: *Parlamentsfeindlichkeit u. Obstruktion (Weltkrieg) Zerfall der Monarchie (1907–1918)*.

A detailed history of the Austrian Social Democratic Labor party.

Camille Huysmans, ses discours prononcés en Hollande du 9 au 31 janvier, 1916, Belgique ₍n.p.₎, ₍1916?₎, 54 pages.

Texts of several speeches delivered in Holland by Camille Huysmans in his capacity as Secretary of the Executive Committee of the Second International.

LA CHESNAIS, P. G. *La paix de Stockholm. Extrait de la Grande Revue*, Paris, 1918, 30 pages.

Attitude of various socialist groups toward the Stockholm Conference of 1917. This volume also contains the text of the manifesto by the Dutch-Scandinavian Committee, dated October 10, 1917.

COMITÉ ORGANISATEUR DE LA CONFÉRENCE SOCIALISTE INTERNATIONALE DE STOCKHOLM. *Stockholm*, Stockholm, 1918, 542 pages.

A valuable collection of documents pertaining to the unofficial socialist conferences held in Stockholm in 1917 together with documents submitted to the committee in charge of calling the Stockholm Conference. The preface, by Camille Huysmans, gives a brief review of the origin of the Stockholm undertaking as well as an evaluation of its achievements.

CONFÉDÉRATION GÉNÉRALE DU TRAVAIL. *XXᵉ Congrès National Corporatif (XIVᵉ de la C.G.T.) tenu à Lyon du 15 au 21 septembre 1919. Compterendu des travaux*, Villeneuve, Saint-Georges, ₍n.d.₎, 422 pages.

DAVID, EDUARD. *Die Sozialdemokratie im Weltkrieg*, Berlin, 1915, 192 pages.

A justification of the German majority socialist point of view. Includes documents pertaining to the German and the international socialist movements during the first year of the World War.

DESTRÉE, J. *Les Socialistes et la guerre européenne 1914–1915*, Brussels, Paris, 1916. 136 pages.

A brief summary of the attitude of the socialists of various countries toward the World War. One chapter is devoted to the socialist peace conferences of 1914–1915.

DRAHN, ERNST, AND SUSANNE LEONHARD. *Unterirdische Literatur im revolutionären Deutschland während des Weltkrieges*, Berlin, Fichtenau, 1920, 200 pages.

A collection of revolutionary propaganda material either published illegally in Germany or smuggled into Germany during the World War.

Contains Bukharin's "Thesen über die sozialistische Revolution und die Aufgaben des Proletariats während seiner Diktatur in Russland," pp. 151–58.

ESSEN, A. M. *Tri Internatsionala* ("Three Internationals"), Moscow, 1926, 252 pages.

A history of the First, Second, and Third Internationals up to 1924 inclusive.

FAINSOD, MERLE. *International Socialism and the World War*, Cambridge, Mass., 1935, 238 pages.

A study of international socialism during the war period and of the establishment of the Communist International.

FRAINA, LOUIS C. *Revolutionary Socialism. A Study in Socialist Reconstruction*. Issued by the Central Executive Committee of the Socialist Propaganda League, New York, [1918], 246 pages.

A statement of the position of the Socialist Propaganda League by one of its leaders.

GANETSKY, YA. "Delegatsiia SDP i L na II sezde RSDRP" ("The Delegation of the Social Democracy of Poland and Lithuania at the Second Congress of the R.S.D.L. Party"), *Proletarskaia Revoliutsiia*, No. 2, 1933, pp. 187–200.

A study, based on personal recollections and documentary material, dealing with the position of the Polish Social Democrats on the question of joining the R.S.D.L. party. The study covers the period just preceding the 1903 Congress of the R.S.D.L. party and describes the conduct of the Polish delegation at that Congress.

GILLIE, D. R. (translator and editor). *Joseph Pilsudski. The Memories of a Polish Revolutionary and Soldier*, London, 1931, 377 pages.

An autobiography by the founder of the Polish Socialist party covering his activities until he became chief of the Polish state. Pilsudski's articles and speeches are supplied with explanatory notes by the translator.

GOLDER, F. A. *Documents of Russian History, 1914–1917.* Translated by Emanuel Aronsberg, New York, London, 1927, 663 pages.

A valuable collection of translated and annotated documents.

GORTER, HERMANN. *Der Imperialismus, der Weltkrieg und die Sozialdemokratie*, Munich, [1919], 133 pages.

An analysis of the causes of the collapse of the Second International written by a revolutionary social democrat a few weeks after the outbreak of the World War.

The author looked for the establishment of a new International devoted to opposition to imperialist war and the realization of socialism.

GRUMBACH, S. (HOMO). *Der Irrtum von Zimmerwald-Kiental. Rede, gehalten am 3. Juni 1916 im Unionsaale des Volkshauses zu Bern*, Bümpliz, Bern, 1916, 95 pages. *L'Erreur de Zimmerwald-Kienthal*, Paris, 1917, 131 pages.

An analysis and criticism of the Zimmerwald movement by one of its most determined opponents.

GRÜNBERG, CARL. *Die Internationale und der Weltkrieg*, Leipzig, 1916, 318 pages. Reprinted from the *Archiv für die Geschichte des Sozialismus und der Arbeiterbewegung* (C. Grünberg, editor), Vol. VI, pp. 373–541; Vol. VII, pp. 99–278.

A very valuable collection of documents on the pro-war and anti-war attitude of various socialist parties during the prewar period and immediately after the declaration of the war. Contains also all the anti-militarist resolutions adopted by the Second International prior to the World War. Published also in Russian.

GUILBEAUX, HENRI. *Wladimir Iljitsch Lenin. Ein treues Bild seines Wesens*, Berlin, 1923, 174 pages.

A brief biography of Lenin by one of his co-workers and admirers.

HAMILTON, MARY AGNES. *Arthur Henderson. A Biography*, London, Toronto, 1938, 461 pages.

Chapter vii deals with the proposed Stockholm Socialist Conference, Henderson's trip to Russia in the spring of 1917, and the events which ultimately led to his resignation from the British Cabinet.

HILL, ELIZABETH, AND DORIS MUDIE (editors). *The Letters of Lenin*, New York, 1937, 499 pages.

A translation of Lenin's letters selected from Volumes XXVIII and XXIX of his *Sochineniia* and from the volume of his letters to relatives published by the Gosizdat in 1931.

HILLQUIT, MORRIS. *Loose Leaves from a Busy Life*, New York, 1934, 339 pages.

The autobiography of a prominent member of the American Socialist party written against the background of the American socialist labor movement prior to, during, and after the World War.

Huitième Congrès Socialiste International tenu à Copenhague du 28 août au 3 septembre 1910. Compte rendu analytique. Publié par le Secrétariat du Bureau Socialiste International, Gand, 1911, 511 pages.

HUMPHREY, A. W. *International Socialism and the War*, London, 1915, 168 pages.

A general outline of the development of the socialist movement from the eighteen-forties to October 1914. Gives the point of view of the main socialist groups of Western Europe and Russia, based solely upon reports in the English newspapers. Owing to lack of information the author frequently draws wrong conclusions.

Illustrierte Geschichte der Deutschen Revolution, Berlin, 1929, 528 pages.

A valuable chronological account of the developments within the Social Democratic party of Germany during the World War, with special emphasis on the activity of the moderate opposition and the revolutionary group (especially Spartakus), supported by excerpts from documents of that period. This account, which ends with March 1920, is a history of the German revolution and is endorsed by the Communist International.

Internationaler Sozialisten-Kongress zu Kopenhagen 28. August bis 3. September 1910, Berlin, 1910, 126 pages.

Internationaler Sozialisten-Kongress zu Stuttgart 18. bis 24. August 1907, Berlin, 1907, 132 pages.

"Iz Arkhivov Karla Libknekhta i Klary Zetkin" ("From the Archives of Karl Liebknecht and Klara Zetkin"), *Bolshevik,* No. 13–14, 1934, pp. 104–107.

Klara Zetkin's letter to Karl Liebknecht written early in 1915, dealing with the calling of the International Socialist Women's Conference in Berne in the spring of 1915; also a reprint of Karl Liebknecht's letter to Klara Zetkin dated November 29, 1915, written from a hospital bed.

"Iz materialov Instituta Marksa-Engelsa-Lenina" ("From the Materials of the Marx-Engels-Lenin Institute"), *Bolshevik,* No. 22, November 30, 1932, pp. 76–96.

Reproduces Lenin's original manuscript commenting on Bukharin's article "K teorii imperialisticheskogo gosudarstva" ("Contribution to the Theory of the Imperialist State"). Contains letters exchanged between Lenin, Zinoviev, and Bukharin in connection with the controversy over the publication of the *Kommunist.*

"Iz perepiski russkogo Biuro TsK s zagranitsei v gody voiny (1915–1916)" ("From the Correspondence of the Russian Bureau of the Central Committee with Organizations Abroad during the War Years [1915–1916]"), *Proletarskaia Revoliutsiia,* No. 102–103, 1930, pp. 177–95.

Eight letters addressed by Elizarova, Secretary of the Bureau of the Bolshevik Central Committee in Russia, to the Central Committee of the R.S.D.L. party (Bolsheviks) in Switzerland, with a preface by A. Elizarova.

Izveshchenie o konferentsii organizatsii R.S.-D.R.P. ("Notice about the Conference of Organizations of the R.S.D.L. Party"). Published by the Organization Committee of the R.S.D.L. party, September 1912, ₍Vienna₎, 53 pages.

A report on the "August" Conference of the R.S.D.L. party in Vienna. Contains resolutions adopted by the Conference.

Jahrbuch der sozialdemokratischen Partei der Schweiz 1915, Zurich, 1916, 187 pages.

Jahrbuch der sozialdemokratischen Partei der Schweiz 1916, Zurich, 1917, 187 pages.

KABAKTSCHIEFF, CHRISTO. *Die Entstehung und Entwicklung der Komintern. Kurzer Abriss der Geschichte der Komintern,* Hamburg, 1929, 174 pages. The Russian edition appeared under the title: *Kak voznik i razvivalsia Kommunisticheskii Internatsional* ("The Origin and Development of the Communist International"), Moscow, Leningrad, 1929, 240 pages.

A brief history of the Communist International through the Sixth Congress. One chapter deals with the formation of the Left wing in the Second International, the Zimmerwald movement during the war, and the origins of the Comintern.

KARDASHEV, D. "K istorii zarozhdeniia biuro komitetov bolshinstva" ("A Contribution to the History of the Origin of the Bureau of the Majority Committees"), *Proletarskaia Revoliutsiia,* No. 10 (93), 1929, pp. 80–95, and No. 1 (96), 1930, pp. 47–67.

The narrative is based on recollections and correspondence of participants.

KAUTSKY, LUISE (editor). *Rosa Luxemburg Letters to Karl and Luise Kautsky from 1896 to 1918.* Translated by Louis P. Lochner, New York, 1925, 238 pages.

A collection of Rosa Luxemburg's letters for the period 1896–1918, with a preface and a postscript by Luise Kautsky.

KHABAS, R. "Sozdanie bolshevistskogo tsentra (B.K.B.) i gazety *Vpered*" ("The Establishment of the Bolshevik Center [The Bureau of the Majority Committees] and of the Newspaper *Vpered*"), *Proletarskaia Revoliutsiia,* No. 11 (34), 1924, pp. 19–38.

This account is based chiefly on recollections of participants. The appendices consist of Lenin's letter of January 4, 1905, pertaining to the organization of the *Vpered,* and of S. Olminsky's recollections on that subject.

KHONIAVKO, I. P. "V podpolie i v emigratsii (1911–1917 g.g.)" ("In the Underground Party Organization and as an Emigré, 1911–1917"), *Proletarskaia Revoliutsiia,* No. 4 (16), 1923, pp. 159–75.

Recollections by a Bolshevik member of the R.S.D.L. party for the period 1911–1915. A valuable account of the situation which prevailed in the Paris Bolshevik group at the outbreak of the World War.

Kriegs- und Friedensprobleme der Arbeiterklasse. Entwurf eines Manifestes. Vorgelegt der zweiten Zimmerwalder Konferenz. Herausgegeben vom Auswärtigen Sekretariat des Organisationskomitees der sozialdem. Arbeiterpartei Russlands. [n.d.], [n.p.], 25 pages.

Contains the draft manifesto submitted by P. Axelrod, S. Lapinski, and L. Martov to the Kienthal Conference and also an excerpt from a declaration "on the war and the Russian Social Democracy" issued by the Petersburg and Moscow organizations of the R.S.D.L. party (Mensheviks).

KRUPSKAIA, N. K. (editor). *Pamiati Inessy Armand* ("In Memory of Inessa Armand"), Moscow, Leningrad, 1926, 107 pages.

A biographical sketch of Inessa Armand by N. K. Krupskaia and various other authors. Valuable for certain excerpts from Inessa Armand's correspondence with Lenin during the World War pertaining to the activity of the Zimmerwald Left.

KRUPSKAYA, NADEZHDA K. *Memories of Lenin.* Translated by E. Verney, New York, [1930–1933], 2 vols.

The first volume covers the period 1894 to 1908. The second volume deals with Lenin's life from 1908 to his return to Russia in 1917. The account is based on personal recollections and Lenin's correspondence.

KRZHIZHANOVSKY, S. "Polskaia sotsial-demokratiia na II sezde R.S.D.R.P." ("The Polish Social Democracy at the Second Congress of the R.S.D.L. Party"), *Borba Klassov,* Nos. 8–9, August–September 1933, pp. 113–21.

An account of the position of the Social Democracy of Poland and Lithuania with respect to the R.S.D.L. party and the controversy regarding the conditions of unification. The account covers the period 1893–1903 and is based on primary and secondary sources.

KRZHIZHANOVSKY, S. "Polskaia sotsial-demokratiia i II sezd RSDRP" ("The Polish Social Democracy and the Second Congress of the R.S.D.L. Party"), *Proletarskaia Revoliutsiia*, No. 2, 1933, pp. 104–35.

A study of the relations between the Social Democracy of Poland (later that of Poland and Lithuania) and the R.S.D.L. party and of the failure to achieve unification. The study covers the period from 1893 to 1903 and is based on documentary material.

LEDER, V. "Natsionalnyi vopros v polskoi i russkoi sotsial-demokratii" ("The National Question in the Polish and Russian Social Democracy"), *Proletarskaia Revoliutsiia*, No. 2–3 (61–62), 1927, pp. 148–208.

A study of the attitude of the Polish Social Democrats toward the self-determination of nations question and of the differences which arose, in this connection, between the Polish and the Russian Social Democrats. The study covers the period from 1893 to 1917, and is based on primary and secondary materials.

LENIN, V. I. *Kommunisticheskii Internatsional. Stati, Rechi, Dokumenty 1914–1923* ("The Communist International. Articles, Speeches, Documents, 1914–1923") (edited by V. Knorin), Moscow, 1934, 2 volumes.

Selections from Lenin's writings for the period 1914–1923, dealing specifically with the Communist International. Volume I covers the period 1914–1919.

LENIN, V. I. *Selected Works*, New York, 1935+; in 12 volumes. Vol. II: *The Struggle for the Bolshevik Party (1900–1904)*; Vol. V: *Imperialism and Imperialist War (1914–1917)*.

For the controversy between the Bolshevik and the Menshevik groups within the R.S.D.L. party see Volume II; Volume V contains Lenin's writings on the issues raised by the World War.

LENIN, V. I. *Selections from Lenin*, New York, ₁1929–30₁, 2 volumes. Vol. I: *The Fight for the Programme. Party Organisation and Tactics. 1893–1904*; Vol. II: *The Bolshevik Party in Action. 1904–1914*.

Translated and authorized selections from Lenin's writings for the period 1893–1914.

LENIN, V. I. *Sochineniia* ("Works") (second edition), Moscow, Leningrad, 1929–1932, 30 volumes.

Lenin's unabridged writings, chronologically arranged, as authorized by the Central Committee of the All-Russian Communist party. The following volumes are cited: Vol. V, 1902–1903; Vol. VI, 1903–1904; Vol. VII, 1904–1905; Vol. VIII, 1905; Vol. XII, 1907–1908; Vol. XIV, 1909–1910; Vol. XVI, 1912–1913; Vol. XVII, 1913–1914; Vol. XIX, 1916–1917; Vol. XXVIII, *Pisma* (Letters), 1895–1910; Vol. XXIX, *Pisma* (Letters), 1911–1922; Vol. XXX, 1899–1921.

Lenin on Britain, London, ₁1934₁, 316 pages.

Selections from Lenin's writings dealing specifically with Great Britain; authorized translations compiled and prefaced by Harry Pollitt.

"Lenin—vozhd VKP (b) (Bibliograficheskie materialy)" ("Lenin—the Leader of the All-Russian Communist Party [Bolsheviks] [Bibliographical Materials]"), *Proletarskaia Revoliutsiia*, No. 3, 1934, pp. 273–94.

A list of titles of articles, recollections, and documents dealing directly with Lenin down to the Revolution of 1917.

Leninskii Sbornik ("Lenin's Miscellany"). Published by the Marx-Engels-Lenin Institute, Moscow, Leningrad, 1924+; 32 volumes published so far. Volumes used: II, V, VI, XI, XIV, XV, XVI, XVII.

Contains original drafts of Lenin's writings and letters to his associates arranged by subject rather than chronologically.

Vols. II, V, VI, XI, XIV, XV, XVI, and XVII contain valuable material on Russian party history and also concerning the Zimmerwald Left.

LENZ, JOSEF. *The Rise and Fall of the Second International*, New York, [c1932], 285 pages. German and Russian editions appeared under the following titles: *Die II Internationale und ihr Erbe 1889–1929*, Hamburg, Berlin, 1930, 302 pages; *Istoriia Vtorogo Internatsionala*, Moscow, 1931, 285 pages.

The author gives a summary of the chief resolutions and proceedings of the Second International from its founding in 1889; discusses the development of Right, Center, and Left tendencies; the Zimmerwald movement, Zimmerwald Left, and their fusion with the Communist International; the Two-and-a-Half International and the fusion with the restored Second International. The book ends with the Brussels Congress of the Second and the Sixth Congress of the Third International and is endorsed by the Communist International.

LLOYD GEORGE, DAVID. *War Memoirs*, London, 1933–1934, 6 volumes.

Volume IV contains a chapter on the proposed Stockholm International Socialist Conference and presents a version of that affair with which several other accounts do not entirely agree.

Londonskii sezd rossiiskoi sots. demokr. rab. partii (sostoiavshiisia v 1907 g.). Polnyi tekst protokolov ("The London Congress of the Russian Social Democratic Labor Party Held in 1907. Complete Text of Protocols"), Paris, 1909, 484 pages.

[LORIOT, F.] *Les socialistes de Zimmerwald et la guerre*. Published by the Comité pour la Reprise des Relations Internationales, Paris, [n.d.], [n.p.].

An analysis of the French socialist majority and minority policy and a statement of the platform of the French Zimmerwaldists by a leader of the Left wing of the Committee for the Resumption of International Relations.

LORWIN, LEWIS L. *Labor and Internationalism*, New York, 1929, 682 pages.

A brief history of the international socialist labor movement from 1830 to 1928, including the First, the Second, the Two-and-a-Half, and the Third Internationals.

LOUIS, PAUL. *La crise du socialisme mondial de la IIe à la IIIe Internationale*, Paris, 1921, 192 pages.

An essay on the collapse of the Second International during the war and its inadequacy after its restoration in 1919, which was responsible for the success and victory of the Third International. The author discusses the importance of the twenty-one conditions of the Second Congress of the Communist International and the splits which these conditions caused in the various parties.

LUTZ, RALPH HASWELL, *Fall of the German Empire 1914–1918*. Translations by David G. Rempel and Gertrude Rendtorff, Stanford University, California, 1932, 2 volumes.

A collection of documents with introductory and explanatory notes.

LUXEMBURG, R. *The Crisis in the German Social Democracy (The Junius' Pamphlet)*, New York, 1918, 128 pages.

A criticism and an analysis of the German socialist majority policy and a statement of the German Left policy in time of war by a member of the German Left. The German original was published in 1916 under the title *Die Krise der Sozialdemokratie* and contained as an appendix the theses drafted by Rosa Luxemburg and adopted by the *Internationale* group in January 1916.

MALATESTA, A. *I socialisti italiani durante la guerra*, Milan, 1926, 303 pages.

A valuable historic review of events within the Italian socialist movement, against the background of the World War and the international socialist movement.

MARTOV, L. *Istoriia Rossiiskoi Sotsial-Demokratii. Period 1898–1907 g.* ("History of Russian Social Democracy 1898–1907"), third edition, Petrograd, Moscow, 1923, 214 pages.

The only available history of the party by a Menshevik.

MARTOV, L. *Spasiteli ili uprazdniteli (Kto i kak razrushal R.S.-D.R.P.)* ("Saviors or Destroyers [Who Destroyed the Russian Social Democratic Labor Party and How It Was Done]"), Paris, 1911, 47 pages.

A justification of so-called "liquidationism" and the Menshevik interpretation of the reasons why the 1910 plenum of the Central Committee of the R.S.D.L. party in Paris failed to re-establish party unity.

MAXE, JEAN. *De Zimmerwald au bolshevisme ou le triomphe du Marxisme pangermaniste. Essai sur les menées internationalistes pendant la guerre 1914–1920*, Paris, 1920, 236 pages.

A pessimistic study based on primary and secondary source material by an opponent of Bolshevism. The author presents the Zimmerwald movement as a defeatist movement initiated chiefly by the Russian Bolsheviks.

MEYER, ERNST (editor). *Spartakus im Kriege. Die illegalen Flugblätter des Spartakusbundes im Kriege*, Berlin, 1927, 232 pages.

A collection of proclamations issued by the Internationale (later the Spartakus) group from 1914 to 1918; with an explanatory introduction by Ernst Meyer.

MIKHAILOV, M. M. "Lenin v borbe s opportunizmom v mezhdunarodnoi sotsial-demokratii (do 1904 goda)" ("Lenin's Struggle against Opportunism within the International Social Democracy [Prior to 1904]"), *Krasnaia Letopis*, No. 1–2 (46–47), 1932, pp. 5–21.

A brief study of Lenin's attitude toward revisionism, and so-called "opportunism" within German Social Democracy. The study is based on primary sources and covers the period 1900–1905.

MIUNTSENBERG, V. (W. MÜNZENBERG). *S Libknekhtom i Leninym. Piatnadtsat let v proletarskom iunosheskom dvizhenii* ("With Liebknecht and Lenin. Fifteen Years in the Proletarian Youth Movement"), second edition, Moscow, Leningrad, 1930, 205 pages.

Recollections of the international socialist youth movement for the period 1906–1921, by one of the organizers of the Communist Youth International.

MÜNZENBERG, WILHELM. *Die sozialistische Jugend-Internationale*, Berlin, [n.d.], 88 pages. (Internationale sozialistische Jugendbibliothek Heft 3.)

A brief and valuable account of events within the international socialist youth movement from 1907 to 1918, by one of the youth movement's most active participants and war-time Secretary of the International Socialist Youth League. The account is reinforced by documentary texts.

NARODETZKI, ANDRÉ. *Devant la guerre; la faillite des trois Internationales. L'Internationale des nations, l'Internationale catholique, l'Internationale ouvrière, leur origine, leur doctrine pacifique, leur fonction et leur action en 1914*, Paris, 1922, 155 pages.

The chapter on the Workers' International deals with the formation of the First International and its activities and the functioning of the Second International up to the outbreak of the war. The account ends with a comparison of the collapses of the First and the Second Internationals, both having been caused by war.

NEVSKY, V. I. *Istoriia R.K.P. (b) Kratkii Ocherk* ("History of the Russian Communist Party [Bolsheviks] Brief Outline"), second edition, Leningrad, 1926, 462 pages.

A valuable account of the Narodnik movement and the beginnings of the social democratic movement in Russia.

Little space is devoted to the Bolshevik party during the war prior to the March Revolution. The Zimmerwald movement and the Zimmerwald Left are barely mentioned.

Obzor deiatelnosti rossiiskoi sotsial-demokraticheskoi rabochei partii za vremia s nachala voiny Rossii s Avstro-Vengriei i Germaniei po iiul 1916 goda ("Review of the Activity of the Russian Social Democratic Labor Party since the outbreak of the War between Russia and Austria-Hungary and Germany to July 1916"), [n.p.], [1916], 102 pages.

An anonymous publication by the Russian Secret Police.

ONEAL, JAMES. *American Communism. A Critical Analysis of Its Origins, Development and Programs,* New York, 1927, 256 pages.

Deals chiefly with the formation of the Communist party in the United States, after 1919. Contains some information on the earlier period.

PAINTER, FLOY RUTH. *That Man Debs and His Life Work,* Indiana University, 1929, 209 pages.

A biography of a leader of the American Socialist party. Chapter iii deals with the World War period.

PALÉOLOGUE, MAURICE. *An Ambassador's Memoirs.* Translated by F. A. Holt, O.B.E., London, 1923–1925, 3 volumes.

A diary covering the period July 1914—May 1917, by the last French Ambassador at the Russian Imperial Court.

PALME-DUTT, R. *The Two Internationals,* London, 1920, 92 pages.

Deals with the situation within the Second International during the World War and its revival in 1919, the formation of the Third International, and the attitude of certain Center parties towards both Internationals. The appendices contain documents of the 1919 Berne Conference of the Socialist International and of the Moscow Congress of the Communist International.

Pamiatniki agitatsionnoi literatury ross. sots. demokr. rab. partii, VI (1914–1917), Period voiny, Vyp. I. Proklamatsii 1914 g. ("Memorials of Agitational Literature of the Russian Social Democratic Labor Party, Volume VI [1914–1917], War Period, Issue One. Proclamations for 1914"), Moscow, Petrograd, 1923, 345 pages.

A valuable collection of Social Democratic proclamations distributed in Russia during the World War, with comments by Russian Secret Police agents. This is a collection of documents from the Secret Police files.

Papers Relating to the Foreign Relations of the United States, 1917, Supplement 2. The World War (United States Department of State), Washington, D.C., 1932, 2 volumes.

The Parliamentary Debates, House of Commons, Fifth Series.

Volumes XCIV, XCVI, and XCVII contain the debate on the Stockholm Conference.

Pendant la Guerre. Le Parti Socialiste, la Guerre et la Paix. Toutes les résolutions et tous les documents du Parti Socialiste de Juillet 1914 à fin 1917, Paris, 1918, 224 pages.

A valuable collection of the chief manifestoes and declarations issued by the French Socialist party for the period 1914–1917. Contains full text of the party's reply to the questionnaire of the Dutch-Scandinavian Committee in Stockholm.

Pervyi Vserossiiskii Sezd Sovetov R.i.S.D. ("The First All-Russian Congress of Soviets of Workers' and Soldiers' Deputies"), edited by V. N. Rakhmetov with a preface by Ya. A. Yakovlev; second volume edited by V. N. Rakhmetov and N. P. Miamlin, Moscow, Leningrad, 1930–1931, 2 volumes.

Petrogradskii Sovet Rabochikh i Soldatskikh Deputatov. Protokoly zasedanii Ispolnitelnogo Komiteta i Biuro I.K. ("The Petrograd Soviet of Workers' and Soldiers' Deputies. Protocols of Meetings of the Executive Committee and of the Bureau of the Executive Committee"), edited by B. Ya. Nalivaisky with a preface by Ya. A. Yakovlev, Moscow, Leningrad, 1925, 374 pages.

Pisma P. B. Akselroda i Yu. O. Martova ("Letters of P. B. Axelrod and Yu. O. Martov"), Berlin, 1924, 367 pages.

A collection of letters exchanged by two prominent Mensheviks from 1901 to 1916.

P.K. and SH. L. "Lenin i mezhdunarodnoe sotsialisticheskoe Biuro v 1905 godu" ("Lenin and the International Socialist Bureau in 1905"), *Krasnaia Letopis,* No. 1 (12), 1925, pp. 116–22.

Contains two letters by Lenin and one by Plekhanov written in the summer of 1905, addressed to the International Socialist Bureau. The letters deal with the Bolshevik-Menshevik controversy.

PLEKHANOV, G. V. *O Voine. Otvet tovarishchu Z. P.* ("On the War. Reply to Comrade Z. P."), Paris, 1914, 32 pages.

A statement of the author's attitude toward the European war, written in the form of a letter, dated October 27, 1914.

POKROVSKY, M. N. (editor). *Ocherki po istorii oktiabrskoi revoliutsii* ("Outline of History of the October Revolution"), Moscow, Leningrad, 1927, 2 volumes.

Articles by various Bolshevik authors on the causes of the Bolshevik Revolution of 1917; the effects of the World War on the labor movement; the March 1917 Revolution and its consequences. Volume I contains D. Baevsky's article: "Partiia v gody imperialisticheskoi voiny" ("The Party during the Years of the Imperialist War"), pp. 333–518, a study based on primary and secondary source materials.

POL, K. "Bolsheviki i dovoennyi II Internatsional" ("The Bolsheviks and the Prewar Second International"), *Proletarskaia Revoliutsiia,* Nos. 2–3 (109–110), 1931, pp. 22–58, and Nos. 4–5 (111–112), 1931, pp. 35–79.

A study, based on primary and secondary source material, of Lenin's evaluation of the international labor movement and of the leaders of the Second International.

The Policy of the International. A Speech of and an Interview with the Secretary of the International, Camille Huysmans, Member of the Belgian Parliament and the Brussels City Council, London, 1916, 31 pages.

Report of an interview with a correspondent of *Le Petit Parisien* held on March 25,

1916, and the speech delivered before the Congress of the Dutch Social Democratic Labor party at Arnhem on January 9, 1916; both represent a statement of the policy of the Executive Committee of the Second International during the first two years of the World War.

POPOV, A. (N. VOROBIEV). "Stranichka vospominanii o rabote v 'Mezhdu-raionke'" ("A Page of Recollections on the Activity in the 'Mezh-raionka'"), *Proletarskaia Revoliutsiia*, No. 10 (22), 1923, pp. 95–111.

Recollections by a member of the "Mezhraionka" organization for the period 1914–1915, dealing chiefly with his trip to Western Europe in behalf of his organization for the purpose of establishing contacts with Plekhanov, Axelrod, and others.

POPOV, N. *Outline History of the Communist Party of the Soviet Union,* Moscow, Leningrad, 1934, 2 volumes.

Volume I covers the history of the R.S.D.L. party from its origin through the November Revolution. Written by a Soviet historian and endorsed by the Soviet government.

POSTGATE, R. W. *The Bolshevik Theory,* London, 1920, 240 pages.

A study of Bolshevik doctrine with valuable appendices which contain translations of documents relating to the First Congress of the Comintern.

POSTGATE, R. W. *The International during the War,* London, 1918.

A brief account, based on primary and secondary sources, of the situation within the international socialist movement during the World War.

POSTGATE, R. W. *The Workers' International,* London, 1921, 125 pages.

A brief account of the First, the Second, and the Third Internationals and the Zimmerwald movement during the World War. Gives a list of all congresses of the First, the Anarchist, and the Second Socialist Internationals.

Prazhskaia konferentsiia RSDRP 1912 goda. Stati i dokumenty ("The Prague Conference of the Russian Social Democratic Labor Party of 1912. Articles and Documents"), [Moscow], 1937, 245 pages.

A collection of articles and letters written by Lenin, Stalin, and Ordzhonikidze in connection with the calling of the Prague Conference of the R.S.D.L. party and its results; also texts of resolutions adopted by the Conference. The book is prefaced and published by the Central Committee of the All Russian Communist party.

Protokoll über die Verhandlungen des Parteitages der sozialdemokratischen Partei Deutschlands. Abgehalten zu Dresden vom 13. bis 20. September 1903, Berlin, 1903, 448 pages.

Protokoll über die Verhandlungen des Parteitages der sozialdemokratischen Partei Deutschlands. Abgehalten zu Hannover vom 9. bis 14. Oktober 1899, Berlin, 1899, 304 pages.

Protokoll über die Verhandlungen des Parteitages der sozialdemokratischen Partei Deutschlands. Abgehalten zu Jena vom 17. bis 23. September 1905, Berlin, 1905, 380 pages.

Protokoly obedinitelnogo sezda rossiiskoi sotsial-demokraticheskoi rabochei partii sostoiavshegosia v Stokgolme v 1906 godu ("Protocols of the Unification Congress of the Russian Social Democratic Labor Party Held in Stockholm in 1906"), Moscow, Leningrad, 1926, 404 pages.

RADEK, K. *Tri Internatsionala* ("Three Internationals"), Simferopol, 1924, 55 pages.

Lectures delivered at the Sverdlov Institute at Moscow. The author argues that the Second International failed because of reformism. The First International was the seed time and the Third International the time of harvest.

Raskol na II sezde R.S.D.R.P. i II Internatsional. Sbornik dokumentov ("The Party Split Which Occurred at the Second Congress of the R.S.D.L. Party and the Second International. Collection of Documents"). Published by the Marx-Engels-Lenin Institute, Moscow, 1933, 159 pages.

A collection of reports, letters, and articles by the leaders of the Bolshevik party, covering the period 1904–1905, in which the Bolshevik stand on the question of the Russian party split was presented to the Executive of the Second International. The appendix contains letters and articles by Bebel, Kautsky, and Luxemburg on the Russian party split.

RAVICH, OLGA. "Fevralskie dni 1917 goda v Shveitsarii" ("The February Days of 1917 in Switzerland"), *Katorga i Ssylka*, No. 1 (30), 1927, pp. 180–86.

An account of the impression produced by the news of the March Revolution of 1917, upon the Bolshevik emigrés in Switzerland and of their return trip to Russia. The article is written exclusively from memory.

RAVICH, OLGA. "Mezhdunarodnaia zhenskaia sotsialisticheskaia konferentsiia, 1915 g." ("The International Socialist Women's Conference in 1915"), *Proletarskaia Revoliutsiia*, No. 10 (45), 1925, pp. 165–77.

Recollections by an active participant of the Russian and international socialist women's movement dealing with preparations for, and the actual proceedings of, the International Socialist Women's Conference at Berne in 1915.

Report of the Annual Conference [of the Independent Labour Party] *Held at Norwich, April 1915*, London, 1915, 127 pages.

Report of the Annual Conference [of the Independent Labour Party] *Held at Leeds, April 1917*, London, May 1917, 96 pages.

Report of the Annual Conference [of the Independent Labour Party] *Held at Leicester, April 1918*, London, 1918, 106 pages.

Report of the Fifteenth Annual Conference of the Labour Party, Bristol, 1916, London, 1916, 148 pages.

Report of Proceedings at the Forty-ninth Annual Trades Union Congress Held in the Palace Hall, Blackpool, on September 3rd to 8th, 1917, London, 1917, 392 pages.

Report of the Sixteenth Annual Conference of the Labour Party, Manchester, 1917, London, 1917, 170 pages.

Report of the Seventeenth Annual Conference of the Labour Party, Nottingham and London, 1918, Westminster, London, 1918, 151 pages.

Report of the Eighteenth Annual Conference of the Labour Party, London: June 1918, London, 1918, 91 pages.

Report of the Nineteenth Annual Conference of the Labour Party, Southport, 1919, London, 1919, 242 pages.

Revoliutsiia 1917 goda (Khronika sobytii) ("Revolution of 1917 [Chronicle of Events]"), Moscow, Petrograd, 1923–1930, 6 volumes.

A day-by-day chronology of the chief events in Russia for 1917. Vol. I, by N. Avdeev, covers January–April; Vol. II, by N. Avdeev, April–May; Vol. III, by Vera Vladimirova, June–July; Vol. IV, by Vera Vladimirova, August–September; Vol. V, by K. Riabinsky, October; and Vol. VI, by I. N. Liubimov, October–December.

RIAZANOV, D. *Mezhdunarodnyi proletariat i voina. Sbornik statei, 1914–1916* ("The International Proletariat and the War. A Miscellany of Articles, 1914–1916"), Moscow, 1919, 107 pages.

A collection of articles written during the first two years of the World War dealing with the division of international social democracy into revolutionary social democrats and social patriots.

RIBOT, ALEXANDRE. *Letters to a Friend. Recollections of My Political Life.* Translated from the French by Herbert Wilson, London, [1926], 318 pages.

Reminiscences of the author's political life for the period August 1914—September 1917.

ROSENBERG, ARTHUR. *A History of Bolshevism from Marx to the First Five Years' Plan.* Translated from the German by Yan F. D. Morrow, London, 1934, 250 pages.

An attempt at an unbiased study and analysis of the development of Bolshevism from its beginning to 1932 written by a former member of the German Communist party. Chapter iv covers the period 1914 to February 1917, and deals with the Bolshevik attitude toward the Second International and participation in the Zimmerwald movement.

ROSMER, ALFRED. *Le mouvement ouvrier pendant la guerre. De l'union sacrée à Zimmerwald,* Paris, 1936, 588 pages.

A valuable account of the labor movement for the period 1913–1915, with special emphasis on the activity of the minority group within the C.G.T.; by one of its wartime leaders. Contains valuable documentary material both in the text and in appendices.

RUTGERS, S. "Vstrechi s Leninym" ("Meeting Lenin"), *Istorik Marksist,* Nos. 2–3 (42–43), 1935, pp. 85–98.

Valuable recollections of a Dutch Communist, who was one of the founders of the Socialist Propaganda League, about his wartime activities in the United States and his later activity in the Communist International.

SAMOILOV, F. N. Vospominaniia ("Recollections"), Moscow, 1922–1927, 4 volumes.

The first three volumes contain an account of Bolshevik activity in the Ivanovo-Voznesensk district for the period 1903–1914. The fourth volume, entitled *Protsess bolshevistskoi fraktsii IV Gosudarstvennoi Dumy* ("The Trial of the Bolshevik Group in the Fourth State Duma"), contains valuable recollections by one of the defendants who, as member of the Fourth State Duma, was accused by the Tsarist government of subversive activity.

SAPOSS, DAVID J. *The Labor Movement in Post-war France,* New York, 1931, 508 pages.

A detailed account of the French Trade Union movement after the World War, preceded by a brief but valuable account of the war period. The study is based on primary and secondary sources.

SCHEIDEMANN, PHILIPP. *The Making of New Germany.* Translated by J. E. Michell, New York, 1929, 2 volumes.

An autobiography by one of the leaders of the Majority Social Democrats in Germany during the World War.

SCHEIDEMANN, P. *Es lebe der Frieden!*, Berlin, 1916, 32 pages.

A statement of the war and peace policy of the majority group of the German Social Democratic party.

SCHENKER, ERNST. *Die sozialdemokratische Bewegung in der Schweiz von ihren Anfängen bis zur Gegenwart,* Appenzell, 1926, 224 pages.

A Ph.D. dissertation, dealing with the development of the social democratic movement in Switzerland between 1830 and 1925.

SCHÜLLER, RICHARD, ALFRED KURELLA, R. CHITAROW. *Geschichte der Kommunistischen Jugend-Internationale,* Berlin, [c1929–1931], three volumes in one. Vol. I by Richard Schüller: *Von den Anfängen der Proletarischen Jugendbewegung bis zur Gründung der KJI.*

A history of the Communist Youth International. Vol. I deals with the formation of the first youth organizations in various Western European countries, the attitude of the Second International toward the socialist youth movement, the formation of the International Socialist Youth League and its gradual transformation during the World War period into the Communist Youth International.

Seconde Conférence Socialiste Internationale de Zimmerwald. Published by the Comité pour la Réprise des Rélations Internationales, Paris, [1916].

Contains R. Grimm's article, "De Zimmerwald à Kienthal," the official report on the Kienthal Conference and its major resolutions, the text of Brizon's speech delivered in the Chamber of Deputies on June 24, 1916, and press comments on the participation of certain members of the Chamber of Deputies in the Kienthal Conference.

SHKLOVSKY, G. "Tsimmervald" ("Zimmerwald"), *Proletarskaia Revoliutsiia,* No. 9 (44), 1925, pp. 73–106.

An account of the events which led to the calling of the Zimmerwald and Kienthal Conferences with an analysis of their proceedings and results. Apparently the article was compiled from information available in Lenin's and Zinoviev's writings; it contains a valuable document: a letter by Zinoviev in which he reports on the meeting of the Enlarged International Socialist Committee, held early in February 1916.

SHLIAPNIKOV, A. "Fevralskaia revoliutsiia i evropeiskie sotsialisty" ("The February Revolution and the European Socialists"), *Krasnyi Arkhiv,* Vol. II (XV), 1926, pp. 61–85; Vol. III (XVI), 1926, pp. 25–43.

This study covers the period from March to August 1917 and deals with the negotiations between the Executive Committee of the Petrograd Soviet of Workers' and Soldiers' Deputies and representatives of international socialism concerning the proposed calling of an international socialist conference. Contains very valuable documents.

SHLIAPNIKOV, A. *Kanun semnadtsatogo goda* ("On the Eve of 1917"), third edition, Moscow, Petrograd, 1923, 2 volumes.

Vol. I is a very valuable account of Bolshevik activity during the war by a member of the Central Committee of the party, who served in those years as a link between the Bolsheviks in Russia and the Bolshevik leaders abroad. Vol. II deals chiefly with the events in Russia and the activity of the Bolsheviks in the navy and among the students. Both volumes contain valuable documentary material.

SLUTSKY, A. "Bolsheviki o germanskoi s.-d. v period ee predvoennogo krizisa" ("The Bolsheviks and German Social Democracy in the Period of the Prewar Crisis"), *Proletarskaia Revoliutsiia,* No. 6 (101), 1930, pp. 38–72.

An analysis of the formation of the Center within German Social Democracy and the attitude of the Bolsheviks to the changes in the ranks of the German Social Democrats and within the International. The author believes that there was a certain amount of vacillation within the ranks of the Bolsheviks during the prewar period and that these vacillations were due to an overestimation of the prestige of German Social Democracy which had a very strong influence upon the Russian Social Democratic movement. The author sees Lenin's achievement largely in his attempt to clarify the Bolshevik attitude toward events in the German Social Democratic movement and to do away with uncertainties and vacillations.

Spartakusbriefe, Berlin, 1920–1921, 2 volumes.

A collection of proclamations and so-called "Political Letters" issued during the years of the World War by the *Internationale* (later the *Spartakus*) group.

STALIN, JOSEPH. *Leninism,* New York, 1928–[33], 2 volumes.

An interpretation of Lenin's doctrine as given in articles, speeches, and lectures written and delivered by the author since Lenin's death. Vol. I contains "The Foundations of Leninism." Vol. II contains the text of the letter addressed to *Proletarskaia Revoliutsiia* presenting the author's point of view on Lenin's stand on the question of Centrism.

STEKLOV, YU. M. *Istoriia rabochego dvizheniia (Tri Internatsionala)* ("The History of the Workers' Movement [Three Internationals]"), Moscow, 1921–?, 3 volumes.

A history of the First, Second, and Third Internationals.

SZMIDT, B. *Socjaldemokracja Królestwa Polskiego i Litwy. Materjaly i dokumenty 1914–1918* ("The Social Democracy of the Kingdom of Poland and Lithuania. Materials and Documents, 1914–1918"), Moscow, 1936, 411 pages.

Articles and texts of resolutions and manifestoes pertaining to the activity of the Social Democracy of Poland and Lithuania and reprinted from the official party publications for the period 1914–1918. Contains valuable information on the Polish Social Democracy's activity in the Zimmerwald movement and on the party split.

TRACHTENBERG, ALEXANDER (editor). *The American Socialists and the War: A Documentary History of the Attitude of the Socialist Party toward War and Militarism since the Outbreak of the Great War.* With an introduction by Morris Hillquit, New York, 1917, 48 pages.

A collection of documents reprinted from the *American Socialist,* the *New York Call,* and official bulletins of the American Socialist party dealing with its attitude toward the World War.

Tretii ocherednoi sezd rossiiskoi sotsial-demokraticheskoi rabochei partii 1905 goda. Polnyi tekst protokolov ("The Third Regular Congress of the Russian Social Democratic Labor Party, 1905. Full Text of Protocols"), Moscow, 1924, 569 pages.

TROTSKY, LEON. *My Life. An Attempt at an Autobiography,* New York, 1930, 599 pages.

An autobiography from childhood to 1929, when Trotsky was deported from Russia. Chapter xix deals with the author's activities in Paris during 1914–1915 and in the Zimmerwald movement.

TROTSKY, L. *Voina i revoliutsiia. Krushenie vtorogo Internatsionala i podgotovka tretego* ("War and Revolution. The Bankruptcy of the Second International and Preparation for the Third"), Petrograd, 1922, 2 volumes.

A collection of articles written and published by the author from August 1914 to May 1917, dealing with the attitude of various socialist groups toward the World War and with connected topics; this also contains a diary of the first days of the war. Most of the articles were published in *Nashe Slovo* and represent the point of view of the group which supported this publication. A section of the second volume contains recollections on the Zimmerwald Conference and articles written during Trotsky's stay in the United States and published in *Novyi Mir*. This volume contains unique descriptive sketches and some biographical information on some outstanding Zimmerwaldists. Included in this collection is the Russian text of Trotsky's *Der Krieg und die Internationale*, which was written by him shortly after the outbreak of the World War and distributed secretly in Western European countries.

TSIAVLOVSKY, M. A. (editor). *Bolsheviki. Dokumenty po istorii bolshevizma s 1903 po 1916 god byvsh. Moskovskago Okhrannago otdeleniia* ("Bolsheviks. Documents of the Former Moscow Secret Police Department Pertaining to the History of Bolshevism from 1903 to 1916"), Moscow, 1918, 246 pages.

A valuable collection of documents consisting of reports by secret police agents, and reports compiled by the Secret Police Department on the basis of information received from various sources and of general reviews of the activity of the Bolshevik party prepared by the Secret Police. Also contains certain valuable biographical data.

Tsimmervaldskaia i Kintalskaia konferentsii Offitsialnye dokumenty ("The Zimmerwald and Kienthal Conferences. Official Documents"), Leningrad, Moscow, 1924, 61 pages.

A Russian edition of the official report of the International Socialist Committee on the Zimmerwald conferences and the chief documents of the Zimmerwald and Kienthal conferences. The preface gives a brief history of the Zimmerwald movement.

L'Ukraine et la Guerre. Lettre ouverte adressée à la 2me conférence socialiste internationale tenue en Hollande en mai 1916, Lausanne, 1916, 55 pages.

Text of the report submitted to the Kienthal Conference by the Editorial Board of the Ukrainian Social Democratic periodical *Borotba.*

VAGANIAN, V. *G. V. Plekhanov. Opyt kharakteristiki sotsialno-politicheskikh vozzrenii* ("G. V. Plekhanov. An Attempt at a Characterization of Social-Political Views"), Moscow, 1924, 697 pages.

One of the best biographies of Plekhanov. Chapter ix gives an account of Plekhanov's activity in the Second International.

VANDERVELDE, EMILE. *La Belgique envahie et le socialisme international.* With a preface by Marcel Sembat, Paris, 1918, 234 pages.

This is a collection of the principal speeches and open letters delivered and written by Vandervelde during the World War, in justification of his pro-Entente attitude.

VANDERVELDE, EMILE. *Three Aspects of the Russian Revolution,* London, 1918, 280 pages.

Impressions of the situation in Russia soon after the March Revolution, by a member of the Belgian Socialist Mission.

VANDERVELDE, EMILE, *Souvenirs d'un militant socialiste,* Paris, [*ca.* 1939], 292 pp.

Reminiscences of the author's early life and his activity, for the period 1881–1919, as member of the Belgian Labor party, Chairman of the International Socialist Bureau, and member of the Belgian Cabinet.

VAVILIN, I. "Bolsheviki i Tsimmervald" ("The Bolsheviks and Zimmerwald"), *Krasnaia Letopis,* No. 2 (59), 1934, pp. 10–23.

A survey of Bolshevik participation in the Zimmerwald movement.

VEILAND, O. "Avgustovskii blok (1911–1914 g.g.)" ("The August Bloc [1911–1914]"), *Proletarskaia Revoliutsiia,* No. 1 (60), 1927, pp. 125–83.

An analysis of the dissensions between the Bolsheviks and the Mensheviks which led to the formation of the August bloc and the election of the Organization Committee. The author gives an account of the August 1912 conference in Vienna and the gradual disintegration of the August bloc.

Voina. Sbornik Statei ("The War. A Miscellany"). Articles by Ida Axelrod, G. Aleksinsky, L. Deutsch, P. Dnevnitsky, Mark Z-r, K. Kakhel, Olgin, and G. V. Plekhanov, Paris, 1915, 106 pages.

A miscellany by several Russian Mensheviks on the topic of war. Contains G. Plekhanov's article "Eshche o voine" ("More about the War") which was written in the form of a letter dated May 8, 1915, and which represents a justification of the author's point of view on the war in answer to criticisms received by him in connection with the publication of his pamphlet *O voine* ("On the War") in 1914.

VOLOSEVICH, V. *Bolshevizm v gody mirovoi voiny* ("Bolshevism during the Years of the World War"), Leningrad, [192?], 146 pages.

A good exposition, by a Bolshevik, of the Bolshevik war-time slogans, with reference to the condition of international socialism during the World War, the Zimmerwald movement, the first slogans of the Third International, and party activity abroad and in Russia up to the overthrow of Tsarism.

Vsesoiuznaia kommunisticheskaia partiia (b) v rezoliutsiiakh i resheniiakh sezdov, konferentsii i plenumov TsK (1898–1935) ("The All-Union Communist Party [Bolsheviks] in Resolutions and Decisions of the Congresses, Conferences, and Plenums of the Central Committee [1898–1935]"), fifth edition, [n.p.], 1936, 2 volumes.

Volume I covers the period 1898–1925.

Vtoroi ocherednoi sezd ross. sots.-dem. rabochei partii. Polnyi tekst protokolov ("The Second Regular Congress of the Russian Social Democratic Labor Party. Full Text of Protocols"). Published by the Central Committee, Geneva, [n.d.], 394 pages.

WALLING, E. *The Socialists and the War. A Documentary Statement of the Position of the Socialists of All Countries; with Special Reference to Their Peace Policy including a Summary of the Revolutionary State Socialist Measures Adopted by the Governments at War,* New York, 1915, 512 pages.

An account of international socialism, from just preceding the World War to 1915. Contains an analysis of the socialists' attitude toward the war, of the socialist peace efforts and their peace policy. The account is reinforced by excerpts from documents.

WARSKI, A. "Sotsial-demokratiia Polshi i Litvy i II sezd RSDRP" ("The Social Democracy of Poland and Lithuania and the Second Congress of the Russian Social Democratic Labor Party"), *Kommunisticheskii Internatsional*, No. 14 (192), April 5, 1929, pp. 30–41, and No. 16–17 (194–195), April 26, 1929, pp. 24–39.

An account of the controversy between the Social Democracy of Poland and Lithuania and the R.S.D.L. party on the question of self-determination of nations. This is an analysis of the Polish point of view by an outstanding member of the Polish Social Democracy, later of the Polish Communist party. The analysis is strongly influenced by later events.

YAROSLAVSKY, E. (editor). *Istoriia V.K.P. (b)* ("History of the All-Russian Communist Party [Bolsheviks]"), Moscow, Leningrad, 1926–1929, 3 volumes.

Volume III contains a history of the Bolshevik movement during the World War and the origin of the Third International, with some information on the Zimmerwald movement.

YURENEV, I. " 'Mezhraionka' (1911–1917 gg.)," *Proletarskaia Revoliutsiia*, No. 1 (24), 1924, pp. 109–39, and No. 2 (25), 1924, pp. 114–43.

Recollections of the activity of the "Mezhraionka" organization from its origin to the March Revolution of 1917, written by one of "Mezhraionka's" most outstanding members.

Zapiski Instituta Lenina ("Notes of the Lenin Institute"), Moscow, 1927, 3 volumes.

Published by the Lenin Institute in Moscow. Volume II contains reprints of articles, speeches, and letters by Lenin, the originals of which are in the Institute's archives, and also recollections about Lenin written by a number of his close associates.

ZETKIN, C. *Von der Internationale des Wortes zur Internationale der Tat*, Hamburg, 1924, 38 pages.

A comparison of the policies of the three Internationals.

ZÉVAÈS, ALEXANDRE. *Le Parti Socialiste de 1904 à 1923*, Paris, 1923, 264 pages.

A general but well-organized review of the developments within the French Socialist party including its relations with the Second and the Third Internationals; supplied with abundant footnotes.

ZINOVIEV, G. *Sochineniia* ("Works"), Moscow, Leningrad, 1923–?. (Number of volumes uncertain.)

Volume V contains the author's articles written during the 1914–1916 period, which deal with the Bolshevik attitude toward the war and the Zimmerwald movement. Volume XV contains the author's recollections of Lenin, more particularly the article, "Lenin i Komintern" ("Lenin and the Comintern").

ZUBOK, L. "U istokov kommunisticheskogo dvizheniia v S. Sh. A." ("At the Source of the Communist Movement in the United States"), *Istorik Marksist*, Nos. 5–6 (45–46), 1935, pp. 39–66.

This article is based on primary and secondary sources and covers the period of the World War. It is valuable because it contains information on the activity of the Russian Bolsheviks in the United States and the effect of the Russian Revolution on the American Socialist movement.

PERIODICALS AND NEWSPAPERS

This list contains those periodicals and newspapers which are cited in footnotes or referred to in the text of this volume.

Appeal to Reason; Girard, Kansas; 1895–1921; weekly, independent radical publication; during World War, anti-militarist; 1917–1919, appeared as *The New Appeal;* 1919, old name resumed; 1921, superseded by *Haldeman-Julius Weekly;* notable editors: J. A. Wayland, Fred D. Warren, Louis Kopelin, and E. Haldeman-Julius.

Arbeiter-Jugend; Berlin; 1909—April 1933; fortnightly; later, monthly; "Vorwärts" publication; by 1923 appeared with subtitle *Monatsschrift des Verbandes der sozialistischen Arbeiterjugend Deutschlands* and was published by "Arbeiter-Jugend" Verlag; after 1926, subtitle became *Monatsschrift der sozialistichen Arbeiterjugend;* supplements were issued under titles *Die Arbeitergemeinschaft* and *Kultur und Leben;* responsible editors: Karl Korn, G. Ollenhauer, Gustav Weber, and Fritz Ohlig; notable contributors: Eduard David, Artur Crispien, and Hans Vogel.

Die Arbeiterpolitik: Wochenschrift für wissenschaftlichen Sozialismus; Bremen; 1916–1919; weekly; published by the so-called Bremen Left Radicals, i.e., Left-wing adherents of German Social Democratic party; notable contributors: K. Radek, Henri Guilbeaux, J. Borchardt, M. Bronski, N. Bukharin, and G. Zinoviev.

Arbeiter-Zeitung: Zentralorgan der deutschen Sozialdemokratie in Oesterreich; Vienna; 1889 + ; succeeded *Die .Gleichheit;* July 12—October 11, 1889, fortnightly; October 18, 1889—October 24, 1890, weekly; October 31, 1893—December 30, 1894, twice weekly; after January 1, 1895, daily; after April 12, 1919, subtitle altered to *Zentralorgan der Sozialdemokratie Deutschösterreichs;* notable editors: Rudolf Pokorny, Victor Adler, Friedrich Austerlitz, Max Winter, Karl Hans Sailer, and Oskar Pollak; 1933, transferred to Brno, Czechoslovakia, where it was published after February 25, 1934, weekly by Foreign Delegation of Austrian Social Democratic Labor party with subtitle *Organ der österreichischen Sozialisten;* editors: Julius Deutsch and Otto Bauer.

Avanti; Giornale del Partito socialista; Rome, Milan, Turin, Paris; December 25, 1896 + ; daily; central organ of the Italian Socialist party; reflected always the point of view predominant in the party; the changes in party policy were usually accompanied by changes of editors; notable editors: Bissolati, Enrico Ferri, Claudio Treves, Mussolini, and G. Serrati; October 1911, transferred to Milan; during World War circulation rose to 200,000 copies and the newspaper was published simultaneously in three editions—in Rome, Milan, and Turin; decidedly anti-war and Zimmerwaldist; after the party split in 1922, became the organ of the intransigent wing of the Italian Socialist party; 1926, suppressed by the Fascist regime; transferred to Paris where it has been published since 1927 as a weekly, at times irregular; editor, A. Balabanoff.

La Bataille syndicaliste; Paris, Bordeaux; April 27, 1911—December 15, 1920; daily; official organ of the Confédération Générale du Travail; after the outbreak of the World War defensist, strongly supporting government by which it was subsidized; September 26, 1915, as result of declining circulation pronounced bankrupt; October 23, 1915, suspended publication; Desbois and Marcelle Capy represented the anti-war minority on the editorial board; four specimen numbers issued October 5, 21, 25, and 28, 1915; November 3, 1915, publication resumed as *La Bataille: Organe quotidien syndicaliste;* organ of a group of Right syndicalists, majority leaders of the C.G.T., and published entirely on government money.

Berner Tagwacht: Offizielles Publikationsorgan der sozialdemokratischen Partei der Schweiz; Berne; January 4, 1893 + ; succeeded *Schweizer Sozialdemokrat;* 1893—December 1, 1906, twice weekly; later, daily; during World War, Zimmerwaldist; November 13-14, 1918, suppressed by Swiss government and appeared as *Die Rote Fahne;* notable editors: Karl Moor, Robert Grimm, and Hans Vogel.

Bolshevik: politiko-ekonomichcskii dvukhnedelnik TsK VKP (b); ("Bolshevik: Political and Economic Semimonthly Journal of the Central Committee of the All-Russian Communist Party"); Moscow; 1921 + ; notable editors: V. Astrov, N. Bukharin, V. Molotov, and E. Yaroslavsky.

Borba Klassov: Istoricheskii massovyi ezhemesiachnyi zhurnal ("Class Struggle: A Monthly History Journal for the Masses"); Moscow; 1931–1936; organ for propagation of Marxism-Leninism and basic policies of All-Russian Communist party and Communist International on basis of historical development of the class struggle; 1931, subtitle altered to *Istoricheskii massovyi zhurnal obshchestva istorikov Marksistov pri Komakademii Ts. I.K. S.S.S.R.* ("A Monthly History Journal for the Masses of the Society of Marxist Historians Attached to the Communist Academy of the C.E.C. of the U.S.S.R."); 1937 succeeded by *Istoricheskii Zhurnal* ("History Journal"); editors: 1931–1932, M. N. Pokrovsky; after 1932, B. V. Volgin.

Borba: Nefraktsionnyi rabochii zhurnal ("The Struggle: A Nonfactional Workers' Journal"); St. Petersburg; February–July 1914; eight numbers; irregular; Nos. 1, 2, and 5 were confiscated; directed by L. Trotsky; advocated platform of "August bloc" and party unification by creation of a party center; suppressed by government.

Bremer-Bürgerzeitung; 1890—February 3, 1919; daily; organ of German Social Democratic party; during World War, became organ of Bremen-Radical opposition; December 23, 1918, came under control of Independent Social Democratic party and adopted subtitle *Organ des Arbeiter- und Soldatenrats;* notable editors: J. Knief, Hans Donath, Paul Frölich, and Wilhelm Holzmeier.

Bulletin du Département des Rélations Internationales; Stockholm; June–November 1917; mimeographed publication in French, English, and German issued by the Executive Committee of the Petrograd Soviet of Workers' and Soldiers' deputies; contained reprints from *Izvestiia,* messages from the Department of International Relations, and articles on events in Russia; gratis to executives of socialist parties in Western Europe; editor, Yu. S. Weinberg.

Bulletin périodique du Bureau Socialiste International; Brussels; 1909–1913; irregular and undated; eleven numbers; official organ of Executive Committee of International Socialist Bureau; published in German, French, and English.

The Call: An Organ of International Socialism; London; 1916–1920; at first fortnightly; after June 8, 1916, weekly; began as organ of the Left wing of the British Socialist Party; later organ of its Executive Committee.

Chicago Daily Tribune; Chicago, Illinois; 1847 + ; Republican; 1847–1858, published as *Chicago Daily Tribune;* July 1858—October 24, 1860, as *Chicago Press and Tribune;* October 25, 1860—October 6, 1872, as *Chicago Tribune;* thereafter as *Chicago Daily Tribune;* notable managers and editors: Joseph Medill, Dr. C. H. Ray, Horace White, Sidney Howard Gay, Joseph M. Patterson, and Robert R. McCormick.

The Clarion; London; 1891–1932; weekly; after May 1927, monthly; devoted to literature, poetry, and general topics; published by Fabian Society; superseded by *The New Clarion;* notable editors and contributors: Robert Blatchford, A. M. Thompson, Norman Angell, and Ramsay MacDonald.

Contemporary Review; London; 1866 + ; monthly; political journal; Liberal; editors: G. P. Gooch and Rev. John Scott Lidgett.

Critica Sociale: Rivista quindicinale del socialismo ("Social Critique: Quarterly Review of Socialism"); 1891–1926; Milan; quarterly, later semimonthly and at times irregular; 1891, as successor to *Cuore e critica* ("Heart and Critique") appeared as *Critica sociale (Cuore e critica): Rivista di studi sociali, politici e letterari* ("Social Critique [Heart and Critique]: Review of Social, Political, and Literary Studies"); 1892, title changed to *Critica Sociale: Rivista quindicinale di studi sociali, politici, filosofici e letterari* ("Social Critique: Quarterly Review of Social, Political, Philosophical, and Literary Studies"); 1898, subtitle changed to *Rivista quindicinale del socialismo scientifico* ("Quarterly Review of Scientific Socialism"); July 1, 1899, the word "Scientifico" was dropped from the subtitle; editor-in-chief: F. Turati; notable contributors: L. Bissolati, Paul Lafargue, Enrico Ferri, Rosa Luxemburg, K. Kautsky, E. Vandervelde, Arturo Labriola, G. E. Modigliani, Rinaldo Rigola, and R. Abramovich.

Current History Magazine; New York; 1914 + ; semimonthly; from No. 5, Vol. I, monthly; published by The New York Times Co.; from May 1936, by Current History Inc.; from March 1939, by Current History Publishing Corporation. Editors: G. W. Ochs Oakes, M. E. Tracy; among the contributors many well-known American and foreign historians, economists, and writers on public questions.

Delo, see *Nasha Zaria.*

Demain: Pages et documents; Geneva; 1916–1918; monthly; published and edited by Henri Guilbeaux; changed from moderate pacifist to Zimmerwald Left policy.

Den ("The Day"); St. Petersburg; 1912–1918; daily; founded by group of liberals consisting of Left-wing Constitutional Democrats, Right Mensheviks, and Bolsheviks from *Vpered* group; during World War, defensist; after March Revolution, when it came under control of Menshevik Defensists, consistently in favor of coalition with bourgeois-liberal parties; after May 30, 1917, carried subtitle: *Organ sotsialisticheskoi mysli* ("Organ of Socialist Thought"); anti-Bolshevik; May 1918, after attempts to continue publication as *Noch* ("Night"), *Polnoch* ("Midnight"), *Temnaia Noch* ("Dark Night"), etc., suppressed by Soviet authorities; until 1917, edited by I. Kugel, later by A. N. Potresov, P. Maslov, V. Kantorovich, and others.

Difesa delle Lavoratrici ("The Defense of the Working Women"); Milan; ?–1926; organ of the Italian Socialist party; edited by a committee of socialist women.

The Economist; London; 1843 + ; British financial and economic weekly; independent Liberal; favors free trade; notable editors: F. W. Hirst, Hartley Withers, and Sir Walter T. Layton.

Edinstvo ("Unity"); St. Petersburg, Moscow; 1914, 1917–1918; 1914, four numbers published by "Mezhraionka"; reappeared after March Revolution; daily; 189 numbers; published under Plekhanov's personal guidance; other notable editors: V. I. Zasulich, L. G. Deutsch, and G. Aleksinsky; advocated victory over Germany and supported Russian Provisional Government; November 1917, suppressed; soon reappeared under title *Nashe Edinstvo* ("Our Unity") but was again suppressed; 1918, two monthly issues of *Edinstvo* were published in Moscow.

Die Forderung: Organ für sozialistische Endzielpolitik; Zürich; October 13, 1917—March 2, 1918; nine numbers; organ of first group of Swiss Communists; editors: Cilla Itschner and Karl Graf.

Die Freie Jugend: Organ der sozialistischen Jugendorganisation der Schweiz; Zürich; 1911–1918; irregular; successor to *Der Skorpion* and *Der Jugendbursche;* Left Social Democratic; served for enlightenment of socialist youth; devoted to topics of labor movement and socialism; during World War anti-militarist and pacifist; notable editors: Max Bock, W. Münzenberg, Jakob Herzog, Willi Tröstel, and E. Arnold.

Gazeta Robotnicza ("Workers' Newspaper"); Warsaw, Cracow; 1906, 1912–1916, 1918; irregular; May 16—October 1906, fourteen numbers; organ of Warsaw Committee of Social Democracy of Poland and Lithuania; 1912, resumed publication in two separate editions, published respectively by each of the two rival Warsaw Committees (one edition of four numbers endorsed by Main Presidium of party and other edition of eleven numbers by opposition, the so-called Rozlomovists); *Gazeta Robotnicza* (Rozlomovist) became organ of Regional Presidium of Social Democracy of Poland and Lithuania; 1912–1914, Nos. 15 to 23, edited by A. Malecki and

Henryk Kaminski; 1915, No. 24; 1916, No. 25; after the two factions united in 1916, one more issue, No. 1, appeared in August 1918 as organ of Warsaw Committee of Social Democracy of Poland and Lithuania.

Gazette de Soleure or *Solothurner Zeitung: freisinnig-demokratisches Organ des Kantons Solothurn. Tageszeitung für Volkswirtschaft;* Solothurn, Switzerland; 1907 + ; radical; during World War neutral; notable editors G. Vogt and A. F. Bill.

Die Gleichheit: Die Zeitschrift für die Interessen der Arbeiterinnen; Stuttgart; 1891–1921 ? ; fortnightly; later known with subtitle *Zeitschrift für Arbeiterfrauen und Arbeiterinnen;* founded and edited by Klara Zetkin; organ of German socialist women's movement; published news of international socialist women's movement; supplements appeared as *Für unsere Mütter, Für unsere Kinder, Für unsere Mütter und Hausfrauen* and *Die Frau und ihr Haus;* other notable editors: Heinrich Schultz and Marie Juchacz.

Die Glocke: Sozialistische Wochenschrift; Berlin; September 1, 1915—1925; in October 1921, subtitle altered to *Wochenschrift für Politik, Finanz, Wirtschaft u. Kultur;* published by A. Helphand (Parvus); Right Social Democratic; during World War, defensist; notable contributors: Paul Lensch, Haenisch, P. Scheidemann, and F. Ebert.

Golos: ezhednevnaia politicheskaia i obshchestvennaia gazeta ("The Voice: A Daily Political and Social Newspaper"); Paris; September 13, 1914—January 13, 1915; 108 numbers; Nos. 1 to 5 carried title *Nash Golos* ("Our Voice"); established by unemployed Russian printers; organ of a group of Russian Social Democrats–Internationalists from both Menshevik and Bolshevik ranks; notable contributors: Yu. O. Martov, Trotsky, Lozovsky, Manuilsky, Antonov-Ovseenko, Kollontai, and Lunacharsky; anti-war and anti-imperialist; suppressed by French authorities; resumed publication as *Nashe Slovo: obshchestvennaia i politicheskaia gazeta* ("Our Word: A Social and Political Newspaper"); January 29, 1915—October 15, 1916; Paris; 213 numbers; published by same group of Social Democrats–Internationalists; policy tended more to Left than that of *Golos* because of withdrawal of Yu. O. Martov from the editorial board on April 19, 1916, and the growing influence of L. Trotsky; in addition to Russian contributors the paper carried articles by outstanding representatives of the Western European socialist movement; suppressed by French authorities; resumed publication as *Nachalo* ("A Beginning"); Paris; September 30, 1916—March 24, 1917; 147 numbers again published by mixed group of Social Democrats–Internationalists but controlled by Bolshevik-Internationalists, among them Antonov-Ovseenko, who had broken all his ties with Menshevism, Lunacharsky, and Manuilsky.

Golos Sotsial-Demokrata ("The Voice of a Social Democrat"); Geneva, Paris; 1908–1911; twenty-six numbers; June 25, 1911—July 1912, editorial board issued six supplementary numbers under title *Listok Golosa Sotsial-Demokrata* ("A Leaflet of the Voice of a Social Democrat"); monthly; later, irregular; official theoretical and political organ of Russian Mensheviks abroad; notable editors: P. Axelrod, G. V. Plekhanov,

F. Dan, Yu. O. Martov, and A. S. Martynov; because of paper's Right trend Plekhanov withdrew from editorial board in May 1909.

Der Grütlianer; Basel, Luzern, Berne, Zürich; 1851–1925; began as a semi-monthly; gradually its publication increased until it became a daily; editors prior to 1853 in Basel: Schabelitz and Klein; until 1861 in Luzern: Schüpp and Anton Lang; until 1872 in Berne: Arnold Lang and J. Allemann; thereafter published in Zürich; notable editors for the later period: Salomon Bleuler, Reinhold Ruegg, J. Vogelsanger, H. Mettier, Paul Brandt, H. Wirz, E. Walter, and F. Nydegger; organ of the Swiss Grütli Verein which joined the Right wing of the Swiss Social Democratic party from which it was expelled in 1916; thereafter opposed proletarian dictatorship, favored the League of Nations and general disarmament.

Hamburger Echo; Hamburg; 1887–1918; daily; organ of German Social Democratic party; during World War, extreme Right Social Democratic; notable editors: Rense and Hermann Molkenbuhr; notable contributors: P. Lensch, H. Cunow, and Haenisch; came gradually under control of Left wing; November 10, 1918, superseded by *Die Rote Fahne* (Hamburg); editor Paul Frölich; title soon altered to *Hamburger Volkszeitung.*

L'Humanité: Journal socialiste; Paris; 1904 + ; daily; after 1918 irregular; founded by Jean Jaurès; until 1920, central organ of French Socialist party; 1904—July 31, 1914, edited by Jaurès; 1914–1918, controlled by French Majority Socialists; notable editors: Pierre Renaudel and Compère Morel; 1918–1920, controlled by former Socialist minority which during this period constituted the party majority; editors: Jean Longuet, Marcel Cachin, and others; after January 1921, organ of French Communist party; after April 8, 1921, carried subtitle *Journal communiste;* after February 1923, *Organ central du parti communiste (S.F.I.C.);* 1939, suppressed by the government; notable editors: Marcel Cachin, Charles Vaillant-Couturier, and others.

Informatsionnyi Listok Zagranichnoi Organizatsii Bunda ("Information Leaflet of the Organization of the Bund Abroad"); Geneva; June 1911—June 1916; eleven numbers; September 1916, replaced by *Biulleten Zagranichnago Komiteta Bunda* ("Bulletin of the Committee of the Bund Abroad".).

Die Internationale: Eine Zeitschrift für Praxis und Theorie des Marxismus: Berlin; 1915–1935; began with subtitle *Eine Monatsschrift für Praxis und Theorie des Marxismus;* subtitle altered in 1919 to *Eine Wochenschrift . . . .* and in 1920 to *Eine Halbmonatsschrift . . . . ;* after June 24, 1920, all indication of regularity in publication was eliminated from subtitle which became *Eine Zeitschrift . . . . ;* 1924, a supplement appeared at regular intervals under title *Parteiarbeiter: Mitteilungsblatt für Funktionäre;* originally established by Rosa Luxemburg and Franz Mehring; April 1915, first number confiscated and publication suppressed; 1919, resumed publication as organ of Central Committee of German Communist party; autumn 1932 suspended by the German government; April 1935 resumed publication but was soon suppressed; notable editors: Walter Stoecker, August Thalheimer, and Ernst Schneller.

Internationale Korrespondenz (IK); Berlin; September 1914—October 1918; twice weekly; published by Albert Baumeister; organ of Right wing of German Social Democratic party; after 1916, carried subtitle *Über Arbeiterbewegung, Sozialismus und auswärtige Politik.*

Internationales Flugblatt; Zürich; September 1915; one number; organ of Zimmerwald Left group; contained documents presented by this group to Zimmerwald Conference and a preface under the title "Die Zimmerwalder Linke über die Aufgaben der Arbeiterklasse. Zur Einführung."

Internationale sozialistische Kommission: Nachrichtendienst; Stockholm; May 6, 1917—September 1, 1918; 44 numbers; mimeographed publication; official organ of Zimmerwald movement; until June 19, 1917, issued by International Socialist Committee composed of R. Grimm, O. Morgari, Charles Naine, and A. Balabanoff; later issued by Z. Höglund, C. N. Carleson, Ture Nerman, and A. Balabanoff.

Internationale sozialistische Kommission zu Bern: Bulletin; Berne; 1915–1917; six numbers: No. 1, September 21, 1915; No. 2, November 27, 1915; No. 3, February 29, 1916; No. 4, April 22, 1916; No. 5, July 10, 1916; and No. 6, January 6, 1917; official organ of Zimmerwald movement; published in English, German, and French by International Socialist Committee composed of R. Grimm, Charles Naine, O. Morgari, and A. Balabanoff.

The Internationalist; Boston, New York; 1917; irregular; only a few numbers came out; organ of the Socialist Propaganda League; notable editors: S. Rutgers and Fritz Rozin; the first number came out in January 1917, but a few months later the publication was transferred to New York where it was continued as *The New International: A Journal of Revolutionary Socialist Reconstruction;* editor: Louis C. Fraina.

Internatsional i Voina ("The International and the War"); Zürich; 1915; one number; published by the Secretariat of the Organization Committee of the R.S.D.L. Party Abroad; internationalist and pro-Zimmerwald.

Iskra ("The Spark"); Petrograd; October 8 (September 26)—December 17 (4), 1917; weekly; twelve numbers; organ of Menshevik-Internationalists; editor-in-chief: L. Martov; notable editors: Astrov and Martynov.

Iskra: Tsentralnyi Organ Rossiiskoi Sotsial-demokraticheskoi Rabochei Partii ("The Spark: Central Organ of the Russian Social Democratic Labor Party"); Munich, London, Geneva; December 1900—October 1905; 112 numbers; editorial board until August 1903: V. Lenin, L. Martov, A. Potresov, P. Axelrod, V. Zasulich, and G. Plekhanov; transferred to London (1902–1903) and then to Geneva; August–November 1903, edited by V. Lenin and Plekhanov; No. 52, November 7, 1903, was edited by Plekhanov alone; thereafter the newspaper was controlled exclusively by Menshevik section of R.S.D.L. party.

Istorik Marksist ("The Marxist Historian"); Moscow; 1926 + ; 1926–1929, quarterly; 1926, two numbers; 1930, bimonthly; 1931, two numbers; 1932–1934, bimonthly; 1935, monthly; since 1936, bimonthly; 1926–1933, published by Society of Marxist Historians attached to the Communist Academy; since 1934, published by History Institute of the Communist Academy; notable editors: P. O. Gorin, N. M. Lukin, M. N. Pokrovsky, E. Yaroslavsky, A. M. Pankratova, and P. S. Drozdov.

Izvestiia Zagranichnago Sekretariata Organizatsionnogo Komiteta Rossiiskoi Sotsial-demokraticheskoi Rabochei Partii ("News of the Secretariat of the Organization Committee of the Russian Social Democratic Labor Party Abroad"); Zürich; February 22, 1915—February 16, 1917; nine numbers; organ of Menshevik-Internationalists.

Journal of Modern History; Chicago; 1929 + ; a quarterly journal published by the University of Chicago Press in co-operation with the Modern European History Section of the American Historical Association; editor, Bernadotte E. Schmitt; associate editor, Louis Gottschalk.

Jugend-Internationale: Kampforgan der Kommunistischen Jugend-Internationale; Zürich, Berlin, Vienna, Berlin; September 1, 1915—1934; began as an irregular publication under the subtitle *Kampf und Propagandaorgan der internationalen Verbindung sozialistischer Jugendorganisationen;* May 1918, suppressed by the Swiss Federal Council; eleven numbers; No. 11 carried the title *Brot, Frieden und Freiheit;* July 1919 resumed in Berlin and soon became a monthly organ of the Communist Youth International; November 1923—September 1927 in Vienna; later again in Berlin; published in several European languages; notable contributors: N. Bukharin, L. Trotsky, H. Roland-Holst, K. Radek, Karl Kilbom, A. Kollontai, and W. Münzenberg.

Katorga i Ssylka: Istoriko-revoliutsionnyi Vestnik ("Penal Servitude and Exile: Revolutionary History Messenger"); Moscow; 1921-1935; 1921–1924, irregular; 1924, bimonthly; 1925-1927, eight issues a year; 1928–1933, monthly; 1934, bimonthly; 1935, No. 1 (116) is believed to be the last issue; published by All-Union Society of Political Convicts and Exiled Settlers; valuable for documentary material and recollections of political prisoners condemned to penal servitude and exile under Tsarist regime; editor-in-chief, F. Kon.

Klassekampen: Organ for den revolusjonaere ungdom i Norge ("Class Struggle: Organ for the Revolutionary Youth in Norway"); Oslo; 1908 + ; formerly daily, now monthly; organ of Norwegian League of Communist Youth; formerly organ of League of Socialist Youth; during World War, opposed war and policies of majority socialists; opened its pages to Zimmerwald Left ideas; editor: Eugene Olaussen.

Kommunist ("The Communist"); Geneva; September 1915; Nos. 1–2; published jointly by editorial board of *Sotsial Demokrat* and Yu. Piatakov, E. Bosh, and Bukharin; discontinued because of disagreements on editorial board over questions of party theory and character of the periodical.

Kommunisticheskii Internatsional: Organ Ispolnitelnogo Komiteta Kommunisticheskogo Internatsionala ("The Communist International; Organ of the Executive Committee of the Communist International"); Petrograd, Moscow; May 1, 1919 + ; originated as monthly; 1921–1924, irregular; 1925, monthly; September 1926—1929, weekly; 1930–1936, three times per month; since July 1936, monthly; in August 1919, German, French, and English editions began to appear in Berlin, Paris, and London; publication of English edition subsequently transferred to New York; German edition published at first in Berlin, then in Hamburg, and again in Berlin, where it was suppressed in 1933; a Chinese edition began to appear on February 20, 1930, and a Spanish edition in 1933.

Krasnaia Letopis: Istoricheskii Zhurnal Petrogradskogo Biuro Komissii po Istorii Oktiabrskoi Revoliutsii i Rossiiskoi Kommunisticheskoi Partii ("The Red Chronicle: History Journal of the Petrograd Bureau of the Commission for the Study of the History of the October Revolution and the Russian Communist Party"); Leningrad; 1922–1937; bimonthly; later irregular; beginning with No. 1 (16), 1926, subtitle altered to *Istoricheskii Zhurnal Leningradskogo Istparta* ("History Journal of the Leningrad Istpart"); beginning with No. 1 (22), 1927, subtitle dropped; 1935 not published; 1936, Nos. 1 and 2; 1937, No. 3.

Krasnyi Arkhiv: Istoricheskii zhurnal ("Red Archives: History Journal"); 1922; Moscow; devoted to history of the revolutionary movement and of the Soviet Union; 1922–1935, published by the Central Archives of the R.S.F.S.R.; 1936–1937, by the Central Archives of the U.S.S.R. and the R.S.F.S.R.; since 1938 published by the Main Archives of the People's Commissariat for Internal Affairs of the U.S.S.R.

The Labour Leader: A Weekly Journal of Socialism, Trade Unionism and Politics; Manchester; 1889–1922; founded by J. Keir Hardie to succeed *The Miner;* after 1894, weekly; after 1904, organ of Independent Labour party; notable editors: W. C. Anderson, J. R. MacDonald, Bruce Glasier, E. D. Morel, and Norman Angell; 1922, title altered to *The New Leader.*

The Labour Monthly: A Magazine of International Labour; London; 1921+; an independent pro-Communist publication; advocates policy of British Communist party and of Communist International; editor: R. Palme-Dutt; notable contributors: L. Trotsky, V. Lenin, K. Radek, Henri Barbusse, Max Beer, G. D. H. Cole, Bernard Shaw, E. Varga, and Wm. Gallacher.

Leipziger Volkszeitung: die Tageszeitung für die Interessen des werktätigen Volkes; Leipzig; 1893–1933; daily; Left wing newspaper of German Social Democratic party; notable early editors: Franz Mehring, Rosa Luxemburg, Paul Lensch, and Friedrich and Kurt Geyer; gradually came under control of Social Democratic Center; during World War was central organ of moderate opposition which in 1917 constituted Independent Social Democratic party.

Letopis ("The Chronicle"); Petrograd; December 1915—December 1917; monthly; twenty-five numbers; successor of *Sovremennik* ("The Contemporary"); founded by M. Gorky; published by group of Social Democrats–Internationalists; discussed literary, political, and academic topics; antiwar; notable editors: N. Sukhanov, V. Bazarov, and A. Bogdanov; notable contributors: A. Lozovsky, L. Kamenev, M. Pokrovsky, and Martov's partisans on Organization Committee of R.S.D.L. party.

Lichtstrahlen: monatliches Bildungsorgan für denkende Arbeiter; Berlin; September 1913—May 14, 1921; May 1916, superseded by *Leuchtturm: Bildungsorgan für denkende Arbeiter;* apparently only one number; November 1918, resumed publication as *Lichtstrahlen;* Left Social Democratic; anti-war and anti–Majority Socialist in policy; publisher: Julian Borchardt.

Luch ("The Ray"); St. Petersburg; September 29 (16), 1912—July 18 (5), 1913; daily; 237 numbers; began as Right Menshevik paper; membership of editorial board changed a number of times because of arrests and changes in party policies; notable editors: V. Ezhov, F. Dan, N. Garvi, and Eva Broido; suppressed by government; resumed publication as *Zhivaia Zhizn* ("The Active Life"); July 24 (11), 1913—August 14 (1), 1913; St. Petersburg; 19 numbers; presence of F. Dan and L. Martov on editorial board caused change in policy; again suppressed; finally suppressed on eve of World War after appearing as *Novaia Rabochaia Gazeta* ("The New Workers' Newspaper"); August 21 (8), 1913—February 5 (January 23), 1914; 136 numbers; *Severnaia Rabochaia Gazeta* ("The Northern Workers' Newspaper"); February 12 (January 30), 1914—May 14 (1), 1914; 68 numbers; *Nasha Rabochaia Gazeta* ("Our Workers' Newspaper"); May 16 (3), 1914—July 22 (9), 1914; 56 numbers; last editorial board consisted of F. Dan, D. Koltsov, E. Maevsky, L. Martov, and A. Romanov.

The Masses: A Monthly Magazine Devoted to the Interests of the Working People; New York; 1911—December 1917; established by an independent group of Left-wing writers and journalists; 1916, absorbed *The New Review: A Critical Survey of International Socialism* (New York; 1913–1916, monthly); editors: Max Eastman, Floyd Dell, Robert Minor, Joseph Freeman, Arturo Giovannitti, Claude McKay, and Michael Gold; 1917, deprived of second-class mailing privileges; discontinued; superseded by *The Liberator: A Journal of Revolutionary Progress;* New York; March 1918—October 1924; monthly; same editors as *The Masses;* autumn 1924, control passed to American Communist party; editorial board reorganized to include members of Communist party Central Committee as "political editors": Z. Foster, Ludwig Lore, Jay Lovestone, C. Ruthenberg, and M. J. Olgin; former editors, except Max Eastman, retained as "art editors"; discontinued; after merging with *The Labor Herald,* reappeared as *The Workers' Monthly: A Combination of the Labor Herald, Liberator and Soviet Russia Pictorial;* Chicago; *The Masses* was revived as *The New Masses;* New York; February 1927 + ; weekly; established as a Left-wing literary magazine; now follows line of Communist International; notable editors: Theodore Draper, Granville Hicks, Ruth McKenney, Joseph Freeman, Michael Gold, and James Dugan.

Morning Post; London; 1772–1937; Conservative; daily; began as *Morning Post and Daily Advertising Pamphlet;* became leading Right Conservative journal; protectionist, imperialist, Francophile; notable editors: Sir William Hardman, J. Nicol Dunn, Sir Fabian Ware, and H. A. Gwynne; 1937, united with *Daily Telegraph* as *Daily Telegraph and Morning Post.*

Mysl: Politicheskaia, obshchestvennaia i literaturnaia gazeta ("The Thought: A Political, Social, and Literary Newspaper") ; Paris; November 15, 1914—March 14, 1915; daily; 101 numbers; organ of internationalist wing of Socialist Revolutionist party; editor: V. Chernov; suppressed by French authorities; resumed as *Zhizn* ("Life") ; Paris, Geneva; March 21, 1915—June 1916; daily, later weekly, finally regular; retained former subtitle; June 6, 1915, ceased publication in Paris; June 20, 1915, resumed publication in Geneva; editors: V. Chernov and N. I. Rakitnikov.

Nash Golos ("Our Voice") ; September, 1915—May 10, 1916 and 1917; Samara; irregular; 1915–1916, 29 numbers; newspaper published by group of S.D. Mensheviks; served at first as joint organ for defensist and internalist groups of Menshevism; favored both Zimmerwald movement and work in War Industries Committees; gradually became increasingly internationalist; suppressed by government; resumed publication as *Golos Truda* ("The Voice of Labor") of which 2 numbers appeared on June 21, 1916, and July 3, 1916; title altered to *Golos* ("The Voice") ; September 2—October 27, 1916; 4 numbers; after the March Revolution *Nash Golos* was again published in Samara until late in 1917 as organ of Samara Menshevik Committee; early editorial board consisted of A. Kabtsan, B. S. Vasilev, N. Golikov, A. Yugov, and I. S. Belov; spring of 1916, I. Ber (Gurevich) joined editorial board; notable contributors: members of labor group in Central War Industries Committee, Menshevik Duma deputies, P. Axelrod and L. Martov.

Nasha Rabochaia Gazeta, see *Luch.*

Nasha Zaria ("Our Dawn") ; St. Petersburg; January 1910—June 1914; monthly; official theoretical and political organ of Right Menshevism; editor-in-chief: A. N. Potresov; other notable editors: V. O. Levitsky, N. Cherevanin, L. I. Axelrod-Ortodox, and L. Martov; after outbreak of World War, one issue was published in September 1914 (Nos. 7–9) but was confiscated by police; though pro-Entente, journal was suppressed; resumed publication as *Nashe Delo* ("Our Cause") ; July 1915—December 1915; six numbers, of which several were double; publication supervised by Organization Committee of R.S.D.L. party to unite defensist and internationalist wings of Menshevism; editorial board consisted of S. O. Tsederbaum (Ezhov), N. Garvi, Batursky, B. O. Bogdanov, and A. Gorsky; nearly all numbers confiscated; suppressed; resumed publication as *Delo: Ezhenedelnyi sotsial-demokraticheskii zhurnal* ("The Cause: A Weekly Social Democratic Journal") ; Moscow; 1916–1917 and 1918; 1916, ten numbers; 1917, two numbers prior to March Revolution and one (Nos. 3–6) after; decidedly defensist; notable editors: P. P. Maslov and P. N. Kolokolnikov; March 18, 1918—June 1918, Petrograd, Moscow; published by group of united Menshevik defensists and Plekhanov's adherents; editor-in-chief: V. Levitsky.

Nashe Delo, see *Nasha Zaria.*

Nashe Slovo, see *Golos.*

Die Neue Zeit: Wochenschrift der deutschen Sozialdemokratie; Stuttgart; 1883—August 25, 1923; weekly; later fortnightly; first eighteen numbers carried subtitle *Revue des geistigen und öffentlichen Lebens;* during last few years of publication appeared with subtitle *Halbmonatschrift der deutschen Sozialdemokratie;* Marxist organ of German Social Democratic party; gradually changed from Left to Right socialist position; until 1917, edited by Karl Kautsky; 1918–1922, edited by Heinrich Cunow.

Neues Leben: Monatschrift für sozialistische Bildung; Berne; January 1915— December 1917; monthly; organ of Swiss Socialist party, dealing with questions of labor and party organization; internationalist; editors: Robert Grimm and Jakob Lorenz; revived in 1921 as *Rote Revue;* editors: Ernst Nobs and Friedrich Heeb.

The New York Call; New York; May 30, 1908—November 12, 1923; American Socialist daily; September 1923, title altered to *The New York Leader;* editors: C. M. Wright, C. W. Ervin.

New Yorker Volkszeitung; January 8, 1878—October 12, 1932; New York; daily; socialist; published in German by Socialist Co-operative Publishing Association; editor, Ludwig Lore; December 17, 1932, superseded by *Neue Volkszeitung.*

Norddeutsche Allgemeine Zeitung; Berlin; 1861 + ; daily; published in three editions: morning, evening, and national (Reich); founded as independent, democratically inclined, pro-Austrian publication; after 1862, pro-Prussian and under Bismarck's influence; became so-called "Kanzlerblatt"; notable directors: A. Brass, Emil Pindter, Griesemann, W. Lauser, and O. Runge; November 10, 1918, superseded by *Die Internationale;* November 12, 1918, title altered to *Deutsche Allgemeine Zeitung;* came under control of a syndicate which bought it for national government; 1926, sold to a group of bankers and industrialists; notable editors: Fritz Klein and Karl Silex.

La Nouvelle Internationale: Journal des ouvriers socialistes internationalistes; Geneva; May 1, 1917—1921; notable editors: Charles Hubacher and Ernest Brunner; May 1, 1921, superseded by *L'Avant-garde.*

Novaia Rabochaia Gazeta, see *Luch.*

Novyi Mir ("The New World"); New York; 1911–1916; organ of Russian Social Democrats–Internationalists; 1911–1914, weekly; after 1914, three times a week and at times daily; during World War, approached Zimmerwald Left position; after November Revolution, Communist; notable editors: N. Bukharin, L. Trotsky, V. Volodarsky, and I. Chudnovsky.

Ny Tid ("The New Times"); Trondhjem; 1899– ? ; daily; organ of Norwegian Social Democratic party; Left socialist in policy; editor-in-chief: Martin Tranmael; foreign contributors: Elise Ottesen, A. Kollontai, and Karl Kilbom.

Otkliki Bunda ("Echoes of the Bund"); Geneva; 1909–1911; five numbers; irregular; organ of Committee of the Bund Abroad; June 14, 1915, resumption announced, but periodical never reappeared.

Le Petit Parisien; Paris; 1876 + ; daily; one of Paris "Big Five"; independent; Left republican; favored Russo-French alliance; during World War highly anti-German; founded by Louis Andrieux and Jules Roche;

notable editors and contributors: Jean Dupuy, Lieutenant-Colonel Rousset, E. de Feuquières, Le Goffic, Jean Frollo, Jules Destrée, P. Painlevé, and Claude Anet.

Le Peuple: Organe de la Democratie Socialiste; Brussels; December 1885+; daily; central organ of Belgian Labor party; notable editors: Louis Bertrand, J. Wauters, Louis de Brouckère, A. Wauters, and I. Delvigne.

Pikri ("The Thought"); Kutais; 1912–1914; daily; published in Georgian by the Transcaucasian Regional Committee of the R.S.D.L. party.

Politiken ("Politics"); Stockholm; April 27, 1916 + ; every other day; from early 1917, daily; after November 2, 1917, title altered to *Folkets Dagblat Politiken* ("The People's Daily Political News"); began as Left Socialist opposition paper; gradually became Communist; notable editors: T. Nerman, C. N. Carleson, and Karl Kilbom.

Pravda: Organ Tsentralnago Komiteta i Peterburgskago Komiteta R.S.D.-R.P. ("The Truth: Organ of the Central Committee and the Petersburg Committee of the R.S.D.L. Party"); St. Petersburg, Moscow; May 5 (April 22), 1912 + ; daily; until July 18 (5), 1913, 356 numbers; suppressed; first editorial board: N. G. Poletaev, I. P. Pokrovsky, V. M. Molotov, F. F. Raskolnikov, K. S. Eremeev, and K. N. Samoilova; notable contributors: V. D. Bonch-Bruevich, V. M. Velichkina, V. I. Lenin, and G. Zinoviev; July 26 (13)—August 14 (1), 1913, published as *Rabochaia Pravda* ("The Workers' Truth"); 17 numbers; suppressed; editorial board: K. S. Eremeev, M. S. Olminsky, M. A. Savelev, K. N. Samoilova, and M. Chernomazov; August 14 (1)—September 20 (7), 1913, published as *Severnaia Pravda* ("The Northern Truth"); 31 numbers; suppressed; September 24 (11)—October 22 (9), 1913, published as *Pravda Truda* ("The Truth of Labor"); 20 numbers; October 14 (1), 1913, because of anticipated suppression another edition of *Pravda* was started under the title *Za Pravdu* ("For the Truth"); *Pravda Truda,* however, appeared on October 14 (1), 21 (8), and 22 (9); December 18 (5), 1913, *Za Pravdu* was suppressed after 52 numbers had appeared; December 20 (7), 1913—February 3 (January 21), 1914, published as *Proletarskaia Pravda* ("The Proletarian Truth"); (34 numbers; suppressed; February 4 (January 22)—June 3 (May 21), 1914, published as *Put Pravdy* ("The Path of Truth"); 92 numbers; suppressed; June 4 (May 22), 1914, replaced by *Rabochii* ("The Workman"), a periodical, which on that day came out in the form of a newspaper; June 5 (May 23)—July 21 (8), 1914, published as *Trudovaia Pravda* ("The Labor Truth"); 35 numbers; suppressed; March 18 (5), 1917, resumed publication as *Pravda: Organ Tsentralnago Komiteta i Peterburgskago Komiteta R.S.D.R.P.* ("The Truth: Organ of the Central Committee and the Petersburg Committee of the R.S.D.L. Party"); July 18 (5), 1917, editorial office raided and paper suppressed; 99 numbers: July 19 (6), 1917, reappeared as *Listok "Pravdy"* ("The Leaflet of 'the Truth'"); one number.

August 5 (July 23)—August 22 (9), 1917, functions of *Pravda* assumed by *Rabochii i Soldat: Tsentralnyi Organ R.S.D.R.P.* ("The

Worker and the Soldier: Central Organ of the R.S.D.L. Party"), former organ of the Military Organization of the party now transformed into its central organ; 15 numbers; editorial staff: N. Podvoisky, V. Nevsky, A. Zalezhsky, B. Shumiatsky, and A. S. Kiselev; suppressed; August 26 (13)—September 6 (August 24), 1917, published as *Proletarii: Tsentralnyi Organ R.S.D.R.P.* ("The Proletarian: Central Organ of the R.S.D.L. Party"); 10 numbers; suppressed; September 7 (August 25)— September 15 (2), 1917, published as *Rabochii: Tsentralnyi Organ R.S.D.R.P.* ("The Workman: Central Organ of the R.S.D.L. Party"); 12 numbers; suppressed; September 16 (3)—November 8 (October 26), 1917, published as *Rabochii Put: Tsentralnyi Organ R.S.D.R.P.* ("The Workers' Path: The Central Organ of the R.S.D.L. Party"); 45 numbers; additional notable editors for 1917: Avilov, Kamenev, Stalin, and Lenin; November 9 (October 27) resumed original name *Pravda* with subtitle *Tsentralnyi Organ R.S.D.R.P.;* March 9 (February 24), 1918, subtitle altered to *Tsentralnyi Organ Kommunisticheskoi partii (bolshevikov)* ("Central Organ of the Communist Party [Bolsheviks]"); after March 12 (February 27), 1918, subtitle altered to *Organ Tsentralnago Komiteta Ross. Komm. partii (bolshevikov)* ("Organ of the Central Committee of the Russian Communist Party [Bolsheviks]"); March 23 (10)— March 26 (13), 1918, subtitle was *Organ Tsentralnago i Peterburgskago Komiteta Ross. Kommunist. partii (bolshevikov)* ("Organ of the Central Committee and the Petersburg Committee of the Russian Communist Party [Bolsheviks]"); March 27 (14)—April 1 (March 19), 1918, *Pravda* appeared with the subtitle *(Petrogradskaia Pravda) Organ Tsentralnago i Petrogr. Komit. Ross. Kommunisticheskoi partii (bolshevikov)* ("[Petrograd Truth] Organ of the Central and Petrograd Committees of the Russian Communist Party [Bolsheviks]"); April 2 (March 20), a new paper appeared in Petrograd under the title of *Petrogradskaia Pravda: Organ Peterburgskago Komiteta Ross. Komm. partii (bolshevikov)* ("The Petrograd Truth: Organ of the Petersburg Committee of the Russian Communist Party [Bolsheviks]");[1] functions of the old *Pravda* had been assumed on March 29 (16), 1918, by *Pravda: Organ Tsentralnago i Moskovskago Komiteta Ross. Komm. partii (bolshevikov)* ("The Truth: Organ of the Central and the Moscow Committees of the Russian Communist Party [Bolsheviks]"); Moscow; August 1918, subtitle altered to *Organ Tsentralnago Komiteta, Mosk. Kom., i Mosk. Okr. Kom. RKP (bolshevikov)* ("Organ of the Central Committee, the Moscow Committee, and the Moscow Regional Committee of the Russian Communist Party [Bolsheviks]"); after July 12, 1919, the abbreviation *Gub.* ("Gubernia") was substituted for the abbreviation *Okr.* ("Regional"); August 14, 1920, subtitle became *Organ Tsentralnago Komiteta i Moskovskago Komiteta RKP (bolshevikov)* ("Organ of the Central Committee and the Moscow Committee of the Russian Communist Party [Bolsheviks]"); January 3, 1924, *RKP* in the subtitle was replaced by *VKP*

---

[1] For the history of this paper see *Petrogradskaia Pravda* in *The Bolsheviks and World Revolution.*

("All-Russian Communist Party"); notable editors since 1918: N. Bukharin, G. I. Krumin, and M. A. Savelev.

Pravda: Rabochaia Gazeta ("The Truth: A Workers' Newspaper"); Lvov, Vienna; October 16, 1908—May 6 (April 23), 1912; 25 numbers; Nos. 1 and 2 carried additional subtitle *Organ Ukrainskago Soiuza "Spilki"* ("Organ of the Ukrainian 'Spilka' League"); Nos. 1 and 2 appeared in Lvov, later issues in Vienna where paper was published by a group of Russian Non-factional Social Democratic writers, headed by L. Trotsky, supported "August bloc."

Preussische Jahrbücher; Berlin; 1858–1935; monthly; political, literary, and historical journal; liberal; notable editors: Rudolf Haym, A. Flögel, Hans Delbrück, Walter Schotte, Walter Heynen, and Emil Daniels.

Proletarii: Organ Mosk. SPb. i Mosk. Okr. Komitetov R.S.D.R.P. ("Proletarian: Organ of the Moscow, the St. Petersburg, and the Moscow Regional Committees of the R.S.D.L. Party"); Moscow, Viborg, Geneva, Paris; September 3 (August 21), 1906—December 11 (November 28), 1909; 50 numbers; Bolshevik; first published illegally in Russia and Finland; subtitle soon altered to *Organ Mosk. SPb. Mosk. Okr. Kazansk. Kursk. i Permsk. komitetov R.S.D.R.P.* ("Organ of the Moscow, the St. Petersburg, the Moscow Regional, Kazan, Kursk, and Perm Committees of the R.S.D.L. Party"); February 26 (13), 1908, continued in Geneva with the following subtitle: *Organ S. Peterburgskago i Moskovskago komitetov, R.S.D.R.P.* ("Organ of the St. Petersburg and Moscow Committees of the R.S.D.L. Party"); from January 21 (8), 1909, in Paris; notable editors: V. I. Lenin, A. A. Bogdanov, I. F. Dubrovinsky, G. E. Zinoviev, L. Kamenev, and I. P. Goldenberg.

Proletarii; Le Prolétaire: Tsentralnyi Organ Rossiiskoi Sotsial-demokraticheskoi Rabochei Partii ("The Proletarian: Central Organ of the Russian Social Democratic Labor Party"); Geneva; May 27 (14)—November 25 (12), 1905; irregular; 26 numbers; responsible editor: V. I. Lenin; notable contributors: V. V. Vorovsky, N. S. Olminsky, A. V. Lunacharsky, V. A. Karpinsky, and I. Teodorovich.

Proletarskaia Revoliutsiia: Istoricheskii Zhurnal Istparta ("The Proletarian Revolution: A History Journal of the Istpart"); Moscow; 1921–1936; monthly; later semiannual; originally publication of Research Committee on Party History attached to Central Committee of All-Russian Communist party; with last issue for 1924, subtitle dropped; October 1928–June 1931, published by Lenin Institute; discontinued; 1933, resumed publication as organ of Marx-Engels-Lenin Institute; 1933, Nos. 1 and 2; 1934, Nos. 3 and 4; 1935, Nos. 5 and 6; 1936, No. 7.

Prosveshchenie: Obshchestvenno-politicheskii i literaturnyi zhurnal marksistskogo.napravleniia ("Education: A Social-Political and Literary Journal of Marxist Orientation"); St. Petersburg; December 1911—October 1917; irregular; organ of Bolshevik section of R.S.D.L. party; July 1914, suppressed by government; 1917, resumed with a double number for September–October; editors: A. I. Elizarova, M. S. Olminsky, Skrypnik,

Riabinin, and L. Kamenev; notable contributors: N. I. Bukharin, V. Lenin, Yu. Steklov, N. K. Krupskaia, and D. B. Riazanov.

Przegląd Socjal Demokratyczny ("Social Democratic Review"); Cracow; 1902–1904, 1908–1910; until 1903, semimonthly; later monthly; official organ of Social Democracy of Poland and Lithuania; edited by its Main Presidium; notable editors: J. Tyszka, R. Luxemburg, J. Marchlewski, and A. Warski.

Rabochaia Gazeta ("Workers' Newspaper"); Paris; November 12 (October 30), 1910—August 12 (July 30), 1912; nine numbers; at first joint organ of certain Bolsheviks and party Mensheviks; January 1912, made by Bolsheviks central organ of R.S.D.L. party; party Mensheviks continued to contribute; notable editors: Lenin, Zinoviev, and Kamenev.

Rabochaia Gazeta: Organ Organizatsionnogo Komiteta i Peterburgskoi Organizatsii R.S.D.R.P. ("Workers' Newspaper: Organ of the Organization Committee and the Petersburg Organization of the R.S.D.L. Party"); Petrograd; March 7, 1917—November 20, 1917; daily; at first joint organ of Menshevik-Defensists and Internationalists; editorial board included Batursky, Ermansky, and Gorev; May 1917, editorial board consisting of Garvi, Gorev, and Cherevanin, all defensists, elected; May 21, 1917, name of Petersburg Organization, which at that time was internationalist, was dropped by request from subtitle; October 1917, editorial board composed of F. I. Dan, B. I. Gorev, and G. M. Ehrlich, all Menshevik-Defensists, elected; after split within Defensist group in November 1917, control passed gradually to internationalists; newspaper suppressed by Soviet government for noncompliance with decree on nationalization of advertisements; though persecuted by government, Mensheviks continued to publish a central organ under various names until March 1919.

Rabochaia Mysl: Gazeta Peterburgskikh rabochikh ("Workers' Thought: Newspaper of the Petersburg Workers"); St. Petersburg and outside Russia; 1897–1902; sixteen numbers; organ of Right wing of R.S.D.L. party; supported "economism"; notable editors: K. M. Takhtarev and A. A. Yakubov.

Rabochee Delo: Organ Soiuza Russkikh Sotsial-demokratov ("Workers' Cause: Organ of the League of Russian Social Democrats"); Geneva; April 1899—February 1902; irregular; twelve numbers; organ of League of Russian Social Democrats; sympathetic toward "economism"; 1900–1901, eight numbers of *Listok Rabochego Dela* ("The Workers' Cause Leaflet") were issued as supplements; notable editors: B. Krichevsky, P. Teplov, and Ivanshin.

Rabochie Vedomosti ("Workers' Records"); Petrograd; 1916; organ of "Mezhraionka" group and Union of Textile Workers; three numbers: No. 1, August 1916, and Nos. 2–3 (double issue), October–November 1916; notable editors: Yurenev and A. Popov.

Rabotnitsa: Organ Tsentralnago Komiteta R.S.D.R.P. (b) ("The Working Woman: Organ of the Central Committee of the R.S.D.L. Party [Bolsheviks]"); Petrograd; February 23, 1914—January 26, 1918; irregular;

twenty numbers in all; June 26, 1914—May 10, 1917, not published; devoted chiefly to the socialist women's movement; notable editors and contributors: N. K. Krupskaia, Aleksandra Kollontai, and Z. Lilina.

Rech ("Speech"); Petrograd; 1906–1918; daily; central organ of Constitutional Democratic party; suppressed after unsuccessful attempts to circulate it as *Nasha Rech* ("Our Speech"), *Svobodnaia Rech* ("Free Speech"), *Vek* ("Century"), *Novaia Rech* ("New Speech"), and *Nash Vek* ("Our Century"); notable editors: I. V. Hessen and P. N. Miliukov; notable contributors: I. I. Petrunkevich, V. D. Nabokov, and A. I. Kaminka.

Revoliutsiia Prava ("The Revolution of the Law"); Moscow; 1927–1929, published by the "Section on the Theory of Law and State of the Communist Academy"; came out after 1930 under the title *Sovetskoe gosudarstvo i revoliutsiia prava* ("Soviet State and the Revolution of the Law") and after 1932 under the title *Sovetskoe gosudarstvo* ("Soviet State"); beginning with 1930 has been published by the Institute of Soviet Construction and Law.

Die Rote Fahne: Zentralorgan der Kommunistischen Partei Deutschlands (Sektion der Kommunistischen Internationale); Berlin; November 9, 1918–1933; daily; at times irregular; 1921–1922, twice a day; January 15—February 3, March 3—April 11, 1919, not published; resumed publication in Leipzig; May 9, 1919, completely suppressed by Noske; December 12, 1919, reappeared in Berlin; commenced publication in 1918 with subtitle *Ehemaliger Berliner Lokal-Anzeiger;* after November 18, 1918, carried subtitle *Zentralorgan des Spartakusbundes;* September 19, 1920, subtitle altered to *Zentralorgan der Kommunistischen Partei Deutschlands (Sektion der III. Kommunistischen Internationale);* September 23, 1920, numeral "III." dropped; January 1, 1921—August 27, 1921, subtitle was *Zentralorgan der Vereinigten Kommunistischen Partei Deutschlands (Sektion der Kommunistischen Internationale);* thereafter the newspaper appeared with subtitle adopted on September 23, 1920; founded by R. Luxemburg and Karl Liebknecht, who were also its editors; other notable editors: Leo Jogiches (Tyszka), Bruno Schäfer, and E. Meyer.

Russische Korrespondenz "Prawda"; Stockholm; June 16 (3)—November 16 (3), 1917; semiweekly; 33 numbers; mimeographed; published by Bureau of Central Committee of R.S.D.L. party (Bolsheviks) abroad; presented Russian revolutionary events from Bolshevik point of view; editor: Karl Radek.

Sbornik Sotsial-Demokrata, Tsentralnogo Organa Rossiiskoi Sotsial-Demokraticheskoi Rabochei Partii ("A Miscellany of the *Sotsial-Demokrat,* Central Organ of the Russian Social-Democratic Labor Party"); Geneva; No. 1, October 1916; No. 2, December 1916; published by Central Committee of R.S.D.L. party; editors: V. Lenin and G. Zinoviev.

La Sentinelle: Quotidien socialiste; Chaux-de-Fonds; 1890+; prior to 1912, weekly or three times per week; founded as organ of Association of Workers' Societies; later became political organ of Neuchâtel group of Swiss Social Democratic party; 1907–1911, not published; December 18, 1915, above subtitle adopted; previous subtitle was *Journal d'infor-mation et d'annonces: Organe des socialistes du Jura;* Left-wing organ; during World War, Francophile; supported Zimmerwald movement.

Social Demokratas ("Social Democrat"); issued in England; 1915–1916; number of issues uncertain; organ of a group of Lithuanian Social Democrats; at first centrist, later revolutionary internationalist; editor: V. S. Mickiewicz-Kapsukas.

Social-Demokraten: Organ för Sveriges Socialdemokratiska arbetareparti ("The Social Democrat: Organ of the Swedish Social Democratic Labor Party"); Stockholm; 1885 + ; daily; central organ of Swedish Social Democratic Labor party; moderately reformist; during World War, Majority Socialist; notable editors: Hjalmar Branting, C. N. Carleson, J. A. Engberg, and Fredrik Ström.

Socialist Review: A Monthly Review of Modern Thought; Manchester, London; 1908–1934; organ of Independent Labour party; subtitle varied in accordance with frequency of publication; 1908–1914, monthly; 1914–1921, quarterly; after 1922, monthly; notable editors: J. R. MacDonald, Bruce Glasier, John Strachey, and Clifford Allen.

Sotsial-Demokrat ("The Social Democrat"); Moscow; March 1917—March 1918; daily; organ of Moscow Committee of R.S.D.L. party (Bolsheviks); fused with *Pravda;* notable editors: Solts, Olminsky, Lukon, Bukharin, Osinsky, and Meshchersky.

Sotsial-Demokrat: Literaturno-politicheskoe obozrenie ("The Social Democrat: Literary and Political Review"); Geneva; 1890–1892; four numbers; journal of "Emancipation of Labor" group.

Sotsial-Demokrat: Tsentralnyi Organ Rossiiskoi Sotsial-demokraticheskoi Rabochei Partii ("The Social Democrat: Organ of the Russian Social Democratic Labor Party"); Vilna, Paris, Geneva; 1908–1917; irregular; No. 1, published in Vilna, suppressed and confiscated by police; 1909, resumed publication in Paris; notable editors: V. Lenin, L. Martov, G. Zinoviev, L. Kamenev, and Marchlewski; 1910, came entirely under control of Bolshevik section of party; editors: V. Lenin, G. Zinoviev, and L. Kamenev; November 1, 1914—January 31, 1917, Nos. 33 to 58 published in Geneva; editors: V. Lenin and G. Zinoviev.

Sovremennik ("The Contemporary"); St. Petersburg; 1911–1915; monthly; dealt with literature, politics, history, sociology, and fine arts; on the whole a radical publication, at first strongly favoring Socialist Revolutionist and later Marxist policies; established by P. I. Pevin; A. V. Amfiteatrov acted as editor-in-chief until late 1911, after which he served as a contributor; other notable editors and contributors: M. M. Koialovich, V. A. Tikhonov, Maxim Gorky, V. S. Miroliubov, V. M. Chernov, V. V. Vodovozov, E. A. Liatsky, V. Ya. Bogucharsky, E. Kuskova, S. N. Prokopovich, V. B. Stankevich, N. Sukhanov.

Sozialistische Monatshefte: Internationale Revue des Sozialismus; Berlin; 1897–1933; monthly; successor to *Der sozialistische Akademiker;* originally organ of revisionist wing of German Social Democratic party;

later organ of Right wing of party; notable editors: Berthold Heymann, Hugo Warszawski, Oscar Richter, Ella Bormann, and Josef Bloch; notable contributors: Heine, Lensch, and Haenisch.

Spartak ("Spartacus"); Moscow; May 20—October 29, 1917; ten numbers; semimonthly; popular theoretical journal of Moscow Regional Committee and Moscow District Committee of R.S.D.L. party (Bolsheviks); Left-Bolshevik policy; editor: N. Bukharin; notable contributors: M. Olminsky, N. Meshcheriakov, I. Stepanov-Skvortsov, N. Osinsky, and E. Yaroslavsky.

Sprawa Robotnicza ("The Workers' Cause"); Paris; 1893–1896; twenty-six numbers; organ of the Social Democracy of the Kingdom of Poland; notable editors: J. Tyszka, Rosa Luxemburg, A. Warski, and J. Marchlewski.

Stormklockan ("Alarm-Bell"); Stockholm; 1908+; weekly, at times daily; originally organ of Swedish Socialist Youth League; now of Communist Youth League; during World War, represented Left wing of Swedish Social Democratic Labor party and served as tribune for Zimmerwald Left ideas; anti-war; favored disarmament; for brief period late in 1929 appeared as daily organ of Swedish Communist party; 1930, returned to previous status as organ of Swedish Communist Youth League; notable editors: Z. Höglund, Hjalmar Viksten, Erik Hedén, Ture Nerman, and Karl Kilbom.

Strakhovanie Rabochikh ("The Workers' Insurance"); St. Petersburg, Moscow; December 1912—July 1918; begun as monthly; from autumn 1913 to outbreak of World War, semimonthly; during World War, monthly; early in 1918, moved from Petrograd to Moscow; organ of Menshevik section of R.S.D.L. party; devoted chiefly to workers' insurance and sick benefit funds; notable editors: B. Batursky and S. M. Schwartz; notable contributors: G. O. Bienstock, N. Morozov, M. L. Kheisin, S. O. Tsederbaum, A. Kabtsan, and P. K. Gribkov.

The Times; London; 1785 + ; daily; began as *The Daily Universal Register Printed Logographically by His Majesty's Patent;* 1788, assumed present title; independent conservative; leading British newspaper; notable owners: John Walter, John Walter, Jr., Lord Northcliffe, John Walter IV, J. J. Astor; notable editors: John Walter, John Thaddeus Delane, George Earle Buckle, Geoffrey Dawson.

De Tribune ("The Tribune"); Amsterdam; October 19, 1907—April 19, 1937; at first weekly, later daily; founded as organ of extreme Left wing of Dutch Social Democratic Labor party; notable organizers, editors, and contributors: V. Van Ravesteijn, D. J. Wijnkoop, Hermann Gorter, A. Pannekoek, and Roland Holst; 1909 became organ of Social Democratic party of Holland; 1919 came under control of Dutch Communist party; April 19, 1937, title altered to *Het Volksdagblad: Dagblad voor Nederland.*

La Vie ouvrière: Revue syndicaliste bi-mensuelle; Paris; 1909+; semimonthly, later weekly; central organ of Confédération Générale du Travail; 1914, suppressed; not published during World War; 1919, resumed publication as organ of C.G.T. minority; later became organ of Confédération Générale du Travail Unitaire; notable editor: Pierre Monatte.

Volia Naroda ("The Will of the People"); Petrograd; April 20, 1917—February 1918; daily; organ of Right Socialist Revolutionists; supported Provisional Government and its foreign policy; finally suppressed by Soviet Government after several attempts to continue publication as *Volia* ("The Will"), *Volia Volnaia* ("The Free Will"), and *Volia Strany* ("The Will of the Country"); notable editors: E. Breshko-Breshkovskaia, A. A. Argunov, and V. S. Miroliubov; notable contributors: De Brouckère, Emile Vandervelde, Albert Thomas, V. Chernov.

Het Volk ("The People"); Amsterdam; 1900 + ; daily; official organ of Dutch Social Democratic Labor party; after 1927, twice daily except Sunday; after 1931, joint organ of Social Democratic Labor party and Netherlands Federation of Trade Unions; notable editors: P. J. Troelstra, J. J. de Roode, W. H. Vliegen, and J. F. Ankersmit.

Volksrecht: Sozialdemokratisches Tagblatt; Zürich; April 1898 + ; daily; official organ of Swiss national and Zürich canton Social Democratic party organizations; during World War, Left Social Democratic; close to revolutionary Marxism; notable editors: Ernst Nobs, J. Schmid, and Friedrich Heeb.

Volksstimme; Chemnitz; 1891–1933; daily; during the World War, organ of the extreme Right of the German Social Democratic party; notable editors: Gustav Noske and E. Heilmann.

Volkszeitung, see *New Yorker Volkszeitung.*

Voprosy Strakhovaniia: Rabochii Zhurnal ("Insurance Problems: Workers' Journal"); St. Petersburg; October 1913—1918; monthly; Bolshevik; organ of workers' insurance campaign launched as a result of government insurance law of June 23, 1912; publication interrupted soon after outbreak of World War but resumed more or less regularly in February 1915; notable editors and contributors: A. N. Vinokurov, S. S. Danilov, P. Stuchka, and N. A. Skrypnik.

Vorbote: Internationale Marxistische Rundschau; Berne; 1916; No. 1, January; No. 2, April; organ of Zimmerwald Left group; publishers and editors: H. Roland-Holst and A. Pannekoek; notable contributors: V. Lenin, G. Zinoviev, K. Radek, and D. Wijnkoop.

Vorwärts: Berliner Volksblatt: Zentralorgan der sozialdemokratischen Partei Deutschlands; Berlin; 1891–1933; daily; superseded *Berliner Volksblatt;* prior to October 1916, controlled by Left and later by Center groups; after October 1916, controlled by Majority Socialists; notable editors: Wilhelm Liebknecht, R. Hilferding, Ernst Meyer, Friedrich Stampfer, and Kurt Geyer; after suppression under Nazi regime, transferred to Karlsbad, Czechoslovakia, and published there after June 18, 1933, as *Neuer Vorwärts: Sozialdemokratisches Wochenblatt;* after January 17, 1938, published in Paris.

Vozrozhdenie: Zhurnal obshchestvenno-politicheskii, kulturno-filosofskii i literaturno-khudozhestvennyi ("Renaissance: A Social-Political, Cultural-Philosophic, and Artistic-Literary Journal"); Moscow, St. Petersburg; December 1908—July 1910; at first monthly; 1910, fortnightly; 1908, one number; 1909, twelve numbers; 1910, eleven numbers; Editor D. Topuridze secured collaboration of a group of Social Democrats including L. Martov, F. Dan, Yu. Steklov, and G. Tsiperovich; early in 1910, journal came under control of Moscow Menshevik group and became political and theoretical organ of Menshevism; subtitle was dropped; notable editors and contributors: V. Ezhov, V. Mirov, A. Kollontai, K. Zalevsky, L. Martov, Astrov, A. Martynov, Yu. Larin, and F. Dan; suppressed by government; succeeded by *Zhizn* ("Life") and *Delo Zhizni* ("Life's Cause").

Vpered ("Forward"); Paris; June 1910—May 1911; irregular; four numbers; organ of *Vpered* group, so-called Left Bolsheviks; notable editors and contributors: A. V. Lunacharsky, A. Bogdanov, G. Aleksinsky, and M. N. Pokrovsky.

Vpered: En Avant ("Forward"); Geneva; January 4 (December 22, 1904)— May 18 (5), 1905; weekly; eighteen numbers; Bolshevik organ of Bureau of the Majority's Committees; important in organization and ideological formation of Bolshevism; notable editors: V. Lenin, Olminsky, Vorovsky, A. V. Lunacharsky, A. Bogdanov, V. D. Bonch-Bruevich.

Za Partiiu ("For the Party"); Paris; April 29 (16), 1912—February 1914; irregular; five numbers; organ of Plekhanov's group and Party-Bolsheviks; notable editors: G. Plekhanov, Charles Rappoport, Babin, Vladimirov, Liubimov, and Lozovsky.

Di Zait; St. Petersburg; January 2, 1913 (December 20, 1912)—May 18 (5), 1914; weekly; 60 numbers; Yiddish organ of the Bund; suppressed by government, July 4 (June 21), 1914; reappeared as *Unser Zait;* 6 numbers; July 26 (13), 1914, completely suppressed; notable editors: D. Zaslavsky, M. Rafes, Ehrlich, V. Medem, Abramovich (Rein), and E. Frumkina.

Zhizn, see *Mysl.*

BIOGRAPHICAL NOTES

PARTY ABBREVIATIONS

C.G.T. .... Confédération Générale du Travail
Comintern .... Third or Communist International
I.L. party .... Independent Labour Party
I.S.B. .... International Socialist Bureau
I.S.C. .... International Socialist Committee
I.S.D. party .... Independent Social Democratic Party
R.S.D.L. party .... Russian Social Democratic Labor Party
R.S.F.S.R. .... Russian Socialist Federated Soviet Republic
S.D. party .... Social Democratic Party
S.L. party .... Socialist Labor Party
U.S.S.R. .... Union of Socialist Soviet Republics

ABRAMOVICH, A. E. (1888–   ). Member of R.S.D.L. party; Bolshevik; during World War, member of Chaux-de-Fonds section of party; after 1917, active in the Ukraine; later, official of Comintern.

ABRAMOVICH, RAFAIL ABRAMOVICH (REIN; MOVICH) (1879–   ). Member of the Bund, Right wing; during World War, Centrist and émigré; 1917, returned to Russia; re-elected to Bund Central Committee and Central Committee of United R.S.D.L. party; 1920, opposed Bund's fusion with Russian Communist party; a founder of Social Democratic Bund and *Sotsialisticheskii Vestnik.*

ADLER, FRIEDRICH (1879–   ). Son of Victor Adler; 1907–1911, lecturer in physics, Zürich University; 1911–1916, Secretary of Austrian S.D.L. party and editor of *Der Kampf;* during World War, pacifist and member of moderate Left wing of party; 1916, shot Count Stürgkh; condemned to death, later amnestied; 1919, member of National Assembly; Vice-Chairman of S.D.L. party; 1921–1922, Secretary of "Two-and-a-Half" International; after 1923, Secretary of Labor and Socialist International; since 1934 émigré.

ADLER, VICTOR (1852–1918). Founder and leader of Austrian S.D.L. party; 1889–1918, member of I.S.B.; founder of *Arbeiter-Zeitung;* after 1906, member of Reichsrat; advocate of national autonomy; anti-militarist; during World War, defensist; 1918, Minister of Foreign Affairs.

AFFOLTER, HANS (1870–   ). Lawyer; member of Swiss S.D. party, Left Wing; 1911, elected to National Council; occupied various responsible positions; during World War, internationalist.

AHSIS, *see* Rozin, Fritz.

ALBARDA, JOHAN WILLEM (1877–   ). Teacher; member of Dutch S.D.L. party; after 1913, member of States-General; 1914, co-opted to Executive Committee of I.S.B.; 1917, member of Dutch-Scandinavian Committee at Stockholm; 1925, Chairman of labor deputies in States-General.

ALBISSER, JOSEF (1868–   ). Lawyer; founder and member of Swiss S.D. party; active in trade union and workers' insurance movement; 1914, attended Italo-Swiss Socialist Conference, Lugano.

ALEKSANDR, *see* Shliapnikov, Aleksandr Gavrilovich.

ALEKSANDRA MIKHAILOVNA, *see* Kollontai, Aleksandra Mikhailovna.

ALEKSANDROV, *see* Semashko, Nikolai Aleksandrovich.

ALEKSANDROVA, EKATERINA MIKHAILOVNA (SOFIIA ALEKSEEVNA; STEIN) (1864–   ). Member of "People's Will" party; wife of Olminsky; joined *Iskra* group; attended Second Congress of R.S.D.L. party; member of Central Committee; 1912, contributor to *Pravda* (Vienna); advocate of party unity; represented Vienna *Pravda* group on Menshevik Organization Committee.

ALEKSEEV, N. A. (ANDREEV; UGRIUMYI) (1873–   ). Member of R.S.D.L. party; Bolshevik; 1905, Secretary of Bureau of Presidium at Third Party Congress; 1911–1917, active as physician in Siberia; 1917, member of Irkutsk United Social Democratic organization; 1919, Chairman of Kirensk Revolutionary Committee; 1922, returned to Moscow; occupied responsible positions in public education system and in Comintern; later, lecturer on party history at Second Moscow University.

ALEKSINSKY, GRIGORII ALEKSEEVICH (1879–   ). After 1905, member of R.S.D.L. party; Bolshevik; deputy to Second State Duma; escaped abroad after arrest of Social Democratic group; ultimatist; joined *Vpered* group and lectured at Capri party school; head of editorial boards of *Vpered* and *Na temy dnia;* during World War, socialist defensist of pro-Entente orientation; contributor to Paris *Prizyv;* 1917, returned to Russia and joined *Edinstvo* group; 1918, arrested by Vecheka; escaped abroad; contributor to Burtsev's *Obshchee Delo* (Paris).

ALEXANDER II (1818–1881). Tsar of Russia from 1855 to 1881.

ALEXANDER III (1845–1894). Tsar of Russia from 1881 to 1894.

ALLEN, CLIFFORD (BARON ALLEN of Hurtwood) (1889–1939). Member of British I.L. party; 1911–1915, with *Daily Citizen;* 1916–1917, three times imprisoned as conscientious objector; 1920, I.L. party delegate to Soviet Russia; 1922–1926, Treasurer and Chairman of I.L. party; 1924–1929, director of *Daily Herald;* 1924–1926, member of Executive of Labor and Socialist International; 1932, created baron.

ANDERSON, WILLIAM C. (1878–1919). Member of British I.L. party; 1914–1918, member of Parliament; 1915, attended Inter-Allied Socialist Conference in London; throughout World War, loyal to internationalist policy of I.L. party; opposed both military and industrial conscription.

ANDREEV, LEONID NIKOLAEVICH (1871–1919). Writer and playwright; during 1905 revolution associated with revolutionary groups; February 1905, Central Committee of R.S.D.L. party arrested at his home; during World War, defensist and member of editorial board of *Russkaia Volia;* after Bolshevik Revolution emigrated to Finland; hostile to Soviet government.

ANGELICA, *see* Balabanoff, Angelica.

ANSEELE, EDOUARD (1856–1938). Member of Belgian S.L. party; reformist; editor of a number of socialist papers; since 1894, Member of Parliament; active in Second International; devoted himself to promotion of co-operative movement; 1918–1921, member of Belgian cabinet.

ANTONOV-BRITTMAN, *see* Popov, A. N.

ARMAND, INESSA (ELIZAVETA FEDOROVNA PETROVA) (1875–1920). Member of R.S.D.L. party; Bolshevik; active party worker in Russia and abroad; 1914, attended Brussels Conference of I.S.B.; during World War, close associate of Lenin; attended Zimmerwald and Kienthal conferences; active in women's and socialist youth international movements; 1917, returned to Russia and held responsible positions.

ARMUZZI, DOMENICO. Migrated from Italy to Switzerland; fruit store proprietor; member of Executive of Italian Socialist party in Switzerland.

ASQUITH, HERBERT HENRY (EARL OF OXFORD AND ASQUITH) (1852–1928). British statesman; leader of Liberal party; 1908–1916, Prime Minister.

AUSTERLITZ, FRIEDRICH (1862–1931). Member of Austrian S.D.L. party; after 1895, editor of *Arbeiter-Zeitung;* member of Reichsrat for Vienna; during World War, defensist; 1919, member of Austrian National Assembly; later, member of Nationalrat.

AVENARIUS, RICHARD (1843–1896). German philosopher.

AVRAMOV, ROMAN. 1908, represented Bulgarian "Narrow" Socialists at meeting of I.S.B.; soon withdrew from party activity.

AXELROD, IDA ISAAKOVNA (died 1917). Literary critic; member of "People's Will" party; 1893, emigrated to Switzerland; joined "Emancipation of Labor" group and the R.S.D.L. party; contributed to *Berner Tagwacht, Neue Zeit, Vorwärts,* and *Leipziger Volkszeitung;* 1917, returned to Russia.

AXELROD, PAVEL BORISOVICH (1850–1928). Began revolutionary activity as student; forced to emigrate; joined Bakuninists; returned to Russia; joined "Black Partition" group; again forced to emigrate; became Marxist; helped to organize "Emancipation of Labor" group; 1895–1896, member of League of Russian Social Democrats; opposed economism; editor of *Iskra;* contributor to *Sotsial-Demokrat* and author of a number of books on socialism and labor movement; after 1903 Menshevik; editor of *Golos Sotsial-Demokrata;* Right Zimmerwaldist; 1917, no part in revolution; opposed Soviet government; died an émigré.

BADAEV, ALEKSEI EGOROVICH (1883–). Locksmith; member of R.S.D.L. party; Bolshevik; 1912, member of Fourth State Duma; 1914, arrested; 1915, exiled to Turukhan Krai; 1917, active in Petrograd; later, member of Central Committee of Russian Communist party and of Central Executive Committee of U.S.S.R. and President of Moscow Consumers' Co-operatives.

BAGROVSKY. Member of R.S.D.L. party; Bolshevik; 1915–1916, member of Bukharin-Piatakov group in Stockholm; supervised transport of revolutionary literature into Russia; soon expelled from party under suspicion as provocateur.

BALABANOFF, ANGELICA (1878–). 1900, joined Italian Socialist party; well known in socialist movements of practically every European country; at one time member of I.S.B.; 1912–1914, co-editor of *Avanti!;* contributed to Marxist publications in Germany, Switzerland, and Scandinavian countries; pacifist; 1915–1919, member of Zimmerwald I.S.C.; responsible Secretary of Zimmerwald movement and editor of its *Bulletin;* spring, 1917, in Russia; after Grimm affair returned to Stockholm and prepared Third Zimmerwald Conference; went to Switzerland; 1918, expelled from Switzerland and returned to Russia; 1919, Secretary of Comintern; acting Commissar of Foreign Affairs in Ukrainian Soviet government; 1920, resigned; 1922, left Russia; now Secretary of International Bureau of Socialist Parties and Secretary of Italian Socialist party; editor of *Avanti!* (Paris).

BANG, NINA (1866–1928). Member of Executive of Danish S.D. party; contributor to *Social-Demokraten* (Copenhagen); 1918, member of Riksdag; later held prominent positions in Danish government.

BARSOV, *see* Tskhakaia, Mikhail Grigorievich.

BAUER, OTTO (1881–1938). Leader and theoretician of Austrian S.D.L. party; founder of *Der Kampf;* contributor to *Neue Zeit;* before 1914, Left wing;

drafted in World War; 1915–1917, war prisoner in Russia; 1918, Undersecretary and soon Secretary of State for Foreign Affairs; opposed Comintern and took part in organizing Two-and-a-Half International; 1919, delegate to St. Germain; held other responsible positions; 1934, forced to emigrate and deprived of Austrian citizenship; author of a number of books on socialism.

BEBEL, AUGUST (1840–1913). Wood turner; prominent member of German S.D. party and its chairman for many years; Left wing; fought revisionism and ministerialism in party and in Second International; prominent leader of Second International; during last few years of life, took more moderate stand; author of numerous books and pamphlets.

BELENIN, *see* Shliapnikov, Aleksandr Gavrilovich.

BELENKY, GRIGORII YAKOVLEVICH (1885–   ). 1901, joined R.S.D.L. party; Bolshevik; several times arrested and exiled; 1912, escaped to Paris; during World War, Secretary of Paris section of Bolsheviks; 1917, returned to Russia; took part in Bolshevik revolution; occupied various responsible positions; 1926, in ranks of Trotsky opposition.

BER, I., *see* Gurevich, Boris Naumovich.

BERGER, VICTOR LOUIS (1860–1929). Member of American Socialist party and Chairman of its Executive; 1911, member of the United States Congress; 1918, re-elected but denied seat because he opposed war with Germany; 1918–1919, tried for antiwar speeches and sentenced to twenty years' imprisonment; 1921, decision reversed by Supreme Court; 1922, re-elected to Congress; 1928, defeated; 1892–1898, editor of *Vorwärts;* edited also *Social Democratic Herald* and *Milwaukee Leader.*

BERNSTEIN, EDUARD (1850–1932). Right wing member of German S.D. party; 1881–1901, in exile; studied Marxism; 1899, advanced theory of revisionism in *Die Voraussetzungen des Sozialismus und die Aufgaben der Sozialdemokratie;* contributed to *Neue Zeit;* 1902–1906, 1912–1918, 1920–1928, member of Reichstag; leader of Second International; during World War pacifist-centrist; one of the founders of "Arbeitsgemeinschaft" group and German I.S.D. party; 1919, returned to S.D. party.

BERZIN, JAN ANTONOVICH (WINTER; PAVLOV) (1881–   ). 1902, joined Lettish S.D. party; during 1905 revolution, active in the Baltic; repeatedly arrested; 1907, Secretary of Petersburg Committee of R.S.D.L. party; 1908, emigrated; member of Zimmerwald Left; 1916–1917, in the United States; editor of *Strahdneeks* (Roxbury, Mass.) and contributor to *Novyi Mir* (New York); 1917, returned to Russia; member of Central Committee of R.S.D.L. party and Lettish S.D. party; 1918–1927, Soviet representative to various European countries; held responsible posts with Soviet government; Director of Central Archives Department (Moscow); editor of *Krasnyi Arkhiv.*

BETHMANN-HOLLWEG, THEOBALD VON (1856–1921). 1909–1917, Chancellor of German Empire and Prussian Prime Minister.

BIENSTOCK, GRIGORII OSIPOVICH (GRIGORII OSIPOV) (1885–   ). Lawyer; 1904, member of R.S.D.L. party; 1906, joined Mensheviks; 1914–1916, in Western Europe; Menshevik-Internationalist; 1916, mobilized in Russia; 1917, member of the Petrograd Soviet; co-editor of *Internatsional;* December 1918, left Russia illegally; 1919, returned to Russia and joined Right Mensheviks; since 1922, abroad; contributed to Russian and German socialist press in Western Europe; author of a number of books and pamphlets.

BISMARCK, OTTO, PRINCE VON (1815–1898). 1862, head of Prussian Cabinet and Minister of Foreign Affairs; 1871–1890, first Imperial Chancellor.

BISSOLATI, LEONIDA (1857–1920). Lawyer and journalist; member of Italian Socialist party; one of the earliest Italian Marxists; 1896–1903, 1908–1910, editor of *Avanti!;* contributor to *Critica Sociale;* 1912, expelled from party for approval of Tripolitan War; later, leader of interventionalist Reform Socialists in Chamber of Deputies; 1914–1918, member of cabinet.

BLAGOEV, DMITRII (1859–1924). Came to Russia from Bulgaria as child; 1884, founded first S.D. group in Petersburg; 1885, arrested and deported to Bulgaria, where he organized groups for study and spread of socialist ideas; later, leader of revolutionary "Narrow" Socialists who (1919) formed Bulgarian Communist party; adherent of Zimmerwald movement and of Comintern.

BLANC, ALEXANDRE (1874–1924). French Socialist; during World War, minority Socialist; member of Chamber of Deputies; 1916, attended Kienthal Conference.

BLANQUI, LOUIS AUGUSTE (1805–1881). French revolutionary Communist, advocate of the dictatorship of the proletariat; member of the Paris Commune.

BLOCH, ROSA. Member of Swiss S.D. party; 1917, attended Third Zimmerwald Conference, Stockholm.

BOBROV, *see* Natanson, Mark Andreevich.

BOGDANOV, *see* Malinovsky, Aleksandr Aleksandrovich.

BONCH-BRUEVICH, VLADIMIR DMITRIEVICH (1873–). Historian of Sectarian movement in Russia; member of "Emancipation of Labor" group and later of R.S.D.L. party; Bolshevik; contributed to and helped to publish practically every Bolshevik newspaper; 1917, Executive Secretary of Council of People's Commissars; later occupied responsible posts with Soviet government.

BONDFIELD, MARGARET (1873–). British trade unionist; prominent in women's socialist movement; member of I.L. party; 1923, Member of Parliament; Parliamentary Secretary to Ministry of Labor in MacDonald government.

BORCHARDT, JULIAN (1868–1932). Member of German S.D. party, Left wing; 1908–1913, deputy to Prussian Landtag; during World War, publisher of *Lichtstrahlen;* member of Zimmerwald Left; 1916–1918, founder and member of International Socialists of Germany; later, nonpartisan.

BORGBJERG, FREDERICK (1866–). Member of Danish S.D. party; contributor to *Social-Demokraten* (Copenhagen); since 1898, member of Riksdag; occupied various responsible government positions; 1917, visited Russia to persuade Russian socialists to attend International Socialist Congress in Stockholm.

BORISOV, M. Member of the Bund; contributed to Bund periodicals; July 1914, attended conference called in Brussels by I.S.B.

BOSH, EVGENIIA BOGDANOVNA (1879–1925). Member of R.S.D.L. party; Bolshevik; active in the Ukraine; 1912, exiled to Siberia; soon escaped to the United States; 1915, in Switzerland; attended conference of Bolshevik sections in Berne; 1916, moved to Sweden; member of Bukharin-Piatakov group and of editorial staff of *Kommunist;* later, active in civil war in the Ukraine; failing health caused her to commit suicide.

BOURDERON, ALBERT (1858–1930). Member of French Socialist party and of Executive of C.G.T.; Secretary of Coopers' Union; 1915, attended Zimmerwald Conference; one of organizers of Comité pour la Reprise des Relations Internationales; 1916, moved toward Centrist group; justified participation of socialists in bourgeois government; gradually broke completely with Zimmerwald movement.

BRANTING, KARL HJALMAR (1860–1925). Member of Swedish S.D.L. party and leader of its Right wing; 1886–1917, editor of *Social-Demokraten* (Stockholm); 1896, elected to Riksdag; 1915, organized Conference of Socialists of Neutral Countries in Copenhagen; 1917, presided over socialist discussions in Stockholm; 1919, Chairman of Berne Conference of Second International; several times Prime Minister of Sweden, which he represented at League of Nations.

BRAUN, ADOLF. Writer; member of Austrian S.D.L. party; 1910, attended International Socialist Congress, Copenhagen.

BRIAND, ARISTIDE (1862–1932). Member of French Socialist party; 1902, elected to Chamber of Deputies; after 1909, several times Prime Minister; 1925–1932, French representative at League of Nations.

BRILLIANT, *see* Sokolnikov, Grigorii Yakovlevich.

BRIZON, PIERRE (1878–1923). Member of French Socialist party; during World War adhered to minority; 1916, attended Kienthal Conference; joined Comité pour la Reprise des Relations Internationales as Right Zimmerwaldist; editor of *La Vague;* 1921, joined French Communist party but soon withdrew.

BRONSKI, MIECZYSLAW (1882–   ). 1902, joined Social Democracy of Poland and Lithuania; 1906, on editorial board of *Czerwony Sztandar* in Warsaw; 1907, after spending year in prison emigrated to Switzerland; member of Zürich organization of Swiss S.D. party; member of Zimmerwald Left; 1917, went to Russia; after Bolshevik Revolution, occupied responsible positions in Soviet government; later, professor of political economy and member of Communist Academy.

BRONSTEIN, NATALIIA GRIGORIEVNA (IRINA IZOLSKAIA). Wife of S. Yu. Semkovsky (Bronstein).

DE BROUCKÈRE, LOUIS (1870–1951). Belgian professor; member of Belgian S.L. party; early fought against ministerialism; during World War, social patriot; member of Executive of Second International; several times member of Belgian cabinet and Belgian delegate to League of Nations.

BRUNNER. Swiss worker in Geneva; co-operated with Russian Bolsheviks.

BRUNS. Member of Dutch S.D.L. party; July–August, 1916, attended Conference of Socialists of Neutral Countries at The Hague.

BUKHARIN, NIKOLAI IVANOVICH (NOTA BENE) (1888–1938). 1906, joined R.S.D.L. party; Bolshevik; 1911, forced to emigrate to Western Europe; party theoretician and journalist; wrote for Russian and Western European Left Socialist press; 1914, in Switzerland; 1915, went to Sweden; editor of *Kommunist* (Geneva); deported to Norway; 1916–1917, in New York where he published *Novyi Mir*; 1917, returned to Russia; occupied responsible party posts; spring, 1918, Left Communist; published *Spartak* and *Kommunist* (Moscow); 1918–1929, editor of *Pravda;* 1919–1929, member of Executive Committee of Comintern; 1929, expelled from Politburo; executed.

BURIANOV, ANDREI FADDEEVICH (1880–   ). Member of R.S.D.L. party; member of Menshevik S.D. group in Fourth State Duma; vacillated in political orientation; 1914, withdrew from Duma group and joined Plekhanov's group.

CACHIN, MARCEL (1869–1958). Member of French Socialist party; formerly manual laborer; graduate of University of Bordeaux; after 1910, member of Chamber of Deputies; during World War, majority socialist; under influence of Russian events rapidly changed orientation; since 1918, director of *L'Humanité;* after 1920, leader of French Communist party; in Chamber of Deputies until defeat in 1932; 1935, elected to Senate as Popular Front candidate.

CARLESON, CARL NATANAEL (1865–). Teacher; member of Swedish S.D.L. party; 1888, began to contribute to *Social-Demokraten* (Stockholm); 1892–1896, 1908–1910, editor of its foreign section; substituted for Branting as chief editor; gradually moved toward Left; 1917, one of the founders of Left S.D. party; 1918, one of the organizers of Swedish Communist party; 1917–1918, chief editor of *Politiken;* 1922, withdrew from Communist party; independent author and lecturer.

CATANESI, AMADEO (–1915). Secretary of Italian Socialist Youth League; contributor to *Avanguardia;* killed in World War.

CAVAIGNAC, LOUIS (1802–1857). French general; 1848, War Minister in Provisional Government of Second French Republic; held dictatorial powers; 1849, Chairman of Council of Ministers; candidate for president of Second Republic; defeated; withdrew from politics after Louis Bonaparte's coup d'état.

CECIL, EDGAR ALGERNON ROBERT (VISCOUNT CECIL of Chelwood) (1864–). British statesman; 1915–1916, Under-Secretary of Foreign Affairs; 1916–1918, Minister of Blockade.

CETON, J. Member of Dutch S.D. party; party Secretary.

CHERNOV, VIKTOR MIKHAILOVICH (GARDENIN) (1876–1952). Member of the Socialist–Revolutionist party; its foremost theoretician; member of its Central Committee and editor of *Revoliutsionnaia Rossiia;* during the World War, internationalist; attended the Zimmerwald Conference; belonged to the Zimmerwald Center; 1917, member of Kerensky government; after Bolshevik Revolution, in ranks of anti-Soviet forces; author of many works.

CHKHEIDZE, NIKOLAI SEMENOVICH (1864–1926). Georgian member of R.S.D.L. party; Menshevik; member of Third and Fourth State Dumas; Chairman of Social Democratic Duma group; favored participation of workers in War-Industries Committees; 1917, member of Provisional Committee of State Duma and first Chairman of Petrograd Soviet; 1918, Chairman of Georgian Constituent Assembly; 1921, emigrated; ended life by suicide.

CHKHENKELI, AKAKII IVANOVICH (1874–). Lawyer; Georgian member of R.S.D.L. party; Menshevik; member of Third and Fourth State Dumas; 1914, attended Brussels Conference called by I.S.B.; 1918–1921, Minister of Foreign Affairs in Georgian Democratic Republic.

CHRISTIAN, ERNST, SR. Member of Norwegian Socialist Youth League.

CHRISTIANSEN, CHR. (1895–). Danish writer on youth movement and education; 1915, attended International Socialist Youth Conference in Berne; editor of *Socialisten;* occupied various important posts in the field of labor education.

COHN, OSCAR (1869–). Lawyer; member of German S.D. party; 1912–1918, member of Reichstag; since 1917, Independent Social Democrat; 1918, member of National Assembly; after 1919, active in Jewish affairs; joined Poale Zion.

COMPÈRE-MOREL, ADÉODAT CONSTANT ADOLPHE (1872–). Member of French Socialist party; at first Guesdist; contributed to French Left Socialist press; editor of a number of socialist publications; during World War, moved to Right wing; defensist.

CONSTANTINE I (1868–1923). Eldest son of George I of Greece; March 1913—June 1917, December 1920—September 1922, King of Greece.

CONSTANTINESCU, ALEXANDER. Rumanian Left-wing Socialist; 1917, delegate to Third Zimmerwald Conference, Stockholm.

CORNELISSEN, CHRISTIAN. Dutch anarchist; during World War, defensist; contributed to *La Bataille Syndicaliste.*

CUNOW, HEINRICH (1862–1936). Professor in Berlin University; member of German S.D. party; writer; member of editorial boards of chief Social Democratic papers; 1917, editor of *Neue Zeit;* during World War on extreme Right wing.

CZERNIN, COUNT OTTOKAR (1872–1932). Austrian statesman; Bohemian by birth; 1912, member of Austrian Upper House; 1916–1918, Minister of Foreign Affairs; 1920–1923, Member of Nationalrat.

DABROWSKI, *see* Stein, BRONISLAW.

DALIN, *see* Levin, David Yulievich.

DAN, FEDOR ILICH (GURVICH) (1871–1947). Physician; formerly member of League of Struggle for the Liberation of the Working Class; later, member of R.S.D.L. party; several times arrested and exiled; permanent member of Menshevik Central Committee; after 1905 revolution, Right Menshevik; during World War, Centrist; 1917, member of Petrograd Soviet and of editorial staff of *Izvestiia;* later active on behalf of his party; 1919–1920, held position in Narkomzdrav; since 1922, émigré; member of editorial board of *Sotsialisticheskii Vestnik.*

DANNEBERG, ROBERT (1885–   ). Member of Austrian S.D.L. party; active in Socialist Youth movement; 1907–1915, Secretary of Socialist Youth International.

DANSKY, *see* Komarowski, K. A.

DÄTTWYLER, MAX. Member of Swiss S.D. party; pacifist.

DAVID, EDUARD (1863–1930). Member of German S.D. party; after 1903, Reichstag member; advocate of revisionism; during World War, majority socialist; 1919–1920, Minister without portfolio; first president of National Assembly; 1922–1927, representative of central government in Darmstadt.

DAVIDOVICH, D. Member of Jewish Socialist Territorialist Labor party of America; summer, 1917, took part in negotiations with Dutch-Scandinavian Committee in Stockholm.

DEBS, EUGENE VICTOR (1855–1926). American labor leader; 1897, turned socialist and helped to organize American Socialist party; several times imprisoned; repeatedly candidate of his party for President of the United States; 1907–1913, on editorial staff of *Appeal to Reason;* 1914–1917, editor of *National Rip-Saw* (St. Louis); nationally known speaker in interest of socialist movement; 1915, Chancellor of People's College (Fort Scott, Kansas); opposed entrance of the United States into World War; 1918, sentenced to ten years' imprisonment for violation of Espionage Act; 1921, pardoned; up to time of death continued activity on behalf of Socialist party.

DIAMAND, HERMANN (1860–1931). Polish-Galician Socialist; 1907–1918, deputy to Austrian Reichsrat from 'Galicia.

DIETRICH. Young German Social Democrat; 1915, attended International Socialist Youth Conference at Berne.

DNEPROV, MENSHEVIK, *see* Martynov, Aleksandr Samoilovich.

DOLECKI, JAKÓB (FENIGSTEIN) (1888–   ). 1904, joined Social Democracy of Poland and Lithuania; 1907–1911, active in Russian and Polish S.D. organizations in Western Europe; later active in Warsaw and Lodz; 1913–1914, Secretary of Regional Presidium of Social Democracy of Poland and Lithuania; July 1914, present at I.S.B. Conference in Brussels; 1917, member of Central Committee of Social Democracy of Poland and Lithuania; editor of *Tribuna;* 1918–1919, in Minsk; member of Central Committee of Communist party of Lithuania and White Russia; acting Chairman of Council of People's Commissars of Lithuania and White Russia; member of Presidium of Central Executive Committee of Lithuania and White Russia; after 1921, held responsible positions in U.S.S.R.

DOLGOLEVSKY, MOISHA, *see* Bukharin, N. I.

DOMSKI, L., *see* Stein, Henryk.

DREYFUS, ALFRED (1859–1935). Captain in French army; prominent figure and innocent victim in "Dreyfus affair"; accused by French General Staff of stealing military secrets.

DUBREUILH, LOUIS (1862–1924). Member of French Socialist party; General Secretary of French Section of Second International; during World War, majority socialist contributor to a number of socialist publications.

DUBROVINSKY, YOSIF FEDOROVICH (INNOKENTII) (1877–1913). Member of R.S.D.L. party and of its Central Committee; Bolshevik; 1905, arrested but soon released; active in 1905 revolution; 1906–1907, under arrest; helped to prepare Fifth Party Congress but was prevented from attending it; re-elected by that congress to Central Committee; contributor to *Proletarii;* advocate of party unity; returned to Russia to restore Russian section of Central Committee in Moscow but was arrested and exiled to Turukhansk region for four years; ended life by suicide.

DUGONI, ENRICO. Member of Italian Socialist party; active among agricultural workers; Member of Italian Chamber of Deputies; 1916, attended Kienthal Conference; 1920, member of Italian commission sent to Soviet Russia.

DUMAS, CHARLES (1883–   ). After 1902, member of French Socialist party; contributor to *Populaire du Centre* and to various other French and foreign socialist publications; during World War, acted as Guesde's secretary.

DUNCAN, JAMES (1857–1928). Several times Vice-President of American Federation of Labor; 1917, member of the Root Mission to Russia.

DUNCKER, KÄTHE. Member of German S.D. party; during World War, member of *Internationale* group; 1917, represented this group at Third Zimmerwald Conference; later Communist.

DZIERZYNSKI, FELIKS (1877–1926). Originally member of Main Presidium of Social Democracy of Poland and Lithuania; 1906, member of Central Committee of R.S.D.L. party; many times arrested; 1912, sentenced to nine years of penal labor; 1917–1926, member of Central Committee of R.S.D.L. party; during Bolshevik Revolution, member of Military Revolutionary Committee; later Chairman of O.G.P.U.

EBERT, FRIEDRICH (1870–1925). Member of German S.D. party; 1912, elected to Reichstag; 1913, Chairman of party Executive; during World War on Right wing of party; supported national defense; 1918, member of Council of People's Commissars; 1919–1925, President of German Republic.

EGOROV. Possibly a pseudonym of G. I. Safarov.

EGOROV, NIKOLAI MAXIMOVICH. "Mezhraionka" member; member of Social Democratic group in Third State Duma.

EHRLICH, HENRIK (1882–   ). Lawyer; after 1905 revolution, connected with the Bund; 1909, Chairman of Bund's Central Committee in Petersburg; prominent Menshevik; 1917, member of Petrograd Soviet; member of its delegation to England, France, and Italy; 1917–1918, active in Menshevik central organizations; 1918, went to Warsaw; contributed to Bundist press; since 1921, co-editor of Jewish *Volkszeitung* (Warsaw).

ELIZAROVA, ANNA ILINICHNA (JAMES) (1864–1935). Lenin's sister; active member of R.S.D.L. party; Bolshevik; took part in organization of *Iskra;* during

World War, in charge of party correspondence with Bureau of Central Committee Abroad; 1916, arrested and exiled to Astrakhan Gubernia; 1917, secretary of editorial board of *Pravda;* also edited *Tkach;* engaged in educational and child-welfare work.

ELM, ADOLF VON (1857–1916). Tobacco worker; member of German S.D. party, Right wing; leader of co-operative movement; 1878–1882, in the United States; 1894–1906, Reichstag member; contributed to *Sozialistische Monatshefte.*

ENGELS, FRIEDRICH (1820–1895). Friend and collaborator of Karl Marx.

ERMANSKY, OSIP ARKADIEVICH (1866–   ). 1899–1902, active in Social Democratic movement in South Russia; Chairman of League of Southern Organizations; 1903, joined Mensheviks; 1905, active in Moscow; advocate of party unity; contributed to various Menshevik publications; opposed World War; 1917, Menshevik-Internationalist; on editorial staff of *Rabochaia Gazeta;* 1918, member of Central Committee of United R.S.D.L. party (Mensheviks); 1920, member of Moscow Soviet; 1921, joined Russian Communist party; member of Communist Academy until 1930, when he was expelled; present status unknown.

ERWIG, JOHANNES. Member of Socialist Youth League of Norway; 1917, attended Third Zimmerwald Conference, Stockholm.

ESSEN, ALEKSANDR MAGNUSOVICH (STEPANOV) (1880–1930). Member of R.S.D.L. party; Bolshevik; 1905, member and representative abroad of Bureau of Majority Committees; member of Petersburg Committee; 1906, member of Moscow Party Committee; 1907–1917, took no part in party activities; after 1917, active in Georgia where he joined internationalists; 1920, joined Russian Communist party; 1923–1925, head of Tiflis Polytechnical Institute; later occupied various responsible posts in Soviet government; author of many books.

FÄHNDRICH, M. Member of Swiss S.D. party; during World War, Secretary of its Executive.

FAIRCHILD, EDWIN CHARLES (1874–   ). Lecturer in economics and philosophy; once member of British I.L. party; later member of British Socialist party; 1916–1919, editor of *The Call;* 1919, resigned from British Socialist party.

DE FALCO, GIUSEPPE. Writer; Italian Socialist; September 1914, attended Italo-Swiss Socialist Conference, Lugano.

FERRI, MARIO. Member of Swiss S.D. party; member of National Council from Tessin; 1914, attended Italo-Swiss Socialist Conference, Lugano.

FIGNER, VERA NIKOLAEVNA (1852–1942). Formerly member of "Land of Freedom" group and later of "People's Will" party; outstanding revolutionary terrorist; 1883, arrested; imprisoned for twenty years in Schlüsselburg fortress; 1904, exiled to Archangel Gubernia; 1906–1915, in Western Europe; worked with Socialist-Revolutionists; 1915, on arrival in Russia arrested and exiled to Nizhni Novgorod; 1916, permitted to reside in Petrograd; 1917, in charge of relief work among former political exiles; later, devoted herself exclusively to literary activity; 1935, reported arrested by Soviet authorities.

FIMMEN, EDO (1881–1943). 1915–1919, Secretary of Federation of Dutch Trade Unions; 1916, among Dutch delegation to Conference of Socialists of Neutral Countries, The Hague.

FISCHER, RICHARD (1855–1926). Member of German S.D. party; editor of a number of socialist publications; 1880–1890, in Switzerland and England; 1890–1893, party secretary; 1902 became manager of *Vorwärts;* 1919–1920, member of National Assembly; after 1920, member of Reichstag.

FLEISSNER, HERMANN (1865–   ). Writer; member of German S.D. party; member of Reichstag from Saxony; during World War, in Haase-Ledebour group and subsequently German I.S.D. party; 1920–1924, Minister in Saxony.

FLEROVSKY, IVAN PETROVICH. Rural teacher; member of R.S.D.L. party; Bolshevik; 1908–1909, arrested for conducting propaganda among workers and exiled to Archangel; 1913, as moderate Bolshevik joined "Mezhraionka" in St. Petersburg; 1917–1918, active in Petrograd and Kronstadt; author of recollections pertaining to the 1918 mutinies in the navy; later, active in institutions of people's economy; as an early dissentient with official Russian Communist party policy he disappeared.

FLIECHEK. Dutch Social Democrat; January, 1915, attended International Socialist Conference at Copenhagen.

FOKIN, IGNATII IVANOVICH (IGNAT) (1889–1919). Draftsman; member of R.S.D.L. party; Bolshevik; several times arrested for revolutionary propaganda; outstanding member of Petersburg Committee; 1915, member of Bureau of Central Committee; 1917, exiled to Siberia shortly before March revolution; took part in Bolshevik Revolution; Chairman of Briansk Soviet; died on way to Briansk after attending Eighth Congress of Russian Communist party.

FOMIN, VALENTIN (V. OLGIN). Member of R.S.D.L. party; 1909–1912, Plekhanovist; 1917, member of Central Committee of *Edinstvo* group; 1918, attended Ufa State Conference; 1918–1919, leader of Omsk Committee of *Edinstvo;* supported Kolchak; now émigré.

FORSTNER. Lieutenant in German army who figured in "Zabern incident," November 1913.

FRIMU, J. C. Manual laborer; member of Rumanian S.D. party; 1917, delegate to Third Zimmerwald Conference, Stockholm; imprisoned on return to Rumania; later, fatally wounded during a workers' demonstration.

FRÖLICH, PAUL (1884–1953). Member of German S.D. party; 1910–1914, editor of *Hamburger Echo;* during World War with Left Radical opposition; 1914–1916, editor of *Bremer Bürgerzeitung;* 1916, attended Kienthal Conference; 1916–1918, one of publishers of *Arbeiterpolitik;* 1918, founder of *Rote Fahne* (Hamburg); 1919–1924, member of German Communist party; 1921–1924, 1928–1930, member of Reichstag; 1928, expelled from Communist party as a dissentient; 1933, confined in a concentration camp; 1938, expelled from Germany.

FÜRSTENBERG, PRINCE MAXIMILIAN EGON (1863–   ). Member of Prussian and Austrian upper houses; Vice-President of the Austrian Upper House; personally close to Kaiser Wilhelm.

GALERKA, *see* Olminsky, Mikhail Stepanovich.

GALPERIN, LEV EFIMOVICH (KONIAGA, VORON) (1872–   ). Member of R.S.D.L. party from its origin; *Iskra* agent in Russia; active in Caucasus; Bolshevik; was co-opted to Central Committee; favored party unity; 1905, arrested; after 1906, took no active part in party work; engaged in literary work; held position with People's Commissariat of Commerce.

GARAMI, ERNŐ (1876–   ). Journalist; member of Hungarian S.D. party; moderate Social Democrat; 1915, representative at Vienna Conference of Socialists of Central Powers; after revolution, Minister of Commerce in Károlyi cabinet; 1919, left Hungary but returned after downfall of Soviet government; now émigré.

GARDENIN, *see* Chernov, Viktor Mikhailovich.

GARIBALDI, GIUSEPPE (1807–1882). Italian liberator and statesman.

GINZBURG, BORIS ABRAMOVICH (D. KOLTSOV) (1863–1920). Formerly member of League of Russian Social Democrats Abroad; later, member of "Emancipation of Labor" group and subsequently of R.S.D.L. party; 1903, sided with Mensheviks; contributed to most Menshevik publications; moved to extreme Right wing; 1914–1917, defensist; 1918–1919, worked in Central Union of Consumers' Associations.

GIRSH, P. L. (LIBMAN; LEMANSKY) (1882–   ). Member of the Bund; 1902, left Russia because of police persecution; after 1911, member of Bund's Committee Abroad; on Bund's Right wing; 1913–1914, in Russia; edited *Di Zait;* 1914, left Russia; during World War, Centrist; 1915, delegated to Zimmerwald Conference without voting powers.

GLASIER, JOHN BRUCE (1859–1920). Prominent member of British I.L. party; 1905–1909, editor of *Labour Leader;* 1913–1917, editor of *Socialist Review.*

GOLDENBERG, YOSIF PETROVICH (MESHKOVSKY) (1873–1922). Member of the R.S.D.L. party; Bolshevik; 1907–1909, member of Central Committee; 1910–1914, in exile; during World War, Menshevik and defensist; 1917, among delegation which went abroad to prepare for calling of International Socialist Conference in Stockholm; 1918–1919, moved toward Left; 1920, admitted to Russian Communist party; 1921, returned to Russia.

GOLDFARB, MAX. Member of American Socialist party; 1917, in spite of refusal of passport by the United States government, reached Stockholm, where he claimed to represent his party at international socialist meetings.

GOLDMAN, MIKHAIL ISAAKOVICH (LIEBER) (1880–1937). Member of Bund and of its Central Committee; belonged to its Right wing and was on extreme Right of R.S.D.L. party; during World War, defensist; 1917, member of first All-Russian Central Executive Committee; anti-Bolshevik; 1934, deported by Soviet government to Volga region.

GOMPERS, SAMUEL (1850–1924). 1881–1924, President of American Federation of Labor.

GORBUNOV. Believed to be a pseudonym adopted for use abroad by a Russian workman from St. Petersburg; member of R.S.D.L. party; Menshevik; 1910 and later, in Zürich; member of Zürich group of aid to the R.S.D.L. party; 1912, represented Petersburg Initiative group of R.S.D.L. party at Basel Congress of Second International; his real name cannot be established.

GORDON. Printer; member of the Bund; during World War, in Scandinavian countries; deported with Bukharin by Swedish government for revolutionary propaganda.

GORKY, MAXIM (ALEKSEI MAXIMOVICH PESHKOV) (1868–1936). Russian author and playwright; Social Democrat; sympathized with the Bolsheviks, whom he helped financially and otherwise; 1908–1910, sided with the *Vpered* group and organized the party school at Capri; during the World War, internationalist; proponent of party unity; publisher of *Novaia Zhizn;* 1917, opposed Bolshevik dictatorship; late 1918, abandoned fight against the Bolsheviks and enthusiastically co-operated with them in the field of enlightenment, although politically he was unreconciled to Bolshevik tactics; 1921, left Russia on account of ill health; 1928, in Russia; made member of the Communist Academy and elected to the Central Executive Committee; 1929–1932, again in Italy, returning to Russia to become one of the most esteemed and celebrated personalities in the Soviet Union.

GORTER, HERMANN (1864–1927). Poet; 1897, joined Dutch S.D.L. party; 1907, founded *De Tribune;* 1909, expelled from party with other Tribunists and joined new S.D. party of Holland; during World War, anti-militarist; 1917–1918, led

Left wing of S.D. party; 1918–1921, Communist; 1921, withdrew from Communist party of Holland and formed Dutch Communist Labor party.

GOTZ, ABRAM RAFAILOVICH (1882–1937). Member of Russian Socialist-Revolutionist party and of its Central Committee; Vice-Chairman of first All-Russian Central Executive Committee; later member of Committee to Save the Country and the Revolution; 1920–1925, imprisoned; pardoned; 1925–1936, active in various agricultural institutions in Siberia; several times arrested; 1936, placed under arrest and brought to Moscow, apparently under accusation of maintaining contact with Right Socialist-Revolutionists, which was one point raised by prosecution during Bukharin-Rykov trial in Moscow.

GRABER, ERNEST PAUL (1875–   ). Teacher; member of Swiss S.D. party; 1915–1919, editor of *La Sentinelle* with which he was connected until 1925; occupied responsible party posts; 1916, attended Kienthal Conference; after 1912, member of National Council.

GRAVE, JEAN. French anarchist; co-editor of *Le Révolté;* author of a number of works on anarchism.

GREGORY, *see* Zinoviev, Grigorii Evseevich.

GREULICH, HERMANN (1842–1925). Member of Swiss S.D. party, Right wing; formerly member of Grütli Verein; 1869–1880, editor of *Züricher Tagwacht;* co-editor of *Volksrecht* (Zürich); occupied prominent party posts; during World War, fought Zimmerwald movement.

GRIGORII, *see* Zinoviev, Grigorii Evseevich.

GRIMM, ROBERT (1881–1958). Member of Swiss S.D. party; 1909–1918, 1928–1932, editor of *Berner Tagwacht;* contributed to *Neues Leben;* 1911, elected to National Council; during World War, moderate socialist-internationalist; 1915–1917, Chairman of International Socialist Committee; 1917, went to Russia; deported and forced to resign from the I.S.C.; rehabilitated by Swiss party; 1918, member of Olten Committee; 1920, one of organizers of Two-and-a-Half International; later returned to Second International and was repeatedly member of its Executive.

GRUMBACH, SOLOMON (HOMO) (1884–   ). Formerly member of German S.D. party; revisionist; 1908, joined French Socialist party; contributed to *L'Humanité;* on Right wing of party; 1914–1918, in Switzerland; pro-Entente; severe opponent of Zimmerwald movement; 1928, elected to Chamber of Deputies by Upper Alsace.

GUESDE, JULES BASILE (1845–1922). Member of French Socialist party; once Left-wing leader; fought reformism and ministerialism; 1893–1921, member of Chamber of Deputies; during World War, advocated *l'Union sacrée;* August 1914—October 1915, Minister without portfolio.

GUILBEAUX, HENRI (1885–1938). Formerly anarcho-syndicalist; member of French Socialist party; during World War, pacifist; publisher of *Demain* in Switzerland; affiliated with Left Zimmerwaldists and took part in Zimmerwald movement; 1917, favored Bolshevik Revolution in Russia; attended First, Second, and Fifth Congresses of Comintern; 1919, sentenced to death in absentia by French court for high treason; 1924, amnestied; meanwhile worked in Berlin as correspondent for *L'Humanité;* later turned against Soviet Russia; contributed to nationalist and anti-Semitic publications.

GUREVICH, BORIS NAUMOVICH (I. BER). Member of R.S.D.L. party; Menshevik; during World War, internationalist; 1914–1915, on editorial staffs of *Golos* and *Nashe Slovo;* 1915–1916, on editorial boad of *Nash Golos* (Samara); 1917, with Menshevik Central organization; later, leader of Kharkov Mensheviks;

on extreme Left of Menshevik-Internationalists; since 1921, under arrest and in exile.

GUREVICH, EMMANUIL LVOVICH (E. SMIRNOV) (1866–   ). Formerly of "People's Will" party; 1901, joined R.S.D.L. party; contributed to both legal and illegal Russian Social Democratic press; founder of S.D. *Borba* group; after 1903, sided with Mensheviks; later, on extreme Right wing.of Menshevism; during World War, defensist; 1917, Soviet delegate to Stockholm and member of Russian-Dutch-Scandinavian Committee; editor of *Vlast Naroda;* now nonpartisan; member of Marx-Engels-Lenin Institute (Moscow).

GUTOVSKY, VIKENTII ANITSETOVICH (E. MAEVSKY; SIMONOV) (1865–1918). Member of R.S.D.L. party; Menshevik; 1899, as adherent of *Rabochee Znamia* exiled to Siberia; organizer of Siberian Social Democratic League; active in 1905 revolution; later, extreme Right Menshevik; during World War, defensist; 1918, editor of *Vlast Naroda* (Cheliabinsk); opposed Kolchak; shot by army officers.

GVOZDEV, KUZMA ANTONOVICH (1883–   ). Railroad worker; 1903–1907, with Socialist-Revolutionists; 1905, headed a railroad strike committee; several times arrested and exiled; after 1914, member of R.S.D.L. party; Menshevik; defensist; headed labor group in Central War Industries Committee; January 1917, arrested with others of this group; after March revolution, member of Executive Committee of Petrograd Soviet; Minister of Labor in Coalition Government; after Bolshevik revolution, opposed Bolsheviks; later, withdrew from active politics and occupied posts in central trade union offices and Supreme Council of People's Economy.

HAASE, HUGO (1863–1919). Member of German S.D. party and of I.S.B.; 1897–1918, member of Reichstag; 1916, headed "Arbeitsgemeinschaft" and later one of leaders of I.S.D. party; member of its Executive; 1918, member of Council of People's Commissars; assassinated.

HANECKI, JAKÓB (FIRSTENBERG) (1879–   ). Formerly member of Main Presidium of Social Democracy of Poland and Lithuania; 1912–1916, member of Regional Presidium of that party; 1907, elected to Central Committee of R.S.D.L. party; 1913, attended Poronino Conference; 1912, present at Basel Congress of Second International; 1914, attended Brussels Unification Conference called by I.S.B.; during World War, member of Zimmerwald Left; 1917, member of Bureau of Central Committee of R.S.D.L. party in Stockholm; later held responsible posts with Soviet government.

HANSEN, ARVID (1894–   ). Member of Swedish S.D.L. party; during World War, member of Swedish Left S.D.L. party; contributed to Russian Bolshevik and Zimmerwald Left publications; later member of Swedish Communist party and chief editor of its pub'ications.

HARDIE, JAMES KEIR (1856–19.'5). Founder and leader of Scottish Labour party, later of British I.L. party; Member of Parliament; prominent in Second International; at outbreak of World War, pacifist.

HEDEN, ERIK. Member of Swedish S.D.L. party; during World War, on Left wing; 1917, member of Swedish Left S.D.L. party; anti-militarist; charged with high treason and imprisoned for many months; contributor to *Politiken, Stormklockan,* and other Left socialist publications.

HEINE, WOLFGANG (1861–   ). Lawyer; member of German S.D. party; revisionist; contributor to *Sozialistische Monatshefte;* during World War, majority socialist; after 1918, in Prussian government.

HELPHAND, ALEXANDER L. (PARVUS) (1867–1924). Once engaged in revolutionary activity in Russia; forced to flee to Germany; after 1891, member of German S.D. party; fought reformism; 1905, took part in revolutionary movement in Russia; imprisoned and exiled to Siberia; 1906, escaped to Germany; contributed to various Social Democratic publications; 1910–1914, in Balkans as German exile; enriched himself by speculating on war deliveries; on return to Germany joined ranks of extreme Right Social Democrats; gave financial support to *Internationale Korrespondenz;* published *Die Glocke;* founder of Institute for the Study of the Consequences of the War.

HENDERSON, ARTHUR (1863–1935). British trade unionist; leader of British Labour party and its Secretary for nearly twenty-three years; repeatedly Member of Parliament; during World War, member of British ministry; 1917, forced to resign because of stand on Stockholm Socialist Peace Conference; in later years, held ministerial posts in Labor government; outstanding figure at many international peace and disarmament conferences.

HERVÉ, GUSTAVE (1871–1944). Lawyer; journalist; member of French Socialist party; on extreme Left; 1906, founded *La Guerre sociale;* fought imperialism and militarism; after 1914, turned nationalist and in his paper, renamed *La Victoire,* advocated complete destruction of enemy coalition; withdrew from French Socialist party.

HERZOG, JAKOB. Member of Swiss S.D. party; member of Swiss socialist youth organization, Left wing; founder of *Die Forderung;* October 1918, expelled from party for breach of discipline and formed first group of Swiss Communists.

HILLQUIT, MORRIS (1869–1933). 1888, became socialist; successful lawyer and leader of American Socialist party for many years; member of I.S.B.; anti-Communist and critic of Bolsheviks.

HINDENBURG, PAUL VON (1847–1934). Field Marshal of German armies; 1925–1934, President of German Republic.

HODGE, JOHN (1855–1937). Prominent in British trade union movement; Member of Parliament; 1915, Chairman of Labour party group in House of Commons; 1916–1919, member of British ministry.

HOFER, ADOLF (died soon after 1918). Landowner; member of the German S.D. party; 1913–1918, member of Prussian Landtag; after 1917, member of the I.S.D. party; delegate to Third Zimmerwald Conference, Stockholm.

HOFFMANN, ADOLF (1858–1930). Member of German S.D. party; member of Prussian Landtag; later, member of Reichstag; during World War, in Haase-Ledebour group; 1915–1916, attended both Zimmerwald and Kienthal conferences; after 1917, member of I.S.D. party; 1918–1919, Prussian Minister of Education; 1920–1921, member of Communist party; 1921–1922, again in the ranks of the I.S.D. party; after 1922, member of the S.D. party.

HOFFMANN, HERMANN ARTHUR (1857–). Lawyer; 1896–1911, member of Swiss State Council; 1911, elected to Federal Council; 1914–1917, in charge of its political division; resigned over "Grimm affair."

HÖGLUND, CARL ZETH KONSTANTIN (1884–1956). Member of Swedish S.D.L. party; 1904–1905, on staff of *Ny Tid;* 1908–1911, member of party Executive; 1908–1918, editor of *Stormklockan;* 1919–1924, editor of *Folkets Dagblad;* 1924–1925, editor of *Nya Politiken;* 1915–1917, member of Lower House of Riksdag; during World War leader of Left wing of S.D.L. party; anti-militarist; imprisoned on charge of high treason; 1917, leader of Left S.D.L. party; 1918, Communist; 1924, attempted to create own party but failed; returned to ranks of S.D.L. party and regained some of former party positions.

HOMO, *see* Grumbach, Solomon.

How, James Eads (1869–1930). Born in St. Louis, Missouri; attended Harvard University two years; worked in the yards of the Wabash Railway; studied three years at Meadville Theological Seminary and one year at Manchester College, Oxford; later studied medicine but did not practice; organized, directed, and financed the Brotherhood of the Daily Life; attended the Third Zimmerwald Conference as representative of this organization.

Huber, Johannes (1879–   ). Lawyer; member of Swiss S.D. party; moderate socialist; held responsible positions; 1918–1919, supported Olten Committee in charge of general strike.

Huysmans, Camille (1871–   ). Professor at Brussels University; member of Belgian S.L. party; 1905–1921, Secretary of I.S.B.; since 1910, Member of Chamber of Deputies; 1925–1927, Minister of Arts and Sciences; 1933, Mayor of Antwerp; 1936–, President of the Chamber of Deputies.

Hyndman, Henry Mayers (1842–1921). 1881, founder of London Democratic Federation; after 1911, leader of British Socialist party; 1900–1910, member of I.S.B.; at outbreak of World War, turned nationalist; editor of *Justice;* 1916, formed National Socialist party.

Iglesias, Pablo. Spanish socialist; active in international labor movement.

Ilich or Ilyich, *see* Lenin, Vladimir Ilich.

Ilin. Unidentified; 1915, attended Berne Conference of Bolshevik groups and was elected to Revisory Commission of Committee of Organizations Abroad.

Ilin, V., *see* Lenin, Vladimir Ilich

Inessa, *see* Armand, Inessa.

Inkpin, Albert (1884–   ). 1913–1920, General Secretary of British Socialist party; editor of *The Call*; 1920–1922, General Secretary of Communist party of Great Britain.

Izolskaia, Irina, *see* Bronstein, Nataliia Grigorievna.

Jagiello, Evgenii Ossipovich (1874–   ). Member of the Polish Socialist party (Levitsa); member of Fourth State Duma; his election was cause of controversy between Bolshevik and Menshevik groups in Duma.

James, *see* Elizarova, Anna Ilinichna.

Jaurès, Jean Auguste (1859–1914). Professor of philosophy at Toulouse; French Socialist party leader; after 1885, member of Chamber of Deputies; 1904–1914, founder and editor of *L'Humanité;* on Right wing of French Socialist party and Second International; anti-militarist and advocate of ministerialism; favored Franco-German alliance; wrote numerous books on French revolution and socialism; assassinated on eve of World War.

Jouhaux, Leon (1878–1953). After 1909, Secretary of C.G.T.; leader of its majority during World War; later served as Vice-President of Amsterdam International; held posts with League of Nations.

Jowett, Frederick William (1864–1944). Formerly textile worker; journalist; influential member of British I. L. party; Member of Parliament.

Junius, *see* Luxemburg, Rosa.

Kaclerović, Triša (1879–   ). Lawyer; one of the founders of Serbian S.D. party; 1908–1921, member of Skupshchina; anti-militarist; 1916, attended Kienthal Conference; 1921, Chairman of Club of Communist Deputies; upon suppression of Serbian Communist party, returned for a time to trade union activities, then formed Independent Labor party; edited and contributed to various Left socialist publications.

KAMENEV, LEV BORISOVICH (ROSENFELD) (1883–1936). 1901, joined R.S.D.L. party; Bolshevik; 1908, arrested and emigrated to Western Europe; contributed to *Proletarii* and *Sotsial-Demokrat;* 1914, deported to Russia for illegal activity; November 1914, arrested together' with Bolshevik Duma deputies; exiled to Siberia; 1917, on editorial board of *Pravda*; member of Central Committee; during November revolution, opposed Lenin's tactics; 1918–1926, Chairman of Moscow Soviet; took part in major activities of Soviet government; later occupied responsible posts in government; 1927, expelled from party; 1928, reinstated; 1932, once more expelled; 1936, executed.

KAMINSKAIA, ANNA (DOMSKAIA; NÉE SOPHIE UNSCHLICHT). 1915, represented the Regional Presidium of Social Democracy of Poland and Lithuania at the International Socialist Women's Conference at Berne; later prominent in Polish Communist movement; as member of the Trotsky opposition was imprisoned by Soviet government.

KAMSKY, *see* Obukhov, V. M.

KARAKHAN, LEV MIKHAILOVICH (1889–1937). 1904, joined R.S.D.L. party; later "Mezhraionka" member; 1917, joined Bolsheviks; well-known Soviet diplomat; executed.

KARPELES, BENNO. Member of Austrian S.D.L. party; engaged in co-operative trade union movement; 1910, member of subcommission on question of co-operatives at International Socialist Congress, Copenhagen.

KARPINSKY, V. A. (1880–   ). Member of R.S.D.L. party; Bolshevik; 1904, emigrated to Western Europe where he worked in party organizations; manager of party library and party archives in Geneva; 1914–1917, helped to publish *Sotsial-Demokrat* and to distribute the Bolshevik press; December 1917, after winding up all party affairs returned to Russia and held various responsible party positions.

KARPOV, LEV YAKOVLEVICH (VLADIMIR) (1879–1921). Chemical engineer; active in formation of Northern League of Workers; 1905, member of Central Committee of R.S.D.L. party; arrested but soon released; took part in organizing *Vpered*; 1906, in charge of organizing a laboratory of explosives; Secretary of Moscow Committee; carried on propaganda among students; 1907, deported to Kiev; returned to Moscow illegally; soon withdrew from political activity; 1917, active in organizing Supreme Council of Public Economy; founder of its Chemical Department.

KASPAROV, VLADIMIR (SLAVA) (1884–1917). Member of R.S.D.L. party; Bolshevik; 1905–1906, active in Caucasus; during World War, in Switzerland; took part in activity of Bolshevik groups abroad.

KATAYAMA, SEN (1859–1933). 1901, one of the founders of the S.D. party of Japan; 1904, represented his party at the Amsterdam International Socialist Congress; 1912, imprisoned for nine months; 1914, emigrated to the United States; 1919, organized a Japanese Communist group in New York; 1921, organized an American Bureau of the Communist and the Red Trade Union Internationals in Mexico; elected to the Executive Committee of the Comintern; 1929, elected to the Presidium of the Executive Committee of the Comintern.

KATIN-YARTSEV, V. N. (1875–1928). Physician; member of R.S.D.L. party; once member of League of Struggle for the Liberation of the Working Class; 1897, arrested and sentenced to solitary confinement in Petropavlovsk fortress; 1899, exiled for five years to Yakutsk region; 1906–1908, nonfactional S.D.; during World War, defensist; 1917, member of *Edinstvo* group; member of Petrograd Soviet; contributor to *Den*; remained until death in Soviet Russia.

KAUTSKY, KARL (1854–1938). Marxist theoretician in German S.D. party; influential member of Second International; founder and editor of *Neue Zeit*; helped to draft Erfurt program; during World War peace proponent; joined Right wing of German I.S.D. party; one of organizers of Two-and-a-Half International; 1922, favored fusion with Second International; rejoined German S.D. party; prolific writer on socialism and Marxist interpretation.

KERENSKY, ALEKSANDR FEDOROVICH (1881–   ). Lawyer; formerly Socialist-Revolutionist; Trudovik leader in Fourth State Duma; February–May, 1917, Minister of Justice; May–September, 1917, Minister of War and Navy; July–November, 1917, Prime Minister of Russian Provisional Coalition government; editor of *Novaia Rossiia*, Paris.

KERR, CHARLES. American publisher of Marx and other socialist and radical writers.

KESKULA. Estonian; 1915–1916, living in Stockholm.

KHARITONOV, M. M. (1887–   ). Member of R.S.D.L. party; Bolshevik; 1912, emigrated to Western Europe; member of Zürich Bolshevik group and of Swiss S.D. party; after Bolshevik revolution, held high posts in Soviet military service and in Bolshevik party; 1924–1925, member of Central Committee of Russian Communist party; 1925, joined the Trotsky opposition; expelled from party but soon reinstated; later occupied responsible Soviet government posts.

KHARLAKOV. Bulgarian S.D.; autumn, 1917, in Stockholm, where he took part in meetings of International Socialist Committee.

KHAUSTOV, VALENTIN IVANOVICH (1884–   ). Member of R.S.D.L. party; Menshevik; member of Fourth State Duma; 1914, read S.D. declaration in Duma stating group's refusal to vote war credits; after 1917, withdrew from party activity.

KIEVSKY, P., *see* Piatakov, Georgii Leonidovich.

KIRKOV, G. Bulgarian S.D.; "Narrow" Socialist; member of Zimmerwald movement; 1917, in Stockholm.

KLÖTI, EMIL (1877–   ). Lawyer; member of Swiss S.D. party; during World War on Right wing; member of party Executive.

KOBETSKY, MIKHAIL (1881–   ). 1903, joined R.S.D.L. party; Bolshevik; 1908, forced to emigrate to Denmark; after 1917, held responsible posts in Bolshevik party and Comintern.

KOLAROV, VASIL (1877–   ). Member of Bulgarian S.D.L. party; "Narrow" Socialist; after 1905, member of its Executive; 1913–1923, member of Bulgarian parliament; 1907, 1910, attended both Stuttgart and Copenhagen congresses of Second International; 1915, represented "Narrow" Socialists at Zimmerwald Conference; since 1919, Political Secretary of Bulgarian Communist party; official of Comintern.

KOLLONTAI, ALEKSANDRA MIKHAILOVNA (1872–   ). Member of R.S.D.L. party; formerly Menshevik; well known in European women's socialist movement; during World War in Scandinavia; internationalist; contributed to *Golos* and *Nashe Slovo* (Paris); moved toward Left and co-operated with Russian Bolsheviks; 1917, returned to Russia and officially joined Bolsheviks; held high Soviet and party positions.

KOLTSOV, *see* Ginzburg, Boris Abramovich.

KOMAROWSKI, K. A. (DANSKY) (1883–   ). Member of Polish Socialist party (Levitsa); 1911, joined R.S.D.L. party; Bolshevik; active in workers' insurance movement; 1913–1914, accused by extreme Right wing of R.S.D.L. party of simultaneously contributing to Marxist and bourgeois press.

KON, FELIKS (1864–   ). Formerly member of Polish "Proletarjat"; later, member of Polish Socialist party; 1906, joined "Levitsa"; member of its Central Committee; 1907–1917, in Western Europe; joined Zimmerwald movement; 1917, returned to Russia; 1918, joined Polish Communist party; 1919, active in the Ukraine; 1920, member of Military Revolutionary Committee during Soviet-Polish war; later, active in Comintern; author of numerous books and pamphlets.

KORITSCHONER, FRANZ (1891–   ). Member of Austrian S.D.L. party, Left wing; during World War, internationalist; 1916, attended Kienthal Conference; after 1918, Austrian Communist; contributor to and co-editor of *Die Rote Fahne* (Vienna).

KORNBLUM. Member of R.S.D.L. party; Bolshevik; during World War, in Switzerland; 1915, attended Berne Conference of Bolshevik Organizations Abroad.

KOSOVSKY, V. (M. YA. LEWINSON) (1867–   ). One of the founders of the Bund; member of its Central Committee; 1900, emigrated to Western Europe; in R.S.D.L. party among Right Mensheviks; contributed to *Nasha Zaria, Luch* and Jewish socialist press; during World War, justified the viewpoint of German majority socialists; advocated restoration of Second International; at present member of Bund organization in Warsaw.

KRASIN, LEONID BORISOVICH (ZIMIN) (1870–1926). Engineer; member of R.S.D.L. party; Bolshevik; member of Central Committee; advocate of party unity; 1908, emigrated to Western Europe; joined *Vpered* group; 1917, returned to Russia; held many responsible posts in Soviet government.

KROGH, HELGE (1889–   ). Writer, playwright, and critic; member of the Norwegian S.D. party.

KROKHMAL, VIKTOR NIKOLAEVICH (FOMIN) (1873–1930). Lawyer; member of R.S.D.L. party; Menshevik; once member of *Iskra;* until 1907, member of Central Committee; during years of reaction abstained from party activity but as lawyer served party continuously; later resumed activity in *Rabochaia Gazeta* and various commissions attached to Social Democratic Duma group; 1917, member of Central Committee, from which he resigned in November after opposing any concessions to Bolshevism; arrested several times as Right Menshevik; escaped further persecution because of personal friendship with Dzierzynski, after whose death he was again placed under arrest.

KROPOTKIN, PETR, PRINCE (1842–1921). Russian nobleman; scientist; well-known anarchist.

KROTOVSKY, YU., *see* Yurenev, Konstantin Konstantinovich.

KRUPSKAIA, NADEZHDA KONSTANTINOVNA (SABLINA) (1869–1939). Took part in formation of Petersburg League of Struggle for.the Liberation of the Working Class; 1896, arrested and exiled to Minusinsk; there married Lenin; 1901, emigrated; Secretary of *Iskra* and later of Bureau of Central Committee of R.S.D.L. party abroad; 1905–1908 in Russia; 1908–1917, again abroad; 1917, returned to Russia with Lenin, and engaged in her special field, labor education, holding responsible government positions; member of Supreme Council.

KRYLENKO, NIKOLAI VASILEVICH (ABRAM) (1885–   ). Member of R.S.D.L. party; Bolshevik; party agitator; several times arrested and exiled; 1911, contributed to *Zvezda* and *Pravda*; 1914–1915, in Switzerland; Bukharin's partisan; attended Berne Conference of Bolshevik Organizations Abroad; soon returned to Russia where he was arrested and drafted; 1917, active in army committees; delegate to first All-Russian Congress of Soviets; later, member of Military Revolutionary Committee; Supreme Commander of Red army; headed Commissariat of Justice and held other responsible posts in Soviet government.

KUDASHEV, NIKOLAI ALEKSANDROVICH, PRINCE (1859–1925). 1911–1915, Russian ambassador to Belgium; last Russian imperial ambassador to China.

KUNFI, ZSIGMOND (1879–   ). Journalist; member of Hungarian S.D. party, Left wing; 1918, Minister of Education; 1919, People's Commissar of Education and Culture in Hungarian Soviet government; later, on editorial staff of *Arbeiter-Zeitung* (Vienna).

KURSKY, S. (FRANZ). Member of the Bund; after 1900, in Western Europe; member of Bund's Committee Abroad; represented Bund at a number of international conferences; custodian of Bund archives.

KUZMA, *see* Liakhotsky, Kuzma.

KUZNETSOV, NIKOLAI VASILEVICH (SAPOZHKOV). Member of R.S.D.L. party; Bolshevik; 1910–1914, member of Paris Bolshevik section; at outbreak of World War, enlisted in French army.

KVIATKOVSKY, A. A. (ANDREI) (1878–   ). Member of R.S.D.L. party; Bolshevik; several times arrested for illegal party activity; 1907, withdrew from political activity and took up work in a commercial enterprise; 1917, active in All-Russian Union of Towns; later Chairman of Presidium of "Arcos"; not a Communist.

LAFONT, ERNEST (1879–   ). Lawyer; formerly member of French Socialist party; majority socialist; 1917, as member of Chamber of Deputies went to Russia; returned to France converted to support proposed international socialist conference at Stockholm; now leader of neo-Socialist group.

LAFONTAINE, HENRI (1854–   ). Member of Belgian S.L. party; professor at University of Brussels; after 1892, president of International Peace Bureau; after 1895, member of Belgian Senate; headed International Bibliographical Institute (Brussels) and International Press Bureau.

LANDSBERG, OTTO (1869–   ). Member of German S.D. party; majority socialist; member of Reichstag; 1918–1919, member of Council of People's Commissars; 1919–1920, Minister of Justice and member of National Assembly; 1920–1922, ambassador to Belgium; 1924–1933, again in Reichstag.

LANG, OTTO. Member of Swiss S.D. party, Right wing; 1917, on commission, appointed by I.S.C. to investigate Grimm affair.

LAPINSKI, *see* Lewinson, Pawel.

LARIN, YU., *see* Lurie, Mikhail Aleksandrovich.

LAW, ANDREW BONAR (1858–1923). British statesman; 1911–1921, leader of Unionist party; 1916–1919, member of War Cabinet; 1922–1923, Prime Minister.

LAZZARI, COSTANTINO (1857–1928). One of the oldest members of Italian Socialist party; leader of its Left wing; fought Turati's revisionism; 1912, elected party Secretary; noncommittal on Italian participation in World War; 1915, attended Zimmerwald Conference; belonged to Center; favored Bolshevik revolution in Russia; opposed certain conditions imposed by Comintern and was expelled together with Italian Socialist party; 1919, elected to Chamber of Deputies; for protesting against restoration of capital punishment was expelled from Chamber; retired; after political persecution, died in Rome.

LEDEBOUR, GEORG (1850–1947). Member of German S.D. party; 1900–1918, 1920–1924, member of Reichstag; during World War opposed majority socialist policy; 1915, attended Zimmerwald Conference; belonged to Zimmerwald Right; 1917, joined I.S.D. party; 1919, member of Revolutionary Committee (Berlin) during "Spartakus" uprising; opponent of proletarian dictatorship; refused to return to ranks of Second International; organized small group of his own, the so-called "Socialist League"; now in Switzerland.

LEE, ALGERNON (1873–). Journalist; member of Executive of American Socialist party; editor of a number of socialist papers; Educational Director of Rand School of Social Sciences; attended a number of international socialist conferences and congresses as representative of his party.

LEGIEN, KARL (1861–1920). After 1890, head of German Federation of Trade Unions; member of German S.D. party; reformist; member of Reichstag; 1914–1918, extreme Right Socialist; 1919–1920, member of National Assembly.

LEMANSKY, P., *see* Girsh, P. L.

LENGNIK, FRIDRIKH VILGELMINOVICH (VASILEV; KURZ) (1873–). Once member of League of Struggle for the Liberation of the Working Class; member of R.S.D.L. party; Bolshevik; member of Central Committee; during preparations for Third Party Congress (1905), prominent figure in R.S.D.L. party; several times arrested and forced to go abroad; after 1917, active in Commissariat of Education and held responsible positions with Soviet government.

LENIN, N., *see* Lenin, Vladimir Ilich.

LENIN, VLADIMIR ILICH (ULIANOV, NIKOLAI LENIN, KARPOV, V. ILIN, K. TULIN) (1870–1924). Leader and organizer of Russian Bolshevik party; its foremost theoretician.

LENSCH, PAUL (1873–1926). Member of German S.D. party, Left wing; 1905–1913, editor of *Leipziger Volkszeitung*; after outbreak of World War, moved to extreme Right of party; edited *Deutsche Allgemeine Zeitung*; 1922, expelled from party; author of several books on German Social Democracy.

LENSKI, *see* Leszczyński, Juljan.

LESZCZYŃSKI, JULJAN (LENSKI). Originally member of Rozlomovist section of Social Democracy of Poland and Lithuania; 1913, attended Poronino Conference of R.S.D.L. party; 1918, joined Communist party of Poland; 1924–1925, arrested in Warsaw, but with aid of plenipotentiary representative of Soviet Russia escaped to Moscow via Danzig; later, guided from Moscow activities of Polish Communist party; member of its Central Committee; late 1937, arrested in Moscow together with the other members of Central Committee of Polish Communist party; his fate is not known.

LEVA, *see* Vladimirov, Miron Konstantinovich.

LEVI, PAUL (1883–1930). Lawyer; member of German S.D. party; during World War in ranks of extreme Left opposition; member of "Spartakus" League and later of German Communist party; 1915, believed to have attended Zimmerwald Conference under pseudonym of "Hartstein"; 1917–1918, member of the Executive of the "Spartakus" group; 1919–21, member of Central Committee of the German Communist party; 1921, expelled from German Communist party after he accused its Central Committee of Bakuninism; soon joined I.S.D. party and together with Right wing of that party returned to S.D. party; there he organized a Left group; editor of *Sozialistische Politik und Wirtschaft;* after 1928, one of editors of *Der Klassenkampf.*

LEVIN, DAVID YULIEVICH (DALIN) (1888–). Member of R.S.D.L. party; Right Menshevik; 1910–1917, in England and Scandinavian countries; contributed to *Nasha Zaria*; during World War, Menshevik-Internationalist; December 1917, elected to Central Committee of United S.D.L. party; since 1921, émigré; 1922–1934, on editorial staff of *Sotsialisticheskii Vestnik.*

LEWINSON, PAWEL (STANISLAW LAPINSKI) (1879–). 1906–1918, leader of Polish Socialist party (Levitsa); took part in Zimmerwald movement; outstanding member of Polish Communist party; 1938, reported arrested in Moscow with other members of Central Committee of his party.

LIADOV, *see* Mandelstamm, Martyn Nikolaevich.

LIAKHOTSKY, KUZMA (–1917). Ukrainian by birth; owner of a small printing shop in Geneva, where most Russian Bolshevik publications of 1914–1917 were set in type.

LIAN, OLE Z. Member of Norwegian S.D. party; 1915, took part in preparations for Copenhagen Conference of Socialists of Neutral Countries; 1917, member of Dutch-Scandinavian Committee (Stockholm).

LIBMAN, *see* Girsh, P. L.

LIEBER, *see* Goldman, Mikhail Isaakovich.

LIEBKNECHT, KARL (1871–1919). Member of German S.D. party, Left wing; member of Reichstag and Prussian Landtag; a founder of Youth International; determined anti-militarist; advocate of civil war vs. civil peace; first to oppose war credits in Reichstag; 1915, one of organizers of *Internationale* group, later of "Spartakus" League; drafted; May 1916—November 1918, arrested and imprisoned for antiwar activities; January 1919, assassinated.

LILINA, ZLATA YONOVNA (ZINAIDA, ZINA) (1881–1929). Member of R.S.D.L. party; Bolshevik; after 1908, in Western Europe; active in women's socialist movement; contributed to *Pravda* and *Rabotnitsa*; during World War, on Committee of Propaganda among Prisoners of War organized by Central Committee of party; 1917, returned to Russia; headed child welfare work and held other responsible posts in Soviet government.

LIMANOWSKI, BOLESLAW (1835–1935). After early 'sixties, in revolutionary movement in Lithuania; one of founders of Polish Socialist party.

LINDHAGEN, CARL (1876–1950). Lawyer; formerly a Liberal; since 1909, member of Swedish S.D. party; 1897–1917, member of Riksdag; after 1919, member of Upper House; during World War, as pacifist joined Zimmerwald movement; 1917, joined Left S.D. party; later, member of Communist party of Sweden and Comintern; withdrew from both and formed group of his own, advocating Christian Communism.

LINDQUIST, HERMANN. Member of Swedish S.D. party; 1915, took part in preparations for Copenhagen Conference of Socialists of Neutral Countries; 1917, on Dutch-Scandinavian Committee (Stockholm).

LINDSTRÖM, JEORJ. Member of Swedish S.D.L. party; Left wing; took part in discussions conducted by I.S.C. in Stockholm and also in Third Zimmerwald Conference.

LITVINOV, MAXIM MAXIMOVICH (MAXIMOVICH, MAXIMOV) (1876–1951). Member of R.S.D.L. party from its origin; worked alternately in Russia and abroad; during World War in England; official Bolshevik delegate to I.S.B.; after November revolution Soviet plenipotentiary representative to Great Britain; 1918, returned to Russia; 1918–1930, Acting People's Commissar of Foreign Affairs; 1930–1939, People's Commissar of Foreign Affairs.

LLOYD GEORGE, DAVID (1863–   ). British statesman; 1915–1916, Minister of Munitions; 1916–1922, Prime Minister.

LONGMAN, MARY. During World War, Secretary of Women's Labour League, which was affiliated with British Labour party.

LONGUET, JEAN (1876–1938). Member of French Socialist party; 1914–1918, leader of party minority; editor of *Le Populaire*; 1914–1919, member of Chamber of Deputies; 1918–1921, editor of *L'Humanité*; one of the organizers of Two-and-a-Half International; later returned to ranks of Second International.

LORE, LUDWIG. German-American journalist; during the World War active in the American Socialist party, Left wing; editor, *New Yorker Volkszeitung*; now columnist on foreign affairs, *New York Post* and contributor to *The Nation, The New Republic, Current History,* and other periodicals.

LORIOT, FERNAND (1870–1933). Teacher; member of French Socialist party; 1915–1919, leader of Left wing of Comité pour la Reprise des Relations Internationales; supporter of Zimmerwald Left in France; 1919, Secretary of Comité de la Troisième Internationale; later, leader of French Communist party; 1927, broke with Communist party.

LOZOVSKY, A. (SOLOMON ABRAMOVICH DRIDZO) (1878–   ). Member of R.S.D.L. party; Bolshevik; took part in 1905 revolution; arrested a number of times; 1906, escaped abroad; 1909–1917, in Paris; member of French Socialist party; active in French trade unions; during World War, internationalist; on editorial staff of *Golos, Nashe Slovo* and *Nachalo*; 1917, elected Secretary of All-Russian Central Council of Trade Unions; 1918, expelled from Russian Communist party because of differences over tactics with respect to trade unions; 1918–1919, S.D. Internationalist; rejoined Communist party; one of the organizers of Red Trade Union International; since 1921, its General Secretary.

LUNACHARSKY, ANATOLII VASILEVICH (VOINOV) (1875–1933). Dramatist; member of R.S.D.L. party; Bolshevik; after 1905, attended all party congresses; 1906, emigrated; one of the organizers of *Vpered* group; active in party schools at Capri and Bologna; during World War, internationalist; contributor to *Golos* and *Nashe Slovo* in Paris; 1917, joined "Mezhraionka," and later Bolsheviks; 1917–1929, Commissar of Education; later, Chairman of Committee for Research and Educational Institutions; 1933, appointed ambassador to Spain.

LURIE, MIKHAIL ALEKSANDROVICH (YU. LARIN) (1882–1932). Member of R.S.D.L. party; Menshevik; one of the organizers of first trade unions in Russia; 1913, arrested; until 1917, in Western Europe; Menshevik-Internationalist; after March revolution, returned to Russia; joined Bolsheviks and worked for Soviet government in economic field.

LUTERAAN. Member of Socialist Youth Organization of Holland; 1915, attended International Socialist Youth Conference at Berne.

LUXEMBURG, ROSA (JUNIUS) (1870–1919). Born in Poland; after 1883 active in S.D. party of Poland; after 1897, with Left-wing German labor movement; opposed revisionism; brilliant journalist and polemical writer; opposed German Right and Center and certain Bolshevik theories; during World War imprisoned for internationalist, anti-militarist activities; helped to found and issue *Die Internationale*; active leader and agitator of "Spartakus" League; opposed early formation of Comintern; member of first editorial board of *Die Rote Fahne*; January 15, 1919, arrested and assassinated.

LUZZATO, MRS. Member of Austrian S.D.L. party; during World War, in ranks of extreme opposition within party which rallied around Karl Marx Club (Vienna); 1917, delegate to Third Zimmerwald Conference; author of *Entwicklung und Wesen des Sozialismus* (Vienna, 1910).

MACDONALD, JAMES RAMSAY (1866–1937). Until 1930, leader of British I.L. party; prominent in Second International; 1906–1918, 1922–1937, Member of Parliament; moderate socialist; during World War pacifist; at one time editor of *Socialist Review;* 1924, 1929–1931, head of Labour government; 1931–1935, head of National government; leader of National Labour group; editor of its *News Letter.*

MACH, ERNST (1838–1916). Austrian physicist and philosopher; advocate of a theory of knowledge similar to that of Avenarius.

MCLEAN, JOHN (1878–1923). Scottish teacher; member of British Socialist party, Left wing; publisher of *Vanguard;* during World War, arrested and imprisoned for antiwar activities; active leader of shop-steward movement and organizer of a number of serious strikes in Glasgow district; 1918, Soviet Russian Consul in Glasgow, but not recognized by British government.

MADSEN, CARL F. (1889–). Shoemaker; member of Danish S.D. party; active in Danish trade union movement; 1915, took part in preparations for Copenhagen Conference of Socialists of Neutral Countries; 1917, member of Dutch-Scandinavian Committee (Stockholm).

MAEVSKY, E., *see* Gutovsky, Vikentii Anitsetovich.

MAISKY, IVAN MIKHAILOVICH (LIAKHOVETSKY; V. MAISKY) (1884–). Economist; member of R.S.D.L. party; Menshevik.; during World War, shared viewpoint of Menshevik Organization Committee; after 1917, member of Menshevik Central Committee; during civil war, in ranks of anti-Bolshevik forces; later joined Russian Communist party and held responsible posts in Soviet government; after 1933, ambassador at London.

MAKADZIUB, MARK SAULOVICH (PANIN). Member of R.S.D.L. party; Menshevik; member of Organization Committee; after 1905 revolution, moved to extreme Right wing of Menshevism; contributor to *Nasha Zaria*; 1913, began to withdraw from party activity; until 1917, worked in a commercial enterprise in Perm; member of special commission appointed for calling Menshevik Unification Congress (August 1917); member of Russian-Dutch-Scandinavian Committee, Stockholm; after Bolshevik revolution worked in Soviet institutions in charge of fuel purveyance and later in lumber export institutions of Soviet Russia abroad.

MALECKI, A. (1879–). Formerly member of Social Democracy of Poland and Lithuania; member of its Main Presidium: spent most of his life in Western Europe; joined the Rozlomovists; edited *Gazeta Robotnicza*; member of Regional Presidium of Social Democracy of Poland and Lithuania; active in Second International; since 1921, in Russia; 1922–1925, on Executive Committee of Comintern; engaged in teaching.

MALINOVSKY, ALEKSANDR ALEKSANDROVICH (BOGDANOV; RIADOVOI; SYSOIKA) (1873–1928). Physician; philosopher; follower of Mach; member of R.S.D.L. party; Bolshevik; moved to Left wing of Bolsheviks; joined *Vpered* group; 1917, not participant in Bolshevik revolution; active in field of proletarian culture; engaged in scientific research.

MALINOVSKY, ROMAN VATSLAVOVICH (1878–1918). Member of R.S.D.L. party; member of Fourth State Duma; secret police agent; 1914, dismissed from Secret Police staff; resigned from State Duma; went abroad; 1915, joined Russian volunteer army in France; returned to Russia; shot by decision of Supreme Soviet Tribunal.

MALVY, LOUIS (1875–). French statesman; 1914–1917, Minister of the Interior; 1918, tried on high treason charges, and sentenced to five years' exile by High Court; after 1924, member of Chamber of Deputies and again held high posts in French government.

DE MAN, HENRI (1885–1953). Professor of social psychology at the University of Brussels; member of the Belgian Labor party and its Vice-President; 1935, became Minister of Public Works and Unemployment in Van Zeeland Cabinet; Director of Belgian Labor Research Bureau.

MANDELSTAMM, MARTYN NIKOLAEVICH (LIADOV; RUSALKA; LIDIN) (1872–). 1893, one of the organizers of first Moscow workers' union; exiled for five years;

member of R.S.D.L. party; Bolshevik; 1898–1909, attended all congresses and conferences of R.S.D.L. party; 1904, attended Amsterdam International Socialist Congress; until 1911, with *Vpered* group; after March revolution, Acting Chairman of Baku Soviet; 1918, captured by Turks; 1920, returned to Moscow; held responsible positions in administration of Soviet industry; 1929, member of Council of Lenin Institute.

MANKOV, IVAN NIKOLAEVICH (1881–   ). Member of R.S.D.L. party; Menshevik; member of Fourth State Duma; during World War, defensist; 1915, expelled from Duma Social Democratic group for voting war credits; 1917, withdrew from political activities.

MANNERHEIM, KARL GUSTAV EMIL (1867–   ). Formerly Russian army officer; served in Russo-Japanese and World War; 1918, Commander-in-Chief of White Forces in Finnish civil war; 1918–1919, Regent in Finland; later Finnish Field Marshal.

MANUILSKY, DMITRII ZAKHARIEVICH (BEZRABOTNYI) (1883–   ). Member of R.S.D.L. party; Bolshevik; 1905, party agitator; arrested and exiled after Kronstadt uprising; 1907, escaped from prison and went to Western Europe; moved to Left wing of Bolshevism; member of *Vpered* group; during World War, internationalist; contributed to *Golos* and *Nashe Slovo* (Paris); 1917, member of "Mezhraionka" in Russia; joined Bolshevik party; Commissar of Krasnoe Selo; after holding a number of responsible posts with Soviet government, ordered to the Ukraine; after 1920, member of Central Committee of Ukrainian Communist party; since 1924, member of Presidium of Executive Committee of Comintern.

MARCHLEWSKI, JULJAN (J. KARSKI) (1866–1925). Member of both German and Polish S.D. parties; on Left wing of German Social Democrats; contributor to *Vorwärts, Neue Zeit,* and *Leipziger Volkszeitung;* 1905, active in revolutionary movement in Warsaw; 1906–1907, arrested and imprisoned; during World War, again active in German movement; one of organizers of *Internationale* group; later one of the organizers of "Spartakus" League; 1916–1918, confined to a concentration camp in Germany; 1918, exchanged for a German prisoner of war in Soviet Russia; 1919, took part in Ruhr uprising; active member of Comintern; 1920, Chairman of Revolutionary Committee of Poland; later devoted himself to scientific research.

MARCK, CH. Unidentified; contributor to *La Bataille.*

MARKOV, NIKOLAI EVGENIEVICH (MARKOV II) (1866–   ). Large Russian landowner; member of Third and Fourth State Dumas; member of League of the Russian People.

MARTOV, L. (YULII OSIPOVICH TSEDERBAUM; YU. MARTOV; EGOROV) (1873–1923). Formerly member of Petersburg League of Struggle for the Liberation of the Working Class; exiled for three years; collaborated in founding and editing *Iskra* and *Zaria;* member of R.S.D.L. party; Menshevik; during World War, internationalist; adherent of Zimmerwald; after March revolution, headed Menshevik-Internationalists; 1921, left Russia; editor of Menshevik *Sotsialisticheskii Vestnik* (Paris).

MARTOV, YU., *see* Martov, L.

MARTYNOV, ALEKSANDR SAMOILOVICH (PIKER) (1865–   ). Once member of "People's Will" party; 1899, joined R.S.D.L. party; member of editorial staff of *Yuzhnyi Rabochii;* 1903, sided with Mensheviks; 1913, as member of Organization Committee signed statement presented to London Conference of I.S.B., using pseudonym "Dneprov"; during World War, internationalist; 1917, elected to Menshevik Central Committee; 1918, went to the Ukraine and withdrew from party activity; later became a Bolshevik; 1923, admitted to Russian Communist party; since 1924, member of editorial board of *Kommunisticheskii Internatsional.*

MARX, KARL HEINRICH (1818–1883). Founder of scientific socialism.

MASLOV, PETER PAVLOVICH (1867–1946). Russian economist; Marxist; specialist on agrarian questions; member of R.S.D.L. party; Menshevik; after 1905 revolution, on extreme Right wing of Menshevism; during World War, defensist; after 1917, gave up political activity.

MAXIMOV, *see* Litvinov, Maxim Maximovich.

MAXIMOVICH, *see* Litvinov, Maxim Maximovich.

MAYÉRAS, BARTHÉLEMY (1879–   ). Member of French Socialist party; 1914–1919, member of Chamber of Deputies; during World War, one of the leaders of moderate minority socialists; founder of *Le Populaire du Centre.*

MEDEM, VLADIMIR DAVYDOVICH (GOLDBLAT) (1879–1923). Author; member of the Bund, Right wing; after 1903, member of the Bund Committee Abroad; after 1906, member of Central Committee; shortly before outbreak of World War, imprisoned; 1915, released by Germans; until 1920, active in Poland; 1921–1923, in New York; contributed to Jewish *Vorwärts.*

MEHRING, FRANZ (1846–1919). German revolutionary Marxist; editor of *Leipziger Volkszeitung* and *Neue Zeit;* at outbreak of World War helped to organize *Internationale* group; later member of "Spartakus" League. Approved Bolshevik revolution in Russia; author of four-volume history of German S.D. party.

MERKEL (SKARE; SAUER). Member of Lettish S.D. party; prior to World War, lived in Brussels; acted for Secretariat of Menshevik Organization Committee.

MERRHEIM, ARTHUR CHARLES (1881–1925). Member of C.G.T.; Secretary of French Metal Workers' Union; 1915, joined Zimmerwald movement; one of the organizers of Comité pour la Reprise des Relations Internationales; adhered to its Right wing; 1918, returned to ranks of C.G.T. majority and joined Amsterdam Trade Union International.

MEYER, ERNST (1888–   ). Member of German S.D. party, Left wing adherent; during World War, member of *Internationale* group; later member of "Spartakus" League; after 1918, member of German Communist party.

MGELADZE, VLAS D. (TRIA) (1868–   ). Georgian member of R.S.D.L. party; Menshevik; 1905, active in Persia; 1912, one of delegates to August Conference from Transcaucasian Regional Committee; during World War, associated with League for the Liberation of the Ukraine; after 1917, member of Georgian Menshevik government.

MICKIEWICZ-KAPSUKAS, VIKENTII SEMENOVICH (1880–1935). After 1903, member of S.D. party of Lithuania; 1908–1913, while serving term of penal labor, became acquainted with Bolsheviks whom he joined in 1915; during World War, in England and the United States; member of Zimmerwald Left; after Bolshevik revolution, Commissar of Head Treasury in Petrograd; after 1918, member of Central Committee of Communist party of Lithuania; 1919, member of Central Executive Committee of Lithuania and White Russia; later active in Comintern.

MILIUKOV, PAVEL NIKOLAEVICH (1859–1943). Historian; formerly professor at Moscow University; leader of Constitutional Democrats; member of Third and Fourth State Dumas; March–May, 1917, Minister of Foreign Affairs; during civil war, with anti-Bolshevik forces; after 1921 in Western Europe; editor of *Poslednie Novosti* (Paris).

MILLERAND, ALEXANDRE (1859–1943). French newspaper owner and publisher; 1885, elected to Chamber of Deputies; 1899–1902, Minister of Commerce in Waldeck-Rousseau cabinet; 1904, expelled from French Socialist party; 1909–1920, held office in various governments; September 1920—June 1924, President of French Republic.

MINEV, S. Member of Bulgarian S.D.L. party; "Narrow" Socialist; during World War, in Switzerland; 1915, attended International Socialist Youth Conference and took part in Zimmerwald movement.

MODIGLIANI, GIUSEPPE EMANUELE (1868–1947). Lawyer; member of Italian Socialist party; reformist; 1913–1926, Member of Chamber of Deputies; 1915–1916, took part in Zimmerwald movement and attended its conferences; belonged to Zimmerwald Center; after 1922, member of Unitary Socialist party of Italy; now in exile.

MODRÁČEK, FRANTIŠEK (1871–   ). Once anarchist; member of Czech S.D. party; turned from Marxism to revisionism; 1907–1918, member of Austrian Reichsrat; 1917–1922, contributor to *Socialistické Listy;* 1918, founded Socialist Labor party; after 1920, member of Czech parliament; 1923, expelled from Socialist Labor party; joined S.D. party.

MOLKENBUHR, HERMANN (1851–1927). Worker in a cigarette factory; member of German S.D. party, Left wing; 1881–1884, in the United States; after 1904, Secretary of party Presidium; member of I.S.B.; repeatedly elected to Reichstag; during World War, majority socialist; 1919–1920, member of National Assembly.

MÖLLER, GUSTAV (1883–   ). Member of Swedish S.D.L. party; 1917, member of Dutch-Scandinavian Committee; since 1919, member of Riksdag; member of Executive of Labor and Socialist International; served several times in Swedish cabinet.

MOLOTOV, VIACHESLAV MIKHAILOVICH (SKRIABIN) (1890–   ). Member of R.S.D.L. party; Bolshevik; 1913–1917, lived and worked on illegal status in Petrograd; arrested but soon escaped from exile in Irkutsk Gubernia; 1917, member of Petersburg Committee; member of Executive Committee of Petrograd Soviet; during Bolshevik revolution, member of Military Revolutionary Committee; held responsible posts with Soviet government; since 1931, Chairman of Council of People's Commissars; since 1939, also Commissar of Foreign Affairs.

MONATTE, PIERRE. French anarcho-syndicalist; Left-wing leader of C.G.T.; editor of *La Vie ouvrière;* 1915, joined Comité pour la Reprise des Relations Internationales; drafted to active army; 1920–1925, member of French Communist party; one of editors of *L'Humanité;* 1925, expelled from Communist party; editor of *La Révolution Proletaire.*

MONITOR. Member of German S.D. party; majority socialist; contributor to *Preussische Jahrbücher.*

MOOR, KARL (1853–   ). Member of Swiss S.D. party; 1895–1907, editor of *Berner Tagwacht;* 1907–1911, party Secretary for Berne canton; member of Berne Great Council; advocate of women's suffrage; after 1917, spent most of his time in Soviet Russia.

MORGARI, ODINO (1860–   ). Member of Italian Socialist party; member of Chamber of Deputies; for many years editor of *Sempre Avanti!* and of *Seme;* after 1908, editor-in-chief of *Avanti!*; joined Zimmerwald movement and attended all its conferences in Switzerland; elected member of International So-

cialist Committee; belonged to Zimmerwald Center; 1917–1919, advocate of
proletarian revolution; turned against proletarian dictatorship; 1920, emigrated
to Paris where he is in ranks of Right socialists.

MOUTET, MARIUS (1876–   ). Lawyer; member of French Socialist party; 1917,
went to Russia to convert Russian socialists to Entente socialist viewpoint but
was converted himself in favor of calling an international socialist congress;
later, member of French cabinet.

MOVSHOVICH, M. I. (VLADIMIR). Member of R.S.D.L. party; Bolshevik; several
times arrested; 1911, emigrated to Switzerland; Secretary of Lausanne section
of Bolsheviks; on return to Russia, active in trade union work.

MÜLLER, GUSTAV (1860–1921). Member of Swiss S.D. party, Right wing; member of National Council and of Berne municipal and canton elective bodies; during World War, Colonel in Swiss artillery.

MÜLLER, HERMANN (1877–1931). Member of German S.D. party and of its Executive; during World War, majority socialist; editor of *Vorwärts;* representative at Stockholm; 1919, Minister of Foreign Affairs and signatory of Versailles
treaty; twice Chancellor of German Republic; 1930, resigned Chancellorship;
later, socialist leader in Reichstag.

MÜNZENBERG, WILLI (1889–   ). Shoe factory worker; engaged in youth movement in Germany; 1914–1921, Secretary of International Socialist Youth
League; later, Secretary of Communist Youth League.

MURANOV, MATVEI KONSTANTINOVICH (1873–   ). Member of R.S.D.L. party;
Bolshevik; early in his revolutionary activity, exiled; member of Fourth State
Duma; November 1914, arrested, tried, and exiled with entire Bolshevik Duma
group; 1917, returned from Siberia and held high posts with Soviet government; now reported "missing."

MUSATTI, ELIA (1869–1936). Member of Italian Socialist party, Left wing; after
1912, member of party Executive; Member of Parliament; resigned in protest
against Tripolitan war; took part in Zimmerwald movement and attended its
conferences; 1922, joined Unitary Socialist party of Italy.

MUSSOLINI, BENITO (1883–1945). Born and reared in revolutionary milieu of Ro-
magna, Italy; member of Italian Socialist party; to escape military service, went
to Switzerland; 1912–1914, editor of *Avanti!;* ardent opponent of war to moment
when he was forced by unanimous vote of party Executive to resign post for
revealing pro-Entente sympathies; 1914, founded *Il Popolo d'Italia* in which he
advocated Italy's intervention in World War against Germany; 1918, led "Bolshevist" movement in Italy in favor of expropriation of factories by working
people; March 1919, founded first "Fascio di Combatimente" (Milan); since
November 1, 1922, Premier with dictatorial powers.

N. I., *see* Bukharin, Nikolai Ivanovich.

NADEZHDA KONSTANTINOVNA, *see* Krupskaia, Nadezhda Konstantinovna.

NAINE, CHARLES (1874–1926). Leader of Neûchatel group of Swiss S.D. party;
editor of *La Sentinelle;* 1906–1910, member of Neûchatel Great Council; after
1911, member of National Council; during World War, internationalist; took
part in Zimmerwald movement; elected member of International Socialist Committee.

NATANSON, MARK ANDREEVICH (BOBROV) (1850–1919). Member of revolutionary
movement from 'sixties; one of founders of "Land and Freedom" group; later,
joined "People's Will" group and took part in organizing "People's Right"
party; several times arrested and exiled; member of Central Committee of

Socialist-Revolutionist party from its origin; after 1905, Left wing; during World War, internationalist; attended Zimmerwald Conference; after 1917, Left Socialist-Revolutionist; 1918, headed "Revolutionary Communists."

NĚMEC, ANTONÍN (1858–1926). Journalist; member of Czech S.D. party; editor of *Rovnost;* after 1894, edited *Dělnické Listy* (Vienna) and after 1897 edited *Právo Lidu* (Prague); after 1904, Czech representative on I.S.B.; 1907–1918, deputy in Austrian Reichsrat; 1918–1920, member of Czech Revolutionary National Assembly; 1920–1925, deputy in Czechoslovak parliament; after 1925 honorary Chairman of Czech S.D. party.

NERMAN, TURE (1886–). Member of Swedish Socialist Youth League; member of its Central Committee; 1912, as such took part in Basel International Socialist Congress; 1915, attended Zimmerwald Conference; 1916, first editor of *Politiken;* 1919, editor of *Stormklockan;* 1918–1924, member of Swedish Communist party and of Comintern; 1924, withdrew from Communist party.

NICHOLAS II (1868–1918); last Tsar of Russia.

NICOD, RENÉ (1881–). 1898, joined French Socialist party; during World War, party Secretary of Ain Department; one of leaders of Left opposition against majority socialist policy.

NICOLET, EMIL (1879–1921). Member of Swiss S.D. party; after 1907, member of Geneva Great Council; after 1919, member of National Council; during World War, favored national defense.

NIEUWENHUIS, FERDINAND DOMELA (1846–1919). Author; originally Dutch Social Democrat; member of States General; after 1894, in ranks of anarchists.

NIK, IV., *see* Bukharin, Nikolai Ivanovich.

NILSSEN, MAGNUS (1871–1947). Member of Norwegian S.D. party; 1906–1924, and after 1928, member of Storting; 1915, took part in preparations for Copenhagen Conference of Socialists of Neutral Countries; 1917, member of Dutch-Scandinavian Committee (Stockholm).

NISSEN, EGEDE. Member of Norwegian S.D. party; 1905, co-operated with Russian revolutionaries in transport of illegal literature into Russia through Finland; 1917, attended Third Zimmerwald Conference; Communist member of Storting.

NOBS, ERNST (1886–). Teacher; journalist; member of Swiss S.D. party; since 1915, editor of *Volksrecht* (Zürich); took part in Zimmerwald movement; 1920, withdrew from party because of disagreement with Comintern's conditions of admission; returned to ranks of Second International.

NOGIN, VIKTOR PAVLOVICH (MAKAR) (1879–1924). Member of R.S.D.L. party; Bolshevik; formerly member of League of Struggle for the Liberation of the Working Class; *Iskra* agent; many times arrested and exiled; 1917, Chairman of Moscow Soviet; elected to Central Committee of party; 1917–1918, Commissar of Commerce and Industry and Assistant Commissar of Labor; later, took charge of textile industry.

NOSKOV, VLADIMIR ALEKSANDROVICH (BORIS; GLEBOV; MA.) (1878–1913). Member of R.S.D.L. party; 1903, elected to Central Committee by Second Party Congress; favored party unity; 1905, arrested with other Central Committee members; on release withdrew from party activity; committed suicide.

NOTA BENE, *see* Bukharin, Nikolai Ivanovich.

NOTZ. Member of German socialist youth organization in Stuttgart.

OBUKHOV, V. M. (KAMSKY; VOLGIN). Member of the R.S.D.L. party; Bolshevik.

ODIER, EDOUARD (1844–1919). Lawyer; Swiss diplomat; 1906–1918, ambassador to Russia.

O'GRADY, SIR JAMES (1866–   ). British trade unionist; member of British Labour party; Member of Parliament; spring, 1917, went to Russia on behalf of British government; late in 1919, was instrumental in negotiations concerning repatriation of all British subjects in Soviet Russia.

OLAUSSEN, ANSGAR EUGENE (1887–   ). Factory worker; member of Norwegian Socialist Youth League; 1915, as such took part in Berne Conference of International Socialist Youth; participant in Zimmerwald movement.

OLGA, see Ravich, S. N.

OLGIN, see Fomin, Valentin.

OLJELUND, LARS IVAN (1892–   ). Member of Left opposition within Swedish S.D.L. party; anti-militarist; during World War arrested and charged with high treason; imprisoned.

OLMINSKY, MIKHAIL STEPANOVICH (GALERKA; ALEKSANDROV) (1863–1933). Member of "People's Will" party; 1894–1903, imprisoned and exiled; 1904, joined Bolsheviks abroad; during World War, internationalist; after March revolution, chief editor of *Pravda;* later, member of editorial board of *Sotsial-Demokrat;* elected to Constituent Assembly; 1924, head of Istpart; later, connected with Lenin Institute (Moscow).

ORDZHONIKIDZE, GRIGORII KONSTANTINOVICH (SERGO) (1886–1937). Feldscher by education; Georgian member of R.S.D.L. party; Bolshevik; took part in 1905 revolution in Caucasus; 1905–1907, arrested several times; exiled to Siberia but fled abroad; active in preparations for Prague party conference at which he was elected to Central Committee; 1912, on return to Russia arrested for flight from Siberian exile; 1915, after serving term in Schlüsselburg, exiled to Yakutsk; after March revolution, member of Yakutsk Executive Committee; later, of Petersburg Committee; after Bolshevik revolution, Extraordinary Commissar of the Ukraine, South Russia, and North Caucasus; took part in civil war; Chairman of Caucasian Revolutionary Committee; 1920–1921, worked for establishment of Soviet power in Georgia and Armenia; for many years member of Central Committee of Russian Communist party; held high posts in Soviet government.

ORLOVSKY, see Vorovsky, Vatslav Vatslavovich.

OSIPOV, G. I., see Zalkind, Rozaliia Samoilovna.

PANIN, see Makadziub, Mark Saulovich.

PANNEKOEK, ANTONIE (1873–   ). Professor of astronomy; originally member of Dutch S.D.L. party, Left wing; after 1909, member of S.D. party of Holland (Tribunists); during World War, member of Zimmerwald Left; published Zimmerwald Left periodical, *Vorbote;* 1918, formed Communist party of Holland; 1919, joined Comintern, from which he withdrew the following year.

PARVUS, see Helphand, Alexander L.

PAVEL BORISOVICH, see Axelrod, Pavel Bonsovich.

PELUSO, EDMONDO. Member of Portuguese Socialist movement; during World War, Social Democratic newspaper correspondent in Switzerland; later, Communist and official of Comintern.

PETROVA, see Armand, Inessa.

PETROVSKY, GRIGORII IVANOVICH (1877–   ). Metal worker; member of R.S.D.L. party; Bolshevik; 1905, member of Ekaterinoslav Soviet of Workers'

Deputies; member of Fourth State Duma; 1914, arrested; 1915, exiled to Siberia; 1917, Commissar of Yakutsk region; after Bolshevik revolution, People's Commissar of the Interior; 1919, Chairman of Ukrainian Central Executive Committee; later held important party and government posts; now Vice-Chairman of Presidium of Supreme Council.

PFLÜGER, PAUL BERNARD (1865–   ). Formerly member of Grütli Verein; later, member of Swiss S.D. party, Right wing; 1911–1918, member of National Council; during World War, favored national defense.

PHILLIPS, MARION (1881–1932). Economist; member of British Labour party; 1913, General Secretary of Women's Labour League; after 1914, member of Central Committee on Women's Training and Employment; 1918–1919, member of Consumers' Council of Ministry of Food; Secretary of Joint Standing Committee of Industrial Women's Organizations; editor of *The Labour Woman;* contributor to various socialist and labor publications and author of several books; 1929, Member of Parliament.

PIATAKOV, GEORGII LEONIDOVICH (P. KIEVSKY; YURII N. LIALIN) (1890–1937). Formerly an anarchist; after 1910, member of R.S.D.L. party; Bolshevik; 1912, exiled to Siberia; 1914, escaped through Japan and the United States to Europe; 1915, attended Berne Conference of sections of Russian Bolsheviks abroad; disagreed with Lenin on a number of questions and began to issue *Kommunist,* thus involving himself in a controversy with members of the Central Committee; 1916, moved to Sweden; 1917, returned to Russia; Chief Commissar of State Bank; 1918, headed first Ukrainian Soviet government; leader of Left Communists during Brest-Litovsk negotiations; later, occupied a number of responsible posts in central Soviet government; expelled from party for supporting Trotsky; 1929, readmitted; executed.

PILSUDSKI, JÓZEF (1867–1935). Polish nationalist and statesman; founder of Polish Socialist party; 1908, organized secret military organization which later became Polish Legion; 1918, chief of independent Polish state; 1919–1920, Commander of Polish armies in Soviet-Polish war; made first Marshal of Poland; 1926, after retirement of three years returned to political activity and leadership in the Polish state.

PLATTEN, FRITZ (1883–1942). Member of Swiss S.D. party; 1905, took part in revolutionary movement in Russia; during World War, Left wing Social Democrat; until 1919, party Secretary; joined Zimmerwald movement; co-operated with Zimmerwald Left; 1917, aided Russian socialist émigrés to return to Russia via Germany and accompanied them on this trip; 1918–1919, 1921–1922, member of National Council; 1919, attended first congress of Comintern; since 1923 in Soviet Russia; active in Kolkhoz movement.

PLEKHANOV, GEORGII VALENTINOVICH (1856–1918). Pioneer and brilliant exponent of Marxism in Russia; member of "Chernyi Peredel"; 1883, organizer of "Emancipation of Labor" group; 1889, participated in formation of Second International; until 1913, represented R.S.D.L. party on I.S.B.; opposed economism; favored party unity after Bolshevik-Menshevik split; opposed "liquidationism"; 1909, formed group of party-Mensheviks; during World War, pro-Entente defensist; 1917, returned to Russia; supported continuation of war and collaboration with Liberals; opposed Bolsheviks; author of twenty-four volumes on economic, social, and political questions.

POINCARÉ, RAYMOND NICHOLAS LANDRY (1860–1934). 1913–1920, President of French Republic.

POKROVSKY, MIKHAIL NIKOLAEVICH (1868–1932). Historian; Marxist; member of R.S.D.L. party; Bolshevik; 1905, active in organizing armed insurrection;

1906–1907, member of Moscow Committee; elected to Central Committee; emigrated to Western Europe; joined *Vpered* group from which he withdrew in 1911; during World War, internationalist; 1917, returned to Russia; Chairman of Moscow Soviet; during Brest-Litovsk negotiations, Left Communist; 1918–1932, Assistant Commissar of education and editor of a number of Soviet historical publications.

POPOV, ALEKSANDR LVOVICH (N. VOROBIEV). Related to owners of Russian tea firm; nonfactional Social Democrat; connected with "Mezhraionka"; gave financial support to various Social Democratic organizations; after 1920, worked in archives of People's Commissariat of Foreign Affairs; contributor to *Krasnyi Arkhiv* and *Proletarskaia Revoliutsiia*.

POPOV, A. N. (ANTONOV; BRITTMAN) (–1915). Member of R.S.D.L. party; Bolshevik; 1906–1907, connected with Kronstadt party military organization; arrested and exiled abroad where he became member of Committee of Organizations Abroad; 1907–1908, underwent party trial over affair of Kronstadt military organization; acquitted; died in Western Europe.

POPOV, I. F. (1886–   ). Member of R.S.D.L. party; Bolshevik; 1907–1908, arrested and exiled for revolutionary activity among students; escaped; 1908–1914, in Brussels; represented Central Committee of party in I.S.B.; 1915, withdrew from active party work; 1918, returned to Russia from German captivity; later, active in workers' and peasants' inspection.

POPOVIĆ, DUŠAN (1884–1919). Member of Serbian S.D. party; editor and contributor to *Radnichki Noviny;* founder of *Borba;* during World War, contributed to Western European socialist press; 1917, came to Stockholm and took part in discussions organized by Russian-Dutch-Scandinavian Committee.

POSTOLOVSKY, D. S. (MIKHAILOV; ALEKSANDROV; DIUBUA; VADIM) (1876–   ). Member of R.S.D.L. party from its origin; Bolshevik; always worked in close contact with central party institutions; active in 1905 revolution; advocate of party unity; December 1905, arrested; subsequently withdrew from party activity; 1917, member of Petrograd Soviet; member of *Novaia Zhizn* group; later joined Russian Communist party; worked in Commission on Legislation and similar legislative institutions of Soviet government.

POTRESOV, ALEKSANDR NIKOLAEVICH (STAROVER) (1869–1934). Journalist and early Marxist; once member of League of Struggle for the Liberation of the Working Class; later, member of R.S.D.L. party; Menshevik; 1900, forced to emigrate; 1905, in Russia; later, on extreme Right of Menshevism; on editorial board of *Nasha Zaria;* during World War, defensist; 1917, contributed to *Den;* author of many works on socialism; died in Western Europe.

PRAMPOLINI, CAMILLO (1859–1930). Member of Italian Socialist party, Right wing; editor of *Lotta di classe;* advocate and outstanding leader of co-operative movement; during World War, pacifist; 1916, attended Kienthal Conference; editor of *La Giustizia;* author of numerous socialist propaganda pamphlets.

PRESSEMANE, ADRIEN (1879–1929). Member of French Socialist party; editor of *Populaire du Centre;* member of Chamber of Deputies; during World War, minority socialist.

PROUDHON, PIERRE-JOSEPH (1809–1865). French revolutionary writer; author of *Qu'est-ce que la propriété?* and a forerunner of the anarchists.

QUESSEL, LUDWIG (1872–1931). Member of German S.D. party; revisionist; during World War, majority socialist; 1912–1918, 1920–1930, member of Reichstag; 1919–1920, member of Weimar National Assembly.

RADEK, KARL BERNGARDOVICH (PARABELLUM) (1885–   ). 1908, after several years of activity in Galician and Polish socialist labor movement joined German S.D. party; connected with Left wing; during World War, revolutionary internationalist; member of Rozlomovists of Social Democracy of Poland and Lithuania; on editorial staff of *Gazeta Robotnicza;* collaborated with Russian Bolsheviks in Zimmerwald movement and contributed to publications of Zimmerwald Left; 1917, forbidden by Provisional government to enter Russia; in Stockholm, member of Bureau of Bolshevik Central Committee Abroad and its spokesman at international socialist discussions; after Bolshevik revolution, went to Russia and joined the Bolshevik party; 1918, Left Communist; December 1918, entered Germany illegally; attended First Congress of German Communist party; after January uprising of Spartakists, arrested by German authorities; 1919, released; returned to Russia; until 1924, member of Executive Committee of Comintern; member of Central Committee of Russian Communist party; 1927, expelled from the party for supporting Trotsky; 1930, readmitted; editor of *Izvestiia;* Stalin's spokesman in field of international Communist labor movement; 1937, tried and sentenced to ten years' imprisonment.

RAFFIN-DUGENS, JEAN PIERRE (1861–   ). Formerly manual laborer; later, teacher; member of French Socialist party; 1910–1919, member of Chamber of Deputies; during World War, minority socialist; edited *Droit du Peuple, Le Populaire,* and *Le Populaire du Centre;* 1921, joined French Communist party.

RAKOVSKY, CHRISTIAN (1873–   ). Member of Rumanian S.D. party; during World War, internationalist; took part in Zimmerwald movement; belonged to Zimmerwald Center; 1916, imprisoned by Rumanian government for antiwar propaganda; 1917, released by Russian soldiers from Jassy prison; went to Russia; joined Russian Communist party; 1918–1919, held responsible Soviet posts in the Ukraine; later held Soviet diplomatic posts in Western Europe; 1928, expelled from Russian Communist party for supporting Trotsky; exiled; 1934, reinstated; 1938, sentenced to a term in prison.

RAPPOPORT, CHARLES (1865–   ). Formerly member of "People's Will" party; 1902, joined R.S.D.L. party; after emigrating to France, devoted himself entirely to French Socialist movement; joined French Socialist party; at first Guesdist; later socialist reformist; wrote for French press and *Neue Zeit* and *Sotsial-Demokrat;* during World War, in ranks of party minority; later joined French Communist party and served as correspondent for *Izvestiia* (Moscow).

RATTI, CELESTINO. Member of Executive of Italian Socialist party; member of editorial staff of *Avanti!*

RAVICH, OLGA, *see* Ravich, S. N.

RAVICH, S. N. (OLGA KARPINSKAIA). Member of R.S.D.L. party; Bolshevik; during World War, in Switzerland; member of Geneva section of Bolsheviks; active in publishing and distributing Bolshevik literature; 1917, returned to Russia; active in field of public education; since 1925, in ranks of opposition; 1938, said to have been deported by Soviet authorities.

REINSTEIN, BORIS. Member of American Socialist Labor party; 1917, managed to reach Stockholm though refused passport by the United States government; took part in Zimmerwald conferences at Stockholm; went to Soviet Russia; later, member of International Propaganda Committee; 1919, attended First Congress of Comintern.

RENAUDEL, PIERRE (1871–1935). Member of French Socialist party, Left wing; editor of *Le Peuple* and on editorial staff of *La Vie socialiste;* during World War leader of majority socialists; 1914–1918, editor of *L'Humanité;* 1914–1919 and after 1924, member of Chamber of Deputies.

RENNER, KARL (RUDOLF SPRINGER) (1870–1950). Member of Austrian S.D.L. party; revisionist; after 1907, member of Reichsrat; student of nationalities question; during World War, defensist; 1918, first Chancellor of the Austrian Republic; one of signatories of Treaty of St. Germain.

REPETTO. 1916, represented Argentine socialist movement at Conference of Socialists of Neutral Countries at The Hague.

RIADOVOI, *see* Malinovsky, Aleksandr Aleksandrovich.

RIAZANOV, DAVID BORISOVICH (GOLDENDACH; BUKVOED) (1870–1933). Member of R.S.D.L. party; one of founders of S.D. *Borba* group; author and publisher of numerous works on Marxism; organizer of Russian trade unions; several times arrested and forced to emigrate; during World War, in France; contributed to *Golos* and *Nashe Slovo;* internationalist and anti-defensist; opposed slogan of "defeat of the fatherland in the imperialist war"; 1917, returned to Russia; joined "Mezhraionka"; July 1917, joined Bolshevik party; 1918, in charge of Central Archives and member of Collegium of People's Commissariat of Education; 1919, organized Communist Academy; later, organized Marx-Engels-Lenin Institute (Moscow), of which he was director; 1929, elected to Academy of Science; 1931, expelled from party and exiled.

RIBOT, ALEXANDRE (1842–1923). French statesman; lawyer; moderate republican; after 1878, in Chamber of Deputies; several times member of Cabinet and Prime Minister; March–September, 1917, Prime Minister and Minister of Foreign Affairs.

RIGOLA, RINALDO (1864–   ). Italian trade unionist; formerly an anarchist; later, member of Italian Socialist party, Left wing; gradually moved to Right wing; Secretary of Confederazione Generale del Lavoro; contributor to *Avanti!* and *Tempo;* after establishment of Italian Fascism, publisher of *Problemi del Lavoro* (Milan).

RIMATHÉ, ANTON DE ZIZERS (1874–   ). Member of Swiss S.D. party; 1916–1919, member of National Council.

ROBMANN, AGNES. Member of Swiss S.D. party; member of Swiss delegation at Kienthal Conference.

DE ROCHEFORT, HENRY (1830–1913). Journalist; Left-wing leader of French Republican party; publisher of *La Lanterne, La Marseillaise,* and later *L'Intransigeant;* ardent foe of Napoleon III; sympathized with the Paris Commune; arrested, tried, and exiled; 1880, returned to France; 1885–1889, member of Chamber of Deputies.

RODZIANKO, MIKHAIL VLADIMIROVICH (1859–1924). Member of Octobrist party; after 1907, member of State Duma; 1912–1917, its Chairman; after Bolshevik revolution, émigré.

ROLAND-HOLST, HENRIETTE (1869–1952). Poet and author; member of Dutch S.D.L. party, Left wing; founder of Revolutionary Socialist League of Holland; during World War, internationalist; active propagandist of anti-militarism; 1916, joined S.D. party and Zimmerwald Left; publisher of *Vorbote;* 1918, joined Dutch Communist party; 1924, withdrew and formed Independent Communist party; advocated Christian socialism.

ROMANOV, ALEKSEI BOGDANOVICH (NIKITIN). Printer; member of R.S.D.L. party; Menshevik; trade unionist; 1914, member of Petersburg Initiative group; on editorial staff of *Rabochaia Gazeta;* delegate to Brussels Unification Conference.

ROMM, MAXIM. Russian political exile in the United States; treasurer for funds contributed to aid revolutionary groups in Russia and political refugees regardless of party affiliation; active in the American socialist movement.

DE ROODE, J. J. Member of Dutch S.D.L. party; 1907–1920, editor of *Het Volk*.

ROOT, ELIHU (1845–1937). American lawyer and statesman; 1917, head of special diplomatic mission to Russia.

ROSMER, ALFRED (1877–). French syndicalist; leader of minority of C.G.T.; contributor to *La Vie Ouvrière* and *Bataille Syndicaliste;* during World War, joined Zimmerwald movement; later, member of Comité de la Troisième Internationale; 1920, joined French Communist party; co-editor of *L'Humanité;* once active in Comintern; no longer Communist, at present not a member of any political party; member of Fédération du Livre.

ROTTER, MAX. Member of Swiss S.D. party; pacifist; October–November, 1917, connected with labor disturbances in Switzerland.

ROZANOV, VLADIMIR NIKOLAEVICH (1876–). Member of R.S.D.L. party; Menshevik; member of Central Committee; during World War, internationalist; 1917, revolutionary defensist; later active in People's Commissariat of Health.

ROZIN, FRITZ (AHSIS) (1870–1919). Member of the Lettish S.D. party; Lettish S.D. member of the Central Committee of the R.S.D.L. party; 1907, arrested and sentenced to penal labor in Siberia; escaped to the United States, where he edited a Lettish Social Democratic paper; 1917, attended the Third Zimmerwald Conference at Stockholm; 1918–1919, in Moscow, Commissar for the Lettish National Affairs; member of the Presidium of the Socialist Academy and Chairman of the Executive Committee of the Soviet of Workers, Landless and Sharpshooters' Deputies in Latvia.

ROZMIROVICH, ELENA FEDOROVNA (1866–). Member of R.S.D.L. party; Bolshevik; 1909, forced to emigrate; after several years of party activity in Western Europe returned to Russia; after 1913, Secretary of Bolshevik section of Social Democratic Duma group and of Russian Bureau of Central Committee; contributed to a number of Bolshevik periodicals; 1914, forced to emigrate again; active in Switzerland; 1917, returned to Russia; editor of *Soldatskaia Pravda;* later held important positions in Soviet government.

RUBANOVICH, ILIIA ADOLFOVICH (1860–1920). Member of Russian Socialist-Revolutionist party from its origin; member of I.S.B.; 1907–1909, edited *La Tribune Russe* (Paris); during World War, social patriot.

RUDOLPH I (1218–1291). 1273–1291, German King.

RÜHLE, OTTO (1874–). Member of German S.D. party; after 1912, member of Reichstag; during World War, internationalist; voted against war credits in Reichstag; 1919, joined German Communist party; later, Left Communist; 1920, one of the founders and leaders of German Communist Labor party.

RUMIANTSEV, PETR PETROVICH (SCHMIDT) (1870–1925). Statistician; writer; member of R.S.D.L. party; Bolshevik; member of Bureau of Majority Committees; 1905, co-opted to Central Committee; contributor to Bolshevik press; after 1907, gave up party activity.

RUSANOV, NIKOLAI SERGEEVICH (TARASOV; KUDRIN) (1859–). Once member of "People's Will" party; later, member of Russian Socialist-Revolutionist party; spent many years outside Russia; 1901, editor of *Vestnik Russkoi Revoliutsii,* and later contributed to *Revoliutsionnaia Rossiia* and *Russkoe Bogatstvo;* 1917, on editorial staff of *Delo Naroda;* now émigré.

RUSSELL, CHARLES EDWARD (1860–1941). Journalist; member of American Socialist party; 1917, member of the Root mission sent to Russia.

RUTGERS, S. J. Member of the Dutch S.D. party; during the World War, in the United States where he helped to organize the Socialist Propaganda League and edited a Lettish Social Democratic newspaper; after 1917 went to Russia and as a member of the Dutch Communist party took part in the activities of the Comintern.

RYKOV, ALEKSEI IVANOVICH (1881–1938). Member of R.S.D.L. party; Bolshevik; attended a number of party conferences and congresses; several times imprisoned and exiled; 1917, member of Presidium of Moscow Soviet; member of Council of People's Commissars; later, occupied a number of important posts in Soviet government; 1924–1929, Chairman of Council of People's Commissars; 1929, expelled from party for belonging to Right opposition; 1931, readmitted; after 1931, Commissar of Post, Telegraph, and Radio; 1938, executed.

SABLINA, see Krupskaia, Nadezhda Konstantinovna.

SAFAROV, GEORGII IVANOVICH (1891–   ). Member of R.S.D.L. party; Bolshevik; several times arrested and exiled for party activity; member of Petersburg Committee and Northern Regional Bureau; after 1912, in Switzerland; 1915–1916, organized in France a Left group of workers at St. Nazaire; 1916, deported from France to Switzerland, where he took part in Bolshevik party activity; 1917, returned to Russia; 1918, Left Communist; editor of *Leningradskaia Pravda;* 1927, expelled from party as oppositionist; 1928, readmitted; after 1929, an official of the Comintern; 1935, arrested in connection with Kirov's assassination and sentenced to a long term in prison.

SALTER, MRS. ADA. Member of British I.L. party; 1915, attended Berne International Conference of Socialist Women.

SAMOILOV, FEDOR NIKITICH (1882–   ). Textile worker; member of R.S.D.L. party; Bolshevik; member of Fourth State Duma; 1914, in Switzerland on account of bad health; November 1914, arrested with other Bolshevik Duma deputies and exiled to Siberia; after return from Siberia in 1917, held responsible posts in Ivanovo-Voznesensk and in Central Soviet institutions.

SAMUELSON, OSKAR. Member of Swedish S.D.L. party and of Swedish Socialist youth organization; during World War, on Left wing; 1917, attended Third Zimmerwald Conference, Stockholm.

SANDERS, WILLIAM STEPHEN (1871–   ). Member of Fabian Society; 1914–1920, its Secretary; Member of Parliament; 1913–1915, member of National Executive of British Labour party; served in World War; spring, 1917, on delegation to Russia; 1920–1929, on staff of International Labor Office (Geneva); 1930–1931, with War Office.

SAPOZHKOV, see Kuznetsov, Nikolai Vasilevich.

SAUMONEAU, LOUISE (1875–   ). Teacher; member of French Socialist party; during World War, member of Comité pour la Reprise des Relations Internationales; carried on active antiwar propaganda among women; editor of *Femme Socialiste;* later a Communist.

SAVELEV. Unidentified; 1916, represented internationalist wing of Russian Socialist-Revolutionists at Kienthal Conference in Switzerland.

SCHEIDEMANN, PHILIPP (1865–1939). Member of German S.D. party; after 1912, in party Presidium; 1903–1918, 1920–1933, member of Reichstag; during World War, majority socialist leader; 1918, Under-Secretary of State without portfolio; 1919, first Chancellor of German Republic; refused to sign Versailles treaty and resigned; resumed party activities; émigré since 1933.

SCHENKEL, HANS (1869–1926). Member of Swiss S.D. party; member of Winterthur Great Council; 1913–1917, member of National Council; author of a number of works on education and political economy.

SCHERRER, HEINRICH (1847–1919). Lawyer; formerly member of Grütli Verein; member of Swiss S.D. party, Right wing; 1902, elected to National Council; later, member of the State Council.

SCHLEIFER. A Swiss working woman in Geneva; co-operated with Geneva section of Russian Bolsheviks.

SCHLESINGER, THERESE. Member of Austrian S.D.L. party; author of various pamphlets on labor movement and of articles in *Neue Zeit, Der Kampf,* and *Arbeiter-Zeitung;* during World War in ranks of opposition; member of Karl Marx Club (Vienna); 1917, delegate to Third Zimmerwald Conference.

SCHMID, ARTHUR. Member of Swiss S.D. party; during World War, on its Left wing.

SCHMID, JACQUES (1882–). Member of Swiss S.D. party, moderate socialist; editor of several Swiss S.D. papers; after 1912, member of Solothurn Great Council and Olten municipal council; after 1917, member of National Council.

SCHMIDT, *see* Rumiantsev, Petr Petrovich.

SELIGER, JOSEF (1870–1920). Member of German S.D. party in Czechoslovakia; 1907–1918, member of Austrian Reichsrat; 1920, elected to Czech parliament.

SEMASHKO, NIKOLAI ALEKSANDROVICH (ALEKSANDROV) (1874–). Physician; member of R.S.D.L. party; Bolshevik; 1905–1917, in Western Europe; active in organizations of Russian Bolsheviks abroad; 1917, one of Bolshevik delegates to Third Zimmerwald Conference, Stockholm; 1918–1930, People's Commissar of Health; later, member of Presidium of All-Russian Central Executive Committee.

SEMBAT, MARCEL (1862–1922). Member of French Socialist party; after 1893, member of Chamber of Deputies; during World War, majority socialist; 1914–1916, Minister of Public Works.

SEMENOV, N. N. Member of R.S.D.L. party; Bolshevik; 1905, attended Third Congress of R.S.D.L. party under pseudonym of "Valerianov."

SEMKOVSKY, SEMEN YULEVICH (BRONSTEIN) (1882–). Journalist; member of R.S.D.L. party; Menshevik; 1907, emigrated and joined Trotsky's *Pravda* (Vienna); wrote also for Polish, Austrian, and American socialist publications; 1912, active in calling August Conference; Menshevik representative on I.S.B.; 1914, attended Unification Conference at Brussels; organizer of Secretariat of Organization Committee Abroad; editor of its organ; 1917, returned to Russia; member of Menshevik Central Committee; editor of its organs; 1920, withdrew from Menshevik ranks; became a Communist; later, member of All-Ukrainian Central Executive Committee; teacher in several Ukrainian universities.

SERRATI, GIACINTO MENOTTI (1874–1926). Member of Italian Socialist party, Left wing; 1914–1920, editor of *Avanti!;* took active part in Zimmerwald movement and attended its conferences; favored joining Comintern; 1920, attended Second Congress of Communist International but disagreed with its policy of effecting party divisions; subsequently expelled with Italian Socialist party from Comintern; 1924, with his followers joined Italian Communist party.

SHAGOV, NIKOLAI ROMANOVICH (1882–1918). Manual laborer; member of R.S.D.L. party; Bolshevik; member of Fourth State Duma; contributed to *Pravda;* 1914, arrested with Bolshevik Duma group; 1915, exiled to Siberia where he became insane.

SHENKMAN. Member of R.S.D.L. party; 1917–1918, active in Kazan; later, Chairman of Council of People's Commissars of Tartar Republic; shot at time of surrender of Kazan.

SHERMAN, CHARLES O. One of the leaders of the Industrial Workers of the World.

SHKLOVSKY, GRIGORII LVOVICH (1875–   ). Member of R.S.D.L. party; Bolshevik; originally active in White Russia; many times arrested and exiled; 1908, escaped from exile and went to Switzerland; 1912, Bolshevik delegate to Basel International Socialist Congress; 1915, attended Berne Conference of Bolshevik Organizations Abroad; elected to Committee of Organizations Abroad; 1917, returned to Russia; active in Bolshevik revolution; 1918, with Soviet diplomatic corps in Switzerland; until 1925, connected with People's Commissariat of Foreign Affairs; 1928, removed from his duties for supporting Trotsky; since 1929, connected with Chemical Syndicate and related institutions.

SHLIAPNIKOV, ALEKSANDR GAVRILOVICH (BELENIN) (1884–   ). Metal worker; member of R.S.D.L. party; Bolshevik; agitator in large steel works in Petersburg; 1908–1914, in Western Europe; during World War, made several trips into Russia on commission from Bureau of Central Committee Abroad; organized Russian Bureau of Central Committee in Petrograd; 1914, represented Russian Bolsheviks at Congress of Swedish S.D.L. party at Stockholm; organized transport of illegal Bolshevik literature into Russia through Finland; 1917, member of Executive Committee of Petrograd Soviet; Commissar of Labor; took active part in civil war; later held responsible posts in Soviet government; now reported "missing."

SHVEDCHIKOV, KONSTANTIN MATVEEVICH (1884–   ). Printer; member of R.S.D.L. party; Bolshevik; propagandist; active in 1905 revolution; many times imprisoned and exiled; 1917, manager of *Pravda;* held responsible posts with Commissariat of Foreign Trade; in charge of Soviet cinema industry.

SIGG, JEAN (1865–1922). Member of Swiss S.D. party and of its Executive; Right wing; 1890–1919, deputy in Geneva Great Council; 1898–1921, Labor Secretary for French Switzerland; 1912–1920, deputy in National Council; 1920–1922, member of the State Council.

SILVIN, MIKHAIL ALEKSANDROVICH (BEM) (1874–   ). Once member of League of Struggle for the Emancipation of the Working Class; member of R.S.D.L. party; member of Central Committee; 1908, withdrew from political activity; after 1917, worked in People's Commissariat of Education but did not join Russian Communist party; engaged in workers' insurance activity since 1923.

SINGER, PAUL (1844–1911). Member of German S.D. party, Left wing; member of party Presidium and frequently chairman of party congresses; German representative on I.S.B.; 1884–1911, member of Reichstag.

SIROLA, YRJÖ (1876–1936). Member of Finnish S.D. party; its General Secretary; its representative in Second International; 1905–1917, in the United States; collaborated in Finnish socialist press; 1917, returned to Finland; Left wing; since 1918, member of Finnish Communist party; People's Commissar of Foreign Affairs in Finnish Red Government; later, People's Commissar of Education in Karelian Autonomous Soviet Socialist Republic.

DE SISMONDI, SIMON (1773–1842). Swiss economist and historian; Utopian socialist.

ŠKATULA, EMANUEL (1878–   ). Author and translator; member of the Czech S.D. party; 1899–1908, Secretary of the Czech Trade Union Federation; 1908–1919, Secretary of the S.D. party; 1920–1922, Secretary of the Workers'

Academy and of the Social Institute of the Czechoslovak Republic; edited and contributed to *Právo Lidu* and many other publications.

SKOBELEV, MIKHAIL IVANOVICH (1885–1930). Member of R.S.D.L. party; Menshevik; represented Transcaucasia in Fourth State Duma; during World War, Centrist; 1917, member of Executive Committee of Petrograd Soviet; member of Second Provisional Coalition Government; worked for a short time with Soviet government; then emigrated to Paris where he was instrumental in establishment of Soviet trade relations with France; 1922, joined Russian Communist party and returned to Russia where he held responsible positions.

SKOULOUDIS, STEPHEN (1836–1928). Greek statesman; 1915–1916, Prime Minister of Greece.

SKOVNO, A. Member of R.S.D.L. party; Bolshevik; during World War, in Western Europe; 1917, returned to Russia with Lenin.

SKRYPNIK, NIKOLAI ALEKSEEVICH (1872–1933). Member of R.S.D.L. party; Bolshevik; several times imprisoned and exiled; 1913–1914, one of the editors of *Voprosy Strakhovaniia* and *Pravda;* leader of workers' insurance group in Petrograd; 1917, member of Central Council of factory and shop committees in Petrograd; later, member of Military Revolutionary Committee; 1917–1918, active in the Ukraine; Chairman of Ukrainian Soviet government; later, held other important posts in Ukrainian government and was member of Central Executive Committee of U.S.S.R.; committed suicide.

SLAVA, *see* Kasparov, Vladimir.

SMIRNOV, E., *see* Gurevich, Emmanuil Lvovich.

SOBELSOHN, *see* Radek, Karl Berngardovich.

SÖDERBERG, ERNST JULIUS (1871–1919). Member of Swedish S.D.L. party; engaged in trade union work; 1917, member of Dutch-Scandinavian Committee, Stockholm.

SOKOLNIKOV, GRIGORII YAKOVLEVICH (BRILLIANT; VIKTORENOK) (1888–). Member of R.S.D.L. party; Bolshevik; 1905–1907, active in Moscow party organization; 1909, emigrated to Western Europe; during World War, internationalist; 1917, returned to Russia; editor of *Pravda;* 1918, Chairman of Soviet delegation to Brest-Litovsk; during civil war, filled responsible posts at front; after 1922, People's Commissar of Finance; held other high positions in Soviet government; 1937, reported sentenced to a long prison term.

SONNINO, BARON SIDNEY (1847–1922). Italian statesman; 1914–1919, Minister of Foreign Affairs.

STADTHAGEN, ARTHUR (1857–1917). Lawyer; member of German S.D. party; member of Reichstag; during World War, with minority socialists; 1917, joined I.S.D. party.

STAHL, LIUDMILA (1872–1939). Member of R.S.D.L. party; Bolshevik; many times arrested and exiled; 1905, member of Odessa Party Committee; after another arrest emigrated to Paris; joined French Socialist party and was active in Bolshevik group in Paris; one of the leaders of the women's socialist movement; contributor to *Rabotnitsa;* 1917, on return to Russia devoted herself to work among women.

STALIN, YOSIF VISSARIONOVICH (DZHUGASHVILI) (1879–1953). Since 1898 Georgian member of the R.S.D.L. party; Bolshevik; after 1905 took part in all party congresses; many times arrested; 1913–1917, in Siberian exile; on return to Petrograd edited *Pravda;* 1917–1923, People's Commissar for Affairs of Nationalities; 1917–23, Commissar of Workers' Inspection and Control; active in Red army during civil war; 1920–23, member of Revolutionary Military Soviet; after 1922, General Secretary of Central Committee; since 1925 member of Executive Committee of Comintern; after 1927, member of All-Russian Central Executive Committee; now member of Presidium of Supreme Council; leader of the Communist party of the Soviet Union and most influential personality in the Soviet regime.

STARK, LEONID NIKOLAEVICH (1889–   ). Son of an admiral, member of R.S.D.L. party; Bolshevik; member of Petersburg Committee; 1916–1917, founder of Bolshevik publishing house "Volna"; 1915–1917, friendly with the provocateur, Chernomazov; subsequently disappeared from party arena; later, completely rehabilitated by Bolsheviks; during civil war, worked in military-sanitary department; later, held several Soviet diplomatic posts.

STAROVER, see Potresov, Aleksandr Nikolaevich.

STAUNING, THORVALD AUGUST MARINUS (1873–1942). Member and leader of Danish S.D. party; reformist; after 1906, member of Riksdag; 1916–1920, Minister without portfolio; after 1924, repeatedly Prime Minister.

STEIN, BRONISLAW (DĄBROWSKI; KRAJEWSKI; BRONISLAW KAMINSKI). One of the Kaminski-Stein brothers; during World War, on Left Wing of Social Democracy of Poland and Lithuania; took part in International Socialist Youth movement and Zimmerwald movement; after 1918, member of Polish Communist party; active in Soviet Russia; expelled from party for supporting Trotsky; 1931, readmitted; 1938, placed under arrest.

STEIN, HENRYK (L. DOMSKI; HENRYK KAMINSKI) (1883–   ). Member of Social Democracy of Poland and Lithuania; several times imprisoned and exiled; 1908–1915, in Western Europe; on editorial boards of Polish Social Democratic newspapers; after 1912, editor of *Gazeta Robotnicza* (Cracow); member of Regional Presidium of Social Democracy of Poland and Lithuania; contributed to Russian Bolshevik publications; later elected to Main Presidium of party; after December 1918, member of Central Committee of Polish Communist party; 1925, removed from his party posts for Left deviation; 1928, expelled for supporting Trotsky; 1930, readmitted.

STEKLOV, YURII MIKHAILOVICH (1873–   ). Member of R.S.D.L. party; Bolshevik; several times arrested and exiled; one of founders of *Borba* publishing house; 1917, revolutionary defensist; close to *Novaia Zhizn* group; member of Executive Committee of Petrograd Soviet; later, editor of *Izvestiia* and repeatedly elected to Central Executive Committee; held other responsible editorial posts and headed committee in charge of controlling institutions of learning; author of works on history of socialism.

STEPANOV, see Essen, Aleksandr Magnusovich.

STOINOV, N. Russian Social Democrat; Plekhanovist; later, member of "Mezhraionka."

STOLYPIN, PETR ARKADIEVICH (1863–1911). 1906–1911, Chairman of Council of Ministers and Minister of the Interior of Imperial Russia.

STRÖM, OTTO FREDRIK (1880–   ). Member of Swedish S.D.L. party; editor and contributor to many Scandinavian socialist newspapers; 1911–1916, party Secretary; 1916–1921, and after 1930, member of Lower Chamber of Riksdag; 1916–1918, Secretary of Left S.D.L. party; 1918–1919, editor of *Folkets Dagblad;* 1921–1924, Secretary of Swedish Communist party; later, returned to S.D.L. party and was editor of *Social-Demokraten* (Stockholm).

STUDER, FRIEDRICH (FRITZ) (1873–   ). Lawyer; member of Swiss S.D. party; after 1901, member of Winterthur Great Council; 1911–1916, Chairman of S.D. party.

STURM. Member of German socialist youth organization in Göttingen.

SÜDEKUM, ALBERT OSKAR WILHELM (1871–   ). Member of German S.D. party; revisionist; 1900–1918, member of Reichstag; during World War, majority socialist; 1918–1920, Prussian Minister of Finance.

THALHEIMER, BERTHA. Sister of August Thalheimer, one of the former leaders of German Communist party.

THOMAS, ALBERT (1878–1932). Member of French Socialist party; after 1904, on editorial staff of L'Humanité; 1910–1914, 1919–1921, member of Chamber of Deputies; 1914–1917, member of French Cabinet; spring, 1917, visited Russia; prominent in Second International; after 1920, Director of International Labor Office (Geneva).

THORNE, WILLIAM JAMES (1857–   ). British trade unionist; member of British Labour party; Member of Parliament; after 1894, member of Parliamentary Committee of Trade Union Congress.

TINEV, KATERINA. Member of Bulgarian S.D.L. party; "Narrow" Socialist.

TISZA, COUNT STEPHEN (1861–1918). Hungarian statesman; 1913–1917, Prime Minister; later active at front and in diplomatic service; assassinated by soldiers.

TRANMAEL, MARTIN. Norwegian trade union leader; Left member of Norwegian S.D. party; member of Storting; during World War Zimmerwaldist; chief editor of Ny Tid Drontheim).

TRAUTMANN, WILLIAM ERNEST. One of the organizers of the Industrial Workers of the World; 1900–1905, editor of Brauer Zeitung.

TREVES, CLAUDIO (1869–1933). Author; member of Italian Socialist party; 1906–1926, Member of Chamber of Deputies; 1908–1912, editor of Avanti!; Left reformist; during World War, Centrist; 1927–1933, émigré.

TRIER, GERSON (1851–   ). Teacher; member of Danish S.D. party; member of its Presidium; during World War, internationalist; 1916, withdrew from party in opposition to its policy favoring participation of socialists in bourgeois cabinets.

TROELSTRA, PIETER JELLES (1860–1930). One of the founders of Dutch S.D.L. party; 1897–1925, member of States-General; 1900–1903, first editor of Het Volk; member of I.S.B.; during World War, defensist; 1925, retired from politics.

TROIANOVSKY, ALEKSANDR ANTONOVICH (1881–1955). Member of R.S.D.L. party; since 1904, Bolshevik; contributed to a number of Bolshevik publications; after 1908, in Western Europe; during World War, stood in opposition to antiwar, defeatist policy of Bolshevik Central Committee; 1917–1921, with Mensheviks; 1923, joined Russian Communist party; 1924–1927, with People's Commissariat for Foreign Trade; 1928–1933, Soviet ambassador to Japan; 1933–1938, ambassador to the United States.

TROTSKY, LEV DAVYDOVICH (BRONSTEIN; ANTID OTO) (1879–1940). Member of R.S.D.L. party; Menshevik; 1902, forced to go to Western Europe; 1905, Chairman of Petersburg Soviet; exiled to Siberia, but escaped; 1908–1912, publisher of Pravda (Vienna); one of the organizers of August bloc; during World War, internationalist; on editorial staff of Nashe Slovo; took part in Zimmerwald movement; 1916, expelled from France; through Spain reached New York; on editorial staff of Novyi Mir (New York); 1917, returned to

Russia; member of "Mezhraionka"; July 1917, joined Bolsheviks; Chairman of Petrograd Soviet; later, Commissar of Foreign Affairs; 1918–1925, Commissar of War; member of Political Bureau; 1926, expelled from Bureau; 1927, expelled from party; since 1929, exiled from Soviet Russia.

TSERETELI, IRAKLII GEORGIEVICH (1882–1959). Georgian member of R.S.D.L. party; Menshevik; 1907, member of Second State Duma and Chairman of Social Democratic Duma group; November 1907—March 1917, imprisoned and exiled to Siberia; 1917, member of Petrograd Soviet; Minister of the Interior in Provisional government; 1918, in Georgia; after 1919, émigré.

TSKHAKAIA, MIKHAIL GRIGORIEVICH (BARSOV) (1865–   ). Caucasian member of R.S.D.L. party; Bolshevik; active in underground party work in the Caucasus; attended several party congresses; 1905–1917, in Western Europe; 1917, returned to Russia; carried on party activity in the Caucasus; attended Democratic Conference and took part in Bolshevik revolution; 1919–1920, imprisoned by Mensheviks; later, held responsible positions with Soviet government.

TULIAKOV, IVAN NIKITICH (1877–1920?). Manual laborer; member of R.S.D.L. party; Menshevik; member of Fourth State Duma; prior to 1914, on extreme Right wing of Menshevism; during World War, Zimmerwaldist.

TURATI, FILIPPO (1857–1932). Lawyer; writer and poet; member of Italian Socialist party; one of first Italian Marxists; Member of Chamber of Deputies; editor of *Critica Sociale* and *Avanti!*; 1899–1901, imprisoned for provoking riots in Milan; during World War, opposed Italian intervention; believed in parliamentarism and social reform; foe of Soviet system; 1922, joined Unitary Socialist party; 1926, escaped from Italy and lived as émigré in Paris.

TUTSOWICZ, DIMITRIJE (1881–1914). Member of Serbian S.D. party; wrote widely for Serbian and foreign socialist press; editor of *Radnichki Novina* and *Borba;* translator of works of Marx; killed on battlefield.

TYSZKA, JAN (LEO JOGICHES; LEV GROZOWSKI) (1867–1919). Member and founder of Polish S.D. party; member of its Central Committee; later, member of Main Presidium of Social Democracy of Poland and Lithuania; imprisoned and exiled for revolutionary activity; Polish member of Central Committee of R.S.D.L. party; after 1910, in Germany; member of German S.D. party, Left wing; one of organizers of *Internationale* group; later, member of "Spartakus" League; imprisoned by German government; 1918, released; took part in revolution; one of organizers of German Communist party; March 1919, imprisoned and executed without trial.

ULIANOV V., *see* Lenin, V. I.

URITSKY, MIKHAIL SOLOMONOVICH (1873–1918). Member of R.S.D.L. party; Menshevik; took part in 1905 revolution; many times arrested and exiled; 1914, went to Western Europe; internationalist; contributor to *Nashe Slovo* (Paris); 1917, returned to Russia; joined Bolshevik party; member of Military Revolutionary Committee; Chairman of Petrograd Cheka; assassinated.

UTIN, NIKOLAI ISAAKOVICH (1845–1883). Son of a banker; 1862, member of Central Committee of "Land and Freedom" group; 1863, emigrated; joined First International; Secretary of its Russian section in Geneva; member of editorial board of *Narodnoe Delo;* fought Bakunin in First International; about 1875, withdrew from revolutionary activity.

VAILLANT, EDOUARD (1840–1915). French socialist; member of French Commune; editor of *L'Homme Libre;* after 1893, member of Chamber of Deputies; outstanding member of First and later Second International; together with Guesde fought Millerandism and Jaurèsism; one of the founders of Socialist party of

France (Revolutionary Alliance); 1905, after party unification, joined Jaurès group of French Socialist party and fought Guesdism; ardent antimilitarist; at outbreak of World War, favored defense against German aggression.

VALERIANOV, see Semenov, N. N.

VANDERVELDE, EMILE (1866–1938). Member of Belgian S.L. party; after 1894, Member of Parliament; Chairman of I.S.B.; during World War, Minister of State in Belgian cabinet; believed in Entente cause; later, held various cabinet positions; author of several books on socialism.

VAN KOL, HENDRIK (1851–1925). Member of Dutch S.D.L. party; revisionist; 1897–1918, member of States-General.

VAN ZUTPHEN. Member of Dutch S.D.L. party; 1916, attended Conference of Socialists of Neutral Countries at The Hague.

VASILEV, see Lengnik, Fridrikh Vilgelminovich.

VÄSTBERG, JOHAN MAURITZ. Member of Swedish S.D.L. party; during World War as members of Swedish Youth League supported minority socialists; contributed to *Politiken*.

VIDNES, JAKOB LAURENTIUS (1875–   ). Member of Norwegian S.D. party; 1912–1918, member of its Executive; contributor to *Social-Demokraten* (Stockholm) and after 1912, its editor; 1915, active in preparing for Copenhagen Conference of socialists of neutral countries; 1917, member of Dutch-Scandinavian Committee, Stockholm.

VIKTORENOK, see Sokolnikov, Grigorii Yakovlevich.

VISSCHER, J. Formerly member of Dutch S.D.L. party; during World War, in ranks of opposition to majority policy; member of Revolutionary Socialist League of Holland.

VLADIMIR ILICH or VLADIMIR ILYICH, see Lenin, Vladimir Ilich.

VLADIMIROV, MIRON KONSTANTINOVICH (LEVA) (1879–1925). Member of R.S.D.L. party; Bolshevik; member of Polesian Committee; many times arrested and exiled; 1908–1917, after escape from exile lived in Western Europe; 1911, lectured at Paris party school; became a Plekhanovist; during World War, contributed to *Nashe Slovo* (Paris); 1917, returned to Russia; was readmitted to Bolshevik party; held various responsible posts in Soviet government including that of Acting Chairman of Supreme Council of People's Economy.

VLADIMIRSKY, MIKHAIL FEDOROVICH (KAMSKY) (1874–1951). Physician; member of R.S.D.L. party; Bolshevik; engaged in party activity, chiefly in Moscow; several times arrested and exiled; 1906–1917, forced to stay in France; member of Paris section of Russian Bolsheviks; member of Bolshevik Committee of Organizations Abroad; 1914, attended Unification Conference at Brussels; 1917, returned to Russia; was active in the Ukraine and held various responsible posts, including that of Commissar of Public Health in R.S.F.S.R.

VLASOV. Unidentified; Russian Socialist-Revolutionist; 1916, attended Kienthal Conference.

VLIEGEN, WILLEM HUBERT (1862–1947). Member of Dutch S.D.L. party; 1907–1919, one of the editors of *Het Volk*; after 1909, member of States-General; 1915, alternate member of Executive Committee of I.S.B.; 1916, attended Conference of Socialists of Neutral Countries at The Hague; 1917, alternate member of Russian-Dutch-Scandinavian Committee, Stockholm.

VOGEL, HANS. Member of Swiss S.D. party, Left wing; member of editorial staff of *Volksrecht* (Zürich); editor of *Berner Tagwacht*.

VOLLMAR, GEORG (1850–1922). Member of German S.D. party, Right wing; revisionist; after 1881, almost continuously member of Reichstag; active in Second International.

VOROVSKY, VATSLAV VATSLAVOVICH (YU. ADAMOVICH; P. ORLOVSKY; FAVN; M. SCHWARZ) (1871–1923). Publicist; in revolutionary movement from 1890; member of R.S.D.L. party; Bolshevik; 1917, member of Bureau of Central Committee Abroad; 1918, represented R.S.F.S.R. in Switzerland; 1921, in Italy; delegate to Lausanne Conference where he was assassinated.

WAIBEL, ANTON. German anarchist, living in Switzerland.

WALDECK-ROUSSEAU, PIERRE MARIE (1846–1904). Lawyer; 1879, member of Chamber of Deputies; 1894, member of Senate; 1881–1899, in various governments; 1899–1902, Prime Minister and Minister of the Interior.

WALECKI, MAXIMILIAN GUSTAVOVICH (MAX HORWITZ) (1877–   ). Mathematician; 1895, joined Polish Socialist party; later engaged in party activity in Warsaw; member of Warsaw Committee; repeatedly arrested and exiled; August 1914, attended last pre-war meeting of I.S.B.; 1906–1918, member of Executive of Polish Socialist party (Levitsa); forced to escape to Switzerland; took part in Zimmerwald movement; 1917, one of editors of *Volksrecht* (Zürich); since November 1918, in Poland; one of the organizers of Polish Communist party; Polish representative in Comintern; member of Russian Communist party; 1938, reported under arrest.

WARDLE, GEORGE JAMES (1865–   ). British trade unionist; member of British Labour party; 1906–1920, Member of Parliament.

WARSKI, *see* Warszawski, Adolf.

WARSZAWSKI, ADOLF (WARSKI) (1868–   ). Member of Social Democracy of Poland and Lithuania and its Main Presidium; editor of *Przegląd Socyal Demokratyczny*; contributor to numerous socialist publications; 1907, elected member of Central Committee of R.S.D.L. party; close to Bolsheviks; during World War, internationalist; joined Zimmerwald Left; 1916, returned to Poland where he was arrested; 1918, one of the founders of Polish Communist party; 1924–1925, not in ranks of Communists; since 1926, Communist deputy in Polish parliament.

WEBB, BEATRICE POTTER (BARONESS PASSFIELD) (1858–   ). Wife of Sidney Webb; writer on labor and social questions; member of Fabian Society; engaged in study of social and industrial labor conditions; served on numerous government committees.

WEINBERG, YULII STANISLAVOVICH. Member of Social Democracy of Poland and Lithuania; on eve of World War, exiled to Siberia; there adhered to group of Siberian S.D. Zimmerwaldists and contributed to their press; member of Petrograd Soviet delegation to Stockholm; recalled; returned to Siberia.

WELTMANN, MIKHAIL LAZAREVICH (M. P. PAVLOVICH) (1871–1927). Economist and historian, chiefly interested in study of Oriental culture; member of R.S.D.L. party; Menshevik; 1905–1906, outstanding member of Petersburg Military Organization of party; during World War, in France; contributed to *Golos* and *Nashe Slovo;* during Bolshevik revolution, fought in ranks of Bolsheviks, whom he soon joined officially; active in People's Commissariat of Foreign Affairs; attended Brest-Litovsk Peace Conference as expert; later, held responsible military posts at Southern Front; after 1921, in People's Commissariat for Affairs of Nationalities; later Dean of Institute for the Study of Oriental Culture and professor at Military Academy; author of important works on imperialism.

WENCKOWSKI. Member of Social Democracy of Poland and Lithuania; Rozlomovist; attended Poronino Conference.

WENGELS, ROBERT. Member of German I.S.D. party; 1917, attended Third Zimmerwald Conference in Stockholm.

WIBAUT, F. (1859–). Journalist and large businessman; member of Dutch S.D.L. party; member of its Executive; later, member of S.D. party of Holland; 1910, delegate to Copenhagen International Socialist Congress; during World War, occupied Centrist position; gradually moved to extreme Right of labor movement.

WIJNKOOP, DAVID (1877–1941). Member of Dutch S.D.L. party, Left wing; 1909, one of the founders of S.D. party of Holland; 1918–1925, member of States-General; 1919, joined Comintern; later withdrew from Communist ranks.

WILHELM II (1859–). 1888–1918, German Emperor and King of Prussia.

WILLE, ULRICH (1848–1925). Author; after 1869, in Swiss army; 1900–1914, professor in École Polytechnique Fédérale; after August 4, 1914, General in Swiss army.

WILLIAMS, RUSSELL. Journalist; member of British I.L. party.

WILSON, WOODROW (1862–1924). 1913–1921, President of the United States.

WINTER, see Berzin, Jan Antonovich.

WURM, EMMANUEL (1857–1920). Member of German S.D. party; publisher and editor of a number of socialist publications, including Neue Zeit; 1890–1906, 1912–1918, member of Reichstag; during World War, member of moderate opposition; after 1917, member of I.S.D. party; November and December, 1918, Prussian Food Minister.

YONOV, FISHEL MARKOVICH (KOIGEN) (1870–1923). Member of the Bund; its representative at several congresses of R.S.D.L. party; favored party unity; during World War, at head of Left wing; internationalist; joined Communist Bund and subsequently Russian Communist party.

YURENEV, KONSTANTIN KONSTANTINOVICH (1889–). Member of R.S.D.L. party; Bolshevik; 1913–1917, Mezhraionka member; member of Executive Committee of Petrograd Soviet; joined Bolshevik party; held responsible posts in Soviet government and filled several Soviet diplomatic positions in foreign countries.

YURII, see Piatakov, Georgii Leonidovich.

YURKEVICH, L. (L. RYBALKA). Member of Central Committee of Ukrainian S.D.L. party; 1913–1914, contributed to Dzvin; during World War, published Borotba (Lausanne); took part in Zimmerwald movement, together with Borotba group, which adhered to Zimmerwald Right; wrote articles in support of defeatist slogan and opposed League for the Liberation of the Ukraine.

ZAIMIS, ALEXANDER (1855–). Greek statesman; 1915–1917, Prime Minister of Greece.

ZALEZHSKY, VLADIMIR NIKOLAEVICH (1880–). Member of R.S.D.L. party; Bolshevik; carried on party activity in all parts of Russia; 1912–1917, imprisoned and exiled; 1917, member of Petersburg Committee; later, active in Finland; took part in civil war; later devoted himself to literary activity and teaching.

ZALKIND, ROZALIIA SAMOILOVNA (ZEMLIACHKA; G. I. OSIPOV; BERLIN) (1875–). Member of R.S.D.L. party; Bolshevik; one of the most active party organizers and agitators; member of Bureau of Majority Committees;

1905, delegate to Third Party Congress from Petersburg Committee; during December uprising, Secretary of Moscow Committee; 1908–1914, forced to live abroad; returned to Russia; member of Bureau of Central Committee in Russia; after 1917, again in Moscow Committee; 1918, took part in civil war at Southern Front; Secretary of Crimean Regional Bureau; later, occupied responsible party posts in various parts of Russia and was a member of Central Control Committee.

ZALUTSKY, PETR ANTONOVICH (1887–   ). Formerly member of Russian Socialist-Revolutionist party; 1907, joined R.S.D.L. party in Harbin; active in Vladivostok; several times arrested and exiled; after 1911, in Petersburg; organized publication of *Zvezda* and *Pravda;* during World War, member of Petersburg Committee and of Russian Bureau of Central Committee; 1917, member of Petrograd Soviet; active among soldiers' deputies; member of Petrograd Military Revolutionary Committee and active at civil war fronts; repeatedly member of Central Committee; held high party posts in Soviet government; 1927, expelled from party for supporting Trotsky; 1928, readmitted; headed Elektrostroi in Kashir.

ZASULICH, VERA IVANOVNA (1851–1919). Once Narodnik partisan; became Social Democrat; 1869–1875, exiled for revolutionary activity; 1878, attempted to assassinate Trepov, Petersburg Governor, but was acquitted by jury; 1880, emigrated; took part in formation of Emancipation of Labor group; 1900, joined editorial staff of *Iskra;* 1903, Menshevik; during World War, social patriot; 1917, one of *Edinstvo* group.

ZETKIN, KLARA (1857–1933). Member of German S.D. party; Left wing; active in international women's movement; during World War, internationalist; member of "Internationale" group; later, member of "Spartakus" League; editor of *Gleichheit;* 1918, joined German Communist party; member of its Central Committee; later, member of Executive Committee of Comintern; Communist member of Reichstag; after 1924, spent most of her time in Russia where she died.

ZHORDANIIA, NOI NIKOLAEVICH (AN; KOSTROV) (1870–   ). Georgian member of R.S.D.L. party; Menshevik; attended a number of party congresses and conferences; after 1907, member of Central Committee; during World War, defensist; 1918–1920, headed Georgian Menshevik government; 1921, escaped to France.

ZIETZ, LUISE (1865–1922). Member of German S.D. party and of its Presidium; active in women's socialist movement; during World War, sided with minority socialists; 1917, joined I.S.D. party; served as its Secretary; 1919–1920, member of National Assembly; later, member of Reichstag.

ZINOVIEV, GRIGORII EVSEEVICH (SKOPIN; RADOMYSLSKY) (1883–1936). Member of R.S.D.L. party; Bolshevik; active in 1905 revolution; member of Petersburg Committee; 1906, forced to emigrate to Western Europe; 1908, returned to Russia for revolutionary activity but was arrested and left Russia; edited and contributed to many Bolshevik publications; member of Central Committee; during World War, in Switzerland; together with Lenin led Zimmerwald Left; 1917, returned to Russia; opposed Lenin on question of armed insurrection; Chairman of Petrograd Soviet; 1919–1926, Chairman of Executive Committee of Comintern; 1927, expelled from party for supporting Trotsky; 1928, readmitted; 1928–1934, Chairman of Tsentro-Soiuz; charged with conspiracy to murder Kirov; 1935, tried and sentenced to ten years' imprisonment; 1936, tried again; executed.

ZURABOV, ARSHAK GERASIMOVICH (1873–1919). Caucasian member of R.S.D.L. party; Menshevik; contributed to Georgian and Armenian Social Democratic press; 1907, elected deputy to State Duma; served four-year term in Petropavlovsk fortress; 1912, elected member of Menshevik Organization Committee; during World War, internationalist; 1917, returned to Russia; member of Transcaucasian Diet and member of Executive Committee of Tiflis Soviet; 1918, moved toward Left and opposed Georgian Menshevik government; exiled to Erivan where he died.

GENERAL INDEX

A

Abramovich, A. E., 558, 619, 771
Abramovich, R. A., 616, 619, 771
Adler, Friedrich, 255, 660, 673, 771
Adler, Victor, 56, 68, 69, 166, 287, 293, 443, 658, 771
Adlers, 444, 659
Affolter, Hans, 548 n., 553, 771
Agent provocateur, 126, 249
Ahsis, see Rozin, F.
Albanian question, 82
Albarda, J. W., 259, 464, 590, 597, 771
Albisser, J., 263, 771
Aleksandr, see Shliapnikov, A. G.
Aleksandra Mikhailovna, see Kollontai, A. M.
Aleksandrov, see Semashko, N. A.
Aleksandrova, E. M., 47 n., 772
Alekseev, N. A., 40 n., 772
Aleksinsky, G. A., 18, 104, 117 n., 126, 163, 164, 165, 205, 206, 207, 772
Alexander II, 5, 772
Alexander III, 5, 772
Algeciras conference, 51
All Jewish Workers' League of Lithuania, Poland, and Russia, see Bund
Allen, C., 406, 772
Alsace-Lorraine question, 360, 365, 511–512, 513, 589, 593, 606, 653
American Federation of Labor, 588, 598, 606, 607
American internationalists, see Socialist Propaganda League; American Socialist party, New York opposition
American Socialist Labor party, 61 n., 568, 577, 588; and Zimmerwald movement, 364, 369, 565, 630; see also Socialist Labor party of North America
American Socialist parties, and Bolsheviks, 565–67, 572, 577, 580; and the party split, 407 (see also Socialist Propaganda League); and the war, 135, 461, 569
American Socialist party, 61 n., 568–569, 574, 588; convention (St. Louis, 1917), 569, 577; German group, 369, 566, 568; National Executive Com-

mittee, 257, 583–84; New York opposition, 567, 568; and resumption of international socialist relations, 257, 258, 260, 264, 583–84, 598, 600; and Zimmerwald movement, 364, 369, 565, 566 n., 568, 609; see also Socialist Propaganda League
"Amnesty," mutual, theory of, 166, 167, 169, 222, 381, 388
Amsterdam Congress (1904), see Second International Congresses, 1904, at Amsterdam
Anarchists, 7, 149, 489
Anarcho-syndicalists, 147, 155
Anderson, W. C., 273, 277, 656, 772
Andreev, L. N., 47 n., 772
Angelica, see Balabanoff, A.
Annexations, forced, 220, 235, 242, 266, 269, 270, 281, 299, 312, 328, 381 n., 393, 399, 402, 403, 404, 411, 421, 422, 423, 425, 430, 431, 453, 467, 508, 515–16, 522, 526, 586, 695; see also Peace: without annexations and indemnities
Anseele, E., 70, 105, 772
Antonov-Brittman, see Popov, A. N.
Appeal to Reason, 407 n., 571, 750
Arbeiter-Jugend, 305, 750
Arbeiterpolitik, Die, 567 n., 750
Arbeiter-Zeitung, 284 n., 443, 750
Arbeitsgemeinschaft group, 497, 545, 578 n., 580 n.; see also German S.D. Party Center; Haase-Bernstein-Kautsky group; Haase-Ledebour-Kautsky group; German Social Democratic Party Opposition
Arbitration, compulsory, international courts of, 59, 70, 73, 263, 265, 269, 279, 281, 285, 396, 402, 411, 415–16, 425, 442, 449, 450, 458, 461, 490, 499, 679
Archiv für die Geschichte des Sozialismus und der Arbeiterbewegung, 398 n., 615 n., 617 n., 630 n., 631 n., 648 n., 650 n., 656 n., 665 n., 666 n., 667 n., 668 n., 674 n., 676 n., 677 n., 678 n., 681 n., 684 n., 686 n., 689 n., 730, 734
Armaments, 58, 59, 72, 73, 150; limitation of, 263, 265, 285, 415–16, 422, 494

cialist party, Zimmerwald opposition of
French Socialist Party National Council, 313, 414, 467, 590
Frieden, Brot und Freiheit, 685
Frimu, J. C., 674, 781
Frölich, P., 407, 410, 411, 781
Fürstenberg, Prince Maximilian, 617 n., 781

G

Galerka, *see* Olminsky, M. S.
Galperin, L. E., 47 n., 781
Garami, E., 284, 781
Gardenin, *see* Chernov, V. M.
Garibaldi, G., 523 n., 781
Gazeta Robotnicza, 240, 244, 335 n., 507, 515 n., 518, 530, 531, 753–54
General Staff, German, 249
Geneva Conference (1905) of R.S.D.L. party, 13
German fleet, mutiny of, 666
German Independent Social Democratic party, 663, 675 n.; All German Women's Committee, 668, 689, 691; and Stockholm Conference project of, 600, 630, 638, 640, 650, 660–62; and Zimmerwald movement, 609, 637, 664, 666, 667, 674
German Social Democratic party, 3, 42–43, 61 n., 88, 454, 532; and co-operatives, 70, 77; and the general strike, 22–23, 56–57; Reichstag group, 42 n., 133, 414, 433, 440, 457, 578 n.; and R.S.D.L. party unity, 20, 23–25, 27, 32–35, 40–42, 48–49, 89, 93–94; split of, 405; and trade unions, 62–63; and war and militarism, 24, 54–57, 59, 60
German Social Democratic Party Center, 20, 24, 52, 54–55, 59–60, 133, 154, 320, 339, 352, 424, 573; *see also Arbeitsgemeinschaft* group; Centrism; Kautsky, K.
German Social Democratic Party Congresses: 1875, at Gotha, 3; 1899, at Hanover, 76; 1903, at Dresden, 10–11, 42; 1907, at Essen, 63; 1910, at Magdeburg, 23; 1911, at Jena, 24, 25 n., 56–57
German Social Democratic Party Left (*see also* German S.D. Party Opposition, Württemberg; Bremen Left Radicals; *Internationale* group; Inter-

national Socialists of Germany; *Lichtstrahlen* group), 20, 24–25, 56–57, 133, 146, 154, 198, 206, 217, 321 n., 317, 318, 414, 439, 563, 580; and Third International, 290, 328, 337, 339, 340, 379, 440; and the Zimmerwald movement, 314, 320, 337, 338, 339, 342, 362, 407–8, 426
German Social Democratic Party Majority, 336, 437, 439, 563, 573, 575, 592, 622, 648, 649; and resumption of international socialist relations, 264, 284, 287; and socialist defensism, 133, 140–41, 153–54, 157, 160, 161, 194, 196, 283, 285, 343, 352, 363–64, 387; and the Zimmerwald movement, 321, 363–64, 384 n., 455
Peace, 381, 593; civil, 532
War aims, 453; and British memorandum on, 606
German Social Democratic Party Minority, *see* German Social Democratic Party Left; German Social Democratic Party Opposition
German Social Democratic Party Opposition, 277, 370 n., 439–41, 456, 461, 575; Württemberg, 336–38, 370; *see also Arbeitsgemeinschaft* group; German Social Democratic Party Center; Haase - Ledebour - Kautsky group; Haase-Bernstein-Kautsky group
German Social Democratic Party Presidium, 32, 33, 35, 41, 48, 196, 414, 439, 580 n., 648
German Social Democratic Party Right, 10–11, 20, 22–24, 42, 51–52, 54–55, 59–61, 526; *see also* German Social Democratic Party Majority
Ginzburg, B. A., 50, 782
Girsh, P. L., 320, 324 n., 341, 505, 526, 782
Glasier, B., 273, 274, 277, 321, 570, 583, 656, 782
Gleichheit, Die, 689–90, 754
Glocke, Die, 524 n., 754
Goldenberg, Y. P., 597, 600, 630, 637, 665, 782
Goldfarb, M., 598, 782
Goldman, M. I., 592, 619, 782
Golos, 162, 172, 195, 203, 204, 205, 258 n., 259 n., 754
Golos Sotsial-Demokrata, 17, 19, 80 n., 119 n., 755

bourgeoisie of other countries), 180 n., 185, 206, 224, 232, 525; Russo-Japanese, 55, 84, 87, 267

Civil (war against the bourgeoisie of one's own country), 87, 141–43, 150 n., 152, 154–56, 158, 163, 168, 175, 183, 184, 186, 188–90, 197–98, 202, 220–21, 227–28, 239, 286, 290–91, 294, 314–17, 326 n., 327, 345–46, 351, 353, 355, 404–5, 407, 411, 475, 490, 493, 542, 570, 581, 657, 697; Finland, 685, 696, 698; Russia, 692

War aims, 589, 591, 602, 620, 622, 626, 645; of the American Federation of Labor, 606–7; British Memorandum on, 605–7

War credits, 58, 73, 141, 153–54, 160, 163, 184, 185, 188, 198, 270, 280, 283–84, 291, 294, 314, 324 n., 331, 334, 338–39, 343, 345, 350, 352, 354, 357, 371, 378, 381, 387–88, 393–94, 410, 413, 421, 428, 433–34, 436, 440–41, 457, 549, 557 n., 634, 661, 668

War Industries Committees, 193, 211, 252, 381, 382, 386, 403, 497, 573–74

Wardle, G. J., 600, 814

Warski, *see* Warszawski, A.

Warszawski, A., 310, 312, 314, 320, 333, 341, 408, 442, 446, 503, 505, 506, 814

Washington International Socialist Conference, 1914, proposed, 258

Webb, Beatrice, 374, 814

Weinberg, Y. S., 599, 814

Weltmann, M. L., 162 n., 814

Wenckowski, 505, 815

Wengels, Robert, 674, 815

Wibaut, F., 259, 264, 464, 590, 597, 815

Wijnkoop, D., 196, 235 n., 317, 318, 319, 349, 373, 398 n., 815

Wilhelm II, 142, 151, 262, 409, 462, 530, 701, 815

Wille, Ulrich, 457, 815

Williams, Russell, 406, 573, 815

Winter, *see* Berzin, J. A.

Wilson, Woodrow, 466, 470, 485, 568, 591, 598 n., 815

Women's Bureau, Socialist International, 191, 287, 291–92

Women's Council, International Socialist, British, 288

Women's International Peace Congress, The Hague (1915), 294

Women's International Socialist Conferences, *see* International Socialist Women's Conferences

Women's movement, international socialist, 290, 292–94, 299–300, 636–37, 688–91

Women's Socialist International, 287, 689

Women's Socialist Organizations, International Secretariat of, *see* Women's Bureau, socialist international

Workers' "Circles" (Russian), 6

Workers' International, *see* Second International

Working class action, anti-war (preventive), 58, 63, 81, 85, 87 (*see also* Peace, action for)

Working day, eight-hour, 111, 143 n., 151 n., 156, 159, 183, 211, 212, 398, 540, 678

World revolution, 63

Württemberg Social Democrats, *see* German Social Democratic party Opposition, Württemberg

Wurm, E., 23, 71, 76, 77, 815

Y

Yonov, F. M., 105, 815

Youth International, 301, 303, 306, 378, 408, 535; *see also* Youth League, International Socialist

Youth League, International Socialist, Bureau of, 192, 301, 302, 303, 307

Youth League, International Socialist, Conferences: 1910, at Copenhagen, 301, 307, 308; 1912, at Basel, 308; 1915, at Berne, 192, 261, 286, 301–8

Youth League, International Socialist, Left, 146

Youth League, International Socialist, Secretariat in Switzerland, 302, 307

Youth Leagues, Socialist: Austrian, 303; Dutch, 304; French, 303; German, 301, 303, 305; Italian, 302; Spanish (Madrid), 369; Swiss, 225, 303, 540

Danish, 304; and Zimmerwald movement, 369, 609, 675 n.

Norwegian, 208 n., 225, 304, 491, 492; and the Zimmerwald movement, 214, 217, 341–42, 369, 559–60, 609, 674; *see also* Norwegian S.D. Party Left